MICROECONOMICS

Fourth Canadian Edition

Paul Krugman
Robin Wells
Iris Au
Jack Parkinson

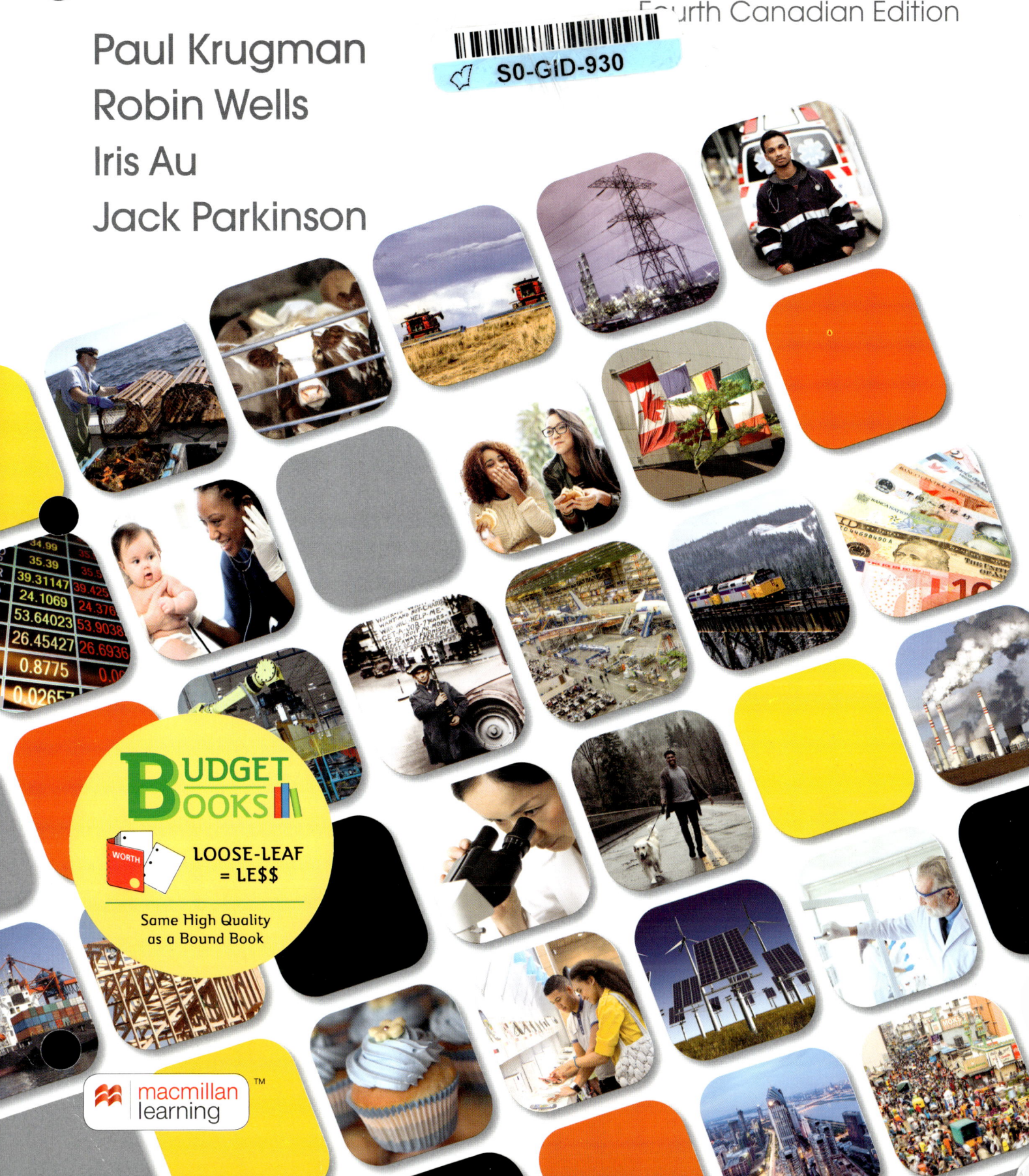

macmillan learning

Brief Contents

NEW Achieve for *Microeconomics*

Engage Every Student

Achieve is a comprehensive set of interconnected teaching and assessment tools. It incorporates the most effective elements from Macmillan's market-leading solutions in a single, easy-to-use platform. Our resources were co-designed with instructors and students, using a foundation of learning research and rigorous testing.

Everything You Need in a Single Learning Path

Achieve is an online learning system that supports students and instructors at every step, from the first point of contact with new content to demonstrating mastery of concepts and skills. Powerful resources including an integrated e-book, robust homework, and a wealth of interactives create an extraordinary learning resource for students.

Learning Objectives Provide Powerful Insights

Every asset you can assign in Achieve is tagged to a learning objective. Insights and reporting help instructors and students understand how they are performing against objectives, enabling more efficient and effective interventions.

PRE-CLASS

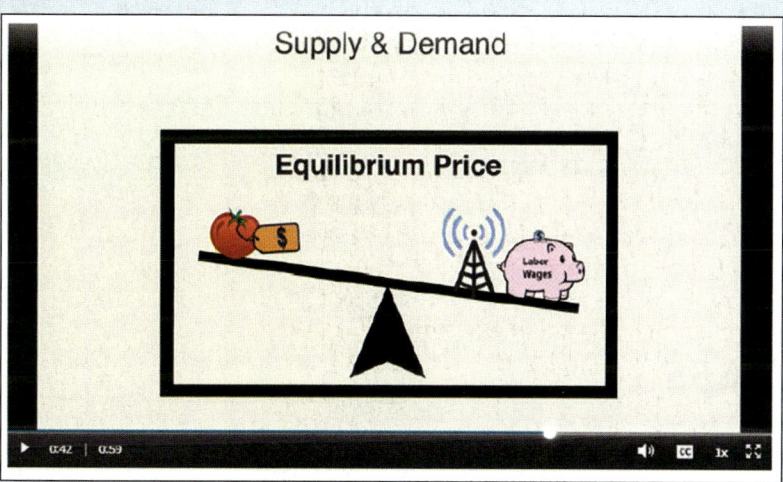

▲ **Pre-Class Tutorials with Bridge Questions** Developed by two pioneers in active-learning methods—Eric Chiang, Florida Atlantic University, and José Vazquez, University of Illinois at Urbana-Champaign—pre-class tutorials foster basic understanding of core economic concepts before students ever set foot in class. Students watch pre-lecture videos and complete bridge questions that prepare them to engage in class. Instructors receive data about student comprehension that can inform the lecture preparation.

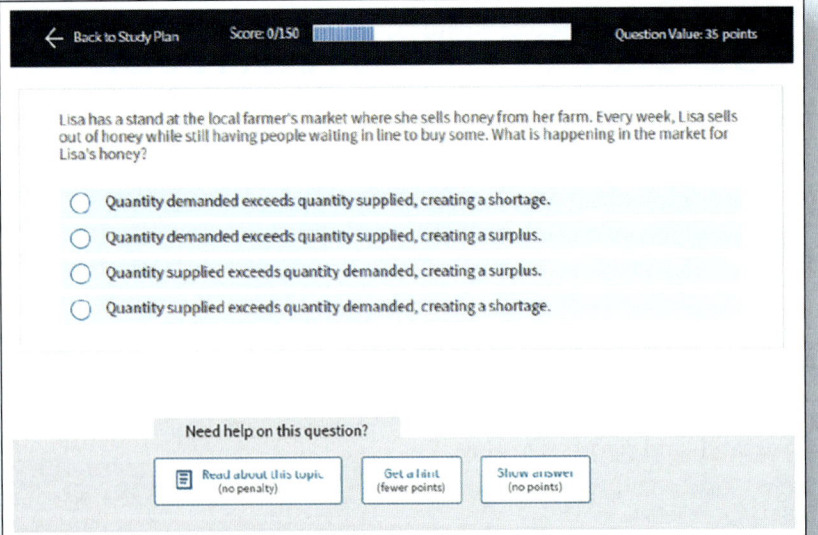

◀ LearningCurve Adaptive Quizzing With a game-like interface, this popular and effective quizzing engine offers students a low-stakes way to brush up on concepts and help identify knowledge gaps. Questions are linked to relevant e-book sections, providing both the incentive to read and a framework for an efficient reading experience.

IN-CLASS

▶ Instructor Activity Guides The guides provide instructors with a structured plan to facilitate an activity that encourages student engagement in both face-to-face and remote learning courses. Each guide is based on a single topic and allows students to participate through questions, group work, presentations, and/or simulations. The guide displays the activity type, estimated prep and class time, implementation instructions, suggestions for remote implementation where applicable, and Learning Objectives and Bloom's level for ease of use. Our Instructor Activity Guides encourage engagement from a Pre-Class Reflection question to prime student interest and offer follow-up iClicker questions to measure comprehension.

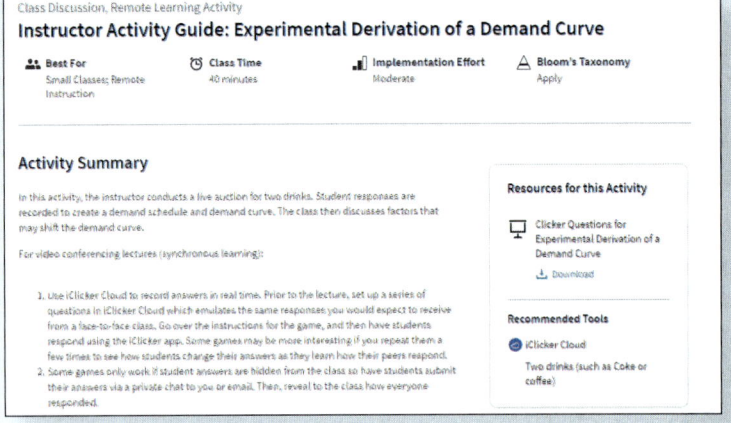

POST-CLASS

Interactive E-Book The Achieve e-book allows students to highlight and take notes; instructors can choose to assign sections of the e-book as part of their course assignments. The e-book includes step-by-step graphs for complex figures.

Step-by-Step Graphs Available in the e-book, step-by-step graphs mirror how an instructor constructs graphs in the classroom. By breaking down the process into its components, these graphs create more manageable "chunks" for students to understand each step of the process.

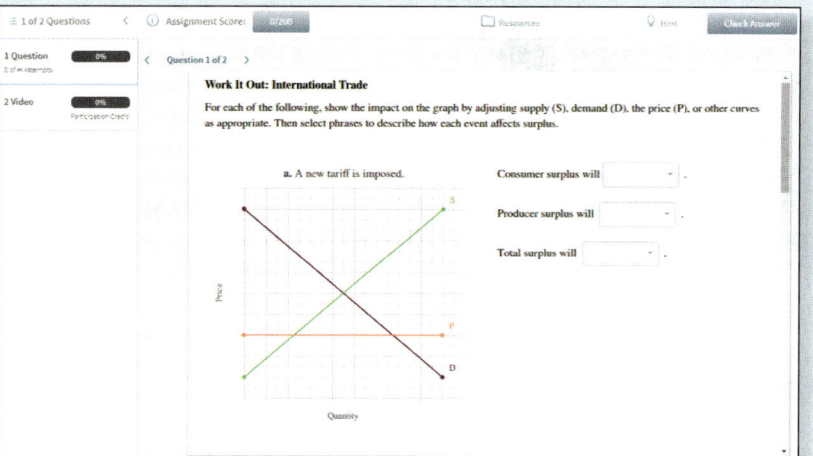

◀ Work It Out These skill-building activities pair sample end-of-chapter problems with targeted feedback and video explanations to help students solve problems step by step. This approach allows students to work independently, tests their comprehension of concepts, and prepares them for class and exams.

▶ End-of-Chapter Questions Developed by economists active in the classroom, these multistep questions are adapted from problems found in the text. Each problem is paired with rich feedback for incorrect and correct responses that guide students through the process of problem solving. These questions also feature our user-friendly graphing tool, designed so students focus entirely on economics and not on how to use the application.

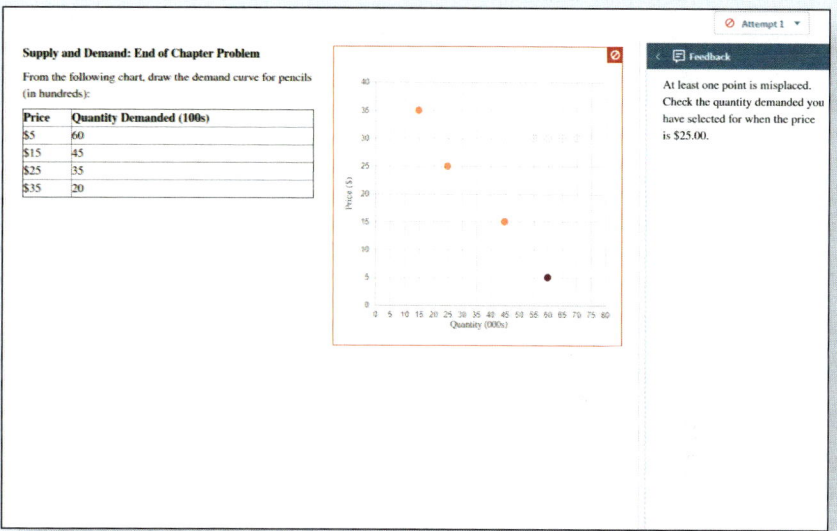

EconoFact Analysis Macmillan Learning has partnered with EconoFact to bring incisive and accessible analysis of current economic and policy trends into the economics classroom. The EconoFact Network provides even-handed and timely analysis of economic issues drawing on relevant data, historical experience, and well-regarded economic frameworks presented in the form of a short memo. In Achieve, instructors can access in-class activity guides to help integrate the memos into their own lectures. Instructors can also access and assign assessment on each memo that starts with basic reading comprehension and builds up to applying the analytical tools students have learned in their course to the economic or policy issue covered in the memo.

Homework Curated homework problems feature algorithmically generated variables and our user-friendly graphing tool. These problems are multistep with a variety of answer inputs—each with detailed and targeted feedback specific to that answer.

Practice Quizzes Designed to be used as a study tool, these quizzes feature questions from the Test Bank and allow for multiple attempts as students familiarize themselves with content.

Powerful Support for Instructors

Test Bank This comprehensive Test Bank contains multiple-choice and short-answer questions to help instructors assess students' comprehension, interpretation, and ability to synthesize.

Lecture Slides These brief, interactive, and visually interesting slides are designed to hold students' attention in class with graphics and animations demonstrating key concepts and real-world examples.

Clicker Slides These slides contain questions to incorporate active learning in the classroom. Students can participate by using the iClicker app on their smartphone or laptop.

iClicker Integration With Achieve's seamless integration with iClicker, you can help any student participate—in the classroom or virtually. iClicker's attendance feature gets students in class, then instructors can choose from flexible polling and quizzing options to engage,

check understanding, and get feedback from students in real time. iClicker also allows students to participate using laptops, mobile devices, or iClicker remotes—whichever each student prefers. Additionally, we offer Instructor Activity Guides and book-specific iClicker question slides within Achieve to make the most out of your class time. It's no surprise that over a decade after being founded by educators, iClicker still leads the market. And thousands of instructors continue to give every student a voice with our simple, award-winning student engagement solutions.

Instructor's Resource Manual The Instructor's Resource Manual offers instructors teaching materials and tips to enhance the classroom experience, along with chapter objectives, outlines, and a breakdown of the large library of MRU videos.

Solutions Manual The Solutions Manual contains detailed solutions to all end-of-chapter problems from the textbook.

Gradebook Assignment scores are collected into a comprehensive gradebook providing instructors' reporting on individuals and overall course performance.

LMS Integration LMS Integration is included so that all students' scores in Achieve can easily integrate into a school's learning management system and that an instructor's gradebook and roster are always in sync.

Customer Support Our Achieve Client Success Specialist Team—dedicated platform experts—provides collaboration, software expertise, and consulting to tailor each course to fit your instructional goals and student needs. Start with a demo at a time that works for you to learn more about how to set up your customized course. Talk to your sales representative or visit https://www.macmillanlearning.com/college/ca/contact-us/training-and-demos for more information.

Pricing and bundling options are available at the Macmillan student store: store.macmillanlearning.com/

WHAT'S NEW IN THIS EDITION?

There are 44 new opening stories, Business Cases, and Economics in Action applications in this edition—fully one-third of these stories are new, ensuring that the Fourth Edition is truly current and relevant. Many other stories have been updated and refreshed.

Rawpixel.com/Shutterstock

7 New Opening Stories

Mastering Textbook Economics
A Bronx Tale
"Shine Bright Like a Diamond"
Deflating the Bread Dough
The Food Court of Canada
Free Medication for Ontario's Youth
Extreme Weather

Michael Nagle/Bloomberg/Getty Images

9 New Business Cases

Ticket Prices and Music's Reigning Couple
A Market Disruptor Gets Disrupted by the Market
A Welcome Tax Hike: Microsoft Raises Its Internal Carbon Tax
The Rise of the Machine at Amazon
Retail Wars: Big Box Stores in the Age of Amazon
Harry's and the Dollar Shave Club Nick the Profits of Schick and Gillette
Xcel Energy Goes for a Win-Win
Saving the "Beast": Ecotourism Protects the Jaguars of Brazil
Walmart Revolutionizes Its Labour Practices

Smileus/Shutterstock

28 New Economics in Action Applications

The Cost of Marriage: China's One-Child Policy Creates Millions of Lonely Bachelors
Wait, Then Hurry Up, and Wait Again
When Economists Agree
The Plunging Cost of Solar Panels
Holy Guacamole
Is Facebook Really Free?
The Rise and Fall of the Unpaid Intern
How Price Controls in Venezuela Proved Disastrous
A Global Commodities Glut
The China Shock
The Steel Tariffs of 2018–2019
Trade War, What Is It Good For?
In Praise of Hard Deadlines
How the Sharing Economy Reduces Fixed Cost
Pay-for-Delay Runs Out of Time
A Global Pork Shortage Hits Chinese Diners Hard
Are Antitrust Policy Makers Behind the Digital Times?
Is It a Beer-opoly or Not?
The Case Against Chocolate Producers Melts
The Ups and Downs of a Cartel: OPEC Hits the Skids on U.S. Shale Oil
The Price Wars of Christmas: Amazon and Walmart Slug It Out
Over 3,500 Economists Agree: Tax Greenhouse Gas Emissions
Canadian Infrastructure Is "At Risk"
Saving the Oceans with ITQs
Welfare State Programs and Poverty Rates in the Great Recession 2008–2010
The Not-So Melancholy Danes
Marginal Productivity and the Minimum Wage Puzzle
The Real Housewives of the United States

MICROECONOMICS

MICROECONOMICS

Fourth Canadian Edition

Paul Krugman
Graduate Center of the City University of New York

Robin Wells

Iris Au
University of Toronto, Scarborough

Jack Parkinson
University of Toronto, Scarborough

worth publishers
Macmillan Learning
New York

Senior Vice President, Social Sciences: **Charles Linsmeier**

Program Director, Social Sciences: **Shani Fisher**

Senior Executive Program Manager: **Simon Glick**

Senior Development Editor: **Lukia Kliossis**

Director of Media Editorial and Assessment, Social Sciences: **Noel Hohnstine**

Senior Assessment Editor: **Joshua Hill**

Media Editor: **Stephany Harrington**

Assistant Editor: **Amanda Gaglione**

Marketing Manager: **Clay Bolton**

Marketing Assistant: **Steven Huang**

Director, Content Management Enhancement: **Tracey Kuehn**

Senior Managing Editor: **Lisa Kinne**

Senior Content Project Manager: **Martha Emry**

Content Project Manager: **Jogender Taneja, Lumina Datamatics, Inc.**

Director of Design, Content Management: **Diana Blume**

Design Services Manager: **Natasha A. S. Wolfe**

Interior Design: **Lumina Datamatics, Inc.**

Senior Design Manager and Cover Design: **John Callahan**

Illustrations: **Network Graphics**

Illustration Coordinator: **Janice Donnola**

Executive Permissions Editor: **Cecilia Varas**

Assistant Director, Process Workflow: **Susan Wein**

Senior Workflow Project Manager: **Paul Rohloff**

Production Supervisor: **Lawrence Guerra**

Media Project Manager: **Jason Perkins**

Composition: **Lumina Datamatics, Inc.**

Printing and Binding: **LSC Communications**

See page xxx for cover credits information.
Page xxx is an extension of this copyright page.

ISBN-13: 978-1-319-24531-3
ISBN-10: 1-319-24531-5

Library of Congress Control Number: 2020943048

Printed in the United States of America

1   2   3   4   5   6   25   24   23   22   21   20

Worth Publishers
One New York Plaza
Suite 4600
New York, NY 10004-1562
www.macmillanlearning.com

Engaging Students in the Study of *Microeconomics*

We are committed to the belief that students learn best from a complete textbook program built around narratives, steeped in real life and current events, with a strong emphasis on global matters and with proven technology that supports student success.

Narrative Approach

This is a textbook built around narratives and stories, many pulled from real life. In every chapter, stories are used to teach core concepts and motivate learning. We believe that the best way to introduce concepts and reinforce them is through memorable, real-world stories; students simply relate more easily to them.

Global Focus

This book is unrivalled in the attention paid to global matters. We have thoroughly integrated an international perspective into the text, in the numerous applications, cases, and stories and, of course, in the data-based Global Comparison feature.

Technology That Builds Success

Microeconomics is not just a textbook. With Achieve, it has evolved to become a complete program with interactive features designed and built to extend the goals of the text. This program encourages even stronger student engagement, mastery of the material, and success in the course.

What's New in the Sixth Edition?

Technology that offers the best value and price. Because students' needs are changing, our most powerful learning option is now our most affordable. Achieve is a new digital solution that brings all of the best aspects of Krugman/Wells and Macmillan's digital resources together in one place. Built on best practices in learning science, Achieve provides students with robust tools to succeed in economics while giving instructors insights into their students' understanding and performance.

Current events framed by the world's best communicators of economics. No other text stays as fresh as this one. This edition includes essential coverage of the global effects of the coronavirus pandemic. For this edition, we've also added cutting-edge online features, including EconoFact Analysis with memos and Bloomberg Analysis with videos. These activities pair journalistic takes on pressing issues with questions based on Bloom's taxonomy. This complements the text's unparalleled coverage of current topics: sustainability, the economic impact of technology, pressing policy debates, and much more.

A richer commitment to broadening students' understanding of the global economy. With unparalleled insight and clarity, the authors use their hallmark narrative approach to take students outside of the classroom and into our global world, starting in Chapter 1 with a new principle on how increases in the economy's potential lead to economic growth over time. To reflect our rapidly changing world, there is an expanded section on market power and the digital economy and an incisive new look at externalities.

About the Authors

PAUL KRUGMAN, recipient of the 2008 Nobel Memorial Prize in Economic Sciences, is a faculty member of the Graduate Center of the City University of New York, associated with the Luxembourg Income Study, which tracks and analyzes income inequality around the world. Prior to that, he taught at Princeton University for 14 years. He received his BA from Yale and his PhD from MIT. Before Princeton, he taught at Yale, Stanford, and MIT. He also spent a year on the staff of the U.S. Council of Economic Advisers in 1982–1983. His research has included pathbreaking work on international trade, economic geography, and currency crises. In 1991, Krugman received the American Economic Association's John Bates Clark medal. In addition to his teaching and academic research, Krugman writes extensively for nontechnical audiences. He is a regular op-ed columnist for the *New York Times*. His best-selling trade books include *End This Depression Now!*, *The Return of Depression Economics and the Crisis of 2008*, a history of recent economic troubles and their implications for economic policy, and *The Conscience of a Liberal*, a study of the political economy of economic inequality and its relationship with political polarization from the Gilded Age to the present. His earlier books, *Peddling Prosperity* and *The Age of Diminished Expectations*, have become modern classics.

ROBIN WELLS was a Lecturer and Researcher in Economics at Princeton University. She received her BA from the University of Chicago and her PhD from the University of California at Berkeley; she then did postdoctoral work at MIT. She has taught at the University of Michigan, the University of Southampton (United Kingdom), Stanford, and MIT.

Ligaya Franklin

IRIS AU is an Associate Professor, Teaching Stream in Economics at the University of Toronto Scarborough (UTSC). She received her BA, MA, and PhD from Simon Fraser University. She taught at Simon Fraser University and Kwantlen University College (now known as Kwantlen Polytechnic University) before joining UTSC. Currently, she teaches introductory and intermediate macroeconomics, international finance, international financial management, economics of public policy, and topics on financial crises on a regular basis.

Bradley T. Smith

JACK PARKINSON is an Associate Professor, Teaching Stream in Economics at the University of Toronto Scarborough (UTSC). He received his Hons. BA from Western University and his MA and PhD from the University of Toronto. He has worked as a corporate tax policy analyst for the Ontario Ministry of Finance while teaching during his lunchtime or evenings. Over the past 20 years he has taught on all three campuses of the University of Toronto. Currently, he teaches introductory microeconomics, intermediate and advanced macroeconomics, money and banking, economics of organization, and applied economic statistics.

Vision and Story of *Microeconomics*

This is a book about economics as the study of what people do and how they interact, a study very much informed by real-world experience. These words, this spirit, have served as a guiding principle for us in every edition.

FROM PAUL AND ROBIN

While we were driven to write this book by many small ideas about particular aspects of economics, we also had one big idea: an economics textbook should be built around narratives, many of them pulled from real life, and it should never lose sight of the fact that economics is, in the end, a set of stories about what people do.

Many of the stories economists tell take the form of models—for whatever else they are, economic models are stories about how the world works. But we believe that student understanding of and appreciation for models are greatly enhanced if they are presented, as much as possible, in the context of stories about the real world that both illustrate economic concepts and touch on the concerns we all face living in a world shaped by economic forces. In 2020, the interplay between economics and our everyday lives became clearer than ever as the coronavirus pandemic affected us all, worldwide.

You'll find a rich array of stories in every chapter, in the chapter openers, Economics in Actions, For Inquiring Minds, Global Comparisons, and Business Cases. As always, we include many new stories and update others. We also integrate an international perspective throughout, more extensively than ever before. We have a new focus on how increases in the economy's potential leads to long-run growth, highlighted as a principle in Chapter 1 then throughout the text. An overview of the types of narrative-based features in the text is on p. xi.

We also include pedagogical features that reinforce learning. For example, each major section ends with three related elements devised with the student in mind: (1) the Economics in Actions: a real-world application to help students achieve a fuller understanding of concepts they just read about; (2) a Quick Review of key ideas in list form; and (3) Check Your Understanding self-test questions with answers at the back of the book. Our thought-provoking end-of-chapter problems are another strong feature. The Work It Out feature appears in all end-of-chapter problem sets, offering students online tutorials that guide them step-by-step through solving key problems. Discovering Data exercises offer students the opportunity to use interactive graphs to analyze interesting economic questions. An overview of the text's tools for learning is on p. xvii.

Students also benefit from Achieve, where all of our impressive digital resources are found in one platform. These include several exciting new digital features, such as step-by-step graphs and EconoFact Analysis, as well as adaptive quizzing, tutorials, Bloomberg videos, graphing questions, and data-analysis questions. All have been devised with the goal of supporting instructor teaching and student learning in principles of economics courses.

We hope your experience with this text is a good one. Thank you for introducing it into your classroom.

Vision and Story of *Microeconomics*

FROM IRIS AND JACK

We are just as excited to be working on the Fourth Canadian Edition as we were several years ago when we initially adapted the latest edition of Paul and Robin's wonderful book for the Canadian market. The U.S. edition of the text, which started out as a top-tier product, has only improved with each new edition, and we hope that the Canadian edition follows in its footsteps.

We believe the narrative approach adopted by Paul and Robin is an excellent way to expose students to the beauty of economics and its power to explain and understand the world we all live in.

Many of the narratives contained in the chapter opening stories, Economics in Action, Global Comparisons, and Business Cases have been altered, sometimes significantly, so as to infuse them with up-to-date content relevant to Canadians. Of course Canadians, living in an open economy that is quite dependent on trade, are used to thinking about global economic issues and linkages. With that in mind, a few of the narratives have not changed much from what appeared in the sixth U.S. edition. Throughout we have taken great care whenever altering the text so as to maintain the quality of the underlying narratives.

Chapter 7 in particular was revised to deal specifically with the major types of taxes collected by different levels of government in Canada. Chapter 18, which provides a discussion of the welfare state, covers the material from a Canadian perspective. The chapter also covers our health care system, comparing it to other systems around the world. We have revised the Canadian examples to reflect the latest developments in our economy.

We are extremely pleased to be able to do our part to bring these narratives to a Canadian audience. If, after reading this text, some students decide that economics is really interesting and go on to take additional economics courses, we would be happy. But most importantly, we hope that all students feel this text greatly enhances and assists their study of economics.

Engaging Students with a Narrative Approach

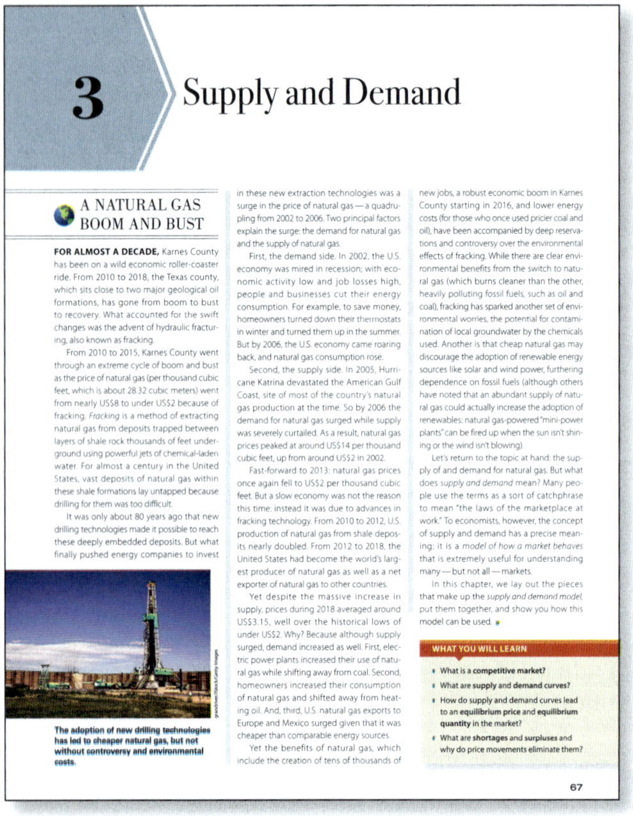
3 Supply and Demand

A NATURAL GAS BOOM AND BUST

FOR ALMOST A DECADE, Karnes County has been on a wild economic roller-coaster ride. From 2010 to 2018, the Texas county, which sits close to two major geological oil formations, has gone from boom to bust to recovery. What accounted for the swift changes was the advent of hydraulic fracturing, also known as fracking.

From 2010 to 2015, Karnes County went through an extreme cycle of boom and bust as the price of natural gas (per thousand cubic feet, which is about 28.32 cubic meters) went from nearly US$8 to under US$2 because of fracking. *Fracking* is a method of extracting natural gas from deposits trapped between layers of shale rock thousands of feet underground using powerful jets of chemical-laden water. For almost a century in the United States, vast deposits of natural gas within these shale formations lay untapped because drilling for them was too difficult.

It was only about 80 years ago that new drilling technologies made it possible to reach these deeply embedded deposits. But what finally pushed energy companies to invest in these new extraction technologies was a surge in the price of natural gas—a quadrupling from 2002 to 2006. Two principal factors explain the surge: the demand for natural gas and the supply of natural gas.

First, the demand side. In 2002, the U.S. economy was mired in recession; with economic activity low and job losses high, people and businesses cut their energy consumption. For example, to save money, homeowners turned down their thermostats in winter and turned them up in the summer. But by 2006, the U.S. economy came roaring back, and natural gas consumption rose.

Second, the supply side. In 2005, Hurricane Katrina devastated the American Gulf Coast, site of most of the country's natural gas production at the time. So by 2006 the demand for natural gas surged while supply was severely curtailed. As a result, natural gas prices peaked at around US$14 per thousand cubic feet, up from around US$2 in 2002.

Fast-forward to 2013: natural gas prices once again fell to US$2 per thousand cubic feet. But a slow economy was not the reason this time: instead it was due to advances in fracking technology. From 2010 to 2012, U.S. production of natural gas from shale deposits nearly doubled. From 2012 to 2018, the United States had become the world's largest producer of natural gas as well as a net exporter of natural gas to other countries.

Yet despite the massive increase in supply, prices during 2018 averaged around US$3.15, well over the historical lows of under US$2. Why? Because although supply surged, demand increased as well. First, electric power plants increased their use of natural gas while shifting away from coal. Second, homeowners increased their consumption of natural gas and shifted away from heating oil. And, third, U.S. natural gas exports to Europe and Mexico surged given that it was cheaper than comparable energy sources.

Yet the benefits of natural gas, which include the creation of tens of thousands of new jobs, a robust economic boom in Karnes County starting in 2016, and lower energy costs (for those who once used pricier coal and oil), have been accompanied by deep reservations and controversy over the environmental effects of fracking. While there are clear environmental benefits from the switch to natural gas (which burns cleaner than the other, heavily polluting fossil fuels, such as oil and coal), fracking has sparked another set of environmental worries, the potential for contamination of local groundwater by the chemicals used. Another is that cheap natural gas may discourage the adoption of renewable energy sources like solar and wind power, furthering dependence on fossil fuels (although others have noted that an abundant supply of natural gas could actually increase the adoption of renewables: natural gas-powered "mini-power plants" can be fired up when the sun isn't shining or the wind isn't blowing).

Let's return to the topic at hand: the supply of and demand for natural gas. But what does *supply and demand* mean? Many people use the terms as a sort of catchphrase to mean "the laws of the marketplace at work." To economists, however, the concept of supply and demand has a precise meaning: it is a *model of how a market behaves* that is extremely useful for understanding many—but not all—markets.

In this chapter, we lay out the pieces that make up the *supply and demand model*, put them together, and show you how this model can be used.

The adoption of new drilling technologies has led to cheaper natural gas, but not without controversy and environmental costs.

WHAT YOU WILL LEARN

- What is a **competitive market?**
- What are **supply and demand curves?**
- How do supply and demand curves lead to an **equilibrium price** and **equilibrium quantity** in the market?
- What are **shortages** and **surpluses** and why do price movements eliminate them?

67

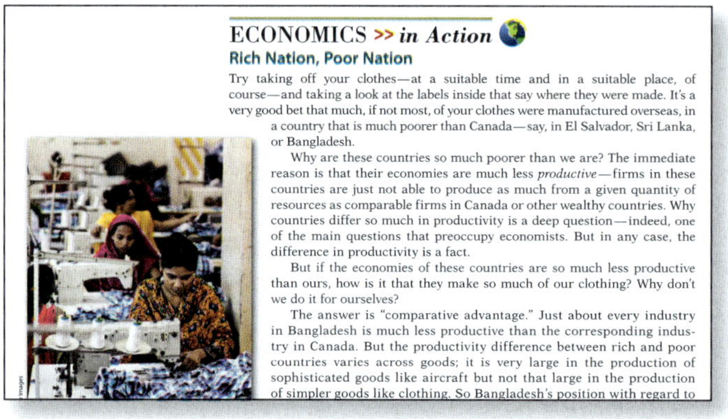
ECONOMICS >> in Action

Rich Nation, Poor Nation

Try taking off your clothes—at a suitable time and in a suitable place, of course—and taking a look at the labels inside that say where they were made. It's a very good bet that much, if not most, of your clothes were manufactured overseas, in a country that is much poorer than Canada—say, in El Salvador, Sri Lanka, or Bangladesh.

Why are these countries so much poorer than we are? The immediate reason is that their economies are much less *productive*—firms in these countries are just not able to produce as much from a given quantity of resources as comparable firms in Canada or other wealthy countries. Why countries differ so much in productivity is a deep question—indeed, one of the main questions that preoccupy economists. But in any case, the difference in productivity is a fact.

But if the economies of these countries are so much less productive than ours, how is it that they make so much of our clothing? Why don't we do it for ourselves?

The answer is "comparative advantage." Just about every industry in Bangladesh is much less productive than the corresponding industry in Canada. But the productivity difference between rich and poor countries varies across goods; it is very large in the production of sophisticated goods like aircraft but not that large in the production of simpler goods like clothing. So Bangladesh's position with regard to

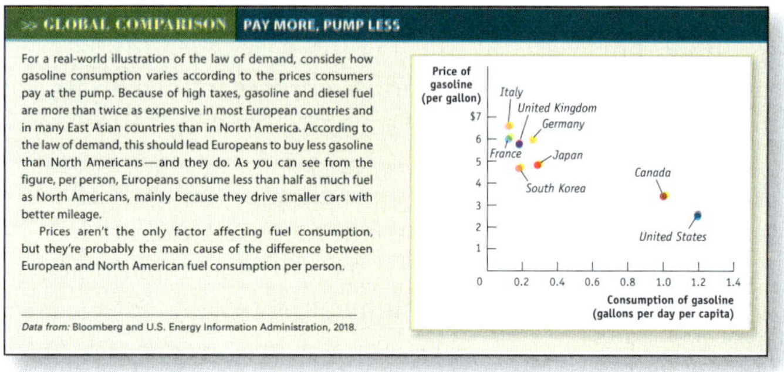
GLOBAL COMPARISON PAY MORE, PUMP LESS

For a real-world illustration of the law of demand, consider how gasoline consumption varies according to the prices consumers pay at the pump. Because of high taxes, gasoline and diesel fuel are more than twice as expensive in most European countries and in many East Asian countries than in North America. According to the law of demand, this should lead Europeans to buy less gasoline than North Americans—and they do. As you can see from the figure, per person, Europeans consume less than half as much fuel as North Americans, mainly because they drive smaller cars with better mileage.

Prices aren't the only factor affecting fuel consumption, but they're probably the main cause of the difference between European and North American fuel consumption per person.

Data from: Bloomberg and U.S. Energy Information Administration, 2018.

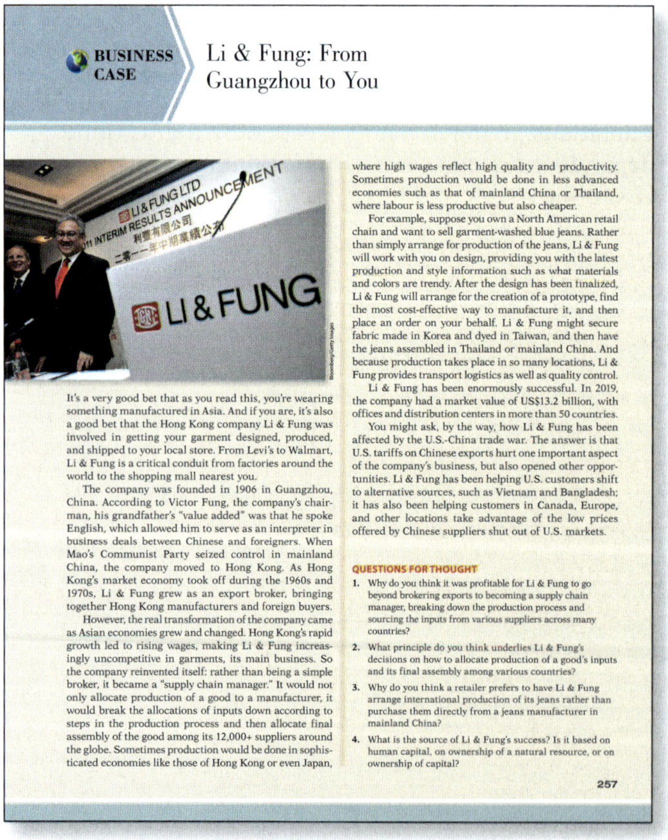
BUSINESS CASE

Li & Fung: From Guangzhou to You

It's a very good bet that as you read this, you're wearing something manufactured in Asia. And if you are, it's also a good bet that the Hong Kong company Li & Fung was involved in getting your garment designed, produced, and shipped to your local store. From Levi's to Walmart, Li & Fung is a critical conduit from factories around the world to the shopping mall nearest you.

The company was founded in 1906 in Guangzhou, China. According to Victor Fung, the company's chairman, his grandfather's "value added" was that he spoke English, which allowed him to serve as an interpreter in business deals between Chinese and foreigners. When Mao's Communist Party seized control in mainland China, the company moved to Hong Kong. As Hong Kong's market economy took off during the 1960s and 1970s, Li & Fung grew as an export broker, bringing together Hong Kong manufacturers and foreign buyers.

However, the real transformation of the company came as Asian economies grew and changed. Hong Kong's rapid growth led to rising wages, making Li & Fung increasingly uncompetitive in garments, its main business. So the company reinvented itself: rather than being a simple broker, it became a "supply chain manager." It would not only allocate production of a good to a manufacturer, it would break the allocations of inputs down according to steps in the production process and then allocate final assembly of the good among its 12,000+ suppliers around the globe. Sometimes production would be done in sophisticated economies like those of Hong Kong or even Japan, where high wages reflect high quality and productivity. Sometimes production would be done in less advanced economies such as that of mainland China or Thailand, where labour is less productive but also cheaper.

For example, suppose you own a North American retail chain and want to sell garment-washed blue jeans. Rather than simply arrange for production of the jeans, Li & Fung will work with you on design, providing you with the latest production and style information such as what materials and colors are trendy. After the design has been finalized, Li & Fung will arrange for the creation of a prototype, find the most cost-effective way to manufacture it, and then place an order on your behalf. Li & Fung might secure fabric made in Korea and dyed in Taiwan, and then have the jeans assembled in Thailand or mainland China. And because production takes place in so many locations, Li & Fung provides transport logistics as well as quality control.

Li & Fung has been enormously successful. In 2019, the company had a market value of US$13.2 billion, with offices and distribution centers in more than 50 countries.

You might ask, by the way, how Li & Fung has been affected by the U.S.-China trade war. The answer is that U.S. tariffs on Chinese exports hurt one important aspect of the company's business, but also opened other opportunities. Li & Fung has been helping U.S. customers shift to alternative sources, such as Vietnam and Bangladesh; it has also been helping customers in Canada, Europe, and other locations take advantage of the low prices offered by Chinese suppliers shut out of U.S. markets.

QUESTIONS FOR THOUGHT

1. Why do you think it was profitable for Li & Fung to go beyond brokering exports to becoming a supply chain manager, breaking down the production process and sourcing the inputs from various suppliers across many countries?
2. What principle do you think underlies Li & Fung's decisions on how to allocate production of a good's inputs and its final assembly among various countries?
3. Why do you think a retailer prefers to have Li & Fung arrange international production of its jeans rather than purchase them directly from a jeans manufacturer in mainland China?
4. What is the source of Li & Fung's success? Is it based on human capital, on ownership of a natural resource, or on ownership of capital?

257

- To engage students, every chapter begins with a compelling story. **What You Will Learn** questions help students focus on key concepts in the chapter.
- So students can immediately see economic concepts applied in the real world, **Economics in Action** applications appear throughout chapters.
- To provide students with an international perspective, the **Global Comparison** feature uses data and graphs to illustrate why countries reach different economic outcomes.
- So students can see key economic principles applied to real-life business situations, each chapter concludes with a **Business Case.**

Engaging Students with Effective Tools for Learning

ECONOMICS >> in Action
Trade War, What Is It Good For?

There are, as we've seen, a number of reasons countries sometimes impose tariffs and other restrictions on imports, and these measures often hurt other countries as well as domestic consumers. However, we generally only use the term *trade war* when hurting foreigners isn't a side effect of tariffs, but their purpose—that is, when tariffs are imposed to inflict damage on another country in an attempt to force it to make concessions of some kind.

A classic example is the "chicken war" that broke out between the United States and Europe more than half a century ago. In 1964, the U.S. imposed a 25% tariff on imports of light trucks—a category that today includes most pickups and SUVs. The purpose of the tariff was to put pressure on the European community to eliminate a tariff it had placed on U.S. exports of frozen chicken, which surged with the rise of factory farming. Incredibly, this dispute was never resolved: that 25% tariff remains in place.

Historically, however, trade wars in which countries try to inflict pain have been fairly rare. Before the 1930s, Canada, the United States, and other countries generally ignored the effects of their trade policies on other countries; since World War II trade wars have mostly been prevented by international trade agreements.

That may, however, be changing. Since 2017 the U.S. government has imposed tariffs on a wide variety of goods and trading partners, with the explicit aim of forcing other countries to change their policies, and some of the countries have responded with tariffs of their own that are explicitly meant to cause pain in the U.S.

We have already discussed the steel tariffs the U.S. recently imposed on Canada and Mexico, at least partly intended to force our neighbours into agreeing to revise the North American Free Trade Agreement. Those tariffs, however, pale in significance compared with the 25% tariff the U.S. government imposed on $250 billion worth of Chinese exports in 2019—almost half of what China sells to the United States—with a threat to expand the tariffs to the rest of China's exports unless China meets policy demands that include protecting U.S. intellectual property and reducing China's trade surplus with the United States.

China has, in turn, retaliated by imposing tariffs on U.S. products, especially agricultural goods, in a clear attempt to raise the political costs of current U.S. policy, for example by hurting U.S. farmers.

What is happening now, in other words, really is a trade war in the classic sense. At the time of writing it was unclear when or how this trade war might be resolved. And the case of the "chicken war" of 1964 suggests that the effects of the current trade conflict might last for a very long time.

In 2019, the United States and China engaged in a classic trade war by levying tariffs on each other's exports.

>> Quick Review

- The three major justifications for trade protection are national security, job creation, and the infant industry argument.

- Despite the deadweight losses, import protections are often imposed because groups representing import-competing industries are more influential than groups of consumers.

- To further trade liberalization, countries engage in **international trade agreements.** An important purpose of these agreements is to head off the possibility of **trade wars.** Some agreements are among a small number of countries, such as the **North American Free Trade Agreement (NAFTA)** and the **European Union (EU).** The

- To reinforce learning, sections within chapters conclude with three tools: an application of key concepts in the **Economics in Action;** a **Quick Review** of key concepts; and a comprehension check with **Check Your Understanding** questions. Solutions for these questions appear at the back of the text.

- **Pitfalls** teach students to identify and avoid common misconceptions about economic concepts.

- End-of-chapter **Work It Out** skill-building problems provide interactive step-by-step help with solving select problems from the text.

PITFALLS

DEMAND VERSUS QUANTITY DEMANDED

When economists say "an increase in demand," they mean a rightward shift of the demand curve, and when they say "a decrease in demand," they mean a leftward shift of the demand curve — that is, when they're being careful.

In ordinary speech most of us, professional economists included, use the word *demand* casually. For example, an economist might say "the demand for air travel has doubled over the past 20 years, partly because of falling airfares" when they really mean that the *quantity demanded* has doubled.

It's OK to be a bit sloppy in ordinary conversation. But when you're doing economic analysis, it's important to make the distinction between changes in the quantity demanded, which involve movements along a demand curve, and shifts of the demand curve (see Figure 3-3). Sometimes students end up writing something like this: "If demand increases, the price will go up, but that will lead to a fall in demand, which pushes the price down . . ." and then go around in circles.

By making a clear distinction between changes in *demand*, which mean shifts of the demand curve, and changes in *quantity demanded*, which means movement along the demand curve, you can avoid a lot of confusion.

WORK IT OUT

20. The accompanying table gives the annual Canadian demand and supply schedules for pickup trucks.

Price of truck	Quantity of trucks demanded (millions)	Quantity of trucks supplied (millions)
$20,000	20	14
25,000	18	15
30,000	16	16
35,000	14	17
40,000	12	18

a. Plot the demand and supply curves using these schedules. Indicate the equilibrium price and quantity on your diagram.

b. Suppose the tires used on pickup trucks are found to be defective. What would you expect to happen in the market for pickup trucks? Show this on your diagram.

c. Suppose that Transport Canada imposes costly regulations on manufacturers that cause them to reduce supply by one-third at any given price. Calculate and plot the new supply schedule and indicate the new equilibrium price and quantity on your diagram. ◼

Acknowledgements

We must thank the many people at Worth Publishers for their work on this edition: Chuck Linsmeier, Shani Fisher, Simon Glick, Lukia Kliossis, Stephany Harrington, Amanda Gaglione, and Joshua Hill in editorial. We thank Clay Bolton and Travis Long for their enthusiastic and tireless advocacy of this book. Many thanks to the incredible production, design, photo, and media production teams: Tracey Kuehn, Lisa Kinne, Susan Wein, Paul Rohloff, Martha Emry, Diana Blume, Natasha Wolfe, Cecilia Varas, Richard Fox, and Jason Perkins.

We are also indebted to the following reviewers for their suggestions and advice on the Sixth American Edition:

Brandon Addison, *Providence Christian College*

Gabriel Azarlian, *California State University, Northridge*

Nestor Azcona, *Providence College*

Christopher Blake, *Oxford College of Emory University*

Bruce Brown, *Santa Monica College*

Terry Brownschidle, *Rider University*

Don Carlson, *Williams College*

Humza Chohan, *Coastline Community College*

Brandyn Churchill, *Vanderbilt University*

Charlie Cowell, *Western Iowa Tech Community College*

Meredith Crane, *Cincinnati State Technical & Community College*

Finley Edwards, *Baylor University*

Wayne Edwards, *University of Vermont*

Cynthia Foreman, *Clark College*

Julie Gonzalez, *University of California, Santa Cruz*

Robert Gordon, *Northwestern University*

Timothy Haase, *Ramapo College of New Jersey*

Niree Kodaverdian, *Pomona College*

Janet Koscianski, *Shippensburg University of Pennsylvania*

Zhen Li, *Albion College*

Lok Man Lo, *San Francisco State University*

Mark Miller, *Ramapo College of New Jersey*

Margaret Morgan-Davie, *Hamilton College*

Michael Nichols, *Baker College of Jackson*

Sanjay Paul, *Elizabethtown College*

Michael Polcen, *Northern Virginia Community College, Loudon*

Collin Rabe, *University of Richmond*

Edward Raupp, *Great Bay Community College*

Jack Reardon, *University of Wisconsin, Eau Claire*

Jeff Sarbaum, *University of North Carolina, Greensboro*

Angela Seidel, *St. Francis University*

Ali Shahnawaz, *California State University, Chico*

Jeffrey Stewart, *University of Dayton*

John Tarchick, *Wayne State University*

John Vahaly, *University of Louisville*

Yongqing Wang, *University of Wisconsin, Milwaukee at Waukesha*

Anne M. Wenzel, *San Francisco State University*

Deborah Wright, *Southeastern Community College*

Luo Yilan, *Cerritos College*

We would also like thank the following reviewers for their input on the Fourth Canadian Edition:

Kam Chu, *Memorial University*

Phil Ghayad, *Dawson College*

Gubhinder Kundhi, *Memorial University*

Moshe Lander, *Concordia University, Sir George Williams*

Tom Porter, *University of Saskatchewan*

Terri Rizzo, *Lakehead University*

Medoune Seck, *John Abbott College*

Organization of This Book

To help plan your course, we've listed what we consider to be core and optional chapters, with descriptions about the coverage in each.

Optional

Introduction: An Engine for Growth and Discovery
Initiates students into the study of economics using China's Pearl River Delta as the motivating story. Includes basic terms and explains the difference between microeconomics and macroeconomics.

Core

1. First Principles
Outlines 12 principles underlying the study of economics: principles of individual choice, interaction between individuals, and economy-wide interaction.

2. Economic Models: Trade-offs and Trade
Employs two economic models—the production possibilities frontier and comparative advantage—as an introduction to gains from trade and international comparisons. Also introduces the circular-flow diagram.

Optional

2 Appendix: Graphs in Economics
A comprehensive review of graphing and math skills for students who would find this background helpful.

Core

3. Supply and Demand
Covers the essentials of supply, demand, market equilibrium, surplus, and shortage.

Optional

3 Appendix: The Algebra of Demand, Supply, and Equilibrium
Offers a mathematical approach to the concepts of demand and supply, using algebra to determine the equilibrium price and quantity.

Core

4. Consumer and Producer Surplus
Introduces market efficiency, the ways markets fail, the role of prices as signals, and property rights.

5. Price Controls and Quotas: Meddling with Markets
Covers market interventions and their consequences: price and quantity controls, inefficiency, and deadweight loss.

6. Elasticity
Introduces the various elasticity measures and explains how to calculate and interpret them, including price, cross-price and income elasticity of demand, and price elasticity of supply.

Optional

6 Appendix: The Algebra of Elasticity
Offers a mathematical approach to the various elasticity resources.

Core

7. Taxes
Covers basic tax analysis along with a review of the burden of taxation and considerations of equity versus efficiency. The structure of taxation, tax policy, and public spending are also discussed.

Optional

8. International Trade
An examination of comparative advantage, tariffs and quotas, the politics of trade protection and international trade agreements, and the controversy over imports from low-wage countries. With new coverage of hyperglobalization, the EU and Brexit, outsourcing, and reshoring.

Core

9. Decision Making by Individuals and Firms
Focuses on marginal analysis ("either–or" and "how much" decisions) and the concept of sunk cost, with detailed coverage of behavioural economics, showing the limitations of rational thought.

Optional

9 Appendix: How to Make Decisions Involving Time: Understanding Present Value
Expands on the coverage in the chapter by examining why decisions involving time are different and how to make them.

Core

10. The Rational Consumer
Provides a complete treatment of consumer behaviour for those who don't cover indifference curves. Includes the budget line, optimal consumption choice, diminishing marginal utility, and substitution effects.

Optional

10 Appendix: Consumer Preferences and Consumer Choice
Offers detailed treatment for those who wish to cover indifference curves.

Core

11. Behind the Supply Curve: Inputs and Costs
Develops the production function and the various cost measures of the firm, including discussion of the difference between average cost and marginal cost.

Optional

11 Appendix: Inverse Relationships Between Productivity and Cost
A derivation of the relationships between (1) the marginal product of labour and marginal cost and (2) the average product of labour and average cost.

Contents

PART 2 Supply and Demand

Photo Credits

Front Cover

Credits are listed left to right.

First Row: Lobster Fishing: All Canada Photos/Alamy; Cows: Stockbyte/Photodisc; Combines: Teri Virbickis/Getty; Powerlines: Steve Allen/Stockbyte/Getty Images; Paramedic: Granger Wootz/Getty Images

Second Row: Currency exchange: Bankoo/Shutterstock; Baby at doctor's office: FatCamera/Getty; Friends eating burgers: PeopleImages/Getty; Flags: Design Pics Inc/Alamy

Third Row: Robot: iStockphoto/Thinkstock; Depression-era worker: akg-images/The Image Works; Plane factory: Vince Streano/Getty Images; Train: Robert McGouey/Alamy Stock photo; Currency: Lucia Pitter/Shutterstock

Fourth Row: Cargo ship: EvrenKalinbacak/Shutterstock; Construction workers: mikeledray/Shutterstock; Looking through microscope: Tetra Images/AGE Fotostock; Walking dog: Gregory Whitaker/EyeEm/Getty Images; Smoke stacks: iStockphoto/Thinkstock

Fifth Row: Cupcakes: Tobias Titz/AGE Fotostock; Couple shopping for phones: Juice Images/AGE Fotostock; Solar panels: iurii/Shutterstock; Scientist in lab: Kasipat Phonlamai/EyeEm/Getty Images

Sixth Row: Shenzhen at night: zhangyang13576997233/Shutterstock; Busy market: Peter Adams/Getty Images

Back Cover

First Row: Stacked wood: Fedor Selivanov/Shutterstock; Electric car charging: Oscar Bjarnason/Getty Images; Stacked copper wires: Arsel Ozgurdal/Shutterstock; Night traffic: Artens/Shutterstock; Warehouse employee: JulieanneBirch/Getty Images; Soy bean farm: Fotokostic/Shutterstock

Second Row: Engineers: Maskot/Getty Images; Fish: John_Walker/Shutterstock; Recording concert: Wittybear/Shutterstock; Printing U.S. money: matthiashaas/Thinkstock; Graduates: Prasit Rodphan/Shutterstock

Third Row: Fruit stand: Richard A McMillin/Shutterstock; Diamonds: The Adventurer/Shutterstock; Canadian Currency: Feng Yu/Alamy; Shopping outdoors: Peathegee Inc/AGE Fotostock; Fracking: CSP_LonnyGarris/AGE Fotostock

Fourth Row: Sushi: Ipatov/Shutterstock

Introduction: An Engine for Growth and Discovery

A DAY IN THE MEGACITY

LONDON, NEW YORK, AND TOKYO have something in common: they are megacities — huge metropolitan complexes that contain tens of millions of people and are spread over immense tracts of land. While most people are familiar with these megacities, not everyone knows about the biggest of them all: the vast urban complex known as China's Pearl River Delta (the PRD). Roughly the same size as the province of Nova Scotia,

Xinhua/Alamy Stock Photo

Thirty years ago China was very poor with a backward economy. Now it produces sophisticated goods for the world, allowing it to deliver relatively comfortable incomes to many of its people.

the PRD is home to more than 65 million people. Driving across the PRD (as one of the authors has done), with its endless succession of factories, office buildings, and apartment towers, is an unforgettable — and very long — experience.

What are all those people doing? A significant percentage of them are engaged in producing goods for world markets, especially, but by no means only, electronic components: just about every smartphone, tablet, and computer contains components produced in the PRD. But the megacity's residents are consumers as well as producers. While the wage of an average worker in the PRD is relatively low by Canadian standards, overall wages and income are high enough to support a vast retail sector, ranging from mom-and-pop local stores to shops selling expensive luxury goods.

But not so long ago, neither the PRD nor the economic dynamism it embodies was visible. As recently as 1980, 800 million people in China subsisted on less than US$1.50 a day. The average Chinese citizen more or less had enough to eat and a roof over their head, but not much more than that. In fact, the standard of living wasn't much higher than it had been centuries earlier. And from 1959 to 1961, in what is now known as "The Great Leap Backward," the Chinese government got the economy so wrong that millions of Chinese died from man-made famine.

However, in the years since 1980, Chinese incomes have soared more than twentyfold in real terms as the poverty rate (percentage of the population subsisting on less than US$1.90 a day) has fallen from 88% in 1981 to 0.7% in 2015. The rise of the PRD is one chapter of an incredible success story in which hundreds of millions of Chinese have been lifted out of abject poverty over the past few decades. Never in human history have so many seen so much progress.

Although this is a remarkable story, it is not entirely unprecedented. From 1840

to 1910, British workers also experienced a marked rise in their standard of living. And this success was repeated soon afterward in Canada, setting the stage for the high levels of prosperity we now enjoy. Commenting on how English workers were lifted out of poverty, the great economist Alfred Marshall made an observation that is equally relevant for Chinese workers today: "The hope that poverty and ignorance may gradually be extinguished, derives indeed much support from the steady progress of the working classes during the nineteenth century."

These unprecedented sets of events have touched our lives today in a dizzying number of ways. You are using smartphones, tablets, and laptops that are manufactured in the PRD as you pursue a first-rate education in Canada, one of the richest countries in the world.

What can economics say about all of this? Quite a lot, it turns out. What you will learn from this book is how these momentous changes, which lifted hundreds of millions of people out of poverty, are related to a simple, but very important, set of questions involving economics. Among these questions are:

- How does our economic system work? That is, how does it manage to deliver the goods?

- When and why does our economic system sometimes go astray, leading people into counterproductive behaviour?

- Why are there ups and downs in the economy? That is, why does the economy sometimes have a bad year?

- Why is the long run mainly a story of ups rather than downs? That is, why has China, like Great Britain, the United States, and Canada, become much richer over time?

Let's take a look at these questions and offer a brief preview of what you will learn in this book. ●

An **economy** is a system for coordinating society's productive activities.

Economics is the social science that studies the production, distribution, and consumption of goods and services.

A **market economy** is an economy in which decisions about production and consumption are made by individual producers and consumers.

The Invisible Hand

The massive industrial and consumer complex that is today's Pearl River Delta is quite a new creation. As recently as 1980 much of the region was an economic backwater; the nucleus, Shenzhen, was then a small and very poor fishing village. How did this backwater turn into the electronics workshop of the world, making it a dynamic creator of wealth?

To achieve the level of prosperity we have in Canada, a level the average resident of the PRD can only now begin to aspire to, you need a well-functioning system for coordinating productive activities—the activities that create the goods and services people want and get them to the people who want them. That kind of system is what we mean when we talk about the **economy.** And **economics** is the social science that studies the production, distribution, and consumption of goods and services.

An economy succeeds to the extent that it, literally, delivers the goods. And as we've discussed, over the past 30 years the Chinese economy has achieved a spectacular increase in the amount of goods it delivers both to its own citizens and to the rest of the world.

So China's economy must be doing something right, and we might want to compliment the people in charge. But guess what? There isn't anyone in charge—not anymore.

In the 1970s, before the PRD began its incredible rise, China was a *command economy* in which decisions about what factories would produce and what goods would be delivered to households were made by government officials. But experience shows that command economies don't work very well. Producers in command economies like China before 1980 or the Soviet Union before 1991 routinely found themselves unable to produce because they did not have crucial raw materials, or if they succeeded in producing, they found nobody wanted their products. Consumers were often unable to find necessities like toilet paper or milk. Command economies are infamous for long lines at shops. And as we mentioned, from 1959 to 1961, the Chinese government got its command economy terribly wrong, inflicting enormous hardship and causing millions of unnecessary deaths.

In 1978, the Chinese government finally admitted that its economic model wasn't working, and began a remarkable transformation into a **market economy,** one in which production and consumption are the result of decentralized decisions by many firms and individuals. Canada has a market economy. And in today's China there is no central authority telling people what to produce or where to ship it. Each individual producer makes what they think will be most profitable; each consumer buys what they choose. It's important to realize, however, that the Chinese government intervenes in markets much more than the Canadian government does; in particular, while China's government rarely tells producers what to produce, it often tells banks how much to lend and to whom.

If you had never seen a market economy in action, you might imagine that it would be chaotic. After all, nobody is in charge. But market economies are able to coordinate even highly complex activities and reliably provide consumers with the goods and services they want. Indeed, people quite casually trust their lives to the market system: residents of any major city would starve in days if the unplanned yet somehow orderly actions of thousands of businesses did not deliver a steady supply of food. Surprisingly, the unplanned "chaos" of a market economy turns out to be far more orderly than the planning of a command economy. And that's why almost every country in the world—North Korea and Cuba are the only exceptions—has become a market economy.

In 1776, in a famous passage in his book *The Wealth of Nations,* the pioneering Scottish economist Adam Smith wrote about how individuals, in pursuing their own interests, often end up serving the interests of society as a whole. Of a businessman whose pursuit of profit makes the nation wealthier, Smith wrote: "[H]e intends

A booming marketplace in today's China.

only his own gain, and he is in this, as in many other cases, led by an invisible hand to promote an end which was no part of his intention." Ever since, economists have used the term **invisible hand** to refer to the way a market economy manages to harness the power of self-interest for the good of society.

The study of how individuals make decisions and how these decisions interact is called **microeconomics.** One of the key themes in microeconomics is the validity of Adam Smith's insight: individuals pursuing their own interests often do promote the interests of society as a whole.

So the answer to our first question—"How does our economic system manage to deliver the goods?"—is that we rely on the virtues of a market economy and the power of the invisible hand.

But the invisible hand isn't always our friend. It's also important to understand when and why the individual pursuit of self-interest can lead to counterproductive behaviour.

|| My Benefit, Your Cost

In most ways, life in the PRD is immensely better than it was in 1980. Two things have, however, gotten much worse: traffic congestion and air quality. At rush hour, the average speed on the PRD's roads is only around 19 kilometers an hour and the air is seriously unhealthy much of the year.

Why do these problems represent failures of the invisible hand? Consider the case of traffic congestion.

When traffic is congested, each driver is imposing a cost on all the other drivers on the road—she is literally getting in their way (and they are getting in her way). This cost can be substantial: the Toronto Board of Trade estimates the productivity loss as a result of traffic congestion in the city at $6 billion annually. However, according to the C.D. Howe Institute, the annual cost could shoot up to $7.5 to $11 billion if taking the social costs into consideration. Yet when deciding whether or not to drive, commuters have no incentive to take the costs they impose on others into account.

Traffic congestion is a familiar example of a much broader problem: **market failure,** which happens when the individual pursuit of one's own interest, instead of promoting the interests of society as a whole, actually makes society worse off. Another important example of market failure is air pollution, which is all too visible, literally, in the PRD. Water pollution and the overexploitation of natural resources such as fish and forests reflect the same problem.

The environmental costs of self-interested behaviour can sometimes be huge. And as the world becomes more crowded and the environmental footprint of human activity continues to grow, issues like climate change and ocean acidification will become increasingly important.

The good news, as you will learn if you study microeconomics, is that economic analysis can be used to diagnose cases of market failure. And often, economic analysis can also be used to devise solutions for the problem.

|| Good Times, Bad Times

China has become an enormous economic powerhouse in the last 30 years. (And, depending upon the data source used, China and the United States vie for top place among the world's economies.) One somewhat ironic consequence of China's rise is that people around the world get nervous at any signs of trouble in Chinese industry, because it's such a big source of demand for raw materials. And in 2020, there was a lot to be nervous about. Many economic indicators pointed to a sharp slowdown in the economy.

World History Archive/Alamy Stock Photo

According to Adam Smith, a market economy manages to harness the power of self-interest for the common good.

The **invisible hand** refers to the way in which the individual pursuit of self-interest can lead to good results for society as a whole.

Microeconomics is the branch of economics that studies how people make decisions and how these decisions interact.

When the individual pursuit of self-interest leads to bad results for society as a whole, there is **market failure.**

ECONOMICS 101

©Dave Carpenter/Cartoonstock

DAVE Carpenter

"Remember, an economic boom is usually followed by an economic kaboom."

Such troubled periods are a regular feature of modern economies. The fact is that the economy does not always run smoothly: it experiences fluctuations, a series of ups and downs. By middle age, a typical Canadian will have experienced two or three downs, known as **recessions.** The Canadian economy experienced serious recessions beginning in 1982, 1990, and 2008. During a severe recession, hundreds of thousands of workers may be laid off.

Like market failure, recessions are a fact of life; but also like market failure, they are a problem for which economic analysis offers some solutions. Recessions are one of the main concerns of the branch of economics known as **macroeconomics,** which is concerned with the overall ups and downs of the economy. If you study macroeconomics, you will learn how economists explain recessions and how government policies can be used to minimize the damage from economic fluctuations.

Despite the occasional recession, however, over the long run the stories of all major economies contain many more ups than downs. And that long-run ascent is the subject of our final question.

‖ Onward and Upward

The overall standard of living of the average resident of the PRD, while immensely higher than it was in 1980, is still pretty low by Canadian standards. But then, Canada wasn't always as rich as it is today. Indeed, at the beginning of the twentieth century, most Canadians lived under conditions that we would now think of as extreme poverty. Only 10% of homes had flush toilets or central heating, even fewer had electricity, and almost nobody had a car, let alone a washing machine or air conditioning. But over the course of the following century Canada achieved a remarkable rise in living standards that ultimately led to the great wealth that we see around us today.

Such comparisons are a stark reminder of how much lives around the world have been changed by **economic growth,** the increasing ability of the economy to produce goods and services, leading to higher living standards. Why does the economy grow over time? And why does economic growth occur faster in some places and times than in others? These are key questions for economics, because economic growth is a good thing, for many, as residents of the PRD can attest, and most of us want more of it. But economic growth does come with some costs.

Specifically, despite benefiting the vast majority of people, economic growth has always created losers as well as winners as fast-growing, emerging sectors of the economy eclipse those of the past. For example, the gleaming towers built in the PRD, along with newly constructed dams, displaced many Chinese, a number of them farmers who lost their land and livelihoods.

The environment is another potential loser, unless attention is paid to the question of how to achieve *sustainable long-run economic growth*, which is economic growth over the long term that balances protection of the environment with improved living standards for current and future generations. Today, the goal of balancing the production of goods and services with the health of the environment is a hotly debated policy topic. Economic analysis has a key role to play here because environmental degradation is often a result of market failure.

‖ An Engine for Discovery

We hope we have convinced you that what the great economist Alfred Marshall called the "ordinary business of life," the economic actions and transactions that go on every day not just in the PRD but around the world, is really quite

A **recession** is a downturn in the economy.

Macroeconomics is the branch of economics that is concerned with overall ups and downs in the economy.

Economic growth is the growing ability of the economy to produce goods and services, leading to higher living standards.

extraordinary, if you stop to think about it, and that it can lead us to ask some very interesting and important questions.

In this book, we will describe the answers economists have given to these questions. But this book, like economics as a whole, isn't a list of answers: it's an introduction to a discipline, a way to address questions like those we asked earlier. Or as Alfred Marshall put it: "Economics . . . is not a body of concrete truth, but an engine for the discovery of concrete truth."

So let's turn the key and start the ignition.

KEY TERMS

Economy, p. 2
Economics, p. 2
Market economy, p. 2

Invisible hand, p. 3
Microeconomics, p. 3
Market failure, p. 3

Recession, p. 4
Macroeconomics, p. 4
Economic growth, p. 4

.1 ❭ First Principles

THERE WAS A TIME when most of the world's college students were located in wealthy Western nations. Today, however, the number of college and university students in developing countries like China and India is rapidly overtaking the number in Canada and Western Europe. In fact, China already has more students enrolled in college and university than Canada does.

And what are these students studying? A variety of subjects, of course. But regardless of the region of the world, a lot of students will be studying economics.

You might wonder, however, whether the economics being taught at, say, Shanghai

Regardless of where in the world you study, the basic principles of economics are the same.

University or the University of Mumbai bears much resemblance to the economics being taught in Canadian colleges and universities. After all, there are big differences between nations in levels of income, political institutions, and the problems they face. Doesn't this mean that the economics in these countries is different, too?

The answer is, yes and no. "Yes," because different circumstances and history affect what both students and practitioners need to know. That's why there are international editions of this textbook. Despite the close ties and similarities between Canada and the United States, Canada is different enough to warrant our own edition with explanations about our own economic issues and institutions.

The answer is also "no" because much of the material covered in basic economics is the same wherever you are around the world. The reason for this is that all economics is based on a set of common principles that apply to many different issues, regardless of the particular setting.

Some of these principles involve *individual choice* — for economics is, first of all, about the choices that individuals make. Do you save your money and take the bus or do you buy a car? Do you keep your old phone or upgrade to a new one? These decisions involve *making a choice* from among a limited number of alternatives — limited because no one can have everything that they want. Every question in economics at its most basic level involves individuals making choices.

But to understand how an economy works, you need to understand more than how individuals make choices. None of us are like Robinson Crusoe, living alone on an island. Every person must make decisions in an environment that is shaped by the decisions of others. So in this chapter we will learn about four principles of economics that guide the choices made by individuals.

Indeed, in a modern economy even the simplest decisions you make — say, what to have for breakfast — are shaped by the decisions of thousands of other people, from the banana grower in Costa Rica who decided to grow the fruit you eat to the farmer in Saskatchewan who provided the wheat in your bread.

Because each of us in a market economy depends on so many others — and they, in turn, depend on us — our choices interact. So although all economics at a basic level is about individual choice, in order to understand how market economies behave we must also understand *economic interaction* — how my choices affect your choices, and vice versa. To that end, in this chapter you will study the four principles that govern how individual choices interact in the economy.

Although many important economic interactions can be understood by looking at the markets for individual goods (like the market for wheat), when we consider the economy as a whole, we see that it is composed of an enormous number of markets for individual goods, and these many markets interact. As a result, the larger economy experiences ups and downs. In order to understand economy-wide interactions, in this chapter we will study the three principles that underlie their behaviour.

These eleven principles are the basis of all economic analysis. They form the common ground of economics. And they apply just as much in Shanghai or Mumbai as they do in Vancouver or Calgary. ●

WHAT YOU WILL LEARN

- What four principles guide the choices made by individuals?
- What four principles govern how individual choices interact?
- What three principles illustrate economy-wide interactions?

Principles That Underlie Individual Choice: The Core of Economics

Every economic issue involves, at its most basic level, **individual choice**—decisions by an individual about what to do and what not to do. In fact, you might say that it isn't economics if it isn't about choice.

Take Walmart or Amazon. There are thousands of different products available, and it is extremely unlikely that you—or anyone else—could afford to buy everything you might want to have. And anyway, there's only so much space in your dorm room or apartment. So will you buy another bookcase or a mini-refrigerator? Given limitations on your budget and your living space, you must choose which products to buy and which to leave on the shelf.

The fact that those products are on the shelf in the first place involves choice—the store manager chose to put them there, and the manufacturers of the products chose to produce them. All economic activities involve individual choice.

Four economic principles underlie the economics of individual choice, as shown in Table 1-1. We'll now examine each of these principles.

Principle #1: Choices Are Necessary Because Resources Are Scarce

You can't always get what you want. Many of us would like to have a big beautiful house or apartment in a great location, a new car or two, and vacations in exotic locations each year. But even in a rich country like Canada, not many families can afford all that. So they must make choices—like whether to travel by train through the Rockies this year or buy a better car, or whether to move to the city where housing is expensive, or accept a longer commute in order to live where housing prices are cheaper.

Limited income isn't the only thing that keeps us from having everything we want. Time is also in limited supply: there are only 24 hours in a day. Choosing to spend time on one activity means choosing not to spend time on something else—studying for an exam means forgoing a night spent watching a movie. Indeed, many people faced with the limited number of hours in the day are willing to trade money for time. For example, local convenience stores typically charge higher prices than a regular supermarket. But they fulfill a valuable role by catering to time-pressed customers who would rather pay more than travel farther to the supermarket.

This leads us to our first principle of individual choice:

> *People must make choices because resources are scarce.*

A **resource** is anything that can be used to produce something else. Lists of the economy's resources usually begin with land, labour (the time of workers), capital (machinery, buildings, and other man-made productive assets), and human capital (the educational achievements and skills of workers). A resource is **scarce** when there's not enough of the resource available to satisfy all the ways a society wants to use it.

There are many scarce resources. These include natural resources that come from the physical environment, such as minerals, lumber, and petroleum. There is also a limited quantity of human resources, such as labour, skill, and intelligence. And in a growing world economy with a rapidly increasing human population, even clean air and water have become scarce resources.

Just as individuals must make choices, the scarcity of resources means that society as a whole must make choices. One way a society with a market economy makes choices is by allowing them to emerge from many individual choices. For example, Canadians as a group have only so many hours in a week. How many of those hours will be spent travelling to supermarkets to get lower prices, rather than saving time by shopping at local convenience stores? The answer is the sum of individual decisions: each of the millions of individuals in the economy makes

---

TABLE 1-1 Principles of Individual Choice
1. People must make choices because resources are scarce.
2. The opportunity cost of an item—what you must give up in order to get it—is its true cost.
3. "How much" decisions require making trade-offs at the margin: comparing the costs and benefits of doing a little bit more of an activity versus doing a little bit less.
4. People respond to incentives, exploiting opportunities to make themselves better off.

Ben Heys/Shutterstock

Resources are scarce.

Individual choice is the decision by an individual of what to do, which necessarily involves a decision of what not to do.

A **resource** is anything that can be used to produce something else.

Resources are **scarce**—not enough of the resources are available to satisfy all the various ways a society wants to use them.

a choice about where to shop, and the overall choice is simply the sum of those individual decisions.

Principle #2: The True Cost of Something Is Its Opportunity Cost

It is the last term before you graduate, and your class schedule allows you to take only one elective. There are two, however, that you really want to take: Data Visualization Basics and Introduction to Chinese.

Suppose you decide to take the Intro to Chinese course. What's the cost of that decision? It is, primarily, the fact that you can't take the Data Visualization class, your next best alternative choice. Economists call that kind of cost—what you must give up in order to get an item you want—the **opportunity cost** of that item. This leads us to our second principle of individual choice:

> *The opportunity cost of an item—what you must give up in order to get it—is its true cost.*

So the opportunity cost of taking the Intro to Chinese class includes the benefit you would have derived from the Data Visualization class.

The concept of opportunity cost is crucial to understanding individual choice because, in the end, all costs are opportunity costs. That's because every choice you make means forgoing some other alternative.

Sometimes critics claim that economists are concerned only with costs and benefits that can be measured in dollars and cents. But that is not true. Much economic analysis involves cases like our electives example, where it costs no extra tuition to take one elective course instead of another—that is, there is no direct monetary cost. Nonetheless, the elective you choose has an opportunity cost—the other desirable elective course that you must forgo because time limits permit you to take only one. More specifically, the opportunity cost of a choice is what you forgo by not choosing your next best alternative.

You might think that opportunity cost is an add-on—that is, something *additional* to the monetary cost of an item. But it isn't. Suppose that an elective class costs an additional $750. Now there is a monetary cost to taking Intro to Chinese. Is the opportunity cost of taking that course something separate from that monetary cost?

Yes, it is. Consider that you will have to spend that $750 no matter which class you take. So what you give up to take Intro to Chinese is still the Data Visualization class—you have to spend that $750 either way. But what if the Data Visualization class is free? In that case, what you give up to take the Intro to Chinese class is the benefit from the data visualization class *plus* the benefit you could have gained from spending the $750 on other things.

Either way, the real cost of taking your preferred class is what you must give up to get it. As you expand the set of decisions that underlie each choice—whether to take an elective or not, whether to finish this term or not, whether to drop out or not—you'll realize that all costs are ultimately opportunity costs.

Sometimes the money you have to pay for something is a good indication of its opportunity cost. But many times it is not.

One very important example of how poorly monetary cost can indicate opportunity cost is the cost of attending college or university. Tuition and housing are major monetary expenses for most students; but even if they were free, attending college or university would still be an expensive proposition because most post-secondary students, if they were not in college or university, would have a job. By going to college or university, then, students *forgo* the income they could have earned if they had worked instead. This means that the opportunity cost of attending a post-secondary institution is what you pay for tuition and housing plus the forgone income you would have earned in a job.

It's easy to see that the opportunity cost of going to a post-secondary institution is especially high for people who could be earning a lot during what

The real cost of an item is its **opportunity cost:** what you must give up in order to get it.

Mark Zuckerberg, founder of Facebook, understood the concept of opportunity cost.

Justin Sullivan/Getty Images

You make a **trade-off** when you compare the costs with the benefits of doing something.

Decisions about whether to do a bit more or a bit less of an activity are **marginal decisions.**

The study of such decisions is known as **marginal analysis.**

would otherwise have been their college or university years. That is why star athletes and successful entrepreneurs often skip or drop out of college or university.

Principle #3: "How Much" Is a Decision at the Margin

Some of the decisions we make involve an "either–or" choice—for example, you decide either to go to college or university or to begin working; you decide either to take economics or something else. But other important decisions involve "how much" choices—for example, if you are taking both economics and chemistry this semester, you must decide how much time to spend studying for each. When it comes to understanding "how much" decisions, economics has an important insight to offer: "how much" is a decision made at the margin.

Suppose you are taking both economics and chemistry. And suppose you are a pre-med student, so your grade in chemistry matters more to you than your grade in economics. Should you spend *all* your study time on chemistry and wing it on the economics exam? Probably not; even if you think your chemistry grade is more important, you should put some effort into studying economics.

Spending more time studying chemistry involves a benefit (a higher expected grade in that course) and a cost (you could have spent that time doing something else, such as studying to get a higher grade in economics). That is, your decision involves a **trade-off**—a comparison of costs and benefits.

How do you decide this kind of "how much" question? The typical answer is that you make the decision a bit at a time, by asking how you should spend the next hour. If both exams are the next day, you will spend the night reviewing your notes for both courses. At 6:00 P.M., you decide that it's a good idea to spend at least an hour on each course. At 8:00 P.M., you decide you need to spend another hour on each course. At 10:00 P.M., you are getting tired and figure you have one more hour to study before bed. Do you study chemistry or economics? If you are pre-med, it's likely to be chemistry; if you are a business major, it's likely to be economics.

Note how you've made the decision to allocate your time: at each point the question is whether or not to spend *one more hour* on either course. In deciding whether to spend that hour studying chemistry, you weigh the costs (an hour forgone of studying economics or an hour forgone of sleeping) versus the benefits (a likely increase in your chemistry grade). As long as the benefit of studying chemistry for one more hour outweighs the cost, you should choose to study for that additional hour.

Decisions of this type—whether to do a bit more or a bit less of an activity, like what to do with your next hour, your next dollar, and so on—are **marginal decisions.** This brings us to our third principle of individual choice:

> *"How much" decisions require making trade-offs at the margin: comparing the costs and benefits of doing a little bit more of an activity versus doing a little bit less.*

The study of such decisions is known as **marginal analysis.** Many of the questions that we face in real life involve marginal analysis: How many minutes should I exercise? How many hours should I work? What is an acceptable rate of negative side effects from a new medicine? Marginal analysis plays a central role in economics because it is the key to deciding "how much" of an activity to do.

Principle #4: People Respond to Incentives, Exploiting Opportunities to Make Themselves Better Off

While listening to the news one day, the authors heard a great tip about cheap parking in New York City. At the time, garages in the Wall Street area charged as much as US$30 per day. But according to this news report, some people had found a better way: instead of parking in a garage, they had their oil changed at the Jiffy Lube for US$19.95—and they keep your car all day!

It's a great story, but unfortunately it turned out not to be true—in fact, there is no Jiffy Lube in New York City. But if there were, you can be sure there would be a lot of oil changes there. Why? Because when people are offered opportunities to make themselves better off, they take them—and if they could find a way to park their car all day for US$19.95 rather than US$30, they would.

In this example, economists say that people are responding to an **incentive**—an opportunity to make themselves better off, which leads to our fourth principle of individual choice:

> *People respond to incentives, exploiting opportunities to make themselves better off.*

When you try to predict how individuals will behave in an economic situation, it is a very good bet that they will respond to incentives—that is, exploit opportunities to make themselves better off. Furthermore, individuals will *continue* to exploit these opportunities until they have been fully exhausted. If there really were a Jiffy Lube and an oil change really were a cheap way to park your car, we can safely predict that before long the waiting list for oil changes would be weeks, if not months.

In fact, the principle that people will exploit opportunities to make themselves better off is the basis of *all* predictions by economists about individual behaviour.

In fact, economists tend to be skeptical of any attempt to change behaviour that *doesn't* change incentives. For example, a plan aimed at reducing traffic in New York City that doesn't offer New York City-bound drivers an incentive, like a financial reward, for not driving, or that isn't accompanied by a penalty for driving, is unlikely to succeed. Likewise, a plan that calls on manufacturers to reduce pollution voluntarily probably won't be effective. In contrast, a plan that gives them a financial reward to reduce pollution is a lot more likely to succeed because it has changed their incentives.

So are we ready to do economics? Not yet—because most of the interesting things that happen in the economy are the result not merely of individual choices but of the way in which individual choices interact.

An **incentive** is anything that offers rewards to people to change their behaviour.

An incentive that cuts waste: Shoppers switch to reusable shopping bags when charged a fee for disposable bags at checkout.

ECONOMICS >> *in Action*
The Cost of Marriage: China's One-Child Policy Creates Millions of Lonely Bachelors

China is the most populous country on Earth, with over 1,420,000,000 people, as of 2019. That's over *one billion four hundred twenty million* people. And trends in Chinese demographics have shifted the cost of marriage over time—specifically, the cost of finding a bride for Chinese bachelors.

In the 1970s, China was very poor and had an already large and growing population. Concerned that it would be unable to adequately provide care for so many people, the Chinese government introduced a one-child policy that restricted most couples to only one child and imposed penalties on those who defied the mandate. By 2016, the average number of children per Chinese woman had fallen to 1.6, from more than 5 before the policy was introduced in 1978.

But the one-child policy has led to an unfortunate unintended consequence on the balance between the sexes in the population. Until recently, China was overwhelmingly rural. Because of the physical demands of farming, sons were strongly preferred over daughters. In addition, tradition dictated that sons, not daughters, took care of elderly parents. The effect of the one-child policy was to greatly increase the perceived cost to a Chinese family of a female child. As a result, while some female infants were given up for adoption abroad, many simply "disappeared" during the first year of life, victims of neglect and mistreatment

The cost of finding a bride is quite high for millions of men in China.

as Chinese families were determined that their only child be a son. The Nobel-prize winning economist Amartya Sen calculated that there were millions of "missing women" in Asia due to the perceived higher cost of female children, with estimates running from 45 million to 100 million missing women.

The number of boys in China has outpaced the number of girls for 20 years. Today, there are nearly 34 million *excess* males in the population compared to females. That's 90% of the entire population of Canada—men who will never find wives from among their fellow Chinese.

As of 2018, within the age group of 15- to 29-year-olds, there are 112 men for every 100 women, with projections that there will be as many as 190 young men per 100 young women by 2050. So, although the Chinese government officially ended the one-child policy in 2015, the consequences will endure for decades.

Not surprisingly, some Chinese bachelors are eager to meet eligible women from abroad—particularly from nearby countries such as Vietnam, Laos, and Cambodia that don't have a problem with gender imbalance. And enterprising eligible women from those countries are coming to China to find husbands. Marriage brokers have sprung up in these countries to address the situation in China. For example, one Chinese bachelor, Liu Hua, found happiness with Lili, a Cambodian woman who came to China to find a husband. Before meeting Lili, Liu lived in a village with 60 bachelors and only 2 single women. He ended up paying deposits ranging from $6635 to $53,075 to three families in nearby villages for the opportunity to date their daughters (not all of which was refunded when the matches didn't work out). He eventually paid a $19,900 broker's fee to marry Lili. Happily married, they now have two children—a boy *and* a girl.

>> Quick Review

- All economic activities involve **individual choice.**

- People must make choices because **resources** are **scarce.**

- The real cost of something is its **opportunity cost**—what you must give up to get it. All costs are opportunity costs. Monetary costs are sometimes a good indicator of opportunity costs, but not always.

- Many choices involve not *whether* to do something but *how much* of it to do. "How much" choices call for making a **trade-off** at the margin. The study of **marginal decisions** is known as **marginal analysis.**

- Because people exploit opportunities to make themselves better off, **incentives** can change people's behaviour.

>> Check Your Understanding 1-1

Solutions appear at back of book.

1. Explain how each of the following illustrates one of the four principles of individual choice.
   a. You are on your third trip to a restaurant's all-you-can-eat dessert buffet and are feeling very full. Although it would cost you no additional money, you forgo a slice of coconut cream pie but have a slice of chocolate cake.
   b. Even if there were more resources in the world, there would still be scarcity.
   c. Different teaching assistants teach several Economics 101 tutorials. Those taught by the teaching assistants with the best reputations fill up quickly, with spaces left unfilled in the ones taught by assistants with poor reputations.
   d. To decide how many hours per week to exercise, you compare the health benefits of one more hour of exercise to the effect on your grades of one less hour spent studying.

2. You make $45,000 per year at your current job with Whiz Kids Consultants. You are considering a job offer from Brainiacs, Inc., that will pay you $50,000 per year. Which of the following are elements of the opportunity cost of accepting the new job at Brainiacs, Inc.?
   a. The increased time spent commuting to your new job
   b. The $45,000 salary from your old job
   c. The more spacious office at your new job

‖ Interaction: How Economies Work

An economy is a system for coordinating the productive activities of many people. In a market economy like we live in, coordination takes place without any coordinator: each individual makes their own choices.

Yet those choices are by no means independent of one another: each individual's opportunities, and hence choices, depend to a large extent on the choices made by other people. So to understand how a market economy behaves, we have to examine this **interaction** in which my choices affect your choices, and vice versa.

When studying economic interaction, we quickly learn that the end result of individual choices may be quite different from what any one individual intends. Consider the case of North American farmers, who, over the past century have adopted new farming techniques and crop strains that have reduced their costs and increased their yields. The end result of each farmer trying to increase their own income has actually been to drive many farmers out of business. Because Canadian farmers have been so successful at producing larger yields, agricultural prices have steadily fallen, reducing the incomes of many farmers, and as a result fewer people find farming worth doing. That is, an individual farmer who plants a better variety of corn is better off, but when many farmers plant a better variety of corn, the result may be to make farmers as a group worse off.

There are four principles underlying the economics of interaction. These principles are summarized in Table 1-2 and we will now examine each one.

TABLE 1-2 **Principles of Interaction of Individual Choices**
5. There are gains from trade.
6. Markets move toward equilibrium.
7. Resources should be used efficiently to achieve society's goals.
8. Markets usually lead to efficiency, but when they don't, government intervention can improve society's welfare.

Principle #5: There Are Gains from Trade

Why do the choices I make interact with the choices you make? A family could try to take care of all its own needs—growing its own food, sewing its own clothing, providing itself with entertainment. But trying to live that way would be very hard.

The key to a much better standard of living for everyone is **trade,** in which people divide tasks among themselves and each person provides a good or service that other people want in return for different goods and services that he or she wants.

The reason we have an economy, not many self-sufficient individuals, is that there are **gains from trade:** by dividing tasks and trading, two people (or 7.8 billion people) can each get more of what they want than they could get by being self-sufficient. This leads us to our fifth principle:

"I hunt and she gathers—otherwise, we couldn't make ends meet."

There are gains from trade.

Gains from trade arise from this division of tasks, which economists call **specialization**—a situation in which different people each engage in a different task, specializing in those tasks that they are good at performing. The advantages of specialization, and the resulting gains from trade, were the starting point for Adam Smith's 1776 book *The Wealth of Nations,* which many regard as the beginning of economics as a discipline.

Smith's book begins with a description of an eighteenth-century pin factory where, rather than each of the 10 workers making a pin from start to finish, each worker specialized in one of the many steps in pin-making:

> One man draws out the wire, another straights it, a third cuts it, a fourth points it, a fifth grinds it at the top for receiving the head; to make the head requires two or three distinct operations; to put it on, is a particular business, to whiten the pins is another; it is even a trade by itself to put them into the paper; and the important business of making a pin is, in this manner, divided into about eighteen distinct operations. . . . Those ten persons, therefore, could make among them upwards of forty-eight thousand pins in a day. But if they had all wrought separately and independently, and without any of them having been educated to this particular business,

Interaction of choices—my choices affect your choices, and vice versa—is a feature of most economic situations. The results of this interaction are often quite different from what the individuals intend.

In a market economy, individuals engage in **trade:** they provide goods and services to others and receive goods and services in return.

There are **gains from trade:** people can get more of what they want through trade than they could if they tried to be self-sufficient.

An increase in output is due to **specialization:** each person specializes in the task that they are good at performing.

they certainly could not each of them have made twenty, perhaps not one pin a day. . . .

The same principle applies when we look at how people divide tasks among themselves and trade in an economy. *The economy, as a whole, can produce more when each person specializes in a task and trades with others.*

The benefits of specialization are the reason a person typically chooses only one career. It takes many years of study and experience to become a physician or a commercial pilot. Many physicians might well have had the potential to become excellent pilots, and vice versa. But it is very unlikely that anyone who decided to pursue both careers would be as good at both as someone who decided at the beginning to specialize in a single field. So it is to everyone's advantage that individuals specialize in their careers.

Markets allow a physician and a pilot to specialize in their own fields. Because markets for commercial flights and for medical care exist, a physician is assured that she can find a flight and a pilot is assured that he can find a physician. As long as individuals know that they can find the goods and services they want in the market, they are willing to forgo self-sufficiency and to specialize. But what assures people that markets will deliver what they want? The answer to that question leads us to our next principle of how individual choices interact.

Principle #6: Markets Move Toward Equilibrium

It's a busy afternoon at the supermarket; there are long lines at the checkout counters. Then one of the previously closed cash registers opens. What happens right away, of course, is a rush to that register. After a couple of minutes, however, things will have settled down. Shoppers will have rearranged themselves so that the line at the newly opened register is about the same length as the lines at all the other registers.

How do we know this? We know from our fourth principle that people will exploit opportunities to make themselves better off. People will rush to the newly opened register to save time standing in line. The rushing around will stop when shoppers can no longer improve their position by switching lines—that is, when the opportunities to make themselves better off have all been exploited.

A story about supermarket checkout lines may seem to have little to do with how individual choices interact, but in fact it illustrates an important principle. A situation in which individuals cannot make themselves better off by doing something different—the situation in which all the checkout lines are the same length—is what economists call an **equilibrium.** An economic situation is in equilibrium when no individual would be better off doing something different.

Recall the story about the mythical Jiffy Lube, where it was supposedly cheaper to leave your car for an oil change than to pay for parking. If the opportunity had really existed and people were still paying US$30 to park in garages, the situation would *not* have been an equilibrium. And that should have been a giveaway that the story couldn't be true. In reality, people would have seized an opportunity to park cheaply, just as they seize opportunities to save time at the checkout line. And in so doing they would have eliminated the opportunity! Either it would have become very hard to get an appointment for an oil change or the price of a lube job would have increased to the point that it was no longer an attractive option (unless you really needed an oil change). This brings us to our sixth principle:

> *Because people respond to incentives, markets move toward equilibrium.*

As we will see, markets usually reach equilibrium through changes in prices, which rise or fall until no opportunities for individuals to make themselves better off remain.

The concept of equilibrium is extremely helpful in understanding economic interactions because it provides a way to cut through the sometimes complex

Witness equilibrium in action on the checkout line.

An economic situation is in **equilibrium** when no individual would be better off doing something different.

details of those interactions. To understand what happens when a new line opens at a supermarket, you don't need to worry about exactly how shoppers rearrange themselves, which register just opened, and so on. What you need to know is that any time there is a change, the situation will move to an equilibrium.

The fact that markets move toward equilibrium is why we can depend on them to work in a predictable way. In fact, we can trust markets to supply us with the essentials of life. For example, people who live in cities can be sure that the supermarket shelves will always be fully stocked. Why? Because if some merchants who distribute food *didn't* make deliveries, a big profit opportunity would be created for any merchant who did—and there would be a rush to supply food, just like the rush to a newly opened cash register.

So the market ensures that food will always be available for city dwellers. And, returning to our fifth principle, this allows city dwellers to be city dwellers—to specialize in doing city jobs rather than living on farms and growing their own food.

A market economy, as we have seen, allows people to achieve gains from trade. But how do we know how well such an economy is doing? The next principle gives us a standard to use in evaluating an economy's performance.

Principle #7: Resources Should Be Used Efficiently to Achieve Society's Goals

You are attending a lecture in a classroom that is too small for the number of students—many of your fellow classmates are standing or sitting on the floor—despite the fact that large, empty classrooms are available nearby. You would be correct to say that this is no way to run a college or university. Economists would call this an *inefficient* use of resources. But if an inefficient use of resources is undesirable, just what does it mean to use resources *efficiently*?

You might imagine that the efficient use of resources has something to do with money, maybe that it is measured in dollars-and-cents terms. But in economics, as in life, money is only a means to other ends. The measure that economists really care about is not money but people's happiness or welfare. Economists say that *an economy's resources are used efficiently when they are used in a way that has fully exploited all opportunities to make everyone better off.* Put another way: an economy is **efficient** if it takes all opportunities to make some people better off without making other people worse off.

In our classroom example, there clearly was a way to make everyone better off—move the lecture to a larger room. Students attending the lecture would be made better off without hurting anyone else at the school. This result would be an efficient use of the school's resources. Assigning the course to the smaller classroom was an inefficient use of those resources.

When an economy is efficient, it is producing the maximum gains from trade possible given the resources available. Why? Because there is no way to rearrange how resources are used so that everyone can be made better off. When an economy is efficient, one person can be made better off by rearranging how resources are used *only* by making someone else worse off.

In our example, if all larger classrooms were already occupied, the school would actually have been run efficiently: to make your class better off by moving it to a larger classroom would displace other students already in a larger room. Those students would be made worse off by a move.

We can now state our seventh principle:

> **Resources should be used as efficiently as possible to achieve society's goals.**

Should policy makers always strive to achieve economic efficiency? Well, not quite, because efficiency is only a means to achieving society's goals. Sometimes efficiency may conflict with a goal that society has deemed worthwhile to achieve. For example, in most societies, people also care about issues of fairness, or **equity.**

Sometimes equity trumps efficiency.

An economy is **efficient** if it takes all opportunities to make some people better off without making other people worse off.

Equity means that everyone gets their fair share. Since people can disagree about what's "fair," equity isn't as well defined a concept as efficiency.

And there is typically a trade-off between equity and efficiency: policies that promote equity often come at a cost of decreased efficiency in the economy, and vice versa.

To see this, consider the case of disabled-designated parking spaces in public parking lots. Many people have difficulty walking due to age or disability, so it seems only fair to assign closer parking spaces specifically for their use. You may have noticed, however, that a certain amount of inefficiency is involved. To ensure that a parking space is always available should a disabled person want one, there are typically more such spaces available than there are disabled people who want one. As a result, desirable parking spaces are unused. (And the temptation for nondisabled people to use them is so great that drivers must be dissuaded by fear of getting a ticket.)

So, short of hiring parking valets to allocate spaces, there is a conflict between *equity*, making life "fairer" for disabled people, and *efficiency*, making sure that all opportunities to make people better off have been fully exploited by never letting close-in parking spaces go unused.

Exactly how far policy makers should go in promoting equity over efficiency is a difficult question that goes to the heart of the political process. As such, it is not a question that economists can answer. What is important for economists, however, is always to seek to use the economy's resources as efficiently as possible in the pursuit of society's goals, whatever those goals may be.

Principle #8: Markets Usually Lead to Efficiency, But When They Don't, Government Intervention Can Improve Society's Welfare

There is no branch of the Canadian government entrusted with ensuring the general economic efficiency of our market economy—we don't have agents tasked with checking that brain surgeons aren't plowing fields or that Manitoba farmers aren't trying to grow wheat. The government doesn't need to enforce the efficient use of resources, because in most cases the invisible hand does the job. As explained in the Introduction, the *invisible hand* refers to how a market economy harnesses the power of self-interest for the good of society.

The incentives built into a market economy ensure that resources are usually put to good use and that opportunities to make people better off are not wasted. If a college or university were known for its habit of crowding students into small classrooms while large classrooms went unused, its enrollment would soon drop, putting the jobs of its administrators at risk. The "market" for post-secondary students would respond in a way that induces administrators to run the institution efficiently.

A detailed explanation of why markets are usually very good at making sure that resources are used efficiently will have to wait until we have studied how markets actually work. But the most basic reason is that in a market economy, in which individuals are free to choose what to consume and what to produce, people normally take opportunities for mutual gain—that is, gains from trade.

If people encounter an opportunity to make themselves better off, they will take advantage of it. And that is exactly what defines efficiency: all the opportunities to make some people better off without making other people worse off have been exploited. We have now arrived at the first half of our eighth principle:

> *Because people exploit gains from trade, markets usually lead to efficiency.*

However, there are exceptions to this principle that markets are generally efficient. In cases of *market failure*, the individual pursuit of self-interest found in markets makes society worse off—that is, the market outcome is inefficient.

Consider the nature of the market failure caused by traffic congestion—commuters driving to work have no incentive to take into account the cost that their actions inflict on other drivers in the form of increased traffic congestion.

Possible remedies to this situation include charging tolls, subsidizing the cost of public transportation, and taxing gasoline sales to individual drivers. These remedies would change the incentives of would-be drivers, motivating them to drive less. But they also share another feature: each relies on government intervention in the market, which leads to the second half of this principle:

> **When markets don't achieve efficiency, government can intervene to improve society's welfare.**

An appropriately designed government policy can sometimes move society closer to an efficient outcome by changing how society's resources are used. And, as we will see next, short of instances of market failure, the general rule is that markets are a remarkably good way of organizing an economy.

ECONOMICS >> *in Action*
Wait, Then Hurry Up, and Wait Again

Many living in the Greater Toronto Area rely on public transit, like buses, subways, and local taxis, for their day-to-day commute. Yet each of these forms of transportation has drawbacks: the subway is often plagued with delays, buses can be slow, and taxis are expensive and might be hard to find during peak hours and/or in bad weather.

Unsurprisingly, the market for transportation changed quite dramatically with the arrival of ride-hailing services like Uber and Lyft and other private transportation companies (PTCs), which have become wildly popular in cities like Toronto and Montreal. Hopping into an Uber has been seen as a way to get where you need to go more quickly. In 2019, there were slightly more than 90,000 ride-hailing drivers (including Uber, Lyft, and other smaller operators) in Toronto, up from about 30,000 three years ago. According to a 2019 study by the City of Toronto, these drivers provide an average of 176,000 rides per day, representing a 180% increase during the same time period. When comparing the travel time on public transit in similar routes, services provided by PTCs could save commuters an average of 5–10 minutes in the downtown core and an average of 8–20 minutes outside the downtown core. Correspondingly, there was a drop in the city's' public transit ridership.

Yet, the popularity of ride-hailing services has created one significant drawback. With more vehicles on the street, traffic congestion has increased. Toronto also indicated that the increasing use by PTCs had caused a 4% increase in travel time in the downtown core, an area in which the majority of PTCs rides occurred, during peak hours between 2017 and 2019. Although these PTCs seem to have a marginal impact on travel time during the study period, the city vows to continue to monitor the impacts of PTC trips on the city's street network.

It's an outcome that traffic planners find predictable. Thanks to the new ride-hailing apps that induce more driving and have led to an influx of new cars on city streets, commuters looking for a quick trip in a cab are finding their travel time has increased, making the bus, subway, or walking appealing travel options once again. With commuting times more or less back where they started before ride-hailing services appeared, a new equilibrium has been reached in which travel times across all modes of available transport are unchanged. This predictable outcome resembles what traffic

The fundamental law of traffic congestion is an example of equilibrium in action.

shaunl/Getty Images

planners call the *fundamental law of traffic congestion:* if a city builds more roads, this induces more driving, and this increase in traffic continues until a new equilibrium is reached, with commuting times more or less back where they started. Whether it's a new ride-hailing app or newly built roads that induces more driving, the ultimate result is that a new equilibrium is reached in which travel times across all modes of transportation are unchanged.

For those who hoped that ride-hailing services would make commuting faster and easier, this result is discouraging. It is, however, a good illustration of the importance of thinking about equilibrium.

>> Check Your Understanding 1-2

Solutions appear at back of book.

1. Explain how each of the following illustrates one of the four principles of interaction.
   a. At a college tutoring co-op, students can arrange to provide tutoring in subjects they are good in (like economics) in return for receiving tutoring in subjects they struggle with (like philosophy).
   b. The local municipality imposes a law that requires bars and nightclubs near residential areas to keep their noise levels below a certain threshold.
   c. To provide better care for low-income patients, the local municipality has decided to close some underutilized neighbourhood clinics and shift funds to the main hospital.
   d. On Amazon, books of a given title with approximately the same level of wear and tear sell for about the same price.

2. Which of the following describes an equilibrium situation? Which does not? Explain your answer.
   a. The restaurants across the street from the university dining hall serve better-tasting and cheaper meals than those served at the university dining hall. The vast majority of students continue to eat at the dining hall.
   b. You currently take the subway to work. Although taking the bus is cheaper, the ride takes longer. So you are willing to pay the higher subway fare in order to save time.

|| Economy-Wide Interactions

The economy as a whole—the macroeconomy—has its ups and downs. For example, late in 2008 the Canadian economy entered a severe recession in which almost half a million people lost their jobs, while those who remained employed saw their wages stagnate. It took 26 months—until January 2011—for the number of Canadians employed to return to its pre-recession level.

Over time, the behaviour of the macroeconomy is a lot like a drive through a mountain range. The trip isn't one continuous upward climb to a destination at high altitude. Instead, you will drive over hills and valleys, with short-term ups and downs during your journey, as you slowly, but inevitably, ascend to your destination.

In the short run, the overall economy experiences ups and downs: good economic times (recoveries) alternate with bad economic times (recessions), with a cycle lasting an average of seven to 10 years. However, over the long run, a period of at least 10 years, the economy grows larger and larger. A graph of the total amount of goods and services the economy produces over time would show a line that looks a lot like our car ride: lots of squiggles up and down, but, over time, the line reaches upward.

To understand why the macroeconomy cycles between recessions and recoveries, but also achieves economic growth over time, we need to look at economy-wide interactions. And understanding the big picture of the economy requires three more economic principles, which are summarized in Table 1-3.

TABLE 1-3 Principles of Economy-Wide Interactions

9. One person's spending is another person's income.

10. Overall spending sometimes gets out of line with the economy's productive capacity; when it does, government policy can change spending.

11. Increases in the economy's potential lead to economic growth over time.

Principle #9: One Person's Spending Is Another Person's Income

Starting in mid-2014, the world oil price showed a downward trend. The drop in oil price has an adverse impact on the economy of Alberta. As the oil price drops, producing oil may no longer become as profitable and as attractive as before, and some oil producers in Alberta respond by cutting production and/or shutting down. At first the damage was limited to the oil industry. But over time the slump spread throughout other parts of the Albertan economy, with consumer spending falling across the board.

But why should a fall in oil production mean empty stores in the shopping malls? After all, malls are where families, not workers in the oil industry, do their shopping.

The answer is that the oil price slump led to lower incomes throughout the economy. People who had been employed either directly in the energy sector, producing goods the industry needs (like machinery), or providing services to the industry (like financial services, restaurants near production sites), either lost their jobs or were forced to take pay cuts. And as incomes fell, so did spending by consumers. This example illustrates our ninth principle:

> **One person's spending is another person's income.**

In a market economy, people make a living selling things—including their labour—to other people. If some group in the economy decides, for whatever reason, to spend more, the incomes of other groups will rise. If some group decides to spend less, the incomes of other groups will fall.

And a chain reaction of changes in spending behaviour tends to have repercussions that spread economy-wide. For example, a fall in consumer spending at shopping malls leads to reduced family incomes; families respond by reducing their own spending, which leads to another round of income cuts; and so on. These repercussions play an important role in our understanding of recessions and recoveries.

Principle #10: Overall Spending Sometimes Gets Out of Line with the Economy's Productive Capacity; When It Does, Government Policy Can Change Spending

The coronavirus pandemic of 2020 harkened back to a period in the 1930s, known as the Great Depression. Then, as now, a collapse in spending by consumers and businesses led to a plunge in overall spending. In both periods, the plunge in spending led to very high unemployment.

What economists learned from the Great Depression is that overall spending—the amount of goods and services that consumers and businesses want to buy—sometimes doesn't match the amount of goods and services the economy is capable of producing. In the 1930s, as in 2020, spending fell far short of what was needed to keep Canadian workers employed, and the result was a severe economic slump.

It's also possible for overall spending to be too high. In that case, the economy experiences *inflation*, a rise in prices throughout the economy. This rise in prices occurs when the amount that people want to buy outstrips the supply, leading producers to raise their prices and still find willing buyers.

When the economy experiences either shortfalls in spending or excesses in spending, government policies can be used to address the imbalances, which leads to our tenth principle:

> **Overall spending sometimes gets out of line with the economy's productive capacity; when it does, government policy can change spending.**

The Canadian government spends a lot, on everything from military equipment to health care. Moreover, it can choose to spend more or less, depending upon

With advances in technology and greater resources, Canadian farmers today produce far more than they did 100 years ago.

the state of the economy. Likewise, the government can vary how much it collects in taxes, which in turn affects how much income consumers and businesses have to spend. And the government through the central bank controls the quantity of money in circulation, which gives it another powerful tool with which to affect total spending. Government spending, taxes, and control of money are the tools of *macroeconomic policy*.

Modern governments deploy macroeconomic policy tools in an effort to balance overall spending in the economy, trying to steer it between the perils of recession and inflation. These efforts aren't always successful—recessions still happen, as do periods of inflation. But it's widely believed that aggressive efforts to sustain spending in 2009 and 2010 helped prevent the financial crisis of 2008 from turning into a full-blown depression.

Principle #11: Increases in the Economy's Potential Lead to Economic Growth Over Time

Today's economy is different from the economy of 20 years ago, and drastically different from the economy of a century ago. These changes are due to *economic growth*, the increase in living standards over time. Economic growth has made Canada and other countries far richer over time. Like a car climbing up a mountain range, despite the valleys and hills along the way, the overall path of the economy over time has been upward in the long run, as Figure 1-1 illustrates.

What accounts for this growth over time? It is due to the emergence of new technologies and increases in the resources available for production—resources like land, labour, and machinery. As a result, the economy's *potential*, the total amount of goods and services it can produce, rises and leads to higher living standards. For example, in 1870, most Canadian workers were engaged in farming; that figure was about 2% in 2019. Yet there is a far greater quantity and variety of food available now than almost 150 years ago. The increased mechanization and technological sophistication of agriculture—humongous tractors and satellite imaging—are changes to the

---

FIGURE 1-1 Growth in the Canadian Economy Over Time

The overall path of the Canadian economy from 1870 to 2016 has been upward, with the inevitable short-term ups and downs along the way.

Data from: Maddison Project Database, version 2018.

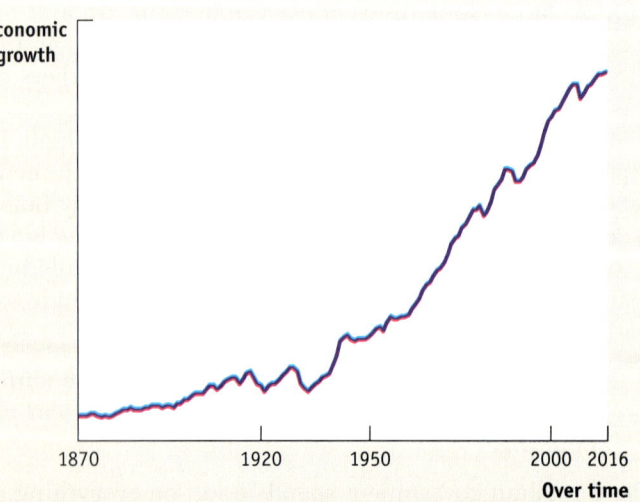

resources available for production. As a result, the economy's potential has risen: Canadian farmers can now produce vastly more than before and Canadian consumers can now consume vastly more than before.

We have now arrived at our eleventh and final principle:

> ### Increases in the economy's potential lead to economic growth over time.

While economic growth has benefited a vast number of people, the increase in living standards are usually unequally distributed among a country's residents in the short term. In fact, at any given time, an increase in the economy's potential typically creates *winners and losers.*

For example, over the past 20 years, technological advancements have revolutionized the way we produce energy in Canada. New drilling techniques have made natural gas abundant, and alternative energy sources such as solar and wind power have emerged. These new sources of energy, which pollute less than older sources such as coal, benefit both the economy and the environment—they are the winners in our example. But at the same time, the reduced demand for coal has hurt communities where mining has been a primary source of employment, creating losers.

Yet, in a dynamic market economy, losers won't always stay losers. Remember Principle #4: People usually respond to incentives. It implies that unemployed coal miners will eventually migrate to other sectors of the economy where they can find work. They may, for example, become solar panel installers. However, because it takes time for workers to make such a transition (and it may be impossible for older workers), we can also see why Principle #9 applies: Government intervention can improve society's welfare. Government assistance programs can provide a cushion for dislocated workers.

In the end, just as increases in an economy's potential lead to economic growth over time, economic growth inevitably leads to fundamental economic and social change. With these changes come questions (and debates) that are as relevant today as they were back in the eighteenth century when Adam Smith penned *The Wealth of Nations*—questions about equity, the role of government, and appropriate macroeconomic policy remedies.

>> Check Your Understanding 1-3

Solutions appear at back of book.

1. Explain how each of the following illustrates one of the three principles of economy-wide interactions.
   a. The price of solar panels has fallen by nearly 99% over the past 40 years. Prices are projected to continue falling over the next 30 years.
   b. The financial crisis of 2008 caused unemployment to soar. In response, the Prime Minister urged Parliament to pass a package of temporary spending increases and tax cuts in early 2009.
   c. With oil prices plummeting, Canadian and U.S. oil companies have been forced to shut down their productive wells. In cities throughout Alberta, North Dakota, Wyoming, Texas, and Alaska, restaurants and other consumer businesses are failing.

>> Quick Review

• In a market economy, one person's spending is another person's income. As a result, changes in spending behaviour have repercussions that spread through the economy.

• Overall spending sometimes gets out of line with the economy's capacity to produce goods and services. When spending is too low, the result is a recession. When spending is too high, it causes inflation.

• When spending is out of line, governments can use macroeconomic policy tools to affect the overall level of spending in an effort to steer the economy between recession and inflation.

• Despite the economy's ups and downs, increases in the economy's potential lead to economic growth in the long term, while creating winners and losers in the short term.

How Priceline Revolutionized the Travel Industry

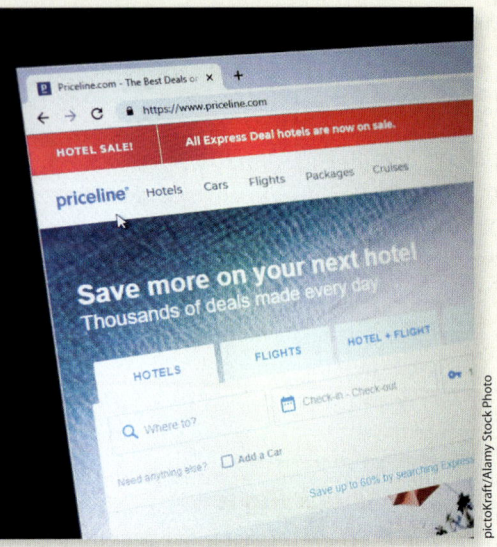

pictoKraft/Alamy Stock Photo

If you bought and held shares of the Priceline Group, the online provider of travel-related reservations and search services, from 2014 to 2019, you would have been one happy camper. During that time, the share price appreciated by 50%, beating the performance of the S&P 500, a widely used overall measure of stock prices, resulting in a company valuation of nearly US$80 billion for the company's stock.

Even more remarkable is the fact that in 2002, the company was in such deep trouble that many doubted it would survive. From 1999 to 2002, Priceline lost 95% of its value, going from a company valuation of US$9 billion to a paltry US$425 million. What went so terribly wrong and then so incredibly right at Priceline?

When the company (originally known as Priceline.com) was formed in 1998, investors were immediately impressed by how it used the internet to revolutionize the travel industry. Before the internet, travellers relied on travel agents and airline staff to book flights and hotels. Information was fragmented and it was difficult to compare prices when shopping for tickets. Because prices were high, far fewer people travelled long distances, for example for the holidays. Priceline's success lay in its ability to spot exploitable opportunities for itself and its customers. The company understood that when a plane departs with empty seats or a hotel has empty beds, there is a cost—the revenue that would have been earned if the seat or bed were filled. Priceline's innovation was to bring airlines and hotels with unsold capacity together with travellers.

It works this way: customers specify the price they are willing to pay for a given trip or hotel, and then Priceline presents them with a list of options from airlines or hotels that are willing to accept that price. Typically, price declines as the trip date nears. Although some travellers like the security of booking their trips well in advance and are willing to pay for that, others are quite happy to wait until the last minute, and risk not getting their first choice flight or hotel in order to benefit from a lower price.

Priceline, then, found a way to make everyone better off—including itself, since it charged a small fee for each trade it facilitated.

Yet, in 2002 the company was at risk of going under. After the terrorist attacks of September 11, 2001, many Canadians and Americans simply stopped flying. As the economy went into a deep slump, airplanes sat empty on the tarmac and the airlines lost billions of dollars. Several major airlines spiralled toward bankruptcy, and Priceline was losing several million U.S. dollars a year.

In order to avert a meltdown of the airline industry, the U.S. Congress passed a US$15 billion aid package that was critical in stabilizing the industry. It was the seed of Priceline's turnaround. The company managed to survive and eventually thrive.

Quick on its feet when it saw its market challenged by newcomers, Expedia and Orbitz, it responded aggressively by moving more of its business toward hotel bookings and into Europe, where the online travel industry was still quite small. Its network was particularly valuable in the European hotel market, composed of many more small hotels compared to the North American market, which is dominated by nationwide chains. The efforts paid off, and by 2003 Priceline was turning a profit. Over the years Priceline expanded by acquiring the travel websites Booking.com, KAYAK, agoda.com, rentalcars.com, and OpenTable, transforming itself into the Priceline Group, with revenue of US$15.1 billion in 2019.

QUESTION FOR THOUGHT

1. Explain how each of the eleven principles of economics is illustrated in this case.

SUMMARY

1. All economic analysis is based on a set of basic principles that apply to three levels of economic activity. First, we study how individuals make choices; second, we study how these choices interact; and third, we study how the economy functions overall.

2. Everyone has to make choices about what to do and what *not* to do. **Individual choice** is the basis of economics—if it doesn't involve choice, it isn't economics.

3. The reason choices must be made is that **resources**— anything that can be used to produce something else—are **scarce.** Individuals are limited in their choices by money and time; economies are limited by their supplies of human and natural resources.

4. Because you must choose among limited alternatives, the true cost of anything is what you must give up to get it—all costs are **opportunity costs.**

5. Many economic decisions involve questions not of "whether" but of "how much"—how much to spend on some good, how much to produce, and so on. Such decisions must be made by performing a **trade-off** *at the margin*—by comparing the costs and benefits of doing a bit more or a bit less. Decisions of this type are called **marginal decisions,** and the study of them, **marginal analysis,** plays a central role in economics.

6. The study of how people *should* make decisions is also a good way to understand actual behaviour. Individuals usually respond to **incentives**—exploiting opportunities to make themselves better off.

7. The next level of economic analysis is the study of **interaction**—how my choices depend on your choices, and vice versa. When individuals interact, the end result may be different from what anyone intends.

8. Individuals interact because there are **gains from trade:** by engaging in the **trade** of goods and services with one another, the members of an economy can all be made better off. **Specialization**—each person specializes in the task they are good at—is the source of gains from trade.

9. Because individuals usually respond to incentives, markets normally move toward **equilibrium**—a situation in which no individual can make themself better off by taking a different action.

10. An economy is **efficient** if all opportunities to make some people better off without making other people worse off are taken. Resources should be used as efficiently as possible to achieve society's goals. But efficiency is not the sole way to evaluate an economy: **equity,** or fairness, is also desirable, and there is often a trade-off between equity and efficiency.

11. Markets usually lead to efficiency, with some well-defined exceptions. But when markets fail and do not achieve efficiency, government intervention can improve society's welfare.

12. Because people in a market economy earn income by selling things, including their own labour, one person's spending is another person's income. As a result, changes in spending behaviour can spread throughout the economy.

13. Overall spending in the economy can get out of line with the economy's productive capacity. Spending below the economy's productive capacity leads to a recession; spending in excess of the economy's productive capacity leads to inflation. When overall spending gets out of line, governments can use macroeconomic policy tools to steer the economy between recession and inflation.

14. Increases in the economy's potential lead to economic growth over time. Although economic growth leads to higher living standards for everyone over time, in the short run, increases in the economy's potential lead to both winners and losers.

KEY TERMS

PROBLEMS

1. In each of the following situations, identify which of the eleven principles is at work:

   a. You choose to purchase your textbooks online rather than pay a higher price for the same books through your college or university bookstore.

   b. On your spring break trip, your budget is limited to $35 a day.

   c. To help reduce traffic congestion, many cities have adopted congestion pricing. Under this program, drivers are charged more to use express lanes during peak rush hour.

   d. The government passes an infrastructure bill to help construction workers who were left jobless after the last recession.

   e. You buy a used textbook from your roommate. Your roommate uses the money to buy songs from iTunes.

   f. You decide how many cups of coffee to have when studying the night before an exam by considering how much more work you can do by having another cup versus how jittery it will make you feel.

   g. There is limited lab space available to do the project required in Chemistry 101. The lab supervisor assigns lab time to each student based on when that student is able to come.

   h. You realize that you can graduate a semester early by forgoing a semester of study abroad.

   i. At the student center, there is a bulletin board on which people advertise used items for sale, such as bicycles. Once you have adjusted for differences in quality, all the bikes sell for about the same price.

   j. You are better at performing lab experiments, and your lab partner is better at writing lab reports. So the two of you agree that you will do all the experiments and she will write up all the reports.

   k. Amazon announces a program to develop a drone delivery system in place of traditional ground shipping.

2. Describe some of the opportunity costs when you decide to do the following:

   a. Attend college or university instead of taking a job

   b. Watch a movie instead of studying for an exam

   c. Ride the bus instead of driving your car

3. Kim needs to buy a textbook for the next economics class. The price at the college bookstore is $65. One website offers it for $55, and another site, for $57. All prices include sales tax. The accompanying table indicates the typical shipping and handling charges for the textbook ordered online.

Shipping method	Delivery time	Charge
Standard shipping	3–7 days	$3.99
Second-day air	2 business days	8.98
Next-day air	1 business day	13.98

   a. What is the opportunity cost of buying online instead of at the bookstore? Note that if you buy the book online, you must wait to get it.

   b. Show the relevant choices for Kim. What determines which of these options Kim will choose?

4. Use the concept of opportunity cost to explain the following:

   a. More people choose to get graduate degrees when the job market is poor.

   b. More people choose to do their own home repairs when the economy is slow and hourly wages are down.

   c. There are more parks in suburban than in urban areas.

   d. Convenience stores, which have higher prices than supermarkets, cater to busy people.

   e. Fewer students enroll in classes that meet before 10:00 A.M.

5. For the following examples, state how you would use the principle of marginal analysis to make a decision:

   a. Deciding how many days to wait before doing your laundry

   b. Deciding how much time to spend researching before writing your term paper

   c. Deciding how many bags of chips to eat

   d. Deciding how many class lectures to skip

6. This morning you made the following individual choices: you bought a bagel and coffee at the local café, you drove to school in your car during rush hour, and you typed your course notes for your roommate because she was texting in class—in return for which she will do your laundry for a month. For each of these actions, describe how your individual choices interacted with the individual choices made by others. Were other people left better off or worse off by your choices in each case?

7. Which of the following situations describes an equilibrium? Which does not? If the situation does not describe an equilibrium, what would an equilibrium look like?

   a. Many people regularly commute from the suburbs to downtown Pleasantville. Due to traffic congestion, the trip takes 30 minutes via highway but only 15 minutes via side streets.

   b. At the intersection of Victoria and Broadway are two gas stations. One station charges 105.9 cents per litre for regular gas and the other charges 102.9 cents per litre. Customers can get service immediately at the first station but must wait in a long line at the second.

   c. Every student enrolled in Economics 101 must also attend a weekly tutorial. This year there are two sections offered: section A and section B, which meet at the same time in adjoining classrooms and are taught by equally competent instructors. Section A is overcrowded, with people sitting on the floor and often unable to see what is written on the board at the front of the room. Section B has many empty seats.

8. For each of the following, explain whether you think the situation is efficient or not. If it is not efficient, why not? What actions would make it efficient?

   a. Electricity is included in the rent at your dorm. Some residents in your dorm leave lights, computers, and appliances on when they are not in their rooms.

   b. Although they cost the same amount to prepare, the cafeteria in your dorm consistently provides too many dishes that diners don't like, such as tofu casserole, and too few dishes that diners do like, such as pad thai.

   c. The enrollment for a particular course exceeds the spaces available. Some students who need to take this course to complete their major are unable to get a space even though others who are taking it as an elective do get a space.

9. Discuss the efficiency and equity implications of each of the following. How would you go about balancing the concerns of equity and efficiency in these areas?

   a. The government pays the full tuition for every college and university student to study whatever subject he or she wishes.

   b. When people lose their jobs, the government provides unemployment benefits (i.e., employment insurance) until they find new ones.

10. Governments often adopt certain policies in order to promote efficiency in society. For each of the following policies, determine what the incentive is and what behaviour the government wishes to promote. In each case, why do you think the market is inefficient and why the government might wish to change people's behaviour, rather than allow their actions to be solely determined by individual choice?

   a. A tax of $5 per pack is imposed on cigarettes.

   b. The government pays parents $100 when their child is vaccinated for measles.

   c. The government pays college and university students to tutor children from low-income families.

   d. The government imposes a tax on the amount of air pollution that a company discharges.

11. In each of the following situations, explain how government intervention could improve society's welfare by changing people's incentives. In what sense is the market going wrong?

   a. Pollution from auto emissions has reached unhealthy levels.

   b. Everyone in Woodville would be better off if streetlights were installed in the town. But no individual resident is willing to pay for installation of a streetlight in front of their house because it is impossible to recoup the cost by charging other residents for the benefit they receive from it.

12. On June 6, 2013, Stephen Poloz, the newly appointed governor of the Bank of Canada, addressed the House of Commons Standing Committee on Finance. In this speech he said, "In the immediate aftermath of the crisis (the Great Recession of 2008), stimulative monetary and fiscal policies proved highly effective in supporting robust growth in domestic demand, particularly household expenditures, which grew to record levels. Yet, as effective as it has been, with domestic demand now slowing, the limits of this growth model are clear." Which two of the three principles of economy-wide interaction are at work in this statement?

13. In 2007, a sharp downturn in the U.S. housing market reduced the income of many who worked in the American home construction industry. In October of that year, a Conference Board of Canada report stated falling house prices in parts of the United States, combined with low savings and rising energy costs, would result in weak U.S. consumer spending. Furthermore, U.S. imports of wood and autos would decline because of the slower U.S. economic growth. With this information, use one of the principles of economy-wide interaction to trace a chain of links that explains how reduced spending for U.S. home purchases is likely to affect the performance of the Canadian economy.

14. In May 2016, a huge wildfire tore through the Fort McMurray region in Alberta. The fire not only caused the mandatory evacuation of about 90,000 residents, but it also caused a loss of $1 billion worth of output due to the shutdown of nearby oil sands facilities, and massive destruction to homes and other properties in Fort McMurray. Thankfully no lives were lost from the fire (two died in traffic accidents during the evacuation) but thousands of homes and other properties were either damaged or destroyed resulting in about $3.6 billion worth of insurance claims. Even those who weren't directly affected by the destruction were hurt because businesses failed or contracted and jobs dried up. Using one of the principles of economy-wide interaction, explain how government intervention can help in this situation.

15. Self-driving cars, also known as autonomous vehicles, will require little or no human input to operate safely. A 2017 federal government report indicated that more than 1.1 million jobs could be lost due to the increased use of autonomous vehicles, and the job losses ranged from truck drivers to taxi drivers and from parking attendants to auto-body shop workers. Another report indicated that these vehicles could save Canadians up to $65 billion in the forms of fewer collisions, less traffic jams, lower fuel costs, and others. Identify the winners and losers in the development of autonomous vehicles.

·2 Economic Models: Trade-offs and Trade

🌎 FROM KITTY HAWK TO C-SERIES (NOW A220)

ON SEPTEMBER 16, 2013, THE CS100, the newest jet in Bombardier's cutting-edge C-Series of aircraft, took its first test flight. It was a game-changing moment: the CS100 is part of a new aerodynamic revolution—an ultra-efficient airplane designed to cut airline operating costs and one of the first to use super-lightweight composite materials. To ensure that the plane was sufficiently lightweight and aerodynamic, it underwent more than 4,500 hours of wind tunnel tests—tests that resulted in subtle design changes that improved its performance, reducing fuel consumption and CO_2 emissions each by 20% compared to existing passenger jets.

The Wright Brothers' model made modern airplanes possible.

The C-Series (now called the A220 after the aircraft program was fully acquired by Airbus in February 2020) is a spectacular advance from the 1903 maiden voyage of the Wright Flyer, the first successful powered airplane flight, in Kitty Hawk, North Carolina. Yet the Bombardier engineers—and all aeronautic engineers—owe an enormous debt to the Wright Flyer's inventors, Wilbur and Orville Wright. What made the Wrights truly visionary was their wind tunnel, an apparatus that let them experiment with many different designs for wings and control surfaces. Doing experiments with a miniature airplane inside a wind tunnel the size of a shipping crate gave the Wright Brothers the knowledge that would make heavier-than-air flight possible.

Some 110 years later, Bombardier tested the design of its C-Series aircraft using more than 20 sophisticated miniature scale models inside state-of-the-art wind tunnel facilities in six countries. It also augmented its wind tunnel testing with leading-edge computational fluid dynamics testing, made possible through the use of super-computers. Thus, while a miniature airplane, whether inside a packing crate, an ultramodern wind tunnel, or a complex simulation scenario, is not the same thing as an actual aircraft in flight, it is clearly a very useful model of a flying plane—a simplified representation of the real thing that can be used to answer crucial questions, such as how much lift a given wing shape will generate at a given airspeed.

Needless to say, testing an airplane design in a wind tunnel or with computer simulations is cheaper and safer than building a full-scale version and hoping it will fly. Likewise, models play a crucial role in almost all scientific research—economics very much included.

In fact, you could say that economic theory consists mainly of a collection of models, a series of simplified representations of economic reality that allow us to understand a variety of economic issues.

In this chapter, we'll look at three economic models that are crucially important in their own right and also illustrate why such models are so useful. We'll conclude with a look at how economists actually use models in their work. ●

WHAT YOU WILL LEARN

- What are economic **models** and why are they so important to economists?
- How do three simple models—the **production possibility frontier, comparative advantage,** and the **circular-flow diagram**—help us understand how modern economies work?
- Why is an understanding of the difference between **positive economics** and **normative economics** important for the real-world application of economic principles?
- Why do economists sometimes disagree?

A **model** is a simplified representation of a real situation that is used to better understand real-life situations.

The **other things equal assumption** means that all other relevant factors remain unchanged.

‖ Models in Economics: Some Important Examples

A **model** is any simplified representation of reality that is used to better understand real-life situations. But how do we create a simplified representation of an economic situation?

One possibility—an economist's equivalent of a wind tunnel—is to find or create a real but simplified economy. Take, for example, an economist who wants to know how an increase in the government-mandated minimum wage would affect the Canadian economy. It would be impossible to do an experiment that involved raising the minimum wage across the country and seeing what happens. Instead, the economist will observe the effects of a smaller economy that is raising its minimum wage (like Manitoba did in October 2019) and then extrapolate those results to the larger Canadian economy.

Another possibility is to simulate the workings of the economy on a computer. For example, when changes in tax law are proposed, government officials use *tax models*—large mathematical computer programs—to assess how the proposed changes would affect different types of people.

Models are important because their simplicity allows economists to focus on the effects of only one change at a time. That is, they allow us to hold everything else constant and study how one change affects the overall economic outcome.

So an important assumption when building economic models is the **other things equal assumption,** which means that all other relevant factors remain unchanged.

But you can't always find or create a small-scale version of the whole economy, and a computer program is only as good as the data it uses. (Programmers have a saying: "garbage in, garbage out.") For many purposes, the most effective form of economic modelling is the construction of "thought experiments": simplified, hypothetical versions of real-life situations.

We used the example of how customers checking out at a supermarket rearrange themselves when a new cash register opens to illustrate the concept of equilibrium in Chapter 1. Although we didn't say it, this is an example of a simple model—an imaginary supermarket, in which many details, like what customers were buying, are ignored. This simple model can be used to answer a "what if" question: for example, what if another cash register were to open?

As this checkout story shows, it is possible to describe and analyze a useful economic model in plain English. However, because much of economics involves changes in quantities—in the price of a product, the number of units produced, or the number of workers employed in its production—economists often find that using some mathematics helps clarify an issue. In particular, a numerical example, a simple equation, or—especially—a graph can be key to understanding an economic concept.

Whatever form it takes, a good economic model can be a tremendous aid to understanding. We'll now look at three simple but important economic models and what they tell us.

- First, we will look at the *production possibility frontier,* a model that helps economists think about the trade-offs every economy faces.
- We then turn to *comparative advantage,* a model that clarifies the principle of gains from trade—trade both between individuals and between countries.
- We will also examine the *circular-flow diagram,* a schematic representation that helps us understand how flows of money, goods, and services are channelled through the economy.

Throughout this chapter, and the entire book, we will make considerable use of graphs to represent mathematical relationships. If you are already familiar with how graphs are used, you can skip the appendix to this chapter, which provides a brief introduction to the use of graphs in economics. If not, this would be a good time to read the appendix on graphing.

Trade-offs: The Production Possibility Frontier

The first principle of economics we introduced in Chapter 1 is that resources are scarce and, as a result, any economy faces trade-offs—whether it's an isolated group of a few dozen hunter-gatherers or the nearly 7.8 billion people making up the twenty-first-century global economy. No matter how light-weight the Bombardier jet is, no matter how efficient their assembly line, producing jets means using resources that therefore can't be used to produce something else.

To think about the trade-offs that face any economy, economists often use the model known as the **production possibility frontier.** The idea behind this model is to improve our understanding of trade-offs by considering a simplified economy that produces only two goods. This simplification enables us to show the trade-off graphically.

Suppose, for a moment, that Canada was a one-company economy, with Bombardier its sole employer and trains and private jets its only products. But there would still be a choice of what kinds of transportation vehicles to produce—say, Toronto Rocket subway trains versus private jets. Figure 2-1 shows a hypothetical production possibility frontier representing the trade-off this one-company economy would face. The frontier—the line in the diagram—shows the maximum quantity of jets that Bombardier can produce per year *given* the quantity of subway trains it produces per year, and vice versa. That is, it answers questions of the form, "What is the maximum quantity of jets that Bombardier can produce in a year if it also produces 21 (or 35, or 70) subway trains that year?"

There is a crucial distinction between points *inside* or *on* the production possibility frontier (the shaded area) and *outside* the frontier. If a production point lies inside or on the frontier—like point *C*, at which Bombardier produces 10 jets and 21 subway trains in a year—it is feasible. After all, the frontier tells us that if Bombardier produces 10 jets, it could also produce a maximum of 35 subway trains that year, so it could certainly make 21 subway trains.

However, a production point that lies outside the frontier—such as the hypothetical production point *D*, where Bombardier produces 20 jets and 70 subway trains—isn't feasible. Bombardier can produce 20 jets and no subway trains, *or* it can produce 70 subway trains and no jets, but it can't do both.

> The **production possibility frontier** illustrates the trade-offs facing an economy that produces only two goods. It shows the maximum quantity of one good that can be produced for any given quantity produced of the other.

FIGURE 2-1 The Production Possibility Frontier

The production possibility frontier illustrates the trade-offs Bombardier faces in producing subway trains and jets. It shows the maximum quantity of one good that can be produced given the quantity of the other good produced. Here, the maximum quantity of subway trains manufactured per year depends on the quantity of jets manufactured that year, and vice versa. Bombardier's feasible production is shown by the area *inside* or *on* the curve. Production at point *C* is feasible but not efficient. Points *A* and *B* are feasible and efficient in production, but point *D* is not feasible.

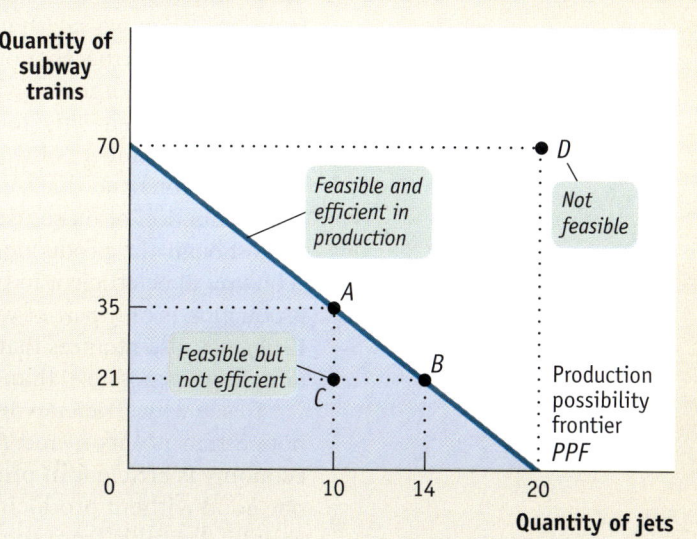

In Figure 2-1 the production possibility frontier intersects the horizontal axis at 20 jets. This means that if Bombardier dedicated all its production capacity to making jets, it could produce 20 jets per year but could produce no subway trains. The production possibility frontier intersects the vertical axis at 70 subway trains. This means that if Bombardier dedicated all its production capacity to making subway trains, it could produce 70 subway trains per year but no jets.

The figure also shows less extreme trade-offs. For example, if Bombardier's managers decide to make 10 jets this year, they can produce at most 35 subway trains; this production choice is illustrated by point *A*. And if Bombardier's managers decide to produce 14 jets, they can make at most 21 subway trains, as shown by point *B*.

Thinking in terms of a production possibility frontier simplifies the complexities of reality. The real-world Canadian economy produces millions of different goods. Even Bombardier can produce more than two different types of planes and trains. Yet it's important to realize that even in its simplicity, this stripped-down model gives us important insights about the real world.

By simplifying reality, the production possibility frontier helps us understand some aspects of the real economy better than we could without the model: efficiency, opportunity cost, and economic growth.

Efficiency First of all, the production possibility frontier is a good way to illustrate the general economic concept of *efficiency*. Recall from Chapter 1 that an economy is efficient if there are no missed opportunities—there is no way to make some people better off without making other people worse off.

One key element of efficiency is that there are no missed opportunities in production—there is no way to produce more of one good without producing less of other goods. As long as Bombardier operates on its production possibility frontier, its production is efficient. At point *A*, 35 subway trains are the maximum quantity feasible given that Bombardier has also committed to producing 10 jets; at point *B*, 21 subway trains are the maximum number that can be made given the choice to produce 14 jets; and so on.

But suppose for some reason that Bombardier was operating at point *C*, making 10 jets and 21 subway trains. In this case, it would not be operating efficiently and would therefore be *inefficient:* it could be producing more of both transportation vehicles.

Although we have used an example of the production choices of a one-firm, two-good economy to illustrate efficiency and inefficiency, these concepts also carry over to the real economy, which contains many firms and produces many goods. If the economy as a whole could not produce more of any one good without producing less of something else—that is, if it is on its production possibility frontier—then we say that the economy is *efficient in production*.

If, however, the economy could produce more of some things without producing less of others—which typically means that it could produce more of everything—then it is inefficient in production. For example, an economy in which large numbers of workers are involuntarily unemployed is clearly inefficient in production. And that's a bad thing because these workers could be employed in the production of more useful goods and services.

Although the production possibility frontier helps clarify what it means for an economy to be efficient in production, it's important to understand that efficiency in production is only *part* of what's required for the economy as a whole to be efficient. Efficiency also requires that the economy allocate its resources so that consumers are as well off as possible. If an economy does this, we say that it is *efficient in allocation*.

To see why efficiency in allocation is as important as efficiency in production, notice that points *A* and *B* in Figure 2-1 both represent situations in which the economy is efficient in production, because in each case it can't produce more of one good without producing less of the other. But these two situations may not be equally desirable from society's point of view. Suppose that society prefers to have more jets and fewer subway trains than at point *A;* say, it prefers to have 14 jets and 21 subway trains, corresponding to point *B*. In this case, point *A* is inefficient in allocation from the point of view of the economy as a whole because it would rather have Bombardier produce at point *B* instead of point *A*.

This example shows that efficiency for the economy as a whole requires *both* efficiency in production and efficiency in allocation: to be efficient, an economy must produce as much of each good as it can given the production of other goods. It must also produce the mix of goods that people want to consume and deliver those goods to the right people. An economy that gives subway trains to airports and private business jets to intercity transit authorities is inefficient, too.

In the real world, command economies, such as the former Soviet Union, are notorious for inefficiency in allocation. For example, it was common for consumers to find stores well stocked with items few people wanted but lacking basics such as soap and toilet paper.

Opportunity Cost   The production possibility frontier is also useful as a reminder of the fundamental point that the true cost of any good isn't the money it costs to buy it, but what must be given up in order to get that good—the *opportunity cost*. If, for example, Bombardier decides to change its production from point *A* to point *B*, it will produce 4 more jets but 14 fewer subway trains. So the opportunity cost of 4 jets is 14 subway trains—the 14 subway trains that must be foregone in order to produce 4 more jets. This means that each jet has an opportunity cost of $^{14}/_4 = ^7/_2$ of a subway train.

Is the opportunity cost of an extra jet in terms of subway trains always the same, no matter how many jets and subway trains are currently produced? In the example illustrated by Figure 2-1, the answer is yes. If Bombardier increases its production of jets from 14 to 20, the number of subway trains it produces falls from 21 to zero. So Bombardier's opportunity cost per additional jet is $^{21}/_6$ or $= 3^1/_2$ subway trains, the same as it was when Bombardier went from 10 jets produced to 14.

However, the fact that in this example the opportunity cost of a jet in terms of a subway train is always the same is a result of an assumption we've made, an assumption that's reflected in how Figure 2-1 is drawn. Specifically, whenever we assume that the opportunity cost of an additional unit of a good doesn't change regardless of the output mix, the production possibility frontier is a straight line.

Moreover, as you might have already guessed, the slope of a straight-line production possibility frontier is equal to the opportunity cost—specifically, the opportunity cost for the good measured on the horizontal axis in terms of the good measured on the vertical axis. In Figure 2-1, the production possibility frontier has a *constant slope* of $-^7/_2$, implying that Bombardier faces a *constant opportunity cost* for 1 jet equal to $3^1/_2$ subway trains. (A review of how to calculate the slope of a straight line is found in this chapter's appendix.) This is the simplest case, but the production possibility frontier model can also be used to examine situations in which opportunity costs change as the mix of output changes.

Figure 2-2 illustrates a different assumption, a case in which Bombardier faces *increasing opportunity cost*. Here, the more jets it produces, the more costly it is to produce yet another jet in terms of foregone production of subway trains. And the same holds true in reverse: the more subway trains Bombardier produces, the more costly it is to produce yet another subway train in terms of foregone production of jets. For example, to go from producing zero jets to producing 10, Bombardier has to forgo producing 10 subway trains. That is, the opportunity cost of those 10 jets is 10 subway trains. But to increase its production of jets to 20—that is, to produce an additional 10 jets—it must forgo producing 60 subway trains, a much higher opportunity cost. As you can see in Figure 2-2, when opportunity costs are increasing rather than constant, the production possibility frontier is a bowed-out curve rather than a straight line.

FIGURE 2-2 Increasing Opportunity Cost

The bowed-out shape of the production possibility frontier reflects increasing opportunity cost. In this example, to produce the first 10 jets, Bombardier must forego producing 10 subway trains. But to produce an additional 10 jets, Bombardier must forego manufacturing 60 more subway trains.

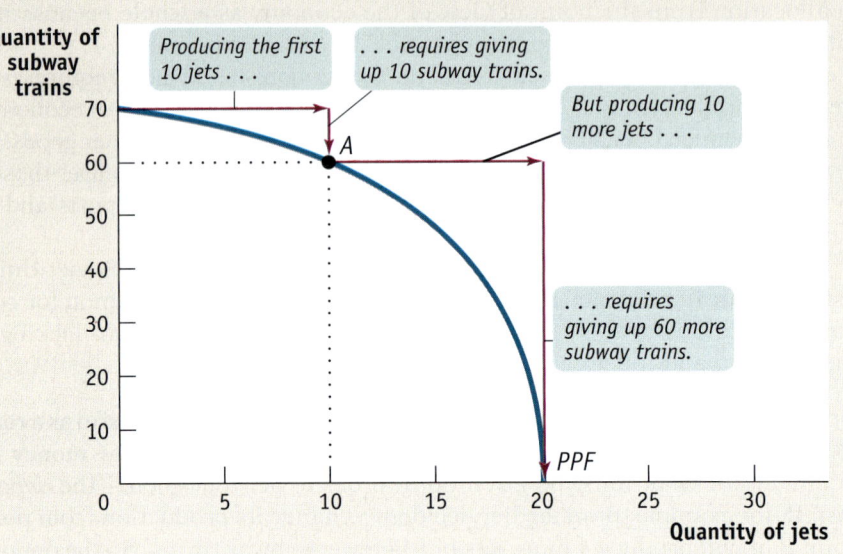

Although it's often useful to work with the simple assumption that the production possibility frontier is a straight line, economists believe that in reality opportunity costs are typically increasing. When only a small amount of a good is produced, the opportunity cost of producing that good is relatively low because the economy needs to use only those resources that are especially well suited for its production.

For example, if an economy grows only a small amount of corn, that corn can be grown in places where the soil and climate are perfect for corn-growing but less suitable for growing anything else, like wheat. So growing that corn involves giving up only a small amount of potential wheat output. Once the economy grows a lot of corn, however, land that is well suited for wheat but isn't so great for corn must be used to produce corn anyway. As a result, the additional corn production involves sacrificing considerably more wheat production. In other words, as more of a good is produced, its opportunity cost typically rises because well-suited inputs are used up and less adaptable inputs must be used instead.

Economic Growth Finally, the production possibility frontier helps us understand what it means to talk about *economic growth*. In the Introduction, we defined the concept of economic growth as *the growing ability of the economy to produce goods and services.* As we saw, economic growth is one of the fundamental features of the real economy. But are we really justified in saying that the economy has grown over time? After all, although the Canadian economy produces more of many things than it did a century ago, it produces less of other things—for example, horse-drawn carriages. Production of many goods, in other words, is actually down. So how can we say for sure that the economy as a whole has grown?

The answer is illustrated in Figure 2-3, where we have drawn two hypothetical production possibility frontiers for the economy. In them we have assumed once again that everyone in the economy works for Bombardier and, consequently, the economy produces only two goods, subway trains and jets. Notice how the two curves are nested, with the one labelled "Original *PPF*" lying completely inside the one labelled "New *PPF*." Now we can see graphically what we mean by economic growth of the economy: economic growth means an *expansion of the economy's production possibilities;* that is, the economy *can* produce more of everything.

For example, if the economy initially produces at point *A* (60 subway trains and 10 jets), economic growth means that the economy could move to point *E* (70 subway trains and 12 jets). *E* lies outside the original frontier; so in the

FIGURE 2-3 Economic Growth

Economic growth results in an *outward shift* of the production possibility frontier because production possibilities are expanded. The economy can now produce more of everything. For example, if production is initially at point *A* (50 subway trains and 10 jets), economic growth means that the economy could move to point *E* (60 subway trains and 12 jets).

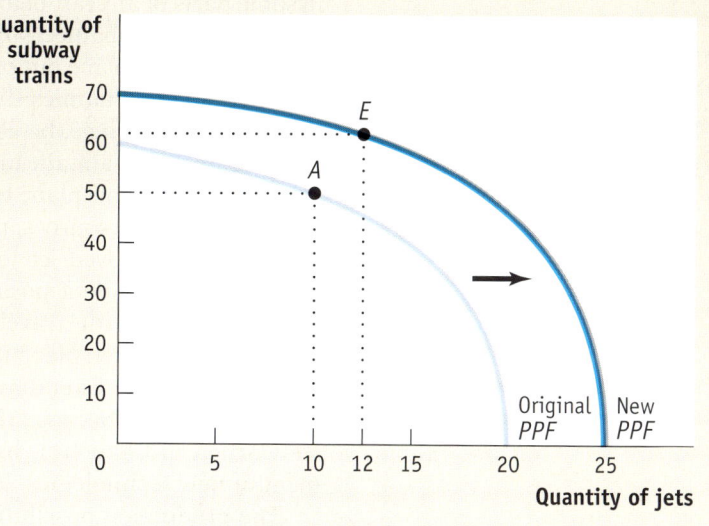

production possibility frontier model, growth is shown as an outward shift of the frontier.

What can lead the production possibility frontier to shift outward? There are basically two sources of economic growth. One is an increase in the economy's **factors of production,** the resources used to produce goods and services. Economists usually use the term *factor of production* to refer to a resource that is not used up in production. For example, in traditional airplane manufacture workers used riveting machines to connect metal sheets when constructing a plane's fuselage; the workers and the riveters are factors of production, but the rivets and the sheet metal are not. Once a fuselage is made, a worker and riveter can be used to make another fuselage, but the sheet metal and rivets used to make one fuselage cannot be used to make another.

Broadly speaking, the main factors of production are the resources: land, labour, physical capital, and human capital. Land is a resource supplied by nature; labour is the economy's pool of workers; physical capital refers to created resources such as machines and buildings; and human capital refers to the educational achievements and skills of the labour force, which enhance its productivity. Of course, each of these is actually a broad category rather than a single factor: land in Labrador is very different from land in Ontario.

To see how adding to an economy's factors of production leads to economic growth, suppose that Bombardier builds another production facility that allows it to increase the number of transportation vehicles—jets or subway trains or both—it can produce in a year. The new production facility is a factor of production, a resource Bombardier can use to increase its yearly output. How many more jets or subway trains of each type Bombardier will produce is a management decision that will depend on, among other things, customer demand. But we can say that Bombardier's production possibility frontier has shifted outward because it can now produce more jets without reducing the number of subway trains it makes, or it can make more subway trains without reducing the number of jets produced.

Factors of production are resources used to produce goods and services.

The four factors of production: land, labour, physical capital, and human capital.

Technology is the technical means for producing goods and services.

The other source of economic growth is progress in **technology,** the technical means for the production of goods and services. Composite materials had been used in some parts of aircraft before the Bombardier C-Series (now A220) was developed. But Bombardier engineers realized that there were large additional advantages to building a whole plane out of composites. The plane would be lighter, stronger, and have better aerodynamics than a plane built in the traditional way. It would there-fore have longer range, be able to carry more people, and use less fuel, in addition to being able to maintain higher cabin pressure. So in a real sense, Bombardier's innovation—a whole plane built out of composites—was a way to do more with any given amount of resources, pushing out the production possibility frontier.

Because improved jet technology has pushed out the production possibility frontier, it has made it possible for the economy to produce more of everything, not just jets and air travel. Over the past 30 years, the biggest technological advances have taken place in information technology, not in construction or food services. Yet some Canadians have chosen to buy bigger houses and eat out more than they used to because the economy's growth has made it possible to do so. As we learned in Chapter 1, increases in the economy's potential, like the development of new technologies, lead to economic growth over time.

The production possibility frontier is a very simplified model of an economy. Yet it teaches us important lessons about real-life economies. It gives us our first clear sense of what constitutes economic efficiency, it illustrates the concept of opportunity cost, and it makes clear what economic growth is all about.

Comparative Advantage and Gains from Trade

Another of the eleven principles of economics described in Chapter 1 is the principle of *gains from trade*—the mutual gains that individuals can achieve by specializing in doing different things and trading with one another. Our second illustration of an economic model is a particularly useful model of gains from trade—trade based on *comparative advantage.*

One of the most important insights in all of economics is that there are gains from trade: it makes sense to produce the things you're especially good at producing and to buy from other people the things you aren't as good at producing. This would be true even if you could produce everything for yourself: even if a brilliant brain surgeon *could* repair her own dripping faucet, it's probably a better idea for her to call in a professional plumber.

How can we model the gains from trade? Let's stay with our aircraft example and once again imagine that Canada is a one-company economy where everyone works for Bombardier, producing airplanes and subway trains. Let's now assume, however, that Canada has the ability to trade with Brazil—another one-company economy where everyone works for the Brazilian aircraft company Embraer, which is, in the real world, a successful producer of jets. (If you fly from one major Canadian city to another, your plane is likely to be a Bombardier, but if you fly into a small city, the odds are good that your plane will be an Embraer.)

In our example, the only two goods produced are subway trains and jets. Both countries could produce both kinds of jets. But as we'll see in a moment, they can gain by producing different things and trading with each other. For the purposes of this example, let's return to the simpler case of straight-line production possibility frontiers. Canada's production possibilities are represented by the production possibility frontier in panel (a) of Figure 2-4, which is similar to the production possibility frontier in Figure 2-1. According to this diagram, Canada can produce 70 subway trains if it makes no jets and can manufacture 20 jets if it makes no subway trains. Recall that this means that the slope of the Canadian production possibility frontier is $-\frac{7}{2}$: its opportunity cost of 1 jet is $\frac{7}{2}$ of a subway train.

Panel (b) of Figure 2-4 shows Brazil's production possibilities. Like Canada, Brazil's production possibility frontier is a straight line, implying a constant opportunity cost of jets in terms of subway trains. Brazil's production possibility

FIGURE 2-4 Production Possibilities for Two Countries

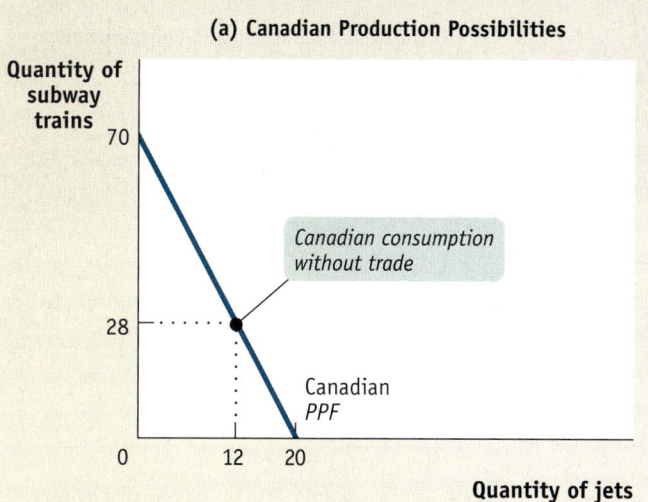

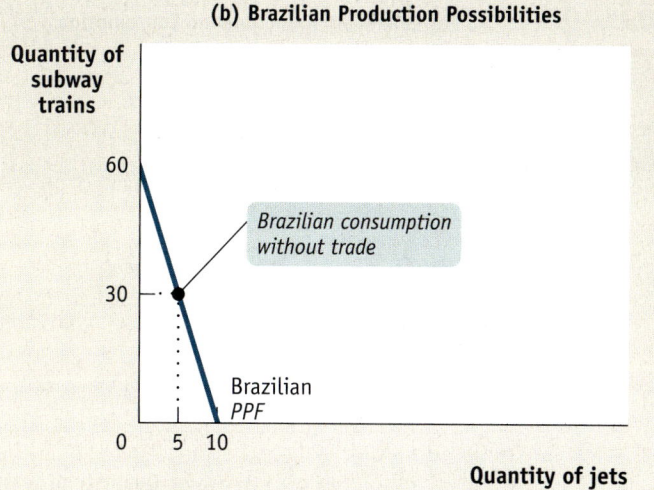

Here, both Canada and Brazil have a constant opportunity cost of jets, illustrated by a straight-line production possibility frontier. For Canada, each jet has an opportunity cost of ⅞ of a subway train. Brazil has an opportunity cost of a jet equal to 6 subway trains.

frontier has a constant slope of –6. Brazil can't produce as much of anything as Canada can: at most it can produce 60 subway trains or 10 jets. But it is relatively better at manufacturing subway trains than Canada; whereas Canada sacrifices ⅔ of a jet per subway train produced, for Brazil the opportunity cost of a subway train is only ⅙ of a jet. Table 2-1 summarizes the two countries' opportunity costs of subway trains and jets.

Now, Canada and Brazil could each choose to make their own subway trains and jets, not trading any of them and consuming only what each produced within its own country. (A country "consumes" an airplane when it is owned by a domestic resident.) Let's suppose that the two countries start out this way and make the consumption choices shown in Figure 2-4: in the absence of trade, Canada produces and consumes 28 subway trains and 12 jets per year, while Brazil produces and consumes 30 subway trains and 5 jets per year.

But is this the best the two countries can do? No, it isn't. Given that the two producers—and therefore the two countries—have different opportunity costs, Canada and Brazil can strike a deal that makes both of them better off.

Table 2-2 shows how such a deal works: Canada specializes in the production of jets, manufacturing 20 per year, and sells 6 to Brazil. Meanwhile, Brazil specializes in the production of subway trains, producing 60 per year, and sells 29 to Canada. The result is shown in Figure 2-5. Canada now consumes more subway trains

TABLE 2-1 Canadian and Brazilian Opportunity Costs of Jets and Subway Trains

	Canadian opportunity cost	Brazilian opportunity cost
1 subway train	⅔ jet > ⅙ jet	
1 jet	½ subway trains < 6 subway trains	

TABLE 2-2 How Canada and Brazil Gain from Trade

		Without trade		With trade		Gains from trade
		Production	Consumption	Production	Consumption	
Canada	Subway trains	28	28	0	29	+1
	Jets	12	12	20	14	+2
Brazil	Subway trains	30	30	60	31	+1
	Jets	5	5	0	6	+1

FIGURE 2-5 **Comparative Advantage and Gains from Trade**

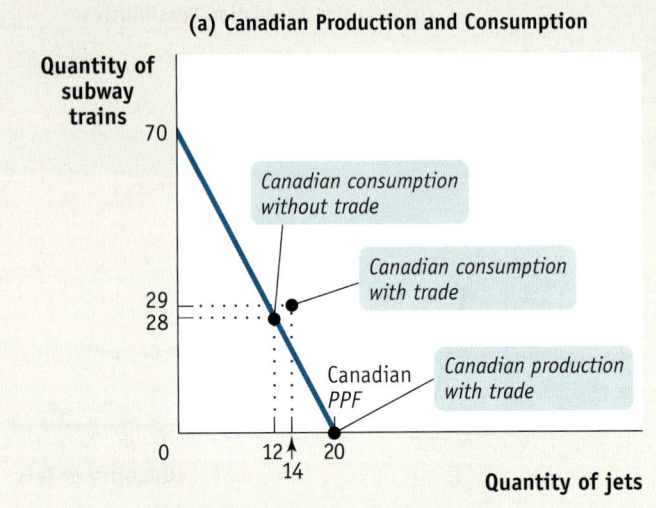

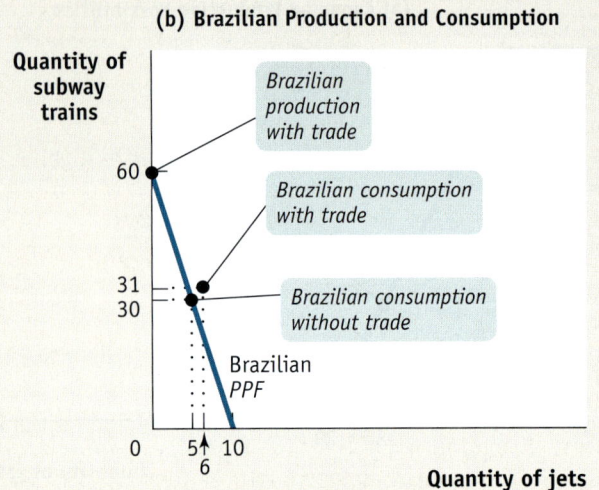

By specializing and trading, Canada and Brazil can produce and consume more of both jets and subway trains. Canada specializes in manufacturing jets, its comparative advantage, and Brazil — which has an *absolute* disadvantage in both goods but a *comparative* advantage in subway trains — specializes in manufacturing subway trains. With trade, both countries can consume more of both goods than either could without trade.

and jets than before: instead of 28 subway trains and 12 jets, it now consumes 29 subway trains and 14 jets. Brazil also consumes more, going from 30 subway trains and 5 jets to 31 subway trains and 6 jets. As Table 2-2 also shows, both Canada and Brazil reap gains from trade, consuming more of both types of transportation vehicle than they would have without trade.

Both countries are better off when they each specialize in what they are good at and trade. It's a good idea for Canada to specialize in the production of jets because its opportunity cost of a jet is smaller than Brazil's: $\frac{7}{2} < 6$. Correspondingly, Brazil should specialize in the production of subway trains because its opportunity cost of a subway train is smaller than Canada's: $\frac{1}{6} < \frac{2}{7}$.

What we would say in this case is that Canada has a comparative advantage in the production of jets and Brazil has a comparative advantage in the production of subway trains. A country has a **comparative advantage** in producing something if the opportunity cost of that production is lower for that country than for other countries. The same concept applies to firms and people: a firm or an individual has a comparative advantage in producing something if its or their opportunity cost of production is lower than for others.

One point of clarification before we proceed further. You may have wondered why Canada traded 6 jets to Brazil in return for 29 subway trains. Why not some other deal, like trading 6 jets for 20 subway trains? The answer to that question has two parts. First, there may indeed be other trades that Canada and Brazil might agree to. Second, there are some deals that we can safely rule out — one like 6 jets for 20 subway trains.

To understand why, reexamine Table 2-1 and consider Canada first. Without trading with Brazil, the Canadian opportunity cost of a subway train is $\frac{2}{7}$ of a jet. So it's clear that Canada will not accept any trade that requires it to give up more than $\frac{2}{7}$ of a jet for a subway train. Trading 6 jets in return for 20 subway trains would require Canada to pay an opportunity cost of $\frac{6}{20} = \frac{3}{10}$ of a jet for a subway train. Because $\frac{3}{10}$ is greater than $\frac{2}{7}$, this is a deal that Canada would reject. Similarly, Brazil won't accept a trade that gives it less than 6 subway trains for a jet.

A country has a **comparative advantage** in producing a good or service if its opportunity cost of producing the good or service is lower than other countries' cost. Likewise, an individual has a comparative advantage in producing a good or service if their opportunity cost of producing the good or service is lower than it is for other people.

The point to remember is that Canada and Brazil will be willing to trade only if the "price" of the good each country obtains in the trade is less than its own opportunity cost of producing the good domestically. Moreover, this is a general statement that is true whenever two parties—countries, firms, or individuals—trade voluntarily.

While our story clearly simplifies reality, it teaches us some very important lessons that apply to the real economy, too.

First, the model provides a clear illustration of the gains from trade: through specialization and trade, both countries produce more and consume more than if they were self-sufficient.

Second, the model demonstrates a very important point that is often overlooked in real-world arguments: each country has a comparative advantage in producing something. This applies to firms and people as well: *everyone has a comparative advantage in something, and everyone has a comparative disadvantage in something.*

Crucially, in our example it doesn't matter if, as is probably the case in real life, Canadian workers are just as good as or even better than Brazilian workers at producing subway trains and jets. Suppose that Canada is actually better than Brazil at production of both types of transportation vehicles. In that case, we would say that Canada has an **absolute advantage** in both subway train and jet production: in an hour, a Canadian worker can produce more of either a subway train or jet than a Brazilian worker. You might be tempted to think that in that case Canada has nothing to gain from trading with the less productive Brazil.

But we've just seen that Canada can indeed benefit from trading with Brazil because *comparative, not absolute, advantage is the basis for mutual gain.* It doesn't matter whether it takes Brazil more resources than Canada to make a subway train; what matters for trade is that for Brazil the opportunity cost of a subway train is lower than the Canadian opportunity cost. So Brazil, despite its absolute disadvantage, even in subway trains, has a comparative advantage in the manufacture of subway trains. Meanwhile Canada, which can use its resources most productively by manufacturing jets, has a comparative *dis*advantage in manufacturing subway trains.

A country has an **absolute advantage** in producing a good or service if the country can produce more output per worker than other countries. Likewise, an individual has an absolute advantage in producing a good or service if they are better at producing it than other people. Having an absolute advantage is not the same thing as having a comparative advantage.

Comparative Advantage and International Trade, in Reality

Look at the label on a manufactured good sold in Canada, and there's a good chance you will find that it was produced in some other country—in China, or Japan, or even in the United States. On the other side, many Canadian industries sell a large fraction of their output overseas. This is particularly true of agriculture, high technology, and entertainment.

PITFALLS

MISUNDERSTANDING COMPARATIVE ADVANTAGE

Students do it, pundits do it, and politicians do it all the time: they confuse *comparative advantage* with *absolute advantage*. For example, back in the 1980s, when the North American economy seemed to be lagging behind that of Japan, news commentators could be heard warning that if we didn't improve our productivity, we would soon have no comparative advantage in anything.

What those commentators meant was that we would have no *absolute advantage* in anything—that there might come a time when

the Japanese were better at everything than we were. (It didn't turn out that way, but that's another story.) And they had the idea that in that case we would no longer be able to benefit from trade with Japan.

But just as Brazil, in our example, was able to benefit from trade with Canada (and vice versa) despite the fact that Canada was absolutely better at manufacturing both jets and subway trains, in real life, nations can still gain from trade even if they are less productive in all industries than the countries they trade with.

Should all this international exchange of goods and services be celebrated, or is it cause for concern? Politicians and the public often question the desirability of international trade, arguing that the nation should produce goods for itself rather than buying them from foreigners. Industries around the world demand protection from foreign competition: Japanese farmers want to keep out Canadian rice, Canadian steelworkers want to keep out European steel. And these demands are often supported by public opinion.

Economists, however, have a very positive view of international trade. Why? Because they view it in terms of comparative advantage. As we learned from our example of Canadian jets and Brazilian subway trains, international trade benefits both countries. Each country can consume more than if it doesn't trade and remains self-sufficient. Moreover, these mutual gains don't depend on each country being better than other countries at producing one kind of good. Even if one country has, say, higher output per worker in both industries—that is, even if one country has an absolute advantage in both industries—there are still gains from trade. The following Global Comparison illustrates just this point.

GLOBAL COMPARISON   PAJAMA REPUBLICS

A terrible industrial disaster made headlines when a building that housed five clothing factories collapsed in Bangladesh in 2013, killing more than a thousand garment workers trapped inside. Attention soon focused on the substandard working conditions in those factories, as well as the many violations of building codes and safety procedures—including those required by Bangladeshi law—that set the stage for the tragedy.

While this disaster provoked a justified outcry, it also highlighted the remarkable rise of Bangladesh's clothing industry, which has become a major player in world markets—second only to China in total exports—and a desperately needed source of income and employment in a very poor country.

It's not that Bangladesh has especially high productivity in clothing manufacturing. In fact, estimates by the consulting firm McKinsey & Company suggest that it's about a quarter less productive than China. Rather, it has even lower productivity in other industries, giving it a comparative advantage in clothing manufacturing. This is typical in poor countries, which often rely heavily on clothing exports during the early phases of their economic development. An official from one such country once joked, "We are not a banana republic—we are a pajama republic."

The figure plots the per capita income of several such "pajama republics" (the total income of the country divided by the size of the population) against the share of total exports accounted for by clothing; per capita income is measured as a percentage of the

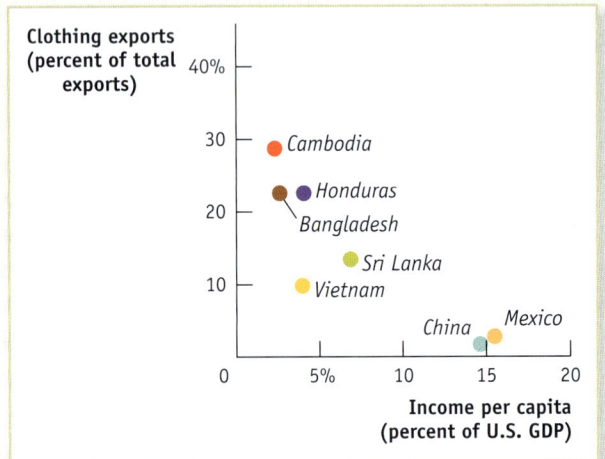

U.S. level in order to give you a sense of just how poor these countries are. As you can see, they are very poor indeed—and the poorer they are, the more they depend on clothing exports.

It's worth pointing out, by the way, that relying on clothing exports is not necessarily a bad thing, despite tragedies like the one in Bangladesh. Indeed, Bangladesh, although still desperately poor, is more than four and a half times as rich as it was two decades ago, when it began its dramatic rise as a clothing exporter. (Also see the upcoming Economics in Action on Bangladesh.)

Data from: The World Bank.

Transactions: The Circular-Flow Diagram

Trade takes the form of **barter** when people directly exchange goods or services that they have for goods or services that they want.

The model economies that we've studied so far—each containing only one firm—are huge simplifications. We've also greatly simplified trade between Canada and Brazil, assuming that they engage only in the simplest of economic transactions, **barter,** in which one party directly trades a good or service for another good or service without using money. In a modern economy, simple barter is rare: usually people trade goods or services for money—pieces of coloured paper with no inherent value—and then trade those pieces of coloured paper for the goods or services they want. That is, they sell goods or services and buy other goods or services.

And they both sell and buy a lot of different things. The Canadian economy is a vastly complex entity, with more than a million workers employed by thousands of companies, producing thousands of different goods and services. Yet you can learn some very important things about the economy by considering the simple graphic shown in Figure 2-6, the **circular-flow diagram.** This diagram represents the transactions that take place in an economy by two kinds of flows around a circle: flows of physical things such as goods, services, labour, or raw materials in one direction, and flows of money that pay for these physical things in the opposite direction. In this case the physical flows are shown in blue, the money flows in green.

The simplest circular-flow diagram illustrates an economy that contains only two kinds of inhabitants: **households** and **firms.** A household consists of either an individual or a group of people (usually, but not necessarily, a family) that share their income. A firm is an organization that produces goods and services for sale—and that employs members of households.

As you can see in Figure 2-6, there are two kinds of markets in this simple economy. On the left side, there are **markets for goods and services** in which households buy the goods and services they want from firms. This produces a flow of goods and services to households and a return flow of money to firms.

On the right side, there are **factor markets** in which firms buy the resources they need to produce goods and services. Recall from earlier that the main factors of production are land, labour, physical capital, and human capital.

The factor market most of us know best is the labour market, in which workers sell their services. In addition, we can think of households as owning and selling the other factors of production to firms. For example, when a firm buys physical capital in the form of machines, the payment ultimately goes to the households that own the machine-making firm. In this case, the transactions occur in the *capital market,* the market in which capital is bought and sold. As we'll examine in detail later, factor markets ultimately determine an economy's **income distribution,** how the total income created in an economy is allocated between less-skilled workers, highly skilled workers, and the owners of capital and land.

The **circular-flow diagram** represents the transactions in an economy by flows around a circle.

A **household** is a person or a group of people that share their income.

A **firm** is an organization that produces goods and services for sale.

Firms sell goods and services that they produce to households in **markets for goods and services.**

Firms buy the resources they need to produce goods and services in **factor markets.**

An economy's **income distribution** is the way in which total income is divided among the owners of the various factors of production.

FIGURE 2-6 The Circular-Flow Diagram

This diagram represents the flows of money and of goods and services in the economy. In the markets for goods and services, households purchase goods and services from firms, generating a flow of money to the firms and a flow of goods and services to the households. The money flows back to households as firms purchase factors of production from the households in factor markets.

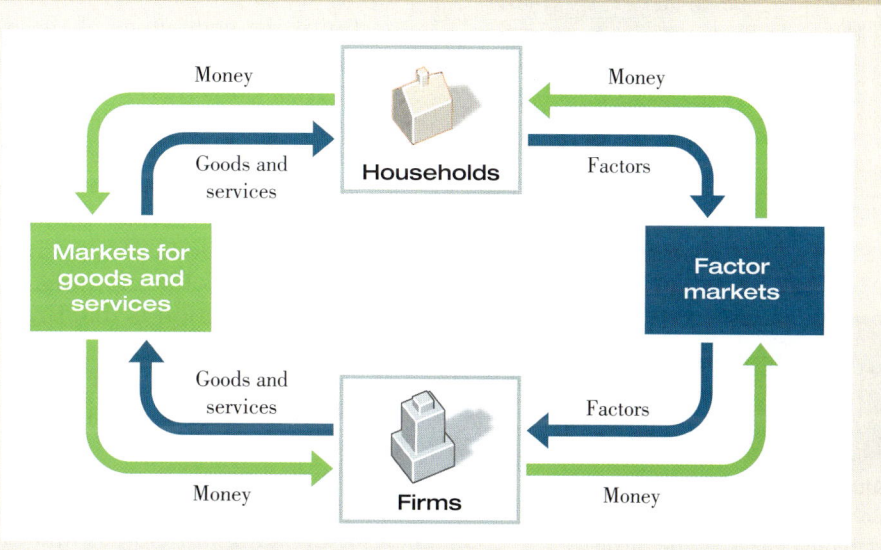

The circular-flow diagram ignores a number of real-world complications in the interests of simplicity. A few examples:

- In the real world, the distinction between firms and households isn't always that clear-cut. Consider a small, family-run business—a farm, a shop, a small hotel. Is this a firm or a household? A more complete picture would include a separate box for family businesses.

- Many of the sales that firms make are not to households but to other firms; for example, steel companies sell mainly to other companies such as auto manufacturers, not to households. A more complete picture would include these flows of goods, services, and money within the business sector.

- The figure doesn't show the government, which in the real world diverts quite a lot of money out of the circular flow in the form of taxes but also injects a lot of money back into the flow in the form of spending.

Figure 2-6, in other words, is by no means a complete picture either of all the types of inhabitants of the real economy or of all the flows of money and physical items that take place among these inhabitants.

Despite its simplicity, however, the circular-flow diagram is a very useful aid to thinking about the economy.

ECONOMICS >> *in Action*
Rich Nation, Poor Nation

Try taking off your clothes—at a suitable time and in a suitable place, of course—and taking a look at the labels inside that say where they were made. It's a very good bet that much, if not most, of your clothes were manufactured overseas, in a country that is much poorer than Canada—say, in El Salvador, Sri Lanka, or Bangladesh.

Why are these countries so much poorer than we are? The immediate reason is that their economies are much less *productive*—firms in these countries are just not able to produce as much from a given quantity of resources as comparable firms in Canada or other wealthy countries. Why countries differ so much in productivity is a deep question—indeed, one of the main questions that preoccupy economists. But in any case, the difference in productivity is a fact.

But if the economies of these countries are so much less productive than ours, how is it that they make so much of our clothing? Why don't we do it for ourselves?

The answer is "comparative advantage." Just about every industry in Bangladesh is much less productive than the corresponding industry in Canada. But the productivity difference between rich and poor countries varies across goods; it is very large in the production of sophisticated goods like aircraft but not that large in the production of simpler goods like clothing. So Bangladesh's position with regard to clothing production is like Brazil's position with respect to producing subway trains; it's not as (absolutely) good at it as Canada, but it's the thing Brazil does comparatively well.

Although Bangladesh is at an absolute disadvantage compared with Canada in almost everything, it has a comparative advantage in clothing production. This means that both Canada and Bangladesh are able to consume more because they specialize in producing different things, with Bangladesh supplying our clothes and Canada supplying Bangladesh with more sophisticated goods.

Jeff Holt/Bloomberg via Getty Images

Although less productive than the Canadian economy, Bangladesh's economy has a comparative advantage in clothing production.

>> Check Your Understanding 2-1
Solutions appear at back of book.

1. True or false? Explain your answer.
   a. An increase in the amount of resources available to Bombardier for use in producing private business jets and subway trains does not change its production possibility frontier.
   b. A technological change that allows Bombardier to build more subway trains for any amount of private business jets built results in a change in its production possibility frontier.
   c. The production possibility frontier is useful because it illustrates how much of one good an economy must give up to get more of another good regardless of whether resources are being used efficiently.

2. In Italy, an automobile can be produced by 8 workers in one day and a washing machine by 3 workers in one day. In Canada, an automobile can be produced by 6 workers in one day and a washing machine by 2 workers in one day.
   a. Which country has an absolute advantage in the production of automobiles? In washing machines?
   b. Which country has a comparative advantage in the production of washing machines? In automobiles?
   c. What pattern of specialization results in the greatest gains from trade between the two countries?

3. Using Table 2-1, explain why Canada and Brazil are willing to engage in a trade of 7 jets for 29 subway trains.

4. Use the circular-flow diagram to explain how an increase in the amount of money spent by households results in an increase in the number of jobs in the economy. Describe in words what the circular-flow diagram predicts.

Using Models

We have now seen how economic analysis is mainly a matter of creating models that draw on a set of basic principles but add some more specific assumptions that allow the modeller to apply those principles to a particular situation. But what do economists actually *do* with their models?

Positive versus Normative Economics

Imagine that you are an economic adviser to the premier of your province. What kinds of questions might the premier ask you to answer?

Well, here are three possible questions:

1. How much revenue will the provincial gasoline tax yield next year?
2. How much would that revenue increase if the tax were raised by 5 percentage points?
3. Should the government increase the tax, bearing in mind that the tax increase will raise much needed revenue and reduce traffic and air pollution, but will impose some financial hardship on frequent commuters and the trucking industry?

There is a big difference between the first two questions and the third one. The first two are questions about facts. Your forecast of next year's gasoline tax collection will be proved right or wrong when the numbers actually come in. Your estimate of the impact of a change in the tax is a little harder to check—revenue depends on other factors besides the tax, and it may be hard to disentangle the causes of any change in revenue. Still, in principle there is only one right answer.

But the question of whether gasoline tax should be raised may not have a "right" answer—two people who agree on the effects of a higher tax could still

Positive economics is the branch of economic analysis that describes the way the economy actually works.

Normative economics makes prescriptions about the way the economy should work.

A **forecast** is a simple prediction of the future.

disagree about whether raising the tax is a good idea. For example, someone who takes public transit or walks to work probably won't care about the increased gasoline tax but may care about the reduced traffic and pollution. However, a regular car commuter may have the opposite priorities.

This example highlights a key distinction between two roles of economic analysis. Analysis that tries to answer questions about the way the world works, which have definite right and wrong answers, is known as **positive economics.** In contrast, analysis that involves saying how the world *should* work is known as **normative economics.** To put it another way, positive economics is about description; normative economics is about prescription.

Positive economics occupies most of the time and effort of the economics profession. And models play a crucial role in almost all positive economics. As we mentioned earlier, the Canadian government uses a computer model to assess proposed changes in national tax policy, and many provincial governments have similar models to assess the effects of their own tax policy.

It's worth noting that there is a subtle but important difference between the first and second questions we imagined the premier asking. Question 1 asked for a simple prediction about next year's revenue—a **forecast.** Question 2 was a "what if" question, asking how revenue would change if the tax law were changed. Economists are often called upon to answer both types of questions, but models are especially useful for answering "what if" questions.

The answers to such questions often serve as a guide to policy, but they are still predictions, not prescriptions. That is, they tell you what will happen if a policy were changed; they don't tell you whether or not that result is good.

Suppose your economic model tells you that the premier's proposed increase in gasoline taxes will raise property values in communities near the highway but will hurt people who must use the highway to get to work. Does that make this proposed tax increase a good idea or a bad one? It depends on whom you ask. As we've just seen, someone who is very concerned with the communities near the road will support the increase, but someone who is very concerned with the welfare of drivers will feel differently. That's a value judgment—it's not a question of economic analysis.

Still, economists often do engage in normative economics and give policy advice. How can they do this when there may be no "right" answer?

One answer is that economists are also citizens, and we all have our opinions. But economic analysis can often be used to show that some policies are clearly better than others, regardless of anyone's opinions.

Suppose that policies A and B achieve the same goal, but policy A makes everyone better off than policy B—or at least makes some people better off without making other people worse off. Then A is clearly more efficient than B. That's not a value judgment: we're talking about how best to achieve a goal, not about the goal itself.

For example, two different policies have been used to help low-income families obtain housing: rent control, which limits the rents landlords are allowed to charge, and rent subsidies, which provide families with additional money to pay rent. Almost all economists agree that subsidies are the more efficient policy. And so the great majority of economists, whatever their personal politics, favour subsidies over rent control.

When policies can be clearly ranked in this way, then economists generally agree. But it is no secret that economists sometimes disagree.

‖ When and Why Economists Disagree

Economists have a reputation for arguing with each other. Where does this reputation come from, and is it justified?

One important answer is that media coverage tends to exaggerate the real differences in views among economists. If nearly all economists agree on an issue—for example, the proposition that rent controls lead to housing shortages—reporters and editors are likely to conclude that it's not a story worth covering, leaving the professional consensus unreported. But an issue on which prominent economists take opposing sides—for example, whether cutting taxes right now would help the economy—makes a news story worth reporting. So you hear much more about the areas of disagreement within economics than you do about the large areas of agreement.

It is also worth remembering that economics is, unavoidably, often tied up in politics. On a number of issues powerful interest groups know what opinions they want to hear; they therefore have an incentive to find and promote economists who profess those opinions, giving these economists a prominence and visibility out of proportion to their support among their colleagues.

While the appearance of disagreement among economists exceeds the reality, it remains true that economists often *do* disagree about important things. For example, some well-respected economists argue vehemently that the Canadian government should replace the income tax with a *value-added tax* (a national sales tax, which is the main source of government revenue in many European countries). Other equally respected economists disagree. Why this difference of opinion?

One important source of differences lies in values: as in any diverse group of individuals, reasonable people can differ. In comparison to an income tax, a value-added tax typically falls more heavily on people of modest means. So an economist who values a society with more social and income equality for its own sake will tend to oppose a value-added tax. An economist with different values will be less likely to oppose it.

A second important source of differences arises from economic modelling. Because economists base their conclusions on models, which are simplified representations of reality, two economists can legitimately disagree about which simplifications are appropriate—and therefore arrive at different conclusions.

Suppose that the Canadian government were considering introducing a value-added tax. Economist A may rely on a model that focuses on the administrative costs of tax systems—that is, the costs of monitoring, processing papers, collecting the tax, and so on. This economist might then point to the well-known high costs of administering a value-added tax and argue against the change. But economist B may think that the right way to approach the question is to ignore the administrative costs and focus on how the proposed law would change savings behaviour. This economist might point to studies suggesting that value-added taxes promote higher consumer saving, a desirable result.

Because the economists have used different models—that is, made different simplifying assumptions—they arrive at different conclusions. And so the two economists may find themselves on different sides of the issue.

ECONOMICS >> *in Action*
When Economists Agree

"If all the economists in the world were laid end to end, they still couldn't reach a conclusion," goes an economist joke. But do economists really disagree that much? Not according to an ongoing survey. The Booth School of Business at the University of Chicago has assembled a panel of 51 economists, all with exemplary professional reputations, representing a mix of regions, schools, and political

These four economists are on the panel (clockwise from top left): Cecilia Rouse of Princeton, David Cutler of Harvard, Hilary Hoynes of University of California, Berkeley, and Raj Chetty of Harvard.

affiliations. They are regularly polled on questions of policy or political interest, often ones on which there are bitter divides among politicians or the general public.

Yet the survey shows much more agreement among economists than rumour would have it, even on supposedly controversial topics. For example, 85% of the panel agreed that trade with China makes most Americans better off and nearly the same percentage agreed that Americans who work in the production of competing goods, like clothing, are made worse off by trade with China. Roughly the same percentage (82%) disagreed with the proposition that rent control increases the supply of quality, affordable housing.

In the first case, the panel overwhelmingly agreed with a position widely considered liberal in American politics, while in the second case they agreed with one widely considered politically conservative.

Disagreements tended to involve untested economic policies. There was, for example, an almost even split over whether new policies adopted by the Federal Reserve, the U.S. central bank, aimed at boosting the economy during the deep recession of 2007 to 2009 would work. Ideology played a limited role in these disagreements: Economists known to be liberals did have slightly different positions, on average, from those known to be conservatives, but the differences weren't nearly as large as those among the general public.

So economists do disagree quite a lot on some issues, especially in macroeconomics. But there is a large area of common ground.

>> Quick Review

• **Positive economics** — the focus of most economic research — is the analysis of the way the world works, in which there are definite right and wrong answers. It often involves making **forecasts. Normative economics,** which makes prescriptions about how things *ought to be,* inevitably involves value judgments.

• Economists do disagree — though not as much as legend has it — for two main reasons. One, they may disagree about which simplifications to make in a model. Two, economists may disagree — like everyone else — about values.

>> Check Your Understanding 2-2

Solutions appear at back of book.

1. Which of the following is a positive statement? Which is a normative statement?
   a. Society should take measures to prevent people from engaging in dangerous personal behaviour.
   b. People who engage in dangerous personal behaviour impose higher costs on society through higher medical costs.
2. True or false? Explain your answer.
   a. Policy choice A and policy choice B attempt to achieve the same social goal. Policy choice A, however, results in a much less efficient use of resources than policy choice B. Therefore, economists are more likely to agree on choosing policy choice B.
   b. When two economists disagree on the desirability of a policy, it's typically because one of them has made a mistake.

Efficiency, Opportunity Cost, and the Logic of Lean Production

Dan Lamont/Alamy

In January 2020, the Boeing 777X, an update to the widely popular 777, took its maiden flight. The 777X was the product of what Boeing calls its *advanced manufacturing* process. With it, Boeing extended its extremely successful process known as *lean production* to newer production methods, such as robotics.

Lean manufacturing, pioneered by Toyota Motors of Japan, is based on the practice of having parts arrive on the factory floor just as they are needed for production. This reduces the amount of parts Boeing holds in inventory as well as the amount of the factory floor needed for production. To help move from lean production to advanced manufacturing Boeing has turned to Toyota, hiring some of its top engineers.

Boeing first adopted lean manufacturing in 1999 in the manufacture of the 737, the most popular commercial airplane. By 2005, after constant refinement, it achieved a 50% reduction in the time it takes to produce a plane and a nearly 60% reduction in parts inventory. An important feature is a continuously moving assembly line, moving products from one assembly team to the next at a steady pace and eliminating the need for workers to wander across the factory floor from task to task or in search of tools and parts.

Toyota's lean production techniques have been the most widely adopted, revolutionizing manufacturing worldwide. In simple terms, lean production is focused on organization and communication. Workers and parts are organized so as to ensure a smooth and consistent workflow that minimizes wasted effort and materials. Lean production is also designed to be highly responsive to changes in the desired mix of output—for example, quickly producing more SUVs and fewer sedans according to changes in customer demand.

Toyota's methods were so successful that they transformed the global auto industry and severely threatened once-dominant North American automakers. Until the 1980s, the "Big Three"—Chrysler, Ford, and General Motors—dominated the North American auto industry, with virtually no foreign-made cars sold in North America. In the 1980s, however, Toyotas became increasingly popular due to their high quality and relatively low price—so popular that the Big Three eventually prevailed upon the U.S. government to protect them by restricting the sale of Japanese autos in the United States. A few months later, the Canadian government also imposed a quota on the number of autos Toyota could export to Canada. Over time, Toyota responded by building assembly plants in the United States and Canada, bringing along its lean production techniques, which then spread throughout North American manufacturing.

QUESTIONS FOR THOUGHT

1. What is the opportunity cost associated with having a worker wander across the factory floor from task to task or in search of tools and parts?

2. Explain how lean manufacturing improves the economy's efficiency in allocation.

3. Before lean manufacturing innovations, Japan mostly sold consumer electronics to Canada. How did lean manufacturing innovations alter Japan's comparative advantage vis-à-vis Canada?

4. How do you think the shift in the location of Toyota's production from Japan to Canada has altered the pattern of comparative advantage in automaking between the two countries?

SUMMARY

1. Almost all economics is based on **models,** "thought experiments" or simplified versions of reality, many of which use mathematical tools such as graphs. An important assumption in economic models is the **other things equal assumption,** which allows analysis of the effect of a change in one factor by holding all other relevant factors unchanged.

2. One important economic model is the **production possibility frontier.** It illustrates *opportunity cost* (showing how much less of one good can be produced if more of the other good is produced); *efficiency* (an economy is efficient in production if it produces on the production possibility frontier and efficient in allocation if it produces the mix of goods and services that people want to consume); and *economic growth* (an outward shift of the production possibility frontier). There are two basic sources of growth: an increase in **factors of production**—resources such as land, labour, capital, and human capital, inputs that are not used up in production—and improved **technology.**

3. Another important model is **comparative advantage,** which explains the source of gains from trade between individuals and countries. Everyone has a comparative advantage in something—some good or service in which that person has a lower opportunity cost than everyone else. But it is often confused with **absolute advantage,** an ability to produce a particular good or service better than anyone else. This confusion leads some to erroneously conclude that there are no gains from trade between people or countries.

4. In the simplest economies people **barter**—trade goods and services for one another—rather than trade them for money, as in a modern economy. The **circular-flow diagram** represents transactions within the economy as flows of goods, services, and money between **households** and **firms.** These transactions occur in **markets for goods and services** and **factor markets,** markets for factors of production—land, labour, physical capital, and human capital. The circular-flow diagram is useful in understanding how spending, production, employment, income, and growth are related in the economy. Ultimately, factor markets determine the economy's **income distribution,** how an economy's total income is allocated to the owners of the factors of production.

5. Economists use economic models for both **positive economics,** which describes how the economy works, and for **normative economics,** which prescribes how the economy *should* work. Positive economics often involves making **forecasts.** Economists can determine correct answers for positive questions but typically not for normative questions, which involve value judgments. The exceptions are when policies designed to achieve a certain objective can be clearly ranked in terms of efficiency.

6. There are two main reasons economists disagree. One, they may disagree about which simplifications to make in a model. Two, economists may disagree—like everyone else—about values.

KEY TERMS

Model, p. 28
Other things equal assumption, p. 28
Production possibility frontier, p. 29
Factors of production, p. 33
Technology, p. 34
Comparative advantage, p. 36

Absolute advantage, p. 37
Barter, p. 38
Circular-flow diagram, p. 39
Household, p. 39
Firm, p. 39
Markets for goods and services, p. 39

Factor markets, p. 39
Income distribution, p. 39
Positive economics, p. 42
Normative economics, p. 42
Forecast, p. 42

PRACTICE QUESTIONS

1. Penelope Pundit, an economics reporter, states that the European Union (EU) is increasing its productivity very rapidly in all industries. She claims that this productivity advance is so rapid that output from the EU in these industries will soon exceed that of Canada and, as a result, Canada will no longer benefit from trade with the EU.

   a. Do you think Penelope Pundit is correct or not? If not, what do you think is the source of her mistake?

   b. If the EU and Canada continue to trade, what do you think will characterize the goods that the EU sells to Canada and the goods that Canada sells to the EU?

2. The inhabitants of the fictional economy of Atlantis use money in the form of cowry shells. Draw a circular-flow diagram showing households and firms. Firms produce potatoes and fish, and households buy potatoes and fish. Households also provide the land

and labour to firms. Identify where in the flows of cowry shells or physical things (goods and services, or resources) each of the following impacts would occur. Describe how this impact spreads around the circle.

a. A devastating hurricane floods many of the potato fields.

b. A very productive fishing season yields a very large number of fish caught.

c. The inhabitants of Atlantis discover Shakira and spend several days a month at dancing festivals.

3. An economist might say that colleges and universities "produce" education, using faculty members and students as inputs. According to this line of reasoning, education is then "consumed" by households. Construct a circular-flow diagram to represent the sector of the economy devoted to college and university education: colleges and universities represent firms, and households both consume education and provide faculty and students to colleges and universities. What are the relevant markets in this diagram? What is being bought and sold in each direction? What would happen in the diagram if the government decided to subsidize 50% of all college and university students' tuition?

4. A representative of the Canadian clothing industry made the following statement: "Workers in Asia often work in sweatshop conditions earning only pennies an hour. Canadian workers are more productive and

as a result earn higher wages. In order to preserve the dignity of the Canadian workplace, the government should enact legislation banning imports of low-wage Asian clothing."

a. Which parts of this quote are positive statements? Which parts are normative statements?

b. Is the policy that is being advocated consistent with the preceding statements about the wages and productivities of Canadian and Asian workers?

c. Would such a policy make some Canadians better off without making any other Canadians worse off? That is, would this policy be efficient from the viewpoint of all Canadians?

d. Would Asian workers earning low wages benefit from or be hurt by such a policy?

5. Evaluate the following statement: "It is easier to build an economic model that accurately reflects events that have already occurred than to build an economic model to forecast future events." Do you think this is true or not? Why? What does this imply about the difficulties of building good economic models?

6. Economists who work for the government are often called on to make policy recommendations. Why do you think it is important for the public to be able to differentiate normative statements from positive statements in these recommendations?

PROBLEMS

1. Two important industries on the island of Bermuda are fishing and tourism. According to data from the Food and Agriculture Organization of the United Nations and the Bermuda Department of Statistics, in a single year the 315 registered fishermen in Bermuda caught 497 metric tons of marine fish. And the 2,446 people employed by hotels produced 580,209 hotel stays (measured by the number of visitor arrivals). Suppose that this production point is efficient in production. Assume also that the opportunity cost of 1 additional metric ton of fish is 2,000 hotel stays and that this opportunity cost is constant (the opportunity cost does not change).

a. If all 315 registered fishermen were to be employed by hotels (in addition to the 2,446 people already working in hotels), how many hotel stays could Bermuda produce?

b. If all 2,446 hotel employees were to become fishermen (in addition to the 315 fishermen already working in the fishing industry), how many metric tons of fish could Bermuda produce?

c. Draw a production possibility frontier for Bermuda, with fish on the horizontal axis and hotel stays on the vertical axis, and label Bermuda's actual production point for 2014.

2. According to Statistics Canada, 11.1 million hectares of land in Canada were used for wheat or corn

farming in 2019. Of those 11.1 million hectares, farmers used 9.7 million hectares to grow 1,188.6 million bushels of wheat and 1.4 million hectares of land to grow 527.7 million bushels of corn. Suppose that Canadian wheat and corn farming is efficient in production. At that production point, the opportunity cost of producing 1 additional bushel of wheat is 1.7 fewer bushels of corn. However, because farmers have increasing opportunity costs, additional bushels of wheat have an opportunity cost greater than 1.7 bushels of corn. For each of the following production points, decide whether that production point is (i) feasible and efficient in production, (ii) feasible but not efficient in production, (iii) not feasible, or (iv) unclear as to whether or not it is feasible.

a. Farmers use 2.6 million hectares of land to produce 319 million bushels of wheat, and they use 2.5 million hectares of land to produce 942 million bushels of corn. The remaining 5 million hectares are left unused.

b. From their original production point, farmers transfer 0.6 million hectares of land from corn to wheat production. They now produce 1,218.5 million bushels of wheat and 387.4 million bushels of corn.

c. Farmers reduce their production of wheat to 1,125.6 million bushels and increase their production of corn to 620.7 million bushels. Along the production possibility frontier, the opportunity cost of going from

527.7 million bushels of corn to 620.7 million bushels of corn is 0.666 bushel of wheat per bushel of corn.

3. In the ancient country of Roma, only two goods, spaghetti and meatballs, are produced. There are two tribes in Roma, the Tivoli and the Frivoli. By themselves, the Tivoli each month can produce either 30 kilograms of spaghetti and no meatballs, or 50 kilograms of meatballs and no spaghetti, or any combination in between. The Frivoli, by themselves, each month can produce 40 kilograms of spaghetti and no meatballs, or 30 kilograms of meatballs and no spaghetti, or any combination in between.

   a. Assume that all production possibility frontiers are straight lines. Draw one diagram showing the monthly production possibility frontier for the Tivoli and another showing the monthly production possibility frontier for the Frivoli. Show how you calculated them.

   b. Which tribe has the comparative advantage in spaghetti production? In meatball production?

   In A.D. 100, the Frivoli discover a new technique for making meatballs that doubles the quantity of meatballs they can produce each month.

   c. Draw the new monthly production possibility frontier for the Frivoli.

   d. After the innovation, which tribe now has an absolute advantage in producing meatballs? In producing spaghetti? Which has the comparative advantage in meatball production? In spaghetti production?

4. According to the Canadian International Merchandise Trade Database from Statistics Canada in 2019, Canada sold cereal worth $935.8 million to China and bought cereal worth only $7.4 million from China. During the same year, however, Canada bought $6,275.8 million worth of textiles and textile articles from China but sold only $121.3 million worth of textiles and textile articles to China. Using what you have learned about how trade is determined by comparative advantage, answer the following questions.

   a. Which country has the comparative advantage in cereal production? In production of textiles and textile articles?

   b. Can you determine which country has the absolute advantage in cereal production? In production of textiles and textile articles?

5. You are in charge of allocating residents to your dormitory's baseball and basketball teams. You are down to the last four people, two of whom must be allocated to baseball and two to basketball. The accompanying table gives each person's batting average and free-throw average.

Name	Batting average	Free-throw average
Taylor	70%	60%
Nico	50%	50%
Annie	10%	30%
Ryan	80%	70%

   a. Explain how you would use the concept of comparative advantage to allocate the players. Begin by establishing each player's opportunity cost of free throws in terms of batting average.

   b. Why is it likely that the other basketball players will be unhappy about this arrangement but the other baseball players will be satisfied? Nonetheless, why would an economist say that this is an efficient way to allocate players for your dorm's sports teams?

6. Your roommate plays loud music most of the time; you, however, would prefer more peace and quiet. You suggest that she buy some headphones. She responds that although she would be happy to use headphones, she has many other things that she would prefer to spend her money on right now. You discuss this situation with a friend who is an economics major. The following exchange takes place:

   Friend: How much would it cost to buy headphones?
   You: $15.

   Friend: How much do you value having some peace and quiet for the rest of the semester?
   You: $30.

   Friend: It is efficient for you to buy the headphones and give them to your roommate. You gain more than you lose; the benefit exceeds the cost. You should do that.

   You: It just isn't fair that I have to pay for the headphones when I'm not the one making the noise.

   a. Which parts of this conversation contain positive statements and which parts contain normative statements?

   b. Construct an argument supporting your viewpoint that your roommate should be the one to change her behaviour. Similarly, construct an argument from the viewpoint of your roommate that you should be the one to buy the headphones. If your dormitory has a policy that gives residents the unlimited right to play music, whose argument is likely to win? If your dormitory has a rule that a person must stop playing music whenever a roommate complains, whose argument is likely to win?

7. Are the following statements true or false? Explain your answers.

   a. "When people must pay higher taxes on their wage earnings, it reduces their incentive to work" is a positive statement.

   b. "We should lower taxes to encourage more work" is a positive statement.

   c. Economics cannot always be used to completely decide what society ought to do.

   d. "The system of public education in this country generates greater benefits to society than the cost of running the system" is a normative statement.

   e. All disagreements among economists are generated by the media.

8. The mayor of Gotham City, worried about a potential epidemic of deadly influenza this winter, asks an economic

adviser the following series of questions. Determine whether a question requires the economic adviser to make a positive assessment or a normative assessment.

a. How much vaccine will be in stock in the city by the end of November?

b. If we offer to pay 10% more per dose to the pharmaceutical companies providing the vaccines, will they provide additional doses?

c. If there is a shortage of vaccine in the city, whom should we vaccinate first—the elderly or the very young? (Assume that a person from one group has an equal likelihood of dying from influenza as a person from the other group.)

d. If the city charges $25 per shot, how many people will pay?

e. If the city charges $25 per shot, it will make a profit of $10 per shot, money that can go to pay for inoculating poor people. Should the city engage in such a scheme?

WORK IT OUT

9. Atlantis is a small, isolated island in the South Atlantic. The inhabitants grow potatoes and catch fish. The accompanying table shows the maximum annual output combinations of potatoes and fish that can be produced. Obviously, given their limited resources and available technology, as they use more of their resources for potato production, there are fewer resources available for catching fish.

Maximum annual output options	Quantity of potatoes (kilograms)	Quantity of fish (kilograms)
A	1,000	0
B	800	300
C	600	500
D	400	600
E	200	650
F	0	675

a. Draw a production possibility frontier with potatoes on the horizontal axis and fish on the vertical axis illustrating these options, showing points *A–F*.

b. Can Atlantis produce 500 kilograms of fish and 800 kilograms of potatoes? Explain. Where would this point lie relative to the production possibility frontier?

c. What is the opportunity cost of increasing the annual output of potatoes from 600 to 800 kilograms?

d. What is the opportunity cost of increasing the annual output of potatoes from 200 to 400 kilograms?

e. Can you explain why the answers to parts c and d are not the same? What does this imply about the slope of the production possibility frontier? ■

Graphs in Economics

Getting the Picture

When reading about economics in the *Globe and Mail* or in your economics textbook, you will see many graphs. Visual images can make it much easier to understand verbal descriptions, numerical information, or ideas. In economics, graphs are the type of visual image used to facilitate understanding. So, you need to be familiar with how to interpret and construct these visual aids. This appendix explains how to do this.

Graphs, Variables, and Economic Models

One reason to attend college and university is that a bachelor's degree provides access to higher paying jobs. Additional degrees, such as MBAs or law degrees, increase earnings even more. If you were to read an article about the relationship between educational attainment and income, you would probably see a graph showing the income levels for workers with different amounts of education. And this graph would depict the idea that, in general, more education increases income.

This graph, like most of those in economics, would depict the relationship between two economic variables. A **variable** is a quantity that can take on more than one value, such as the number of years of education a person has, the price of a can of pop, or a household's income.

As you learned in Chapter 2, economic analysis relies heavily on *models*, simplified descriptions of real situations. Most economic models describe the relationship between two variables, simplified by holding constant other variables that may affect the relationship.

For example, an economic model might describe the relationship between the price of a can of pop and the number of cans of pop that consumers will buy, assuming that everything else affecting consumers' purchases of pop stays constant. This type of model can be described mathematically or verbally, but illustrating the relationship in a graph makes it easier to understand, as you'll see next.

How Graphs Work

Most graphs in economics are based on a grid built around two perpendicular lines that show the values of two variables, helping you visualize the relationship between them. Let's see how this works.

Two-Variable Graphs

Figure 2A-1 shows a typical two-variable graph. It illustrates the data in the accompanying table on outside temperature and the number of cans of pop a typical vendor can expect to sell at a baseball stadium during one game. The first column shows the values of outside temperature (the first variable) and the second column shows the values of the number of cans of pop sold (the second variable). Five combinations or pairs of the two variables are shown, each denoted by *A* through *E* in the third column.

A quantity that can take on more than one value is called a **variable.**

FIGURE 2A-1 Plotting Points on a Two-Variable Graph

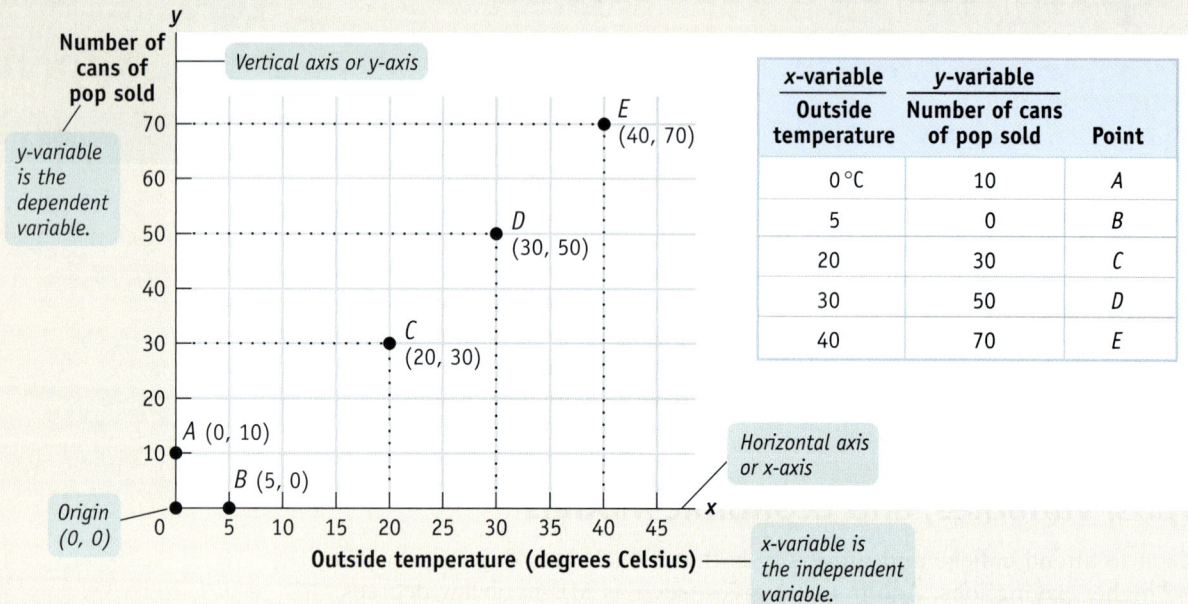

The data from the table are plotted where outside temperature (the independent variable) is measured along the horizontal axis and number of cans of pop sold (the dependent variable) is measured along the vertical axis. Each of the five combinations of temperature and cans of pop sold is represented by a point: A, B, C, D, and E. Each point in the graph is identified by a pair of values. For example, point C corresponds to the pair (20, 30)—an outside temperature of 20°C (the value of the x-variable) and 30 cans of pop sold (the value of the y-variable).

The line along which values of the x-variable are measured is called the **horizontal axis** or **x-axis.** The line along which values of the y-variable are measured is called the **vertical axis** or **y-axis.** The point where the axes of a two-variable graph meet is the **origin.**

A **causal relationship** exists between two variables when the value taken by one variable directly influences or determines the value taken by the other variable. In a causal relationship, the determining variable is called the **independent variable;** the variable it determines is called the **dependent variable.**

Now let's turn to graphing the data in this table. In any two-variable graph, one variable is called the x-variable and the other is called the y-variable. Here we have made outside temperature the x-variable and number of cans of pop sold the y-variable. The solid horizontal line in the graph is called the **horizontal axis** or **x-axis,** and values of the x-variable—outside temperature—are measured along it. Similarly, the solid vertical line in the graph is called the **vertical axis** or **y-axis,** and values of the y-variable—number of cans of pop sold—are measured along it.

At the **origin,** the point where the two axes meet, each variable is equal to zero. As you move rightward from the origin along the x-axis, values of the x-variable are positive and increasing. As you move up from the origin along the y-axis, values of the y-variable are positive and increasing.

You can plot each of the five points A through E on this graph by using a pair of numbers—the values that the x-variable and the y-variable take on for a given point. In Figure 2A-1, at point C, the x-variable takes on the value 20 and the y-variable takes on the value 30. You plot point C by drawing a line straight up from 20 on the x-axis and a horizontal line across from 30 on the y-axis. We write point C as (20, 30). We write the origin as (0, 0).

Looking at point A and point B in Figure 2A-1, you can see that when one of the variables for a point has a value of zero, it will lie on one of the axes. If the value of the x-variable is zero, the point will lie on the vertical axis, like point A. If the value of the y-variable is zero, the point will lie on the horizontal axis, like point B.

Most graphs that depict relationships between two economic variables represent a **causal relationship,** a relationship in which the value taken by one variable directly influences or determines the value taken by the other variable. In a causal relationship, the determining variable is called the **independent variable;** the variable it determines is called the **dependent variable.** In our example of pop sales, the outside temperature is the independent variable.

It directly influences the number of cans of pop that are sold, the dependent variable in this case.

By convention, we put the independent variable on the horizontal axis and the dependent variable on the vertical axis. Figure 2A-1 is constructed consistent with this convention; the independent variable (outside temperature) is on the horizontal axis and the dependent variable (number of cans of pop sold) is on the vertical axis.

An important exception to this convention is in graphs showing the economic relationship between the price of a product and quantity of the product: although price is generally the independent variable that determines quantity, it is always measured on the vertical axis.

> A **curve** is a line on a graph that depicts a relationship between two variables. It may be either a straight line or a curved line. If the curve is a straight line, the variables have a **linear relationship.** If the curve is not a straight line, the variables have a **nonlinear relationship.**

Curves on a Graph

Panel (a) of Figure 2A-2 contains some of the same information as Figure 2A-1, with a line drawn through the points *B*, *C*, *D*, and *E*. Such a line on a graph is called a **curve,** regardless of whether it is a straight line or a curved line. If the curve that shows the relationship between two variables is a straight line, or linear, the variables have a **linear relationship.** When the curve is not a straight line, or nonlinear, the variables have a **nonlinear relationship.**

A point on a curve indicates the value of the *y*-variable for a specific value of the *x*-variable. For example, point *D* indicates that at a temperature of 30°C, a vendor can expect to sell 50 cans of pop. The shape and orientation of a curve reveal the general nature of the relationship between the two variables. The upward tilt of the curve in panel (a) of Figure 2A-2 means that vendors can expect to sell more cans of pop at higher outside temperatures.

FIGURE 2A-2 Drawing Curves

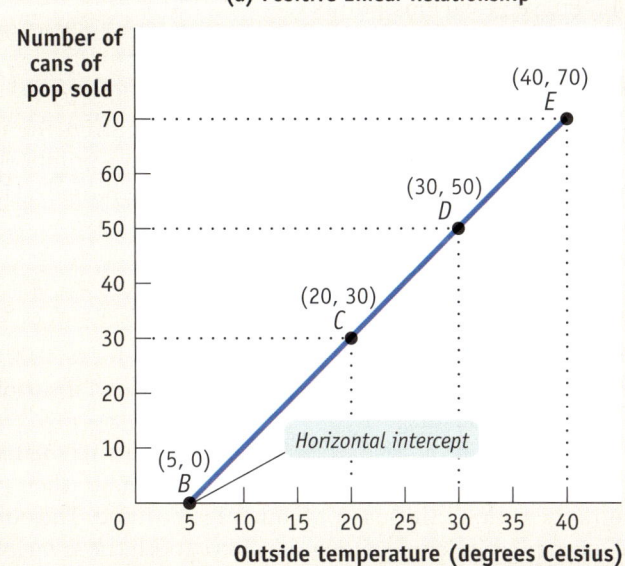
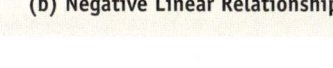
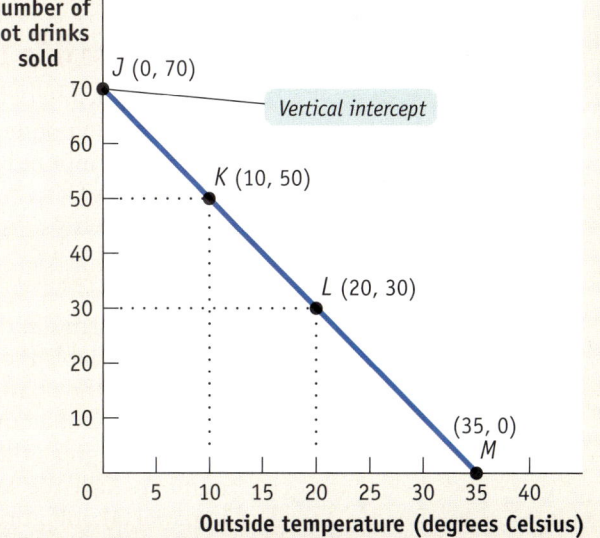

(a) Positive Linear Relationship

(b) Negative Linear Relationship

The curve in panel (a) illustrates the relationship between the two variables, outside temperature and number of cans of pop sold. The two variables have a positive linear relationship: positive because the curve has an upward tilt, and linear because it is a straight line. It implies that an increase in the *x*-variable (outside temperature) leads to an increase in the *y*-variable (number of cans of pop sold). The curve in panel (b) is also a straight line, but it tilts downward.

The two variables here, outside temperature and number of hot drinks sold, have a negative linear relationship: an increase in the *x*-variable (outside temperature) leads to a decrease in the *y*-variable (number of hot drinks sold). The curve in panel (a) has a horizontal intercept at point *B*, where it hits the horizontal axis. The curve in panel (b) has a vertical intercept at point *J*, where it hits the vertical axis, and a horizontal intercept at point *M*, where it hits the horizontal axis.

Two variables have a **positive relationship** when an increase in the value of one variable is associated with an increase in the value of the other variable. It is illustrated by a curve that slopes upward from left to right.

Two variables have a **negative relationship** when an increase in the value of one variable is associated with a decrease in the value of the other variable. It is illustrated by a curve that slopes downward from left to right.

The **horizontal intercept** of a curve is the point at which it hits the horizontal axis; it indicates the value of the *x*-variable when the value of the *y*-variable is zero.

The **vertical intercept** of a curve is the point at which it hits the vertical axis; it shows the value of the *y*-variable when the value of the *x*-variable is zero.

The **slope** of a line or curve is a measure of how steep it is. The slope of a line is measured by "rise over run"—the change in the *y*-variable between two points on the line divided by the change in the *x*-variable between those same two points.

When variables are related this way—that is, when an increase in one variable is associated with an increase in the other variable—the variables are said to have a **positive relationship.** It is illustrated by a curve that slopes upward from left to right. Because this curve is also linear, the relationship between outside temperature and number of cans of pop sold illustrated by the curve in panel (a) of Figure 2A-2 is a positive linear relationship.

When an increase in one variable is associated with a decrease in the other variable, the two variables are said to have a **negative relationship.** It is illustrated by a curve that slopes downward from left to right, like the curve in panel (b) of Figure 2A-2. Because this curve is also linear, the relationship it depicts is a negative linear relationship. Two variables that might have such a relationship are the outside temperature and the number of hot drinks a vendor can expect to sell at a baseball stadium.

Return for a moment to the curve in panel (a) of Figure 2A-2 and you can see that it hits the horizontal axis at point *B*. This point, known as the **horizontal intercept,** shows the value of the *x*-variable when the value of the *y*-variable is zero. In panel (b) of Figure 2A-2, the curve hits the vertical axis at point *J*. This point, called the **vertical intercept,** indicates the value of the *y*-variable when the value of the *x*-variable is zero.

A Key Concept: The Slope of a Curve

The **slope** of a curve is a measure of how steep it is and indicates how sensitive the *y*-variable is to a change in the *x*-variable. In our example of outside temperature and the number of cans of pop a vendor can expect to sell, the slope of the curve would indicate how many more cans of pop the vendor could expect to sell with each 1 degree increase in temperature. Interpreted this way, the slope gives meaningful information. Even without numbers for *x* and *y*, it is possible to arrive at important conclusions about the relationship between the two variables by examining the slope of a curve at various points.

The Slope of a Linear Curve

Along a linear curve, the slope, or steepness, is measured by dividing the *rise* between two points on the curve by the *run* between those same two points. The rise is the amount that *y* changes, and the run is the amount that *x* changes. Here is the formula:

$$\frac{\text{Change in } y}{\text{Change in } x} = \frac{\Delta y}{\Delta x} = \text{Slope}$$

In the formula, the symbol Δ (the Greek uppercase delta) stands for *change in.* When a variable increases, the change in that variable is positive; when a variable decreases, the change in that variable is negative.

The slope of a curve is positive when the rise (the change in the *y*-variable) has the same sign as the run (the change in the *x*-variable). That's because when two numbers have the same sign, the ratio of those two numbers is positive. The curve in panel (a) of Figure 2A-2 has a positive slope: along the curve, both the *y*-variable and the *x*-variable increase.

The slope of a curve is negative when the rise and the run have different signs. That's because when two numbers have different signs, the ratio of those two numbers is negative. The curve in panel (b) of Figure 2A-2 has a negative slope: along the curve, an increase in the *x*-variable is associated with a decrease in the *y*-variable.

Figure 2A-3 illustrates how to calculate the slope of a linear curve. Let's focus first on panel (a). From point *A* to point *B* the value of the *y*-variable changes from

FIGURE 2A-3 Calculating the Slope

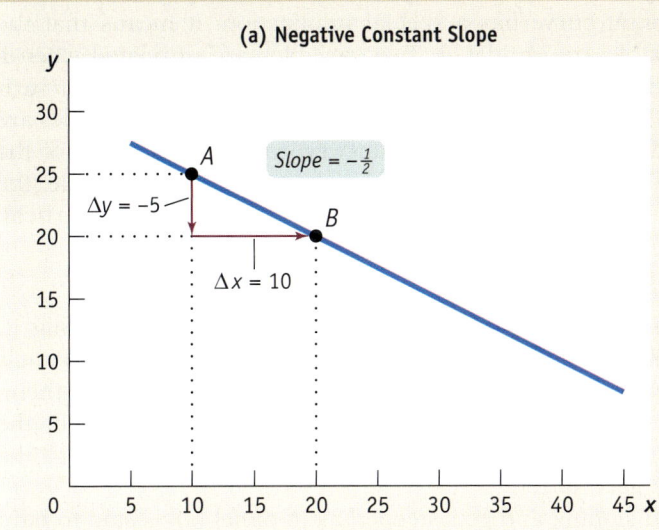

Panels (a) and (b) show two linear curves. Between points *A* and *B* on the curve in panel (a), the change in *y* (the rise) is −5 and the change in *x* (the run) is 10. So the slope from *A* to *B* is $\frac{\Delta y}{\Delta x} = \frac{-5}{10} = -\frac{1}{2} = -0.5$, where the negative sign indicates that the curve is downward sloping. In panel (b), the curve has a slope from *A* to *B* of $\frac{\Delta y}{\Delta x} = \frac{10}{2} = 5$. The slope from *C* to *D* is $\frac{\Delta y}{\Delta x} = \frac{20}{4} = 5$. The slope is positive, indicating that the curve is upward sloping. Furthermore, the slope between *A* and *B* is the same as the slope between *C* and *D*, making this a linear curve. The slope of a linear curve is constant: it is the same regardless of where it is measured along the curve.

25 to 20 and the value of the *x*-variable changes from 10 to 20. So the slope of the line between these two points is:

$$\frac{\text{Change in } y}{\text{Change in } x} = \frac{\Delta y}{\Delta x} = \frac{-5}{10} = -\frac{1}{2} = -0.5$$

Because a straight line is equally steep at all points, the slope of a straight line is the same at all points. In other words, a straight line has a constant slope. You can check this by calculating the slope of the linear curve between points *A* and *B* and between points *C* and *D* in panel (b) of Figure 2A-3.

Between *A* and *B*: $\dfrac{\Delta y}{\Delta x} = \dfrac{10}{2} = 5$

Between *C* and *D*: $\dfrac{\Delta y}{\Delta x} = \dfrac{20}{4} = 5$

Horizontal and Vertical Curves and Their Slopes

When a curve is horizontal, the value of the *y*-variable along that curve never changes—it is constant. Everywhere along the curve, the change in *y* is zero. Now, zero divided by any number is zero. So, regardless of the value of the change in *x*, the slope of a horizontal curve is always zero.

If a curve is vertical, the value of the *x*-variable along the curve never changes—it is constant. Everywhere along the curve, the change in *x* is zero. This means that the slope of a vertical curve is a ratio with zero in the denominator.

A **nonlinear curve** is one in which the slope is not the same between every pair of points.

The **absolute value** of a negative number is the value of the negative number without the minus sign.

A ratio with zero in the denominator is equal to infinity—that is, an infinitely large number. So the slope of a vertical curve is equal to infinity.

A vertical or a horizontal curve has a special implication: it means that the x-variable and the y-variable are unrelated. Two variables are unrelated when a change in one variable (the independent variable) has no effect on the other variable (the dependent variable). Or to put it a slightly different way, two variables are unrelated when the dependent variable is constant regardless of the value of the independent variable. If, as is usual, the y-variable is the dependent variable, the curve is horizontal. If the dependent variable is the x-variable, the curve is vertical.

The Slope of a Nonlinear Curve

A **nonlinear curve** is one in which the slope changes as you move along it. Panels (a), (b), (c), and (d) of Figure 2A-4 show various nonlinear curves. Panels (a) and (b) show nonlinear curves whose slopes change as you move along them, but the slopes always remain positive. Although both curves tilt upward, the curve in panel (a) gets steeper as you move from left to right in contrast to the curve in panel (b), which gets flatter.

A curve that is upward sloping and gets steeper, as in panel (a), is said to have *positive increasing* slope. A curve that is upward sloping but gets flatter, as in panel (b), is said to have *positive decreasing* slope.

When we calculate the slope along these nonlinear curves, we obtain different values for the slope at different points. How the slope changes along the curve determines the curve's shape. For example, in panel (a) of Figure 2A-4, the slope of the curve is a positive number that steadily increases as you move from left to right, whereas in panel (b), the slope is a positive number that steadily decreases.

The slopes of the curves in panels (c) and (d) are negative numbers. Economists often prefer to express a negative number as its **absolute value,** which is the value of the negative number without the minus sign. In general, we denote the absolute value of a number by two parallel bars around the number; for example, the absolute value of -4 is written as $|-4| = 4$.

In panel (c), the absolute value of the slope steadily increases as you move from left to right. The curve therefore has *negative increasing* slope. And in panel (d), the absolute value of the slope of the curve steadily decreases along the curve. This curve therefore has *negative decreasing* slope.

Calculating the Slope Along a Nonlinear Curve

We've just seen that along a nonlinear curve, the value of the slope depends on where you are on that curve. So how do you calculate the slope of a nonlinear curve? We will focus on two methods: the *arc method* and the *point method*.

The Arc Method of Calculating the Slope   An arc of a curve is some piece or segment of that curve. For example, panel (a) of Figure 2A-4 shows an arc consisting of the segment of the curve between points A and B. To calculate the slope along a nonlinear curve using the arc method, you draw a straight line between the two endpoints of the arc. The slope of that straight line is a measure of the average slope of the curve between those two endpoints.

You can see from panel (a) of Figure 2A-4 that the straight line drawn between points A and B increases along the x-axis from 6 to 10 (so that $\Delta x = 4$) as it increases along the y-axis from 10 to 20 (so that $\Delta y = 10$). Therefore the slope of the straight line connecting points A and B is:

$$\frac{\Delta y}{\Delta x} = \frac{10}{4} = 2.5$$

This means that the average slope of the curve between points A and B is 2.5.

FIGURE 2A-4 Nonlinear Curves

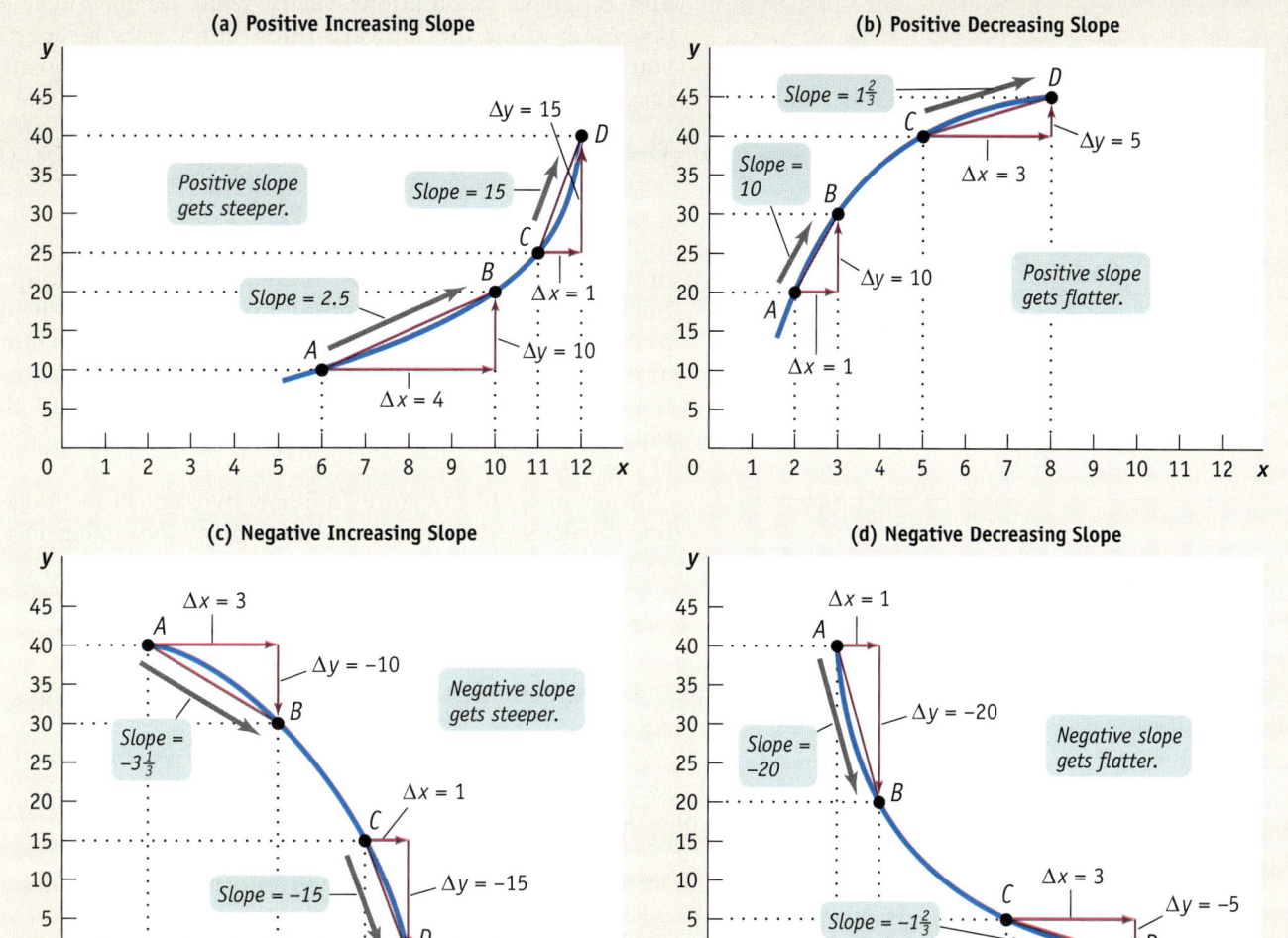

In panel (a), the slope of the curve from A to B is $\frac{y}{x} = \frac{10}{4} = 2.5$, and from C to D it is $\frac{\Delta y}{\Delta x} = \frac{15}{1} = 15$. The slope is positive and increasing; the curve gets steeper as you move to the right. In panel (b), the slope of the curve from A to B is $\frac{\Delta y}{\Delta x} = \frac{10}{1} = 10$, and from C to D it is $\frac{\Delta y}{\Delta x} = \frac{5}{3} = 1\frac{2}{3}$. The slope is positive and decreasing; the curve gets flatter as you move to the right. In panel (c), the slope from A to B is $\frac{\Delta y}{\Delta x} = \frac{-10}{3} = -3\frac{1}{3}$, and from C to D it is $\frac{\Delta y}{\Delta x} = \frac{-15}{1} = -15$. The slope is negative and increasing; the curve gets steeper as

you move to the right. And in panel (d), the slope from A to B is $\frac{\Delta y}{\Delta x} = \frac{-20}{1} = -20$, and from C to D it is $\frac{\Delta y}{\Delta x} = \frac{-5}{3} = -1\frac{2}{3}$. The slope is negative and decreasing; the curve gets flatter as you move to the right. The slope in each case has been calculated by using the arc method—that is, by drawing a straight line connecting two points along a curve. The average slope between those two points is equal to the slope of the straight line between those two points.

Now consider the arc on the same curve between points C and D. A straight line drawn through these two points increases along the x-axis from 11 to 12 ($\Delta x = 1$) as it increases along the y-axis from 25 to 40 ($\Delta y = 15$). So the average slope between points C and D is:

$$\frac{\Delta y}{\Delta x} = \frac{15}{1} = 15$$

FIGURE 2A-5 Calculating the Slope Using the Point Method

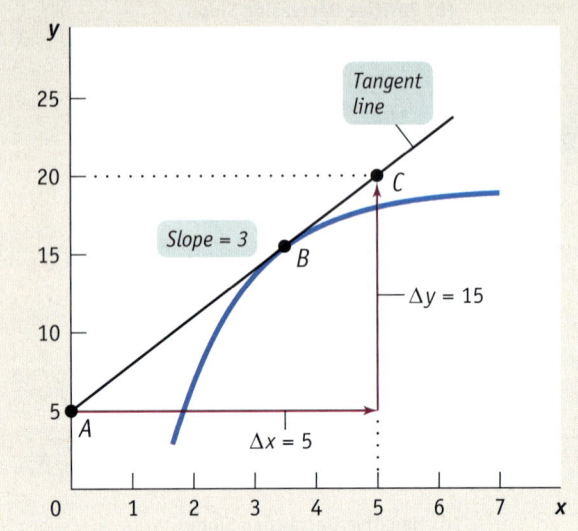

Here a tangent line has been drawn, a line that just touches the curve at point *B*. The slope of this line is equal to the slope of the curve at point *B*. The slope of the tangent line, measuring from *A* to *C*, is $\frac{\Delta y}{\Delta x} = \frac{15}{5} = 3$.

Therefore the average slope between points *C* and *D* is larger than the average slope between points *A* and *B*. These calculations verify what we have already observed—that this upward-tilted curve gets steeper as you move from left to right and therefore has positive increasing slope.

The Point Method of Calculating the Slope The point method calculates the slope of a nonlinear curve at a specific point on that curve. Figure 2A-5 illustrates how to calculate the slope at point *B* on the curve. First, we draw a straight line that just touches the curve at point *B*. Such a line is called a **tangent line:** the fact that it just touches the curve at point *B* and does not touch the curve at any other point on the curve means that the straight line is *tangent* to the curve at point *B*. The slope of this tangent line is equal to the slope of the nonlinear curve at point *B*.

You can see from Figure 2A-5 how the slope of the tangent line is calculated. From point *A* to point *C*, the change in *y* is 15 and the change in *x* is 5, generating a slope of

$$\frac{\Delta y}{\Delta x} = \frac{15}{5} = 3$$

By the point method, the slope of the curve at point *B* is equal to 3.

A natural question to ask at this point is which method should I use—the arc method or the point method—in calculating the slope of a nonlinear curve? The answer depends on the curve itself and the data used to construct it.

Use the arc method when you don't have enough information to be able to draw a smooth curve. For example, suppose that in panel (a) of Figure 2A-4 you have only the data represented by points *A, C,* and *D* and don't have the data represented by point *B* or any of the rest of the curve. Clearly, then, you can't use the point method to calculate the slope at point *B;* you would have to use the arc method to approximate the slope of the curve in this area by drawing a straight line between points *A* and *C*.

But if you have sufficient data to draw the smooth curve shown in panel (a) of Figure 2A-4, then you could use the point method to calculate the slope at point *B*—and at every other point along the curve as well.

Maximum and Minimum Points

The slope of a nonlinear curve can change from positive to negative or vice versa. When the slope of a curve changes from positive to negative, it creates what is called a *maximum* point of the curve. When the slope of a curve changes from negative to positive, it creates a *minimum* point.

Panel (a) of Figure 2A-6 illustrates a curve in which the slope changes from positive to negative as you move from left to right. When *x* is between 0 and 50, the slope of the curve is positive. At *x* equal to 50, the curve attains its highest point—the largest value of *y* along the curve. This point is called the **maximum** of the curve. When *x* exceeds 50, the slope becomes negative as the curve turns downward. Many important curves in economics, such as the curve that represents how the profit of a firm changes as it produces more output, are hill-shaped like this.

In contrast, the curve shown in panel (b) of Figure 2A-6 is U-shaped: it has a slope that changes from negative to positive. At *x* equal to 50, the curve reaches its lowest point—the smallest value of *y* along the curve. This point is called the

A **tangent line** is a straight line that just touches, or is tangent to, a nonlinear curve at a particular point. The slope of the tangent line is equal to the slope of the nonlinear curve at that point.

A nonlinear curve may have a **maximum** point, the highest point along the curve. At the maximum, the slope of the curve changes from positive to negative.

FIGURE 2A-6 Maximum and Minimum Points

(a) Maximum

Maximum point

y increases as x increases.

y decreases as x increases.

(b) Minimum

Minimum point

y decreases as x increases.

y increases as x increases.

Panel (a) shows a curve with a maximum point, the point at which the slope changes from positive to negative. Panel (b) shows a curve with a minimum point, the point at which the slope changes from negative to positive.

minimum of the curve. Various important curves in economics are U-shaped like this.

Calculating the Area Below or Above a Curve

It is useful to know how to measure the size of the area below or above a curve. For the sake of simplicity, we'll only calculate the area below or above a linear curve.

How large is the shaded area below the linear curve in panel (a) of Figure 2A-7? First note that this area has the shape of a right triangle. A right triangle is a triangle that has two sides that make a right angle with each other. We will refer to one of these sides as the *height* of the triangle and the other side as the *base* of the triangle. For our purposes, it doesn't matter which of these two sides we refer to as the base and which as the height.

Calculating the area of a right triangle is straightforward: multiply the height of the triangle by the base of the triangle, and divide the result by 2. The height of the triangle in panel (a) of Figure 2A-7 is 10 − 4 = 6. And the base of the triangle is 3 − 0 = 3. So the area of that triangle is:

$$\frac{6 \times 3}{2} = 9$$

How about the shaded area above the linear curve in panel (b) of Figure 2A-7? We can use the same formula to calculate the area of this right triangle. The height of the triangle is 8 − 2 = 6. And the base of the triangle is 4 − 0 = 4. So the area of that triangle is:

$$\frac{6 \times 4}{2} = 12$$

Graphs That Depict Numerical Information

Graphs are also a convenient way to summarize and display data without assuming some underlying causal relationship. Graphs that simply display numerical information are called *numerical graphs*.

A nonlinear curve may have a **minimum** point, the lowest point along the curve. At the minimum, the slope of the curve changes from negative to positive.

FIGURE 2A-7 Calculating the Area Below and Above a Linear Curve

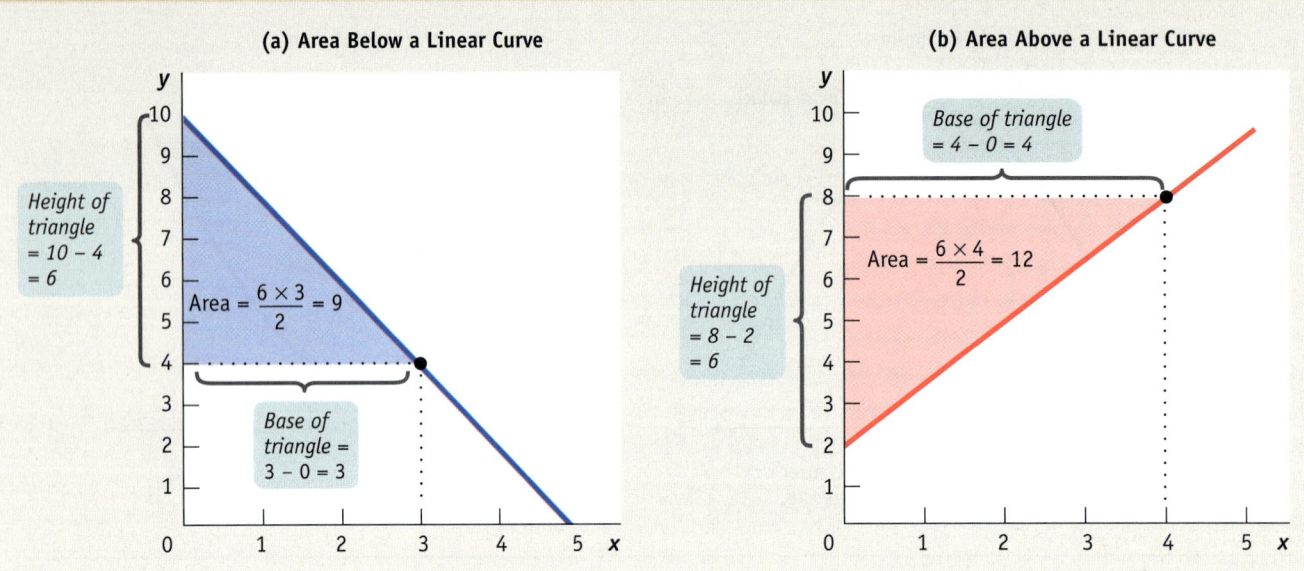

The area above or below a linear curve forms a right triangle. The area of a right triangle is calculated by multiplying the height of the triangle by the base of the triangle, and dividing the result by 2. In panel (a), the area of the shaded triangle is $6 \times \frac{3}{2} = 9$. In panel (b), the area of the shaded triangle is $6 \times \frac{4}{2} = 12$.

Here we will consider four types of numerical graphs: *time-series graphs, scatter diagrams, pie charts,* and *bar graphs.* These are widely used to display real, empirical data about different economic variables because they often help economists and policy makers identify patterns or trends in the economy. But it's important to be aware of both the usefulness and the limitations of numerical graphs to avoid misinterpreting them or drawing unwarranted conclusions from them.

Types of Numerical Graphs

You have probably seen graphs that show what has happened over time to economic variables such as the unemployment rate or stock prices. A **time-series graph** has successive dates on the horizontal axis and the values of a variable that occurred on those dates on the vertical axis.

For example, Figure 2A-8 shows real gross domestic product (GDP) per capita—a rough measure of a country's standard of living—in Canada from 1981 to 2019. A line connecting the points that correspond to real GDP per capita for each calendar quarter during those years gives a clear idea of the overall trend in the standard of living over these years.

Figure 2A-9 is an example of a different kind of numerical graph. It represents information from a sample of 180 countries on the standard of living, again measured by GDP per capita, and the amount of carbon emissions per capita, a measure of environmental pollution. Each point here indicates an average resident's standard of living and their annual carbon emissions for a given country.

The points lying in the upper right of the graph, which show combinations of a high standard of living and high carbon emissions, represent economically advanced countries such as Canada. (The country with the highest carbon

A **time-series graph** has dates on the horizontal axis and values of a variable that occurred on those dates on the vertical axis.

emissions, at the top of the graph, is Qatar.) Points lying in the bottom left of the graph, which show combinations of a low standard of living and low carbon emissions, represent economically less-advanced countries such as Afghanistan and Sierra Leone.

The pattern of points indicates that there is a positive relationship between living standard and carbon emissions per capita: on the whole, people create more pollution in countries with a higher standard of living.

This type of graph is called a **scatter diagram,** in which each point corresponds to an actual observation of the *x*-variable and the *y*-variable. In scatter diagrams, a curve is typically fitted to the scatter of points; that is, a curve is drawn that approximates as closely as possible the general relationship between the variables. As you can see, the fitted line in Figure 2A-9 is upward sloping, indicating the underlying positive relationship between the two variables. Scatter diagrams are often used to show how a general relationship can be inferred from a set of data.

A **pie chart** shows the share of a total amount that is accounted for by various components, usually expressed in percentages. For example, Figure 2A-10 is a pie chart that depicts what percentage of all unemployed in Canada in 2019 came from different age groups. The fraction of unemployed is the highest among people in the 15 to 24 years age group; about 27% of the unemployed in 2019 fell into this age group.

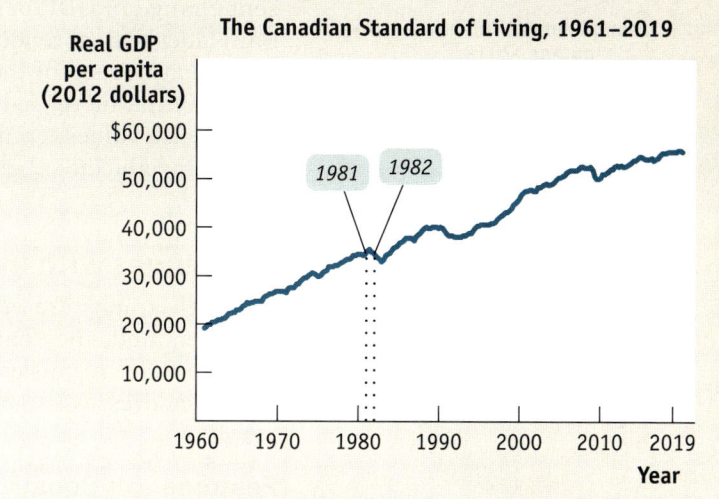

FIGURE 2A-8 Time-Series Graph

Time-series graphs show successive dates on the *x*-axis and values for a variable on the *y*-axis. This time-series graph shows real gross domestic product per capita, a measure of a country's standard of living, in Canada from 1961 to 2019.

Data from: Statistics Canada.

A **scatter diagram** shows points that correspond to actual observations of the *x*- and *y*-variables. A curve is usually fitted to the scatter of points.

A **pie chart** shows how some total is divided among its components, usually expressed in percentages.

FIGURE 2A-9 Scatter Diagram

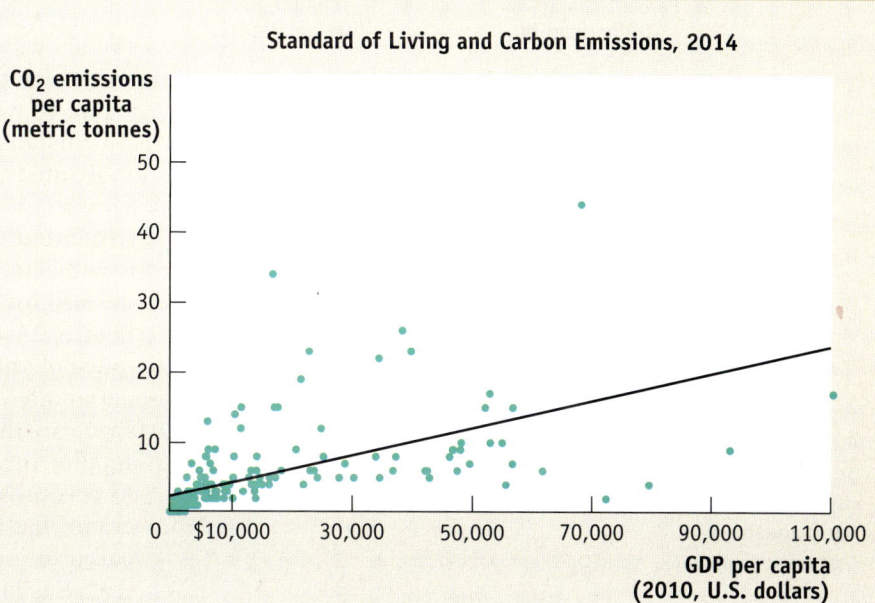

In a scatter diagram, each point represents the corresponding values of the *x*- and *y*-variables for a given observation. Here, each point indicates the GDP per capita and the amount of carbon dioxide emissions per capita for a given country for a sample of 180 countries. The upward-sloping fitted line here is the best approximation of the general relationship between the two variables.

Data from: World Development Indicators.

FIGURE 2A-10 Pie Chart

Unemployment in Canada by Age, 2019

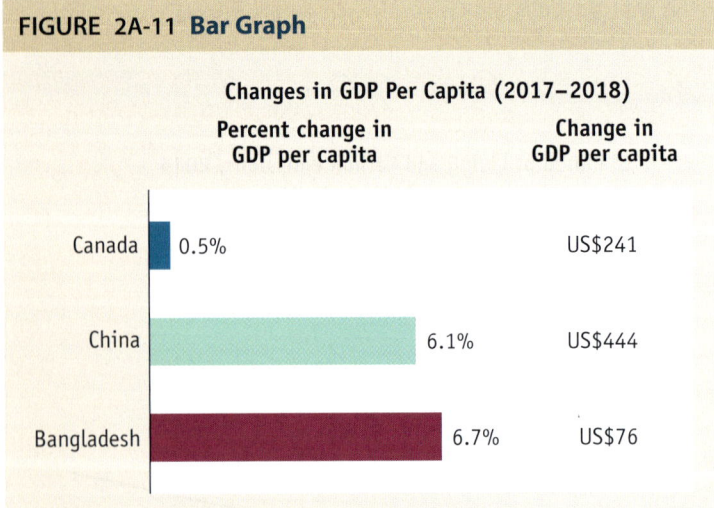

A pie chart shows the percentages of a total amount that can be attributed to various components. This pie chart shows the percentage of the unemployed in Canada in 2019 by age group.
Source: Statistics Canada.

Bar graphs use bars of various heights or lengths to indicate values of a variable. In the bar graph in Figure 2A-11, the bars show the percent change in GDP per capita from 2017 to 2018 for Canada, China, and Bangladesh. Exact values of the variable that is being measured may be written at the end of the bar, as in this figure. For instance, GDP per capita for China increased by 6.1% between 2017 and 2018. But even without the precise values, comparing the heights or lengths of the bars can give useful insight into the relative magnitudes of the different values of the variable.

Challenges with Interpreting Numerical Graphs

Although graphs are visual images that make ideas or information easier to understand, they can be constructed (intentionally or unintentionally) in ways that are misleading and can lead to inaccurate conclusions. This section addresses some difficulties you may have when you are analyzing graphs.

Features of Construction When evaluating a numerical graph, pay close attention to the scale, or size of increments, shown on the axes. Small increments tend to visually exaggerate changes in the variables, whereas large increments tend to visually diminish them. So the scale used in construction of a graph can influence your interpretation of the significance of the changes it illustrates—perhaps in an unwarranted way.

Figure 2A-12 shows real GDP per capita in Canada from 1980 to 1983 using increments of $500. You can see that real GDP per capita fell from $35,231 in the first-quarter of 1980 to $33,008 in the fourth-quarter of 1984. A decrease, sure, but is it as enormous as the scale chosen for the vertical axis makes it seem? It is not.

If you reexamine Figure 2A-8, which shows real GDP per capita in Canada from 1961 to 2019, you will see that it includes the same data shown in Figure 2A-12. But, Figure 2A-8 is constructed with a scale having increments of $10,000 rather than $500. From it you can see that the fall in real GDP per capita from 1981 to 1982 was, in fact, relatively insignificant.

In fact, the story of real GDP per capita—a measure of the standard of living—in Canada is mostly a story of ups, not downs. This comparison shows that if you are not careful to factor in the choice of scale in interpreting graphs, you can arrive at very different, and possibly incorrect, conclusions.

Related to the choice of scale is the use of *truncation* in constructing a graph. An axis is **truncated** when part of the range is omitted. This is indicated by two slashes (//) in the axis near the origin. You can see that the vertical axis of Figure 2A-12 has been truncated—some of the range of values from 0 to $31,500 have been omitted and a // appears in the axis. Truncation saves space in the presentation of a graph and allows smaller increments to be used in constructing it. As a result, changes in the variable depicted on a graph that has been truncated appear larger compared to a graph that has not been truncated and that uses larger increments.

FIGURE 2A-11 Bar Graph

Changes in GDP Per Capita (2017–2018)

	Percent change in GDP per capita	Change in GDP per capita
Canada	0.5%	US$241
China	6.1%	US$444
Bangladesh	6.7%	US$76

A bar graph measures a variable by using bars of various heights or lengths. This bar graph shows the percent change in GDP per capita (measured in constant 2010 US$) for Canada, China, and Bangladesh.
Data from: World Bank, World Development Indicators.

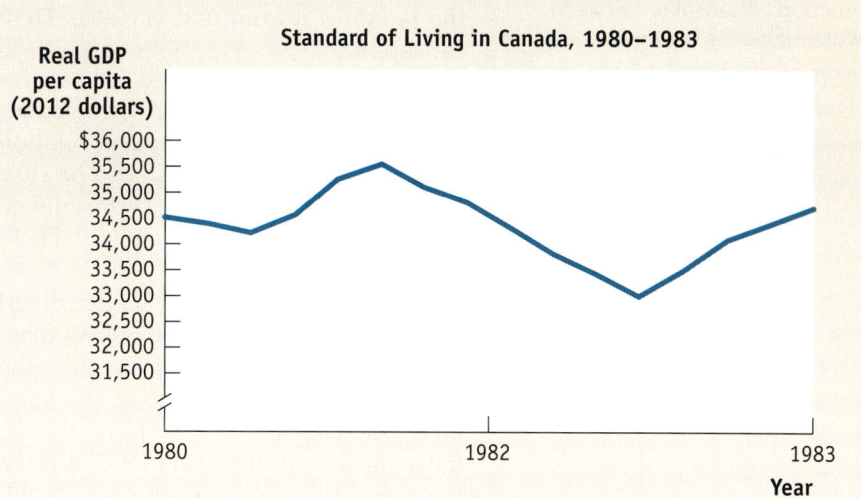

FIGURE 2A-12 Interpreting Graphs: The Effect of Scale

Some of the same data for the years 1981 and 1982 used in Figure 2A-8 are represented here, except that here they are shown using increments of $500 rather than increments of $10,000. As a result of this change in scale, changes in the standard of living look much larger in this figure compared to Figure 2A-8.

Data from: Statistics Canada.

You must also consider exactly what a graph is illustrating. For example, in Figure 2A-11, you should recognize that what is being shown are *percent* changes in GDP per capita, not *numerical* changes. The growth rate for Bangladesh increased by the highest percentage, 6.7% in this example. If you were to confuse numerical changes with percent changes, you would erroneously conclude the country with the greatest change in GDP per capita was Bangladesh.

In fact, a correct interpretation of Figure 2A-11 shows that the greatest percentage increase in GDP per capita was Bangladesh—a growth rate of 6.7%. Although there was a higher percentage increase in GDP per capita for Bangladesh, the dollar increase for Bangladesh from 2017 to 2018 was smaller than the change for Canada, which had the lowest growth rate, leading to a smaller change in GDP per capita for Bangladesh than Canada and China.

Omitted Variables From a scatter diagram that shows two variables moving either positively or negatively in relation to each other, it is easy to conclude that there is a causal relationship. But relationships between two variables are not always due to direct cause and effect. Quite possibly an observed relationship between two variables is due to the *unobserved* effect of a third variable on each of the other two variables.

An unobserved variable that, through its influence on other variables, creates the erroneous appearance of a direct causal relationship among those variables is called an **omitted variable.** For example, in Manitoba, a greater amount of snowfall during a given week will typically cause people to buy more snow shovels. It will also cause people to buy more de-icer fluid. But if you omitted the influence of the snowfall and simply plotted the number of snow shovels sold versus the number of bottles of de-icer fluid sold, you would produce a scatter diagram that showed an upward tilt in the pattern of points, indicating a positive relationship between snow shovels sold and de-icer fluid sold.

To attribute a causal relationship between these two variables, however, is misguided. More snow shovels sold do not cause more de-icer fluid to be sold, or vice versa. They move together because they are both influenced by a third, determining, variable—the weekly snowfall, which is the omitted variable in this case.

A **bar graph** uses bars of varying heights or lengths to show the comparative sizes of different observations of a variable.

An axis is **truncated** when some of the values on the axis are omitted, usually to save space.

An **omitted variable** is an unobserved variable that, through its influence on other variables, creates the erroneous appearance of a direct causal relationship among those variables.

The error of **reverse causality** is committed when the true direction of causality between two variables is reversed.

So before assuming that a pattern in a scatter diagram implies a cause-and-effect relationship, it is important to consider whether the pattern is instead the result of an omitted variable. Or to put it another way: correlation is not causation.

Reverse Causality Even when you are confident that there is no omitted variable and that there is a causal relationship between two variables shown in a numerical graph, you must also be sure to avoid making the mistake of **reverse causality**—coming to an erroneous conclusion about which is the dependent and which is the independent variable by reversing the true direction of causality between the two variables.

For example, imagine a scatter diagram that depicts the grade point averages (GPAs) of 20 of your classmates on one axis and the number of hours that each classmate spends studying on the other. A line fitted between the points will probably have a positive slope, showing a positive relationship between GPA and hours of studying. We could reasonably infer that hours spent studying is the independent variable and that GPA is the dependent variable. But you could make the error of reverse causality: you could infer that a high GPA causes a student to study more, whereas a low GPA causes a student to study less.

As you've just seen, it is important to understand how graphs can mislead or be interpreted incorrectly. Policy decisions, business decisions, and political arguments are often based on interpretation of the types of numerical graphs we've just discussed. Problems of misleading features of construction, omitted variables, and reverse causality can lead to important and undesirable consequences.

PROBLEMS

1. Study the four accompanying diagrams. Consider the following statements and indicate which diagram matches each statement. Which variable would appear on the horizontal and which on the vertical axis? In each of these statements, is the slope positive, negative, zero, or infinity?

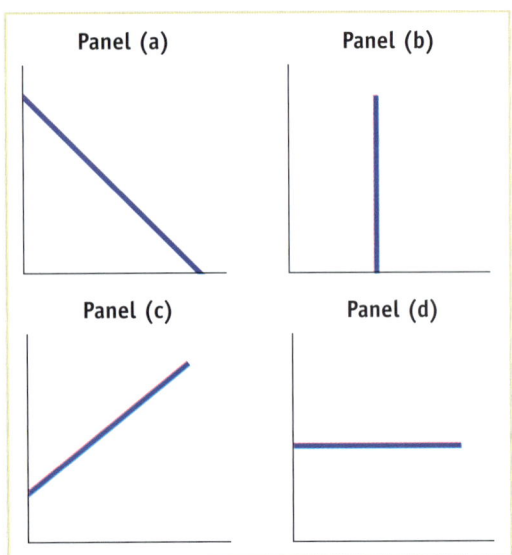

Panel (a)   Panel (b)

Panel (c)   Panel (d)

a. If the price of movies increases, fewer consumers go to see movies.

b. More experienced workers typically have higher incomes than less experienced workers.

c. Whatever the temperature outside, Canadians consume the same number of hot dogs per day.

d. Consumers buy more frozen yogurt when the price of ice cream goes up.

e. Research finds no relationship between the number of diet books purchased and the number of pounds lost by the average dieter.

f. Regardless of its price, Canadians buy the same quantity of salt.

2. In the early 1980s, economist Arthur Laffer argued in favour of lowering income tax rates in order to increase tax revenues. Like most economists, he believed that at tax rates above a certain level, tax revenue would fall because high taxes would discourage some people from working and that people would refuse to work at all if they received no income after paying taxes. This relationship between tax rates and tax revenue is graphically summarized in what is widely known as the Laffer curve. Plot the Laffer curve relationship assuming that it has the shape of a nonlinear curve. The following questions will help you construct the graph.

a. Which is the independent variable? Which is the dependent variable? On which axis do you therefore measure the income tax rate? On which axis do you measure income tax revenue?

b. What would tax revenue be at a 0% income tax rate?

c. The maximum possible income tax rate is 100%. What would tax revenue be at a 100% income tax rate?

d. Estimates now show that the maximum point on the Laffer curve is (approximately) at a tax rate of 80%. For tax rates less than 80%, how would you describe the relationship between the tax rate and tax revenue, and how is this relationship reflected in the slope? For tax rates higher than 80%, how would you describe the relationship between the tax rate and tax revenue, and how is this relationship reflected in the slope?

3. In the accompanying figures, the numbers on the axes have been lost. All you know is that the units shown on the vertical axis are the same as the units on the horizontal axis.

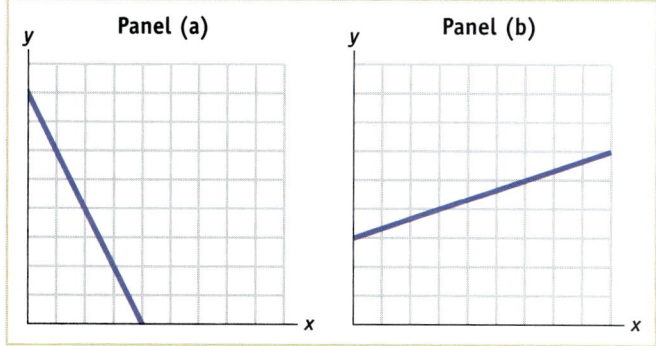

a. In panel (a), what is the slope of the line? Show that the slope is constant along the line.

b. In panel (b), what is the slope of the line? Show that the slope is constant along the line.

4. Answer each of the following questions by drawing a schematic diagram.

a. Taking measurements of the slope of a curve at three points farther and farther to the right along the horizontal axis, the slope of the curve changes from –0.3, to –0.8, to –2.5, measured by the point method. Draw a schematic diagram of this curve. How would you describe the relationship illustrated in your diagram?

b. Taking measurements of the slope of a curve at five points farther and farther to the right along the horizontal axis, the slope of the curve changes from 1.5, to 0.5, to 0, to –0.5, to –1.5, measured by the point method. Draw a schematic diagram of this curve. Does it have a maximum or a minimum?

5. For each of the accompanying diagrams, calculate the area of the shaded right triangle.

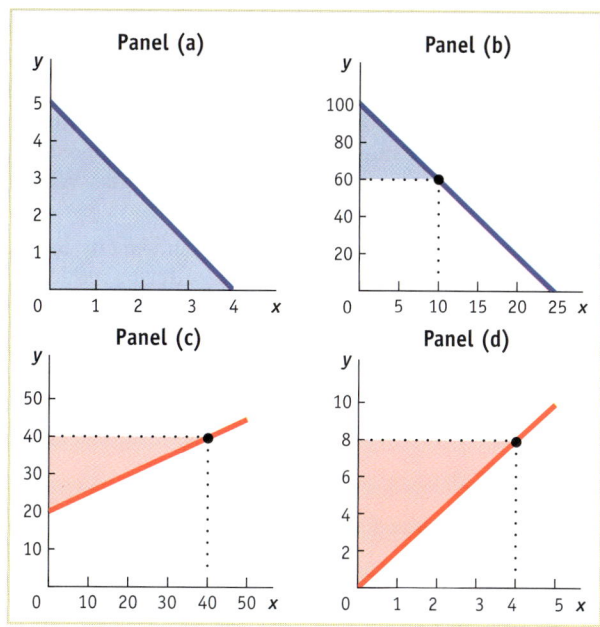

6. The base of a right triangle is 10, and its area is 20. What is the height of this right triangle?

7. The accompanying table shows the relationship between workers' hours of work per week and their hourly wage rate. Apart from the fact that they receive a different hourly wage rate and work different hours, these five workers are otherwise identical.

Name	Quantity of labour (hours per week)	Wage rate (per hour)
Akiko	30	$15
Ben	35	30
Cameron	37	45
Diego	36	60
Emily	32	75

a. Which variable is the independent variable? Which is the dependent variable?

b. Draw a scatter diagram illustrating this relationship. Draw a (nonlinear) curve that connects the points. Put the hourly wage rate on the vertical axis.

c. As the wage rate increases from $15 to $30, how does the number of hours worked respond according to the relationship depicted here? What is the average slope of the curve between Akiko's and Ben's data points using the arc method?

d. As the wage rate increases from $60 to $75, how does the number of hours worked respond according to the relationship depicted here? What is the average slope of the curve between Diego's and Emily's data points using the arc method?

8. An insurance company has found that the severity of property damage in a fire is positively related to the number of firefighters arriving at the scene.

   a. Draw a diagram that depicts this finding with number of firefighters on the horizontal axis and amount of property damage on the vertical axis. What is the argument made by this diagram? Suppose you reverse what is measured on the two axes. What is the argument made then?

   b. Should the insurance company ask the city to send fewer firefighters to any fire in order to reduce its payouts to policy holders?

9. This table illustrates annual salaries and income tax owed by five individuals. Despite receiving different annual salaries and owing different amounts of income tax, these five individuals are otherwise identical.

Name	Annual salary	Annual income tax owed
Mila	$22,000	$3,304
Jayden	63,000	14,317
Aria	3,000	454
Logan	94,000	23,927
Saeed	37,000	7,020

   a. If you were to plot these points on a graph, what would be the average slope of the curve between the points for Jayden's and Logan's salaries and taxes using the arc method? How would you interpret this value for slope?

   b. What is the average slope of the curve between the points for Aria's and Mila's salaries and taxes using the arc method? How would you interpret that value for slope?

   c. What happens to the slope as salary increases? What does this relationship imply about how the level of income taxes affects a person's incentive to earn a higher salary?

WORK IT OUT

10. Studies have found a relationship between a country's yearly rate of economic growth and the yearly rate of increase in airborne pollutants. It is believed that a higher rate of economic growth allows a country's residents to have more cars and travel more, thereby releasing more airborne pollutants.

   a. Which variable is the independent variable? Which is the dependent variable?

   b. Suppose that in the country of Sudland, when the yearly rate of economic growth fell from 3% to 1.5%, the yearly rate of increase in airborne pollutants fell from 6% to 5%. What is the average slope of a nonlinear curve between these points using the arc method?

   c. Assume that when the yearly rate of economic growth rose from 3.5% to 4.5%, the yearly rate of increase in airborne pollutants rose from 5.5% to 7.5%. What is the average slope of a nonlinear curve between these two points using the arc method?

   d. How would you describe the relationship between the two variables here? ■

3 > Supply and Demand

A NATURAL GAS BOOM AND BUST

FOR ALMOST A DECADE, Karnes County has been on a wild economic roller-coaster ride. From 2010 to 2018, the Texas county, which sits close to two major geological oil formations, has gone from boom to bust to recovery. What accounted for the swift changes was the advent of hydraulic fracturing, also known as fracking.

From 2010 to 2015, Karnes County went through an extreme cycle of boom and bust as the price of natural gas (per thousand cubic feet, which is about 28.32 cubic meters) went from nearly US$8 to under US$2 because of fracking. *Fracking* is a method of extracting natural gas from deposits trapped between layers of shale rock thousands of feet underground using powerful jets of chemical-laden water. For almost a century in the United States, vast deposits of natural gas within these shale formations lay untapped because drilling for them was too difficult.

It was only about 80 years ago that new drilling technologies made it possible to reach these deeply embedded deposits. But what finally pushed energy companies to invest

The adoption of new drilling technologies has led to cheaper natural gas, but not without controversy and environmental costs.

in these new extraction technologies was a surge in the price of natural gas — a quadrupling from 2002 to 2006. Two principal factors explain the surge: the demand for natural gas and the supply of natural gas.

First, the demand side. In 2002, the U.S. economy was mired in recession; with economic activity low and job losses high, people and businesses cut their energy consumption. For example, to save money, homeowners turned down their thermostats in winter and turned them up in the summer. But by 2006, the U.S. economy came roaring back, and natural gas consumption rose.

Second, the supply side. In 2005, Hurricane Katrina devastated the American Gulf Coast, site of most of the country's natural gas production at the time. So by 2006 the demand for natural gas surged while supply was severely curtailed. As a result, natural gas prices peaked at around US$14 per thousand cubic feet, up from around US$2 in 2002.

Fast-forward to 2013: natural gas prices once again fell to US$2 per thousand cubic feet. But a slow economy was not the reason this time: instead it was due to advances in fracking technology. From 2010 to 2012, U.S. production of natural gas from shale deposits nearly doubled. From 2012 to 2018, the United States had become the world's largest producer of natural gas as well as a net exporter of natural gas to other countries.

Yet despite the massive increase in supply, prices during 2018 averaged around US$3.15, well over the historical lows of under US$2. Why? Because although supply surged, demand increased as well. First, electric power plants increased their use of natural gas while shifting away from coal. Second, homeowners increased their consumption of natural gas and shifted away from heating oil. And, third, U.S. natural gas exports to Europe and Mexico surged given that it was cheaper than comparable energy sources.

Yet the benefits of natural gas, which include the creation of tens of thousands of

new jobs, a robust economic boom in Karnes County starting in 2016, and lower energy costs (for those who once used pricier coal and oil), have been accompanied by deep reservations and controversy over the environmental effects of fracking. While there are clear environmental benefits from the switch to natural gas (which burns cleaner than the other, heavily polluting fossil fuels, such as oil and coal), fracking has sparked another set of environmental worries, the potential for contamination of local groundwater by the chemicals used. Another is that cheap natural gas may discourage the adoption of renewable energy sources like solar and wind power, furthering dependence on fossil fuels (although others have noted that an abundant supply of natural gas could actually increase the adoption of renewables: natural gas-powered "mini-power plants" can be fired up when the sun isn't shining or the wind isn't blowing).

Let's return to the topic at hand: the supply of and demand for natural gas. But what does *supply and demand* mean? Many people use the terms as a sort of catchphrase to mean "the laws of the marketplace at work." To economists, however, the concept of supply and demand has a precise meaning: it is a *model of how a market behaves* that is extremely useful for understanding many — but not all — markets.

In this chapter, we lay out the pieces that make up the *supply and demand model*, put them together, and show you how this model can be used. •

WHAT YOU WILL LEARN

- What is a **competitive market**?
- What are **supply** and **demand curves**?
- How do supply and demand curves lead to an **equilibrium price** and **equilibrium quantity** in the market?
- What are **shortages** and **surpluses** and why do price movements eliminate them?

A **competitive market** is a market in which there are many buyers and sellers of the same good or service, none of whom can influence the price at which the good or service is sold.

The **supply and demand model** is a model of how a competitive market behaves.

Supply and Demand: A Model of a Competitive Market

Natural gas sellers and natural gas buyers constitute a market—a group of producers and consumers who exchange a good or service for payment. In this chapter, we'll focus on a particular type of market known as a *competitive market*. A **competitive market** is a market in which there are many buyers and sellers of the same good or service. More precisely, the key feature of a competitive market is that no individual's actions have a noticeable effect on the price at which the good or service is sold. It's important to understand, however, that this is not an accurate description of every market.

For example, it's not an accurate description of the market for carbonated soft drinks. That's because in this market, Coca-Cola and Pepsi account for such a large proportion of total sales that they are able to influence the price at which their beverages are bought and sold. But it is an accurate description of the market for natural gas. The global marketplace for natural gas is so huge that even the biggest North American driller for natural gas—ExxonMobil—accounts for such a small share of total global transactions that it is unable to influence the price at which natural gas is bought and sold.

It's a little hard to explain why competitive markets are different from other markets until we've seen how a competitive market works. So let's take a rain check—we'll return to that issue at the end of this chapter. For now, let's just say that it's easier to model competitive markets than other markets. When taking an exam, it's always a good strategy to begin by answering the easier questions. In this book, we're going to do the same thing. So we will start with competitive markets.

When a market is competitive, its behaviour is well described by the **supply and demand model.** And because many markets are competitive, the supply and demand model is a very useful one indeed.

There are five key elements in this model:

- The *demand curve*
- The *supply curve*
- The set of factors that cause the demand curve to shift and the set of factors that cause the supply curve to shift
- The *market equilibrium,* which includes the *equilibrium price* and *equilibrium quantity*
- The way the market equilibrium changes when the supply curve or demand curve shifts

To understand the supply and demand model, we will examine each of these elements.

The Demand Curve

How much natural gas will Canadian consumers want to buy in a given year? You might at first think that we can answer this question by simply adding up the amounts each Canadian household and business consumes in that year. But that's not enough to answer the question, because how much natural gas Canadians want to buy depends on the price of natural gas.

When the price of natural gas falls, as it did from 2006 to 2015, consumers will generally respond to the lower price by using more natural gas—for example, by turning up their thermostats to keep their houses warmer in the winter or switching to vehicles powered by natural gas. In general, the amount of natural gas, or of any good or service that people want to buy, depends upon the price. The higher the price, the less of the good or service people want to purchase; alternatively, the lower the price, the more they want to purchase.

So the answer to the question "How many units of natural gas do consumers want to buy?" depends on the price of a unit of natural gas. If you don't yet know what the price will be, you can start by making a table of how many units of natural gas people would want to buy at a number of different prices. Such a table is known as a *demand schedule*. This, in turn, can be used to draw a *demand curve*, which is one of the key elements of the supply and demand model.

A **demand schedule** shows how much of a good or service consumers will want to buy at different prices.

The Demand Schedule and the Demand Curve

A **demand schedule** is a table showing how much of a good or service consumers will want to buy at different prices. At the right of Figure 3-1, we show a hypothetical demand schedule for natural gas. It's expressed in BTUs (British thermal units), a commonly used measure of quantity of natural gas. It's a hypothetical demand schedule—it doesn't use actual data on Canadian demand for natural gas.

According to the table, if a BTU of natural gas costs $3, consumers will want to purchase 10 trillion BTUs of natural gas over the course of a year. If the price is $3.25 per BTU, they will want to buy only 8.9 trillion BTUs; if the price is only $2.75 per BTU, they will want to buy 11.5 trillion BTUs. The higher the price, the fewer BTUs of natural gas consumers will want to purchase. So, as the price rises,

FIGURE 3-1 The Demand Schedule and the Demand Curve

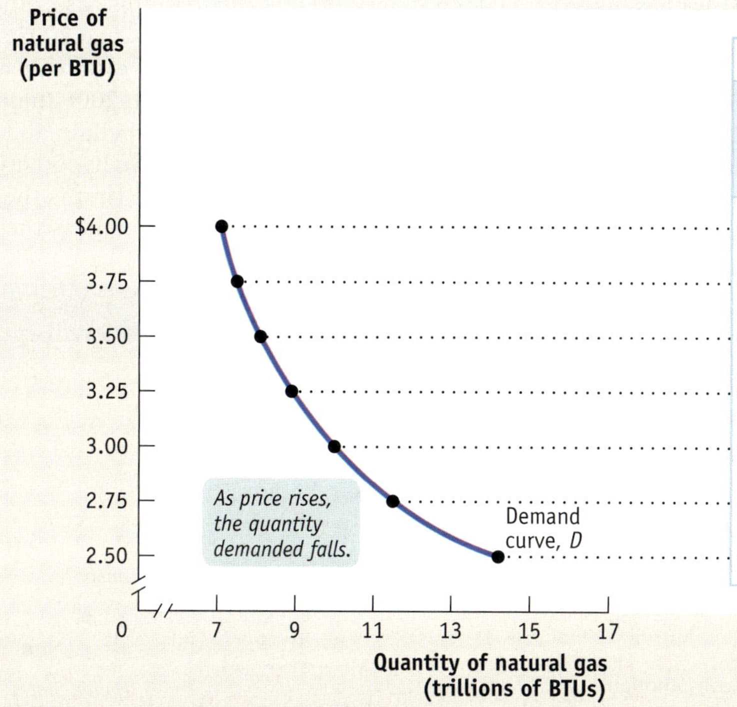

Price of natural gas (per BTU)	Quantity of natural gas demanded (trillions of BTUs)
$4.00	7.1
3.75	7.5
3.50	8.1
3.25	8.9
3.00	10.0
2.75	11.5
2.50	14.2

The demand schedule for natural gas yields the corresponding demand curve, which shows how much of a good or service consumers want to buy at any given price. The demand curve and the demand schedule reflect the law of demand: as price rises, the quantity demanded falls. Similarly, a fall in price raises the quantity demanded. As a result, the demand curve is downward sloping.

The **quantity demanded** is the actual amount of a good or service consumers are willing to buy at some specific price.

A **demand curve** is a graphical representation of the demand schedule. It shows the relationship between quantity demanded and price.

The **law of demand** says that a higher price for a good or service, other things equal, leads people to demand a smaller quantity of that good or service.

the **quantity demanded** of natural gas—the actual amount consumers are willing to buy at some specific price—falls.

The graph in Figure 3-1 is a visual representation of the information in the table. (You might want to review the discussion of graphs in economics in the appendix to Chapter 2.) The vertical axis shows the price of a BTU of natural gas and the horizontal axis shows the quantity of natural gas in trillions of BTUs. Each point on the graph corresponds to one of the entries in the table. The curve that connects these points is a **demand curve.** A demand curve is a graphical representation of the demand schedule, another way of showing the relationship between the quantity demanded and price.

Note that the demand curve shown in Figure 3-1 slopes downward. This reflects the inverse relationship between price and the quantity demanded: a higher price reduces the quantity demanded, and a lower price increases the quantity demanded. We can see this from the demand curve in Figure 3-1. As price falls, we move down the demand curve and quantity demanded increases. And as price increases, we move up the demand curve and quantity demanded falls.

In the real world, demand curves almost always *do* slope downward. (The exceptions are so rare that for practical purposes we can ignore them.) Generally, the proposition that a higher price for a good, *other things equal*, leads people to demand a smaller quantity of that good is so reliable that economists are willing to call it a "law"—the **law of demand.**

Shifts of the Demand Curve

Although natural gas prices in 2006 were higher than they had been in 2002, North American consumption of natural gas was higher in 2006. How can we reconcile this fact with the law of demand, which says that a higher price reduces the quantity demanded, other things equal?

The answer lies in the crucial phrase *other things equal.* In this case, other things weren't equal: the North American economy had changed between 2002 and 2006 in ways that increased the amount of natural gas demanded at any given price. For one thing, the North American economy was much stronger in 2006 than in 2002. Figure 3-2 illustrates this phenomenon using the demand schedule and demand curve for natural gas. (As before, the numbers in Figure 3-2 are hypothetical.)

The table in Figure 3-2 shows two demand schedules. The first is the demand schedule for 2002, the same as shown in Figure 3-1. The second is the demand

For a real-world illustration of the law of demand, consider how gasoline consumption varies according to the prices consumers pay at the pump. Because of high taxes, gasoline and diesel fuel are more than twice as expensive in most European countries and in many East Asian countries than in North America. According to the law of demand, this should lead Europeans to buy less gasoline than North Americans—and they do. As you can see from the figure, per person, Europeans consume less than half as much fuel as North Americans, mainly because they drive smaller cars with better mileage.

Prices aren't the only factor affecting fuel consumption, but they're probably the main cause of the difference between European and North American fuel consumption per person.

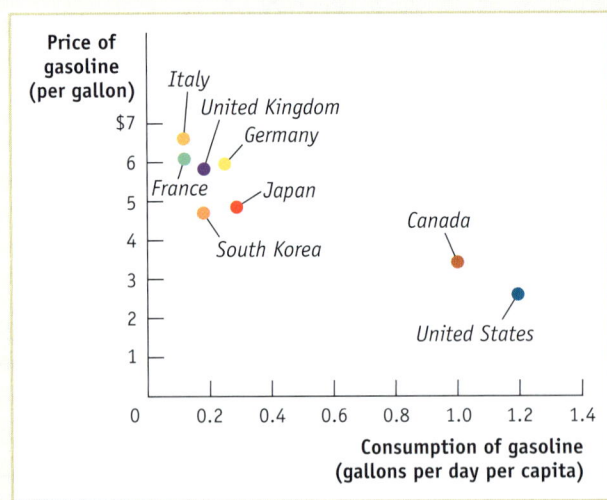

Data from: Bloomberg and U.S. Energy Information Administration, 2018.

FIGURE 3-2 An Increase in Demand

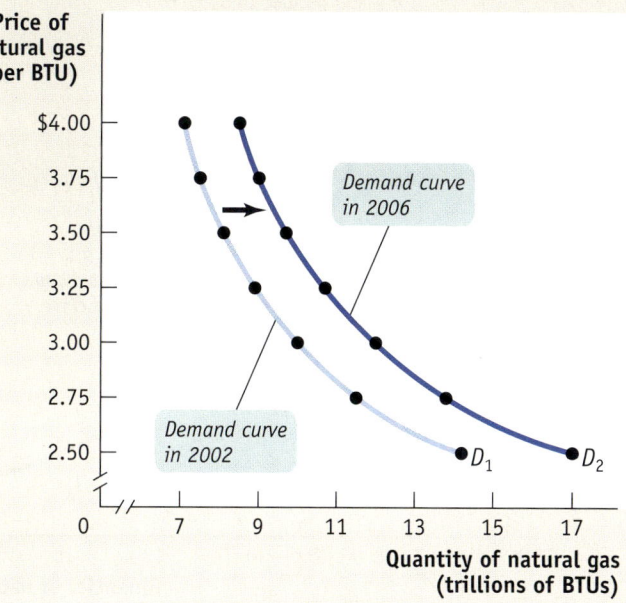

Demand Schedules for Natural Gas		
Price of natural gas (per BTU)	Quantity of natural gas demanded (trillions of BTUs)	
	in 2002	in 2006
$4.00	7.1	8.5
3.75	7.5	9.0
3.50	8.1	9.7
3.25	8.9	10.7
3.00	10.0	12.0
2.75	11.5	13.8
2.50	14.2	17.0

A strong economy is one factor that increases the demand for natural gas — a rise in the quantity demanded at any given price. This is represented by the two demand schedules — one showing the demand in 2002 when the economy was weak, the other showing the demand in 2006, when the economy was strong — and their corresponding demand curves. The increase in demand shifts the demand curve to the right.

schedule for 2006. It differs from the 2002 schedule because of the stronger North American economy, leading to an increase in the quantity of natural gas demanded at any given price. So at each price the 2006 schedule shows a larger quantity demanded than the 2002 schedule. For example, the quantity of natural gas consumers wanted to buy at a price of $3 per BTU increased from 10 trillion to 12 trillion BTUs per year; the quantity demanded at $3.25 per BTU went from 8.9 trillion to 10.7 trillion, and so on.

What is clear from this example is that the changes that occurred between 2002 and 2006 generated a *new* demand schedule, one in which the quantity demanded was greater at any given price than in the original demand schedule. The two curves in Figure 3-2 show the same information graphically. As you can see, the demand schedule for 2006 corresponds to a new demand curve, D_2, that is to the right of the demand schedule for 2002, D_1. This **shift of the demand curve** shows the change in the quantity demanded at any given price, represented by the change in position of the original demand curve D_1 to its new location at D_2.

It's crucial to make the distinction between such shifts of the demand curve and **movements along the demand curve,** changes in the quantity demanded of a good arising from a change in that good's price. Figure 3-3 illustrates the difference.

The movement from point A to point B is a movement along the demand curve: the quantity demanded rises due to a fall in price as you move down D_1. Here, a fall in the price of natural gas from $3.50 to $3 per BTU generates a rise in the quantity demanded from 8.1 trillion to 10 trillion BTUs per year. But the quantity demanded can also rise when the price is unchanged if there is an *increase in demand*—a rightward shift of the demand curve. This is illustrated in Figure 3-3 by the shift of the demand curve from D_1 to D_2. Holding the price constant at $3.50 per BTU, the quantity demanded rises from 8.1 trillion BTUs at point A on D_1 to 9.7 trillion BTUs at point C on D_2.

A **shift of the demand curve** is a change in the quantity demanded at any given price, represented by the shift of the original demand curve to a new position, denoted by a new demand curve.

A **movement along the demand curve** is a change in the quantity demanded of a good arising from a change in the good's price.

FIGURE 3-3 Movement Along the Demand Curve versus Shift of the Demand Curve

The rise in quantity demanded when going from point *A* to point *B* reflects a movement along the demand curve: it is the result of a fall in the price of the good. The rise in quantity demanded when going from point *A* to point *C* reflects a shift of the demand curve: it is the result of a rise in the quantity demanded at any given price.

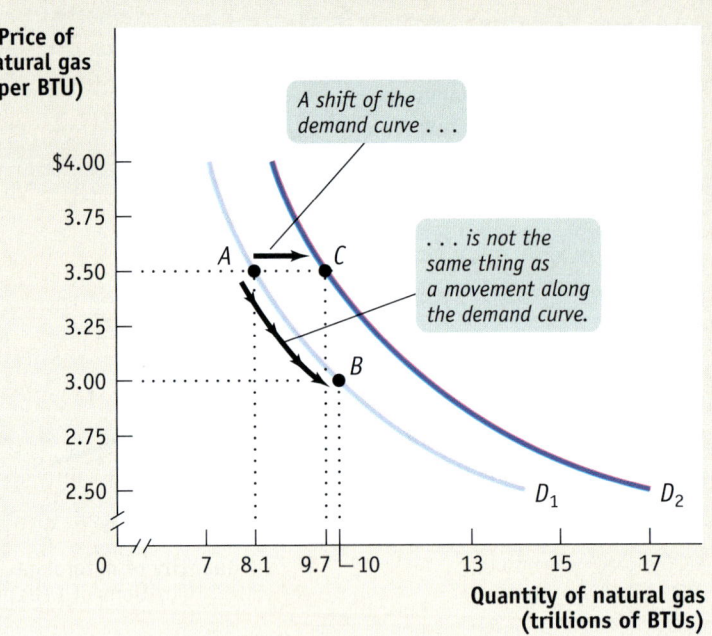

When economists say "the demand for *X* increased" or "the demand for *Y* decreased," they mean that the demand curve for *X* or *Y* shifted—not that the quantity demanded rose or fell because of a change in the price.

Understanding Shifts of the Demand Curve

Figure 3-4 illustrates the two basic ways in which demand curves can shift.

1. When economists talk about an increase in demand, they mean a *rightward* shift of the demand curve: at any given price, consumers demand a larger quantity of the good or service than before. This is shown by the rightward shift of the original demand curve D_1 to curve D_2.

2. When economists talk about a decrease in demand, they mean a *leftward* shift of the demand curve: at any given price, consumers demand a smaller quantity of the good or service than before. This is shown by the leftward shift of the original demand curve D_1 to curve D_3.

What caused the demand curve for natural gas to shift? As we mentioned earlier, the reason was the stronger North American economy in 2006 compared to 2002. If you

---

PITFALLS

DEMAND VERSUS QUANTITY DEMANDED

When economists say "an increase in demand," they mean a rightward shift of the demand curve, and when they say "a decrease in demand," they mean a leftward shift of the demand curve—that is, when they're being careful.

In ordinary speech most of us, professional economists included, use the word *demand* casually. For example, an economist might say "the demand for air travel has doubled over the past 20 years, partly because of falling airfares" when they really mean that the *quantity demanded* has doubled.

It's OK to be a bit sloppy in ordinary conversation. But when you're doing economic analysis, it's important to make the distinction between changes in the quantity demanded, which involve movements along a demand curve, and shifts of the demand curve (see Figure 3-3). Sometimes students end up writing something like this: "If demand increases, the price will go up, but that will lead to a fall in demand, which pushes the price down . . ." and then go around in circles.

By making a clear distinction between changes in *demand,* which mean shifts of the demand curve, and changes in *quantity demanded,* which means movement along the demand curve, you can avoid a lot of confusion.

FIGURE 3-4 **Shifts of the Demand Curve**

Any event that increases demand shifts the demand curve to the right, reflecting a rise in the quantity demanded at any given price. Any event that decreases demand shifts the demand curve to the left, reflecting a fall in the quantity demanded at any given price.

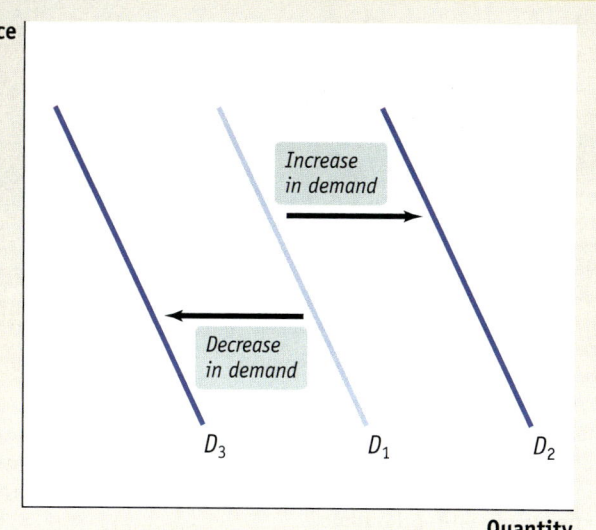

think about it, you can come up with other factors that would be likely to shift the demand curve for natural gas. For example, suppose that the price of heating oil rises. This will induce some consumers, who heat their homes and businesses in winter with heating oil, to switch to natural gas instead, increasing the demand for natural gas.

Economists believe that there are five principal factors that shift the demand curve for a good or service:

- Changes in the prices of related goods or services
- Changes in income
- Changes in tastes
- Changes in expectations
- Changes in the number of consumers

Although this list is not exhaustive, it contains the five most important factors that can shift demand curves. When we say that the quantity of a good or service demanded falls as its price rises, *other things equal,* we are in fact stating that the factors that shift demand are remaining unchanged. Let's now explore how those factors shift the demand curve.

Changes in the Prices of Related Goods or Services Heating oil is what economists call a *substitute* for natural gas. A pair of goods are **substitutes** if a rise in the price of one good (heating oil) makes consumers more likely to buy the other good (natural gas). Substitutes are usually goods that in some way serve a similar function: coffee and tea, muffins and doughnuts, train rides and air flights. A rise in the price of the alternative good induces some consumers to purchase the original good *instead* of the substitute, shifting demand for the original good to the right.

But sometimes a rise in the price of one good makes consumers *less* willing to buy another good. Such pairs of goods are known as **complements.** Complements are usually goods that in some sense are consumed together: smartphones and apps, coffee and a breakfast burrito, cars and gasoline. Because consumers like to consume a good and its complement together, a change in the price of one of the goods will affect the demand for its complement. In particular, when the price of one good rises, the demand for its complement decreases, shifting the demand curve for the complement to the left. So, for example, when the price of gasoline began to rise in 2009 from about $1 per litre to about $1.30 per litre in 2011, the demand for gas-guzzling cars fell.

Two goods are **substitutes** if a rise in the price of one of the goods leads to an increase in the demand for the other good.

Two goods are **complements** if a rise in the price of one good leads to a decrease in the demand for the other good.

Consumption of normal goods increases when incomes increase, benefiting businesses like casual-dining restaurants, but at the expense of fast-food outlets.

Changes in Income Why did the stronger economy in 2006 lead to an increase in the demand for natural gas compared to the demand during the weak economy of 2002? It was because the economy was stronger and consumers had more income, making them more likely to purchase more of *most* goods and services at any given price. For example, with a higher income you are likely to keep your house warmer in the winter than if your income is low.

And, the demand for natural gas, a major source of fuel for electricity-generating power plants, is tied to the demand for other goods and services. For example, businesses must consume power in order to provide goods and services to households. So when the economy is strong and household incomes are high, businesses will consume more electricity and, indirectly, more natural gas.

Why do we say that people are likely to purchase more of *"most* goods," rather than purchase more of *"all* goods"? Most goods are **normal goods**—the demand for them increases when consumer income rises. However, the demand for some products falls when income rises. Goods for which demand decreases when income rises are known as **inferior goods.** Usually an inferior good is considered less desirable than more expensive alternatives—such as a bus ride versus a taxi ride. When they can afford to, people stop buying an inferior good and switch their consumption to the preferred, more expensive alternative. So when a good is inferior, a rise in income shifts the demand curve to the left. And, not surprisingly, a fall in income shifts the demand curve to the right.

One example of the distinction between normal and inferior goods that has drawn attention in the business press is the difference between so-called casual-dining restaurants such as Swiss Chalet or White Spot and fast-food chains such as KFC or McDonald's. When their incomes rise, North Americans tend to eat out more at casual-dining restaurants. However, some of that increased dining out comes at the expense of fast-food venues—to some extent, people visit McDonald's less often once they can afford to move upscale. So casual dining is a normal good, whereas fast-food consumption appears to be an inferior good.

Changes in Tastes Why do people want what they want? Fortunately, we don't need to answer that question—we just need to acknowledge that people have certain preferences, or tastes, that determine what they choose to consume and that these tastes can change. Economists usually lump together changes in demand due to trends, beliefs, cultural shifts, and so on under the heading of changes in tastes or preferences.

For example, once upon a time men wore hats. Up until around World War II, a respectable man wasn't fully dressed unless he wore a dignified hat along with his suit. But the returning troops adopted a more informal style. And U.S. President Eisenhower, who had been supreme commander of Allied Forces before becoming president, often went hatless. After World War II, it was clear that the demand curve for hats had shifted leftward, reflecting a decrease in the demand for hats.

Economists have relatively little to say about the forces that influence consumers' tastes. (Although marketers and advertisers have plenty to say about them!) However, a change in tastes does have a predictable impact on demand. When tastes change in favour of a good, more people want to buy it at any given price, so the demand curve shifts to the right. When tastes change against a good, fewer people want to buy it at any given price, so the demand curve shifts to the left.

When a rise in income increases the demand for a good—the normal case—it is a **normal good.**

When a rise in income decreases the demand for a good, it is an **inferior good.**

Changes in Expectations When consumers have some choice about when to make a purchase, current demand for a good is often affected by expectations about its future price. For example, savvy shoppers often wait for seasonal sales—say, buying next year's holiday decorations during the post-holiday markdowns. In this case, expectations of a future drop in price lead to a decrease in demand today. Alternatively, expectations of a future rise in price are likely to cause an increase in demand today.

In addition, the fall in gas prices in recent years to around $2 per BTU has spurred more consumers to switch to natural gas from other fuel types than when natural gas fell to $2 per BTU in 2002. But why are consumers more willing to switch now? Because in 2002, consumers didn't expect the fall in the price of natural gas to last—and they were right.

In 2002, natural gas prices fell because of the weak economy. That situation changed in 2006 when the economy came roaring back and the price of natural gas rose dramatically. In contrast, consumers have come to expect that the more recent fall in the price of natural gas will not be temporary because it is based on a permanent change: the ability to tap much larger deposits of natural gas.

Expected changes in future income can also lead to changes in demand: if you expect your income to rise in the future, you will typically borrow today and increase your demand for certain goods; if you expect your income to fall in the future, you are likely to save today and reduce your demand for some goods.

Changes in the Number of Consumers Another factor that can cause a change in demand is a change in the number of consumers of a good or service. For example, population growth in North America eventually leads to higher demand for natural gas as more homes and businesses need to be heated in the winter and cooled in the summer.

Let's introduce a new concept: the **individual demand curve,** which shows the relationship between quantity demanded and price for an individual con-sumer. For example, suppose that the Gonzalez family is a consumer of natural gas for heating and cooling their home. Panel (a) of Figure 3-5 shows how many

An **individual demand curve** illustrates the relationship between quantity demanded and price for an individual consumer.

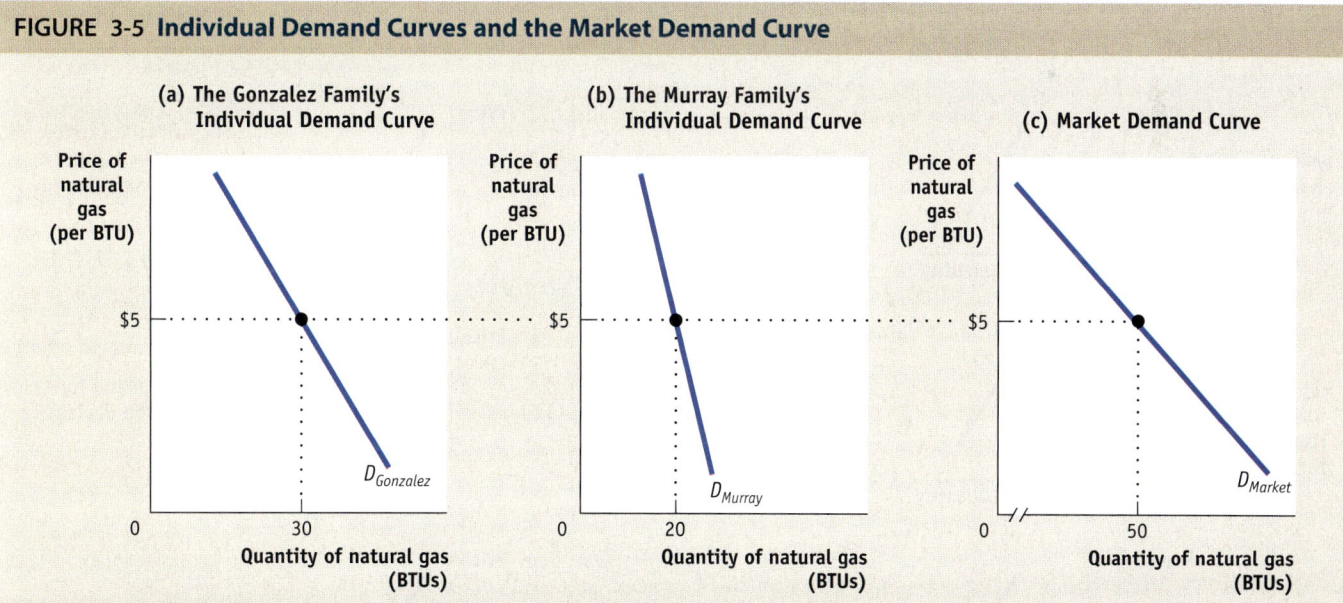

FIGURE 3-5 Individual Demand Curves and the Market Demand Curve

The Gonzalez family and the Murray family are the only two consumers of natural gas in the market. Panel (a) shows the Gonzalez family's individual demand curve: the number of BTUs they will buy per year at any given price. Panel (b) shows the Murray family's individual demand curve. Given that the Gonzalez family and the Murray family are the only two consumers, the *market demand* curve, which shows the quantity of BTUs demanded by all consumers at any given price, is shown in the panel (c). The market demand curve is the *horizontal sum* of the individual demand curves of all consumers. In this case, at any given price, the quantity demanded by the market is the sum of the quantities demanded by the Gonzalez family and the Murray family.

TABLE 3-1 Factors That Shift Demand

When this happens . . .	. . . demand increases	But when this happens . . .	. . . demand decreases
When the price of a substitute rises . . .	. . . demand for the original good increases.	When the price of a substitute falls . . .	. . . demand for the original good decreases.
When the price of a complement falls . . .	. . . demand for the original good increases.	When the price of a complement rises . . .	. . . demand for the original good decreases.
When income rises . . .	. . . demand for a normal good increases.	When income falls . . .	. . . demand for a normal good decreases.
When income falls . . .	. . . demand for an inferior good increases.	When income rises . . .	. . . demand for an inferior good decreases.
When tastes change in favour of a good . . .	. . . demand for the good increases.	When tastes change against a good . . .	. . . demand for the good decreases.
When the price is expected to rise in the future . . .	. . . demand for the good increases today.	When the price is expected to fall in the future . . .	. . . demand for the good decreases today.
When the number of consumers rises . . .	. . . market demand for the good increases.	When the number of consumers falls . . .	. . . market demand for the good decreases.

BTUs of natural gas they will buy per year at any given price. The Gonzalez family's individual demand curve is $D_{Gonzalez}$.

The *market demand curve* shows how the combined quantity demanded by all consumers depends on the market price of the good. (Most of the time when economists refer to the demand curve they mean the market demand curve.) The market demand curve is the *horizontal sum* of the individual demand curves of all consumers in that market.

To see what we mean by the term *horizontal sum,* assume for a moment that there are only two consumers of natural gas, the Gonzalez family and the Murray family. The Murray family consumes natural gas to fuel their natural gas–powered car. The Murray family's individual demand curve, D_{Murray}, is shown in panel (b). Panel (c) shows the market demand curve. At any given price, the quantity demanded by the market is the sum of the quantities demanded by the Gonzalez family and the Murray family. For example, at a price of $5 per BTU, the Gonzalez family demands 30 BTUs of natural gas per year and the Murray family demands 20 BTUs per year. So the quantity demanded by the market is 50 BTUs per year, as seen on the market demand curve, D_{Market}.

Clearly, the quantity demanded by the market at any given price is larger with the Murray family present than it would be if the Gonzalez family were the only consumer. The quantity demanded at any given price would be even larger if we added a third consumer, then a fourth, and so on. So an increase in the number of consumers leads to an increase in demand.

For a review of the factors that shift demand, see Table 3-1.

ECONOMICS >> *in Action*
Beating the Traffic

All big cities have traffic problems, and many local authorities try to discourage driving in the crowded city centre. If we think of an auto trip to the city centre as a good that people consume, we can use the economics of demand to analyze anti-traffic policies.

One common strategy is to reduce the demand for auto trips by lowering the prices of substitutes. Many metropolitan areas subsidize bus and rail service, hoping to lure commuters out of their cars. An alternative is to raise the price of complements: several major North American cities impose high taxes on commercial parking garages and impose short time limits on parking meters, both to raise revenue and to discourage people from driving into the city.

A few major cities—including Singapore, London, Oslo, Stockholm, and Milan—have been willing to adopt a direct and politically controversial approach: reducing congestion by raising the price of driving. Under *congestion pricing*, a charge is imposed on cars entering the city centre during business hours. Drivers buy passes, which are then debited electronically as they drive by monitoring stations. Compliance is monitored with cameras that photograph license plates.

The standard cost of driving into London is currently £11.50 (about $20). Drivers who don't pay and are caught pay a fine of £130 (about $227) for each transgression.

Not surprisingly, studies have shown that after the implementation of congestion pricing, traffic does decrease. In the 1990s, London had some of the worst traffic in Europe. The introduction of its congestion charge in 2003 immediately reduced traffic in the city centre by about 15%. Fifteen years later, by 2018, the policy was still working, as traffic volumes are still 25% lower than they were in the late 1990s. And there has been increased use of substitutes, such as public

Cities can reduce traffic congestion by raising the price of driving.

>> Quick Review

• The **supply and demand model** is a model of a **competitive market** — one in which there are many buyers and sellers of the same good or service.

• The **demand schedule** shows how the **quantity demanded** changes as the price changes. A **demand curve** illustrates this relationship.

• The **law of demand** asserts that a higher price reduces the quantity demanded. Thus, demand curves normally slope downward.

• An increase in demand leads to a rightward **shift of the demand curve:** the quantity demanded rises for any given price. A decrease in demand leads to a leftward shift: the quantity demanded falls for any given price. A change in price results in a change in the quantity demanded and a **movement along the demand curve.**

• The five main factors that can shift the demand curve are changes in (1) the price of a related good, such as a **substitute** or a **complement,** (2) income, (3) tastes, (4) expectations, and (5) the number of consumers.

• The market demand curve is the horizontal sum of the **individual demand curves** of all consumers in the market.

transportation, bicycles, and ride-hailing. From 2001 to 2011, bike trips in London increased by 79%, and bus usage was up by 30%.

And less congestion led not just to fewer accidents, but to a lower *rate* of accidents as fewer cars jostled for space. One study found that from 2000 to 2010 the number of accidents per mile (1.6 kilometers) driven in London fell by 40%. Stockholm experienced effects similar to those in London: traffic fell by 22% in 2013 compared to pre-congestion charge levels, transit times fell by one-third to one-half, and air quality measurably improved. A 2018 article found that serious childhood asthma attacks declined significantly in Stockholm after the congestion charge was imposed.

Congestion pricing is now getting the attention of city planners in North America. New York City will become the first North American city to implement congestion pricing as of 2020, with Vancouver, Montreal, Toronto considering plans to do the same.

>> Check Your Understanding 3-1

Solutions appear at back of book.

1. Explain whether each of the following events represents (i) a *shift of* the demand curve or (ii) a *movement along* the demand curve.
   a. A store owner finds that customers are willing to pay more for umbrellas on rainy days.
   b. When Circus Cruise Lines offered reduced prices for summer cruises in the Caribbean, its number of bookings increased sharply.
   c. People buy more long-stem roses the week of Valentine's Day, even though the prices are higher than at other times during the year.
   d. A sharp rise in the price of gasoline leads many commuters to join carpools in order to reduce their gasoline purchases.

‖ The Supply Curve

Some deposits of natural gas are easier to tap than others. Before the widespread use of fracking, drillers would limit their natural gas wells to deposits that lay in easily reached pools beneath the earth. How much natural gas they would tap from existing wells, and how extensively they searched for new deposits and drilled new wells, depended on the price they expected to get for the natural gas. The higher the price, the more they would tap existing wells as well as drill and tap new wells.

So just as the quantity of natural gas that consumers want to buy depends upon the price they have to pay, the quantity that producers of natural gas, or of any good or service, are willing to produce and sell—the **quantity supplied**—depends upon the price they are offered.

The Supply Schedule and the Supply Curve

The table in Figure 3-6 shows how the quantity of natural gas made available varies with the price—that is, it shows a hypothetical **supply schedule** for natural gas.

A supply schedule works the same way as the demand schedule shown in Figure 3-1: in this case, the table shows the number of BTUs of natural gas producers are willing to sell at different prices. At a price of $2.50 per BTU, producers are willing to sell only 8 trillion BTUs of natural gas per year. At $2.75 per BTU, they're willing to sell 9.1 trillion BTUs. At $3, they're willing to sell 10 trillion BTUs, and so on.

The **quantity supplied** is the actual amount of a good or service people are willing to sell at some specific price.

A **supply schedule** shows how much of a good or service would be supplied at different prices.

FIGURE 3-6 The Supply Schedule and the Supply Curve

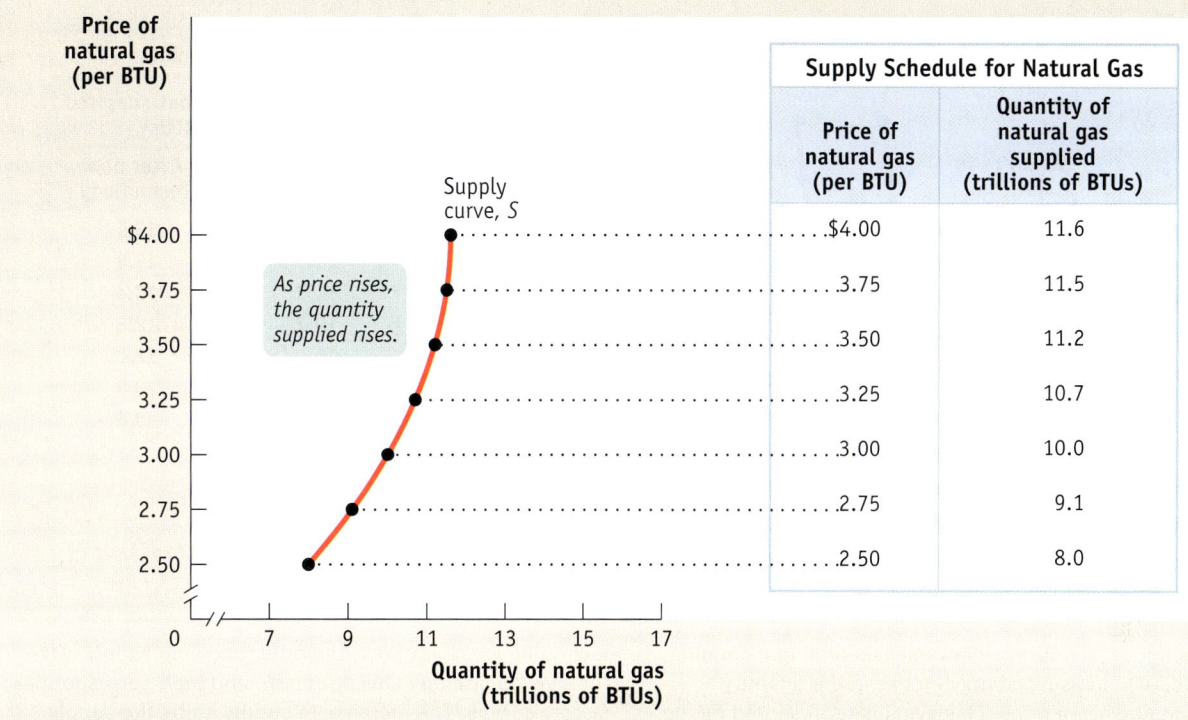

Supply Schedule for Natural Gas	
Price of natural gas (per BTU)	Quantity of natural gas supplied (trillions of BTUs)
$4.00	11.6
3.75	11.5
3.50	11.2
3.25	10.7
3.00	10.0
2.75	9.1
2.50	8.0

The supply schedule for natural gas is plotted to yield the corresponding supply curve, which shows how much of a good producers are willing to sell at any given price. The supply curve and the supply schedule reflect the fact that supply curves are usually upward sloping: the quantity supplied rises when the price rises.

In the same way that a demand schedule can be represented graphically by a demand curve, a supply schedule can be represented by a **supply curve,** as shown in Figure 3-6. Each point on the curve represents an entry from the table.

Suppose that the price of natural gas rises from $3 to $3.25; we can see that the quantity of natural gas that producers are willing to sell rises from 10 trillion to 10.7 trillion BTUs. This is the normal situation for a supply curve, that a higher price leads to a higher quantity supplied. So just as demand curves normally slope downward, supply curves normally slope upward: the higher the price being offered, the more of any good or service producers will be willing to sell.

A **supply curve** shows the relationship between quantity supplied and price.

A **shift of the supply curve** is a change in the quantity supplied of a good or service at any given price. It is represented by the change of the original supply curve to a new position, denoted by a new supply curve.

Shifts of the Supply Curve

As we discussed in the introduction to this chapter, innovations in the technology of drilling natural gas deposits have led to a huge increase in North American (primarily U.S.) production of natural gas. Figure 3-7 illustrates these events in terms of the supply schedule and the supply curve for natural gas. The table in Figure 3-7 shows two supply schedules. The schedule before improved natural gas–drilling technology was adopted is the same one as in Figure 3-6. The second schedule shows the supply of natural gas *after* the improved technology was adopted.

Just as a change in demand schedules leads to a shift of the demand curve, a change in supply schedules leads to a **shift of the supply curve**—a change in the quantity supplied at any given price. This is shown in Figure 3-7 by the shift of the supply curve before the adoption of new natural gas–drilling technology, S_1,

FIGURE 3-7 An Increase in Supply

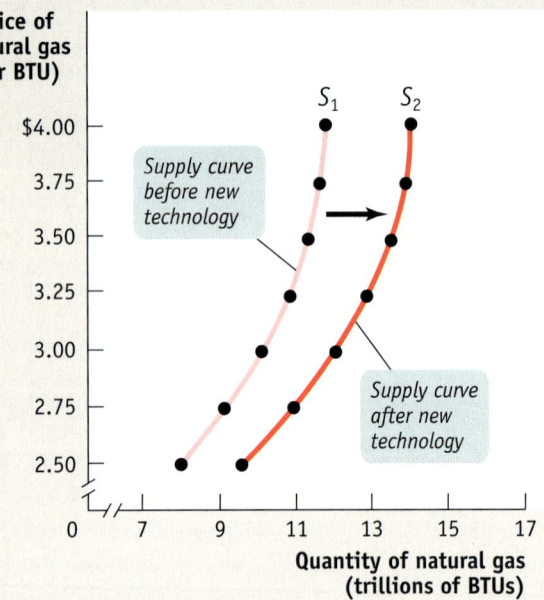

Supply Schedules for Natural Gas		
Price of natural gas (per BTU)	Quantity of natural gas supplied (trillions of BTUs)	
	Before new technology	After new technology
$4.00	11.6	13.9
3.75	11.5	13.8
3.50	11.2	13.4
3.25	10.7	12.8
3.00	10.0	12.0
2.75	9.1	10.9
2.50	8.0	9.6

The adoption of an improved natural gas–drilling technology generated an increase in supply—a rise in the quantity supplied at any given price. This event is represented by the two supply schedules—one showing supply before the new technology was adopted, the other showing supply after the new technology was adopted—and their corresponding supply curves. The increase in supply shifts the supply curve to the right.

A **movement along the supply curve** is a change in the quantity supplied of a good arising from a change in the good's price.

to its new position after the adoption of new natural gas–drilling technology, S_2. Notice that S_2 lies to the right of S_1, a reflection of the fact that quantity supplied rises at any given price.

As in the analysis of demand, it's crucial to draw a distinction between such shifts of the supply curve and **movements along the supply curve**—changes in the quantity supplied arising from a change in price. We can see this difference in Figure 3-8. The movement from point A to point B is a movement along the supply curve: the quantity supplied rises along S_1 due to a rise in price. Here, a rise in price from $3 to $3.50 leads to a rise in the quantity supplied from 10 trillion to 11.2 trillion BTUs of natural gas. But the quantity supplied can also rise when the price is unchanged if there is an increase in supply—a rightward shift of the supply curve. This is shown by the rightward shift of the supply curve from S_1 to S_2. Holding the price constant at $3, the quantity supplied rises from 10 trillion BTUs at point A on S_1 to 12 billion BTUs at point C on S_2.

Understanding Shifts of the Supply Curve

Figure 3-9 illustrates the two basic ways in which supply curves can shift. When economists talk about an "increase in supply," they mean a *rightward* shift of the supply curve: at any given price, producers supply a larger quantity of the good than before. This is shown in Figure 3-9 by the rightward shift of the original supply curve S_1 to S_2. And when economists talk about a "decrease in supply," they mean a *leftward* shift of the supply curve: at any given price, producers supply a smaller quantity of the good than before. This is represented by the leftward shift of S_1 to S_3.

FIGURE 3-8 Movement Along the Supply Curve versus Shift of the Supply Curve

The increase in quantity supplied when going from point *A* to point *B* reflects a movement along the supply curve: it is the result of a rise in the price of a good. The increase in quantity supplied when going from point *A* to point *C* reflects a shift of the supply curve: it is the result of an increase in the quantity supplied at any given price.

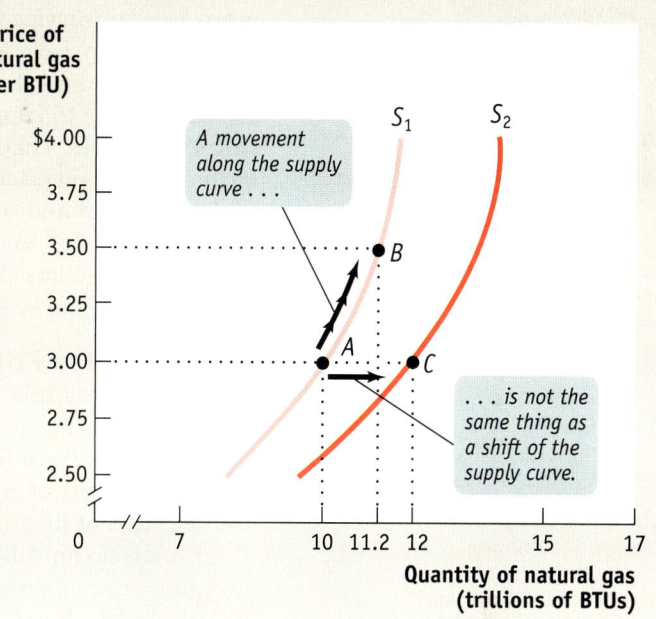

Economists believe that shifts of the supply curve for a good or service are mainly the result of five factors (though, as with demand, there are other possible causes):

- Changes in input prices
- Changes in the prices of related goods or services
- Changes in technology
- Changes in expectations
- Changes in the number of producers

FIGURE 3-9 Shifts of the Supply Curve

Any event that increases supply shifts the supply curve to the right, reflecting a rise in the quantity supplied at any given price. Any event that decreases supply shifts the supply curve to the left, reflecting a fall in the quantity supplied at any given price.

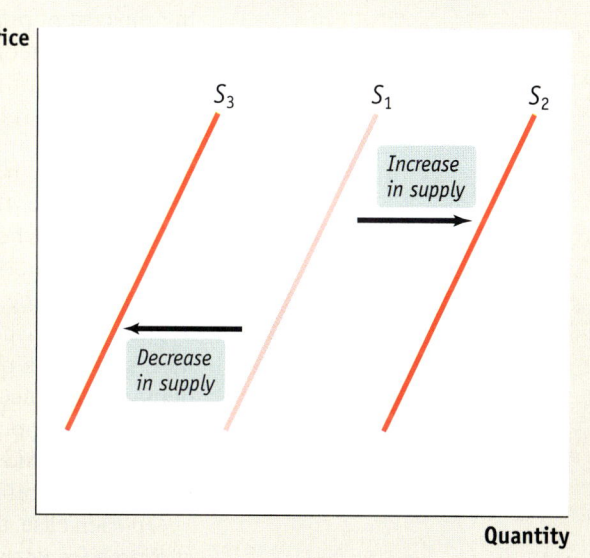

An **input** is a good or service that is used to produce another good or service.

Changes in Input Prices To produce output, you need inputs. For example, to make vanilla ice cream, you need vanilla beans, cream, sugar, and so on. An **input** is any good or service that is used to produce another good or service. Inputs, like outputs, have prices. And an increase in the price of an input makes the production of the final good more costly for those who produce and sell it. So producers are less willing to supply the final good at any given price, and the supply curve shifts to the left. That is, supply decreases. For example, fuel is a major cost for airlines. When oil prices surged in 2007–2008, airlines began cutting back on their flight schedules and some went out of business or merged with larger airlines.

Similarly, a fall in the price of an input makes the production of the final good less costly for sellers. They are more willing to supply the good at any given price, and the supply curve shifts to the right. That is, supply increases.

Changes in the Prices of Related Goods or Services A single producer often produces a mix of goods rather than a single product. For example, an oil refinery produces gasoline from crude oil, but it also produces heating oil and other products from the same raw material. When a producer sells several products, the quantity of any one good it is willing to supply at any given price depends on the prices of its other co-produced goods.

This effect can run in either direction. An oil refiner will supply less gasoline at any given price when the price of heating oil rises, shifting the supply curve for gasoline to the left. But it will supply more gasoline at any given price when the price of heating oil falls, shifting the supply curve for gasoline to the right. This means that gasoline and other co-produced oil products are *substitutes in production* for refiners.

In contrast, due to the nature of the production process, other goods can be *complements in production*. Producers of natural gas often find that natural gas wells also produce oil as a by-product of extraction. The higher the price at which a driller can sell its oil, the more willing it will be to drill natural gas wells and the more natural gas it will supply at any given price. Higher oil prices then lead to more natural gas supplied at any given price because oil and natural gas can be tapped simultaneously. As a result, oil is a complement in the production of natural gas. The reverse is also true: natural gas is a complement in the production of oil.

Changes in Technology As the opening story illustrates, changes in technology affect the supply curve. Technology improvements enable producers to spend less on inputs (in this case, drilling equipment, labour, land purchases, and so on), yet still produce the same amount of output. When a better technology becomes available, reducing the cost of production, supply increases and the supply curve shifts to the right.

Improved technology enabled natural gas producers to more than double output in less than two years. Technology is also the main reason that natural gas has remained relatively cheap, even as demand has grown.

Changes in Expectations Just as changes in expectations can shift the demand curve, they can also shift the supply curve. When suppliers have some choice about when they put their good up for sale, changes in the expected future price of the good can lead a supplier to supply less or more of the good today.

Consider the fact that gasoline and other oil products are often stored for significant periods of time at oil refineries before being sold to consumers. In fact, storage is normally part of producers' business strategy. Knowing that the demand for gasoline peaks in the summer, oil refiners normally store some of their gasoline produced during the spring for summer sale. Similarly, knowing that the demand for heating oil peaks in the winter, they normally store some of their heating oil produced during the fall for winter sale.

In each case, there's a decision to be made between selling the product now versus storing it for later sale. The choice a producer makes depends on a comparison of the current price and the expected future price. This example illustrates how changes in expectations can alter supply: an increase in the anticipated future price of a good or service reduces supply today, a leftward shift of the supply curve. But a fall in the anticipated future price increases supply today, a rightward shift of the supply curve.

Changes in the Number of Producers Just as changes in the number of consumers affect the demand curve, changes in the number of producers affect the supply curve. Let's examine the **individual supply curve,** by looking at panel (a) in Figure 3-10. The individual supply curve shows the relationship between quantity supplied and price for an individual producer. For example, suppose that Canadian Natural Resources Limited is a natural gas producer and that panel (a) of Figure 3-10 shows the quantity of BTUs it will supply per year at any given price. Then $S_{Canadian}$ is its individual supply curve.

The *market supply curve* shows how the combined total quantity supplied by all individual producers in the market depends on the market price of that good. Just as the market demand curve is the horizontal sum of the individual demand curves of all consumers, the market supply curve is the horizontal sum of the individual supply curves of all producers. Assume for a moment that there are only two natural gas producers, Canadian Natural Resources Limited and Encana Corporation. Encana's individual supply curve is shown in panel (b). Panel (c) shows the market supply curve. At any given price, the quantity supplied to the market is the sum of the quantities supplied by Canadian Natural Resources Limited and Encana Corporation. For example, at a price of $1 per BTU, Canadian Natural Resources Limited supplies 200,000 BTUs and Encana Corporation supplies 100,000 BTUs per year, making the quantity supplied to the market 300,000 BTUs.

Clearly, the quantity supplied to the market at any given price is larger when Encana Corporation is also a producer than it would be if Canadian Natural Resources Limited were the only supplier. The quantity supplied at a given price would be even larger if we added a third producer, then a fourth, and so on. So an increase in the number of producers leads to an increase in supply and a rightward shift of the supply curve.

For a review of the factors that shift supply, see Table 3-2.

An **individual supply curve** illustrates the relationship between quantity supplied and price for an individual producer.

FIGURE 3-10 The Individual Supply Curve and the Market Supply Curve

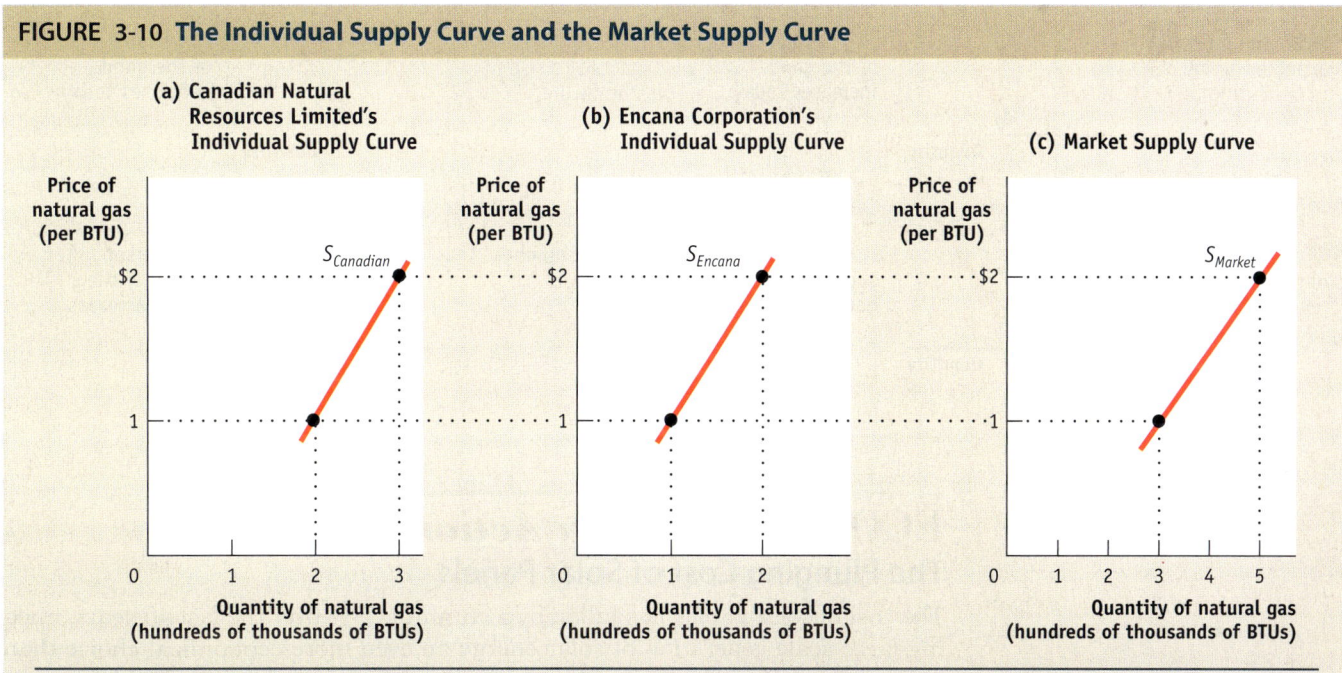

Panel (a) shows the individual supply curve for Canadian Natural Resources Limited, $S_{Canadian}$, the quantity it will sell at any given price. Panel (b) shows the individual supply curve for Encana Corporation, S_{Encana}. The market supply curve, which shows the quantity of natural gas supplied by all producers at any given price is shown in panel (c). The market supply curve is the horizontal sum of the individual supply curves of all producers.

TABLE 3-2 Factors That Shift Supply

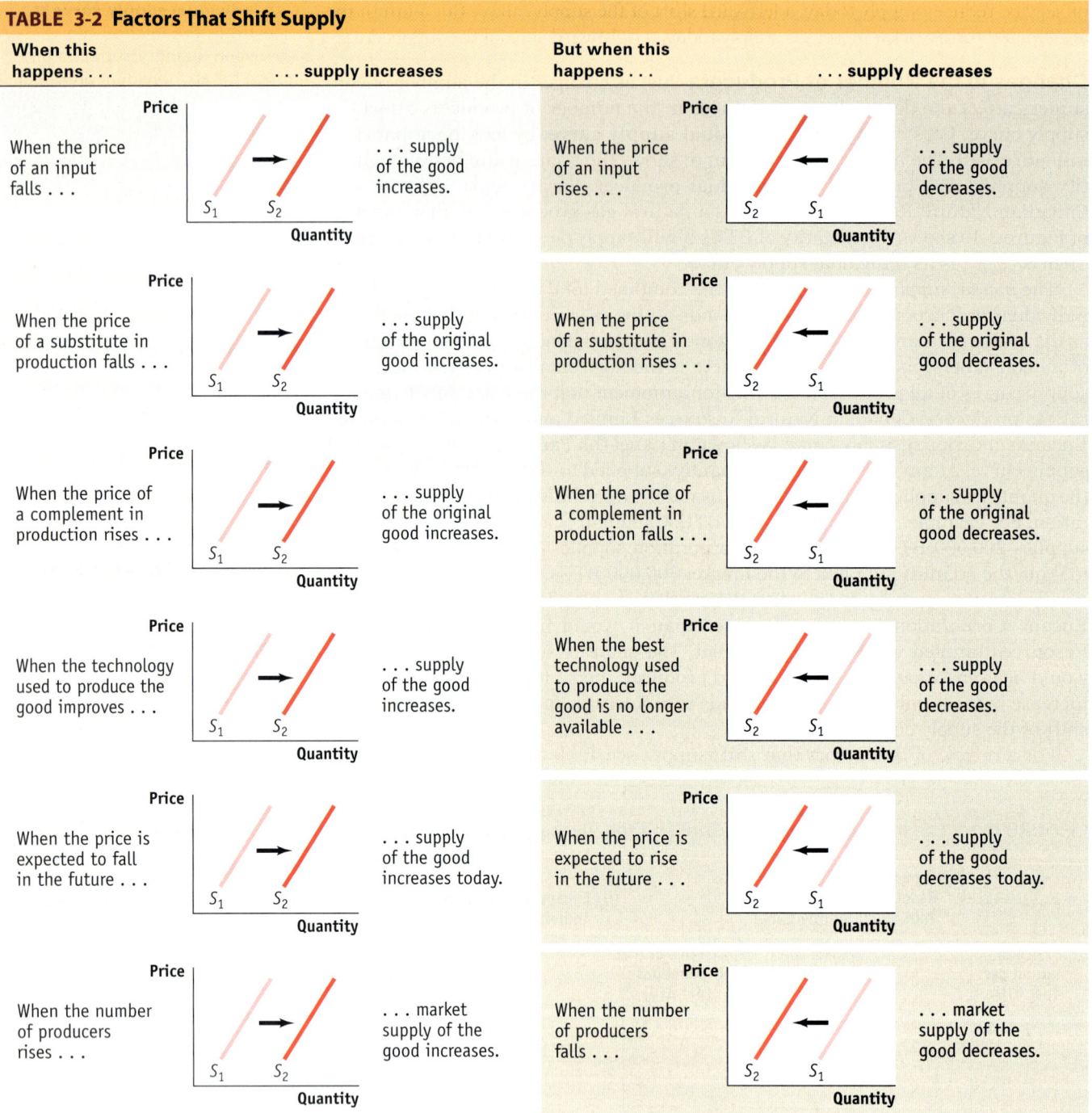

When this happens . . .	. . . supply increases	But when this happens . . .	. . . supply decreases
When the price of an input falls . . .	. . . supply of the good increases.	When the price of an input rises . . .	. . . supply of the good decreases.
When the price of a substitute in production falls . . .	. . . supply of the original good increases.	When the price of a substitute in production rises . . .	. . . supply of the original good decreases.
When the price of a complement in production rises . . .	. . . supply of the original good increases.	When the price of a complement in production falls . . .	. . . supply of the original good decreases.
When the technology used to produce the good improves . . .	. . . supply of the good increases.	When the best technology used to produce the good is no longer available . . .	. . . supply of the good decreases.
When the price is expected to fall in the future . . .	. . . supply of the good increases today.	When the price is expected to rise in the future . . .	. . . supply of the good decreases today.
When the number of producers rises . . .	. . . market supply of the good increases.	When the number of producers falls . . .	. . . market supply of the good decreases.

ECONOMICS >> *in Action*
The Plunging Cost of Solar Panels

The cost of solar panels has fallen by a stunning 99% over the last 40 years, making large-scale generation of solar energy an even more economical choice than more conventional forms of energy, such as coal-generated power. The lower cost of solar panels accounts for the proliferation of skyward-facing blue rectangles visible in many parts of North America. And, the cost of solar panels is projected to keep falling. According to a 2018 study by the Canada Energy Regulator (CER), formerly known as the National Energy Board (NEB), the installation cost of solar panels has dropped dramatically in the past decade. Take residential solar panels as an example, the CER estimated the current cost of a 5 kW residential project was about $16,000, but the cost is expected to drop to $12,975 in next five years and $11,260 in the next 10 years. Technological breakthroughs could result in an even greater decline.

What accounts for the enormous reductions in the cost of solar energy? There are two explanations. First, advances in technology played a major part. Over time, engineers discovered new, more efficient ways to convert solar rays into usable energy. These new technologies allowed solar panel producers to reduce the cost of production, increasing supply, which shifted the supply curve to the right.

The second driver of the plunge in solar panel prices began with an event that actually caused the price to increase: a change in the cost of a key input—polysilicon—that then led to a change in the number of producers.

Until 2008, solar panels were still relatively expensive and the market for them, while growing, was still small. That same year, polysilicon, the main input in solar panels (and, for semiconductor chips), surged to $507 per kilogram, up from around $39 four years earlier. The reason for this price surge—an increase of 1,300%—was that demand for both solar panels and semiconductor chips was growing. As a result, the demand for polysilicon was growing as well. But at the time, the market supply curve for polysilicon remained unchanged, ultimately contributing to the high price of polysilicon and a leftward shift in the supply curve for solar panels.

Although the high price of polysilicon in 2008 initially contributed to higher solar panel prices, it also prompted new polysilicon producers to enter the market, leading to a massive increase in supply. As a result, by 2014, the price of polysilicon had dropped from $507 to under $18 as the market supply curve shifted outward. Solar panel prices then dropped further and sales increased.

The CER projected that solar power will make up 3% of Canada's total electricity generation capacity by 2040, comparing to 0.5% in 2015.

Advances in technology and a change in the number of producers of polysilicon, a key input, contributed to the plunging cost of solar panels.

> ## >> Quick Review
>
> • The **supply schedule** shows how the **quantity supplied** depends on the price. The **supply curve** illustrates this relationship.
>
> • Supply curves are normally upward sloping: at a higher price, producers are willing to supply more of a good or service.
>
> • A change in price results in a **movement along the supply curve** and a change in the quantity supplied.
>
> • Increases or decreases in supply lead to **shifts of the supply curve.** An increase in supply is a rightward shift: the quantity supplied rises for any given price. A decrease in supply is a leftward shift: the quantity supplied falls for any given price.
>
> • The five main factors that can shift the supply curve are changes in (1) **input** prices, (2) prices of related goods or services, (3) technology, (4) expectations, and (5) number of producers.
>
> • The market supply curve is the horizontal sum of the **individual supply curves** of all producers in the market.

>> Check Your Understanding 3-2

Solutions appear at back of book.

1. Explain whether each of the following events represents (i) a *shift of* the supply curve or (ii) a *movement along* the supply curve.
   a. More homeowners put their houses up for sale during a real estate boom that causes house prices to rise.
   b. Many strawberry farmers open temporary roadside stands during harvest season, even though prices are usually low at that time.
   c. Immediately after the school year begins, fast-food chains must raise wages, which represent the price of labour, to attract workers.
   d. Many construction workers temporarily move to areas that have suffered hurricane damage, lured by higher wages.
   e. Since new technologies have made it possible to build larger cruise ships (which are cheaper to run per passenger), Caribbean cruise lines offer more cabins, at lower prices, than before.

‖ Supply, Demand, and Equilibrium

We have now covered the first three key elements in the supply and demand model: the demand curve, the supply curve, and the set of factors that shift each curve. The next step is to put these elements together to show how they can be used to predict the actual price at which the good is bought and sold, as well as the actual quantity transacted.

A competitive market is in equilibrium when price has moved to a level at which the quantity of a good or service demanded equals the quantity of that good or service supplied. The price at which this takes place is the **equilibrium price,** also referred to as the **market-clearing price.** The quantity of the good or service bought and sold at that price is the **equilibrium quantity.**

What determines the price at which a good or service is bought and sold? What determines the quantity transacted of the good or service? In Chapter 1, we learned the general principle that *markets move toward equilibrium,* a situation in which no individual would be better off taking a different action. In the case of a competitive market, we can be more specific: a competitive market is in equilibrium when the price has moved to a level at which the quantity of a good demanded equals the quantity of that good supplied. At that price, no individual seller could make herself better off by offering to sell either more or less of the good and no individual buyer could make himself better off by offering to buy more or less of the good. In other words, at the market equilibrium, price has moved to a level that exactly matches the quantity demanded by consumers to the quantity supplied by sellers.

The price that matches the quantity supplied and the quantity demanded is the **equilibrium price;** the quantity bought and sold at that price is the **equilibrium quantity.** The equilibrium price is also known as the **market-clearing price:** it is the price that "clears the market" by ensuring that every buyer willing to pay that price finds a seller willing to sell at that price, and vice versa. So how do we find the equilibrium price and quantity?

Finding the Equilibrium Price and Quantity

The easiest way to determine the equilibrium price and quantity in a market is by putting the supply curve and the demand curve on the same diagram. Since the supply curve shows the quantity supplied at any given price and the demand curve shows the quantity demanded at any given price, the price at which the two curves cross is the equilibrium price: the price at which quantity supplied equals quantity demanded.

Figure 3-11 combines the demand curve from Figure 3-1 and the supply curve from Figure 3-6. They *intersect* at point *E,* which is the equilibrium of this market; $3 is the equilibrium price and 10 trillion BTUs is the equilibrium quantity.

Let's confirm that point *E* fits our definition of equilibrium. At a price of $3 per BTU, natural gas producers are willing to sell 10 trillion BTUs a year and natural

---

FIGURE 3-11 Market Equilibrium

Market equilibrium occurs at point *E,* where the supply curve and the demand curve intersect. In equilibrium, the quantity demanded is equal to the quantity supplied. In this market, the equilibrium price is $3 per BTU and the equilibrium quantity is 10 trillion BTUs per year.

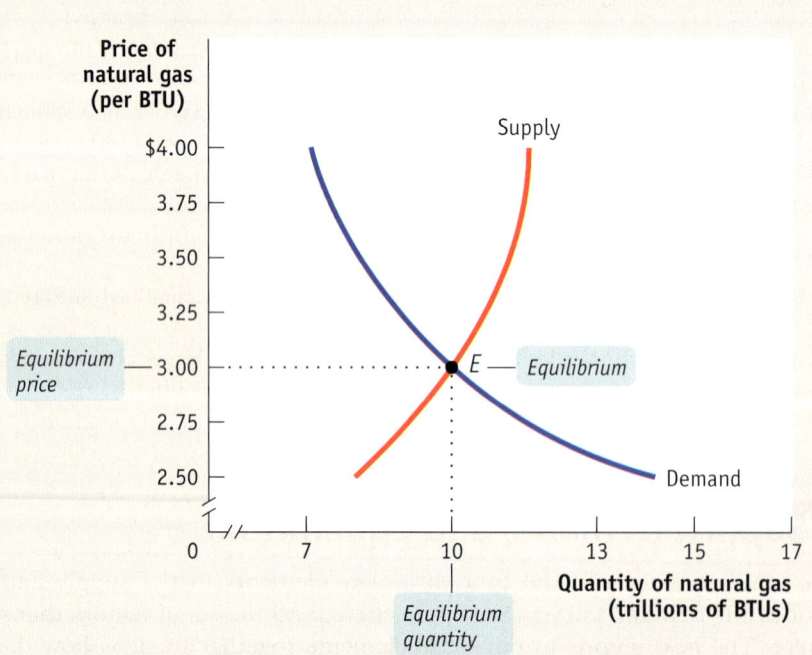

gas consumers want to buy 10 trillion BTUs a year. So at the price of $3 per BTU, the quantity of natural gas supplied equals the quantity demanded. Notice that at any other price the market would not clear: every willing buyer would not be able to find a willing seller, or vice versa. More specifically, if the price were more than $3, the quantity supplied would exceed the quantity demanded; if the price were less than $3, the quantity demanded would exceed the quantity supplied.

The model of supply and demand, then, predicts that given the demand and supply curves shown in Figure 3-11, 10 trillion BTUs would change hands at a price of $3 per BTU. But how can we be sure that the market will arrive at the equilibrium price? We begin by answering three simple questions:

1. Why do all sales and purchases in a market take place at the same price?
2. Why does the market price fall if it is above the equilibrium price?
3. Why does the market price rise if it is below the equilibrium price?

1. Why Do All Sales and Purchases in a Market Take Place at the Same Price?
There are some markets in which the same good can sell for many different prices, depending on who is selling or who is buying. For example, have you ever bought a souvenir in a tourist trap and then seen the same item on sale somewhere else for a lower price? Because tourists don't know which shops offer the best deals and don't have time for comparison shopping, sellers in tourist areas can charge different prices for the same good.

But in any market in which both buyers and sellers have been around for some time, sales and purchases tend to converge at a generally uniform price, so we can safely talk about *the* market price. It's easy to see why. Suppose a seller offered a potential buyer a price noticeably above what the buyer knew other people to be paying. The buyer would clearly be better off shopping elsewhere—unless the seller were prepared to offer a better deal.

Conversely, a seller would not be willing to sell for significantly less than the amount she knew most buyers were paying; she would be better off waiting to get a more reasonable customer. So in any well-established, ongoing market, where both buyers and sellers do not have information limitations, all sellers receive and all buyers pay approximately the same price. This is what we call the *market price*.

2. Why Does the Market Price Fall If It Is Above the Equilibrium Price?
Suppose the supply and demand curves are as shown in Figure 3-11 but the market price is above the equilibrium level of $3—say, $3.50. This situation is illustrated in Figure 3-12. Why can't the price stay there?

As the figure shows, at a price of $3.50 there would be more BTUs of natural gas available than consumers wanted to buy: 11.2 trillion BTUs versus 8.1 trillion BTUs. The difference of 3.1 trillion BTUs is the **surplus**—also known as the *excess supply*—of natural gas at $3.50.

This surplus means that some natural gas producers are frustrated: at the current price, they cannot find consumers who want to buy their natural gas. The surplus offers an incentive for those frustrated would-be sellers to offer a lower price in order to poach business from other producers and entice more consumers to buy. The result of this price cutting will be to push the prevailing price down until it reaches the equilibrium price. So the price of a good will

There is a **surplus** of a good or service when the quantity supplied exceeds the quantity demanded. Surpluses occur when the price is above its equilibrium level.

FIGURE 3-12 Price Above Its Equilibrium Level Creates a Surplus

The market price of $3.50 is above the equilibrium price of $3. This creates a surplus: at a price of $3.50, producers would like to sell 11.2 trillion BTUs but consumers want to buy only 8.1 trillion BTUs, so there is a surplus of 3.1 trillion BTUs. This surplus will push the price down until it reaches the equilibrium price of $3.

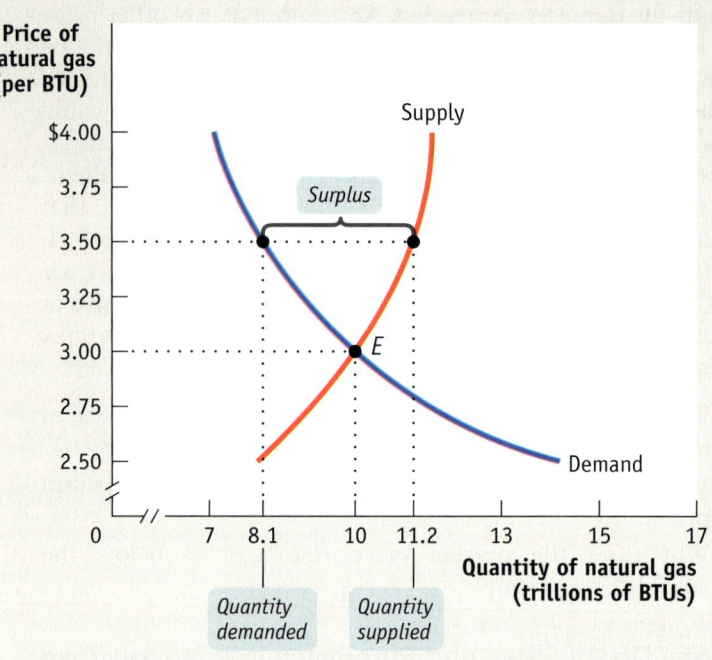

fall whenever there is a surplus—that is, whenever the market price is above its equilibrium level.

3. Why Does the Market Price Rise If It Is Below the Equilibrium Price? Now suppose the price is below its equilibrium level—say, at $2.75 per BTU, as shown in Figure 3-13. In this case, the quantity demanded, 11.5 trillion BTUs, exceeds the quantity supplied, 9.1 trillion BTUs, implying that there are

FIGURE 3-13 Price Below Its Equilibrium Level Creates a Shortage

The market price of $2.75 is below the equilibrium price of $3. This creates a shortage: consumers want to buy 11.5 trillion BTUs, but only 9.1 trillion BTUs are for sale, so there is a shortage of 2.4 trillion BTUs. This shortage will push the price up until it reaches the equilibrium price of $3.

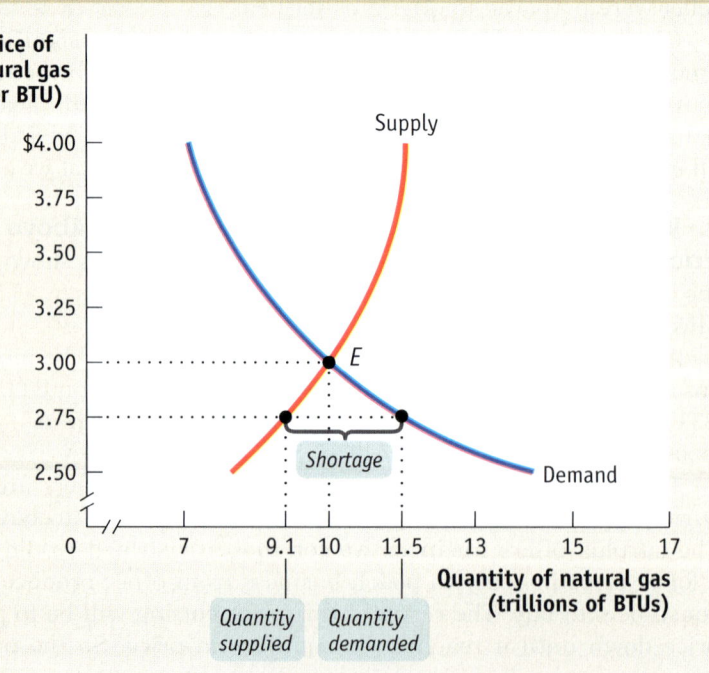

would-be buyers who cannot find natural gas: there is a **shortage,** also known as an *excess demand,* of 2.4 trillion BTUs.

When there is a shortage, there are frustrated would-be buyers—people who want to purchase natural gas but cannot find willing sellers at the current price. In this situation, either buyers will offer more than the prevailing price or sellers will realize that they can charge higher prices. Either way, the result is to drive up the prevailing price.

This bidding up of prices happens whenever there are shortages—and there will be shortages whenever the price is below its equilibrium level. So the market price will always rise if it is below the equilibrium level.

Using Equilibrium to Describe Markets

We have now seen that a market tends to have a single price, the equilibrium price. If the market price is above the equilibrium level, the ensuing surplus leads buyers and sellers to take actions that lower the price. And if the market price is below the equilibrium level, the ensuing shortage leads buyers and sellers to take actions that raise the price. So the market price always *moves toward* the equilibrium price, the price at which there is neither surplus nor shortage.

There is a **shortage** of a good or service when the quantity demanded exceeds the quantity supplied. Shortages occur when the price is below its equilibrium level.

ECONOMICS >> *in Action*
The Price of Admission

The market equilibrium, so the theory goes, is pretty egalitarian because the equilibrium price applies to everyone. That is, all buyers pay the same price—the equilibrium price—and all sellers receive that same price. But is this realistic?

The market for sporting event tickets is an example that seems to contradict the theory—there's one price at the box office, and there's another price (typically much higher) for the same event online where people who already have tickets resell them. For example, compare the box office price for a standing room only ticket to game one of the 2019 NBA finals, in March 2019 to the StubHub.com price for seats in the same location: $756 versus $1,030 (both measured on the day tickets went on sale).

Puzzling as this may seem, there is no contradiction once we take opportunity costs and tastes into account. For major events, buying tickets from the box office can mean waiting in very long "digital" lines. Ticket buyers who use online resellers have decided that the opportunity cost of their time is too high to spend waiting in line. And tickets for major events being sold at face value by online box offices often sell out within minutes. In this case, some people who want to go to the concert badly but have missed out on the opportunity to buy cheaper tickets from the online box office are willing to pay the higher online reseller price.

Not only that, but by comparing prices across sellers for seats close to one another, you can see that markets really do move to equilibrium. For example, for a seat in Row B Courtside North, StubHub's price was $10,889 each while SeatGeek's price for a nearby seat was $11,669 (both sites required buying two tickets). As the competitive market model predicts, units of the same good will end up selling for approximately the same price.

In fact, e-commerce has made markets move to equilibrium more quickly by doing the price comparisons for you. The website SeatGeek compares ticket prices across more than 100 ticket resellers, allowing customers to instantly choose the best deal. Tickets that are priced lower than those of competitors will be snapped up, while higher priced tickets will languish unsold.

Prensa Internacional/ZUMA Press, Inc./Alamy Stock Photo

The competitive market model determines the price you pay for sport event tickets.

And tickets on StubHub can sell for less than the face value for events with little appeal, while they can skyrocket for events in high demand. For example, in 2019, the average ticket price on StubHub for Game 6 of the NBA Finals was about $4,400, with one fan paying nearly $93,000 for a pair of courtside seats to watch the Toronto Raptors win their first NBA championship. Even StubHub's chief executive said the site is "the embodiment of supply-and-demand economics."

So the theory of competitive markets isn't just speculation. If you want to experience it for yourself, try buying tickets to a concert or an NBA championship.

>> **Quick Review**

• Price in a competitive market moves to the **equilibrium price,** or **market-clearing price,** where the quantity supplied is equal to the quantity demanded. This quantity is the **equilibrium quantity.**

• All sales and purchases in a market take place at the same price. If the price is above its equilibrium level, there is a **surplus** that drives the price down to the equilibrium level. If the price is below its equilibrium level, there is a **shortage** that drives the price up to the equilibrium level.

>> **Check Your Understanding** **3-3**

Solutions appear at back of book.

1. In the following three situations, the market is initially in equilibrium. Explain the changes in either supply or demand that result from each event. After each event described below, does a surplus or shortage exist at the original equilibrium price? What will happen to the equilibrium price as a result?
   a. 2017 was a very good year for Ontario wine-grape growers, who produced a bumper crop.
   b. After a blizzard, Ottawa hoteliers often find that many people cancel their upcoming vacations, leaving them with empty hotel rooms.
   c. After a heavy snowfall, many people want to buy second-hand snowblowers at the local home improvement store.

‖ Changes in Supply and Demand

The huge fall in the price of natural gas from US$14 to US$2 per BTU from 2006 to 2013 may have come as a surprise to consumers, but to suppliers it was no surprise at all. Suppliers knew that advances in drilling technology had opened up vast reserves of natural gas that had been too costly to tap in the past. And, predictably, an increase in supply reduces the equilibrium price.

The adoption of improved drilling technology is an example of an event that shifted the supply curve for a good without having an effect on the demand curve. There are many such events. There are also events that shift the demand curve without shifting the supply curve. For example, a medical report that chocolate is good for you increases the demand for chocolate but does not affect the supply. Events often shift either the supply curve or the demand curve, but not both; it is therefore useful to ask what happens in each case.

We have seen that when a curve shifts, the equilibrium price and quantity change. We will now concentrate on exactly how the shift of a curve alters the equilibrium price and quantity.

What Happens When the Demand Curve Shifts

Heating oil and natural gas are substitutes: if the price of heating oil rises, the demand for natural gas will increase, and if the price of heating oil falls, the demand for natural gas will decrease. But how does the price of heating oil affect the *market equilibrium* for natural gas?

Figure 3-14 shows the effect of a rise in the price of heating oil on the market for natural gas. The rise in the price of heating oil increases the demand for natural gas. Point E_1 shows the equilibrium corresponding to the original demand curve, with P_1 the equilibrium price and Q_1 the equilibrium quantity bought and sold.

An increase in demand is indicated by a *rightward* shift of the demand curve from D_1 to D_2. At the original market price P_1, this market is no longer in equilibrium: a shortage occurs because the quantity demanded exceeds the quantity supplied. So the price of natural gas rises and generates an increase in the quantity

FIGURE 3-14 Equilibrium and Shifts of the Demand Curve

The original equilibrium in the market for natural gas is at E_1, at the intersection of the supply curve and the original demand curve, D_1. A rise in the price of heating oil, a substitute, shifts the demand curve rightward to D_2. A shortage exists at the original price, P_1, causing both the price and quantity supplied to rise, a movement along the supply curve. A new equilibrium is reached at E_2, with a higher equilibrium price, P_2, and a higher equilibrium quantity, Q_2. When demand for a good or service increases, the equilibrium price and the equilibrium quantity of the good or service both rise.

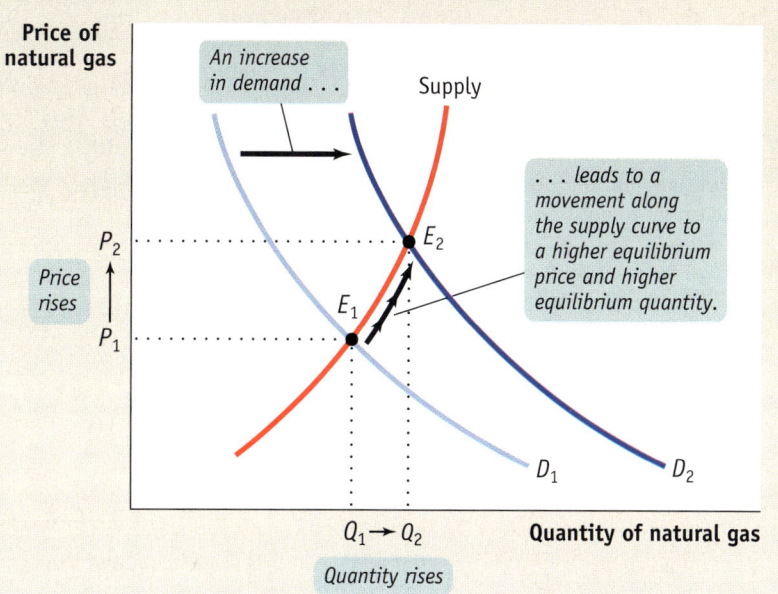

supplied, an upward *movement along the supply curve.* A new equilibrium is established at point E_2, with a higher equilibrium price, P_2, and higher equilibrium quantity, Q_2. This sequence of events reflects a general principle: *When demand for a good or service increases, the equilibrium price and the equilibrium quantity of the good or service both rise.*

What would happen in the reverse case, a fall in the price of heating oil? A fall in the price of heating oil reduces the demand for natural gas, shifting the demand curve to the *left.* At the original price, a surplus occurs as quantity supplied exceeds quantity demanded. The price falls and leads to a decrease in the quantity supplied, resulting in a lower equilibrium price and a lower equilibrium quantity. This illustrates another general principle: *When demand for a good or service decreases, the equilibrium price and the equilibrium quantity of the good or service both fall.*

To summarize how a market responds to a change in demand: *An increase in demand leads to a rise in both the equilibrium price and the equilibrium quantity. A decrease in demand leads to a fall in both the equilibrium price and the equilibrium quantity.*

What Happens When the Supply Curve Shifts

For most goods and services, it is a bit easier to predict changes in supply than changes in demand. Physical factors that affect supply, like weather or the availability of inputs, are easier to get a handle on than the fickle tastes that affect demand. Still, with supply as with demand, what we can best predict are the *effects* of shifts of the supply curve.

As we mentioned in the opening story, improved drilling technology significantly increased the supply of natural gas from 2006 onward. Figure 3-15 shows how this shift affected the market equilibrium. The original equilibrium is at E_1, the point of intersection of the original supply curve, S_1, with an equilibrium price P_1 and equilibrium quantity Q_1. As a result of the improved technology, supply increases and S_1 shifts *rightward* to S_2. At the original price P_1, a surplus of natural gas now exists and the market is no longer in equilibrium. The surplus causes a fall in price and an increase in the quantity demanded, a *downward movement along the demand curve.* The new equilibrium is at E_2, with an equilibrium price P_2 and an equilibrium quantity Q_2. In the new equilibrium

FIGURE 3-15 Equilibrium and Shifts of the Supply Curve

The original equilibrium in the market is at E_1. Improved technology causes an increase in the supply of natural gas and shifts the supply curve rightward from S_1 to S_2. A new equilibrium is established at E_2, with a lower equilibrium price, P_2, and a higher equilibrium quantity, Q_2.

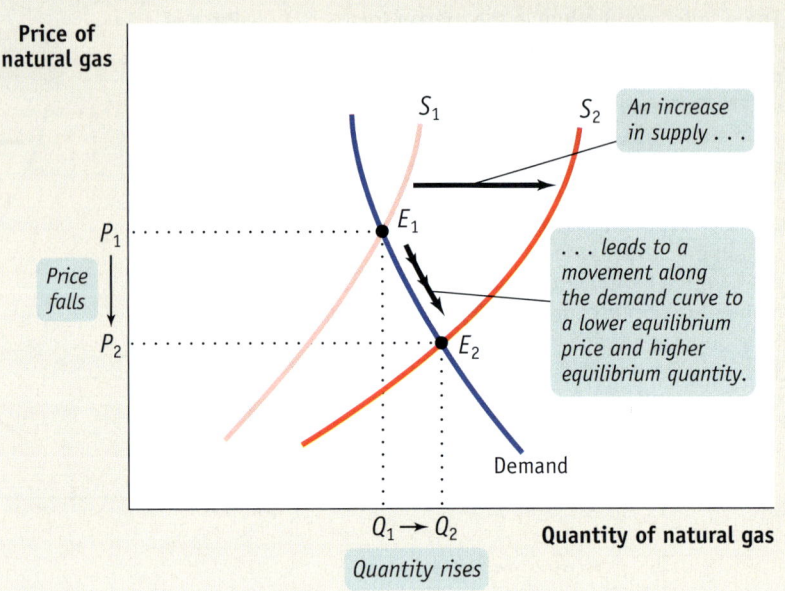

Price of natural gas

S_1 S_2 *An increase in supply . . .*

P_1 ⋯⋯⋯⋯⋯ E_1

Price falls

. . . leads to a movement along the demand curve to a lower equilibrium price and higher equilibrium quantity.

P_2 ⋯⋯⋯⋯⋯ E_2

Demand

$Q_1 \rightarrow Q_2$ **Quantity of natural gas**

Quantity rises

E_2, the price is lower and the equilibrium quantity is higher than before. This can be stated as a general principle: *When supply of a good or service increases, the equilibrium price of the good or service falls and the equilibrium quantity of the good or service rises.*

What happens to the market when supply falls? A fall in supply leads to a *leftward* shift of the supply curve. At the original price a shortage now exists. As a result, the equilibrium price rises and the quantity demanded falls. This describes what happened to the market for natural gas after the Fort McMurray wildfire lead to the shutdown of some refinery plants in 2016. We can formulate a general principle: *When supply of a good or service decreases, the equilibrium price of the good or service rises and the equilibrium quantity of the good or service falls.*

To summarize how a market responds to a change in supply: *An increase in supply leads to a fall in the equilibrium price and a rise in the equilibrium quantity. A decrease in supply leads to a rise in the equilibrium price and a fall in the equilibrium quantity.*

Simultaneous Shifts of Supply and Demand Curves

Finally, it sometimes happens that events shift *both* the demand and supply curves at the same time. This is not unusual; in real life, supply curves and demand curves for many goods and services shift quite often because the economic environment continually changes.

Figure 3-16 illustrates two examples of simultaneous shifts. In both panels there is an increase in supply—that is, a rightward shift of the supply curve from S_1 to S_2—representing, for example, adoption of an improved drilling technology. Notice that the rightward shift in panel (a) is smaller than the one in panel (b): we can suppose that panel (a) represents a small, incremental change in technology while panel (b) represents a big advance in technology.

Both panels show a decrease in demand—that is, a leftward shift from D_1 to D_2. Also notice that the leftward shift in panel (a) is relatively larger than the one in panel (b): we can suppose that panel (a) reflects the effect on demand of a deep recession in the overall economy, while panel (b) reflects the effect of a mild winter.

FIGURE 3-16 Simultaneous Shifts of the Demand and Supply Curves

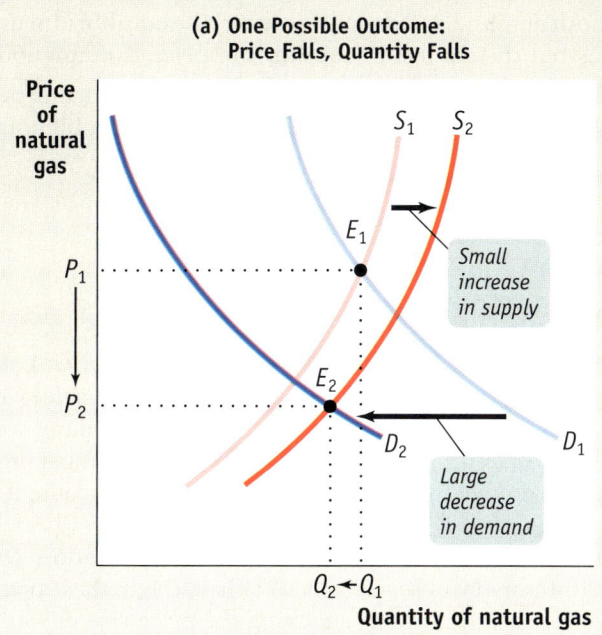

(a) One Possible Outcome: Price Falls, Quantity Falls

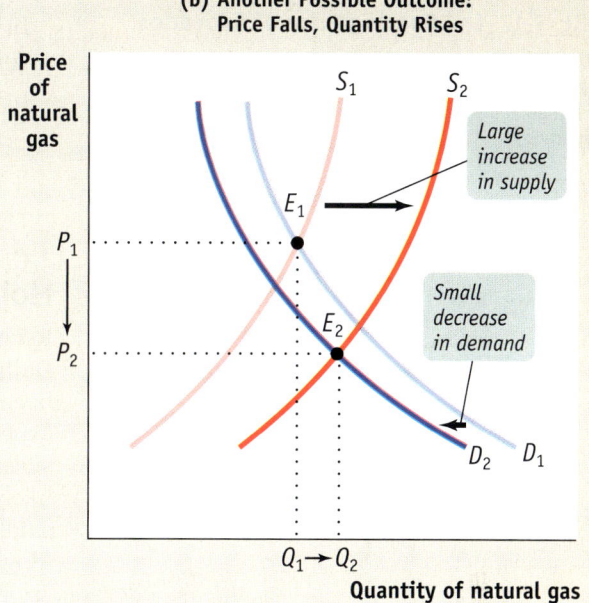

(b) Another Possible Outcome: Price Falls, Quantity Rises

In panel (a) there is a simultaneous leftward shift of the demand curve and a rightward shift of the supply curve. Here the decrease in demand is relatively larger than the increase in supply, so the equilibrium quantity falls as the equilibrium price also falls. In panel (b) there is also a simultaneous leftward shift of the demand curve and rightward shift of the supply curve. Here the increase in supply is large relative to the decrease in demand, so the equilibrium quantity rises as the equilibrium price falls.

In both cases the equilibrium price falls from P_1 to P_2 as the equilibrium moves from E_1 to E_2. But what happens to the equilibrium quantity, the quantity of natural gas bought and sold? In panel (a) the decrease in demand is large relative to the increase in supply, and the equilibrium quantity falls as a result. In panel (b) the increase in supply is large relative to the decrease in demand, and the equilibrium quantity rises as a result. That is, when demand decreases and supply increases, the actual quantity bought and sold can go either way depending on *how much* the demand and supply curves have shifted.

In general, when supply and demand shift in opposite directions, we can't predict what the ultimate effect will be on the quantity bought and sold. What we can say is that a curve that shifts a disproportionately greater distance than the other curve will have a disproportionately greater effect on the quantity bought and sold. That said, we can make the following prediction about the outcome when the supply and demand curves shift in opposite directions:

• When demand decreases and supply increases, the equilibrium price falls but the change in the equilibrium quantity is ambiguous.

• When demand increases and supply decreases, the equilibrium price rises but the change in the equilibrium quantity is ambiguous.

But suppose that the demand and supply curves shift in the same direction. This is what has happened in Canada, as the economy made a gradual recovery from the recession in 2008, resulting in an increase in both demand and supply. Can we safely make any predictions about the changes in price and quantity? In this situation, the change in quantity bought and sold can be predicted, but the change in price is ambiguous. The two possible outcomes when the supply and demand curves shift in the same direction are as follows:

- When both demand and supply increase, the equilibrium quantity rises but the change in equilibrium price is ambiguous.
- When both demand and supply decrease, the equilibrium quantity falls but the change in equilibrium price is ambiguous.

FIGURE 3-17 The Soaring Price of Avocados

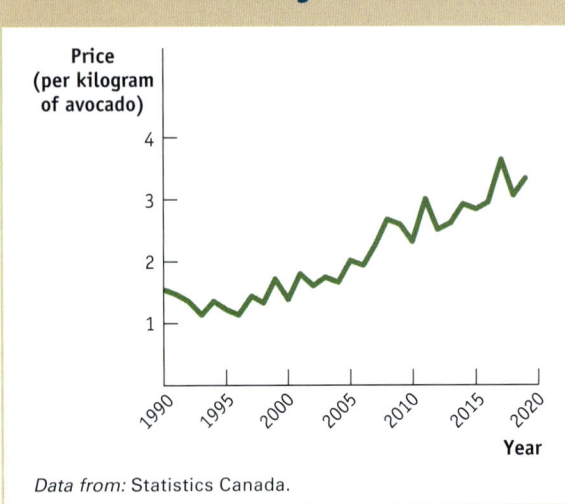

Data from: Statistics Canada.

ECONOMICS >> *in Action*
Holy Guacamole!

Recently Sylvain Charlebois of the Agri-Food Analytics Lab, at Dalhousie University noted that Canadian avocado prices have been high for a while now. "Typically, most Canadians would expect to pay $1 per unit. In the last few months, it's almost impossible to find them below $2. And if you do buy an avocado, it will likely be smaller, darker and much less appetizing," Charlebois said. Commenting on the wholesale price of avocados, David Magaña, an industry observer, said, "This is the highest price in at least a decade, probably more." Yet, however shocking the price rise, it was just the result of the avocado market responding to the forces of supply and demand.

First, you can thank North Americans' fast-growing appetite (demand) for all things avocado: guacamole, avocado toast, and avocado smoothies. In 2019 the average Canadian ate just over 2.5 kilograms of the fruit per year, compared to 0.20 kilograms per capita in 1990. In addition, demand for avocados is growing in other places such as Europe and China. Both of these events shifted the demand curve rightward.

Second, there's supply. In 2019 the California avocado harvest was the smallest in a decade following a severe heatwave, coming in nearly 50% lower than in 2018. In addition, two other major avocado growing areas—Peru and South Africa—experienced year-on-year declines in output. These events shifted the supply curve leftward.

Inevitably, an increase in demand coupled with a sharp fall in supply leads to sharply rising prices for avocados. It's economic logic, after all. Until demand falls, or supply rises, or both, the price of satisfying North America's avocado cravings will remain high, as shown in Figure 3-17.

Unfortunately, there isn't a bright spot on the horizon for avocado lovers. Climate change is impacting winter rainfall in California along with temperature fluctuations that make growing orchard crops, like avocados, a more risky proposition. So you might want to enjoy your avocado toast or tortilla chips and dip while you can.

>> Quick Review

- Changes in the equilibrium price and quantity in a market result from shifts of the supply curve, the demand curve, or both.

- An increase in demand increases both the equilibrium price and the equilibrium quantity. A decrease in demand decreases both the equilibrium price and the equilibrium quantity.

- An increase in supply drives the equilibrium price down but increases the equilibrium quantity. A decrease in supply raises the equilibrium price but reduces the equilibrium quantity.

- Often fluctuations in markets involve shifts of both the supply and demand curves. When they shift in the same direction, the change in equilibrium quantity is predictable but the change in equilibrium price is not. When they shift in opposite directions, the change in equilibrium price is predictable but the change in equilibrium quantity is not. When there are simultaneous shifts of the demand and supply curves, the curve that shifts the greater distance has a greater effect on the change in equilibrium price and quantity.

>> Check Your Understanding 3-4

Solutions appear at back of book.

1. For each of the following, determine (i) the market in question; (ii) whether a shift in demand or supply occurred, the direction of the shift, and what induced the shift; and (iii) the effect of the shift on the equilibrium price and the equilibrium quantity.
   a. As domestic retail gasoline prices fall, more people buy large cars.
   b. As technological innovation has lowered the cost of recycling used paper, fresh paper made from recycled stock is used more frequently.
   c. When a local cable company offers cheaper on-demand films, local movie theatres have more unfilled seats.
2. When a new, faster computer chip is introduced, demand for computers using the older, slower chips decreases. Simultaneously, computer makers increase their

production of computers containing the old chips in order to clear out their stocks of old chips.

a. Draw two diagrams of the market for computers containing the old chips: one in which the equilibrium quantity falls in response to these events and one in which the equilibrium quantity rises.

b. What happens to the equilibrium price in each diagram?

‖ Competitive Markets — and Others

Earlier in this chapter we defined a competitive market and explained that the supply and demand framework is a model of competitive markets. But why does it matter whether or not a market is competitive? Now that we've seen how the supply and demand model works, we can offer some explanation.

To understand why competitive markets are different from other markets, compare the problems facing two individuals: a wheat farmer who must decide whether to grow more wheat and the president of a giant aluminum company—say, Rio Tinto Alcan—who must decide whether to produce more aluminum.

For the wheat farmer, the question is simply whether the extra wheat can be sold at a price high enough to justify the extra production cost. The farmer need not worry about whether producing more wheat will affect the price of the wheat they were already planning to grow. That's because the wheat market is competitive. There are thousands of wheat farmers, and one farmer's decision will not impact the market price.

But for the Alcoa executive, the aluminum market is *not* competitive. There are only a few big producers, including Rio Tinto Alcan, and each of them is well aware that its actions *do* have a noticeable impact on the market price. This adds a whole new level of complexity to the decisions producers have to make. Rio Tinto Alcan can't decide whether or not to produce more aluminum just by asking whether the additional product will sell for more than it costs to make. The company also has to ask whether producing more aluminum will drive down the market price and reduce its *profit*, its net gain from producing and selling its output.

When a market is competitive, individuals can base decisions on less complicated analyses than those used in a noncompetitive market. This in turn means that it's easier for economists to build a model of a competitive market than of a noncompetitive market.

This doesn't mean that economic analysis has nothing to say about noncompetitive markets. On the contrary, economists can offer some very important insights into how other kinds of markets work. But those insights require other models.

Uber Gives Riders a Lesson in Supply and Demand

JEENAH MOON/The New York Times/Redux

Two young entrepreneurs, Garrett Camp and Travis Kalanick, created Uber in 2009 to alleviate a common frustration: how to find a taxi when you need to get somewhere and there aren't any taxis available. In densely populated cities like Toronto, finding a taxi is relatively easy on most days—stand on a corner, stick out your arm, and before long a taxi will stop to pick you up. And you know exactly what taxi fare rates will be before you step into the car, because they are set by city regulators.

But at other times, it can be difficult to find a taxi, and you can wait a very long time for one—for example, on rainy days or during rush hour. As you wait, you will probably notice empty taxis passing you by—drivers who have quit working for the day and are headed home. Moreover, there are times when it is simply impossible to hail a taxi—such as during a snowstorm or on New Year's Eve.

Uber was created to address this problem. Using an app, Uber connects people who want a ride to drivers with cars. It also registers drivers, sets fares, and automatically collects payment from a registered rider's credit card. Uber then keeps 25% of the fare, with the rest going to the driver. As of 2019, Uber was operating in 65 countries and in more than 600 cities, and booked US$11.3 billion in rides.

Studies have shown that Uber fares are either roughly equal to or less than regular taxi fares during normal driving hours. The qualification *during normal driving hours* is important because at other times Uber's rates fluctuate. When there are more people looking for a ride than cars available, Uber uses what it calls *surge pricing:* setting the rate higher until everyone who wants a car at the going price can get one. For example, during a snowstorm or on New Year's Eve, Uber rides cost around 9 to 10 times the standard price. Enraged, some Uber customers have accused it of price gouging.

But according to its founders, Uber's surge pricing is simply a method of keeping customers happy because the surge price is calculated to leave as few people as possible without a ride. As Kalanick explains, "We do not own cars nor do we employ drivers. Higher prices are required to get cars on the road and keep them on the road during the busiest times." However, with more drivers joining Uber's fleet, drivers are finding that it takes longer hours to make sufficient income. So in cities like San Diego, California where passengers have limited access to taxi services, Uber drivers have banded together to take "synchronized breaks" during peak hours, such as Saturday nights. These breaks cause prices to surge, which prompts the drivers to jump into their cars. Clearly these Uber drivers know how supply and demand works.

QUESTIONS FOR THOUGHT

1. What accounts for the fact that before Uber's arrival, there were typically enough taxis available for everyone who wanted one on good weather days, but not enough available on bad weather days?

2. How does Uber's surge pricing solve the problem? Assess Kalanick's claim that the price is set to leave as few people possible without a ride.

3. Use a supply and demand diagram to illustrate how Uber drivers can cause prices to surge by taking coordinated breaks. Why is this strategy unlikely to work in Toronto, a large city with an established fleet of taxis?

SUMMARY

1. The **supply and demand model** illustrates how a **competitive market,** one with many buyers and sellers, none of whom can influence the market price, works.

2. The **demand schedule** shows the **quantity demanded** at each price and is represented graphically by a **demand curve.** The **law of demand** says that demand curves slope downward; that is, a higher price for a good or service leads people to demand a smaller quantity, other things equal.

3. A **movement along the demand curve** occurs when a price change leads to a change in the quantity demanded. When economists talk of increasing or decreasing demand, they mean **shifts of the demand curve**—a change in the quantity demanded at any given price. An increase in demand causes a rightward shift of the demand curve. A decrease in demand causes a leftward shift.

4. There are five main factors that shift the demand curve:
   * A change in the prices of related goods or services, such as **substitutes** or **complements**
   * A change in income: when income rises, the demand for **normal goods** increases and the demand for **inferior goods** decreases
   * A change in tastes
   * A change in expectations
   * A change in the number of consumers

5. The market demand curve for a good or service is the horizontal sum of the **individual demand curves** of all consumers in the market.

6. The **supply schedule** shows the **quantity supplied** at each price and is represented graphically by a **supply curve.** Supply curves usually slope upward.

7. A **movement along the supply curve** occurs when a price change leads to a change in the quantity supplied. When economists talk of increasing or decreasing supply, they mean **shifts of the supply curve**—a change in the quantity supplied at any given price. An increase in supply causes a rightward shift of the supply curve. A decrease in supply causes a leftward shift.

8. There are five main factors that shift the supply curve:
   * A change in **input** prices
   * A change in the prices of related goods and services
   * A change in technology
   * A change in expectations
   * A change in the number of producers

9. The market supply curve for a good or service is the horizontal sum of the **individual supply curves** of all producers in the market.

10. The supply and demand model is based on the principle that the price in a market moves to its **equilibrium price,** or **market-clearing price,** the price at which the quantity demanded is equal to the quantity supplied. This quantity is the **equilibrium quantity.** When the price is above its market-clearing level, there is a **surplus** that pushes the price down. When the price is below its market-clearing level, there is a **shortage** that pushes the price up.

11. An increase in demand increases both the equilibrium price and the equilibrium quantity; a decrease in demand has the opposite effect. An increase in supply reduces the equilibrium price and increases the equilibrium quantity; a decrease in supply has the opposite effect.

12. Shifts of the demand curve and the supply curve can happen simultaneously. When they shift in opposite directions, the change in equilibrium price is predictable but the change in equilibrium quantity is not. When they shift in the same direction, the change in equilibrium quantity is predictable but the change in equilibrium price is not. In general, the curve that shifts the greater distance has a greater effect on the changes in equilibrium price and quantity.

KEY TERMS

PRACTICE QUESTIONS

1. In the market for automobiles explain how demand responds to (i) an increase in the price of automobiles today and (ii) an expected increase in the future price of automobiles.

2. Explain why the following statement is misleading: "Apple increases the supply of watches following an unexpected increase in demand."

3. In each of the following, what is the mistake that underlies the statement? Explain the mistake in terms of supply and demand and the factors that influence them.

   a. Consumers are illogical because they are buying more Starbucks beverages in 2019 despite the fact that Starbucks has raised prices 10 to 30 cents per drink.

   b. Consumers are illogical because they buy less at Cost-U-Less Warehouse Superstore when their incomes go up.

   c. Consumers are illogical for buying an iPhone 11 when an iPhone X costs less.

4. Two students are debating the effects of an expected decline in future home prices. One student claims that a decline in home prices will increase the total quantity of homes while the other student claims that the quantity of homes will decline. Which student is correct? Explain. Be sure to discuss how expected price changes shift demand and/or supply.

PROBLEMS

1. Surveys have found that chocolate is Canadians' favourite ice-cream flavour. For each of the following, indicate the possible effects on demand, supply, or both as well as equilibrium price and quantity of chocolate ice cream.

   a. A severe drought in Ontario causes dairy farmers to reduce the number of milk-producing cattle in their herds by a third. These dairy farmers supply cream that is used to manufacture chocolate ice cream.

   b. A new report by the Canadian Medical Association reveals that chocolate does, in fact, have significant health benefits.

   c. The discovery of cheaper synthetic vanilla flavouring lowers the price of vanilla ice cream.

   d. New technology for mixing and freezing ice cream lowers manufacturers' costs of producing chocolate ice cream.

2. In a supply and demand diagram, draw the shift of the demand curve for hamburgers in your hometown due to the following events. In each case, show the effect on equilibrium price and quantity.

   a. The price of tacos increases.

   b. All hamburger sellers raise the price of their french fries.

   c. Income falls in town. Assume that hamburgers are a normal good for most people.

   d. Income falls in town. Assume that hamburgers are an inferior good for most people.

   e. Hot dog stands cut the price of hot dogs.

3. The market for many goods changes in predictable ways according to the time of year, in response to events such as holidays, vacation times, seasonal changes in production, and so on. Using supply and demand, explain the change in price in each of the following cases. Note that supply and demand may shift simultaneously.

   a. Lobster prices usually fall during the summer peak lobster harvest season, despite the fact that people like to eat lobster during the summer more than at any other time of year.

   b. The price of a Christmas tree is lower after Christmas than before but fewer trees are sold.

   c. The price of a round-trip ticket to Paris on Air France falls by more than $200 after the end of school vacation in September. This happens despite the fact that generally worsening weather increases the cost of operating flights to Paris, and Air France therefore reduces the number of flights to Paris at any given price.

4. Show in a diagram the effect on the demand curve, the supply curve, the equilibrium price, and the equilibrium quantity of each of the following events.

   a. The market for hotel rooms in your town

   Case 1: The wages of housekeepers go up.

   Case 2: A major political convention will be held in your town, attracting many visitors from across the country.

   b. The market for Toronto Raptors cotton T-shirts

   Case 1: The Raptors win the NBA championship.

   Case 2: The price of cotton increases.

   c. The market for bagels

   Case 1: People realize that bagels are high in calories and sugar.

   Case 2: People have less time to cook breakfast in the morning.

   d. The market for the Krugman, Wells, Au, and Parkinson economics textbook

   Case 1: Your professor makes it required reading for all of their students.

   Case 2: Printing costs for textbooks are lowered by the use of synthetic paper.

5. Let's assume that each person in Canada consumes an average of 74 L (litres) of soft drinks at an average price of $0.97 per litre and that the Canadian population is 38 million. Assume that at a price of $0.97 per litre, each individual consumer would demand 92 L of soft drinks. From this information about the individual demand schedule, calculate the market demand schedule for soft drinks for the prices of $0.75 and $0.97 per litre.

6. Suppose that the supply schedule of Nova Scotia lobsters is as follows:

Price of lobster (per pound)	Quantity of lobster supplied (pounds)
$25	800
20	700
15	600
10	500
5	400

Suppose that Nova Scotia lobsters can be sold only in Canada. The Canadian demand schedule for Nova Scotia lobsters is as follows:

Price of lobster (per pound)	Quantity of lobster demanded (pounds)
$25	200
20	400
15	600
10	800
5	1,000

a. Draw the demand curve and the supply curve for Nova Scotia lobsters. What are the equilibrium price and quantity of lobsters?

Now suppose that Nova Scotia lobsters can be sold in France. The French demand schedule for Nova Scotia lobsters is as follows:

Price of lobster (per pound)	Quantity of lobster demanded (pounds)
$25	100
20	300
15	500
10	700
5	900

b. What is the demand schedule for Nova Scotia lobsters now that French consumers can also buy them? Draw a supply and demand diagram that illustrates the new equilibrium price and quantity of lobsters. What will happen to the price at which fishers can sell lobster? What will happen to the price paid by Canadian consumers? What will happen to the quantity consumed by Canadian consumers?

7. Find the flaws in reasoning in the following statements, paying particular attention to the distinction

between shifts of and movements along the supply and demand curves. Draw a diagram to illustrate what actually happens in each situation.

a. "A technological innovation that lowers the cost of producing a good might seem at first to result in a reduction in the price of the good to consumers. But a fall in price will increase demand for the good, and higher demand will send the price up again. It is not certain, therefore, that an innovation will really reduce price in the end."

b. "A study shows that eating a clove of garlic a day can help prevent heart disease, causing many consumers to demand more garlic. This increase in demand results in a rise in the price of garlic. Consumers, seeing that the price of garlic has gone up, reduce their demand for garlic. This causes the demand for garlic to decrease and the price of garlic to fall. Therefore, the ultimate effect of the study on the price of garlic is uncertain."

8. The following table shows a demand schedule for a normal good.

Price	Quantity demanded
$23	70
21	90
19	110
17	130

a. Do you think that the increase in quantity demanded (say, from 90 to 110 in the table) when price decreases (from $21 to $19) is due to a rise in consumers' income? Explain clearly (and briefly) why or why not.

b. Now suppose that the good is an inferior good. Would the demand schedule still be valid for an inferior good?

c. Lastly, assume you do not know whether the good is normal or inferior. Devise an experiment that would allow you to determine which one it was. Explain.

9. In recent years, the number of car producers in China has increased rapidly. In fact, China now has more car brands than the United States. In addition, car sales have climbed every year and automakers have increased their output at even faster rates, causing fierce competition and a decline in prices. At the same time, Chinese consumers' incomes have risen. Assume that cars are a normal good. Draw a diagram of the supply and demand curves for cars in China to explain what has happened in the Chinese car market.

10. Aaron Hank is a star hitter for the Bay City baseball team. He is close to breaking the major league record for home runs hit during one season, and it is widely anticipated that in the next game he will break that record. As a result, tickets for the team's next game have been a hot commodity. But today it is announced that, due to a knee injury, he will not in fact play in the team's next game. Assume that season ticket-holders are able to resell their tickets if they wish. Use supply and demand diagrams to explain your answers to parts a and b.

a. Show the case in which this announcement results in a lower equilibrium price and a lower equilibrium quantity than before the announcement.

b. Show the case in which this announcement results in a lower equilibrium price and a higher equilibrium quantity than before the announcement.

c. What accounts for whether case a or case b occurs?

d. Suppose that a scalper had secretly learned before the announcement that Aaron Hank would not play in the next game. What actions do you think he would take?

11. Fans of music often bemoan the high price of concert tickets. One superstar has argued that it isn't worth hundreds, even thousands, of dollars to see her perform. Let's assume this star sold out arenas around the country at an average ticket price of $75.

a. How would you evaluate the argument that ticket prices are too high?

b. Suppose that due to this star's protests, ticket prices were lowered to $50. In what sense is this price too low? Draw a diagram using supply and demand curves to support your argument.

c. Suppose the superstar really wanted to bring down ticket prices. Since she controls the supply of her services, what would you recommend she do? Explain using a supply and demand diagram.

d. Suppose this performer's next album was a total dud. Do you think she would still have to worry about ticket prices being too high? Why or why not? Draw a supply and demand diagram to support your argument.

e. Suppose the performer announced that her next tour was going to be her last. What effect would this likely have on the demand for and price of tickets? Illustrate with a supply and demand diagram.

12. After several years of decline, the market for handmade acoustic guitars is making a comeback. These guitars are usually made in small workshops employing relatively few highly skilled luthiers. Assess the impact on the equilibrium price and quantity of handmade acoustic guitars as a result of each of the following events. In your answers indicate which curve(s) shift(s) and in which direction.

a. Environmentalists succeed in having the use of Brazilian rosewood banned in Canada, forcing luthiers to seek out alternative, more costly woods.

b. A foreign producer reengineers the guitar-making process and floods the market with identical guitars.

c. Music featuring handmade acoustic guitars makes a comeback as audiences tire of heavy metal and alternative rock music.

d. The country goes into a deep recession and the income of the average Canadian falls sharply. Explain if your answer would change if we were also told that a significant portion of the unemployed were quarantined at home due to a pandemic and some decided to learn how to play a musical instrument like the guitar.

13. *Demand twisters:* Sketch and explain the demand relationship in each of the following statements.

a. I would never buy a Taylor Swift album! You couldn't even give me one for nothing.

b. I generally buy a bit more coffee as the price falls. But once the price falls to $2 per pound, I'll buy out the entire stock of the supermarket.

c. I spend more on orange juice even as the price rises. (Does this mean that I must be violating the law of demand?)

d. Due to a tuition rise, most students at a college find themselves with less disposable income. Almost all of them eat more frequently at the school cafeteria and less often at restaurants, even though prices at the cafeteria have risen, too. (This one requires that you draw both the demand and the supply curves for school cafeteria meals.)

14. Will Shakespeare is a struggling playwright in sixteenth-century London. As the price he receives for writing a play increases, he is willing to write more plays. For the following situations, use a diagram to illustrate how each event affects the equilibrium price and quantity in the market for Shakespeare's plays.

a. The playwright Christopher Marlowe, Shakespeare's chief rival, is killed in a bar brawl.

b. The bubonic plague, a deadly infectious disease, breaks out in London.

c. To celebrate the defeat of the Spanish Armada, Queen Elizabeth declares several weeks of festivities, which involves commissioning new plays.

15. This year, the small town of Middling experiences a sudden doubling of the birth rate. After three years, the birth rate returns to normal. Use a diagram to illustrate the effect of these events on the following:

a. The market for an hour of babysitting services in Middling this year

b. The market for an hour of babysitting services 14 years into the future, after the birth rate has returned to normal, by which time children born today are old enough to work as babysitters

c. The market for an hour of babysitting services 30 years into the future, when children born today are likely to be having children of their own

16. Use a diagram to illustrate how each of the following events affects the equilibrium price and quantity of pizza.

a. The price of mozzarella cheese rises.

b. The health hazards of hamburgers are widely publicized.

c. The price of tomato sauce falls.

d. The incomes of consumers rise, and pizza is an inferior good.

e. Consumers expect the price of pizza to fall next week.

17. Although he was a prolific artist, Pablo Picasso painted only 1,000 canvases during his "Blue Period." Picasso is now dead, and all of his Blue Period works are currently on display in museums and private galleries throughout Europe and North America.

  a. Draw a supply curve for Picasso Blue Period works. Why is this supply curve different from ones you have seen?

  b. Given the supply curve from part a, the price of a Picasso Blue Period work will be entirely dependent on what factor(s)? Draw a diagram showing how the equilibrium price of such a work is determined.

  c. Suppose rich art collectors decide that it is essential to acquire Picasso Blue Period art for their collections. Show the impact of this on the market for these paintings.

18. Draw the appropriate curve in each of the following cases. Is it like or unlike the curves you have seen so far? Explain.

  a. The demand for cardiac bypass surgery, given that the government pays the full cost for any patient

  b. The demand for elective cosmetic plastic surgery, given that the patient pays the full cost

  c. The supply of reprints of Annie Leibovitz photographs

19. In 2018 the price of oil fell to a 14-year low. For drivers, the cost of driving fell significantly as gasoline prices plunged. For the airline industry, the cost of operation also fell significantly because jet fuel is a major expense.

  a. Draw a supply and demand diagram that illustrates the effect of a fall in the price of jet fuel on the supply of air travel.

  b. Draw a supply and demand diagram that illustrates the effect of a fall in the price of oil on the demand for air travel. (*Hint:* think about this in terms of the substitutes for air travel, like driving.)

  c. Put the diagrams from parts a and b together. What happens to the equilibrium price and quantity of air travel?

Despite the fall in the cost of driving, many more Canadians chose to fly to their destinations during 2018 as incomes rose and people splurged on vacations that had been postponed during the Great Recession.

  d. Using your results from part c, modify your diagram to illustrate an outcome in which the equilibrium price of air travel rises as people take more vacations by air.

WORK IT OUT

20. The accompanying table gives the annual Canadian demand and supply schedules for pickup trucks.

Price of truck	Quantity of trucks demanded (millions)	Quantity of trucks supplied (millions)
$20,000	20	14
25,000	18	15
30,000	16	16
35,000	14	17
40,000	12	18

  a. Plot the demand and supply curves using these schedules. Indicate the equilibrium price and quantity on your diagram.

  b. Suppose the tires used on pickup trucks are found to be defective. What would you expect to happen in the market for pickup trucks? Show this on your diagram.

  c. Suppose that Transport Canada imposes costly regulations on manufacturers that cause them to reduce supply by one-third at any given price. Calculate and plot the new supply schedule and indicate the new equilibrium price and quantity on your diagram. ■

The Algebra of Demand, Supply, and Equilibrium

Often algebraic models are employed in economics to convey the essence of what is being investigated. In particular, these models often assume that the curves being studied are nice linear expressions so that our analysis is easier and we don't get bogged down with less important details and end up getting nowhere.

‖ The Demand Curve

The law of demand says that, other things equal, a higher price for a good or service leads people to demand a smaller quantity of that good or service. On a graph, this means the demand curve is a downward-sloping function of the price of the good or service being studied. For each quantity, the demand curve reveals the maximum price consumers are willing (and able) to pay. Similarly, at each level of the price, the demand curve reveals the maximum quantity that consumers are willing (and able) to purchase. In the case of a linear expression, a demand curve in its simplest form would be:

(3A-1) $P = a - b \times Q^d$

where P is the price, Q^d is the quantity, and a and b are positive constants.[1] That $b \times Q^d$ is *subtracted* from a constant tells us the law of demand holds here—as price rises, all else constant, a lower level of quantity is demanded and vice versa (the demand curve slopes downward). The b term describes how sensitive the price is to changes in the quantity demanded (i.e., the slope of the demand curve). If b takes on a larger value, then the demand curve becomes relatively steeper—the same change in quantity results in a larger change in the maximum price consumers are willing to pay. If b takes on a smaller value, the effect is opposite—the demand curve becomes relatively flatter and the same change in quantity results in a smaller change in the maximum price consumers are willing to pay.

Although Equation 3A-1 looks straightforward, there is a lot more going on beneath the surface. The constant a contains information on the factors that shift the demand curve: changes in the price(s) of related goods and services, changes in income, changes in tastes, changes in expectations, and changes in the number of consumers. For example, the annual demand for maple syrup, with the price in dollars per litre and the quantity in millions of litres, may be given by a linear demand curve such as:

$$P = a_0 + a_1 \times P_{corn\ syrup} - a_2 \times P_{pancake\ mix} + a_3 \times Y + a_4 \times Tastes + a_5 \times P^e_{future} + a_6 \times Pop - b \times Q^d$$

with a expanded to include several factors multiplied by constants that are summarized in Table 3A-1. These factors are all multiplied by positive constants that, like b, describe how sensitive the demand curve is to changes in those factors. The constant a_0 picks up the impact of all other determinants of the demand for maple syrup that have been left out of the equation of the demand curve.

---

[1] The price term P should be interpreted as the maximum price consumers are willing to pay (this is sometimes called the *demand price*). Naturally, they would be happy to pay less than this price.

TABLE 3A-1 Variable Factors That Shift Maple Syrup Demand

Factor	Denoted by	Change to the demand curve
Price of corn syrup	$P_{corn\ syrup}$	As the price of a substitute increases (decreases), the demand for maple syrup increases (decreases).
Price of pancake mix	$P_{pancake\ mix}$	As the price of a complement increases (decreases), the demand for maple syrup decreases (increases).
Average consumer income	Y	As the income of consumers increases (decreases), the demand for normal goods increases (decreases) and the demand for inferior goods decreases (increases).[2]
Consumer preference index	$Tastes$	As consumer preference for maple syrup increases (decreases), the demand for maple syrup increases (decreases).
Expected future price	P^e_{future}	As the expected future price of maple syrup increases (decreases), the demand for maple syrup increases (decreases).
Population of potential consumers	Pop	As the population of potential consumers increases (decreases), the demand for maple syrup increases (decreases).

Note that the "other things equal" assumption means that everything in the demand curve equation, except P and Q^d, are being held constant. So, other things equal, when we move along the demand curve as P and Q^d change—the *quantity demanded* either increases or decreases. If one of these other factors does change, then the *entire* demand curve shifts either to the right (up) or left (down)—*demand* either increases or decreases. Figure 3A-1 examines a shift in the demand curve using algebra.

Let us simplify the expanded equation. Suppose the following values apply for factors that affect the demand curve for maple syrup: $P_{corn\ syrup} = \$10$, $P_{pancake\ mix} = \$5$, $Y = \$40$, which represents the average income of a Canadian (in thousands of dollars), $Tastes = 9$, $P^e_{future} = \$20$ (per litre), and $Pop = 34$, which is the population of Canada (in millions of people). Suppose also the values for the constants are $a_0 = \$5$, $a_1 = \$0.25$, $a_2 = \$2$, $a_3 = \$0.5$, $a_4 = \$0.45$, $a_5 = \$1.5$, $a_6 = \$0.05$, and $b = \$1.25$.

Given these assumed values, the demand curve for maple syrup becomes:

$$P = 5 + 0.25(10) - 2(5) + 0.5(40) + 0.45(9) + 1.5(20) + 0.05(34) - 1.25Q^d$$
$$P = 53.25 - 1.25Q^d$$

FIGURE 3A-1 Shifts of the Demand Curve

According to geometry, if the value of *a* increases, then the demand curve should shift up. But in economics, an increase in the value of *a* leads to an increase in demand, which shifts the demand curve to the right. Both interpretations are correct because the new demand curve is shifted to the right and shifted up. In this diagram, the value of *a* changes from 15 to 20.

Note that if demand decreases (i.e., *a* decreases), the demand curve shifts down (or to the left).

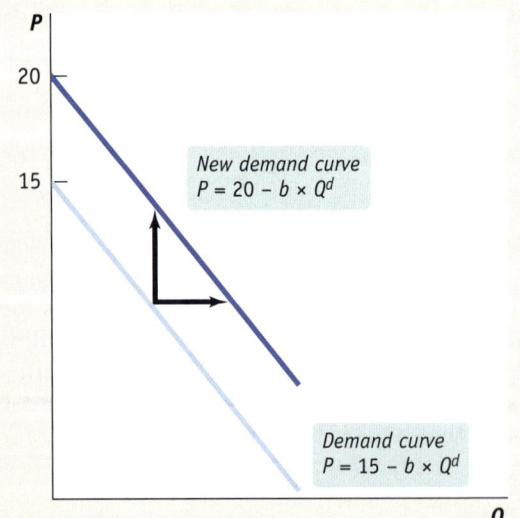

New demand curve
$P = 20 - b \times Q^d$

Demand curve
$P = 15 - b \times Q^d$

---

[2] Here we have assumed that maple syrup is a normal good.

‖ The Supply Curve

Usually, in the short run, other things equal, the supply curve is an upward-sloping function of the price of the good or service being studied. For each level of output, the supply curve reveals the minimum price at which suppliers are willing to sell. Similarly, at each level of the price the supply curve reveals the maximum quantity that suppliers are willing to sell. In the case of linear expressions, a supply curve in its simplest form would be:

(3A-2) $P = c + d \times Q^S$

where P is the price, Q^S is the quantity, and c and d are positive constants.[3] That $d \times Q^S$ is *added* to a constant tells us that as price rises, all else constant, a higher level of quantity is supplied and vice versa (the supply curve slopes upward). The d term describes how sensitive the price is to changes in the quantity supplied (i.e., the slope of the supply curve). If d takes on a larger value then the supply curve becomes relatively steeper—the same change in quantity results in a larger change in the minimum price at which suppliers are willing to sell. If d takes on a smaller value, the effect is opposite—the supply curve becomes relatively flatter and the same change in quantity results in a smaller change in the minimum price at which suppliers are willing to sell.

Again, the simple appearance of Equation 3A-2 hides enormous amounts of information. The constant c contains information on the factors that shift the supply curve: changes in the prices of inputs, changes in the prices of related goods and services, changes in technology, changes in weather, changes in expectations, and changes in the number of producers. For example, the supply of maple syrup, again with the price in dollars per litre and the quantity in millions of litres, might be represented by a linear supply curve such as:

$$P = c_0 + c_1 \times P_{input} + c_2 \times P_{lumber} - c_3 \times P_{tourism} - c_4 \times Tech - c_5 \times Weather$$
$$+ c_6 \times P^e_{future} - c_7 \times N + d \times Q^S$$

with c expanded to include several factors multiplied by constants that are summarized in Table 3A-2. These factors are all multiplied by positive constants that, like d, describe how sensitive the supply curve is to change in those factors. The constant c_0 picks up the impact of all other determinants of the supply of maple syrup that have been left out of the equation of the supply curve. Like the demand curve, if any of these values change, then the

TABLE 3A-2 Variable Factors That Shift Maple Syrup Supply		
Factor	**Denoted by**	**Change to the supply curve**
Input costs	P_{input}	As the price of an input increases (decreases), the supply of maple syrup decreases (increases).
Price of maple lumber	P_{lumber}	As the price of a substitute in production increases (decreases), the supply of maple syrup decreases (increases).
Income from maple farm tourism	$P_{tourism}$	As the income from a complement in production increases (decreases), the supply of maple syrup increases (decreases).
Technology index	$Tech$	As technology improves, the supply of maple syrup increases.
Weather-impact index	$Weather$	As the benefits from the weather increases (decreases), the supply of maple syrup increases (decreases).
Expected future price	P^e_{future}	As the expected future price of maple syrup increases (decreases), the supply of maple syrup decreases (increases).
Number of producers	N	As the number of producers increases (decreases), the supply of maple syrup increases (decreases).

---

[3] The price term P should be interpreted as the minimum price suppliers are willing to charge (this is sometimes called the *supply price*). Naturally, they would be happy to charge more than this price.

FIGURE 3A-2 Shifts of the Supply Curve

As with the demand curve in Figure 3A-1, there are two ways to interpret a shift in the supply curve. In economics, a decrease in the value of c represents an increase in supply, which shifts the supply curve to the right. The shift right can also be seen as a shift down because the constant term decreased. In this diagram, the value of c changes from 10 to 5.

Note that if supply decreases (i.e., c increases), the supply curve shifts up (or to the left).

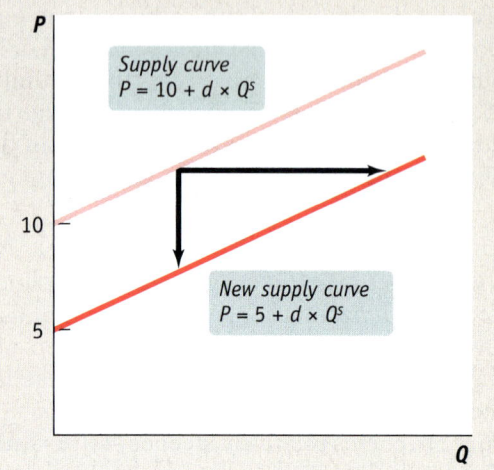

supply curve changes too. Figure 3A-2 examines a shift in the supply curve using algebra.

Suppose that, given a set of values for all the factors and constants, we get the following supply curve for maple syrup:

$$P = 12.75 + 0.25Q^S$$

Before we use the demand and supply curves for maple syrup to find the equilibrium price and quantity, let's look at Figure 3A-3, which provides a visual summary of the demand and supply curves. For a summary of how to interpret points along these curves, see Table 3A-3.

FIGURE 3A-3 Demand and Supply Curves

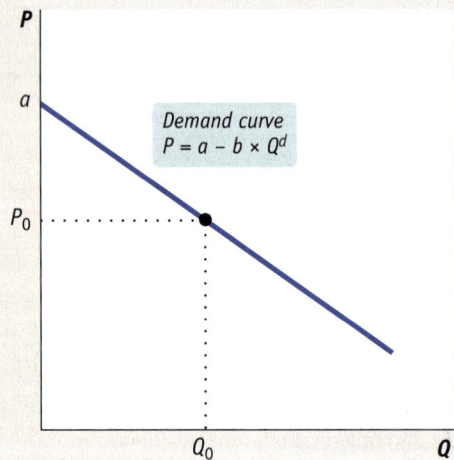

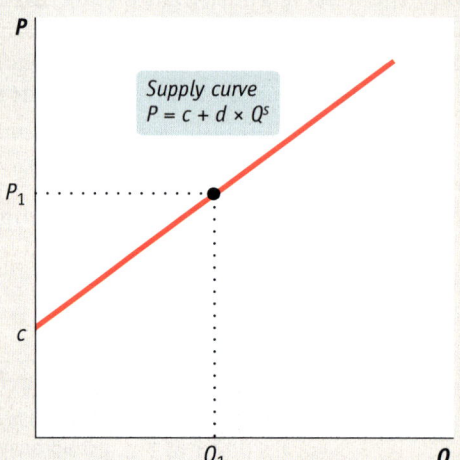

In the demand curve, the term a is the P-axis intercept. This is the lowest price with zero demand. If the price falls below a, then the quantity demanded rises above zero. Similarly, in the supply curve, the term c is the P-axis intercept. This is the price that is so low, the quantity supplied falls to zero.

If the price increases from c, then the quantity supplied rises above zero. The slope of the demand curve is equal to $-b$ and the slope of the supply curve is equal to d. Table 3A-3 provides a summary of alternative interpretations of the points along the demand and supply curves.

TABLE 3A-3 Interpreting Points Along Demand and Supply Curves

Curve	Along the Q-axis	Along the P-axis
Demand Curve	At each given price level, the demand curve reveals the maximum quantity that consumers are willing (and able) to buy.	For each given level of output, the demand curve reveals the maximum price (per unit) consumers are willing (and able) to pay.
	So at the price $P = P_0$, the quantity demanded is equal to $Q^d = Q_0$.	Thus, at the output level $Q = Q_0$, the maximum price consumers are willing to pay is $P = P_0$.
Supply Curve	At each level of the price, the supply curve reveals the maximum quantity that suppliers are willing (and able) to sell.	For each level of output, the supply curve reveals the minimum price (per unit) at which suppliers are willing to sell.
	So at the price $P = P_1$, the quantity supplied is equal to $Q^S = Q_1$.	So at the output level $Q = Q_1$, the minimum price at which suppliers are willing to sell is $P = P_1$.

‖ Market Equilibrium

Along the demand curve, all consumers have voluntarily chosen how much to buy at each specific price to maximize their level of utility or satisfaction. Similarly, along the supply curve all suppliers have voluntarily chosen the quantity they are willing to sell at each specific price to maximize their level of profit. Recall that the market equilibrium occurs where the demand and supply curves intersect. At this intersection, the market outcome is efficient—nobody can be made better off. Figure 3A-4 shows the point of intersection for our maple syrup example.

In the same way we find the intersection of two lines in geometry, we can determine the equilibrium quantity by equating the supply and demand curves. At equilibrium, P^S and P^d should both be equal to the equilibrium price, P^*. Likewise, Q^S and Q^d should both be equal to the equilibrium quantity, Q^*. So in our maple syrup example, we can say:

$$12.75 + 0.25Q^* = 53.25 - 1.25Q^*$$

and solve for Q^*:

$$1.50Q^* = 40.50$$
$$Q^* = 27$$

FIGURE 3A-4 Market Equilibrium for Maple Syrup

By graphing the pair of lines, we can see that they intersect at E^*, the equilibrium. At this point, $Q^* = 27$ (millions of litres) and $P^* = \$19.50$ per litre. We can use these values to check our answer when we solve for the equilibrium price and quantity algebraically.

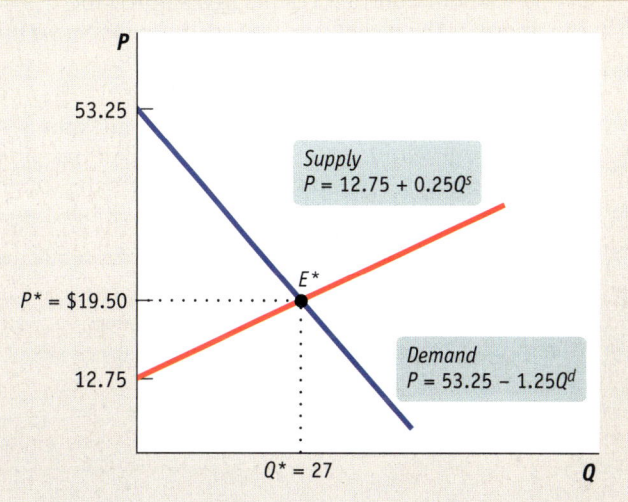

Knowing that the equilibrium quantity is 27 million litres per year, we can now determine the equilibrium price using either the demand curve or the supply curve:

$$P^* = 53.25 - 1.25Q^* \qquad\qquad P^* = 12.75 + 0.25Q^*$$
$$= 53.25 - 1.25(27) \qquad\qquad = 12.75 + 0.25(27)$$
$$= \$19.50 \qquad\qquad\qquad = \$19.50$$

The equilibrium price is \$19.50 per litre of maple syrup.

Since the market is based on voluntary exchanges at the equilibrium point (Q^*, P^*), it is not possible to make either consumers (buyers) or suppliers (sellers) better off without making the other group worse off. For example, consumers would like to buy more maple syrup at a lower price per litre, as this would raise their level of utility or satisfaction. The problem with this is that such a move would result in a reduction in the profits of suppliers, which makes them worse off. Neither group would voluntarily do something that would harm themselves. Thus, once we have arrived at the equilibrium intersection, this outcome is a stable situation—stable until such a time that there is a shift in one or both of the curves. Such shifts drive the market to a new equilibrium.

PROBLEMS

1. Suppose that the demand and supply for maple syrup are given by the following equations?

$$P = 53.25 - 1.25Q^d \qquad \text{Demand Curve}$$
$$P = 12.75 + 0.25Q^S \qquad \text{Supply Curve}$$

In each case below, compute the new equilibrium price and quantity exchanged. Has there been an increase/decrease in demand or supply? An increase/decrease in the quantity supplied or demanded? Show in a diagram the initial and new equilibrium locations.

a. Improved weather conditions shift the supply curve to $P = 5.25 + 0.25Q^S$.

b. Increased use of corn to make gasoline additives causes the price of corn syrup to increase, and as a result, the demand curve shifts to $P = 60 - 1.25Q^d$.

c. A new labour contract results in a significant increase in the wages of workers in the maple syrup industry, causing the supply curve to shift to $P = 15.45 + 0.25Q^S$.

d. The income of consumers rises, which shifts the demand curve to $P = 55.50 - 1.25Q^d$; and at the same time an improvement in technology shifts the supply curve to $P = 7.50 + 0.25Q^S$.

2. Suppose the monthly demand and supply for iPods are given by the following equations:

$$P = 500 - 0.001Q^d \qquad \text{Demand Curve}$$
$$P = 200 + 0.0005Q^S \qquad \text{Supply Curve}$$

a. Use the demand and supply curves to solve for the equilibrium price and quantity. Create a diagram to depict this equilibrium.

b. Rewrite the demand curve as an expression that shows quantity demanded (Q^d) in terms of the price.

c. Rewrite the supply curve as an expression that shows quantity supplied (Q^S) in terms of the price.

d. Use the demand and supply curves you derived in parts (b) and (c) to solve for the equilibrium levels of price and quantity. How does this result differ from part (a)? Briefly explain why this is so.

e. Suppose the introduction of new low-cost smart phones that also play music causes the demand curve for iPods to shift to $P = 425 - 0.001Q^d$. Derive the resulting new equilibrium levels of price and quantity. Show in a diagram this new equilibrium along with the initial equilibrium location. Are Apple shareholders pleased by this outcome? Briefly explain why or why not.

f. Suppose instead that the offshoring of the production of iPods to a lower cost country causes the supply curve to shift to $P = 140 + 0.0005Q^S$. Derive the resulting new equilibrium levels of price and quantity. Show in a diagram this new equilibrium along with the initial equilibrium location. Are Apple shareholders pleased by this outcome? Briefly explain why or why not.

4 Consumer and Producer Surplus

MASTERING TEXTBOOK ECONOMICS

ALTHOUGH YOU ARE JUST BEGINNING your study of economics, chances are that you have already made a number of economic decisions regarding your textbooks — this one included. It is likely you've had several options to choose from. Do you purchase an e-book subscription, a new copy of the actual textbook, or a used copy? Do you rent the book or borrow a copy? According to a publication by Higher Education Strategy Associates (HESA), about 85% of Canadian university students stated that they spent money buying textbooks.

How much am I willing to pay for my textbook?

With so many students choosing to use physical textbooks, there is also a very lively market in used textbooks. And whenever a market exists, it means that people are making decisions. Students who own a physical textbook will make a decision at the end of the course whether or not to keep their books: is the money made by selling their used textbook worth more than keeping the book? Likewise, students looking to purchase a textbook will determine whether the price of a somewhat battered used textbook is low enough that they are better off buying it rather than renting the book, or buying a new book or an e-book subscription.

Both students who sell their books and those who buy them clearly benefit from the existence of the second-hand book market whether it is online, in the college or university bookstore, or elsewhere. But can we put a number on what used textbook sellers and buyers gain from these transactions? Can we answer the question, "How much do the buyers and sellers of textbooks gain from the existence of the used-book market"?

Yes, we can. In this chapter, we will see how to measure benefits, such as those to buyers of used textbooks, from being able to purchase a good — known as *consumer surplus*. And we will see that there is a corresponding measure, *producer surplus,* of the benefits sellers receive from being able to sell a good.

The concepts of consumer surplus and producer surplus are extremely useful for analyzing a wide variety of economic issues. They let us calculate how much benefit producers and consumers receive from the existence of a market. They also allow us to calculate how the welfare of consumers and producers is affected by changes in market prices. Such calculations play a crucial role in evaluating many economic policies.

What information do we need to calculate consumer and producer surplus? Surprisingly, all we need are the demand and supply curves for a good. That is, the supply and demand model isn't just a model of how a competitive market works — it's also a model of how much consumers and producers gain from participating in that market.

So our first step will be to learn how consumer and producer surplus can be derived from the demand and supply curves. We will then see how these concepts can be applied to actual economic issues. ●

WHAT YOU WILL LEARN

- What is **consumer surplus?**
- What is **producer surplus?**
- What is **total surplus,** and why is it used to illustrate the gains from trade in a market?
- What accounts for the importance of **property rights** and economic signals in a well-functioning market?
- Why can a market sometimes fail and be **inefficient?**

Rawpixel.com/Shutterstock

A consumer's **willingness to pay** for a good is the maximum price at which they would buy that good.

|| Consumer Surplus and the Demand Curve

The market in used textbooks is a big business in terms of dollars and cents—estimated to transact over tens of millions of dollars each year. More importantly for us, it is a convenient starting point for developing the concepts of consumer and producer surplus. We'll use the concepts of consumer and producer surplus to understand exactly how buyers and sellers benefit from a competitive market and how big those benefits are. In addition, these concepts play important roles in analyzing what happens when competitive markets don't work well or there is interference in the market.

So let's begin by looking at the market for used textbooks, starting with the buyers. To keep the discussion simple, we'll assume that all transactions are done through the campus bookstore. The key point, as we'll see in a minute, is that the demand curve is derived from their tastes or preferences—and that those same preferences also determine how much they gain from the opportunity to buy used books.

Willingness to Pay and the Demand Curve

A used book is not as good as a new book—it will be battered and coffee-stained, may include someone else's highlighting, and may not be completely up to date. How much this bothers you depends on your preferences. Some potential buyers would prefer to buy the used book even if it is only slightly cheaper than a new one; others would buy the used book only if it is considerably cheaper.

Let's define a potential buyer's **willingness to pay** as the maximum price at which they would buy a good, in this case a used textbook. An individual won't buy the good if it costs more than this amount but they are eager to do so if it costs less. If the price is just equal to an individual's willingness to pay, they are indifferent between buying and not buying. For the sake of simplicity, we'll assume that the individual buys the good in this case.

The table in Figure 4-1 shows five potential buyers of a used book that costs $100 new, listed in order of their willingness to pay. At one extreme is Aisha, who will buy a second-hand book even if the price is as high as $59. Ben is less willing to have a used book and will buy one only if the price is $45 or less. Chloe is willing to pay only $35, and Darsh, only $25. And Elena, who really doesn't like the idea of a used book, will buy one only if it costs no more than $10.

How many of these five students will actually buy a used book? It depends on the price. If the price of a used book is $55, only Aisha buys one; if the price is $40, Aisha and Ben both buy used books, and so on. So the information in the table can be used to construct the *demand schedule* for used textbooks.

We can use this demand schedule to derive the market demand curve shown in Figure 4-1. Because we are considering only a small number of consumers, this curve doesn't look like the smooth demand curves of Chapter 3, where markets contained hundreds or thousands of consumers. Instead, this demand curve is step-shaped, with alternating horizontal and vertical segments. Each horizontal segment—each step—corresponds to one potential buyer's willingness to pay.

However, we'll see shortly that for the analysis of consumer surplus it doesn't matter whether the demand curve is step-shaped, as in this figure, or whether there are many consumers, making the curve smooth.

Willingness to Pay and Consumer Surplus

Suppose that the campus bookstore makes used textbooks available at a price of $30. In that case, Aisha, Ben, and Chloe will buy books. Do they gain from their purchases, and if so, how much?

The answer, shown in Table 4-1, is that each student who purchases a book does achieve a net gain but that the amount of the gain differs among students.

FIGURE 4-1 The Demand Curve for Used Textbooks

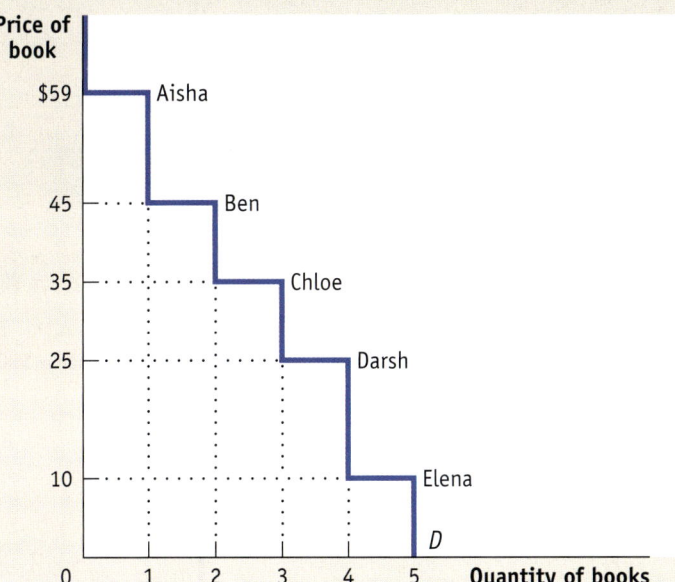

Potential buyers	Willingness to pay
Aisha	$59
Ben	45
Chloe	35
Darsh	25
Elena	10

With only five potential consumers in this market, the demand curve is step-shaped. Each step represents one consumer, and its height indicates that consumer's willingness to pay—the maximum price at which they will buy a used textbook—as indicated in the table. Aisha has the highest willingness to pay at $59, Ben has the next highest at $45, and so on down to Elena with the lowest willingness to pay at $10. At a price of $59, the quantity demanded is one (Aisha); at a price of $45, the quantity demanded is two (Aisha and Ben); and so on until you reach a price of $10, at which all five students are willing to purchase a used textbook.

Aisha would have been willing to pay $59, so her net gain is $59 – $30 = $29. Ben would have been willing to pay $45, so his net gain is $45 – $30 = $15. Chloe would have been willing to pay $35, so her net gain is $35 – $30 = $5. Darsh and Elena, however, won't be willing to buy a used book at a price of $30, so they neither gain nor lose.

The net gain that a buyer achieves from the purchase of a good is called that buyer's **individual consumer surplus.** What we learn from this example is that whenever a buyer pays a price less than their willingness to pay, the buyer achieves some individual consumer surplus.

The sum of the individual consumer surpluses achieved by all the buyers of a good is known as the **total consumer surplus** achieved in the market. In Table 4-1, the total consumer surplus is the sum of the individual consumer surpluses achieved by Aisha, Ben, and Chloe: $29 + $15 + $5 = $49.

Economists often use the term **consumer surplus** to refer to both individual and total consumer surplus. We will follow this practice; it will always be clear in context whether we are referring to the consumer surplus achieved by an individual or by all buyers.

Individual consumer surplus is the net gain to an individual buyer from the purchase of a good. It is equal to the difference between the buyer's willingness to pay and the price paid.

Total consumer surplus is the sum of the individual consumer surpluses of all the buyers of a good in a market.

The term **consumer surplus** is often used to refer both to individual and to total consumer surplus.

TABLE 4-1 Consumer Surplus If the Price of a Used Textbook = $30

Potential buyer	Willingness to pay	Price paid	Individual consumer surplus = Willingness to pay – Price paid
Aisha	$59	$30	$29
Ben	45	30	15
Chloe	35	30	5
Darsh	25	—	—
Elena	10	—	—
All buyers			**Total consumer surplus = $49**

FIGURE 4-2 Consumer Surplus in the Used-Textbook Market

At a price of $30, Aisha, Ben, and Chloe each buy a book but Darsh and Elena do not. Aisha, Ben, and Chloe receive individual consumer surpluses equal to the difference between their willingness to pay and the price, illustrated by the areas of the shaded rectangles. Both Darsh and Elena have a willingness to pay less than $30, so they are unwilling to buy a book in this market; they receive zero consumer surplus. The total consumer surplus is given by the entire shaded area—the sum of the individual consumer surpluses of Aisha, Ben, and Chloe—equal to $29 + $15 + $5 = $49.

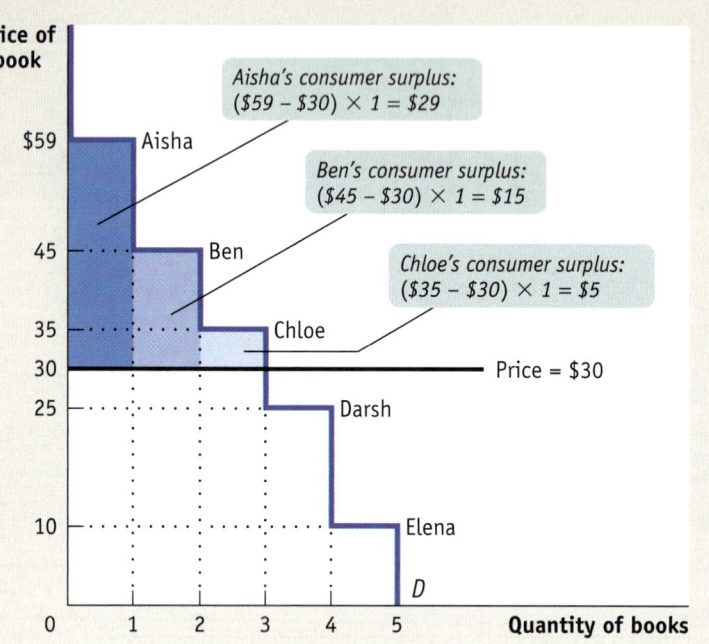

Total consumer surplus can be represented graphically. Figure 4-2 reproduces the demand curve from Figure 4-1. Each step in that demand curve is one book wide and represents one consumer. For example, the height of Aisha's step is $59, her willingness to pay. This step forms the top of a rectangle, with $30—the price she actually pays for a book—forming the bottom. The area of Aisha's rectangle, $($59 − 30) \times 1 = 29, is her consumer surplus from purchasing one book at $30. So the individual consumer surplus Aisha gains is the *area of the dark blue rectangle* shown in Figure 4-2.

In addition to Aisha, Ben and Chloe will also each buy a book when the price is $30. Like Aisha, they benefit from their purchases, though not as much, because they each have a lower willingness to pay. Figure 4-2 also shows the consumer surplus gained by Ben and Chloe; again, this can be measured by the areas of the appropriate rectangles. Darsh and Elena, because they do not buy books at a price of $30, receive no consumer surplus.

The total consumer surplus achieved in this market is just the sum of the individual consumer surpluses received by Aisha, Ben, and Chloe. So total consumer surplus is equal to the combined area of the three rectangles—the entire shaded area in Figure 4-2. Another way to say this is that total consumer surplus is equal to the area below the demand curve but above the price.

Figure 4-2 illustrates the following general principle: *The total consumer surplus generated by purchases of a good at a given price is equal to the area below the demand curve but above that price.* The same principle applies regardless of the number of consumers.

When we consider large markets, this graphical representation of consumer surplus becomes extremely helpful. Consider, for example, the sales of iPhones to millions of potential buyers. Each potential buyer has a maximum price that they are willing to pay. With so many potential buyers, the demand curve will be smooth, like the one shown in Figure 4-3.

Suppose that at a price of $500, a total of 1 million iPhones are purchased. How much do consumers gain from being able to buy those 1 million iPhones? We could answer that question by calculating the individual consumer surplus of

FIGURE 4-3 Consumer Surplus

The demand curve for iPhones is smooth because there are many potential buyers. At a price of $500, 1 million iPhones are demanded. The consumer surplus at this price is equal to the shaded area: the area below the demand curve but above the price. This is the total net gain to consumers generated from buying and consuming iPhones when the price is $500.

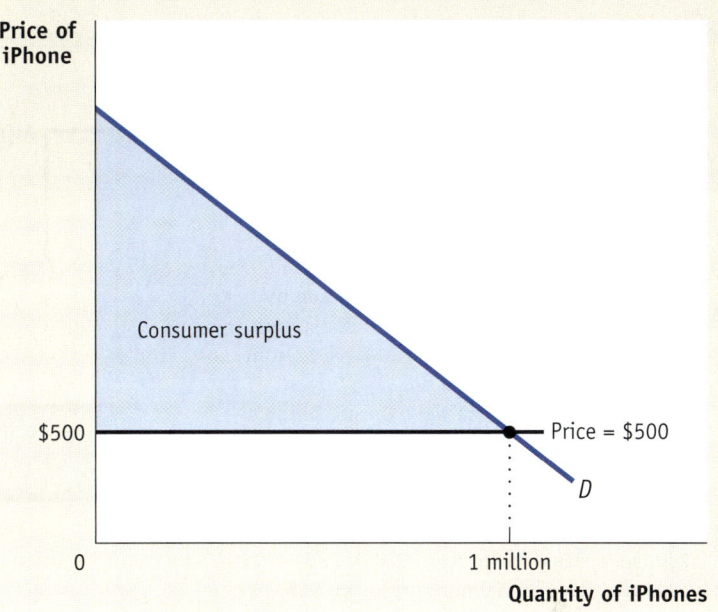

each buyer and then adding these numbers up to arrive at a total. But it is much easier just to look at Figure 4-3 and use the fact that total consumer surplus is equal to the shaded area. As in our original example, consumer surplus is equal to the area below the demand curve but above the price. (To refresh your memory on how to calculate the area of a right triangle, see the appendix to Chapter 2.)

How Changing Prices Affect Consumer Surplus

It is often important to know how much consumer surplus *changes* when the price changes. For example, we may want to know how much consumers are hurt if a flood in cotton-growing areas of Pakistan drives up cotton prices or how much consumers gain if the introduction of fish farming makes salmon steaks less expensive. The same approach we have used to derive consumer surplus can be used to answer questions about how changes in prices affect consumers.

Let's return to the example of the market for used textbooks. Suppose that the bookstore decided to sell used textbooks for $20 instead of $30. How much would this fall in price increase consumer surplus?

The answer is illustrated in Figure 4-4. As shown in the figure, there are two parts to the increase in consumer surplus. The first part, shaded dark blue, is the gain of those who would have bought books even at the higher price of $30. Each of the students who would have bought books at $30—Aisha, Ben, and Chloe—now pays $10 less, and therefore each gains $10 in consumer surplus from the fall in price to $20. So the dark blue area represents the $10 × 3 = $30 increase in consumer surplus to those three buyers.

The second part, shaded light blue, is the gain to those who would not have bought a book at $30 but are willing to pay more than $20. In this case, that gain goes to Darsh, who would not have bought a book at $30 but does buy one at $20. He gains $5—the difference between his willingness to pay of $25 and the new price of $20. So the light blue area represents a further $5 gain in consumer surplus.

The total increase in consumer surplus is the sum of the shaded areas, $35. Likewise, a rise in price from $20 to $30 would decrease consumer surplus by an amount equal to the sum of the shaded areas.

FIGURE 4-4 Consumer Surplus and a Fall in the Price of Used Textbooks

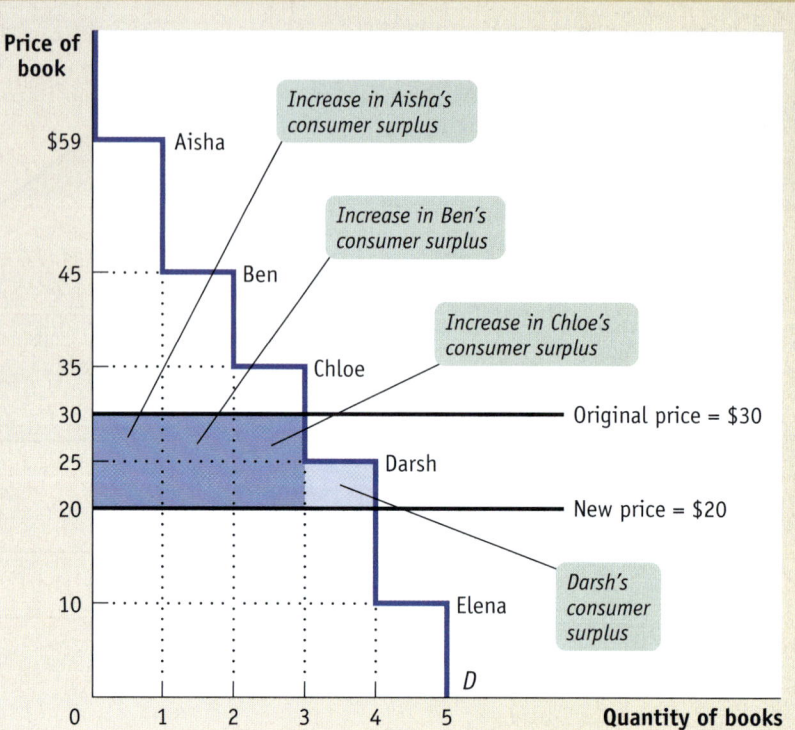

There are two parts to the increase in consumer surplus generated by a fall in price from $30 to $20. The first is given by the dark blue rectangle: each person who would have bought at the original price of $30—Aisha, Ben, and Chloe—receives an increase in consumer surplus equal to the total reduction in price, $10. So the area of the dark blue rectangle corresponds to an amount equal to $3 \times \$10 = \$30$. The second part is given by the light blue area: the increase in consumer surplus for those who would not have bought at the original price of $30 but who buy at the new price of $20—namely, Darsh. Darsh's willingness to pay is $25, so he now receives consumer surplus of $5. The total increase in consumer surplus is $(3 \times \$10) + \$5 = \$35$, represented by the sum of the shaded areas. Likewise, a rise in price from $20 to $30 would decrease consumer surplus by $35, the amount corresponding to the sum of the shaded areas.

Figure 4-4 illustrates that when the price of a good falls, the area under the demand curve but above the price—which we have seen is equal to total consumer surplus—increases. Figure 4-5 shows the same result for the case of a smooth demand curve, the demand for iPhones. Here we assume that the price of iPhones falls from $2,000 to $500, leading to an increase in the quantity demanded from 200,000 to 1 million units.

As in the used-textbook example, we divide the gain in consumer surplus into two parts.

1. The dark blue rectangle in Figure 4-5 corresponds to the dark blue area in Figure 4-4: it is the gain to the 200,000 people who would have bought iPhones even at the higher price of $2,000. As a result of the price reduction, each receives additional surplus of $1,500.

2. The light blue triangle in Figure 4-5 corresponds to the light blue area in Figure 4-4: it is the gain to people who would not have bought the good at the higher price but are willing to do so at a price of $500. For example, the light blue triangle includes the gain to someone who would have been willing to pay $1,000 for an iPhone and therefore gains $500 in consumer surplus when it is possible to buy an iPhone for only $500.

As before, the total gain in consumer surplus is the sum of the shaded areas: the increase in the area under the demand curve but above the price.

What would happen if the price of a good were to rise instead of fall? We would do the same analysis in reverse. Suppose that the price of iPhones rises from $500 to $2,000. This would lead to a fall in consumer surplus, equal to the sum of the shaded areas in Figure 4-5. This loss consists of two parts.

1. The dark blue rectangle represents the loss to consumers who would still buy an iPhone, even at a price of $2,000.

2. The light blue triangle represents the loss to consumers who decide not to buy an iPhone at the higher price.

FIGURE 4-5 A Fall in the Price Increases Consumer Surplus

A fall in the price of an iPhone from $2,000 to $500 leads to an increase in the quantity demanded and an increase in consumer surplus. The change in total consumer surplus is given by the sum of the shaded areas: the total area below the demand curve and between the old and new prices. Here, the dark blue area represents the increase in consumer surplus for the 200,000 consumers who would have bought an iPhone at the original price of $2,000; they each receive an increase in consumer surplus of $1,500. The light blue area represents the increase in consumer surplus for those willing to buy at a price equal to or greater than $500 but less than $2,000. Similarly, a rise in the price of an iPhone from $500 to $2,000 generates a decrease in consumer surplus equal to the sum of the two shaded areas.

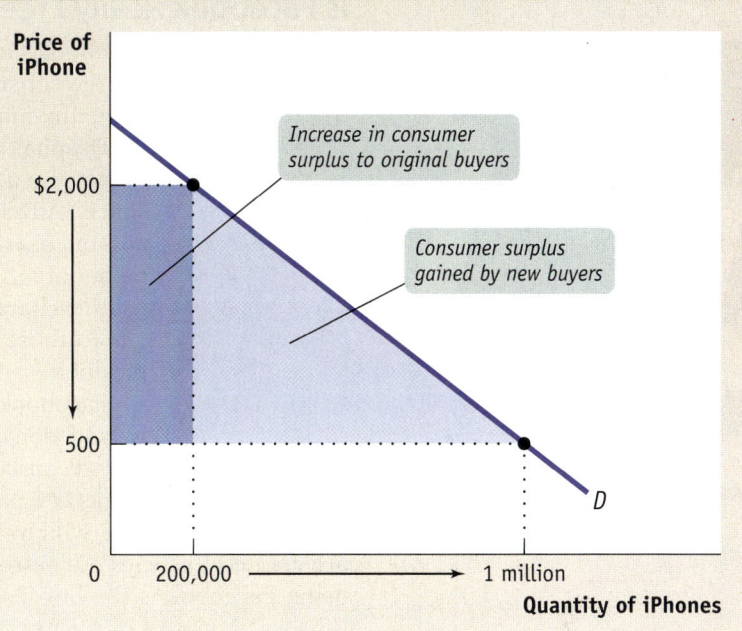

FOR INQUIRING MINDS   A Matter of Life and Death

In 2018, while 2,782 organ transplants were performed in Canada, 223 people died while waiting for a transplant and 4,351 Canadians were wait-listed.

Since the number of people who need organs far exceeds availability, and the demand for organs continues to grow faster than the supply, what is the best way to allocate the available organs? A market isn't feasible. And for understandable reasons, the sale of human body parts is illegal in this country. In the case of the sickest individuals needing a kidney, Canadian transplant hospitals have set up a national wait-list that gives these patients priority. For other organs, and patients needing a kidney who are not extremely ill, there is no single national wait-list. Each province is free to set its own mechanism to allocate donated organs. But a national, coordinated system (excluding Quebec) for handling the donation and transplantation of organs (and tissues) is being developed by Canadian Blood Services.

Under current kidney transplant guidelines, if a donated kidney does not go to a critically ill patient who will die in days without this organ, it goes to the person who has been waiting the longest. This is very similar

to what used to happen in the United States, where the kidney allocation protocol has been devised by the nonprofit group United Network for Organ Sharing (UNOS). According to this kind of system, a donated kidney would go to the person waiting the longest. For example, an available kidney would go to a 75-year-old who has been waiting for two years instead of to a 25-year-old who has been waiting a year, even though the 25-year-old will likely live longer and benefit from the transplanted organ for a longer period of time.

So, in 2013 UNOS formulated a new set of guidelines based on a concept called *net survival benefit*. Available kidneys are ranked according to how long they are likely to last; recipients are ranked according to how long they are likely to live once receiving a kidney. A kidney is then matched to the recipient expected to achieve the greatest survival time from that kidney. That is, a kidney expected to last many decades will be given to a young person, while a kidney with a shorter expected life span will be given to an older recipient.

So what does kidney transplantation have to do with consumer surplus?

The UNOS concept of *net survival benefit* is a lot like individual consumer surplus — the individual consumer surplus generated from getting a new kidney. In essence, UNOS has devised a system that allocates a kidney according to who gets the greatest consumer surplus, thereby maximizing the total consumer surplus from the available pool of kidneys. In terms of results, the UNOS system operates a lot like a competitive market, but without the purchase and sale of kidneys.

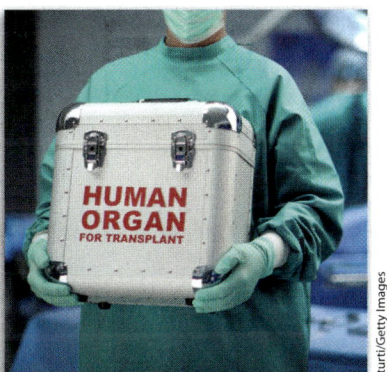

Organ recipients are determined based on who will receive the greatest individual consumer surplus from a transplant.

ECONOMICS >> *in Action*
Is Facebook Really Free?

Valentin Wolf/imageBROKER/Shutterstock

Would you be willing to pay for a version of Facebook without ads?

Facebook earned $93.8 billion in 2019 even though it doesn't charge consumers to use its social media platform. How did the company manage this impressive feat?

Despite being a high-tech company, Facebook earns its money in a rather old-fashioned way: by selling advertising space. Advertisers pay Facebook for the right to place their ads on users' Facebook pages. In addition, Facebook gathers personal information from its users—location, age, gender, and profile characteristics—that allows advertisers to target their ads to those individuals who are more likely to purchase their products.

Facebook offers its platform to users at a zero-price—that is, you don't pay money to access it. Yet there still is still an *effective price* to be paid for its use. Although you don't incur a monetary payment, by using Facebook you release control of personal information, which can cause annoyance and distraction as targeted ads are created to sway your purchasing decisions or views. So the effective price of using Facebook is the burden in terms of annoyance and distraction caused by the loss of control of your personal information.

In the last quarter of 2019 Facebook had an average revenue per user (ARPU) of US$41.41 (i.e., US$13.8 per month) in North America. This means that if Facebook had to offer an ad-free version, it might have to charge its North American users an average price of US$13.8 per month. Would its North American users pay this amount to get access to an ad-free version of Facebook?

How burdensome this effective price is varies from person to person. We can get a sense of the effective price a person incurs when using Facebook by asking how much they are willing to pay for an ad-free version of Facebook. In fact, a recent survey of American Facebook users did just that. This survey revealed that nearly 42% of the users would pay US$5 or less per month to have an ad-free version, about 25% would pay an amount between US$6 and US$10, 22% between US$11 and US$15, and about 12% are willing to pay more than US$15. Thus, for the majority 78% who were willing to pay no more than US$15 for an ad-free Facebook, the effective price of Facebook's data collection and advertisements was very low. These users gained the most consumer surplus from the current zero-price arrangement. In contrast, those who are willing to pay more incurred a higher effective price and therefore gained less consumer surplus.

So is Facebook really free? For the majority of users it is, but for a significant minority of users, it is not.

>> **Quick Review**

• The demand curve for a good is determined by each potential consumer's **willingness to pay.**

• **Individual consumer surplus** is the net gain an individual consumer gets from buying a good.

• The **total consumer surplus** in a given market is equal to the area below the market demand curve but above the price.

• A fall in the price of a good increases **consumer surplus** through two channels: a gain to consumers who would have bought at the original price and a gain to consumers who are persuaded to buy by the lower price. A rise in the price of a good reduces consumer surplus in a similar fashion.

>> **Check Your Understanding** **4-1**

Solutions appear at back of book.

1. Consider the market for cheese-stuffed jalapeno peppers. There are two consumers, Teresa and Azar, and their willingness to pay for each pepper is given in the accompanying table. (Neither is willing to consume more than 4 peppers at any price.) Use the table (i) to construct the demand schedule for peppers for prices of $0.00, $0.10, and so on, up to $0.90, and (ii) to calculate the total consumer surplus when the price of a pepper is $0.40.

Quantity of peppers	Teresa's willingness to pay	Azar's willingness to pay
1st pepper	$0.90	$0.80
2nd pepper	0.70	0.60
3rd pepper	0.50	0.40
4th pepper	0.30	0.30

‖ Producer Surplus and the Supply Curve

Just as some buyers of a good would have been willing to pay more for their purchase than the price they actually pay, some sellers of a good would have been willing to sell it for less than the price they actually receive. So just as there are consumers who receive consumer surplus from buying in a market, there are producers who receive producer surplus from selling in a market.

> A seller's **cost** is the lowest price at which they are willing to sell a good.

Cost and Producer Surplus

Consider a group of students who are potential sellers of used textbooks. Because they have different preferences, the various potential sellers differ in the price at which they are willing to sell their books. The table in Figure 4-6 shows the prices at which several different students would be willing to sell. Andrew is willing to sell the book as long as he can get at least $5; Brianna won't sell unless she can get at least $15; Carlos, unless he can get $25; Desiree, unless she can get $35; and Eli, unless he can get $45.

The lowest price at which a potential seller is willing to sell has a special name in economics: it is called the seller's **cost.** So Andrew's cost is $5, Brianna's is $15, and so on.

Using the term *cost,* which people normally associate with the monetary cost of producing a good, may sound a little strange when applied to sellers of used textbooks. The students don't have to manufacture the books, so it doesn't cost the student who sells a used textbook anything to make that book available for sale, does it?

Yes, it does. A student who sells a book won't have it later, as part of their personal collection. So there is an *opportunity* cost to selling a textbook, even if the owner has completed the course for which it was required. And remember that one of the basic principles of economics is that the true measure of the cost of doing something is always its opportunity cost. That is, the real cost of something is what you must give up to get it.

FIGURE 4-6 The Supply Curve for Used Textbooks

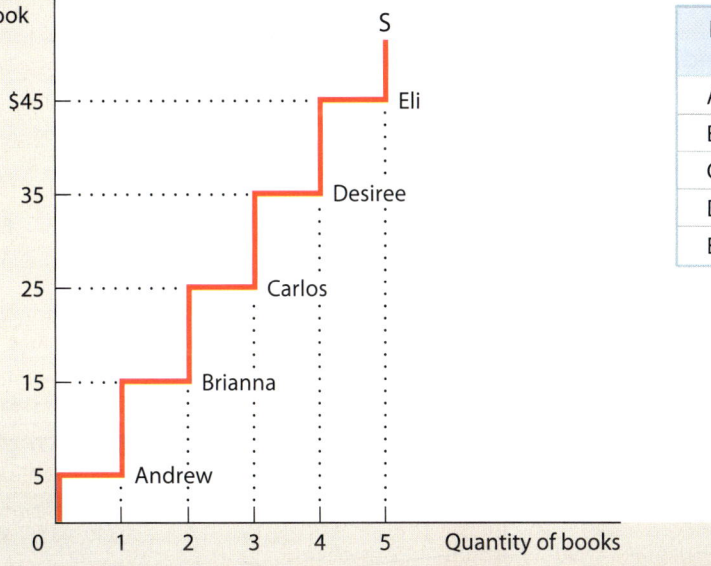

Potential sellers	Cost
Andrew	$5
Brianna	15
Carlos	25
Desiree	35
Eli	45

The supply curve illustrates seller's cost, the lowest price at which a potential seller is willing to sell the good, and the quantity supplied at that price. Each of the five students has one book to sell and each has a different cost, as indicated in the accompanying table. At a price of $5 the quantity supplied is one (Andrew), at $15 it is two (Andrew and Brianna), and so on until you reach $45, the price at which all five students are willing to sell.

Individual producer surplus is the net gain to an individual seller from selling a good. It is equal to the difference between the price received and the seller's cost.

Total producer surplus is the sum of the individual producer surpluses of all the sellers of a good in a market.

Economists use the term **producer surplus** to refer both to individual and to total producer surplus.

So it is good economics to talk of the minimum price at which someone will sell a good as the "cost" of selling that good, even if they don't spend any money to make the good available for sale. Of course, in most real-world markets the sellers are also those who produce the good and therefore *do* spend money to make it available for sale. In this case, the cost of making the good available for sale includes monetary costs, but it may also include other opportunity costs.

Getting back to the example, suppose that Andrew sells his book for $30. Clearly he has gained from the transaction: he would have been willing to sell for only $5, so he has gained $25. This net gain, the difference between the price he actually gets and his cost—the minimum price at which he would have been willing to sell—is known as his **individual producer surplus.**

Just as we derived the demand curve from the willingness to pay of different consumers, we can derive the supply curve from the cost of different producers. The step-shaped curve in Figure 4-6 shows the supply curve implied by the costs shown in the accompanying table. At a price less than $5, none of the students are willing to sell; at a price between $5 and $15, only Andrew is willing to sell, and so on.

As in the case of consumer surplus, we can add the individual producer surpluses of sellers to calculate the **total producer surplus,** the total net gain to all sellers in the market. Economists use the term **producer surplus** to refer to either individual or total producer surplus. Table 4-2 shows the net gain to each of the students who would sell a used book at a price of $30: $25 for Andrew, $15 for Brianna, and $5 for Carlos. The total producer surplus is $25 + $15 + $5 = $45.

TABLE 4-2 Producer Surplus When the Price of a Used Textbook = $30			
Potential seller	Cost	Price received	Individual producer surplus = Price received − Cost
Andrew	$5	$30	$25
Brianna	15	30	15
Carlos	25	30	5
Desiree	35	—	—
Eli	45	—	—
All sellers			**Total producer surplus = $45**

FIGURE 4-7 Producer Surplus in the Used-Textbook Market

At a price of $30, Andrew, Brianna, and Carlos each sell a book but Desiree and Eli do not. Andrew, Brianna, and Carlos get individual producer surpluses equal to the difference between the price and their cost, illustrated here by the shaded rectangles. Desiree and Eli each have a cost that is greater than the price of $30, so they are unwilling to sell a book and so receive zero producer surplus. The total producer surplus is given by the entire shaded area, the sum of the individual producer surpluses of Andrew, Brianna, and Carlos, equal to $25 + $15 + $5 = $45.

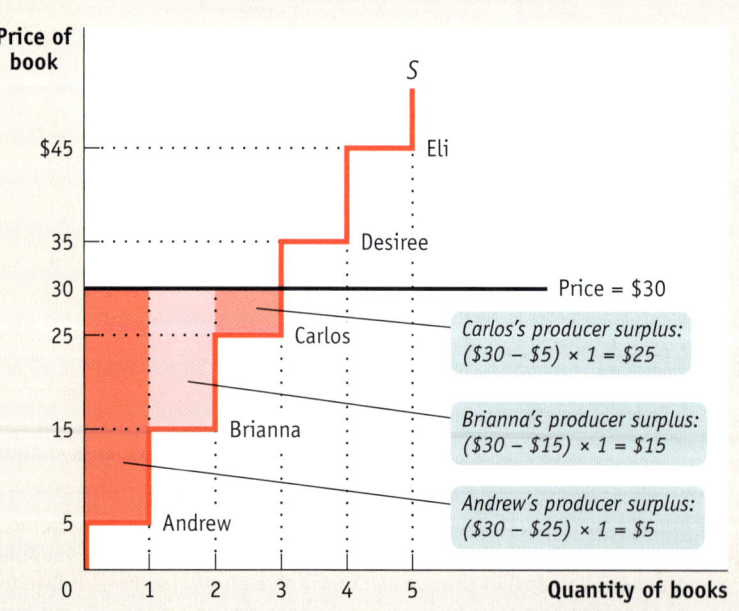

FIGURE 4-8 Producer Surplus

Here is the supply curve for wheat. At a price of $5 per bushel, farmers supply 1 million bushels. The producer surplus at this price is equal to the shaded area: the area above the supply curve but below the price. This is the total gain to producers—farmers in this case—from supplying their product when the price is $5.

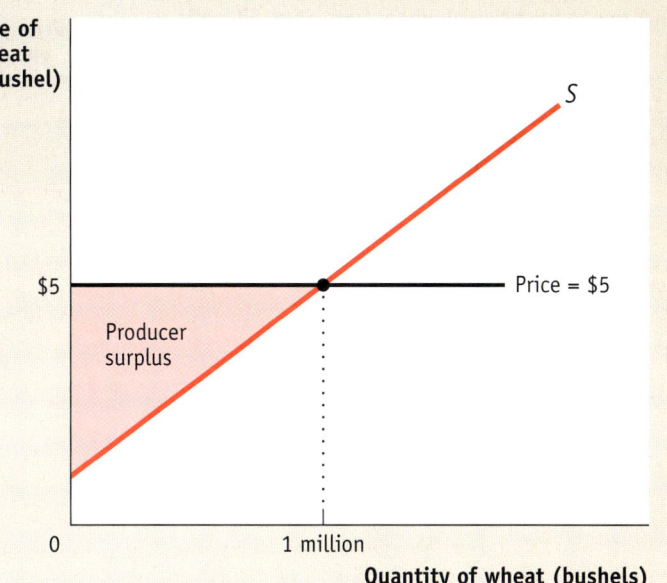

As with consumer surplus, the producer surplus gained by those who sell books can be represented graphically. Figure 4-7 reproduces the supply curve from Figure 4-6. Each step in that supply curve is one book wide and represents one seller. The height of Andrew's step is $5, his cost. This forms the bottom of a rectangle, with $30, the price he actually receives for his book, forming the top. The area of this rectangle, $(\$30 - \$5) \times 1 = \$25$, is his producer surplus. So the producer surplus Andrew gains from selling his book is the *area of the red rectangle* shown in the figure.

Let's assume that the campus bookstore is willing to buy all the used copies of this book that students are willing to sell at a price of $30. Then, in addition to Andrew, Brianna and Carlos will also sell their books. They will also benefit from their sales, though not as much as Andrew, because they have higher costs. Andrew, as we have seen, gains $25. Brianna gains a smaller amount: since her cost is $15, she gains only $15. Carlos gains even less, only $5.

Again, as with consumer surplus, we have a general rule for determining the total producer surplus from sales of a good: *The total producer surplus from sales of a good at a given price is the area above the supply curve but below that price.*

This rule applies both to examples like the one shown in Figure 4-7, where there are a small number of producers and a step-shaped supply curve, and to more realistic examples, where there are many producers and the supply curve is smooth.

Consider, for example, the supply of wheat. Figure 4-8 shows how producer surplus depends on the price per bushel. Suppose that, as shown in the figure, the price is $5 per bushel and farmers supply 1 million bushels. What is the benefit to the farmers from selling their wheat at a price of $5? Their producer surplus is equal to the shaded area in the figure—the area above the supply curve but below the price of $5 per bushel.

How Changing Prices Affect Producer Surplus

As with the case of consumer surplus, a change in price alters producer surplus. But the effects are opposite. While a fall in price increases consumer surplus, it reduces producer surplus. And a rise in price reduces consumer surplus but increases producer surplus.

FIGURE 4-9 A Rise in the Price Increases Producer Surplus

A rise in the price of wheat from $5 to $7 leads to an increase in the quantity supplied and an increase in producer surplus. The change in total producer surplus is given by the sum of the shaded areas: the total area above the supply curve but between the old and new prices. The red area represents the gain to the farmers who would have supplied 1 million bushels at the original price of $5; they each receive an increase in producer surplus of $2 for each of these bushels. The triangular pink area represents the increase in producer surplus achieved by the farmers who supply the additional 500,000 bushels because of the higher price. Similarly, a fall in the price of wheat from $7 to $5 generates a reduction in producer surplus equal to the sum of the shaded areas.

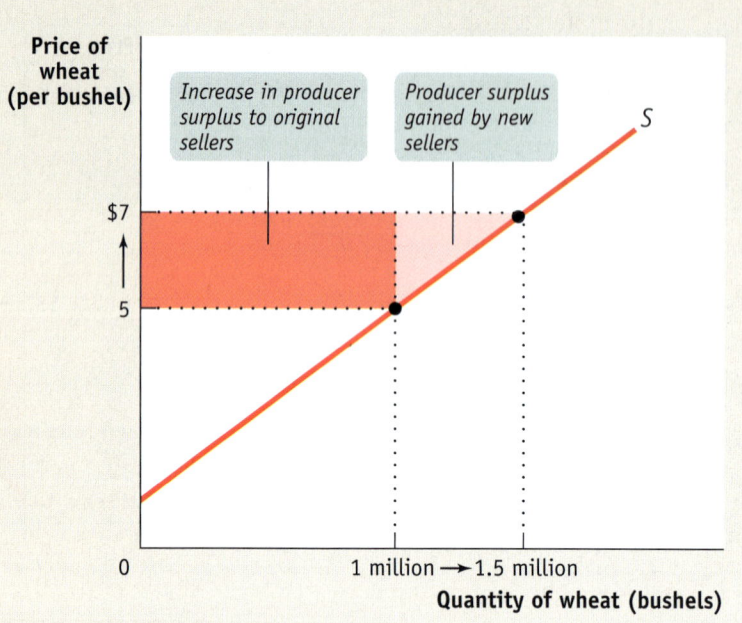

To see this, let's first consider a rise in the price of the good. Producers of the good will experience an increase in producer surplus, though not all producers gain the same amount. Some producers would have produced the good even at the original price; they will gain the entire price increase on every unit they produce. Other producers will enter the market because of the higher price; they will gain only the difference between the new price and their cost.

Figure 4-9 is the supply counterpart of Figure 4-5. It shows the effect on producer surplus of a rise in the price of wheat from $5 to $7 per bushel. The increase in producer surplus is the sum of the shaded areas, which consists of two parts. First, there is a red rectangle corresponding to the gains to those farmers who would have supplied wheat even at the original $5 price. Second, there is an additional pink triangle that corresponds to the gains to those farmers who would not have supplied wheat at the original price but are drawn into the market by the higher price.

If the price were to fall from $7 to $5 per bushel, the story would run in reverse. The sum of the shaded areas would now be the decline in producer surplus, the decrease in the area above the supply curve but below the price. The loss would consist of two parts, the loss to farmers who would still grow wheat at a price of $5 (the red rectangle) and the loss to farmers who cease to grow wheat because of the lower price (the pink triangle).

ECONOMICS >> in Action
High Times Down on the Farm

The price of Saskatchewan farmland is very sensitive to changes in the world economy—specifically, changes in world supply and demand for food commodities. In fact, from 2000 to 2018, the price of Saskatchewan farmland had a spectacular upward run, with the average price of farmland hitting an all-time record high of $1,454 per acre in 2018. That year, the price was more than 2.6 times the 2010 price and more than 4.3 times the 2000 price.

Figure 4-10 shows the explosive increase in the price of Saskatchewan farmland during these years. And there was no mystery as to why farmland prices rose so dramatically: it was all about the high prices being paid for grains like wheat and oilseed crops such as canola. According to Statistics Canada, from 2010 to 2018, the price of grains jumped by 28% and oilseed by 19%.

The escalating Saskatchewan farmland prices also reflect shifts in the world economy. Higher demand for food in rising-income economies like China and India have lifted the prices of Saskatchewan food products to higher levels. An escalating trade dispute between the United States and China also benefited Canadian wheat farmers. In light of the dispute, China switched some of its wheat purchases from the United States to Canada, increasing the demand for Canadian wheat.

So a person who buys farmland in Saskatchewan buys the producer surplus generated by that acre of land. And higher long-term prices for wheat and oilseed, which raise the producer surplus of Saskatchewan farmers, will make Saskatchewan farmland more valuable.

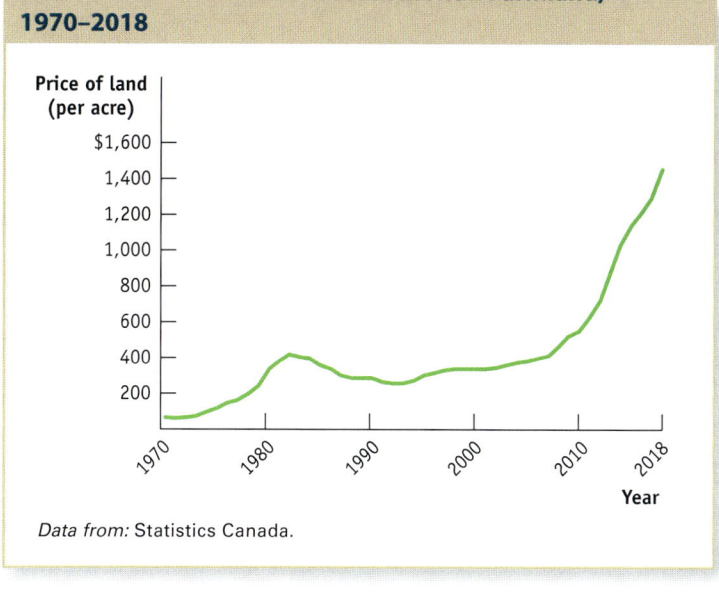

FIGURE 4-10 The Price of Saskatchewan Farmland, 1970–2018

Data from: Statistics Canada.

>> Check Your Understanding 4-2

Solutions appear at back of book.

1. Consider again the market for cheese-stuffed jalapeno peppers. There are two producers, Cara and Jamie, and their costs of producing each pepper are given in the accompanying table. (Neither is willing to produce more than 4 peppers at any price.)

Quantity of peppers	Cara's cost	Jamie's cost
1st pepper	$0.10	$0.30
2nd pepper	0.10	0.50
3rd pepper	0.40	0.70
4th pepper	0.60	0.90

   a. Use the accompanying table to construct the supply schedule for peppers for prices of $0.00, $0.10, and so on, up to $0.90.

   b. Calculate the total producer surplus when the price of a pepper is $0.70.

Consumer Surplus, Producer Surplus, and the Gains from Trade

One of the eleven core principles of economics is that markets are a remarkably effective way to organize economic activity: they generally make society as well off as possible given the available resources. The concepts of consumer surplus and producer surplus can help us deepen our understanding of why this is so.

The Gains from Trade

Let's return to the market in used textbooks but now consider a much bigger market—say, one at a large university. There are many potential buyers and sellers, so the market is competitive. Let's line up incoming students who are

FIGURE 4-11 Total Surplus

In the market for used textbooks, the equilibrium price is $30 and the equilibrium quantity is 1,000 books. Consumer surplus is given by the blue area, the area below the demand curve but above the price. Producer surplus is given by the red area, the area above the supply curve but below the price. The sum of the blue and the red areas is total surplus, the total benefit to society from the production and consumption of the good.

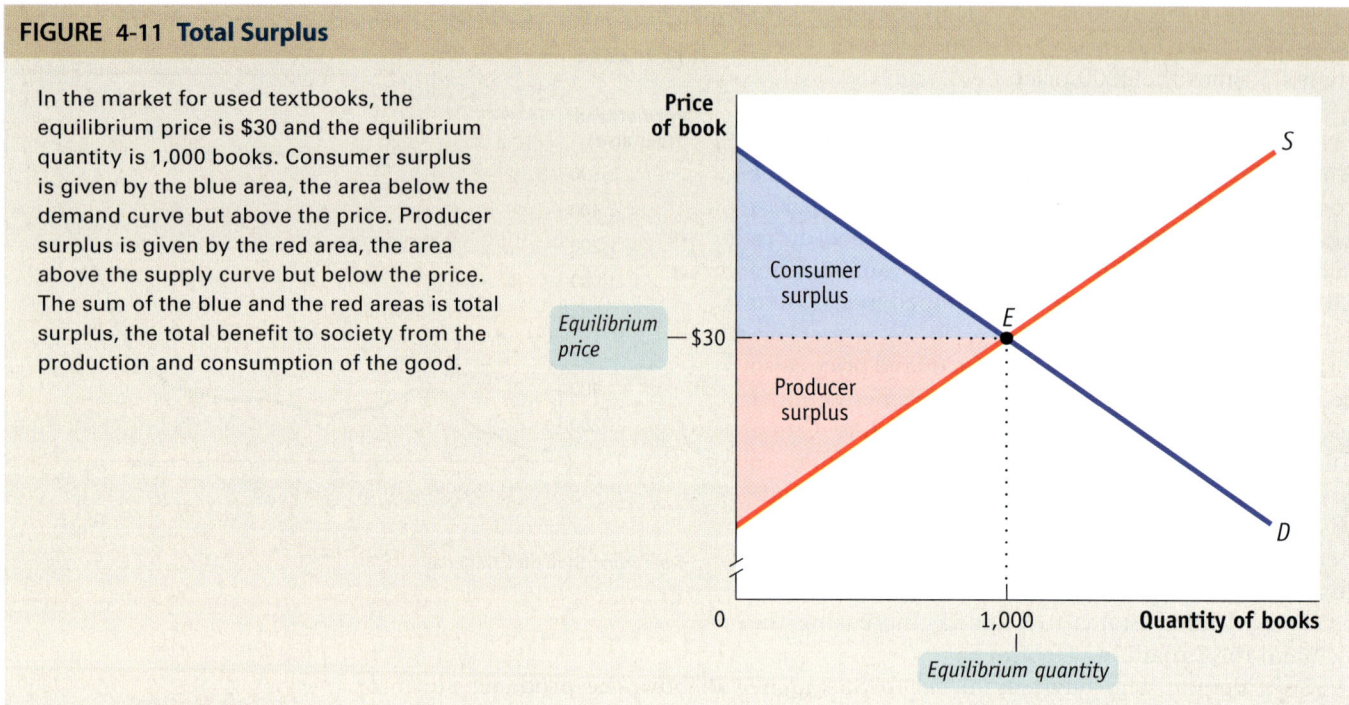

The **total surplus** generated in a market is the total net gain to consumers and producers from trading in the market. It is the sum of the producer and the consumer surplus.

potential buyers of a book in order of their willingness to pay, so that the entering student with the highest willingness to pay is potential buyer number 1, the student with the next highest willingness to pay is number 2, and so on. Then we can use their willingness to pay to derive a demand curve like the one in Figure 4-11.

Similarly, we can line up outgoing students, who are potential sellers of the book, in order of their cost—starting with the student with the lowest cost, then the student with the next lowest cost, and so on—to derive a supply curve like the one shown in the same figure.

As we have drawn the curves, the market reaches equilibrium at a price of $30 per book, and 1,000 books are bought and sold at that price. The two shaded triangles show the consumer surplus (blue) and the producer surplus (red) generated by this market. The sum of consumer and producer surplus is known as the **total surplus** generated in a market.

The striking thing about this picture is that both consumers and producers gain. Both are made better off because there is a market in this good. This should come as no surprise—it illustrates another core principle of economics: *There are gains from trade.* Gains from trade are the reason everyone is better off participating in a market economy than they would be if each individual tried to be self-sufficient.

But are we as well off as we could be? This brings us to the question of the efficiency of markets.

The Efficiency of Markets

Markets produce gains from trade, but in Chapter 1 we made an even bigger claim: that markets are usually *efficient*. That is, once the market has produced its gains from trade, there is no way to make some people better off without making other people worse off, except under some well-defined conditions.

The analysis of consumer and producer surplus helps us understand why markets are usually efficient. To gain more intuition into why this is so, consider the fact that market equilibrium is just *one* way of deciding who consumes the good and who sells the good. There are other possible ways of making that decision.

Consider, again, the case of kidney transplants, in which a decision must be made about who receives one. It is not possible to use a market to decide because in this situation, human organs are involved. In Canada, the decision on who gets available kidneys depends on the time the recipient is on the wait list and how sick they are. This might be considered an inefficient method. In the United States, to address this kind of inefficiency, the UNOS now uses a new system, based on *net survival benefit,* a concept an awful lot like consumer surplus that, although not a market system, succeeds in reproducing the efficiency of one.

To further our understanding of why markets usually work so well, imagine a committee charged with improving on the market equilibrium by deciding who gets and who gives up a used textbook. The committee's ultimate goal is to bypass the market outcome and devise another arrangement, one that would produce higher total surplus.

Let's consider the three ways in which the committee might try to increase the total surplus:

1. Reallocate consumption among consumers
2. Reallocate sales among sellers
3. Change the quantity traded

Reallocate Consumption Among Consumers The committee might try to increase total surplus by selling books to different consumers. Figure 4-12 shows why this will result in lower surplus compared to the market equilibrium outcome. Here we have smooth demand and supply curves because there are many buyers and sellers. Points *A* and *B* show the positions on the demand curve of two potential buyers of used books, Ana and Braxton. As we can see from the figure, Ana is willing to pay $35 for a book, but Braxton is willing to pay only $25. Since the market equilibrium price is $30, under the market outcome Ana buys a book and Braxton does not.

Now suppose the committee reallocates consumption. This would mean taking the book away from Ana and giving it to Braxton. Since the book is worth $35 to Ana but only $25 to Braxton, this change *reduces total consumer surplus* by

---

FIGURE 4-12 Reallocating Consumption Lowers Consumer Surplus

Ana (point *A*) has a willingness to pay of $35. Braxton (point *B*) has a willingness to pay of only $25. At the market equilibrium price of $30, Ana purchases a book but Braxton does not. If we rearrange consumption by taking a book from Ana and giving it to Braxton, consumer surplus declines by $10, and, as a result, total surplus declines by $10.

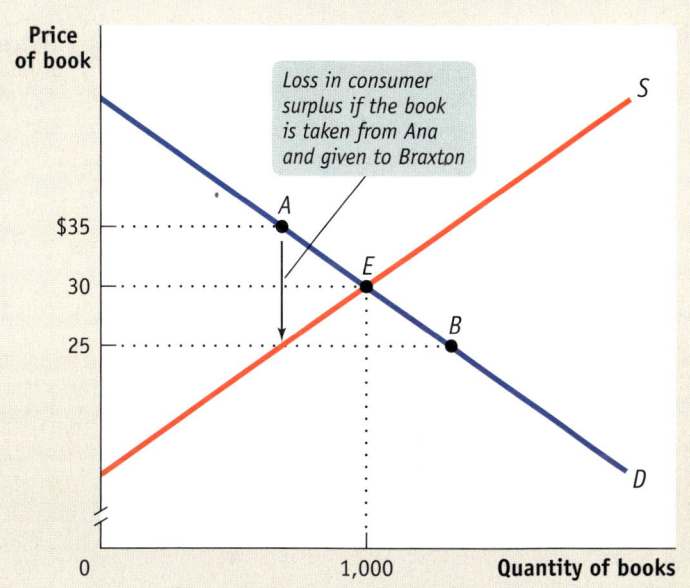

$35 – $25 = $10. Moreover, this result doesn't depend on which two students we pick. Every student who buys a book at the market equilibrium has a willingness to pay of $30 or more, and every student who doesn't buy a book has a willingness to pay of less than $30.

So reallocating the good among consumers always means taking a book away from a student who values it more and giving it to one who values it less. This necessarily reduces total consumer surplus.

Reallocate Sales Among Sellers The committee might try to increase total surplus by altering who sells their books, taking sales away from sellers who would have sold their books at the market equilibrium and instead compelling those who would not have sold their books at the market equilibrium to sell them.

Figure 4-13 shows why this will result in lower surplus. Here points *X* and *Y* show the positions on the supply curve of Xavier, who has a cost of $25, and Yvette, who has a cost of $35. At the equilibrium market price of $30, Xavier would sell his book but Yvette would not sell hers. If the committee reallocated sales, forcing Xavier to keep his book and Yvette to sell hers, total producer surplus would be reduced by $35 – $25 = $10.

Again, it doesn't matter which two students we choose. Any student who sells a book at the market equilibrium has a lower cost than any student who keeps a book. So reallocating sales among sellers necessarily increases total cost and reduces total producer surplus.

Change the Quantity Traded The committee might try to increase total surplus by compelling students to trade either more books or fewer books than the market equilibrium quantity.

Figure 4-14 shows why this will result in lower surplus. It shows all four students: potential buyers Ana and Braxton, and potential sellers Xavier and Yvette. To reduce sales, the committee will have to prevent a transaction that would have occurred in the market equilibrium—that is, prevent Xavier from selling to Ana. Since Ana is willing to pay $35 and Xavier's cost is $25, preventing this transaction reduces total surplus by $35 – $25 = $10.

FIGURE 4-13 Reallocating Sales Lowers Producer Surplus

Yvette (point *Y*) has a cost of $35, $10 more than Xavier (point *X*), who has a cost of $25. At the market equilibrium price of $30, Xavier sells a book but Yvette does not. If we rearrange sales by preventing Xavier from selling his book and compelling Yvette to sell hers, producer surplus declines by $10 and, as a result, total surplus declines by $10.

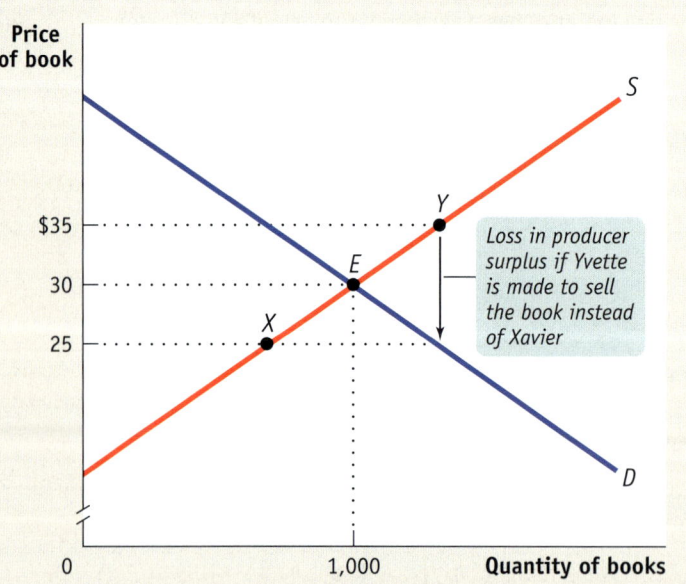

FIGURE 4-14 Changing the Quantity Lowers Total Surplus

If Xavier (point *X*) were prevented from selling his book to someone like Ana (point *A*), total surplus would fall by $10, the difference between Ana's willingness to pay ($35) and Xavier's ($25). This means that total surplus falls whenever fewer than 1,000 books—the equilibrium quantity—are transacted. Likewise, if Yvette (point *Y*) were compelled to sell her book to someone like Braxton (point *B*), total surplus would also fall by $10, the difference between Yvette's cost ($35) and Braxton's willingness to pay ($25). This means that total surplus falls whenever more than 1,000 books are transacted. These two examples show that at market equilibrium, all mutually beneficial transactions—and only mutually beneficial transactions—occur.

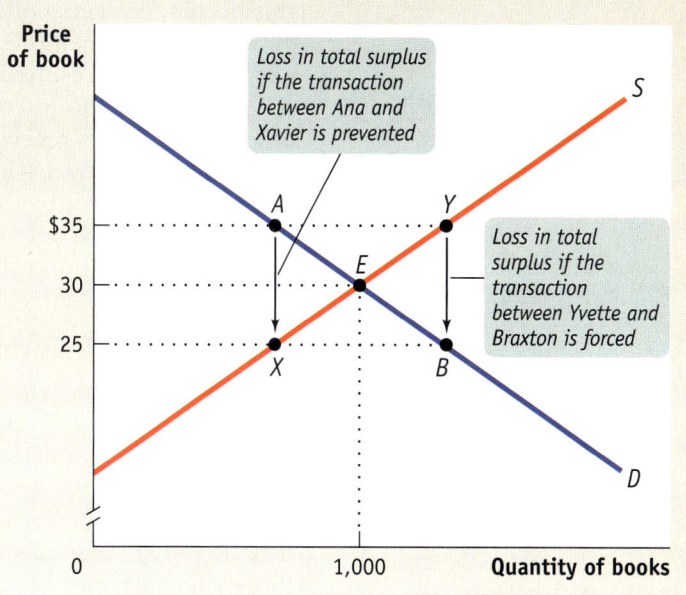

Once again, this result doesn't depend on which two students we pick: any student who would have sold the book at the market equilibrium has a cost of $30 or less, and any student who would have purchased the book at the market equilibrium has a willingness to pay of $30 or more. So preventing any sale that would have occurred in the market equilibrium necessarily reduces total surplus.

Finally, the committee might try to increase sales by forcing Yvette, who would not have sold her book at the market equilibrium, to sell it to someone like Braxton, who would not have bought a book at the market equilibrium. Because Yvette's cost is $35, but Braxton is only willing to pay $25, this transaction reduces total surplus by $10. And once again it doesn't matter which two students we pick—anyone who wouldn't have bought the book has a willingness to pay of less than $30, and anyone who wouldn't have sold has a cost of more than $30.

The key point to remember is that once this market is in equilibrium, there is no way to increase the gains from trade. Any other outcome reduces total surplus. We can summarize our results by stating that an efficient market performs four important functions:

1. It allocates consumption of the good to the potential buyers who most value it, as indicated by the fact that they have the highest willingness to pay.
2. It allocates sales to the potential sellers who most value the right to sell the good, as indicated by the fact that they have the lowest cost.
3. It ensures that every consumer who makes a purchase values the good more than every seller who makes a sale, so that all transactions are mutually beneficial.
4. It ensures that every potential buyer who doesn't make a purchase values the good less than every potential seller who doesn't make a sale, so that no mutually beneficial transactions are missed.

As a result of these four functions, *any way of allocating the good other than the market equilibrium outcome lowers total surplus.*

There are three caveats, however. First, although a market may be efficient, it isn't necessarily *fair.* In fact, fairness, or *equity,* is often in conflict with efficiency. We'll discuss this in the next section.

The second caveat is that markets sometimes *fail*. As mentioned in Chapter 1, under some well-defined conditions, markets can fail to deliver efficiency. When this occurs, markets no longer maximize total surplus.

Third, even when the market equilibrium maximizes total surplus, this does not mean that it results in the best outcome for every *individual* consumer and producer. Other things equal, each buyer would like to pay a lower price and each seller would like to receive a higher price. So if the government were to intervene in the market—say, by lowering the price below the equilibrium price to make consumers happy or by raising the price above the equilibrium price to make producers happy—the outcome would no longer be efficient. Although some people would be happier, total surplus would be lower.

Equity and Efficiency

For many patients who need kidney transplants, the new UNOS guidelines, covered earlier, were unwelcome news. Unsurprisingly, those who have been waiting years for a transplant have found the guidelines, which give precedence to younger patients, . . . well . . . unfair. And the guidelines raise other questions about fairness: Why limit potential transplant recipients to Americans? Why include younger patients with other chronic diseases? Why not give precedence to those who have made recognized contributions to society? And so on.

The point is that efficiency is about *how to achieve goals, not what those goals should be*. For example, UNOS decided that its goal is to maximize the life span of kidney recipients. Some might have argued for a different goal, and efficiency does not address which goal is the best. *What efficiency does address is the best way to achieve a goal once it has been determined*—in this case, using the UNOS concept of net survival benefit.

It's easy to get carried away with the idea that markets are always right and that economic policies that interfere with efficiency are bad. But that would be misguided because there is another factor to consider: society cares about equity, or what's "fair."

There is often a trade-off between equity and efficiency: policies that promote equity often come at the cost of decreased efficiency, and policies that promote efficiency often result in decreased equity. So it's important to realize that a society's choice to sacrifice some efficiency for the sake of equity, however it defines equity, is a valid one. And it's important to understand that fairness, unlike efficiency, can be very hard to define. Fairness is a concept about which well-intentioned people often disagree.

Artazum/Shutterstock

Owners use marketplaces like Airbnb to turn unused resources into cash.

ECONOMICS >> *in Action*
Take the Keys, Please

"Airbnb was really born from a math problem," said its co-founder, Joe Gebbia. "We quit our jobs to be entrepreneurs, and the landlord raised our rent beyond our means. And so we had a math problem to solve. It just so happened that that coming weekend, a design conference came to San Francisco that just wiped out the hotels in the city. We connected the dots. We had extra space in our apartment. So thus was born the air bed-and-breakfast."

From that bout of desperation-induced ingenuity sprang a company that is now the largest single source of lodging in the world. As of 2019, 500 million people searching for a bed have availed themselves of Airbnb's marketplace and, on average, more than 2 million people stay at an Airbnb rental each night worldwide. The website now lists 7 million hosts in over 220 countries and regions, including 4,000 castles and 2,400 tree houses.

Airbnb is the most famous and successful purveyor in what is called "the sharing economy": companies that provide a marketplace in which people can share the use of goods. And there is a dizzying array of others: Turo and Getaround let you rent cars from their owners; Boatbound facilitates boat rentals, Desktime offers office space for rent, JustPark provides parking spaces, and Rent the Runway offers designer clothing.

What's motivating all this sharing? Well, it isn't an outbreak of altruism—it's plain dollars and cents. If there are unused resources sitting around, why not make money by renting them to someone else? As Judith Chevalier, a Yale School of Management economist, says, "These companies let you wring a little bit of value out of . . . goods that are just sitting there." And generating a bit more surplus from your possessions leads to a more efficient use of those resources. As a result, says Arun Sundararajan, a professor at the NYU Stern School of Business, "That makes it possible for people to rethink the way they consume."

>> Check Your Understanding 4-3

Solutions appear at back of book.

1. Using the tables in Check Your Understanding 4-1 and 4-2, find the equilibrium price and quantity in the market for cheese-stuffed jalapeno peppers. What is total surplus in the equilibrium in this market, and who receives it?

2. Show how each of the following three actions reduces total surplus:
   a. Having Azar consume one fewer pepper, and Teresa one more pepper, than in the market equilibrium
   b. Having Cara produce one fewer pepper, and Jamie one more pepper, than in the market equilibrium
   c. Having Azar consume one fewer pepper, and Cara produce one fewer pepper, than in the market equilibrium

3. Suppose UNOS decides to further alter its guidelines for the allocation of donated kidneys, no longer relying solely on the concept of net survival benefit but also giving preference to patients with small children. If "total surplus" in this case is defined to be the total life span of kidney recipients, is this new guideline likely to reduce, increase, or leave total surplus unchanged? How might you justify this new guideline?

>> Quick Review

- **Total surplus** measures the gains from trade in a market.

- Markets are efficient except under some well-defined conditions. We can demonstrate the efficiency of a market by considering what happens to total surplus if we start from the equilibrium and reallocate consumption, reallocate sales, or change the quantity traded. Any outcome other than the market equilibrium reduces total surplus, which means that the market equilibrium is efficient.

- Because society cares about equity, government intervention in a market that reduces efficiency while increasing equity can be justified.

‖ A Market Economy

As we learned earlier, in a market economy decisions about production and consumption are made via markets. In fact, the economy as a whole is made up of many *interrelated markets*. Up until now, to learn how markets work, we've been examining a single market—the market for used textbooks. But in reality, consumers and producers do not make decisions in isolated markets. For example, a student's decision in the market for used textbooks might be affected by how much interest must be paid on a student loan; thus, the decision in the used textbook market would be influenced by what is going on in the market for money.

We know that an efficient market equilibrium maximizes total surplus—the gains to buyers and sellers in that market. Is there a comparable result for an economy as a whole, an economy composed of a vast number of individual markets? The answer is yes, but with qualifications.

When each and every market in the economy maximizes total surplus, the economy as a whole is efficient. This is a very important result: just as it is impossible to make someone better off without making other people worse off in a single market when it is efficient, the same is true when each and every market in that economy

Property rights are the rights of owners of valuable items, whether resources or goods, to dispose of those items as they choose.

An **economic signal** is any piece of information that helps people make better economic decisions.

is efficient. However, it is important to realize that this is a *theoretical* result: it is virtually impossible to find an economy in which every market is efficient.

For now, let's examine why markets and market economies typically work so well. Once we understand why, we can then briefly address why markets sometimes get it wrong.

Why Markets Typically Work So Well

Economists have written volumes about why markets are an effective way to organize an economy. In the end, well-functioning markets owe their effectiveness to two powerful features: *property rights* and the role of prices as *economic signals*.

Property Rights By **property rights** we mean a system in which valuable items in the economy have specific owners who can dispose of them as they choose. In a system of property rights, by purchasing a good you receive *ownership rights*: the right to use and dispose of the good as you see fit. Property rights are what make the mutually beneficial transactions in the used-textbook market, or any market, possible.

To see why property rights are crucial, imagine that students do not have full property rights in their textbooks and are prohibited from reselling them when the semester ends. This restriction on property rights would prevent many mutually beneficial transactions. Some students would be stuck with textbooks they will never reread when they would be much happier receiving some cash instead. Other students would be forced to pay full price for brand-new books when they would be happier getting slightly battered copies at a lower price.

Price is the most important economic signal in a market economy.

Economic Signals Once a system of well-defined property rights is in place, the second necessary feature of well-functioning markets—prices as economic signals—can operate. An **economic signal** is any piece of information that helps people and businesses make better economic decisions. For example, business forecasters say that sales of cardboard boxes are a good early indicator of changes in industrial production: if businesses are buying lots of cardboard boxes, you can be sure that they will soon increase their production.

But prices are far and away the most important signals in a market economy, because they convey essential information about other people's costs and their willingness to pay. If the equilibrium price of used books is $30, this in effect tells everyone both that there are consumers willing to pay $30 and up and that there are potential sellers with a cost of $30 or less. The signal given by the market price ensures that total surplus is maximized by telling people whether to buy books, sell books, or do nothing at all.

Each potential seller with a cost of $30 or less learns from the market price that it's a good idea to sell their book; if they have a higher cost, it's a good idea to keep it. Likewise, each consumer willing to pay $30 or more learns from the market price that it's a good idea to buy a book; if they are unwilling to pay $30, then it's a good idea not to buy a book.

This example shows that the market price "signals" to consumers with a willingness to pay equal to or more than the market price that they should buy the good, just as it signals to producers with a cost equal to or less than the market price that they should sell the good. And since, in equilibrium, the quantity demanded equals the quantity supplied, all willing consumers will find willing sellers.

Prices can sometimes fail as economic signals. Sometimes a price is not an accurate indicator of how desirable a good is. When there is uncertainty about the quality of a good, price alone may not be an accurate indicator of the value of the good. For example, you can't infer from the price alone whether a used car is good or a "lemon." In fact, a well-known problem in economics is "the market for lemons," a market in which prices don't work well as economic signals.

A Few Words of Caution

Markets are an amazingly effective way to organize economic activity. But as we've seen, markets can sometimes get it wrong. We first learned about this in Chapter 1 in our eighth principle: *When markets don't achieve efficiency, government intervention can improve society's welfare.*

When markets are **inefficient,** there are missed opportunities—ways in which production or consumption can be rearranged that would make some people better off without making other people worse off. In other words, there are gains from trade that go unrealized: total surplus could be increased. And when a market or markets are inefficient, the economy in which they are embedded is also inefficient.

Markets can be rendered inefficient for a number of reasons. Two of the most important are a lack of property rights and inaccuracy of prices as economic signals. When a market is inefficient, we have a **market failure.** We will examine various types of market failure in later chapters. For now, let's review the three main ways in which markets sometimes fall short of efficiency.

1. *Market Power:* Markets can fail due to *market power,* which occurs when a firm has the ability to raise the market price. In this case, the assumption that underlies supply and demand analysis—that no one can have a noticeable effect on the market price—is no longer valid. As we'll see in Chapter 13, the presence of market power leads to inefficiency as the firm manipulates the market price in order to increase profits and thereby prevents mutually beneficial trades from occurring.

2. *Externalities:* Markets can fail due to *externalities,* which arise when actions have side effects on the welfare of others. The most common example of an externality is pollution. Because the market price doesn't capture the negative effect pollution has on others, the market outcome is inefficient. In Chapter 16, we'll learn more about externalities and how societies try to cope with them.

3. *Public Goods, Common Resources, and Private Information:* Markets can fail when the nature of the good makes it unsuitable for efficient allocation by a market. This is true for *public goods* like national defence. Because it cannot be bought and sold by people, national defence cannot be allocated efficiently by a market. It is also true for *common resources,* like the fish in our oceans. Markets generally fail in these cases due to incomplete property rights. Markets will also fail when some people possess information about goods that others don't have, as in the market for used cars that we just discussed. In Chapters 17 and 20, we will learn about how society copes in these situations.

But even with these limitations, it's remarkable how well markets work at maximizing gains from trade.

> A market or an economy is **inefficient** if there are missed opportunities: some people could be made better off without making other people worse off.
>
> **Market failure** occurs when a market fails to be efficient.

ECONOMICS >> *in Action*
A Great Leap—Backward

Of any country in the world, China is perhaps the one most associated with free wheeling markets. From the endless street markets for food in Shanghai, to the bustling export-goods markets in Guangzhou that specialize in everything from eyeglasses to electronics, to the massive mall in Shenzhen where you can

Although some aspects of central planning remain, China's economy has moved closer to a free-market system.

find finely tailored custom suits and fake designer bags, the shopping possibilities in China are endless.

Yet, not so long ago, China was a country almost completely lacking in markets. That's because until the 1980s, China was largely a *planned economy* in which a central planner, rather than markets, made consumption and production decisions. Russia, many Eastern European countries, and several Southeast Asian countries once had planned economies. In addition, India and Brazil once had significant parts of their economies under central planning.

Planned economies are notorious for their inefficiency, and probably the most compelling example of that is the so-called Great Leap Forward, an ambitious economic plan instituted in China during the late 1950s by its leader Mao Zedong. Its intention was to speed up the country's industrialization. Key to this plan was a shift from urban to rural manufacturing: farming villages were supposed to start producing heavy industrial goods such as steel. Unfortunately, the plan backfired.

Diverting farmers from their usual work led to a sharp fall in food production. Meanwhile, because raw materials for steel, such as coal and iron ore, were sent to ill-equipped and inexperienced rural producers rather than to urban factories, industrial output declined as well. The plan, in short, led to a fall in the production of everything in China.

Because China was a very poor country to start with, the results were catastrophic. The famine that followed is estimated to have reduced China's population by as much as 30 million.

China's transition to a free-market system has put it on the path to greater economic growth, increased wealth, and led to the emergence of a middle class. But some aspects of central planning still remain, largely in the allocation of financial capital and in state-owned enterprises. As a result, significant central planning inefficiencies persist. In addition, as it transitions to a free-market system, China is now experiencing excessive pollution, an inefficiency arising from market failure. Many economists have observed that these inefficiencies must be addressed if China is to sustain its rapid growth and satisfy the aspirations of billions of Chinese in a sustainable way.

>> Quick Review

• In a market economy, markets are interrelated. When each and every market in an economy is efficient, the economy as a whole is efficient. But in the real world, some markets in a market economy will almost certainly fail to be efficient.

• A system of **property rights** and the operation of prices as **economic signals** are two key factors that enable a market to be efficient. But under conditions in which property rights are incomplete or prices give inaccurate economic signals, markets can fail.

• Under certain conditions, **market failure** occurs and the market is **inefficient:** gains from trade are unrealized. The three principal causes of market failure are market power, externalities, and a good that, by its nature, makes it unsuitable for a market to allocate efficiently.

>> Check Your Understanding 4-4

Solutions appear at back of book.

1. In some jurisdictions that are rich in natural resources, such as oil, the law separates the right to above-ground use of the land from the right to drill below ground (called "mineral rights"). Someone who owns both the above-ground rights and the mineral rights can sell the two rights separately. Explain how this division of the property rights enhances efficiency compared to a situation in which the two rights must always be sold together.

2. Suppose that in the market for used textbooks the equilibrium price is $30, but it is mistakenly announced that the equilibrium price is $300. How does this affect the efficiency of the market? Be specific.

3. What is wrong with the following statement? "Markets are always the best way to organize economic activity. Any policies that interfere with markets reduce society's welfare."

Ticket Prices and Music's Reigning Couple, Beyoncé and Jay-Z

Larry Busacca/FW18/Getty Images

Beyoncé and Jay-Z are the reigning couple of music, estimated to be worth US$1.4 billion. And a good chunk of that money was earned by touring. In 2018, their "On the Run II Tour" grossed a staggering US$253 million with nearly 2.2 million tickets sold. The couple also had a very profitable year in 2014 when their initial "On the Run Tour" grossed over US$100 million. One music industry expert noted that no one should be surprised by this. "With nearly 200 million records sold between them and 36 total Grammys, Beyoncé and Jay-Z are a creative force to be reckoned with. When their talents are combined, the sky is the limit—at least as far as ticket prices are concerned." And, the market seems to agree. TicketIQ estimated that the average online reseller ticket price for the 2018 tour was US$403.

Yet, despite the high demand for tickets to their performances, Beyoncé and Jay-Z receive significantly less than this amount for an average ticket. Why? Omar Al-Joulani, the producer of the tour explained that tickets are priced to be *inclusive*. At the BC Place event in Vancouver, British Columbia in 2018, the average price for direct-sale tickets was about US$112. Al-Joulani continued: "Our strategy was to price tickets so that wherever you were on that ticket chain you had an opportunity to attend the show."

So if you were able to obtain a ticket from a direct seller, you could have made a pretty penny by reselling your ticket at the market price. Perhaps this was Beyoncé's and Jay-Z's way of sharing the wealth as well as their music.

QUESTIONS FOR THOUGHT

1. Use the concepts of consumer surplus and producer surplus to analyze the exchange between Beyoncé and Jay-Z and their fans in the absence of ticket resellers. (That is, assume that everyone buys a ticket directly and goes to the concert.) Draw a diagram to illustrate.

2. Referring to the diagram drawn in response to question 1, explain the effect of resellers on the allocation of consumer surplus and producer surplus among Beyoncé and Jay-Z and their fans.

SUMMARY

1. The **willingness to pay** of each individual consumer determines the demand curve. When price is less than or equal to the willingness to pay, the potential consumer purchases the good. The difference between willingness to pay and price is the net gain to the consumer, the **individual consumer surplus.**

2. **Total consumer surplus** in a market, the sum of all individual consumer surpluses in a market, is equal to the area below the market demand curve but above the price. A rise in the price of a good reduces consumer surplus; a fall in the price increases consumer surplus. The term **consumer surplus** is often used to refer to both individual and total consumer surplus.

3. The **cost** of each potential producer, the lowest price at which they are willing to supply a unit of a particular good, determines the supply curve. If the price of a good is above a producer's cost, a sale generates a net gain to the producer, known as the **individual producer surplus.**

4. **Total producer surplus** in a market, the sum of the individual producer surpluses in a market, is equal to the area above the market supply curve but below the price. A rise in the price of a good increases producer surplus; a fall in the price reduces producer surplus. The term **producer surplus** is often used to refer to both individual and total producer surplus.

5. **Total surplus,** the total gain to society from the production and consumption of a good, is the sum of consumer and producer surplus.

6. Usually markets are efficient and achieve the maximum total surplus. Any possible reallocation of consumption or sales, or a change in the quantity bought and sold, reduces total surplus. However, society also cares about equity. So government intervention in a market that reduces efficiency but increases equity can be a valid choice by society.

7. An economy composed of efficient markets is also efficient, although this is virtually impossible to achieve in reality. The keys to the efficiency of a market economy are **property rights** and the operation of prices as **economic signals.** Under certain conditions, **market failure** occurs, making a market **inefficient.** The three principal causes of market failure are market power, externalities, and a good which, by its nature, makes it unsuitable for a market to allocate efficiently.

KEY TERMS

Willingness to pay, p. 110
Individual consumer surplus, p. 111
Total consumer surplus, p. 111
Consumer surplus, p. 111
Cost, p. 117

Individual producer surplus, p. 118
Total producer surplus, p. 118
Producer surplus, p. 118
Total surplus, p. 122
Property rights, p. 128

Economic signals, p. 128
Inefficient, p. 129
Market failure, p. 129

PRACTICE QUESTIONS

1. Assume that due to a decrease in demand, the average domestic airline fare decreased from $375 in the third quarter of 2019 to $360 in the fourth quarter of the same year, a decrease of $15. The number of passenger tickets sold in the third quarter was 185 million, and it was 175 million in the fourth quarter. Over the same period, the airlines' costs remained roughly the same: the price of jet fuel averaged around $2 per gallon in both quarters, and airline pilots' salaries remained roughly the same, averaging $117,000 per year in 2019.

   Using this information, determine precisely how much producer surplus has decreased as a result of the $15 decrease in the average fare. If you cannot be precise, determine whether it will be less than, or more than, a specific amount?

2. The outbreak of COVID-19 can be considered the most severe public health crisis in the century since the Spanish flu (also known as the 1918 flu pandemic). With the spread of the virus, we saw many residents scrambling to stock up basic necessities including toilet paper, hand sanitizer, disinfecting wipes, face masks, bread, etc., across Canada and in other countries. Given limited supplies, a high-end grocery chain store in Toronto was found charging $30 for a package of Lysol disinfecting wipes which normally sell for $5, an act known as price gouging. Explain how price gouging can result in an increase in consumer surplus.

3. In the early 1990s, the Chrysler Corporation released the best-selling SUV, the Jeep Grand Cherokee. At the time of release, the Grand Cherokee came in three different models, each model offering unique features. Today, the Grand Cherokee is sold in 10 unique models. Why do firms provide unique models and how does increasing the number of models affect producer surplus?

PROBLEMS

1. Determine the amount of consumer surplus generated in each of the following situations.

   a. Bo goes to the clothing store to buy a new T-shirt, for which he is willing to pay up to $10. He picks out one he likes with a price tag of exactly $10. When he is paying for it, he learns that the T-shirt has been discounted by 50%.

   b. Alberto goes to the music store hoping to find a used copy of The Tragically Hip's *Yer Favourites* for up to $30. The store has one copy of the record selling for $30, which he purchases.

   c. After soccer practice, Stephany is willing to pay $2 for a bottle of mineral water. The 7-Eleven sells mineral water for $2.25 per bottle, so she declines to purchase it.

2. Determine the amount of producer surplus generated in each of the following situations.

   a. Conner lists his old Lionel electric trains on eBay. He sets a minimum acceptable price, known as his reserve price, of $75. After five days of bidding, the final high bid is exactly $75. He accepts the bid.

   b. So-Hee advertises her car for sale in the used-car section of the student newspaper for $2,000, but she is willing to sell the car for any price higher than $1,500. The best offer she gets is $1,200, which she declines.

   c. Sanjay likes his job so much that he would be willing to do it for free. However, his annual salary is $80,000.

3. There are six potential consumers of computer games, each willing to buy only one game. Consumer 1 is willing to pay $40 for a computer game, consumer 2 is willing to pay $35, consumer 3 is willing to pay $30, consumer 4 is willing to pay $25, consumer 5 is willing to pay $20, and consumer 6 is willing to pay $15.

   a. Suppose the market price is $29. What is the total consumer surplus?

   b. The market price decreases to $19. What is the total consumer surplus now?

   c. When the price falls from $29 to $19, how much does each consumer's individual consumer surplus change? How does total consumer surplus change?

4. a. In an auction, potential buyers compete for a good by submitting bids. Adam Galinsky, a social psychologist at Northwestern University, compared eBay auctions in which the same good was sold. He found that, on average, the larger the number of bidders, the higher the sales price. For example, in two auctions of identical iPads, the one with the larger number of bidders brought a higher selling price. According to Galinsky, this explains why smart sellers on eBay set absurdly low opening prices (the lowest price that the seller will accept), such as 1 cent for a new iPad. Use the concepts of consumer and producer surplus to explain Galinsky's reasoning.

   b. You are considering selling your first car. If the car is in good condition, it is worth a lot; if it is in poor condition, it is useful only as scrap. Assume that your car is in excellent condition but that it costs a potential buyer $40 for a CARFAX report to determine the car's condition. Use what you learned in part a to explain whether or not you should pay for the CARFAX report and share the results with all interested buyers.

5. The accompanying table shows the supply and demand schedules for used copies of the third edition of this textbook. The supply schedule is derived from offers at Amazon. The demand schedule is hypothetical.

Price of book	Quantity of books demanded	Quantity of books supplied
$55	50	0
60	35	1
65	25	3
70	17	3
75	14	6
80	12	9
85	10	10
90	8	18
95	6	22
100	4	31
105	2	37
110	0	42

   a. Calculate consumer and producer surplus at the equilibrium in this market.

   b. Now the fourth edition of this textbook becomes available. As a result, the willingness to pay off each potential buyer for a second-hand copy of the third edition falls by $20. In a table, show the new demand schedule and again calculate consumer and producer surplus at the new equilibrium.

6. On Thursday nights, a local restaurant has a pasta special. Ari likes the restaurant's pasta, and his willingness to pay for each serving is shown in the accompanying table.

Quantity of pasta (servings)	Willingness to pay for pasta (per serving)
1	$10
2	8
3	6
4	4
5	2
6	0

   a. If the price of a serving of pasta is $4, how many servings will Ari buy? How much consumer surplus does he receive?

b. The following week, Ari is back at the restaurant again, but now the price of a serving of pasta is $6. By how much does his consumer surplus decrease compared to the previous week?

c. One week later, he goes to the restaurant again. He discovers that the restaurant is offering an "all-you-can-eat" special for $25. How much pasta will Ari eat, and how much consumer surplus does he receive now?

d. Suppose you own the restaurant and Ari is a typical customer. What is the highest price you can charge for the "all-you-can-eat" special and still attract customers?

7. You are the manager of Fun World, a small amusement park. The accompanying diagram shows the demand curve of a typical customer at Fun World.

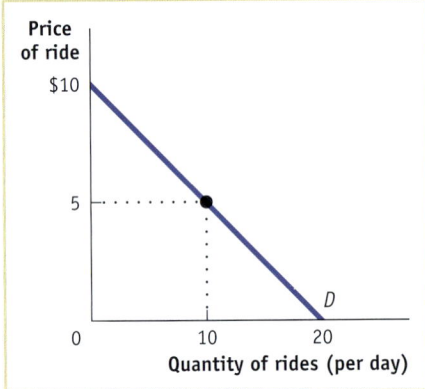

a. Suppose that the price of each ride is $5. At that price, how much consumer surplus does an individual consumer get? (Recall that the area of a right triangle is ½ × the height of the triangle × the base of the triangle.)

b. Suppose that Fun World considers charging an admission fee, even though it maintains the price of each ride at $5. What is the maximum admission fee it could charge? (Assume that all potential customers have enough money to pay the fee.)

c. Suppose that Fun World lowered the price of each ride to zero. How much consumer surplus does an individual consumer get? What is the maximum admission fee Fun World could charge?

8. The accompanying diagram illustrates a taxi driver's individual supply curve (assume that each taxi ride is the same distance).

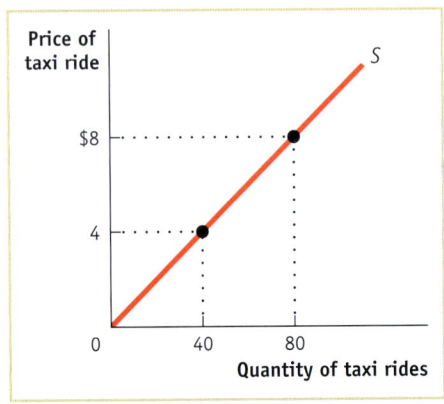

a. Suppose the city sets the price of taxi rides at $4 per ride, and at $4 the taxi driver is able to sell as many taxi rides as he desires. What is this taxi driver's producer surplus? (Recall that the area of a right triangle is ½ × the height of the triangle × the base of the triangle.)

b. Suppose that the city keeps the price of a taxi ride set at $4, but it decides to charge taxi drivers a "licensing fee." What is the maximum licensing fee the city could extract from this taxi driver?

c. Suppose that the city allowed the price of taxi rides to increase to $8 per ride. Again assume that, at this price, the taxi driver sells as many rides as he is willing to offer. How much producer surplus does an individual taxi driver now get? What is the maximum licensing fee the city could charge this taxi driver?

9. Spotify, Pandora, and Google Play are some of the more popular music streaming services. These companies offer free access to music. For a small monthly fee users can purchase premium access and listen to millions of songs on demand and ad free. But not all artists are fans of free streaming music. Taylor Swift's move to prevent Spotify from playing her 2014 release, *1989*, for free, made headlines. When Spotify refused to restrict access to only paying customers, Swift would not allow the company to play her music for free. She is not alone. Adele, Dr. Dre, Garth Brooks, and Coldplay have all had run-ins with free streaming services.

a. If music lovers obtain music and video content via free music streaming services, instead of buying it directly or paying for premium access, what would the record companies' producer surplus be from music sales? What are the implications for record companies' incentive to produce music content in the future?

b. If Taylor Swift and other artists were not allowed to pull their music from the free streaming services, what would happen to mutually beneficial transactions (the producing and buying of music) in the future?

10. Music artists sometimes use novel approaches to address ticket reselling. For example, on the first day that tickets for Adele's highly anticipated U.S. concert tour went on sale at Ticketmaster on a first come, first served basis. Throughout the day, a record 10 million people tried to purchase the 750,000 tickets available. In an attempt to prevent ticket scalping, Adele and Ticketmaster limited buyers to four tickets per concert and required that premium seat holders present the credit card used to purchase tickets to get into the concert. Despite these attempts to restrict resale, tickets on secondary sites like StubHub were selling for 10 times their face value.

a. Draw a supply and demand diagram that depicts the market for Adele concert tickets. Assume all tickets cost $150. Label the equilibrium price, quantity, and resulting shortage.

b. In your diagram, highlight or label the areas that correspond to consumer surplus, producer surplus, and total surplus.

c. Use your diagram to explain how reselling tickets on secondary sites can increase consumer surplus.

11. Uber has long been criticized for its use of surge pricing, setting prices based on current supply and demand factors, which, at times, results in a sudden and drastic increase in prices. In a *Wall Street Journal* article, the CEO of Uber was asked if we are seeing the end of surge pricing. His response: ". . . at the end of the day, Friday night is three or five times bigger than a Sunday night in any city around the world. And if you've got enough supply on the system so that we were perfectly supplied on a Friday night for as much demand as a city could ever throw at us, then the rest of the week you have drivers not making a living."

a. Draw a demand and supply graph for Uber rides in Calgary on a Sunday night. How does demand change on a Friday night? How does the supply of Uber rides change? Label the shortage of Uber cars that results on a Friday night without surge pricing.

b. In your diagram, show what happens to consumer and producer surplus on a Friday night without surge pricing.

c. Using your diagram explain how surge pricing changes consumer and producer surplus.

12. Hollywood screenwriters negotiate a new agreement with movie producers stipulating that they will receive 10% of the revenue from every rental of a movie they wrote. They have no such agreement for movies shown on on-demand television.

a. When the new writers' agreement comes into effect, what will happen in the market for movie rentals—that is, will supply or demand shift, and how? And, as a result, how will consumer surplus in the market for movie rentals change? Illustrate with a diagram. Will the writers' agreement be popular with consumers who rent movies?

b. Consumers consider movie rentals and on-demand movies substitutable to some extent. When the new writers' agreement comes into effect, what will happen in the market for on-demand movies—that is, will supply or demand shift, and how? And, as a result, how will producer surplus in the market for on-demand movies change? Illustrate with a diagram. Will the writers' agreement be popular with the cable television companies that show on-demand movies?

c. Consumers have shifted their movie-watching preferences from Redbox rentals to streaming services like Netflix and Amazon Prime. What has happened in the market for movie rentals after the shift in movie preferences? How has producer surplus in the market for movie rentals changed? Illustrate with a diagram. Use your diagram to explain how the shift to streaming movies affects movie rental companies and Hollywood screenwriters.

WORK IT OUT

13. The accompanying diagram shows the demand and supply curves for taxi rides in Montreal.

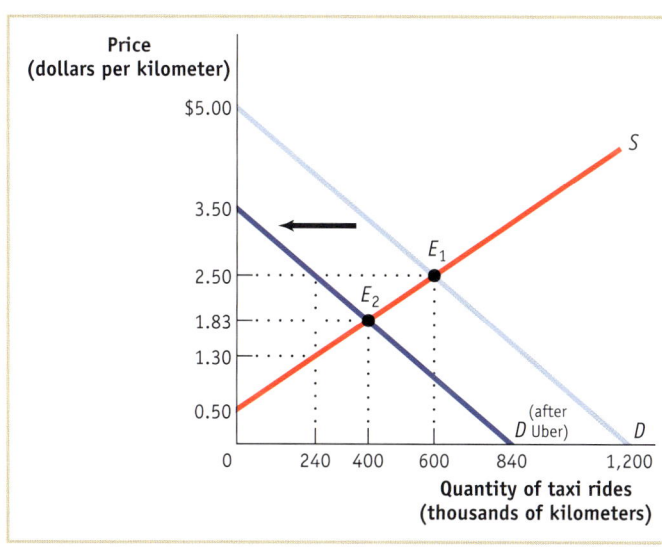

a. At E_1 the market is at equilibrium with 600 thousand kilometers of rides of rides transacted at an equilibrium price of $2.50. Calculate consumer surplus, producer surplus, and total surplus at E_1.

b. Uber's entry into the market reduces the quantity of rides demanded from taxis by 30% at every price, shifting the demand curve leftward. Assume that Montreal lawmakers respond by imposing a regulated price of $2.50 per kilometer. Calculate consumer surplus, producer surplus, and total surplus for the taxi market after Uber has entered the market.

c. After complaints from riders, Montreal removes the regulated price of $2.50 per kilometer. What happens to the equilibrium price and quantity? How will taxi drivers and riders be affected? ◼

5 Price Controls and Quotas: Meddling with Markets

BIG CITY, NOT SO BRIGHT IDEAS

IN 2017, a 25-year-old tenant received unexpected bad news that the rent for her one-bedroom apartment in Toronto's Queen West neighbourhood was going to increase from $1,275 per month to $1,700 per month in 90 days. Situations like this are the norm, as a recent CBC article noted that one-bedroom apartments in downtown Toronto go for $2,000 per month.

In Toronto, an affordable and available rental apartment is hard to find.

Jay Lazarin/iStock/Getty Images Plus

In April 2017, Ontario put its Fair Housing Plan into effect, which expanded rent control to include apartments built after 1991. The legislation hasn't passed yet, but it likely will. The law will also prevent landlords from raising rents more than the rate of inflation, and caps rent increases at 2.5% even if the rate of inflation is higher.

So, how was this news received? Renters are unsurprisingly happy, but the rental industry is concerned as it fears investors will stop buying apartments and landlords will sell their units.

Rent control is a type of *market intervention,* a policy imposed by government to prevail over the market forces of supply and demand — in this case, over the market forces of the supply and demand for Toronto rental apartments.

Although rent-control laws were introduced during World War II in many major Canadian and American cities to protect the interests of tenants, the problems they create have led most cities to discard them. New York City and San Francisco are notable American exceptions, although rent control covers only a small and diminishing proportion of rental apartments in these cities. In much of Canada, rent controls have been eliminated or, in fact, never existed in the first place. Where they still do exist, in British Columbia, Manitoba, Ontario, Québec, and Prince Edward Island, rent controls are significantly weaker than they were several decades ago. However, the Fair Housing Plan in Ontario will make the impact of rent control more widespread in the province.

In Chapter 3, we learned the principle that a market moves to equilibrium — the market price rises or falls to the level at which the quantity of a good that people are willing to supply is equal to the quantity that other people demand. However, when governments intervene in markets, they try to defy that principle.

As we will learn in this chapter, when a government tries to dictate either a market price or a market quantity that's different from the equilibrium price or quantity, the market strikes back in predictable ways. The shortage of apartments is one example of what happens when the logic of the market is defied: a market intervention like rent control keeps the price of apartment rentals below market equilibrium level, creating a shortage and other serious problems. And, as we'll see, those problems inevitably create winners and losers.

Our ability to predict what will happen when governments try to defy supply and demand shows the power and usefulness of supply and demand analysis.

We will also examine another form of market intervention used in Toronto and other cities — a licencing system for taxis that reduces the number of taxis offering rides below the market equilibrium level. Originally intended to protect the interests of both drivers and customers, like rent control, it led to a shortage of taxis. Although in recent years, the rise of companies like Uber has upended market interventions in the taxi industry and moved it closer to market equilibrium. We address this development in the chapter and in the Business Case at end of chapter.

Although there are specific winners and losers from market intervention, we will learn how and why society as a whole loses — a result that has led economists to be generally skeptical of market interventions except in certain well-defined situations. ●

WHAT YOU WILL LEARN

- What is a market intervention and why are **price controls** and **quantity controls** the two main forms it takes?
- Why do price and quantity controls create **deadweight losses**?
- Who benefits and who loses from market interventions?
- Why are economists often skeptical of market interventions? And why do governments undertake market interventions even though they create losses to society?

Price controls are legal restrictions on how high or low a market price may go. They can take two forms: a **price ceiling,** a maximum price sellers are allowed to charge for a good or service, or a **price floor,** a minimum price buyers are required to pay for a good or service.

Why Governments Control Prices

As we know from Chapter 3, a market moves to equilibrium—the market price moves to the level at which the quantity supplied equals the quantity demanded. But this equilibrium price does not necessarily please either buyers or sellers.

After all, buyers would always like to pay less if they could. Sometimes they can make a strong moral or political case for this, such as when the equilibrium rental rates are not affordable for an average working person. In that case, a government might well be under pressure to impose limits on the rents landlords can charge.

Similarly, sellers would always like to get higher prices. Sometimes they can make a strong moral or political case for this, such as when the equilibrium wage rate for a worker who sells their labour in the labour market results in an income below the poverty level. In that case, a government might well be pressured to require employers to pay a rate no lower than some specified minimum wage.

So there are often strong political demands for governments to intervene in markets with powerful interests often making a compelling case that market intervention in their favour is "fair." When a government intervenes to regulate prices, we say that it imposes **price controls.** These controls typically take the form either of an upper limit, a **price ceiling,** or a lower limit, a **price floor.**

However, it's not that easy to tell a market what to do. When a government tries to legislate prices—whether it legislates them down by imposing a price ceiling or up by imposing a price floor—there are certain predictable and unpleasant side effects.

Yet, there are two important caveats to consider. First, we assume in this chapter that the markets in question are efficient before price controls are imposed. But markets can sometimes be inefficient—for example, a market dominated by a monopolist, a single seller that has the power to influence the market price. When markets are inefficient, price controls don't necessarily cause problems and can potentially move markets closer to efficiency. Second, short-term price controls in response to shortages caused by natural disasters can be justified on the basis of equity and social welfare. For example, during the coronavirus pandemic of 2020, a shortage of ventilators necessary to keep people alive would have led to skyrocketing prices in a free market, thereby making them only available to the well-off. So the government acted to allocate ventilators according to need, making for a far more equitable allocation of life and death.

Price Ceilings

Aside from rent control, there are other price ceilings in Canada today. Currently there exists some form of price controls in Canadian markets for pharmaceutical drugs, electricity, basic residential phone services, and agricultural commodities (such as eggs, chicken, turkey, and dairy). At times, price ceilings have been widespread. They are typically imposed during crises—wars, harvest failures, natural disasters—because these events often lead to sudden price increases that hurt many people but produce big gains for a lucky few.

The Canadian government imposed ceilings on many prices during World War II: the war sharply increased demand for raw materials (such as aluminum and steel) and necessities (such as rentals, sugar, milk, and coal), and price controls prevented those with access to these goods and services from earning huge profits. World oil prices spiked in 1979–1980 due to uncertainty caused by the Iranian revolution and the outbreak of war between Iran and Iraq (both large oil-producing nations). Price controls on oil were imposed in 1980, when Prime Minister Pierre Trudeau's government introduced the National Energy Program to help Canada achieve energy self-sufficiency, redistribute the wealth from nonrenewable energy production to all parts of the country, and increase Canadian ownership of the oil industry.

You can rent a one-bedroom apartment in Toronto on fairly short notice—if you are able and willing to pay several thousand dollars a month and live in a less desirable area. Yet some people pay only a small fraction of this for comparable apartments, and others pay hardly more for bigger apartments in the most desirable locations.

Aside from producing great deals for some renters, however, what are the broader consequences of Toronto's rent-control system? To answer this question, we turn to the model we developed in Chapter 3: the supply and demand model.

Modelling a Price Ceiling

To see what can go wrong when a government imposes a price ceiling on an efficient market, consider Figure 5-1, which shows a simplified model of the market for apartments in a large city. For the sake of simplicity, we imagine that all apartments are exactly the same and would rent for the same price in an unregulated market.

The table in Figure 5-1 shows the demand and supply schedules; the demand and supply curves are shown on the left. We show the quantity of apartments on the horizontal axis and the monthly rent per apartment on the vertical axis. You can see that in an unregulated market the equilibrium would be at point *E*: 2 million apartments would be rented for $1,000 each per month.

Now suppose that the government imposes a price ceiling, limiting rents to a price below the equilibrium price—say, no more than $800.

FIGURE 5-1 **The Market for Apartments in the Absence of Price Controls**

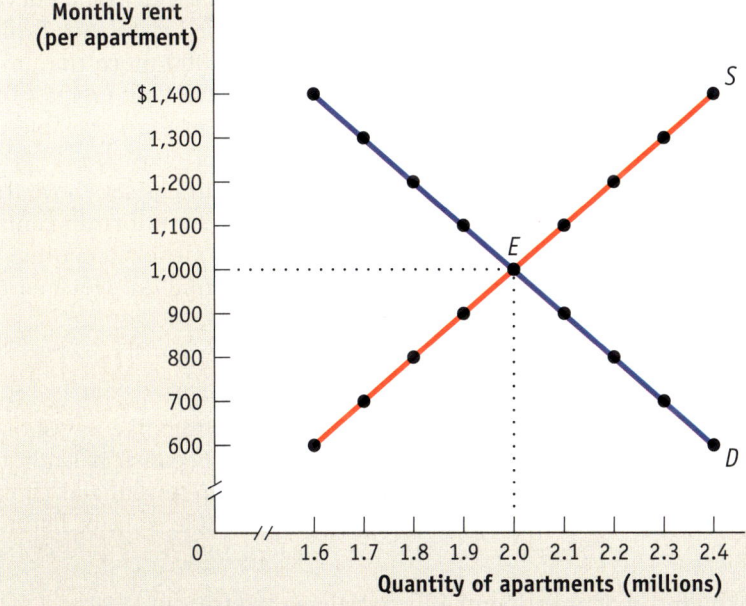

Monthly rent (per apartment)	Quantity of apartments (millions)	
	Quantity demanded	Quantity supplied
$1,400	1.6	2.4
1,300	1.7	2.3
1,200	1.8	2.2
1,100	1.9	2.1
1,000	2.0	2.0
900	2.1	1.9
800	2.2	1.8
700	2.3	1.7
600	2.4	1.6

Without government intervention, the market for apartments reaches equilibrium at point *E* with a market rent of $1,000 per month and 2 million apartments rented.

FIGURE 5-2 The Effects of a Price Ceiling

The black horizontal line represents the government-imposed price ceiling on rents of $800 per month. This price ceiling reduces the quantity of apartments supplied to 1.8 million, point *A,* and increases the quantity demanded to 2.2 million, point *B.* This creates a persistent shortage of 400,000 units: 400,000 people who want apartments at the legal rent of $800 but cannot get them.

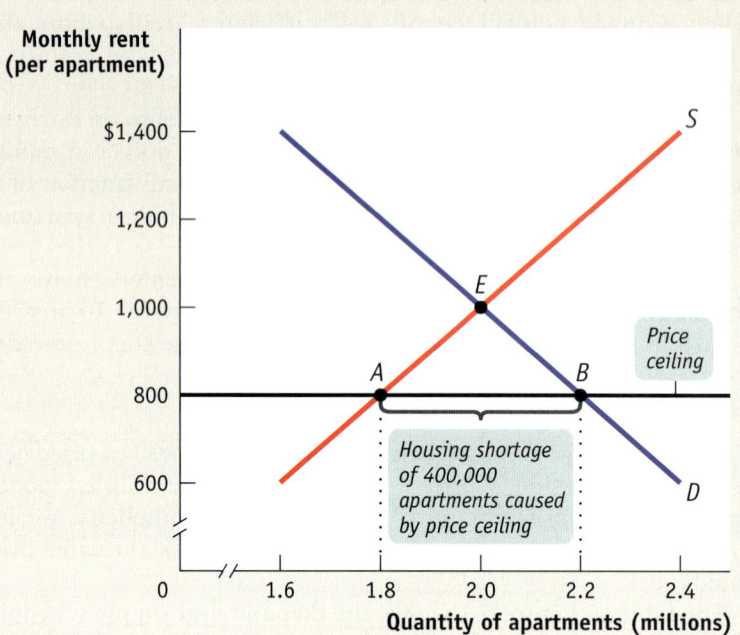

Figure 5-2 shows the effect of the price ceiling, represented by the line at $800. At the enforced rental rate of $800, landlords have less incentive to offer apartments, so they won't be willing to supply as many as they would at the equilibrium rate of $1,000. They will choose point *A* on the supply curve, offering only 1.8 million apartments for rent, 200,000 fewer than in the unregulated market.

At the same time, more people will want to rent apartments at a price of $800 than at the equilibrium price of $1,000; as shown at point *B* on the demand curve, at a monthly rent of $800 the quantity of apartments demanded rises to 2.2 million, 200,000 more than in the unregulated market and 400,000 more than are actually available at the price of $800. So there is now a persistent shortage of rental housing: at that price, 400,000 more people want to rent than are able to find apartments.

Do price ceilings always cause shortages? No. If a price ceiling is set above the equilibrium price, it won't have any effect. Suppose that the equilibrium rental rate on apartments is $1,000 per month and the city government sets a ceiling of $1,200. Who cares? In this case, the price ceiling won't be *binding*—it won't actually constrain market behaviour—and it will have no effect.

How a Price Ceiling Causes Inefficiency

The housing shortage shown in Figure 5-2 is not merely annoying: like any shortage induced by price controls, it can be seriously harmful because it leads to inefficiency. In other words, there are gains from trade that go unrealized.

Rent control, like all price ceilings, creates inefficiency in at least four distinct ways.

1. It reduces the quantity of apartments rented below the efficient level.
2. It typically leads to inefficient allocation of apartments among would-be renters.
3. It leads to wasted time and effort as people search for apartments.
4. It leads landlords to maintain apartments in inefficiently low quality or condition.

In addition to inefficiency, price ceilings give rise to illegal behaviour as people try to circumvent them. We'll now look at each of these inefficiencies caused by price ceilings.

Inefficiently Low Quantity In Chapter 4, we learned that the market equilibrium of an efficient market leads to the "right" quantity of a good or service being bought and sold—that is, the quantity that maximizes the sum of producer and consumer surplus. Because rent controls reduce the number of apartments supplied, they reduce the number of apartments rented, too.

Figure 5-3 shows the implications for total surplus. Recall that total surplus is the sum of the area above the supply curve and below the demand curve. If the only effect of rent control was to reduce the number of apartments available, it would cause a loss of surplus equal to the area of the shaded triangle in the figure.

The area represented by that triangle has a special name in economics, **deadweight loss:** the lost surplus associated with the transactions that no longer occur due to the market intervention. In this example, the deadweight loss is the lost surplus associated with the apartment rentals that no longer occur due to the price ceiling, a loss that is experienced by both disappointed renters and frustrated landlords. Economists often call triangles like the one in Figure 5-3 a *deadweight-loss triangle.*

Deadweight loss is a key concept in economics, one that we will encounter whenever an action or a policy leads to a reduction in the quantity transacted below the efficient market equilibrium quantity. It is important to realize that deadweight loss is a *loss to society*—it is a reduction in total surplus, a loss in surplus that accrues to no one as a gain. It is not the same as a loss in surplus to one person that then accrues as a gain to someone else, what an economist would call a *transfer* of surplus from one person to another. In the next section, we look at how a price ceiling can create deadweight loss as well as a transfer of surplus between renters and landlords.

Deadweight loss is the loss in total surplus that occurs whenever an action or a policy reduces the quantity transacted below the efficient market equilibrium quantity.

FIGURE 5-3 A Price Ceiling Causes Inefficiently Low Quantity

A price ceiling reduces the quantity supplied below the market equilibrium quantity, leading to a deadweight loss. The area of the shaded triangle corresponds to the amount of total surplus lost due to the inefficiently low quantity transacted.

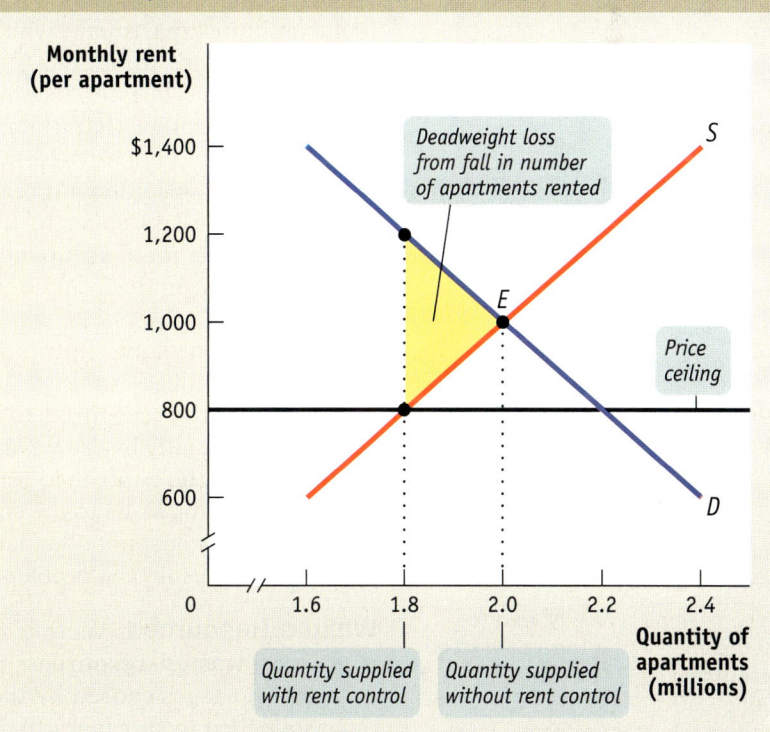

Deadweight loss is not the only type of inefficiency that arises from a price ceiling. The types of inefficiency created by rent control go beyond reducing the quantity of apartments available. These additional inefficiencies—inefficient allocation to consumers, wasted resources, and inefficiently low quality—lead to a loss of surplus over and above the deadweight loss.

Inefficient Allocation to Consumers Rent control doesn't just lead to too few apartments being available. It can also lead to misallocation of the apartments that are available: people who badly need a place to live may not be able to find an apartment, but some apartments may be occupied by people with much less urgent needs.

In the case shown in Figure 5-2, 2.2 million people would like to rent an apartment at $800 per month, but only 1.8 million apartments are available. Of those 2.2 million who are seeking an apartment, some want one badly and are willing to pay a high price to get it. Others have a less urgent need and are only willing to pay a low price, perhaps because they have alternative housing.

An efficient allocation of apartments would reflect these differences: people who really want an apartment will get one and people who aren't all that eager to find an apartment won't. In an inefficient distribution of apartments, the opposite will happen: some people who are not especially interested in finding an apartment will get one and others who are very eager to find an apartment won't.

Because people usually get apartments through luck or personal connections under rent control, it generally results in an **inefficient allocation to consumers** of the few apartments available.

To see the inefficiency involved, consider the plight of the Lees, a family with young children who have no alternative housing and would be willing to pay up to $1,500 for an apartment—but are unable to find one. Also consider George, a retiree who lives most of the year in Florida but still has a lease on the New York City apartment he moved into 40 years ago. George pays $800 per month for this apartment, but if the rent were even slightly more—say, $850—he would give it up and stay with his children when he visits New York City.

This allocation of apartments—George has one and the Lees do not—is a missed opportunity: there is a way to make the Lees and George both better off at no additional cost. The Lees would be happy to pay George, say, $1,200 a month to sublease his apartment, which he would happily accept since the apartment is worth no more than $849 a month to him. George would prefer the money he gets from the Lees to keeping his apartment; the Lees would prefer to have the apartment rather than the money. So both would be made better off by this transaction—and nobody else would be made worse off.

Generally, if people who really want apartments could sublease them from people who are less eager to live there, both those who gain apartments and those who trade their occupancy for money would be better off. However, subletting is illegal under rent control because it would occur at prices above the price ceiling.

The fact that subletting is illegal doesn't mean it never happens. In fact, chasing down illegal subletting is a major business for New York City private investigators who are hired to prove that the legal tenants in rent-controlled apartments actually live somewhere else, and have sublet their apartments at two or three times the controlled rent.

This subletting leads to the emergence of a black market, which we will discuss shortly. For now, just note that landlords and legal agencies actively discourage the practice. As a result, the problem of inefficient allocation of apartments remains.

Wasted Resources Another reason a price ceiling causes inefficiency is that it leads to **wasted resources:** people expend money, effort, and time to cope with the shortages caused by the price ceiling. Back in 1979, U.S. price controls on gasoline led to shortages that forced millions of Americans to wait in lines at gas stations for hours each week. The opportunity cost of the time spent in gas

A price ceiling like rent control leads to inefficiency in the market for rental apartments.

Price ceilings often lead to inefficiency in the form of **inefficient allocation to consumers:** some people who want the good badly and are willing to pay a high price don't get it, and some who care relatively little about the good and are only willing to pay a low price do get it.

Price ceilings typically lead to inefficiency in the form of **wasted resources:** people expend money, effort, and time to cope with the shortages caused by the price ceiling.

FOR INQUIRING MINDS   Mumbai's Rent-Control Millionaires

Mumbai, India, like Toronto, has rent-controlled apartments. Currently, about 60% of apartments in Mumbai's city centre are rent-controlled. Although Mumbai is half a world away from Toronto, the economics of rent control works just the same: rent control leads to shortages, low quality, inefficient allocation to consumers, wasted resources, and black markets.

Mumbai landlords, who often pay more in taxes and maintenance than what they receive in rent, sometimes simply abandon their properties to decay. And a black market in rent-controlled apartments thrives in Mumbai as old tenants sell the right to occupy apartments to new tenants.

And, like many major cities, Toronto included, Mumbai has its "rent-control millionaires." One renter, Mea Kadwani, lived in a 2,600 square foot apartment paying just US$26.51 per month in an area where apartments not under rent control often go for US$2651.20 a month. He refused to leave when his roof collapsed, and after three years of negotiations was paid US$3.3 million by a developer to vacate the apartment so that a luxury building could be constructed.

With its shortage of land for development, and its desirability as a place to live for the rapidly expanding number of high-income Indians, Mumbai has thousands of rent-controlled tenants who have become millionaires upon vacating their apartments.

lines—the wages not earned, the leisure time not enjoyed—constituted wasted resources from the point of view of consumers and of the economy as a whole.

Because of rent control, the Lees will spend all their spare time for several months searching for an apartment, time they would rather have spent working or in family activities. That is, there is an opportunity cost to the Lees' prolonged search for an apartment—the leisure or income they had to forgo.

If the market for apartments worked freely, the Lees would quickly find an apartment at the equilibrium rent of $1,000, leaving them time to earn more or to enjoy themselves—an outcome that would make them better off without making anyone else worse off. Again, rent control creates missed opportunities.

Inefficiently Low Quality   Yet another way a price ceiling creates inefficiency is by causing goods to be of inefficiently low quality. **Inefficiently low quality** means that sellers offer low-quality goods at a low price even though buyers would rather have higher quality and would be willing to pay a higher price for it.

Again, consider rent control. Landlords have no incentive to provide better conditions because they cannot raise rents to cover their repair costs but are able to find tenants easily. In many cases, tenants would be willing to pay much more for improved conditions than it would cost for the landlord to provide them—for example, upgrading an outdated electrical system that cannot safely run air conditioners or computers. But any additional payment for such improvements would be legally considered a rent increase, which is prohibited.

Indeed, rent-controlled apartments are notoriously badly maintained, rarely painted, subject to frequent electrical and plumbing problems, sometimes even hazardous to inhabit. This whole situation is a missed opportunity—some tenants would be happy to pay for better conditions, and landlords would be happy to provide them for payment. But such an exchange would occur only if the market were allowed to operate freely.

Black Markets   In addition to these four inefficiencies there is a final aspect of price ceilings: the incentive they provide for illegal activities, specifically the emergence of **black markets.** We have already described one kind of black market activity—illegal subletting by tenants. But it does not stop there. Clearly, there is a temptation for a landlord to say to a potential tenant, "Look, you can have the place if you slip me an extra few hundred in cash each month"—and for the tenant to agree if they are one of those people who would be willing to pay much more than the maximum legal rent.

So, what's wrong with black markets? In general, it's a bad thing if people break any law, because it encourages disrespect for the law in general. Worse yet, in this case illegal activity worsens the position of those who are honest. If the Lees are scrupulous about upholding the rent-control law but other people—who

Price ceilings often lead to inefficiency in that the goods being offered are of **inefficiently low quality:** sellers offer low-quality goods at a low price even though buyers would prefer a higher quality at a higher price.

A **black market** is a market in which goods or services are bought and sold illegally—either because it is illegal to sell them at all or because the prices charged are legally prohibited by a price ceiling.

may need an apartment less than the Lees—are willing to bribe landlords or grab illegal sublets, the Lees may never find an apartment.

Yet black markets can diminish *some* of the inefficiency of rent control. For example, if George allows the Lees to sublet his rent-controlled apartment (a black market deal since it is illegal), society is better off (as are the Lees) than if there were no deal. But in the end, society as a whole is made worse off by the presence of a black market relative to a market that is completely free of rent control.

Winners, Losers, and Rent Control

We've just seen how price controls can lead to inefficiencies. These inefficiencies, in turn, create winners and losers as some people benefit from policies like rent control while others are made worse off.

Using consumer and producer surplus, we can graphically evaluate the winners and the losers from rent control. Panel (a) of Figure 5-4 shows the consumer surplus and producer surplus in the equilibrium of the unregulated market for apartments before rent control. Recall that the *consumer surplus,* represented by the area below the demand curve and above the price, is the total net gain to consumers in the market equilibrium. Likewise, *producer surplus,* represented by the area above the supply curve and below the price, is the total net gain to producers in the market equilibrium.

Panel (b) of this figure shows the consumer and producer surplus in the market after the price ceiling of $800 has been imposed. As you can see, for consumers who can still obtain apartments under rent control, consumer surplus has increased. These renters are clearly winners: they obtain an apartment at $800, paying $200 less than the unregulated market price. These people receive a direct transfer of surplus from landlords in the form of lower rent.

FIGURE 5-4 Winners and Losers from Rent Control

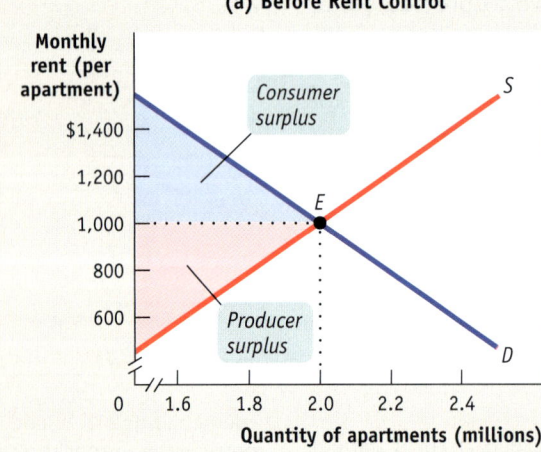

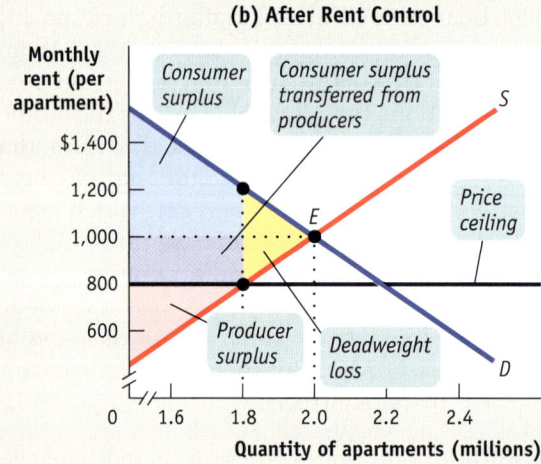

Price ceilings like rent control reduce total surplus. Panel (a) shows the producer and consumer surplus created in the unregulated market for apartments. Total surplus is greatest at the market equilibrium: a monthly rent of $1,000 and a quantity of 2.0 million apartments transacted. Panel (b) shows the producer and consumer surplus in the market after a price ceiling of $800 is imposed, resulting in a fall in total surplus. At the mandated rent of $800, landlords reduce the quantity of apartments supplied from 2.0 million to 1.8 million.

For renters who can find an apartment, their consumer surplus has increased. This increase in consumer surplus is a direct transfer from landlords, represented by the purple-shaded rectangle. However, consumer surplus declines for those who are now unable to rent an apartment. Their loss, as well as the loss to landlords from renting fewer apartments, is represented by the deadweight-loss triangle shaded in yellow. The deadweight loss represents the total loss to society from the imposition of rent control.

But not all renters win: there are fewer apartments to rent now than if the market had remained unregulated, making it hard, if not impossible, for some to find a place to call home.

Without direct calculation of the surpluses gained and lost, it is generally unclear whether renters as a whole are made better or worse off by rent control. What we can say is that the greater the deadweight loss—the larger the reduction in the quantity of apartments rented—the more likely it is that renters as a whole lose.

However, we can say unambiguously that landlords are worse off: producer surplus has clearly decreased. Landlords who continue to rent out their apartments get $200 a month less in rent, and others withdraw their apartments from the market altogether. The deadweight-loss triangle, shaded yellow in panel (b), represents the value lost to both renters and landlords from rentals that essentially vanish thanks to rent control.

So Why Are There Price Ceilings?

We have seen three common results of price ceilings:

- A persistent shortage of the good
- Inefficiency arising from this persistent shortage in the form of inefficiently low quantity (deadweight loss), inefficient allocation of the good to consumers, resources wasted in searching for the good, and the inefficiently low quality of the good offered for sale
- The emergence of illegal, black market activity

Given these unpleasant consequences of price ceilings, why do governments still sometimes impose them? Why does rent control, in particular, persist in New York City?

One answer is that although price ceilings may have adverse effects, they do benefit some people. In practice, New York City's rent-control rules—which are more complex than our simple model—hurt most residents but give a small minority of renters much cheaper housing than they would get in an unregulated market. And those who benefit from the controls are typically better organized and more vocal than those who are harmed by them.

Also, when price ceilings have been in effect for a long time, buyers may not have a realistic idea of what would happen without them. In our earlier example, the rental rate in an unregulated market (Figure 5-1) would be only 25% higher than in the regulated market (Figure 5-2): $1,000 instead of $800. But how would renters know that? Indeed, they might have heard about black market transactions at much higher prices—the Lees or some other family paying George $1,200 or more—and would not realize that these black market prices are much higher than the price that would prevail in a fully unregulated market.

A last answer is that government officials often do not understand supply and demand analysis! It is a great mistake to suppose that economic policies in the real world are always sensible or well informed.

ECONOMICS >> *in Action*
How Price Controls in Venezuela Proved Disastrous

By all accounts, Venezuela is a rich country as one of the world's top producers of oil. But despite its wealth, price controls have so distorted its economy that the country is struggling to feed its citizens and provide health care. Necessities like toilet paper, rice, coffee, corn, flour, milk, and meat are chronically lacking. Hospitals operate without basic supplies and with broken equipment.

Venezuela's food shortages show how price controls disproportionately hurt the people they were designed to benefit.

Today, Venezuelans line up for hours to purchase price-controlled goods at state-run stores but often came away empty handed. "Empty shelves and no one to explain why a rich country has no food. It's unacceptable," said Jesús López, a 90-year-old farmer.

The origins of the shortages can be traced to policies espoused by Venezuela's former president, Hugo Chávez. First elected in 1998 on a platform that promised to favour the poor and working classes over the country's economic elite, Chávez implemented price controls on basic foodstuffs. Prices were set so low that farmers reduced production, so that by 2006, shortages were severe. As a result, Venezuela went from being self-sufficient in food in 1998 to importing more than 70% of its food. By 2019, researchers had documented widespread weight loss and increasing malnutrition among the Venezuelan population.

At the same time, generous government programs for the poor and working class created higher demand. The reduced supply of goods due to price controls combined with higher demand led to sharply rising prices for black market goods that, in turn, generated even greater demand for goods sold at the controlled prices. Smuggling became rampant, as a bottle of milk sold across the border in Colombia for seven or eight times the controlled price in Venezuela. Not surprisingly, fresh milk was rarely seen in Venezuelan markets.

The irony of the situation is that the policies put in place to help the poor and working classes have disproportionately hurt them. In 2019, the minimum monthly wage allowed Venezuelans to afford only 24 eggs, three-quarters of a pizza, or half a burger on the black market. People were spending up to 12 hours at a time in line to purchase basic foodstuffs. As one shopper in a low-income area said, "It fills me with rage to have to spend the one free day I have wasting my time for a bag of rice. I end up paying more at the resellers [the black market]. In the end, all these price controls proved useless."

The lack of basic necessities—food and medicine—coupled with soaring crime led to a mass exodus of more than 3 million people from Venezuela to neighbouring countries in 2019. As one woman said, "I'm leaving with nothing. But I have to do this. Otherwise, we will just die hungry here."

>> Quick Review

- **Price controls** take the form of either legal maximum prices—**price ceilings**—or legal minimum prices—**price floors.**

- A price ceiling below the equilibrium price benefits successful buyers but causes predictable adverse effects such as persistent shortages, which lead to four types of inefficiencies: **deadweight loss, inefficient allocation to consumers, wasted resources,** and **inefficiently low quality.**

- A deadweight loss is a loss of total surplus that occurs whenever a policy or action reduces the quantity transacted below the efficient market equilibrium level.

- Price ceilings also lead to **black markets,** as buyers and sellers attempt to evade the price controls.

- Price ceilings can be justified when the market is inefficient or when a natural disaster leads to shortages that, if left to a free market, would greatly diminish equity and social welfare.

>> Check Your Understanding 5-1

Solutions appear at back of book.

1. On game days, homeowners near Middletown University's stadium used to rent parking spaces in their driveways to fans at a going rate of $11. A new town ordinance now sets a maximum parking fee of $7. Use the accompanying supply and demand diagram to explain how each of the following corresponds to a price-ceiling concept.

   a. Some homeowners now think it's not worth the hassle to rent out spaces.

   b. Some fans who used to carpool to the game now drive alone.

   c. Some fans can't find parking and leave without seeing the game.

   Explain how each of the following adverse effects arises from the price ceiling.

   d. Some fans now arrive several hours early to find parking.

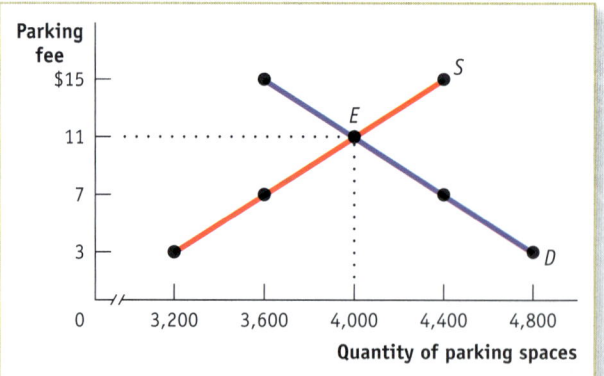

   e. Friends of homeowners near the stadium regularly attend games, even if they aren't big fans. But some serious fans have given up because of the parking situation.

   f. Some homeowners rent spaces for more than $7 but pretend that the buyers are nonpaying friends or family.

2. True or false? Explain your answer. A price ceiling below the equilibrium price of an otherwise efficient market does the following:

   a. Increases quantity supplied

   b. Makes some people who want to consume the good worse off

   c. Makes all producers worse off

3. Which of the following create deadweight loss? Which do not and are simply a transfer of surplus from one person to another? Explain your answer.

   a. You have been evicted from your rent-controlled apartment after the landlord discovered your pet boa constrictor. The apartment is quickly rented to someone else at the same price. You and the new renter do not necessarily have the same willingness to pay for the apartment.

   b. In a contest, you won a ticket to a concert. But you can't go because you have an exam the next day, and the terms of the contest do not allow you to sell the ticket or give it to someone else. Would your answer to this question change if you could not sell the ticket but could give it to someone else?

   c. Your school's dean of students, who is a proponent of a low-fat diet, decrees that ice cream can no longer be served on campus.

   d. Your ice-cream cone falls on the ground and your dog eats it. (Take the liberty of counting your dog as a member of society, and assume that, if it could, your dog would be willing to pay the same amount for the ice-cream cone as you.)

‖ Price Floors

Sometimes governments intervene to push market prices up instead of down. *Price floors* have been widely legislated for agricultural products, such as wheat and milk, as a way to support the incomes of farmers. Historically, there were also price floors—legally mandated minimum prices—on such services as trucking and air travel, although these were phased out by most governments in the 1970s.

   If you have ever worked in a fast-food restaurant, you are likely to have encountered a price floor: governments in Canada, the United States, and many other countries maintain a lower limit on the hourly wage rate of a worker's labour; that is, a floor on the price of labour called the **minimum wage.**

The **minimum wage** is a legal floor on the wage rate, which is the market price of labour.

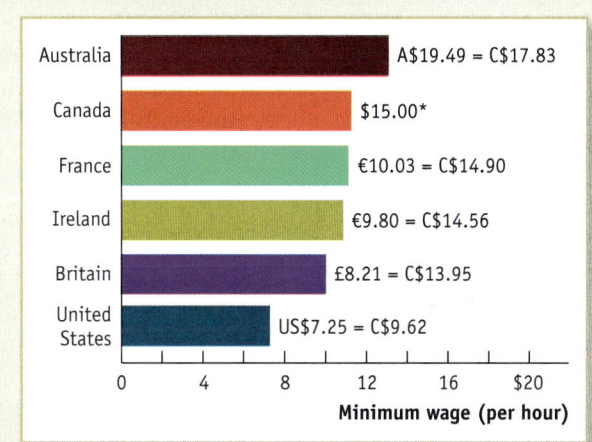

> ### 🌐 GLOBAL COMPARISON   CHECK OUT THE UNITED STATES' LOW, LOW WAGES!
>
> The minimum wage rate in Canada, as you can see in this graph, is actually quite high compared with that in other rich countries. Since minimum wages are set in national currency—the British minimum wage is set in British pounds, the French minimum wage is set in euros, and so on—the comparison depends on the exchange rate on any given day. As of 2019, Australia had a minimum wage nearly twice as high as the U.S. rate, with France, Canada, and Ireland not far behind.
>
> You can see one effect of this difference in the supermarket checkout line. In the United States, there is usually someone to bag your groceries—someone typically paid the minimum wage or at best, slightly more. In Canada and Europe, where hiring a bagger is a lot more expensive, you're almost always expected to do the bagging yourself.
>
> *Data from:* Organization for Economic Cooperation and Development (OECD).
> *The Canadian minimum wage varies by province from $11.32 in Saskatchewan to $15 in Alberta.

FIGURE 5-5 The Market for Butter in the Absence of Government Controls

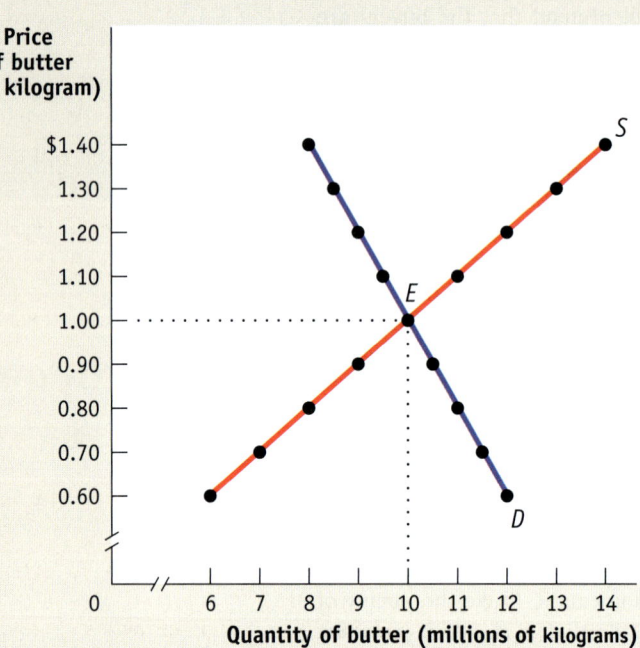

Price of butter (per kilogram)	Quantity of butter (millions of kilograms)	
	Quantity demanded	Quantity supplied
$1.40	8.0	14.0
1.30	8.5	13.0
1.20	9.0	12.0
1.10	9.5	11.0
1.00	10.0	10.0
0.90	10.5	9.0
0.80	11.0	8.0
0.70	11.5	7.0
0.60	12.0	6.0

Without government intervention, the market for butter reaches equilibrium at a price of $1 per kilogram with 10 million kilograms of butter bought and sold.

Just like price ceilings, price floors are intended to help some people but generate predictable and undesirable side effects. Figure 5-5 shows hypothetical supply and demand curves for butter. Left to itself, the market would move to equilibrium at point *E,* with 10 million kilograms of butter bought and sold at a price of $1 per kilogram.

Now suppose that the government, in order to help dairy farmers, imposes a price floor on butter of $1.20 per kilogram. Its effects are shown in Figure 5-6, where the line at $1.20 represents the price floor. At a price of $1.20 per kilogram, producers would want to supply 12 million kilograms (point *B* on the supply curve) but consumers would want to buy only 9 million kilograms (point *A* on the demand curve). So the price floor leads to a persistent surplus of 3 million kilograms of butter.

Does a price floor always lead to an unwanted surplus? No. Just as in the case of a price ceiling, the floor may not be binding—that is, it may be irrelevant. If the equilibrium price of butter is $1 per kilogram but the floor is set at only $0.80, the floor has no effect.

But suppose that a price floor is binding: what happens to the unwanted surplus? The answer depends on government policy. In the case of agricultural price floors, governments buy up unwanted surplus. As a result, the government, for example, has at times found itself warehousing thousands of tons of butter, cheese, and other farm products. The government then has to find a way to dispose of these unwanted goods.

Some countries pay exporters to sell products at a loss overseas; this is standard procedure for the European Union. Sometimes Canada gives surplus food away as foreign aid to less-developed countries. In some cases, governments have actually destroyed the surplus production.

When the government is not prepared to purchase the unwanted surplus, a price floor means that would-be sellers cannot find buyers. This is what happens

FIGURE 5-6 The Effects of a Price Floor

The black horizontal line represents the government-imposed price floor of $1.20 per kilogram of butter. The quantity of butter demanded falls to 9 million kilograms, and the quantity supplied rises to 12 million kilograms, generating a persistent surplus of 3 million kilograms of butter.

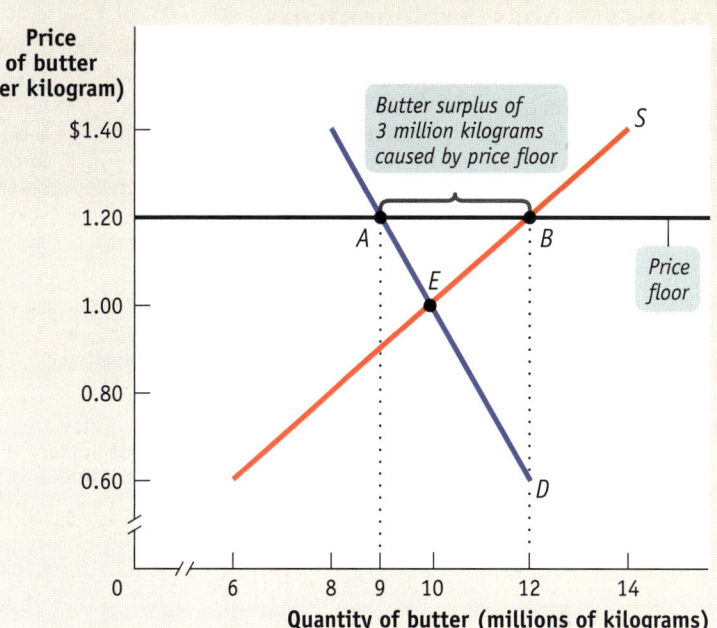

when there is a price floor on the wage rate paid for an hour of labour, the minimum wage: when the minimum wage is above the equilibrium wage rate, some people who are willing to work—that is, sell labour—cannot find buyers—that is, employers—willing to give them jobs.

How a Price Floor Causes Inefficiency

The persistent surplus that results from a price floor creates missed opportunities—inefficiencies—that resemble those created by the shortage that results from a price ceiling. Like a price ceiling, a price floor creates inefficiency in at least four ways:

1. It creates deadweight loss by reducing the quantity transacted to below the efficient level.
2. It leads to an inefficient allocation of sales among sellers.
3. It leads to a waste of resources.
4. It leads to sellers providing an inefficiently high-quality level.

In addition to inefficiency, like a price ceiling, a price floor leads to illegal behaviour as people break the law to sell below the legal price.

Inefficiently Low Quantity Because a price floor raises the price of a good to consumers, it reduces the quantity of that good demanded; because sellers can't sell more units of a good than buyers are willing to buy, a price floor reduces the quantity of a good bought and sold below the market equilibrium quantity and leads to a deadweight loss. Notice that this is the *same* effect as a price ceiling. You might be tempted to think that a price floor and a price ceiling have opposite effects, but both have the effect of reducing the quantity of a good bought and sold (see the accompanying Pitfalls).

Since the equilibrium of an efficient market maximizes the sum of consumer and producer surplus, a price floor that reduces the quantity below the equilibrium quantity reduces total surplus. Figure 5-7 shows the implications for total

PITFALLS

CEILINGS, FLOORS, AND QUANTITIES

A price ceiling pushes the price of a good *down*. A price floor pushes the price of a good *up*. So it's easy to assume that the effects of a price floor are the opposite of the effects of a price ceiling. In particular, if a price ceiling reduces the quantity of a good bought and sold, doesn't a price floor increase the quantity?

No, it doesn't. In fact, both floors and ceilings reduce the quantity bought and sold. Why? When the quantity of a good supplied isn't equal to the quantity demanded, the actual quantity sold is determined by the "short side" of the market—whichever quantity is less. If sellers don't want to sell as much as buyers want to buy, it's the sellers who determine the actual quantity sold, because buyers can't force unwilling sellers to sell. If buyers don't want to buy as much as sellers want to sell, it's the buyers who determine the actual quantity sold, because sellers can't force unwilling buyers to buy.

FIGURE 5-7 A Price Floor Causes Inefficiently Low Quantity

A price floor reduces the quantity demanded below the market equilibrium quantity and leads to a deadweight loss.

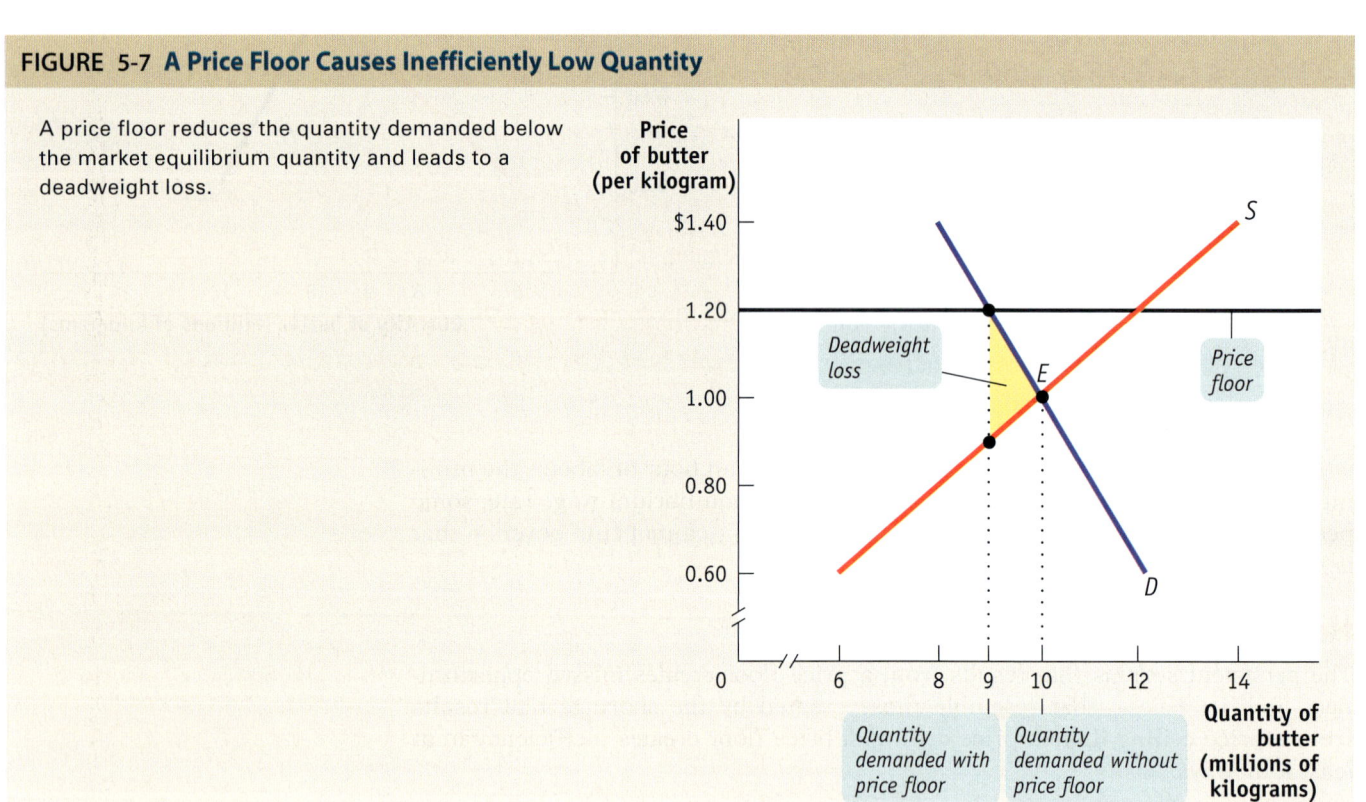

---

surplus of a price floor on the price of butter. Total surplus is the sum of the area above the supply curve and below the demand curve.

By reducing the quantity of butter sold, a price floor causes a deadweight loss equal to the area of the shaded triangle in the figure. As in the case of a price ceiling, however, deadweight loss is only one of the forms of inefficiency that the price control creates.

Inefficient Allocation of Sales Among Sellers Like a price ceiling, a price floor can lead to *inefficient allocation*—in this case, an **inefficient allocation of sales among sellers:** sellers who are willing to sell at the lowest price are unable to make sales, while sales go to sellers who are only willing to sell at a higher price.

One example of the inefficient allocation of selling opportunities caused by a price floor is the "two-tier" labour market found in many European countries that emerged in the 1980s and persists to this day. A high minimum wage led to a two-tier labour system, composed of the fortunate who had good jobs in the formal labour market, and the rest who were locked out without any prospect of ever finding a good job.

Price floors can lead to **inefficient allocation of sales among sellers:** sellers who are willing to sell at the lowest price are unable to make sales, while sales go to sellers who are only willing to sell at a higher price.

Either unemployed or underemployed in dead-end jobs in the black market for labour, the unlucky ones are disproportionately young, from the ages of 18 to early 30s. Although eager for good jobs in the formal sector and willing to accept less than the minimum wage—that is, willing to sell their labour for a lower price—it is illegal for employers to pay them less than the minimum wage. For example, in 2019, unemployment for young Italian workers stood at nearly 20%.

The inefficiency of unemployment and underemployment is compounded as generations of young people are unable to get adequate job training, develop careers, and save for their future. These young people are also more likely to engage in crime. The worst hit countries—such as Greece, Spain, Italy, and France—have seen many of their best and brightest young people emigrate, leading to a permanent reduction in the future performance of their economies.

Wasted Resources Also like a price ceiling, a price floor generates inefficiency by *wasting resources*. The most graphic examples involve government purchases of the unwanted surpluses of agricultural products caused by price floors. The surplus production is sometimes destroyed, which is pure waste; in other cases, the stored produce goes, as officials euphemistically put it, "out of condition" and must be thrown away.

Price floors also lead to wasted time and effort. Consider the minimum wage. Would-be workers who spend many hours searching for jobs, or waiting in line in the hope of getting jobs, play the same role in the case of price floors as hapless families searching for apartments in the case of price ceilings.

Inefficiently High Quality Again like price ceilings, price floors lead to inefficiency in the quality of goods produced.

We saw that when there is a price ceiling, suppliers produce products that are of inefficiently low quality: buyers prefer higher-quality products and are willing to pay for them, but sellers refuse to improve the quality of their products because the price ceiling prevents their being compensated for doing so. This same logic applies to price floors, but in reverse: suppliers offer goods of **inefficiently high quality.**

How can this be? Isn't high quality a good thing? Yes, but only if it is worth the cost. Suppose that suppliers spend a lot to make goods of very high quality but that this quality isn't worth much to consumers, who would rather receive the money spent on that quality in the form of a lower price. This represents a missed opportunity: suppliers and buyers could make a mutually beneficial deal in which buyers got goods of lower quality for a much lower price.

A good example of the inefficiency of excessive quality comes from the days when transatlantic airfares were set artificially high by international treaty. Forbidden to compete for customers by offering lower ticket prices, airlines instead offered expensive services, like lavish in-flight meals that went largely uneaten—an especially wasteful practice, considering that what passengers really wanted was less food and lower airfares.

Since the deregulation of North American airlines in the 1970s, Canadian passengers have experienced a large decrease in ticket prices accompanied by a decrease in the quality of in-flight service—smaller seats, lower-quality food, and so on. Everyone complains about the service—but thanks to lower fares, the number of people flying on Canadian carriers has grown over 400% since airline deregulation.

Illegal Activity In addition to the four inefficiencies we analyzed, like price ceilings, price floors provide incentives for illegal activity. For example, in countries where the minimum wage is far above the equilibrium wage rate, workers desperate for jobs sometimes agree to work off the books for employers who conceal their employment from the government—or bribe the government inspectors. This practice, known in Europe as *black labour,* is especially common in Southern European countries such as Italy and Spain.

Price floors often lead to inefficiency in that goods of **inefficiently high quality** are offered: sellers offer high-quality goods at a high price, even though buyers would prefer a lower quality at a lower price.

So Why Are There Price Floors?

To sum up, a price floor creates various negative side effects:

- A persistent surplus of the good
- Inefficiency arising from the persistent surplus in the form of inefficiently low quantity (deadweight loss), inefficient allocation of sales among sellers, wasted resources, and an inefficiently high level of quality offered by suppliers
- The temptation to engage in illegal activity, particularly bribery and corruption of government officials

So why do governments impose price floors when they have so many negative side effects? The reasons are similar to those for imposing price ceilings. Government officials often disregard warnings about the consequences of price floors either because they believe that the relevant market is poorly described by the supply and demand model or, more often, because they do not understand the model. Above all, just as price ceilings are often imposed because they benefit some influential buyers of a good, price floors are often imposed because they benefit some influential sellers.

ECONOMICS >> *in Action*
The Rise and Fall of the Unpaid Intern

Aaron Bacall/www.Cartoonstock.com

"We have an opening for a part-time unpaid intern, which could lead to a full-time unpaid internship."

The best-known example of a price floor is the minimum wage. Most economists believe, however, that the minimum wage has relatively little effect on the overall job market in Canada and the United States, mainly because the floor is set so low. In the 1960s, the minimum wage was more than half the average wage of Canadian blue-collar workers; by 2015, the number had fallen to 44% (compared to about 30% in the United States). In fact, about 10% of all Canadian workers are paid the minimum wage. However, there is one sector of these job markets where it appears that the minimum wage can indeed be binding: the market for interns.

Starting in 2011, a spate of lawsuits in the United States brought by former unpaid interns claiming they were cheated out of wages brought the matter to public attention. A common thread in these complaints was that interns were assigned grunt work with no educational value, such as tracking lost cell phones. In other cases, unpaid interns complained that they were given the work of full-salaried employees. And by 2015, many of those lawsuits proved successful: Condé Nast Publications settled for US$5.8 million, Sirius SatelliteXM Radio settled for US$1.3 million, and Viacom Media settled for US$7.2 million. Even the Olsen twins had to cough up US$140,000 in payments to unpaid interns for their fashion company, Dualstar Entertainment, in 2017.

As a result, in 2018 the U.S. Department of Labor issued new rules stating that unless their programs can clearly demonstrate an educational component such as course credit, companies have to pay their interns minimum wage or shut down their programs altogether. Even though few similar lawsuits in Canada have been successful, governments here have moved to adopt and enforce the same kind of rules limiting unpaid internships to educational training situations. All other interns are considered employees guaranteeing them at least the minimum wage.

Some observers worry that the end of the unpaid internship means that programs that once offered valuable training will be lost. But as one American lawyer commented, "The law says that when you work, you have to get paid [at least the minimum wage]."

>> *Check Your Understanding* 5-2

Solutions appear at back of book.

1. The provincial legislature mandates a price floor for gasoline of P_F per litre. Assess the following statements and illustrate your answer using the figure provided.

   a. Proponents of the law claim it will increase the income of gas station owners. Opponents claim it will hurt gas station owners because they will lose customers.

   b. Proponents claim consumers will be better off because gas stations will provide better service. Opponents claim consumers will be generally worse off because they prefer to buy gas at cheaper prices.

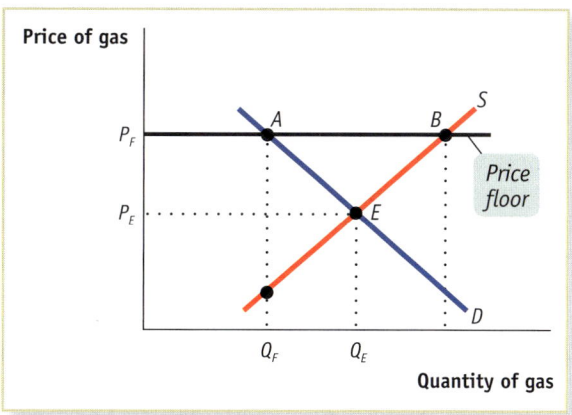

   c. Proponents claim that they are helping gas station owners without hurting anyone else. Opponents claim that consumers are hurt and will end up doing things like buying gas in a nearby province, on the black market, and even over the border in the United States.

>> *Quick Review*

• The most familiar price floor is the **minimum wage.** Price floors are also commonly imposed on agricultural goods.

• A price floor above the equilibrium price benefits successful sellers but causes predictable adverse effects such as a persistent surplus, which leads to four kinds of inefficiencies: deadweight loss from inefficiently low quantity, **inefficient allocation of sales among sellers,** wasted resources, and **inefficiently high quality.**

• Price floors encourage illegal activity, such as workers who work off the books, often leading to official corruption.

‖ Controlling Quantities

In Toronto, standard taxi licences come in the form of a special numbered plate that must be affixed to the cab. Fifteen hundred of these standard taxi licences were issued in 1953. Over time, the taxi licencing rules were changed first to allow these licences to be sold on the open market—making them a capital asset for the licence holder, rather than the issuer. Later, the leasing of taxi licences was allowed. The limited supply of licences coupled with the transferability and leasing options resulted in the market price of a taxi plate rising significantly while encouraging the decline in taxicab quality. Many plate owners leased out their licences, rather than drive their own cab. These owners sought to maximize their leasing revenues by setting lease fees as a high percentage of the driver's revenue, which encouraged drivers to keep operating costs as low as possible. Of course, low operating costs meant that cab maintenance was minimized and replacement of the cars was usually delayed as long as legally permitted. Many customers complained about cars in bad or unsafe condition operated by overworked, stressed-out drivers.

In 1998, the city decided to introduce a new class of licence with the sale of 1,400 new Ambassador taxi licences, and going forward, no new standard licences would ever be issued. Unlike a standard licence, Ambassador licences can't be sold, leased, or otherwise transferred—licence holders are the owner and operator of the taxi—and the licence remains the property of the city. The aim was to allow these drivers to be entrepreneurs who cared about the quality of their car since they couldn't lease from some other party—so if everything worked as intended quality in the market would rise. By 2018, there were about 5,500 taxi licences in Toronto of both types.

Yet restrictions on the number of taxis induced people to try to circumvent them, eventually leading to the emergence of mobile-app-based car services like Uber and Lyft. Their cars aren't hailed from the street like taxis—in fact, their drivers are forbidden from picking up riders from the street. Instead, riders arrange trips on their smartphones, directing available drivers to their location. Of course, the ubiquity of smartphones also contributed to the emergence of these car services.

A **quantity control,** or **quota,** is an upper limit on the quantity of some good that can be bought or sold. The total amount of the good that can be legally transacted is the **quota limit.**

A **licence** gives its owner the right to supply a good.

The entrance of Uber in 2013 and Lyft four years later have fundamentally altered the market for car rides in Toronto and most other major cities. But let's postpone the discussion of those effects until we learn more about how the market worked when only licenced taxicabs could operate.

A taxi licence is a form of **quantity control,** or **quota,** by which the government regulates the quantity of a good that can be bought and sold rather than the price at which it is transacted. It is another way that government intervenes in markets along with price ceilings and price floors. The total amount of the good that can be transacted under the quantity control is called the **quota limit.** Typically, the government limits quantity in a market by issuing **licences;** only people with a licence can legally supply the good.

The city government of Toronto limited the number of taxi rides that can be sold by limiting the number of taxis to only those who hold licence. More generally, quantity controls, or quotas, set an upper limit on the quantity of a good that can be transacted. For example, quotas have been used frequently to limit the size of the catch of endangered fish stocks. In this case, quotas are implemented for good economic reasons: to protect endangered fish stocks.

But some quotas are implemented for bad economic reasons, typically for the purpose of enriching the quota holder. For example, quantity controls introduced to address a temporary problem such as assuring that only safe and clean taxis are allowed to operate, become difficult to remove later, once the problem has disappeared, because quota holders benefit from them and exert political pressure.

The Anatomy of Quantity Controls

Before the arrival of Uber and Lyft, a Toronto taxi licence was worth a lot of money—averaging several hundred thousand dollars. To understand why a Toronto taxi licence was worth so much money in those days, we consider a simplified version of the market for taxi rides, shown in Figure 5-8. Just as we assumed in the analysis of rent control that all apartments are the same, we now

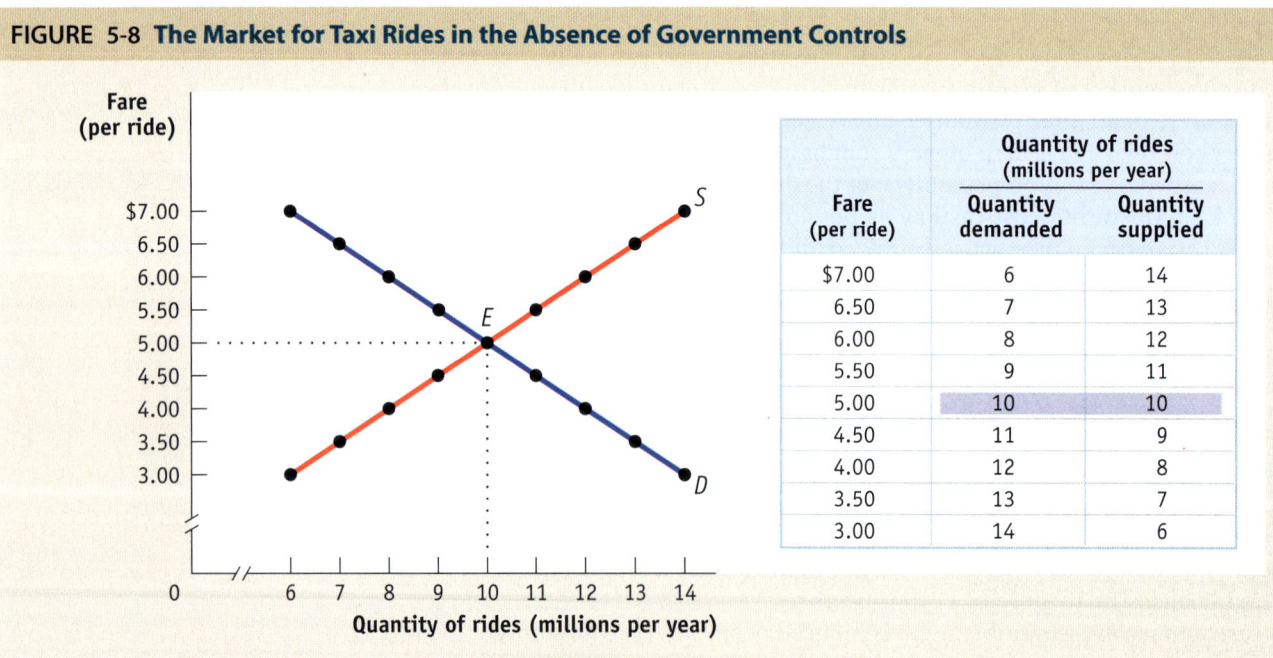

FIGURE 5-8 The Market for Taxi Rides in the Absence of Government Controls

Fare (per ride)	Quantity of rides (millions per year)	
	Quantity demanded	Quantity supplied
$7.00	6	14
6.50	7	13
6.00	8	12
5.50	9	11
5.00	10	10
4.50	11	9
4.00	12	8
3.50	13	7
3.00	14	6

Without government intervention, the market reaches equilibrium with 10 million rides taken per year at a fare of $5 per ride.

suppose that all taxi rides are the same—ignoring the real-world complication that some taxi rides are longer, and so more expensive, than others.

The table in the figure shows supply and demand schedules. The equilibrium—indicated by point *E* in the figure and by the shaded entries in the table—is a fare of $5 per ride, with 10 million rides taken per year. (You'll see in a minute why we present the equilibrium this way.)

In this example, the Toronto licence system limits the number of taxis, but each taxi driver can offer as many rides as they can manage. To simplify our analysis, however, we will assume that a licence system limits the number of taxi rides that can legally be given to 8 million per year.

Until now, we have derived the demand curve by answering questions of the form: "How many taxi rides will passengers want to take if the price is $5 per ride?" But it is possible to reverse the question and ask instead: "At what price will consumers want to buy 10 million rides per year?" The price at which consumers want to buy a given quantity—in this case, 10 million rides at $5 per ride—is the **demand price** of that quantity. You can see from the demand schedule in Figure 5-8 that the demand price of 6 million rides is $7 per ride, the demand price of 7 million rides is $6.50 per ride, and so on.

Similarly, the supply curve represents the answer to questions of the form: "How many taxi rides would taxi drivers supply at a price of $5 each?" But we can also reverse this question to ask: "At what price will suppliers be willing to supply 10 million rides per year?" The price at which suppliers will supply a given quantity—in this case, 10 million rides at $5 per ride—is the **supply price** of that quantity. We can see from the supply schedule in Figure 5-8 that the supply price of 6 million rides is $3 per ride, the supply price of 7 million rides is $3.50 per ride, and so on.

Now we are ready to analyze a quota. We have assumed that the city government limits the quantity of taxi rides to 8 million per year. Licences, each of which carries the right to provide a certain number of taxi rides per year, are made available to selected people in such a way that a total of 8 million rides will be provided. Licence-holders may then either drive their own taxis or rent their licences to others for a fee.

Figure 5-9 shows the resulting market for taxi rides, with the black vertical line at 8 million rides per year representing the quota limit. Because the quantity of rides is limited to 8 million, consumers must be at point *A* on the demand curve, corresponding to the shaded entry in the demand schedule: the demand price of 8 million rides is $6 per ride. Meanwhile, taxi drivers must be at point *B* on the supply curve, corresponding to the shaded entry in the supply schedule: the supply price of 8 million rides is $4 per ride.

But how can the price received by taxi drivers be $4 when the price paid by taxi riders is $6? The answer is that in addition to the market in taxi rides, there is also a market in licences. Licence-holders may not always want to drive their taxis: they may be ill or on vacation. Those who do not want to drive their own taxis will sell the right to use the licence to someone else.

So we need to consider two sets of transactions here, and so two prices: (1) the transactions in taxi rides and the price at which these will occur, and (2) the transactions in licences and the price at which these will occur. It turns out that since we are looking at two markets, the $4 and $6 prices will both be right.

To see how this all works, consider two imaginary Toronto taxi drivers, Ali and Jean. Ali has a licence but can't use it because he's recovering from a severely sprained wrist. So he's looking to rent his licence out to someone else. Jean doesn't have a licence but would like to rent one. Furthermore, at any point in time there are many other people like Jean who would like to rent a licence. Suppose Ali agrees to rent his licence to Jean. To make things simple, assume that any driver can give only one ride per day and that Ali is renting his licence to Jean for one day. What rental price will they agree on?

The **demand price** of a given quantity is the price at which consumers will demand that quantity.

The **supply price** of a given quantity is the price at which producers will supply that quantity.

FIGURE 5-9 Effect of a Quota on the Market for Taxi Rides

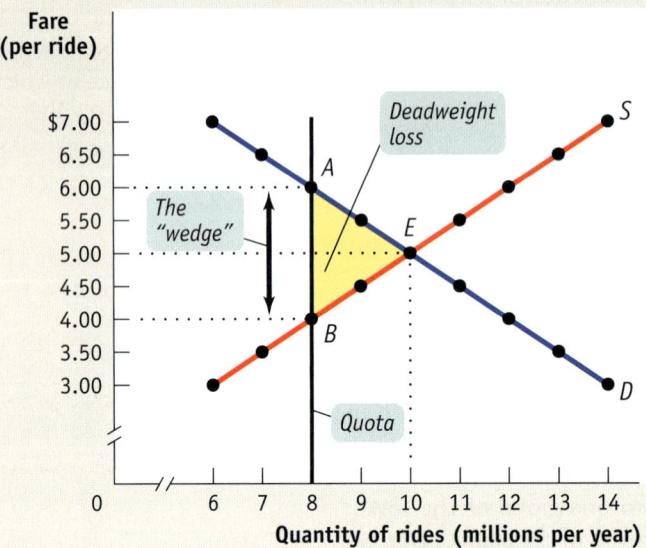

Fare (per ride)	Quantity of rides (millions per year)	
	Quantity demanded	Quantity supplied
$7.00	6	14
6.50	7	13
6.00	8	12
5.50	9	11
5.00	10	10
4.50	11	9
4.00	12	8
3.50	13	7
3.00	14	6

The table shows the demand price and the supply price corresponding to each quantity: the price at which that quantity would be demanded and supplied, respectively. The city government imposes a quota of 8 million rides by selling licences for only 8 million rides, represented by the black vertical line. The price paid by consumers rises to $6 per ride, the demand price of 8 million rides, shown by point A.

The supply price of 8 million rides is only $4 per ride, shown by point B. The difference between these two prices is the quota rent per ride, the earnings that accrue to the owner of a licence. The quota rent drives a wedge between the demand price and the supply price. And since the quota discourages mutually beneficial transactions, it creates a deadweight loss equal to the shaded triangle.

A quantity control, or quota, drives a **wedge** between the demand price and the supply price of a good; that is, the price paid by buyers ends up being higher than that received by sellers.

The difference between the demand and supply price at the quota limit is the **quota rent,** the earnings that accrue to the licence-holder from ownership of the right to sell the good. It is equal to the market price of the licence when the licences are traded.

To answer this question, we need to look at the transactions from the viewpoints of both drivers. Once she has the licence, Jean knows she can make $6 per day—the demand price of a ride under the quota. And she is willing to rent the licence only if she makes at least $4 per day—the supply price of a ride under the quota. So Ali cannot demand a rent of more than $2—the difference between $6 and $4. And if Jean offered Ali less than $2—say, $1.50—there would be other eager drivers willing to offer him more, up to $2. So, in order to get the licence, Jean must offer Ali at least $2. Since the rent can be no more than $2 and no less than $2, it must be exactly $2.

It is no coincidence that $2 is exactly the difference between $6, the demand price of 8 million rides, and $4, the supply price of 8 million rides. In every case in which the supply of a good is legally restricted, there is a **wedge** between the demand price of the quantity transacted and the supply price of the quantity transacted.

This wedge, illustrated by the double-headed arrow in Figure 5-9, has a special name: the **quota rent.** It is the earnings that accrue to the licence-holder from ownership of a valuable commodity, the licence. In the case of Ali and Jean, the quota rent of $2 goes to Ali because he owns the licence, and the remaining $4 from the total fare of $6 goes to Jean.

Figure 5-9 also illustrates the quota rent in the market for Toronto taxi rides. The quota limits the quantity of rides to 8 million per year, a quantity at which the demand price of $6 exceeds the supply price of $4. The wedge between these two prices, $2, is the quota rent that results from the restrictions placed on the quantity of taxi rides in this market.

But wait a second. What if Ali doesn't rent out his licence? What if he uses it himself? Doesn't this mean that he gets a price of $6? No, not really. Even if Ali doesn't rent out his licence, he could have rented it out, which means that the licence has an *opportunity cost* of $2: if Ali decides to use his own licence and drive his own taxi rather than renting his licence to Jean, the $2 represents his opportunity cost of not renting out his licence. That is, the $2 quota rent is now the rental income he forgoes by driving his own taxi.

In effect, Ali is in two businesses—the taxi-driving business and the licence-renting business. He makes $4 per ride from driving his taxi and $2 per ride from renting out his licence. It doesn't make any difference that in this particular case he has rented his licence to himself! So under quantity controls, the licence is a valuable asset regardless of whether the licence owner uses it or rents it out to others. In 2013, before the rise of Uber and Lyft eliminated the quantity control, Toronto taxi licences sold for about $360,000, and a Vancouver taxi licence could sell for over $800,000. Notice, by the way, that quotas—like price ceilings and price floors—don't always have a real effect. If the quota were set at 12 million rides—that is, above the equilibrium quantity in an unregulated market—it would have no effect because it would not be binding.

The Costs of Quantity Controls

Like price controls, quantity controls can have some predictable and undesirable side effects. The first is the by-now-familiar problem of inefficiency due to missed opportunities: quantity controls create deadweight loss by preventing mutually beneficial transactions from occurring, transactions that would benefit both buyers and sellers.

Looking back at Figure 5-9, you can see that starting at the quota limit of 8 million rides, Torontonians would be willing to pay at least $5.50 per ride when 9 million rides are offered, 1 million more than the quota, and that taxi drivers would be willing to provide those rides as long as they got at least $4.50 per ride. These are rides that would have taken place if there were no quota limit.

The same is true for the next 1 million rides: Torontonians would be willing to pay at least $5 per ride when the quantity of rides is increased from 9 to 10 million, and taxi drivers would be willing to provide those rides as long as they got at least $5 per ride. Again, these rides would have occurred without the quota limit.

Only when the market has reached the unregulated market equilibrium quantity of 10 million rides are there no "missed-opportunity rides." The quota limit of 8 million rides has caused 2 million "missed-opportunity rides."

Generally, *as long as the demand price of a given quantity exceeds the supply price, there is a deadweight loss.* A buyer would be willing to buy the good at a price that the seller would be willing to accept, but such a transaction does not occur because it is forbidden by the quota. The deadweight loss arising from the 2 million in missed-opportunity rides is represented by the shaded triangle in Figure 5-9.

And because there are transactions that people would like to make but are not allowed to, quantity controls generate an incentive to circumvent them. In the days before Uber and Lyft, a substantial number of unlicenced taxis simply defied the law and picked up passengers without a licence. These unregulated, unlicenced taxis contributed to a disproportionately large share of accidents.

However, Uber and Lyft cars legally circumvent the restriction that a car without a licence can't be hailed from the street. According to the City of Toronto, as of June 2019, there were about 90,000 ride-hailing drivers working in the city (most of them work for Uber and Lyft), significantly more than 12,000 licenced taxi drivers.

Clearly, the quantity restriction on taxicabs has been substantially undermined. In effect, the quota line in Figure 5-9 has shifted rightward, closer to the equilibrium quantity, with the entry of Uber and Lyft.

In the past few years, as quota rents to owners of a taxi licence have fallen, the prices of taxi licences have fallen significantly as well. In 2018, prices for Toronto taxi licences dropped to about $33,000, a steep fall from the $336,000 pricetag five years earlier. In sum, quantity controls typically create the following undesirable side effects:

- Deadweight loss because some mutually beneficial transactions don't occur
- Incentives for illegal activities

ECONOMICS >> *in Action*
The Lobsters of Atlantic Canada

Forget the various finned species of fish, when it comes to Canada's fisheries sector, lobster truly is the "King of Seafood." This industry employs thousands of people in New Brunswick, Newfoundland and Labrador, Nova Scotia, Prince Edward Island, and Québec, and contributed more than $2.5 billion in export sales in 2019. According to the federal government, our lobsters are exported to more than 50 countries worldwide and are one of the exports most closely associated with Canada.

But all is not well in this fishery; it has experienced ups and downs. While the number of lobster fishing licences is limited, the fishery has been hit by several negative shocks in recent years. First, usually about 80% of Canadian lobster exports go to the United States, but demand there has softened since its economy experienced a recession starting in 2007. This situation is worsened by the appreciation of the Canadian dollar against the U.S. dollar at that time, which put additional downward pressure on the value of Canadian exports. At the same time, landings of lobster in Atlantic Canada and the United States (mostly in the state of Maine) have risen almost 50% in the past 12 years. Catches in 2012 and 2013 were described as the best seen in years.

So demand is down and supply is up, together these have resulted in the prices plummeting from about $8 per pound in 2005 to about $4 per pound in 2013. Low prices hurt more than just fishers who have difficulty in covering their expenses when prices were so low; it also affected other parts of the economy. When the fishers are barely or just making enough to cover their costs, they are going to keep going with what they have and will reduce spending on replacing their boats and equipment and on other goods and services. Thus, low lobster prices will have an effect on everybody in the community whether they are car dealers, boat builders, restaurant owners, or others.

All Canada Photos/Alamy

The limited number of lobster fishing licences protects the lobster population and the economic lives of lobster fishers.

Of course, limiting the number of lobster-fishing licences is a form of a quota, as under current rules, each owner-operator is allotted a certain number of traps. But unfortunately, with low demand and high supply between 2007 and 2013, this quota has become a non-binding constraint. As a result, the price of lobster is not supported above the current low level that occurs at the intersection of the supply and demand curves.

The continuation of such low prices has led to calls for the introduction of either new rules that would effectively lower the quota or measures geared towards finding additional demand in other markets at home or abroad, so as to help raise the price of lobster. One way the government has reacted to this situation is via the Atlantic Lobster Sustainability Measures Program, which is buying back and retiring about 600 lobster-fishing licences. This measure removed more than 200,000 traps from the water by March 2014.

In the coming years, Canadian lobster fishers have finally caught a break as the price of lobster seems to have bottomed out over the past few years. Contributing factors included a stronger and growing demand for lobster from Asian countries (China in particular), the depreciation of the Canadian dollar, and the levelling off of the lobster harvest (partly due to the reduction of the number of fishing licences). With a growing demand and a reduction in supply, it was not surprising to see the lobster price rise, reaching record highs. Unfortunately, the coronavirus pandemic in early 2020 hit the industry hard. With travel restrictions and lockdowns in place, the demand for lobster dropped dramatically in China. Fishers saw the shore price, or price paid to lobster fishers for their catch, fall from $10.50 per pound to $8 per pound in February 2020. Lockdowns then began spreading to other parts of the world to fight the spread of the virus, so this downward trend is expected to continue. Once again, the quota might become a non-binding one.

Notice, by the way, that this is an example of a proposed quota that is probably justified by broader economic and environmental considerations—unlike the taxicab quota, which has long since lost any economic rationale. Still, whatever its rationale, the proposed Atlantic Canada lobster quota would work the same way as any other quota.

Once the quota system is established with a binding quota, then many boat owners will stop fishing for lobsters. They will realize that rather than operating a boat, it is more profitable to sell or rent their licences to someone else. The value of a licence required to fish for lobsters will easily be worth more than the boat itself.

>> Check Your Understanding 5-3

Solutions appear at back of book.

1. Suppose that the supply and demand for taxi rides is given by Figure 5-8 but the quota is set at 6 million rides instead of 8 million. Find the following and indicate them on Figure 5-8.
   a. The price of a ride
   b. The quota rent
   c. The deadweight loss
   d. Suppose the quota limit on taxi rides is increased to 9 million. What happens to the quota rent? To the deadweight loss?
2. Assume that the quota limit is 8 million rides. Suppose demand decreases due to a decline in tourism. What is the smallest parallel leftward shift in demand that would result in the quota no longer having an effect on the market? Illustrate your answer using Figure 5-8.

>> Quick Review

• **Quantity controls,** or **quotas,** are government-imposed limits on how much of a good may be bought or sold. The quantity allowed for sale is the **quota limit.** The government then issues a **licence** — the right to sell a given quantity of a good under the quota.

• When the quota limit is smaller than the equilibrium quantity in an unregulated market, the **demand price** is higher than the **supply price** — there is a **wedge** between them at the quota limit.

• This wedge is the **quota rent,** the earnings that accrue to the licence-holder from ownership of the right to sell the good — whether by actually supplying the good or by renting the licence to someone else. The market price of a licence equals the quota rent.

• Like price controls, quantity controls create deadweight loss and encourage illegal activity.

A Market Disruptor Gets Disrupted by the Market

Michael Nagle/Bloomberg/Getty Images

August 8, 2019, was a grim day at the San Francisco headquarters of Uber, the global leader in ride-hailing companies. That day it announced a staggering loss of US$5.2 billion in just the previous 3 months. This was in addition to the loss of more than US$1 billion in the first quarter of the year. Equally ominous was news of a significant drop in the annual growth rate in the number of rides provided. These results led some observers to question the company's long-term viability.

For a company that had been the darling of the high-tech business world, this day was a spectacular humbling. Investors had believed that only one company—namely Uber—would come to dominate the ride-hailing industry, ultimately making it very profitable. What had gone so wrong?

Uber was the brainchild of two friends, Travis Kalanick and Garret Camp, conceived after a difficult search for a taxi in Paris. When it launched in 2010 in San Francisco, Uber was the first company to enable ride hailing via a smartphone app. It provided easy access to lower-priced cab rides. Uber expanded rapidly, eventually extending its reach to over 600 cities worldwide. The company focused, in particular, on expansion in cities where the existing taxi market was highly regulated and restricted. Ridership grew explosively, so that by 2019 Uber was completing nearly 14 million rides each day.

But Uber's success did not go unnoticed. Seeing the opportunity to make money, some people wanted to become Uber drivers, while others wanted to start up rival companies. In 2012, for example, Lyft launched a competing service. In Latin America, China, and India, home-grown challengers emerged. Uber responded by rolling out costly initiatives. For example, to keep its ridership high, Uber began subsidizing rides—that is, it provided discount codes and coupons that lowered the price of rides below the actual cost of providing them.

Whether Uber can get back on track—turning its losses around, recapturing its high growth rates of the past, and fulfilling its early promise—remains to be seen.

QUESTIONS FOR THOUGHT

1. How did quantity controls for taxi rides contribute to Uber's high rates of growth in its early years?

2. Based on what you've learned in the chapter, explain whether Uber's recent difficulties were predictable or the result of bad luck.

3. How likely is it that Uber can regain its past high rates of growth?

4. How has the allocation of surplus changed in this market over time? Who benefited when Uber began competing with existing taxi companies? Who benefited when rival ride-hailing companies began competing with Uber?

SUMMARY

1. Even when a market is efficient, governments often intervene to pursue greater fairness or to please a powerful interest group. Interventions can take the form of **price controls** or quantity controls, both of which generate predictable and undesirable side effects consisting of various forms of inefficiency and illegal activity.

2. A **price ceiling,** a maximum market price below the equilibrium price, benefits successful buyers but creates persistent shortages. Because the price is maintained below the equilibrium price, the quantity demanded is increased and the quantity supplied is decreased compared to the equilibrium quantity. This leads to predictable problems: inefficiencies in the form of **deadweight loss** from inefficiently low quantity, **inefficient allocation to consumers, wasted resources,** and **inefficiently low quality.** It also encourages illegal activity as people turn to **black markets** to get the good. Because of these problems, price ceilings have generally lost favour as an economic policy tool. However, price ceilings can be justified when the market is inefficient or when a natural disaster leads to shortages that, if left to a free market, would greatly diminish equity and social welfare.

3. A **price floor,** a minimum market price above the equilibrium price, benefits successful sellers but creates persistent surplus. Because the price is maintained above the equilibrium price, the quantity demanded is decreased and the quantity supplied is increased compared to the equilibrium quantity. This leads to predictable problems: inefficiencies in the form of deadweight loss from inefficiently low quantity, **inefficient allocation of sales among sellers,** wasted resources, and **inefficiently high quality.** It also encourages illegal activity and black markets. The most well-known kind of price floor is the **minimum wage,** but price floors are also commonly applied to agricultural products.

4. **Quantity controls,** or **quotas,** limit the quantity of a good that can be bought or sold. The quantity allowed for sale is the **quota limit.** The government issues **licences** to individuals, the right to sell a given quantity of the good. The owner of a licence earns a **quota rent,** earnings that accrue from ownership of the right to sell the good. It is equal to the difference between the **demand price** at the quota limit, what consumers are willing to pay for that quantity, and the **supply price** at the quota limit, what suppliers are willing to accept for that quantity. Economists say that a quota drives a **wedge** between the demand price and the supply price; this wedge is equal to the quota rent. Quantity controls lead to deadweight loss in addition to encouraging illegal activity.

KEY TERMS

Price controls, p. 138
Price ceiling, p. 138
Price floor, p. 138
Deadweight loss, p. 141
Inefficient allocation to consumers, p. 142
Wasted resources, p. 142

Inefficiently low quality, p. 143
Black market, p. 143
Minimum wage, p. 147
Inefficient allocation of sales among sellers, p. 150
Inefficiently high quality, p. 151
Quantity control, p. 154

Quota, p. 154
Quota limit, p. 154
Licence, p. 154
Demand price, p. 155
Supply price, p. 155
Wedge, p. 156
Quota rent, p. 156

PRACTICE QUESTIONS

1. Suppose a city government is considering adopting legislation capping housing rents in the city. Explain how the proposed policy will affect landlords, renters, and the quality of rental units available.

2. In your province, the minimum wage is $14 per hour. Yet, you notice that many fast-food restaurants have posted help wanted signs for jobs paying $15 per hour. What does this tell you about the minimum wage and the availability of restaurant work in your town?

3. Many of British Columbia's residents and politicians are concerned about the declining salmon population,

a primary food source for local wildlife, including the endangered orca whale. To protect the salmon population from overfishing, politicians are considering two policies. The first is a binding price ceiling in the market for salmon. The second policy is a quota: permits would be sold to those who fish commercially in order to restrict their salmon catch. As events have unfolded, it's become clear that politicians tend to favour the quota system, while those who catch fish for a living prefer a price ceiling. Why do you think this is the case?

PROBLEMS

1. In order to ingratiate himself with voters, the mayor of Gotham City decides to lower the price of taxi rides. Assume, for simplicity, that all taxi rides are the same distance and therefore cost the same. The accompanying table shows the demand and supply schedules for taxi rides.

Fare (per ride)	Quantity of rides (millions per year)	
	Quantity demanded	Quantity supplied
$7.00	10	12
6.50	11	11
6.00	12	10
5.50	13	9
5.00	14	8
4.50	15	7

a. Assume that there are no restrictions on the number of taxi rides that can be supplied (there is no licence system). Find the equilibrium price and quantity.

b. Suppose that the mayor sets a price ceiling at $5.50. How large is the shortage of rides? Illustrate with a diagram. Who loses and who benefits from this policy?

c. Suppose that the stock market crashes and, as a result, people in Gotham City are poorer. This reduces the quantity of taxi rides demanded by 6 million rides per year at any given price. What effect will the mayor's new policy have now? Illustrate with a diagram.

d. Suppose that the stock market rises and the demand for taxi rides returns to normal (that is, returns to the demand schedule given in the table). The mayor now decides to ingratiate himself with taxi drivers. He announces a policy in which operating licences are given to existing taxi drivers; the number of licences is restricted such that only 10 million rides per year can be given. Illustrate the effect of this policy on the market, and indicate the resulting price and quantity transacted. What is the quota rent per ride?

2. In the mid-eighteenth century, the government of New France (modern-day Québec) controlled the price of bread, which was set at a predetermined price below the free market price.

a. Draw a diagram showing the effect of the policy. Did the policy act as a price ceiling or a price floor?

b. What kinds of inefficiencies were likely to have arisen when the controlled price of bread was above the market price? Explain in detail.

One year during this period, a poor wheat harvest caused a leftward shift in the supply of bread and therefore an increase in its market price. Montreal bakers found that the controlled price of bread in Montreal was below the market price.

c. Draw a diagram showing the effect of the price control on the market for bread during this one-year period. Did the policy act as a price ceiling or a price floor?

d. What kinds of inefficiencies do you think occurred during this period? Explain in detail.

3. The Canadian Dairy Commission (CDC) administers the price floor for butter, which was set at $8 per kilogram in 2018. At that price, according to data from the CDC, the quantity of butter supplied in 2018 was 154 million kilograms, and the quantity demanded was 124.4 million kilograms. To support the price of butter at the price floor, the CDC therefore had to buy up 33.6 million kilograms of butter. The accompanying diagram shows supply and demand curves illustrating the market for butter.

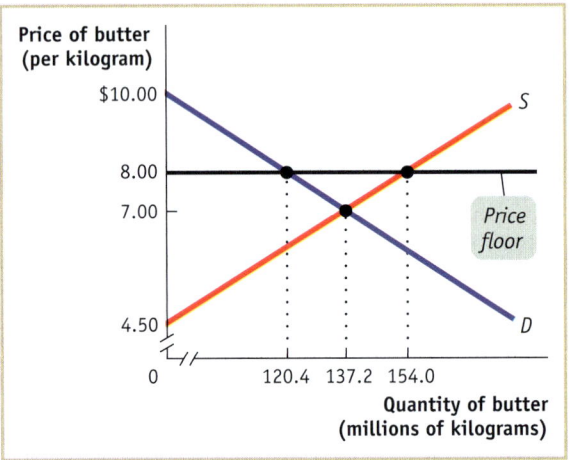

a. In the absence of a price floor, how much consumer surplus is created? How much producer surplus? What is the total surplus?

b. With the price floor at $8 per kilogram of butter, consumers buy 120.4 million kilograms of butter. How much consumer surplus is created now?

c. With the price floor at $8 per kilogram of butter, producers sell 154 million kilograms of butter (some to consumers and some to the CDC). How much producer surplus is created now?

d. How much money does the CDC spend on buying up surplus butter?

e. Suppose the federal government covers the cost of surplus butter using tax revenue, as they do in the United States. As a result, total surplus (producer plus consumer) is reduced by the amount the CDC spent on buying surplus butter. Using your answers for parts b–d, what is the total surplus when there is a price floor? How does this compare to the total surplus without a price floor from part a?

Note: In reality, with the help of provincial marketing boards, the CDC uses a number of supply management techniques to help ensure that it is not buying butter and ultimately destroying it. The CDC and the marketing boards set the price floor based on supplier costs so that suppliers can earn a fair rate of return and use production quotas to attempt to limit supply. The CDC buys and sells butter at the support price to eliminate seasonal price fluctuations; any surplus butter bought one year is sold in the following year when demand is firmer. This eliminates the need for the CDC to use government tax revenue to subsidize its buying activities. Part e of this question asks you to imagine that this is not how the CDC actually operates.

4. The accompanying table shows hypothetical demand and supply schedules for milk per year. The Canadian government decides that the incomes of dairy farmers should be maintained at a level that allows the traditional family dairy farm to survive. So it implements a price floor of $1 per pint by buying surplus milk until the market price is $1 per pint.

Price of milk (per pint)	Quantity of milk (millions of pints per year)	
	Quantity demanded	Quantity supplied
$1.20	550	850
1.10	600	800
1.00	650	750
0.90	700	700
0.80	750	650

a. In a diagram, show the deadweight loss from the inefficiently low quantity bought and sold.

b. How much surplus milk will be produced as a result of this policy?

c. What will be the cost to the government of this policy?

d. Since milk is an important source of protein and calcium, the government decides to provide the surplus milk it purchases to elementary schools at a price of only $0.60 per pint. Assume that schools will buy any amount of milk available at this low price. But parents now reduce their purchases of milk at any price by 50 million pints per year because they know their children are getting milk at school. How much will the dairy program now cost the government?

e. Explain how inefficiencies in the form of inefficient allocation to sellers and wasted resources arise from this policy.

5. European governments tend to make greater use of price controls than does the Canadian government. For example, the French government sets minimum starting yearly wages for new hires who have completed *le bac*, a certification roughly equivalent to a high school diploma. The demand schedule for new hires with *le bac* and the supply schedule for similarly credentialled new job seekers are given in the accompanying table. The price here—given in euros, the currency used in France—is the same as the yearly wage.

Wage (per year)	Quantity demanded (new job offers per year)	Quantity supplied (new job seekers per year)
€45,000	200,000	325,000
40,000	220,000	320,000
35,000	250,000	310,000
30,000	290,000	290,000
25,000	370,000	200,000

a. In the absence of government interference, what are the equilibrium wage and number of graduates hired per year? Illustrate with a diagram. Will there be anyone seeking a job at the equilibrium wage who is unable to find one—that is, will there be anyone who is involuntarily unemployed?

b. Suppose the French government sets a minimum yearly wage of €35,000. Is there any involuntary unemployment at this wage? If so, how much? Illustrate with a diagram. What if the minimum wage is set at €40,000? Also illustrate with a diagram.

c. Given your answer to part b and the information in the table, what do you think is the relationship between the level of involuntary unemployment and the level of the minimum wage? Who benefits from such a policy? Who loses? What is the missed opportunity here?

6. In many European countries, high minimum wages have led to high levels of unemployment and under-employment, and a two-tier labour system. In the formal labour market, workers have good jobs that pay at least the minimum wage. In the informal, or black market for labour, workers have poor jobs and receive less than the minimum wage.

a. Draw a demand and supply diagram showing the effect of the imposition of a minimum wage on the overall market for labour, with wage on the vertical axis and hours of labour on the horizontal axis. Your supply curve should represent the hours of labour offered by workers according to the wage, and the demand curve should represent the hours of labour demanded by employers according to the wage. On your diagram show the deadweight loss from the imposition of a minimum wage. What type of shortage is created? Illustrate on your diagram the size of the shortage.

b. Assume that the imposition of the high minimum wage causes a contraction in the economy so that employers in the formal sector cut their production and their demand for workers. Illustrate the effect of this on the overall market for labour. What happens to the size of the deadweight loss? The shortage? Illustrate with a diagram.

c. Assume that the workers who cannot get a job paying at least the minimum wage move into the informal labour market where there is no minimum wage. What happens to the size of the informal market for labour as a result of the economic contraction? What happens to the equilibrium wage in the informal labour market? Illustrate with a supply and demand diagram for the informal market.

7. For the last 75 years, the Canadian government has used price supports to provide income assistance to Canadian farmers. To implement these price supports, at times the government has used price floors, which it maintains by buying up the surplus farm products. At other times, it has used target prices, a policy by which the government gives the farmer an amount equal to the difference between the market price and the target price for each unit sold. Consider the market for corn depicted in the accompanying diagram.

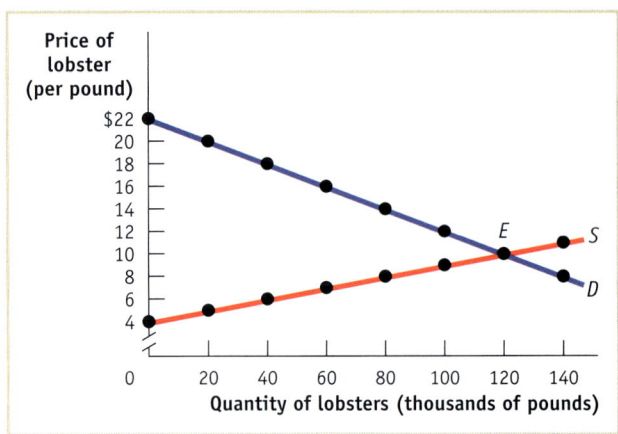

Price of corn (per bushel) / Quantity of corn (bushels)

a. If the government sets a price floor of $5 per bushel, how many bushels of corn are produced? How many are purchased by consumers? By the government? How much does the program cost the government? How much revenue do corn farmers receive?

b. Suppose the government sets a target price of $5 per bushel for any quantity supplied up to 1,000 bushels. How many bushels of corn are purchased by consumers and at what price? By the government? How much does the program cost the government? How much revenue do corn farmers receive?

c. Which of these programs (in parts a and b) costs corn consumers more? Which program costs the government more? Explain.

d. Is one of these policies less inefficient than the other? Explain.

8. The waters off the North Atlantic coast were once teeming with fish. But because of overfishing by the commercial fishing industry, the stocks of fish became seriously depleted. In 1991, the International Commission for the Conservation of Atlantic Tunas (ICCAT) implemented a quota to allow swordfish stocks to recover. The quota limited the amount of swordfish caught per year by all Canadian-licenced fishing boats to 2 million kilograms. As soon as the Canadian fishing fleet had met the quota limit, the swordfish catch was closed down for the rest of the year. The accompanying table gives the hypothetical demand and supply schedules for swordfish caught in Canada per year.

Price of swordfish (per kilogram)	Quantity of swordfish (millions of kilograms per year)	
	Quantity demanded	Quantity supplied
$40	1	10
36	2	8
32	3	6
28	4	4
26	5	2

a. Use a diagram to show the effect of the quota on the market for swordfish in 1991. In your diagram, illustrate the deadweight loss from inefficiently low quantity.

b. How do you think fishers will change how they fish in response to this policy?

9. In the Atlantic provinces and Québec, you must have a licence to harvest lobster commercially; these licences are issued yearly. The federal Department of Fisheries and Oceans Canada is concerned about the dwindling supplies of lobsters found off our coast. This department has decided to place a yearly quota of 80,000 pounds of lobsters harvested in all Canadian waters. It has also decided to give licences this year only to those fishers who had licences last year. The accompanying diagram shows the demand and supply curves for Canadian lobsters.

Price of lobster (per pound) / Quantity of lobsters (thousands of pounds)

a. In the absence of government restrictions, what are the equilibrium price and quantity?

b. What is the *demand price* at which consumers wish to purchase 80,000 pounds of lobsters?

c. What is the *supply price* at which suppliers are willing to supply 80,000 pounds of lobsters?

d. What is the *quota rent* per pound of lobster when 80,000 pounds are sold? Illustrate the quota rent and the deadweight loss on the diagram.

e. Explain a transaction that benefits both buyer and seller but is prevented by the quota restriction.

10. The Venezuelan government has imposed a price ceiling on the retail price of roasted coffee beans.

The accompanying diagram shows the market for coffee beans. In the absence of price controls, the equilibrium is at point E, with an equilibrium price of P_E and an equilibrium quantity bought and sold of Q_E.

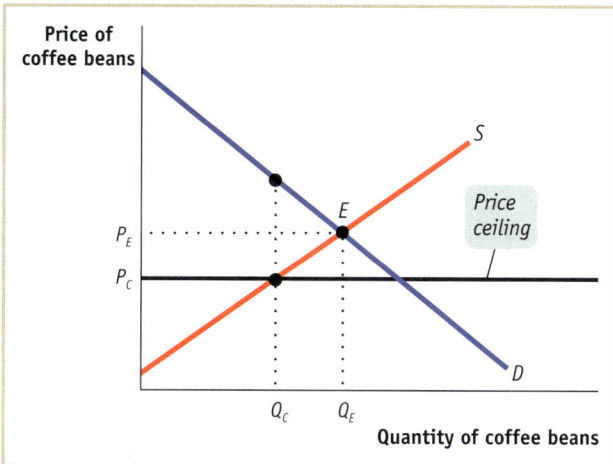

a. Show the consumer and producer surplus before the introduction of the price ceiling.

After the introduction of the price ceiling, the price falls to P_C and the quantity bought and sold falls to Q_C.

b. Show the consumer surplus after the introduction of the price ceiling (assuming that the consumers with the highest willingness to pay get to buy the available coffee beans; that is, assuming that there is no inefficient allocation to consumers).

c. Show the producer surplus after the introduction of the price ceiling (assuming that the producers with the lowest cost get to sell their coffee beans; that is, assuming that there is no inefficient allocation of sales among producers).

d. Using the diagram, show how much of what was producer surplus before the introduction of the price ceiling has been transferred to consumers as a result of the price ceiling.

e. Using the diagram, show how much of what was total surplus before the introduction of the price ceiling has been lost. That is, how great is the deadweight loss?

11. Many university and college students attempt to land internships before graduation to burnish their resumes, gain experience in a chosen field, or try out possible careers. The hope shared by all of these prospective interns is that they will find internships that pay more than typical summer jobs, such as waiting tables or flipping burgers.

a. With wage measured on the vertical axis and number of hours of work on the horizontal axis, draw a supply and demand diagram for the market for interns in which the minimum wage is non-binding at the market equilibrium.

b. Assume that a market downturn reduces the demand for interns by employers. However, many students are willing and eager to work in unpaid internships. As a result, the new market equilibrium wage is equal to zero. Draw another supply and demand diagram to illustrate this new market equilibrium. As in Figure 5-7, include a shaded triangle that represents the deadweight loss from the minimum wage. Using the diagram, explain your findings.

12. This question uses the algebraic method of determining equilibrium from Appendix 3A. In Canada, producers of milk, poultry, and eggs are protected by government-imposed supply management rules. This supply management system is made up of a combination of import controls, production planning quotas, and minimum prices for these products.

Suppose, for simplicity, the Canadian market for turkeys is described by the following demand and supply curves:

$$P = 30 - 0.125Q^d \quad \text{Demand Curve}$$
$$P = 1.48 + 0.03Q^S \quad \text{Supply Curve,}$$

where Q represents the monthly quantity of turkey in thousands of kilograms and the price P is the price per kilogram.

a. Suppose Canada does not have any supply management for turkey farmers. Derive the equilibrium price and quantity of turkey. Draw a diagram representing the market for turkey. Clearly label the equilibrium price and quantity.

b. Suppose, to support the incomes of farmers who raise turkeys, the government imposes a price floor for turkeys at $9 per kilogram. Determine the resulting price paid by consumers, quantity of turkeys exchanged, and the price received by suppliers in equilibrium. Sketch this into your diagram from part a.

c. Briefly explain how this price floor supports the income of farmers.

d. Why might the government need to also impose limitations on the quantity of turkeys imported? Explain.

e. Show that the imposition of a production quota of 168,000 kilograms of turkey per month results in the same price paid by consumers as the price floor in part b. What are the resulting demand price, supply price, and quota rent?

f. Would the government (or a supply management authority) need to have the means to impose penalties for violating the price floor and/or the supply quota? Explain why or why not.

g. Would farmers who were unable to get a turkey production quota licence be pleased by this supply management system? Explain why or why not. Suppose if they wish, these farmers could rent a production quota licence from another farmer who was awarded one. Would this make these other farmers extremely happy? Explain why or why not.

WORK IT OUT

13. Suppose it is decided that rent control in a city will be abolished and that market rents will now prevail. Assume that all rental units are identical and so are offered at the same rent. To address the plight of residents who may be unable to pay the market rent, an income supplement will be paid to all low-income households equal to the difference between the old controlled rent and the new market rent.

    a. Use a diagram to show the effect on the rental market of the elimination of rent control. What will happen to the quality and quantity of rental housing supplied?

    b. Use a second diagram to show the additional effect of the income-supplement policy on the market. What effect does it have on the market rent and quantity of rental housing supplied in comparison to your answers to part a?

    c. Are tenants better or worse off as a result of these policies? Are landlords better or worse off? Is society as a whole better or worse off?

    d. From a political standpoint, why do you think cities have been more likely to resort to rent control rather than a policy of income supplements to help low-income people pay for housing? ◾

.6 > Elasticity

TAKEN FOR A RIDE

IF YOU ARE EXPERIENCING a true emergency, you aren't likely to quibble about the price of an ambulance ride to the nearest emergency room. But what if it isn't an emergency? Take the case of Gavin Baumbach, a student from the University of King's College, Nova Scotia, who caught the flu. He lived in residence and called his don-on-duty for help, who in turn called for emergency service. Shaken, he took the ride and, within several minutes, he was at the hospital. Later, he found out that his trip to the hospital cost him $711 (Nova Scotian residents are charged $146 per ambulance ride; but non-Nova Scotians are charged $711 per ambulance ride, and the cost can easily go up to more than $1,000 for non-Canadians). Stunned by the bill, Baumbach struggled to find a way to pay it. It turned out his university's health plan would only cover the first $500. For the remaining amount, he had to borrow money from his parents. "I'm living off of student loans, I couldn't afford that," Baumbach said.

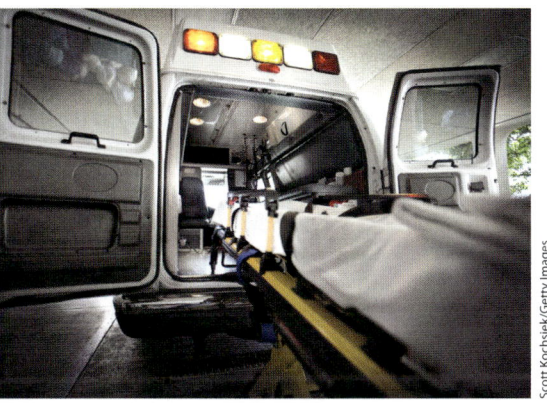

Scott Kochsiek/Getty Images

The demand for ambulance rides to the hospital is relatively unresponsive to the price.

Gavin's experience is by no means unique. Although ambulances are often requested by a bystander or a 911 dispatcher, it is the patient who receives the bill. Undoubtedly, in a true medical emergency, a patient feels fortunate when an ambulance pulls up. But in nonemergency cases, like Gavin's, many patients feel obliged to get into the ambulance once it arrives. And just like Gavin, they are uninformed about the cost of the ride to the hospital. While many people have (both public and private) health insurance that will cover some or all the cost of the ambulance service, the patient is ultimately responsible for paying the rest.

In Canada, paramedics and ambulance services are not mentioned in the Canada Health Act and are therefore not an insured service. Provinces and territories can choose to subsidize the cost of these services and, to some extent, all provincial and territorial governments do. Depending on the nature of services provided (emergency vs. nonemergency, for example), charges for an ambulance ride vary wildly across the country. Charges to patients range from $45 to several hundred dollars. In some provinces, like Manitoba, Saskatchewan, and Quebec, the fee structure includes a fixed amount plus a per-kilometer fee. The cost of an air ambulance ride is much higher. A pregnant Albertan was charged $30,000 for air ambulance service after she went into labour in Ontario two months before her baby's due date.

What accounts for the extreme variation in the cost of ambulance services? How are these services able to charge hundreds of dollars, regardless of whether an ambulance is actually needed? The answer to these questions is *price unresponsiveness:* in the heat of the moment, many consumers — particularly those with true emergencies — are *unresponsive* to the price of an ambulance. Ambulance operators judge correctly that a significant number of patients won't ask "How much is this ride to the emergency room going to cost?" before getting onboard. In other words, a large increase in the price of an ambulance ride leaves the quantity demanded by a significant number of consumers relatively unchanged.

Let's consider a very different scenario. Suppose that the maker of a particular brand of breakfast cereal decided to charge 10 times the original price. It would be extremely difficult, if not impossible, to find consumers willing to pay the much higher price. In other words, consumers of breakfast cereal are much more responsive to price than the consumers of ambulance rides.

But how do we define *responsiveness?* Economists measure responsiveness of consumers to price with a particular number, called the *price elasticity of demand*. In this chapter, we will show how the price elasticity of demand is calculated and why it is the best measure of how the quantity demanded responds to changes in price. We will then see that the price elasticity of demand is only one of a family of related concepts, including the *income elasticity of demand, cross-price elasticity of demand,* and *price elasticity of supply.* ●

WHAT YOU WILL LEARN

- Why is **elasticity** used to measure the response to changes in prices or income?
- What are the different elasticity measures and what do they mean?
- What factors influence the size of these various elasticities?
- Why is it vitally important to determine the size of the relevant elasticity before setting prices or government fees?

The **price elasticity of demand** is the ratio of the percent change in the quantity demanded to the percent change in the price as we move along the demand curve. (Given the demand curve is usually downward sloping, when interpreting the price elasticity of demand, we only look at the absolute value.)

‖ Defining and Measuring Elasticity

In order for investors to know whether they can earn significant profits in the ambulance business, they need to know the *price elasticity of demand* for ambulance rides. With this information, investors can accurately predict whether or not a significant rise in the price of an ambulance ride results in an increase in revenue.

Calculating the Price Elasticity of Demand

Figure 6-1 shows a hypothetical demand curve for an ambulance ride. At a price of $200 per ride, consumers would demand 10 million rides per year (point *A*); at a price of $210 per ride, consumers would demand 9.9 million rides per year (point *B*).

Figure 6-1, then, tells us the change in the quantity demanded for a particular change in the price. But how can we turn this into a measure of price responsiveness? The answer is to calculate the *price elasticity of demand*.

The **price elasticity of demand** is the ratio of the *percent change in quantity demanded* to the *percent change in price* as we move along the demand curve. As we'll see later in this chapter, the reason economists use percent changes is to obtain a measure that doesn't depend on the units in which a good is measured (say, a 1-km ambulance trip versus a 10-km ambulance trip). But before we get to that, let's look at how elasticity is calculated.

To calculate the price elasticity of demand, we first calculate the *percent change in the quantity demanded* and the corresponding *percent change in the price* as we move along the demand curve. These are defined as follows:

(6-1) $\%$ change in quantity demanded $= \dfrac{\text{Change in quantity demanded}}{\text{Initial quantity demanded}} \times 100$

and

(6-2) $\%$ change in price $= \dfrac{\text{Change in price}}{\text{Initial price}} \times 100$

In Figure 6-1, we see that when the price rises from $200 to $210, the quantity demanded falls from 10 million to 9.9 million rides, yielding a change in the

---

FIGURE 6-1 The Demand for Ambulance Rides

At a price of $200 per ambulance ride, the quantity of ambulance rides demanded is 10 million per year (point *A*). When price rises to $210 per ambulance ride, the quantity demanded falls to 9.9 million ambulance rides per year (point *B*).

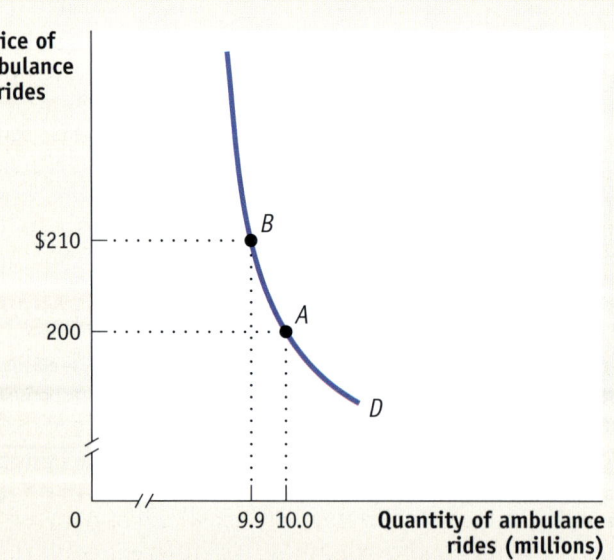

quantity demanded of 0.1 million rides. So the percent change in the quantity demanded is:

$$\% \text{ change in quantity demanded} = \frac{9.9 \text{ million rides} - 10 \text{ million rides}}{10 \text{ million rides}} \times 100$$

$$= \frac{-0.1 \text{ million rides}}{10 \text{ million rides}} \times 100 = -1\%$$

The initial price is $200 and the change in the price is $10, so the percent change in price is:

$$\% \text{ change in price} = \frac{\$210 - \$200}{\$200} \times 100 = \frac{\$10}{\$200} \times 100 = 5\%$$

To calculate the price elasticity of demand, we find the ratio of the percent change in the quantity demanded to the percent change in the price:

(6-3) $\text{Price elasticity of demand} = \dfrac{\% \text{ change in quantity demanded}}{\% \text{ change in price}}$

In Figure 6-1, the price elasticity of demand is therefore:

$$\text{Price elasticity of demand} = \frac{1\%}{5\%} = 0.2$$

Notice that the minus sign that appeared in the calculation of the percent change in the quantity demanded has been dropped when we calculate this last equation, the price elasticity of demand. Why have we done this? The *law of demand* says that demand curves are downward sloping, so price and quantity demanded always move in opposite directions. In other words, a positive percent change in price (a rise in price) leads to a negative percent change in the quantity demanded; a negative percent change in price (a fall in price) leads to a positive percent change in the quantity demanded. This means that the price elasticity of demand is, in strictly mathematical terms, a negative number.

However, it is inconvenient to repeatedly write a minus sign. So when economists talk about the price elasticity of demand, they usually drop the minus sign and report the *absolute value* of the price elasticity of demand. In this case, for example, economists would usually say "the price elasticity of demand is 0.2," taking it for granted that you understand they mean *minus* 0.2. We follow this convention here.

The larger the price elasticity of demand, the more responsive the quantity demanded is to the price. When the price elasticity of demand is large—when consumers change their quantity demanded by a large percentage compared to the percent change in the price—economists say that demand is highly elastic.

As we'll see shortly, a price elasticity of 0.2 indicates a small response of quantity demanded to price. That is, the quantity demanded will fall by a relatively small amount when price rises. This is what economists call *inelastic* demand. And inelastic demand is exactly what enables an ambulance operator to increase the total amount earned by raising the price of an ambulance ride.

An Alternative Way to Calculate Elasticities: The Midpoint Method

Price elasticity of demand compares the *percent change in quantity demanded* with the *percent change in price*. When we look at some other elasticities, which we will do shortly, we'll learn why it is important to focus on percent changes. But at this point we need to discuss a technical issue that arises when you calculate percent changes in variables.

The best way to understand the issue is with a real example. Suppose you were trying to estimate the price elasticity of demand for gasoline by comparing gasoline prices and consumption in different countries. Because of higher taxes, gasoline usually costs more in Canada than in the United States (approximately

The **midpoint method** is a technique for calculating the percent change. In this approach, we calculate changes in a variable compared with the average, or midpoint, of the starting and final values.

$0.34 more per litre in the last quarter of 2019). So what is the percentage difference between Canadian and American gas prices?

Well, it depends on which way you measure it. In the last quarter of 2019, the average price of a litre of gas in Canada was about $1.34 while the average price of a litre of gas in the United States was closer to $1.00 (both measured in Canadian dollars). Because the price of a litre of gas in Canada was $0.34 higher than in the United States, it was 34% ($0.34/$1.00 × 100%) higher. Because the price of gasoline in the United States was $0.34 lower, it was 25% ($0.34/$1.34 × 100%) lower.

This is a nuisance: we'd like to have a percent measure of the difference in prices that doesn't depend on which way you measure it. To avoid computing different elasticities for rising and falling prices we use the *midpoint method*.

The **midpoint method** replaces the usual definition of the percent change in a variable, X, with a slightly different definition:

(6-4) $\% \text{ change in } X = \dfrac{\text{Change in } X}{\text{Average value of } X} \times 100$

where the average value of X is defined as:

$$\text{Average value of } X = \dfrac{\text{Starting value of } X + \text{Final value of } X}{2}$$

When calculating the price elasticity of demand using the midpoint method, both the percent change in the price and the percent change in the quantity demanded are found using this method. To see how this method works, suppose you have the following data for some good:

Situation	Price	Quantity demanded
A	$0.90	1,100
B	$1.10	900

To calculate the percent change in quantity going from situation A to situation B, we compare the change in the quantity demanded—a fall of 200 units—with the *average* of the quantity demanded in the two situations. So we calculate:

$$\% \text{ change in quantity demanded} = \dfrac{(900 - 1{,}100)}{(1{,}100 + 900)/2} \times 100 = \dfrac{-200}{1{,}000} \times 100 = -20\%$$

In the same way, we calculate:

$$\% \text{ change in price} = \dfrac{(\$1.10 - \$0.90)}{(\$0.90 + \$1.10)/2} \times 100 = \dfrac{\$0.20}{\$1.00} \times 100 = 20\%$$

So in this case we would calculate the price elasticity of demand to be:

$$\text{Price elasticity of demand} = \dfrac{\% \text{ change in quantity demanded}}{\% \text{ change in price}} = \dfrac{20\%}{20\%} = 1$$

again dropping the minus sign.

The important point is that we would get the same result, a price elasticity of demand of 1, whether we go up the demand curve from situation A to situation B or down the demand curve from situation B to situation A.

To arrive at a more general formula for price elasticity of demand, suppose that we have data for two points on a demand curve. At point 1 the quantity demanded and price are (Q_1, P_1); at point 2 they are (Q_2, P_2). Then the formula for calculating the price elasticity of demand is:

(6-5) $\text{Price elasticity of demand} = \dfrac{\dfrac{Q_2 - Q_1}{(Q_1 + Q_2)/2}}{\dfrac{P_2 - P_1}{(P_1 + P_2)/2}}$

As before, when finding a price elasticity of demand calculated by the midpoint method, we drop the minus sign and use the absolute value.

ECONOMICS >> *in Action*

Estimating Elasticities

You might think it's easy to estimate price elasticities of demand from real-world data: just compare percent changes in prices with percent changes in quantities demanded. Unfortunately, it's rarely that simple because changes in price aren't the only thing affecting changes in the quantity demanded: other factors—such as changes in income, changes in tastes, and changes in the prices of other goods—shift the demand curve, thereby changing the quantity demanded at any given price.

To estimate price elasticities of demand, economists must use careful statistical analysis to separate the influence of the change in price, holding other things equal.

Economists have estimated price elasticities of demand for a number of goods and services. Table 6-1 summarizes some of these and shows a wide range of price elasticities. There are some goods, like gasoline in the short run and post-secondary education, for which demand hardly responds at all to changes in the price. There are other goods, such as airline travel for leisure, or Coke and Pepsi, for which the quantity demanded is very sensitive to the price.

Notice that Table 6-1 is divided into two parts: inelastic and elastic demand. We'll explain the significance of that division in the next section.

TABLE 6-1 Some Estimated Price Elasticities of Demand	
Good	**Price elasticity of demand**
Inelastic demand	
Post-secondary education	0.14–0.29
Gasoline (short-run)	0.25
Gasoline (long-run)	0.57–0.74
Airline travel (business, short-haul)	0.70
Elastic demand	
Non-alcoholic beverages	1.14
Housing	1.2
Airline travel (leisure, short-haul)	1.52
Coke/Pepsi	3.3

>> Check Your Understanding 6-1

Solutions appear at back of book.

1. The price of strawberries falls from $1.50 to $1.00 per carton and the quantity demanded goes from 100,000 to 200,000 cartons. Use the midpoint method to find the price elasticity of demand.

2. At the present level of consumption, 4,000 movie tickets, and at the current price, $10 per ticket, the price elasticity of demand for movie tickets is 1. Using the midpoint method, calculate the percentage by which the owners of movie theatres must reduce price in order to sell 5,000 tickets.

3. The price elasticity of demand for ice-cream sandwiches is 1.2 at the current price of $0.50 per sandwich and the current consumption level of 100,000 sandwiches. Calculate the change in the quantity demanded when price rises by $0.05. Use Equations 6-1 and 6-2 to calculate percent changes and Equation 6-3 to relate price elasticity of demand to the percent changes.

>> Quick Review

• The **price elasticity of demand** is equal to the percent change in the quantity demanded divided by the percent change in the price as you move along the demand curve, and dropping any minus sign.

• In practice, percent changes are best measured using the **midpoint method,** in which the percent changes are calculated using the average of starting and final values.

‖ Interpreting the Price Elasticity of Demand

In a true emergency, a patient is unlikely to question the price of the ambulance ride to the hospital. But even in a nonemergency, like Gavin's case, patients are often unlikely to respond to an increase in the price of an ambulance by reducing their quantity demanded, because they are not aware of the cost. As a result, investors in private ambulance companies see profit-making opportunities in delivering ambulance services, because the price elasticity of demand is small. But what does that mean? How low does a price elasticity have to be for us to classify it as low? How high does it have to be for us to consider it high? And what determines whether the price elasticity of demand is high or low anyway?

To answer these questions, we need to look more deeply at the price elasticity of demand.

Demand is **perfectly inelastic** when the quantity demanded does not respond at all to changes in the price. When demand is perfectly inelastic, the demand curve is a vertical line.

Demand is **perfectly elastic** when any price increase will cause the quantity demanded to drop to zero. When demand is perfectly elastic, the demand curve is a horizontal line.

How Elastic Is Elastic?

As a first step toward classifying price elasticities of demand, let's look at the extreme cases.

First, consider the demand for a good when people pay no attention to the price—say, snake anti-venom. Suppose that consumers will buy 1,000 doses of anti-venom per year regardless of the price. In this case, the demand curve for anti-venom would look like the curve shown in panel (a) of Figure 6-2: it would be a vertical line at 1,000 doses of anti-venom. Since the percent change in the quantity demanded is zero for *any* change in the price, the price elasticity of demand in this case is zero. The case of a zero price elasticity of demand is known as **perfectly inelastic demand.**

The opposite extreme occurs when even a tiny rise in the price will cause the quantity demanded to drop to zero or even a tiny fall in the price will cause the quantity demanded to get extremely large.

Panel (b) of Figure 6-2 shows the case of pink tennis balls; we suppose that tennis players really don't care what colour their balls are and that other colours, such as neon green and vivid yellow, are available at $5 per dozen balls. In this case, consumers will buy no pink balls if they cost more than $5 per dozen but will buy only pink balls if they cost less than $5. The demand curve will therefore be a horizontal line at a price of $5 per dozen balls. As you move back and forth along this line, there is a change in the quantity demanded but no change in the price. Roughly speaking, when you divide a number by zero, you get infinity, denoted by the symbol ∞. So a horizontal demand curve implies an infinite price elasticity of demand. When the price elasticity of demand is infinite, economists say that demand is **perfectly elastic.**

The price elasticity of demand for the vast majority of goods is somewhere between these two extreme cases. Economists use one main criterion for classifying these intermediate cases: they ask whether the price elasticity of demand is

FIGURE 6-2 Two Extreme Cases of Price Elasticity of Demand

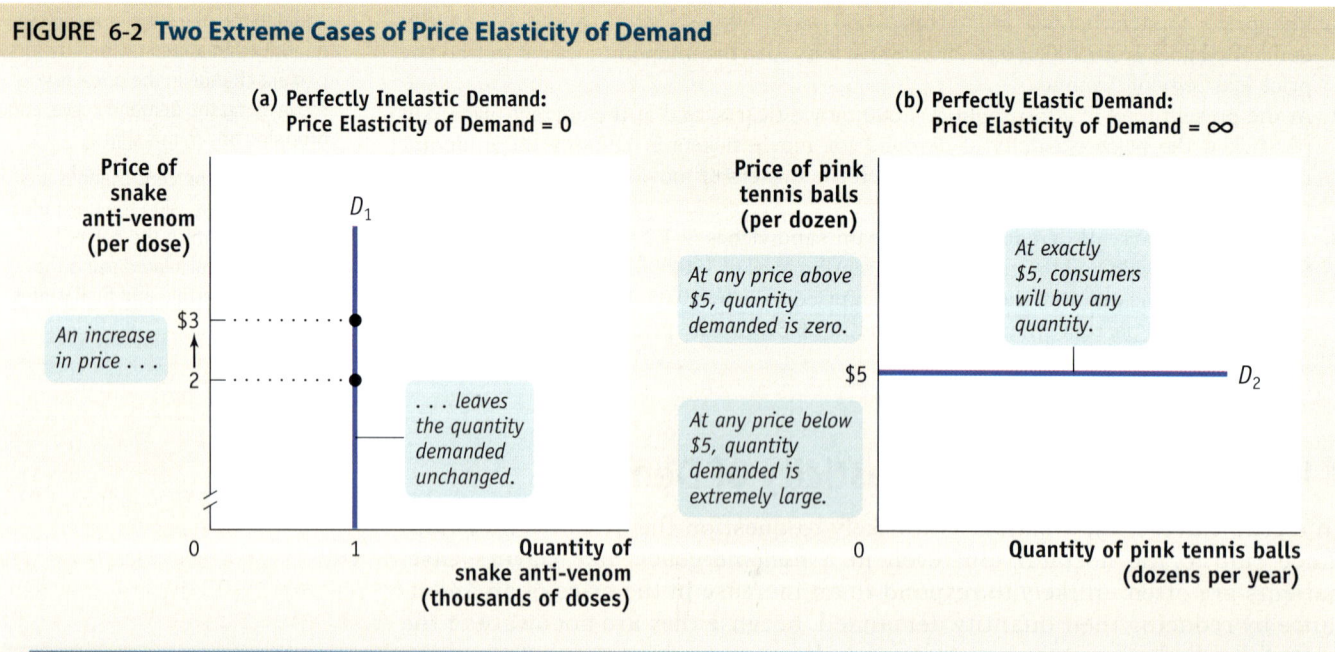

Panel (a) shows a perfectly inelastic demand curve, which is a vertical line. The quantity of snake anti-venom demanded is always 1,000 doses, regardless of price. As a result, the price elasticity of demand is zero—the quantity demanded is unaffected by the price. Panel (b) shows a perfectly elastic demand curve, which is a horizontal line. At a price of $5, consumers will buy any quantity of pink tennis balls, but they will buy none at a price above $5. If the price falls below $5, they will buy an extremely large number of pink tennis balls and none of any other colour.

greater than or less than 1. When the price elasticity of demand is greater than 1, economists say that demand is **elastic.** When the price elasticity of demand is less than 1, they say that demand is **inelastic.** The borderline case is **unit-elastic demand,** where the price elasticity of demand is—surprise—exactly 1.

To see why a price elasticity of demand equal to 1 is a useful dividing line, let's consider a hypothetical example: a toll bridge operated by the provincial ministry of transportation. Other things equal, the number of drivers who use the bridge depends on the toll, the price the provincial ministry of transportation charges vehicles to cross the bridge: the higher the toll, the fewer the drivers who use the bridge.

Figure 6-3 shows three hypothetical demand curves—one in which demand is unit-elastic, one in which it is inelastic, and one in which it is elastic. In each case, point A shows the quantity demanded if the toll is $0.90 and point B shows the quantity demanded if the toll is $1.10. An increase in the toll from $0.90 to $1.10 is an increase of 20% if we use the midpoint method to calculate percent changes.

Panel (a) shows what happens when the toll is raised from $0.90 to $1.10 and the demand curve is unit-elastic. Here the 20% price rise leads to a fall in the quantity of cars using the bridge each day from 1,100 to 900, which is a 20%

> Demand is **elastic** if the price elasticity of demand is greater than 1, **inelastic** if the price elasticity of demand is less than 1, and **unit-elastic** if the price elasticity of demand is exactly 1.

FIGURE 6-3 Unit-Elastic Demand, Inelastic Demand, and Elastic Demand

(a) Unit-Elastic Demand: Price Elasticity of Demand = 1

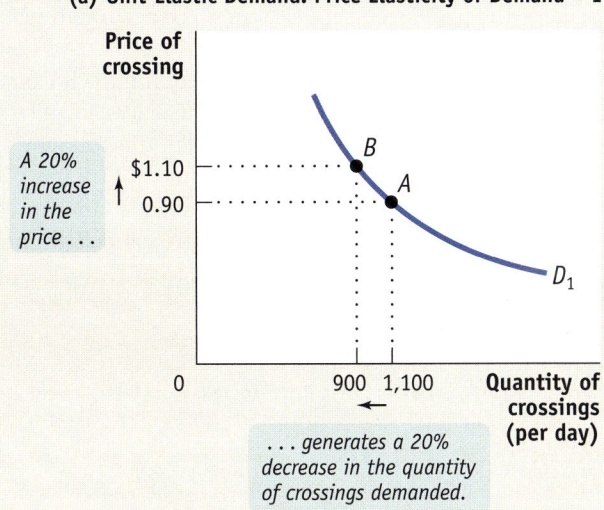

A 20% increase in the price . . .

. . . generates a 20% decrease in the quantity of crossings demanded.

(b) Inelastic Demand: Price Elasticity of Demand = 0.5

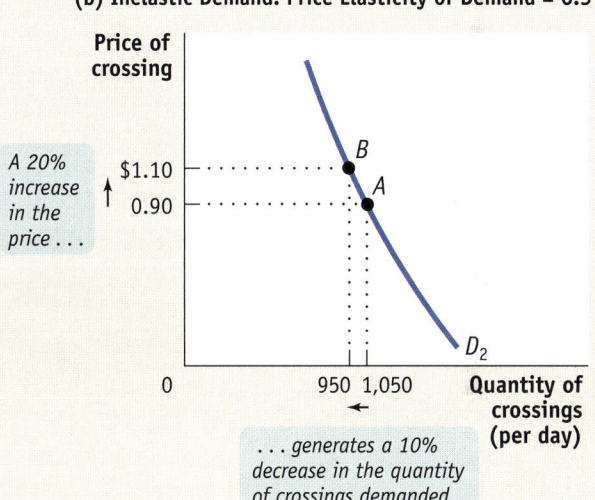

A 20% increase in the price . . .

. . . generates a 10% decrease in the quantity of crossings demanded.

(c) Elastic Demand: Price Elasticity of Demand = 2

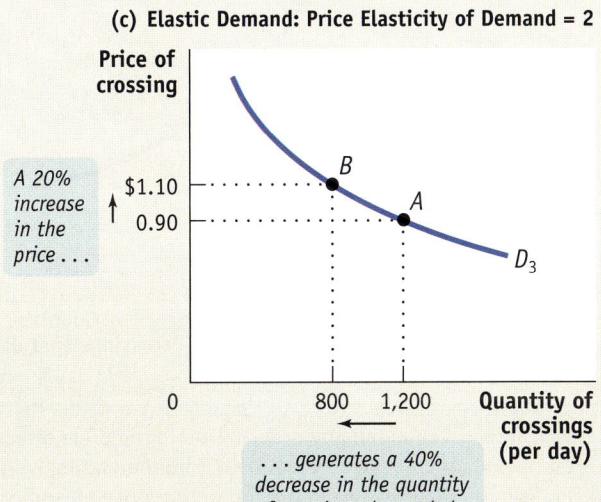

A 20% increase in the price . . .

. . . generates a 40% decrease in the quantity of crossings demanded.

Panel (a) shows a case of unit-elastic demand: a 20% increase in price generates a 20% decline in quantity demanded, implying a price elasticity of demand of 1. Panel (b) shows a case of inelastic demand: a 20% increase in price generates a 10% decline in quantity demanded, implying a price elasticity of demand of 0.5. A case of elastic demand is shown in panel (c): a 20% increase in price causes a 40% decline in quantity demanded, implying a price elasticity of demand of 2. All percentages are calculated using the midpoint method.

The **total revenue** is the total value of sales of a good or service. It is equal to the price multiplied by the quantity sold.

decline (again using the midpoint method). So the price elasticity of demand is 20%/20% = 1.

Panel (b) shows a case of inelastic demand when the toll is raised from $0.90 to $1.10. The same 20% price rise reduces the quantity demanded from 1,050 to 950. That's only a 10% decline, so in this case the price elasticity of demand is 10%/20% = 0.5.

Panel (c) shows a case of elastic demand when the toll is raised from $0.90 to $1.10. The 20% price increase causes the quantity demanded to fall from 1,200 to 800—a 40% decline, so the price elasticity of demand is 40%/20% = 2.

Why does it matter whether demand is unit-elastic, inelastic, or elastic? Because this classification predicts how changes in the price of a good will affect the *total revenue* earned by producers from the sale of that good. In many real-life situations, it is crucial to know how price changes affect total revenue. **Total revenue** is defined as the total value of sales of a good or service, equal to the price multiplied by the quantity sold.

(6-6) Total revenue = Price × Quantity sold

Total revenue has a useful graphical representation that can help us understand why knowing the price elasticity of demand is crucial when we ask whether a price rise will increase or reduce total revenue. Panel (a) of Figure 6-4 shows the same demand curve as panel (a) of Figure 6-3. We see that 1,100 drivers will use the bridge if the toll is $0.90. So the total revenue at a price of $0.90 is $0.90 × 1,100 = $990. This value is equal to the area of the green rectangle, which is drawn with the bottom left corner at the point (0, 0) and the top right corner at (1,100, 0.90). In general, the total revenue at any given price is equal to the area of a rectangle whose height is the price and whose width is the quantity demanded at that price.

To get an idea of why total revenue is important, consider the following scenario. Suppose that the toll on the bridge is currently $0.90 but that the provincial ministry of transportation must raise extra money for road repairs. One way to do this is to raise the toll on the bridge. But this plan might backfire, since a higher toll

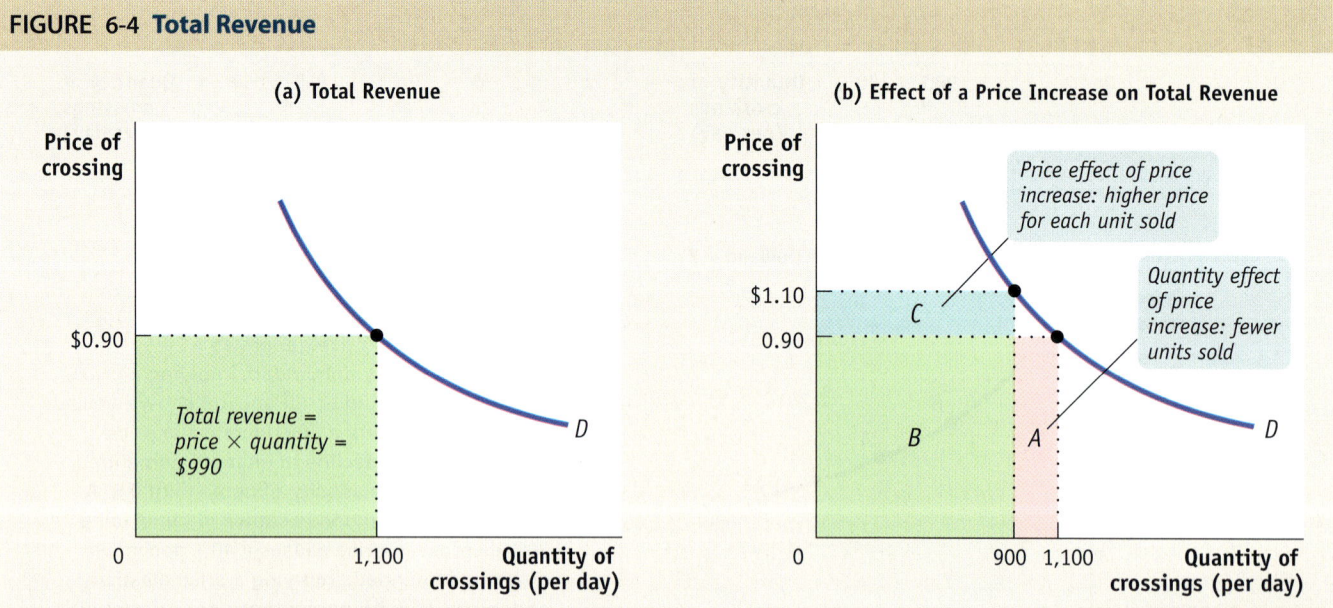

FIGURE 6-4 **Total Revenue**

(a) Total Revenue

Price of crossing

$0.90

Total revenue = price × quantity = $990

D

0   1,100   Quantity of crossings (per day)

(b) Effect of a Price Increase on Total Revenue

Price of crossing

Price effect of price increase: higher price for each unit sold

$1.10

0.90

C

Quantity effect of price increase: fewer units sold

B   A

D

0   900 1,100   Quantity of crossings (per day)

The green rectangle in panel (a) shows the total revenue generated from 1,100 drivers who each pay a toll of $0.90. Panel (b) shows how total revenue is affected when the price increases from $0.90 to $1.10. Due to the quantity effect, total revenue falls by area *A*. Due to the price effect, total revenue increases by the area *C*. In general, the overall effect can go either way, depending on the price elasticity of demand.

will reduce the number of drivers who use the bridge. And if traffic on the bridge dropped a lot, a higher toll would actually reduce total revenue instead of increasing it. So it's important for the provincial ministry of transportation to know how drivers will respond to a toll increase.

We can see graphically how the toll increase affects total bridge revenue by examining panel (b) of Figure 6-4. At a toll of $0.90, total revenue is given by the sum of the areas *A* and *B*. After the toll is raised to $1.10, total revenue is given by the sum of areas *B* and *C*. So when the toll is raised, revenue represented by area *A* is lost but revenue represented by area *C* is gained.

These two areas have important interpretations. Area *C* represents the revenue gain that comes from the additional $0.20 paid by drivers who continue to use the bridge. That is, the 900 drivers who continue to use the bridge contribute an additional $0.20 × 900 = $180 per day to total revenue, represented by area *C*. But 200 drivers who would have used the bridge at a price of $0.90 no longer do so, generating a loss to total revenue of $0.90 × 200 = $180 per day, represented by area *A*. (In this particular example, because demand is unit-elastic—the same as in panel (a) of Figure 6-3—the rise in the toll has no effect on total revenue; areas *A* and *C* are the same size.)

Except in the rare case of a good with perfectly elastic or perfectly inelastic demand, when a seller raises the price of a good, two countervailing effects are present:

- *A price effect:* After a price increase, each unit sold sells at a higher price, which tends to raise revenue.

- *A quantity effect:* After a price increase, fewer units are sold, which tends to lower revenue.

But then, you may ask, what is the ultimate net effect on total revenue: does it go up or down? The answer is that, in general, the effect on total revenue can go either way—a price rise may either increase total revenue or lower it. If the price effect, which tends to raise total revenue, is the stronger of the two effects, then total revenue goes up. If the quantity effect, which tends to reduce total revenue, is the stronger, then total revenue goes down. And if the strengths of the two effects are exactly equal—as in our toll bridge example, where a $180 gain offsets a $180 loss—total revenue is unchanged by the price increase.

The price elasticity of demand tells us what happens to total revenue when price changes: its size determines which effect—the price effect or the quantity effect—is stronger. Specifically:

- If demand for a good is *unit-elastic* (the price elasticity of demand is 1), an increase in price does not change total revenue. In this case, the quantity effect and the price effect exactly offset each other.

- If demand for a good is *inelastic* (the price elasticity of demand is less than 1), a higher price increases total revenue. In this case, the quantity effect is weaker than the price effect.

- If demand for a good is *elastic* (the price elasticity of demand is greater than 1), an increase in price reduces total revenue. In this case, the quantity effect is stronger than the price effect.

Table 6-2 shows how the effect of a price increase on total revenue depends on the price elasticity of

The provincial ministry of transportation uses the price elasticity of demand to calculate the change in revenue from higher tolls.

TABLE 6-2 **Price Elasticity of Demand and Total Revenue**		
	Price of toll = $0.90	**Price of toll = $1.10**
Unit-elastic demand (price elasticity of demand = 1)		
Quantity demanded	1,100	900
Total revenue	$990	$990
Inelastic demand (price elasticity of demand = 0.5)		
Quantity demanded	1,050	950
Total revenue	$945	$1,045
Elastic demand (price elasticity of demand = 2)		
Quantity demanded	1,200	800
Total revenue	$1,080	$880

demand, using the same data as in Figure 6-3. An increase in the price from $0.90 to $1.10 leaves total revenue unchanged at $990 when demand is unit-elastic. When demand is inelastic, the quantity effect is dominated by the price effect; the same price increase leads to an increase in total revenue from $945 to $1,045. And when demand is elastic, the quantity effect dominates the price effect; the price increase leads to a decline in total revenue from $1,080 to $880.

The price elasticity of demand also predicts the effect of a *fall* in price on total revenue. When the price falls, the same two countervailing effects are present, but they work in the opposite direction as compared to the case of a price rise. There is the price effect of a lower price per unit sold, which tends to lower revenue. This is countered by the quantity effect of more units sold, which tends to raise revenue. Which effect dominates depends on the price elasticity. Here is a quick summary:

- When demand is *unit-elastic,* the two effects exactly balance; so a fall in price has no effect on total revenue.
- When demand is *inelastic,* the quantity effect is dominated by the price effect; so a fall in price reduces total revenue.
- When demand is *elastic,* the quantity effect dominates the price effect; so a fall in price increases total revenue.

Price Elasticity Along the Demand Curve

Suppose an economist says that "the price elasticity of demand for coffee is 0.25." What they mean is that *at the current price* the elasticity is 0.25. In the previous discussion of the toll bridge, what we were really describing was the elasticity *at the toll price* of $0.90. Why this qualification? Because for the vast majority of demand curves, the price elasticity of demand at one point along the curve is different from the price elasticity of demand at other points along the same curve.

To see this, consider the table in Figure 6-5, which shows a hypothetical demand schedule. It also shows in the last column the total revenue generated at each price and quantity combination in the demand schedule. The upper panel of the graph in Figure 6-5 shows the corresponding demand curve. The lower panel illustrates the same data on total revenue: the height of the bar at each quantity demanded—which corresponds to a particular price—measures the total revenue generated at that price.

In Figure 6-5, you can see that when the price is low, raising the price increases total revenue: starting at a price of $1, raising the price to $2 increases total revenue from $9 to $16. This means that when the price is low, demand is inelastic. Moreover, you can see that demand is inelastic on the entire section of the demand curve from a price of $0 to a price of $5.

When the price is high, however, raising it further reduces total revenue: starting at a price of $8, raising the price to $9 reduces total revenue, from $16 to $9. This means that when the price is high, demand is elastic. Furthermore, you can see that demand is elastic over the section of the demand curve from a price of $5 to $10.

For the vast majority of goods, the price elasticity of demand changes along the demand curve. So whenever you measure a good's elasticity, you are really measuring it at a particular point or section of the good's demand curve.

What Factors Determine the Price Elasticity of Demand?

Investors in private ambulance companies believe that the price elasticity of demand for an ambulance ride is low for two important reasons. First, in many if not most cases, an ambulance ride is a medical necessity. Second, in an emergency

FIGURE 6-5 **The Price Elasticity of Demand Changes Along the Demand Curve**

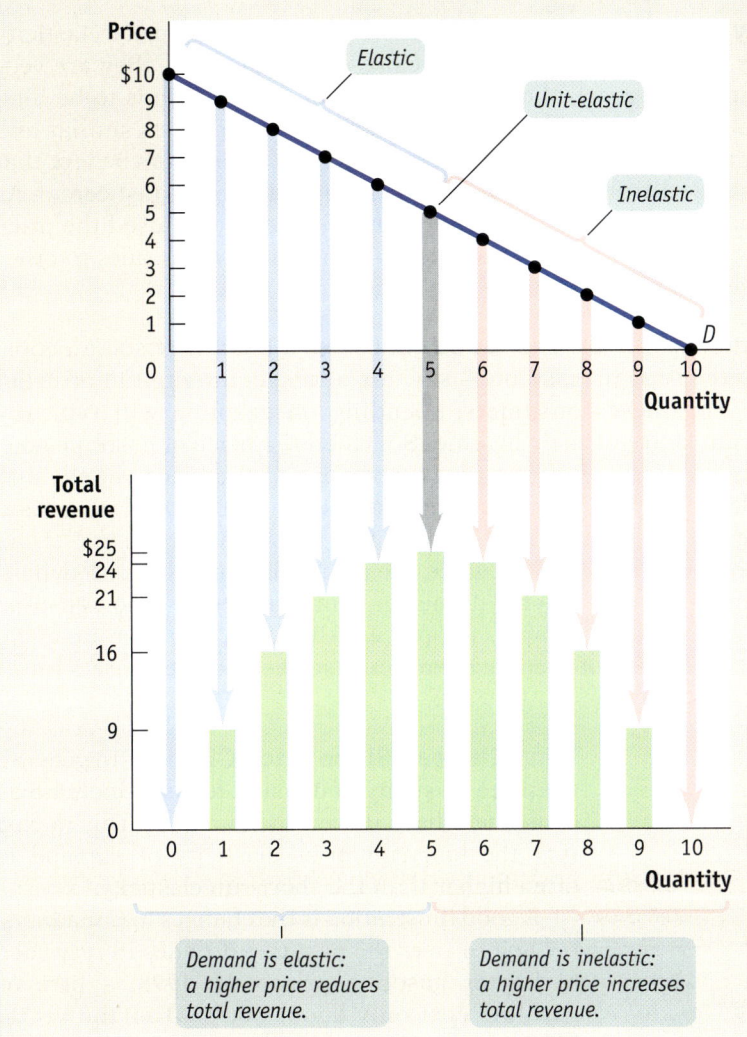

Demand Schedule and Total Revenue for a Linear Demand Curve		
Price	Quantity demanded	Total revenue
$0	10	$0
1	9	9
2	8	16
3	7	21
4	6	24
5	5	25
6	4	24
7	3	21
8	2	16
9	1	9
10	0	0

Demand is elastic: a higher price reduces total revenue.

Demand is inelastic: a higher price increases total revenue.

The upper panel of the graph shows a demand curve corresponding to the demand schedule in the table. The lower panel shows how total revenue changes along that demand curve: at each price and quantity combination, the height of the bar represents the total revenue generated. You can see that at a low price, raising the price increases total revenue. So demand is inelastic at low prices. At a high price, however, a rise in price reduces total revenue. So demand is elastic at high prices.

there really is no substitute for the standard of care that an ambulance provides. And even among ambulances there are typically no substitutes because in any given geographical area there is usually only one ambulance provider. The exceptions are very densely populated areas, but even in those locations an ambulance dispatcher is unlikely to give you a choice of ambulance providers with an accompanying price list.

In general, there are four main factors that determine elasticity: whether a good is a necessity or luxury, the availability of close substitutes, the share of income a consumer spends on the good, and how much time has elapsed since a change in price. We'll briefly examine each of these factors.

Whether the Good Is a Necessity or a Luxury As our opening story illustrates, the price elasticity of demand tends to be low if a good is something you must have, like a life-saving ambulance ride to the hospital. The price elasticity of demand tends to be high if the good is a luxury—something you can easily live without. For example, most people would consider a 98-inch ultra-high-definition TV a luxury—nice to have, but something they can live without. Therefore, the price elasticity of demand for it will be much higher than for a life-saving ambulance ride to the hospital.

The Availability of Close Substitutes As we just noted, the price elasticity of demand tends to be low if there are no close substitutes or if they are very difficult to obtain. In contrast, the price elasticity of demand tends to be high if there are other readily available goods that consumers regard as similar and would be willing to consume instead. For example, most consumers believe that there are fairly close substitutes to their favourite brand of breakfast cereal. As a result, if the maker of a particular brand of breakfast cereal raised the price significantly, that maker is likely to lose much—if not all—of its sales to other brands whose prices have not risen.

Share of Income Spent on the Good Consider a good that some people consume frequently, such as gasoline—say, for a long commute to and from work every day. For these consumers, spending on gasoline will typically absorb a significant share of their income. So, when the price of gasoline goes up, these consumers are likely to be very responsive to the price change and have a higher elasticity of demand. Why? Because when the good absorbs a significant share of these consumers' income, it is worth their time and effort to find a way to reduce their demand when the price goes up—such as switching to car-pooling instead of driving alone. In contrast, people who consume gasoline infrequently—for example, people who walk to work or take the bus—will have a low share of income spent on gasoline and therefore a lower elasticity of demand.

"*Three hundred dollars' of regular.*"

Time Elapsed Since Price Change In general, the price elasticity of demand tends to increase as consumers have more time to adjust. This means that the long-run price elasticity of demand is often higher than the short-run elasticity.

A good illustration is the changes in Canadians' behaviour over the past two decades in response to higher gasoline prices. In 1998, a litre of gasoline cost only about $0.55. Over the years, however, gasoline prices steadily rose, so that by 2008 a litre of gas cost over $1.15 in Canada. Initially, consumption fell very little because there were no close substitutes for gasoline and driving cars was necessary for people to carry out the ordinary tasks of life. Over time, however, Canadians changed their habits by driving less, getting a more fuel-efficient car, and using other modes of transportation like buses or bicycles in ways that enabled them to gradually reduce their gasoline consumption. This confirms that the long-run price elasticity of demand for gasoline is indeed much larger than the short-run elasticity.

Gas prices dropped a bit from 2014 to 2016, with the average price down from $1.28 per litre to $1.00 per litre. Not surprisingly, gasoline consumption then started to rise again from 42.7 billion litres in 2014 to 45.1 billion litres, as consumers switched back to their gas-guzzlers. As the economy was doing well in 2017 and 2018, gasoline prices inched up. Higher gasoline prices and improved fuel efficiency of new cars combined to render Canadian consumption virtually flat during 2017 and 2018, a situation that persisted until the sharp fall in demand caused by the coronavirus pandemic in 2020.

ECONOMICS >> *in Action*
Responding to Your Tuition Bill

If it seems like the cost of post-secondary education keeps going up—it's because it has. According to Statistics Canada, the average undergraduate tuition fee in Canada increased from $4,400 in the 2006–2007 academic year to $6,463 in the 2019–2020 year, which was a total increase of 47% in 14 years (during that period, there was a tuition freeze in Quebec and there was a 10% reduction in tuition in Ontario in the 2019–2020 academic year, making the national rise in tuition lower than it would have been otherwise). Over the same time period, the overall price level, measured by the CPI, increased by a total of only 25%. An important question for educators and policy makers is whether the rise in tuition deters people from going to university. And if so, by how much?

Several studies have shown that tuition increases lead to consistently negative effects on enrolment numbers, with estimates of the price elasticity of demand ranging from 0.14 to 0.29. So a 10% rise in university tuition leads to a fall in enrolment of approximately 1.4% (10 × 0.14) to 2.9% (10 × 0.29). One study found that funding from the provincial governments in the form of financial aid has a relatively large impact on enrolment. The study found that when student aid funding from the provincial government drops by 10%, university enrolment falls by 2.5%.

These results indicate that both rising tuition costs and cuts to government-provided student aid adversely affect university enrolment. This should not be surprising because a rise in tuition and/or a drop in financial aid increase the net cost of a university education. Indeed, studies show that young people who have a binding budget constraint will be most affected by tuition hikes and/or cuts to government-provided student aid, as they have difficulty in financing their university education on their own. Thus, an increase in tuition (and/or cuts to student aid) is more of a barrier to access to post-secondary education for students who qualify for financial aid than for students from more affluent families (who do not qualify for student aid and pay full tuition). Students on financial aid may be more responsible to the full cost of tuition due to fear of losing their grant money or concerns about the cost of paying back their student loans.

In conclusion, an increase in tuition is also more of a barrier for students receiving financial aid than for students paying full tuition. Financial aid recipients may be more responsive to the full cost of tuition for fear of losing their grant money or out of concern about the cost of paying back their student loans.

Students receiving financial aid are more responsive to the price of tuition than students who do not.

>> Check Your Understanding 6-2

Solutions appear at back of book.

1. For each case, choose the condition that characterizes demand: elastic demand, inelastic demand, or unit-elastic demand.
   a. Total revenue decreases when price increases.
   b. The additional revenue generated by an increase in quantity sold is exactly offset by revenue lost from the fall in price received per unit.
   c. Total revenue falls when output increases.
   d. Producers in an industry find they can increase their total revenues by coordinating a reduction in industry output.
2. What is the elasticity of demand for the following goods? Explain. What is the shape of the demand curve?
   a. Demand for a blood transfusion by an accident victim
   b. Demand by students for green erasers

>> Quick Review

- Demand is **perfectly inelastic** if it is completely unresponsive to price. It is **perfectly elastic** if it is infinitely responsive to price.

- Demand is **elastic** if the price elasticity of demand is greater than 1. It is **inelastic** if the price elasticity of demand is less than 1. It is **unit-elastic** if the price elasticity of demand is exactly 1.

- When demand is elastic, the quantity effect of a price increase dominates the price effect and **total revenue** falls. When demand is inelastic, the quantity effect is dominated by the price effect and total revenue rises.

- Because the price elasticity of demand can change along the demand curve, economists refer to a particular point on the demand curve when speaking of the price elasticity of demand.

- Ready availability of close substitutes makes demand for a good more elastic, as does a longer length of time elapsed since the price change. Demand for a necessity is less elastic, and demand for a luxury good is more elastic. Demand tends to be inelastic for goods that absorb a small share of a consumer's income and elastic for goods that absorb a large share of income.

The **cross-price elasticity of demand** between two goods measures the effect of the change in one good's price on the quantity demanded of the other good. It is equal to the percent change in the quantity demanded of one good divided by the percent change in the other good's price.

‖ Other Demand Elasticities

The quantity of a good demanded depends not only on the price of that good but also on other variables. In particular, demand curves shift because of changes in the prices of related goods and changes in consumers' incomes. It is often important to have a measure of these other effects, and the best measures are—you guessed it—elasticities. Specifically, we can best measure how the demand for a good is affected by prices of other goods using a measure called the *cross-price elasticity of demand,* and we can best measure how demand is affected by changes in income using the *income elasticity of demand.*

The Cross-Price Elasticity of Demand

In Chapter 3, you learned that the demand for a good is often affected by the prices of other, related goods—goods that are substitutes or complements. There you saw that a change in the price of a related good shifts the demand curve of the original good, reflecting a change in the quantity demanded at any given price. The strength of such a "cross" effect on demand can be measured by the **cross-price elasticity of demand,** defined as the ratio of the percent change in the quantity demanded of one good to the percent change in the price of the other. Like the price elasticity of demand, the cross-price elasticity is calculated using the midpoint method.

(6-7) Cross-price elasticity of demand between goods A and B

$$= \frac{\% \text{ change in quantity of A demanded}}{\% \text{ change in price of B}}$$

When two goods are substitutes, like hot dogs and hamburgers, the cross-price elasticity of demand is positive: a rise in the price of hot dogs increases the demand for hamburgers—that is, it causes a rightward shift of the demand curve for hamburgers. If the goods are close substitutes, the cross-price elasticity will be positive and large. If they are not close substitutes, the cross-price elasticity will be positive and small. So when the cross-price elasticity of demand is positive, its size is a measure of how closely substitutable the two goods are.

When two goods are complements, like hot dogs and hot dog buns, the cross-price elasticity is negative: a rise in the price of hot dogs decreases the demand for hot dog buns—that is, it causes a leftward shift of the demand curve for hot dog buns. As with substitutes, the size of the cross-price elasticity of demand between two complements tells us how strongly complementary they are: if the cross-price elasticity is only slightly below zero, they are weak complements; if it is very negative, they are strong complements.

Note that in the case of the cross-price elasticity of demand, the sign (plus or minus) is very important: it tells us whether the two goods are complements or substitutes. So we cannot drop the minus sign as we did for the price elasticity of demand.

Our discussion of the cross-price elasticity of demand is a useful place to return to a point we made earlier: elasticity is a *unit-free* measure—that is, it doesn't depend on the units in which goods are measured.

To see how this could be a potential problem, suppose someone told you that "if the price of hot dog buns rises by $0.30, Canadians will buy 1 million fewer hot dogs this year." If you've ever bought hot dog buns, you'll immediately wonder: is that a $0.30 increase in the price *per bun,* or is it a $0.30 increase in the price *per package?* Buns are usually sold in packages of eight. It makes a big difference what units we are talking about! However, if someone says that the cross-price elasticity of demand between buns and hot dogs is –0.3, it doesn't matter whether buns are sold individually or by the package. Thus, elasticity is defined as a ratio of percent changes, as a way of making sure that confusion over units doesn't arise.

The Income Elasticity of Demand

The **income elasticity of demand** is a measure of how much the demand for a good is affected by changes in consumers' incomes. It allows us to determine whether a good is a normal or inferior good as well as to measure how intensely the demand for the good responds to changes in income.

(6-8) Income elasticity of demand $= \dfrac{\%\ \text{change in quantity demanded}}{\%\ \text{change in income}}$

Just as the cross-price elasticity of demand between two goods can be either positive or negative, depending on whether the goods are substitutes or complements, the income elasticity of demand for a good can also be either positive or negative. Recall from Chapter 3 that goods can be either *normal goods,* for which demand increases when income rises, or *inferior goods,* for which demand decreases when income rises. These definitions relate directly to the sign of the income elasticity of demand:

- When the income elasticity of demand is positive, the good is a normal good. In this case, the quantity demanded at any given price increases as income increases. Correspondingly, the quantity demanded at any given price decreases as income falls.

- When the income elasticity of demand is negative, the good is an inferior good. In this case, the quantity demanded at any given price decreases as income increases. Likewise, the quantity demanded at any given price increases as income falls.

> The **income elasticity of demand** is the percent change in the quantity of a good demanded when a consumer's income changes divided by the percent change in the consumer's income.

🌐 **GLOBAL COMPARISON**   **FOOD'S BITE IN WORLD BUDGETS**

The income elasticity of demand for food is less than 1 — it is income-inelastic. As consumers grow richer, other things equal, spending on food rises less than income.

Given these facts, we would expect to find that people in poor countries spend a larger share of their income on food than people in rich countries. And that's exactly what the data show. In this graph, we compare per capita income — a country's total income, divided by the population — with the share of income that is spent on food. (To make the graph a manageable size, per capita income is measured as a percentage of U.S. per capita income.)

In very poor countries like Pakistan, people spend a large percent of their income on food. In middle-income countries, like Israel and Mexico, the share of spending that goes to food is much lower. And it's lower still in rich countries like Canada and the United States.

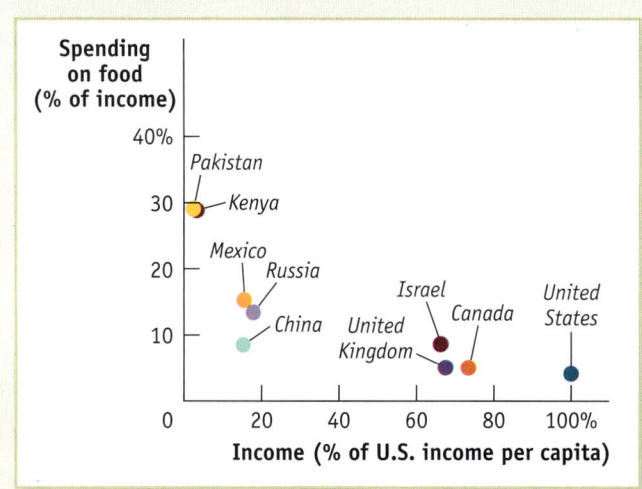

Data from: USDA and IMF, World Economic Outlook.

The demand for a good is **income-elastic** if the income elasticity of demand for that good is greater than 1.

The demand for a good is **income-inelastic** if the income elasticity of demand for that good is positive but less than 1.

Economists often use estimates of the income elasticity of demand to predict which industries will grow most rapidly as the incomes of consumers grow over time. In doing this, they often find it useful to make an additional distinction among normal goods, identifying which normal goods are *income-elastic* and which are *income-inelastic*.

- The demand for a good is **income-elastic** if the income elasticity of demand for that good is greater than 1. When income rises, the demand for income-elastic goods rises *faster* than income. Luxury goods such as second homes and international travel tend to be income-elastic.

- The demand for a good is **income-inelastic** if the income elasticity of demand for that good is positive but less than 1. When income rises, the demand for income-inelastic goods rises, but more slowly than income. Necessities such as food and clothing tend to be income-inelastic.

ECONOMICS >> *in Action*
Spending It

Governments around the world carry out extensive surveys of how families spend their incomes. This is not just a matter of intellectual curiosity. Quite a few government benefit programs involve some adjustment for changes in the cost of living. To estimate those changes, the government must know how people spend their money. But an additional payoff to these surveys is data on the income elasticity of demand for various goods.

What stands out from these studies? The classic result is that the income elasticity of demand for "food eaten at home" is considerably less than 1: as a family's income rises, the share of its income spent on food prepared at home falls. Correspondingly, the lower a family's income, the higher the share of income spent on food consumed at home.

In poor countries, many families spend more than half their income on food consumed at home. Although the income elasticity of demand for "food eaten at home" is estimated at less than 0.5 in Canada, the income elasticity of demand for "food eaten away from home" (restaurant meals) is estimated to be much higher—close to 1.

Judging from the activity at this busy McDonald's in Saigon, incomes are rising in Vietnam.

Paula Bronstein/Getty Images

Families with higher incomes eat out more often and at fancier places. In 1981, about 14% of Canadian income was spent on food consumed at home, a number that dropped to slightly less than 9% in 2018. But over the same time period, the share of Canadian income spent on food consumed away from home has stayed constant at 7%. In fact, a sure sign of rising income levels in developing countries is the arrival of fast-food restaurants that cater to newly affluent customers. For example, McDonald's can now be found in Hanoi, Jakarta, and Mumbai.

There is one clear example of an inferior good found in the surveys: rental housing. Families with higher income actually spend less on rent than families with lower income, because they are much more likely to own their own homes. And the category identified as "other housing"—which basically means second homes—is highly income-elastic. Only higher-income families can afford a luxury like a vacation home, so "other housing" has an income elasticity of demand greater than 1.

>> *Check Your Understanding* **6-3**
Solutions appear at back of book.

1. After Charlotte's income increased from $12,000 to $18,000 a year, her purchases of movie downloads increased from 10 to 40 downloads a year. Calculate Charlotte's income elasticity of demand for movies using the midpoint method.

2. Expensive restaurant meals are income-elastic goods for most people, including Sanjay. Suppose his income falls by 10% this year. What can you predict about the change in Sanjay's consumption of expensive restaurant meals?

3. As the price of margarine rises by 20%, a manufacturer of baked goods increases its quantity of butter demanded by 5%. Calculate the cross-price elasticity of demand between butter and margarine. Are butter and margarine substitutes or complements for this manufacturer?

‖ The Price Elasticity of Supply

A fundamental characteristic of any market for ambulance services, no matter where it is located, is limited supply. For example, it would have been much harder to charge Gavin Baumbach $711 for a short ride to the hospital if there had been many ambulance providers cruising nearby and offering a lower price. But there are good economic reasons why there are not: who among those experiencing a true health emergency would trust their health and safety to a low-price ambulance? And who would want to be a supplier, paying the expense of providing quality ambulance services, without being able to charge high prices to recoup costs? Not surprisingly, then, in most locations there is only one ambulance provider available.

In sum, a critical element in the ability of ambulance providers to charge high prices is limited supply: a low responsiveness in the quantity of output supplied to the higher prices charged for an ambulance ride. To measure the response of ambulance providers to price changes, we need a measure parallel to the price elasticity of demand—the *price elasticity of supply,* as we'll see next.

Measuring the Price Elasticity of Supply

The **price elasticity of supply** is defined the same way as the price elasticity of demand, although since it is always positive there is no minus sign to be eliminated:

(6-9) Price elasticity of supply $= \dfrac{\%\ \text{change in quantity supplied}}{\%\ \text{change in price}}$

It can also be calculated using the midpoint method. The only difference is that now we consider movements along the supply curve rather than movements along the demand curve.

Suppose that the price of tomatoes rises by 10%. If the quantity of tomatoes supplied also increases by 10% in response, the price elasticity of supply of tomatoes is 1 (10%/10%) and supply is unit-elastic. If the quantity supplied increases by 5%, the price elasticity of supply is 0.5 and supply is inelastic; if the quantity increases by 20%, the price elasticity of supply is 2 and supply is elastic.

As in the case of demand, the extreme values of the price elasticity of supply have a simple graphical representation. Panel (a) of Figure 6-6 shows the supply of cell phone frequencies, the portion of the radio spectrum that is suitable for sending and receiving cell phone signals. Governments own the right to sell the use of this part of the radio spectrum to cell phone operators inside their borders. But governments can't increase or decrease the number of cell phone frequencies that they have to offer—for technical reasons, the quantity of frequencies suitable for cell phone operation is a fixed quantity.

The **price elasticity of supply** is a measure of the responsiveness of the quantity of a good supplied to the price of that good. It is the ratio of the percent change in the quantity supplied to the percent change in the price as we move along the supply curve.

FIGURE 6-6 Two Extreme Cases of Price Elasticity of Supply

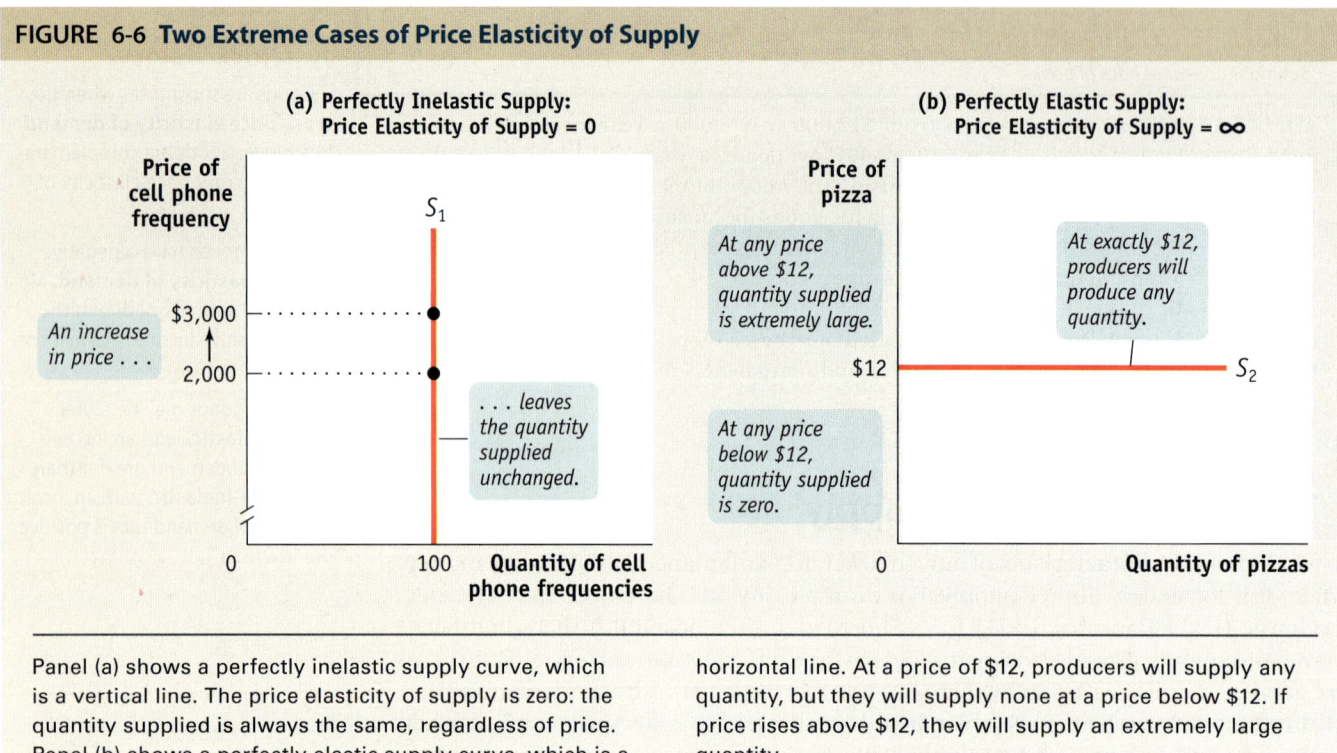

Panel (a) shows a perfectly inelastic supply curve, which is a vertical line. The price elasticity of supply is zero: the quantity supplied is always the same, regardless of price. Panel (b) shows a perfectly elastic supply curve, which is a horizontal line. At a price of $12, producers will supply any quantity, but they will supply none at a price below $12. If price rises above $12, they will supply an extremely large quantity.

There is **perfectly inelastic supply** when the price elasticity of supply is zero, so that changes in the price of the good have no effect on the quantity supplied. A perfectly inelastic supply curve is a vertical line.

There is **perfectly elastic supply** when even a tiny increase or reduction in the price will lead to very large changes in the quantity supplied, so that the price elasticity of supply is infinite. A perfectly elastic supply curve is a horizontal line.

So the supply curve for cell phone frequencies is a vertical line, which we have assumed is set at the quantity of 100 frequencies. As you move up and down that curve, the change in the quantity supplied by the government is zero, whatever the change in price. So panel (a) illustrates a case in which the price elasticity of supply is zero. This is a case of **perfectly inelastic supply.**

Panel (b) shows the supply curve for pizza. We suppose that it costs $12 to produce a pizza, including all opportunity costs. At any price below $12, it would be unprofitable to produce pizza and all the pizza parlours in Canada would go out of business. Alternatively, there are many producers who could operate pizza parlours if they were profitable. The ingredients—flour, tomatoes, and cheese—are plentiful. And if necessary, more tomatoes could be grown, more milk could be produced to make mozzarella, and so on. So any price above $12 would elicit an extremely large quantity of pizzas supplied. The implied supply curve is therefore a horizontal line at $12.

Since even a tiny increase in the price would lead to a huge increase in the quantity supplied, the price elasticity of supply would be more or less infinite. This is a case of **perfectly elastic supply.**

As our cell phone frequencies and pizza examples suggest, real-world instances of both perfectly inelastic and perfectly elastic supply are easy to find—much easier than their counterparts in demand.

What Factors Determine the Price Elasticity of Supply?

Our examples tell us the main determinant of the price elasticity of supply: the availability of inputs. In addition, as with the price elasticity of demand, time may also play a role in the price elasticity of supply. Here we briefly summarize the two factors.

The Availability of Inputs The price elasticity of supply tends to be large when inputs are readily available and can be shifted into and out of production at a relatively low cost. It tends to be small when inputs are difficult to obtain—and can be shifted into and out of production only at a relatively high cost. In the case of ambulance services, the high cost of providing quality ambulance services is the crucial element in keeping the elasticity of supply very low.

Time The price elasticity of supply tends to grow larger as producers have more time to respond to a price change. This means that the long-run price elasticity of supply is often higher than the short-run elasticity.

The price elasticity of the supply of pizza is very high because the inputs needed to expand the industry are readily available. The price elasticity of cell phone frequencies is zero because an essential input—the radio spectrum—cannot be increased at all.

Many industries are like pizza production and have large price elasticities of supply: they can be readily expanded because they don't require any special or unique resources. In contrast, the price elasticity of supply is usually substantially less than perfectly elastic for goods that involve limited natural resources: minerals like gold or copper, agricultural products like coffee that flourish only on certain types of land, and renewable resources like ocean fish that can only be exploited up to a point without destroying the resource.

But given enough time, producers are often able to significantly change the amount they produce in response to a price change, even when production involves a limited natural resource or a very costly input. Agricultural markets provide a good example. When Canadian farmers receive much higher prices for a given commodity, like wheat (because of a drought in a big wheat-producing country like Australia), in the next planting season they are likely to switch their acreage planted from other crops to wheat.

For this reason, economists often make a distinction between the short-run elasticity of supply, usually referring to a few weeks or months, and the long-run elasticity of supply, usually referring to several years. In most industries, the long-run elasticity of supply is larger than the short-run elasticity.

ECONOMICS >> *in Action*
A Global Commodities Glut

The rapidly growing Chinese economy has been a voracious consumer of commodities—metals, foodstuffs, and fuel—as its economy rapidly expanded to become a global manufacturing powerhouse. As China's demand for commodities to support its transformation soared, the countries providing those commodities also saw their incomes soar.

However, when the Chinese economy faltered in 2016, the commodities boom came to an abrupt end. Global commodity producers saw the demand for their goods fall dramatically, just as many of them were investing in costly projects to increase supplies. For example, Chile, the world's major copper producer, had undertaken a massive expansion of its copper mines, digging up 1.7 billion tons of material as copper prices plummeted around the world. India was building railroad lines to connect its underused coal mines to the export market just as a worldwide glut of coal opened up. And Australia was planning to increase its natural gas production by 150% just as natural gas companies around the world went bankrupt due to shrinking fuel demand and plunging prices.

Commodity producers, who had greatly expanded capacity to supply a booming Chinese economy, faltered badly when the Chinese economy slumped in 2016.

Because these countries had invested many billions of dollars into increasing their supply capacity over several years, they could not simply shut down production. So production continued, worsening the existing glut of commodities.

What the commodity producers appear to have forgotten is the logic of the price elasticity of supply: combine persistently high prices with the easy availability of inputs to increase supply capacity (in this case, the chief input was financial capital), and the predictable result is a big increase in the supply of commodities—a rightward shift of the supply curve.

Also predictable is that once the growth in demand for the commodities slowed down, a steep drop in prices would follow. As one commodities expert at the Council on Foreign Relations said, "Producers ended up being their own worst enemies. No one ever worried they would produce too much, but that is exactly what has happened and gotten them into this mess."

• The **price elasticity of supply** is the percent change in the quantity supplied divided by the percent change in the price.

• Under **perfectly inelastic supply,** the quantity supplied is completely unresponsive to price and the supply curve is a vertical line. Under **perfectly elastic supply,** the supply curve is horizontal at some specific price. If the price falls below that level, the quantity supplied is zero. If the price rises above that level, the quantity supplied is extremely large.

• The price elasticity of supply depends on the availability of inputs, the ease of shifting inputs into and out of alternative uses, and the period of time that has elapsed since the price change.

>> **Check Your Understanding** 6-4

Solutions appear at back of book.

1. Using the midpoint method, calculate the price elasticity of supply for web-design services when the price per hour rises from $100 to $150 and the number of hours transacted increases from 300,000 to 500,000. Is supply elastic, inelastic, or unit-elastic?
2. Are each of the following statements true or false? Explain.
   a. If the demand for milk rose, then, in the long run, milk drinkers would be better off if supply were elastic rather than inelastic.
   b. Long-run price elasticities of supply are generally larger than short-run price elasticities of supply. As a result, the short-run supply curves are generally flatter than the long-run supply curves.
   c. When supply is perfectly elastic, changes in demand have no effect on price.

|| An Elasticity Menagerie

We've just run through quite a few different elasticities. Table 6-3 summarizes all of them and their implications.

TABLE 6-3 An Elasticity Menagerie

Price elasticity of demand = $\dfrac{\text{\% change in quantity demanded}}{\text{\% change in price}}$ (dropping the minus sign)	
0	**Perfectly inelastic:** price has no effect on quantity demanded (vertical demand curve).
Between 0 and 1	**Inelastic:** a rise in price increases total revenue.
Exactly 1	**Unit-elastic:** changes in price have no effect on total revenue.
Greater than 1, less than ∞	**Elastic:** a rise in price reduces total revenue.
∞	**Perfectly elastic:** any rise in price causes quantity demanded to fall to 0. Any fall in price leads to an infinite quantity demanded (horizontal demand curve).
Cross-price elasticity of demand = $\dfrac{\text{\% change in quantity demanded of \textit{one good}}}{\text{\% change in price of \textit{another good}}}$	
Negative	**Complements:** quantity demanded of one good falls when the price of another rises.
Positive	**Substitutes:** quantity demanded of one good rises when the price of another rises.
Income elasticity of demand = $\dfrac{\text{\% change in quantity demanded}}{\text{\% change in income}}$	
Negative	**Inferior good:** quantity demanded falls when income rises.
Positive, less than 1	**Normal good, income-inelastic:** quantity demanded rises when income rises, but not as rapidly as income.
Greater than 1	**Normal good, income-elastic:** quantity demanded rises when income rises, and more rapidly than income.
Price elasticity of supply = $\dfrac{\text{\% change in quantity supplied}}{\text{\% change in price}}$	
0	**Perfectly inelastic:** price has no effect on quantity supplied (vertical supply curve).
Greater than 0, less than ∞	ordinary upward-sloping supply curve.
∞	**Perfectly elastic:** any fall in price causes quantity supplied to fall to 0. Any rise in price elicits an infinite quantity supplied (horizontal supply curve).

The Airline Industry: Fly Less and Charge More

Michael Wheatley/Alamy

The Canadian airline industry is characterized by a duopoly—Air Canada and WestJet—which capture 80% of the domestic air travel. In 2018, the market shares of Air Canada and WestJet in the domestic market were 46% and 34% respectively. This figure was much higher in comparison to domestic air travel in the United States and Europe. From 2012 until 2019, the Canadian airline industry was profitable every year.

However, it wasn't always like this. The Canadian airline industry suffered heavy losses for decades as smaller regional airlines were either driven out of businesses or acquired by larger airlines. For instance, Air Canada incurred an after-tax net loss of $1,025 million in 2008 but managed to reduce its losses and turned in a net after-tax profit of $131 million in 2012.

How did the Canadian airline industry achieve such a dramatic turnaround? Simple: fly less and charge more. The catalyst was a particularly nasty recession in 2008, which pushed the Canadian and the global airline industry to the edge of disaster. When the economy cratered, people stopped flying. Airlines were forced to significantly slash their capacity—flying fewer planes—to match the lower demand for seats. Smaller carriers such as Zoom Airlines, saddled with years of losses, were no longer viable. As a result, starting in 2010, flights became a lot more crowded. Air Canada reported a load factor of 82% while WestJet had a load factor of 80%.

Airlines also began charging more: beginning in 2010, the industry enjoyed several years of significant fare increases. One way the airlines accomplished this was by varying ticket prices according to the day and time of departure, as well as the day the ticket was purchased. For example, Wednesday became the cheapest day to fly, with Friday and Saturday the most expensive. The least expensive flight of the day is the first flight of the morning (the one that requires you to get up at 4 A.M.). Buying tickets on Tuesdays at 3 P.M. Eastern Standard Time results in the cheapest fares, while tickets purchased on the weekend cost the most.

And it didn't stop there, as every beleaguered traveller knows. Airlines began imposing new fees and increased old ones—fees for food, blankets, baggage, the right to board first or choose your seat in advance, and so on. These fees are now a major source of airline revenue, all while providing a seemingly ever-shrinking amount of leg room. Calin Rovinescu, the CEO of Air Canada, claimed that these ancillary fees will not go away soon because they represent a good share of the firm's profit. One airline industry researcher, commenting on the long-term profitability of airlines, said: "The wild card is always capacity discipline. All it takes is one carrier to begin to add capacity aggressively, and then we follow and we undo all the good work that's been done."

QUESTIONS FOR THOUGHT

1. How would you describe the price elasticity of demand for airline flights given the information in this case? Explain.

2. Using the concept of elasticity, explain why airlines would create such great variations in the price of a ticket depending on when it is purchased and the day and time the flight departs. Assume that some people are willing to spend time shopping for deals as well as fly at inconvenient times, but others are not.

3. Using the concept of elasticity, explain why airlines have imposed fees on things such as checked bags. Why might they try to hide or disguise fees?

4. Use an elasticity concept to explain under what conditions the airline industry will be able to maintain its high profitability in the future. Explain.

SUMMARY

1. Many economic questions depend on the size of consumer or producer responses to changes in prices or other variables. *Elasticity* is a general measure of responsiveness that can be used to answer such questions.

2. The **price elasticity of demand**—the percent change in the quantity demanded divided by the percent change in the price (dropping the minus sign)—is a measure of the responsiveness of the quantity demanded to changes in the price. In practical calculations, it is usually best to use the **midpoint method,** which calculates percent changes in prices and quantities based on the average of starting and final values.

3. The responsiveness of the quantity demanded to price can range from **perfectly inelastic demand,** where the quantity demanded is unaffected by the price, to **perfectly elastic demand,** where there is a unique price at which consumers will buy as much or as little as they are offered. When demand is perfectly inelastic, the demand curve is a vertical line; when it is perfectly elastic, the demand curve is a horizontal line.

4. The price elasticity of demand is classified according to whether it is more or less than 1. If it is greater than 1, demand is **elastic;** if it is less than 1, demand is **inelastic;** if it is exactly 1, demand is **unit-elastic.** This classification determines how **total revenue,** the total value of sales, changes when the price changes. If demand is elastic, total revenue falls when the price increases and rises when the price decreases. If demand is inelastic, total revenue rises when the price increases and falls when the price decreases. If demand is unit-elastic, total revenue is unchanged by a change in price.

5. The price elasticity of demand depends on whether there are close substitutes for the good in question (it

is higher), whether the good is a necessity (it is lower) or a luxury (it is higher), the share of income spent on the good (it is higher), and the length of time that has elapsed since the price change (it is higher).

6. The **cross-price elasticity of demand** measures the effect of a change in one good's price on the quantity demanded of another good. The cross-price elasticity of demand can be positive, in which case the goods are substitutes, or negative, in which case they are complements.

7. The **income elasticity of demand** is the percent change in the quantity of a good demanded when a consumer's income changes divided by the percent change in income. The income elasticity of demand indicates how intensely the demand for a good responds to changes in income. It can be negative; in that case the good is an inferior good. Goods with positive income elasticities of demand are normal goods. If the income elasticity is greater than 1, a good is **income-elastic;** if it is positive and less than 1, the good is **income-inelastic.**

8. The **price elasticity of supply** is the percent change in the quantity of a good supplied divided by the percent change in the price. If the quantity supplied does not change at all, we have an instance of **perfectly inelastic supply;** the supply curve is a vertical line. If the quantity supplied is zero below some price but infinite above that price, we have an instance of **perfectly elastic supply;** the supply curve is a horizontal line.

9. The price elasticity of supply depends on the availability of resources to expand production and on time. It is higher when inputs are available at relatively low cost and the longer the time elapsed since the price change.

KEY TERMS

Price elasticity of demand, p. 168
Midpoint method, p. 170
Perfectly inelastic demand, p. 172
Perfectly elastic demand, p. 172
Elastic demand, p. 173

Inelastic demand, p. 173
Unit-elastic demand, p. 173
Total revenue, p. 174
Cross-price elasticity of demand, p. 180
Income elasticity of demand, p. 181

Income-elastic demand, p. 182
Income-inelastic demand, p. 182
Price elasticity of supply, p. 183
Perfectly inelastic supply, p. 184
Perfectly elastic supply, p. 184

PRACTICE QUESTIONS

1. You recently came across the following headlines:

   i. "Private schools cut tuition and fail to reach enrollment goals"

   ii. "University of British Columbia raises tuition on out-of-province students, still at capacity"

   What does each statement say about the elasticity of demand for university tuition? Is each statement

   consistent with what you learned about the factors that determine elasticity?

2. You and your classmate were discussing some recent observations on your campus. Using the concepts of elasticity, how would you explain each of these situations:

   i. Textbook prices at the campus bookstore are 20% to 30% more expensive than online retailers.

ii. You notice that at the restaurant where you wait tables, the bar gives away free salty snacks like popcorn and peanuts.

iii. The athletics department charges lower prices for hockey tickets to students than those to the general public.

iv. Parking prices increased 25% for the school year and you still have difficulty finding an open spot.

3. There is a debate about whether sterile hypodermic needles should be passed out free of charge in cities with high drug use. Proponents argue that doing so will reduce the incidence of diseases, such as HIV/AIDS, that are often spread by needle sharing among drug users. Opponents believe that doing so will encourage more drug use by reducing the risks of this behaviour. As an economist asked to assess the policy, you must know the following: (i) how responsive the spread of diseases like HIV/AIDS is to the price of sterile needles and (ii) how responsive drug use is to the price of sterile needles. Assuming that you know these two things, use the concepts of price elasticity of demand for sterile needles and the cross-price elasticity between drugs and sterile needles to answer the following questions.

a. In what circumstances do you believe this is a beneficial policy?

b. In what circumstances do you believe this is a bad policy?

PROBLEMS

1. Do you think the price elasticity of demand for Ford sport-utility vehicles (SUVs) will increase, decrease, or remain the same when each of the following events occurs? Explain your answer.

a. Other car manufacturers, such as General Motors, decide to make and sell SUVs.

b. SUVs produced outside North America are banned from the North American market.

c. Due to ad campaigns, Canadians believe that SUVs are much safer than ordinary passenger cars.

d. The time period over which you measure the elasticity lengthens. During that longer time, new models such as four-wheel-drive cargo vans appear.

2. The following table shows the quantity demanded and the average price of wheat flour in Canada between 2018 and 2019.

	2018	2019
Quantity demanded (thousand kg)	2,152,650	2,263,310
Average price (per kg)	$1.86	$1.81

a. Using the midpoint method, calculate the price elasticity of demand for flour.

b. What is the total revenue for Canadian flour suppliers in 2018 and 2019?

c. Did the price change increase or decrease the total revenue of Canadian flour suppliers? How could you have predicted this from your answer to part a?

3. The accompanying table gives part of the supply schedule for personal computers in Canada.

Price of computer	Quantity of computers supplied
$1,100	12,000
900	8,000

a. Calculate the price elasticity of supply when the price increases from $900 to $1,100 using the midpoint method. Is it elastic, inelastic, or unit-elastic?

b. Suppose firms produce 1,000 more computers at any given price due to improved technology. As price increases from $900 to $1,100, is the price elasticity of supply now greater than, less than, or the same as it was in part a?

c. Suppose a longer time period under consideration means that the quantity supplied at any given price is 20% higher than the figures given in the table. As price increases from $900 to $1,100, is the price elasticity of supply now greater than, less than, or the same as it was in part a?

4. The accompanying table lists the cross-price elasticities of demand for several goods, where the percent quantity change is measured for the first good of the pair, and the percent price change is measured for the second good.

Good	Cross-price elasticities of demand
Air-conditioning units and kilowatts of electricity	−0.34
Coke and Pepsi	+0.63
High-fuel-consuming sport-utility vehicles (SUVs) and gasoline	−0.28
McDonald's burgers and Burger King burgers	+0.82
Butter and margarine	+1.54

a. Explain the sign of each of the cross-price elasticities. What does it imply about the relationship between the two goods in question?

b. Compare the absolute values of the cross-price elasticities and explain their magnitudes. For example, why is the cross-price elasticity of McDonald's burgers and Burger King burgers less than the cross-price elasticity of butter and margarine?

c. Use the information in the table to calculate how a 5% increase in the price of Pepsi affects the quantity of Coke demanded.

d. Use the information in the table to calculate how a 10% decrease in the price of gasoline affects the quantity of SUVs demanded.

5. What can you conclude about the price elasticity of demand in each of the following statements?

a. "The pizza delivery business in this town is very competitive. I'd lose half my customers if I raised the price by as little as 10%."

b. "I owned both of the two John Lennon autographed lithographs in existence. I sold one on eBay for a high price. But when I sold the second one, the price dropped by 80%."

c. "My economics professor has chosen to use the Krugman/Wells/Au/Parkinson textbook for this class. I have no choice but to buy this book."

d. "I always spend a total of exactly $10 per week on coffee."

6. Take a linear demand curve like that shown in Figure 6-5, where the range of prices for which demand is elastic and inelastic is labelled. In each of the following scenarios, the supply curve shifts. Show along which portion of the demand curve (that is, the elastic or the inelastic portion) the supply curve must have shifted in order to generate the event described. In each case, show on the diagram the quantity effect and the price effect.

a. Recent attempts by the Colombian army to stop the flow of illegal drugs into the United States have actually benefited drug dealers.

b. New construction increased the number of seats in the football stadium and resulted in greater total revenue from box-office ticket sales.

c. A fall in input prices has led to higher output of Porsches. But total revenue for the Porsche company has declined as a result.

7. The accompanying table shows the price and yearly quantity of souvenir T-shirts demanded in the town of Crystal Lake according to the average income of the tourists visiting.

Price of T-shirt	Quantity of T-shirts demanded when average tourist income is $20,000	Quantity of T-shirts demanded when average tourist income is $30,000
$4	3,000	5,000
5	2,400	4,200
6	1,600	3,000
7	800	1,800

a. Using the midpoint method, calculate the price elasticity of demand when the price of a T-shirt rises from $5 to $6 and the average tourist income is $20,000. Also calculate it when the average tourist income is $30,000.

b. Using the midpoint method, calculate the income elasticity of demand when the price of a T-shirt is $4 and the average tourist income increases from $20,000 to $30,000. Also calculate it when the price is $7.

8. A recent study determined the following elasticities for Honda Civics:

Price elasticity of demand = 2

Income elasticity of demand = 1.5

The supply of Civics is elastic. Based on this information, are the following statements true or false? Explain your reasoning.

a. A 10% increase in the price of a Civic will reduce the quantity demanded by 20%.

b. An increase in consumer income will increase the price and quantity of Civics sold.

9. In each of the following cases, do you think the price elasticity of supply is (i) perfectly elastic; (ii) perfectly inelastic; (iii) elastic, but not perfectly elastic; or (iv) inelastic, but not perfectly inelastic? Explain using a diagram.

a. An increase in demand this summer for luxury cruises leads to a huge jump in the sales price of a cabin on the *Queen Mary 2*.

b. The price of a kilowatt of electricity is the same during periods of high electricity demand as during periods of low electricity demand.

c. Fewer people want to fly during February than during any other month. The airlines cancel about 10% of their flights as ticket prices fall about 20% during this month.

d. Owners of vacation homes in Nova Scotia rent them out during the summer. Due to the soft economy this year, a 30% decline in the price of a vacation rental leads more than half of homeowners to occupy their vacation homes themselves during the summer.

10. Use an elasticity concept to explain each of the following observations.

a. During economic booms, the number of new personal care businesses, such as gyms and tanning salons, is proportionately greater than the number of other new businesses, such as grocery stores.

b. Cement is the primary building material in Mexico. After new technology makes cement cheaper to produce, the supply curve for the Mexican cement industry becomes relatively flatter.

c. Some goods that were once considered luxuries, like a cell phone, are now considered virtual necessities. As a result, the demand curve for cell phone services has become steeper over time.

d. Consumers in a less developed country like Guatemala spend proportionately more of their income on equipment for producing things at home, like sewing machines, than consumers in a more developed country like Canada.

11. Taiwan is a major world supplier of semiconductor chips. A recent earthquake severely damaged the production facilities of Taiwanese chip-producing companies, sharply reducing the amount of chips they could produce.

a. Assume that the total revenue of a typical non-Taiwanese chip manufacturer rises due to these events. In terms of an elasticity, what must be true for this to happen? Illustrate the change in total revenue with a diagram, indicating the price effect and the quantity effect of the Taiwan earthquake on this company's total revenue.

b. Now assume that the total revenue of a typical non-Taiwanese chip manufacturer falls due to these events. In terms of an elasticity, what must be true for this to happen? Illustrate the change in total revenue with a diagram, indicating the price effect and the quantity effect of the Taiwan earthquake on this company's total revenue.

12. Worldwide, the average coffee grower has increased the amount of acreage under cultivation over the past few years. The result has been that the average coffee plantation produces significantly more coffee than it did 10 to 20 years ago. Unfortunately for the growers, however, this has also been a period in which their total revenues have plunged. In terms of an elasticity, what must be true for these events to have occurred? Illustrate these events with a diagram, indicating the quantity effect and the price effect that gave rise to these events.

13. Anindya Sen and May Luong studied the relationship between the price of beer and rates of sexually transmitted infections (STIs) in Canada. Their result indicated that there is a significant relationship between beer price and STI rates. Their findings suggest that "higher beer prices do result in lower STI rates and price elasticities within a range of –0.6 to –1.4." According to this estimate of the cross-price elasticity of demand by Sen and Leong, are beer and STIs complements or substitutes? Explain.

14. The U.S. government is considering reducing the amount of carbon dioxide that firms are allowed to produce by issuing a limited number of tradable allowances for carbon dioxide (CO_2) emissions. In a recent report, the U.S. Congressional Budget Office (CBO) argues that "most of the cost of meeting a cap on CO_2 emissions would be borne by consumers, who would face persistently higher prices for products such as electricity and gasoline . . . poorer households would bear a larger burden relative to their income than wealthier households would." What assumption about one of the elasticities you learned about in this chapter has to be true for poorer households to be disproportionately affected?

15. According to data from auto sales data website, Good Car Bad Car, Canadian sales of the fuel-efficient Toyota Prius (including all different types) rose from 7,977 vehicles sold in 2017 to 9,174 in 2018. Over the same period, according to data from Statistics Canada, the average price of regular gasoline rose from $1.12 to $1.26 per litre. Using the midpoint method, calculate the cross-price elasticity of demand between Toyota Prii (the official plural of "Prius" is "Prii") and regular gasoline. According to your estimate of the cross-price elasticity, are the two goods complements or substitutes? Does your answer make sense?

WORK IT OUT

16. Nile.com, the online bookseller, wants to increase its total revenue. One strategy is to offer a 10% discount on every book it sells. Nile.com knows that its customers can be divided into two distinct groups according to their likely responses to the discount. The accompanying table shows how the two groups respond to the discount.

	Group A (sales per week)	Group B (sales per week)
Volume of sales before the 10% discount	1.55 million	1.50 million
Volume of sales after the 10% discount	1.65 million	1.70 million

a. Using the midpoint method, calculate the price elasticities of demand for group A and group B.

b. Explain how the discount will affect total revenue from each group.

c. Suppose Nile.com knows which group each customer belongs to when they log on and can choose whether or not to offer the 10% discount. If Nile.com wants to increase its total revenue, should discounts be offered to group A or to group B, to neither group, or to both groups? ■

The Algebra of Elasticity

As we have noted our simple algebraic models often use nice linear expressions so that our analysis is easy, yet still contains the essence of supply and demand.

‖ Price Elasticity of Demand

Let's return to our example from Appendix 3A, the demand for maple syrup, to look at the algebra of elasticity. There, we started with a very simple linear demand curve in its simplest form:

(3A-1) $P = a - b \times Q^d$

where P denotes the price (in dollars per litre), Q^d denotes the quantity (in millions of litres), and a and b are positive constants.

If we isolate Q^d as a function of the other terms, we get:

(6A-1) $Q^d = \dfrac{a}{b} - \dfrac{1}{b} \times P$

According to this equation, if the price of maple syrup increases by \$1 per litre (i.e., $\Delta P = 1$), then the quantity of maple syrup demanded decreases by $\dfrac{1}{b}$ (i.e., $\Delta Q^d = -\dfrac{1}{b}$). Therefore, the ratio $\dfrac{\Delta Q^d}{\Delta P}$ is equal to $-\dfrac{1}{b}$, a fact we will need to use later.

Now we can look more closely at the price elasticity of demand, which for the midpoint method was expressed in Equation 6-5 as:

(6-5) Price elasticity of demand $= \dfrac{\dfrac{Q_2 - Q_1}{(Q_1 + Q_2)/2}}{\dfrac{P_2 - P_1}{(P_1 + P_2)/2}}$

This equation can be simplified after rewriting it using algebraic terms such as ΔQ^d for the change in $Q^d = Q_2 - Q_1$, ΔP for the change in $P = P_2 - P_1$, and using the values P and Q^d instead of the midpoint values:

(6A-2) Price elasticity of demand $= \dfrac{\dfrac{Q_2 - Q_1}{(Q_1 + Q_2)/2}}{\dfrac{P_2 - P_1}{(P_1 + P_2)/2}} = \dfrac{\left(\dfrac{\Delta Q^d}{Q^d}\right)}{\left(\dfrac{\Delta P}{P}\right)} = \left(\dfrac{\Delta Q^d}{\Delta P}\right) \times \left(\dfrac{P}{Q^d}\right)$

When interpreting the price elasticity of demand, we only look at the absolute value, so we can redefine the price elasticity of demand, E_d, as:

(6A-3) $E_d = \left\lvert \left(\dfrac{\Delta Q^d}{\Delta P}\right) \times \left(\dfrac{P}{Q^d}\right) \right\rvert = \left\lvert \left(-\dfrac{1}{b}\right) \times \left(\dfrac{P}{Q^d}\right) \right\rvert = \left(\dfrac{1}{b}\right) \times \left(\dfrac{P}{Q^d}\right)$

This formula for the price elasticity of demand comes in handy when analyzing a graph of the demand curve. As we move along the demand curve in Figure 6A-1, b remains constant but the ratio of P divided by Q^d varies. Therefore the price elasticity of demand varies as we move along a linear demand curve. The ratio

FIGURE 6A-1 Price Elasticity Along a Linear Demand Curve

Price elasticity varies along the demand curve. A line with a slope b that passes through the origin will intersect the demand curve. At the point of intersection, price elasticity is 1 (the unit-elastic point). To the left of the point, price elasticity is greater than 1. To the right, price elasticity is less than 1.

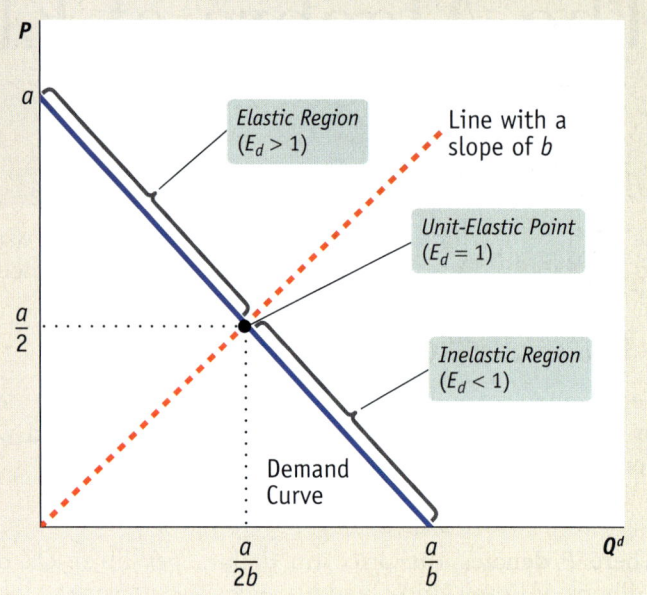

P/Q^d is the slope of the line passing through the origin and the point (Q^d, P) on the demand curve (because the rise of the line is P and the run is Q^d). When the slope of the line is equal to b, the point at which this line intersects the demand curve has a price elasticity of demand of one—the unit-elastic point. All lines steeper than this one intersect at points on the demand curve with a price elasticity of demand greater than one—the region of elastic demand points. Similarly, the points on the demand curve that lie below the unit-elastic point have price elasticity of demand less than one—the inelastic points.

These regions can be determined algebraically by first substituting $P = a - b \times Q^d$ into Equation 6A-2 to express E_d in terms of a, b, and Q^d:

$$\textbf{(6A-4)} \quad E_d = \left(\frac{1}{b}\right) \times \left(\frac{P}{Q^d}\right) = \left(\frac{1}{b}\right) \times \left(\frac{a - b \times Q^d}{Q^d}\right)$$

$$= \left(\frac{a - b \times Q^d}{b \times Q^d}\right) = \left(\frac{a}{b \times Q^d}\right) - 1$$

Notice that by carefully selecting values of Q^d, we can generate values of E_d that are less than, greater than, or equal to 1.

$$\text{If } Q^d = \left(\frac{a}{2 \times b}\right), \text{ then } E_d = \left(\frac{a}{b \times Q^d}\right) - 1 = 2 - 1 = 1$$

$$\text{If } Q^d < \left(\frac{a}{2 \times b}\right), \text{ then } E_d = \left(\frac{a}{b \times Q^d}\right) - 1 > 1$$

$$\text{If } Q^d > \left(\frac{a}{2 \times b}\right), \text{ then } E_d = \left(\frac{a}{b \times Q^d}\right) - 1 < 1$$

‖ Income Elasticity of Demand

The income elasticity of demand measures how sensitive the demand curve is to changes in consumers' incomes by measuring how far the demand curve parallel shifts along the quantity axis as consumers' incomes change. More precisely, it measures the percentage change in quantity demand per percentage change in income. To examine income algebraically, we need to revisit the expanded version of Equation 3A-1 from Appendix 3A:

$$P = a_0 + a_1 \times P_{corn\ syrup} - a_2 \times P_{pancake\ mix} + a_3 \times Y + a_4 \times Tastes + a_5$$
$$\times P_{future}^e + a_6 \times Pop - b \times Q^d$$

TABLE 6A-1 **Variable Factors That Shift Maple Syrup Demand**	
Factor	**Denoted by**
Price of corn syrup	$P_{corn\ syrup}$
Price of pancake mix	$P_{pancake\ mix}$
Average consumer income	Y
Consumer preference index	$Tastes$
Expected future price	P_{future}^e
Population of potential consumers	Pop

where P denotes the price, Q^d denotes the quantity, and the other terms are positive constants. Table 6A-1 summarizes the factors in this equation. For the income elasticity of demand, we are dealing with the Y term, average consumer income.

If we isolate Q^d as a function of the other terms, we get:

(6A-5) $Q^d = \left(\dfrac{a_0}{b}\right) + \left(\dfrac{a_1}{b}\right) \times P_{corn\ syrup} - \left(\dfrac{a_2}{b}\right) \times P_{pancake\ mix} + \left(\dfrac{a_3}{b}\right) \times Y$

$+ \left(\dfrac{a_4}{b}\right) \times Tastes + \left(\dfrac{a_5}{b}\right) \times P_{future}^e + \left(\dfrac{a_6}{b}\right) \times Pop - \left(\dfrac{1}{b}\right) \times P$

As we noticed in Equation 6A-1, according to Equation 6A-5, if the average consumer income increases by \$1 (i.e., $\Delta Y = 1$), then the quantity demanded for maple syrup will increase by $\dfrac{a_3}{b}$ (i.e., $\Delta Q^d = \dfrac{a_3}{b}$). Therefore, the ratio $\dfrac{\Delta Q^d}{\Delta Y}$ is equal to $\dfrac{a_3}{b}$. So, using the general demand curve given above, we get:

(6A-6) Income elasticity of demand $= E_{Inc} = \left(\dfrac{\Delta Q^d}{\Delta Y}\right) \times \left(\dfrac{Y}{Q^d}\right) = \left(\dfrac{a_3}{b}\right) \times \left(\dfrac{Y}{Q^d}\right)$

We know that b, Y, and Q^d are all positive, so a_3 determines whether the income elasticity of demand is positive or negative:

If $a_3 > 0$, then $E_{Inc} = \left(\dfrac{a_3}{b}\right) \times \left(\dfrac{Y}{Q}\right) > 0$

If $a_3 < 0$, then $E_{Inc} = \left(\dfrac{a_3}{b}\right) \times \left(\dfrac{Y}{Q}\right) < 0$

So if $a_3 > 0$, this good is a normal good (like maple syrup) because an increase in income results in an increase in demand. Similarly, if $a_3 < 0$, this good is an inferior good because an increase in income results in a decrease in demand.

‖ Cross-Price Elasticity of Demand

The cross-price elasticity of demand measures how sensitive the demand curve is to changes in the price of some other good or service by measuring how far the demand curve shifts along the quantity axis as the other price changes. More precisely it measures the percentage change in quantity demand per percentage change in the other goods price. Using the general demand curve given above in Equation (6A-5) we get:

(6A-7) Cross-price elasticity of demand $= E_{cross\text{-}price} = \left(\dfrac{\Delta Q^d}{\Delta P_{corn\ syrup}}\right) \times \left(\dfrac{P_{corn\ syrup}}{Q^d}\right)$

$= \left(\dfrac{a_1}{b}\right) \times \left(\dfrac{P_{corn\ syrup}}{Q^d}\right)$

Again, analyzing Equation 6A-5 reveals that when the price of corn syrup increases by \$1 (i.e., $\Delta P_{corn\ syrup} = 1$), then the quantity of maple syrup demanded increases by $\dfrac{a_1}{b}$ (i.e., $\Delta Q^d = \dfrac{a_1}{b}$). Therefore, the ratio $\dfrac{\Delta Q^d}{\Delta P_{corn\ syrup}}$ is equal to $\dfrac{a_1}{b}$.

Since $b, P_{corn\ syrup}$, and Q^d are all positive, a_1 determines whether the cross-price elasticity of demand is positive or negative:

$$\text{If } a_1 > 0, \text{ then } E_{cross\text{-}price} = \left(\frac{a_1}{b}\right) \times \left(\frac{P_{corn\ syrup}}{Q^d}\right) > 0$$

$$\text{If } a_1 < 0, \text{ then } E_{cross\text{-}price} = \left(\frac{a_1}{b}\right) \times \left(\frac{P_{corn\ syrup}}{Q^d}\right) < 0$$

So if $a_1 > 0$, the other good is a substitute (as corn syrup is for maple syrup) and an increase in the price of the second good causes an increase in demand for the first good. Similarly, if $a_1 < 0$, the other good is a complement (as pancake mix is for maple syrup) and an increase in the price of the second good causes a decrease in demand for the first good.

‖ Elasticity of Supply

In the case of linear expressions, a supply curve in its simplest form would be:

(6A-8) $P = c + d \times Q^S$

or

(6A-9) $Q^S = \left(\frac{c}{d}\right) + \left(\frac{1}{d}\right) \times P$

where P denotes the price, Q^S denotes the quantity, and c and d are positive constants. Continuing with the maple syrup example, if the price of maple syrup increases by \$1 per litre (i.e., $\Delta P = 1$), then the quantity supplied will increase by $\frac{1}{d}$ (i.e., $\Delta Q^S = -\frac{1}{d}$). Therefore, the ratio $\frac{\Delta Q^S}{\Delta P}$ is equal to $\frac{1}{d}$.

Now we can look more closely at the price elasticity of supply:

(6A-10) $E_S = \text{Elasticity of supply} = \left(\frac{\Delta Q^S}{\Delta P}\right) \times \left(\frac{P}{Q^S}\right)$

$$= \left(\frac{1}{d}\right) \times \left(\frac{P}{Q^S}\right) = \left(\frac{1}{d}\right) \times \left(\frac{c + d \times Q^S}{Q^S}\right) = \left(\frac{c + d \times Q^S}{d \times Q^S}\right) = \left(\frac{c}{d \times Q^S}\right) + 1$$

Notice:

- If $c = 0$, then the supply curve goes through the origin and the price elasticity of supply is equal to one.
- If $c > 0$, then the supply curve intersects along the P-axis and the price elasticity of supply is greater than one (elastic supply).
- If $c < 0$, then the supply curve intersects along the Q^S-axis and the price elasticity of supply is less than one (inelastic supply).
- If $c \neq 0$, as we move along the supply curve c and d remain constant but Q^S varies. Therefore the price elasticity of supply varies as we move along a linear supply curve that does not pass through the origin.

PROBLEMS

1. This question uses the algebraic method of determining equilibrium from Appendix 3A. Suppose that the demand and supply for maple syrup is given by the following equations:

$$P = 53.25 - 1.25Q^d \qquad \text{Demand Curve}$$
$$P = 12.75 + 0.25Q^S \qquad \text{Supply Curve}$$

a. Solve for the equilibrium price and quantity. Determine the price elasticity of demand and supply in equilibrium.

b. Determine the unit-elastic point for this demand curve.

c. Given $P_{pancake\ mix} = 12$ and $a_2 = -1.8$ (the coefficient of the price of pancake mix in the expanded demand curve), determine the cross-price elasticity of demand at the equilibrium point.

d. The incomes of consumers rise, which shift the demand curve to $P = 55.50 - 1.25Q^d$ and at the same time an improvement in technology shifts the supply curve to $P = 7.50 + 0.25Q^S$. Solve for the new equilibrium price and quantity. Determine the price elasticity of demand and supply at this new equilibrium.

2. This question uses the algebraic method of determining equilibrium from Appendix 3A. Suppose the monthly demand and supply for iPods are given by the following equations:

$$P = 500 - 0.001Q^d \qquad \text{Demand Curve}$$
$$P = 200 + 0.0005Q^S \qquad \text{Supply Curve}$$

a. Use the supply and demand curves given above to solve for the equilibrium levels of price and quantity. Determine the price elasticity of demand and supply in equilibrium.

b. Given $Y = 40,000$ and $a_3 = 0.004$ (the coefficient of the average consumer index from the expanded demand curve), determine the income elasticity of demand at the equilibrium point.

c. Suppose instead that the offshoring of the production of tablets to a lower-cost country causes the supply curve to shift to $P = 140 + 0.0005Q^S$. Derive the resulting new equilibrium levels of price and quantity. Determine the price elasticity of demand and supply at this new equilibrium.

7 Taxes

AN ABORIGINAL TAX CONFLICT

IN THE SUMMER OF 1990, Mohawks from the Kanesatake reserve near Montreal held marches and erected a peaceful blockade to protest the planned expansion of a golf course in Oka, Québec. The Mohawks claimed the golf course expansion would further encroach on their land. Early in the 78-day standoff, after the arrival of supporters from the Akwesasne reserve, police attacked the barricade with tear gas and flash grenades. Gunfire soon erupted and officer Corporal Marcel Lemay was killed.

CP Photo/Tom Hanson

Taxation was one of the issues behind the 1990 Oka conflict in Québec.

What was the fighting about? Land claims, certainly, but also taxes. Most bands of Aboriginal Canadians have signed treaties with the federal government recognizing them as distinct nations within Canada, exempt from taxation. The government has a bad record of not fully honouring treaties, which has led to frequent disputes over territory. For some Mohawk reserves, issues related to taxation were never far away.

You could say the Oka conflict started with the Akwesasne reserve, which overlaps parts of Ontario, Québec, and New York state. This was the centre of "tax-based" conflicts related to gambling and smuggling, starting in the 1980s. According to one source, by the spring of 1990, Akwesasne had become the fourth-largest gambling centre in North America. More than a dozen casinos were bringing in millions of dollars, paying no taxes, and were not accountable to anyone, including Mohawk leaders. The smuggling business and sale of tax-free cigarettes were similarly large-scale, very profitable, and depriving governments of many millions in tax revenue.

In early 1990, divisions within the Akwesasne reserve led to anti-casino blockades erected by Mohawks, violence, several killings, and the eventual intervention from Canadian and U.S. police forces. The casinos and alleged smuggling operations were shut down. A few months later, those on the losing side, eager to repair their image and regain strength within the Mohawk reserves, happily sent weapons and manpower to Oka.

And tax and land disputes continue. The sale of tax-free cigarettes remains a thriving business, providing impoverished people with income, but possibly dodging tax laws. In 1994, a Revenue Canada building in downtown Toronto was occupied for over a month by protesters reacting to a government plan to tax Aboriginal people and businesses for any income earned for work off-reserve (even if the employer was on a reserve).

There are two main morals to this story. One, taxes are necessary: all governments need money to function. Without taxes, governments could not provide the services we want, from national defence to public parks. But taxes have a cost that normally exceeds the money actually paid to the government. That's because taxes distort incentives to engage in mutually beneficial transactions.

And that leads us to the second moral: making tax policy isn't easy—in fact, if you are a politician, it can be dangerous to your professional health. But the story also illustrates some crucial issues in tax policy—issues that economic models help clarify.

One principle used for guiding tax policy is efficiency: taxes should be designed to distort incentives as little as possible. But efficiency is not the only concern when designing tax rates. As the government learned from the Revenue Canada occupation, it's also important that a tax be seen as fair. Tax policy always involves striking a balance between the pursuit of efficiency and the pursuit of perceived fairness.

In this chapter, we will look at how taxes affect efficiency and fairness as well as raise revenue for the government. ●

WHAT YOU WILL LEARN

- How do taxes affect supply and demand?
- What factors determine who bears the burden of a tax?
- What are the costs and benefits of a tax, and why is the cost greater than the tax revenue generated?

- What is the difference between **progressive** and **regressive taxes**?
- Why is there a **trade-off between equity and efficiency** in the design of a tax system?
- How is the Canadian tax system structured?

An **excise tax** is a tax on sales of a good or service.

The Economics of Taxes: A Preliminary View

To understand the economics of taxes, it's helpful to look at a simple type of tax known as an **excise tax**—a tax charged on each unit of a good or service that is sold. Most tax revenue in Canada comes from other kinds of taxes, which we'll describe later in the chapter. But excise taxes are common. For example, there are excise taxes on gasoline, cigarettes, and fuel-inefficient vehicles, and many local governments impose excise taxes on services such as hotel room rentals. The lessons we'll learn from studying excise taxes apply to other, more complex taxes as well.

The Effect of an Excise Tax on Quantities and Prices

Suppose that the supply and demand for hotel rooms in the city of Potterville are as shown in Figure 7-1. We'll make the simplifying assumption that all hotel rooms are the same. In the absence of taxes, the equilibrium price of a room is $80 per night and the equilibrium quantity of hotel rooms rented is 10,000 per night.

Now suppose that Potterville's government imposes an excise tax of $40 per night on hotel rooms—that is, every time a room is rented for the night, the owner of the hotel must pay the city $40. For example, if a customer pays $80, $40 is collected as a tax, leaving the hotel owner with only $40. As a result, hotel owners are less willing to supply rooms at any given price.

What does this imply about the supply curve for hotel rooms in Potterville? To answer this question, we must compare the incentives of hotel owners *pre*-tax (before the tax is levied) to their incentives *post*-tax (after the tax is levied).

From Figure 7-1 we know that pre-tax, hotel owners are willing to supply 5,000 rooms per night at a price of $60 per room. But after the $40 tax per room is levied, they are willing to supply the same amount, 5,000 rooms, only if they receive $100 per room—$60 for themselves plus $40 paid to the city as tax. This is shown by point *A*. In other words, for hotel owners to be willing to supply the

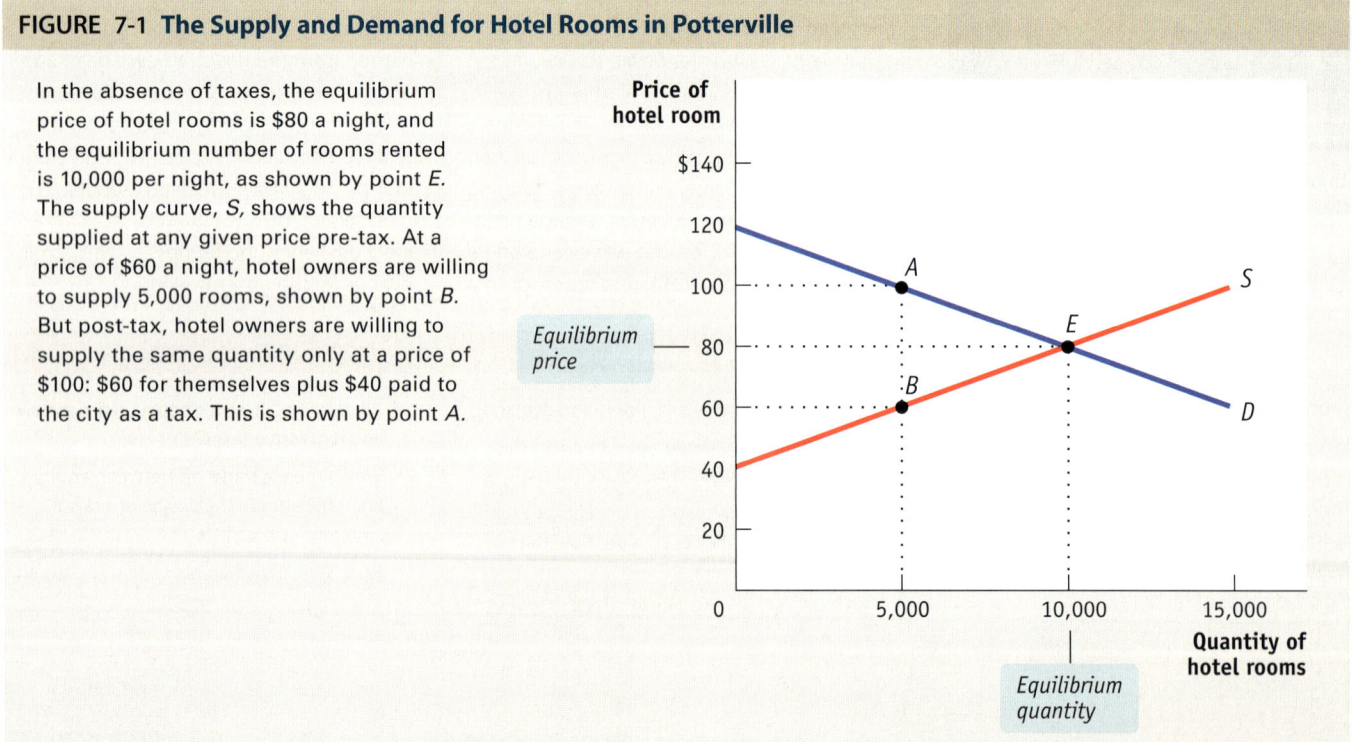

FIGURE 7-1 The Supply and Demand for Hotel Rooms in Potterville

In the absence of taxes, the equilibrium price of hotel rooms is $80 a night, and the equilibrium number of rooms rented is 10,000 per night, as shown by point *E*. The supply curve, *S*, shows the quantity supplied at any given price pre-tax. At a price of $60 a night, hotel owners are willing to supply 5,000 rooms, shown by point *B*. But post-tax, hotel owners are willing to supply the same quantity only at a price of $100: $60 for themselves plus $40 paid to the city as a tax. This is shown by point *A*.

same quantity post-tax as they would have pre-tax, they must receive an additional $40 per room, the amount of the tax.

This implies that the post-tax supply curve shifts up, decreasing by the amount of the tax compared to the pre-tax supply curve. At every quantity supplied, the supply price—the price that producers must receive to produce a given quantity—has increased by $40.

The upward shift of the supply curve caused by the tax is shown in Figure 7-2, where S_1 is the pre-tax supply curve and S_2 is the post-tax supply curve. As you can see, as a result of the tax the market equilibrium moves from E, at the equilibrium price of $80 per room and 10,000 rooms rented each night, to A, at a market price of $100 per room and only 5,000 rooms rented each night. A is, of course, on both the demand curve D and the new supply curve S_2.

Although $100 is the demand price (P_C) of 5,000 rooms—but in effect hotel owners receive only $60 ($P_P$), because they must pay $40 of it in tax. From the point of view of hotel owners, it is as if they were on their original supply curve at point B.

Let's check this again. How do we know that 5,000 rooms will be supplied at a price of $100? Because the price net of tax ($P_P = P_C - T$) is $60, and according to the original supply curve, 5,000 rooms will be supplied at a price of $60, as shown by point B in Figure 7-2.

Does this look familiar? It should. In Chapter 5, we described the effects of a quota on sales: a quota *drives a wedge* between the price paid by consumers and the price received by producers. An excise tax does the same thing. As a result of this wedge, consumers pay more (P_c) and producers receive less (P_P), with the gap being the tax wedge (T), so that $P_C = P_P + T$.

In our example, consumers—people who rent hotel rooms—end up paying $100 a night, $20 more than the pre-tax price of $80. At the same time, producers—the hotel owners—receive a price net of tax of $60 per room, $20 less than the pre-tax price. In addition, the tax creates missed opportunities: 5,000 potential consumers who would have rented hotel rooms—those willing to pay $80 but not $100 per night—are discouraged from doing so. Correspondingly, 5,000 rooms that would have been made available by hotel owners if they received $80 are not offered when they receive only $60. Like a quota, this tax leads to inefficiency by

FIGURE 7-2 An Excise Tax Imposed on Hotel Owners

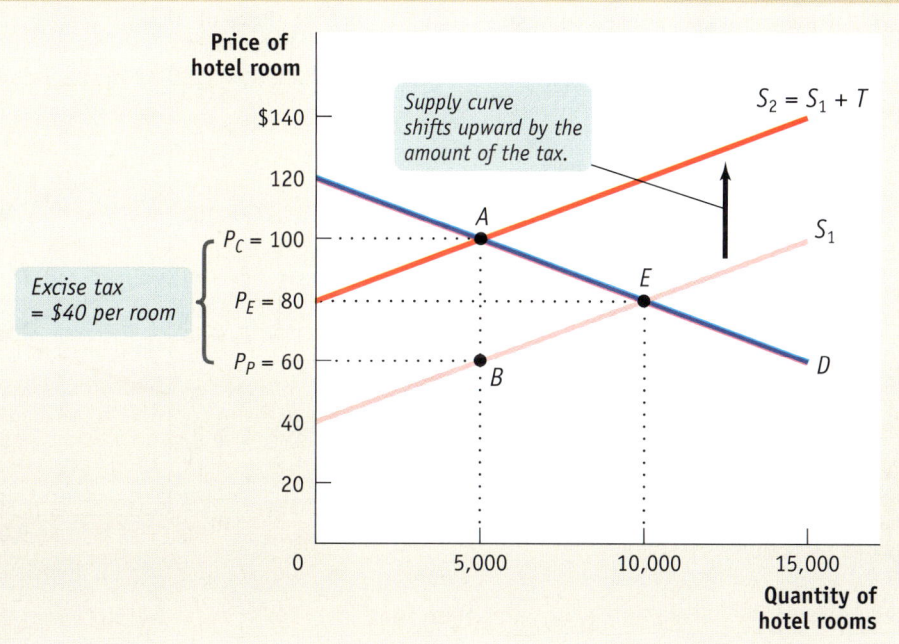

A $40 per room tax imposed on hotel owners shifts the supply curve from S_1 to S_2, an upward shift of $T = $40. The equilibrium price of hotel rooms rises from $80 to $100 per night, and the equilibrium quantity of rooms rented falls from 10,000 to 5,000. Although hotel owners pay the tax, they actually bear only half the burden: the price they receive net of tax falls only $20, from $80 to $60. Guests who rent rooms bear the other half of the burden, because the price they pay rises $20, from $80 to $100.

The **incidence** of a tax is a measure of who really pays it.

distorting incentives and creating missed opportunities for mutually beneficial transactions.

It's important to recognize that as we've described it, Potterville's hotel tax is a tax on the hotel owners, not their guests—it's a tax on the producers, not the consumers. Yet the price received by producers, net of tax (P_P) falls by only $20, half the amount of the tax, and the price paid by consumers (P_C) rises by $20. In effect, half the tax is being paid by consumers.

What would happen if the city levied a tax on consumers instead of producers? That is, suppose that instead of requiring hotel owners to pay $40 a night for each room they rent, the city required hotel *guests* to pay $40 for each night they stayed in a hotel. The answer is shown in Figure 7-3. If a hotel guest must pay a tax of $40 per night, then the price for a room paid by that guest must be reduced by $40 for the quantity of hotel rooms demanded post-tax to be the same as that demanded pre-tax. Thus, the demand curve shifts *downward* by the amount of the tax from D_1 to $D_2 = D - T$.

At every quantity demanded, the demand price—the price that consumers must be offered to demand a given quantity—has fallen by $40. This shifts the equilibrium from E to B, where the market price of hotel rooms is $60 and 5,000 hotel rooms are rented. In effect, hotel guests pay $100 when the tax is included. So from the point of view of guests, it is as if they were on their original demand curve at point A.

If you compare Figures 7-2 and 7-3, you will immediately notice that they show equivalent outcomes. In both cases consumers pay $100 (= P_C), producers receive $60 (= P_P) and 5,000 hotel rooms are bought and sold. *In fact, it doesn't matter who officially pays the tax—the outcome is the same.*

This insight illustrates a general principle of the economics of taxation: the **incidence** of a tax—who really bears the burden of the tax—is typically not a question you can answer by asking who writes the cheque to the government. In this particular case, a $40 tax on hotel rooms is reflected in a $20 increase in the price paid by consumers and a $20 decrease in the price received by producers. Here, regardless of whether the tax is levied on consumers or producers, the incidence of the tax is evenly split between them.

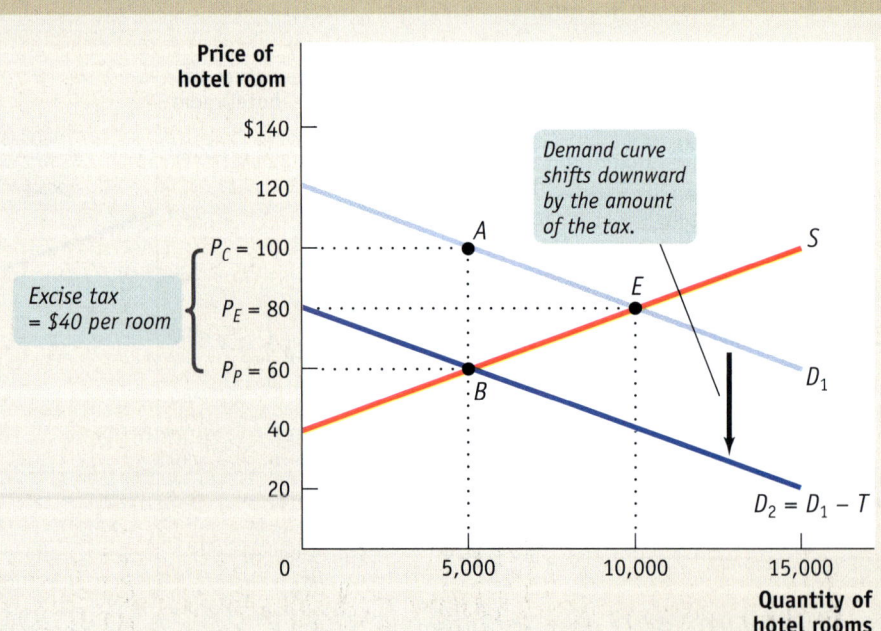

FIGURE 7-3 An Excise Tax Imposed on Hotel Guests

A $40 per room tax imposed on hotel guests shifts the demand curve from D_1 to D_2, a downward shift of $40. The equilibrium price of hotel rooms falls from $80 to $60 per night, and the quantity of rooms rented falls from 10,000 to 5,000. Although in this case the tax is officially paid by consumers, while in Figure 7-2 the tax was paid by producers, the outcome is the same: after taxes, hotel owners receive $60 per room but guests pay $100. This illustrates a general principle: *The incidence of an excise tax doesn't depend on whether consumers or producers officially pay the tax.*

Price Elasticities and Tax Incidence

We've just learned that the incidence of an excise tax doesn't depend on who officially pays it. In the example shown in Figures 7-1 through 7-3, a tax on hotel rooms falls equally on consumers and producers, no matter who the tax is levied on.

But it's important to note that this 50–50 split between consumers and producers is a result of our assumptions in this example. In the real world, the incidence of an excise tax usually falls unevenly between consumers and producers, as one group bears more of the burden than the other.

What determines how the burden of an excise tax is allocated between consumers and producers? The answer is that it depends on the shapes of the supply and the demand curves. *More specifically, the incidence of an excise tax depends on the price elasticity of supply and the price elasticity of demand.* We first look at a case in which consumers pay most of an excise tax, then at a case in which producers pay most of the tax.

When an Excise Tax Is Paid Mainly by Consumers Figure 7-4 shows an excise tax that falls mainly on consumers: an excise tax on gasoline, which we set at $0.25 per litre. (There really is a federal excise tax on gasoline, though it is actually only about $0.10 per litre in Canada. Finally, the GST/HST, and, if applicable, provincial sales taxes also apply to gasoline sales.) According to Figure 7-4, in the absence of the tax, gasoline would sell for $1.05 per litre.

Two key assumptions are reflected in the shapes of the supply and demand curves in Figure 7-4.

1. The price elasticity of demand for gasoline is assumed to be very low, so the demand curve is relatively steep. Recall that a low price elasticity of demand means that the quantity demanded changes little in response to a change in price—a feature of a steep demand curve.

2. The price elasticity of supply of gasoline is assumed to be very high, so the supply curve is relatively flat. A high price elasticity of supply means that the quantity supplied changes a lot in response to a change in price—a feature of a relatively flat supply curve.

We have learned that an excise tax drives a wedge, equal to the size of the tax, between the price paid by consumers and the price received by producers. This wedge drives the price paid by consumers up and the price received by producers

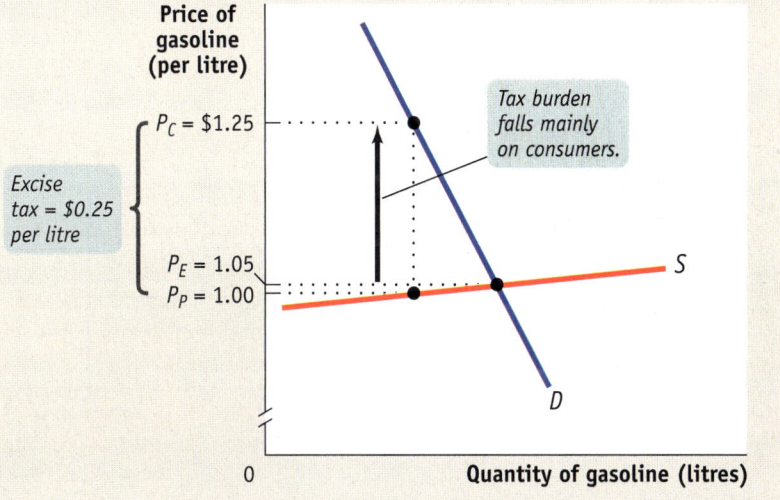

FIGURE 7-4 An Excise Tax Paid Mainly by Consumers

The relatively steep demand curve here reflects a low price elasticity of demand for gasoline. The relatively flat supply curve reflects a high price of elasticity of supply. The pre-tax price of a litre of gasoline is $1.05, and a tax of $0.25 per litre is imposed. The price paid by consumers rises by $0.20 to $1.25, reflecting the fact that most of the burden of the tax falls on consumers. Only a small portion of the tax is borne by producers: the price they receive falls by only $0.05 to $1.00.

down. But as we can see from Figure 7-4, in this case those two effects are very unequal in size. The price received by producers falls only slightly, from $1.05 to $1.00, but the price paid by consumers rises by a lot, from $1.05 to $1.25. In this case, consumers bear the greater share of the tax burden.

This example illustrates another general principle of taxation: *When the price elasticity of demand is low and the price elasticity of supply is high, the burden of an excise tax falls mainly on consumers.* Why? A low price elasticity of demand means that consumers have few substitutes, and therefore little alternative to buying higher-priced gasoline. In contrast, a high price elasticity of supply results from the fact that producers have many production substitutes for their gasoline (that is, other uses for the crude oil from which gasoline is refined).

This gives producers much greater flexibility in refusing to accept lower prices for their gasoline. And, not surprisingly, the party with the least flexibility—in this case, consumers—gets stuck paying most of the tax. This is a good description of how the burden of the most significant excise taxes actually collected in Canada today, such as those on cigarettes and alcoholic beverages, is allocated between consumers and producers.

When an Excise Tax Is Paid Mainly by Producers Figure 7-5 shows an example of an excise tax paid mainly by producers, a $5.00 per day tax on downtown parking in a small city. In the absence of the tax, the market equilibrium price of parking is $6.00 per day.

We've assumed in this case that the price elasticity of supply is very low because the lots used for parking have very few alternative uses. This makes the supply curve for parking spaces relatively steep. The price elasticity of demand, however, is assumed to be high: substitutes are readily available as consumers can easily switch from the downtown spaces to other parking spaces a few minutes' walk from downtown, spaces that are not subject to the tax. This makes the demand curve relatively flat.

The tax drives a wedge between the price paid by consumers and the price received by producers. In this example, however, the tax causes the price paid by consumers to rise only slightly, from $6.00 to $6.50, but causes the price received by producers to fall a lot, from $6.00 to $1.50. In the end, consumers bear only $0.50 of the $5.00 tax burden, with producers bearing the remaining $4.50.

Again, this example illustrates a general principle: *When the price elasticity of demand is high and the price elasticity of supply is low, the burden of an excise*

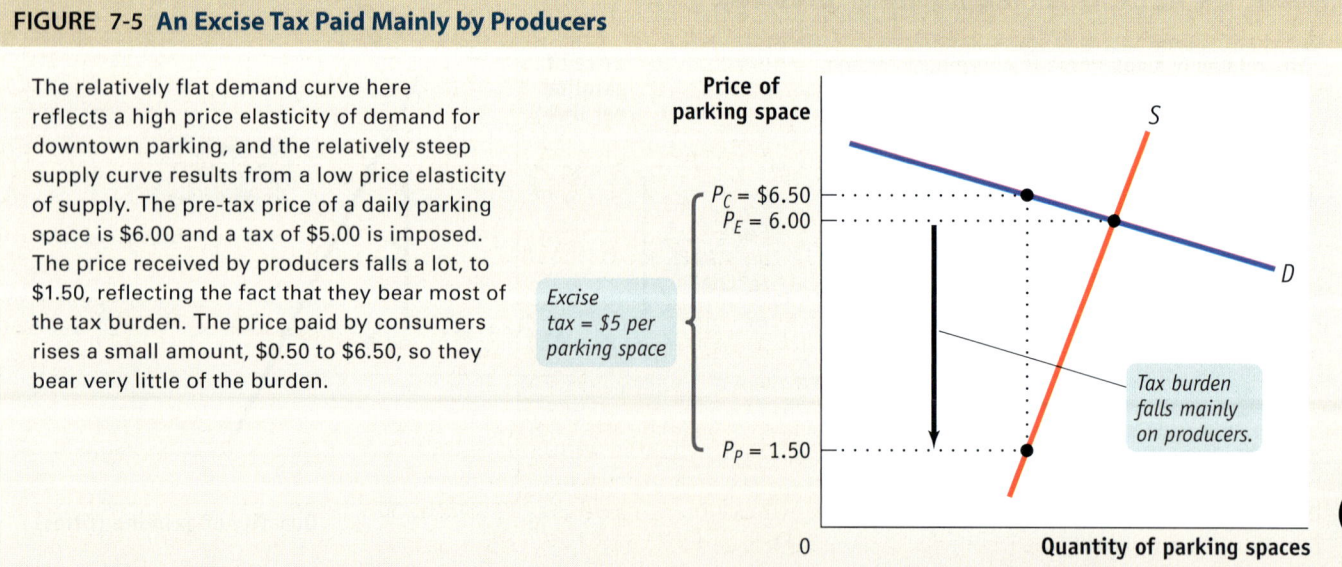

FIGURE 7-5 An Excise Tax Paid Mainly by Producers

The relatively flat demand curve here reflects a high price elasticity of demand for downtown parking, and the relatively steep supply curve results from a low price elasticity of supply. The pre-tax price of a daily parking space is $6.00 and a tax of $5.00 is imposed. The price received by producers falls a lot, to $1.50, reflecting the fact that they bear most of the tax burden. The price paid by consumers rises a small amount, $0.50 to $6.50, so they bear very little of the burden.

Price of parking space

$P_C = \$6.50$
$P_E = 6.00$

Excise tax = $5 per parking space

$P_P = 1.50$

S

D

Tax burden falls mainly on producers.

0   Quantity of parking spaces

tax falls mainly on producers. A real-world example is a tax on purchases of existing houses. Before the recession hit Canada in 2008, the cash-strapped city of Toronto implemented a municipal land transfer tax to raise revenue. A land transfer tax is collected as a percentage of the price at which a residential or commercial property sells.

To politicians, the idea was simple: homes sales were strong and in the preceding years prices had steadily risen. The tax rate was designed to rise somewhat as the price increased, so to some degree the higher the price paid the more tax paid in both relative and absolute terms. So besides helping the city meet its budgetary needs, the tax was intended to be paid mostly by well-off outsiders moving into desirable locations and purchasing homes from the less well-off original occupants. But this ignores the fact that the price elasticity of demand for houses in Toronto is often high, because potential buyers can choose to move to other towns. Furthermore, the price elasticity of supply is often low because most sellers must sell their houses due to job transfers or to provide funds for their retirement. So taxes on home purchases are actually paid mainly by the less well-off sellers—not, as Toronto officials may have imagined, by wealthy buyers.

Putting It All Together   We've just seen that when the price elasticity of supply is high and the price elasticity of demand is low, an excise tax falls mainly on consumers. And when the price elasticity of supply is low and the price elasticity of demand is high, an excise tax falls mainly on producers. This leads us to the general rule: *When the price elasticity of demand is higher than the price elasticity of supply, an excise tax falls mainly on producers. When the price elasticity of supply is higher than the price elasticity of demand, an excise tax falls mainly on consumers.*

So elasticity—not who officially pays the tax—determines the incidence of an excise tax.

ECONOMICS >> *in Action*
Who Pays Canada's Payroll Taxes?

Anyone who works for an employer receives a paycheque that itemizes not only the wages paid but also the money deducted from the paycheque for various taxes. For most people, one of the big deductions is for Canada's various payroll taxes. Nationally, these payroll taxes fund the Canada Pension Plan (CPP), a pension plan for Canada's workers (workers in Québec contribute to the Québec Pension Plan (QPP)), and Employment-Insurance (EI), an insurance program that provides assistance to many of Canada's workers during periods of unemployment. At the provincial level, payroll taxes exist to fund worker compensation systems for injured workers and, in some cases, to help fund provincial health and education spending.

Contrary to widely held beliefs, for many Canadians it's payroll taxes, not the income tax, that takes the biggest bite from their paycheques.

In 2020, most Canadian workers paid 6.83% of about the first $58,700 of their earnings in CPP (5.25%) and EI (1.58%) contributions. But this isn't even the half of it: each employer is required to pay an amount equal to the CPP contributions and 1.4 times the EI contributions of its employees. And when it comes to the various other provincial payroll taxes, the employer is expected to pay the entire amount.

How should we think about Canada's payroll taxes? Are they really shared by workers and employers? We can use our previous analysis to answer that question because payroll taxes are like an excise tax—a tax on the sale and purchase of labour. A portion of it is a tax levied on the sellers—that is, workers. The rest is a tax levied on the buyers—that is, employers.

But we already know that the incidence of a tax does not really depend on who actually makes out the cheque. Almost all economists agree that payroll taxes are more costly for workers than for their employers. The reason for this conclusion lies in a comparison of the price elasticities of the supply of labour by households and the demand for labour by firms. Evidence indicates that the price elasticity of demand for labour is quite high, at least 3. That is, an increase in average wages of 1% would lead to at least a 3% decline in the number of hours of work demanded by employers. Labour economists believe, however, that the price elasticity of supply of labour is very low. The reason is that although a fall in the wage rate reduces the incentive to work more hours, it also makes people poorer and less able to afford leisure time. The strength of this second effect is shown in the data: the number of hours people are willing to work falls very little—if at all—when the wage per hour goes down.

Our general rule of tax incidence says that when the price elasticity of demand is much higher than the price elasticity of supply, the burden of an excise tax falls mainly on the suppliers. So the burden of Canada's payroll taxes falls mainly on the suppliers of labour, that is, workers—even though on paper most of these taxes are paid by employers. Payroll taxes are largely borne by workers in the form of lower wages, rather than by employers in the form of lower profits.

This conclusion tells us something important about the Canadian tax system: payroll taxes, rather than the much-maligned income tax, are the main tax burden on families in the lower half of the income distribution. For most workers, payroll taxes amount to more than 14.3% of all wages and salaries up to about $58,700 per year (note that $6.83\% + 5.25\% + 1.4 \times 1.58\% = 14.292\%$). Thus, the great majority of workers in Canada pay about 14.3% of their wages in federal payroll taxes and more when taking the provincial payroll taxes into consideration.

Meanwhile, only middle- and high-income Canadian families pay more than 15% of their income in income tax. In fact, according to the Fraser Institute, the average Canadian household earned an income of $88,865 in 2018, and they paid $39,399 in taxes—more than their spending on housing, food, and clothing combined. Of the total taxes paid, average household paid $12,242 in income taxes and $7,475 in payroll and health taxes, which represented 31.2% and 19% of the total taxes paid. So for the average family, payroll taxes represent their second largest tax burden.

>> Quick Review

• An **excise tax** drives a wedge between the price paid by consumers and that received by producers, leading to a fall in the quantity transacted. It creates inefficiency by distorting incentives and creating missed opportunities.

• The **incidence** of an excise tax doesn't depend on who the tax is officially levied on. Rather, it depends on the price elasticities of demand and of supply.

• The higher the price elasticity of supply and the lower the price elasticity of demand, the heavier the burden of an excise tax on consumers. The lower the price elasticity of supply and the higher the price elasticity of demand, the heavier the burden on producers.

>> Check Your Understanding 7-1

Solutions appear at back of book.

1. Consider the market for butter, shown in the accompanying figure. The government imposes an excise tax of $0.30 per kilogram of butter. What is the price paid by consumers post-tax? What is the price received by producers post-tax? What is the quantity of butter transacted? How is the incidence of the tax allocated between consumers and producers? Show this on the figure.

2. The demand for economics textbooks is very inelastic, but the supply is somewhat elastic. What does this imply about the incidence of an excise tax? Illustrate with a diagram.

3. True or false? When a substitute for a good is readily available to consumers, but it is difficult for producers to adjust the quantity of the good produced, then the burden of a tax on the good falls more heavily on producers. Explain your answer.

4. The supply of bottled spring water is very inelastic, but the demand for it is somewhat elastic. What does this imply about the incidence of a tax? Illustrate with a diagram.

5. True or false? Other things equal, consumers would prefer to face a less elastic supply curve for a good or service when an excise tax is imposed. Explain your answer.

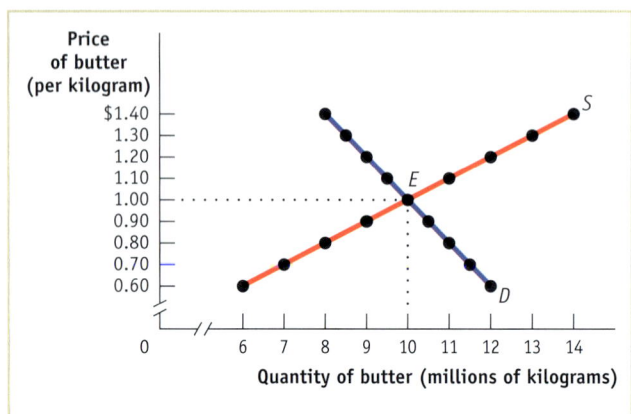

‖ The Benefits and Costs of Taxation

When a government is considering whether to impose a tax or how to design a tax system, it has to weigh the benefits of a tax against its costs. We don't usually think of a tax as something that provides benefits, but governments need money to provide things people want, such as building infrastructure and health care for those unable to afford it. The benefit of a tax is the revenue it raises for the government to pay for these services. Unfortunately, this benefit comes at a cost—a cost that is normally greater than the amount consumers and producers pay. Let's look first at what determines how much money a tax raises, then at the costs a tax imposes.

The Revenue from an Excise Tax

How much revenue does the government collect from an excise tax? In our hotel tax example, the revenue is equal to the area of the shaded rectangle in Figure 7-6. To see why this area represents the revenue collected by a $40 tax on hotel rooms, notice that the height of the rectangle is $40, equal to the tax per room. It is also, as we've seen, the size of the wedge that the tax drives between the supply price (the price received by producers) and the demand price (the price paid by consumers). Meanwhile, the width of the rectangle is 5,000 rooms, equal to the equilibrium quantity of rooms given the $40 tax. With that information, we can make the following calculations.

The tax revenue collected is:

$$\text{Tax revenue} = \$40 \text{ per room} \times 5{,}000 \text{ rooms} = \$200{,}000$$

The area of the shaded rectangle is:

$$\text{Area} = \text{Height} \times \text{Width} = \$40 \text{ per room} \times 5{,}000 \text{ rooms} = \$200{,}000$$

or

$$\text{Tax revenue} = \text{Area of shaded rectangle}$$

This is a general principle: *The revenue collected by an excise tax is equal to the area of the rectangle whose height is the tax wedge between the supply and demand curves and whose width is the quantity transacted under the tax.*

"*What taxes would you like to see imposed on other people?*"

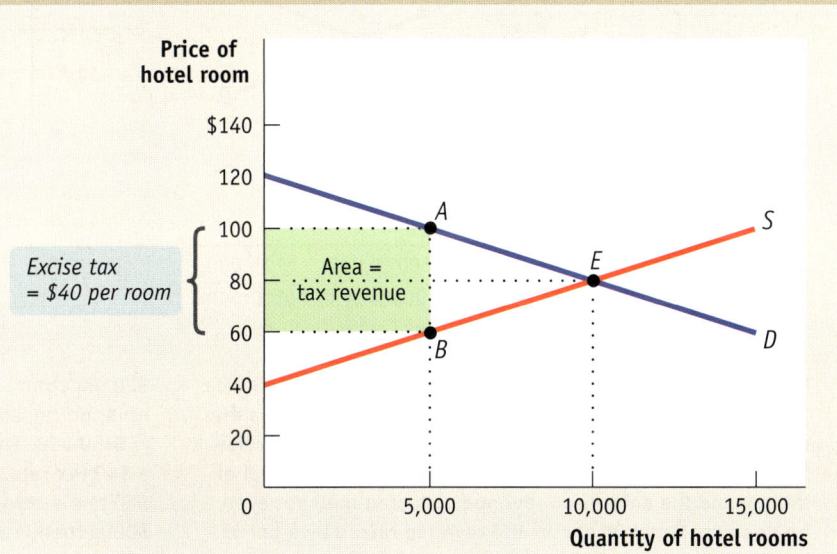

FIGURE 7-6 The Revenue from an Excise Tax

The revenue from a $40 excise tax on hotel rooms is $200,000, equal to the tax rate, $40—the size of the wedge that the tax drives between the supply price and the demand price—multiplied by the number of rooms rented, 5,000. This is equal to the area of the shaded rectangle.

A **tax rate** is the amount of tax people are required to pay per unit of whatever is being taxed.

Tax Rates and Revenue

In Figure 7-6, $40 per room is the *tax rate* on hotel rooms. A **tax rate** is the amount of tax levied per unit of the taxed item. Sometimes tax rates are defined in terms of dollar amounts per unit of a good or service; for example, a federal excise tax of $2.48 per pack of cigarettes sold. In other cases, they are defined as a percentage of the price; for example, the (federal) payroll tax is 14.3% of a worker's earnings up to $58,700 in 2020.

There's obviously a relationship between tax rates and revenue. That relationship is not, however, one-for-one. In general, doubling the excise tax rate on a good or service won't double the amount of revenue collected, because the tax increase will reduce the quantity of the good or service transacted. And the relationship between the level of the tax and the amount of revenue collected may not even be positive: in some cases, raising the tax rate actually *reduces* the amount of revenue the government collects.

We can illustrate these points using our hotel room example. Figure 7-6 showed the revenue the government collects from a $40 tax on hotel rooms. Figure 7-7 shows the revenue the government would collect from two alternative tax rates—a lower tax of only $20 per room and a higher tax of $60 per room.

Panel (a) of Figure 7-7 shows the case of a $20 tax, equal to half the tax rate illustrated in Figure 7-6. At this lower tax rate, 7,500 rooms are rented, generating tax revenue of:

$$\text{Tax revenue} = \$20 \text{ per room} \times 7{,}500 \text{ rooms} = \$150{,}000$$

Recall that the tax revenue collected from a $40 tax rate is $200,000. So the revenue collected from a $20 tax rate, $150,000, is only 75% of the amount collected when the tax rate is twice as high ($150,000/$200,000 × 100 = 75%). To put

FIGURE 7-7 Tax Rates and Revenue

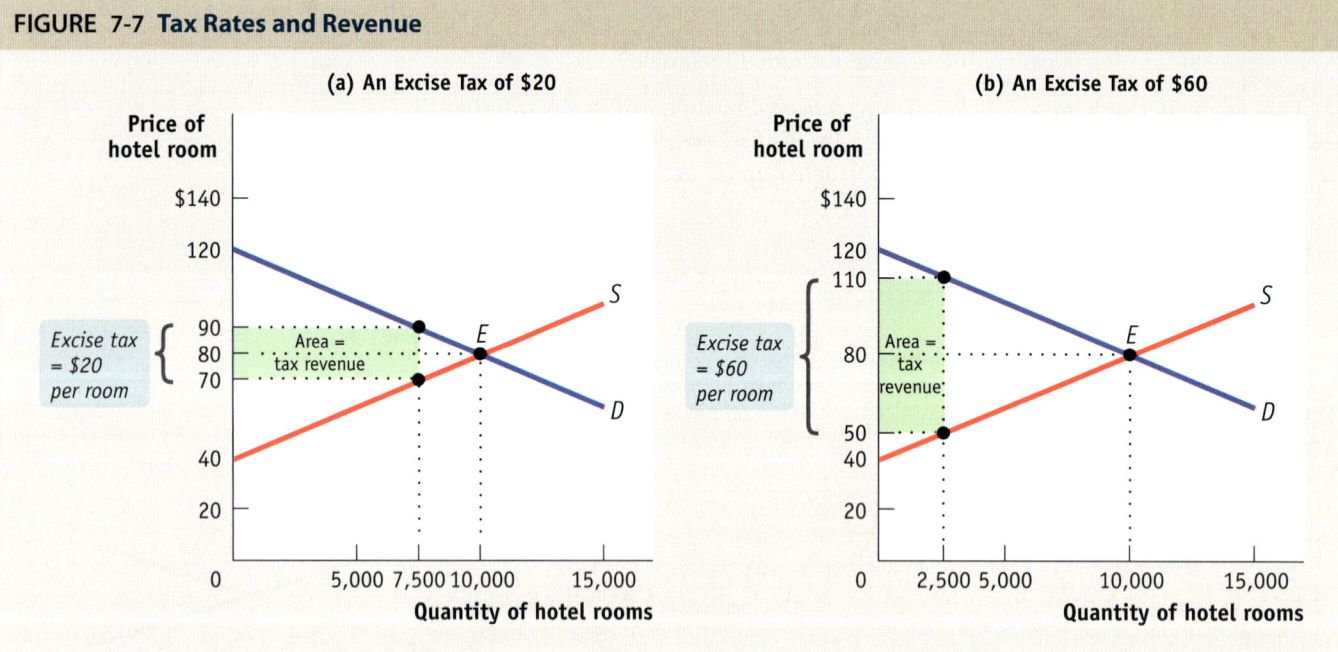

In general, doubling the excise tax rate on a good or service won't double the amount of revenue collected, because the tax increase will reduce the quantity of the good or service bought and sold. And the relationship between the level of the tax and the amount of revenue collected may not even be positive. Panel (a) shows the revenue raised by a tax of $20 per room, only half the tax rate in Figure 7-6. The tax revenue raised, equal to the area of the shaded rectangle, is $150,000. That is 75% of $200,000, the revenue raised by a $40 tax rate. Panel (b) shows that the revenue raised by a $60 tax is also $150,000. So raising the tax rate from $40 to $60 actually reduces tax revenue.

it another way, a 100% increase in the tax rate from $20 to $40 per room leads to only a one-third, or 33.3%, increase in revenue, from $150,000 to $200,000 (($200,000 − $150,000)/$150,000 × 100 = 33.3%).

Panel (b) depicts what happens if the tax rate is raised from $40 to $60 per room, leading to a fall in the number of rooms rented from 5,000 to 2,500. The revenue collected at a $60 per room tax rate is:

$$\text{Tax revenue} = \$60 \text{ per room} \times 2{,}500 \text{ rooms} = \$150{,}000$$

This is also *less* than the revenue collected by a $40 per room tax. So raising the tax rate from $40 to $60 actually reduces revenue. More precisely, in this case raising the tax rate by 50% (($60 − $40)/$40 × 100 = 50%) lowers the tax revenue by 25% (($150,000 − $200,000)/$200,000 × 100 = −25%). Why did this happen? Because the fall in tax revenue caused by the reduction in the number of rooms rented more than offset the increase in the tax revenue caused by the rise in the tax rate. In other words, setting a tax rate so high that it deters a significant number of transactions will likely lead to a fall in tax revenue.

One way to think about the revenue effect of increasing an excise tax is that the tax increase affects tax revenue in two ways. On one side, the tax increase means that the government raises more revenue for each unit of the good sold, which other things equal would lead to a rise in tax revenue. On the other side, the tax increase reduces the quantity of sales, which other things equal would lead to a fall in tax revenue. The end result depends both on the price elasticities of supply and demand and on the initial level of the tax.

If the price elasticities of both supply and demand are low, the tax increase won't reduce the quantity of the good sold very much, so tax revenue will definitely rise. If the price elasticities are high, the result is less certain; if they are high enough, the tax reduces the quantity sold so much that tax revenue falls. Also, if the initial tax rate is low, the government doesn't lose much revenue from the decline in the quantity of the good sold, so the tax increase will definitely increase tax revenue. If the initial tax rate is high, the result is again less certain. Tax revenue is likely to fall or rise very little from a tax increase only in cases in which the price elasticities are high and there is already a high tax rate.

The possibility that a higher tax rate can reduce tax revenue, and the corresponding possibility that cutting taxes can increase tax revenue, is a basic principle of taxation that policy makers take into account when setting tax rates. That is, when considering a tax created for the purpose of raising revenue (in contrast to taxes created to discourage undesirable behaviour, known as *sin taxes*), a well-informed policy maker won't impose a tax rate so high that cutting the tax would increase revenue.

In the real world, however, policy makers aren't always well informed, but they usually aren't complete fools either. That's why it's very hard to find real-world examples in which raising a tax reduced revenue or cutting a tax increased revenue. Nonetheless, the theoretical possibility that a tax reduction increases tax revenue has played an important role in the folklore of North American politics. Kevin Milligan from the University of British Columbia estimates that if Canada's personal income tax rate were to hit 57% (don't worry, we aren't there yet) then an increase in the tax rate would lower tax revenue. As explained in For Inquiring Minds, an economist who sketched out the figure of a revenue-increasing income tax reduction had a significant impact on the economic policies adopted in the United States in the 1980s.

The Costs of Taxation

What is the cost of a tax? Is it the money taxpayers pay to the government? In other words, is the cost of a tax the tax revenue collected? The answer to this question is actually more complex. Suppose the government uses the tax revenue to provide services that taxpayers want. Or that it just hands the tax revenue right back to taxpayers. Could we say in those cases that the tax didn't actually cost anything?

FOR INQUIRING MINDS French Tax Rates and *L'Arc Laffer*

One afternoon in 1974, the American economist Arthur Laffer drew on a napkin a diagram that came to be known as the *Laffer curve*. According to this diagram, raising tax rates initially increases tax revenue, but beyond a certain level a continued rise in tax rates causes tax revenues to fall as people forgo economic activity. Correspondingly, a reduction in tax rates from that threshold results in an increase in economic activity as more people are willing to undertake economic transactions.

Although not a new idea, Laffer's diagram captured the American political debate at the time. In 1981, newly elected American President Ronald Reagan enacted tax cuts with the promise that they would pay for themselves — that is, that the tax

cuts would increase economic activity so much that the federal government's revenue would not fall.

Very few economists now believe that Reagan's tax cuts actually increased government revenue because, on the whole, American tax rates were simply not high enough to provide a significant deterrent to economic activity. Yet there is a theoretical case that the Laffer curve does exist at high tax rate levels. And the case of the French tax hike appears to present a real-world illustration.

A 1997 change to the French tax law significantly raised taxes on wealthy French citizens. Moreover, unlike in the United States, it is relatively easy for a French person to move to a neighbouring country, such as Belgium

or Switzerland, with much lower taxes on the wealthy.

The matter exploded in a public fracas between France's most celebrated president, Francois Hollande, and one of the country's most celebrated actors, Gerard Depardieu, when Hollande announced a 75% tax rate on incomes over US$1.2 million to close a huge government deficit. It is estimated that several hundred billion dollars in assets left France, along with French citizens who chose to leave the country to escape higher tax rates. Among them was Depardieu, who renounced his French citizenship and decamped for Belgium. In addition, bankruptcies of businesses accelerated and firms slashed investment. Then, in 2015, the policy was abandoned and the tax rate on high incomes returned to its previous level.

No, we could not—because a tax, like a quota, prevents mutually beneficial transactions from occurring. Consider Figure 7-6 once more. Here, with a $40 tax on hotel rooms, guests pay $100 per room but hotel owners receive only $60 per room. Because of the wedge created by the tax, we know that some transactions don't occur that would have occurred without the tax.

For example, we know from the supply and demand curves that there are some potential guests who would be willing to pay up to $90 per night and some hotel owners who would be willing to supply rooms if they received at least $70 per night. If these two sets of people were allowed to trade with each other without the tax, they would engage in mutually beneficial transactions—hotel rooms would be rented.

But such deals would be illegal, because the $40 tax would not be paid. In our example, 5,000 potential hotel room rentals that would have occurred in the absence of the tax, to the mutual benefit of guests and hotel owners, do not take place because of the tax. Specifically, 5,000 (the number of lost rentals) is equal to 10,000 (the equilibrium quantity at an untaxed rate of $80) minus 5,000 (the rooms that are rented with the tax).

So an excise tax imposes costs over and above the tax revenue collected in the form of inefficiency, which occurs because the tax discourages mutually beneficial transactions. As we learned in Chapter 5, the cost to society of this kind of inefficiency—the value of the forgone mutually beneficial transactions—is called the *deadweight loss*. While all real-world taxes impose some deadweight loss, a badly designed tax imposes a larger deadweight loss than a well-designed one.

To measure the deadweight loss from a tax, we turn to the concepts of producer and consumer surplus. Figure 7-8 shows the effects of an excise tax on consumer and producer surplus. In the absence of the tax, the equilibrium is at E and the equilibrium price and quantity are P_E and Q_E, respectively. An excise tax drives a wedge equal to the amount of the tax between the price received by producers and the price paid by consumers, reducing the quantity sold. In this case, where the tax is T dollars per unit, the quantity sold falls to Q_T. The price paid by consumers rises to P_C, the demand price of the reduced quantity, Q_T, and the price received by producers falls to P_P, the supply price of that quantity. The difference between these prices, $P_C - P_P$, is equal to the excise tax, T.

FIGURE 7-8 A Tax Reduces Consumer and Producer Surplus

Before the tax, the equilibrium price and quantity are P_E and Q_E, respectively. After an excise tax of T per unit is imposed, the price to consumers rises to P_C and consumer surplus falls by the sum of the dark blue rectangle, labelled A, and the light blue triangle, labelled B. The tax also causes the price to producers to fall to P_P; producer surplus falls by the sum of the red rectangle, labelled C, and the pink triangle, labelled F. The government receives revenue from the tax equal to $Q_T \times T$, which is given by the sum of the areas A and C. Areas B and F represent the losses to consumer and producer surplus that are not collected by the government as revenue. They are the deadweight loss to society of the tax.

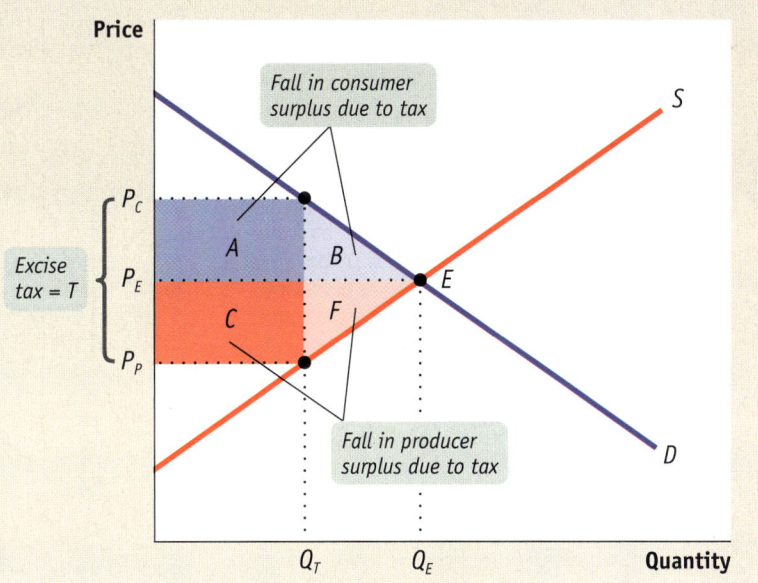

Using the concepts of producer and consumer surplus, we can show exactly how much surplus producers and consumers lose as a result of the tax. From Figure 4-5 we learned that a fall in the price of a good generates a gain in consumer surplus that is equal to the sum of the areas of a rectangle and a triangle. Similarly, a price increase causes a loss to consumers that is represented by the sum of the areas of a rectangle and a triangle. So it's not surprising that in the case of an excise tax, the rise in the price paid by consumers causes a loss equal to the sum of the areas of a rectangle and a triangle: the dark blue rectangle labelled A and the area of the light blue triangle labelled B in Figure 7-8.

Meanwhile, the fall in the price received by producers leads to a fall in producer surplus. This, too, is equal to the sum of the areas of a rectangle and a triangle. The loss in producer surplus is the sum of the areas of the red rectangle labelled C and the pink triangle labelled F in Figure 7-8.

Of course, although consumers and producers are hurt by the tax, the government gains revenue. The revenue the government collects is equal to the tax per unit sold, T, multiplied by the quantity sold, Q_T. This revenue is equal to the area of a rectangle Q_T wide and T high. And we already have that rectangle in the figure: it is the sum of rectangles A and C. So the government gains part of what consumers and producers lose from an excise tax.

But it is important to note that a portion of the loss to producers and consumers from the tax is not offset by a gain to the government—specifically, the two triangles B and F. The deadweight loss caused by the tax is equal to the combined area of these two triangles. It represents the total surplus lost to society because of the tax—that is, the amount of surplus that would have been generated by transactions that now do not take place because of the tax.

Figure 7-9 replicates Figure 7-8 but without the rectangles A (the surplus shifted from consumers to the government) and C (the surplus shifted from producers to the government) and shows only the deadweight loss, here drawn as a triangle shaded yellow. The base of that triangle is equal to the tax wedge, T; the height of the triangle is equal to the reduction in the quantity transacted due to the tax, $Q_E - Q_T$. Clearly, the larger the tax wedge and the larger the reduction in the quantity transacted, the greater the inefficiency from the tax.

FIGURE 7-9 The Deadweight Loss of a Tax

A tax leads to a deadweight loss because it creates inefficiency: some mutually beneficial transactions never take place because of the tax — namely, the transactions $Q_E - Q_T$. The yellow area here represents the value of the deadweight loss: it is the total surplus that would have been gained from the $Q_E - Q_T$s transactions. If the tax had not discouraged transactions — had the number of transactions remained at Q_E because of either perfectly inelastic supply or perfectly inelastic demand — no deadweight loss would have been incurred.

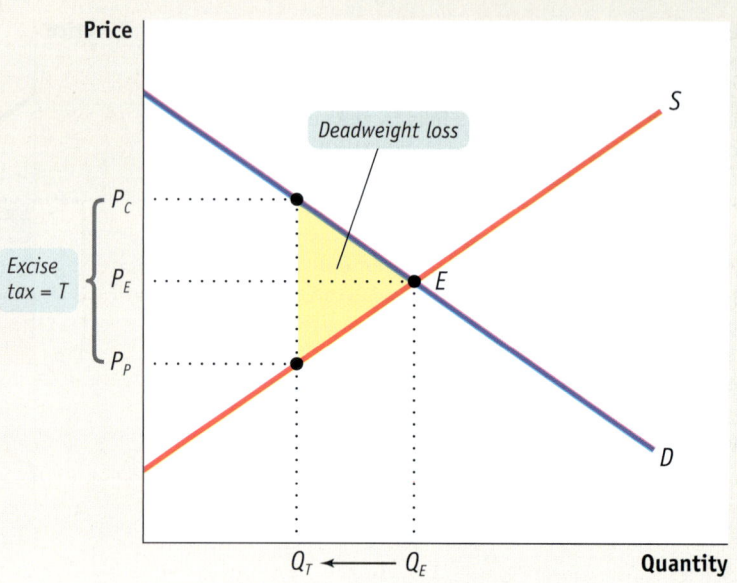

But also note an important, contrasting point: if the excise tax somehow *didn't* reduce the quantity bought and sold in this market — if Q_T remained equal to Q_E after the tax was levied — the yellow triangle would disappear and the deadweight loss from the tax would be zero. This observation is simply the flip-side of the principle found earlier in the chapter: a tax causes inefficiency because it discourages mutually beneficial transactions between buyers and sellers. So if a tax does not discourage transactions, which would be true if either supply or demand were perfectly inelastic, it causes no deadweight loss. In this case, the tax simply shifts surplus straight from consumers and producers to the government.

Using a triangle to measure deadweight loss is a technique used in many economic applications. For example, triangles are used to measure the deadweight loss produced by types of taxes other than excise taxes. They are also used to measure the deadweight loss produced by monopoly, another kind of market distortion. And deadweight-loss triangles are often used to evaluate the benefits and costs of public policies besides taxation — such as whether to impose stricter safety standards on a product.

In considering the total amount of inefficiency caused by a tax, we must also take into account something not shown in Figure 7-9: the resources actually used by the government to collect the tax, and by taxpayers to pay it, over and above the amount of the tax. These lost resources are called the **administrative costs** of the tax. The most familiar administrative cost of the Canadian tax system is the time individuals spend filling out their income tax forms or the money they pay for tax return preparation services like those provided by companies like H&R Block. (The latter is considered an inefficiency from the point of view of society because resources spent on return preparation could be used for other, non-tax-related purposes.)

Society ultimately pays the administrative costs of taxes.

The **administrative costs** of a tax are the resources used for its collection, for the method of payment, and for any attempts to evade the tax.

Included in the administrative costs that taxpayers incur are resources used to evade the tax, both legally and illegally. The costs of operating the Canada Revenue Agency, the arm of the federal government tasked with collecting the federal income tax, are actually quite small in comparison to the administrative costs paid by taxpayers.

So we get:

$$\text{Total inefficiency of tax} = \text{Deadweight loss} + \text{Administrative costs}$$

The general rule for economic policy is that, other things equal, a tax system should be designed to minimize the total inefficiency it imposes on society. In practice, other considerations also apply, but this principle nonetheless gives valuable guidance. Administrative costs are usually well known, more or less determined by the current technology of collecting taxes (for example, filing paper returns versus filing electronically).

But how can we predict the size of the deadweight loss associated with a given tax? Not surprisingly, as in our analysis of the incidence of a tax, the price elasticities of supply and demand play crucial roles in making such a prediction.

Elasticities and the Deadweight Loss of a Tax

We know that the deadweight loss from an excise tax arises because it prevents some mutually beneficial transactions from occurring. In particular, the producer and consumer surplus that is forgone because of these missing transactions is equal to the size of the deadweight loss itself. This means that the larger the number of transactions that are prevented by the tax, the larger the deadweight loss.

This fact gives us an important clue in understanding the relationship between elasticity and the size of the deadweight loss from a tax. Recall that when demand or supply is elastic, the quantity demanded or the quantity supplied is relatively responsive to changes in the price. So a tax imposed on a good for which either demand or supply, or both, is elastic will cause a relatively large decrease in the quantity transacted and a relatively large deadweight loss. In addition, the greater the elasticity of either demand or supply, the greater the deadweight loss from a tax. Correspondingly, a tax imposed when demand or supply, or both, is inelastic will cause a relatively small decrease in the quantity transacted and a relatively small deadweight loss.

The four panels of Figure 7-10 illustrate the positive relationship between a good's price elasticity of either demand or supply and the deadweight loss from taxing that good. Each panel represents the same amount of tax imposed but on a different good; the size of the deadweight loss is given by the area of the shaded triangle. In panel (a), the deadweight-loss triangle is large because demand for this good is relatively elastic—a large number of transactions fail to occur because of the tax. In panel (b), the same supply curve is drawn as in panel (a), but demand for this good is relatively inelastic; as a result, the triangle is small because only a small number of transactions are forgone. Likewise, panels (c) and (d) contain the same demand curve but different supply curves. In panel (c), an elastic supply curve gives rise to a large deadweight-loss triangle, but in panel (d) an inelastic supply curve gives rise to a small deadweight-loss triangle.

The implication of this result is clear: if you want to minimize the efficiency costs of taxation, you should choose to tax only those goods for which demand or supply, or both, is relatively inelastic. For such goods, a tax has little effect on behaviour because behaviour is relatively unresponsive to changes in the price. In the extreme case in which demand is perfectly inelastic (a vertical demand curve), the quantity demanded is unchanged by the imposition of the tax. As a result, the tax imposes no deadweight loss. Similarly, if supply is perfectly inelastic (a vertical supply curve), the quantity supplied is unchanged by the tax and there is also no deadweight loss.

So if the goal in choosing whom to tax is to minimize deadweight loss, then taxes should be imposed on goods and services that have the most inelastic response—that is, goods and services for which consumers or producers will change their behaviour the least in response to the tax. (Unless they have a tendency to revolt, of course.) And this lesson carries a flip-side: using a tax to purposely decrease the amount of a harmful activity, such as underage drinking, will have the most impact when that activity is elastically demanded or supplied.

FIGURE 7-10 Deadweight Loss and Elasticities

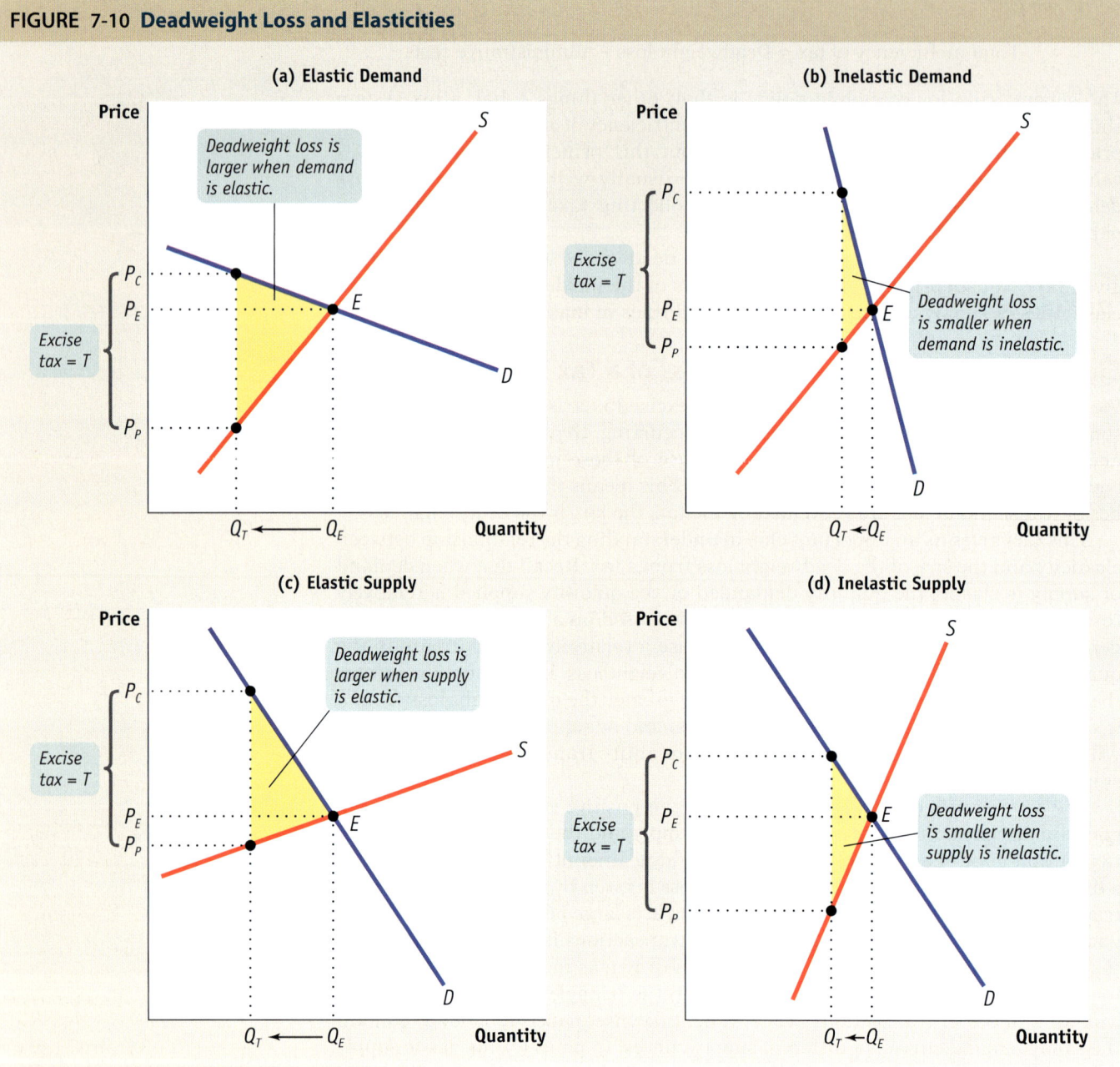

Demand is elastic in panel (a) and inelastic in panel (b), but the supply curves are the same. Supply is elastic in panel (c) and inelastic in panel (d), but the demand curves are the same. The deadweight losses are larger in panels (a) and (c) than in panels (b) and (d) because the greater the price elasticity of demand or supply, the greater the tax-induced fall in the quantity transacted. In contrast, the lower the price elasticity of demand or supply, the smaller the tax-induced fall in the quantity transacted and the smaller the deadweight loss.

ECONOMICS >> *in Action*
Taxing Tobacco

One of the most important excise taxes in Canada is the tax on cigarettes. At the time of writing, the federal government imposes a tax of $2.48 for a pack of 20 cigarettes; provincial and territorial governments impose taxes that range from $2.98 a pack in Québec to $6.00 a pack in Manitoba; and throughout the country, the GST/HST applies on top of these excise taxes (in Manitoba and Saskatchewan the provincial sales tax (PST) also applies on top of the excise tax). The combined tax on a pack of cigarettes varies from $9.78 per pack in Québec to $14.07 a pack in Nova Scotia. In general, tax rates on cigarettes have increased over time, because more and more governments have seen them not just as a source of revenue but as a way to discourage smoking. But the rise in cigarette taxes has not been gradual. Usually, once a government decides to raise cigarette taxes, it raises them a lot—which provides economists with useful data on what happens when there is a big tax increase.

Table 7-1 shows the results of increases in cigarette taxes between 2015 and 2017. The price of cigarettes increased across the country. It was not surprising that sales fell in each case, just as our analysis predicts. However, the federal government experienced a drop in tax revenue, while the provincial governments of New Brunswick and Ontario found their tax revenue rose. The difference might be due to the difference in the elasticity of demand for cigarettes at the national level and the provincial level (in this case, the elasticity of demand for cigarettes is lower at the provincial level).

TABLE 7-1 Results of Increases in Cigarette Taxes

Jurisdiction	Total increase in tax (per pack)	New jurisdiction tax (per pack)	Change in quantity transacted	Change in tax revenue
Canada (federal)	$0.053	$2.156	−6.62%	−2.58%
New Brunswick	$1.304	$5.104	−19.16%	2.69%
Ontario	$0.500	$3.295	−6.62%	1.47%

Data from: Health Canada and smoke-free.ca.

>> Check Your Understanding 7-2

Solutions appear at back of book.

1. The accompanying table shows five consumers' willingness to pay for one can of diet pop each, as well as five producers' costs of selling one can of diet pop each. Each consumer buys at most one can of pop; each producer sells at most one can of pop. The government asks your advice about the effects of an excise tax of $0.40 per can of diet pop. Assume that there are no administrative costs from the tax.

Consumer	Willingness to pay	Producer	Cost
Ana	$0.70	Zachary	$0.10
Brianna	0.60	Yves	0.20
Chizuko	0.50	Xavier	0.30
Dylan	0.40	William	0.40
Ella	0.30	Vern	0.50

   a. Without the excise tax, what is the equilibrium price and the equilibrium quantity of pop transacted?
   b. The excise tax raises the price paid by consumers post-tax to $0.60 and lowers the price received by producers post-tax to $0.20. With the excise tax, what is the quantity of pop transacted?
   c. Without the excise tax, how much individual consumer surplus does each of the consumers gain? How much with the tax? How much total consumer surplus is lost as a result of the tax?
   d. Without the excise tax, how much individual producer surplus does each of the producers gain? How much with the tax? How much total producer surplus is lost as a result of the tax?
   e. How much government revenue does the excise tax create?
   f. What is the deadweight loss from the imposition of this excise tax?
2. In each of the following cases, focus on the price elasticity of demand and use a diagram to illustrate the likely size—small or large—of the deadweight loss resulting from a tax. Explain your reasoning.
   a. Gasoline
   b. Milk chocolate bars

>> Quick Review

• An excise tax generates tax revenue equal to the **tax rate** times the number of units of the good or service transacted but reduces consumer and producer surplus.

• The government tax revenue collected is less than the loss in total surplus because the tax creates inefficiency by discouraging some mutually beneficial transactions.

• The difference between the tax revenue from an excise tax and the reduction in total surplus is the deadweight loss from the tax. The total amount of inefficiency resulting from a tax is equal to the deadweight loss plus the **administrative costs** of the tax.

• The larger the number of transactions prevented by a tax, the larger the deadweight loss. As a result, taxes on goods with a greater price elasticity of supply or demand, or both, generate higher deadweight losses. There is no deadweight loss when the number of transactions is unchanged by the tax. (That is, when supply or demand is perfectly inelastic.)

According to the **benefits principle** of tax fairness, those who benefit from public spending should bear the burden of the tax that pays for that spending.

According to the **ability-to-pay principle** of tax fairness, those with greater ability to pay a tax should pay more tax.

‖ Tax Fairness and Tax Efficiency

We've just seen how economic analysis can be used to determine the inefficiency caused by a tax. It's clear that, other things equal, policy makers should choose a tax that creates less inefficiency over a tax that creates more. But that guideline still leaves policy makers with wide discretion in choosing what to tax and, consequently, who bears the burden of the tax. How should they exercise this discretion?

One answer is that policy makers should make the tax system fair. But what exactly does fairness mean? Moreover, however you define fairness, how should policy makers balance considerations of fairness versus considerations of efficiency?

Two Principles of Tax Fairness

Fairness, like beauty, is often in the eyes of the beholder. When it comes to taxes, however, most debates about fairness rely on one of two principles of tax fairness: the *benefits principle* and the *ability-to-pay principle*.

The Benefits Principle According to the **benefits principle** of tax fairness, those who benefit from public spending should bear the burden of the tax that pays for that spending. For example, those who benefit from a road should pay for that road's upkeep, those who fly on airplanes should pay for air traffic control, and so on. The benefits principle is the basis for some parts of the Canadian tax system. For example, the federal Gas Tax Fund specifically reserves a portion of federal taxes collected on the sale of gasoline and diesel fuel for the maintenance and improvement of municipal infrastructure projects. In this way, motorists who benefit from the highway system also pay for it.

The benefits principle is attractive from an economic point of view because it matches well with one of the major justifications for public spending—the theory of *public goods,* which explains why government action is sometimes needed to provide people with goods that markets alone would not provide, goods like national defence or a sewer system. If that's the role of government, it seems natural to charge each person in proportion to the benefits they get from those goods.

Practical considerations, however, make it impossible to base the entire tax system on the benefits principle. It would be too cumbersome to have a specific tax for each of the many distinct programs that the government offers. Also, attempts to base taxes on the benefits principle often conflict with the other major principle of tax fairness: the *ability-to-pay principle.*

The Ability-to-Pay Principle According to the **ability-to-pay principle,** those with greater ability to pay a tax should pay more. This principle is usually interpreted to mean that high-income individuals should pay more in taxes than low-income individuals. Often the ability-to-pay principle is used to argue not only that high-income individuals should pay more taxes but also that they should pay a higher *percentage* of their income in taxes. We'll consider the issue of how taxes vary as a percentage of income later.

Canadian municipal property taxes are levied as a percentage of the value of a property. But the fact that one house is worth $500,000 while another is worth $250,000 does not imply that the former creates a burden on municipal services that is twice as large. The tax violates the benefits principle of tax fairness. Also, just because a senior citizen owns a home worth $500,000 does not imply they have the ability-to-pay a large property tax amount. So this tax also violates the ability-to-pay principle, which may force "lucky" seniors, who have had the good fortune to see their home value rise significantly over time, to sell their homes so as to live within their income.

Equity versus Efficiency

Canadian taxes on the manufacture and retail sale of alcohol are complex. In general, most provinces require makers to have a special manufacturer licence, the cost of which is a flat fee or tax paid by both large and small producers. This is an example of a **lump-sum tax,** a tax that is the same regardless of any actions people take. In this case, the large producers pay the same amount of tax regardless of how many litres they produce.

Lump-sum taxes are widely perceived to be much less fair than a tax that is proportional to the amount of the transaction. Small producers may feel that they should pay less tax than much larger producers pay. If the fixed licencing fee is set quite high, then some smaller producers may find their profit-maximizing response is to shut down their firm.

But provincial and territorial alcohol taxes applied on retail sales are usually levied on what is essentially a per-litre basis, which definitely distorts incentives to engage in mutually beneficial transactions and creates deadweight loss. Because of these alcohol sales taxes, some producers will reduce how much alcohol they make, with some forgoing production altogether. The result, surely, is a lower production of alcohol and less income earned by manufacturers and employees in the alcohol sector because of these sales taxes.

In contrast, a lump-sum tax does not distort incentives. Because under a lump-sum tax people have to pay the same amount of tax regardless of their actions, it does not lead them to change their actions and therefore causes no deadweight loss. So lump-sum taxes, although unfair, are better than other taxes at promoting economic efficiency.

A tax system can be made fairer by moving it in the direction of the benefits principle or the ability-to-pay principle. But this will come at a cost because the tax system will now tax people more heavily based on their actions, increasing the amount of deadweight loss. This observation reflects a general principle that we learned in Chapter 1: there is often a trade-off between equity and efficiency.

Here, unless a tax system is badly designed, it can be made fairer only by sacrificing efficiency. Conversely, it can be made more efficient only by making it less fair. This means that there is normally a **trade-off between equity and efficiency** in the design of a tax system.

It's important to understand that economic analysis cannot say how much weight a tax system should give to equity and how much to efficiency. That choice is a value judgment, one we make through the political process.

> A **lump-sum tax** is the same for everyone, regardless of any actions people take.
>
> In a well-designed tax system, there is a **trade-off between equity and efficiency:** the system can be made more efficient only by making it less fair, and vice versa.

ECONOMICS >> *in Action*
Federal Tax Philosophy

What is the principle underlying the federal tax system? (By federal, we mean taxes collected by the federal government, as opposed to the taxes collected by provincial, territorial, and local governments.) The answer is that it depends on the tax.

The best-known federal tax, accounting for about half of all federal revenue, is the personal income tax. The structure of the income tax reflects the ability-to-pay principle: families with low incomes pay little or no income tax. In fact, some families pay negative income tax: a program known as the Working Income Tax Benefit "tops up," or adds to, the earnings of low-wage workers. Meanwhile, those with high incomes not only pay a lot of income tax but also must pay a larger share of their income in income taxes than the average family.

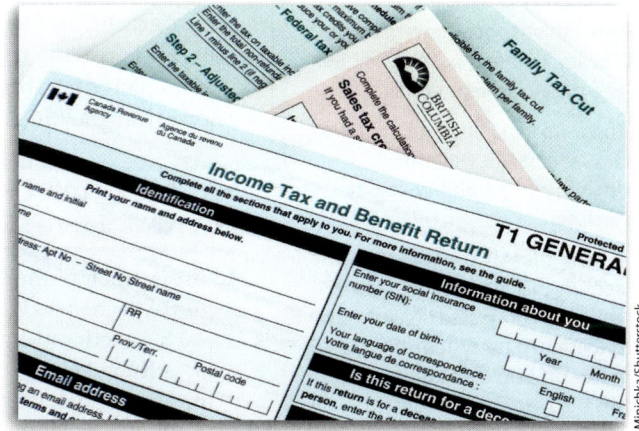

Every year, Canadians use the T1 Schedule 1 form to calculate the amount of federal taxes they owe.

Alongside the personal income tax system that generally flows money from individuals to governments in the form of tax payments is a system of government personal transfer payments that flow money in the other direction. Since transfers flow from governments at all levels to individuals, they are like a tax but with a negative (tax) rate. Major federal transfer programs exist for old age security benefits and for children's benefits payments. In 2018–2019, almost $54.4 billion in regular and supplemental Old Age Security (OAS) payments were paid to Canadian seniors. This far eclipsed the $23.9 billion in government transfers in the form of children's benefits payments made to assist people with the cost of raising a young family.

These transfer payments are financed out of general government revenues and have built-in reductions. In order to qualify either for a larger amount or even a payment at all, the potential recipient must have an income below some set threshold. This ensures that larger payments are directed to those who need them the most, while keeping transfer program expenses down, which helps keep the program affordable.

Table 7-2 illustrates which families earn income in the country and bear the burden of income taxes (to the federal and provincial/territorial governments). The table divides Canadian families into percentiles, based on after-tax income: the top 1% refers to the families at the very top end of the income distribution earning so much income that the remaining 99% of families earn a lower amount of income, the top 5% is the richest 5 percent in terms of total income (not wealth), and so on. The second column shows the share of total Canadian pre-tax (and pre-transfer) income received by income group.

As you can see, low-income families earn little income and pay even less income tax. Even middle-income families paid a substantially smaller share of total income tax collected than their share of total income. The families falling in the lower (or poorest) half of the income distribution only earned 17.8% of all income even though they represent 50% of all families, they also paid a much smaller share of the total income taxes paid (4.8%) compared to their share of total income. In contrast, the top 1% of families by income earned 9.9% of all income (ten times their percentage in the population) and paid 21.1% of all income taxes paid to governments.

Government programs that distribute transfer payments to individuals and families often are designed so that the size of transfer payments made increases the lower the income of the recipient or is reduced the higher the income of intended recipient. This sort of design results in poorer (richer) families receiving a larger (smaller) share of transfer payments (than their share of the population). If we combine the impacts of the design of the income tax and government transfer programs the result is to lower the after-tax and transfer income of richer families while raising the after-tax and transfer income of poorer families. In essence income is redistributed from families at the top end of the income distribution to poorer families in the bottom half.

TABLE 7-2 Share of Pre-Tax Income and Income Tax, by Income Group in 2017

Income group	Percent of total income received before tax and transfer	Percent of total personal income tax paid
Top 1%	9.9%	21.1%
Top 5%	23.0	40.6
Top 10%	34.2	54.1
Top 50%	82.2	95.2
Bottom 50%	17.8	4.8

Data from: Statistics Canada.

>> Quick Review

• Other things equal, government tax policy aims for tax efficiency. But it also tries to achieve tax fairness.

• There are two important principles of tax fairness: the **benefits principle** and the **ability-to-pay principle.**

• A lump-sum tax is efficient because it does not distort incentives, but it is generally considered unfair. In any well-designed tax system, there is a **trade-off between equity and efficiency.** How the tax system should weight equity and efficiency is a value judgment to be decided by the political process.

>> Check Your Understanding 7-3

Solutions appear at back of book.

1. Assess each of the following taxes in terms of the benefits principle versus the ability-to-pay principle. What, if any, actions are distorted by the tax? Assume for simplicity in each case that the purchaser of the good bears 100% of the burden of the tax.
   a. A federal tax of $500 for each new car purchased that finances highway safety programs
   b. A local tax of 20% on hotel rooms that finances local government expenditures
   c. A local tax of 1% on the assessed value of homes that finances local schools
   d. A 1% sales tax on food that pays for government food safety regulation and inspection programs

‖ Understanding the Tax System

An excise tax is the easiest tax to analyze, making it a good vehicle for understanding the general principles of tax analysis. However, in Canada today, excise taxes are actually a relatively minor source of government revenue. In this section, we develop a framework for understanding more general forms of taxation and look at some of the major taxes used in Canada.

Tax Bases and Tax Structure

Every tax consists of two pieces: a *base* and a *structure*. The **tax base** is the measure or value that determines how much tax an individual or firm pays. It is usually a monetary measure, like income or property value. The **tax structure** specifies how the tax depends on the tax base. It is usually expressed in percentage terms; for example, homeowners in some areas might pay yearly property taxes equal to 2% of the value of their homes.

Some important taxes and their tax bases are as follows:

- **Income tax:** a tax that depends on the income of an individual or family from wages and investments
- **Payroll tax:** a tax that depends on the earnings an employer pays to an employee
- **Sales tax:** a tax that depends on the value of goods sold (also known as an excise tax)
- **Profits tax:** a tax that depends on a firm's profits (also known as the corporate income tax)
- **Property tax:** a tax that depends on the value of property, such as the value of a home
- **Wealth tax:** a tax that depends on an individual's wealth

Once the tax base has been defined, the next question is how the tax depends on the base. The simplest tax structure is a **proportional tax,** also sometimes called a *flat tax,* which is the same percentage of the base regardless of the taxpayer's income or wealth. For example, a property tax that is set at 2% of the value of the property, whether the property is worth $10,000 or $10,000,000, is a proportional tax.

Many taxes, however, are not proportional. Instead, different people pay different percentages, usually because the tax law tries to incorporate either the benefits principle or the ability-to-pay principle.

Because taxes are ultimately paid out of income, economists classify taxes according to how they vary with the income of individuals. A tax that rises *more* than in proportion to income, so that high-income taxpayers pay a larger percentage of their income than low-income taxpayers, is a **progressive tax.** A tax that rises *less* than in proportion to income, so that higher-income taxpayers pay a smaller percentage of their income than low-income taxpayers, is a **regressive tax.** A proportional tax on income would be neither progressive nor regressive.

The Canadian tax system contains a mixture of progressive and regressive taxes, though it is somewhat progressive overall.

Equity, Efficiency, and Progressive Taxation

Most, though not all, people view a progressive tax system as fairer than a regressive system. The reason is the ability-to-pay principle: a high-income family that pays 35% of its income in taxes is still left with a lot more money than a low-income family that pays only 15% in taxes. But attempts to make taxes strongly progressive run up against the trade-off between equity and efficiency.

To see why, consider a hypothetical example, illustrated in Table 7-3. We assume that there are two kinds of people in the

The **tax base** is the measure or value, such as income or property value, that determines how much tax an individual or firm pays.

The **tax structure** specifies how the tax depends on the tax base.

An **income tax** is a tax on an individual's or family's income.

A **payroll tax** is a tax on the earnings an employer pays to an employee.

A **sales tax** is a tax on the value of goods sold.

A **profits tax** is a tax on a firm's profits; also known as a corporate income tax.

A **property tax** is a tax on the value of property, such as the value of a home.

A **wealth tax** is a tax on an individual's wealth.

A **proportional tax** is the same percentage of the tax base regardless of the taxpayer's income or wealth.

A **progressive tax** takes a larger share of the income of high-income taxpayers than of low-income taxpayers.

A **regressive tax** takes a smaller share of the income of high-income taxpayers than of low-income taxpayers.

TABLE 7-3 Proportional versus Progressive Taxes in Taxmania

Pre-tax income	After-tax income with proportional taxation	After-tax income with progressive taxation
$40,000	$30,000	$40,000
$80,000	$60,000	$50,000

The **marginal tax rate** is the percentage of an increase in income that is taxed away.

nation of Taxmania: half of the population earns $40,000 a year and half earns $80,000, so the average income is $60,000 a year. We also assume that the Taxmanian government needs to collect 25% of that income—$15,000 a year per person—in taxes.

One way to raise this revenue would be through a proportional tax that takes 25% of everyone's income. The results of this proportional tax are shown in the second column of Table 7-3: after taxes, lower-income Taxmanians would be left with an income of $30,000 a year and higher-income Taxmanians, $60,000.

Even this system might have some negative effects on incentives. Suppose, for example, that finishing college improves a Taxmanian's chance of getting a higher-paying job. Some people who would invest time and effort in going to college in hopes of raising their income from $40,000 to $80,000, a $40,000 gain, might not bother if the potential gain is only $30,000, the after-tax difference in pay between a lower-paying and higher-paying job.

But a strongly progressive tax system could create a much bigger incentive problem. Suppose that the Taxmanian government decided to exempt the poorer half of the population from all taxes but still wanted to raise the same amount of revenue. To do this, it would have to collect $30,000 from each individual earning $80,000 a year. As the third column of Table 7-3 shows, people earning $80,000 would then be left with income after taxes of $50,000—only $10,000 more than the after-tax income of people earning half as much. In effect, 75% of their income over $40,000 has been taxed away. This would greatly reduce the incentive for people to invest time and effort to raise their earnings.

The point here is that any income tax system will tax away part of the gain an individual gets by moving up the income scale, reducing the incentive to earn more. But a progressive tax takes away a larger share of the gain than a proportional tax, creating a more adverse effect on incentives. In comparing the incentive effects of tax systems, economists often focus on the **marginal tax rate:** the percentage of an increase in income that is taxed away. In this example, the marginal tax rate on income above $40,000 is 25% with proportional taxation but 75% with progressive taxation.

Our hypothetical example is much more extreme than the reality of progressive taxation in Canada today—although in previous decades the marginal tax rates paid by high earners were very high indeed. In 1949, the top marginal tax rate for Canadian taxpayers was 84%. However, these have moderated over time as concerns arose about the severe incentive effects of extremely progressive taxes. In short, the ability-to-pay principle pushes governments toward a highly progressive tax system, but efficiency considerations push them the other way.

Taxes in Canada

Table 7-4 shows the revenue raised by major taxes in Canada in 2018. Some of the taxes are collected by the federal government and the others by provincial, territorial, and local governments.

There is a major tax corresponding to five of the six tax bases we identified earlier. There are income taxes, payroll taxes, sales taxes, (corporate) profits taxes, and property taxes, all of which play an important role in the overall tax system. The only item missing is a wealth tax. In fact, most Canadian provinces and territories do have a wealth tax, called *probate fees*, which depend on the value of someone's estate after they die.

Probate fees are charged by the provincial court to recognize the validity of a deceased person's will and the appointment of the executor. When the court grants letters of probate, this notifies the public that the will is adequate and that it was not being challenged. Thus, probate protects the executor and all parties who received an inheritance payment under the will from future legal challenges or claims. These fees vary significantly from province to province; in Québec, probate costs about $100, while in Ontario, probate fees depend on the size of the estate rising to 15% of the value of the estate above $51,000. The deceased's assets are deemed to have been sold on the day of the death, and any tax owing from this sale is payable through the regular income tax system on a final tax return. There is one important exception when someone dies: the assets can be passed, tax-free, to a spouse.

In addition to the taxes shown, provincial, territorial, and local governments collect substantial revenue from other sources as varied as driver's licence fees and sewer charges. These fees and charges are an important part of the tax burden, but they are very difficult to summarize or analyze.

TABLE 7-4 Major Taxes in Canada, 2018

Federal taxes (billions)		Provincial, territorial, and local taxes (billions)	
Personal income	$173.3	Personal and corporate income	$136.1
Corporate profits	50.4	Payroll	15.1
Employment-Insurance (payroll)	22.3	Sales	115.2
CPP/QPP (payroll)	65.5	Property	12.5
Sales	57.2		

Data from: Statistics Canada.

Are the taxes in Table 7-4 progressive or regressive? It depends on the tax. The personal income tax is strongly progressive. The payroll tax, except for the CPP and EI portions are paid only on earnings up to about $55,000, is somewhat regressive. Sales taxes are generally regressive, because higher-income families save more of their income and thus spend a smaller share of it on taxable goods than do lower-income families. In addition, there are other taxes principally levied at the provincial and local level that are typically quite regressive: it costs the same amount to renew a driver's licence no matter what your income is.

Overall, the Canadian income tax system is quite progressive. The third column of Table 7-5 shows the share of all income earned by different percentiles of income earners. The fourth column of this table shows that as we move higher up the income distribution, the share of income tax paid declines more slowly than the share of income earned does. In 2017, the people in the top half of the income distribution earned 82% of all income earned, but paid 95% of all income taxes. The table shows in Canada, the income tax system is indeed progressive, with low-income families paying a relatively small share of their income in income taxes and high-income families paying a greater share of their income.

Since the mid- to late-1990s, the federal government and most provincial governments have cut income taxes for most families. The largest cuts, both as a share of income and as a share of taxes collected, have gone to families with high incomes. Although the Trudeau government's 2016 budget raised taxes on higher-income families, overall, the personal income tax system is less progressive (at the time of writing) than it was before the mid-1990s because the share of income paid by high-income families has fallen relative to the share paid by middle- and low-income families.

And the overall tax system is likely even less progressive than in the past. The reduction of the GST from 7% to 5% helped make the tax system less regressive (or more progressive). But, increases in payroll tax rates and other fees charged by governments make the tax system more regressive. Also, corporate tax rates have fallen very significantly since the mid-1990s. Of course people with higher incomes are more likely to own a greater fraction of Canada's corporations than

TABLE 7-5 Distribution of Income Earned and Income Tax Paid, 2017

Income group	Average income earned	Share of income	Share of federal, provincial and territorial income taxes paid
Top 0.01% of earners	$5,550,400	1.1%	2.6%
Top 0.1% of earners	1,624,600	3.4	7.9
Top 1% of earners	477,700	9.9	21.1
Top 5% of earners	222,800	23	40.6
Top 10% of earners	165,300	34.2	54.1
Top 50% of earners	79,500	82.2	95.2

Data from: Statistics Canada.

lower-income people. So you could argue that corporate tax cuts also make the tax system more regressive.

In summary, the Canadian tax system is somewhat progressive, with the richest tenth of the population paying a somewhat higher share of income in taxes than families in the middle and the poorest Canadians paying considerably less. Although our tax system is progressive, the degree of progressiveness varies with the nature of the taxes. The federal income tax is more progressive than payroll taxes. And personal income taxation is more progressive than sales and property taxes.

Different Taxes, Different Principles

Why are some taxes progressive but others regressive? Can't the government make up its mind?

There are two main reasons for the mixture of regressive and progressive taxes in the Canadian system: the difference between levels of government and the fact that different taxes are based on different principles.

Provincial and especially local governments generally do not make much effort to apply the ability-to-pay principle. This is largely because they are subject to *tax competition:* a province or local government that imposes high taxes on people with high incomes faces the prospect that those people may move to other locations where taxes are lower. This is much less of a concern at the national level, although a handful of very rich people have given up their Canadian citizenship to avoid paying Canadain taxes.

Although the federal government is in a better position than provincial or local governments to apply principles of fairness, it applies different principles to different taxes. We saw an example of this in the preceding Economics in Action. The most important tax, the federal income tax, is strongly progressive, reflecting the ability-to-pay principle. But the second most important tax, the federal payroll tax, is somewhat regressive, because most of it is linked to specific programs—CPP and EI—and, reflecting the benefits principle, is levied more or less in proportion to the benefits received from these programs.

Provincial and especially local governments generally do not make as much effort to apply the ability-to-pay principle. This is largely because they are subject to *tax competition:* a province or local government that imposes high taxes on people with high incomes faces the prospect that those people may move to other locations where taxes are lower. This is much less of a concern at the national level, although a handful of very rich people have given up their Canadian citizenship to avoid paying Canadian taxes.

GLOBAL COMPARISON   YOU THINK YOUR TAXES ARE HIGH?

Everyone, everywhere complains about taxes. But citizens of Canada actually have less to complain about than citizens of some other wealthy countries.

To assess the overall level of taxes, economists usually calculate taxes as a share of *gross domestic product* or *GDP*—the total value of goods and services produced in a country. By this measure, as you can see in the accompanying figure, in 2017, Canadian taxes were near the middle of the scale. But our neighbour, the United States, has significantly lower taxes. Tax rates in Europe, where governments need a lot of revenue to pay for extensive benefits such as guaranteed health care and generous unemployment benefits, are about 40% higher than in Canada.

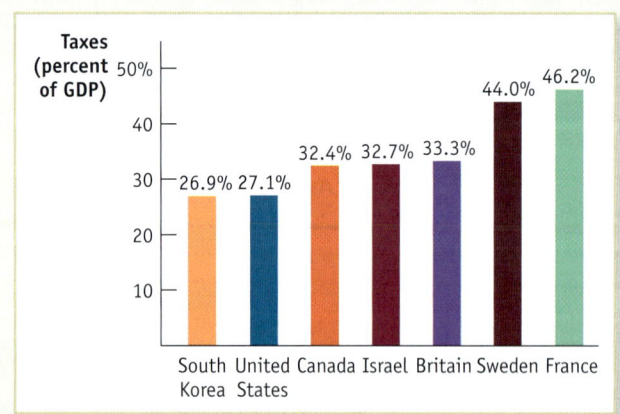

Data from: OECD.

FOR INQUIRING MINDS   Taxing Income versus Taxing Consumption

The Canadian government taxes people mainly on the money they *make,* not on the money they spend on consumption. Yet most tax experts argue that this policy badly distorts incentives. Someone who earns income and then invests that income for the future gets taxed twice: once on the original sum and again on any earnings made from the investment.

So a system that taxes income rather than consumption discourages people from saving and investing, instead providing an incentive to spend their income today. And encouraging savings and investing is an important policy goal for two reasons. First, empirical evidence shows that Canadians tend to save too little for retirement and health care expenses in their later years.

Second, savings and investment both contribute to economic growth.

Moving from a system that taxes income to one that taxes consumption would solve this problem. In fact, the governments of many countries get much of their revenue from a value-added tax, or VAT, which acts like a national sales tax. In some countries, VAT rates are very high; in Sweden, for example, the rate is 25%.

Canada has taken mixed steps towards taxing consumption instead of income. The introduction of tax-free savings accounts (TFSA) helps to reduce the double-taxation issue, as any income earned on assets held in a TSFA is exempt from taxation. Also, the federal government does have a value-added tax (VAT) in the Goods and

Services Tax (GST). Several provinces integrated this national VAT with a provincial VAT to form a single Harmonized Sales Tax (HST) that, like the GST, applies on the sale of most goods and services. Alberta and the three territories only have the GST. Other provinces have the GST along with a provincial retail sales tax that does not function like a value-added tax, but does tax the consumption of many goods. Value-added taxes have two main negative qualities. One is that it is difficult, though not impossible, to make a consumption tax progressive. The other is that a VAT typically has very high administrative costs. So with our low GST/HST rates, Canadians are left with all of the bad parts of a VAT and fewer of the benefits.

Although the federal government is in a better position than provincial or local governments to apply principles of fairness, it applies different principles to different taxes. We saw an example of this in the preceding Economics in Action. The most important tax, the federal income tax, is strongly progressive, reflecting the ability-to-pay principle. But the federal payroll taxes, the second most important tax, are somewhat regressive, because most of this tax revenue is linked to specific programs—CPP and EI—and, reflecting the benefits principle, payroll taxes are levied more or less in proportion to the benefits received from these programs.

ECONOMICS >> *in Action*
Provincial Tax Choices

While federal taxes are strongly progressive, and provincial and local taxes are generally regressive, there is wide variation in tax systems across provinces.

You can see how big these differences can get by comparing the effective provincial income tax rates for 2017 in Alberta and Québec, shown in Figure 7-11.

FIGURE 7-11 Effective Provincial Personal Income Tax Rates by Income Category in Alberta and Québec, in 2017

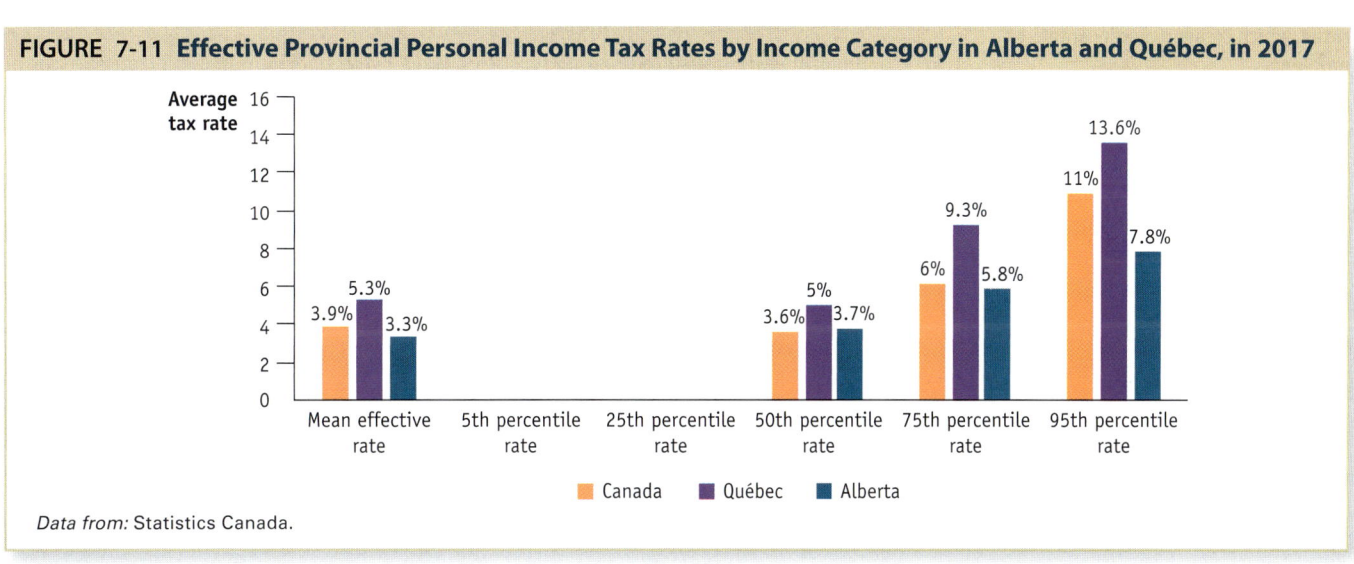

Data from: Statistics Canada.

Alberta's effective provincial personal income tax rate is represented by the blue bars, Québec's effective provincial personal income tax rate is represented by the purple bars (for comparison, the average effective provincial income tax rate for all of Canada is represented by the orange bars).

For a family or individual tax filer, the effective provincial income tax rate is the total provincial income taxes paid divided by their income (including transfers from governments). This picks up the impact of differing provincial income tax rates as well as any differences in credits, deductions, or other benefits that may exist at the provincial level. Families in the first 25th percentile of tax filers have an effective provincial tax rate of 0%. Families at the 50th percentile of incomes face an effective provincial income tax rate of 5% in Québec, which is higher than the 3.7% effective rate faced by similar families in Alberta. Families at the 95th percentile of incomes face an effective rate of 13.6% in Québec which is substantially higher than the 7.8% effective rate faced by families at the 95th percentile of incomes in Alberta.

Alberta has a relatively small government compared to Québec, so that average tax rate as a percentage of income is lower. But the two provinces also make very different choices about how to collect revenue. In 2017, Alberta imposed an income tax that is 10% of the first $126,625 of income and reaches 15% for income over $303,900. Québec, in 2017, imposed a tax rate of 15% on the first $42,705 of income and their rate reaches 25.75% for income over $103,915.

It is worth noting that Figure 7-11 ignores the differences in other taxes collected in Alberta and Québec. Provincial differences in other taxes do exist and can also be significant. For example, Alberta has no provincially levied sales tax whereas Québec imposes a provincial sales tax of 9.975%. The result is that the difference in the overall provincial tax burden is wider than the gap shown in Figure 7-11.

This comparison teaches us that tax policy isn't one-dimensional. There are many choices involved in setting up a tax system and keeping taxes low for some people may involve making them higher for others.

>> Quick Review

- Every tax consists of a **tax base** and a **tax structure.**

- Among the types of taxes are **income taxes, payroll taxes, sales taxes, profits taxes, property taxes,** and **wealth taxes.**

- Tax systems are classified as being **proportional, progressive,** or **regressive.**

- Progressive taxes are often justified by the ability-to-pay principle. But strongly progressive taxes lead to high **marginal tax rates,** which create major incentive problems.

- Canada has a mixture of progressive and regressive taxes. However, the overall structure of taxes is progressive.

>> Check Your Understanding 7-4

Solutions appear at back of book.

1. An income tax taxes 1% of the first $10,000 of income and 2% on all income above $10,000.
   a. What is the marginal tax rate for someone with income of $5,000? How much total tax does this person pay? How much is this as a percentage of their income?
   b. What is the marginal tax rate for someone with income of $20,000? How much total tax does this person pay? How much is this as a percentage of their income?
   c. Is this income tax proportional, progressive, or regressive?

2. When comparing households at different income levels, economists find that consumption spending grows more slowly than income. Assume that when income grows by 50%, from $10,000 to $15,000, consumption grows by 25%, from $8,000 to $10,000. Compare the percent of income paid in taxes by a family with $15,000 in income to that paid by a family with $10,000 in income under a 1% tax on consumption purchases. Is this a proportional, progressive, or regressive tax?

3. True or false? Explain your answers.
   a. Payroll taxes do not affect a person's incentive to take a job because they are paid by employers.
   b. A lump-sum tax is a proportional tax because it is the same amount for each person.

A Welcome Tax Hike: Microsoft Raises Its Internal Carbon Tax

Chona Kasinge/Bloomberg/Getty Images

Microsoft hiked a tax—on itself. In April of 2019, the company announced that it would nearly double its internal carbon tax, from $8 to $15 per metric ton of carbon dioxide. While the company has made steady progress toward its corporate goal of cutting carbon emissions by 75% by 2030, "the magnitude and speed of the world's environmental changes have made it increasingly clear that we must do more," in the words of Microsoft's president, Brad Smith. The company now vows to reach its goal seven years earlier, in 2023.

Microsoft's various business units—such as its Intelligent Cloud Division—are assessed on their performance by senior management each quarter (every three months). One of the major factors in the performance review is quarterly profit—that is, how much did the business unit earn over and above its costs. So it might be surprising to learn that one type of cost that Microsoft's business units must pay is a tax: a carbon tax that is levied internally by Microsoft on its own units. Microsoft began implementing an internal carbon tax in 2012, and since then the policy has quickly grown in popularity. Today, well over 1,400 firms and organizations—from Google, Disney, and ExxonMobil to Yale University—levy an internal carbon tax on their operations.

A *carbon tax* is a tax on a good or service assessed according to the amount of carbon dioxide created by the production of that good or service. Carbon dioxide is one of the main pollutants behind global climate change. A Microsoft business unit determines its carbon tax levy by calculating the total amount of energy that it consumes for its operations—such as the energy consumed for its office space, data centres, or business travel. Next, the amount of energy consumed is converted into metric tons of carbon—the amount of carbon emissions generated by the unit's consumption of energy. Microsoft's Environmental Sustainability Team then calculates each unit's carbon tax. It is a substantial sum: even before the 2019 tax hike, Microsoft collected approximately US$30 million in carbon tax revenue from its business units.

The carbon tax revenue is placed in a fund that pays for a range of clean energy projects within Microsoft. For example, at its corporate headquarters in Redmond, Washington, carbon tax revenue paid for a data collection and software system that optimized energy use across 125 buildings, leading to huge cost and carbon-emissions savings. In just its first three years, the carbon tax system led to a US$10 million savings for Microsoft through reduced energy consumption and a 7.5 million metric ton reduction in carbon emissions.

Although the internal carbon tax scheme reduces the company's profit in the short run, Microsoft's shareholders support the scheme. They believe that reducing energy consumption in the long run will lead to higher future profits. For example, through research and development generated by their own internal carbon tax program, Microsoft has developed important skills and technology, particularly in the area of artificial intelligence. That new capability is now being used to create similar programs for its customers who also want to reduce their carbon emissions and save energy. In the words of Smith, "Already we're helping empower our customers and partners with new technology to help them drive efficiencies, transform their businesses, and create their own solutions to create a more sustainable planet."

QUESTIONS FOR THOUGHT

1. To save energy and reduce carbon emissions, why do you think that Microsoft instituted a tax rather than issuing a company-wide directive?

2. How is Microsoft behaving like a government? Why is this preferable to business units acting independently?

3. What trade-offs should Microsoft consider in determining the size of the carbon tax? What happens if the tax is too high? Too low?

4. What does this case tell you about the relationship between an objective and the size of the tax created to achieve that objective? Should they be determined independently or jointly?

SUMMARY

1. **Excise taxes**—taxes on the purchase or sale of a good—raise the price paid by consumers and reduce the price received by producers, driving a wedge between the two. The **incidence** of the tax—how the burden of the tax is divided between consumers and producers—does not depend on who officially pays the tax.

2. The incidence of an excise tax depends on the price elasticities of supply and demand. If the price elasticity of demand is higher than the price elasticity of supply, the tax falls mainly on producers; if the price elasticity of supply is higher than the price elasticity of demand, the tax falls mainly on consumers.

3. The tax revenue generated by a tax depends on the **tax rate** and on the number of taxed units transacted. Excise taxes cause inefficiency in the form of deadweight loss because they discourage some mutually beneficial transactions. Taxes also impose **administrative costs:** resources used to collect the tax, to pay it (over and above the amount of the tax), and to evade it.

4. An excise tax generates revenue for the government but lowers total surplus. The loss in total surplus exceeds the tax revenue, resulting in a deadweight loss to society. This deadweight loss is represented by a triangle, the area of which equals the value of the transactions discouraged by the tax. The greater the elasticity of demand or supply, or both, the larger the deadweight loss from a tax. If either demand or supply is perfectly inelastic, there is no deadweight loss from a tax.

5. An efficient tax minimizes both the sum of the deadweight loss due to distorted incentives and the administrative costs of the tax. However, tax fairness is also a goal of tax policy.

6. There are two major principles of tax fairness, the **benefits principle** and the **ability-to-pay principle.** The most efficient tax, a **lump-sum tax,** does not distort incentives but performs badly in terms of fairness. The fairest taxes in terms of the ability-to-pay principle, however, distort incentives the most and perform badly on efficiency grounds. So in a well-designed tax system, there is a **trade-off between equity and efficiency.**

7. Every tax consists of a **tax base,** which defines what is taxed, and a **tax structure,** which specifies how the tax depends on the tax base. Different tax bases give rise to different taxes—the **income tax, payroll tax, sales tax, profits tax, property tax,** and **wealth tax.** A **proportional tax** is the same percentage of the tax base for all taxpayers.

8. A tax is **progressive** if higher-income people pay a higher percentage of their income in taxes than lower-income people and **regressive** if they pay a lower percentage. Progressive taxes are often justified by the ability-to-pay principle. However, a highly progressive tax system significantly distorts incentives because it leads to a high **marginal tax rate,** the percentage of an increase in income that is taxed away, on high earners. The Canadian tax system is progressive overall, although it contains a mixture of progressive and regressive taxes.

KEY TERMS

Excise tax, p. 200
Incidence, p. 202
Tax rate, p. 208
Administrative costs, p. 212
Benefits principle, p. 216
Ability-to-pay principle, p. 216
Lump-sum tax, p. 217

Trade-off between equity and
   efficiency, p. 217
Tax base, p. 219
Tax structure, p. 219
Income tax, p. 219
Payroll tax, p. 219
Sales tax, p. 219

Profits tax, p. 219
Property tax, p. 219
Wealth tax, p. 219
Proportional tax, p. 219
Progressive tax, p. 219
Regressive tax, p. 219
Marginal tax rate, p. 220

PRACTICE QUESTIONS

1. A province needs to raise money, and the premier has a choice of imposing an excise tax of the same amount on one of two previously untaxed goods: restaurant meals or gasoline. Both the demand for and the supply of restaurant meals are more elastic than the demand for and the supply of gasoline. If the premier wants to minimize the deadweight loss caused by the tax, which good should be taxed? For each good, draw a diagram that illustrates the deadweight loss from taxation.

2. Assume that demand for gasoline is inelastic and supply is relatively elastic. The government imposes a sales tax on gasoline. The tax revenue is used to fund research into clean fuel alternatives to gasoline, which will improve the air we all breathe.

   a. Who bears more of the burden of this tax, consumers or producers? Show in a diagram who bears how much of the burden.

   b. Is this tax based on the benefits principle or the ability-to-pay principle? Explain.

3. You are advising the government on how to pay for national defence. There are two proposals for a tax system to fund national defence. Under both proposals, the tax base is an individual's income. Under proposal A, all citizens pay exactly the same lump-sum tax, regardless of income. Under proposal B, individuals with higher incomes pay a greater proportion of their income in taxes.

  a. Is the tax in proposal A progressive, proportional, or regressive? What about the tax in proposal B?

  b. Is the tax in proposal A based on the ability-to-pay principle or on the benefits principle? What about the tax in proposal B?

  c. In terms of efficiency, which tax is better? Explain.

4. You work for the Economic Advisory Council, providing economic advice to the prime minister. The prime minister wants to overhaul the income tax system and asks your advice. Suppose that the current income tax system consists of a proportional tax of 10% on all income and that there is one person in the country who earns $110 million; everyone else earns less than $100 million. The prime minister proposes a tax cut targeted at the very rich so that the new tax system would consist of a proportional tax of 10% on all income up to $100 million and a marginal tax rate of 0% (no tax) on income above $100 million. You are asked to evaluate this tax proposal.

  a. For incomes of $100 million or less, is this proposed tax system progressive, regressive, or proportional? For incomes of more than $100 million? Explain.

  b. Would this tax system create more or less tax revenue, other things equal? Is this tax system more or less efficient than the current tax system? Explain.

PROBLEMS

1. To help fund airport security, Canada imposes the Air Travellers Security Charge (ATSC), an excise tax on the sale of domestic airline tickets. In 2015, the total excise tax was $14.25 per round-trip domestic airline ticket. According to Statistics Canada, 79.5 million passengers travelled on domestic airline trips that year at an average price of $278.80 per trip. The accompanying table shows the supply and demand schedules for airline trips. The quantity demanded at the average price of $278.80 is actual data; the rest is hypothetical:

Price of trip	Quantity of trips demanded (millions)	Quantity of trips supplied (millions)
$380.00	77.7	94.1
278.80	79.5	89.3
271.80	85.5	85.5
263.84	88.5	79.5
273.20	93.0	77.7

  a. What is the revenue in 2015 from this excise tax?

  b. Suppose that on January 1, 2017, the total excise tax increases to $17 per ticket. Assume the supply and demand schedules have not changed. What is the quantity of tickets transacted now? What is the average ticket price now? What will be the 2017 revenue of the ATSC?

  c. Does this increase in the excise tax increase or decrease the revenue of the ATSC?

2. Suppose the federal government begins to levy a tax on sales of luxury cars. For simplicity, assume that the tax was an excise tax of $6,000 per car. The accompanying figure shows hypothetical demand and supply curves for luxury cars.

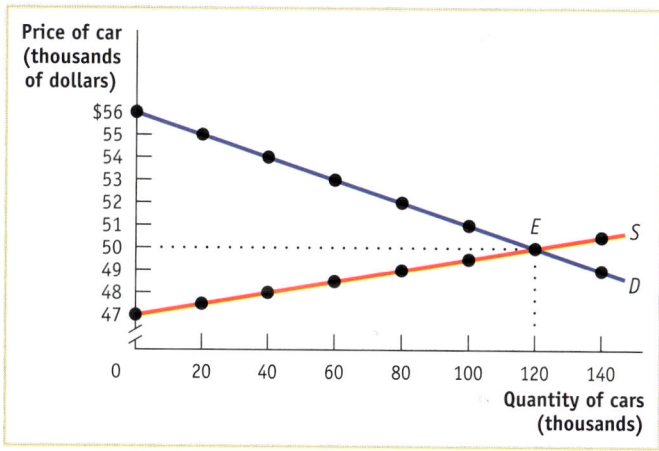

  a. Under the tax, what is the price paid by consumers? What is the price received by producers? What is the government tax revenue from the excise tax?

  Over time, the tax on luxury automobiles is slowly phased out. Suppose that the excise tax falls from $6,000 per car to $4,500 per car.

  b. After the reduction in the excise tax from $6,000 to $4,500 per car, what is the price paid by consumers? What is the price received by producers? What is tax revenue now?

  c. Compare the tax revenue created by the taxes in parts a and b. What accounts for the change in tax revenue from the reduction in the excise tax?

3. All provinces impose excise taxes on gasoline. According to the Alberta Treasury Board and Finance, Alberta imposes an excise tax of $0.09 per litre of gasoline. In 2012, gasoline sales in Alberta totalled 6 billion litres. What was Alberta's tax revenue from the gasoline excise tax? If Alberta doubled the excise tax, would tax revenue double? Why or why not?

4. In Canada, each provincial and territorial government can impose its own excise tax on the sale of cigarettes. Suppose that in the province of Upper Canada, the provincial government imposes a tax of $2.00 per pack sold within the province. In contrast, the neighbouring province of Lower Canada imposes no excise tax on cigarettes. The provinces pre-tax price of a pack of cigarettes is $1.00 in both provinces. A person bringing cigarettes from Lower Canada to Upper Canada is expected to pay $2.00 per pack at the border. Assume that the total cost to a resident of Upper Canada to smuggle a pack of cigarettes from Lower Canada is $1.85 per pack (the cost of time, gasoline, etc.). Assume that the supply curve for cigarettes is neither perfectly elastic nor perfectly inelastic.

a. Draw a diagram of the supply and demand curves for cigarettes in Upper Canada showing a situation in which it makes economic sense for a person to smuggle a pack of cigarettes from Lower Canada to Upper Canada. Explain your diagram.

b. Draw a corresponding diagram showing a situation in which it does not make economic sense for a person to smuggle a pack of cigarettes from Lower Canada to Upper Canada. Explain your diagram.

c. Suppose the demand for cigarettes in Upper Canada is perfectly inelastic. Draw a corresponding diagram to indicate how the cost of smuggling a pack of cigarettes could go until a person no longer found it profitable to smuggle? Explain your diagram.

d. Still assume that demand for cigarettes in Upper Canada is perfectly inelastic and that all smokers in Upper Canada are smuggling their cigarettes at a cost of $1.85 per pack, so no tax is paid. Is there any inefficiency in this situation? If so, how much per pack? Suppose chip-embedded cigarette packaging makes it impossible to smuggle cigarettes across the state border. Is there any inefficiency in this situation? If so, how much per pack?

5. In each of the following cases involving taxes, explain: (i) whether the incidence of the tax falls more heavily on consumers or producers, (ii) why government revenue raised from the tax is not a good indicator of the true cost of the tax, and (iii) how deadweight loss arises as a result of the tax.

a. The government imposes an excise tax on the sale of all college and university textbooks. Before the tax was imposed, 1 million textbooks were sold every year at a price of $50. After the tax is imposed, 600,000 books are sold yearly; students pay $55 per book, $30 of which publishers receive.

b. The government imposes an excise tax on the sale of all airline tickets. Before the tax was imposed, 3 million airline tickets were sold every year at a price of $500. After the tax is imposed, 1.5 million tickets are sold yearly; travellers pay $550 per ticket, $450 of which the airlines receive.

c. The government imposes an excise tax on the sale of all toothbrushes. Before the tax, 2 million toothbrushes were sold every year at a price of $1.50. After the tax is imposed, 800,000 toothbrushes are sold every year; consumers pay $2 per toothbrush, $1.25 of which producers receive.

6. The accompanying diagram shows the market for cigarettes. The current equilibrium price per pack is $4, and every day 40 million packs of cigarettes are sold. In order to recover some of the health care costs associated with smoking, the government imposes a tax of $2 per pack. This will raise the equilibrium price to $5 per pack and reduce the equilibrium quantity to 30 million packs.

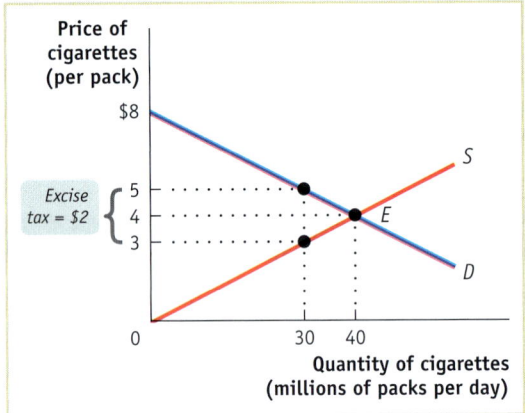

The economist working for the tobacco lobby claims that this tax will reduce consumer surplus for smokers by $40 million per day, since 40 million packs now cost $1 more per pack. The economist working for the lobby for sufferers of second-hand smoke argues that this is an enormous overestimate and that the reduction in consumer surplus will be only $30 million per day, since after the imposition of the tax only 30 million packs of cigarettes will be bought and each of these packs will now cost $1 more. They are both wrong. Why? Include a calculation of consumer surplus before and after the tax in your answer.

7. Consider the original market for pizza in Lafacville, illustrated in the accompanying table. Lafacville officials decide to impose an excise tax on pizza of $4 per pizza.

Price of pizza	Quantity of pizza demanded	Quantity of pizza supplied
$10	0	6
9	1	5
8	2	4
7	3	3
6	4	2
5	5	1
4	6	0
3	7	0
2	8	0
1	9	0

a. What is the quantity of pizza bought and sold after the imposition of the tax? What is the price paid by consumers? What is the price received by producers?

b. Calculate the consumer surplus and the producer surplus after the imposition of the tax. By how much has the imposition of the tax reduced consumer surplus? By how much has it reduced producer surplus?

c. How much tax revenue does Lafacville earn from this tax?

d. Calculate the deadweight loss from this tax.

8. A province needs to raise money and the finance minister has a choice of imposing an excise tax of the same amount on one of two previously untaxed goods: the province can tax sales of either restaurant meals or gasoline. Both the demand for and the supply of restaurant meals are more elastic than the demand for and the supply of gasoline. If the finance minister wants to minimize the deadweight loss caused by the tax, which goods should be taxed? For each good, draw a diagram that illustrates the deadweight loss from taxation.

9. Assume that the demand for gasoline is inelastic and supply is relatively elastic. The government imposes a sales tax on gasoline. The tax revenue is used to fund research into clean air alternatives to gasoline, which will improve the air we all breathe.

a. Who bears more of the burden of this tax, consumers or producers? Show in a diagram who bears how much of the excess burden.

b. Is this tax based on the benefits principle or the ability-to-pay principle? Explain.

10. Assess the following four tax policies in terms of the benefits principle versus the ability-to-pay principle.

a. A tax on gasoline that finances maintenance of provincial roads

b. An 8% tax on imported goods valued in excess of $800 per household brought in on passenger flights

c. Airline-flight landing fees that pay for air traffic control

d. A reduction in the amount of income tax paid based on the number of dependent children in the household.

11. You are advising the government on how to pay for national defence. There are two proposals for a tax system to fund national defence. Under both proposals, the tax base is an individual's income. Under proposal A, all citizens pay exactly the same lump-sum tax, regardless of income. Under proposal B, individuals with higher incomes pay a greater proportion of their income in taxes.

a. Is the tax in proposal A progressive, proportional, or regressive? What about the tax in proposal B?

b. Is the tax in proposal A based on the ability-to-pay principle or on the benefits principle? What about the tax in proposal B?

c. In terms of efficiency, which tax is better? Explain.

12. Each of the following tax proposals has income as the tax base. In each case, calculate the marginal tax rate for each level of income. Then calculate the percentage of income paid in taxes for an individual with a pre-tax income of $5,000 and for an individual with a pre-tax income of $40,000. Classify the tax as being proportional, progressive, or regressive. (*Hint:* You can calculate the marginal tax rate as the percentage of an additional $1 in income that is taxed away.)

a. All income is taxed at 20%.

b. All income up to $10,000 is tax-free. All income above $10,000 is taxed at a constant rate of 20%.

c. All income between $0 and $10,000 is taxed at 10%. All income between $10,000 and $20,000 is taxed at 20%. All income higher than $20,000 is taxed at 30%.

d. Each individual who earns more than $10,000 pays a lump-sum tax of $10,000. If the individual's income is less than $10,000, that individual pays in taxes exactly what their income is.

e. Of the four tax policies, which is likely to cause the worst incentive problems? Explain.

13. In Transylvania, the basic income tax system is fairly simple. The first 40,000 sylvers (the official currency of Transylvania) earned each year are free of income tax. Any additional income is taxed at a rate of 25%. In addition, every individual pays a social security tax, which is calculated as follows: all income up to 80,000 sylvers is taxed at an additional 20%, but there is no additional social security tax on income above 80,000 sylvers.

a. Calculate the marginal tax rates (including income tax and social security tax) for Transylvanians with the following levels of income: 20,000 sylvers, 40,000 sylvers, and 80,000 sylvers. (*Hint:* You can calculate the marginal tax rate as the percentage of an additional 1 sylver in income that is taxed away.)

b. Is the income tax in Transylvania progressive, regressive, or proportional? Is the social security tax progressive, regressive, or proportional?

c. Which income group's incentives are most adversely affected by the combined income and social security tax systems?

14. Suppose the government decides to levy a small excise tax on consumers in a perfectly competitive market in which the elasticity of demand is greater than the elasticity of supply. Who will bear more of the tax burden: the suppliers or the consumers? Explain why.

15. In extreme cases, the supply or demand curve can be either vertical (perfectly inelastic) or horizontal (perfectly elastic). In such extreme situations the burden of a per-unit excise tax falls entirely on one side of the market. Using a diagram in each case, explain why each of the following scenarios occurs.

a. A horizontal demand curve results in the suppliers bearing the entire burden of an excise tax.

b. A horizontal supply curve results in the consumers bearing the entire burden of an excise tax.

c. A vertical demand curve results in the consumers bearing the entire burden of an excise tax.

d. A vertical supply curve results in the suppliers bearing the entire burden of an excise tax.

e. A vertical supply or demand curve results no deadweight loss when an excise tax is imposed.

16. This question uses the algebraic method to solve problems from Appendix 3A and Appendix 6A. Suppose that the demand and supply for maple syrup are given by the following equations:

$$P = 53.25 - 1.25Q^d \qquad \text{Demand Curve}$$
$$P = 12.75 + 0.25Q^S \qquad \text{Supply Curve}$$

where Q is the quantity in millions of litres and P is the price per litre. The federal government is considering imposing an excise tax equal to $1.50 a litre.

a. Determine the price and quantity in the initial equilibrium where no tax is charged.

b. Solve for the new equilibrium quantity, the price paid by consumers, the price received by producers (excluding the tax), the tax revenue collected, and the buyer's and seller's shares of the tax burden.

c. How do your answers to parts (a) and (b) change after the income of consumers rises, shifting the demand curve to $P = 55.50 - 1.25Q^d$?

d. How do your answers to parts (a) and (b) change if instead an improvement in technology shifts the supply curve to $P = 7.50 + 0.25Q^S$?

e. How do your answers to parts (a) and (b) change if instead an improvement in technology shifts the supply curve to $P = 11.25 + 0.15Q^S$? (*Hint:* Round your price and quantity figures to 2 decimal places.)

17. This question uses the algebraic method to solve problems from Appendix 3A and Appendix 6A. Suppose the monthly demand and supply for tablets are given by the following equations:

$$P = 500 - 0.001Q^d \qquad \text{Demand Curve}$$
$$P = 200 + 0.0005Q^S \qquad \text{Supply Curve}$$

a. Use the demand and supply curves to solve for the equilibrium price and quantity. Create a diagram to depict this equilibrium.

b. Suppose the government is considering introducing a tax on electronics that would add $50 to the cost of an tablets. Solve for the new equilibrium quantity, the price paid by consumers, the price received by producers (excluding the tax), the tax revenue collected, and the buyer's and seller's shares of the tax burden.

c. How did the consumer surplus, producer surplus, and total economic surplus change?

d. What is the deadweight loss created by the tax? How much comes from consumers? How much from producers?

18. You work for the Saskatoba Treasury Board and Finance, providing economic advice to the finance minister. The premier wants to overhaul the personal income tax system and asks your advice. The current income tax system in Saskatoba consists of a proportional tax of 10% on all income. Suppose there is one person in the province who earns $110 million; everyone else earns less than $100 million. The premier proposes a tax cut targeted at the very rich so that the new tax system would consist of a proportional tax of 10% on all income up to $100 million and a marginal tax rate of 0% (no tax) on income above $100 million. You are asked to evaluate this tax proposal.

a. For incomes of $100 million or less, is this tax system progressive, regressive, or proportional? For incomes of more than $100 million? Explain.

b. Would this tax system create more or less tax revenue, other things equal? Is this tax system more or less efficient than the current tax system? Explain.

WORK IT OUT

19. The Canadian government would like to help the North American auto industry compete against overseas automakers that sell trucks in Canada. It can do this by imposing an excise tax on each foreign truck sold in Canada. The hypothetical pre-tax demand and supply schedules for imported trucks are given in this table.

Price of imported truck	Quantity of imported trucks (thousands)	
	Quantity demanded	Quantity supplied
$32,000	100	400
31,000	200	350
30,000	300	300
29,000	400	250
28,000	500	200
27,000	600	150

a. In the absence of government interference, what is the equilibrium price of an imported truck? The equilibrium quantity? Illustrate with a diagram.

b. Assume that the government imposes an excise tax of $3,000 per imported truck. Illustrate the effect of this excise tax in your diagram from part a. How many imported trucks are now purchased and at what price? How much does the foreign automaker receive per truck?

c. Calculate the government revenue raised by the excise tax in part b. Illustrate it on your diagram.

d. How does the excise tax on imported trucks benefit North American automakers? Whom does it hurt? How does inefficiency arise from this government policy? ■

8 International Trade

THE EVERYWHERE PHONE

WHAT DO CANADIANS DO with their time? The answer is that they largely spend it staring at small screens. In 2018, the average Canadian spent six minutes shy of three hours a day looking at a smartphone (especially an iPhone) or a tablet. A forecast by eMarketer showed that by 2020, Canadians will spend more time on mobile devices than on TV.

Bloomberg/Getty Images

Raphye Alexius/Cultura Creative (RF)/Alamy

The production and consumption of smartphones are examples of today's hyperglobal world with its soaring levels of international trade.

Where do these small screens come from? Specifically, where does an iPhone come from?

Apple, which sells the iPhone, is an American company. But if you said that iPhones come from America, you're mostly wrong: Apple develops products, but contracts almost all of the manufacturing of those products to other companies that are mainly located overseas. But it's not really right to answer "China," either, even though that's where iPhones are assembled. Assembly is the last phase of iPhone production, in which the pieces are put together in the familiar metal-and-glass case.

In fact, a study of the iPhone X estimated that of the average wholesale price of about US$800 per phone, less than US$25 stayed in the Chinese economy. A substantially larger amount went to South Korean manufacturers, who supplied the display and memory chips. There were also substantial outlays for raw materials, which are sourced all over the world. And the biggest share of the price — more than half — consisted of Apple's profit margin, which was largely a reward for research, development, and design.

So where do iPhones come from? Lots of places. And the case of the iPhone isn't unusual: the car you drive, the clothing you wear, even the food you eat are generally the end products of complex supply chains that span the globe. Large-scale international trade like this isn't new. It was fairly common by the early twentieth century. In recent decades, however, new technologies for transportation and communication have interacted with pro-trade policies to produce an era of *hyperglobalization* in which international trade has soared thanks to complex chains of production like the one that puts an iPhone in front of your nose.

These global supply chains make the world economy much more productive and, as a result, richer than it would be if each country tried to be self-sufficient. And it isn't just the world as a whole that benefits from international trade: it's almost certain that every country benefits, too. But international trade is nonetheless controversial, because it sometimes hurts particular groups *within* countries. For these reasons, we must have a full picture of international trade to understand how national economies work.

This chapter examines the economics of international trade. We start from the model of comparative advantage, which, as we saw in Chapter 2, explains why there are gains from international trade. We will briefly recap that model here, then turn to a more detailed examination of the causes and consequences of globalization. ●

WHAT YOU WILL LEARN

- What is comparative advantage and why does it lead to international trade?
- What are the sources of comparative advantage?
- Who gains and who loses from international trade?

- Why do **trade protections** like **tariffs** and **import quotas** create inefficiency?
- Why do governments engage in trade protection and how do **international trade agreements** counteract this?

Goods and services purchased from other countries are **imports;** goods and services sold to other countries are **exports.**

Globalization is the phenomenon of growing economic linkages among countries.

Comparative Advantage and International Trade

Canada buys smartphones—and many other goods and services—from other countries. At the same time, it sells many goods and services to other countries. Goods and services purchased from abroad are **imports;** goods and services sold abroad are **exports.**

As illustrated by the opening story, international trade plays an increasingly important role in the world economy. Panel (a) of Figure 8-1 shows the ratio of goods crossing national borders to *world GDP*—the total value of goods and services produced in the world as a whole—since 1870. As you can see, the long-term trend has been upward, although there have been some periods of declining trade—for example, the sharp but brief dip in trade during the global financial crisis of 2008 and its aftermath.

Panel (b) illustrates imports and exports as a percentage of GDP for a number of countries. It shows that foreign trade is significantly more important for many countries, like Canada, than it is for the United States.

Foreign trade isn't the only way countries interact economically. In the modern world, investors from one country often invest funds in another nation; many companies are multinational, with subsidiaries operating in several countries; and a growing number of people work in a country different from the one in which they were born. The growth of all these forms of economic linkages among countries is often called **globalization.**

Globalization isn't a new phenomenon. As you can see from panel (a) of Figure 8-1, there was rapid growth in trade between 1870 and the beginning of World War I, as railroads and steamships effectively made shipping goods long distances faster and cheaper, effectively shrinking the world. This growth of trade

FIGURE 8-1 The Growing Importance of International Trade

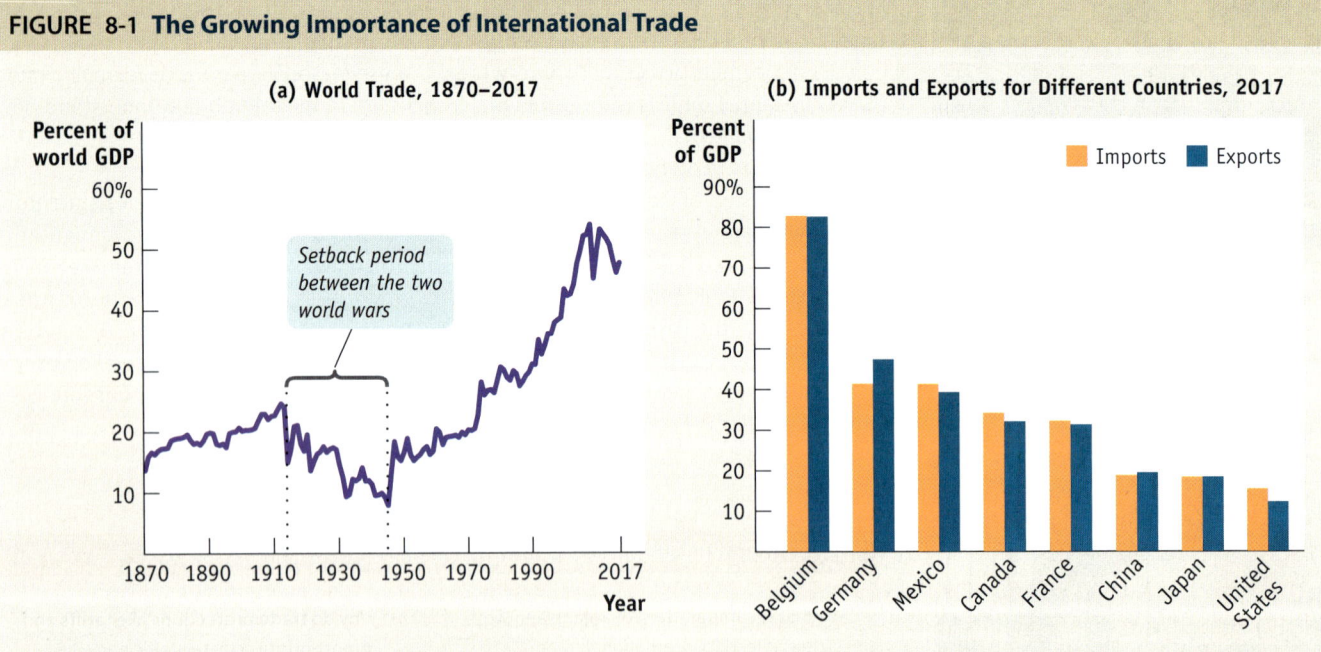

Panel (a) shows the long-term history of the ratio of world trade to world production. The trend has been generally upward, thanks to technological progress in transportation and communication, although there was a long setback during the period between the two world wars. Panel (b) demonstrates that international trade is significantly more important to many countries, like Canada, than it is to the United States.

Data from: [panel (a)] Klasing, M. J., and P. Milionis, "Quantifying the Evolution of World Trade, 1870–1949," *Journal of International Economics* (2013); and Feenstra, Robert C., Robert Inklaar, and Marcel P. Timmer, "The Next Generation of the Penn World Table" *American Economic Review* 105, no. 10 (2015): 3150–3182, available for download at www.ggdc.net/pwt; [panel (b)] World Development Indicators.

was accompanied by large-scale international investment and migration. However, globalization went into reverse for almost 40 years after World War I, as governments imposed limits on trade. And by several measures, globalization didn't return to 1913 levels until the 1980s.

Since then, however, there has been a further dramatic increase in international linkages, sometimes referred to as **hyperglobalization.** The manufacture of iPhones and other high-tech goods, which often involve supply chains of production that span the globe, are an example of hyperglobalization. Each stage of a good's production takes place in a different country—all made possible by advances in communication and transportation technology. (For a real-life example, see this chapter's business case.)

Hyperglobalization is the phenomenon of extremely high levels of international trade.

One big question in international economics is whether hyperglobalization will continue in the decades ahead. As you can see from looking closely at Figure 8-1, the big rise in the ratio of exports to world GDP levelled off around 2005. Since then, many reports have appeared about companies deciding that the money they saved by buying goods from suppliers thousands of miles away is more than offset by the disadvantages of long shipping times and other inconveniences. (Even now, it takes around two weeks for a container ship from China to arrive in British Columbia, and a month to reach the East Coast.) As a result, there has been some move toward *reshoring,* bringing production closer to markets.

Thanks to cheap and fast ways of transporting goods, extremely high levels of international trade are a feature of today's economy.

More recently, international disputes over trade have heated up, and governments may once again impose the kind of restrictions on trade that caused globalization to decline after World War I. Also, the outbreak of the coronavirus pandemic in early 2020 resulted in lockdowns and a significant disruption of the supply chain, as a result firms are rethinking the benefits of outsourcing. Some firms are considering relocating some production facilities as means to minimize future production disruptions. Although international trade is likely to remain important to world economies, it is possible that hyperglobalization may become less prevalent than it is today.

To understand why international trade occurs and why economists believe it is beneficial to the economy, we will first review the concept of comparative advantage.

Production Possibilities and Comparative Advantage, Revisited

To produce phones, any country must use resources—land, labour, and capital—that could have been used to produce other things. The opportunity cost of that phone is the potential production of other goods a country must forgo to produce it.

In some cases, it's easy to see why the opportunity cost of producing a good is especially low in a given country. Consider, for example, shrimp—much of which now comes from seafood farms in Vietnam and Thailand. It's a lot easier to produce shrimp in Vietnam, where the climate is nearly ideal and there's plenty of coastal land suitable for shellfish farming, than it is in Canada.

Conversely, other goods are not produced as easily in Vietnam as in Canada. For example, Vietnam doesn't have the base of skilled workers and technological know-how that makes Canada so good at producing high-technology goods. So the opportunity cost of a tonne of shrimp, in terms of other goods such as aircraft, is much less in Vietnam than it is in Canada.

In other cases, the trade-off is less obvious. For example, it is as easy to assemble smartphones in Canada as in China. And Chinese electronics workers are, if anything, less productive than their Canadian counterparts. But Chinese workers are even less productive than Canadian workers in other areas, such as automobile and chemical production. So we say that China has a comparative advantage in producing smartphones. Let's repeat the definition of comparative advantage from Chapter 2: *A country has a comparative advantage in producing a good or service if the opportunity cost of producing the good or service is lower for that country than for other countries.*

The **Ricardian model of international trade** analyzes international trade under the assumption that opportunity costs are constant.

Employing a Chinese worker to assemble phones is more productive than employing a Canadian worker to assemble phones because the Canadian worker can be even more productively employed elsewhere. That is, the opportunity cost of smartphone assembly in China is less than it is in Canada.

Notice that we said the opportunity cost of phone *assembly*. As we've seen, most of the value of a "Chinese made" phone actually comes from other countries. For the sake of exposition, however, let's ignore that complication and consider a hypothetical case in which China makes phones from scratch.

Figure 8-2 provides a hypothetical numerical example of comparative advantage in international trade. We assume that only two goods are produced and consumed, phones and trucks. (In reality, Canada doesn't export many trucks to China, but we use this as a hypothetical good traded. The associated quantities below are purely fictional to help make the point about the impact (gains) from international trade.) And we assume that there are only two countries in the world, Canada and China. The figure shows hypothetical production possibility frontiers for Canada and China.

As in Chapter 2, we simplify the model by assuming that the production possibility frontiers are straight lines, as shown in Figure 2-1, rather than the more realistic bowed-out shape in Figure 2-2. The straight-line shape implies that the opportunity cost of a phone in terms of trucks in each country is constant—it does not depend on how many units of each good the country produces. The analysis of international trade under the assumption that opportunity costs are constant, which makes production possibility frontiers straight lines, is known as the **Ricardian model of international trade,** named after the English economist David Ricardo, who introduced this analysis in the early nineteenth century.

In Figure 8-2 we show a situation in which Canada can produce 10,000 trucks if it produces no phones, or 10 million phones if it produces no trucks. Thus, the slope of the Canadian production possibility frontier, or *PPF,* is −10,000/10 = − 1,000. That is, to produce an additional million phones, Canada must forgo the production of 1,000 trucks. Likewise, to produce one more truck, Canada must forgo 1,000 phones (equal to 1 million phones divided by 1,000 trucks).

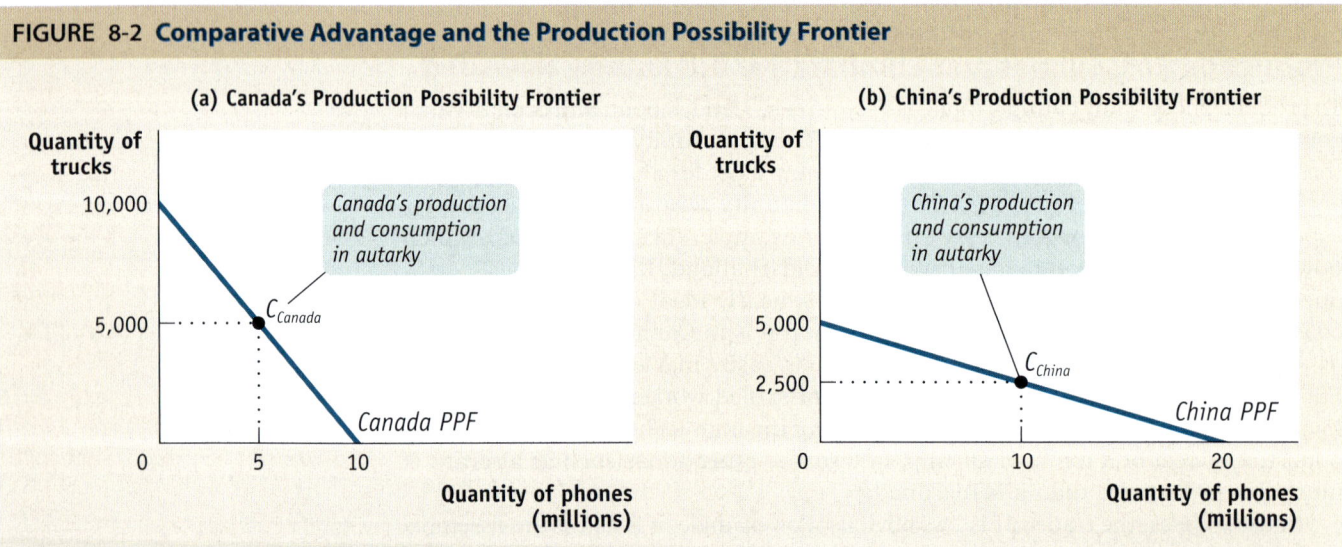

FIGURE 8-2 Comparative Advantage and the Production Possibility Frontier

The Canadian opportunity cost of 1 million phones in terms of trucks is 1,000: for every 1 million phones, 1,000 trucks must be forgone. The Chinese opportunity cost of 1 million phones in terms of trucks is 250: for every additional 1 million phones, only 250 trucks must be forgone. As a result, Canada has a comparative advantage in truck production, and China has a comparative advantage in phone production. In autarky, each country is forced to consume only what it produces: 5,000 trucks and 5 million phones for Canada; 2,500 trucks and 10 million phones for China.

Similarly, China can produce 5,000 trucks if it produces no phones or 20 million phones if it produces no trucks. Thus, the slope of China's *PPF* is −5,000/200 = −250. That is, to produce an additional million phones, China must forgo the production of 250 trucks. Likewise, to produce one more truck, China must forgo 4,000 phones (1 million phones divided by 250 trucks).

Historically, countries have almost always traded with each other. Yet economists find it helpful as a first step to illustrate the choices a country would make if it were unable to engage in international trade. Economists use the term **autarky** to refer to a situation in which a country does not trade with other countries. In our example, we assume that in autarky Canada chooses to produce and consume 5 million phones and 5,000 trucks. We also assume that in autarky China produces 10 million phones and 2,500 trucks.

The trade-offs facing the two countries when they don't trade are summarized in Table 8-1. As you can see, Canada has a comparative advantage in the production of trucks because it has a lower opportunity cost in terms of phones than China has: producing a truck costs Canada only 1,000 phones, while it costs China 4,000 phones. Correspondingly, China has a comparative advantage in phone production: 1 million phones costs only 250 trucks, while it costs Canada 1,000 trucks.

As we learned in Chapter 2, each country can do better by engaging in trade than it could by not trading. A country can accomplish this by specializing in the production of the good in which it has a comparative advantage and exporting that good, while importing the good in which it has a comparative disadvantage.

Let's see how this works.

> **Autarky** is a situation in which a country does not trade with other countries.

TABLE 8-1 Canadian and Chinese Opportunity Costs of Phones and Trucks

	Canadian Opportunity Cost		Chinese Opportunity Cost
1 million phones	1,000 trucks	>	250 trucks
1 truck	1,000 phones	<	4,000 phones

The Gains from International Trade

Figure 8-3 illustrates how both countries can gain from specialization and trade, by showing a hypothetical rearrangement of production and consumption that allows *each* country to consume more of *both* goods. Again, panel (a) represents Canada and panel (b) represents China. In each panel we indicate again the autarky production and consumption assumed in Figure 8-2.

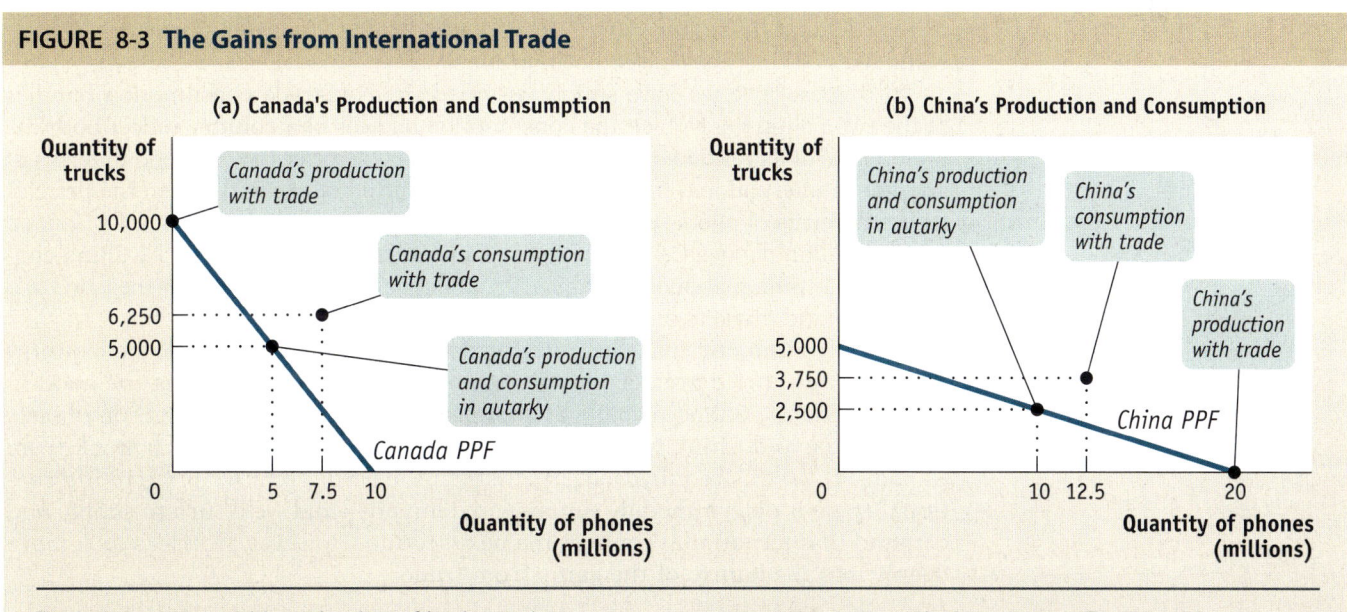

FIGURE 8-3 The Gains from International Trade

(a) Canada's Production and Consumption

Canada's production with trade

Canada's consumption with trade

Canada's production and consumption in autarky

Canada PPF

(b) China's Production and Consumption

China's production and consumption in autarky

China's consumption with trade

China's production with trade

China PPF

Trade increases world production of both goods, allowing both countries to consume more. Here, each country specializes its production as a result of trade: Canada concentrates on producing trucks, and China concentrates on producing phones. Total world production of both goods rises, which means that it is possible for both countries to consume more of both goods.

TABLE 8-2 How Canada and China Gain from Trade

		In Autarky		With Trade		
		Production	Consumption	Production	Consumption	Gains from trade
Canada	Million phones	5	5	0	7.5	+2.5
	Trucks	5,000	5,000	10,000	6,250	+1,250
China	Million phones	10	10	20	12.5	+2.5
	Trucks	2,500	2,500	0	3,750	+1,250

Once trade becomes possible, however, everything changes. With trade, each country can move to producing only the good in which it has a comparative advantage—trucks for Canada and phones for China. Because the world production of both goods is now higher than in autarky, trade makes it possible for each country to consume more of both goods.

Table 8-2 sums up the changes as a result of trade and shows why both countries can gain. The left part of the table shows the autarky situation, before trade, in which each country must produce the goods it consumes. The right part of the table shows what happens as a result of trade. After trade, Canada specializes in the production of trucks, producing 10,000 trucks and no phones; China specializes in the production of phones, producing 20 million phones and no trucks.

The result is a rise in total world production of both goods. As you can see in the table, there are gains from trade to both countries:

- Canada can consume both more trucks (1,250 more) and phones (2.5 million more) than before, even though it no longer produces phones, because it can import phones from China.

- China can also consume more of both goods (1,250 more trucks and 2.5 million more phones), even though it no longer produces trucks, because it can import trucks from Canada.

The key to this mutual gain is the fact that trade liberates both countries from self-sufficiency—from the need to produce the same mixes of goods they consume. Because each country can concentrate on producing the good in which it has a comparative advantage, total world production rises, making a higher standard of living possible in both nations.

In this example we have simply assumed the post-trade consumption bundles of the two countries. In fact, the consumption choices of a country reflect both the preferences of its residents and the *relative prices*—the prices of one good in terms of another in international markets. Although we have not explicitly given the price of trucks in terms of phones, that price is implicit in our example: China sells Canada the 7.5 million phones Canada consumes in return for the 3,750 trucks China consumes, so 1 million phones are traded for 500 trucks. This tells us that the price of a truck on world markets must be equal to the price of 2,000 phones.

One requirement that the relative price must satisfy is that no country pays a relative price greater than its opportunity cost of obtaining the good in autarky. That is, Canada won't pay more than 1,000 trucks for 1 million phones from China, and China won't pay more than 4,000 phones for each truck from Canada. Once this requirement is satisfied, the actual relative price in international trade is determined by supply and demand—and we'll turn to supply and demand in international trade in the next section. However, first let's look more deeply into the nature of the gains from trade.

Comparative Advantage versus Absolute Advantage

It's easy to accept the idea that Vietnam and Thailand have a comparative advantage in shrimp production: they have a tropical climate that's better suited to shrimp farming than the climate of Canada, and they have a lot of usable coastal area. So Canada imports shrimp from Vietnam and Thailand. But as we have seen in the case of cell phone assembly, the gains from trade often depend on *comparative advantage,* rather than on absolute advantage. It would take less labour to assemble a phone in Canada than in China. That is, the productivity of Chinese electronics workers is less than that of their Canadian counterparts. But what determines comparative advantage is not the amount of resources used to produce a good but the opportunity cost of that good—in this case, the quantity of other goods forgone in order to produce a phone. And the opportunity cost of phones is lower in China than in Canada.

The tropical climates of Vietnam and Thailand give them a comparative advantage in shrimp production.

Here's how it works: Chinese workers have low productivity compared with Canadian workers in the electronics industry. But Chinese workers have even lower productivity compared with Canadian workers in other industries. Because Chinese labour productivity in industries other than electronics is relatively very low, producing a phone in China, even though it takes a lot of labour, does not require forgoing the production of large quantities of other goods.

In Canada, the opposite is true: very high productivity in other industries (such as automobiles) means that assembling electronic products in Canada, even though it doesn't require much labour, requires sacrificing lots of other goods. So the opportunity cost of producing electronics is less in China than in Canada. Despite its lower labour productivity, China has a comparative advantage in the production of many consumer electronics, although Canada has an absolute advantage.

The source of China's comparative advantage in consumer electronics is reflected in global markets by the wages Chinese workers are paid. That's because a country's wage rates, in general, reflect its labour productivity. In countries where labour is highly productive in many industries, employers are willing to pay high wages to attract workers, so competition among employers leads to an overall high wage rate. In countries where labour is less productive, competition for workers is less intense and wage rates are correspondingly lower.

As the Global Comparison shows, there is indeed a strong relationship between overall levels of productivity and wage rates around the world. Because China has generally low productivity, it has a relatively low wage rate. Low wages, in turn, give China a cost advantage in producing goods where its productivity is only moderately low, like consumer electronics. As a result, it's cheaper to produce these goods in China than in Canada.

Popular Misconceptions Arising from Misunderstanding Comparative Advantage

The kind of trade that takes place between low-wage, low-productivity economies like China and high-wage, high-productivity economies like Canada gives rise to two common misperceptions:

- The *pauper labour fallacy* is the belief that when a country with high wages imports goods produced by workers who are paid low wages, it must hurt the standard of living of workers in the importing country.

- The *sweatshop labour fallacy* is the belief that trade must be bad for workers in poor exporting countries because those workers are paid very low wages by our standards.

Both fallacies miss the nature of gains from trade: it's to the advantage of both countries if the poorer, lower-wage country exports goods in which it has a comparative advantage, even if its cost advantage in these goods depends on low wages. That is, both countries are able to achieve a higher standard of living through trade.

It's particularly important to understand that buying a good made by someone who is paid much lower wages than most Canadian workers doesn't necessarily

GLOBAL COMPARISON PRODUCTIVITY AND WAGES AROUND THE WORLD

Is it true that both the pauper labour argument and the sweatshop labour argument are fallacies? Yes, it is. The real explanation for low wages in poor countries is low overall productivity.

The graph shows estimates of labour productivity, measured by the value of output (GDP) per worker, and wages, measured by the hourly compensation of the average worker, for several countries in 2018. Both productivity and wages (a common form of measurement for international comparisons) are expressed as percentages of U.S. productivity and wages; for example, productivity and wages in Canada were 81% and 75% respectively, of their U.S. levels. You can see the strong positive relationship between productivity and wages. The relationship isn't perfect. For example, Iceland has higher wages than its productivity might lead you to expect. But simple comparisons of wages give a misleading sense of labour costs in poor countries: their low wage advantage is mostly offset by low productivity.

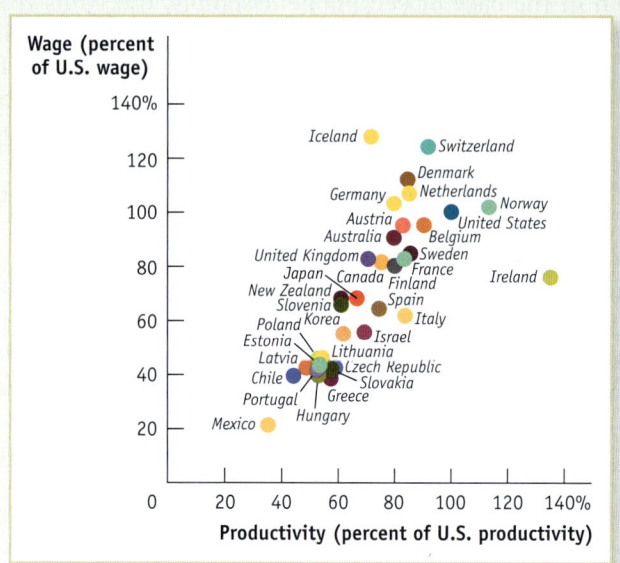

Data from: The OECD and the World Bank, World Development Indicators.

imply that you're taking advantage of that person. It depends on the alternatives. Because workers in poor countries have low productivity across the board, they are offered low wages whether they produce goods exported to Canada or goods sold in local markets. A job that looks terrible by rich-country standards can be a step up for someone in a poor country.

International trade that depends on low-wage exports can nonetheless raise the exporting country's standard of living. This is especially true of very-low-wage nations. For example, Bangladesh and similar countries would be much poorer than they are—their citizens might even be starving—if they weren't able to export goods such as clothing based on their low wage rates.

Sources of Comparative Advantage

International trade is driven by comparative advantage, but where does comparative advantage come from? Economists who study international trade have found three main sources of comparative advantage: international differences in *climate*, international differences in *factor endowments*, and international differences in *technology*.

Differences in Climate One key reason the opportunity cost of producing shrimp in Vietnam and Thailand is less than in Canada is that shrimp need warm water—Vietnam has plenty of that, but Canada doesn't. In general, differences in climate play a significant role in international trade. Tropical countries export tropical products like coffee, sugar, bananas, and shrimp. Countries in the temperate zones export crops like wheat and corn. Some trade is even driven by the difference in seasons between the northern and southern hemispheres: winter deliveries of Chilean grapes have become commonplace in Canadian, U.S., and European supermarkets.

Differences in Factor Endowments Canada does more trade with the United States than with any other country (the European Union and China come in second and third respectively). Among other things, Canada sells the United States a lot of forest products—lumber and products derived from lumber, like pulp

A greater endowment of forestland gives Canada a comparative advantage in forest products.

Johner Images/Alamy

and paper. These exports don't reflect the special skill of Canadian lumberjacks. Canada has a comparative advantage in forest products because its forested area is much greater compared to the size of its labour force than the ratio of forest-land to the labour force in the United States.

Forestland, like labour and capital, is a *factor of production:* an input used to produce goods and services. (Recall from Chapter 2 that the factors of production are land, labour, physical capital, and human capital.) Due to history and geogra-phy, the mix of available factors of production differs among countries, providing an important source of comparative advantage. The relationship between com-parative advantage and factor availability is described in an influential model of international trade, the *Heckscher–Ohlin model,* developed by two Swedish econ-omists in the first half of the twentieth century.

Two key concepts in the model are *factor abundance* and *factor intensity.* Fac-tor abundance refers to how large a country's supply of a factor is relative to its supply of other factors. **Factor intensity** refers to the ranking of goods according to which factor is used in relatively greater quantities in production compared to other factors. So oil refining is a capital-intensive good because it tends to use a high ratio of capital to labour, but phone production is a labour-intensive good because it tends to use a high ratio of labour to capital.

According to the **Heckscher–Ohlin model,** *a country that has an abundant supply of a factor of production will have a comparative advantage in goods whose production is intensive in that factor.* So a country that has a relative abundance of capital will have a comparative advantage in capital-intensive industries such as oil refining, but a country that has a relative abundance of labour will have a comparative advantage in labour-intensive industries such as phone production.

The basic intuition behind this result is simple and based on opportunity cost.

- The opportunity cost of a given factor—the value that the factor would gener-ate in alternative uses—is low for a country when it is relatively abundant in that factor.
- Relative to Canada, China has an abundance of low-skilled labour.
- As a result, the opportunity cost of the production of low-skilled, labour-intensive goods is lower in China than in Canada.

World trade in clothing is the most dramatic example of the validity of the Heckscher–Ohlin model in practice. Clothing production is a labour-intensive activity: it doesn't take much physical capital, nor does it require a lot of human capital in the form of highly educated workers. So you would expect labour-abundant countries such as China and Bangladesh to have a comparative advan-tage in clothing production. And they do.

The fact that international trade is the result of differences in factor endow-ments helps explain another fact: international specialization of production is often *incomplete.* That is, a country often maintains some domestic production of a good that it imports. A good example is British trade in oil. Britain imports most of the petroleum it consumes, mainly from Norway, which has huge off-shore reserves. But Britain has some offshore reserves of its own, mostly off the coast of Scotland, so it's a significant oil producer itself.

In our supply and demand analysis in the next section, we'll consider incom-plete specialization by a country to be the norm. We should emphasize, however, that the fact that countries often incompletely specialize does not in any way change the conclusion that there are gains from trade.

Differences in Technology In the 1970s and 1980s, Japan became by far the world's largest exporter of automobiles, selling large numbers to consumers in North America and the rest of the world. Japan's comparative advantage in automobiles

The **factor intensity** of a good is a measure of which factor is used in relatively greater quantities than other factors in production.

According to the **Heckscher–Ohlin model,** a country has a comparative advantage in a good whose production is intensive in the factors that are abundantly available in that country.

wasn't the result of climate. Nor can it easily be attributed to differences in factor endowments: aside from a scarcity of land, Japan's mix of available factors is quite similar to that in other advanced countries. Instead, Japan's comparative advantage in automobiles was based on the superior production techniques developed by its manufacturers, which allowed them to produce more cars with a given amount of labour and capital than their North American or European counterparts.

Japan's comparative advantage in automobiles was a case of comparative advantage caused by differences in technology — the techniques used in production.

The causes of differences in technology are somewhat mysterious. Sometimes they seem to be based on knowledge accumulated through experience — for example, Switzerland's comparative advantage in watches reflects a long tradition of watchmaking. Sometimes they are the result of a set of innovations that for some reason occur in one country but not in others.

Technological advantage, however, is often transitory. By adopting *lean production* (techniques designed to improve manufacturing productivity through increased efficiency) North American auto manufacturers closed much of the gap in productivity with their Japanese competitors. Similarly, government support of research and development has helped the Canadian and European aircraft industry to close a similar gap with the U.S. aircraft industry. At any given point in time, however, differences in technology are a major source of comparative advantage.

ECONOMICS >> *in Action*
How Hong Kong Lost Its Shirts

The rise of Hong Kong was one of the most improbable-sounding economic success stories of the twentieth century. When a communist regime took over China in 1949, Hong Kong — which was at that time still a British colony — became in effect a city without a hinterland, largely cut off from economic relations with the territory just over the border. Until that point the people of Hong Kong had made a living largely by serving as a point of entry into China. However, after the city became cut off from China, it did not languish. Instead, Hong Kong prospered to such an extent that today the city—now returned to China, but governed as a special administrative region—has a GDP per capita comparable to that of the United States.

Much of Hong Kong's ascent was the result of its clothing industry. In 1980, Hong Kong's garment and textile sectors employed almost 450,000 workers, close to 20% of total employment on the island. These workers overwhelmingly made apparel — shirts, trousers, dresses, and more—for export, especially to the United States.

More recently, the Hong Kong clothing industry has fallen sharply—in fact, it has almost disappeared and along with it, Hong Kong's apparel exports. Figure 8-4 shows Hong Kong's share of U.S. apparel imports since 1989, along with the share of a relative newcomer to the industry, Bangladesh. As you can see, Hong Kong has more or less dropped off the chart, while Bangladesh's share has risen significantly.

Why did Hong Kong lose its comparative advantage in making clothing? It wasn't because the city's garment workers became less productive. Instead, it was because the city got better at other things. Apparel production is a labour-intensive, relatively low-tech industry; comparative advantage in that industry has historically always rested with poor, labour-abundant economies. Hong Kong no longer fits that description; Bangladesh does. Hong Kong's garment industry was a victim of the city's success.

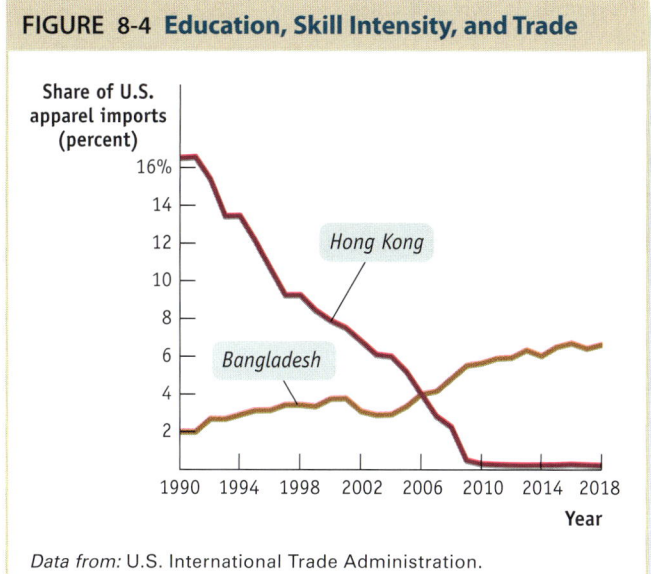

FIGURE 8-4 Education, Skill Intensity, and Trade

Share of U.S. apparel imports (percent)

Data from: U.S. International Trade Administration.

>> Check Your Understanding 8-1

Solutions appear at back of book.

1. In Canada, the opportunity cost of 1 tonne of corn is 50 bicycles. In China, the opportunity cost of 1 bicycle is 0.01 tonne of corn.
   a. Determine the pattern of comparative advantage.
   b. In autarky, Canada can produce 200,000 bicycles if no corn is produced, and China can produce 3,000 tonnes of corn if no bicycles are produced. Draw each country's production possibility frontier assuming constant opportunity cost, with tonnes of corn on the vertical axis and bicycles on the horizontal axis.
   c. With trade, each country specializes its production. Canada consumes 1,000 tonnes of corn and 200,000 bicycles; China consumes 3,000 tonnes of corn and 100,000 bicycles. Indicate the production and consumption points on your diagrams, and use them to explain the gains from trade.
2. Explain the following patterns of trade using the Heckscher–Ohlin model.
   a. France exports wine to Canada, and Canada exports lumber to France.
   b. Brazil exports shoes to Canada, and Canada exports shoe-making machinery to Brazil.

‖ Supply, Demand, and International Trade

Simple models of comparative advantage are helpful for understanding the fundamental causes of international trade. However, to analyze the effects of international trade at a more detailed level and to understand trade policy, it helps to return to the supply and demand model. We'll start by looking at the effects of imports on domestic producers and consumers, then turn to the effects of exports.

>> Quick Review

• **Imports** and **exports** account for a growing share of the Canadian economy and the economies of many other countries.

• The growth of international trade and other international linkages is known as **globalization.** Extremely high levels of international trade are known as **hyperglobalization.**

• International trade is driven by comparative advantage. **The Ricardian model of international trade** shows that trade between two countries makes both countries better off than they would be in **autarky** — that is, there are gains from international trade.

• The main sources of comparative advantage are international differences in climate, factor endowments, and technology.

• The **Heckscher–Ohlin model** shows how comparative advantage can arise from differences in factor endowments: goods differ in their **factor intensity,** and countries tend to export goods that are intensive in the factors they have in abundance.

The **domestic demand curve** shows how the quantity of a good demanded by domestic consumers depends on the price of that good.

The **domestic supply curve** shows how the quantity of a good supplied by domestic producers depends on the price of that good.

The **world price** of a good is the price at which that good can be bought or sold abroad.

The Effects of Imports

Figure 8-5 shows the Canadian market for phones, ignoring international trade for a moment. It introduces a few new concepts: the *domestic demand curve*, the *domestic supply curve*, and the domestic or autarky price.

The **domestic demand curve** shows how the quantity of a good demanded by residents of a country depends on the price of that good. Why "domestic"? Because people living in other countries may demand the good, too. Once we introduce international trade, we need to distinguish between purchases of a good by domestic consumers and purchases by foreign consumers. So the domestic demand curve reflects only the demand of residents of our own country.

Similarly, the **domestic supply curve** shows how the quantity of a good supplied by producers inside our own country depends on the price of that good. Once we introduce international trade, we need to distinguish between the supply of domestic producers and foreign supply—supply brought in from abroad.

In autarky, with no international trade in phones, the equilibrium in this market would be determined by the intersection of the domestic demand and domestic supply curves, point A. The equilibrium price of phones would be P_A, and the equilibrium quantity of phones produced and consumed would be Q_A. As always, both consumers and producers gain from the existence of the domestic market. In autarky, consumer surplus would be equal to the area of the blue-shaded triangle in Figure 8-5. Producer surplus would be equal to the area of the red-shaded triangle. And total surplus would be equal to the sum of these two shaded triangles.

Now let's imagine opening up this market to imports. To do this, we must make an assumption about the supply of imports. The simplest assumption, which we will adopt here, is that unlimited quantities of phones can be purchased from abroad at a fixed price. The price at which a good can be bought or sold abroad is known as the **world price.** Figure 8-6 shows a situation in which the world price of a phone, P_W, is lower than the price of a phone that would prevail in the domestic market in autarky, P_A.

Given that the world price is below the domestic price of a phone, it is profitable for importers to buy phones abroad and resell them domestically. The imported phones increase the supply of phones in the domestic market, driving

---

FIGURE 8-5 **Consumer and Producer Surplus in Autarky**

In the absence of trade, the domestic price is P_A, the autarky price at which the domestic supply curve and the domestic demand curve intersect. The quantity produced and consumed domestically is Q_A. Consumer surplus is represented by the blue-shaded area, and producer surplus is represented by the red-shaded area.

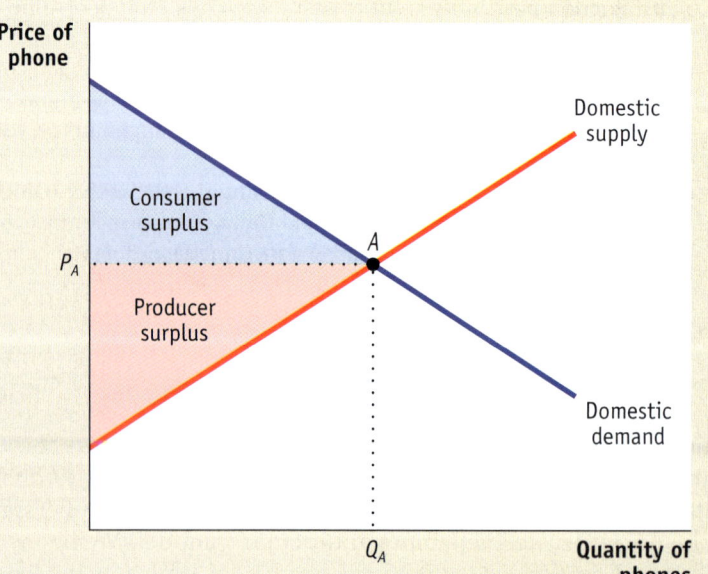

down the domestic market price. Phones will continue to be imported until the domestic price falls to a level equal to the world price.

The result is shown in Figure 8-6. Because of imports, the domestic price of a phone falls from P_A to P_W. The quantity of phones demanded by domestic consumers rises from Q_A to Q_D, and the quantity supplied by domestic producers falls from Q_A to Q_S. The difference between the domestic quantity demanded and the domestic quantity supplied, $Q_D - Q_S$, is filled by imports.

Now let's turn to the effects of imports on consumer surplus and producer surplus. Because imports of phones lead to a fall in their domestic price, consumer surplus rises and producer surplus falls. Figure 8-7 shows how this works. We label four areas: W, X, Y, and Z. The autarky consumer surplus we identified in Figure 8-5 corresponds to W, and the autarky producer surplus corresponds to the sum of X and Y. The fall in the domestic price to the world price leads to an increase in consumer surplus; it increases by X and Z, so consumer surplus now equals the sum of W, X, and Z. At the same time, producers lose X in surplus, so producer surplus now equals only Y.

The table in Figure 8-7 summarizes the changes in consumer and producer surplus when the phone market is opened to imports. Consumers gain surplus equal to the areas $X + Z$. Producers lose surplus equal to X. So the sum of producer and consumer surplus—the total surplus generated in the phone market—increases by Z. As a result of trade, consumers gain and producers lose, but the gain to consumers exceeds the loss to producers.

This is an important result. We have just shown that opening up a market to imports leads to a net gain in total surplus, which is what we should have expected given the proposition that there are gains from international trade.

However, we have also learned that although the country as a whole gains, some groups—in this case, domestic producers of phones—lose as a result of international trade. As we'll see shortly, the fact that international trade creates losers as well as winners is crucial for understanding the politics of trade policy.

We turn next to the case in which a country exports a good.

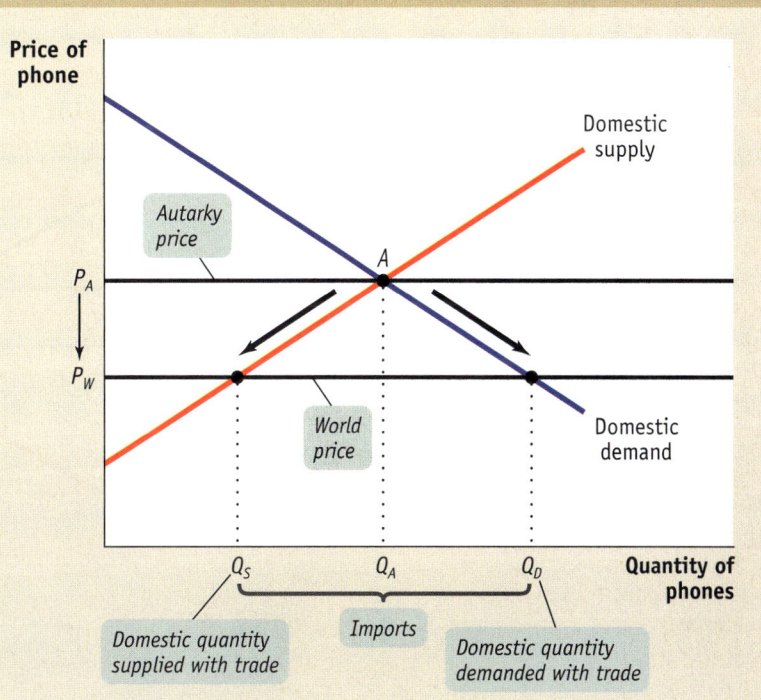

FIGURE 8-6 The Domestic Market with Imports

Here the world price of phones, P_W, is below the autarky price, P_A. When the economy is opened to international trade, imports enter the domestic market, and the domestic price falls from the autarky price, P_A, to the world price, P_W. As the price falls, the domestic quantity demanded rises from Q_A to Q_D and the domestic quantity supplied falls from Q_A to Q_S. The difference between domestic quantity demanded and domestic quantity supplied at P_W, the quantity $Q_D - Q_S$, is filled by imports.

FIGURE 8-7 The Effects of Imports on Surplus

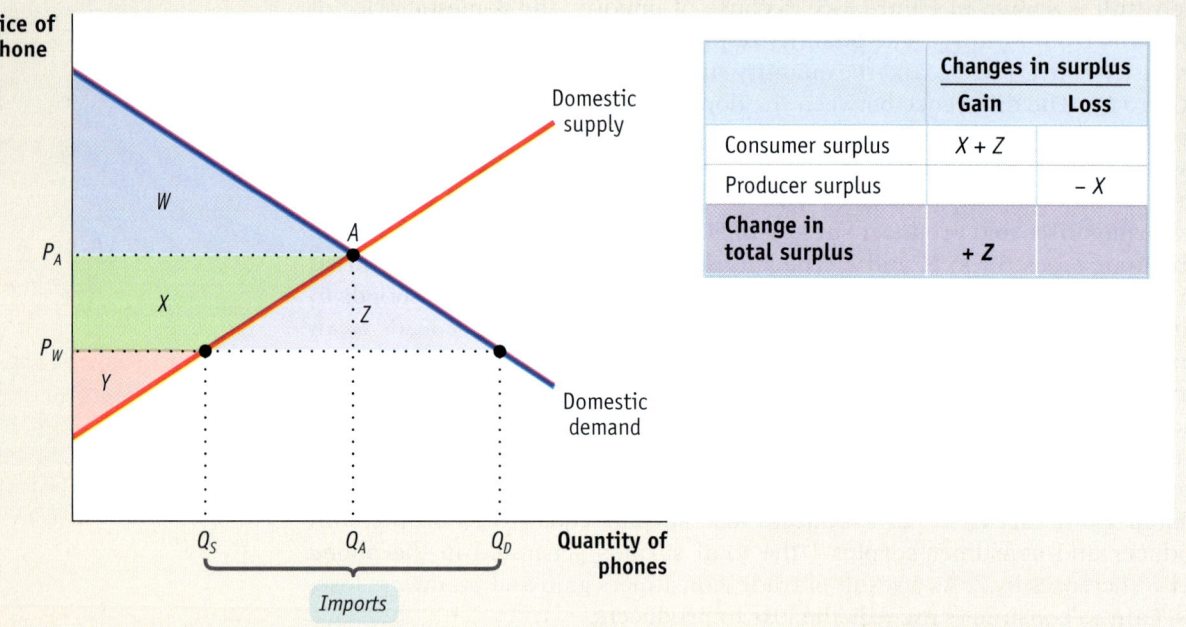

	Changes in surplus	
	Gain	Loss
Consumer surplus	X + Z	
Producer surplus		– X
Change in total surplus	**+ Z**	

When the domestic price falls to P_W as a result of international trade, consumers gain additional surplus (areas $X + Z$) and producers lose surplus (area X). Because the gains to consumers outweigh the losses to producers, there is an increase in the total surplus in the economy as a whole (area Z).

The Effects of Exports

Figure 8-8 shows the effects on a country when it exports a good, in this case trucks. For this example, we assume that unlimited quantities of trucks can be sold abroad at a given world price, P_W, which is higher than the price that would prevail in the domestic market in autarky, P_A.

FIGURE 8-8 The Domestic Market with Exports

Here the world price, P_W, is greater than the autarky price, P_A. When the economy is opened to international trade, some of the domestic supply is now exported. The domestic price rises from the autarky price, P_A, to the world price, P_W. As the price rises, the domestic quantity demanded falls from Q_A to Q_D and the domestic quantity supplied rises from Q_A to Q_S. The portion of domestic production that is not consumed domestically, $Q_S - Q_D$, is exported.

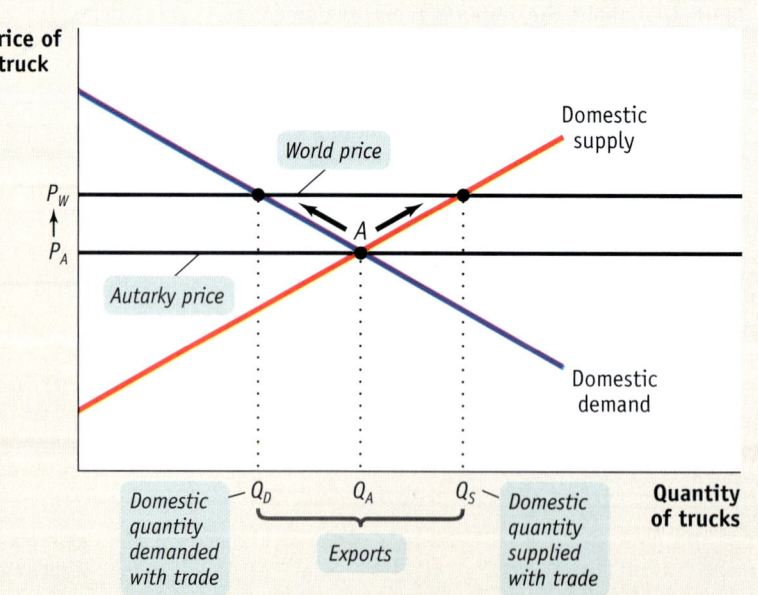

The higher world price makes it profitable for exporters to buy trucks domestically and sell them overseas. The purchases of domestic trucks drive the domestic price up until it is equal to the world price. As a result, the quantity demanded by domestic consumers falls from Q_A to Q_D and the quantity supplied by domestic producers rises from Q_A to Q_S. This difference between domestic production and domestic consumption, $Q_S - Q_D$, is exported.

Like imports, exports lead to an overall gain in total surplus for the exporting country but also create losers as well as winners. Figure 8-9 shows the effects of truck exports on producer and consumer surplus. In the absence of trade, the price of each truck would be P_A. Consumer surplus in the absence of trade is the sum of areas W and X, and producer surplus is area Y. As a result of trade, price rises from P_A to P_W, consumer surplus falls to W, and producer surplus rises to $Y + X + Z$. So producers gain $X + Z$, consumers lose X, and, as shown in the table accompanying the figure, the economy as a whole gains total surplus in the amount of Z.

We have learned, then, that imports of a particular good hurt domestic producers of that good but help domestic consumers, whereas exports of a particular good hurt domestic consumers of that good but help domestic producers. In each case, the gains are larger than the losses.

International Trade and Wages

So far we have focused on the effects of international trade on producers and consumers in a particular industry. For many purposes this is a very helpful approach. However, producers and consumers are not the only parts of society affected by trade; the owners of factors of production are also affected. In particular, the owners of labour, land, and capital employed in producing goods that are exported, or goods that compete with imported goods, can be deeply affected by trade.

FIGURE 8-9 The Effects of Exports on Surplus

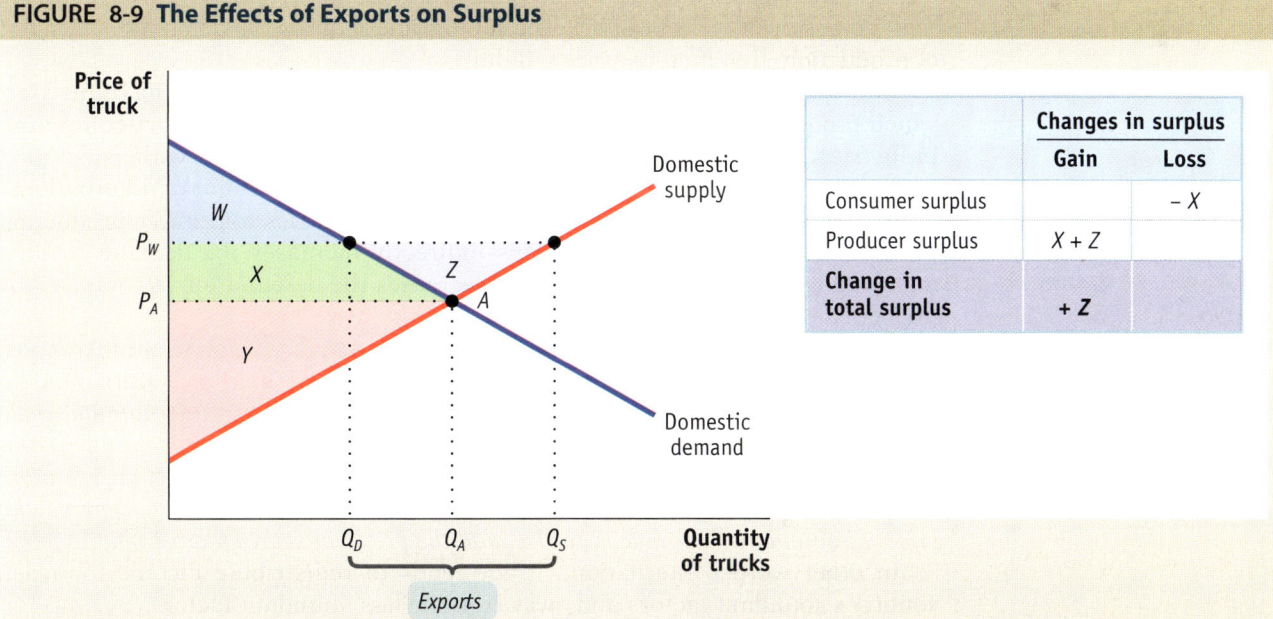

	Changes in surplus	
	Gain	Loss
Consumer surplus		$-X$
Producer surplus	$X + Z$	
Change in total surplus	$+ Z$	

When the domestic price rises to P_W as a result of trade, producers gain additional surplus (area $X + Z$) but consumers lose surplus (area X). Because the gains to producers outweigh the losses to consumers, there is an increase in the total surplus in the economy as a whole (area Z).

Exporting industries produce goods and services that are sold abroad.

Import-competing industries produce goods and services that are also imported.

Moreover, the effects of trade aren't limited to just those industries that export or compete with imports because *factors of production can often move between industries.* So now we turn our attention to the long-run effects of international trade on income distribution—how a country's total income is allocated among its various factors of production.

To begin our analysis, consider the position of Mia, who is initially employed as an accountant in an industry that is shrinking as a result of growing international trade. Suppose, for example, that she works in the Canadian apparel (clothing) industry, which formerly employed tens of thousands of people but has largely been displaced by imports from low-wage countries. Mia is likely to find a new job in another industry, such as health care, which has been expanding rapidly over time. How will the move affect her earnings?

The answer is, there probably won't be much effect. According to government collected data, accountants earn roughly the same amount in health care that they do in what's left of the apparel industry—about $58,000 a year. So we shouldn't think of Mia as a producer of apparel who is hurt by competition from imports. Instead, we should think of her as a worker with particular skills who is affected by imports—mainly by the extent to which those imports change the wages of accountants in the economy as a whole.

The wage rate of accountants is a *factor price*—the price employers have to pay for the services of a factor of production. One key question about international trade is how it affects factor prices—not just narrowly defined factors of production like accountants, but broadly defined factors such as capital, unskilled labour, and college- or university-educated labour.

Earlier in this chapter we described the Heckscher–Ohlin model of trade, which states that comparative advantage is determined by a country's factor endowment. This model also suggests how international trade affects factor prices in a country: compared to autarky, international trade tends to raise the prices of factors that are abundantly available and reduce the prices of factors that are scarce.

We won't work this out in detail, but the idea is simple. The prices of factors of production, like the prices of goods and services, are determined by supply and demand. If international trade increases the demand for a factor of production, that factor's price will rise; if international trade reduces the demand for a factor of production, that factor's price will fall.

Now think of a country's industries as consisting of both **exporting industries,** which produce goods and services that are sold abroad, and **import-competing industries,** which produce goods and services that compete with goods and services that are imported from abroad. Compared with autarky, international trade leads to higher production in exporting industries and lower production in import-competing industries. This indirectly increases the demand for factors used by exporting industries and decreases the demand for factors used by import-competing industries.

In addition, the Heckscher–Ohlin model shows that a country tends to export goods that are intensive in factors that are abundant in that country and to import goods that are intensive in factors that are scarce. *So international trade tends to increase the demand for factors that are more abundant in a country compared with other countries, and to decrease the demand for factors that are more scarce in a country compared with other countries. As international trade grows, the prices of abundant factors tend to rise, and the prices of scarce factors tend to fall.*

In other words, international trade tends to redistribute income toward a country's abundant factors and away from its less abundant factors.

Canada's non-commodity exports tend to be human-capital-intensive (such as high-tech design and television and movie productions) while Canadian imports tend to be unskilled-labour-intensive (such as phone assembly and clothing production). This suggests that the effect of international trade on Canadian factor markets is to raise the wage rate of highly educated Canadian workers and reduce the wage rate of unskilled Canadian workers.

This effect has been a source of much concern in recent years. Wage inequality—the gap between the wages of high-paid and low-paid workers—has increased substantially over the last 40 years. Some economists believe that growing international trade is an important factor in that trend. If international trade has the effects predicted by the Heckscher–Ohlin model, its growth raises the wages of highly educated North American workers, who already have relatively high wages, and lowers the wages of less educated North American workers, who already have relatively low wages.

But keep in mind another phenomenon: trade reduces the income inequality between countries as poor countries improve their standard of living by exporting to rich countries.

The effects of trade on wages in Canada have generated considerable controversy in recent years. Most economists who have studied the issue agree that growing imports of labour-intensive products from newly industrializing economies, and the export of high-technology goods in return, have helped cause a widening wage gap between highly educated and less educated workers in Canada. However, most economists believe that it is only one of several forces explaining the growth in Canadian wage inequality.

ECONOMICS >> *in Action*
The China Shock

If you go into a Walmart or other large store and look at the labels on the products, it can seem as if everything is made in China these days. That's not really true, but we do buy a lot from China, which supplies 12.5% of Canada's imported goods in 2019 (just behind the United States).

This is a fairly recent phenomenon. Imports from China, though growing, were low until the late 1990s when they took a great leap upward. The share of Chinese goods in Canada's total merchandise imports was 2.8% in 1999. This share has tended to increase over time and is up more than fourfold in the last two decades. The surge in Chinese imports corresponded to a change in the structure of the global economy—in particular, a transfer of production and transportation technology from advanced countries to China. China's admittance to the World Trade Organization, a global institution for regulating international trade, in 2001 also contributed to the surge, known as the *China Shock*.

We have seen that international trade often creates losers as well as winners. In this case, the surge in imports from China was good for Canadian consumers, who paid less for many goods. The price of clothing, in particular, fell about 17.5%; between 2001 and 2011, the overall consumer prices rose about 22.6%. It was, however, hard on some Canadian industries. Producers of clothing, manufacturing goods, and some electronic goods, suddenly faced greatly increased competition. The losers were Canadian companies that produced those goods, many of which were forced to close plants, and their laid-off workers.

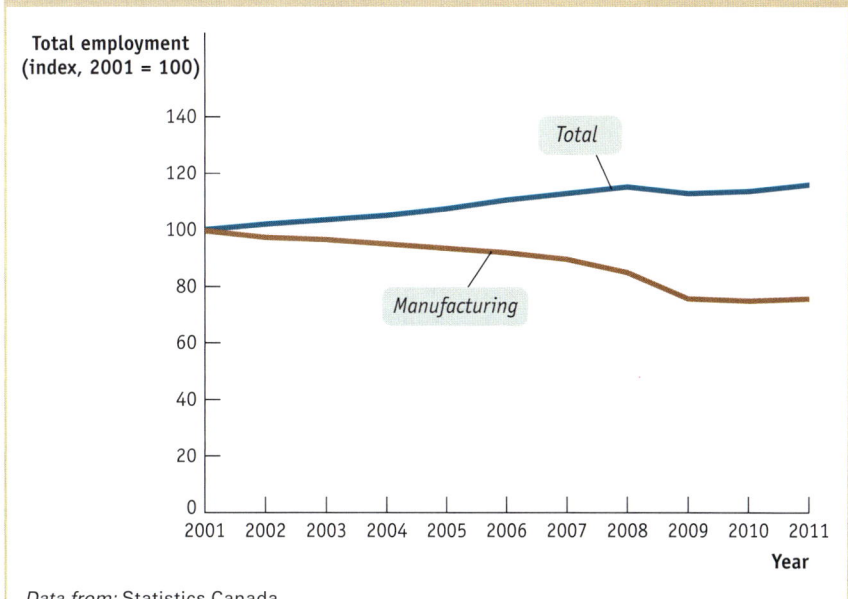

FIGURE 8-10 The Effect of Chinese Imports on Employment in the Canadian Manufacturing Industry

Data from: Statistics Canada.

A 2017 report by Alexander Murray at the Centre for the Study of Living Standards estimated the effects of the China Shock on the level of employment in Canada. The report indicated that Canada experienced a net loss of 105,000 manufacturing jobs due to the increased presence of Chinese imports from 2001 to 2011, which accounts for one-fifth of the total job manufacturing job losses in the country during the same period. Luckily, these job losses were offset by job gains elsewhere: overall Canada's employment rose by 2.04 million over the period as shown in Figure 8-10. But the communities experiencing job gains weren't the same as those experiencing job losses, and some communities were hard hit. Once again, trade creates winners and losers.

>> *Check Your Understanding* **8-2**
Solutions appear at back of book.

1. Due to a strike by truckers, trade in food between Canada and Mexico is halted. In autarky, the price of Mexican grapes is lower than that of Canadian grapes. Using a diagram of Canada's domestic demand curve and Canada's domestic supply curve for grapes, explain the effect of the strike on the following.
   a. Canadian grape consumers' surplus
   b. Canadian grape producers' surplus
   c. Canadian total surplus
2. What effect do you think the strike will have on Mexican grape producers? Mexican grape pickers? Mexican grape consumers? Canadian grape pickers?

‖ The Effects of Trade Protection

Ever since David Ricardo laid out the principle of comparative advantage in the early nineteenth century, most economists have advocated **free trade.** That is, they have argued that government policy should not attempt either to reduce or to increase the levels of exports and imports that occur naturally as a result of supply and demand.

Despite the free-trade arguments of economists, however, many governments use taxes and other restrictions to limit imports. Less frequently, governments offer subsidies to encourage exports. Policies that limit imports, usually with the goal of protecting domestic producers in import-competing industries from foreign competition, are known as **trade protection** or simply as **protection.**

Let's look at the two most common protectionist policies, *tariffs* and *import quotas,* then turn to the reasons governments follow these policies.

The Effects of a Tariff

A **tariff** is a form of excise tax, levied only on sales of imported goods. For example, the Canadian government could declare that anyone bringing phones for sale into the country must pay a tariff of $100 per unit. In the distant past, tariffs were an important source of government revenue because they were relatively easy to collect. But in the modern world, tariffs are usually intended to discourage imports and protect import-competing domestic producers, and not levied as a source of government revenue.

A tariff raises both the price received by domestic producers and the price paid by domestic consumers. Suppose, for example, that our country imports phones, and a phone costs $200 on the world market. As we saw earlier, under free trade the domestic price would also be $200. But if a tariff of $100 per unit is imposed, the domestic price will rise to $300, because it won't be profitable to import phones unless the price in the domestic market is high enough to compensate importers for the cost of paying the tariff.

FIGURE 8-11 The Effect of a Tariff

A tariff raises the domestic price of the good from P_W to P_T. The domestic quantity demanded shrinks from Q_D to Q_{DT}, and the domestic quantity supplied increases from Q_S to Q_{ST}. As a result, imports—which had been $Q_D - Q_S$ before the tariff was imposed—shrink to $Q_{DT} - Q_{ST}$ after the tariff is imposed.

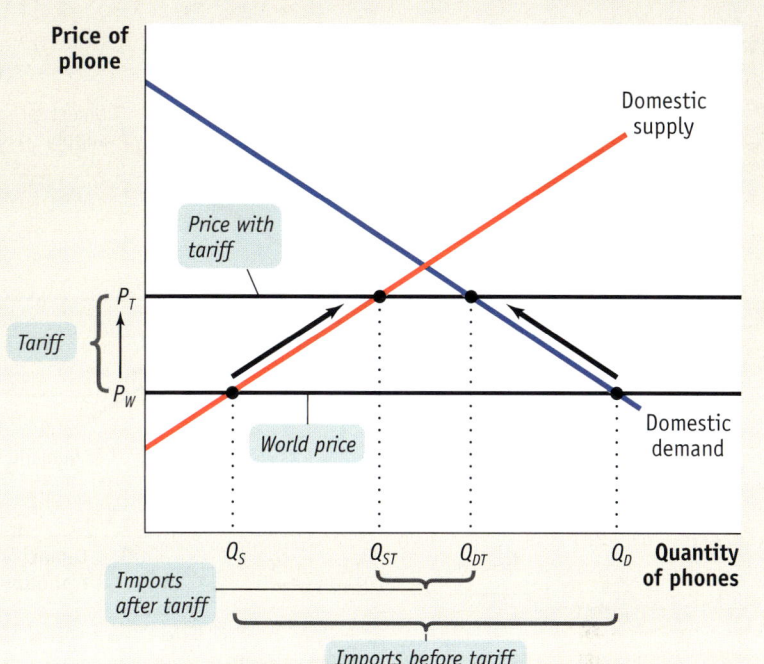

Figure 8-11 illustrates the effects of a tariff on imports of phones. As before, we assume that P_W is the world price of a phone. Before the tariff is imposed, imports have driven the domestic price down to P_W, so that pre-tariff domestic production is Q_S, pre-tariff domestic consumption is Q_D, and pre-tariff imports are $Q_D - Q_S$.

Now suppose that the government imposes a tariff on each phone imported. As a consequence, it is no longer profitable to import phones unless the domestic price received by the importer is greater than or equal to the world price plus the tariff. So the domestic price rises to P_T, which is equal to the world price, P_W, plus the tariff. Domestic production rises to Q_{ST}, domestic consumption falls to Q_{DT}, and imports fall to $Q_{DT} - Q_{ST}$.

A tariff, then, raises domestic prices, leading to increased domestic production and reduced domestic consumption compared to the situation under free trade. Figure 8-12 shows three effects:

1. The higher domestic price increases producer surplus, a gain equal to area *A*.
2. The higher domestic price reduces consumer surplus, a reduction equal to the sum of areas *A, B, C,* and *D*.
3. The tariff yields revenue to the government. How much revenue? The government collects the tariff—which, remember, is equal to the difference between P_T and P_W on each of the $Q_{DT} - Q_{ST}$ units imported. So total revenue is $(P_T - P_W) \times (Q_{DT} - Q_{ST})$. This is equal to area *C*.

The welfare effects of a tariff are summarized in the table in Figure 8-12. Producers gain, consumers lose, and the government gains. But consumer losses are greater than the sum of producer and government gains, leading to a net reduction in total surplus equal to areas $B + D$.

An excise tax creates inefficiency, or deadweight loss, because it prevents mutually beneficial trades from occurring. In the case of a tariff, the deadweight loss imposed on society is equal to the loss in total surplus represented by areas $B + D$.

FIGURE 8-12 A Tariff Reduces Total Surplus

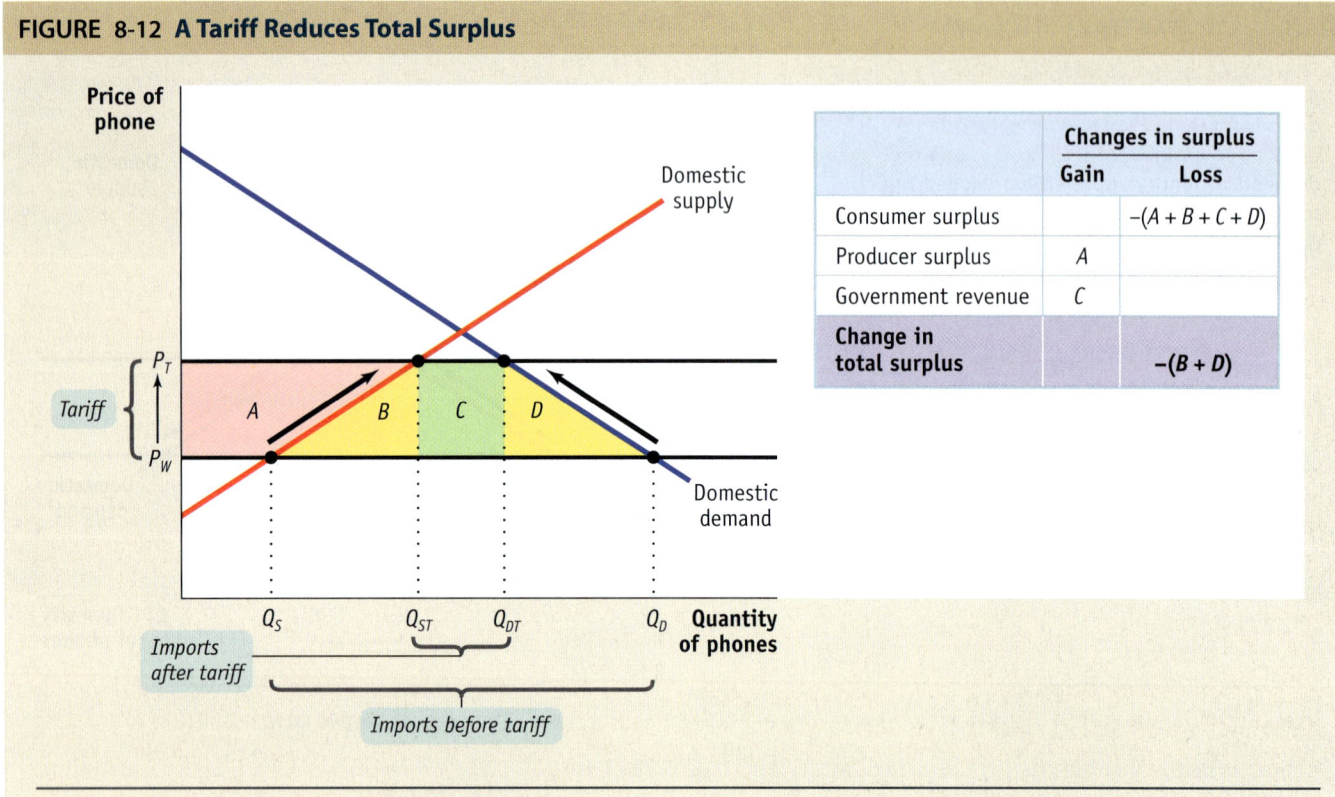

	Changes in surplus	
	Gain	Loss
Consumer surplus		$-(A + B + C + D)$
Producer surplus	A	
Government revenue	C	
Change in total surplus		$-(B + D)$

When the domestic price rises as a result of a tariff, producers gain additional surplus (area A), the government gains revenue (area C), and consumers lose surplus (areas $A + B + C + D$). Because the losses to consumers outweigh the gains to producers and the government, the economy as a whole loses surplus (areas B and D).

Tariffs generate deadweight losses because they create inefficiencies in two ways:

1. Some mutually beneficial trades go unexploited: some consumers who are willing to pay more than the world price, P_W, do not purchase the good, even though P_W is the true cost of a unit of the good to the economy. The cost of this inefficiency is represented in Figure 8-12 by area D.

2. The economy's resources are wasted on inefficient production: some producers whose cost exceeds P_W produce the good, even though an additional unit of the good can be purchased abroad for P_W. The cost of this inefficiency is represented in Figure 8-12 by area B.

The Effects of an Import Quota

An **import quota,** another form of trade protection, is a legal limit on the quantity of a good that can be imported. For example, a Canadian import quota on Chinese phones might limit the quantity imported each year to 50 million units. Import quotas are usually administered through licences: a number of licences are issued, each giving the licence-holder the right to import a limited quantity of the good each year.

A quota on sales has the same effect as an excise tax, with one difference: the money that would otherwise have accrued to the government as tax revenue under an excise tax becomes licence-holders' revenue under a quota—also known as quota rents. (*Quota rent* is defined in Chapter 5.) Similarly, an import quota has the same effect as a tariff, with one difference: the money that would otherwise have been government revenue becomes quota rents to licence-holders.

Look again at Figure 8-12. An import quota that limits imports to $Q_{DT} - Q_{ST}$ will raise the domestic price of phones by the same amount as the tariff we considered previously. That is, it will raise the domestic price from P_W to P_T. However, area C will now represent quota rents rather than government revenue.

An **import quota** is a legal limit on the quantity of a good that can be imported.

Who receives import licences and so collects the quota rents? In the case of Canadian import protection, the answer may surprise you: the most important import licences—mainly for agricultural products, like eggs, milk, and cheese, and also to a lesser extent for clothing and automobiles—are granted to foreign governments.

Because the quota rents for most Canadian import quotas go to foreigners, the cost to the nation of such quotas is larger than that of a comparable tariff (a tariff that leads to the same level of imports). In Figure 8-12, the net loss to Canada from such an import quota would be equal to areas $B + C + D$, the difference between consumer losses and producer gains.

ECONOMICS >> *in Action*
The Steel Tariffs of 2018–2019

U.S. law grants the president authority to impose tariffs unilaterally, without going to U.S. Congress, under certain circumstances. This authority was intended to allow prompt responses to trade challenges without opening up a political process that, history shows, tends to be rife with special-interest politics. In general, U.S. presidents have used this authority sparingly. However, in 2018 President Donald Trump moved to impose high tariffs on multiple countries and multiple products, with the most dramatic move being a 25% tariff on steel imports from all major suppliers, of which Canada was the most important. In July 2018, in response to the American tariffs, the Canadian government imposed retaliatory tariffs on $12 billion worth of goods imported from the United States, including a 25% on imported American steel.

Some of the U.S. president's statements seemed to imply that he believed foreign exporters, not American consumers, would be paying these tariffs. Market data, however, showed a sharp rise in U.S. steel prices as the tariffs went into effect, while world prices were mostly flat. Figure 8-13 shows one example, the price of hot rolled band—a form of steel that is sold to manufacturers of products that use steel. The figure includes data from late 2017 until July 2019. The tariffs were phased in over the course of 2018, then removed in 2019 after the United States, Canada, and Mexico reached a new trade agreement.

As you can see, after the tariffs took effect, the U.S. price soared above the world price; then U.S. prices fell sharply when the tariffs were removed.

Who gained and who lost from the steel tariffs? U.S. steel companies clearly benefited, as higher prices raised their profits. They also responded to the higher prices by reopening some closed production facilities and planning some expansion of their capacity.

At least initially, however, U.S. steel workers didn't seem to be sharing much of the benefit: their wages weren't rising much more than those of workers in other industries.

On the other side, higher steel prices in the United States hurt steel users. Ordinary Americans, of course, don't buy steel directly. The metal is used, instead, to make a variety of manufactured goods, such as cars—and U.S. companies that buy steel complained bitterly about higher costs, assigning the tariff partial responsibility for some plant closings and layoffs. They also passed at least some of the tariff on to their customers in the form of higher prices.

The U.S. steel tariffs of 2018, then, played out pretty much the way standard analysis would have predicted. Producers of import-competing goods—U.S. steel

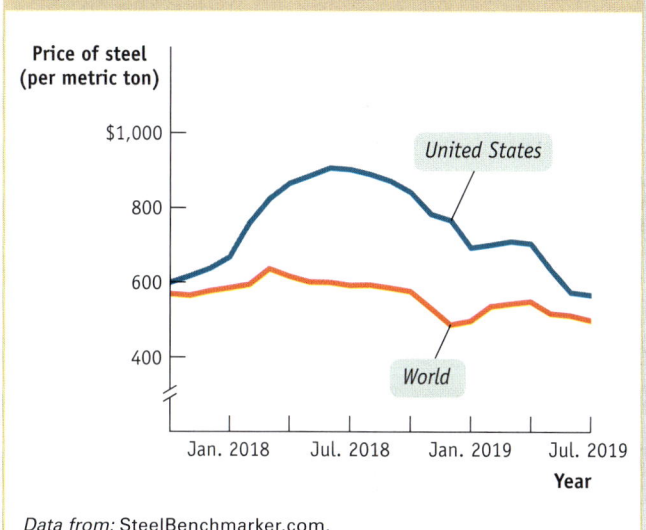

FIGURE 8-13 Tariffs and Steel Prices, United States and the World

Data from: SteelBenchmarker.com.

companies gained. Consumers—manufacturers who use steel, and ultimately, the buyers of these manufacturers' goods—were hurt.

>> Check Your Understanding 8-3

Solutions appear at back of book.

1. Suppose the world price of butter is $0.50 per kilogram and the domestic price in autarky is $1.00 per kilogram. Use a diagram similar to Figure 8-10 to show the following.
   a. If there is free trade, domestic butter producers want the government to impose a tariff of no less than $0.50 per kilogram. Compare the outcome with a tariff of $0.25 per kilogram.
   b. What happens if a tariff greater than $0.50 per kilogram is imposed?
2. Suppose the government imposes an import quota rather than a tariff on butter. What quota limit would generate the same quantity of imports as a tariff of $0.50 per kilogram?

‖ The Political Economy of Trade Protection

We have seen that international trade produces mutual benefits to the countries that engage in it. We have also seen that tariffs and import quotas, although they produce winners as well as losers, reduce total surplus. Yet many countries continue to impose tariffs and import quotas as well as to enact other protectionist measures.

To understand why trade protection takes place, we will first look at some common justifications for protection. Then we will look at the politics of trade protection. Finally, we will look at an important feature of trade protection in today's world: tariffs and import quotas are the subject of international negotiation and are policed by international organizations.

Arguments for Trade Protection

Advocates for tariffs and import quotas offer three common arguments:

1. The *national security* argument is based on the proposition that overseas sources of goods are vulnerable to disruption in times of international conflict. A country should protect domestic suppliers of crucial goods with the aim to be self-sufficient in the production of those goods. The shortages of personal protective equipment during the coronavirus pandemic has led some to question why more of these goods are not domestically made. Currently, Canada imposes import restrictions on agricultural products to protect Canadian farmers, ensure a stable domestic supply of food, and prevent large price fluctuations.

2. The *job creation* argument points to the additional jobs created in import-competing industries as a result of trade protection. Economists argue that these jobs are offset by the jobs lost elsewhere, such as industries that use imported inputs and now face higher input costs. But noneconomists don't always find this argument persuasive.

3. The *infant industry* argument, often raised in newly industrializing countries, holds that new industries require a temporary period of trade protection to get established. For example, in the 1950s many countries in Latin America imposed tariffs and import quotas on manufactured goods, in an effort to switch from their traditional role as exporters of raw materials to a new status as industrial countries.

   In theory, the argument for infant industry protection can be compelling, particularly in high-tech industries that increase a country's overall skill level. Reality, however, is more complicated: it is most often industries that are politically influential that gain protection. In addition, governments tend to be poor predictors of the best emerging technologies. Finally, it is often very difficult to wean an industry from protection when it should be mature enough to stand on its own.

The Politics of Trade Protection

In reality, much trade protection has little to do with the arguments just described. Instead, it reflects the political influence of import-competing producers.

We've seen that a tariff or import quota leads to gains for import-competing producers and losses for consumers. Producers, however, usually have much more influence over trade policy decisions. The producers who compete with imports of a particular good are usually a smaller, more cohesive group than the consumers of that good.

An example is the import quota on eggs. This quota hurts millions of Canadian consumers, but by and large they don't even know it exists. Meanwhile, it benefits about 1,100 Canadian egg farmers, who are very aware of these benefits and hire lobbyists to keep those benefits coming.

It would be nice to say that the main reason trade protection isn't more extensive is that economists have convinced governments of the virtues of free trade. A more important reason, however, is the role of *international trade agreements*.

International Trade Agreements and the World Trade Organization

When a country engages in trade protection, it hurts two groups. We've already addressed the adverse effect on domestic consumers, but protection also hurts foreign export industries. This means that countries care about one anothers' trade policies: the Canadian lumber industry, for example, has a strong interest in keeping U.S. tariffs on forest products low.

Because countries care about one anothers' trade policies, they enter into **international trade agreements:** treaties in which a country promises to engage in less trade protection against the exports of another country in return for a promise by the other country to do the same for its own exports. International trade agreements are especially important as a way to head off potential **trade wars,** in which countries impose tariffs and other protectionist measures against other countries' products in an attempt to force them to make policy concessions. Most world trade is now governed by such agreements.

Some international trade agreements involve just two countries or a small group of countries. For example, in 1993 the United States, Canada, and Mexico joined together in the **North American Free Trade Agreement,** or **NAFTA.** By 2008, NAFTA had removed most barriers to trade among the three nations. In 2018, the countries negotiated a revised agreement, the United States-Mexico-Canada Agreement or USMCA, which made some changes but kept the main structure of NAFTA intact. For accuracy's sake, we will refer to the current trade agreement as **NAFTA-USMCA.**

Most European countries are part of an even more comprehensive agreement, the **European Union,** or **EU.** Unlike members of NAFTA-USMCA, the 27 members of the EU agree to charge the same tariffs on goods imported from non-EU countries. The EU also sets rules on policies other than trade, most notably requiring that each member nation freely accept migrants from any other member, while collecting fees from member nations to pay for things like agricultural subsidies. These rules and fees are often unpopular and controversial. In June 2016, Britain held a referendum on whether to leave the EU—a proposal popularly known as *Brexit* (short for "British exit"), which was approved by a narrow majority of voters. In October 2016, Canada and the European Union (EU) signed the Comprehensive Economic and Trade Agreement (CETA), which was the Canada's biggest bilateral trade agreement since NAFTA. In CETA, both parties agreed to remove 98% of the preexisting tariffs between themselves. The agreement went into effect in September 2017. Negotiations over the details of Britain's exit from the EU, and its future relationship with it, were still in progress as this book went to press.

There are also global trade agreements covering most of the world. Such global agreements are overseen by the **World Trade Organization,** or **WTO,** an

International trade agreements are treaties in which a country promises to engage in less trade protection against the exports of other countries in return for a promise by other countries to do the same for its own exports.

In a **trade war,** countries deliberately try to impose pain on their trading partners, as a way to extract policy concessions.

The **North American Free Trade Agreement,** or **NAFTA,** is a trade agreement among the United States, Canada, and Mexico. The current version of the agreement is **NAFTA-USMCA.**

The **European Union,** or **EU,** is a customs union among 27 European nations.

The **World Trade Organization,** or **WTO,** oversees international trade agreements and rules on disputes between countries over those agreements.

international organization composed of member countries—164 of them currently, accounting for the bulk of world trade. The WTO plays two roles:

1. It provides the framework for the massively complex negotiations involved in a major international trade agreement (the full text of the last major agreement, approved in 1994, was 24,000 pages long).

2. The WTO resolves disputes between its members that typically arise when one country claims that another country's policies violate its previous agreements.

An example of the WTO at work is the ongoing softwood lumber trade dispute between Canada and the United States. The United States lumber industry argues that the stumpage, a fee that provincial governments set and charge logging companies for the right to harvest lumber from public land (the logging right), was too low and has viewed it as a subsidy to Canadian-based lumber producers. In response to these complaints from the U.S. lumber industry, the U.S. Department of Commerce imposed a 27% duty on Canadian softwood lumber in 2002. Like previous episodes of softwood lumber disputes, Canada appealed this 27% duty to NAFTA and WTO panels. In the 2006 Softwood Lumber Agreement, the United States was to remove the countervailing and antidumping duties, and to return over US$4 billion in duties collected from Canadian exporters since 2002. The Softwood Lumber Agreement expired on October 12, 2015, and this led to the renewal of the softwood dispute between Canada and the United States as the U.S. Lumber Coalition claimed that the Canadian stumpage fees charged was below the market rate and thus unfair to the U.S. lumber firms. The U.S. commerce department again imposed tariffs that averaged about 27%. In February 2020, the U.S. Department of Commerce announced that starting in August (of that year) it would significantly lower the tariff rates applied to 4.32% to 15.84% (depending on the exporting company).

The WTO rules do allow trade protection under certain circumstances. One such circumstance occurs when the foreign competition is "unfair" under certain technical criteria. Trade protection is also allowed as a temporary measure when a sudden surge of imports threatens to disrupt a domestic industry. For example, although China, South Korea, and Vietnam are members of the WTO, in 2018 Canada imposed tariffs on cold-rolled steel imports from these countries arguing that these items were unfairly subsidized. This gave exporters from these countries an unfair advantage in the Canadian market at the expense of firms producing such steel in Canada.

The WTO is sometimes, with great exaggeration, described as a world government. In fact, it has no army, no police, and no direct enforcement power. The grain of truth in that description is that when a country joins the WTO, it agrees to accept the organization's judgments—and these judgments apply not only to tariffs and import quotas but also to domestic policies that the organization considers trade protection disguised under another name. So in joining the WTO a country does give up some of its sovereignty.

Challenges to Globalization

The forward march of globalization over the past century is generally considered a major political and economic success because it has brought rising living standards to hundreds of millions of people. But it is also true that many people, including some economists and policy makers, are having second thoughts about globalization. These second thoughts arise largely from the decline of manufacturing in richer countries and *offshore outsourcing* that jeopardizes the jobs of non-manufacturing workers, once considered immune from foreign competition.

The Decline of Manufacturing

We have seen that international trade has an effect on factor prices, particularly wages. Forty years ago, Canadian imports from poorer countries consisted mostly of raw materials and goods that depended upon the climate, like bananas and coffee beans. So Canadian wages were relatively unaffected by international trade. But that is no longer the case. Today many of the manufactured goods consumed in Canada are imported from poorer countries. As a result, international trade now has a much larger effect on income inequality in Canada.

Trade with Asia has raised the greatest concerns among those who study the effect of international trade on wage levels in rich countries. China, despite its rapid economic growth and rising wages in recent years, is still a very low-wage country compared with Canada. Its hourly compensation in manufacturing is approximately 26% of the Canadian level. Other manufacturing exporters, such as India, Bangladesh, and Vietnam, have wage levels less than half of China's. As we discussed earlier in the chapter, it's clear that imports from these countries have placed downward pressure on the wages of less skilled Canadian workers and possibly contributed to income inequality.

Outsourcing

Chinese exports to Canada overwhelmingly consist of labour-intensive manufactured goods. However, some Canadian workers have also found themselves facing a new form of international competition. *Outsourcing,* in which a company hires another company to perform a task, such as running the corporate computer system, is a long-standing business practice. Until recently, however, outsourcing was normally done locally, with a company hiring another company in the same city or country.

Now, modern telecommunications increasingly make it possible to engage in **offshore outsourcing,** in which businesses hire people in another country to perform various tasks. The classic example is call centers: the person answering the phone when you call a company's help line may well be in India, which has taken the lead in attracting offshore outsourcing. Offshore outsourcing has also spread to fields such as software design and even health care: the radiologist examining your X-rays, like the person giving you computer help, may be on another continent.

The threat of offshore outsourcing differs from the threat posed by large-scale imports of manufactured goods from poorer countries. By and large, offshore outsourcing hits higher-skilled Canadian workers who imagined their jobs were safe from foreign competition. An example is Canadian computer programmers, many of whom have their jobs outsourced to India or Eastern Europe. Although offshore outsourcing still accounts for a relatively small portion of international trade, some economists have warned that millions or even tens of millions of workers in rich countries may face unpleasant surprises in the not-too-distant future—workers such as bookkeepers, claims adjusters, and mortgage processors.

Do these challenges of globalization undermine the argument that international trade is a good thing? The great majority of economists would argue that the gains from trade protection still exceed the losses. However, as international trade has grown and job losses in vulnerable sectors have mounted, the politics of international trade has become increasingly difficult and has led to calls for protectionist trade policies. In this debate it's important to understand that government programs, such as unemployment benefits, easily accessible health care, and retraining projects, can reduce the opposition to free trade by helping cushion the losses of those hurt by trade.

Offshore outsourcing takes place when businesses hire people in another country to perform various tasks.

Offshore outsourcing has the potential to disrupt the job prospects of millions of Canadian workers.

Julian Abram Wainwright/Bloomberg via Getty Images

In 2019, the United States and China engaged in a classic trade war by levying tariffs on each other's exports.

ECONOMICS >> *in Action*
Trade War, What Is It Good For?

There are, as we've seen, a number of reasons countries sometimes impose tariffs and other restrictions on imports, and these measures often hurt other countries as well as domestic consumers. However, we generally only use the term *trade war* when hurting foreigners isn't a side effect of tariffs, but their purpose—that is, when tariffs are imposed to inflict damage on another country in an attempt to force it to make concessions of some kind.

A classic example is the "chicken war" that broke out between the United States and Europe more than half a century ago. In 1964, the U.S. imposed a 25% tariff on imports of light trucks—a category that today includes most pick-ups and SUVs. The purpose of the tariff was to put pressure on the European community to eliminate a tariff it had placed on U.S. exports of frozen chicken, which surged with the rise of factory farming. Incredibly, this dispute was never resolved: that 25% tariff remains in place.

Historically, however, trade wars in which countries try to inflict pain have been fairly rare. Before the 1930s, Canada, the United States, and other countries generally ignored the effects of their trade policies on other countries; since World War II trade wars have mostly been prevented by international trade agreements.

That may, however, be changing. Since 2017 the U.S. government has imposed tariffs on a wide variety of goods and trading partners, with the explicit aim of forcing other countries to change their policies, and some of the countries have responded with tariffs of their own that are explicitly meant to cause pain in the U.S.

We have already discussed the steel tariffs the U.S. recently imposed on Canada and Mexico, at least partly intended to force our neighbours into agreeing to revise the North American Free Trade Agreement. Those tariffs, however, pale in significance compared with the 25% tariff the U.S. government imposed on $250 billion worth of Chinese exports in 2019—almost half of what China sells to the United States—with a threat to expand the tariffs to the rest of China's exports unless China meets policy demands that include protecting U.S. intellectual property and reducing China's trade surplus with the United States.

China has, in turn, retaliated by imposing tariffs on U.S. products, especially agricultural goods, in a clear attempt to raise the political costs of current U.S. policy, for example by hurting U.S. farmers.

What is happening now, in other words, really is a trade war in the classic sense. At the time of writing it was unclear when or how this trade war might be resolved. And the case of the "chicken war" of 1964 suggests that the effects of the current trade conflict might last for a very long time.

>> *Quick Review*

• The three major justifications for trade protection are national security, job creation, and the infant industry argument.

• Despite the deadweight losses, import protections are often imposed because groups representing import-competing industries are more influential than groups of consumers.

• To further trade liberalization, countries engage in **international trade agreements.** An important purpose of these agreements is to head off the possibility of **trade wars.** Some agreements are among a small number of countries, such as the **North American Free Trade Agreement (NAFTA)** and the **European Union (EU).** The current version of NAFTA is known as **NAFTA-USMCA.** The **World Trade Organization (WTO)** oversees global trade agreements and referees trade disputes between members.

• Resistance to globalization has emerged in response to a surge in imports of manufacturing goods from poorer countries and the threat of **offshore outsourcing** many jobs that were once considered safe from foreign competition.

>> *Check Your Understanding* 8-4

Solutions appear at back of book.

1. In 2017, the United States imposed a tariff on steel imports from a number of countries including Canada. Steel is an input in a large number and variety of U.S. industries. Explain why political lobbying to eliminate these tariffs is more likely to be effective than political lobbying to eliminate tariffs on consumer goods such as sugar or clothing.

2. Over the years, the WTO has increasingly found itself adjudicating trade disputes that involve not just tariffs or quota restrictions but also restrictions based on quality, health, and environmental considerations. Why do you think this has occurred? What method would you, as a WTO official, use to decide whether a quality, health, or environmental restriction is in violation of a free-trade agreement?

Li & Fung: From Guangzhou to You

Bloomberg/Getty Images

It's a very good bet that as you read this, you're wearing something manufactured in Asia. And if you are, it's also a good bet that the Hong Kong company Li & Fung was involved in getting your garment designed, produced, and shipped to your local store. From Levi's to Walmart, Li & Fung is a critical conduit from factories around the world to the shopping mall nearest you.

The company was founded in 1906 in Guangzhou, China. According to Victor Fung, the company's chairman, his grandfather's "value added" was that he spoke English, which allowed him to serve as an interpreter in business deals between Chinese and foreigners. When Mao's Communist Party seized control in mainland China, the company moved to Hong Kong. As Hong Kong's market economy took off during the 1960s and 1970s, Li & Fung grew as an export broker, bringing together Hong Kong manufacturers and foreign buyers.

However, the real transformation of the company came as Asian economies grew and changed. Hong Kong's rapid growth led to rising wages, making Li & Fung increasingly uncompetitive in garments, its main business. So the company reinvented itself: rather than being a simple broker, it became a "supply chain manager." It would not only allocate production of a good to a manufacturer, it would break the allocations of inputs down according to steps in the production process and then allocate final assembly of the good among its 12,000+ suppliers around the globe. Sometimes production would be done in sophisticated economies like those of Hong Kong or even Japan,

where high wages reflect high quality and productivity. Sometimes production would be done in less advanced economies such as that of mainland China or Thailand, where labour is less productive but also cheaper.

For example, suppose you own a North American retail chain and want to sell garment-washed blue jeans. Rather than simply arrange for production of the jeans, Li & Fung will work with you on design, providing you with the latest production and style information such as what materials and colors are trendy. After the design has been finalized, Li & Fung will arrange for the creation of a prototype, find the most cost-effective way to manufacture it, and then place an order on your behalf. Li & Fung might secure fabric made in Korea and dyed in Taiwan, and then have the jeans assembled in Thailand or mainland China. And because production takes place in so many locations, Li & Fung provides transport logistics as well as quality control.

Li & Fung has been enormously successful. In 2019, the company had a market value of US$13.2 billion, with offices and distribution centers in more than 50 countries.

You might ask, by the way, how Li & Fung has been affected by the U.S.-China trade war. The answer is that U.S. tariffs on Chinese exports hurt one important aspect of the company's business, but also opened other opportunities. Li & Fung has been helping U.S. customers shift to alternative sources, such as Vietnam and Bangladesh; it has also been helping customers in Canada, Europe, and other locations take advantage of the low prices offered by Chinese suppliers shut out of U.S. markets.

QUESTIONS FOR THOUGHT

1. Why do you think it was profitable for Li & Fung to go beyond brokering exports to becoming a supply chain manager, breaking down the production process and sourcing the inputs from various suppliers across many countries?

2. What principle do you think underlies Li & Fung's decisions on how to allocate production of a good's inputs and its final assembly among various countries?

3. Why do you think a retailer prefers to have Li & Fung arrange international production of its jeans rather than purchase them directly from a jeans manufacturer in mainland China?

4. What is the source of Li & Fung's success? Is it based on human capital, on ownership of a natural resource, or on ownership of capital?

SUMMARY

1. International trade is of growing importance to Canada and of even greater importance to other countries. International trade, like trade among individuals, arises from comparative advantage: the opportunity cost of producing an additional unit of a good is lower in some countries than in others. Goods and services purchased from abroad are **imports;** those sold abroad are **exports.** Foreign trade, like other economic linkages between countries, has been growing rapidly, a phenomenon called **globalization. Hyperglobalization,** the phenomenon of extremely high levels of international trade, has occurred as advances in communication and transportation technology have allowed supply chains of production to span the globe.

2. The **Ricardian model of international trade** assumes that opportunity costs are constant. It shows that there are gains from trade: two countries are better off with trade than in **autarky.**

3. In practice, comparative advantage reflects differences between countries in climate, factor endowments, and technology. The **Heckscher–Ohlin model** shows how differences in factor endowments determine comparative advantage: goods differ in **factor intensity,** and countries tend to export goods that are intensive in the factors they have in abundance.

4. The **domestic demand curve** and the **domestic supply curve** determine the price of a good in autarky. When international trade occurs, the domestic price is driven to equality with the **world price,** the price at which the good is bought and sold abroad.

5. If the world price is below the autarky price, a good is imported. This leads to an increase in consumer surplus, a fall in producer surplus, and a gain in total surplus. If the world price is above the autarky price, a good is exported. This leads to an increase in producer surplus, a fall in consumer surplus, and a gain in total surplus.

6. International trade leads to expansion in **exporting industries** and contraction in **import-competing industries.** This raises the domestic demand for abundant factors of production, reduces the demand for scarce factors, and so affects factor prices, such as wages.

7. Most economists advocate **free trade,** but in practice many governments engage in **trade protection.** The two most common forms of **protection** are tariffs and quotas. In rare occasions, export industries are subsidized.

8. A **tariff** is a tax levied on imports. It raises the domestic price above the world price, hurting consumers, benefiting domestic producers, and generating government revenue. As a result, total surplus falls. An **import quota** is a legal limit on the quantity of a good that can be imported. It has the same effects as a tariff, except that the revenue goes not to the government but to those who receive import licences.

9. Although several popular arguments have been made in favour of trade protection, in practice the main reason for protection is probably political: import-competing industries are well organized and well informed about how they gain from trade protection, while consumers are unaware of the costs they pay. Still, North American trade is fairly free, mainly because of the role of **international trade agreements,** in which countries agree to reduce trade protection against one another's exports. Trade agreements also help prevent **trade wars.** The **North American Free Trade Agreement (NAFTA), NAFTA-USMCA,** and the **European Union (EU)** cover a small number of countries. In contrast, the **World Trade Organization (WTO)** covers a much larger number of countries, accounting for the bulk of world trade. It oversees trade negotiations and adjudicates disputes among its members.

10. In the past few years, many concerns have been raised about the effects of globalization. One issue is the increase in income inequality due to the surge in manufacturing imports from poorer countries over the past 20 years particularly countries in Asia. Another concern is the increase in **offshore outsourcing,** as many jobs that were once considered safe from foreign competition have been moved abroad.

KEY TERMS

PRACTICE QUESTIONS

1. Evaluate the following statement: is it true, false, or uncertain? "The United States can produce more tomatoes and avocados compared to Mexico, therefore there is no need for the United States to trade with Mexico for these goods."

2. In the context of supply and demand under international trade, when will a country decide to export a particular good? Import a good? Who gains and loses under each decision?

3. In 2018, the United States announced 25% tariffs on avocados imported from Mexico and that the higher price of avocados would be paid entirely by Mexico. Supporters of the tariff claimed that the increased price would be paid Mexico. Evaluate the validity of this claim. (*Hint:* Use a figure in the chapter to support your conclusion.)

PROBLEMS

1. Both Canada and the United States produce lumber and footballs with constant opportunity costs. The United States can produce either 10 tonnes of lumber and no footballs, or 1,000 footballs and no lumber, or any combination in between. Canada can produce either 8 tonnes of lumber and no footballs, or 400 footballs and no lumber, or any combination in between.

   a. Draw the U.S. and Canadian production possibility frontiers in two separate diagrams, with footballs on the horizontal axis and lumber on the vertical axis.

   b. In autarky, if the United States wants to consume 500 footballs, how much lumber can it consume? Label this point *A* in your diagram. Similarly, if Canada wants to consume 1 tonne of lumber, how many footballs can it consume in autarky? Label this point *C* in your diagram.

   c. Which country has the absolute advantage in lumber production?

   d. Which country has the comparative advantage in lumber production?

   Suppose each country specializes in the good in which it has the comparative advantage, and there is trade.

   e. How many footballs does the United States produce? How much lumber does Canada produce?

   f. Is it possible for the United States to consume 500 footballs and 7 tonnes of lumber? Label this point *B* in your diagram. Is it possible for Canada at the same time to consume 500 footballs and 1 tonne of lumber? Label this point *D* in your diagram.

2. For each of the following trade relationships, explain the likely source of the comparative advantage of each of the exporting countries.

   a. Canada exports software to Venezuela, and Venezuela exports oil to Canada.

   b. Canada exports airplanes to China, and China exports clothing to Canada.

   c. Canada exports wheat to Colombia, and Colombia exports coffee to Canada.

3. Innovation, Science and Economic Development Canada (ISED) provides statistics on Canada's imports and exports on its website. The following steps will take you to the foreign trade statistics. Use them to answer the questions below.

   i. Go to ISED's website at www.ic.gc.ca.

   ii. At the top of the page, there is a drop-down tab labelled "Business," look for and click the sub-heading "International trade and investment," and then select "Trade data and market intelligence," and then pick "Import and export trade data."

   iii. Once you reach the Trade Data Online page, click on "Search by industry."

   iv. In the drop-down menu "Trade Type," select "Total Exports" if you are looking for data on exports or "Total Imports" if you are looking for data on imports.

   v. In the drop-down menu "Trading Partner," select "TOP 10 countries."

   vi. In the drop-down menu "Time Period," select "Specific Year(s)" and choose the year(s) you want. Try 2019 and any other year you want.

   vii. In the drop-down menu "Industry Options," select "Browse List of Industries."

   viii. In the drop-down menu "Browse for an industry," select the good or service you are interested in, or use the North American Industry Classification System (NAICS) code, then hit "View Industries."

   ix. In the "Industry List," choose the industry you are interested in and hit "Add to Selected Industries."

   x. Click on "Run Report."

   a. Look up recent data for Canadian imports of clothing accessories and other clothing manufacturing (NAICS code 3159). From which country do we import the most clothing accessories? Which of the three sources of comparative advantage (climate, factor endowments, and technology) accounts for that country's comparative advantage in clothing accessories?

   b. Look up recent data for Canadian imports of fruits (NAICS code 1113). From which country do we import the most fruit? Which of the three sources of comparative advantage (climate, factor endowments, and technology) accounts for that country's comparative advantage in fruit?

c. Look up recent data for Canadian imports of industrial machinery (NAICS code 3332). From which country do we import the most industrial machinery? Which of the three sources of comparative advantage (climate, factor endowments, and technology) accounts for that country's comparative advantage in industrial machinery?

4. According to data from Statistics Canada, since 2000, the value of Canadian imports of men's and boy's apparel from China has increased $382 million in 2000 to $969 million in 2019. What prediction does the Heckscher–Ohlin model make about the wages received by labour in China?

5. Shoes are labour-intensive and satellites are capital-intensive to produce. Canada has abundant capital. China has abundant labour. According to the Heckscher–Ohlin model, which good will China export? Which good will Canada export? In Canada, what will happen to the price of labour (the wage) and to the price of capital?

6. Before the North American Free Trade Agreement (NAFTA) gradually eliminated import tariffs on goods, the autarky price of tomatoes in Mexico was below the world price and in Canada was above the world price. Similarly, the autarky price of poultry in Mexico was above the world price and in Canada was below the world price. Draw diagrams with domestic supply and demand curves for each country and each of the two goods. (You will need to draw four diagrams, total.) As a result of NAFTA, Canada now imports tomatoes from Mexico and Canada now exports poultry to Mexico. How would you expect the following groups to be affected?

a. Mexican and Canadian consumers of tomatoes. Illustrate the effect on consumer surplus in your diagram.

b. Mexican and Canadian producers of tomatoes. Illustrate the effect on producer surplus in your diagram.

c. Mexican and Canadian tomato workers.

d. Mexican and Canadian consumers of poultry. Illustrate the effect on consumer surplus in your diagram.

e. Mexican and Canadian producers of poultry. Illustrate the effect on producer surplus in your diagram.

f. Mexican and Canadian poultry workers.

7. The accompanying table indicates the Canadian domestic demand schedule and domestic supply schedule for commercial jet airplanes. Suppose that the world price of a commercial jet airplane is $100 million.

Price of jet (millions)	Quantity of jets demanded	Quantity of jets supplied
$120	100	1,000
110	150	900
100	200	800
90	250	700
80	300	600
70	350	500
60	400	400
50	450	300
40	500	200

a. In autarky, how many commercial jet airplanes does Canada produce, and at what price are they bought and sold?

b. With trade, what will the price for commercial jet airplanes be? Will Canada import or export airplanes? How many?

8. The accompanying table shows the Canadian domestic demand schedule and domestic supply schedule for apples. Suppose that the world price of apples is $0.30 per apple.

Price of apple	Quantity of apples demanded (thousands)	Quantity of apples supplied (thousands)
$1.00	2	11
0.90	4	10
0.80	6	9
0.70	8	8
0.60	10	7
0.50	12	6
0.40	14	5
0.30	16	4
0.20	18	3

a. Draw the Canadian domestic supply curve and domestic demand curve.

b. With free trade, how many apples will Canada import or export?

Suppose that the Canadian government imposes a tariff on apples of $0.20 per apple.

c. How many apples will Canada import or export after introduction of the tariff?

d. In your diagram, shade the gain or loss to the economy as a whole from the introduction of this tariff.

9. The Canadian domestic demand schedule and domestic supply schedule for apples was given in Problem 8. Suppose that the world price of apples is $0.30. Canada introduces an import quota of 3,000 apples and assigns the quota rents to foreign apple exporters.

a. Draw the domestic demand and supply curves.

b. What will the domestic price of apples be after introduction of the quota?

c. Illustrate the area representing the quota rent on your graph. What is the value of the quota rents that foreign exporters of apples receive?

10. The Observatory of Economic Complexity (OEC) is a data visualization that models international trade data among countries. Go to the website at atlas.media.mit.edu to answer the following questions.

a. Start by selecting "Countries" and enter "Canada" in the search bar. In 2017, what was the largest exported good (in dollars) for Canada? What was the value of exports for "Planes, Helicopters, and/or Spacecraft"? What was the largest imported good for Canada?

b. Repeat the steps above for Brazil. In 2017, what was the largest exported good for Brazil? What was the value of exports for, "Planes, Helicopters, and/or Spacecraft"? What was the largest imported good for the Brazil?

c. On the top right search bar enter "Brazil" under the "visualizations" column on the right then pick "Where does Brazil export to? (2017)." On the new page, locate "Canada" in the visualization generated for Brazil and click on it and select "What does Canada import from Brazil? (2017)." What is the total value of Brazilian exports to Canada? What is Brazil's largest exported good (in dollars) bought by Canadians? What type of goods does Brazil generally export to Canada? What is the value of exports related to "Planes, Helicopters, and/or Spacecraft"?

d. Now repeat the steps from part c for exports from Canada to Brazil. Change "Country" to "Canada," change "Partner" to "Brazil," and select "Build Visualization." What is the total value of exports from Canada to Brazil? What is Canada's largest export (in dollars) to Brazil? What types of goods does Canada export to Brazil? What is the value of exports related to "Planes, Helicopters, and/or Spacecraft"?

11. Comparative advantage creates an opportunity for less productive economies like Bangladesh to trade with more productive economies like Canada. Using the OEC website from Problem 10 how much did Bangladesh export to Canada? What was its largest export to Canada? In general, what type of goods did Bangladesh export to Canada?

12. Once again, using the OEC website from Problems 10 and 11, identify which country has a comparative advantage for each of the following goods. For each good, include the country's share of global exports and the total dollar value of that share.

a. Computers
b. Maple syrup
c. Soybeans
d. Cocoa beans
e. Beer

13. Over the past five years the United States has become the world's largest producer of natural gas. But gas producers have struggled to find methods to liquefy natural gas so that it can be exported across the Atlantic. Enter Cheniere Energy, a Houston-based natural gas company that has developed a natural gas export terminal located on the Sabine Pass leading into the Gulf of Mexico. The terminal will give U.S. companies access to markets all over the world.

a. Explain how the development of a natural gas export terminal will affect the market for natural gas in the United States.

b. Assuming natural gas prices are US$3.00 per BTU, illustrate the effect of an export terminal on the demand for natural gas in the United States. Explain your findings.

c. Assuming natural gas prices in Europe are US$6.00 per BTU, draw a diagram to illustrate how the development of a natural gas terminal in the United States will affect supply and demand in the natural gas market for Europe. Explain your findings.

d. How will the exporting of natural gas from the United States to Europe affect consumers and producers in both places?

14. In Canada, producers of milk, poultry, and eggs are protected by government-imposed supply management rules. This supply management system is made up of a combination of import controls, production planning quotas, and minimum prices for these products.

a. Suppose the goal of the government is to design a supply management system for agricultural products that works to support the incomes of farmers. Explain how the use of production quotas and/or price floors would help to achieve this goal. Briefly explain who benefits and who loses under such a system and why this is so.

b. Why might the supply management system use a combination of a price floor and a production quota?

c. One important facet of this supply management system are restrictions limiting the import of agricultural products. Explain why such import limits are necessary.

d. Suppose European and American farmers are subsidized by their governments in a way that reduces the farmers' costs. Would the existence of such subsidies strengthen or weaken the need for Canadian import restrictions (to protect the incomes of Canadian farmers)? Explain why or why not.

15. The accompanying diagram illustrates the Canadian domestic demand curve and domestic supply curve for beef.

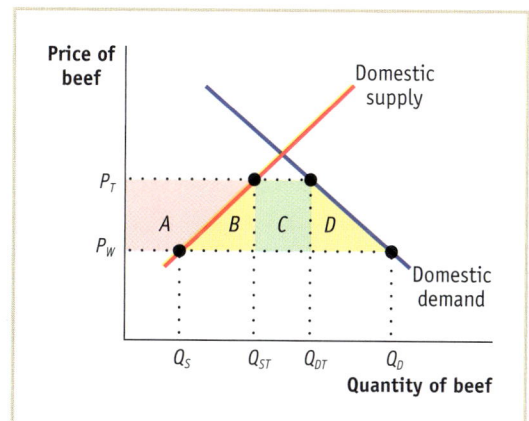

The world price of beef is P_W. Canada currently imposes an import tariff on beef, so the price of beef is P_T. Parliament decides to eliminate the tariff. In terms of the areas marked in the diagram, answer the following questions.

a. With the elimination of the tariff what is the gain/loss in consumer surplus?

b. With the elimination of the tariff what is the gain/loss in producer surplus?

c. With the elimination of the tariff what is the gain/loss to the government?

d. With the elimination of the tariff what is the gain/loss to the economy as a whole?

16. As Canada has opened up to trade, it has lost many of its low-skill manufacturing jobs, but it has gained jobs in high-skill industries, such as the software industry. Explain whether Canada as a whole has been made better off by trade.

17. Canada is highly protective of its agricultural (food) industry, imposing import tariffs, and sometimes quotas, on imports of agricultural goods. This chapter presented three arguments for trade protection. For each argument, discuss whether it is a valid justification for trade protection of Canadian agricultural products.

18. In World Trade Organization (WTO) negotiations, if a country agrees to reduce trade barriers (tariffs or quotas), it usually refers to this as a *concession* to other countries. Do you think that this terminology is appropriate?

19. Producers in import-competing industries often make the following argument: "Other countries have an advantage in production of certain goods purely because workers abroad are paid lower wages. In fact, North American workers are much more productive than foreign workers. So import-competing industries need to be protected." Is this a valid argument? Explain your answer.

WORK IT OUT

20. Assume Saudi Arabia and Canada face the production possibilities for oil and cars shown in the accompanying table.

Saudi Arabia		Canada	
Quantity of oil (millions of barrels)	Quantity of cars (millions)	Quantity of oil (millions of barrels)	Quantity of cars (millions)
0	4	0	10.0
200	3	100	7.5
400	2	200	5.0
600	1	300	2.5
800	0	400	0

a. What is the opportunity cost of producing a car in Saudi Arabia? In Canada? What is the opportunity cost of producing a barrel of oil in Saudi Arabia? In Canada?

b. Which country has the comparative advantage in producing oil? In producing cars?

c. Suppose that in autarky, Saudi Arabia produces 200 million barrels of oil and 3 million cars; and

suppose that Canada produces 300 million barrels of oil and 2.5 million cars. Without trade, can Saudi Arabia produce more oil *and* more cars? Without trade, can Canada produce more oil *and* more cars?

Suppose now that each country specializes in the good in which it has the comparative advantage, and the two countries trade. Also assume that for each country the value of imports must equal the value of exports.

d. What is the total quantity of oil produced? What is the total quantity of cars produced?

e. Is it possible for Saudi Arabia to consume 400 million barrels of oil and 5 million cars and for Canada to consume 400 million barrels of oil and 5 million cars?

f. Suppose that, in fact, Saudi Arabia consumes 300 million barrels of oil and 4 million cars and Canada consumes 500 million barrels of oil and 6 million cars. How many barrels of oil does Canada import? How many cars does Canada export? Suppose a car costs $10,000 on the world market. How much, then, does a barrel of oil cost on the world market? ∎

Decision Making by Individuals and Firms

MAKING DECISIONS IN GOOD TIMES AND BAD

WHEN MACKENZIE MCQUADE graduated from university with a degree in biology, she found a job right away. This experience was a surprise to her because just four years earlier, her older brother, Adam, had endured a very different experience. Graduating in 2010, Adam had earned a similar degree, but he had a very hard time finding a job. By the time he left school, he had been rejected by more than a dozen companies. Stressed out and nervous, he finally landed a position that forced him to move to another city. Many in the dismal 2010 job market chose yet another option: they went back to school. That year, colleges and universities across the country reported a surge in applications for all sorts of degree programs.

The differing fortunes of Mackenzie and Adam weren't due to Mackenzie being any more able than Adam. Rather, they were the result of economic fluctuations. Unfortunately for Adam, he graduated during a very tough job market, when the unemployment rate was nearly 8.1%, the second worst it had been in the past 15 years. Mackenzie, however, graduated at a time when the job market had improved considerably. In fact, two years later, in 2016, the unemployment rate in Canada was down to 7%, below the average of the past 40 years. Graduating seniors were among the luckiest newly minted job seekers in decades. But despite the improved job market, the picture was less than rosy: in 2014, the same year that Mackenzie found her job, 10.7% of young people aged 20 to 24 were unemployed.

Regardless of the circumstances, millions of people every year make decisions about their careers. Mackenzie, with several job offers, had to decide which job to take. Adam had to decide whether to take a not-so-great job that forced him to move, or to take a gamble and continue looking. And millions have made the decision to go back to school rather than endure a low-paying, dead-end job or a prolonged job search.

This chapter is about the economics of making decisions: how to make a decision that results in the best possible — often called *optimal* — economic outcome. Economists have formulated principles or methods of decision making that lead to optimal outcomes, regardless of whether the decision maker is an individual or a firm.

We'll start by examining the decision problem of an individual and learn about the three different types of economic decisions, each with a corresponding principle of decision making that leads to the best possible economic outcome. With this chapter we'll come to understand why economists consider decision making to be the very essence of microeconomics.

Despite the fact that people should use the principles of economic decision making to achieve optimal economic outcomes, they sometimes fail to do so. In other words, people are not always rational decision makers. For example, a shopper may knowingly spend more on gasoline in pursuit of a bargain than they save. Yet economists have discovered that people are *irrational in predictable ways*. A discussion of *behavioural economics*, the branch of economics that studies predictably irrational behaviour, concludes this chapter. ●

Ackerman + Gruber

Due to economic fluctuations, siblings Mackenzie and Adam McQuade had very different experiences landing their first jobs after graduating from university.

WHAT YOU WILL LEARN

- Why does good decision making depend on accurately defining costs and benefits?
- What is the difference between **explicit** and **implicit** costs?
- What is the difference between **accounting profit** and **economic profit,** and why is economic profit the correct basis for decisions?
- What are the three types of economic decisions?
- Why do people behave in irrational yet predictable ways sometimes?
- Why are decisions involving time different, and how they should be made? (In this chapter's appendix.)

An **explicit cost** is a cost that requires an outlay of money.

An **implicit cost** does not require an outlay of money. It is measured by the value, in dollar terms, of benefits that are forgone.

Costs, Benefits, and Profits

In making any type of decision, it's critical to define the costs and benefits of that decision accurately. If you don't know the costs and benefits, it is nearly impossible to make a good decision. So that is where we begin.

An important first step is to recognize the role of *opportunity cost*, a concept we first encountered in Chapter 1, where we learned that opportunity costs arise because *resources are scarce*. Because resources are scarce, the true cost of anything is what you must give up to get it—its opportunity cost.

Whether you decide to continue in school for another year or leave to find a job, each choice has costs and benefits. Because your time—a resource—is scarce, you cannot be both a full-time student and a full-time worker. If you choose to be a full-time student, the opportunity cost of that choice is the income you would have earned at a full-time job. And there may be additional opportunity costs, such as the value of the experience you would have gained by working.

When making decisions, it is crucial to think in terms of opportunity cost, because the opportunity cost of an action is often considerably more than the cost of any outlays of money.

Economists use the concepts of *explicit costs* and *implicit costs* to compare the relationship between opportunity costs and monetary outlays. We'll discuss these two concepts first. Then we'll define the concepts of *accounting profit* and *economic profit*, which are *ways of measuring whether the benefit of an action is greater than the cost*. Armed with these concepts for assessing costs and benefits, we will be in a position to consider our first principle of economic decision making: how to make "either–or" decisions.

Explicit versus Implicit Costs

Suppose that, like Adam McQuade, you face two choices upon graduation: take a less-than-ideal job, or return to school for another year to get a graduate degree.

In order to make that decision correctly, you need to know the cost of an additional year of school.

Here is where it is important to remember the concept of opportunity cost: the cost of the year spent getting an advanced degree includes what you forgo by not taking a job for that year. The opportunity cost of an additional year of school, like any cost, can be broken into two parts: the *explicit* cost of the year's schooling and the *implicit* cost.

An **explicit cost** is a cost that requires an outlay of money. For example, the explicit cost of the additional year of schooling includes tuition. An **implicit cost,** though, does not involve an outlay of money. Instead, it is measured by the value, in dollar terms, of the benefits that are forgone. For example, the implicit cost of the year spent in school includes the income you would have earned if you had taken a job instead.

A common mistake, both in economic analysis and in life—whether individual or business—is to ignore implicit costs and focus exclusively on explicit costs. But often the implicit cost of an activity is quite substantial—indeed, sometimes it is much larger than the explicit cost.

Table 9-1 gives a breakdown of hypothetical explicit and implicit costs associated with spending an additional year in school instead of taking a job. The explicit cost consists of tuition, books, supplies, and a computer for doing assignments—all of which require you to spend money. The implicit cost is the salary you would have earned if you had taken a job instead. As you can see, the total opportunity cost of attending an additional year of schooling is $44,500, the sum of

TABLE 9-1 Opportunity Cost of an Additional Year of School			
Explicit cost		**Implicit cost**	
Tuition	$7,000	Forgone salary	$35,000
Books and supplies	1,000		
Computer	1,500		
Total explicit cost	**9,500**	**Total implicit cost**	**35,000**
Total opportunity cost = Total explicit cost + Total implicit cost = $44,500			

the total implicit cost—$35,000 in forgone salary, and the total explicit cost—$9,500 in outlays on tuition, supplies, and a computer. Because the implicit cost is more than three times as much as the explicit cost, ignoring the implicit cost could lead to a seriously misguided decision. This example illustrates a general principle: *the opportunity cost of any activity is equal to its explicit cost plus its implicit cost.*

A slightly different way of looking at the implicit cost in this example can deepen our understanding of opportunity cost:

- The forgone salary is the cost of using your own resources—your time—in going to school rather than working.
- The use of your time for more schooling, despite the fact that you don't have to spend any money on it, is still costly to you.

This explanation illustrates an important aspect of opportunity cost:

- In considering the cost of an activity, you should include the cost of using any of your own resources for that activity. You can calculate the cost of using your own resources by determining what they would have earned in their next best use.

Understanding the role of opportunity costs makes clear the reason for the surge in school applications in 2009 and 2010: a rotten job market. Starting in the fall of 2008, the Canadian job market deteriorated sharply as the economy entered a severe recession. By 2010, the job market was still quite weak; although job openings had begun to reappear, a relatively high proportion of those openings were for jobs with low wages and no benefits. As a result, the opportunity cost of another year of schooling had declined significantly, making spending another year at school a much more attractive choice than when the job market was strong.

> **Accounting profit** is equal to revenue minus explicit cost.

‖ Accounting Profit versus Economic Profit

Let's return to Adam McQuade and imagine that he faces the choice of either completing a two-year full-time graduate program to become a pharmacist, or spending two years working. We'll assume that in order to be certified as a pharmacist, he must complete the entire two-year graduate program. Which choice should he make?

To get started, let's consider what Adam gains by getting the degree—what we might call his revenue from the pharmacology degree. Once he has completed the degree two years from now, he will receive earnings from the degree valued today at $600,000 over the rest of his lifetime. In contrast, if he doesn't get the degree and instead takes the job currently offered to him, two years from now his future lifetime earnings will be valued today at $500,000. The cost of the tuition for his pharmacology degree is $40,000, which he pays for with a student loan that costs him $4,000 in interest.

At this point, what he should do might seem obvious: if he chooses the pharmacology degree, he gets a lifetime increase in the value of earnings of $600,000 − $500,000 = $100,000, and he pays $40,000 in tuition plus $4,000 in interest. That means he makes a profit of $100,000 − $40,000 − $4,000 = $56,000 by getting his pharmacology degree. This $56,000 is Adam's **accounting profit** from obtaining the degree: his revenue minus his explicit cost. In this example his explicit cost of getting the pharmacology degree is $44,000, the amount of his tuition plus student loan interest.

"I've done the numbers, and I will marry you."

Although accounting profit is a useful measure, it would be misleading for Adam to use it alone in making his decision. To make the right decision, the one that leads to the best possible economic outcome for him, he needs to calculate his **economic profit**—the revenue he receives from the pharmacology degree minus his opportunity cost of staying in school (which is equal to his explicit cost *plus* his implicit cost of staying in school). In general, the economic profit of a given project will be less than the accounting profit because there are almost always implicit costs in addition to explicit costs.

When economists use the term *profit,* they are referring to *economic* profit, not *accounting* profit. This will be our convention in the rest of the book: when we use the term *profit,* we mean economic profit.

How does Adam's economic profit from staying in school differ from his accounting profit? We've already encountered one source of the difference: his two years of forgone job earnings. This is an implicit cost of going to school full time for two years. We assume that the value today of Adam's forgone earnings for the two years is $57,000.

Once we factor in Adam's implicit costs and calculate his economic profit, we see that he is better off not getting a degree in pharmacology. You can see this in Table 9-2: his economic profit from getting the pharmacology degree is –$1,000. In other words, he incurs an *economic loss* of $1,000 if he gets the degree. Clearly, he is better off going to work now.

Let's consider a slightly different scenario to make sure that the concepts of opportunity costs and economic profit are well understood. Let's suppose that Adam does not have to take out $40,000 in student loans to pay his tuition. Instead, he can pay for it with an inheritance from his grandmother. As a result, he doesn't have to pay $4,000 in interest. In this case, his accounting profit is $60,000 rather than $56,000. Would the right decision now be for him to get the pharmacology degree? Wouldn't the economic profit of the degree now be $60,000 – $57,000 = $3,000?

The answer is no, because in this scenario Adam is using his own *capital* to finance his education, and the use of that capital has an opportunity cost even when he owns it.

Capital is the total value of the assets of an individual or a firm. An individual's capital usually consists of cash in the bank, stocks, bonds, and the ownership value of real estate such as a house. In the case of a business, capital also includes its equipment, its tools, and its inventory of unsold goods and used parts. (Economists like to distinguish between *financial assets,* such as cash, stocks, and bonds, and *physical assets,* such as buildings, equipment, tools, and inventory.)

The point is that even if Adam owns the $40,000, using it to pay tuition incurs an opportunity cost—what he forgoes in the next best use of that $40,000. If he hadn't used the money to pay his tuition, his next best use of the money would have been to deposit it in a bank to earn interest.

To keep things simple, let's assume that he earns $4,000 on that $40,000 once it is deposited in a bank. Now, rather than pay $4,000 in explicit costs in the form of student loan interest, Adam pays $4,000 in implicit costs from the forgone interest he could have earned.

This $4,000 in forgone interest earnings is what economists call the **implicit cost of capital**—the income the owner of the capital could have earned if the capital had been employed in its next best alternative use. The net effect is that it makes no difference whether Adam finances his tuition with a student loan or by using his own funds. This comparison reinforces how carefully you must keep track of opportunity costs when making a decision.

TABLE 9-2 Adam's Economic Profit from Acquiring a Pharmacology Degree

Value of increase in lifetime earnings	$100,000
Explicit cost:	
Tuition	–40,000
Interest paid on student loan	–4,000
Accounting Profit	**56,000**
Implicit cost:	
Value of income forgone during 2 years spent in school	–57,000
Economic Profit	**–1,000**

Economic profit is equal to revenue minus the opportunity cost of resources used. It is usually less than the accounting profit.

Capital is the total value of assets owned by an individual or firm—physical assets plus financial assets.

The **implicit cost of capital** is the opportunity cost of the use of one's own capital—the income earned if the capital had been employed in its next best alternative use.

Making "Either–Or" Decisions

An "either–or" decision is one in which you must choose between two activities. That's in contrast to a "how much" decision, which requires you to choose how much of a given activity to undertake. For example, Adam faced an "either–or" decision: to spend two years in graduate school to obtain a degree in pharmacology, or to work. In contrast, a "how much" decision would be deciding how many hours to study or how many hours to work at a job. Table 9-3 contrasts a variety of "either–or" and "how much" decisions.

According to the **principle of "either–or" decision making,** when faced with an "either–or" choice between two activities, choose the one with the positive economic profit.

In making economic decisions, as we have already emphasized, it is vitally important to calculate opportunity costs correctly. The best way to make an "either–or" decision, the method that leads to the best possible economic outcome, is the straightforward **principle of "either–or" decision making.** According to this principle, *when making an "either–or" choice between two activities, choose the one with the positive economic profit.*

Let's examine Adam's dilemma from a different angle in order to understand how this principle works. If he takes the job he is currently offered, the value of his total lifetime earnings is $57,000 (the value today of his earnings over the next two years) + $500,000 (the value today of his total lifetime earnings thereafter) = $557,000. If he gets his pharmacology degree instead and works as a pharmacist, the value today of his total lifetime earnings is $600,000 (value today of his lifetime earnings after two years in school) − $40,000 (tuition) − $4,000 (interest payments) = $556,000. The economic profit from taking the job versus becoming a pharmacist is $557,000 − $556,000 = $1,000.

So the right choice for Adam is to begin work immediately, which gives him an economic profit of $1,000, rather than become a pharmacist, which would give him an economic profit of −$1,000. In other words, by becoming a pharmacist he loses the $1,000 economic profit he would have gained by starting work immediately.

In making "either–or" decisions, mistakes most commonly arise when people or businesses use their own assets in projects rather than rent or borrow assets. That's because they fail to account for the implicit cost of using self-owned capital. This would have been true of Adam, if he were to use his own savings to pay the tuition for pharmacology school. In contrast, when they rent or borrow assets, these rental or borrowing costs show up as explicit costs. If, for example, a restaurant owns its equipment and tools, it would have to compute its implicit cost of capital by calculating how much the equipment could be sold for and how much could be earned by using those funds in the next best alternative project.

In addition, businesses run by the owner (an *entrepreneur*) often fail to calculate the opportunity cost of the owner's time in running the business. In that way, small businesses often underestimate their opportunity costs and overestimate their economic profit of staying in business.

Are we implying that the hundreds of thousands who chose to go back to school rather than find work in 2010 were misguided? Not necessarily. As we mentioned before, the poor job market of 2010

TABLE 9-3 "Either–Or" versus "How Much" Decisions	
"Either–or" decisions	**"How much" decisions**
Tide or Cheer?	How many days before you do your laundry?
Buy a car or not?	How many kilometres do you go before an oil change in your car?
An order of nachos or a sandwich?	How many jalapenos on your nachos?
Run your own business or work for someone else?	How many workers should you hire in your company?
Prescribe drug A or drug B for your patients?	How much should a patient take of a drug that generates side effects?
Graduate school or not?	How many hours to study?

PITFALLS

WHY ARE THERE ONLY TWO CHOICES?

In "either–or" decision making, we have assumed that there are only two activities to choose from. But, what if, instead of just two alternatives, there are three or more? Does the principle of "either–or" decision making still apply?

Yes, it does. That's because any choice between three (or more) alternatives can always be boiled down to a series of choices between two alternatives. Here's an illustration using three alternative activities: A, B, or C. (Remember that this is an "either–or" decision: you can choose only one of the three alternatives.)

Let's say you begin by considering A versus B: in this comparison, A has a positive economic profit but B yields an economic loss. At this point, you should discard B as a viable choice because A will always be superior to B. The next step is to compare A to C: in this comparison, C has a positive economic profit but A yields an economic loss. You can now discard A because C will always be superior to A. You are now done: since A is better than B, and C is better than A, C is the correct choice.

greatly diminished the opportunity cost of forgone wages for many students, making continuing their education the optimal choice for them.

xavieranau/Getty Images

Deciding to rent out a spare room is the right choice when the rent exceeds the opportunity cost of your privacy.

ECONOMICS >> *in Action*
Airbnb and the Rising Cost of Privacy

One of the benefits of getting older is having the higher income to acquire a place of one's own and the privacy that comes with it. No longer will you be forced to endure a messy roommate or wait to use the bathroom. But in many places across the country, that's changing as more people share their homes and apartments with strangers. You can thank websites like Airbnb and VRBO for the change and for the loss of privacy.

It's simply a matter of opportunity cost. The rise of space-sharing websites makes it easy to rent out your extra living space for cash. If you live in an area where there is high demand for short-term stays—like Vancouver, Toronto, or Niagara Falls—renting out your spare room can be very lucrative. In Vancouver or Toronto a private room (shared bathroom) rents for $50 to $100 per night, while in Niagara Falls a private bedroom (shared bathroom) could easily rent for more than $100 per night. So in many places the opportunity cost of an empty spare room—that is, the opportunity cost of your privacy—has risen substantially.

Not surprisingly, builders have taken notice of the trend and are constructing homes with rentable spaces. In one survey, 35% of young adults said that they wanted to be able to rent out space in their homes at least part time. According to Aaron Zifkin, Airbnb's country manager for Canada, more than half of the people that post their homes on Airbnb do so as this helps to payoff their mortgages, or their daily expenses.

>> Quick Review

- All costs are opportunity costs. They can be divided into **explicit costs** and **implicit costs.**

- An activity's **accounting profit** is not necessarily equal to its **economic profit.**

- Due to the **implicit cost of capital**—the opportunity cost of using self-owned **capital**—and the opportunity cost of one's own time, economic profit is often substantially less than accounting profit.

- The **principle of "either–or" decision making** says that when making an "either–or" choice between two activities, choose the one with the positive economic profit.

>> *Check Your Understanding* 9-1

Solutions appear at back of book.

1. Marisol and Logan run a furniture-refinishing business from their home. Which of the following represent an explicit cost of the business and which represent an implicit cost?
   a. Supplies such as paint stripper, varnish, polish, sandpaper, and so on
   b. Basement space that has been converted into a workroom
   c. Wages paid to a part-time helper
   d. A van that they inherited and use only for transporting furniture
   e. The job at a larger furniture restorer that Marisol gave up in order to run the business

2. Assume that Adam has a third alternative to consider: entering a two-year apprenticeship program for skilled machinists that would, upon completion, make him a licenced machinist. During the apprenticeship, he earns a reduced salary of $15,000 per year. At the end of the apprenticeship, the value of his lifetime earnings is $725,000. What is Adam's best career choice?

3. Suppose you have three alternatives—A, B, and C—and you can undertake only one of them. In comparing A versus B, you find that B has an economic profit and A yields an economic loss. But in comparing A versus C, you find that C has an economic profit and A yields an economic loss. How do you decide what to do?

‖ Making "How Much" Decisions: The Role of Marginal Analysis

Although many decisions in economics are "either–or," many others are "how much." Not many people will give up their cars if the price of gasoline goes up, but many people will drive less. How much less? A rise in corn prices won't necessarily persuade a lot of people to take up farming for the first time, but it will persuade farmers who were already growing corn to plant more. How much more?

Recall from our principles of microeconomics that "how much" is a decision at the margin. So to understand "how much" decisions, we will use an approach known as *marginal analysis.* Marginal analysis involves comparing the benefit of doing a little bit more of some activity with the cost of doing a little bit more of that activity. The benefit of doing a little bit more of something is what economists call its *marginal benefit,* and the cost of doing a little bit more of something is what they call its *marginal cost.*

Why is this called "marginal" analysis? A margin is an edge; what you do in marginal analysis is push out the edge a bit and see whether that is a good move. We will study marginal analysis by considering a hypothetical decision of how many years of school to complete. We'll consider the case of Alexa, who studies computer science in the hopes of becoming an app designer. Since there are a wide variety of topics that can be learned one year at a time (programming, hardware, applications, user interface), at the end of each year Alexa can decide whether to continue her studies or not.

Unlike Adam, who faced an "either–or" decision of whether to get a pharmacology degree or not, Alexa faces a "how much" decision of how many years to study computer science. For example, she could study one more year, or five more years, or any number of years in between. We'll begin our analysis of Alexa's decision problem by defining Alexa's *marginal cost* of another year of study.

The **marginal cost** of producing a good or service is the additional cost incurred by producing one more unit of that good or service.

Marginal Cost

We'll assume that each additional year of schooling costs Alexa $10,000 in explicit costs—tuition, interest on a student loan, and so on. In addition to the explicit costs, she also has an implicit cost—the income forgone by spending one more year in school.

Unlike Alexa's explicit costs, which are constant (that is, the same each year), Alexa's implicit cost changes each year. That's because each year she spends in school leaves her better trained than the year before; and the better trained she is, the higher the salary she can command. Consequently, the income she forgoes by not working rises each additional year she stays in school. In other words, the greater the number of years Alexa has already spent in school, the higher her implicit cost of another year of school.

Table 9-4 contains the data on how Alexa's cost of an additional year of schooling changes as she completes more years. The second column shows how her total cost of schooling changes as the number of years she has completed increases. For example, Alexa's first year has a total cost of $30,000: $10,000 in explicit costs of tuition and the like as well as $20,000 in forgone salary.

The second column also shows that the total cost of attending two years is $70,000: $30,000 for her first year plus $40,000 for her second year. During her second year in school, her explicit costs have stayed the same ($10,000) but her implicit cost of forgone salary has gone up to $30,000. That's because she's a more valuable worker with one year of schooling under her belt than with no schooling.

Likewise, the total cost of three years of schooling is $130,000: $30,000 in explicit cost for three years of tuition plus $100,000 in implicit cost of three years of forgone salary. The total cost of attending four years is $220,000, and $350,000 for five years.

The change in Alexa's total cost of schooling when she goes to school an additional year is her *marginal cost* of the one-year increase in years of schooling. In general, the **marginal cost** of producing a good or service (in this case, producing one's own education) is the additional cost incurred by producing one more unit of that good or

TABLE 9-4 Alexa's Marginal Cost of Additional Years in School

Quantity of schooling (years)	Total cost	Marginal cost
0	$0	
		$30,000
1	30,000	
		40,000
2	70,000	
		60,000
3	130,000	
		90,000
4	220,000	
		130,000
5	350,000	

Production of a good or service has **increasing marginal cost** when each additional unit costs more to produce than the previous one.

The **marginal cost curve** shows how the cost of producing one more unit depends on the quantity that has already been produced.

Production of a good or service has **constant marginal cost** when each additional unit costs the same to produce as the previous one.

Production of a good or service has **decreasing marginal cost** when each additional unit costs less to produce than the previous one.

service. The arrows, which zigzag between the total costs in the second column and the marginal costs in the third column, are there to help you to see how marginal cost is calculated from total cost.

Similarly, total cost can be calculated from marginal cost: the total cost of a given quantity is the sum of the marginal costs of that quantity and of all of the previous ones. So the total cost of three years of schooling is $30,000 + $40,000 + $60,000 = $130,000; that is, the marginal cost of year 1 plus the marginal cost of year 2 plus the marginal cost of year 3.

As already mentioned, the third column of Table 9-4 shows Alexa's marginal costs of more years of schooling, which have a clear pattern: they are increasing. They go from $30,000 to $40,000, to $60,000, to $90,000, and finally to $130,000 for the fifth year of schooling. That's because each year of schooling would make Alexa a more valuable and highly paid employee if she were to work. As a result, forgoing a job becomes much more costly as she becomes more educated. This is an example of what economists call **increasing marginal cost,** which occurs when each unit of a good costs more to produce than the previous unit.

Figure 9-1 shows the **marginal cost curve,** a graphical representation of Alexa's marginal costs. The height of each shaded bar corresponds to the marginal cost of a given year of schooling. The red line connecting the dots at the midpoint of the top of each bar is Alexa's marginal cost curve. Alexa has an upward-sloping marginal cost curve because she has increasing marginal cost of additional years of schooling.

Although increasing marginal cost is a frequent phenomenon in real life, it's not the only possibility. **Constant marginal cost** occurs when the cost of producing an additional unit is the same as the cost of producing the previous unit. Plant nurseries, for example, typically have constant marginal cost—the cost of growing one more plant is the same, regardless of how many plants have already been produced. With constant marginal cost, the marginal cost curve is a horizontal line.

There can also be **decreasing marginal cost,** which occurs when marginal cost falls as the number of units produced increases. With decreasing marginal cost, the marginal cost line is downward sloping. Decreasing marginal cost is often due to *learning effects* in production: for complicated tasks, such as assembling a new model of a car, workers are often slow and mistake-prone when

FIGURE 9-1 Marginal Cost

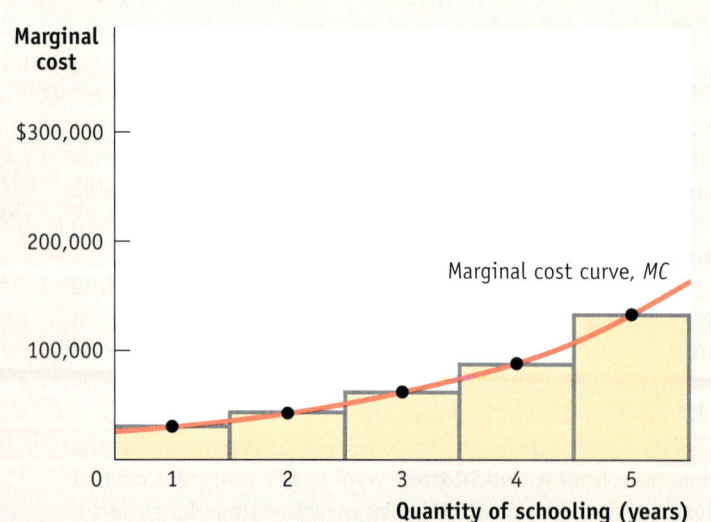

The height of each shaded bar corresponds to Alexa's marginal cost of an additional year of schooling. The height of each bar is higher than the preceding one because each year of schooling costs more than the previous years. As a result, Alexa has increasing marginal cost and the marginal cost curve, the line connecting the midpoints at the top of each bar, is upward sloping.

PITFALLS

TOTAL COST VERSUS MARGINAL COST

It can be easy to conclude that marginal cost and total cost must always move in the same direction. That is, if total cost is rising, then marginal cost must also be rising. Or if marginal cost is falling, then total cost must be falling as well. But the following example shows that this conclusion is wrong.

Let's consider the example of auto production, which is likely to involve learning effects. Suppose that for the first batch of cars of a new model, each car costs $10,000 to assemble. As workers gain experience with the new model, they become better at production. As a result, the per-car cost of assembly falls to $8,000 for the second batch. For the third batch, the per-car assembly cost falls again to $6,500 as workers continue to gain expertise. For the fourth batch, the per-car cost of assembly falls to $5,000 and remains constant for the rest of the production run.

In this example, marginal cost is *decreasing* over batches one through four, falling from $10,000 to $5,000. However, it's important to note that total cost is still *increasing* over the entire production run because marginal cost is greater than zero.

To see this point, assume that each batch consists of 100 cars. Then the total cost of producing the first batch is 100 × $10,000 = $1,000,000. The total cost of producing the first and second batches of cars is $1,000,000 + (100 × $8,000) = $1,800,000. Likewise, the total cost of producing the first, second, and third batches is $1,800,000 + (100 × $6,500) = $2,450,000, and so on. As you can see, although marginal cost is decreasing over the first few batches of cars, total cost is increasing over the same batches.

This shows us that total cost and marginal cost can sometimes move in opposite directions. So it is wrong to assert that they always move in the same direction. What we can assert is that *total cost increases whenever marginal cost is positive,* regardless of whether marginal cost is increasing or decreasing.

---

assembling the earliest units, making for higher marginal cost on those units. But as workers gain experience, assembly time and the rate of mistakes fall, generating lower marginal cost for later units. As a result, overall production has decreasing marginal cost.

Finally, for the production of some goods and services the shape of the marginal cost curve changes as the number of units produced increases. For example, auto production is likely to have decreasing marginal costs for the first batch of cars produced as workers iron out kinks and mistakes in production. Then production has constant marginal costs for the next batch of cars as workers settle into a predictable pace.

But at some point, as workers produce more cars, marginal cost begins to increase as they run out of factory floor space and the auto company incurs costly overtime wages. This gives rise to what we call a "swoosh"-shaped marginal cost curve—a topic we discuss in Chapter 11. For now, we'll stick to the simpler example of an increasing marginal cost curve.

Marginal Benefit

Alexa benefits from higher lifetime earnings as she completes more years of school. Exactly how much she benefits is shown in Table 9-5. Column 2 shows Alexa's total benefit according to the number of years of school completed, expressed as the value of her lifetime earnings. The third column shows Alexa's *marginal benefit* from an additional year of schooling. In general, the **marginal benefit** of producing a good or service is the additional benefit earned from producing one more unit.

As in Table 9-4, the data in the third column of Table 9-5 show a clear pattern. However, this time the numbers are decreasing rather than increasing. The first year of schooling gives Alexa a $300,000 increase in the value of her lifetime earnings. The second year also gives her a positive return, but the size of that return has fallen to $150,000; the third year's return is also positive, but its size has fallen yet again to $90,000; and so on. In other words, the more years of school that Alexa has already completed, the smaller the increase in the value of her lifetime earnings from attending one more year.

The **marginal benefit** of a good or service is the additional benefit derived from producing one more unit of that good or service.

TABLE 9-5 Alexa's Marginal Benefit of Additional Years in School

Quantity of schooling (years)	Total benefit	Marginal benefit
0	$0	
		$300,000
1	300,000	
		150,000
2	450,000	
		90,000
3	540,000	
		60,000
4	600,000	
		50,000
5	650,000	

FIGURE 9-2 Marginal Benefit

The height of each shaded bar corresponds to Alexa's marginal benefit of an additional year of schooling. The height of each bar is lower than the one preceding it because an additional year of schooling has decreasing marginal benefit. As a result, Alexa's marginal benefit curve, the curve connecting the midpoints at the top of each bar, is downward sloping.

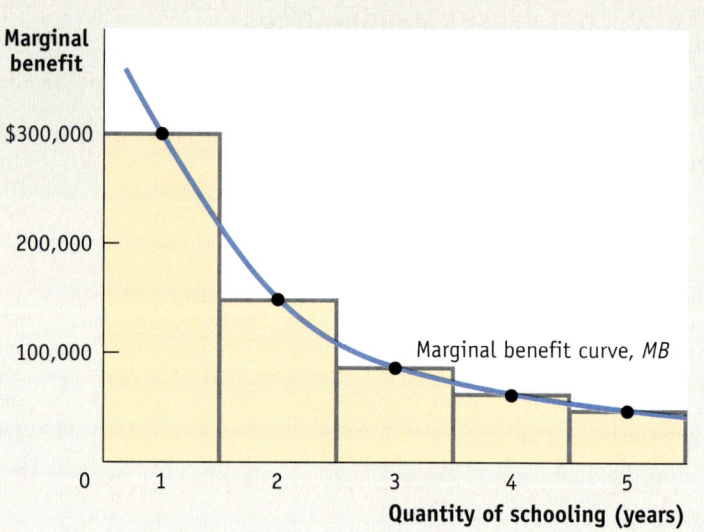

There is **decreasing marginal benefit** from an activity when each additional unit of the activity yields less benefit than the previous unit.

The **marginal benefit curve** shows how the benefit from producing one more unit depends on the quantity that has already been produced.

Alexa's schooling decision has what economists call **decreasing marginal benefit:** each additional year of school yields a smaller benefit than the previous year. Or, to put it slightly differently, with decreasing marginal benefit, the benefit from producing one more unit of the good or service falls as the quantity already produced rises.

Just as marginal cost can be represented by a marginal cost curve, marginal benefit can be represented by a **marginal benefit curve,** shown in blue in Figure 9-2. Alexa's marginal benefit curve slopes downward because she faces decreasing marginal benefit from additional years of schooling.

Not all goods or activities exhibit decreasing marginal benefit. In fact, there are many goods for which the marginal benefit of production is constant—that is, the additional benefit from producing one more unit is the same regardless of the number of units already produced. In later chapters, we will see that the shape of a firm's marginal benefit curve from producing output has important implications for how that firm behaves within its industry. We'll also see why constant marginal benefit is considered the norm for many important industries.

Now we are ready to see how the concepts of marginal benefit and marginal cost are brought together to answer the question of how many years of additional schooling Alexa should undertake.

Marginal Analysis

Table 9-6 shows the marginal cost and marginal benefit numbers from Tables 9-4 and 9-5. It also adds an additional column: the additional profit to Alexa from staying in school one more year, equal to the difference between the marginal benefit and the marginal cost of that additional year in school. (Remember that it is Alexa's economic profit that we care about, not her accounting profit.) We can now use Table 9-6 to determine how many additional years of schooling Alexa should undertake in order to maximize her total profit.

TABLE 9-6 Alexa's Profit from Additional Years of Schooling

Quantity of schooling (years)	Marginal benefit	Marginal cost	Additional profit
0			
	$300,000	$30,000	$270,000
1			
	150,000	40,000	110,000
2			
	90,000	60,000	30,000
3			
	60,000	90,000	–30,000
4			
	50,000	130,000	–80,000
5			

First, imagine that Alexa chooses not to attend any additional years of school. We can see from column 4 that this is a mistake if Alexa wants to achieve the highest total profit from her schooling—the sum of the additional profits generated by another year of schooling. If she attends one additional year of school, she increases the value of her lifetime earnings by $270,000, the profit from the first additional year attended.

Now, let's consider whether Alexa should attend the second year of school. The additional profit from the second year is $110,000, so Alexa should attend the second year as well. What about the third year? The additional profit from that year is $30,000; so, yes, Alexa should attend the third year as well.

What about a fourth year? In this case, the additional profit is negative: it is −$30,000. Alexa loses $30,000 of the value of her lifetime earnings if she attends the fourth year. Clearly, Alexa is worse off by attending the fourth additional year rather than taking a job. And the same is true for the fifth year as well: it has a negative additional profit of −$80,000.

What have we learned? That Alexa should attend three additional years of school and stop at that point. Although the first, second, and third years of additional schooling increase the value of her lifetime earnings, the fourth and fifth years diminish it. So three years of additional schooling lead to the quantity that generates the maximum possible total profit. It is what economists call the **optimal quantity**—the quantity that generates the maximum possible total profit.

Figure 9-3 shows how the optimal quantity can be determined graphically. Alexa's marginal benefit and marginal cost curves are shown together. If Alexa chooses fewer than three additional years (that is, years 0, 1, or 2), she will choose a level of schooling at which her marginal benefit curve lies *above* her marginal cost curve. She can make herself better off by staying in school.

If instead she chooses more than three additional years (years 4 or 5), she will choose a level of schooling at which her marginal benefit curve lies *below* her

> The **optimal quantity** is the quantity that generates the highest possible total profit.

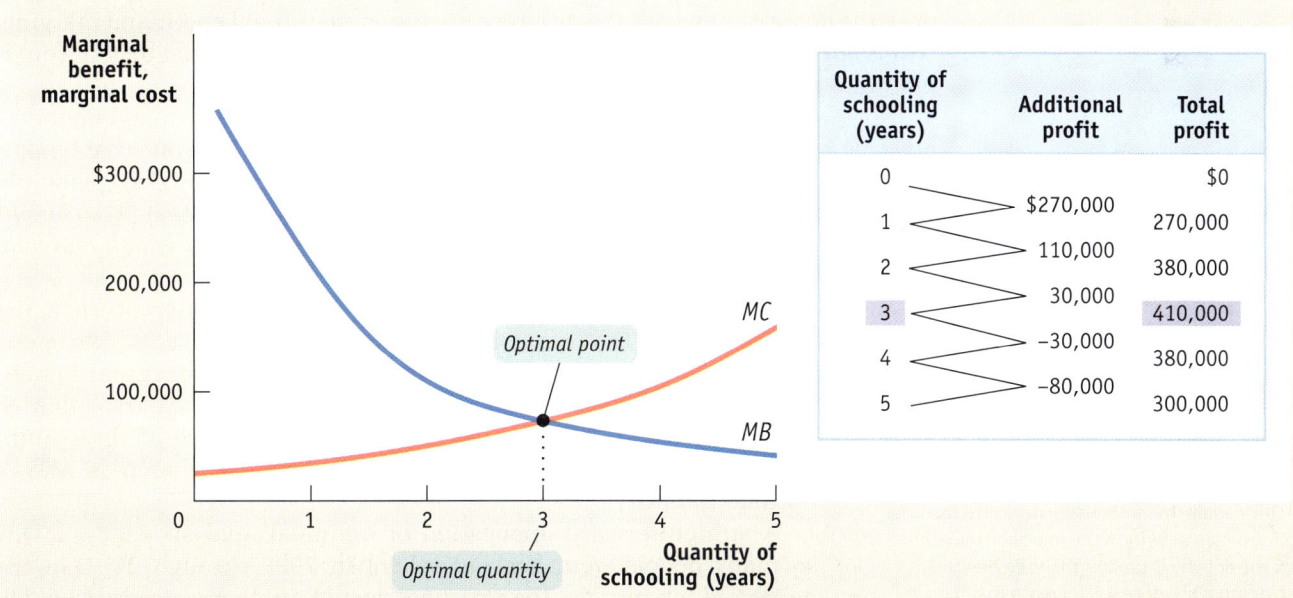

FIGURE 9-3 Alexa's Optimal Quantity of Years of Schooling

Quantity of schooling (years)	Additional profit	Total profit
0		$0
	$270,000	
1		270,000
	110,000	
2		380,000
	30,000	
3		410,000
	−30,000	
4		380,000
	−80,000	
5		300,000

The optimal quantity is the quantity that generates the highest possible total profit. It is the quantity at which marginal benefit is greater than or equal to marginal cost. Equivalently, it is the quantity at which the marginal benefit and marginal cost curves intersect. Here, they intersect at 3 additional years of schooling. The table confirms that 3 is indeed the optimal quantity: it leads to the maximum total profit of $410,000.

According to the **profit-maximizing principle of marginal analysis,** when faced with a profit-maximizing "how much" decision, the optimal quantity is the largest quantity at which the marginal benefit is greater than or equal to marginal cost.

marginal cost curve. She can make herself better off by choosing not to attend the additional year of school and taking a job instead.

The table in Figure 9-3 confirms our result. The second column repeats information from Table 9-6, showing Alexa's marginal benefit minus marginal cost—the additional profit per additional year of schooling. The third column shows Alexa's total profit for different years of schooling. The total profit, for each possible year of schooling, is simply the sum of numbers in the second column up to and including that year.

For example, Alexa's profit from additional years of schooling is $270,000 for the first year and $110,000 for the second year. So the total profit for two additional years of schooling is $270,000 + $110,000 = $380,000. Similarly, the total profit for three additional years is $270,000 + $110,000 + $30,000 = $410,000. Our claim that three years is the optimal quantity for Alexa is confirmed by the data in the table in Figure 9-3: at three years of additional schooling, Alexa reaps the greatest total profit, $410,000.

Alexa's decision problem illustrates how you go about finding the optimal quantity when the choice involves a small number of quantities. (In this example, one through five years.) With small quantities, the rule for choosing the optimal quantity is: *increase the quantity as long as the marginal benefit from one more unit is greater than the marginal cost, but stop before the marginal benefit becomes less than the marginal cost.*

In contrast, when a "how much" decision involves relatively large quantities, the rule for choosing the optimal quantity simplifies to this: *The optimal quantity is the quantity at which marginal benefit is equal to marginal cost.*

To see why this is so, consider the example of a farmer who finds that his optimal quantity of wheat produced is 5,000 bushels. Typically, he will find that in going from 4,999 to 5,000 bushels, his marginal benefit is only very slightly greater than his marginal cost—that is, the difference between marginal benefit and marginal cost is close to zero. Similarly, in going from 5,000 to 5,001 bushels, his marginal cost is only very slightly greater than his marginal benefit—again, the difference between marginal cost and marginal benefit is very close to zero.

So a simple rule for him in choosing the optimal quantity of wheat is to produce the quantity at which the difference between marginal benefit and marginal cost is approximately zero—that is, the quantity at which marginal benefit equals marginal cost.

Now we are ready to state the general rule for choosing the optimal quantity—one that applies for decisions involving either small quantities or large quantities. This general rule is known as the **profit-maximizing principle of marginal analysis:** *When making a profit-maximizing "how much" decision, the optimal quantity is the largest quantity at which marginal benefit is greater than or equal to marginal cost.*

Graphically, the optimal quantity is the quantity of an activity at which the marginal benefit curve intersects the marginal cost curve. For example, in Figure 9-3 the marginal benefit and marginal cost curves cross each other at three years—that is, marginal benefit equals marginal cost at the choice of three additional years of schooling, which we have already seen is Alexa's optimal quantity.

A straightforward application of marginal analysis explains why so many people went back to school in 2009 through 2012: in the depressed job market, the marginal cost of another year of school fell because the opportunity cost of forgone wages had fallen.

A straightforward application of marginal analysis can also explain many facts, such as why average new house sizes are typically larger in Australia, Canada, and the United States than those in countries with smaller land mass (as we explain in the Global Comparison).

PITFALLS

MUDDLED AT THE MARGIN

The idea of setting marginal benefit equal to marginal cost sometimes confuses people. Aren't we trying to maximize the *difference* between benefits and costs? Yes. And don't we wipe out our gains by setting benefits and costs equal to each other? Yes. But that is not what we are doing. Rather, what we are doing is setting *marginal,* not *total,* benefit and cost equal to each other.

Once again, the point is to maximize the total profit from an activity. If the marginal benefit from the activity is greater than the marginal cost, doing a bit more will increase that gain. If the marginal benefit is less than the marginal cost, doing a bit less will increase the total profit. *So only when the marginal benefit and marginal cost are equal is the difference between total benefit and total cost at a maximum.*

GLOBAL COMPARISON   HOUSE SIZES AROUND THE WORLD

Although people in North America usually think they have the biggest of everything, when it comes to house size, Australia takes first place. In 2015, the average new house size in Australia was 2,303 square feet, compared to 2,164 square feet in the United States. Close behind was Canada, with an average new house size of 1,948 square feet, followed by the other countries listed in the figure.

The larger homes can be explained by the lower average prices for land in those countries. Compared to countries like Germany or Japan, Australia, the United States, and Canada have much more land relative to the size of their populations. This greater supply of land leads to lower average prices, and hence lower costs for building bigger houses.

The figure also shows how the forces of supply and demand determine opportunity cost, which then drives consumer choice. The blue bars measure the average new house size per country, while the green bars measure the country land size. As you can see, there is a strong positive relationship between house size and country land size.

But you can also see that there is not a perfect one-to-one relationship between house size and land size. The most notable anomaly is China, with the largest land mass and the second-to-smallest average new house size, a result that is also consistent with opportunity cost. Compared to the residents of the other countries in the sample, and despite rapidly rising incomes, Chinese residents are still significantly poorer. Although, given how poor China was 20 years ago, it's an extraordinary achievement that the average new Chinese house is only 20% smaller than one in the United Kingdom.

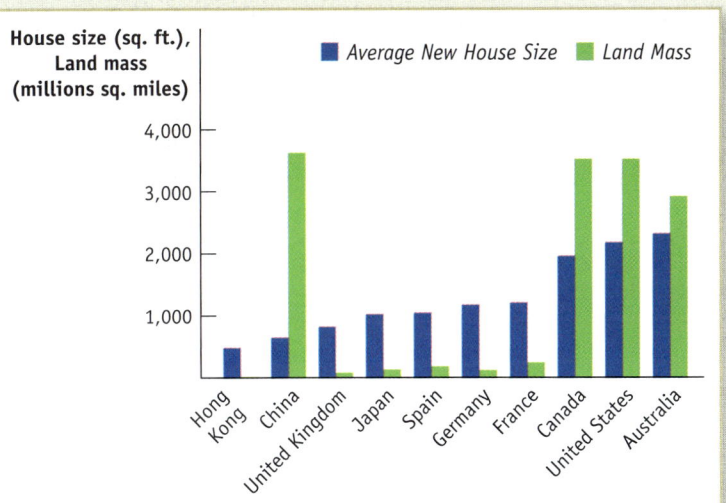

Data from: Shrink That Footprint, www.shrinkthatfootprint.com.

A Principle with Many Uses

The profit-maximizing principle of marginal analysis can be applied to just about any "how much" decision in which you want to maximize the total profit for an activity. It is equally applicable to production decisions, consumption decisions, and policy decisions. Furthermore, decisions where the benefits and costs are not expressed in dollars and cents can also be made using marginal analysis (as long as benefits and costs can be measured in some type of common units). Table 9-7 includes three examples of decisions that are suitable for marginal analysis.

A Preview: How Consumption Decisions Are Different

We've established that marginal analysis is an extraordinarily useful tool. It is used in "how much" decisions that are applied to both consumption choices and to profit maximization. Producers use it to make optimal production decisions at the margin and individuals use it to make optimal consumption decisions at the margin. But consumption decisions differ from production decisions. Why the difference? Because when individuals make choices, they face a limited amount of income. As a result, when they choose more of one good to consume (say, new clothes), they must choose less of another good (say, restaurant dinners).

In contrast, decisions that involve maximizing profit by producing a good or service—such as years of education or tonnes of wheat—are not affected by income limitations. For example, in Alexa's case, she is not limited by income because she can always borrow to pay for another year of school. In the next chapter, we will see how consumption decisions differ from—yet are similar to—production decisions.

TABLE 9-7 Making Decisions Using Marginal Analysis

The "how much" decision to be made	Applying marginal analysis	Arriving at the optimal quantity
The retailer PalMart must decide on the size of the new store it is constructing in Beijing.	PalMart must compare the marginal benefit of enlarging the store by 1 square foot (the value of the additional sales it makes from that additional square foot of floor space) to the marginal cost (the cost of constructing and maintaining the additional square foot).	The optimal store size for PalMart is the largest size at which marginal benefit is greater than or equal to marginal cost.
A physician must decide whether or not to increase the dosage of a drug in light of possible side effects.	The physician must consider the marginal cost, in terms of side effects, of increasing the dosage of a drug versus the marginal benefit of improving health by increasing the dosage.	The optimal dosage level is the largest level at which the marginal benefit of disease amelioration is greater than or equal to the marginal cost of side effects.
A farmer must decide how much fertilizer to apply.	More fertilizer increases crop yield but also costs more.	The optimal amount of fertilizer is the largest quantity at which the marginal benefit of higher crop yield is greater than or equal to the marginal cost of purchasing and applying more fertilizer.

ECONOMICS >> *in Action*
The Cost of a Life

What's the marginal benefit to society of saving a human life? You might be tempted to answer that human life is infinitely precious. But in the real world, resources are scarce, so we must decide how much to spend on saving lives since we cannot spend infinite amounts. After all, we could surely reduce highway deaths by dropping the speed limit on interstates to 60 kilometers per hour, but the cost of a lower speed limit—in time and money—is more than most people are willing to pay.

Generally, people are reluctant to talk in a straightforward way about comparing the marginal cost of a life saved with the marginal benefit—it sounds too callous. Sometimes, however, the question becomes unavoidable.

For example, the cost of saving a life became an object of intense discussion in the United Kingdom after a horrible train crash near London's Paddington Station killed 31 people. There were accusations that the British government was spending too little on rail safety. However, the government estimated that improving rail safety would cost an additional $6 million per life saved. But if that amount was worth spending—that is, if the estimated marginal benefit of saving a life exceeded $6 million—then the implication was that the British government was spending far too little on rail safety.

In contrast, the estimated marginal cost per life saved through highway improvements was only $1.5 million, making it a much better deal than saving lives through greater rail safety. More recently, a 2013 train derailment in Lac-Megantic, Quebec caused explosions and fire that killed 47 people. According to reports, one possible contributing factor in this disaster was the exemption the rail company had received that allowed it to use a one-person crew rather than the usual minimum two-person crew. This exemption allowed the rail company to park an unattended train loaded with highly flammable crude oil several kilometers uphill from the town. This exemption, used to save a few hundred dollars per train shipment, resulted in all these deaths, the destruction of most of the town's downtown, and the release of about 7.6 million liters of crude oil. The exemption is no longer permitted on trains carrying dangerous materials in Canada.

>> *Check Your Understanding* 9-2

Solutions appear at back of book.

1. For each of the "how much" decisions listed in Table 9-3, describe the nature of the marginal cost and of the marginal benefit.

2. Suppose that Alexa's school charges a fixed fee of $70,000 for four years of schooling. If Alexa drops out before she finishes those four years, she still has to pay the $70,000. Alexa's total cost for different years of schooling is now given by the data in the accompanying table. Assume that Alexa's total benefit and marginal benefit remain as reported in Table 9-5.

   Use this information to calculate (i) Alexa's new marginal cost, (ii) her new profit, and (iii) her new optimal years of schooling. What kind of marginal cost does Alexa now have—constant, increasing, or decreasing?

Quantity of schooling (years)	Total cost
0	$0
1	90,000
2	120,000
3	170,000
4	250,000
5	370,000

>> *Quick Review*

• A "how much" decision is made by using marginal analysis.

• The **marginal cost** of producing a good or service is represented graphically by the **marginal cost curve.** An upward-sloping marginal cost curve reflects **increasing marginal cost. Constant marginal cost** is represented by a horizontal marginal cost curve. A downward-sloping marginal cost curve reflects **decreasing marginal cost.**

• The **marginal benefit** of producing a good or service is represented by the **marginal benefit curve.** A downward-sloping marginal benefit curve reflects **decreasing marginal benefit.**

• The **optimal quantity,** the quantity which generates the highest possible total profit, is found by applying the **profit-maximizing principle of marginal analysis,** according to which the optimal quantity is the largest quantity at which marginal benefit is greater than or equal to marginal cost. Graphically, it is the quantity at which the marginal cost curve intersects the marginal benefit curve.

‖ Sunk Costs

When making decisions, knowing what to ignore can be as important as what to include. Although we have devoted much attention in this chapter to costs that are important to take into account when making a decision, some costs should be ignored when doing so. We will now focus on the kinds of costs that people should ignore when making decisions—what economists call *sunk costs*—and why they should be ignored.

To gain some intuition, consider the following scenario. You own a car that is a few years old, and you have just replaced the brake pads at a cost of $250. But then you find out that the entire brake system is defective and also must be replaced. This will cost you an additional $1,500. Alternatively, you could sell the car and buy another of comparable quality, but with no brake defects, by spending an additional $1,600. What should you do: fix your old car, or sell it and buy another?

Some might say that you should take the latter option. After all, this line of reasoning goes, if you repair your car, you will end up having spent $1,750: $1,500 for the brake system and $250 for the brake pads. If instead you sell your old car and buy another, you would spend only $1,600.

But this reasoning, although it sounds plausible, is wrong. It is wrong because the $250 for the brake pads has already been spent. That $250 cannot be recovered; therefore, it should be ignored and should have no effect on your decision whether or not to repair your car and keep it.

From a rational viewpoint, the real cost at this time of repairing and keeping your car is $1,500, not $1,750. So the correct decision is to repair your car and keep it rather than spend $1,600 on a new car.

In this example, the $250 that has already been spent and cannot be recovered is what economists call a **sunk cost.** Sunk costs should be ignored in making decisions about future actions because they have no influence on their actual costs and benefits. Once something can't be recovered, it is irrelevant in making decisions about what to do in the future.

It is often psychologically hard to ignore sunk costs. And if, in fact, you haven't yet incurred the costs, then you should take them into consideration. That is, if you had known at the beginning that it would cost $1,750 to repair your car, then the right choice at that time would have been to buy a new car for $1,600. But once you have already paid the $250 for brake pads, you should no longer include it in your decision making about your next actions. It may be hard to accept that "bygones are bygones," but it is the right way to make a decision.

The $250 already spent on brake pads is irrelevant because it is a sunk cost.

A **sunk cost** is a cost that has already been incurred and is nonrecoverable. A sunk cost should be ignored in decisions about future actions.

ECONOMICS >> *in Action*
Biotech: The World's Biggest Loser

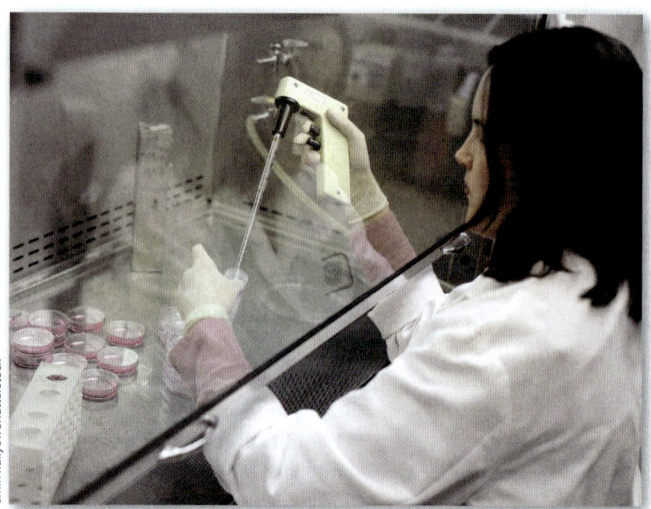

emin kuliyev/Shutterstock

The biotech industry has been built on the premise that sunk costs don't matter.

Biotech firms use cutting-edge bioengineering techniques to discover new therapies to combat disease. But the vast majority of projects that they undertake end in failure. Medscape Medical News estimated that only one out of 5,000 to 10,000 drugs examined in early trials ever makes it to the consumer. And in 2016 it was estimated that over 90% of publicly traded biotech companies would lose money in the upcoming year.

So if there is any industry that exemplifies the principle that sunk costs don't matter, it is the biotech industry. According to Arthur Levinson, chairman of Genentech, one of the largest and most successful of these firms, biotechnology has been "one of the biggest money-losing industries in the history of mankind." It is estimated that the industry has lost well over US$100 billion since 1976. (Yes, that's *billion*.)

How, then, do biotech companies survive? It is thanks to savvy investors who know that although thousands of experimental drugs will fail, a tiny minority will succeed. And when they do, the returns will be enormous. These investors ignore past losses—which are sunk costs—and focus, instead, on a company's technical ability and the breadth of the drugs in their development pipeline.

The drug company Xoma is a case in point. Since its founding in 1981, Xoma has accumulated losses of more than US$1 billion. Yet investors have been willing to provide it with more money year after year because Xoma possesses a very promising antibody technology and, of course, because shrewd investors understand the principle of sunk costs.

>> **Quick Review**

• **Sunk costs** should be ignored in decisions regarding future actions. Because they have already been incurred and are nonrecoverable, they have no effect on future costs and benefits.

>> *Check Your Understanding* 9-3
Solutions appear at back of book.

1. You have decided to go into the ice-cream business and have bought a used ice-cream truck for $8,000. Now you are reconsidering. What is your sunk cost in the following scenarios?
   a. The truck cannot be resold.
   b. The truck can be resold, but only at a 50% discount.
2. You have gone through two years of medical school but are suddenly wondering whether you would be happier as a musician. Which of the following statements are potentially valid arguments and which are not?
   a. "I can't give up now, after all the time and money I've put in."
   b. "If I had thought about it from the beginning, I never would have gone to med school, so I should give it up now."
   c. "I wasted two years, but never mind—let's start from here."
   d. "My parents would kill me if I stopped now." (*Hint:* We're discussing your decision-making ability, not your parents'.)

‖ Behavioural Economics

Most economic models assume that people make choices based on achieving the best possible economic outcome for themselves. Human behaviour, however, is often not so simple. Rather than acting like economic computing machines, people often make choices that fall short—sometimes far short—of the greatest possible economic outcome, or payoff. **Behavioural economics** is a branch of economics that combines economic modelling with insights from human psychology in order to understand how people actually—instead of theoretically—make economic choices. Behavioural economics has become very influential over the past 20 years by delivering insights that allow economists to more accurately model decision making in certain circumstances.

First, we should note that, despite the assumptions of most economic models, sometimes it is *rational* for people to make choices that do not lead to the highest possible monetary payoff. These choices are rational when people value something other than a monetary payoff. For example, Alexa may decide to study computer science for two years rather than three years, the optimal number that maximizes her earnings, because she wants to spend some time travelling. This is a rational choice if Alexa values travel more than she values the additional income that another year of school would provide. As we'll discuss shortly, there are many examples of rational choices that don't maximize monetary payoffs.

Yet it's well documented that people also engage in *irrational* behaviour, choosing an option that leaves them worse off than other available options. The study of irrational economic behaviour was largely pioneered by Daniel Kahneman and Amos Tversky. Kahneman won the 2002 Nobel Prize in economics for his work integrating insights from the psychology of human judgment and decision making into economics. Their work and the insights of others into why people often behave irrationally are having a significant influence on how economists analyze financial markets, labour markets, and other economic concerns.

Rational, but Human, Too

If you are **rational,** you will choose the available option that leads to the outcome you most prefer. But is the outcome you most prefer always the same as the one that gives you the highest possible monetary payoff? No. It can be entirely rational to choose an option that gives you a lower monetary payoff because you care about something other than the size of the monetary payoff. There are four principal reasons why people might prefer a lower monetary payoff: concerns about fairness, nonmonetary rewards, bounded rationality, and risk aversion.

Concerns About Fairness In social situations, people often care about fairness as well as about the size of the economic payoff to themselves. For example, no law requires you to tip your server when you go to a restaurant. But concern for fairness leads most people to leave a tip (unless they've had outrageously bad service) because a tip is seen as fair compensation for good service according to society's norms. Tippers are reducing their own monetary payoff in order to be fair to restaurant servers. A related behaviour is gift-giving: if you care about another person's welfare, it's rational for you to reduce your monetary payoff in order to give that person a gift.

Nonmonetary Rewards More than older generations, young people today seem to understand the meaning of an old saying, "There's more to life than dollars and cents." And despite the fact that economists spend their careers tracking dollars and cents, they would all agree. **Nonmonetary rewards** typically take the form of "feel-good" experiences, such as vacation travel, quality time spent with family and friends, playing a sport, or volunteering at a local soup kitchen. A recent report showed that 9 out of 10 millennials (those born between 1981 and 1996) would take a pay cut to work at a company with similar values to their own, whereas only 9% of baby boomers would do the same. In contrast to activities that lead to higher monetary payoffs that are used for consuming more goods and services, nonmonetary rewards directly generate feelings of satisfaction.

Behavioural economics is a branch of economics that combines economic modelling with insights from human psychology to understand how people actually make decisions.

A **rational** decision maker chooses the available option that leads to the outcome they most prefer.

Nonmonetary rewards are benefits or payoffs that are not financial in nature; examples include increased leisure time and "feel-good" experiences.

A decision maker operating with **bounded rationality** makes a choice that is close to but not exactly the one that leads to the best possible economic outcome.

Risk aversion is the willingness to sacrifice some economic payoff in order to avoid a potential loss.

An **irrational** decision maker chooses an option that leaves her worse off than choosing another available option.

The desire for nonmonetary rewards can, in fact, be explained by economics. It is an outcome of the *principle of diminishing marginal utility*, a concept covered in Chapter 10. Simply stated, according to the principle of diminishing marginal utility, the satisfaction gained by consuming one more unit of a good falls as the amount of the good already consumed rises. For example, your first pair of Converse sneakers may have felt very special. However, by the time you purchase your ninth pair, another pair doesn't feel so special. So instead of working to earn money in order to buy the tenth pair, you choose a feel-good experience instead: for example, you quit your regular job and take a position leading backpacking tours in return for room and board.

Surveys show that once people acquire enough goods to live comfortably, they increasingly prefer noneconomic rewards over higher monetary payoffs. According to a recent survey by the travel website Expedia, this is particularly true for millennials: "Millennials are leading the charge in placing a newfound value on experiences, more than things."

Bounded Rationality Being an economic computing machine—choosing the option that gives you the best economic payoff—can require a fair amount of work: sizing up the options, computing the opportunity costs, calculating the marginal amounts, and so on. The mental effort required has its own opportunity cost. This realization led economists to the concept of **bounded rationality**—making a choice that is close to but not exactly the one that leads to the highest possible payoff because the effort of finding the best payoff is too costly. In other words, bounded rationality is the "good enough" method of decision making.

For example, you may have many criteria, and many options, to consider when making a choice about what to eat during your lunch break. What's convenient? What's fastest? What's affordable? What's healthy? What will be most satisfying? Selecting the optimal outcome—the one that will meet all of these criteria—would probably cost more economic computing power than you are willing to devote to the task. And so, you'll opt for a "good enough" option—one that will satisfy one or two of these criteria, and get on with your day. Behavioural economists have studied the concept of bounded rationality and found that we often make choices in this way. And businesses and policy makers can appeal to this tendency to influence our choices, as we'll learn later in the chapter.

Risk Aversion Because life is uncertain and the future unknown, sometimes a choice comes with significant risk. Although you may receive a high payoff if things turn out well, the possibility also exists that things may turn out badly and leave you worse off.

So even if you think a choice will give you the best payoff of all your available options, you may forgo it because you find the possibility that things could turn out badly too, well, risky. This is called **risk aversion**—the willingness to sacrifice some potential economic payoff in order to avoid a potential loss. (We'll discuss risk in detail in Chapter 20.) Because risk makes most people uncomfortable, it's rational for them to give up some potential economic gain in order to avoid it. In fact, if it weren't for risk aversion, there would be no such thing as insurance.

Irrationality: An Economist's View

Sometimes, though, instead of being rational, people are **irrational**—they make choices that leave them worse off than if they had chosen another available option. Is there anything systematic that economists and psychologists can say about economically irrational behaviour? Yes, because most people are irrational in predictable ways. People's irrational behaviour *typically* stems from seven

mistakes they make when thinking about economic decisions. The mistakes are listed in Table 9-8, and we will discuss each in turn.

Misperceptions of Opportunity Cost As we discussed at the beginning of this chapter, people tend to ignore opportunity costs when they are nonmonetary—that is, opportunity costs that don't involve an outlay of cash. Another common misperception of opportunity cost leads to the **sunk cost fallacy:** making a decision based on the belief that a sunk cost is an opportunity cost. But as we know from the previous section, a sunk cost is not an opportunity cost. Once an outlay is unrecoverable (sunk), it is no longer an opportunity cost and should be ignored in future decision making. For example, many university students refuse to withdraw from a course even when they are unlikely to complete it with a passing grade. Often, this is because they are falling prey to the sunk cost fallacy by including the cost of tuition—which has already been spent and cannot be refunded—in their analysis. A better analysis would ignore this sunk cost, and focus on the opportunity cost of remaining in the course, which includes time and effort that might be better spent studying for other courses.

TABLE 9-8 **The Seven Common Mistakes in Economic Decision Making**
1. Misperceptions of opportunity cost
2. Overconfidence
3. Unrealistic expectations about future behaviour
4. Counting dollars unequally
5. Loss aversion
6. Framing bias
7. Status quo bias

Overconfidence It's a function of ego: we tend to think we know more than we actually do. And even if alerted to how widespread overconfidence is, people tend to think that it's someone else's problem, not theirs. (Certainly not yours or mine!)

For example, one study asked students to estimate how long it would take them to complete their thesis "if everything went as well as it possibly could" and "if everything went as poorly as it possibly could." The results: the typical student thought it would take them 33.9 days to finish, with an average estimate of 27.4 days if everything went well and 48.6 days if everything went poorly. In fact,

The **sunk cost fallacy** is the mistaken belief that a sunk cost represents an opportunity cost.

Mental accounting is the habit of mentally assigning dollars to different accounts so that some dollars are worth more than others.

Loss aversion is an oversensitivity to loss, leading to unwillingness to recognize a loss and move on.

the average time it took to complete a thesis was much longer, 55.5 days. Students were, on average, from 14% to 102% more confident than they should have been about the time it would take to complete their theses.

Overconfidence can cause problems with meeting deadlines. But it can cause far more trouble by having a strong adverse effect on people's financial health. Overconfidence often persuades people that they are in better financial shape than they actually are. It can also lead to bad investment and spending decisions. For example, nonprofessional investors who engage in a lot of speculative investing—such as quickly buying and selling stocks—on average have significantly worse results than professional brokers because of their misguided faith in their ability to spot a winner. Similarly, overconfidence can lead people to make a large spending decision, such as buying a car, without doing research on the pros and cons, relying instead on anecdotal evidence. Even worse, people tend to remain overconfident because they remember their successes, and explain away or forget their failures.

Unrealistic Expectations About Future Behaviour Another form of overconfidence is being overly optimistic about your future behaviour: tomorrow you'll study, tomorrow you'll give up ice cream, tomorrow you'll spend less and save more, and so on. Of course, as we all know, when tomorrow arrives, it's still just as hard to study or give up something that you like as it is right now.

Strategies that keep a person on the straight-and-narrow over time are often, at their root, ways to deal with the problem of unrealistic expectations about one's future behaviour. Examples are automatic payroll deduction savings plans, diet plans with prepackaged foods, and mandatory attendance at study groups. By providing a way for someone to commit today to an action tomorrow, such plans counteract the habit of pushing difficult actions off into the future.

A dollar is a dollar, whether you pay it in cash or with your credit card.

Counting Dollars Unequally Have you ever spent more on something when paying with a credit card than you would have if you had to pay with cash? Or noticed that students who get an allowance from their parents are less careful with their money than those who live on their own earnings? Both of these scenarios are examples of **mental accounting**, which is the habit of mentally assigning dollars to different accounts, making some dollars worth more than others.

By spending more with a credit card, you are in effect treating dollars in your wallet as more valuable than dollars on your credit card balance, although in reality they count equally in your budget. Likewise, if you spend more from an allowance than you would from your own earnings, you are treating dollars you earned as more valuable than dollars your parents give you. Both of these examples stem from the failure to understand that, regardless of the form it comes in, a dollar is a dollar.

Loss Aversion **Loss aversion** is an oversensitivity to loss, leading to an unwillingness to recognize a loss and move on. In fact, in the lingo of financial markets, "selling discipline"—being able and willing to quickly acknowledge when a stock you've bought is a loser and sell it—is a highly desirable trait to have.

Many investors, though, are reluctant to acknowledge that they've lost money on a stock and won't make it back. Although it's rational to sell the stock at that point and redeploy the remaining funds, most people find it so painful to admit a loss that they avoid selling for much longer than they should. According to Daniel Kahneman and Amos Tversky, most people feel the misery of losing $100 about twice as keenly as they feel the pleasure of gaining $100.

Loss aversion can help explain why sunk costs are so hard to ignore: ignoring a sunk cost means recognizing that the money you spent is unrecoverable and therefore lost.

Framing Bias Have you ever wondered why, in a discount store like Walmart, prices are rarely in whole numbers like $1.00 or $2.00? Instead, prices almost always end in the number "99"—such as $0.99 or $1.99? The reason why is due to what economists call **framing bias:** the tendency to make a decision based upon how the choices are presented, or framed, rather than upon a comparison of their true values. By offering prices that end in the number 99 rather than the next whole number, Walmart is exploiting shoppers' framing bias. The company knows that it will make many more sales of an item if it is priced at $0.99 rather than $1.00 because shoppers irrationally perceive $0.99 to be a much more attractive deal than $1.00. Essentially, this is a mental shortcut that people often take when faced with a lot of data, as noted in the bounded rationality discussion earlier in this chapter.

Limited-time sales like Labour Day sales and Black Friday sales are another example of how retailers take advantage of shoppers' framing bias. Retailers know that, overall, shoppers will buy more when prices are perceived to be low for a limited amount of time compared to a policy of keeping prices at a constant, low level. Retailers are exploiting shoppers' irrational perception that "I had better buy a lot now, because prices will never be this low again."

Framing isn't only about prices. Advertisers know that you are much more likely to buy a medicine if the advertisement says "effective in 75% of cases" than if it says "ineffective in 25% of cases," although both statements are equally true.

Retailers also make use of shoppers' tendency to engage in what social scientists call *anchoring*, making decisions according to some perceived benchmark or reference point. For example, retailers attempt to influence shoppers' belief about whether they are getting a good deal by showing both the full price (the anchor) and the discounted price.

Status Quo Bias Another irrational behaviour is **status quo bias,** the tendency to avoid making a decision altogether. A well-known example is the way that employees make decisions about investing in their employer-directed retirement accounts. With a retirement saving account, employees can, through payroll deductions, set aside part of their salary tax-free, a practice that saves a significant amount of money every year in taxes. Some companies operate on an opt-in basis: employees have to actively choose to participate in a retirement saving account. Other companies operate on an opt-out basis: employees are automatically enrolled in a retirement saving account unless they choose to opt out.

If everyone behaved rationally, then the proportion of employees enrolled in retirement saving accounts at opt-in companies would be roughly equal to the proportion enrolled at opt-out companies. In other words, your decision about whether to participate in a retirement saving account should be independent of the default choice at your company. But, in reality, when companies switch to automatic enrollment and an opt-out system, employee enrollment rises dramatically. Clearly, people tend to just go with the status quo. Yet, rational people know that, in the end, the act of not making a choice is still a choice.

Why do people exhibit status quo bias? Some claim it's a form of "decision paralysis": when given more options, people find it harder to make a decision. Others claim it's due to loss aversion and the fear of regret, to thinking that "if I do nothing, then I won't have to regret my choice." Irrational, yes. But not altogether surprising. The recognition of status quo bias has led to the practice of incorporating **nudges** into the status quo choices in order to "nudge" people to make more rational choices. Automatic enrollment into a retirement saving account is a classic example of a nudge.

However, rational people know that, in the end, the act of not making a choice is still a choice.

Rational Models for Irrational People?

So why do economists still use models based on rational behaviour when people are at times manifestly irrational? For one thing, models based on rational behaviour still provide robust predictions about how people behave in most markets.

Framing bias is the tendency to make decisions based upon how choices are presented rather than on a comparison of their true values.

The **status quo bias** is the tendency to avoid making a decision and sticking with the status quo.

A **nudge** is a formulation of the status quo choice intended to shift people to more rational choices when they are prone to status quo bias.

For example, the great majority of farmers will use less fertilizer when it becomes more expensive—a result consistent with rational behaviour.

Another explanation is that sometimes market forces can compel people to behave more rationally over time. For example, if you are a small-business owner who persistently exaggerates your abilities or refuses to acknowledge that your favourite line of items is a loser, then sooner or later you will be out of business unless you learn to correct your mistakes. As a result, it is reasonable to assume that when people are disciplined for their mistakes, as happens in most markets, rationality will win out over time.

Finally, economists depend on the assumption of rationality for the simple but fundamental reason that it makes modelling so much simpler. Remember that models are built on generalizations, and it's much harder to extrapolate from messy, irrational behaviour. Even behavioural economists, in their research, search for *predictably* irrational behaviour in an attempt to build better models of how people behave. Clearly, there is an ongoing dialogue between behavioural economists and the rest of the economics profession, and economics itself has been irrevocably changed by it.

ECONOMICS >> *in Action*
In Praise of Hard Deadlines

Dan Ariely, a professor of psychology and behavioural economics, likes to do experiments with his students that help him explore the nature of irrationality. In his book *Predictably Irrational,* Ariely describes an experiment that gets to the heart of procrastination and ways to address it.

At the time, Ariely was teaching the same subject matter to three different classes, but he gave each class different assignment schedules. The grade in all three classes was based on three equally weighted papers.

Students in the first class were required to choose their own personal deadlines for submitting each paper. Once set, the deadlines could not be changed. Late papers would be penalized at the rate of 1% of the grade for each day late. Papers could be turned in early without penalty but also without any advantage, since Ariely would not grade papers until the end of the semester.

Students in the second class could turn in the three papers whenever they wanted, with no preset deadlines, as long as it was before the end of the term. Again, there would be no benefit for early submission.

Students in the third class faced what Ariely called the "dictatorial treatment." He established three hard deadlines at the fourth, eighth, and twelfth weeks.

So which classes do you think achieved the best and the worst grades? As it turned out, the class with the least flexible deadlines—the one that received the dictatorial treatment—got the best grades. The class with complete flexibility got the worst grades. And the class that got to choose its deadlines performed in the middle.

Ariely learned two simple things about overconfidence from these results. First—no surprise—students tend to procrastinate. Second, hard, equally spaced deadlines are the best cure for procrastination.

But the biggest revelation came from the class that set its own deadlines. The majority of those students spaced their deadlines far apart and got grades as good as those of the students under the dictatorial treatment. Some, however, did not space their deadlines far enough apart, and a few did not space them out at all. These last two groups did less well, putting the average of the entire class below the average of the class with the least flexibility. As Ariely notes, without well-spaced deadlines, students procrastinate and the quality of their work suffers.

This experiment provides two important insights:

1. People who acknowledge their tendency to procrastinate are more likely to use tools for committing to a path of action.
2. Providing those tools allows people to make themselves better off.

If you procrastinate, hard deadlines, as irksome as they may be, are truly for your own good.

>> Check Your Understanding 9-4
Solutions appear at back of book.

1. Which of the types of irrational behaviour are suggested by the following events?
   a. Although the housing market has fallen and Jenny wants to move, she refuses to sell her house for any amount less than what she paid for it.
   b. When Leo shops, he likes to take advantage of the "two-for-one" or "three-for-two" offers that stores frequently display. As a result, he often buys more than he needs and ends up giving much of it away.
   c. Danilo has just started his first job and deliberately decided to opt out of the company's savings plan. His reasoning is that he is very young and there is plenty of time in the future to start saving. Why not enjoy life now?
   d. Emma's company requires employees to download and fill out a form if they want to participate in the company-sponsored savings plan. One year after starting the job, Emma had still not submitted the form needed to participate in the plan.
2. How would you determine whether a decision you made was rational or irrational?

>> Quick Review

• **Behavioural economics** combines economic modelling with insights from human psychology in order to understand how people actually make decisions.

• **Rational** behaviour leads to the most preferred outcome for a person given all the available choices. Due to **bounded rationality, risk aversion, nonmonetary rewards,** and concerns about fairness, it may be rational to choose outcomes with lower economic payoffs compared to other available choices.

• **Irrational** behaviour leads to an outcome that leaves a person worse off than they would be if they chose another available option. Common types of irrational behaviour are misperceptions of opportunity costs, overconfidence, **mental accounting,** unrealistic expectations about the future, **loss aversion, framing bias,** and **status quo bias.** The **sunk cost fallacy** is an example of the misperception of opportunity cost. **Nudges** are frequently incorporated into status quo choices to induce more rational behaviour.

Costco Canada Wins over Customers

Oleksiy Maksymenko Photography/Alamy

In 2017, an article by Hollie Shaw entitled "How Costco Canada Breaks Retail Rules to Win" appeared in the *Financial Post*. The article outlines some of the strategies that allowed Costco to become Canada's most trusted food and drug retailer with the highest level of customer satisfaction of all retailers.

To be able to shop there, Costco charges an annual membership fee that starts at $60. It turns out that charging such a fee is not only treated by consumers as a sunk cost, it builds a bond, a feeling of belonging, to an exclusive club. So rather than driving customers away, the fee has attracted a growing membership base.

Another strategy Costco has adopted is to limit the number of different goods it carries for sale at any one point in time. Studies of consumer behaviour have found that people find it much easier to make a choice when not faced with too many options. This strategy is clearly working for Costco, as in 2019 its revenue had risen to over $28 billion at 100 warehouse locations in Canada. Also, according to a study by the Bank of Montreal, Costco's share of Canada's grocery market rose from 9% in 2013 to 11% in 2017.

A third Costco strategy is to have about half of its product menu change every few weeks and to bring in some items temporarily for limited-time sales road shows. Having a portion of its goods available for an unknown or limited time creates a sense of scarcity. This feeling of scarcity can motivate people to buy an item now for fear of missing out if they wait. In the end, the consumer may end up with a deal, but they also might end up with an item they really truly don't need. This works out well for the seller who, as a result, has earned more revenue.

Finally, Costco has also been able to be successful with the assistance of a generous return policy, high quality offerings, everyday low prices, and weekly markdowns of selected merchandise. Taken together, Costco Canada's strategies have allowed the company to earn revenues that are one fifth as large as Costco earns in the United States.

QUESTIONS FOR THOUGHT

1. Give an example of a type of rational decision making illustrated by this case and explain your choice.

2. Give an example of a type of irrational decision making illustrated by this case and explain your choice.

3. What purpose does Costco's generous return policy serve? What do you predict would happen if it dropped this policy? Would you predict its competitors—say, the local supermarket or The Bay—would adopt the same policy?

SUMMARY

1. All economic decisions involve the allocation of scarce resources. Some decisions are "either–or" decisions, in which the question is whether or not to do something. Other decisions are "how much" decisions, in which the question is how much of a resource to put into a given activity.

2. The cost of using a resource for a particular activity is the opportunity cost of that resource. Some opportunity costs are **explicit costs;** they involve a direct outlay of money. Other opportunity costs, however, are **implicit costs;** they involve no outlay of money but are measured by the dollar value of the benefits that are forgone. Both explicit and implicit costs should be taken into account in making decisions. Many decisions involve the use of **capital** and time, for both individuals and firms. So they should base decisions on **economic profit,** which takes into account implicit costs such as the opportunity cost of time and the **implicit cost of capital.** Making decisions based on **accounting profit** can be misleading. It is often considerably larger than economic profit because it includes only explicit costs and not implicit costs.

3. According to the **principle of "either–or" decision making,** when faced with an "either–or" choice between two activities, one should choose the activity with the positive economic profit.

4. A "how much" decision is made using marginal analysis, which involves comparing the benefit to the cost of doing an additional unit of an activity. The **marginal cost** of producing a good or service is the additional cost incurred by producing one more unit of that good or service. The **marginal benefit** of producing a good or service is the additional benefit earned by producing one more unit. The **marginal cost curve** is the graphical illustration of marginal cost, and the **marginal benefit curve** is the graphical illustration of marginal benefit.

5. In the case of **constant marginal cost,** each additional unit costs the same amount to produce as the previous unit. However, marginal cost and marginal benefit typically depend on how much of the activity has already been done. With **increasing marginal cost,** each unit costs more to produce than the previous unit and is represented by an upward-sloping marginal cost curve. With **decreasing marginal cost,** each unit costs less to produce than the previous unit, leading to a downward-sloping marginal cost curve. In the case of **decreasing marginal benefit,** each additional unit produces a smaller benefit than the unit before.

6. The **optimal quantity** is the quantity that generates the highest possible total profit. According to the **profit-maximizing principle of marginal analysis,** the optimal quantity is the quantity at which marginal benefit is greater than or equal to marginal cost. It is the quantity at which the marginal cost curve and the marginal benefit curve intersect.

7. A cost that has already been incurred and that is nonrecoverable is a **sunk cost.** Sunk costs should be ignored in decisions about future actions because they have no effect on future benefits and costs. The **sunk cost fallacy** is the mistaken belief that sunk costs should be counted in making a decision.

8. **Behavioural economics,** a branch of economics that has become very influential in the past 20 years, combines economic modelling with insights from psychology to understand how people actually make decisions.

9. With **rational** behaviour, individuals will choose the available option that leads to the outcome they most prefer. However, it may be rational to choose an outcome with a lower economic payoff. The four principal reasons why are concerns over fairness, **nonmonetary rewards,** bounded rationality, and risk aversion. **Bounded rationality** occurs because the effort needed to find the best economic payoff is costly. **Risk aversion** causes individuals to sacrifice some economic payoff in order to avoid a potential loss.

10. An **irrational** choice leaves a person worse off than if they had chosen another available option. There are seven common forms that irrational behaviour takes: misperceptions of opportunity cost; overconfidence; unrealistic expectations about future behaviour; **mental accounting,** in which dollars are valued unequally; **loss aversion,** an oversensitivity to loss; **framing bias,** in which decisions are made based upon how choices are presented rather than on their true value; and **status quo bias,** avoiding a decision by sticking with the status quo. **Nudges,** changes to the status quo in order to induce more rational choices, are frequently used.

KEY TERMS

Profit-maximizing principle of marginal analysis, p. 274

Sunk cost, p. 277

Behavioural economics, p. 279

Rational, p. 279

Nonmonetary rewards, p. 279

Bounded rationality, p. 280

Risk aversion, p. 280

Irrational, p. 280

Sunk cost fallacy, p. 281

Mental accounting, p. 282

Loss aversion, p. 282

Framing bias, p. 283

Status quo bias, p. 283

Nudges, p. 283

PRACTICE QUESTIONS

1. A study on student loan default rates by the Brookings Institution found an interesting correlation. Generally, students that needed to borrow more money to attend a four-year institution were less likely to default than students with a lower level of debt. Students that started college in 2003 borrowed an average of US$15,000 and had a default rate of 17.1%. Breaking down the data, students that completed a four-year bachelor's degree borrowed an average of US$25,000 but had a significantly lower default rate of only 5.6%. Whereas, students that dropped out of college only borrowed US$7,500 but had a default rate that was more than four times greater, 23.9%. Use the concept of marginal analysis to explain the student loan default rate data above.

2. Discuss how each of the following statements represent framing bias:

   i. Financial advisors will provide guidance on retirement and savings options for a small fee. They often promote their investing abilities over other advisors. The stock market has fallen 5% for the year but you see an ad for a financial advisor, "our investments have outperformed our competitors by 2%." Why doesn't the advisor want to advertise their actual return?

   ii. A recent study found that high school seniors and college students were less likely to attend a four-year institution when offered a financial aid package that included the word "loan" when compared with a financially equivalent package that omitted the word "loan." In fact, when using the term "loan," students were 10% less likely to attending that particular university.

3. You and your roommate are in a dilemma. You are both taking economics and accounting and have an economics exam tomorrow afternoon. You're worried that you won't have enough study time and are debating skipping accounting to use the time to study for the exam. You're not worried about your accounting grade, but your roommate is still trying to convince you to not skip accounting because you've already paid your tuition. Explain how your roommate is guilty of committing a sunk cost fallacy.

PROBLEMS

1. Jackie owns and operates a website design business. To keep up with new technology, she spends $5,000 per year upgrading her computer equipment. She runs the business out of a room in her home. If she didn't use the room as her business office, she could rent it out for $2,000 per year. Jackie knows that if she didn't run her own business, she could return to her previous job at a large software company that would pay her a salary of $60,000 per year. Jackie has no other expenses.

   a. How much total revenue does Jackie need to make in order to break even in the eyes of her accountant? That is, how much total revenue would give Jackie an accounting profit of just zero?

   b. How much total revenue does Jackie need to make in order for her to want to remain self-employed? That is, how much total revenue would give Jackie an economic profit of just zero?

2. You own and operate a bike store. Each year, you receive revenue of $200,000 from your bike sales, and it costs you $100,000 to obtain the bikes. In addition, you pay $20,000 for electricity, taxes, and other expenses per year. Instead of running the bike store, you could become an accountant and receive a yearly salary of $40,000. A large clothing retail chain wants to expand and offers to rent the store from you for $50,000 per year. How do you explain to your friends

that despite making a profit, it is too costly for you to continue running your store?

3. Suppose you have just paid a nonrefundable fee of $1,000 for your meal plan for this academic term. This allows you to eat dinner in the cafeteria every evening.

   a. You are offered a part-time job in a restaurant where you can eat for free each evening. Your parents say that you should eat dinner in the cafeteria anyway, since you have already paid for those meals. Are your parents right? Explain why or why not.

   b. You are offered a part-time job in a different restaurant where, rather than being able to eat for free, you receive only a large discount on your meals. Each meal there will cost you $2; if you eat there each evening this semester, it will add up to $200. Your roommate says that you should eat in the restaurant since it costs less than the $1,000 that you paid for the meal plan. Is your roommate right? Explain why or why not.

4. You have bought a $10 ticket in advance for the university soccer game, a ticket that cannot be resold. You know that going to the soccer game will give you a benefit equal to $20. After you have bought the ticket, you hear that there will be a professional baseball postseason game at the same time. Tickets to the baseball

game cost $20, and you know that going to the baseball game will give you a benefit equal to $35. You tell your friends the following: "If I had known about the baseball game before buying the ticket to the soccer game, I would have gone to the baseball game instead. But now that I already have the ticket to the soccer game, it's better for me to just go to the soccer game." Are you making the correct decision? Justify your answer by calculating the benefits and costs of your decision.

5. Amy, Bill, and Carla all mow lawns for money. Each of them operates a different lawn mower. The accompanying table shows the total cost to Amy, Bill, and Carla of mowing lawns.

Quantity of lawns mowed	Amy's total cost	Bill's total cost	Carla's total cost
0	$0	$0	$0
1	20	10	2
2	35	20	7
3	45	30	17
4	50	40	32
5	52	50	52
6	53	60	82

a. Calculate Amy's, Bill's, and Carla's marginal costs, and draw each of their marginal cost curves.

b. Who has increasing marginal cost, who has decreasing marginal cost, and who has constant marginal cost?

6. You are the manager of a gym, and you have to decide how many customers to admit each hour. Assume that each customer stays exactly one hour. Customers are costly to admit because they inflict wear and tear on the exercise equipment. Moreover, each additional customer generates more wear and tear than the customer before. As a result, the gym faces increasing marginal cost. The accompanying table shows the marginal costs associated with each number of customers per hour.

Quantity of customers per hour	Marginal cost of customer
0	
1	$14.00
2	14.50
3	15.00
4	15.50
5	16.00
6	16.50
7	17.00

a. Suppose that each customer pays $15.25 for a one-hour workout. Use the profit-maximizing principle of marginal analysis to find the optimal number of customers that you should admit per hour.

b. You increase the price of a one-hour workout to $16.25. What is the optimal number of customers per hour that you should admit now?

7. Georgia and Lauren are economics students who go to a karate class together. Both have to choose how many classes to go to per week. Each class costs $20. The accompanying table shows Georgia's and Lauren's estimates of the marginal benefit that each of them gets from each class per week.

Quantity of classes	Lauren's marginal benefit of each class	Georgia's marginal benefit of each class
0		
1	$23	$28
2	19	22
3	14	15
4	8	7

a. Use marginal analysis to find Lauren's optimal number of karate classes per week. Explain your answer.

b. Use marginal analysis to find Georgia's optimal number of karate classes per week. Explain your answer.

8. The Canadian National Advisory Committee on Immunization (NACI) recommended against vaccinating the whole population against the smallpox virus because the vaccination has undesirable, and sometimes fatal, side effects. Suppose the accompanying table gives the data that are available about the effects of a smallpox vaccination program.

Percent of population vaccinated	Deaths due to smallpox	Deaths due to vaccination side effects
0%	200	0
10	180	4
20	160	10
30	140	18
40	120	33
50	100	50
60	80	74

a. Calculate the marginal benefit (in terms of lives saved) and the marginal cost (in terms of lives lost) of each 10% increment of smallpox vaccination. Calculate the net increase in human lives for each 10% increment in population vaccinated.

b. Using marginal analysis, determine the optimal percentage of the population that should be vaccinated.

9. Paige delivers pizza using her own car, and she is paid according to the number of pizzas she delivers. The accompanying table shows Paige's total benefit

and total cost when she works a specific number of hours.

Quantity of hours worked	Total benefit	Total cost
0	$0	$0
1	30	10
2	55	21
3	75	34
4	90	50
5	100	70

a. Use marginal analysis to determine Paige's optimal number of hours worked.

b. Calculate the total profit to Paige from working 0 hours, 1 hour, 2 hours, and so on. Now suppose Paige chooses to work for 1 hour. Compare her total profit from working for 1 hour with her total profit from working the optimal number of hours. How much would she lose by working for only 1 hour?

10. Assume De Beers is the sole producer of diamonds. When it wants to sell more diamonds, it must lower its price in order to induce shoppers to buy more. Furthermore, each additional diamond that is produced costs more than the previous one due to the difficulty of mining for diamonds. De Beers's total benefit schedule is given in the accompanying table, along with its total cost schedule.

Quantity of diamonds	Total benefit	Total cost
0	$0	$0
1	1,000	50
2	1,900	100
3	2,700	200
4	3,400	400
5	4,000	800
6	4,500	1,500
7	4,900	2,500
8	5,200	3,800

a. Draw the marginal cost curve and the marginal benefit curve and, from your diagram, graphically derive the optimal quantity of diamonds to produce.

b. Calculate the total profit to De Beers from producing each quantity of diamonds. Which quantity gives De Beers the highest total profit?

11. In each of the following examples, explain whether the decision is rational or irrational. Describe the type of behaviour exhibited.

a. Madison likes to give her best friend Mikayla gift cards that Mikayla can use at her favourite stores. Mikayla often forgets to use the cards before their expiration date or loses them, but she is careful with her own cash.

b. The Western Canada Theatre, in Kamloops, British Columbia, offers Pay-What-You-Can matinees to ensure everyone can experience live theatre. This payment system allows patrons to pay any amount they like for a seat, instead of the fixed price, although the usual prices are publicized as a point of comparison.

c. Dominic has just gotten his teaching degree and has two job offers. One job, replacing a teacher who has gone on leave, will last only two years. It is at a prestigious high school, and he will be paid $35,000 per year. He thinks he will probably be able to find another good job in the area after the two years are up but isn't sure. The other job, also at a high school, pays $25,000 per year and is virtually guaranteed for five years; after those five years, he will be evaluated for a permanent teaching position at the school. About 75% of the teachers who start at the school are hired for permanent positions. Dominic takes the five-year position at $25,000 per year.

d. Kimora has planned a trip to Florida during spring break in March. She has several school projects due after her return. Rather than do them in February, she figures she can take her books with her to Florida and complete her projects there.

e. Sahir overpaid when buying a used car that has turned out to be a lemon. He could sell it for parts, but instead he lets it sit in his garage and deteriorate.

f. Barry considers himself an excellent investor in stocks. He selects new stocks by finding ones with characteristics similar to those of his previous winning stocks. He chalks up losing trades to ups and downs in the macroeconomy.

12. You have been hired as a consultant by a company to develop the company's retirement plan, taking into account different types of predictably irrational behaviour commonly displayed by employees. State at least two types of irrational behaviour employees might display with regard to the retirement plan and the steps you would take to forestall such behaviour.

WORK IT OUT

13. Hiro owns and operates a small business that provides economic consulting services. During the year he spends $57,000 on travel to clients and other expenses. In addition, he owns a computer that he uses for business. If he didn't use the computer, he could sell it and earn yearly interest of $100 on the money created through this sale. Hiro's total revenue for the year is $100,000. Instead of working as a consultant for the year, he could teach economics at a small local college and make a salary of $50,000.

a. What is Hiro's accounting profit?

b. What is Hiro's economic profit?

c. Should Hiro continue working as a consultant, or should he teach economics instead? ■

How to Make Decisions Involving Time: Understanding Present Value

As we learned in Chapter 9, the basic rule to follow when deciding whether or not to undertake a project is to compare the benefits of the project with its costs—explicit as well as implicit—and choose the course of action with the higher economic profit.

But many economic decisions involve choices in which the benefits and the costs arrive at different times, making comparisons between those choices more difficult. For example, the decision about whether to go back to school and get an advanced degree or to get a job, is one of those types of comparisons. If you, Alexa, or Adam choose to get an advanced degree, the costs—forgone wages, tuition, and books—are incurred immediately, while the benefits—higher earnings—are reaped in the future. In other cases, the benefits of a project come earlier than the costs, such as taking out a loan to pay for a vacation that must be repaid in the future. So how should we make decisions when time is a factor?

The economically correct way is to use a concept called *present value*. Using present value calculations allows you to convert costs and/or benefits that arrive in the future into a value today. This way, we can always compare projects that occur over time by comparing their values today. You might wonder why you didn't see present value calculations when we analyzed the decisions in Chapter 9. The fact is that present value was used, but implicitly. For example, statements like "he will receive earnings from the degree valued today at $600,000 over the rest of his lifetime" mean that the future benefits had already been converted into a value today—that value being $600,000.

Now let's see exactly how present value works.

How to Calculate the Present Value of a One-Year Project

Suppose that you will graduate exactly one year from today and you will need $1,000 to rent your first apartment. In order to have $1,000 one year from now, how much do you need today? It's not $1,000, and the reason why has to do with the *interest rate*. The **interest rate,** which we will denote by r, is the price charged a borrower for borrowing money expressed as a percentage of the amount borrowed. And let's use X to denote the amount you need today in order to have $1,000 one year from now. If you put X in the bank today and earn an interest rate r on it, then after one year the bank will pay you $X \times (1 + r)$. If the amount paid to you by the bank one year from now is $1,000, then the amount you need to deposit with the bank today is given by the following equation:

(9A-1) $X \times (1 + r) = \$1,000$

You can apply some basic algebra to find that:

(9A-2) $X = \$1,000/(1 + r)$

When someone borrows money for a year, the **interest rate** is the price, calculated as a percentage of the amount borrowed, charged by the lender.

The **present value** of X is the amount of money needed today in order to receive X at a future date given the interest rate.

So the amount you need today to be assured of having $1,000 one year from now, X, is equal to $1,000 divided by $(1+r)$. Notice that the value of X depends on the interest rate, r, which is always greater than zero. This fact implies that X is always less than $1,000. For example, if $r = 5\%$ (that is, $r = 0.05$), then $X = \$1,000/1.05 = \$952.38$. In other words, $952.38 is the value today of receiving $1,000 one year from now given an interest rate of 5%.

Now we can define the **present value** of X: it is the amount of money needed today in order to receive X in the future given the interest rate. In this example, $952.38 is the present value of $1,000 today given an interest rate of 5%.

The concept of present value is very useful when making decisions that require paying upfront costs now for benefits that arrive in the future. Say you had two options, A and B: the choice of taking a one-year job that pays $10,000 immediately (option A) or taking a one-year course that costs $1,000 now but allows you to earn a one-time payment of $12,000 one year from now (option B). Which one should you take?

On the one hand, the present value of option A is simply $10,000 because you receive its payoff immediately. On the other hand, the present value of option B, with an interest rate of 5%, is:

(9A-3) $\$12,000/1.05 - \$1,000 = \$11,429 - \$1,000 = \$10,429$

Since the present value of option B ($10,429) is greater than the present value of option A ($10,000), you should choose option B.

This example illustrates a general principle: when evaluating choices where the costs and/or benefits arrive over time, make your choice by converting the payoffs into their present values and choose the one with the highest present value. Next we will see how to use present value when projects have a time span of more than one year.

How to Calculate the Present Value of Multiyear Projects

Let's represent the value of $1 to be received two years from now as $X_{2\text{yrs}}$. If you lend out $X_{2\text{yrs}}$ today for two years, you will receive:

(9A-4) $X_{2\text{yrs}} \times (1+r)$ at the end of one year

which you then reinvest to receive:

(9A-5) $X_{2\text{yrs}} \times (1+r) \times (1+r) = X_{2\text{yrs}} \times (1+r)^2$ at the end of two years

From Equation 9A-5 we can calculate how much you would have to lend today in order to receive $1 two years from now:

(9A-6) $X_{2\text{yrs}}(1+r)^2 = \$1$

To solve for $X_{2\text{yrs}}$, divide both sides of Equation 9A-6 by $(1+r)^2$ to arrive at:

(9A-7) $X_{2\text{yrs}} = \$1/(1+r)^2$

For example, if $r = 0.10$, then $X_{2\text{yrs}} = \$1/(1.10)^2 = \$1/1.21 = \$0.83$.

Equation 9A-7 points the way toward the general expression for present value, where $1 is paid after N years. It is:

(9A-8) $X_{N\text{yrs}} = \$1/(1+r)^N$

In other words, the present value of $1 to be received N years from now is equal to $\$1/(1+r)^N$.

How to Calculate the Present Value of Projects with Revenues and Costs

Now let's suppose you have to choose which one of three projects to undertake. Project A gives you an immediate payoff of $100. Project B costs you $10 now and pays $115 a year from now. Project C gives you an immediate payoff of $119 but requires you to pay $20 a year from now. We will assume that $r = 0.10$.

In order to compare these three projects, you must evaluate costs and revenues that are expended or realized at different times. It is here, of course, that the concept of present value is extremely handy: by using present value to convert any dollars realized in the future into today's value, you can factor out differences in time. Once differences in time are factored out, you can compare the three projects by calculating each one's *net present value,* the present value of current and future revenues minus the present value of current and future costs. The best project to undertake is the one with the highest net present value.

Table 9A-1 shows how to calculate the net present value of each of the three projects. The second and third columns show how many dollars are realized and when they are realized; costs are indicated by a minus sign. The fourth column shows the equations used to convert the flows of dollars into their present value, and the fifth column shows the actual amounts of the total net present value for each of the three projects.

For instance, to calculate the net present value of project B, you need to calculate the present value of $115 received one year from now. The present value of $1 received one year from now is $\$1/(1+r)$. So the present value of $115 received one year from now is $\$115 \times 1/(1+r) = \$115/(1+r)$. The net present value of project B is the present value of current and future revenues minus the present value of current and future costs: $-\$10 + \$115/(1+r)$.

From the fifth column, we can immediately see that, at an interest rate of 10%, project C is the best project. It has the highest net present value, $100.82, which is higher than the net present value of project A ($100) and much higher than the net present value of project B ($94.55).

This example shows how important the concept of present value is. If we had failed to use the present value calculations and had instead simply added up the revenues and costs, we would have been misled into believing that project B was the best project and C was the worst one.

TABLE 9A-1 The Net Present Value of Three Hypothetical Projects

Project	Dollars realized today	Dollars realized one year from today	Present value formula	Net present value given $r = 0.10$
A	$100	—	$100	$100.00
B	−$10	$115	$-\$10 + \$115/(1+r)$	$94.55
C	$119	−$20	$\$119 - \$20/(1+r)$	$100.82

PROBLEMS

1. Suppose that a major city's main thoroughfare, which is also an highway, will be completely closed to traffic for two years, from January 2018 to December 2019, for reconstruction at a cost of $535 million. If the construction company were to keep the highway open for traffic during construction, the highway recon-struction project would take much longer and be more expensive. Suppose that construction would take four years if the highway were kept open, at a total cost of $800 million. The provincial department of transpor-tation had to make its decision in 2017, one year before the start of construction (so that the first payment was one year away). So the department of transportation had the following choices:

   (i) Close the highway during construction, at an annual cost of $267.5 million per year for two years.

   (ii) Keep the highway open during construction, at an annual cost of $200 million per year for four years.

   a. Suppose the interest rate is 10%. Calculate the pres-ent value of the costs incurred under each plan. Which reconstruction plan is less expensive?

   b. Now suppose the interest rate is 80%. Calculate the present value of the costs incurred under each plan. Which reconstruction plan is now less expensive?

2. You have won the lottery. There are two ways in which you can receive your prize. You can either have $1 million in cash now, or you can have $1.2 million that is paid out as follows: $300,000 now, $300,000 in one year's time, $300,000 in two years' time, and $300,000 in three years' time. The interest rate is 20%. How would you prefer to receive your prize?

3. The drug company Pfizer is considering whether to invest in the development of a new cancer drug. Devel-opment will require an initial investment of $10 mil-lion now; beginning one year from now, the drug will generate annual profits of $4 million for three years.

   a. If the interest rate is 12%, should Pfizer invest in the development of the new drug? Why or why not?

   b. If the interest rate is 8%, should Pfizer invest in the development of the new drug? Why or why not?

The Rational Consumer

THE ABSOLUTE LAST BITE

A POPULAR STYLE OF RESTAURANT, found in many towns across Canada, is the all-you-can-eat buffet. For example, at locations of the Mandarin Restaurant in Southern Ontario, for $26.99 at dinner you can choose from a wide variety of items, such as egg rolls, prime rib, and sushi, all in unlimited quantities.

Paula Solloway/Alamy Stock Photo

When is more of a good thing too much?

But why hasn't the owner of Mandarin been eaten out of business by customers? In other words, what prevents the average customer from wolfing down an amount of food costing far more than $26.99 — say 10 servings of prime rib?

The answer is that even though every once in a while some customers will take advantage of the offer and pile their plates high with 10 servings of prime rib, it's a rare occurrence in real life. That's because the average person knows that, while 1 or 2 servings of prime rib is a treat, 10 servings is likely to lead to an upset stomach. In fact, any sensible person who pays for an all-you-can-eat meal wants to make the

most of it, but making the most of it means knowing when one more bite would be one bite too many.

Notice that last sentence. We said that customers in a restaurant want to "make the most" of their meal; that sounds as if they are trying to maximize something. And we also said that they will stop when consuming one more bite would be a mistake; they are making a marginal decision.

But it is a marginal decision that also involves a person's tastes. While economists can't say much about where tastes come from, they can say a lot about how a rational individual uses marginal analysis to satisfy their tastes. And that is in fact the way that economists think about consumer choice. They work with a model of a *rational consumer* — a consumer who knows what they want and makes the most of the available opportunities.

In this chapter, we will show how to analyze the decisions of a rational consumer. We will begin by showing how the concept of *utility* — a measure of consumer satisfaction — allows us to think about rational consumer choice.

We will then look at how *budget constraints* determine what a consumer can afford to buy and how marginal analysis can be used to determine the consumption choice that maximizes utility.

Finally, we will see how this analysis can be used to understand the law of demand and why the demand curve slopes downward.

For those interested in a more detailed treatment of consumer behaviour and coverage of indifference curves, see the appendix that follows this chapter. ●

WHAT YOU WILL LEARN

- What factors determine how consumers spend their income?
- Why do economists use the concept of **utility** to describe people's tastes?
- Why does the **principle of diminishing marginal utility** accurately describe consumer behaviour?
- What is the **optimal consumption bundle** and why do we use marginal analysis to determine it?
- How do **income** and **substitution effects** show the effects of changes in income and prices on consumers' choices?

The **utility** of a consumer is a measure of the satisfaction the consumer derives from consumption of goods and services.

An individual's **consumption bundle** is the collection of all the goods and services consumed by that individual.

An individual's **utility function** gives the total utility generated by their consumption bundle.

A **util** is a unit of utility.

Utility: Getting Satisfaction

When analyzing consumer behaviour, we're talking about people trying to get satisfaction—that is, about subjective feelings. Yet there is no simple way to measure subjective feelings. How much satisfaction do I get from my third egg roll? Is it less or more than yours? Does it even make sense to ask the question?

Luckily, we don't need to make comparisons between your feelings and mine. All that is required to analyze consumer behaviour is to suppose that each individual is trying to maximize some personal measure of the satisfaction gained from consumption of goods and services. That measure is known as the consumer's **utility,** a concept we use to understand behaviour but don't expect to measure in practice. Nonetheless, we'll see that the assumption that consumers maximize utility helps us think clearly about consumer choice.

Utility and Consumption

An individual's utility depends on everything that individual consumes, from apples to Ziploc bags. The set of all the goods and services an individual consumes is known as the individual's **consumption bundle.** The relationship between an individual's consumption bundle and the total amount of utility it generates for that individual is known as the **utility function.** The utility function is a personal matter; two people with different tastes will have different utility functions. Someone who actually likes to consume 20 egg rolls in a sitting must have a utility function that looks different from that of someone who would rather stop at 3 egg rolls.

So we can think of consumers as using consumption to "produce" utility, much in the same way as in later chapters we will think of producers as using inputs to produce output. However, it's obvious that people do not have a little computer in their heads that calculates the utility generated by their consumption choices. Nonetheless, people must make choices, and they usually base them on at least a rough attempt to decide which choice will give them greater satisfaction. I can have either a Coke or lemonade with my dinner. Which will I enjoy more? I can go backpacking through Europe this summer or save the money toward buying a new car. Which will make me happier?

The concept of a utility function is just a way of representing the fact that when people consume, they take into account their preferences and tastes in a more or less rational way.

How do we measure utility? For the sake of simplicity, it is useful to suppose that we can measure utility in hypothetical units called—what else?—**utils.**

Figure 10-1 illustrates a utility function. It shows the total utility that Cassie, who likes egg rolls, gets from an all-you-can-eat buffet. We suppose that her consumption bundle consists of a Coke plus a number of egg rolls to be determined. The table that accompanies the figure shows how Cassie's total utility depends on the number of egg rolls; the curve in panel (a) of the figure shows that same information graphically.

Cassie's utility function slopes upward over most of the range shown, but it gets flatter as the number of egg rolls consumed increases. And in this example it eventually turns downward. According to the information in the table in Figure 10-1, 9 egg rolls is an egg roll too many. Adding that additional egg roll actually makes Cassie worse off: it would lower her total utility. If she's rational, of course, Cassie will realize that and not consume the ninth egg roll.

So when Cassie chooses how many egg rolls to consume, she will make this decision by considering the *change* in her total utility from consuming one more egg roll. This illustrates the general point: to maximize *total* utility, consumers must focus on *marginal* utility.

FIGURE 10-1 Cassie's Total Utility and Marginal Utility

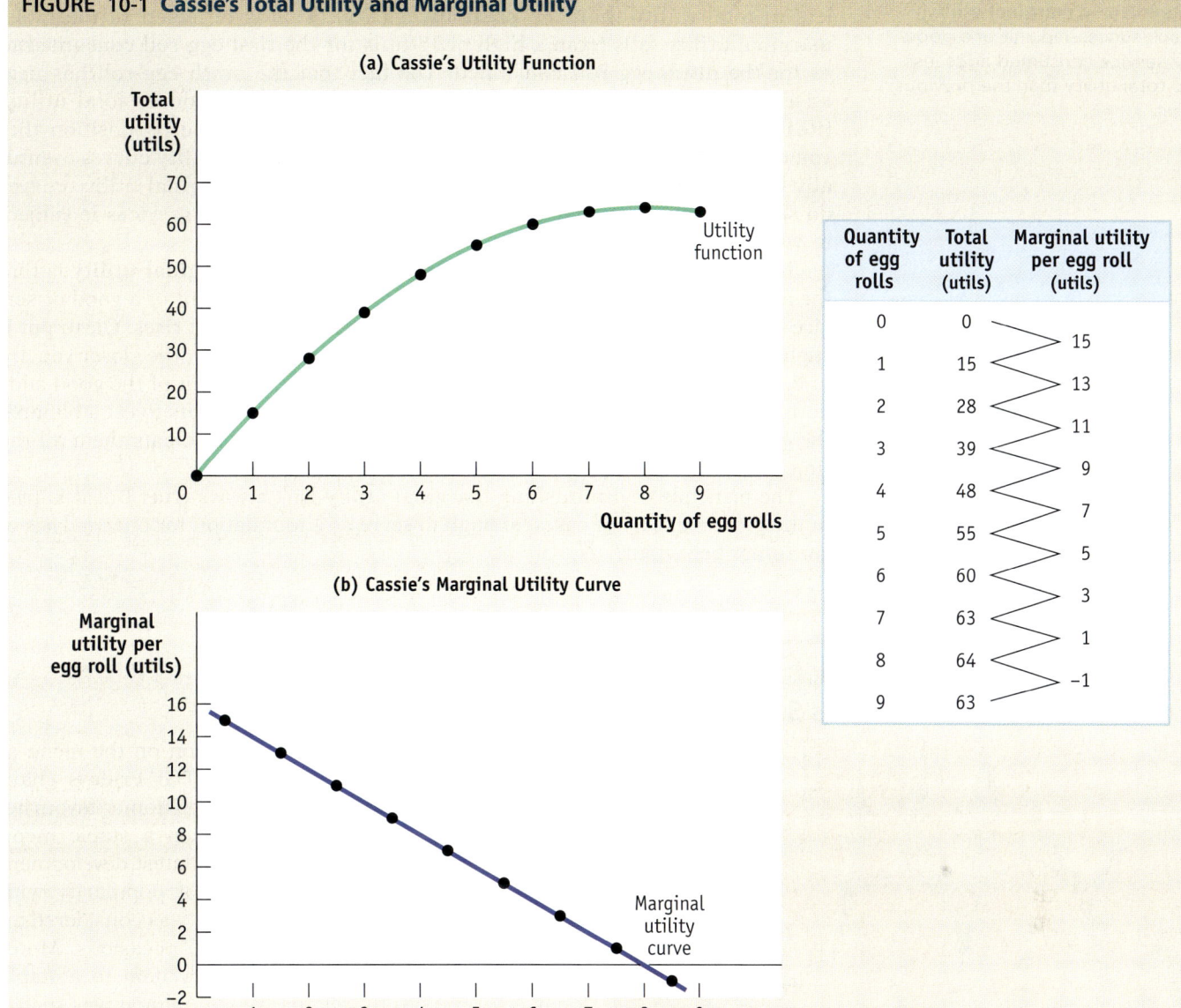

Quantity of egg rolls	Total utility (utils)	Marginal utility per egg roll (utils)
0	0	
		15
1	15	
		13
2	28	
		11
3	39	
		9
4	48	
		7
5	55	
		5
6	60	
		3
7	63	
		1
8	64	
		−1
9	63	

Panel (a) shows how Cassie's total utility depends on her consumption of egg rolls. It increases until it reaches its maximum utility level of 64 utils at 8 egg rolls consumed and decreases after that. Marginal utility is calculated in the table. Panel (b) shows the marginal utility curve, which slopes downward due to diminishing marginal utility. That is, each additional egg roll gives Cassie less additional utility than the previous egg roll.

The Principle of Diminishing Marginal Utility

In addition to showing how Cassie's total utility depends on the number of egg rolls she consumes, the table in Figure 10-1 also shows the **marginal utility** generated by consuming each additional egg roll—that is, the *change* in total utility from consuming one additional egg roll. Panel (b) shows the implied **marginal utility curve.** Following our practice in Chapter 9 with the marginal benefit curve, the marginal utility curve is constructed by plotting points at the midpoint of the unit intervals.

The **marginal utility** of a good or service is the change in total utility generated by consuming one additional unit of that good or service. The **marginal utility curve** shows how marginal utility depends on the quantity of a good or service consumed.

According to the **principle of diminishing marginal utility,** each successive unit of a good or service consumed adds less to total utility than the previous unit.

The marginal utility curve slopes downward: each successive egg roll adds less to total utility than the previous egg roll. This is reflected in the table: marginal utility falls from a high of 15 utils for the first egg roll consumed to −1 for the ninth egg roll consumed. The fact that the ninth egg roll has negative marginal utility means that consuming it actually reduces total utility. (Restaurants that offer all-you-can-eat meals depend on the proposition that you can have too much of a good thing.) Not all marginal utility curves eventually become negative. But it is generally accepted that marginal utility curves do slope downward—that consumption of most goods and services is subject to *diminishing marginal utility.*

The basic idea behind the **principle of diminishing marginal utility** is that the additional satisfaction a consumer gets from one more unit of a good or service declines as the amount of that good or service consumed rises. Or, to put it slightly differently, the more of a good or service you consume, the closer you are to being *satiated*—reaching a point at which an additional unit of the good adds nothing to your satisfaction. For someone who almost never gets to eat a banana, the occasional banana is a marvelous treat. For someone who eats them all the time, a banana is just, well, a banana.

The principle of diminishing marginal utility isn't always true. But it is true in the great majority of cases, enough to serve as a foundation for our analysis of consumer behaviour.

ECONOMICS >> *in Action*
Is Salmon a Luxury? It Depends

Diminishing marginal utility and changes in supply have put salmon on a culinary roller-coaster.

These days, it's common to find salmon on the menu at local restaurants. For example, the TGI Fridays chain touts its "simply grilled salmon," as a customer favourite. However, salmon has not always been a staple menu item in Canada. This trend is just the latest development in salmon's long roller-coaster ride of popularity with Canadian diners. In the 1950s, salmon was considered an expensive luxury, reserved for special occasions. Moreover, the turn from yesterday's luxury item to a staple today is a reversal. In Colonial times, salmon was such a cheap and plentiful fish that servants had clauses in their contracts stipulating that salmon could not be served to them more than a certain number of times a week.

What's behind the extreme changes in salmon's status? The answer is diminishing marginal utility coupled with changes in supply. In the unspoiled nature during the Colonial times, salmon was so plentiful that the fish glutted rivers, lakes, and streams. But by the 1980s, pollution and overfishing threatened salmon with extinction. As a *New York Times* article from 1981 stated, "Only in the last 25 years, because of dwindling numbers, has salmon climbed the culinary scale to become a luxury."

Since then, salmon supply has made a massive comeback, thanks to the advances made by aquaculture, commonly known as fish farming. In 1982, 13,265 tonnes of fish-farmed salmon was produced worldwide. By 2015, that number had increased 1500% to well over 2 million tonnes.

So in Colonial times, when salmon was extraordinarily plentiful and eaten all the time, diminishing marginal utility made one more serving of salmon a low marginal utility event. And, in the 1980s, when salmon was near extinction, its rarity made one more serving a high marginal utility event. Now that supplies are somewhat plentiful again, salmon is neither a luxury nor a food to be avoided. Instead, it falls somewhere in between—an appealing option to be found on the menu at restaurants near you.

>> Check Your Understanding 10-1

Solutions appear at back of book.

1. Explain why a rational consumer who has diminishing marginal utility for a good would not consume an additional unit when it generates negative marginal utility, even when that unit is free.

2. Marta drinks three cups of coffee a day, for which she has diminishing marginal utility. Which of her three cups generates the greatest increase in total utility? Which generates the least?

3. In each of the following cases, determine if the consumer experiences diminishing marginal utility. Explain your answer.
   a. The more Mabel exercises, the more she enjoys each additional visit to the gym.
   b. Although Mei's collection of vinyl records is huge, her enjoyment from buying another album has not changed as her collection has grown.
   c. When Dexter was a struggling student, his enjoyment from a good restaurant meal was greater than it is now that he can afford to have them more frequently.

>> Quick Review
• **Utility** is a measure of a consumer's satisfaction from consumption, expressed in units of **utils.** Consumers try to maximize their utility. A consumer's **utility function** shows the relationship between the **consumption bundle** and the total utility it generates.

• To maximize utility, a consumer considers the **marginal utility** from consuming one more unit of a good or service, illustrated by the **marginal utility curve.**

• In the consumption of most goods and services, and for most people, the **principle of diminishing marginal utility** holds: each successive unit consumed adds less to total utility than the previous unit.

‖ Budgets and Optimal Consumption

The principle of diminishing marginal utility explains why most people eventually reach a limit, even at an all-you-can-eat buffet where the cost of another egg roll is measured only in future indigestion. Under ordinary circumstances, however, it costs some additional resources to consume more of a good, and consumers must take that cost into account when making choices.

What do we mean by cost? As always, the fundamental measure of cost is *opportunity cost.* Because the amount of money a consumer can spend is limited, a decision to consume more of one good is also a decision to consume less of some other good.

Budget Constraints and Budget Lines

Consider Sammy, whose appetite is exclusively for egg rolls and Coke. He has a weekly income of $20 and since, given his appetite, more of either good is better than less, he spends all of it on egg rolls and Coke. We will assume that egg rolls cost $4 per roll and Coke costs $2 per bottle. What are his possible choices?

Whatever Sammy chooses, we know that the cost of his consumption bundle cannot exceed his income, the amount of money he has to spend. That is:

(10-1) Expenditure on egg rolls + Expenditure on Coke ≤ Total income

Consumers always have limited income, which constrains how much they can consume. So the requirement illustrated by Equation 10-1—that a consumer must choose a consumption bundle that costs no more than their income—is known as the consumer's **budget constraint.** It's a simple way of saying that a consumer can't spend more than the total amount of income available to them. In other words, consumption bundles are affordable when they obey the budget constraint. We call the set of all of Sammy's affordable consumption bundles his **consumption possibilities.** In general, whether or not a particular consumption bundle is included in a consumer's consumption possibilities depends on the consumer's income and the prices of goods and services.

Figure 10-2 shows Sammy's consumption possibilities. The quantity of egg rolls in his consumption bundle is measured on the horizontal axis and the

A **budget constraint** requires that the cost of a consumer's consumption bundle be no more than the consumer's income.

A consumer's **consumption possibilities** is the set of all consumption bundles that can be consumed given the consumer's income and prevailing prices.

FIGURE 10-2 The Budget Line

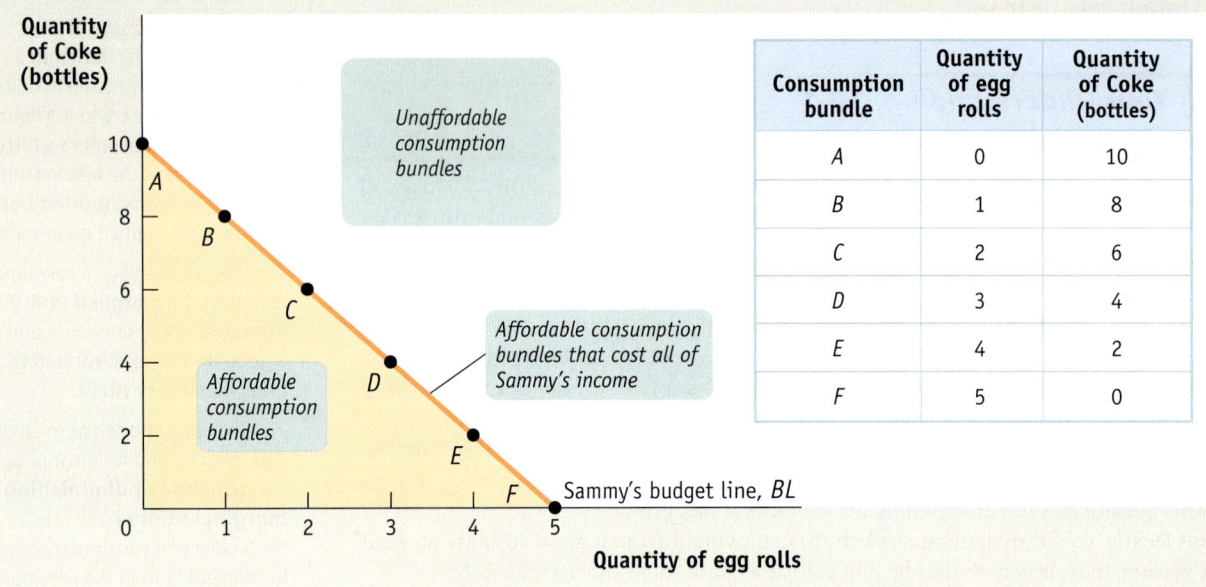

Consumption bundle	Quantity of egg rolls	Quantity of Coke (bottles)
A	0	10
B	1	8
C	2	6
D	3	4
E	4	2
F	5	0

The *budget line* represents the consumption bundles available to Sammy when he spends all of his income. Also, it is the boundary between the set of affordable consumption bundles (the *consumption possibilities*) and unaffordable ones. Given that egg rolls cost $4 per roll and Cokes cost $2 per bottle, if Sammy spends all of his income on egg rolls (bundle *F*), he can purchase 5 egg rolls. If he spends all of his income on Cokes (bundle *A*), he can purchase 10 bottles of Coke.

quantity of Cokes on the vertical axis. The downward-sloping line connecting points *A* through *F* shows which consumption bundles are affordable and which are not. Every bundle on or inside this line (the shaded area) is affordable; every bundle outside this line is unaffordable.

As an example of one of the points, let's look at point *C*, representing 2 egg rolls and 6 Cokes, and check whether it satisfies Sammy's budget constraint. The cost of bundle *C* is 6 bottles of Coke × $2 per bottle + 2 egg rolls × $4 per roll = $12 + $8 = $20. So bundle *C* does indeed satisfy Sammy's budget constraint: it costs no more than his weekly income of $20. In fact, bundle *C* costs exactly as much as Sammy's income. By doing the arithmetic, you can check that all the other points lying on the downward-sloping line are also bundles at which Sammy spends all of his income.

The downward-sloping line has a special name, the **budget line.** It shows all the consumption bundles available to Sammy when he spends all of his income. It's downward sloping because when Sammy is consuming all of his income, say consuming at point *A* on the budget line, then in order to consume more egg rolls he must consume fewer Cokes—that is, he must move to a point like *B*. In other words, when Sammy chooses a consumption bundle that is on his budget line, the opportunity cost of consuming more egg rolls is consuming fewer Cokes, and vice versa. As Figure 10-2 indicates, any consumption bundle that lies above the budget line is unaffordable.

Do we need to consider the other bundles in Sammy's consumption possibilities, the ones that lie *within* the shaded region in Figure 10-2 bounded by the budget line? The answer is, for all practical situations, no: as long as Sammy continues to get positive marginal utility from consuming either good (in other words, Sammy doesn't get *satiated*)—and he doesn't get any utility from saving income rather than spending it—then he will always choose to consume a bundle that lies on his budget line and not within the shaded area.

Given his $20 per week budget, which point on his budget line will Sammy choose?

A consumer's **budget line** shows the consumption bundles available to a consumer who spends all of their income.

Optimal Consumption Choice

Sammy will choose a consumption bundle that lies on his budget line. That's the best he can do given his budget constraint. We want to find the consumption bundle—the point on the budget line—that maximizes Sammy's total utility. This bundle is Sammy's **optimal consumption bundle,** the consumption bundle that maximizes his total utility given the budget constraint.

A consumer's **optimal consumption bundle** is the consumption bundle that maximizes the consumer's total utility given their budget constraint.

Table 10-1 shows how much utility Sammy gets from consuming different amounts of egg rolls and Cokes. As you can see, Sammy has a healthy appetite; the more of either good he consumes, the higher his utility. (Although the quantities are not so large that an additional egg roll or Coke would give him *negative utility,* meaning they wouldn't be rational to consume.)

TABLE 10-1 Sammy's Utility from Egg Roll and Coke Consumption

Utility from egg roll consumption		Utility from Coke consumption	
Quantity of egg rolls	Utility from egg rolls (utils)	Quantity of Coke (bottles)	Utility from Cokes (utils)
0	0	0	0
1	15	1	11.5
2	25	2	21.4
3	31	3	29.8
4	34	4	36.8
5	36	5	42.5
		6	47.0
		7	50.5
		8	53.2
		9	55.2
		10	56.7

But because he has a limited budget, he must make a trade-off: the more egg rolls he consumes, the fewer bottles of Coke, and vice versa. That is, he must choose a point on his budget line.

Table 10-2 shows how Sammy's total utility varies for the different consumption bundles along his budget line. Each of the six possible consumption bundles, *A* through *F* from Figure 10-2, is listed in the first column. The second column shows the number of egg rolls consumed corresponding to each bundle. The third column shows the utility Sammy gets from consuming those egg rolls. The fourth column shows the quantity of Cokes Sammy can afford *given* the level of egg roll consumption. This quantity goes down as the number of egg rolls consumed goes up, because he is sliding down the budget line. The fifth column shows the utility he gets from consuming those Cokes. And the final column shows his *total utility.* In this example, Sammy's total utility is the sum of the utility he gets from egg rolls and the utility he gets from Cokes.

TABLE 10-2 Sammy's Budget and Total Utility

Consumption bundle	Quantity of egg rolls	Utility from egg rolls (utils)	Quantity of Coke (bottles)	Utility from Cokes (utils)	Total utility (utils)
A	0	0	10	56.7	56.7
B	1	15	8	53.2	68.2
C	2	25	6	47.0	72.0
D	3	31	4	36.8	67.8
E	4	34	2	21.4	55.4
F	5	36	0	0	36.0

Figure 10-3 gives a visual representation of the data in Table 10-2. Panel (a) shows Sammy's budget line, to remind us that when he decides to consume more egg rolls he is also deciding to consume fewer Cokes. Panel (b) then shows how his total utility depends on that choice. The horizontal axis in panel (b) has two sets of labels: it shows both the quantity of egg rolls, increasing from left to right, and the quantity of Cokes, increasing from right to left.

The reason we can use the same axis to represent consumption of both goods is, of course, the budget line: the more egg rolls Sammy consumes, the fewer bottles of Coke he can afford, and vice versa.

Clearly, the consumption bundle that makes the best of the trade-off between egg roll consumption and Coke consumption, the optimal consumption bundle, is the one that maximizes Sammy's total utility. That is, Sammy's optimal consumption bundle puts him at the highest point of the total utility curve.

FIGURE 10-3 Optimal Consumption Bundle

Panel (a) shows Sammy's budget line and his six possible consumption bundles. Panel (b) shows how his total utility is affected by his consumption bundle, which must lie on his budget line. The quantity of egg rolls is measured from left to right on the horizontal axis, and the quantity of Cokes is measured from right to left. His total utility is maximized at bundle *C*, the highest point on his utility function, where he consumes 2 egg rolls and 6 bottles of Coke. This is Sammy's *optimal consumption bundle.*

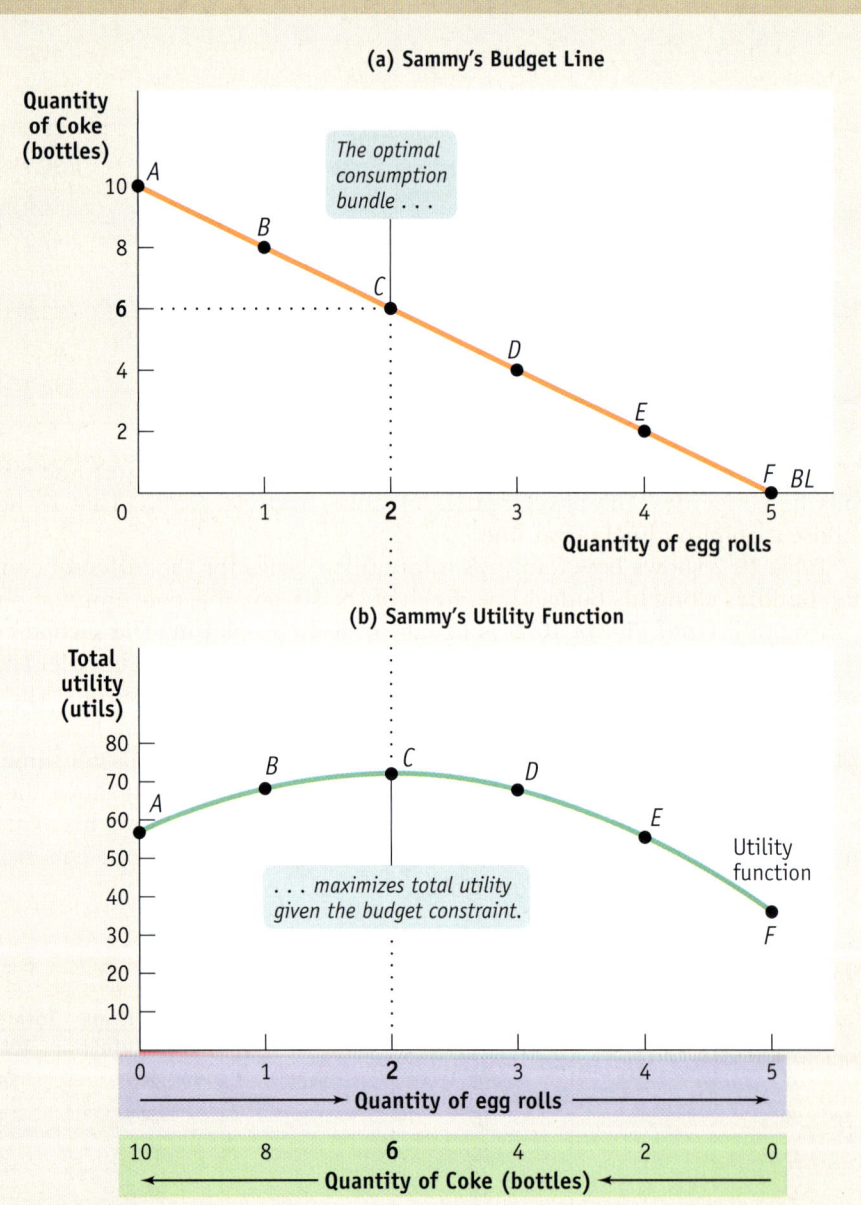

FOR INQUIRING MINDS   Food for Thought on Budget Constraints

Budget constraints aren't just about money. In fact, there are many other budget constraints affecting our lives. You face a budget constraint if you have a limited amount of closet space for your clothes. All of us face a budget constraint on time: there are only so many hours in the day. And people trying to lose weight or improve their health often face a budget constraint on the foods they eat.

The WW (formerly Weight Watchers) diet program is designed to formalize people's food budgets, in order to help them achieve or maintain a healthy weight. The WW plan assigns each food a specific number of points based on calories, saturated fat, sugar, and protein content. For example, a 4-ounce scoop of premium ice cream might be 8 points, a slice of cheese pizza with a medium crust

7 points; most fruits are zero points per serving. Members are allowed a maximum number of points (their points budget) each day but are free to choose which foods they eat.

In other words, someone on the WW plan is just like a consumer choosing a consumption bundle: points are the equivalent of prices, and the overall point limit is the equivalent of total income.

As always, we can find the highest point of the curve by direct observation. We can see from Figure 10-3 that Sammy's total utility is maximized at point *C*, his optimal consumption bundle, which contains 2 egg rolls and 6 bottles of Coke. Here we've solved Sammy's optimal consumption choice problem by calculating and comparing the utility generated by each bundle. But since it is a "how much" problem, marginal analysis will give us greater insight than direct calculation. So in the next section we turn to representing and solving the optimal consumption choice problem with marginal analysis.

ECONOMICS >> *in Action*
The Great Condiment Craze

Have you ever found yourself overwhelmed in the grocery store, trying to decide which mustard to choose? Your grandparents probably never had that problem. In their day, the only kind of mustard available in Canadian grocery stores was a runny, fluorescent yellow concoction packaged in plastic squeeze bottles. Ditto for ketchup and mayonnaise—what little selection there was, tasted the same.

No longer. Canadians have developed an intense liking for condiments—in a dizzying array of varieties. Who wants plain mustard when you can get mustard flavoured with roasted garlic, apricot, or even bourbon/molasses? Likewise, would you like saffron and garlic mayonnaise or sriracha mayonnaise on your sandwich? The sale of mayonnaise and spoonable salad dressing reached $241.82 million in 2019, making this the top selling condiment category in Canada. Mexican salsa dips and ketchup followed with sales of $204.37 million and $147.83 million respectively. Over the next five years, sales are projected to grow faster than the previous five years.

Changing tastes and budgets drove the Canadians condiment craze.

So what happened? Tastes changed and budgets changed. Mass media, immigration, and global trade mean that Canadians are continuously exposed to different cultures and cuisines, making them more willing to try—or even seek out—new flavours. Not only are people wanting to try more flavours, with growing incomes, but many Canadians also have the financial ability to spend more on higher quality condiments that aren't runny and fluorescent yellow. The explosion of varieties also stems from the fact that it's fairly easy to make bottled condiments. This enables smaller companies to experiment with exotic flavours, finding the ones that appeal to consumers' increasingly sophisticated tastes. Eventually, the flavours that attract a significant following are picked up by the larger companies such as Kraft. As one industry analyst put it, "People want cheaper, more specialized gourmet products. It's like fashion."

>> Quick Review

• The **budget constraint** requires that a consumer's total expenditure be no more than their income. The set of consumption bundles that satisfy the budget constraint is the consumer's **consumption possibilities.**

• A consumer who spends all of their income chooses a point on their **budget line.** The budget line slopes downward because on the budget line a consumer must consume less of one good in order to consume more of another.

• The consumption choice that maximizes total utility given the consumer's budget constraint is the **optimal consumption bundle.** It must lie on the consumer's budget line.

>> Check Your Understanding 10-2

Solutions appear at back of book.

1. In the following two examples, find all the consumption bundles that lie on the consumer's budget line. Illustrate these consumption possibilities in a diagram and draw the budget line through them.

   a. The consumption bundle consists of movie tickets and buckets of popcorn. The price of each ticket is $10.00, the price of each bucket of popcorn is $5.00, and the consumer's income is $20.00. In your diagram, put movie tickets on the vertical axis and buckets of popcorn on the horizontal axis.

   b. The consumption bundle consists of underwear and socks. The price of each pair of underwear is $4.00, the price of each pair of socks is $2.00, and the consumer's income is $12.00. In your diagram, put pairs of socks on the vertical axis and pairs of underwear on the horizontal axis.

‖ Spending the Marginal Dollar

As we've just seen, we can find Sammy's optimal consumption choice by finding the total utility he receives from each consumption bundle on his budget line and then choosing the bundle at which total utility is maximized. But we can use marginal analysis instead, turning Sammy's problem of finding his optimal consumption choice into a "how much" problem.

To do this, think about choosing an optimal consumption bundle as a problem of *how much to spend on each good.* That is, to find the optimal consumption bundle with marginal analysis, ask whether Sammy can make himself better off by spending a little bit more of his income on egg rolls and less on Cokes, or by doing the opposite—spending a little bit more on Cokes and less on egg rolls. In other words, the marginal decision is a question of how to *spend the marginal dollar*—how to allocate an additional dollar between egg rolls and bottles of Coke in a way that maximizes utility.

Our first step in applying marginal analysis is to ask if Sammy is made better off by spending an additional dollar on either good; and if so, by how much is he better off. To answer this question we must calculate the **marginal utility per dollar** spent on either egg rolls or Cokes—how much additional utility Sammy gets from spending an additional dollar on either good.

Marginal Utility per Dollar

We've already introduced the concept of *marginal utility,* the additional utility a consumer gets from consuming one more unit of a good or service; now let's see how this concept can be used to derive the related measure of marginal utility per dollar.

Table 10-3 shows how to calculate the marginal utility per dollar spent on egg rolls and Cokes, respectively.

In panel (a) of the table, the first column shows different possible amounts of egg roll consumption. The second column shows the utility Sammy derives from each amount of egg roll consumption; the third column then shows the marginal utility, the increase in utility Sammy gets from consuming an additional egg roll. Panel (b) provides the same information for Cokes. The next step is to derive marginal utility *per dollar* for each good. To do this, we must divide the marginal utility of the good by its price in dollars.

To see why we must divide by the price, compare the third and fourth columns of panel (a). Consider what happens if Sammy increases his egg roll consumption from 2 rolls to 3 rolls. As we can see, this increase in egg roll consumption raises his total utility by 6 utils. But he must spend $4 for that additional roll, so the increase in his utility per additional dollar spent on egg rolls is 6 utils/$4 = 1.5 utils per dollar.

The **marginal utility per dollar** spent on a good or service is the additional utility from spending one more dollar on that good or service.

TABLE 10-3 Sammy's Marginal Utility per Dollar

	(a) Egg rolls (price = $4 per roll)				(b) Cokes (price = $2 per bottle)		
Quantity of egg rolls	Utility from egg rolls (utils)	Marginal utility per roll (utils)	Marginal utility per dollar (utils/$)	Quantity of Coke (bottles)	Utility from Cokes (utils)	Marginal utility per bottle of Coke (utils)	Marginal utility per dollar (utils/$)
0	0			0	0		
		15	3.75			11.5	5.75
1	15			1	11.5		
		10	2.50			9.9	4.95
2	25			2	21.4		
		6	1.50			8.4	4.20
3	31			3	29.8		
		3	0.75			7.0	3.50
4	34			4	36.8		
		2	0.50			5.7	2.85
5	36			5	42.5		
						4.5	2.25
				6	47.0		
						3.5	1.75
				7	50.5		
						2.7	1.35
				8	53.2		
						2.0	1.00
				9	55.2		
						1.5	0.75
				10	56.7		

Similarly, if he increases his egg roll consumption from 3 rolls to 4 rolls, his marginal utility is 3 utils but his marginal utility per dollar is 3 utils/$4 = 0.75 util per dollar. Notice that because of diminishing marginal utility, Sammy's marginal utility per egg roll falls as the quantity of rolls he consumes rises. As a result, his marginal utility per dollar spent on egg rolls also falls as the quantity of rolls he consumes rises.

So the last column of panel (a) shows how Sammy's marginal utility per dollar spent on egg rolls depends on the quantity of rolls he consumes. Similarly, the last column of panel (b) shows how his marginal utility per dollar spent on Coke depends on the quantity of bottles of Coke he consumes. Again, marginal utility per dollar spent on each good declines as the quantity of that good consumed rises, due to diminishing marginal utility.

We will use the symbols MU_r and MU_c to represent the marginal utility per egg roll and bottle of Coke, respectively. And we will use the symbols P_r and P_c to represent the price of egg rolls (per roll) and the price of Coke (per bottle). Then the marginal utility per dollar spent on egg rolls is MU_r/P_r and the marginal utility per dollar spent on Cokes is MU_c/P_c. In general, the additional utility generated from an additional dollar spent on a good is equal to:

(10-2) Marginal utility per dollar spent on a good
= Marginal utility of one unit of the good/Price of one unit of the good
= MU_{Good}/P_{Good}

Now let's see how this concept helps us find the consumer's optimal consumption bundle using marginal analysis.

Optimal Consumption

Let's consider Figure 10-4. As in Figure 10-3, we can measure both the quantity of egg rolls and the quantity of bottles of Coke on the horizontal axis due to the budget constraint. Along the horizontal axis of Figure 10-4—also as in Figure 10-3—the quantity of egg rolls increases as you move from left to right, and the quantity of Cokes increases as you move from right to left. The curve labelled MU_r/P_r in Figure 10-4 shows Sammy's marginal utility per dollar spent on egg rolls as derived in Table 10-3. Likewise, the curve labelled MU_c/P_c shows his marginal utility per dollar spent on Cokes. Notice that the two curves, MU_r/P_r and MU_c/P_c, cross at the optimal consumption bundle, point *C*, consisting of 2 egg rolls and 6 bottles of Coke.

Moreover, Figure 10-4 illustrates an important feature of Sammy's optimal consumption bundle: when Sammy consumes 2 egg rolls and 6 bottles of Coke, his marginal utility per dollar spent is the same, 2, for both goods. That is, at the optimal consumption bundle $MU_r/P_r = MU_c/P_c = 2$.

This isn't an accident. Consider another one of Sammy's possible consumption bundles—say, *B* in Figure 10-3, at which he consumes 1 egg roll and 8 bottles of Coke. The marginal utility per dollar spent on each good is shown by points B_r and B_c in Figure 10-4. At that consumption bundle, Sammy's marginal utility per dollar spent on egg rolls would be approximately 3, but his marginal utility per dollar spent on Cokes would be only approximately 1. This shows that he has made a mistake: he is consuming too many Cokes and not enough egg rolls.

How do we know this? If Sammy's marginal utility per dollar spent on egg rolls is higher than his marginal utility per dollar spent on Cokes, he has a simple way to make himself better off while staying within his budget: spend $1 less on Cokes and $1 more on egg rolls. We can illustrate this with points B_r and B_c in Figure 10-4. By spending an additional dollar on egg rolls, he gains the amount of utility given by B_r, about 3 utils. By spending $1 less on Cokes, he loses the amount of utility given by B_c, only about 1 util.

Because his marginal utility per dollar spent is higher for egg rolls than for Cokes, reallocating his spending toward egg rolls and away from Cokes would

---

FIGURE 10-4 Marginal Utility per Dollar

Sammy's optimal consumption bundle is at point *C*, where his marginal utility per dollar spent on egg rolls, MU_r/P_r, is equal to his marginal utility per dollar spent on Cokes, MU_c/P_c. This illustrates the *utility-maximizing principle of marginal analysis*: at the optimal consumption bundle, the marginal utility per dollar spent on each good and service is the same. At any other consumption bundle on Sammy's budget line, such as bundle *B* in Figure 10-3, represented here by points B_r and B_c, consumption is not optimal: Sammy can increase his utility at no additional cost by reallocating his spending.

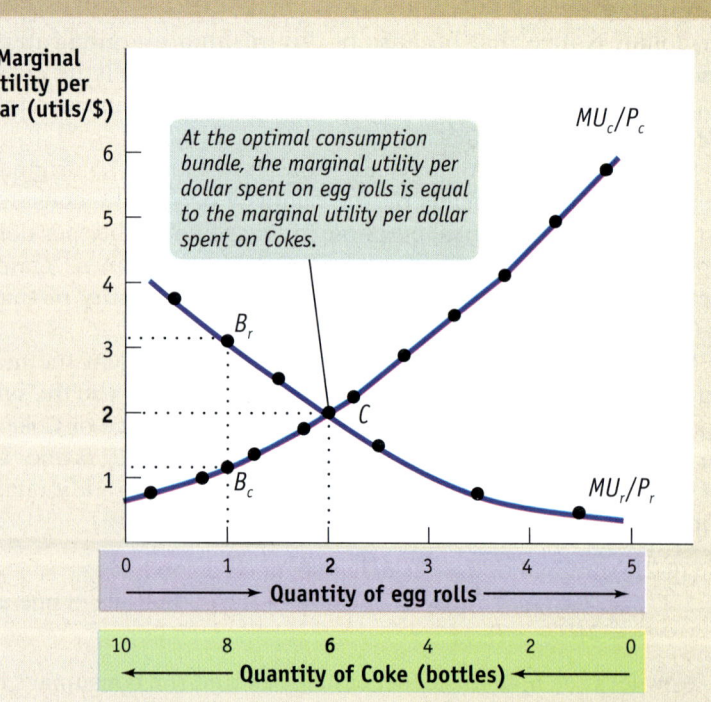

THE RIGHT MARGINAL COMPARISON

Marginal analysis solves "how much" decisions by weighing costs and benefits at the margin: the *benefit* of doing a little bit more versus the *cost* of doing a little bit more. However, the form of the marginal analysis can differ, depending upon whether you are making a production decision that maximizes profits or a consumption decision that maximizes utility. Let's review that difference by returning to an example from Chapter 9.

In Chapter 9, Alexa's decision was a production decision because the problem she faced was maximizing the profit from years of schooling. The optimal quantity of years that maximized her profit was found using marginal analysis: at the optimal quantity, the marginal benefit of another year of schooling was equal to its marginal cost. Alexa did not face a budget constraint because she could always borrow to finance another year of school.

But if you were to extend the way we solved Alexa's production problem to Sammy's consumption problem without any change in form, you might be tempted to say that Sammy's optimal consumption bundle is the one at which the marginal utility of egg rolls is equal to the marginal utility of Cokes, or that the marginal utility of egg rolls is equal to the price of egg rolls. But both those statements would be wrong because they don't properly account for Sammy's budget constraint.

In general, unlike producers, consumers face budget constraints. Consuming more of one good requires consuming less of another. So the consumer's objective is to maximize the utility their limited budget can deliver. The right way to find the optimal consumption bundle is to set the *marginal utility per dollar* equal for each good in the consumption bundle.

When this condition is satisfied, the "bang per buck" is the same across all the goods and services consumed. Only then is there no way to rearrange consumption and get more utility from one's budget.

---

increase his total utility. But if his marginal utility per dollar spent on Cokes is higher, he can increase his utility by spending less on egg rolls and more on Cokes. So if Sammy has in fact chosen his optimal consumption bundle, his marginal utility per dollar spent on egg rolls and Cokes must be equal.

This is a general principle, which we call the **utility-maximizing principle of marginal analysis:** when a consumer maximizes utility in the face of a budget constraint, the marginal utility per dollar spent on each good or service in the consumption bundle is the same. That is, for any two goods r and c the **optimal consumption rule** says that at the optimal consumption bundle:

$$\text{(10-3)} \quad \frac{MU_r}{P_r} = \frac{MU_c}{P_c}$$

It's easiest to understand this rule using examples in which the consumption bundle contains only two goods, but it applies no matter how many goods or services a consumer buys: in the optimal consumption bundle, the marginal utilities per dollar spent for each and every good or service in that bundle are equal.

ECONOMICS >> *in Action*
Buying Your Way Out of Temptation

It might seem odd to pay more to get less. But snack food companies have discovered that consumers are indeed willing to pay more for smaller portions, and that exploiting this trend is a recipe for success. A company executive explained why small packages are popular—they help consumers control portions without having to spend time packaging individual servings themselves. "The irony," said David Adelman, a food industry analyst, "is if you take Wheat Thins or Goldfish, buy a large-size box, count out the items and put them in a Ziploc bag, you'd have essentially the same product." He estimates that snack packs are about 20% more profitable for snack makers than larger packages.

In this case, consumers are making a calculation: the extra utility gained from not having to count out individual portions themselves is worth the extra cost. As one shopper said, "They're pretty expensive, but they're worth it. It's individually packaged for the amount I need, so I don't go overboard." So it's clear that consumers aren't being irrational here. Rather, they're being entirely rational: in addition to their snack, they're buying a little hand-to-mouth restraint.

According to the **utility-maximizing principle of marginal analysis,** the marginal utility per dollar spent must be the same for all goods and services in the optimal consumption bundle.

The **optimal consumption rule** says that (1) the optimal consumption bundle is on the budget line (i.e., our whole budget is spent); and (2) the marginal utility per dollar spent on each good in the bundle is equal.

>> Quick Review

• According to the **utility-maximizing principle of marginal analysis,** the **marginal utility per dollar** — the marginal utility of a good divided by its price — is the same for all goods in the optimal consumption bundle.

• According to the **optimal consumption rule** the optimal consumption bundle (1) is on the budget line; and (2) the marginal utility per dollar spent on each good in the bundle is equal.

• Whenever marginal utility per dollar is higher for one good than for another good, the consumer should spend $1 more on the good with the higher marginal utility per dollar and $1 less on the other. By doing this the consumer will move closer to their optimal consumption bundle. Their optimal consumption bundle is achieved when the marginal utility per dollar is equal across all goods he consumes.

>> Check Your Understanding 10-3
Solutions appear at back of book.

1. In Table 10-3 you can see that marginal utility per dollar spent on egg rolls and marginal utility per dollar spent on Cokes are equal when Sammy increases his consumption of egg rolls from 3 to 4 rolls and his consumption of Cokes from 9 to 10 bottles. Explain why this is not Sammy's optimal consumption bundle. Illustrate your answer using the budget line in Figure 10-3.

2. Explain what is faulty about the following statement, using data from Table 10-3: "In order to maximize utility, Sammy should consume the bundle that gives him the maximum marginal utility per dollar for each good."

‖ From Utility to the Demand Curve

We have now analyzed the optimal consumption choice of a consumer with a given amount of income who faces one particular set of prices — in our Sammy example, $20 of income per week, $4 per egg roll, and $2 per bottle of Coke.

But the main reason for studying consumer behaviour is to go behind the market demand curve — to explain how the utility-maximizing behaviour of individual consumers leads to the downward slope of the market demand curve.

Marginal Utility, the Substitution Effect, and the Law of Demand

Suppose that the price of egg rolls, P_r, rises. The price increase doesn't change the marginal utility a consumer gets from an additional egg roll, MU_r, at any given level of egg roll consumption. However, it does reduce the marginal utility *per dollar spent* on egg rolls, MU_r/P_r. And the decrease in marginal utility per dollar spent on egg rolls gives the consumer an incentive to consume fewer egg rolls when the price of egg rolls rises.

To see why, recall the utility-maximizing principle of marginal analysis: a utility-maximizing consumer chooses a consumption bundle for which the marginal utility per dollar spent on all goods is the same. If the marginal utility per dollar spent on egg rolls falls because the price of egg rolls rises, the consumer can increase their utility by purchasing fewer egg rolls and more of other goods.

The opposite happens if the price of egg rolls falls. In that case the marginal utility per dollar spent on egg rolls, MU_r/P_r, increases at any given level of egg roll consumption. As a result, a consumer can increase their utility by purchasing more egg rolls and less of other goods when the price of egg rolls falls.

So when the price of a good increases, an individual will normally consume less of that good and more of other goods. Correspondingly, when the price of a good decreases, an individual will normally consume more of that good and less of other goods. This explains why the individual demand curve, which relates an individual's consumption of a good to the price of that good, normally slopes downward — that is, it obeys the law of demand. And since — as we learned in Chapter 3 — the market demand curve is the horizontal sum of all the individual demand curves of consumers, it, too, will slope downward.

An alternative way to think about why demand curves slope downward is to focus on opportunity costs. When the price of egg rolls decreases, an individual doesn't have to give up as many units of other goods in order to buy one more egg roll. So consuming egg rolls becomes more attractive. Conversely, when the price of a good increases, consuming that good becomes a less attractive use of resources, and the consumer buys less.

This effect of a price change on the quantity consumed is always present. It is known as the **substitution effect** — the change in the quantity consumed as the consumer substitutes other goods that are now relatively cheaper in place of the good that has become relatively more expensive. When a good absorbs only a small share of the consumer's spending, the substitution effect provides

The **substitution effect** of a change in the price of a good is the change in the quantity of that good consumed as the consumer substitutes other goods that are now relatively cheaper in place of the good that has become relatively more expensive.

the complete explanation of why the consumer's individual demand curve slopes downward. Therefore, when a good absorbs only a small share of the average consumer's spending, the substitution effect provides the sole explanation of why the market demand curve slopes downward.

However, some goods, such as housing, absorb a large share of a typical consumer's spending. For such goods, the story behind the individual demand curve and the market demand curve becomes slightly more complicated.

The Income Effect

For the vast majority of goods, the slopes of the individual and market demand curves are completely determined by the substitution effect. There are, however, some goods, like food or housing, that account for a substantial share of many consumers' spending. In such cases another effect, called the *income effect,* also comes into play.

Consider the case of a family that spends half its income on rental housing. Now suppose that the price of housing increases everywhere. This will have a substitution effect on the family's demand: other things equal, the family will have an incentive to consume less housing—say, by moving to a smaller apartment—and more of other goods. But the family will also, in a real sense, be made poorer by that higher housing price—its income will buy less housing than before.

The amount of income adjusted to reflect its true purchasing power is often termed "real income," in contrast to "money income" or "nominal income," which has not been adjusted. And this reduction in a consumer's real income will have an additional effect, beyond the substitution effect, on the family's consumption bundle, including its consumption of housing.

The change in the quantity of a good consumed that results from a change in the overall purchasing power of the consumer due to a change in the price of that good is known as the **income effect** of the price change. In this case, a change in the price of a good effectively changes a consumer's income because it alters the consumer's purchasing power. Along with the substitution effect, the income effect is another means by which changes in prices alter consumption choices.

It's possible to give more precise definitions of the substitution effect and the income effect of a price change, and we do this in the appendix to this chapter. For most purposes, however, there are only two things you need to know about the distinction between these two effects.

1. For the great majority of goods and services, the income effect is not important and has no significant effect on individual consumption. So most market demand curves slope downward solely because of the substitution effect.

2. When it matters at all, the income effect usually reinforces the substitution effect. That is, when the price of a good that absorbs a substantial share of income rises, consumers of that good become a bit poorer because their purchasing power falls.

As we learned in Chapter 3, the vast majority of goods are *normal goods,* goods for which demand decreases when income falls. So this effective reduction in income leads to a reduction in the quantity demanded and reinforces the substitution effect.

However, in the case of an *inferior good,* a good for which demand increases when income falls, the income and substitution effects work in opposite directions. Although the substitution effect tends to produce a decrease in the quantity of any good demanded as its price increases, in the case of an inferior good the income effect of a price increase tends to produce an *increase* in the quantity demanded.

As a result, it is possible that preferences and income effects can combine to generate a kind of inferior good in which the distinction between income and substitution effects is important. The most extreme example of this is a **Giffen good,** a good that has an upward-sloping demand curve.

Until recently, Giffen goods were treated as a hypothetical case—theoretically possible, but not observed in reality. However, a recent examination of the consumption patterns of Chinese peasants documents a real-world example of a

The **income effect** of a change in the price of a good is the change in the quantity of that good consumed that results from a change in the consumer's purchasing power due to the change in the price of the good.

A **Giffen good** is a hypothetical inferior good for which the income effect outweighs the substitution effect and the demand curve slopes upward.

Giffen good: consumption of rice and noodles, staples in the diet of Chinese peasants, goes up as the price of rice and noodles goes up. Because cheap food like rice and noodles helps these peasants reach a certain required minimum amount of daily calories, it is a necessary part of the diet. But when the price of rice or noodles goes up, more expensive foods like meat or fish have to be forgone. As a result, peasants eat more rice and noodles when the prices go up.

Admittedly, this is a rare case; it's likely to arise only when consumers are very poor and one good, a necessity, accounts for a large part of their budget. So as a practical matter, Giffen goods aren't a subject we need to worry about when discussing the demand for most goods. Typically, income effects are important only for a very limited number of goods.

ECONOMICS >> *in Action*
Lower Gasoline Prices and the Urge to Splurge

For Canadian consumers, 2015 was a year to indulge the urge to splurge, made possible by plunging gasoline prices. From early 2014 to late 2015, gas prices fell nearly 40% to 45% in major urban centres. According to Statistics Canada, this translated into a windfall of approximately $400 for the average Canadian family.

Consumers spent about 80% of their windfall, saving the remaining 20%. Fast-food chains like McDonald's, Wendy's, or Taco Bell, often located near gas stations and which cater to lower-income consumers, were the biggest beneficiaries of this spending as people chose to eat out more frequently or added extras like bacon to their burgers.

This should come as no surprise as low-income households experienced the largest *income effect* from the fall in gas prices—gasoline purchases accounted for a significant share of household spending, especially for households whose pre-tax income fell in the lowest 20%. Those households experienced the largest percentage increase in their average income from the fall in gas prices, and as a result they actually increased their total dollar spending on gasoline. Higher income households in the other four quintiles saw their average income increase by much less in percentage terms, and on average those households lowered their total dollar spending on gasoline.

And data indicate that the *substitution effect*—lower gas prices leading to purchases of more gas and less of other goods—also affected consumers' choices. Not only did people buy more gasoline, they bought higher grades of gasoline. Predictably, gas-guzzling SUVs saw an uptick in sales. But interestingly, the sales of electric vehicles, which use much less gas per kilometre, continued to grow in 2015 (up about 32%) after rising sharply from 2011 to 2013, a period of high gas prices, but still represent less than half a percent of all sales.

>> *Check Your Understanding* 10-4
Solutions appear at back of book.

1. In each of the following cases, state whether the income effect, the substitution effect, or both are significant. In which cases do they move in the same direction? In opposite directions? Why?
   a. Orange juice represents a small share of Clare's spending. She buys more lemonade and less orange juice when the price of orange juice goes up. She does not change her spending on other goods.
   b. Apartment rents have risen dramatically this year. Since rent absorbs a major part of her income, Delia moves to a smaller apartment. Assume that rental housing is a normal good.
   c. The cost of a semester-long meal ticket at the student cafeteria rises, representing a significant increase in living costs. Assume that cafeteria meals are an inferior good.
2. In the example described in Question 1c, how would you determine whether or not cafeteria meals are a Giffen good?

>> *Quick Review*

• Most goods absorb only a small fraction of a consumer's spending. For such goods, the **substitution effect** of a price change is the only important effect of the price change on consumption. It causes individual demand curves and the market demand curve to slope downward.

• When a good absorbs a large fraction of a consumer's spending, the **income effect** of a price change is present in addition to the substitution effect.

• For normal goods, demand rises when a consumer is richer and falls when a consumer is poorer, so that the income effect reinforces the substitution effect. For inferior goods, demand rises when a consumer is poorer and falls when a consumer is richer, so that the income and substitution effects move in opposite directions.

• In the rare case of a **Giffen good,** a type of inferior good, the income effect is so strong that the demand curve slopes upward.

Beyond Impossible: McDonald's and Burger King's Beef-Free Battle

After decades of dependable growth, the fortunes of McDonald's have been on a roller coaster for the past several years. During the Great Recession, McDonald's had outperformed other fast-food restaurants and chain restaurants, such as TGI Friday's, as price-conscious customers were drawn to McDonald's "Dollar Menu." However, by 2013 the Dollar Menu was no longer profitable. When it was replaced with the "Dollar Menu and More," which included items costing up to $5, customer reaction was definitely not positive: from 2014 to 2015 revenue fell by 7.4% and, for the first time ever, McDonald's closed more restaurants than it opened in the United States. As Steve Easterbrook, CEO of McDonald's said at the time, "As we moved away from the Dollar Menu, we didn't replace it with offers of an equivalent form of value. And customers have voted with their feet."

McDonald's tried to lure back customers with its 2016 "McPick 2 Menu" in the United States, which allowed customers to pick two items for $2. Canada had its own version of "McPick" in which customers were allowed to buy some classic items at lower prices. But as the economy slowly recovered, McDonald's found itself struggling to keep its price-conscious customers, while at the same time losing ground to the quickest growing segment of the restaurant industry: fast-casual restaurants that cater to customers with higher incomes. Fast-casual chains such as Chipotle and Panera offer a healthier menu using fresh ingredients, customizable, build-your-own selections, and a more comfortable dining environment. While the average McDonald's combo meal costs from $8.50 to $10.50 in Canada, the the typical Chipotle customer spends $15 for a meal in Canada. Despite their lower cost, McDonald's healthier menu options haven't sold particularly well because health-conscious customers tend to view McDonald's as the place to go for a quick burger and fries.

McDonald's also was caught flat-footed by the success of Burger King's plant-based Impossible Whopper burger in 2019. Costing US$1 more than a regular beef burger, Impossible Burgers are completely meat-free, yet re-create the taste and feel of a beef burger. As the CEO of Restaurant Brands International, the parent company of Burger King, said, sales of the Impossible Whopper have been "highly incremental and have attracted new types of guests into our restaurant. We see a lot of millennial and Gen Z customers who tend to really connect with the message around sustainability." The strong demand for the Impossible Whopper lifted Burger's King sales by nearly 11% in late 2019 while McDonald's comparable sales grew by less than 5% over the same period.

McDonald's is now playing catch-up, rolling out its own plant-based Beyond Burger, called PLT, in selected markets. So the question in the minds of industry analysts is this: having succeeded in dominating the price-conscious but low-profitability segment of the food market, can McDonald's now transform itself in the minds of health-conscious and environmentally conscious customers who are willing to pay more for healthier and more sustainable food? Can it go beyond its identity as a place to buy a cheap beef burger and fries?

QUESTIONS FOR THOUGHT

1. How does the McPick promotion resemble a consumer's optimal choice problem?

2. Give an example of a normal good and an inferior good mentioned in this case. Cite examples of income and substitution effects from the case.

3. Give an example of differences in consumer preferences illustrated by the case.

SUMMARY

1. Consumers maximize a measure of satisfaction called **utility.** Each consumer has a **utility function** that determines the level of total utility generated by their **consumption bundle,** the goods and services that are consumed. We measure utility in hypothetical units called **utils.**

2. A good's or service's **marginal utility** is the additional utility generated by consuming one more unit of the good or service. We usually assume that the **principle of diminishing marginal utility** holds: consumption of another unit of a good or service yields less additional utility than the previous unit. As a result, the **marginal utility curve** slopes downward.

3. A **budget constraint** limits a consumer's spending to no more than their income. It defines the consumer's **consumption possibilities,** the set of all affordable consumption bundles. A consumer who spends all of their income will choose a consumption bundle on the **budget line.** An individual chooses the consumption bundle that maximizes total utility, the **optimal consumption bundle.**

4. We use marginal analysis to find the optimal consumption bundle by analyzing how to allocate the marginal dollar. According to the **utility-maximizing principle of marginal analysis,** at the optimal consumption bundle the **marginal utility per dollar** spent on each good and service—the marginal utility of a good divided by its price—is the same.

5. Changes in the price of a good affect the quantity consumed in two possible ways: the **substitution effect** and the **income effect.** Most goods absorb only a small share of a consumer's spending; for these goods, only the substitution effect—buying less of the good that has become relatively more expensive and more of goods that are now relatively cheaper—is significant. It causes the individual and the market demand curves to slope downward. When a good absorbs a large fraction of spending, the income effect is also significant: an increase in a good's price makes a consumer poorer, but a decrease in price makes a consumer richer. This change in purchasing power makes consumers demand less or more of a good, depending on whether the good is normal or inferior. For normal goods, the substitution and income effects reinforce each other. For inferior goods, however, they work in opposite directions. The demand curve of a **Giffen good** slopes upward because it is an inferior good in which the income effect outweighs the substitution effect. However, Giffen goods are exceedingly rare: they are likely to arise only when consumers are very poor and one good, a necessity, absorbs a large share of their budget.

KEY TERMS

Utility, p. 296
Consumption bundle, p. 296
Utility function, p. 296
Util, p. 296
Marginal utility, p. 297
Marginal utility curve, p. 297

Principle of diminishing marginal utility, p. 298
Budget constraint, p. 299
Consumption possibilities, p. 299
Budget line, p. 300
Optimal consumption bundle, p. 301
Marginal utility per dollar, p. 304

Utility-maximizing principle of marginal analysis, p. 307
Optimal consumption rule, p. 307
Substitution effect, p. 308
Income effect, p. 309
Giffen good, p. 309

PRACTICE QUESTIONS

1. For each of the following situations, decide whether Al has diminishing marginal utility. Explain.

   a. The more economics classes Al takes, the more he enjoys the subject. And the more classes he takes, the easier each one gets, making him enjoy each additional class even more than the one before.

   b. Al likes loud music. In fact, according to him, "the louder, the better." Each time he turns the volume up a notch, he adds 5 utils to his total utility.

   c. Al enjoys watching reruns of the *X-Files*. He claims that these episodes are always exciting, but he does admit that the more times he sees an episode, the less exciting it gets.

   d. Al loves toasted marshmallows. The more he eats, however, the fuller he gets and the less he enjoys each additional marshmallow. And there is a point at which he becomes satiated: beyond that point, more marshmallows actually make him feel worse rather than better.

2. Use the concept of marginal utility to explain the following. Newspaper vending machines are designed so that once you have paid for one paper, you could take more than one paper at a time. But pop vending machines, once you have paid for one pop dispense only one pop at a time.

3. You and your roommate both enjoy Breyer's cookie dough ice cream. At the campus store you can buy a pint of ice cream for $3. In your last visit to the store, you noticed Breyer's ice cream was on sale for 50% off. You are excited for the sale and stock up on pints of ice cream but to your surprise, your roommate purchases fewer pints of Breyer's, opting instead to purchase more of Ben and Jerry's ice cream. Explain how each decision relates to concepts of income and substitution effects.

4. Many universities and colleges offer on-campus meal plans that allow students to purchase a set number of meals per week; the meals are nonrefundable. Most students purchase a meal plan that allows students to eat 20 meals per week at on-campus dining locations. Toward the end of the week you notice most students eating off campus despite not using all of their on-campus meals. Use the concept of marginal utility to explain student's behaviour for spending money to eat off campus instead of consuming "free" on-campus meals.

PROBLEMS

1. Bruno can spend his income on two different goods: smoothies and energy bars. For each of the following three situations, decide if the given consumption bundle is within Bruno's consumption possibilities. Then decide if it lies *on* the budget line or not.

   a. Smoothies cost $2 each, and energy bars cost $3 each. Bruno has income of $60. He is considering a consumption bundle containing 15 smoothies and 10 energy bars.

   b. Smoothies cost $2 each, and energy bars cost $5 each. Bruno has income of $110. He is considering a consumption bundle containing 20 smoothies and 10 energy bars.

   c. Smoothies cost $3 each, and energy bars cost $10 each. Bruno has income of $50. He is considering a consumption bundle containing 10 smoothies and 3 energy bars.

2. Bruno, the consumer in Problem 1, is best friends with Ruby who shares Bruno's love for energy bars and smoothies. The accompanying table shows Ruby's utilities from smoothies and energy bars.

Quantity of smoothies	Utility from smoothies (utils)	Quantity of energy bars	Utility from energy bars (utils)
0	0	0	0
1	32	2	28
2	60	4	52
3	84	6	72
4	104	8	88
5	120	10	100

The price of an energy bar is $2, the price of a smoothie is $4, and Ruby has $20 of income to spend.

   a. Which consumption bundles of energy bars and smoothies can Ruby consume if she spends all her income? Illustrate Ruby's budget line with a diagram, putting smoothies on the horizontal axis and energy bars on the vertical axis.

   b. Calculate the marginal utility of each energy bar and the marginal utility of each smoothie. Then calculate the marginal utility per dollar spent on energy bars and the marginal utility per dollar spent on smoothies.

   c. Draw a diagram like Figure 10-4 in which both the marginal utility per dollar spent on energy bars and the marginal utility per dollar spent on smoothies are illustrated. Draw the quantity of energy bars increasing from left to right, and the quantity of smoothies increasing from right to left. Using this diagram and the utility-maximizing principle of marginal analysis, predict which bundle—from all the bundles on her budget line—Ruby will choose.

3. For each of the following situations, decide whether the bundle Lakshani is considering is optimal or not. If it is not optimal, how could Lakshani improve her overall level of utility? That is, determine which good she should spend more on and which good she should spend less on.

   a. Lakshani has $200 to spend on sneakers and sweaters. Sneakers cost $50 per pair, and sweaters cost $20 each. She is thinking about buying 2 pairs of sneakers and 5 sweaters. She tells her friend that the additional utility she would get from the second pair of sneakers is the same as the additional utility she would get from the fifth sweater.

   b. Lakshani has $5 to spend on pens and pencils. Each pen costs $0.50 and each pencil costs $0.10. She is thinking about buying 6 pens and 20 pencils. The last pen would add five times as much to her total utility as the last pencil.

   c. Lakshani has $50 per season to spend on tickets to hockey games and tickets to soccer games. Each hockey ticket costs $10 and each soccer ticket costs $5. She is thinking about buying 3 hockey tickets and 2 soccer tickets. Her marginal utility from the third hockey ticket is twice as much as her marginal utility from the second soccer ticket.

4. Cal "Cool" Cooper has $200 to spend on Nikes and sunglasses.

   a. Each pair of Nikes costs $100 and each pair of sunglasses costs $50. Which bundles lie on Cal's budget line? Draw a diagram like Figure 10-4 in which both the marginal utility per dollar spent on Nikes and the marginal utility per dollar spent on sunglasses are illustrated. Draw the quantity of Nikes increasing from left to right, and the quantity of sunglasses increasing from right to left. Use this diagram and the optimal consumption rule to decide how Cal should allocate his money. That is, from all the bundles on his budget line, which bundle will Cal choose? The accompanying table gives his utility of Nikes and sunglasses.

Quantity of Nikes (pairs)	Utility from Nikes (utils)	Quantity of sunglasses (pairs)	Utility from sunglasses (utils)
0	0	0	0
1	400	2	600
2	700	4	700

b. The price of a pair of Nikes falls to $50 each, but the price of sunglasses remains at $50 per pair. Which bundles lie on Cal's budget line? Draw a diagram like Figure 10-4 in which both the marginal utility per dollar spent on Nikes and the marginal utility per dollar spent on sunglasses are illustrated. Use this diagram and the utility-maximizing principle of marginal analysis to decide how Cal should allocate his money. That is, from all the bundles on his budget line, which bundle will Cal choose? The accompanying table gives his utility of Nikes and sunglasses.

Quantity of Nikes (pairs)	Utility from Nikes (utils)	Quantity of sunglasses (pairs)	Utility from sunglasses (utils)
0	0	0	0
1	400	1	325
2	700	2	600
3	900	3	825
4	1,000	4	700

c. How does Cal's consumption of Nikes change as the price of Nikes falls? In words, describe the income effect and the substitution effect of this fall in the price of Nikes, assuming that Nikes are a normal good.

5. Damien Matthews is a busy actor. He allocates his free time to watching movies and working out at the gym. The accompanying table shows his utility from the number of times per week he watches a movie or goes to the gym.

Quantity of gym visits per week	Utility from gym visits (utils)	Quantity of movies per week	Utility from movies (utils)
1	100	1	60
2	180	2	110
3	240	3	150
4	280	4	180
5	310	5	190
6	330	6	195
7	340	7	197

Damien has 14 hours per week to spend on watching movies and going to the gym. Each movie takes

2 hours and each gym visit takes 2 hours. (*Hint:* Damien's free time is analogous to income he can spend. The hours needed for each activity are analogous to the price of that activity.)

a. Which bundles of gym visits and movies can Damien consume per week if he spends all his time either going to the gym or watching movies? Draw Damien's budget line in a diagram with gym visits on the horizontal axis and movies on the vertical axis.

b. Calculate the marginal utility of each gym visit and the marginal utility of each movie. Then calculate the marginal utility per hour spent at the gym and the marginal utility per hour spent watching movies.

c. Draw a diagram like Figure 10-4 in which both the marginal utility per hour spent at the gym and the marginal utility per hour spent watching movies are illustrated. Draw the quantity of gym visits increasing from left to right, and the quantity of movies increasing from right to left. Use this diagram and the utility-maximizing principle of marginal analysis to decide how Damien should allocate his time.

6. Anna Jenniferson is an actress who currently spends several hours each week watching movies and going to the gym. She likes watching movies much more than going to the gym. In fact, she says that if she had to give up seeing 1 movie, she would need to go to the gym twice to make up for the loss in utility from not seeing the movie. A movie takes 2 hours, and a gym visit also lasts 2 hours. Should Anna watch more movies or spend more time at the gym?

7. Sven is a low-income student who covers most of his dietary needs by eating cheap breakfast cereal, since it contains most of the important vitamins. As the price of cereal increases, he decides to buy even less of other foods and even more breakfast cereal to maintain his intake of important nutrients. This makes breakfast cereal a Giffen good for Sven. Describe in words the substitution effect and the income effect from this increase in the price of cereal. In which direction does each effect move, and why? What does this imply for the slope of Sven's demand curve for cereal?

8. In each of the following situations, describe the substitution effect and, if it is significant, the income effect. In which direction does each of these effects move? Why?

a. Ed spends a large portion of his income on his children's education. Because tuition fees rise, one of his children has to withdraw from post-secondary education.

b. Homer spends much of his monthly income on home mortgage payments. The interest on his adjustable-rate mortgage falls, lowering his mortgage payments, and Homer decides to move to a larger house.

c. Pam thinks that Spam is an inferior good. Yet as the price of Spam rises, she decides to buy less of it.

9. Restaurant meals and housing (measured in the number of rooms) are the only two goods that Neha buys. She has income of $1,000. Initially, she buys a consumption bundle such that she spends exactly half her income on restaurant meals and the other half of her income on housing. Then her income increases by 50%, but the price of restaurant meals increases by 100% (it doubles). The price of housing remains the same. After these changes, if she wanted to, could Neha still buy the same consumption bundle as before?

10. Scott finds that the higher the price of orange juice, the more money he spends on orange juice. Does that mean that Scott has discovered a Giffen good?

11. Margo's marginal utility of one dance lesson is 100 utils per lesson. Her marginal utility of a new pair of dance shoes is 300 utils per pair. The price of a dance lesson is $50 per lesson. She currently spends all her income, and she buys her optimal consumption bundle. What is the price of a pair of dance shoes?

12. According to data from Statistics Canada, the average retail price of regular gasoline rose from 62.1 cents in 1997 to 104.2 cents in 2016, a 67.8% increase.

a. Other things equal, describe the effect of this price increase on the quantity of gasoline demanded. In your explanation, make use of the utility-maximizing principle of marginal analysis and describe income and substitution effects.

In fact, however, other things were not equal. Over the same time period, the prices of other goods and services rose as well. According to data from Statistics Canada, the overall price of a bundle of goods and services consumed by an average consumer rose by 42%.

b. Taking into account the rise in the price of gasoline and in overall prices, other things equal, describe the effect on the quantity of gasoline demanded.

However, this is not the end of the story. Between 1997 and 2016, the typical consumer's nominal income increased, too: Statistics Canada reports that the median weekly wage of Canadian workers rose from $522.34 in 1997 to $807.60 in 2016, an increase of 54.6%.

c. Taking into account the rise in the price of gasoline, in overall prices, and in consumers' incomes, describe the effect on the quantity of gasoline demanded.

WORK IT OUT

13. Brenda likes to have bagels and coffee for breakfast. The accompanying table shows Brenda's total utility from various consumption bundles of bagels and coffee.

Consumption bundle		Total utility (utils)
Quantity of bagels	Quantity of coffee (cups)	
0	0	0
0	2	28
0	4	40
1	2	48
1	3	54
2	0	28
2	2	56
3	1	54
3	2	62
4	0	40
4	2	66

Suppose Brenda knows she will consume 2 cups of coffee for sure. However, she can choose to consume different quantities of bagels: she can choose either 0, 1, 2, 3, or 4 bagels.

a. Calculate Brenda's marginal utility from bagels as she goes from consuming 0 bagels to 1 bagel, from 1 bagel to 2 bagels, from 2 bagels to 3 bagels, and from 3 bagels to 4 bagels.

b. Draw Brenda's marginal utility curve of bagels. Does Brenda have diminishing marginal utility of bagels? Explain.

c. Brenda has $8 of income to spend on bagels and coffee. Bagels cost $2 each, and coffee costs $2 per cup. Which bundles are on Brenda's budget line? For each of these bundles, calculate the level of utility (in utils) that Brenda enjoys. Which bundle is her optimal bundle?

d. The price of bagels increases to $4, but the price of coffee remains at $2 per cup. Which bundles are now on Brenda's budget line? For each bundle, calculate Brenda's level of utility (in utils). Which bundle is her optimal bundle? ■

Consumer Preferences and Consumer Choice

Different people have different preferences. And for any given person, there will be different consumption bundles that yield the same total utility. This insight leads to the concept of *indifference curves*, a useful way to represent individual preferences. In this appendix, we will look closely at indifference curves.

Using indifference curves to analyze consumer behaviour will serve us in three ways.

1. Indifference curves show how diminishing marginal utility determines the trade-off a consumer makes between consuming more of one good and less of another.

2. They provide a framework for a more in-depth analysis of income and substitution effects—how changes in price and income alter the optimal consumption bundle.

3. Indifference curves allow us to illustrate differences in tastes between two people, and how those differences in tastes lead to different optimal consumption bundles.

Indifference curves, then, allow us to get a deeper understanding of what it means to be a rational consumer.

Mapping the Utility Function

In Chapter 10, we introduced the concept of a utility function, which determines a consumer's total utility given their consumption bundle. In Figure 10-1, we saw how Cassie's total utility changed as we changed the quantity of egg rolls consumed, holding fixed the quantities of other items in her bundle. That is, in Figure 10-1, we showed how total utility changed as consumption of only *one* good changed. But we also learned in Chapter 10, from our example of Sammy, that finding the optimal consumption bundle involves the problem of how to allocate the last dollar spent between *two* goods, egg rolls and bottles of Coke.

In this appendix, we will extend the analysis by learning how to express total utility as a function of consumption of two goods. In this way we will deepen our understanding of the trade-off involved when choosing the optimal consumption bundle and of how the optimal consumption bundle itself changes in response to changes in the prices of goods. In order to do that, we now turn to a different way of representing a consumer's utility function, based on the concept of *indifference curves*.

Indifference Curves

Ingrid is a consumer who buys only two goods: housing, measured in the number of rooms, and restaurant meals. How can we represent her utility function in a way that takes account of her consumption of both goods?

One way is to draw a three-dimensional picture. Figure 10A-1 shows a three-dimensional *utility hill*. The distance along the horizontal axis measures the quantity of housing Ingrid consumes in terms of numbers of rooms; the distance along the vertical axis measures the number of restaurant meals she consumes. The altitude or height of the hill at each point is indicated by a contour line, along which the height of the hill is constant. For example, point *A*, which corresponds

FIGURE 10A-1 Ingrid's Utility Function

The three-dimensional hill shows how Ingrid's total utility depends on her consumption of housing and restaurant meals. Point *A* corresponds to consumption of 3 rooms and 30 restaurant meals. The consumption bundle yields Ingrid 450 utils, corresponding to the height of the hill at point *A*. The lines running around the hill are contour lines, along which the height is constant. Every point on a given contour line generates the same level of utility. So point *B*, corresponding to 6 rooms and 15 restaurants, generates the same level of utility as point *A*, 450 utils, since they lie on the same contour line.

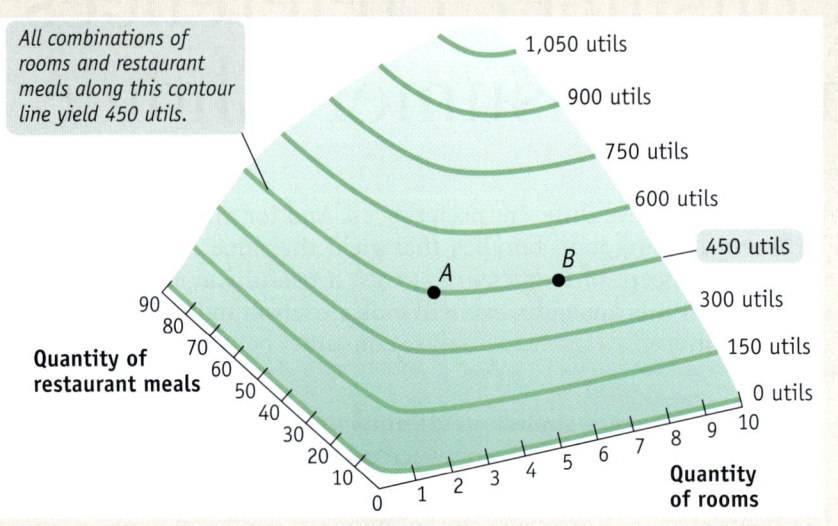

All combinations of rooms and restaurant meals along this contour line yield 450 utils.

to a consumption bundle of 3 rooms and 30 restaurant meals, lies on the contour line labelled 450. So the total utility Ingrid receives from consuming 3 rooms and 30 restaurant meals is 450 utils.

A three-dimensional picture like Figure 10A-1 helps us think about the relationship between consumption bundles and total utility. But anyone who has ever used a topographical map to plan a hiking trip knows that it is possible to represent a three-dimensional surface in only two dimensions. A topographical map doesn't offer a three-dimensional view of the terrain; instead, it conveys information about altitude solely through the use of contour lines.

The same principle can be applied to representing the utility function. In Figure 10A-2, Ingrid's consumption of rooms is measured on the horizontal axis and her consumption of restaurant meals on the vertical axis. The curve here

FIGURE 10A-2 An Indifference Curve

An indifference curve is a contour line along which total utility is constant. In this case, we show all the consumption bundles that yield Ingrid 450 utils. Consumption bundle *A*, consisting of 3 rooms and 30 restaurant meals, yields the same total utility as bundle *B*, consisting of 6 rooms and 15 restaurant meals. That is, Ingrid is indifferent between bundle *A* and bundle *B*.

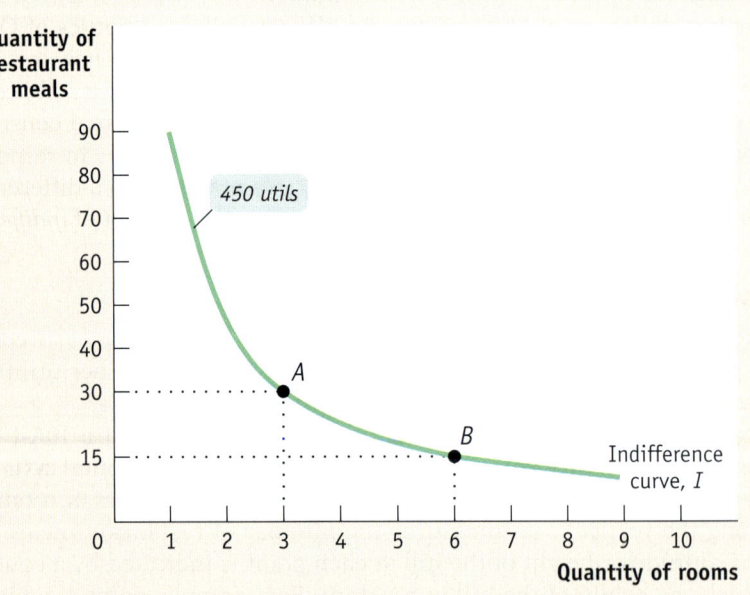

corresponds to the contour line in Figure 10A-1, drawn at a total utility of 450 utils. This curve shows all the consumption bundles that yield a total utility of 450 utils. One point on that contour line is *A*, a consumption bundle consisting of 3 rooms and 30 restaurant meals. Another point on that contour line is *B*, a consumption bundle consisting of 6 rooms but only 15 restaurant meals. Because *B* lies on the same contour line, it yields Ingrid the same total utility—450 utils—as *A*. We say that Ingrid is *indifferent* between *A* and *B*: because bundles *A* and *B* yield the same total utility level, Ingrid is equally well off with either bundle.

A contour line that maps consumption bundles yielding the same amount of total utility is known as an **indifference curve.** An individual is always indifferent between any two bundles that lie on the same indifference curve. For a given consumer, there is an indifference curve corresponding to each possible level of total utility. For example, the indifference curve in Figure 10A-2 shows consumption bundles that yield Ingrid 450 utils; different indifference curves would show consumption bundles that yield Ingrid 400 utils, 500 utils, and so on.

A collection of indifference curves that represents a given consumer's entire utility function, with each indifference curve corresponding to a different level of total utility, is known as an **indifference curve map.** Figure 10A-3 shows three indifference curves—I_1, I_2, and I_3—from Ingrid's indifference curve map, as well as several consumption bundles, *A*, *B*, *C*, and *D*. The accompanying table lists each bundle, its composition of rooms and restaurant meals, and the total utility it yields.

Because bundles *A* and *B* generate the same number of utils, 450, they lie on the same indifference curve, I_2. Although Ingrid is indifferent between *A* and *B*, she is certainly not indifferent between *A* and *C:* as you can see from the table, *C* generates only 391 utils, a lower total utility than *A* or *B*. So Ingrid prefers consumption bundles *A* and *B* to bundle *C*. This is represented by the fact that

An **indifference curve** is a line that shows all the consumption bundles that yield the same amount of total utility for an individual.

The entire utility function of an individual can be represented by an **indifference curve map,** a collection of indifference curves in which each curve corresponds to a different total utility level.

FIGURE 10A-3 An Indifference Curve Map

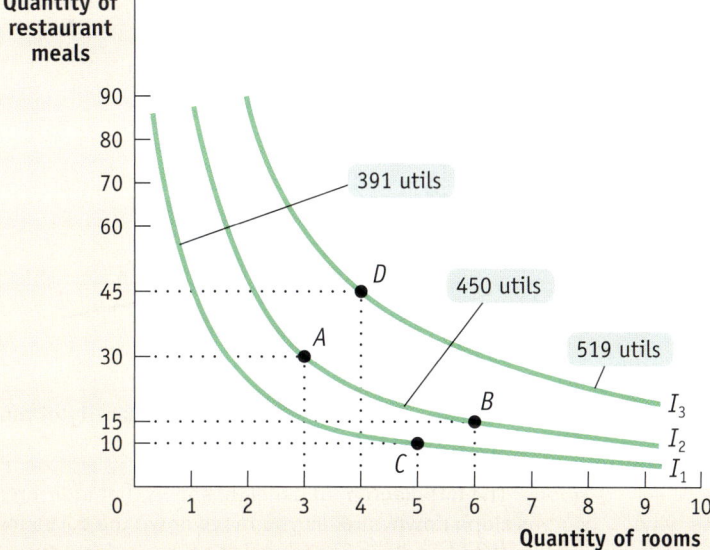

Consumption bundle	Quantity of rooms	Quantity of meals	Total utility (utils)
A	3	30	450
B	6	15	450
C	5	10	391
D	4	45	519

The utility function can be represented in greater detail by increasing the number of indifference curves drawn, each corresponding to a different level of total utility. In this figure, bundle *C* lies on an indifference curve corresponding to a total utility of 391 utils. As in Figure 10A-2, bundles *A* and *B* lie on an indifference curve corresponding to a total utility of 450 utils. Bundle *D* lies on an indifference curve corresponding to a total utility of 519 utils. Ingrid prefers any bundle on I_2 to any bundle on I_1, and she prefers any bundle on I_3 to any bundle on I_2.

C is on indifference curve I_1, and I_1 lies below I_2. Bundle *D*, though, generates 519 utils, a higher total utility than *A* and *B*. It is on I_3, an indifference curve that lies above I_2. Clearly, Ingrid prefers *D* to either *A* or *B*. And, even more strongly, she prefers *D* to *C*.

Properties of Indifference Curves

No two individuals have the same indifference curve map because no two individuals have the same preferences. But economists believe that, regardless of the person, every indifference curve map has two general properties. These are illustrated in panel (a) of Figure 10A-4:

FIGURE 10A-4 Properties of Indifference Curves

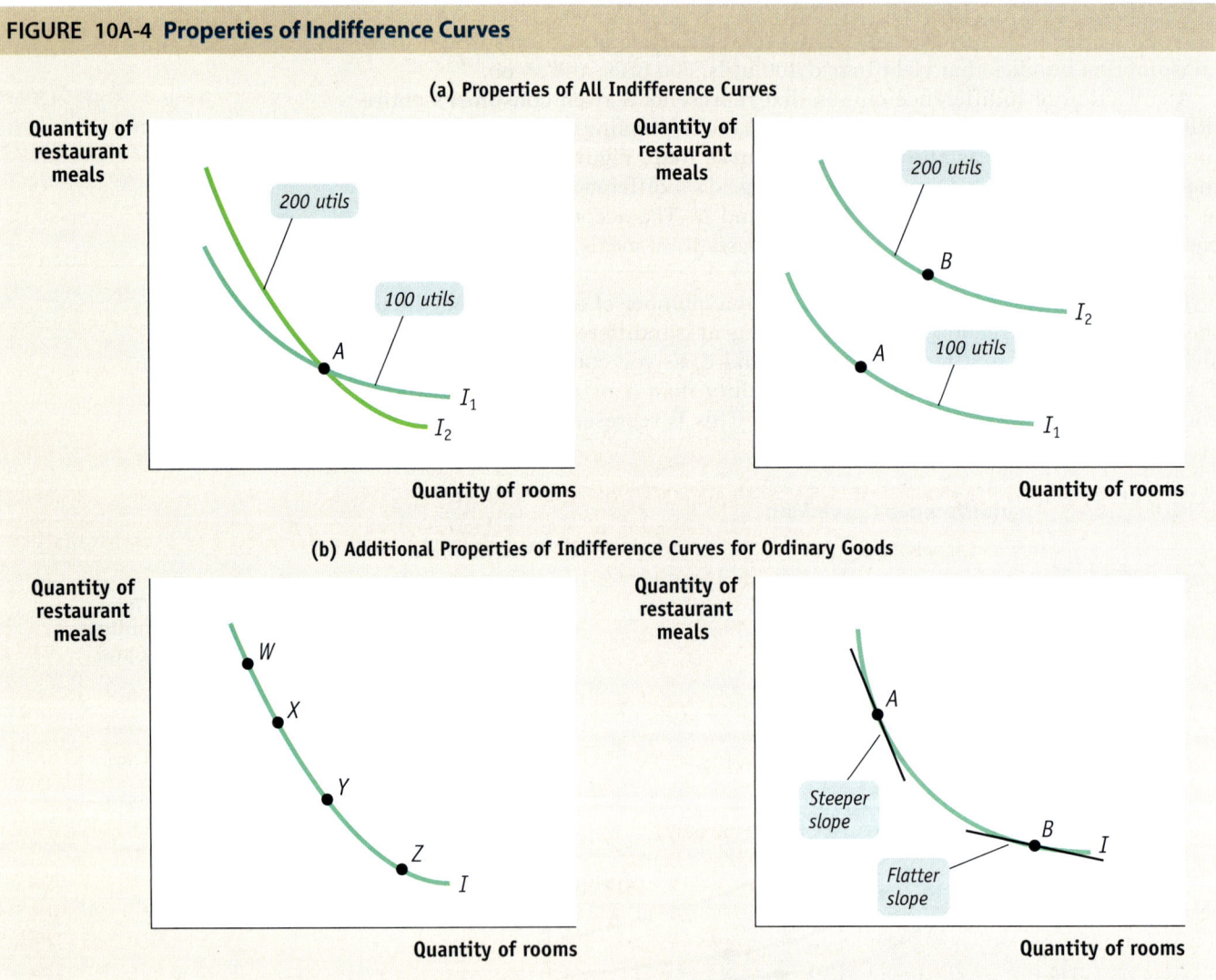

Panel (a) represents two general properties that all indifference curve maps share. The left diagram shows why indifference curves cannot cross: if they did, a consumption bundle such as *A* would yield both 100 and 200 utils, a contradiction. The right diagram of panel (a) shows that indifference curves that are farther out yield higher total utility: bundle *B*, which contains more of both goods than bundle *A*, yields higher total utility. Panel (b) depicts two additional properties of indifference curves for ordinary goods. The left diagram of panel (b) shows that indifference curves slope downward: as you move down the curve from bundle *W* to bundle *Z*, consumption of rooms increases. To keep total utility constant, this must be offset by a reduction in quantity of restaurant meals. The right diagram of panel (b) shows a convex-shaped indifference curve. The slope of the indifference curve gets flatter as you move down the curve to the right, a feature arising from diminishing marginal utility.

- *Indifference curves never cross.* Suppose that we tried to draw an indifference curve map like the one depicted in the left diagram in panel (a), in which two indifference curves cross at *A*. What is the total utility at *A*? Is it 100 utils or 200 utils? Indifference curves cannot cross because each consumption bundle must correspond to a unique total utility level—not, as shown at *A*, two different total utility levels.

- *The farther out an indifference curve lies—the farther it is from the origin—the higher the level of total utility it indicates.* The reason, illustrated in the right diagram in panel (a), is that we assume that more is better—we consider only the consumption bundles for which the consumer is not satiated. Bundle *B*, on the outer indifference curve, contains more of both goods than bundle *A* on the inner indifference curve. So *B*, because it generates a higher total utility level (200 utils), lies on a higher indifference curve than *A*.

Furthermore, economists believe that, for most goods, consumers' indifference curve maps also have two additional properties. They are illustrated in panel (b) of Figure 10A-4:

- *Indifference curves slope downward.* Here, too, the reason is that more is better. The left diagram in panel (b) shows four consumption bundles on the same indifference curve: *W*, *X*, *Y*, and *Z*. By definition, these consumption bundles yield the same level of total utility. But as you move along the curve to the right, from *W* to *Z*, the quantity of rooms consumed increases. The only way a person can consume more rooms without gaining utility is by giving up some restaurant meals. So the indifference curve must slope downward.

- *Indifference curves have a convex shape.* The right diagram in panel (b) shows that the slope of each indifference curve changes as you move down the curve to the right: the curve gets flatter. If you move up an indifference curve to the left, the curve gets steeper. So the indifference curve is steeper at *A* than it is at *B*. When this occurs, we say that an indifference curve has a *convex* shape—it is bowed-in toward the origin. This feature arises from diminishing marginal utility, a principle we discussed in Chapter 10. Recall that when a consumer has diminishing marginal utility, consumption of another unit of a good generates a smaller increase in total utility than the previous unit consumed. In the next section, we will examine in detail how diminishing marginal utility gives rise to convex-shaped indifference curves.

Goods that satisfy all four properties of indifference curve maps are called *ordinary goods*. The vast majority of goods in any consumer's utility function fall into this category. In the next section, we will define ordinary goods and see the key role that diminishing marginal utility plays for them.

Indifference Curves and Consumer Choice

At the beginning of the last section, we used indifference curves to represent the preferences of Ingrid, whose consumption bundles consist of rooms and restaurant meals. Our next step is to show how to use Ingrid's indifference curve map to find her utility-maximizing consumption bundle given her budget constraint, the fact that she must choose a consumption bundle that costs no more than her total income.

It's important to understand how our analysis here relates to what we did in Chapter 10. We are not offering a new theory of consumer behaviour in this appendix—just as in Chapter 10, consumers are assumed to maximize total utility. In particular, we know that consumers will follow the *optimal consumption rule* from Chapter 10: the optimal consumption bundle lies on the budget line, and the marginal utility per dollar is the same for every good in the bundle.

But as we'll see shortly, we can derive this optimal consumer behaviour in a somewhat different way—a way that yields deeper insights into consumer choice.

The Marginal Rate of Substitution

The first element of our approach is a new concept, the *marginal rate of substitution*. The essence of this concept is illustrated in Figure 10A-5.

Recall from the last section that for most goods, consumers' indifference curves are downward sloping and convex. Figure 10A-5 shows such an indifference curve. The points labelled *V, W, X, Y,* and *Z* all lie on this indifference curve—that is, they represent consumption bundles that yield Ingrid the same level of total utility. The table accompanying the figure shows the components of each of the bundles.

As we move along the indifference curve from *V* to *Z*, Ingrid's consumption of housing steadily increases from 2 rooms to 6 rooms, her consumption of restaurant meals steadily decreases from 30 meals to 10 meals, and her total utility is kept constant. As we move down the indifference curve, then, Ingrid is trading more of one good in place of less of the other, with the *terms* of that trade-off—the ratio of additional rooms consumed to restaurant meals sacrificed—chosen to keep her total utility constant.

Notice that the quantity of restaurant meals that Ingrid is willing to give up in return for an additional room changes along the indifference curve. As we move from *V* to *W*, housing consumption rises from 2 to 3 rooms and restaurant meal consumption falls from 30 to 20—a trade-off of 10 restaurant meals for 1 additional room. But as we move from *Y* to *Z*, housing consumption rises from 5 to 6 rooms and restaurant meal consumption falls from 12 to 10, a trade-off of only 2 restaurant meals for an additional room.

To put it in terms of slopes, the slope of the indifference curve between *V* and *W* is −10: the change in restaurant meal consumption, −10, divided by the change in housing consumption, 1. Similarly, the slope of the indifference curve between *Y* and *Z* is −2. So the slope decreases and the indifference curve gets flatter as we

FIGURE 10A-5 The Changing Slope of an Indifference Curve

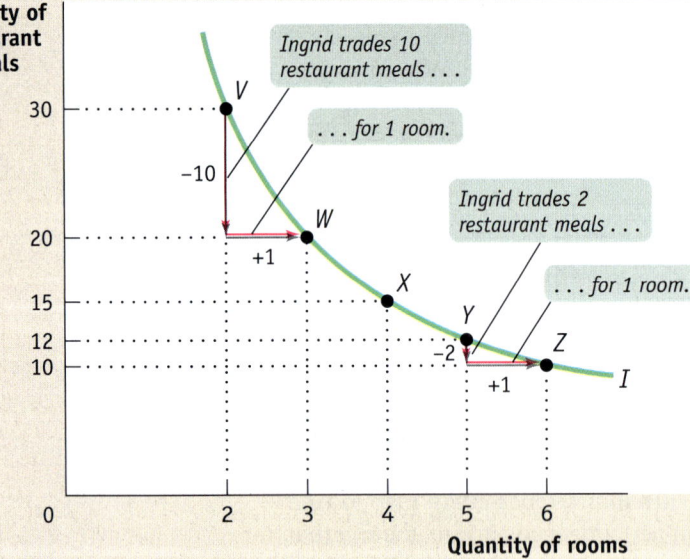

Consumption bundle	Quantity of rooms	Quantity of restaurant meals
V	2	30
W	3	20
X	4	15
Y	5	12
Z	6	10

This indifference curve is downward sloping and convex, implying that restaurant meals and rooms are ordinary goods for Ingrid. As Ingrid moves down her indifference curve from *V* to *Z*, she trades reduced consumption of restaurant meals for increased consumption of housing. However, the terms of that trade-off change. As she moves from *V* to *W*, she is willing to give up 10 restaurant meals in return for 1 more room. As her consumption of rooms rises and her consumption of restaurant meals falls, she is willing to give up fewer restaurant meals in return for each additional room. The flattening of the slope as you move from left to right arises from diminishing marginal utility.

move down it to the right—that is, it has a convex shape, one of the four properties of an indifference curve for ordinary goods.

Why does the trade-off change in this way? Let's think about it intuitively, then work through it more carefully. When Ingrid moves down her indifference curve, whether from V to W or from Y to Z, she gains utility from her additional consumption of housing but loses an equal amount of utility from her reduced consumption of restaurant meals. But at each step, the initial position from which Ingrid begins is different. At V, Ingrid consumes only a small quantity of rooms; because of diminishing marginal utility, her marginal utility per room at that point is high. At V, then, an additional room adds a lot to Ingrid's total utility. But at V she already consumes a large quantity of restaurant meals, so her marginal utility of restaurant meals is low at that point. This means that it takes a large reduction in her quantity of restaurant meals consumed to offset the increased utility she gets from the extra room of housing.

At Y, in contrast, Ingrid consumes a much larger quantity of rooms and a much smaller quantity of restaurant meals than at V. This means that an additional room adds fewer utils, and a restaurant meal forgone costs more utils, than at V. So Ingrid is willing to give up fewer restaurant meals in return for another room of housing at Y (where she gives up 2 meals for 1 room) than she is at V (where she gives up 10 meals for 1 room).

Now let's express the same idea—that the trade-off Ingrid is willing to make depends on where she is starting from—by using a little math. We do this by examining how the slope of the indifference curve changes as we move down it.

Moving down the indifference curve—reducing restaurant meal consumption and increasing housing consumption—will produce two opposing effects on Ingrid's total utility: lower restaurant meal consumption will reduce her total utility, but higher housing consumption will raise her total utility. And since we are moving down the indifference curve, these two effects must exactly cancel out:

Along the indifference curve:
(10A-1) (Change in total utility due to lower restaurant meal consumption) +
(Change in total utility due to higher housing consumption) = 0

or, rearranging terms,

Along the indifference curve:
(10A-2) −(Change in total utility due to lower restaurant meal consumption) =
(Change in total utility due to higher housing consumption)

Let's now focus on what happens as we move only a short distance down the indifference curve, trading off a small increase in housing consumption in place of a small decrease in restaurant meal consumption. Following our notation from Chapter 10, let's use MU_R and MU_M to represent the marginal utility of rooms and restaurant meals, respectively, and ΔQ_R and ΔQ_M to represent the changes in room and meal consumption, respectively.

In general, the change in total utility caused by a small change in consumption of a good is equal to the change in consumption multiplied by the *marginal utility* of that good. This means that we can calculate the change in Ingrid's total utility generated by a change in her consumption bundle using the following equations:

(10A-3) Change in total utility due to a change in restaurant meal
consumption = $MU_M \times \Delta Q_M$

and

(10A-4) Change in total utility due to a change in housing consumption
= $MU_R \times \Delta Q_R$

So we can write Equation 10A-2 in symbols as:

(10A-5) *Along the indifference curve:* $-MU_M \times \Delta Q_M = MU_R \times \Delta Q_R$

Note that the left-hand side of Equation 10A-5 has a minus sign; it represents the loss in total utility from decreased restaurant meal consumption. This must equal the gain in total utility from increased room consumption, represented by the right-hand side of the equation.

What we want to know is how this translates into the slope of the indifference curve. To find the slope, we divide both sides of Equation 10A-5 by ΔQ_R, and again by $-MU_M$, in order to get the ΔQ_M, ΔQ_R terms on one side and the MU_R, MU_M terms on the other. This results in:

(10A-6) *Along the indifference curve:* $\dfrac{\Delta Q_M}{\Delta Q_R} = -\dfrac{MU_R}{MU_M}$

The left-hand side of Equation 10A-6 is the slope of the indifference curve; it is the rate at which Ingrid is willing to trade rooms (the good on the horizontal axis) in place of restaurant meals (the good on the vertical axis) without changing her total utility level. The right-hand side of Equation 10A-6 is minus the ratio of the marginal utility of rooms to the marginal utility of restaurant meals—that is, the ratio of what she gains from one more room to what she gains from one more meal.

Putting all this together, we see that Equation 10A-6 shows that, along the indifference curve, the quantity of restaurant meals Ingrid is willing to give up in return for a room, $\Delta Q_M / \Delta Q_R$, is exactly equal to minus the ratio of the marginal utility of a room to that of a meal, $-MU_R / MU_M$. Only when this condition is met will her total utility level remain constant as she consumes more rooms and fewer restaurant meals.

Economists have a special name for the ratio of the marginal utilities found in the right-hand side of Equation 10A-6: it is called the **marginal rate of substitution,** or **MRS,** of rooms (the good on the horizontal axis) in place of restaurant meals (the good on the vertical axis). That's because as we slide down Ingrid's indifference curve, we are substituting more rooms in place of fewer restaurant meals in her consumption bundle. As we'll see shortly, the marginal rate of substitution plays an important role in finding the optimal consumption bundle.

Recall that indifference curves get flatter as you move down them to the right. The reason, as we've just discussed, is diminishing marginal utility: as Ingrid consumes more housing and fewer restaurant meals, her marginal utility from housing falls and her marginal utility from restaurant meals rises. So her marginal rate of substitution, which is equal to minus the slope of her indifference curve, falls as she moves down the indifference curve.

The flattening of indifference curves as you slide down them to the right—which reflects the same logic as the principle of diminishing marginal utility—is known as the principle of **diminishing marginal rate of substitution.** It says that an individual who consumes only a little bit of good A and a lot of good B will be willing to trade a lot of B in return for one more unit of A; an individual who already consumes a lot of A and not much B will be less willing to make that trade-off.

We can illustrate this point by referring back to Figure 10A-5. At point V, a bundle with a high proportion of restaurant meals to rooms, Ingrid is willing to forgo 10 restaurant meals in return for 1 room. But at point Y, a bundle with a low proportion of restaurant meals to rooms, she is willing to forgo only 2 restaurant meals in return for 1 room.

From this example we can see that, in Ingrid's utility function, rooms and restaurant meals possess the two additional properties that characterize ordinary goods. Ingrid requires additional rooms to compensate her for the loss of a meal, and vice versa; so her indifference curves for these two goods slope

The **marginal rate of substitution,** or **MRS,** of good R in place of good M is equal to MU_R/MU_M, the ratio of the marginal utility of R to the marginal utility of M.

The principle of **diminishing marginal rate of substitution** states that the more of good R a person consumes in proportion to good M, the less M they are willing to substitute for another unit of R.

downward. And her indifference curves are convex: the slope of her indifference curve—*minus* the marginal rate of substitution—becomes flatter as we move down it. In fact, an indifference curve is convex only when it has diminishing marginal rate of substitution—these two conditions are equivalent.

With this information, we can define **ordinary goods,** which account for the great majority of goods in any consumer's utility function. A pair of goods are ordinary goods in a consumer's utility function if they possess two properties: the consumer requires more of one good to compensate for less of the other, and the consumer experiences a diminishing marginal rate of substitution when substituting one good in place of the other.

Next we will see how to determine Ingrid's optimal consumption bundle using indifference curves.

> Two goods, *R* and *M*, are **ordinary goods** in a consumer's utility function when (1) the consumer requires additional units of *R* to compensate for less *M*, and vice versa; and (2) the consumer experiences a diminishing marginal rate of substitution when substituting one good in place of another.

The Tangency Condition

Now let's put some of Ingrid's indifference curves on the same diagram as her budget line, to illustrate an alternative way of representing her optimal consumption choice. Figure 10A-6 shows Ingrid's budget line, *BL*, when her income is $2,400 per month, housing costs $150 per room each month, and restaurant meals cost $30 each. What is her optimal consumption bundle?

To answer this question, we show several of Ingrid's indifference curves: I_1, I_2, and I_3. Ingrid would like to achieve the total utility level represented by I_3, the highest of the three curves, but she cannot afford to because she is constrained by her income: no consumption bundle on her budget line yields that much total utility. But she shouldn't settle for the level of total utility generated by *B*, which lies on I_1: there are other bundles on her budget line, such as *A*, that clearly yield higher total utility than *B*.

In fact, *A*—a consumption bundle consisting of 8 rooms and 40 restaurant meals per month—is Ingrid's optimal consumption choice. The reason is that *A* lies on the highest indifference curve Ingrid can reach given her income.

At the optimal consumption bundle *A*, Ingrid's budget line *just touches* the relevant indifference curve—the budget line is *tangent* to the indifference curve.

FIGURE 10A-6 **The Optimal Consumption Bundle**

The budget line, *BL,* shows Ingrid's possible consumption bundles given an income of $2,400 per month, when rooms cost $150 per month and restaurant meals cost $30 each. I_1, I_2, and I_3 are indifference curves. Consumption bundles such as *B* and *C* are not optimal because Ingrid can move to a higher indifference curve. The optimal consumption bundle is *A*, where the budget line is just tangent to the highest possible indifference curve.

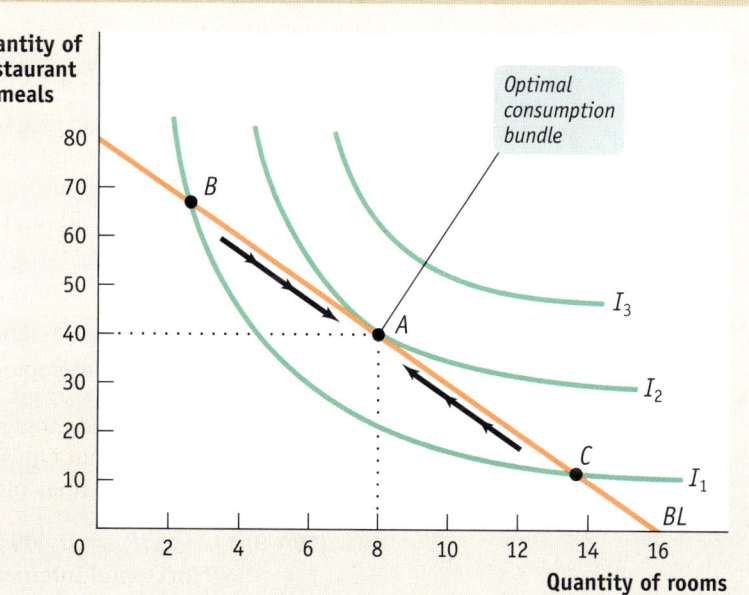

The **tangency condition** between the indifference curve and the budget line holds when the indifference curve and the budget line just touch. This condition determines the optimal consumption bundle when the indifference curves have the typical convex shape.

This **tangency condition** between the indifference curve and the budget line applies to the optimal consumption bundle when the indifference curves have the typical convex shape: *at the optimal consumption bundle, the budget line just touches—is tangent to—the indifference curve.*

To see why, let's look more closely at how we know that a consumption bundle that *doesn't* satisfy the tangency condition can't be optimal. Reexamining Figure 10A-6, we can see that the consumption bundles B and C are both affordable because they lie on the budget line. However, neither is optimal. Both of them lie on the indifference curve I_1, which cuts through the budget line at both points. But because I_1 cuts through the budget line, Ingrid can do better: she can move down the budget line from B or up the budget line from C, as indicated by the arrows. In each case, this allows her to get onto a higher indifference curve, I_2, which increases her total utility.

Ingrid cannot, however, do any better than I_2: any other indifference curve either cuts through her budget line or doesn't touch it at all. And the bundle that allows her to achieve I_2 is, of course, her optimal consumption bundle.

The Slope of the Budget Line

Figure 10A-6 shows us how to use a graph of the budget line and the indifference curves to find the optimal consumption bundle, the bundle at which the budget line and the indifference curve are tangent. But rather than rely on drawing graphs, we can determine the optimal consumption bundle by using a bit of math.

As you can see from Figure 10A-6, at A, the optimal consumption bundle, the budget line, and the indifference curve have the same slope. Why? Because two curves can only touch each other if they have the same slope at their point of tangency. Otherwise, they would cross each other somewhere. And we know that if we are on an indifference curve that crosses the budget line (like I_1 in Figure 10A-6), we can't be on the indifference curve that contains the optimal consumption bundle (like I_2).

So we can use information about the slopes of the budget line and the indifference curve to find the optimal consumption bundle. To do that, we must first analyse the slope of the budget line, a fairly straightforward task. We know that Ingrid will get the highest possible utility by spending all of her income and consuming a bundle on her budget line. So we can represent Ingrid's budget line, the consumption bundles available to her when she spends all of her income, with the equation:

(10A-7) $(Q_R \times P_R) + (Q_M \times P_M) = N$

where N stands for Ingrid's income. To find the slope of the budget line, we divide its vertical intercept (where the budget line hits the vertical axis) by its horizontal intercept (where it hits the horizontal axis). The vertical intercept is the point at which Ingrid spends all her income on restaurant meals and none on rooms (that is, $Q_R = 0$). In that case, the number of restaurant meals she consumes is:

(10A-8) $Q_M = N/P_M = \$2,400/(\$30 \text{ per meal}) = 80 \text{ meals}$
     $= \text{Vertical intercept of budget line}$

At the other extreme, Ingrid spends all her income on rooms and none on restaurant meals (so that $Q_M = 0$). This means that at the horizontal intercept of the budget line, the number of rooms she consumes is:

(10A-9) $Q_R = N/P_R = \$2,400/(\$150 \text{ per room}) = 16 \text{ rooms}$
     $= \text{Horizontal intercept of budget line}$

Now we have the information needed to find the slope of the budget line. It is:

(10A-10) Slope of budget line = –(Vertical intercept)/(Horizontal intercept)

$$= -\frac{\dfrac{N}{P_M}}{\dfrac{N}{P_R}} = -\frac{P_R}{P_M}$$

Notice the minus sign in Equation 10A-10; it's there because the budget line slopes downward. The quantity P_R/P_M is known as the **relative price** of rooms in terms of restaurant meals, to distinguish it from an ordinary price in terms of dollars. In this example, it is equal to $150/$30 = 5. Because buying one more room requires Ingrid to give up P_R/P_M quantity of restaurant meals, or 5 meals, we can interpret the relative price P_R/P_M as the rate at which a room trades for restaurant meals in the market; it is the price—in terms of restaurant meals—Ingrid has to "pay" to get one more room.

Looking at this another way, the slope of the budget line—minus the relative price—tells us the opportunity cost of each good in terms of the other. The relative price illustrates the opportunity cost to an individual of consuming one more unit of one good in terms of how much of the other good in their consumption bundle must be forgone. This opportunity cost arises from the consumer's limited resources—their limited budget.

It's useful to note that Equations 10A-8, 10A-9, and 10A-10 give us all the information we need about what happens to the budget line when relative price or income changes. From Equations 10A-8 and 10A-9, we can see that a change in income, N, leads to a parallel shift of the budget line: both the vertical and horizontal intercepts will shift. That is, how far out the budget line is from the origin depends on the consumer's income. If a consumer's income rises, the budget line moves outward. If the consumer's income shrinks, the budget line shifts inward. In each case, the slope of the budget line stays the same because the relative price of one good in terms of the other does not change.

In contrast, a change in the relative price P_R/P_M will lead to a change in the slope of the budget line. We'll analyze these changes in the budget line and how the optimal consumption bundle changes when the relative price changes or when income changes in greater detail later in the appendix.

Prices and the Marginal Rate of Substitution

Now we're ready to bring together the slope of the budget line and the slope of the indifference curve to find the optimal consumption bundle. From Equation 10A-6, we know that the slope of the indifference curve at any point is equal to minus the marginal rate of substitution:

(10A-11) Slope of indifference curve $= -\dfrac{MU_R}{MU_M}$

As we've already noted, at the optimal consumption bundle the slope of the budget line and the slope of the indifference curve are equal. We can write this formally by putting Equations 10A-10 and 10A-11 together, which gives us the **relative price rule** for finding the optimal consumption bundle:

(10A-12) *At the optimal consumption bundle:* $-\dfrac{MU_R}{MU_M} = -\dfrac{P_R}{P_M}$

or $\dfrac{MU_R}{MU_M} = \dfrac{P_R}{P_M}$

The **relative price** of good R in terms of good M is equal to P_R/P_M, the rate at which R trades for M in the market.

The **relative price rule** says that at the optimal consumption bundle, the marginal rate of substitution between two goods is equal to their relative price.

FIGURE 10A-7 Understanding the Relative Price Rule

The *relative price* of rooms in terms of restaurant meals is equal to minus the slope of the budget line. The *marginal rate of substitution* of rooms in place of restaurant meals is equal to minus the slope of the indifference curve. The *relative price rule* says that at the optimal consumption bundle, the marginal rate of substitution must equal the relative price. This point can be demonstrated by considering what happens when the marginal rate of substitution is not equal to the relative price. At consumption bundle B, the marginal rate of substitution is larger than the relative price; Ingrid can increase her total utility by moving down her budget line, BL. At C, the marginal rate of substitution is smaller than the relative price, and Ingrid can increase her total utility by moving up the budget line. Only at A, where the relative price rule holds, is her total utility maximized given her budget constraint.

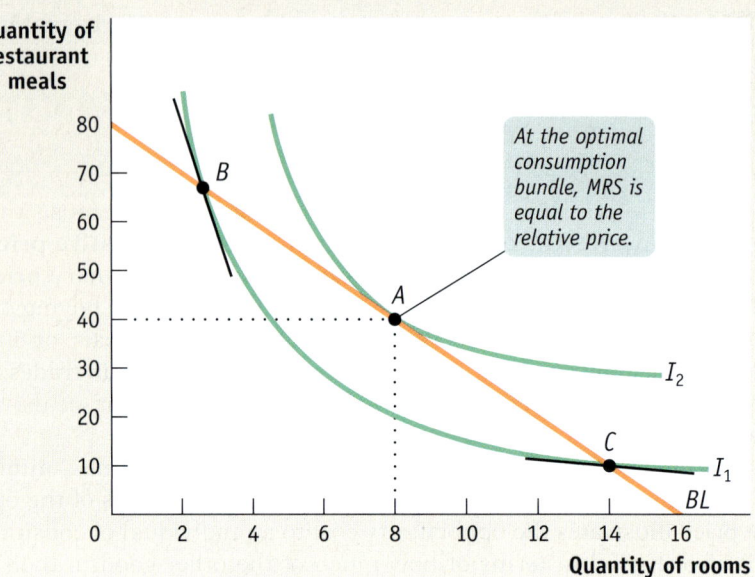

At the optimal consumption bundle, MRS is equal to the relative price.

That is, at the optimal consumption bundle, the marginal rate of substitution between any two goods is equal to the ratio of their prices. Or to put it in a more intuitive way, at Ingrid's optimal consumption bundle, the rate at which she would trade a room in exchange for having fewer restaurant meals along her indifference curve, MU_R/MU_M, is equal to the rate at which rooms are traded for restaurant meals in the market, P_R/P_M.

What would happen if this equality did not hold? We can see by examining Figure 10A-7. There, at point B, the slope of the indifference curve, $-MU_R/MU_M$, is greater in absolute value than the slope of the budget line, $-P_R/P_M$. This means that, at B, Ingrid values an additional room in place of meals *more* than it costs her to buy an additional room and forgo some meals. As a result, Ingrid would be better off moving down her budget line toward A, consuming more rooms and fewer restaurant meals—and because of that, B could not have been her optimal bundle!

Likewise, at C, the slope of Ingrid's indifference curve is less than the slope of the budget line. The implication is that, at C, Ingrid values additional meals in place of a room *more* than it costs her to buy additional meals and forgo a room. Again, Ingrid would be better off moving along her budget line—consuming more restaurant meals and fewer rooms—until she reaches A, her optimal consumption bundle.

But suppose that we do the following transformation to the last term of Equation 10A-12: divide both sides by P_R and multiply both by MU_M. Then the relative price rule becomes (from Chapter 10, Equation 10-3):

(10A-13) *Optimal consumption rule:* $\dfrac{MU_R}{P_R} = \dfrac{MU_M}{P_M}$

So using either the optimal consumption rule (from Chapter 10) or the relative price rule (from this appendix), we find the same optimal consumption bundle.

Preferences and Choices

Now that we have seen how to represent the optimal consumption choice in an indifference curve diagram, we can turn briefly to the relationship between consumer preferences and consumer choices.

When we say that two consumers have different preferences, we mean that they have different utility functions. This in turn means that they will have indifference curve maps with different shapes. And those different maps will translate into different consumption choices, even among consumers with the same income and who face the same prices.

To see this, suppose that Ingrid's friend Lars also consumes only housing and restaurant meals. However, Lars has a stronger preference for restaurant meals and a weaker preference for housing. This difference in preferences is shown in Figure 10A-8, which shows *two* sets of indifference curves: panel (a) shows Ingrid's preferences and panel (b) shows Lars's preferences. Note the difference in their shapes.

Suppose, as before, that rooms cost $150 per month and restaurant meals cost $30. Let's also assume that both Ingrid and Lars have incomes of $2,400 per month, giving them identical budget lines. Nonetheless, because they have different preferences, they will make different consumption choices, as shown in Figure 10A-8. Ingrid will choose 8 rooms and 40 restaurant meals; Lars will choose 4 rooms and 60 restaurant meals.

FIGURE 10A-8 Difference in Preferences

Ingrid and Lars have difference preferences, reflected in the different shapes of their indifference curve maps. So they will choose different consumption bundles even when they have the same possible choices. Both of them have an income of $2,400 per month and face prices of $30 per meal and $150 per room. Panel (a) shows Ingrid's consumption choice: 8 rooms and 40 restaurant meals. Panel (b) shows Lars's choice: even though he has the same budget line, he consumes fewer rooms (4) and more restaurant meals (60).

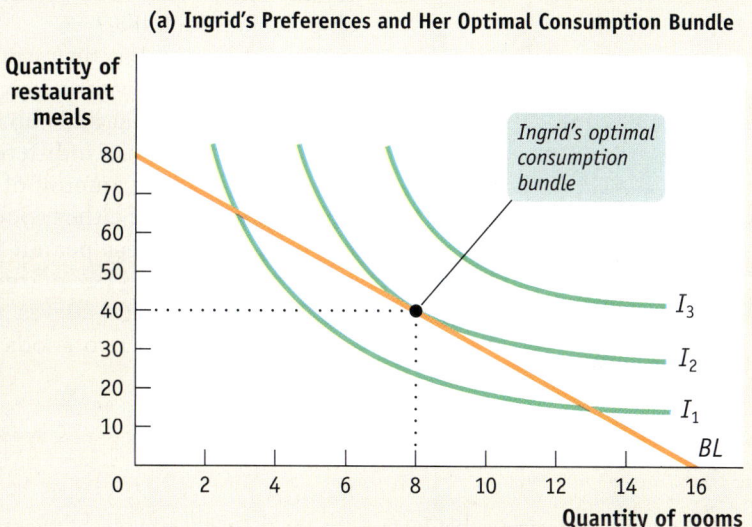

(a) Ingrid's Preferences and Her Optimal Consumption Bundle

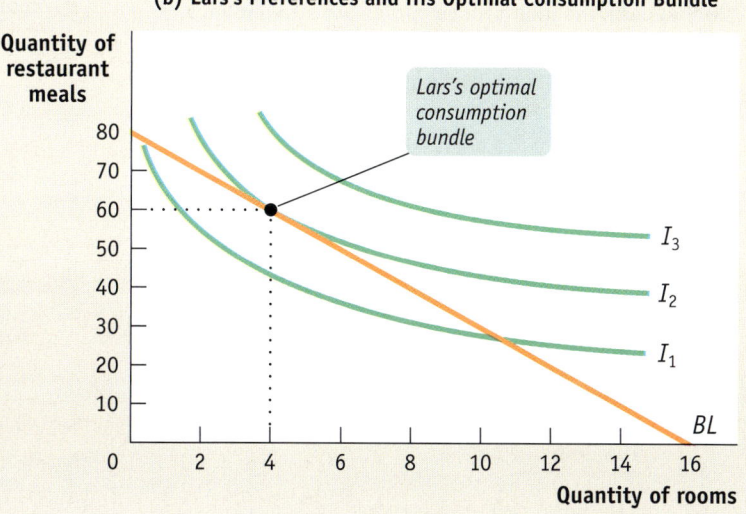

(b) Lars's Preferences and His Optimal Consumption Bundle

Two goods are **perfect substitutes** if the marginal rate of substitution of one good in place of the other good is constant, regardless of how much of each an individual consumes.

Using Indifference Curves: Substitutes and Complements

Now let's apply indifference curve analysis to deepen our understanding of how a consumer classifies different goods based upon their preferences. First, we'll consider the distinction between *substitutes* and *complements*.

Back in Chapter 3, we pointed out that the price of one good often affects the demand for another but that the direction of this effect can go either way: a rise in the price of tea increases the demand for coffee, but a rise in the price of cream reduces the demand for coffee. Tea and coffee are substitutes; cream and coffee are complements.

But what determines whether two goods are substitutes or complements? It depends on the shape of a consumer's indifference curves. This relationship can be illustrated with two extreme cases: the cases of *perfect substitutes* and *perfect complements*.

Perfect Substitutes

Consider Cokie, who likes cookies. She isn't particular: it doesn't matter to her whether she has 3 peanut butter cookies and 7 chocolate chip cookies, or vice versa. What would her indifference curves between peanut butter and chocolate chip cookies look like?

The answer is that they would be straight lines like I_1 and I_2 in Figure 10A-9. For example, I_1 shows that any combination of peanut butter cookies and chocolate chip cookies that adds up to 10 cookies yields Cokie the same utility.

A consumer whose indifference curves are straight lines is always willing to substitute the same amount of one good in place of one unit of the other, regardless of how much of either good they consume. Cokie, for example, is always willing to accept one less peanut butter cookie in exchange for one more chocolate chip cookie, making her marginal rate of substitution *constant*.

When indifference curves are straight lines, we say that goods are **perfect substitutes.** When two goods are perfect substitutes, there is only one relative

---

FIGURE 10A-9 Perfect Substitutes

Two goods are perfect substitutes when the marginal rate of substitution does not depend on the quantities consumed. In that case, the indifference curves are straight lines.

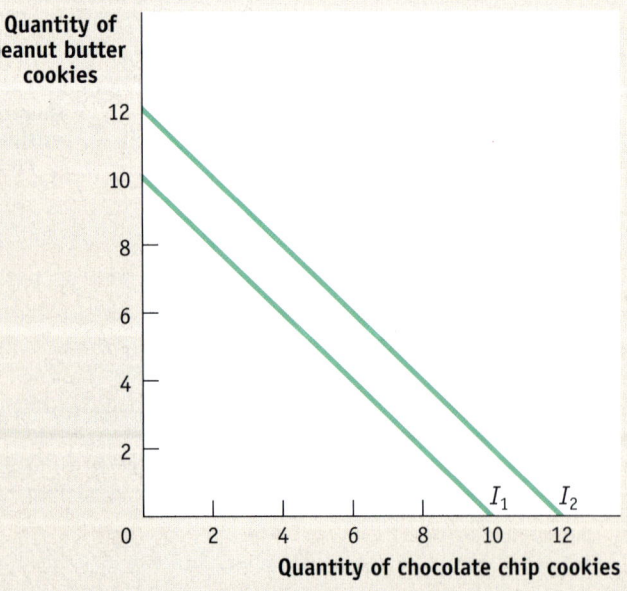

FIGURE 10A-10 Consumer Choice Between Perfect Substitutes

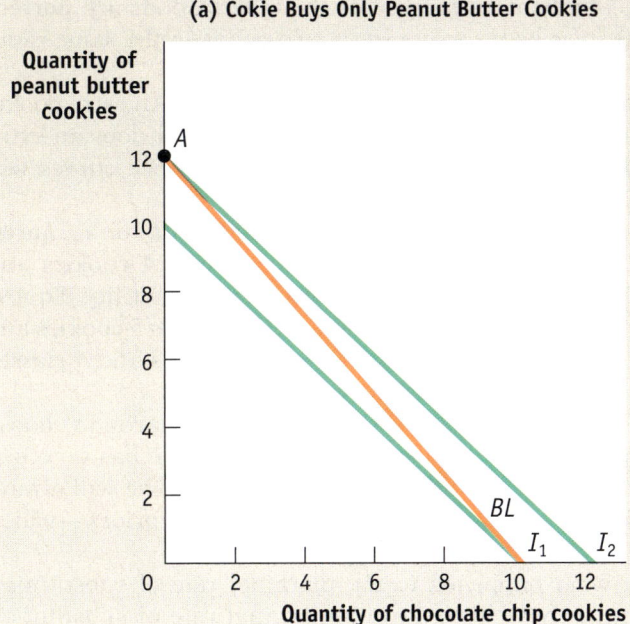

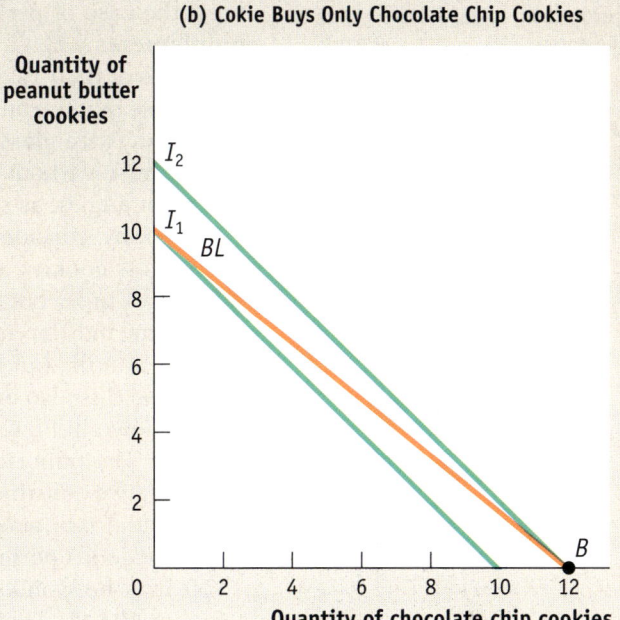

When two goods are perfect substitutes, small price changes lead to large changes in the consumption bundle. In panel (a), the relative price of chocolate chip cookies is slightly higher than the marginal rate of substitution of chocolate chip cookies in place of peanut butter cookies; this is enough to induce Cokie to choose consumption bundle *A*, which consists entirely of peanut butter cookies. In panel (b), the relative price of chocolate chip cookies is slightly lower than the marginal rate of substitution of chocolate chip cookies in place of peanut butter cookies; this induces Cokie to choose bundle *B*, consisting entirely of chocolate chip cookies.

price at which consumers will be willing to purchase both goods; a slightly higher or lower relative price will cause consumers to buy only one of the two goods.

Figure 10A-10 illustrates this point. The indifference curves are the same as those in Figure 10A-9, but now we include Cokie's budget line, *BL*. In each panel, we assume that Cokie has $12 to spend. In panel (a), we assume that chocolate chip cookies cost $1.20 and peanut butter cookies cost $1.00. Cokie's optimal consumption bundle is then at point *A*: she buys 12 peanut butter cookies and no chocolate chip cookies. In panel (b), the situation is reversed: chocolate chip cookies cost $1.00 and peanut butter cookies cost $1.20. In this case, her optimal consumption is at point *B*, where she consumes only chocolate chip cookies.

Why does such a small change in the price cause Cokie to switch all her consumption from one good to the other? Because her marginal rate of substitution is constant and therefore doesn't depend on the composition of her consumption bundle. If the relative price of chocolate chip cookies is more than the marginal rate of substitution of chocolate chip cookies in place of peanut butter cookies, she buys only peanut butter cookies; if it is less, she buys only chocolate chip. And if the relative price of chocolate chip cookies is equal to the marginal rate of substitution, Cokie can maximize her utility by buying any bundle on her budget line. That is, she will be equally happy with any combination of chocolate chip cookies and peanut butter cookies that she can afford. As a result, in this case we cannot predict which particular bundle she will choose among all the bundles that lie on her budget line.

Two goods are **perfect complements** when a consumer wants to consume the goods in the same ratio regardless of their relative price.

Perfect Complements

The case of perfect substitutes represents one extreme form of consumer preferences; the case of perfect complements represents the other. Goods are **perfect complements** when a consumer wants to consume two goods in the same ratio, regardless of their relative price.

Suppose that Aaron likes cookies and milk—but only together. An extra cookie without an extra glass of milk yields no additional utility; neither does an extra glass of milk without another cookie. In this case, his indifference curves will form right angles, as shown in Figure 10A-11.

To see why, consider the three bundles labelled *A*, *B*, and *C*. At *B*, on I_4, Aaron consumes 4 cookies and 4 glasses of milk. At *A*, he consumes 4 cookies and 5 glasses of milk; but the extra glass of milk adds nothing to his utility. So *A* is on the same indifference curve as *B*, I_4. Similarly, at *C* he consumes 5 cookies and 4 glasses of milk, but this yields the same total utility as 4 cookies and 4 glasses of milk. So *C* is also on the same indifference curve, I_4.

Also shown in Figure 10A-11 is a budget line that would allow Aaron to choose bundle *B*. The important point is that the slope of the budget line has no effect on his relative consumption of cookies and milk. This means that he will always consume the two goods in the same proportions regardless of prices—which makes the goods perfect complements.

You may be wondering what happened to the marginal rate of substitution in Figure 10A-11. That is, exactly what is Aaron's marginal rate of substitution between cookies and milk, given that he is unwilling to make any substitutions between them? The answer is that in the case of perfect complements, the marginal rate of substitution is *undefined* because an individual's preferences don't allow *any* substitution between goods.

Less Extreme Cases

There are real-world examples of pairs of goods that are very close to being perfect substitutes. For example, the list of ingredients on a package of Bisquick pancake mix says that it contains "soybean and/or cottonseed oil": the producer uses whichever is cheaper, since consumers can't tell the difference. There are other pairs of goods that are very close to being perfect complements—for example, cars and tires.

FIGURE 10A-11 Perfect Complements

When two goods are perfect complements, a consumer wants to consume the goods in the same ratio regardless of their relative price. Indifference curves take the form of right angles. In this case, Aaron will choose to consume 4 glasses of milk and 4 cookies (bundle *B*) regardless of the slope of the budget line passing through *B*. The reason is that neither an additional glass of milk without an additional cookie (bundle *A*) nor an additional cookie without an additional glass of milk (bundle *C*) adds to his total utility.

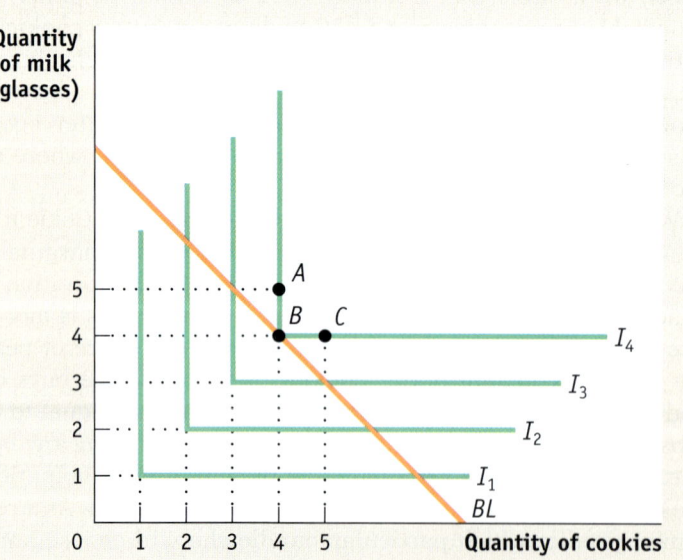

In most cases, however, the possibilities for substitution lie somewhere between these extremes. In some cases it isn't easy to be sure whether goods are substitutes or complements.

‖ Prices, Income, and Demand

Let's return now to Ingrid's consumption choices. In the situation we've considered, her income was $2,400 per month, housing cost $150 per room, and restaurant meals cost $30 each. Her optimal consumption bundle, as seen in Figure 10A-7, contained 8 rooms and 40 restaurant meals.

Let's now ask how her consumption choice would change if either the rent per room or her income changed. As we'll see, we can put these pieces together to deepen our understanding of consumer demand.

The Effects of a Price Increase

Suppose that for some reason there is a sharp increase in housing prices. Ingrid must now pay $600 per room instead of $150. Meanwhile, the price of restaurant meals and her income remain unchanged. How does this change affect her consumption choices?

When the price of rooms rises, the relative price of rooms in terms of restaurant meals rises; as a result, Ingrid's budget line changes (for the worse—but we'll get to that). She responds to that change by choosing a new consumption bundle.

Figure 10A-12 shows Ingrid's original (BL_1) and new (BL_2) budget lines—again, under the assumption that her income remains constant at $2,400 per month. With housing costing $150 per room and a restaurant meal costing $30, her budget line, BL_1, intersected the horizontal axis at 16 rooms and the vertical axis at 80 restaurant meals. After the price of a room rises to $600 per room, the budget line, BL_2, still hits the vertical axis at 80 restaurant meals, but it hits the horizontal axis at only 4 rooms. That's because we know from Equation (10A-9) that the new horizontal intercept of the budget line is now $2,400/$600 = 4. Her budget line has rotated inward and become steeper, reflecting the new, higher relative price of a room in terms of restaurant meals.

FIGURE 10A-12 Effects of a Price Increase on the Budget Line

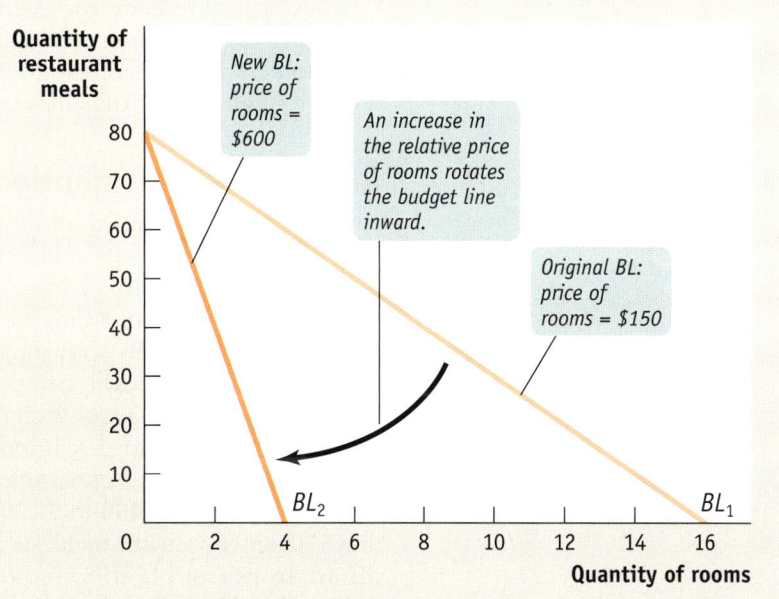

An increase in the price of rooms, holding the price of restaurant meals constant, increases the relative price of rooms in terms of restaurant meals. As a result, Ingrid's original budget line, BL_1, rotates inward to BL_2. Her maximum possible purchase of restaurant meals is unchanged, but her maximum possible purchase of rooms is reduced.

FIGURE 10A-13 Responding to a Price Increase

Ingrid responds to the higher relative price of rooms by choosing a new consumption bundle with fewer rooms and more restaurant meals. Her new optimal consumption bundle, *C*, contains 1 room instead of 8 and 60 restaurant meals instead of 40.

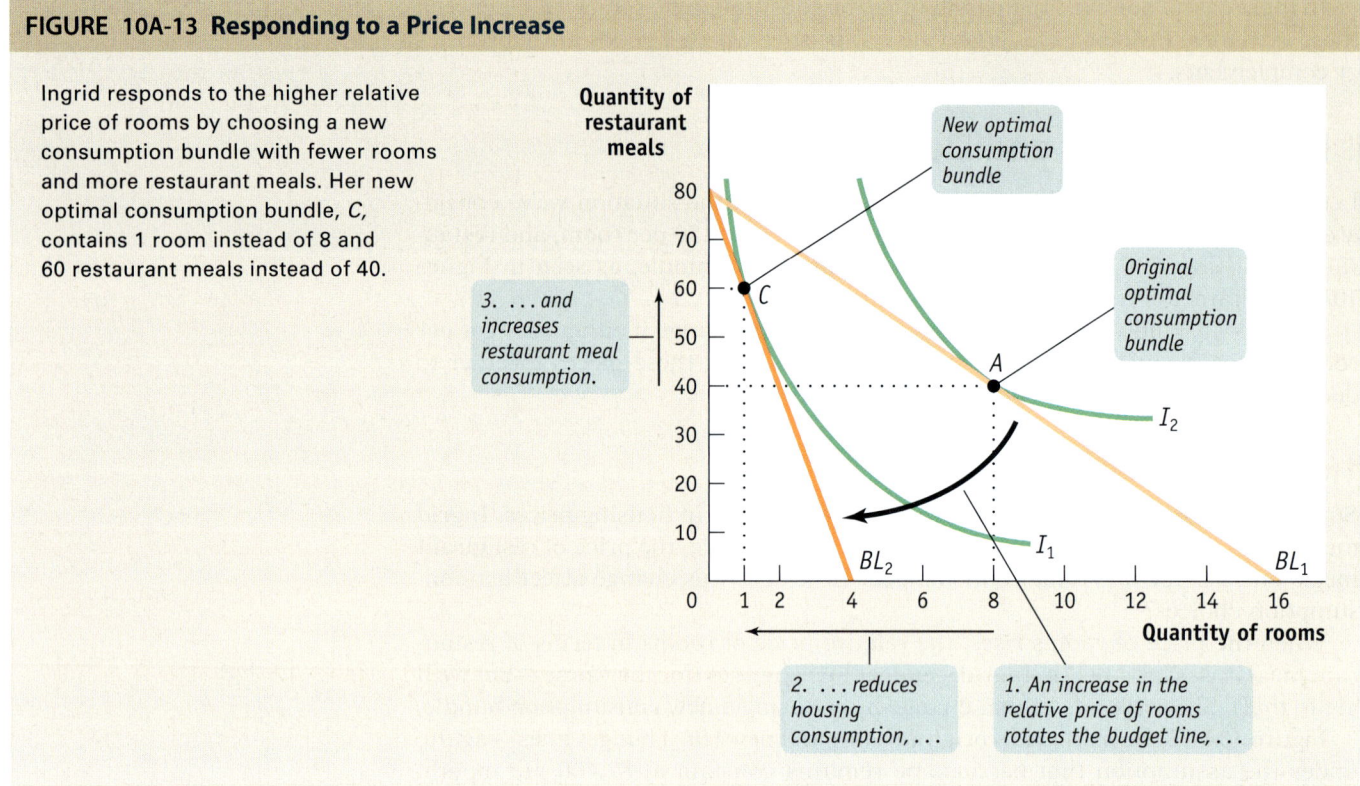

Figure 10A-13 shows how Ingrid responds to her new circumstances. Her original optimal consumption bundle consists of 8 rooms and 40 meals. After her budget line rotates in response to the change in relative price, she finds her new optimal consumption bundle by choosing the point on *BL₂* that brings her to as high an indifference curve as possible. At the new optimal consumption bundle, she consumes fewer rooms and more restaurant meals than before: 1 room and 60 restaurant meals.

Why does Ingrid's consumption of rooms fall? Part—but only part—of the reason is that the rise in the price of rooms reduces her purchasing power, making her poorer. That is, the higher relative price of rooms rotates her budget line inward toward the origin, reducing her consumption possibilities and putting her on a lower indifference curve. In a sense, when she faces a higher price of housing, it's as if her income declined.

To understand this effect, and to see why it isn't the whole story, let's consider a different change in Ingrid's circumstances: a change in her income.

Income and Consumption

In Chapter 3, we learned about the individual demand curve, which shows how a consumer's consumption choice will change as the price of one good changes, holding income and the prices of other goods constant. That is, movement along the individual demand curve primarily shows the substitution effect, as we learned in Chapter 10—how quantity consumed changes in response to changes in the *relative price* of the two goods. But we can also ask how the consumption choice will change if *income* changes, holding relative price constant.

Before we proceed, it's important to understand how a change in income, holding relative price constant, affects the budget line. Suppose that Ingrid's income fell from $2,400 to $1,200 and we hold prices constant at $150 per room and $30 per restaurant meal. As a result, the maximum number of rooms she can afford drops from 16 to 8, and the maximum number of restaurant meals drops from 80 to 40. In other words, Ingrid's consumption possibilities have shrunk,

FIGURE 10A-14 **Effect of a Change in Income on the Budget Line**

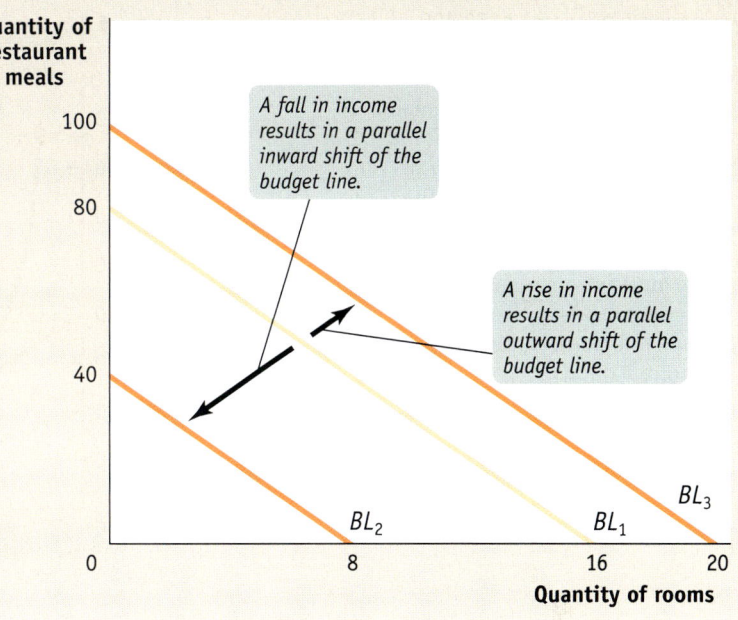

When relative prices are held constant, the budget line shifts parallel in response to changes in income. For example, if Ingrid's income falls from $2,400 to $1,200, she is clearly worse off: her budget line shifts inward from BL_1 to its new position at BL_2. In contrast, if Ingrid's income rises from $2,400 to $3,000, she is clearly better off: her budget line shifts outward from BL_1 to its new position at BL_3.

A fall in income results in a parallel inward shift of the budget line.

A rise in income results in a parallel outward shift of the budget line.

as shown by the parallel inward shift of the budget line in Figure 10A-14 from BL_1 to BL_2. It's a parallel shift because the slope of the budget line—the relative price—remains unchanged when income changes.

Alternatively, suppose Ingrid's income rises from $2,400 to $3,000. She can now afford a maximum of 20 rooms or 100 meals, leading to a *parallel outward shift* of the budget line—the shift from BL_1 to BL_3 in Figure 10A-14. In this case, Ingrid's consumption possibilities have expanded.

Now we are ready to consider how Ingrid responds to a direct change in income—that is, a change in her income level holding relative price constant. Figure 10A-15 compares Ingrid's budget line and optimal consumption choice at an income of $2,400 per month ($BL_1$) with her budget line and optimal consumption choice at an income of $1,200 per month ($BL_2$), keeping prices constant at $150 per room and $30 per restaurant meal. Point *A* is Ingrid's optimal consumption bundle at an income of $2,400, and point *B* is her optimal consumption bundle at an income of $1,200. In each case, her optimal consumption bundle is given by the point at which the budget line is tangent to the indifference curve. As you can see, at the lower income her budget line shifts inward compared to her budget line at the higher income but maintains the same slope because relative price has not changed.

This means that she must reduce her consumption of either housing or restaurant meals, or both. As a result, she is at a lower level of total utility, represented by a lower indifference curve.

As it turns out, Ingrid chooses to consume less of both goods when her income falls: as her income goes from $2,400 to $1,200, her consumption of housing falls from 8 to 4 rooms and her consumption of restaurant meals falls from 40 to 20. This is because in her utility function both goods are *normal goods,* as defined in Chapter 3: goods for which demand increases when income rises and for which demand decreases when income falls.

Although most goods are normal goods, we also pointed out in Chapter 3 that some goods are *inferior goods,* goods for which demand moves in the opposite direction to the change in income: demand decreases when income rises, and demand increases when income falls. An example might be second-hand furniture. Whether a good is an inferior good depends on the consumer's indifference

FIGURE 10A-15 Income and Consumption: Normal Goods

At a monthly income of $2,400, Ingrid chooses bundle A, consisting of 8 rooms and 40 restaurant meals. When relative price remains unchanged, a fall in income shifts her budget line inward to BL_2. At a monthly income of $1,200, she chooses bundle B, consisting of 4 rooms and 20 restaurant meals. Since Ingrid's consumption of both restaurant meals and rooms falls when her income falls, both goods are normal goods.

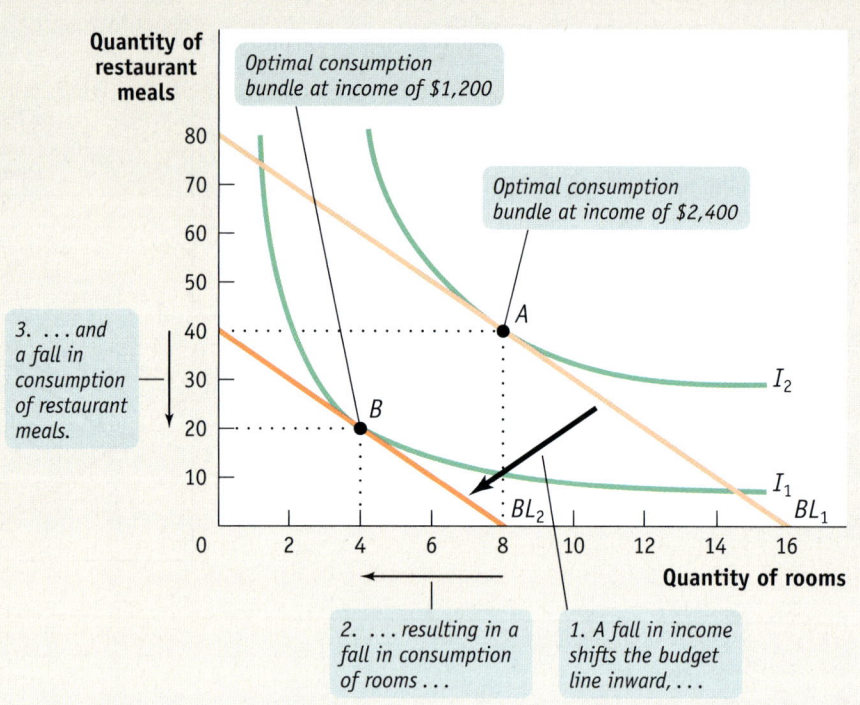

curve map. Figure 10A-16 illustrates such a case, where second-hand furniture is measured on the horizontal axis and restaurant meals are measured on the vertical axis. Note that when Ingrid's income falls from $2,400 ($BL_1$) to $1,200 ($BL_2$), and her optimal consumption bundle goes from D to E, her consumption of second-hand furniture increases—implying that second-hand furniture is an inferior good. Simultaneously, her consumption of restaurant meals decreases—implying that restaurant meals are a normal good.

FIGURE 10A-16 Income and Consumption: An Inferior Good

When Ingrid's income falls from $2,400 to $1,200, her optimal consumption bundle changes from D to E. Her consumption of second-hand furniture increases, implying that second-hand furniture is an inferior good. In contrast, her consumption of restaurant meals falls, implying that restaurant meals are a normal good.

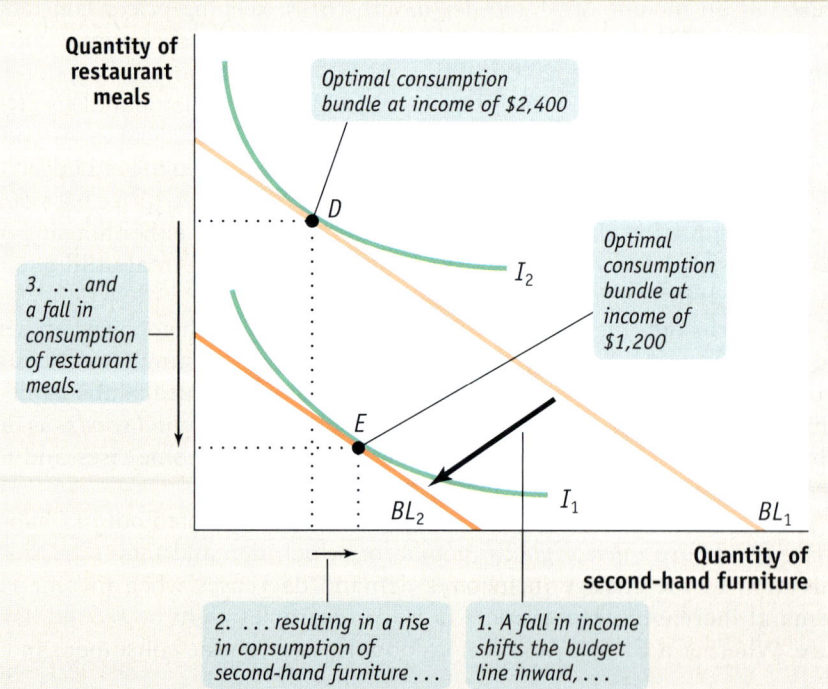

Income and Substitution Effects

Now that we have examined the effects of a change in income, we can return to the issue of a change in price—and show in a more specific way that the effect of a higher price on demand has an income component.

Figure 10A-17 shows, once again, Ingrid's original (BL_1) and new (BL_2) budget lines and consumption choices with a monthly income of $2,400. At a housing price of $150 per room, Ingrid chooses the consumption bundle at A; at a housing price of $600 per room, she chooses the consumption bundle at C.

Let's notice again what happens to Ingrid's budget line after the increase in the price of housing. It continues to hit the vertical axis at 80 restaurant meals; that is, if Ingrid were to spend all her income on restaurant meals, the increase in the price of housing would not affect her. But the new budget line hits the horizontal axis at only 4 rooms. So the budget line has rotated, *shifting inward* and *becoming steeper,* as a consequence of the rise in the relative price of rooms.

We already know what happens: Ingrid's consumption of housing falls from 8 rooms to 1 room. But the figure suggests that there are *two* reasons for the fall in Ingrid's housing consumption. One reason she consumes fewer rooms is that, because of the higher relative price of rooms, the opportunity cost of a room measured in restaurant meals—the quantity of restaurant meals she must give up to consume an additional room—has increased. This change in opportunity cost, which is reflected in the steeper slope of the budget line, gives her an incentive to substitute restaurant meals in place of rooms in her consumption. She now consumes more restaurant meals: 60 instead of 40.

But the other reason Ingrid consumes fewer rooms after their price increases is that the rise in the price of rooms makes her *poorer.* True, her money income hasn't changed. But she must pay more for rooms, and as a result her budget line has rotated inward. So she cannot reach the same level of total utility as before, meaning that her real income has fallen. That is why she ends up on a lower indifference curve.

In the real world, these effects—an increase in the price of a good raises its opportunity cost and also makes consumers poorer—usually go together. But in our imagination we can separate them. In Chapter 10, we introduced

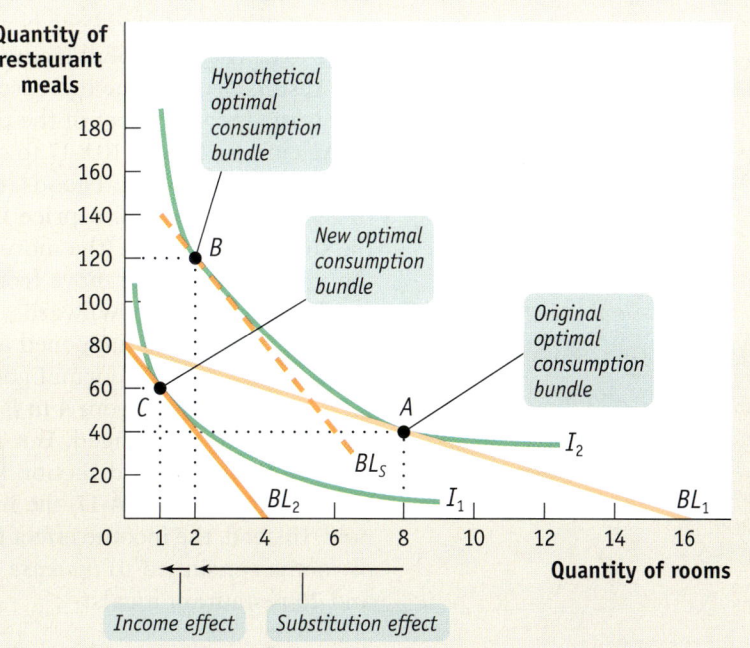

FIGURE 10A-17 Income and Substitution Effects

The movement from Ingrid's original optimal consumption bundle when the price of rooms is $150, A, to her new optimal consumption bundle when the price of rooms is $600, C, can be decomposed into two parts. The movement from A to B—the movement along the original indifference curve, I_2, as relative price changes—is the pure substitution effect. It captures how her consumption would change if she were given a hypothetical increase in income that just compensates her for the increase in the price of rooms, leaving her total utility unchanged. The movement from B to C, the change in consumption when we remove that hypothetical income compensation, is the income effect of the price increase—how her consumption changes as a result of the fall in her purchasing power.

the distinction between the *substitution effect* of a price change (the change in consumption that arises from the substitution of the good that is now relatively cheaper in place of the good that is now relatively more expensive) and the *income effect* (the change in consumption caused by the change in purchasing power arising from a price change). Now we can show these two effects more clearly.

To isolate the substitution effect, let's temporarily change the story about why Ingrid faces an increase in rent: it's not that housing has become more expensive, it's the fact that she has moved from Winnipeg to Vancouver, where rents are higher. But let's consider a hypothetical scenario—let's suppose momentarily that she earns more in Vancouver and that the higher income is just enough to *compensate* her for the higher price of housing, so that her total utility is exactly the same as before.

Figure 10A-17 shows her situation before and after the move. The bundle labelled *A* represents Ingrid's original consumption choice: 8 rooms and 40 restaurant meals. When she moves to Vancouver, she faces a higher price of housing, so her budget line becomes steeper. But we have just assumed that her move increases her income by just enough to compensate for the higher price of housing—that is, just enough to let her reach the original indifference curve. So her new *hypothetical* optimal consumption bundle is at *B*, where the steeper dashed hypothetical budget line (BL_S) is just tangent to the original indifference curve (I_2). By assuming that we have compensated Ingrid for the loss in purchasing power due to the increase in the price of housing, we isolate the *pure substitution effect* of the change in relative price on her consumption.

At *B*, Ingrid's consumption bundle contains 2 rooms and 120 restaurant meals. This costs $4,800 (2 rooms at $600 each, and 120 meals at $30 each). So if Ingrid faces an increase in the price of housing from $150 to $600 per room, but also experiences a rise in her income from $2,400 to $4,800 per month, she ends up with the same level of total utility.

The movement from *A* to *B* is the pure substitution effect of the price change. It is the effect on Ingrid's consumption choice when we change the relative price of housing while keeping her total utility constant.

Now that we have isolated the substitution effect, we can bring back the income effect of the price change. That's easy: we just go back to the original story, in which Ingrid faces an increase in the price of housing *without* any rise in income. We already know that this leads her to *C* in Figure 10A-17. But we can think of the move from *A* to *C* as taking place in two steps. First, Ingrid moves from *A* to *B*, the substitution effect of the change in relative price. Then we take away the extra income needed to keep her on the original indifference curve, causing her to move to *C*. The movement from *B* to *C* is the additional change in Ingrid's demand that results because the increase in housing prices actually reduces her utility. So this is the income effect of the price change.

We can use Figure 10A-17 to confirm that rooms are a normal good in Ingrid's preferences. For normal goods, the income effect and the substitution effect work in the same direction: a price increase induces a fall in quantity consumed by the substitution effect (the move from *A* to *B*) and a fall in quantity consumed by the income effect (the move from *B* to *C*). That's why demand curves for normal goods always slope downward.

What would have happened as a result of the increase in the price of housing if, instead of being a normal good, rooms had been an inferior good for Ingrid? First, the movement from *A* to *B* depicted in Figure 10A-17, the substitution effect, would remain unchanged. But an income change causes quantity consumed to move in the opposite direction for an inferior good. So the movement from *B* to *C* shown in Figure 10A-17, the income effect for a normal good, would no longer hold. Instead, the income effect for an inferior good would cause Ingrid's quantity of rooms consumed to *increase* from *B*—say, to a bundle consisting of 3 rooms and 20 restaurant meals.

In the end, the demand curves for inferior goods normally slope downward: if Ingrid consumes 3 rooms after the increase in the price of housing, it is still 5 fewer rooms than she consumed before. So although the income effect moves in the opposite direction of the substitution effect in the case of an inferior good, in this example the substitution effect is stronger than the income effect.

But what if there existed a type of inferior good in which the income effect is so strong that it dominates the substitution effect? Would a demand curve for that good then slope upward—that is, would quantity demanded increase when price increases? The answer is yes: you have encountered such a good already—it is called a *Giffen good*, and it was described in Chapter 10. As we noted there, Giffen goods are rare creatures, but they cannot be ruled out.

Is the distinction between income and substitution effects important in practice? For analyzing the demand for goods, the answer is that it usually isn't that important. However, in Chapter 19, we'll discuss how individuals make decisions about how much of their labour to supply to employers. In that case income and substitution effects work in opposite directions, and the distinction between them becomes crucial.

PRACTICE QUESTIONS

1. The four properties of indifference curves for ordinary goods illustrated in Figure 10A-4 rule out certain indifference curves. Determine whether those general properties allow each of the following indifference curves. If not, state which of the general principles rules out the curves.

a.

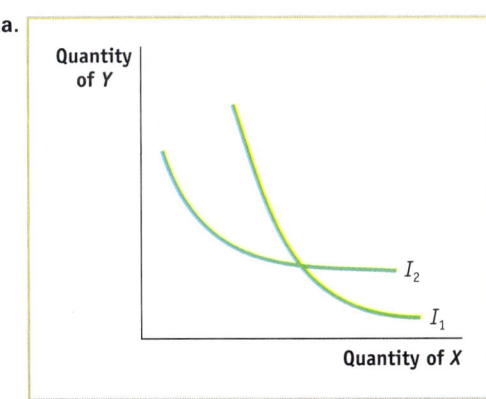

b.

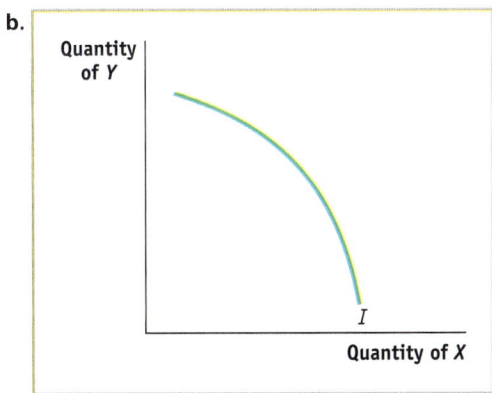

c.

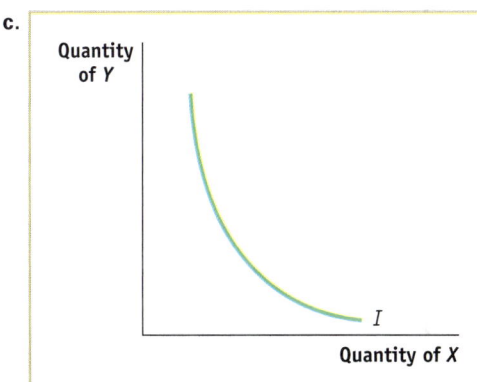

d.

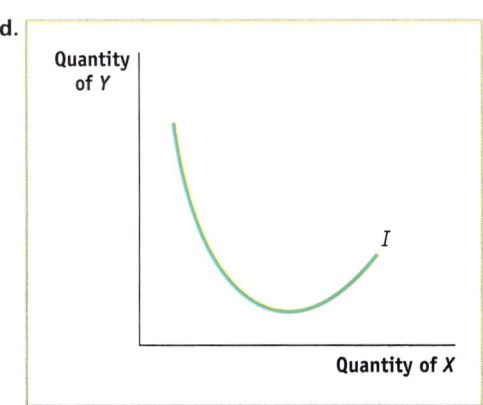

2. Ralph and Lauren are talking about how much they like going to the gym and how much they like eating out at their favourite restaurant and they regularly do some of each. A session at the gym costs the same as a meal at the restaurant. Ralph says that, for his current consumption of gym sessions and restaurant meals,

he values 1 more meal twice as much as he values 1 more session at the gym. Lauren is studying economics, and she tells him that his current consumption bundle cannot be optimal.

a. Is Lauren right? Why or why not? Draw a diagram of Ralph's budget line and the indifference curve that he is on by making his current consumption choice. Place restaurant meals on the horizontal axis and gym sessions on the vertical axis.

b. How should Ralph adjust his consumption so that it is optimal? Illustrate an optimal choice in your diagram.

3. For Norma, both nachos and french fries are normal goods. They are also ordinary goods for Norma. The price of nachos rises, but the price of french fries remains unchanged.

a. Can you determine definitively whether she consumes more or fewer nachos? Explain with a diagram, placing nachos on the horizontal axis and french fries on the vertical axis.

b. Can you determine definitively whether she consumes more or less french fries? Explain with a diagram, placing nachos on the horizontal axis and french fries on the vertical axis.

4. Pam spends her money on bread and Spam, and her indifference curves obey the four properties of indifference curves for ordinary goods. Suppose that, for Pam, Spam is an inferior, but not a Giffen, good; bread is a normal good. Bread costs $2 per loaf, and Spam costs $2 per can. Pam has $20 to spend.

a. Draw a diagram of Pam's budget line, placing Spam on the horizontal axis and bread on the vertical axis. Suppose her optimal consumption bundle is 4 cans of Spam and 6 loaves of bread. Illustrate that bundle and draw the indifference curve on which it lies.

b. The price of Spam falls to $1; the price of bread remains the same. Pam now buys 7 loaves of bread and 6 cans of Spam. Illustrate her new budget line and new optimal consumption bundle in your diagram. Also draw the indifference curve on which this bundle lies.

c. In your diagram, show the income and substitution effects from this fall in the price of Spam. Remember that Spam is an inferior good for Pam.

5. Katya commutes to work. She can either use public transport or her own car. Her indifference curves obey the four properties of indifference curves for ordinary goods.

a. Draw Katya's budget line with car travel on the vertical axis and public transport on the horizontal axis. Suppose that Katya consumes some of both goods. Draw an indifference curve that helps you illustrate her optimal consumption bundle.

b. Now the price of public transport falls. Draw Katya's new budget line.

c. For Katya, public transport is an inferior, but not a Giffen, good. Draw an indifference curve that illustrates her optimal consumption bundle after the price of public transport has fallen. Is Katya consuming more or less public transport?

d. Show the income and substitution effects from this fall in the price of public transport.

6. Carmen consumes nothing but cafeteria meals and music albums. Her indifference curves exhibit the four general properties of indifference curves. Cafeteria meals cost $5 each, and albums cost $10. Carmen has $50 to spend.

a. Draw Carmen's budget line and an indifference curve that illustrates her optimal consumption bundle. Place cafeteria meals on the horizontal axis and albums on the vertical axis. You do not have enough information to know the specific tangency point, so choose one arbitrarily.

b. Now Carmen's income rises to $100. Draw her new budget line on the same diagram, as well as an indifference curve that illustrates her optimal consumption bundle. Assume that cafeteria meals are an inferior good.

c. Can you draw an indifference curve showing that cafeteria meals and albums are both inferior goods?

PROBLEMS

1. For each of the following situations, draw a diagram containing three of Isabella's indifference curves.

a. For Isabella, cars and tires are perfect complements, but in a ratio of 1:4; that is, for each car, Isabella wants exactly four tires. Be sure to label and number the axes of your diagram. Place tires on the horizontal axis and cars on the vertical axis.

b. Isabella gets utility only from her caffeine intake. She can consume Valley Dew or cola, and Valley Dew contains twice as much caffeine as cola.

Be sure to label and number the axes of your diagram. Place cola on the horizontal axis and Valley Dew on the vertical axis.

c. Isabella gets utility from consuming two goods: leisure time and income. Both have diminishing marginal utility. Be sure to label the axes of your diagram. Place leisure on the horizontal axis and income on the vertical axis.

d. Isabella can consume two goods: skis and bindings. For each ski she wants exactly one binding. Be sure to label and number the axes of your diagram. Place bindings on the horizontal axis and skis on the vertical axis.

   e. Isabella gets utility from consuming pop. But she gets no utility from consuming water: any more, or any less, water leaves her total utility level unchanged. Be sure to label the axes of your diagram. Place water on the horizontal axis and pop on the vertical axis.

2. Use the four properties of indifference curves for ordinary goods illustrated in Figure 10A-4 to answer the following questions.

   a. Can you rank the following two bundles? If so, which property of indifference curves helps you rank them?

   Bundle *A:* 2 movie tickets and 3 cafeteria meals

   Bundle *B:* 4 movie tickets and 8 cafeteria meals

   b. Can you rank the following two bundles? If so, which property of indifference curves helps you rank them?

   Bundle *A:* 2 movie tickets and 3 cafeteria meals

   Bundle *B:* 4 movie tickets and 3 cafeteria meals

   c. Can you rank the following two bundles? If so, which property of indifference curves helps you rank them?

   Bundle *A:* 12 videos and 4 bags of chips

   Bundle *B:* 5 videos and 10 bags of chips

   d. Suppose you are indifferent between the following two bundles:

   Bundle *A:* 10 breakfasts and 4 dinners

   Bundle *B:* 4 breakfasts and 10 dinners

   Now compare bundle *A* and the following bundle:

   Bundle *C:* 7 breakfasts and 7 dinners

   Can you rank bundle *A* and bundle *C*? If so, which property of indifference curves helps you rank them? (*Hint:* It may help if you draw this, placing dinners on the horizontal axis and breakfasts on the vertical axis. And remember that breakfasts and dinners are ordinary goods.)

3. Restaurant meals and housing (measured by the number of rooms) are the only two goods that Neha can buy. She has income of $1,000, and the price of each room is $100. The relative price of 1 room in terms of restaurant meals is 5. How many restaurant meals can she buy if she spends all her money on them?

4. Answer the following questions based on two assumptions: (1) Inflation increases the prices of all goods by 20%. (2) Ina's income increases from $50,000 to $55,000.

   a. Has Ina's budget line become steeper, less steep, or equally as steep?

   b. Has Ina's budget line shifted outward, inward, or not at all?

5. Kory has an income of $50, which she can spend on two goods: music albums and cups of hot chocolate. Both are normal goods for her. Each album costs $10, and each cup of hot chocolate costs $2. For each of the following situations, decide whether this is Kory's optimal consumption bundle. If not, what should Kory do to achieve her optimal consumption bundle?

   a. Kory is considering buying 4 albums and 5 cups of hot chocolate. At that bundle, her marginal rate of substitution of albums in place of hot chocolate is 1; that is, she would be willing to forgo only 1 cup of hot chocolate to acquire 1 album.

   b. Kory is considering buying 2 albums and 15 cups of hot chocolate. Kory's marginal utility of the second album is 25, and her marginal utility of the fifteenth cup of hot chocolate is 5.

   c. Kory is considering buying 1 album and 10 cups of hot chocolate. At that bundle, her marginal rate of substitution of albums in place of hot chocolate is 5; that is, she would be just willing to exchange 5 cups of hot chocolate for 1 album.

6. Raul has 4 Cal Ripken and 2 Nolan Ryan baseball cards. The prices of these baseball cards are $24 for Cal and $12 for Nolan. Raul, however, would be willing to exchange 1 Cal card for 1 Nolan card.

   a. What is Raul's marginal rate of substitution of Cal Ripken in place of Nolan Ryan baseball cards?

   b. Can Raul buy and sell baseball cards to make himself better off? How?

   c. Suppose Raul has traded baseball cards and after trading still has some of each kind of card. Also, he now no longer wants to make any more trades. What is his marginal rate of substitution of Cal Ripken in place of Nolan Ryan cards now?

7. Sabine can't tell the difference between Coke and Pepsi—the two taste exactly the same to her.

   a. What is Sabine's marginal rate of substitution of Coke in place of Pepsi?

   b. Draw a few of Sabine's indifference curves for Coke and Pepsi. Place Coke on the horizontal axis and Pepsi on the vertical axis.

   c. Sabine has $6 to spend on cola this week. Coke costs $1.50 per bottle and Pepsi costs $1.00. Draw Sabine's budget line for Coke and Pepsi on the same diagram.

   d. What is Sabine's optimal consumption bundle? Show this on your diagram.

   e. If the price of Coke and Pepsi is the same, what combination of Coke and Pepsi will Sabine buy?

8. Gus spends his income on gas for his car and food. The government raises the tax on gas, thereby raising the price of gas. But the government also lowers the income tax, thereby increasing Gus's income. And this rise in income is just enough to place Gus on the same indifference curve as the one he was on before the price of gas rose. Will Gus buy more, less, or the same amount of gas as before these changes? Illustrate your answer with a diagram, placing gas on the horizontal axis and food on the vertical axis.

9. For Crandall, cheese cubes and crackers are perfect complements: he wants to consume exactly 1 cheese cube with each cracker. He has $2.40 to spend on cheese and crackers. One cheese cube costs 20 cents, and 1 cracker costs 10 cents. Draw a diagram, with crackers on the horizontal axis and cheese cubes on the vertical axis, to answer the following questions.

   a. Which bundle will Crandall consume?

   b. The price of crackers rises to 20 cents. How many cheese cubes and how many crackers will Crandall consume?

   c. Show the income and substitution effects from this price rise.

10. The Japanese Ministry of Internal Affairs and Communications collects data on the prices of goods and services in the Ku-area of Tokyo, as well as data on the average Japanese household's monthly income. The accompanying table shows some of this data. (¥ denotes the Japanese currency, the yen.)

Year	Price of eggs (per pack of 10)	Price of tuna (per 100-gram portion)	Average monthly income
2013	¥187	¥392	¥524,810
2015	231	390	524,585

   a. For each of the two years for which you have data, what is the maximum number of packs of eggs that an average Japanese household could have consumed each month? The maximum number of 100-gram portions of tuna? In one diagram, draw the average Japanese household's budget line in 2013 and in 2015. Place the quantity of eggs on the y-axis and the quantity of tuna on the x-axis.

   b. Calculate the relative price of eggs in terms of tuna for each year. Use the relative price rule to determine how the average household's consumption of eggs and tuna would have changed between 2013 and 2015.

WORK IT OUT

11. Tyrone is a utility maximizer. His income is $100, which he can spend on cafeteria meals and on notepads. Each meal costs $5, and each notepad costs $2. At these prices, Tyrone chooses to buy 16 cafeteria meals and 10 notepads.

   a. Draw a diagram that shows Tyrone's choice using an indifference curve and his budget line, placing notepads on the vertical axis and cafeteria meals on the horizontal axis. Label the indifference curve I_1 and the budget line BL_1.

   b. The price of notepads falls to $1; the price of cafeteria meals remains the same. On the same diagram, draw Tyrone's budget line with the new prices and label it BL_H.

   c. Lastly, Tyrone's income falls to $90. On the same diagram, draw his budget line with this income and the new prices and label it BL_2. Is he worse off, better off, or equally as well off with these new prices and lower income than compared to the original prices and higher income? (*Hint:* Determine whether Tyrone can afford to buy his original consumption bundle of 16 meals and 10 notepads with the lower income and new prices.) Illustrate your answer using an indifference curve and label it I_2.

   d. Give an intuitive explanation of your answer to part c. ∎

.11

Behind the Supply Curve: Inputs and Costs

🌎 THE FARMER'S MARGIN

ALTHOUGH LESS THAN 2% OF Canada's population lives on farms, our agricultural sector is immensely productive and feeds much of the world.

How intensively a hectare of land is worked — a decision at the margin — depends on the price of wheat a farmer faces.

If you look at agricultural statistics, however, something may seem a bit surprising: when it comes to yield per hectare, Canadian farmers are often nowhere near the top. Farmers in Western European countries grow about three times as much wheat per hectare as their Canadian counterparts. Are the Europeans better at growing wheat than we are?

No: European farmers are very skillful, but no more so than Canadians. They produce more wheat per hectare because they employ more inputs — more fertilizer and, especially, more labour — per hectare. Of course, this means that European farmers have higher costs than their Canadian counterparts. But because of

government policies, European farmers receive a much higher price for their wheat than Canadian farmers. This gives them an incentive to use more inputs and to expend more effort at the margin to increase the crop yield per hectare.

Notice our use of the phrase "at the margin." Like most decisions that involve a comparison of benefits and costs, decisions about inputs and production involve a comparison of marginal quantities — the marginal cost versus the marginal benefit of producing a bit more from each hectare.

In Chapter 9, we considered the case of Alexa, who had to choose the number of years of schooling that maximized her profit from an education. There we used the profit-maximizing principle of marginal analysis to find the optimal quantity of years of schooling. In this chapter, we will encounter producers who have to make similar "how much" decisions: choosing the quantity of output produced to maximize profit.

Here and in Chapter 12, we will show how marginal analysis can be used to understand these output decisions — decisions that lie behind the supply curve. The first step in this analysis is to show how the relationship between a firm's inputs and its output — its *production function* — determines its *cost curves*, the relationship between cost and quantity of output produced. That is what we will examine in this chapter. In Chapter 12, we will use our understanding of the firm's cost curves to derive the individual and the market supply curves. ●

WHAT YOU WILL LEARN

- What is a firm's **production function**?
- Why is production often subject to **diminishing returns to inputs**?
- What types of costs does a firm face and how does the firm generate its marginal and **average cost** curves?
- Why does a firm's costs differ in the **short run** and in the **long run**?
- What is **increasing returns to scale** and what advantage does it give?

A **production function** is the relationship between the quantity of inputs a firm uses and the quantity of output it produces.

A **fixed input** is an input whose quantity is fixed for a period of time and cannot be varied.

A **variable input** is an input whose quantity the firm can vary at any time.

The **long run** is the time period in which all inputs can be varied.

The **short run** is the time period in which at least one input is fixed.

The **total product curve** shows how the quantity of output depends on the quantity of the variable input, for a given quantity of the fixed input and production technology.

‖ The Production Function

A *firm* is an organization that produces goods or services for sale. To do this, it must transform inputs into output. The quantity of output a firm produces depends on the quantity of inputs; this relationship is known as the firm's **production function.** As we'll see, a firm's production function underlies its *cost curves.* As a first step, let's look at the characteristics of a hypothetical production function.

Inputs and Output

To understand the concept of a production function, let's consider a farm that we assume, for the sake of simplicity, produces only one output, wheat, and uses only two inputs, land and labour. This particular farm is owned by a couple named Riley and Tyler. They hire workers to do the physical labour on the farm. Moreover, we will assume that all potential workers are of the same quality—they are all equally knowledgeable and capable of performing farmwork.

Riley and Tyler's farm sits on 10 hectares of land. No more hectares are available to them, and they are currently unable to either increase or decrease the size of their farm by selling, buying, or leasing hectareage. Land here is what economists call a **fixed input**—an input whose quantity is fixed for a period of time and cannot be varied. Riley and Tyler are, however, free to decide how many workers to hire. The labour provided by these workers is called a **variable input**—an input whose quantity the firm can vary at any time.

In reality, whether or not the quantity of an input is really fixed depends on the time horizon. In the **long run**—that is, given that a long enough period of time has elapsed—firms can adjust the quantity of any input. For example, in the long run, Riley and Tyler can vary the amount of land they farm by buying or selling land. So there are no fixed inputs in the long run.

In contrast, the **short run** is defined as the time period during which at least one input is fixed. Later in this chapter, we'll look more carefully at the distinction between the short run and the long run. But for now, we will restrict our attention to the short run and assume that at least one input is fixed.

Riley and Tyler know that the quantity of wheat they produce depends on the number of workers they hire. Using modern farming techniques, one worker can cultivate the 10-hectare farm, albeit not very intensively. When an additional worker is added, the land is divided equally among all the workers: each worker has 5 hectares to cultivate when 2 workers are employed, each cultivates 3⅓ hectares when 3 are employed, and so on. So as additional workers are employed, the 10 hectares of land are cultivated more intensively and more bushels of wheat are produced.

The relationship between the quantity of labour and the quantity of output, for a given amount of the fixed input and the given production technology (i.e., farming techniques used in this example), constitutes the farm's production function. The production function for Riley and Tyler's farm, where land is the fixed input and labour is a variable input, is shown in the first two columns of the table in Figure 11-1; the diagram there shows the same information graphically. The curve in Figure 11-1 shows how the quantity of output depends on the quantity of the variable input, for a given quantity of the fixed input and the given production technology. It is called the farm's **total product curve.**

The physical quantity of output, bushels of wheat, is measured on the vertical axis; the quantity of the variable input, labour (that is, the number of workers employed), is measured on the horizontal axis. The total product curve here slopes upward, reflecting the fact that more bushels of wheat are produced as more workers are employed.

Although the total product curve in Figure 11-1 slopes upward along its entire length, the slope isn't constant: as you move up the curve to the right, it flattens out. To understand why the slope changes, look at the third column of the table

FIGURE 11-1 **Production Function and Total Product Curve for Riley and Tyler's Farm**

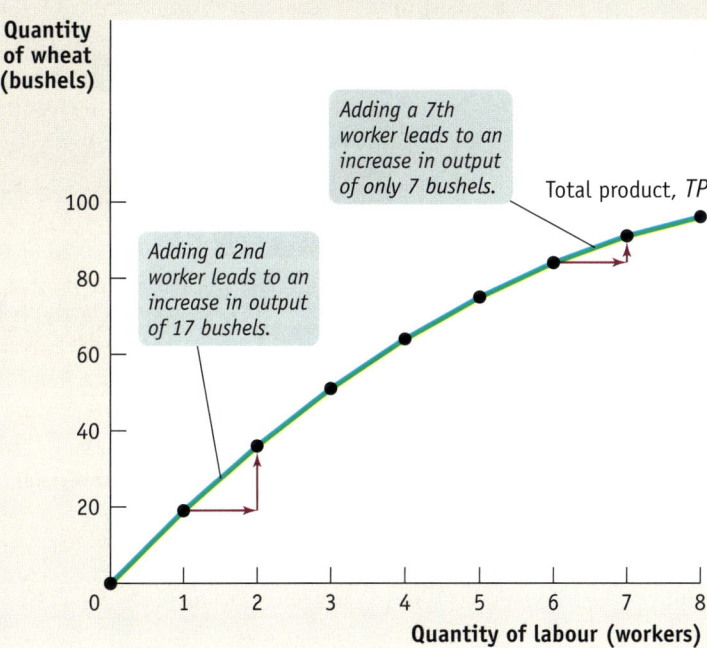

Quantity of labour L (workers)	Quantity of wheat q (bushels)	Marginal product of labour MPL = Δq/ΔL (bushels per worker)
0	0	
		19
1	19	
		17
2	36	
		15
3	51	
		13
4	64	
		11
5	75	
		9
6	84	
		7
7	91	
		5
8	96	

Graph annotations:
Adding a 7th worker leads to an increase in output of only 7 bushels.

Adding a 2nd worker leads to an increase in output of 17 bushels.

Total product, *TP*

The table shows the production function, the relationship between the quantity of the variable input (labour, measured in number of workers) and the quantity of output (wheat, measured in bushels) for a given quantity of the fixed input and production technology. It also calculates the marginal product of labour on Riley and Tyler's farm. The total product curve shows the production function graphically. It slopes upward because more wheat is produced as more workers are employed. It also becomes flatter because the marginal product of labour declines as more and more workers are employed.

in Figure 11-1, which shows the *change in the quantity of output* that is generated by adding one more worker. This is called the *marginal product of labour,* or *MPL:* the additional quantity of output from using one more unit of labour (where one unit of labour is equal to one worker), holding other inputs and the production technology fixed. In general, the **marginal product** of an input is the additional quantity of output that is produced by using one more unit of that input.

In this example, we have data on changes in output at intervals of 1 worker. Sometimes data aren't available in increments of 1 unit—for example, you might have information only on the quantity of output when there are 40 workers and when there are 50 workers. In this case, we use the following equation to calculate the marginal product of labour:

(11-1) $\begin{matrix} \text{Marginal} \\ \text{product} \\ \text{of labour} \end{matrix} = \begin{matrix} \text{Change in quantity of} \\ \text{output produced by one} \\ \text{additional unit of labour} \end{matrix} = \dfrac{\text{Change in quantity of output}}{\text{Change in quantity of labour}}$

Or

$$MPL = \frac{\Delta q}{\Delta L}$$

In this equation, Δ, the Greek uppercase delta, represents the change in a variable.

Now we can explain the significance of the slope of the total product curve: it is equal to the marginal product of labour. The slope of a line is equal to "rise" over "run" (explained in the Chapter 2 graph appendix). This implies that the slope of the total product curve is the change in the quantity of output (the "rise," Δq) divided by the change in the quantity of labour (the "run," ΔL). And this, as we can see from Equation 11-1, is simply the marginal product of labour. So in

The **marginal product** of an input is the additional quantity of output that is produced by using one more unit of that input, holding other inputs and the production technology fixed.

GLOBAL COMPARISON   WHEAT YIELDS AROUND THE WORLD

Wheat yields differ substantially around the world. The disparity between the European Union and Canada that you see in this graph is particularly striking, given that they are both rich economies with comparable agricultural technology. Yet the reason for that disparity is straightforward: differing government policies. In Canada, farmers receive payments from the government to supplement their incomes, but European farmers benefit from price floors. Since European farmers get higher prices for their output than Canadian farmers, they employ more variable inputs and produce significantly higher yields.

Interestingly, in poor countries like Algeria and Ethiopia, foreign aid can lead to significantly depressed yields. Foreign aid from wealthy countries has often taken the form of surplus food, which depresses local market prices, severely hurting the local agriculture that poor countries normally depend on. Charitable organizations like OXFAM have asked wealthy food-producing countries to modify their aid policies — principally, to give aid in cash rather than in food products except in the case of acute food shortages — to avoid this problem.

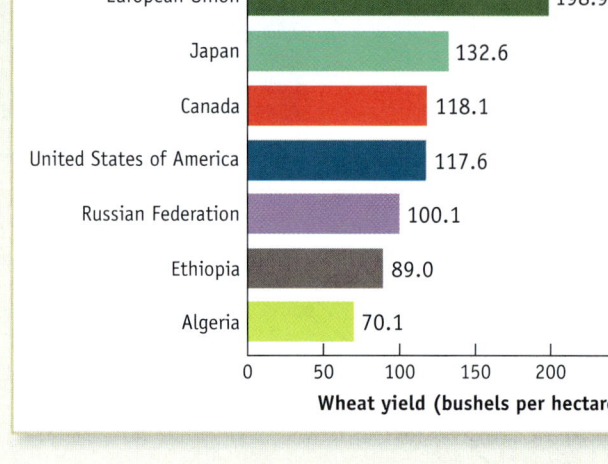

Data from: The Food and Agriculture Organization of the United Nations.

Figure 11-1, the fact that the marginal product of the first worker is 19 also means that the slope of the total product curve in going from 0 to 1 worker is 19. Similarly, the slope of the total product curve in going from 1 to 2 workers is the same as the marginal product of the second worker, 17, and so on.

In this example, the marginal product of labour steadily declines as more workers are hired—that is, each successive worker adds less to output than the previous worker. So as employment increases, the total product curve gets flatter.

Figure 11-2 shows how the marginal product of labour depends on the number of workers employed on the farm. The marginal product of labour, *MPL*, is measured on the vertical axis in units of physical output—bushels of wheat—produced per additional worker, and the number of workers employed is measured on the horizontal axis. You can see from the table in Figure 11-1 that if 5 workers are employed instead of 4, output rises from 64 to 75 bushels; in this case, the marginal product of labour is 11 bushels—the same number found in Figure 11-2. To indicate that 11 bushels is the marginal product when employment rises from 4 to 5, we place the point corresponding to that information halfway between 4 and 5 workers.

In this example, the marginal product of labour falls as the number of workers increases. That is, there are *diminishing returns to labour* on Riley and Tyler's farm. In general, there are **diminishing returns to an input** when an increase in the quantity of that input, holding the quantity of all other inputs fixed and the production technology fixed, reduces that input's marginal product. Due to diminishing returns to labour, the *MPL* curve is negatively sloped.

To grasp why diminishing returns can occur, think about what happens as Riley and Tyler add more and more workers without increasing the number of hectares of land or improving their farming techniques. As the number of workers increases, the land is farmed more intensively and the number of bushels produced increases. But each additional worker is working with a smaller share of the 10 hectares—the fixed input—than the previous worker. As a result, the additional worker cannot produce as much output as the previous worker. So it's not surprising that the marginal product of the additional worker falls.

The crucial point to emphasize about diminishing returns is that, like many propositions in economics, it is an "other things equal" proposition: each

There are **diminishing returns to an input** when an increase in the quantity of that input, holding the levels of all other inputs and the state of technology fixed, leads to a decline in the marginal product of that input.

FIGURE 11-2 Marginal Product of Labour Curve for Riley and Tyler's Farm

The marginal product of labour curve plots each worker's marginal product, the increase in the quantity of output generated by each additional worker, holding other inputs and the production technology fixed. The change in the quantity of output is measured on the vertical axis and the number of workers employed is measured on the horizontal axis. On Riley and Tyler's 10-hectare farm, the first worker employed generates an increase in output of 19 bushels, the second worker generates an increase of 17 bushels, and so on. The curve slopes downward due to diminishing returns to labour.

successive unit of an input will raise production by less than the last *if the quantity of all other inputs and production technology are held fixed.*

What would happen if the levels of other inputs or production technology were allowed to change? You can see the answer illustrated in Figure 11-3. Panel

FIGURE 11-3 Total Product, Marginal Product, and the Fixed Input

(a) Total Product Curves

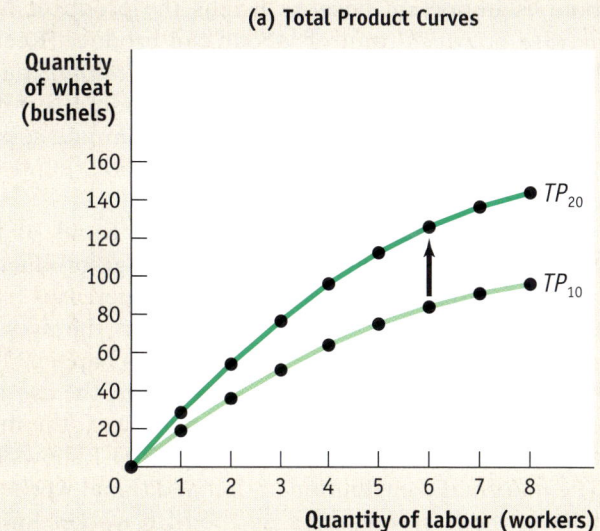

(b) Marginal Product Curves

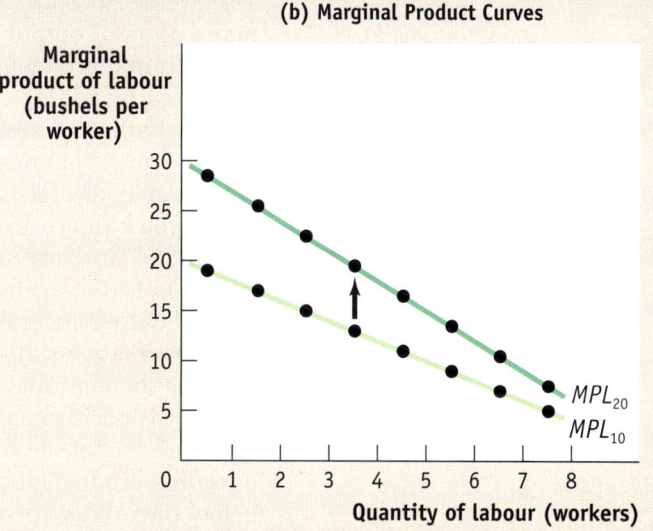

This figure shows how the quantity of output and the marginal product of labour depend on the level of the fixed input and a given state of technology. Panel (a) shows two total product curves for Riley and Tyler's farm, TP_{10} when their farm is 10 hectares and TP_{20} when it is 20 hectares. With more land, each worker can produce more wheat. So an increase in the fixed input shifts the total product curve up from TP_{10} to TP_{20}. This implies that the marginal product of each worker is higher when the farm is 20 hectares than when it is 10 hectares. Panel (b) shows the marginal product of labour curves. The increase in hectareage also shifts the marginal product of labour curve up from MPL_{10} to MPL_{20}. Note that both marginal product of labour curves still slope downward due to diminishing returns to labour. Likewise, if there an in improvement in production technique, both the total product curve and marginal product of labour curve will shift upwards.

(a) shows two total product curves, TP_{10} and TP_{20}. TP_{10} is the farm's total product curve when its total area is 10 hectares (the same curve as in Figure 11-1). TP_{20} is the total product curve when the farm has increased to 20 hectares. Except when 0 workers are employed, TP_{20} lies everywhere above TP_{10} because with more hectares available, any given number of workers produces more output. Panel (b) shows the corresponding marginal product of labour curves. MPL_{10} is the marginal product of labour curve given 10 hectares to cultivate (the same curve as in Figure 11-2), and MPL_{20} is the marginal product of labour curve given 20 hectares.

Both curves slope downward because, in each case, the amount of land is fixed, albeit at different levels. But MPL_{20} lies everywhere above MPL_{10}, reflecting the fact that the marginal product of the same worker is higher when that worker has more of the fixed input to work with.

Figure 11-3 demonstrates a general result: the position of the total product curve of a given input depends on the quantities of other inputs. If you change the quantity of the other inputs or the production technology, both the total product curve and the marginal product curve of the remaining input will shift.

The Average Product of Labour

Riley and Tyler may also be interested in knowing how much wheat is harvested per worker. The *average product of labour*, or *APL*, is the amount of output produced per unit of labour. In general, the **average product** of an input is the amount of output produced per unit of that input employed in the production process:

(11-2) Average product of labour $= \dfrac{\text{Total quantity of output}}{\text{Total quantity of labour employed}}$

or

$$APL = \frac{q}{L}$$

The average product of labour is important because it tells the producer how many units of output the *average* or *typical* unit of labour can produce. Recall, the marginal product of labour shows the *change in the quantity of output* that is generated by adding one more worker. Although these quantities sound similar, they are typically not the same and confusion between them is a common source of errors in economics. Figure 11-4 shows the average product of labour curve for Riley and Tyler's farm compared to the marginal product of labour.

As you can see from the table in Figure 11-4, all other things equal, as the number of workers employed increases, output rises but the average product of labour falls. For example, when the number of workers employed increases from 4 to 5, output increases from 64 bushels to 75 bushels. However, the average product of labour falls from 16 bushels to 15 bushels. Why does this happen? It is because the marginal product is less than the average product; thus, the average product is decreasing. When the number of workers rises from 4 to 5, the marginal product of the fifth worker is 11 bushels (the table in Figure 11-1 shows the marginal product labour). The marginal contribution of that additional worker is below the average productivity of the first 4 workers, so the fifth worker lowers the average product of the whole group. On the farm, the marginal product of labour is less than the average product of labour for all quantities of labour, so the entire average product curve slopes downward.

Our example shows that both marginal product and average product are downward sloping. In practice, however, economists believe that both the marginal product and average product curves often slope *upward* as a firm increases its variable input from some low level (such as zero), sloping downward only at higher levels of this input: so they look like inverted U-shape curves as shown in Figure 11-5.

At a low level of the variable input, the marginal product is increasing because the firm starts with a low number of workers. Adding more workers

The **average product** of an input is the amount of output produced per unit of that input.

FIGURE 11-4 Average and Marginal Product of Labour Curve for Riley and Tyler's Farm

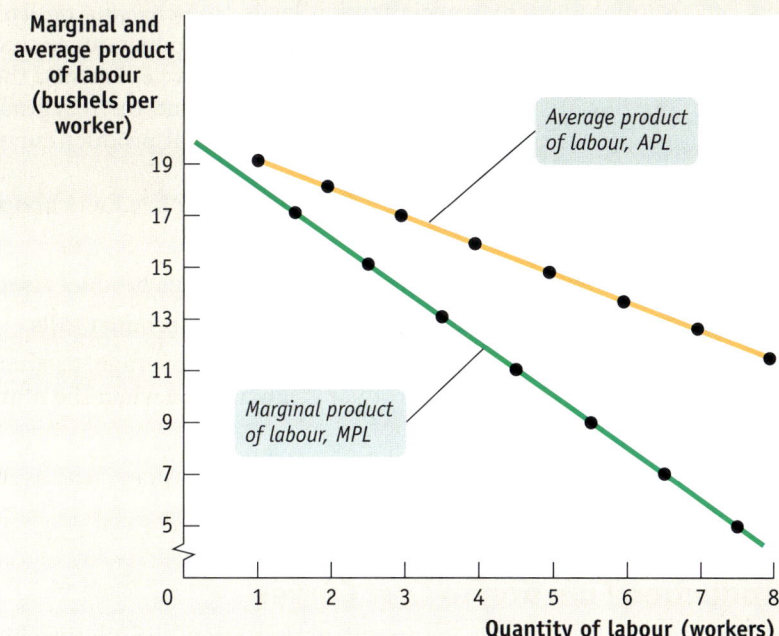

Quantity of labour L (workers)	Quantity of wheat q (bushels)	Marginal product of labour APL = q/L (bushels per worker)
0	0	0
1	19	19
2	36	18
3	51	17
4	64	16
5	75	15
6	84	14
7	91	13
8	96	12

The table shows the production function, the relationship between the quantity of the variable input (labour, measured in number of workers) and the quantity of output (wheat, measured in bushels) for a given quantity of the fixed input and the productive technology. It also calculates the average product of labour on Riley and Tyler's farm. The average product of labour curve shows the average amount of output produced per unit of labour, for a given amount of workers employed. When the farm has one worker, its average product is 19 (the same as the total product). When the farm employs two workers each worker, on average, produces 18 bushels, and so on. The curve slopes downward due to diminishing returns to labour.

in the production process allows these workers to specialize in various tasks. Specialization can allow workers to become more productive, which raises their marginal product. For example, one individual producing salsa would have to perform all the tasks involved: selecting and preparing the ingredients, mixing

FIGURE 11-5 Common Marginal and Average Product of Labour Curves

More realistic marginal product and average product of labour curves look like inverted U-shapes. Starting from a very low input level, the marginal product often rises as the firm employs more of the variable input. That's because hiring additional workers allows greater specialization of their tasks and leads to increasing returns. Once specialization is exhausted, however, diminishing returns to additional workers set in and the marginal product falls. In addition, the average product of labour rises when marginal product exceeds average product, while the average product falls when marginal product is less than average product and average product of labour is maximized when average product equals marginal product.

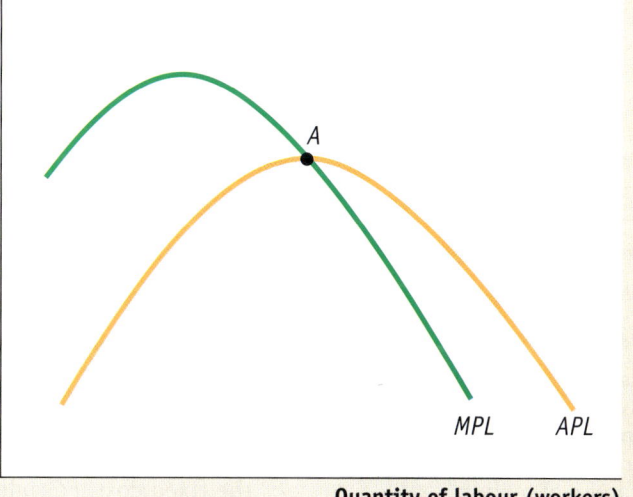

the salsa, bottling and labelling it, packing it into cases, and so on. As more workers are employed, they can divide the tasks, with each worker specializing in one or a few aspects of salsa-making. This specialization leads to *increasing returns* and the hiring of additional workers, resulting in a marginal product curve that initially slopes upward. But once there are enough workers to have exhausted the benefits of specialization, diminishing returns to labour set in and the marginal product curve starts sloping downward. Thus, a typical marginal product curve has an inverted U-shape as shown in Figure 11-5.

By looking at Figure 11-5, you can also observe the following key facts about the relationship between marginal product and average product:

- When marginal product is *greater than* average product, average product rises.
- When marginal product is *less than* average product, average product falls.
- When marginal product is the same as average product, average product remains unchanged. Indeed, the average product is maximized when the marginal product is *equal* to the average product.

As a result, when the marginal product curve has an inverted U-shape, the average product of labour curve also has an inverted U-shape.

From the Production Function to Cost Curves

Once Riley and Tyler know their production function, they know the relationship between inputs of labour and land and output of wheat. But if they want to maximize their profits, they need to translate this knowledge into information about the relationship between the quantity of output and cost. Let's see how they can do this.

To translate information about a firm's production function into information about its costs, we need to know how much the firm must pay for its inputs. We will assume that Riley and Tyler face either an explicit or an implicit cost of $400 for the use of the land. As we learned in Chapter 9, it is irrelevant whether Riley and Tyler must rent the 10 hectares of land for $400 from someone else or whether they own the land themselves and forgo earning $400 from renting it to someone else. Either way, they pay an opportunity cost of $400 by using the land to grow wheat. Moreover, since the land is a fixed input, the $400 Riley and Tyler pay for it is a **fixed cost,** denoted by *FC*—a cost that does not depend on the quantity of output produced (in the short run). In business, fixed cost is often referred to as *overhead cost*.

We also assume that Riley and Tyler must pay each worker $200. Using their production function, Riley and Tyler know that the number of workers they must hire depends on the amount of wheat they intend to produce. So the cost of labour, which is equal to the number of workers multiplied by $200, is a **variable cost,** denoted by *VC*—a cost that depends on the quantity of output produced. It is variable because in order to produce more they have to employ more units of input.

Adding the fixed cost and the variable cost of a given quantity of output gives the **total cost,** or *TC*, of that quantity of output. We can express the relationship among fixed cost, variable cost, and total cost as an equation:

(11-3) Total cost = Fixed cost + Variable cost

Or

$$TC = FC + VC$$

The table in Figure 11-6 shows how total cost is calculated for Riley and Tyler's farm. The second column shows the number of workers employed, *L*. The third column shows the corresponding level of output, *q*, taken from the table in Figure 11-1. The fourth column shows the variable cost, *VC*, equal to the number of workers multiplied by $200, the cost per worker. The fifth column shows the fixed cost, *FC*, which is $400 regardless of how many workers are employed.

A **fixed cost** is a cost that does not depend on the quantity of output produced. It is the cost of the fixed input.

A **variable cost** is a cost that depends on the quantity of output produced. It is the cost of the variable input.

The **total cost** of producing a given quantity of output is the sum of the fixed cost and the variable cost of producing that quantity of output.

FIGURE 11-6 Total Cost Curve for Riley and Tyler's Farm

The table shows the variable cost, fixed cost, and total cost for various output quantities on Riley and Tyler's 10-hectare farm. The total cost curve shows how total cost (measured on the vertical axis) depends on the quantity of output (measured on the horizontal axis). The labelled points on the curve correspond to the rows of the table. The total cost curve slopes upward because the number of workers employed, and hence total cost, increases as the quantity of output increases. The curve gets steeper as output increases due to diminishing returns to labour.

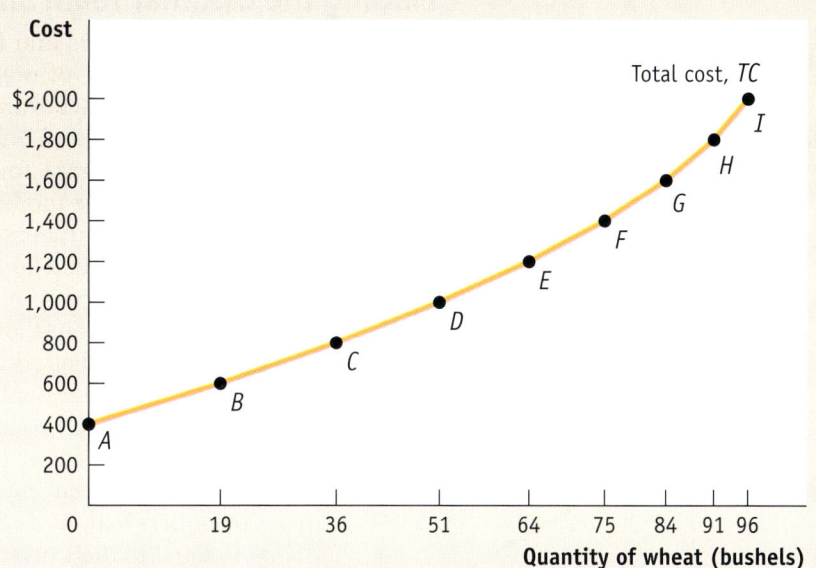

Point on graph	Quantity of labour L (workers)	Quantity of wheat q (bushels)	Variable cost VC	Fixed cost FC	Total cost TC = FC + VC
A	0	0	$0	$400	$400
B	1	19	200	400	600
C	2	36	400	400	800
D	3	51	600	400	1,000
E	4	64	800	400	1,200
F	5	75	1,000	400	1,400
G	6	84	1,200	400	1,600
H	7	91	1,400	400	1,800
I	8	96	1,600	400	2,000

The sixth column shows the total cost of output, *TC*, which is the variable cost plus the fixed cost.

The first column labels each row of the table with a letter, from *A* to *I*. These labels will be helpful in understanding our next step: drawing the **total cost curve,** a curve that shows how total cost depends on the quantity of output.

Riley and Tyler's total cost curve is shown in the diagram in Figure 11-6, where the horizontal axis measures the quantity of output in bushels of wheat and the vertical axis measures total cost in dollars. Each point on the curve corresponds to one row of the table in Figure 11-6. For example, point *A* shows the situation when 0 workers are employed: output is 0, and total cost is equal to fixed cost, $400. Similarly, point *B* shows the situation when 1 worker is employed: output is 19 bushels, and total cost is $600, equal to the sum of $400 in fixed cost and $200 in variable cost.

Like the total product curve, the total cost curve slopes upward: due to the variable cost, the more output produced, the higher the farm's total cost. But unlike the total product curve, which gets flatter as employment rises, the total cost curve gets *steeper*. That is, the slope of the total cost curve is greater as the amount of output produced increases. As we will soon see, the steepening of the total cost curve is also due to diminishing returns to the variable input. Before we can understand this, we must first look at the relationships among several useful measures of cost.

The **total cost curve** shows how total cost depends on the quantity of output.

ECONOMICS >> *in Action*
Finding the Optimal Team Size

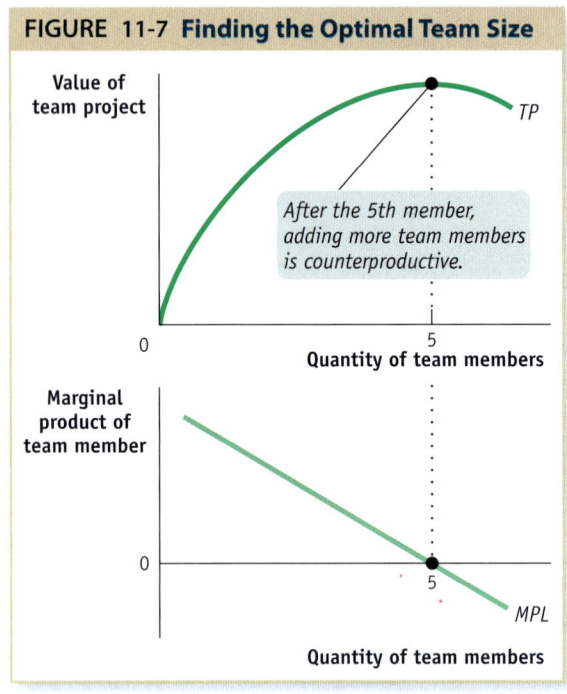

FIGURE 11-7 Finding the Optimal Team Size

After the 5th member, adding more team members is counterproductive.

In both offices and learning environments, team projects are a favourite way of organizing work. They have also been a topic of research. According to one study, the most efficient team size is between 4 and 5 people (4.6 team members, to be exact). Yet researchers have found that project designers routinely create teams that are too large to be efficient. What are project designers failing to understand?

It's true that a larger team has access to more resources, specifically more labour and more human capital. But keep in mind that how large a team should be is a decision at the margin. And studies have shown that adding another person to a team of 5 generally *reduces* the marginal product of existing members. This result is due to a phenomenon called *social loafing:* as the size of the team increases, it's easier to hide individual lack of effort, and the connection between individual effort and reward weakens. So team members loaf. As a result, the marginal product of the 6th member is equal to their personal contribution *minus* the loss due to social loafing that their presence inflicts on other team members.

A larger team must also spend more time coordinating its activities, which reduces the marginal product of each team member. With the addition of each member, team losses get larger. So at some point, team losses from social loafing and coordination costs outweigh the individual contribution made by the 6th team member. This result is well documented among teams of software programmers: at some point, adding another team member reduces the output of the entire team.

This situation is illustrated in Figure 11-7. The top part of the figure shows how the value of the team project varies with the number of team members. Each additional member accomplishes less than the previous one, and beyond a certain point an additional member is actually counterproductive. The bottom part of the figure shows the marginal product of each successive team member, which falls as more team members are employed and eventually becomes negative. In other words, the 6th team member has a negative marginal product.

It appears that project designers are creating teams that are too large by mistakenly focusing on the individual contribution of an additional team member, rather than on the marginal product generated by the *entire* team when another person is added. So, instead of having one large project performed by a team of 10 people, it would be more efficient and productive to split the large project into two smaller projects performed by teams of 5 people. By thinking at the margin, we can understand why, in teamwork, 5 + 5 doesn't equal 10: two teams of 5 people will produce more than one team of 10 people.

>> Quick Review

• The firm's **production function** is the relationship between quantity of inputs and quantity of output. The **total product curve** shows how the quantity of output depends on the quantity of the **variable input** for a given quantity of the **fixed input** and a given state of technology, and its slope is equal to the **marginal product** of the variable input. In the **short run,** the fixed input cannot be varied; in the **long run** all inputs are variable.

• When the levels of all other inputs are fixed, **diminishing returns to an input** may arise, yielding a downward-sloping marginal product curve and a total product curve that becomes flatter as more output is produced.

• The **total cost** of a given quantity of output equals the **fixed cost** plus the **variable cost** of that output. The **total cost curve** becomes steeper as more output is produced due to diminishing returns to the variable input.

>> Check Your Understanding 11-1
Solutions appear at back of book.

1. Bernie's ice-making company produces ice cubes using a 10-tonne machine and electricity. The quantity of output, measured in terms of kilograms of ice, is given in the accompanying table.
   a. What is the fixed input? What is the variable input?
   b. Construct a table showing the marginal product of the variable input. Does it show diminishing returns?

Quantity of electricity (kilowatts per hour)	Quantity of ice (kilograms)
0	0
1	1,000
2	1,800
3	2,400
4	2,800

c. Construct a table showing the average product of the variable input. What happens to the average product as the quantity of variable input used increases?

d. Suppose a 50% increase in the size of the fixed input increases output by 100% for any given amount of the variable input. What is the fixed input now? Construct a table showing the quantity of output, marginal product, and average product in this case.

Two Key Concepts: Marginal Cost and Average Cost

Now that we've learned how to derive a firm's total cost curve from its production function, let's take a deeper look at total cost by deriving two extremely useful measures: *marginal cost* and *average cost*. As we'll see, these two measures of the cost of production have a somewhat surprising relationship to each other. Moreover, they will prove to be vitally important in Chapter 12, where we will use them to analyze the firm's output decision and the market supply curve.

Marginal Cost

We defined *marginal cost* in Chapter 9: it is the change in total cost generated by producing one more unit of output. We've already seen that the marginal product of an input is easiest to calculate if data on output are available in increments of one unit of that input, all other things equal. Similarly, marginal cost is easiest to calculate if data on total cost are available in increments of one unit of output. When the data come in less convenient increments, it's still possible to calculate marginal cost. But for the sake of simplicity, let's work with an example in which the data come in convenient one-unit increments.

Selena's Gourmet Salsas produces bottled salsa and Table 11-1 shows how its costs per day depend on the number of cases of salsa it produces per day. The firm has fixed cost of $108 per day, shown in the second column, which

TABLE 11-1 Costs at Selena's Gourmet Salsas

Quantity of salsa q (cases)	Fixed cost FC	Variable cost VC	Total cost TC = FC + VC	Marginal cost of case MC = ΔTC/Δq
0	$108	$0	$108	
				$12
1	108	12	120	
				36
2	108	48	156	
				60
3	108	108	216	
				84
4	108	192	300	
				108
5	108	300	408	
				132
6	108	432	540	
				156
7	108	588	696	
				180
8	108	768	876	
				204
9	108	972	1,080	
				228
10	108	1,200	1,308	

represents the daily cost of its food-preparation equipment. The third column shows the variable cost, and the fourth column shows the total cost. Panel (a) of Figure 11-8 plots the total cost curve. Like the total cost curve for Riley and Tyler's farm in Figure 11-6, this curve slopes upward, getting steeper as you move up it to the right.

The significance of the slope of the total cost curve is shown by the fifth column of Table 11-1, which calculates *marginal cost*: the additional cost of each additional unit. The general formula for marginal cost is:

$$\textbf{(11-4)} \text{ Marginal cost} = \frac{\text{Change in total cost generated by one additional unit of output}}{} = \frac{\text{Change in total cost}}{\text{Change in quantity of output}}$$

Or

$$MC = \frac{\Delta TC}{\Delta q}$$

As in the case of marginal product, marginal cost is equal to "rise" (the increase in total cost) divided by "run" (the increase in the quantity of output). So just as marginal product is equal to the slope of the total product curve, marginal cost is equal to the slope of the total cost curve.

Now we can understand why the total cost curve gets steeper as we move up it to the right: as you can see in Table 11-1, marginal cost at Selena's Gourmet Salsas rises as output increases. Panel (b) of Figure 11-8 shows the marginal cost curve corresponding to the data in Table 11-1. Notice that, as in Figure 11-2, we plot the marginal cost for increasing output from 0 to 1 case of salsa halfway between 0 and 1, the marginal cost for increasing output from 1 to 2 cases of salsa halfway between 1 and 2, and so on.

Why does the marginal cost curve slope upward? Because there are diminishing returns to inputs in this example. As output increases, the marginal product of the variable input declines. This implies that more and more of the variable

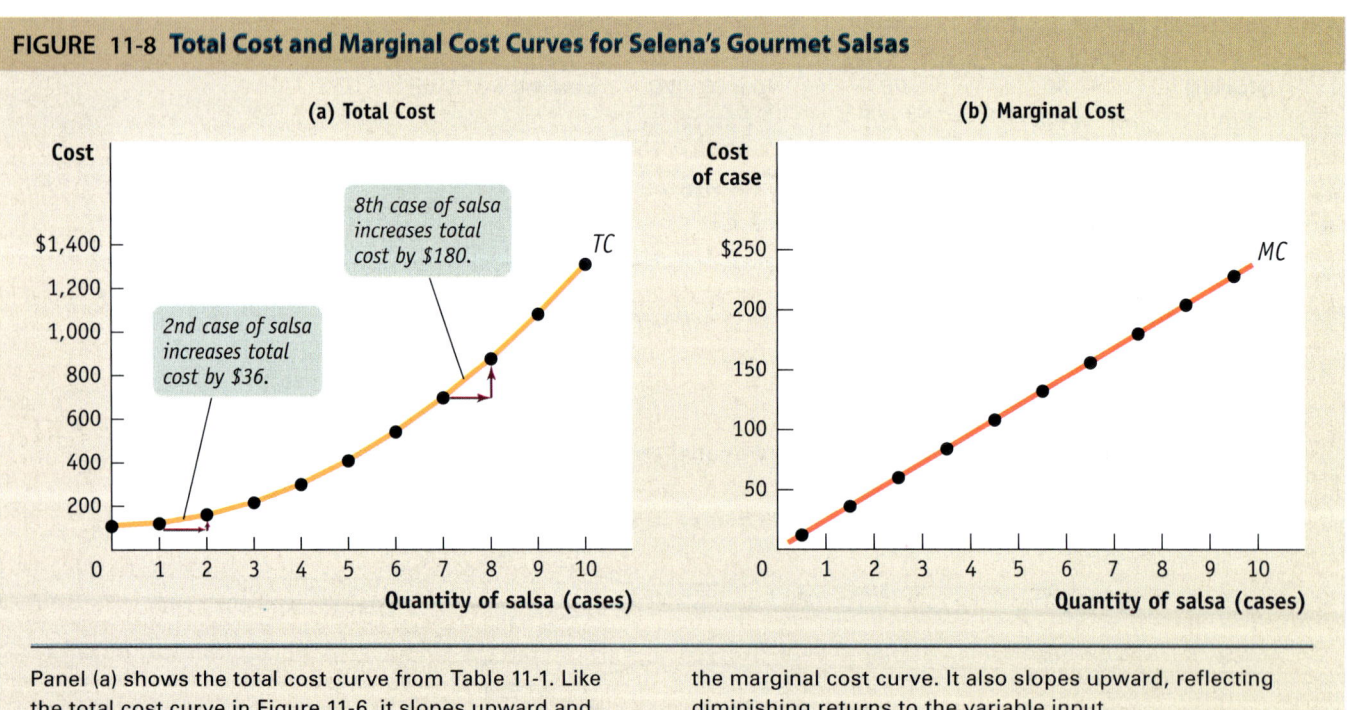

FIGURE 11-8 Total Cost and Marginal Cost Curves for Selena's Gourmet Salsas

Panel (a) shows the total cost curve from Table 11-1. Like the total cost curve in Figure 11-6, it slopes upward and gets steeper as we move up it to the right. Panel (b) shows the marginal cost curve. It also slopes upward, reflecting diminishing returns to the variable input.

input must be used to produce each additional unit of output as the amount of output already produced rises. And since each unit of the variable input must be paid for, the additional cost per additional unit of output also rises.

In addition, recall that the flattening of the total product curve is also due to diminishing returns: the marginal product of an input falls as more of that input is used if the quantities of other inputs are fixed. The flattening of the total product curve as output increases and the steepening of the total cost curve as output increases are just flip-sides of the same phenomenon. That is, as output increases, the marginal cost of output also increases because the marginal product of the variable input decreases.

We will return to marginal cost in Chapter 12, when we consider the firm's profit-maximizing output decision. Our next step is to introduce another measure of cost: *average cost.*

Average Total Cost

In addition to total cost and marginal cost, it's useful to calculate another measure, **average total cost,** often simply called **average cost.** The average total cost is total cost divided by the quantity of output produced; that is, it is equal to total cost per unit of output. If we let *ATC* denote average total cost, the equation looks like this:

(11-5) $ATC = \dfrac{\text{Total cost}}{\text{Quantity of output}} = \dfrac{TC}{q}$

Average total cost is important because it tells the producer how much the *average* or *typical* unit of output costs to produce. Marginal cost, meanwhile, tells the producer how much *one more* unit of output costs to produce. Although they may look very similar, these two measures of cost typically differ.

Table 11-2 uses data from Selena's Gourmet Salsas to calculate average total cost. For example, the total cost of producing 4 cases of salsa is $300, consisting of $108 in fixed cost and $192 in variable cost (from Table 11-1). So the average total cost of producing 4 cases of salsa is $300/4 = $75. You can see from Table 11-2 that as quantity of output increases, average total cost first falls, then rises.

Figure 11-9 plots that data to yield the *average total cost curve,* which shows how average total cost depends on output. As before, cost in dollars is measured on the vertical axis and quantity of output is measured on the horizontal axis. The average total cost curve has a distinctive U shape that corresponds to how average total cost first falls and then rises as output increases. Economists believe that such **U-shaped average total cost curves** are the norm for producers in many industries.

Average total cost, often referred to simply as **average cost,** is total cost divided by quantity of output produced.

A **U-shaped average total cost curve** falls at low levels of output, then rises at higher levels.

Average fixed cost is the fixed cost per unit of output.

Average variable cost is the variable cost per unit of output.

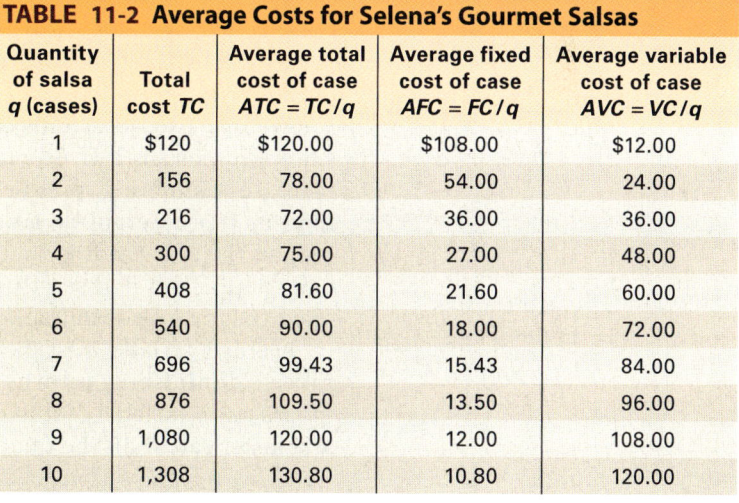

TABLE 11-2 Average Costs for Selena's Gourmet Salsas

Quantity of salsa q (cases)	Total cost TC	Average total cost of case ATC = TC/q	Average fixed cost of case AFC = FC/q	Average variable cost of case AVC = VC/q
1	$120	$120.00	$108.00	$12.00
2	156	78.00	54.00	24.00
3	216	72.00	36.00	36.00
4	300	75.00	27.00	48.00
5	408	81.60	21.60	60.00
6	540	90.00	18.00	72.00
7	696	99.43	15.43	84.00
8	876	109.50	13.50	96.00
9	1,080	120.00	12.00	108.00
10	1,308	130.80	10.80	120.00

To help our understanding of why the average total cost curve is U-shaped, Table 11-2 breaks average total cost into its two underlying components, *average fixed cost* and *average variable cost.* **Average fixed cost,** or *AFC,* is fixed cost divided by the quantity of output, also known as the fixed cost per unit of output. For example, if Selena's Gourmet Salsas produces 4 cases of salsa, average fixed cost is $108/4 = $27 per case. **Average variable cost,** or *AVC,* is variable cost divided by the quantity of output, also known as variable cost per unit of output. At an output of 4 cases, average variable cost is $192/4 = $48 per case.

FIGURE 11-9 Average Total Cost Curve for Selena's Gourmet Salsas

The average total cost curve at Selena's Gourmet Salsas is U-shaped. At low levels of output, average total cost falls because the *spreading effect* of falling average fixed cost dominates the *diminishing returns effect* of rising average variable cost. At higher levels of output, the opposite is true and average total cost rises. At point *M*, corresponding to an output of 3 cases of salsa per day, average total cost is at its minimum level, the minimum average total cost.

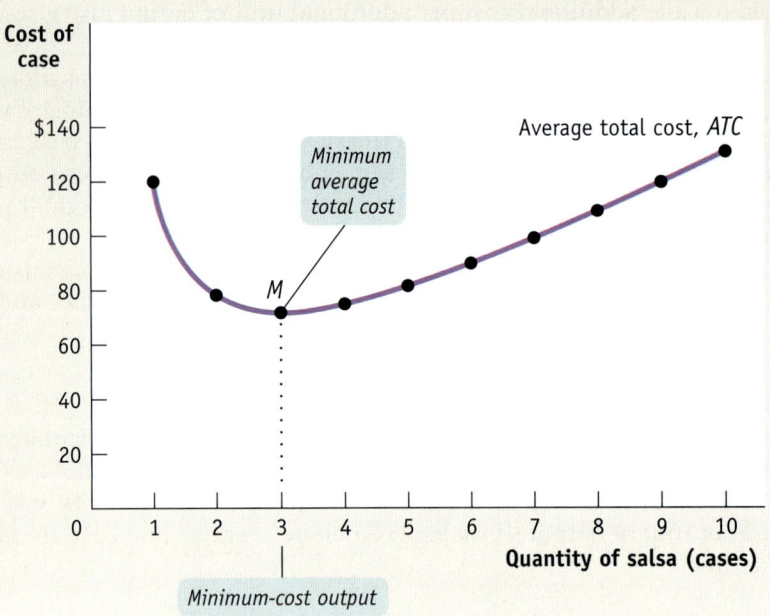

Writing these in the form of equations:

(11-6) $AFC = \dfrac{\text{Fixed cost}}{\text{Quantity of output}} = \dfrac{FC}{q}$

$AVC = \dfrac{\text{Variable cost}}{\text{Quantity of output}} = \dfrac{VC}{q}$

Average total cost is the sum of average fixed cost and average variable cost. It has a U shape because these components move in opposite directions as output rises.

Average fixed cost falls as more output is produced because the numerator (the fixed cost) is a fixed number but the denominator (the quantity of output) increases as more is produced. Another way to think about this relationship is that, as more output is produced, the fixed cost is spread over more units of output; the end result is that the fixed cost *per unit of output*—the average fixed cost—falls. You can see this effect in the fourth column of Table 11-2: average fixed cost drops continuously as output increases.

Average variable cost, however, rises as output increases. As we've seen, this reflects diminishing returns to the variable input: each additional unit of output incurs more variable cost to produce than the previous unit. So variable cost rises at a faster rate than the quantity of output increases.

So increasing output has two opposing effects on average total cost:

1. *The spreading effect.* The larger the output, the greater the quantity of output over which fixed cost is spread, leading to lower average fixed cost.

2. *The diminishing returns effect.* The larger the output, the greater the amount of variable input required to produce additional units, leading to higher average variable cost.

At low levels of output, the spreading effect is very powerful because even small increases in output cause large reductions in average fixed cost. So at low levels of output, the spreading effect dominates the diminishing returns effect and causes the average total cost curve to slope downward. But when output is large, average fixed cost is already quite small, so increasing output further has only a very small spreading effect.

Diminishing returns, however, usually grow increasingly important as output rises. As a result, when output is large, the diminishing returns effect dominates the spreading effect, causing the average total cost curve to slope upward. At the bottom of the U-shaped average total cost curve, point *M* in Figure 11-9, the two effects exactly balance each other. At this point average total cost is at its minimum level, the minimum average total cost.

Figure 11-10 brings together in a single picture four members of the family of cost curves that we have derived from the total cost curve for Selena's Gourmet Salsas: the marginal cost curve (*MC*), the average total cost curve (*ATC*), the average variable cost curve (*AVC*), and the average fixed cost curve (*AFC*). All are based on the information in Tables 11-1 and 11-2. As before, cost is measured on the vertical axis and the quantity of output is measured on the horizontal axis.

Let's take a moment to note some features of the various cost curves.

• Marginal cost slopes upward—the result of diminishing returns that make an additional unit of output more costly to produce than the one before.

• Average variable cost also slopes upward—again, due to diminishing returns—but is flatter than the marginal cost curve. This is because the higher cost of an additional unit of output is averaged across all units, not just the additional units, in the average variable cost measure.

• Average fixed cost slopes downward because of the spreading effect.

• The marginal cost curve intersects the average total cost curve from below, crossing it at its lowest point, point *M* in Figure 11-10. This last feature is our next subject of study.

FIGURE 11-10 Marginal Cost and Average Cost Curves for Selena's Gourmet Salsas

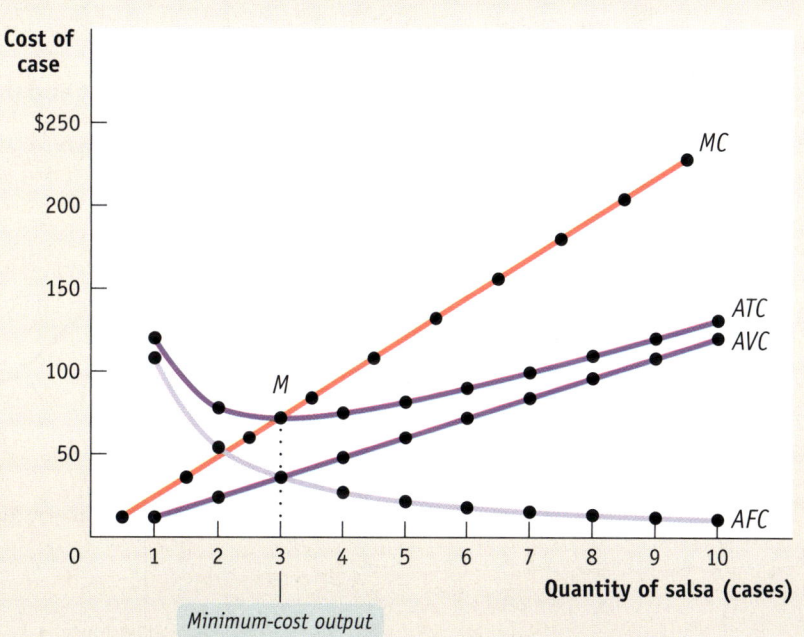

Here we have the family of cost curves for Selena's Gourmet Salsas: the marginal cost curve (*MC*), the average total cost curve (*ATC*), the average variable cost curve (*AVC*), and the average fixed cost curve (*AFC*). Note that the average total cost curve is U-shaped and the marginal cost curve crosses the average total cost curve at the bottom of the U, point *M,* corresponding to the minimum average total cost from Table 11-2 and Figure 11-9.

The **minimum-cost output** is the quantity of output at which average total cost is lowest—the bottom of the U-shaped average total cost curve.

Minimum Average Total Cost

For a U-shaped average total cost curve, average total cost is at its minimum level at the bottom of the U. Economists call the quantity of output that corresponds to the minimum average total cost the **minimum-cost output.** In the case of Selena's Gourmet Salsas, the minimum-cost output is 3 cases of salsa per day.

In Figure 11-10, the bottom of the U is at the level of output at which the marginal cost curve crosses the average total cost curve from below. Is this an accident? No—it reflects three general principles that are always true about a firm's marginal cost and average total cost curves:

1. At the minimum-cost output, average total cost *is equal to* marginal cost.
2. At output less than the minimum-cost output, marginal cost *is less than* average total cost and average total cost is falling.
3. At output greater than the minimum-cost output, marginal cost *is greater than* average total cost and average total cost is rising.

To understand these principles, think about how your grade in one course—say, a 3.0 in sociology—affects your overall grade point average. If your GPA before receiving that grade was more than 3.0, the new grade lowers your average.

Similarly, if marginal cost—the cost of producing one more unit—is less than average total cost, producing that extra unit lowers average total cost. This is shown in Figure 11-11 by the movement from A_1 to A_2. In this case, the marginal cost of producing an additional unit of output is low, as indicated by the point MC_L on the marginal cost curve. When the cost of producing the next unit of output is less than average total cost, increasing production reduces average total cost. So any quantity of output at which marginal cost is less than average total cost must be on the downward-sloping segment of the U.

But if your grade in sociology is more than the average of your previous grades, this new grade raises your GPA. Similarly, if marginal cost is greater than average total cost, producing that extra unit raises average total cost. This is illustrated by the movement from B_1 to B_2 in Figure 11-11, where the marginal cost, MC_H, is higher than average total cost. So any quantity of output at which marginal cost is greater than average total cost must be on the upward-sloping segment of the U.

FIGURE 11-11 The Relationship Between the Average Total Cost and the Marginal Cost Curves

To see why the marginal cost curve (*MC*) must cut through the average total cost curve (*ATC*) at the minimum average total cost (point *M*), corresponding to the minimum-cost output, we look at what happens if marginal cost is different from average total cost. If marginal cost is *less* than average total cost, an increase in output must reduce average total cost, as in the movement from A_1 to A_2. If marginal cost is *greater* than average total cost, an increase in output must increase average total cost, as in the movement from B_1 to B_2.

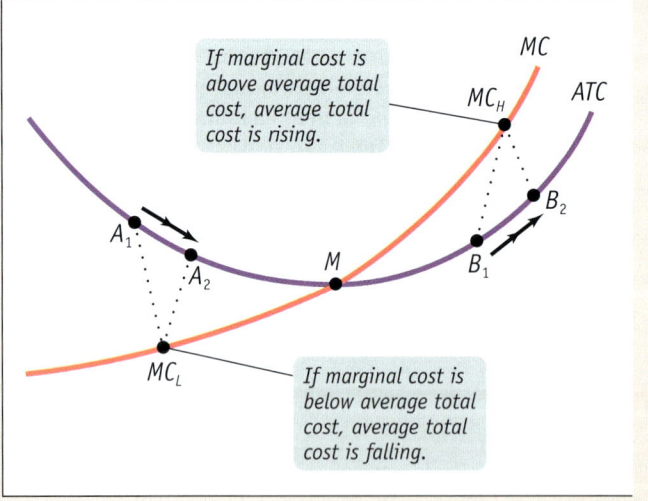

Finally, if a new grade is exactly equal to your previous GPA, the additional grade neither raises nor lowers that average—it stays the same. This corresponds to point *M* in Figure 11-11: when marginal cost equals average total cost, we must be at the bottom of the U, because only at that point is average total cost neither falling nor rising.

Does the Marginal Cost Curve Always Slope Upward?

Up to this point, we have emphasized the importance of diminishing returns, which lead to a marginal product curve that always slopes downward and a marginal cost curve that always slopes upward. In practice, however, economists believe that marginal cost curves often slope *downward* as a firm increases its production from zero up to some low level, sloping upward only at higher levels of production: they look like the curve *MC* in Figure 11-12.

This initial downward slope occurs because a firm often finds that, when it starts with only a very small number of workers, employing more workers and expanding output allows its workers to specialize in various tasks. This, in turn, lowers the firm's marginal cost as it expands output. For example, one individual producing salsa would have to perform all the tasks involved: selecting and preparing the ingredients, mixing the salsa, bottling and labelling it, packing it into cases, and so on. As more workers are employed, they can divide the tasks, with each worker specializing in one or a few aspects of salsa-making.

This specialization leads to *increasing returns* to the hiring of additional workers (i.e., a rising marginal product of labour) and results in a marginal cost curve that initially slopes downward. But once there are enough workers to have completely exhausted the benefits of further specialization, diminishing returns to labour set in and the marginal cost curve changes direction and slopes upward. So typical marginal cost curves actually have the "swoosh" shape shown by *MC* in Figure 11-12. For the same reason, average variable cost curves typically look like *AVC* in Figure 11-12: they are U-shaped rather than strictly upward sloping.

However, as Figure 11-12 also shows, the key features we saw from the example of Selena's Gourmet Salsas remain true: the average total cost curve is U-shaped, and the marginal cost curve passes through the point of minimum average total cost.

FIGURE 11-12 More Realistic Cost Curves

A realistic marginal cost curve has a "swoosh" shape. Starting from a very low output level, marginal cost often falls as the firm increases output. That's because hiring additional workers allows greater specialization of their tasks and leads to increasing returns. Once specialization is achieved, however, diminishing returns to additional workers set in and marginal cost rises. The corresponding average variable cost curve is now U-shaped, like the average total cost curve.

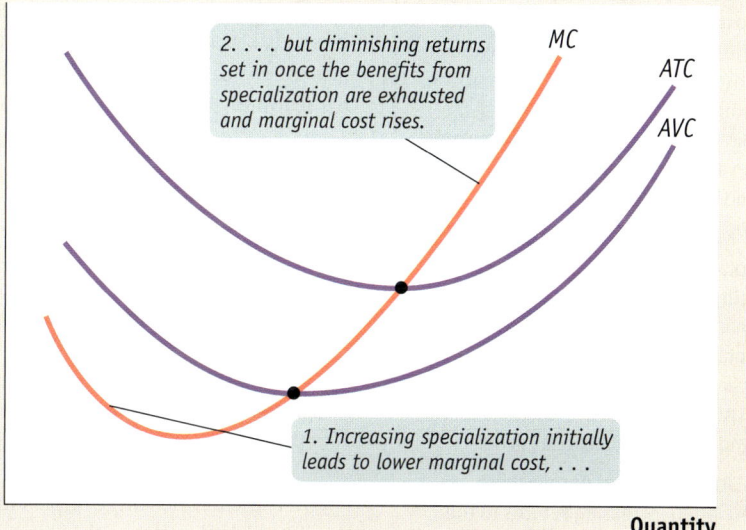

ECONOMICS >> *in Action*
Smart Grid Economics

Astro-0/Getty Images

With SMART Grid technology, consumers save money by basing their demand for electricity on marginal cost rather than average cost.

If you like to listen to music, write term papers, or do laundry in the middle of the night, your local electricity grid would like to thank you. Why? Because you are using electricity when it is least costly to generate.

The problem is that energy cannot be stored efficiently on a large scale. So power plant operators maintain both the main power stations that are designed to run continuously, as well as smaller power plants that operate only during periods of peak demand—such as during daytime working hours or periods of extreme outside temperatures.

According to Natural Resources Canada, the types of available generation such as hydro, fossil fuels, and nuclear power, affect the cost of producing electricity. When the demand for electricity is high in a hot summer afternoon (when air conditioners are running at maximum capacity), less attractive forms of generation must be run to meet higher demand. This leads to higher marginal cost per kilowatt generated than the average cost of generating a kilowatt (that is, cost averaged over kilowatts generated by more cost-effective and less cost-effective forms of generation).

But consumers typically aren't aware that the marginal cost of electricity varies over the course of a day or according to the weather. Instead, consumers see prices on their electricity bills based on the average cost of electricity generation. As a result, electricity demand is inefficient—too high during high marginal cost periods and too low during low marginal cost periods. In the end, consumers end up paying more than they should for their electricity, as utility companies must eventually raise their prices to cover production costs.

To solve this inefficiency, utility companies, appliance manufacturers, and the federal government are working together to develop SMART Grid technologies that help consumers adjust their usage according to the true marginal cost of a kilowatt in real time. "Smart" meters installed in homes allow the price to the consumer to vary according to the true marginal cost, which the consumer can see. And appliances such as dishwashers, refrigerators, dryers, and hot water heaters have been developed to run when electricity rates are lowest.

Studies have consistently shown that when consumers see the real marginal cost fluctuations and are asked to pay accordingly, they scale back their consumption during peak demand times. Clearly, SMART Grid technologies are just an application of smart economics.

>> Quick Review

• Marginal cost is equal to the slope of the total cost curve. Diminishing returns cause the marginal cost curve to slope upward.

• **Average total cost** (or **average cost**) is equal to the sum of **average fixed cost** and **average variable cost**. When the **U-shaped average total cost curve** slopes downward, the spreading effect dominates: fixed cost is spread over more units of output. When it slopes upward, the diminishing returns effect dominates: an additional unit of output requires more variable inputs.

• Marginal cost is equal to average total cost at the **minimum-cost output**. At higher output levels, marginal cost is greater than average total cost and average total cost is rising. At lower output levels, marginal cost is lower than average total cost and average total cost is falling.

• At low levels of output there are often increasing returns to the variable input due to the benefits of specialization, making the marginal cost curve "swoosh"-shaped: initially sloping downward before sloping upward.

>> Check Your Understanding 11-2
Solutions appear at back of book.

1. Aidy's Apple Pies is a roadside business. Aidy must pay $9.00 in rent each day. In addition, it costs her $1.00 to produce the first pie of the day, and each subsequent pie costs 50% more to produce than the one before. For example, the second pie costs $1.00 \times 1.5 = $1.50 to produce, and so on.
   a. Calculate Aidy's marginal cost, variable cost, average total cost, average variable cost, and average fixed cost as her daily pie output rises from 0 to 6. (*Hint:* The variable cost of two pies is just the marginal cost of the first pie, plus the marginal cost of the second, and so on.)
   b. Indicate the range of pies for which the spreading effect dominates and the range for which the diminishing returns effect dominates.
   c. What is Aidy's minimum-cost output? Explain why making one more pie lowers her average total cost when output is lower than the minimum-cost output. Similarly, explain why making one more pie raises Aidy's average total cost when output is greater than the minimum-cost output.

‖ Short-Run versus Long-Run Costs

Up to this point, we have treated fixed cost as completely outside the control of a firm because we have focused on the short run. But as we noted earlier, all inputs are variable in the long run: this means that in the long run fixed cost may also be varied. *In the long run,* in other words, *a firm's fixed cost becomes a variable it can choose.* For example, given time, Selena's Gourmet Salsas can acquire additional food-preparation equipment or dispose of some of its existing equipment.

In this section, we will examine how a firm's costs behave in the short run and in the long run. We will also see that the firm will choose its fixed cost in the long run based on the level of output it expects to produce.

Let's begin by supposing that Selena's Gourmet Salsas is considering whether to acquire additional food-preparation equipment. Acquiring additional machinery will affect its total cost in two ways. First, the firm will have to either rent or buy the additional equipment; either way, that will mean higher fixed cost in the short run. Second, if the workers have more equipment, they will be more productive: fewer workers will be needed to produce any given output, so variable cost for any given output level will be reduced.

The table in Figure 11-13 shows how acquiring an additional machine affects costs. In our original example, we assumed that Selena's Gourmet Salsas had a fixed cost of $108. The left half of the table shows variable cost as well as total cost and average total cost assuming a fixed cost of $108. The average total cost curve for this level of fixed cost is given by ATC_1 in Figure 11-13. Let's compare that to a situation in which the firm buys additional food-preparation equipment, doubling its fixed cost to $216 but reducing its variable cost at any given level of output. The right half of the table shows the firm's variable cost, total cost, and average total cost with this higher level of fixed cost. The average total cost curve corresponding to $216 in fixed cost is given by ATC_2 in Figure 11-13.

From the figure you can see that when output is small, 4 cases of salsa per day or fewer, average total cost is smaller when Selena's Gourmet Salsas forgoes the additional equipment and maintains the lower fixed cost of $108: ATC_1 lies below ATC_2. For example, at 3 cases per day, average total cost is $72 without the additional machinery and $90 with the additional machinery. But as output increases beyond 4 cases per day, the firm's average total cost is lower if it acquires the additional equipment, raising its fixed cost to $216. So, at 9 cases of salsa per day, average total cost is $120 when fixed cost is $108 but only $78 when fixed cost is $216.

Why does average total cost change like this when fixed cost increases? When output is low, the increase in fixed cost from the additional equipment outweighs the reduction in variable cost from higher worker productivity—that is, there are too few units of output over which to spread the additional fixed cost. So if Selena's Gourmet Salsas plans to produce 4 or fewer cases per day, it would be better off choosing the lower level of fixed cost, $108, to achieve a lower average total cost of production. When planned output is high, however, it should acquire the additional machinery.

In general, for each output level there is some choice of fixed cost that minimizes the firm's average total cost for that output level. So when the firm has a desired output level that it expects to maintain over time, it should choose the level of fixed cost optimal for that level—that is, the level of fixed cost that minimizes its average total cost.

Now that we are studying a situation in which fixed cost can change, we need to take time into account when discussing average total cost. All of the average total cost curves we have considered until now are defined for a given level of fixed cost—that is, they are defined for the short run, the period of time over which fixed cost doesn't vary. To reinforce that distinction, for the rest of this chapter we will refer to these average total cost curves as *short-run average total cost curves*.

FIGURE 11-13 Choosing the Level of Fixed Cost for Selena's Gourmet Salsas

For any given level of output, there is a trade-off: a choice between lower fixed cost and higher variable cost, or higher fixed cost and lower variable cost. ATC_1 is the average total cost curve corresponding to a fixed cost of $108; it leads to lower fixed cost and higher variable cost. ATC_2 is the average total cost curve corresponding to a higher fixed cost of $216 but lower variable cost. At low output levels, at 4 or fewer cases of salsa per day, ATC_1 lies below ATC_2: average total cost is lower with only $108 in fixed cost. But as output goes up, average total cost is lower with the higher amount of fixed cost, $216: at more than 4 cases of salsa per day, ATC_2 lies below ATC_1.

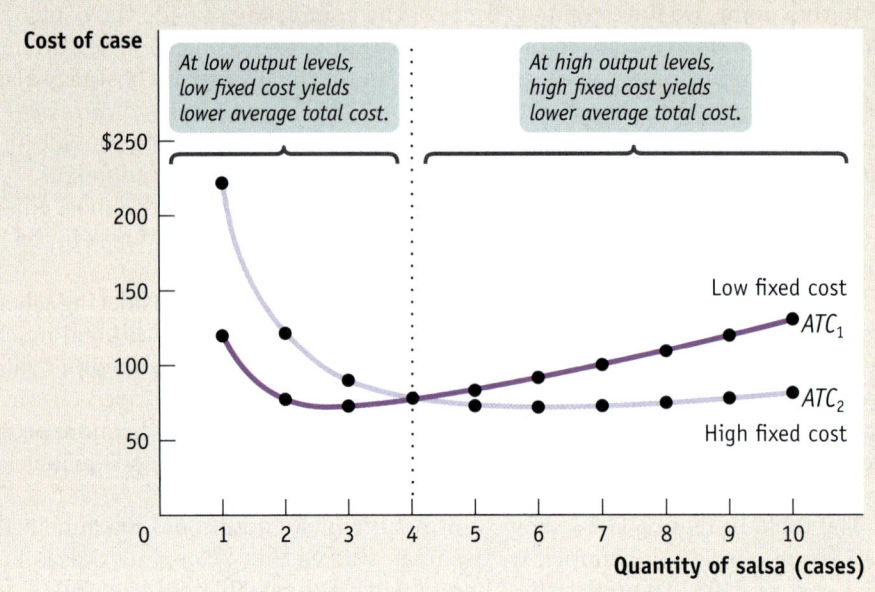

Quantity of salsa (cases)	Low fixed cost (FC = $108)			High fixed cost (FC = $216)		
	High variable cost	Total cost	Average total cost of case ATC_1	Low variable cost	Total cost	Average total cost of case ATC_2
1	$12	$120	$120.00	$6	$222	$222.00
2	48	156	78.00	24	240	120.00
3	108	216	72.00	54	270	90.00
4	192	300	75.00	96	312	78.00
5	300	408	81.60	150	366	73.20
6	432	540	90.00	216	432	72.00
7	588	696	99.43	294	510	72.86
8	768	876	109.50	384	600	75.00
9	972	1,080	120.00	486	702	78.00
10	1,200	1,308	130.80	600	816	81.60

For most firms, it is realistic to assume that there are many possible choices of fixed cost, not just two. The implication: for such a firm, many possible short-run average total cost curves will exist, each corresponding to a different choice of fixed cost and so giving rise to what is called a firm's "family" of short-run average total cost curves.

At any given point in time, a firm will find itself on one of its short-run cost curves, the one corresponding to its current level of fixed cost; a change in output will cause it to move along that curve. If the firm expects that change in output level to be long-standing, then it is likely that the firm's current level of fixed cost is no longer optimal. Given sufficient time, it will want to adjust its fixed cost to a new level that minimizes average total cost for its new output level.

For example, if Selena's Gourmet Salsas had been producing 2 cases of salsa per day with a fixed cost of $108 but found itself increasing its output to 8 cases per day for the foreseeable future, then in the long run it should purchase (or rent) more equipment and increase its fixed cost to a level that minimizes average total cost at the 8-cases-per-day output level.

Suppose we do a thought experiment and calculate the lowest possible average total cost that can be achieved for each output level if the firm were to choose its fixed cost for each output level. Economists have given this thought experiment a name: the *long-run average total cost curve*. Specifically, the **long-run average total cost curve,** or *LRATC,* is the relationship between output and average total cost when fixed cost has been chosen to minimize average total cost *for each level of output*. If there are many possible choices of fixed cost, the long-run average total cost curve will have the familiar, smooth U shape, as shown by *LRATC* in Figure 11-14.

We can now draw the distinction between the short run and the long run more fully. In the long run, when a producer has had time to choose the fixed cost appropriate for its desired level of output, that producer will be at some point on the long-run average total cost curve. But if the output level is altered, the firm will no longer be on its long-run average total cost curve and will instead be moving along its current short-run average total cost curve. It will not be on its long-run average total cost curve again until it readjusts its fixed cost for its new output level.

Figure 11-14 illustrates this point. The curve *ATC₃* shows short-run average total cost if Selena's Gourmet Salsas has chosen the level of fixed cost that minimizes average total cost at an output of 3 cases of salsa per day. This is confirmed by the fact that at 3 cases per day, *ATC₃* touches *LRATC,* the long-run average total cost curve. Similarly, *ATC₆* shows short-run average total cost if Selena's Gourmet Salsas has chosen the level of fixed cost that minimizes average total cost if its output is 6 cases per day. It touches *LRATC* at 6 cases per day. And *ATC₉* shows short-run average total cost if Selena's Gourmet Salsas has chosen the level of fixed cost that minimizes average total cost if its output is 9 cases per day. It touches *LRATC* at 9 cases per day.

Suppose that Selena's Gourmet Salsas initially chose to be on *ATC₆*. If the firm actually produces 6 cases of salsa per day, it will be at point *C* on both its short-run and long-run average total cost curves. Suppose, however, that Selena's Gourmet Salsas ends up producing only 3 cases of salsa per day. In the short run, the firm's average total cost is indicated by point *B* on *ATC₆*; it is no longer on *LRATC*. If managers at Selena's had known that it would be producing only 3 cases per

To understand how firms operate over time, be sure to distinguish between short-run and long-run average costs.

The **long-run average total cost curve** shows the relationship between output and average total cost when fixed cost has been chosen to minimize average total cost for each level of output.

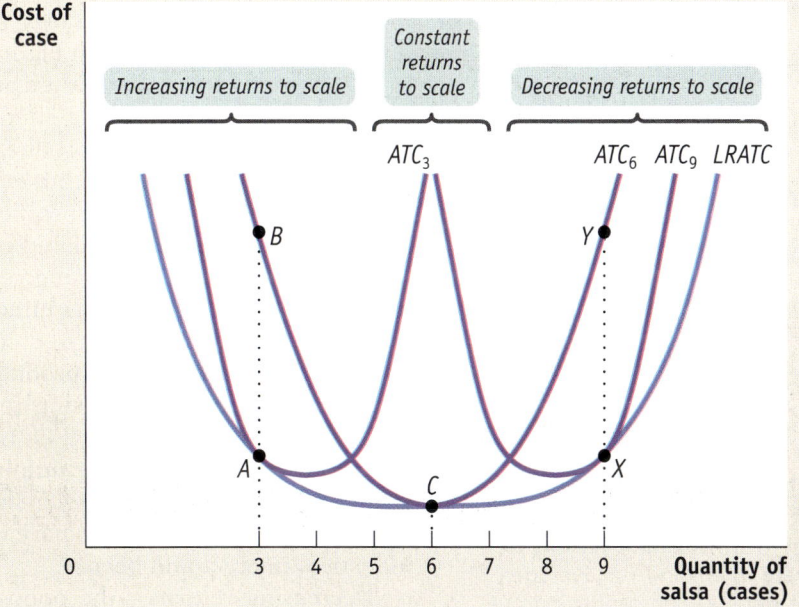

FIGURE 11-14 Short-Run and Long-Run Average Total Cost Curves

Short-run and long-run average total cost curves differ because a firm can choose its fixed cost in the long run. If Selena's Gourmet Salsas has chosen the level of fixed cost that minimizes short-run average total cost at an output of 6 cases, and actually produces 6 cases, then it will be at point *C* on *LRATC* and *ATC₆*. But if the firm produces only 3 cases, it will move to point *B*. If the firm expects to produce only 3 cases for a long time, in the long run it will reduce its fixed cost and move to point *A* on *ATC₃*. Likewise, if it produces 9 cases (putting it at point *Y*) and expects to continue this for a long time, it will increase its fixed cost in the long run and move to point *X* on *ATC₉*.

day, they would have been better off choosing a lower level of fixed cost, the one corresponding to ATC_3, thereby achieving a lower average total cost. They could do this, for example, by selling their production plant and purchasing a smaller one. Then the firm would have found itself at point A on the long-run average total cost curve, which lies below point B.

Suppose, conversely, that Selena's Gourmet Salsas ends up producing 9 cases per day even though it initially chose to be on ATC_6. In the short run, its average total cost is indicated by point Y on ATC_6. But the firm would be better off purchasing/renting more equipment and incurring a higher fixed cost in order to reduce its variable cost and move to ATC_9. This would allow Selena's Gourmet Salsas to reach point X on the long-run average total cost curve, which lies below Y.

The distinction between short-run and long-run average total costs is extremely important in making sense of how real firms operate over time. A company that has to increase output suddenly to meet a surge in demand will typically find that in the short run its average total cost rises sharply because it is hard to get extra production out of existing facilities. But given time to build or rent new factories or add machinery, short-run average total cost falls.

Returns to Scale

What determines the shape of the long-run average total cost curve? The answer is that *scale,* the size of a firm's operations, is often an important determinant of its long-run average total cost of production. Firms that experience scale effects in production find that their long-run average total cost changes substantially depending on the quantity of output they produce. There are **increasing returns to scale** (also known as *economies of scale*) when long-run average total cost declines as output increases.

As you can see in Figure 11-14, Selena's Gourmet Salsas experiences increasing returns to scale over output levels ranging from 0 to 5 cases of salsa per day—the output levels over which the long-run average total cost curve is declining. In contrast, there are **decreasing returns to scale** (also known as *dis-economies of scale*) when long-run average total cost increases as output increases. For Selena's Gourmet Salsas, decreasing returns to scale occur at output levels greater than 7 cases, the output levels over which its long-run average total cost curve is rising.

There is also a third possible relationship between long-run average total cost and scale: firms experience **constant returns to scale** when long-run average total cost is constant as output increases. In this case, the firm's long-run average total cost curve is horizontal over the output levels for which there are constant returns to scale. As you see in Figure 11-14, Selena's Gourmet Salsas has constant returns to scale when it produces anywhere from 5 to 7 cases of salsa per day.

What explains these scale effects in production? The answer ultimately lies in the firm's technology of production. Increasing returns often arise from the increased *specialization* that larger output levels allow—a larger scale of operation means that individual workers can limit themselves to more specialized tasks, becoming more skilled and efficient at doing them.

Another source of increasing returns is very large initial setup cost; in some industries—such as auto manufacturing, electricity generating, or petroleum refining—incurring a high fixed cost in the form of building or renting a plant and equipment necessary to produce any output.

A third source of increasing returns, found in certain high-tech industries such as software development, is that the value of a good or service to an individual increases when a large number of others own or use the same good or service (known as *network externalities*). As we'll see in Chapter 13, where we study monopoly, increasing returns have very important implications for how firms and industries interact and behave.

Decreasing returns—the opposite scenario—typically arise in large firms due to problems of coordination and communication: as the firm grows in size, it

There are **increasing returns to scale** when long-run average total cost declines as output increases.

There are **decreasing returns to scale** when long-run average total cost increases as output increases.

There are **constant returns to scale** when long-run average total cost is constant as output increases.

becomes ever more difficult and so more costly to communicate and to organize its activities. Although increasing returns induce firms to get larger, decreasing returns tend to limit their size. And when there are constant returns to scale, scale has no effect on a firm's long-run average total cost: it is the same regardless of whether the firm produces 1 unit or 100,000 units.

Summing Up Costs: The Short and Long of It

If a firm is to make the best decisions about how much to produce, it has to understand how its costs relate to the quantity of output it chooses to produce. Table 11-3 provides a quick summary of the concepts and measures of cost you have learned about.

TABLE 11-3 Concepts and Measures of Cost			
	Measurement	Definition	Mathematical term
Short run	Fixed cost	Cost that does not depend on the quantity of output produced	FC
	Average fixed cost	Fixed cost per unit of output	$AFC = FC/q$
Short run and long run	Variable cost	Cost that depends on the quantity of output produced	VC
	Average variable cost	Variable cost per unit of output	$AVC = VC/q$
	Total cost	The sum of fixed cost (short run) and variable cost	$TC = FC$ (short run) $+ VC$
	Average total cost (Average cost)	Total cost per unit of output	$ATC = TC/q$
	Marginal cost	The change in total cost generated by producing one more unit of output	$MC = \Delta TC/\Delta q$
Long run	Long-run average total cost	Average total cost when fixed cost has been chosen to minimize average total cost for each level of output	$LRATC$

ECONOMICS >> *in Action*
How the Sharing Economy Reduces Fixed Cost

Turo is a peer-to-peer car-sharing company: it enables people who own cars to rent them to people who want to use a car but prefer not to buy one. Much like Airbnb, the hugely successful peer-to-peer home-sharing company, Turo is an example of a significant and growing phenomenon: the sharing economy. In the sharing economy, technology allows unrelated parties (firms and individuals) to share assets like office space, houses, computing capacity, cars, small jets, financial capital, books, and designer clothes through market transactions. Even the cloud itself, the vast digital network into which you store your photos and your term papers, is a feature of the sharing economy because it allows firms and individuals to rent computing capacity, storage, and software. But what does this have to do with fixed costs? A lot. If the use of an asset can be obtained only when needed, then it goes from incurring a fixed cost to incurring a variable cost.

Let's explain using the example of a car-sharing market, like Turo. Karenna needs to use a car occasionally. Purchasing a car would mean spending a lot of money: even an older used car will cost Karenna a few thousand dollars. That is,

Firms in the sharing economy, like Turo, help convert fixed costs to variable costs and allow for a more efficient use of resources.

Smith Collection/Gado/Getty Images

Karenna has to incur a sizeable fixed cost if she buys a car. And since she needs the car only occasionally, any car she purchased would sit in her driveway for a significant amount of time.

Suppose that instead of purchasing a car, Karenna uses Turo to rent a car when she needs one. Then she incurs a variable cost—the rental rate for the car—instead of a large fixed cost from ownership. By sharing instead of buying a car, Karenna has transformed what would have been a fixed cost into a variable cost.

Now consider Brianna, who owns a car that she rents out to other drivers through the Turo app. Brianna incurred a fixed cost when she bought the car, some of which she can defray by renting out the car when she doesn't need it. However, since people like Brianna regularly rent out their cars, the total number of cars purchased in the economy falls because people like Karenna no longer needs to buy a car in order to consume car rides. As a result, over the entire economy, for a given quantity demanded of car rides, the number of cars falls. Hence the total outlay of fixed costs in the economy falls for a given quantity demanded of car rides.

In effect, by turning the fixed cost of ownership into the variable cost of sharing, the sharing economy allows people to afford more goods and services (such as car rides) than they would have been able to afford otherwise. Likewise, sharing allows people like Brianna to afford assets like a car—assets that may have been previously unaffordable—because she can now use the car to earn income. The sharing economy marketplace makes for a more efficient use of society's resources because it reduces the total amount of fixed costs incurred in order to generate the desired amounts of goods and services.

>> Quick Review

- In the long run, firms choose fixed cost according to expected output. Higher fixed cost reduces average total cost when output is high. Lower fixed cost reduces average total cost when output is low.

- There are many possible short-run average total cost curves, each corresponding to a different level of fixed cost. The **long-run average total cost curve,** *LRATC,* shows average total cost over the long run, when the firm has chosen fixed cost to minimize average total cost for each level of output.

- A firm that has fully adjusted its fixed cost for its output level will operate at a point that lies on both its current short-run and its current long-run average total cost curves. A change in output moves the firm along its current short-run average total cost curve. Once it has readjusted its fixed cost, the firm will operate on a new short-run average total cost curve and on the long-run average total cost curve.

- Scale effects arise from the technology of production. **Increasing returns to scale** tend to make firms larger. **Decreasing returns to scale** tend to limit their size. With **constant returns to scale,** scale has no effect.

>> Check Your Understanding 11-3

Solutions appear at back of book.

1. The accompanying table shows three possible combinations of fixed cost and average variable cost for a single firm. Average variable cost is constant in this example (it does not vary with the quantity of output produced).

Choice	Fixed cost	Average variable cost
1	$8,000	$1.00
2	12,000	0.75
3	24,000	0.25

   a. For each of the three choices, calculate the average total cost of producing 12,000, 22,000, and 30,000 units. For each of these quantities, which choice results in the lowest average total cost?
   b. Suppose that the firm, which has historically produced 12,000 units, experiences a sharp, permanent increase in demand that leads it to produce 22,000 units. Explain how its average total cost will change in the short run and in the long run.
   c. Explain what the firm should do instead if it believes the change in demand indicated in part b is temporary.
2. In each of the following cases, explain what kind of scale effects you think the firm will experience and why.
   a. A telemarketing firm in which employees make sales calls using computers and telephones
   b. An interior design firm in which design projects are based on the expertise of the firm's owner
   c. A diamond-mining company
3. Draw a graph like Figure 11-14 and insert a short-run average total cost curve corresponding to a long-run output choice of 5 cases of salsa per day. Use the graph to show why Selena's Gourmet Salsas should change its fixed cost if it expects to produce only 4 cases per day for a long period of time.

The Rise of the Machine at Amazon

Justin Sullivan/Getty Images

One of the main pillars of Amazon's success is its promise of speedy delivery. For the majority of Prime eligible items, customers receive their orders within two business days. Even better, in select postal codes Amazon can now deliver within 24 hours. And if you happen to live in a major city, odds are that you can receive your delivery in one to two hours. None of its competitors comes close to matching the Amazon's speed. What accounts for Amazon's prodigious delivery abilities?

The answer: robots. Visit an Amazon fulfilment centre and you will see hundreds of them swarming a 125,000 square-foot area, engaged in a finely coordinated dance. They haul shelves of merchandise, weighing up to 700 pounds, and deliver them to human "pickers" who assemble orders, and to human "stockers" who sort incoming inventory.

As of 2019, Amazon had more than 100,000 robots working in its 175 fulfilment centres which shipped out more than 5 billion orders. Before the arrival of robots, human employees did this tedious work, often walking 10 to 15 miles daily, carrying heavy loads. By eliminating the need for humans to walk miles carting merchandise, warehouse operations have become much more efficient. In addition, because robots don't need aisles between shelves like people do, there's more room for merchandise storage in Amazon's fulfilment centres.

Over the past 20 years, Amazon has invested an enormous amount of money perfecting its warehouse management and order fulfilment operations to satisfy customers' desire to receive their items quickly. The company's spokesperson, Phil Hardin, explains the widespread use of robots this way: "It's an investment that has implications for a lot of elements of our cost structure. It has been a great innovation for us, . . . and we think it makes our warehouses more productive." Indeed, some estimates show that, by embracing automation, Amazon has cut the cost of order fulfilment nearly in half.

Amazon's competitors have taken notice. Walmart, for example, also uses robotic systems to speed up delivery times. Robotics companies like Shopify's 6 River Systems have been working with warehouse management companies such as Flowspace to provide order fulfilment services for non-Amazon sellers. However, with Amazon's huge scale advantage, it remains to be seen whether other retailers can ever catch up.

QUESTIONS FOR THOUGHT

1. Describe the shift in Amazon's cost structure based on the concepts from this chapter. Is Amazon on a short-run or long-run cost curve? What are the relevant returns to scale in Amazon's operations?

2. What are the pros and cons of Amazon's strategy?

3. What advantage does a robotic system give Amazon over its rivals? How likely is it that they will catch up with Amazon? What market factors does it depend upon?

SUMMARY

1. The relationship between inputs and output is a producer's **production function.** In the **short run,** the quantity of a **fixed input** cannot be varied but the quantity of a **variable input** can. In the **long run,** the quantities of all inputs can be varied. For a given amount of the fixed input and production technology, the **total product curve** shows how the quantity of output changes as the quantity of the variable input changes. We may also calculate the **marginal product** of an input, the increase in output from using one more unit of that input.

2. There are **diminishing returns to an input** when its marginal product declines as more of the input is used, holding the quantity of all other inputs fixed and a given state of technology.

3. **Total cost,** represented by the **total cost curve,** is equal to the sum of **fixed cost,** which does not depend on output, and **variable cost,** which does depend on output. Due to diminishing returns, marginal cost, the increase in total cost generated by producing one more unit of output, normally increases as output increases.

4. **Average total cost** (also known as **average cost**), total cost divided by quantity of output, is the cost of the average unit of output, and marginal cost is the cost of one more unit produced. Economists believe that **U-shaped average total cost curves** are typical, because average total cost consists of two parts:

   average fixed cost, which falls when output increases (the spreading effect), and **average variable cost,** which rises with output (the diminishing returns effect).

5. When average total cost is U-shaped, the bottom of the U is the level of output at which average total cost is minimized, the point of **minimum-cost output.** This is also the point at which the marginal cost curve crosses the average total cost curve from below. Due to gains from specialization, the marginal cost curve may slope downward initially before sloping upward, giving it a "swoosh" shape.

6. In the long run, a producer can change its fixed input and its level of fixed cost. By accepting higher fixed cost, a firm can lower its variable cost for any given output level, and vice versa. The **long-run average total cost curve** shows the relationship between output and average total cost when fixed cost has been chosen to minimize average total cost at each level of output. A firm moves along its short-run average total cost curve as it changes the quantity of output, and it returns to a point on both its short-run and long-run average total cost curves once it has adjusted fixed cost to its new output level.

7. As output increases, there are **increasing returns to scale** if long-run average total cost declines; **decreasing returns to scale** if it increases; and **constant returns to scale** if it remains constant. Scale effects depend on the technology of production.

KEY TERMS

Production function, p. 344
Fixed input, p. 344
Variable input, p. 344
Long run, p. 344
Short run, p. 344
Total product curve, p. 344
Marginal product, p. 345
Diminishing returns to an input, p. 346

Average product, p. 348
Fixed cost, p. 350
Variable cost, p. 350
Total cost, p. 350
Total cost curve, p. 351
Average total cost, p. 355
Average cost, p. 355
U-shaped average total cost curve, p. 355

Average fixed cost, p. 355
Average variable cost, p. 355
Minimum-cost output, p. 358
Long-run average total cost curve, p. 363
Increasing returns to scale, p. 364
Decreasing returns to scale, p. 364
Constant returns to scale, p. 364

PRACTICE QUESTIONS

1. Explain the difference between diminishing marginal returns to labour and decreasing returns to scale. Provide an example for each case.

2. Many colleges and universities are witnessing a shift in demographics due to women having fewer children today. The Canadian birth rate fell from an average of 1.66 births per woman in 2007 to 1.5 births in 2017. The declining birth rate will reduce the post-secondary age population by about 10% between 2025 and 2029. How will the declining birth rate affect college and university operations? Answer the questions below.

   a. Do higher-education institutions have large or small fixed costs? What are the variable costs for colleges and universities?

   b. Given your answer in part a, how would you describe short-run average total cost?

   c. If colleges and universities are operating where short-run average total costs are minimized, what will happen to the average cost per student of higher education if colleges and universities experience a decline in enrolments?

3. In your economics class, each homework problem set is graded on the basis of a maximum score of 100. You have completed 9 out of 10 of the problem sets for the term, and your current average grade is 88. What range of grades for your 10th problem set will raise your overall average? What range will lower your overall average? Explain your answer.

PROBLEMS

1. Changes in the prices of key commodities have a significant impact on a company's bottom line. For virtually all companies, the price of energy is a substantial portion of their costs. In addition, many industries—such as those that produce beef, chicken, high-fructose corn syrup, and ethanol—are highly dependent on the price of corn. In particular, corn has seen a significant increase in price.

   a. Explain how the cost of energy can be both a fixed cost and a variable cost for a company.

   b. Suppose energy is a fixed cost and energy prices rise. What happens to the company's average total cost curve? What happens to its marginal cost curve? Illustrate your answer with a diagram.

   c. Explain why the cost of corn is a variable cost but not a fixed cost for an ethanol producer.

   d. When the cost of corn goes up, what happens to the average total cost curve of an ethanol producer? What happens to its marginal cost curve? Illustrate your answer with a diagram.

2. Marty's Frozen Yogurt is a small shop that sells cups of frozen yogurt in a university town. Marty owns three frozen-yogurt machines. His other inputs are refrigerators, frozen-yogurt mix, cups, sprinkle toppings, and, of course, workers. He estimates that his daily production function when he varies the number of workers employed (and at the same time, of course, yogurt mix, cups, and so on) is as shown in the accompanying table.

Quantity of labour (workers)	Quantity of frozen yogurt (cups)
0	0
1	110
2	200
3	270
4	300
5	320
6	330

   a. What are the fixed inputs and variable inputs in the production of cups of frozen yogurt?

   b. Draw the total product curve. Put the quantity of labour on the horizontal axis and the quantity of frozen yogurt on the vertical axis.

   c. What is the marginal product of the first worker? The second worker? The third worker? Why does marginal product decline as the number of workers increases?

3. The production function for Marty's Frozen Yogurt is given in Problem 2. Marty pays each of his workers $80 per day. The cost of his other variable inputs is $0.50 per cup of yogurt. His fixed cost is $100 per day.

   a. What is Marty's variable cost and total cost when he produces 110 cups of yogurt? 200 cups? Calculate variable and total cost for every level of output given in Problem 2.

   b. Draw Marty's variable cost curve. On the same diagram, draw his total cost curve.

   c. What is the marginal cost per cup for the first 110 cups of yogurt? For the next 90 cups? Calculate the marginal cost for all remaining levels of output.

4. The production function for Marty's Frozen Yogurt is given in Problem 2. The costs are given in Problem 3.

   a. For each of the given levels of output, calculate the average fixed cost (*AFC*), average variable cost (*AVC*), and average total cost (*ATC*) per cup of frozen yogurt.

   b. On one diagram, draw the *AFC*, *AVC*, and *ATC* curves.

   c. What principle explains why the *AFC* declines as output increases? What principle explains why the *AVC* increases as output increases? Explain your answers.

   d. How many cups of frozen yogurt are produced when average total cost is minimized?

5. Labour costs represent a large percentage of total costs for many firms. According to Trading Economics, Canada's labour costs were up 3.47% in January 2020, compared to January 2019.

   a. When labour costs increase, what happens to average total cost and marginal cost? Consider a case in which labour costs are only variable costs and a case in which they are both variable and fixed costs.

   An increase in labour productivity means each worker can produce more output. Recent data on productivity show that labour productivity in the Canadian business sector grew annually by 1.5% between 1991 and 1999, by 1.0% between 2000 and 2009, and by 0.91% between 2010 and 2019.

   b. When productivity growth is positive, what happens to the total product curve and the marginal product of labour curve? Illustrate your answer with a diagram.

   c. When productivity growth is positive, what happens to the marginal cost curve and the average total cost curve? Illustrate your answer with a diagram.

d. If labour costs are rising over time on average, why would a company want to adopt equipment and methods that increase labour productivity?

6. Magnificent Blooms is a florist specializing in floral arrangements for weddings, graduations, and other events. Magnificent Blooms has a fixed cost associated with space and equipment of $100 per day. Each worker is paid $50 per day. The daily production function for Magnificent Blooms is shown in the accompanying table.

Quantity of labour (workers)	Quantity of floral arrangements
0	0
1	5
2	9
3	12
4	14
5	15

a. Calculate the marginal product of each worker. What principle explains why the marginal product per worker declines as the number of workers employed increases?

b. Calculate the marginal cost of each level of output. What principle explains why the marginal cost per floral arrangement increases as the number of arrangements increases?

7. You have the information shown in the accompanying table about a firm's costs. Complete the missing data.

Quantity of output	TC	MC	ATC	AVC
0	$20		—	—
		$20		
1	?		?	?
		10		
2	?		?	?
		16		
3	?		?	?
		20		
4	?		?	?
		24		
5	?		?	?

8. Evaluate each of the following statements. If a statement is true, explain why; if it is false, identify the mistake and try to correct it.

a. A decreasing marginal product tells us that marginal cost must be rising.

b. An increase in fixed cost increases the minimum-cost output.

c. An increase in fixed cost increases marginal cost.

d. When marginal cost is above average total cost, average total cost must be falling.

9. Sandra and Trey operate a small company that produces souvenir footballs. Their fixed cost is $2,000 per

month. They can hire workers for $1,000 per worker per month. Their monthly production function for footballs is as given in the accompanying table.

Quantity of labour (workers)	Quantity of footballs
0	0
1	300
2	800
3	1,200
4	1,400
5	1,500

a. For each quantity of labour, calculate average variable cost (*AVC*), average fixed cost (*AFC*), average total cost (*ATC*), and marginal cost (*MC*).

b. On one diagram, draw the *AVC*, *ATC*, and *MC* curves.

c. At what level of output is Sandra and Trey's average total cost minimized?

10. You produce widgets. Currently you produce four widgets at a total cost of $40.

a. What is your average total cost?

b. Suppose you could produce one more (the fifth) widget at a marginal cost of $5. If you do produce that fifth widget, what will your average total cost be? Has your average total cost increased or decreased? Why?

c. Suppose instead that you could produce one more (the fifth) widget at a marginal cost of $20. If you do produce that fifth widget, what will your average total cost be? Has your average total cost increased or decreased? Why?

11. Labour costs represent a large percentage of total costs for many firms. According to Trading Economics, Canada's labour costs were up 0.51% in 2016, compared to 2015.

a. When labour costs increase, what happens to average total cost and marginal cost? Consider a case in which labour costs are only variable costs and a case in which they are both variable and fixed costs.

An increase in labour productivity means each worker can produce more output. Recent data on productivity show that labour productivity in the Canadian business sector grew annually by 1.5% between 1991 and 1999, by 1.0% between 2000 and 2009, and by 0.89% between 2016 and 2017.

b. When productivity growth is positive, what happens to the total product curve and the marginal product of labour curve? Illustrate your answer with a diagram.

c. When productivity growth is positive, what happens to the marginal cost curve and the average total cost curve? Illustrate your answer with a diagram.

d. If labour costs are rising over time on average, why would a company want to adopt equipment and methods that increase labour productivity?

12. Daniella owns a small concrete-mixing company. Her fixed cost is the cost of the concrete-batching machinery and her mixer trucks. Her variable cost is the cost of the sand, gravel, and other inputs for producing concrete; the gas and maintenance for the machinery and trucks; and her workers. She is trying to decide how many mixer trucks to purchase. She has estimated the costs shown in the accompanying table based on estimates of the number of orders her company will receive per week.

Quantity of trucks	FC	VC 20 orders	VC 40 orders	VC 60 orders
2	$6,000	$2,000	$5,000	$12,000
3	7,000	1,800	3,800	10,800
4	8,000	1,200	3,600	8,400

a. For each level of fixed cost, calculate Daniella's total cost for producing 20, 40, and 60 orders per week.

b. If Daniella is producing 20 orders per week, how many trucks should she purchase and what will her average total cost be? Answer the same questions for 40 and 60 orders per week.

13. Consider Daniella's concrete-mixing business described in Problem 12. Assume that Daniella purchased 3 trucks, expecting to produce 40 orders per week.

a. Suppose that, in the short run, business declines to 20 orders per week. What is Daniella's average total cost per order in the short run? What will her average total cost per order in the short run be if her business booms to 60 orders per week?

b. What is Daniella's long-run average total cost for 20 orders per week? Explain why her short-run average total cost of producing 20 orders per week when the number of trucks is fixed at 3 is greater than her long-run average total cost of producing 20 orders per week.

c. Draw Daniella's long-run average total cost curve. Draw her short-run average total cost curve if she owns 3 trucks.

14. True or false? Explain your reasoning.

a. The short-run average total cost can never be less than the long-run average total cost.

b. The short-run average variable cost can never be less than the long-run average total cost.

c. In the long run, choosing a higher level of fixed cost shifts the long-run average total cost curve upward.

15. Wolfsburg Wagon (WW) is a small automaker. The accompanying table shows WW's long-run average total cost.

Quantity of cars	LRATC of car
1	$30,000
2	20,000
3	15,000
4	12,000
5	12,000
6	12,000
7	14,000
8	18,000

a. For which levels of output does WW experience increasing returns to scale?

b. For which levels of output does WW experience decreasing returns to scale?

c. For which levels of output does WW experience constant returns to scale?

 **WORK IT OUT**

16. The accompanying table shows a car manufacturer's total cost of producing cars.

Quantity of cars	TC
0	$500,000
1	540,000
2	560,000
3	570,000
4	590,000
5	620,000
6	660,000
7	720,000
8	800,000
9	920,000
10	1,100,000

a. What is this manufacturer's fixed cost?

b. For each level of output, calculate the variable cost (*VC*). For each level of output except zero output, calculate the average variable cost (*AVC*), average total cost (*ATC*), and average fixed cost (*AFC*). What is the minimum-cost output?

c. For each level of output, calculate this manufacturer's marginal cost (*MC*).

d. On one diagram, draw the manufacturer's *AVC*, *ATC*, and *MC* curves. ■

Inverse Relationships Between Productivity and Cost

In this chapter, we mentioned an inverse relationship between marginal product and marginal cost, and between average product and average variable cost. We noted that, all other things equal, when marginal product is rising, the marginal cost is falling. Similarly, we also noted that when the average product is rising, the average variable cost is falling. This appendix uses mathematics to explain these relationships.

Deriving the Inverse Relationships

In the chapter, we defined the marginal product of labour (*MPL*) and the average product of labour (*APL*):

(11-1) $MPL = \dfrac{\Delta q}{\Delta L}$

(11-2) $APL = \dfrac{q}{L}$

Now, let's turn to a firm's costs of production. For any firm, the amount of capital employed in the production process (such as property, machinery, and equipment) is assumed to be constant in the short run. We also assume that the state of production technology is fixed. In the short run, the firm can only adjust the amount of labour employed, the variable input. Since the firm must pay both fixed costs (*FC*) and the variable cost (*VC*) of labour to produce its output, its total cost (*TC*) can be expressed in terms of labour:

(11-3) $TC = FC + VC$

$\qquad = FC + w \times L$

where w is the wage rate page for one unit of labour. For example, suppose the hourly wage at a bakery is $15 and the daily fixed costs total $2,000. We can express the bakery's total cost in terms of the number of hours of labour as:

$$TC = 2,000 + 15 \times L$$

A firm should be interested in minimizing its cost of production for a given level of output. Then, the problem becomes how to minimize *TC*, subject to q.

Recall, marginal cost, *MC*, is the additional cost incurred by producing an additional unit of output. We expressed it as the change in total cost divided by the change in output:

(11-4) $MC = \dfrac{\Delta TC}{\Delta q}$

$\qquad = \dfrac{\Delta(FC + w \times L)}{\Delta q} = \dfrac{\Delta(FC)}{\Delta q} + \dfrac{\Delta(w \times L)}{\Delta q}$

FIGURE 11A-1 Duality Between Productivity and Cost

Due to the inverse relationship between marginal product of labour and marginal cost, and between average product of labour and average variable cost, the marginal cost curve mirrors the marginal product curve while the average variable cost curve mirrors the average product curve. Marginal cost falls when marginal product of labour rises; while marginal cost rises when marginal product of labour falls. When marginal product of labour is maximized (point A), marginal cost reaches its minimum (point A'). Similarly, when average product of labour rises, average variable costs falls; when average product of labour falls, average variable costs rises. When average product of labour is maximized (point B), average variable cost reaches its minimum (point B').

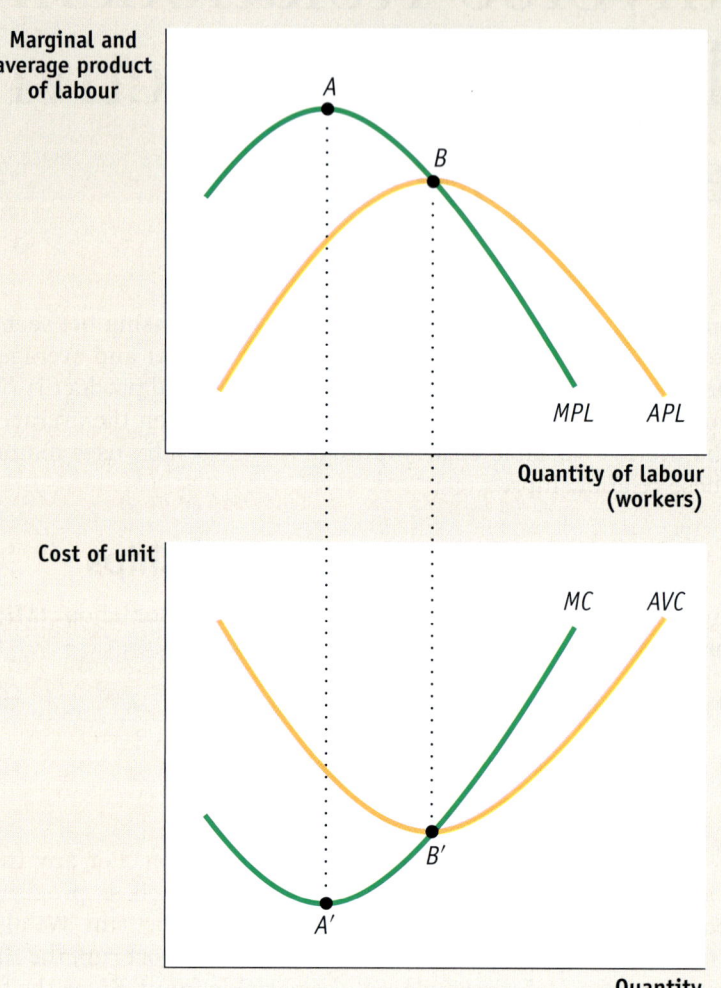

Since fixed costs do not change, ΔFC is zero. The wage is also constant, so the term w can be moved outside of the fraction:

(11A-1) $MC = w \times \dfrac{\Delta L}{\Delta q}$

An example may make this algebra clearer. For the bakery, the change in total cost $(TC = 2,000 + 15 \times L)$ can be separated into the change in the fixed cost ($2,000) plus the change in the variable cost of $15 multiplied by the change in hours of labour. The fixed amount does not change by definition, and only the number of hours of labour changes. At the bakery, the marginal cost is:

$$MC = 15 \times \frac{\Delta L}{\Delta q}$$

Given APL = $\Delta q/\Delta L$ (Equation 11-1), we can rewrite marginal cost (Equation 11A-1) as:

(11A-2) $MC = w \times \dfrac{1}{MPL}$

Now, it is clear that marginal cost falls when marginal product of labour rises; when the marginal product of labour falls, the marginal cost rises. Also, when marginal product is maximized, marginal cost reaches its minimum.

Discovering the inverse relationship between the average product of labour and average variable cost, *AVC*, is somewhat easier. In the chapter, we defined *AVC* as the variable cost per unit of output:

(11-5) $AVC = \dfrac{VC}{q}$

$$= \dfrac{w \times L}{q} = w \times \dfrac{L}{q}$$

Since Equation 11-2 describes *APL* as *q* divided by *L*, we have another inverse relationship. We can rewrite the average variable cost as:

(11A-3) $AVC = w \times \dfrac{1}{APL}$

Now, you can clearly see the inverse relationship between these two concepts. When average product of labour rises, average variable cost falls; when average product of labour falls, average variable cost rises. When average product is maximized, average variable cost reaches its minimum. Figure 11A-1 summarizes these relationships geometrically.

PROBLEMS

1. Magnificent Blooms is a florist specializing in floral arrangements for weddings, graduations, and other events. The daily marginal product of labour and average product of labour are:

$$MPL = 0.25 \times L^{-0.5}$$
$$APL = 0.50 \times L^{-0.5}$$

where *L* is the number of workers used in a day. Each worker is paid $54 per day.

a. If Magnificent Blooms employs 9 workers, what is the average product of labour? What is the marginal product of labour?

b. If Magnificent Blooms increases the number of workers employed, what happens to the marginal product of labour and the average product of labour? Explain.

c. Derive the marginal cost and the average variable cost functions in terms of labour.

d. If Magnificent Blooms needs to make 18 floral arrangements per day, how many workers will it hire? (*Hint:* Use Equation 11-2 with *q* = 18 and solve for *L*.)

e. Determine the marginal cost, the average cost, and average variable cost for 18 floral arrangements per day.

2. Suppose a firm's short-run total costs and marginal costs in dollars are given by:

$$TC = 0.5 \times q^2 + 2.5 \times q + 72$$
$$MC = q + 2.5$$

where *q* is the output per day. The firm has a fixed cost of $40, which is included in the *TC* equation above.

a. Determine this firm's average variable cost and average total cost in terms of *q*.

b. Draw a rough sketch of this firm's average total cost, average variable cost, and marginal cost curves. Put the quantity of output on the horizontal axis and the cost on the vertical axis.

c. Determine the level of output where average total cost is at a minimum. At this level of output, what do average total cost and marginal cost equal? Is this surprising? Explain why or why not.

d. Determine the level of output where average variable cost is at a minimum. At this level of output, what do average variable cost and marginal equal?

Perfect Competition and the Supply Curve

DECK THE HALLS

ONE SURE SIGN it's the holiday season is the sudden appearance of Christmas tree sellers, who set up shop in vacant lots, parking lots, and garden centres all across the country. Until the 1950s, virtually all Christmas trees were obtained by individuals going to local forests to cut down their own. However, by the 1950s increased demand from population growth and diminished supply from the loss of forests created a market opportunity. Seeing an ability to profit by growing and selling Christmas trees, farmers responded.

Joe Raedle/Getty Images

Whether it's Christmas trees or smartphones, how a good is produced determines its cost of production.

So rather than venturing into the forest to cut your own tree, you now have a wide range of tree sizes and varieties to choose from — and they are available close to home. Every year, more than 3 million farmed Christmas trees are sold in Canada. According to Statistics Canada, the sale of Christmas trees reached $114.5 million in 2018, up from $90.1 million a year earlier. In addition, more than half of Christmas tree sales revenue was from exports, mainly to the United States.

Note that the supply of Christmas trees is relatively price inelastic for two reasons: it takes time to acquire land for planting, and it takes time for the trees to grow. However, these limits apply only in the short run. Over time, farms that are already in operation can increase their capacity and new tree farmers can enter the business. And, over time, the trees will mature and be ready to harvest. Additionally, if prices of live trees continue to increase while artificial trees become cheaper, many consumers will buy artificial trees. So the increase in the quantity supplied in response to an increase in price will be much larger in the long run than in the short run.

Where does the supply curve come from? Why is there a difference between the short-run and the long-run supply curve? In this chapter we will use our understanding of costs, developed in Chapter 11, as the basis for an analysis of the supply curve. As we'll see, this will require that we understand the behaviour both of individual firms and of an entire industry, composed of these many individual firms.

Our analysis in this chapter assumes that the industry in question is characterized by *perfect competition*. We begin by explaining the concept of perfect competition, providing a brief introduction to the conditions that give rise to a perfectly competitive industry. We then show how a producer under perfect competition decides how much to produce. Finally, we use the cost curves of the individual producers to derive the *industry supply curve* under perfect competition.

By analyzing the way a competitive industry evolves over time, we will come to understand the distinction between the short-run and long-run effects of changes in demand on a competitive industry — such as, for example, the effect of North America's preference for readily available trees for the holidays on the Christmas tree farming industry. We will conclude with a deeper discussion of the conditions necessary for an industry to be perfectly competitive. •

A **price-taking producer** is a producer whose actions have no effect on the market price of the good or service it sells.

A **price-taking consumer** is a consumer whose actions have no effect on the market price of the good or service that consumer buys.

A **perfectly competitive market** is a market in which all market participants are price-takers.

A **perfectly competitive industry** is an industry in which producers are price-takers.

|| Perfect Competition

Suppose that Yves and Zoe are neighbouring farmers, both of whom grow Christmas trees. Both sell their output to the same set of Christmas tree consumers so, in a real sense, Yves and Zoe compete with each other.

Does this mean that Yves should try to stop Zoe from growing Christmas trees or that Yves and Zoe should form an agreement to grow less? Almost certainly not: there are thousands of Christmas tree farmers, and Yves and Zoe are competing with all those other growers as well as with each other. Because so many farmers sell Christmas trees, if any one of them produced more or less, there would be no measurable effect on market prices.

When people talk about business competition, the image they often have in mind is a situation in which two or three rival firms are intensely struggling for advantage. But economists know that when an industry consists of a few main competitors, it's actually a sign that competition is fairly limited. As the example of Christmas trees suggests, when there is enough competition, it doesn't even make sense to identify your rivals: there are so many competitors that you cannot single out any one of them as a rival.

We can put it another way: Yves and Zoe are **price-taking producers.** A producer is a price-taker when its actions cannot affect the market price of the good or service it sells. As a result, a price-taking producer considers the market price as given. When there is enough competition—when competition is what economists call "perfect"—then every producer is a price-taker.

And there is a similar definition for consumers: a **price-taking consumer** is a consumer who cannot influence the market price of the good or service by their actions. That is, the market price is unaffected by how much or how little of the good the consumer buys.

Defining Perfect Competition

In a **perfectly competitive market,** all market participants, both consumers and producers, are price-takers. That is, neither consumption decisions by individual consumers nor production decisions by individual producers affect the market price of the good.

The supply and demand model, which we introduced in Chapter 3 and have used repeatedly since then, is a model of a perfectly competitive market. It depends fundamentally on the assumption that no individual buyer or seller of a good, such as coffee beans or Christmas trees, believes that it is possible to affect the price at which they can buy or sell the good.

As a general rule, consumers are indeed price-takers. Instances in which consumers are able to affect the prices they pay are rare. It is, however, quite common for producers to have a significant ability to affect the prices they receive, a phenomenon we'll address in the next chapter. So the model of perfect competition is appropriate for some but not all markets. An industry in which producers are price-takers is called a **perfectly competitive industry.** Clearly, some industries aren't perfectly competitive; in later chapters, we'll learn how to analyze industries that don't fit the perfectly competitive model.

Under what circumstances will all producers be price-takers? In the next section, we will find that there are two necessary conditions for a perfectly competitive industry and that a third condition is often present as well.

Two Necessary Conditions for Perfect Competition

The markets for major grains, like wheat and corn, are perfectly competitive: individual wheat and corn farmers, as well as individual buyers of wheat and corn, take market prices as given. In contrast, the markets for some of the food items made from these grains—in particular, breakfast cereals—are by no means perfectly competitive. There is intense competition among cereal brands, but not *perfect* competition. To understand the difference between the market for wheat and the market for shredded wheat cereal is to understand the importance of the two necessary conditions for perfect competition.

First, for an industry to be perfectly competitive, it must contain many producers, none of whom have a large **market share.** A producer's market share is the fraction of the total industry output accounted for by that producer's output. The distribution of market share constitutes a major difference between the grain industry and the breakfast cereal industry. There are thousands of wheat farmers, none of whom account for more than a tiny fraction of total wheat sales.

The breakfast cereal industry, however, is dominated by four producers: General Mills, Post Foods, Kellogg's, and PepsiCo Canada alone account for more than 80% of all cereal sales in Canada. Kellogg's executives know that if they try to sell more cornflakes, they are likely to drive down the market price of cornflakes. That is, they know that their actions influence market prices, simply because they are such a large part of the market that changes in their production will significantly affect the overall quantity supplied. It makes sense to assume that producers are price-takers only when an industry does *not* contain any large producers like Kellogg's.

Second, an industry can be perfectly competitive only if consumers regard the products of all producers as equivalent. This clearly isn't true in the breakfast cereal market: consumers don't consider Cap'n Crunch to be a good substitute for Wheaties. As a result, the maker of Wheaties has some ability to increase its price without fear that it will lose all its customers to the maker of Cap'n Crunch.

Contrast this with the case of a **standardized product,** which is a product that consumers regard as the same good even when it comes from different producers, sometimes known as a **commodity.** Because wheat is a standardized product, consumers regard the output of one wheat producer as a perfect substitute for that of another producer. Consequently, one farmer cannot increase the price for their wheat without losing all sales to other wheat farmers. *So the second necessary condition for a competitive industry is that the industry output is a standardized product* (see the accompanying For Inquiring Minds).

A producer's **market share** is the fraction of the total industry output accounted for by that producer's output.

A good is a **standardized product,** also known as a **commodity,** when consumers regard the products of different producers as the same good.

FOR INQUIRING MINDS   What's a Standardized Product?

A perfectly competitive industry must produce a standardized product. But is it enough for the products of different firms actually to be the same? No: people must also *think* that they are the same. And producers often go to great lengths to convince consumers that they have a distinctive, or *differentiated,* product, even when they don't.

Consider, for example, champagne — not the superexpensive premium champagnes but the more ordinary stuff. Most people cannot tell the difference between champagne actually produced in the Champagne region of France, where the product originated, and similar products from Spain, British Columbia, or Ontario. But the French government has sought and obtained legal protection for the winemakers of Champagne, ensuring that

around the world only bubbly wine from that region can be called champagne. If it's from someplace else, all the seller can do is say that it was produced using the *méthode Champenoise.* This creates a differentiation in the minds of consumers and lets the champagne producers of Champagne charge higher prices.

Similarly, Korean producers of kimchi, the spicy fermented cabbage that is the Korean national side dish, are doing their best to convince consumers that the same product packaged by Japanese firms is just not the real thing. The purpose is, of course, to ensure higher prices for Korean kimchi.

So is an industry perfectly competitive if it sells products that are indistinguishable except in name but that consumers, for whatever reason, don't think

If you can't be persuaded to pay more for Korean kimchi than for Japanese kimchi, then kimchi is a standardized product.

are standardized? No. When it comes to defining the nature of competition, the consumer is always right.

An industry has **free entry and exit** when new producers can easily enter into an industry and existing producers can easily leave that industry.

Free Entry and Exit

All perfectly competitive industries have many producers with small market shares, producing a standardized product. Most perfectly competitive industries are also characterized by one more feature: it is easy for new firms to enter the industry or for firms that are currently in the industry to leave. That is, no obstacles in the form of government regulations or limited access to key resources prevent new producers from entering the market. And no additional costs are associated with shutting down a company and leaving the industry.

Economists refer to the arrival of new firms into an industry as *entry;* they refer to the departure of firms from an industry as *exit.* When there are no obstacles to entry into or exit from an industry, we say that the industry has **free entry and exit.**

Free entry and exit is not strictly necessary for perfect competition. In Chapter 5, we described the case of the Canadian lobster fishery, where regulations place a quota on the number of licences issued, with limits on the number of traps to limit the amount of lobster that can be caught during a season, so entry is limited to established boat owners that have been given licences. Despite this, there are enough boats operating that the lobster fishers are price-takers. But free entry and exit is a key factor in most competitive industries. It ensures that the number of producers in an industry can adjust to changing market conditions. And, in particular, it ensures that producers in an industry cannot act to keep new firms out.

To sum up, then, perfect competition depends on two necessary conditions.

1. The industry must contain many producers, each having a small market share.
2. The industry must produce a standardized product.

In addition, perfectly competitive industries are normally characterized by free entry and exit.

How does an industry that meets these three criteria behave? As a first step toward answering that question, let's look at how an individual producer in a perfectly competitive industry maximizes profit.

ECONOMICS >> *in Action*
Pay-for-Delay Runs Out of Time

Sometimes it is possible to watch as a market becomes perfectly competitive. This is the case in the pharmaceutical industry, when the patent on a popular drug expires and a *generic* rival drug enters the market served by that drug.

Let's start with some background on why the market was originally uncompetitive. A company that develops a new drug is given a *patent,* which gives it a *legal monopoly*—the exclusive right to sell the drug—for 20 years. Legally, no one else can sell the drug without the patent-holder's permission. This allows the developer to recoup the costs of development.

When the patent expires after 20 years, the market is open for entry by other companies to produce and sell *generics,* alternative but medically equivalent versions of the drug. As a result, the price drops dramatically. On average, a generic drug costs about 15% of the price of the equivalent patent-protected drug, which will lose up to 90% of its market share. In the case of Lipitor, Pfizer's blockbuster drug for cholesterol, the generic version was only 8% of the price of Lipitor.

That sequence of events is what is *supposed* to happen. However, makers of the original patent-protected drugs have employed a variety of strategies to block or forestall the entry of generic competitors. A firm applying to Health Canada to market a generic version of a drug must show that

Patents allow drug makers to have a legal monopoly on new medications for 20 years.

it does not infringe on patents filed by brand-name firms. However, brand-name companies can challenge the applications resulting in an automatic 24-month delay. As a result, the original drug maker continues to charge high prices and reap high profits. Another very successful tactic has been *pay-for-delay,* an agreement in which the patent holder pays the generic drug maker to delay the entry of the generic drug in return for compensation. As a result, the patent holder continues to charge high prices, the generic drug maker gets a lucrative payment, and the consumer suffers.

Pay-for-delay agreements have cost North American consumers billions dollars annually from 2005 to 2013. But in 2014, the number of such deals dropped dramatically after the U.S. Supreme Court gave federal regulators the authority to prosecute the deals as anti-competitive. With that authority, the Federal Trade Commission scored a US$1.2 billion settlement from drug maker Teva over allegations it engaged in pay for delay over their sleep-disorder drug Provigl. In recent years, the Canadian Competition Bureau has also taken a keener interest in ensuring such pay to delay agreements do not unfairly limit competition. According to industry observers, increased competition is saving consumers many billions of dollars a year. For the pharmaceutical industry, pay-for-delay has clearly run out of time.

>> Check Your Understanding 12-1

Solutions appear at back of book.

1. In each of the following situations, do you think the industry described will be perfectly competitive or not? Explain your answer.
   a. There are two producers of aluminum in the world, a good sold in many places.
   b. The price of natural gas is determined by global supply and demand. A small share of that global supply is produced by a handful of companies located in the North Sea.
   c. Dozens of designers sell high-fashion clothes. Each designer has a distinctive style and a loyal clientele.
   d. There are many NHL teams in North America, one or two in each major city and each selling tickets to its hometown events.

> ### >> Quick Review
> • Neither the actions of a **price-taking producer** nor those of a **price-taking consumer** can influence the market price of a good.
>
> • In a **perfectly competitive market** all producers and consumers are price-takers. Consumers are almost always price-takers, but this is often not true of producers. An industry in which producers are price-takers is a **perfectly competitive industry.**
>
> • A perfectly competitive industry contains many producers, each of which produces a standardized **product** (also known as a **commodity**) but none of which has a large **market share.**
>
> • Most perfectly competitive industries are also characterized by **free entry and exit.**

‖ Production and Profits

Consider Noelle, who runs a Christmas tree farm. Suppose that the market price of Christmas trees is $72 per tree and that Noelle is a price-taker—she can sell as many as she likes at that price. Then we can use the data in Table 12-1 to find her profit-maximizing level of output by direct calculation.

The first column shows the quantity of output in number of trees, and the second column shows Noelle's total revenue from her output: the market value of trees she produced. Total revenue, *TR,* is equal to the market price multiplied by the quantity of output:

(12-1) $TR = P \times q$

In this example, total revenue is equal to $72 per tree times the quantity of output in trees.

The third column of Table 12-1 shows Noelle's total cost. The fourth column shows her profit, equal to total revenue minus total cost:

(12-2) Profit = $TR - TC$

As indicated by the numbers in the table, profit is maximized at an output of 50 trees, where profit is equal to $720. But we can gain more insight into the profit-maximizing choice of output by viewing it as a problem of marginal analysis, a task we'll do next.

TABLE 12-1 Profit for Noelle's Farm When Market Price Is $72

Quantity of trees q	Total revenue TR	Total cost TC	Profit $TR - TC$
0	$0	$560	–$560
10	720	1,200	–480
20	1,440	1,440	0
30	2,160	1,760	400
40	2,880	2,240	640
50	3,600	2,880	720
60	4,320	3,680	640
70	5,040	4,640	400

Marginal revenue is the change in total revenue generated by an additional unit of output.

According to the **optimal output rule,** profit is maximized by producing the quantity of output at which the marginal revenue of the last unit produced is equal to its marginal cost.

Using Marginal Analysis to Choose the Profit-Maximizing Quantity of Output

Recall from Chapter 9 the *profit-maximizing principle of marginal analysis:* the optimal amount of an activity is the level at which marginal benefit is equal to marginal cost. To apply this principle, consider the effect on a producer's profit of increasing output by one unit. The marginal benefit of that unit is the additional revenue generated by selling it; this measure has a name—it is called the **marginal revenue** of that unit of output. The general formula for marginal revenue is:

(12-3) Marginal revenue = $\dfrac{\text{Change in total revenue generated by one additional unit of output}}{} = \dfrac{\text{Change in total revenue}}{\text{Change in quantity of output}}$

or

$$MR = \frac{\Delta TR}{\Delta q}$$

So Noelle maximizes her profit by producing trees up to the point at which the marginal revenue is equal to marginal cost. We can summarize this as the producer's **optimal output rule:** profit is maximized by producing the quantity at which the marginal revenue of the last unit produced is equal to its marginal cost. That is, $MR = MC$ at the optimal quantity of output.

We can learn how to apply the optimal output rule with the help of Table 12-2, which provides various short-run cost measures for Noelle's farm. The second column contains the farm's variable cost, and the third column shows its total cost of output based on the assumption that the farm incurs a fixed cost of $560. The fourth column shows marginal cost. Notice that, in this example, the marginal cost initially falls but then rises as output increases. This gives the marginal cost curve the "swoosh" shape described in Chapter 11. Shortly it will become clear that this shape has important implications for short-run production decisions.

The fifth column contains the farm's marginal revenue, which has an important feature: Noelle's marginal revenue equal to price is constant at $72 for every output level.

The sixth and final column shows the calculation of the net gain per tree, which is equal to marginal revenue minus marginal cost—or, equivalently in this case, market price minus marginal cost. As you can see, it is positive for the 1st through 50th trees; producing each of these trees raises Noelle's profit. For the 51st through 70th trees, however, net gain is negative: producing them would decrease, not increase, profit. So to maximize profits, Noelle will produce up to the point at which the marginal revenue of the last unit produced is greater than or equal to the marginal cost of the last unit produced; any more reduces her profit. Hence, 50 trees is Noelle's profit-maximizing output.

Because Noelle receives $72 for every tree produced, we know that her farm is a price-taking firm. A price-taking firm cannot influence the market price by its actions. It always takes the market price as given because it cannot lower the market price by selling more or raise the market price by selling less. So, for a price-taking firm, the additional revenue generated by producing one more unit is always the market price. Be sure to keep this fact in mind in future chapters, where

TABLE 12-2 Short-Run Costs for Noelle's Farm

Quantity of trees q	Variable cost VC	Total cost TC	Marginal cost of tree MC = ΔTC/Δq	Marginal revenue of tree MR	Net gain of tree = MR − MC
0	$0	$560			
			$64	$72	$8
10	640	1,200			
			24	72	48
20	880	1,440			
			32	72	40
30	1,200	1,760			
			48	72	24
40	1,680	2,240			
			64	72	8
50	2,320	2,880			
			80	72	−8
60	3,120	3,680			
			96	72	−24
70	4,080	4,640			

FIGURE 12-1 The Price-Taking Firm's Profit-Maximizing Quantity of Output

At the profit-maximizing quantity of output, the market price is equal to marginal cost. It is located at the point where the marginal cost curve crosses the marginal revenue curve, which is a horizontal line at the market price. Here, the profit-maximizing point is at an output of 50 trees, the output quantity at point E.

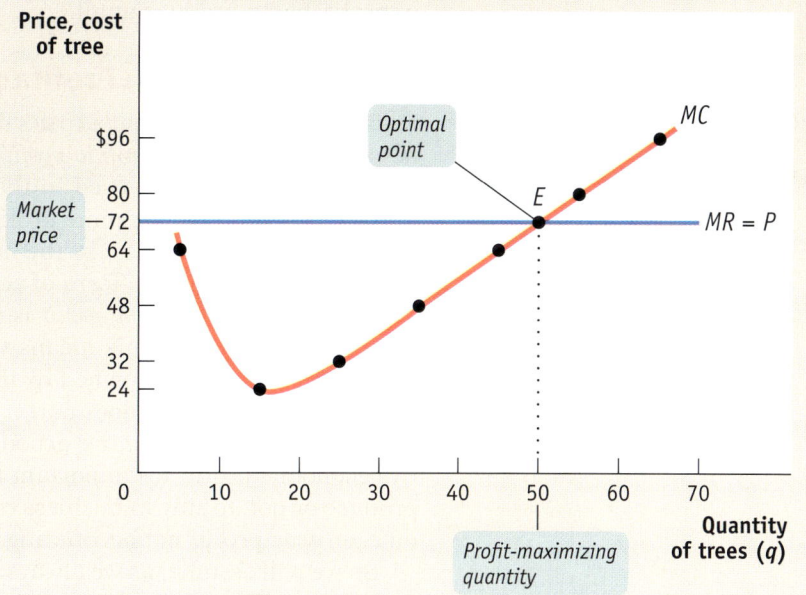

we will learn that marginal revenue is not equal to the market price if the industry is not perfectly competitive. As a result, firms are not price-takers when an industry is not perfectly competitive. For the remainder of this chapter, we will assume that the industry in question is like Christmas tree farming, perfectly competitive.

Figure 12-1 shows that Noelle's profit-maximizing quantity of output is, indeed, 50 trees. The figure shows the marginal cost curve, *MC*, drawn from the data in the fourth column of Table 12-2. As in Chapter 9, we plot the marginal cost of increasing output from 10 to 20 trees halfway between 10 and 20, and so on. The *MC* curve is smooth, allowing us to see how *MC* changes as one more tree is produced. The horizontal line at $72 is Noelle's **marginal revenue curve**.

Note that whenever a firm is a price-taker, its marginal revenue curve is a horizontal line at the market price: it can sell as much as it likes at the market price. Regardless of whether it sells more or less, the market price is unaffected. *In effect, the individual firm faces a horizontal, perfectly elastic demand curve for its output—an individual demand curve for its output that is equivalent to its marginal revenue curve.* The marginal cost curve crosses the marginal revenue curve at point *E* where *MC = MR*. Sure enough, the quantity of output at *E* is 50 trees.

This example illustrates another general rule derived from marginal analysis— the **price-taking firm's optimal output rule,** which says that a price-taking firm's profit is maximized by producing the quantity of output up to the point at which the market price is equal to the marginal cost of the last unit produced. That is, *P = MC at the price-taking firm's optimal quantity of output.* In fact, the price-taking firm's optimal output rule is just an application of the optimal output rule to the particular case of a price-taking firm. Why? Because *in the case of a price-taking firm, marginal revenue is equal to the market price.*

Does this mean that the price-taking firm's production decision can be entirely summed up as "produce up to the point where the marginal cost of production is equal to the price"? No, not quite. Before applying the profit-maximizing principle of marginal analysis to determine how much to produce, a potential producer must as a first step answer an "either–or" question: should it produce at all? If the answer to that question is yes, it then proceeds to the second step—a "how much" decision: maximizing profit by choosing the quantity of output at which marginal cost is equal to price.

PITFALLS

WHAT IF MARGINAL REVENUE AND MARGINAL COST AREN'T EXACTLY EQUAL?

The optimal output rule says that to maximize profit, you should produce the quantity at which marginal revenue is equal to marginal cost. But what do you do if there is no output level at which marginal revenue exactly equals marginal cost? In that case, you produce the largest quantity for which marginal revenue exceeds marginal cost. The simpler version of the optimal output rule applies when production involves large numbers, such as hundreds or thousands of units. In such cases, marginal cost comes in small increments, and there is always a level of output at which marginal cost almost exactly equals marginal revenue.

The **marginal revenue curve** shows how marginal revenue varies as output varies.

According to the **price-taking firm's optimal output rule,** a price-taking firm's profit is maximized by producing the quantity of output at which the market price is equal to the marginal cost of the last unit produced.

To understand why the first step in the production decision involves an "either–or" question, we need to ask how we determine whether it is profitable or unprofitable to produce at all.

When Is Production Profitable?

Recall from Chapter 9 that a firm's decision whether or not to stay in a given business depends on its *economic profit*—the measure of profit based on the opportunity cost of resources used in the business. To put it a slightly different way: in the calculation of economic profit, a firm's total cost incorporates the implicit cost—the benefits forgone in the next best use of the firm's resources—as well as the explicit cost in the form of actual cash outlays.

In contrast, *accounting profit* is profit calculated using only the explicit costs incurred by the firm. This means that economic profit incorporates the opportunity cost of resources owned by the firm and used in the production of output, while accounting profit does not.

A firm may make positive accounting profit while making zero or even negative economic profit. It's important to understand clearly that a firm's decision to produce or not, to stay in business or to close down permanently, should be based on economic profit, not accounting profit.

So we will assume, as we always do, that the cost numbers given in Tables 12-1 and 12-2 include all costs, implicit as well as explicit, and that the profit numbers in Table 12-1 are therefore economic profit. So what determines whether Noelle's farm earns a profit or generates a loss? The answer is that, *given the farm's cost curves, whether or not it is profitable depends on the market price of trees— specifically, whether the market price is more or less than the farm's minimum average total cost.*

TABLE 12-3 Short-Run Average Costs for Noelle's Farm				
Quantity of trees q	Variable cost VC	Total cost TC	Short-run average variable cost of tree AVC = VC/q	Short-run average total cost of tree ATC = TC/q
10	$640.00	$1,200.00	$64.00	$120.00
20	880.00	1,440.00	44.00	72.00
30	1,200.00	1,760.00	40.00	58.67
40	1,680.00	2,240.00	42.00	56.00
50	2,320.00	2,880.00	46.40	57.60
60	3,120.00	3,680.00	52.00	61.33
70	4,080.00	4,640.00	58.29	66.29

In Table 12-3 we calculate short-run average variable cost and short-run average total cost for Noelle's farm. These are short-run values because we take fixed cost as given. (We'll turn to the effects of changing fixed cost shortly.) The short-run average total cost curve, ATC, is shown in Figure 12-2, along with the marginal cost curve, MC, from Figure 12-1. As you can see, average total cost is minimized at point C, corresponding to an output of 40 trees—the *minimum-cost output*—and an average total cost of $56 per tree.

To see how these curves can be used to decide whether production is profitable or unprofitable, recall that profit is equal to total revenue minus total cost, *TR* – *TC*. This means:

- If the firm produces a quantity at which *TR* > *TC*, the firm is profitable.
- If the firm produces a quantity at which *TR* = *TC*, the firm breaks even.
- If the firm produces a quantity at which *TR* < *TC*, the firm incurs a loss.

We can also express this idea in terms of revenue and cost per unit of output. If we divide profit by the number of units of output, *q*, we obtain the following expression for profit per unit of output:

(12-4) Profit/$q = TR/q - TC/q$

TR/*q* is average revenue, which is the market price. *TC*/*q* is average total cost. So a firm is profitable if the market price for its product is more than the average total cost of the quantity the firm produces; a firm loses money if the

FIGURE 12-2 Costs and Production in the Short Run

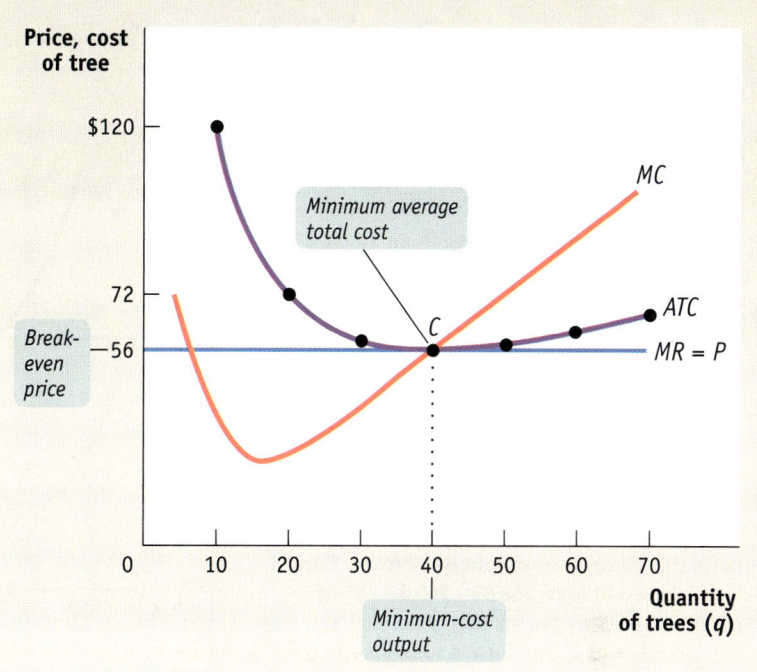

This figure shows the marginal cost curve, *MC*, and the short-run average total cost curve, *ATC*. When the market price is $56, output will be 40 trees (the minimum-cost output), represented by point *C*. The price of $56, equal to the firm's minimum average total cost, is the firm's *break-even price.*

market price is less than average total cost of the quantity the firm produces. This means:

- If the firm produces a quantity at which *P > ATC*, the firm is profitable.
- If the firm produces a quantity at which *P = ATC*, the firm breaks even.
- If the firm produces a quantity at which *P < ATC*, the firm incurs a loss.

Figure 12-3 illustrates this result, showing how the market price determines whether a firm is profitable. It also shows how profits are depicted graphically. Each panel shows the marginal cost curve, *MC*, and the short-run average total cost curve, *ATC*. Average total cost is minimized at point *C*. Panel (a) shows the case we have already analyzed, in which the market price of trees is $72 per tree. Panel (b) shows the case in which the market price of trees is lower, $40 per tree.

In panel (a), we see that at a price of $72 per tree the profit-maximizing quantity of output is 50 trees, indicated by point *E*, where the marginal cost curve, *MC*, intersects the marginal revenue curve—which for a price-taking firm is a horizontal line at the market price. At that quantity of output, average total cost is $57.60 per tree, indicated by point *Z*. Since the price per tree exceeds average total cost per tree, Noelle's farm is profitable.

Noelle's total profit when the market price is $72 is represented by the area of the shaded rectangle in panel (a). To see why, notice that total profit can be expressed in terms of profit per unit:

(12-5) Profit = $TR - TC = (TR/q - TC/q) \times q$

or, equivalently,

Profit = $(P - ATC) \times q$

since *P* is equal to *TR/q* and *ATC* is equal to *TC/q*. The height of the shaded rectangle in panel (a) corresponds to the vertical distance between points *E* and *Z*. It is equal to $P - ATC = \$72.00 - \$57.60 = \$14.40$ per tree. The shaded rectangle has a width equal to the output: $q = 50$ trees. So the area of that rectangle is equal

FIGURE 12-3 **Profitability and the Market Price**

In panel (a), the market price is $72. The farm is profitable because price exceeds minimum average total cost, the break-even price, $56. The farm's optimal output choice is indicated by point E, corresponding to an output of 50 trees. The average total cost of producing 50 trees is indicated by point Z on the ATC curve, corresponding to an amount of $57.60. The vertical distance between E and Z corresponds to the farm's per-unit profit, $72.00 − $57.60 = $14.40. Total profit is given by the area of the shaded rectangle, 50 × $14.40 = $720.00.

In panel (b), the market price is $40; the farm is unprofitable because the price falls below the minimum average total cost, $56. The farm's optimal output choice when producing is indicated by point A, corresponding to an output of 30 trees. The farm's per-unit loss, $58.67 − $40.00 = $18.67, is represented by the vertical distance between A and Y. The farm's total loss is represented by the shaded rectangle, 30 × $18.67 = $560.00 (adjusted for rounding error).

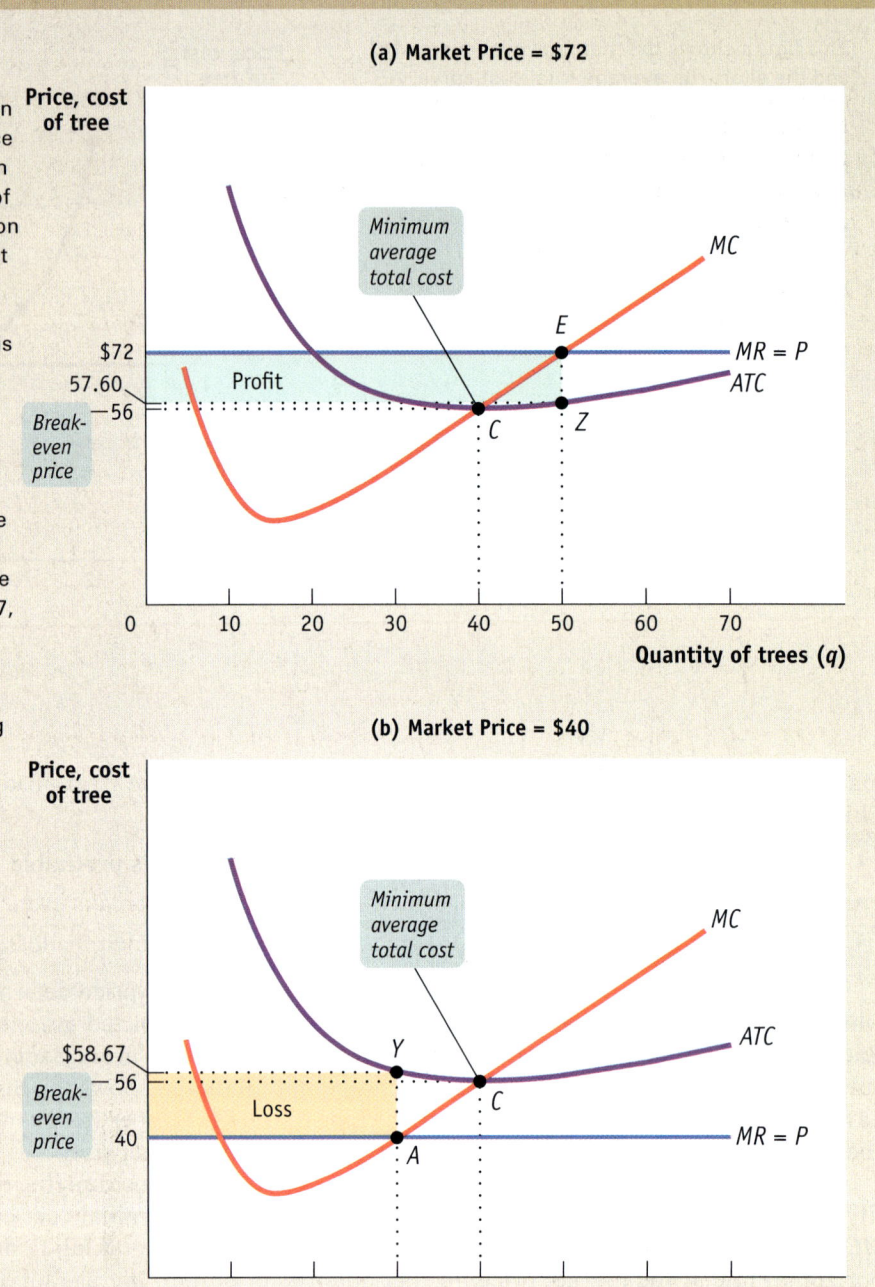

to Noelle's profit: 50 trees × $14.40 profit per tree = $720—the same number we calculated in Table 12-1.

What about the situation illustrated in panel (b)? Here the market price of trees is $40 per tree. Setting price equal to marginal cost leads to a profit-maximizing output of 30 trees, indicated by point A. At this output, Noelle has an average total cost of $58.67 per tree, indicated by point Y. At the profit-maximizing output quantity—30 trees—average total cost exceeds the market price. This means that Noelle's farm generates a loss, not a profit.

How much does she lose by producing when the market price is $40? On each tree she loses $ATC − P = $58.67 − $40.00 = 18.67, an amount corresponding to the vertical distance between points *A* and *Y*. And she would produce 30 trees, which corresponds to the width of the shaded rectangle. So the total value of the losses is $18.67 \times 30 = \$560.00$ (adjusted for rounding error), an amount that corresponds to the area of the shaded rectangle in panel (b).

But how does a producer know, in general, whether or not its business will be profitable? It turns out that the crucial test lies in a comparison of the market price to the producer's *minimum average total cost*. On Noelle's farm, minimum average total cost, which is equal to $56, occurs at an output quantity of 40 trees, indicated by point *C*.

Whenever the market price exceeds minimum average total cost, the producer can find some output level for which the average total cost is less than the market price. In other words, the producer can find a level of output at which the firm makes a profit. So Noelle's farm will be profitable whenever the market price exceeds $56. And she will achieve the highest possible profit by producing the quantity at which marginal cost equals the market price.

Conversely, if the market price is less than minimum average total cost, there is no output level at which price exceeds average total cost. As a result, the firm will be unprofitable at any quantity of output. As we saw, at a price of $40—an amount less than minimum average total cost—Noelle did indeed lose money. By producing the quantity at which marginal cost equals the market price, Noelle did the best she could, but the best that she could do was a loss of $560. Any other quantity would have increased the size of her loss.

The minimum average total cost of a price-taking firm is called its **break-even price,** the price at which it earns zero profit. (Recall that's *economic profit*.) A firm will earn positive profit when the market price is above the break-even price, and it will suffer losses when the market price is below the break-even price. Noelle's break-even price of $56 is the price at point *C* in Figures 12-2 and 12-3.

So the rule for determining whether a producer of a good is profitable depends on a comparison of the market price of the good to the producer's break-even price—its minimum average total cost:

- Whenever the market price exceeds minimum average total cost, the producer is profitable.

- Whenever the market price equals minimum average total cost, the producer breaks even.

- Whenever the market price is less than minimum average total cost, the producer is unprofitable.

The Short-Run Production Decision

You might be tempted to say that if a firm is unprofitable because the market price is below its minimum average total cost, it shouldn't produce any output. In the short run, however, this conclusion isn't right.

In the short run, sometimes the firm should produce even if price falls below minimum average total cost. The reason is that total cost includes *fixed cost*—cost that does not depend on the amount of output produced and can only be altered in the long run.

In the short run, fixed cost must still be paid, regardless of whether or not a firm produces. For example, if Noelle rents a refrigerated truck for the year, she has to pay the rent on the truck regardless of whether she produces any trees. *Since it cannot be changed in the short run, her fixed cost is irrelevant to her decision about whether to produce or shut down in the short run.*

Although fixed cost should play no role in the decision about whether to produce in the short run, other costs—variable costs—do matter. An example of variable costs is the wages of workers who must be hired to help with planting

The **break-even price** of a price-taking firm is the market price at which it earns zero profit.

A firm will cease production in the short run if the market price falls below the **shut-down price,** which is equal to minimum average variable cost.

and harvesting. Variable costs can be saved by *not* producing; so they should play a role in determining whether or not to produce in the short run.

Let's turn to Figure 12-4: it shows both the short-run average total cost curve, *ATC,* and the short-run average variable cost curve, *AVC,* drawn from the information in Table 12-3. Recall that the difference between the two curves—the vertical distance between them—represents average fixed cost, the fixed cost per unit of output, *FC/q.*

Because the marginal cost curve has a "swoosh" shape—falling at first before rising—the short-run average variable cost curve is U-shaped: the initial fall in marginal cost causes average variable cost to fall as well, before rising marginal cost eventually pulls it up again. The short-run average variable cost curve reaches its minimum value of $40 at point *A,* at an output of 30 trees.

We are now prepared to fully analyze the optimal production decision in the short run. We need to consider two cases:

1. When the market price is below minimum average *variable* cost
2. When the market price is greater than or equal to minimum average *variable* cost

When the market price is below minimum average variable cost, the price the firm receives per unit is not covering its variable cost per unit. A firm in this situation should cease production immediately. Why? Because there is no level of output at which the firm's total revenue covers its variable costs—the costs it can avoid by not operating.

In this case the firm maximizes its profits by not producing at all—by, in effect, minimizing its losses. It will still incur a fixed cost in the short run, but it will no longer incur any variable cost. This means that the minimum average variable cost is equal to the **shut-down price,** the price at which the firm ceases production in the short run. In the example of Noelle's tree farm, she will cease production in the short run by laying off workers and halting all planting and harvesting of trees.

When price is greater than minimum average variable cost, however, the firm should produce in the short run. In this case, the firm maximizes profit—or minimizes loss—by choosing the output quantity at which its marginal cost is

---

FIGURE 12-4 The Short-Run Individual Supply Curve

When the market price equals or exceeds Noelle's *shut-down price* of $40, the minimum average variable cost indicated by point *A,* she will produce the output quantity at which marginal cost is equal to price. So at any price equal to or above the minimum average *variable* cost, the short-run individual supply curve is the firm's marginal cost curve; this corresponds to the upward-sloping segment of the individual supply curve. When market price falls below minimum average variable cost, the firm ceases operation in the short run. This corresponds to the vertical segment of the individual supply curve along the vertical axis.

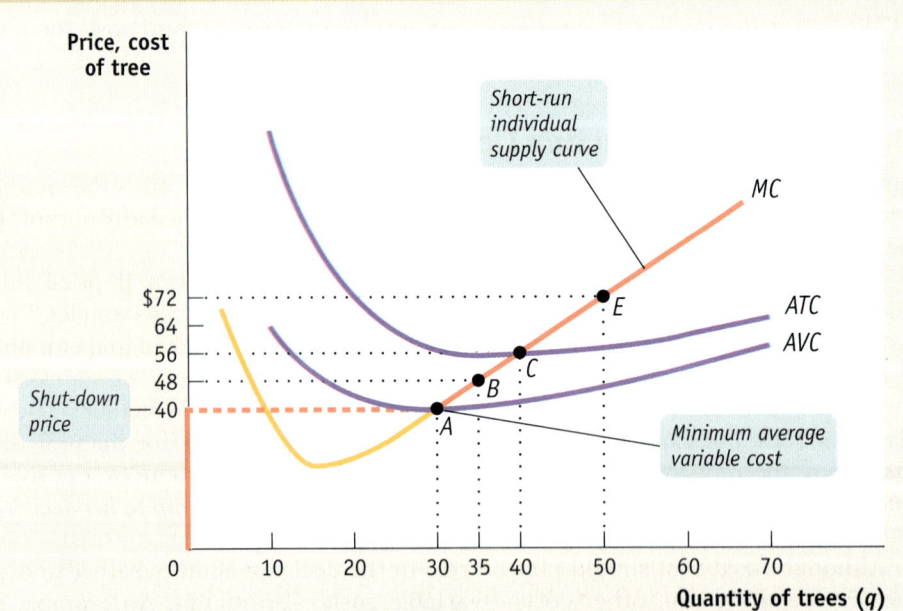

equal to the market price. For example, if the market price of each tree is $72, Noelle should produce at point *E* in Figure 12-4, corresponding to an output of 50 trees. Note that point *C* in Figure 12-4 corresponds to the farm's break-even price of $56 per tree. Since *E* lies above *C*, Noelle's farm will be profitable; she will generate a per-tree profit of $72.00 – $56.00 = $16.00 when the market price is $72.

But what if the market price lies between the shut-down price and the break-even price—that is, between minimum average *variable* cost and minimum average *total* cost? In the case of Noelle's farm, this corresponds to prices anywhere between $40 and $56—say, a market price of $48. At $48, Noelle's farm is not profitable; since the market price is below minimum average total cost, the farm is losing the difference between price and average total cost per unit produced.

Yet even if it isn't covering its total cost per unit, it is covering its variable cost per unit and some—but not all—of its fixed cost per unit. If a firm in this situation shuts down, it would incur no variable cost but would incur the *full* fixed cost. As a result, shutting down generates an even greater loss than continuing to operate.

This means that whenever price lies between minimum average total cost and minimum average variable cost, the firm is better off producing some output in the short run. The reason is that by producing, it can cover its variable cost per unit and at least some of its fixed cost, even though it is incurring a loss. In this case, the firm maximizes profit—that is, minimizes loss—by choosing the quantity of output at which its marginal cost is equal to the market price. So if Noelle faces a market price of $48 per tree, her profit-maximizing output is given by point *B* in Figure 12-4, corresponding to an output of 35 trees.

It's worth noting that the decision to produce when the firm is covering its variable costs but not all of its fixed cost is similar to the decision to ignore *sunk costs*. You may recall from Chapter 9 that a sunk cost is a cost that has already been incurred and cannot be recouped; and because it cannot be changed, it should have no effect on any current decision.

In the short-run production decision, fixed cost is, in effect, like a sunk cost—it has been spent, and it can't be recovered in the short run. This comparison also illustrates why variable cost does indeed matter in the short run: it can be avoided by not producing.

And what happens if market price is exactly equal to the shut-down price, minimum average variable cost? In this instance, the firm is indifferent between producing 30 units or 0 units. As we'll see shortly, this is an important point when looking at the behaviour of an industry as a whole. For the sake of clarity, we'll assume that the firm, although indifferent, does indeed produce output when price is equal to the shut-down price.

Putting everything together, we can now draw the **short-run individual supply curve** of Noelle's farm, the red line in Figure 12-4; it shows how the profit-maximizing quantity of output in the short run depends on the price. As you can see, the curve is in two segments. The upward-sloping red segment starting at point *A* shows the short-run profit-maximizing output when market price is equal to or above the shut-down price of $40 per tree.

As long as the market price is equal to or above the shut-down price, Noelle produces the quantity of output at which marginal cost is equal to the market price. That is, at market prices equal to or above the shut-down price, the firm's short-run supply curve corresponds to its marginal cost curve. But at any market price below minimum average variable cost—in this case, $40 per tree—the firm shuts down and output drops to zero in the short run. This corresponds to the vertical segment of the curve that lies on top of the vertical axis.

Do firms really shut down temporarily without going out of business? Yes. In fact, in some businesses, temporary shut-downs are routine. The most common examples are industries in which demand is highly seasonal, like outdoor amusement parks in climates with cold winters. Such parks would have to offer very

The **short-run individual supply curve** shows how an individual producer's profit-maximizing output quantity depends on the market price, taking fixed cost as given. It is the firm's marginal cost curve at or above its average variable cost curve (and zero output for prices below the minimum of average variable cost).

low prices to entice customers during the colder months—prices so low that the owners would not cover their variable costs (principally wages and electricity). The wiser choice economically is to shut down until warm weather brings enough customers who are willing to pay a higher price.

Changing Fixed Cost

Although fixed cost cannot be altered in the short run, in the long run, firms can acquire or get rid of machines, buildings, and so on. In the long run the level of fixed cost is a matter of choice. We saw in Chapter 11 that a firm will choose the level of fixed cost that minimizes the average total cost for its desired output quantity. Now we will focus on an even bigger question facing a firm when choosing its fixed cost: whether to incur *any* fixed cost at all by remaining in its current business.

In the long run, a producer can always eliminate fixed cost by selling off its plant and equipment (or ending leases for any plant or equipment that is rented). If it does so, of course, it can't ever produce—it has exited the industry. In contrast, a potential producer can take on some fixed cost by acquiring machines and other resources, which puts it in a position to produce—it can enter the industry. In most perfectly competitive industries the set of producers, although fixed in the short run, changes in the long run as firms enter or exit the industry.

Consider Noelle's farm once again. In order to simplify our analysis, we will sidestep the problem of choosing among several possible levels of fixed cost. Instead, we will assume from now on that Noelle has only one possible choice of fixed cost if she operates, the amount of $560, Noelle's minimum average total cost, that was the basis for the calculations in Tables 12-1, 12-2, and 12-3. (With this assumption, Noelle's short-run average total cost curve and long-run average total cost curve are one and the same.) Alternatively, she can choose a fixed cost of zero if she exits the industry.

Suppose that the market price of trees is consistently less than $56 over an extended period of time. In that case, Noelle never fully covers her fixed cost: her business runs at a persistent loss. In the long run, then, she can do better by closing her business and leaving the industry. In other words, *in the long run* firms will exit an industry if the market price is consistently less than their break-even price—their minimum average total cost.

Conversely, suppose that the price of Christmas trees is consistently above the break-even price, $56, for an extended period of time. Because her farm is profitable, Noelle will remain in the industry and continue producing.

But things won't stop there. The Christmas tree industry meets the criterion of *free entry:* there are many potential tree producers because the necessary inputs are easy to obtain. And the cost curves of those potential producers are likely to be similar to those of Noelle, since the technology used by other producers is likely to be very similar to that used by Noelle. If the price is high enough to generate profits for existing producers, it will also attract some of these potential producers into the industry. So *in the long run* a price in excess of $56 should lead to entry: new producers will come into the Christmas tree industry.

As we will see next, exit and entry lead to an important distinction between the *short-run industry supply curve* and the *long-run industry supply curve*.

Summing Up: The Perfectly Competitive Firm's Profitability and Production Conditions

In this chapter, we've studied where the supply curve for a perfectly competitive, price-taking firm comes from. Every perfectly competitive firm makes its production decisions by maximizing profit, and these decisions determine the supply curve. Table 12-4 summarizes the perfectly competitive firm's profitability and production conditions. It also relates them to entry into and exit from the industry.

Buying or selling equipment allows a firm to change its fixed cost.

TABLE 12-4 Summary of the Perfectly Competitive Firm's Profitability and Production Conditions

Profitability condition (minimum *ATC* = break-even price)	Result
P > minimum *ATC*	Firm profitable. Entry into industry in the long run.
P = minimum *ATC*	Firm breaks even. No entry into or exit from industry in the long run.
P < minimum *ATC*	Firm unprofitable. Exit from industry in the long run.

Profitability condition (minimum AVC = shut-down price)	Result
P > minimum *AVC*	Firm produces in the short run. If P < minimum *ATC*, firm covers variable cost and some but not all of fixed cost. If P > minimum *ATC*, firm covers all variable cost and fixed cost.
P = minimum *AVC*	Firm indifferent between producing in the short run or not. Just covers variable cost.
P < minimum *AVC*	Firm shuts down in the short run. Does not cover variable cost.

ECONOMICS >> *in Action*
Farmers Know How

If there is one profession that requires a clear understanding of profit-maximization, it's farming. Farmers must respond to constantly fluctuating prices for their output, as well as constantly changing input prices. Furthermore, the farming industry satisfies the condition of a competitive market because it is composed of thousands of individual, price-taking farmers.

For a good illustration of farmers' economic acumen we can examine Canadian crop prices over the past decade, a period marked by boom and then retrenchment. During this decade, prices for canola rose steadily, reaching an all-time high in 2013 as the price of canola oil rose by 50% and canola seed prices rose by 60%.

This long-term rise was mainly due to two demand-based factors. Crop prices were pushed upward by rapidly rising exports to China and other developing countries. Also, the U.S. Congress passed a mandate to increase the use of corn-based ethanol, a biofuel that is blended into gasoline, as a means of reducing American dependency on imported oil. This caused the price of corn to increase drastically, and this induced farmers to convert their farmland from wheat and canola production to corn production. Buyers of canola oil and seed turned to Canadian farmers for their purchases.

Being smart profit-maximizers, farmers responded by farming their land more intensively—using more fertilizer, for example—and by increasing their hectarage. By 2013, fertilizer prices had increased compared to 2005. And over the decade from 2003 to 2013, the average price of farmland increased by 128%, with some farmland selling for 1.4 times its 2003 price.

Doing this made complete economic sense, as each farmer moved up their individual supply curve. And because the individual supply curve is the marginal cost curve, each farmer's costs also went up as more inputs were employed to produce more output.

By 2016, crop prices fell by 25% for canola oil and 19% for canola seeds from their 2013 high. In 2019, the price of canola oil remained as its 2016 level at $960 per tonne; but the price of canola seeds continued to fall to around $517 per tonne.

Farmers show their economic acumen by moving up and down their supply curves as crop prices change.

The **industry supply curve** shows the relationship between the price of a good and the total output of the industry as a whole.

The **short-run industry supply curve** shows how the quantity supplied by an industry depends on the market price given a fixed number of producers.

Various factors related to both the supply and the demand of farmers' output contributed to this fall. On the demand side, the demand from China dropped partly due to a slowdown of its economy and partly due to a ban on imports of Canadian canola. On the supply side, bumper harvests also sharply depressed crop prices.

Thinking like economists, farmers responded by moving back down their supply curve, withdrawing from production the most expensive land to cultivate and reducing their demand for additional acreage. As a result, from 2012 to 2019 the price of fertilizer has fallen significantly, nearly 50%, from its highs. So if you want to see profit-maximization in action, watch a farmer.

>> Check Your Understanding 12-2

Solutions appear at back of book.

1. Draw a short-run diagram showing a U-shaped average total cost curve, a U-shaped average variable cost curve, and a "swoosh"-shaped marginal cost curve. On it, indicate the range of output and the range of price for which the following actions are optimal.
   a. The firm shuts down immediately.
   b. The firm operates in the short run despite sustaining a loss.
   c. The firm operates while making a profit.
2. Atlantic Canada has a very active lobster industry, which harvests lobsters during the summer months. The rest of the year lobsters can be obtained from other parts of the world, but at a much higher price. Atlantic Canada is also full of "lobster shacks," roadside restaurants serving lobster dishes that are open only during the summer. Explain why it is optimal for lobster shacks to operate only in the summer.

‖ The Industry Supply Curve

Why will an increase in the demand for Christmas trees lead to a large price increase at first but a much smaller increase in the long run? The answer lies in the behaviour of the **industry supply curve**—the relationship between the price and the total output of an industry as a whole. The industry supply curve is what we referred to in earlier chapters as *the* supply curve or the market supply curve. But here we take some extra care to distinguish between the *individual supply curve* of a single firm and the supply curve of the industry as a whole.

As you might guess from the previous section, the industry supply curve must be analyzed in somewhat different ways for the short run and the long run. Let's start with the short run.

The Short-Run Industry Supply Curve

Recall that in the short run the number of producers in an industry is fixed—there is no entry or exit. And you may also remember from Chapter 3 that the market supply curve is the horizontal sum of the individual supply curves of all producers—you find it by summing the total output across all suppliers at every given price. We will do that exercise here under the assumption that all the producers are alike—an assumption that makes the derivation particularly simple. So let's assume there are 100 Christmas tree farms, each with the same costs as Noelle's farm.

Each of these 100 farms will have an individual short-run supply curve like the one in Figure 12-4. At a price below $40, no farms will produce. At a price of $40 or more, each farm will produce the quantity of output at which its marginal cost is equal to the market price. As you can see from Figure 12-4, this will lead each farm to produce 40 trees if the price is $56 per tree, 50 trees if the price is $72, and so on. So if there are 100 tree farms and the price of Christmas trees is $72 per tree, the industry as a whole will produce 5,000 trees, corresponding to 100 farms × 50 trees per farm, and so on. The result is the **short-run industry supply curve,** shown as S in Figure 12-5. This curve shows the quantity that producers will supply at each price, *taking the number of producers as given.*

FIGURE 12-5 **The Short-Run Market Equilibrium**

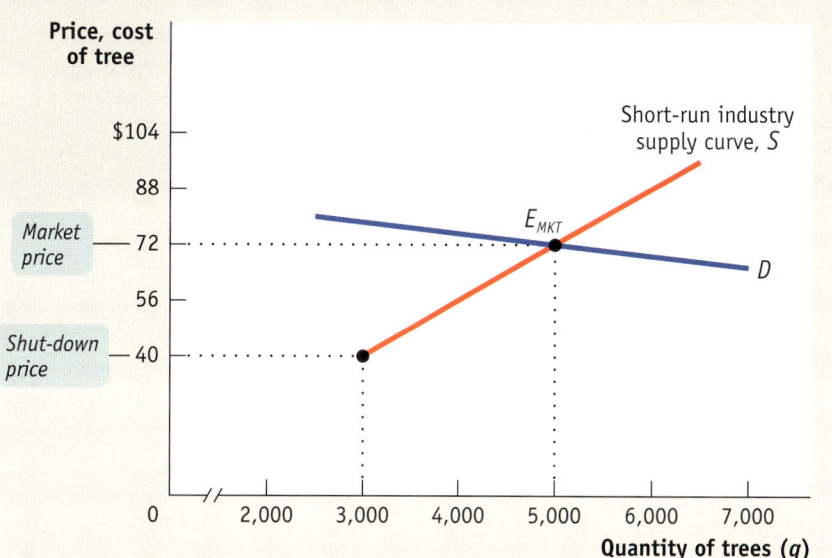

The short-run industry supply curve, S, is the industry supply curve taking the number of producers—here, 100—as given. It is generated by adding together the individual supply curves of the 100 producers. Below the shut-down price of $40, no producer wants to produce in the short run. Above $40, the short-run industry supply curve slopes upward, as each producer increases output as price increases. It intersects the demand curve, D, at point E_{MKT}, the point of short-run market equilibrium, corresponding to a market price of $72 and a quantity of 5,000 trees.

The demand curve *D* in Figure 12-5 crosses the short-run industry supply curve at E_{MKT}, corresponding to a price of $72 and a quantity of 5,000 trees. Point E_{MKT} is a **short-run market equilibrium:** the quantity supplied equals the quantity demanded, taking the number of producers as given. But the long run may look quite different, because in the long run farms may enter or exit the industry.

There is a **short-run market equilibrium** when the quantity supplied equals the quantity demanded, taking the number of producers as given.

The Long-Run Industry Supply Curve

Suppose that in addition to the 100 farms currently in the Christmas tree business, there are many other potential producers. Suppose also that each of these potential producers would have the same cost curves as existing producers like Noelle if they entered the industry.

When will additional producers enter the industry? Whenever existing producers are making a profit—that is, whenever the market price is above the break-even price of $56 per tree, the minimum average total cost of production. For example, at a price of $72 per tree, new firms will enter the industry.

What will happen as additional producers enter the industry? Clearly, the quantity supplied at any given price will increase. The short-run industry supply curve will shift to the right. This will, in turn, alter the market equilibrium and result in a lower market price. Existing firms will respond to the lower market price by reducing their output, but the total industry output will increase because of the larger number of firms in the industry.

Figure 12-6 illustrates the effects of this chain of events on an existing firm and on the market; panel (a) shows how the market responds to entry, and panel (b) shows how an individual existing firm responds to entry. (Note that these two graphs have been rescaled in comparison to Figures 12-4 and 12-5 to better illustrate how profit changes in response to price.) In panel (a), S_1 is the initial short-run industry supply curve, based on the existence of 100 producers. The initial short-run market equilibrium is at E_{MKT}, with an equilibrium market price of $72 and a quantity of 5,000 trees. At this price existing producers are profitable, which is reflected in panel (b): an existing firm makes a total profit represented by the green-shaded rectangle labelled *A* when market price is $72.

These profits will induce new producers to enter the industry, shifting the short-run industry supply curve to the right. For example, the short-run industry supply curve when the number of producers has increased to 167 is S_2. Corresponding to this supply curve is a new short-run market equilibrium labelled

FIGURE 12-6 The Long-Run Market Equilibrium

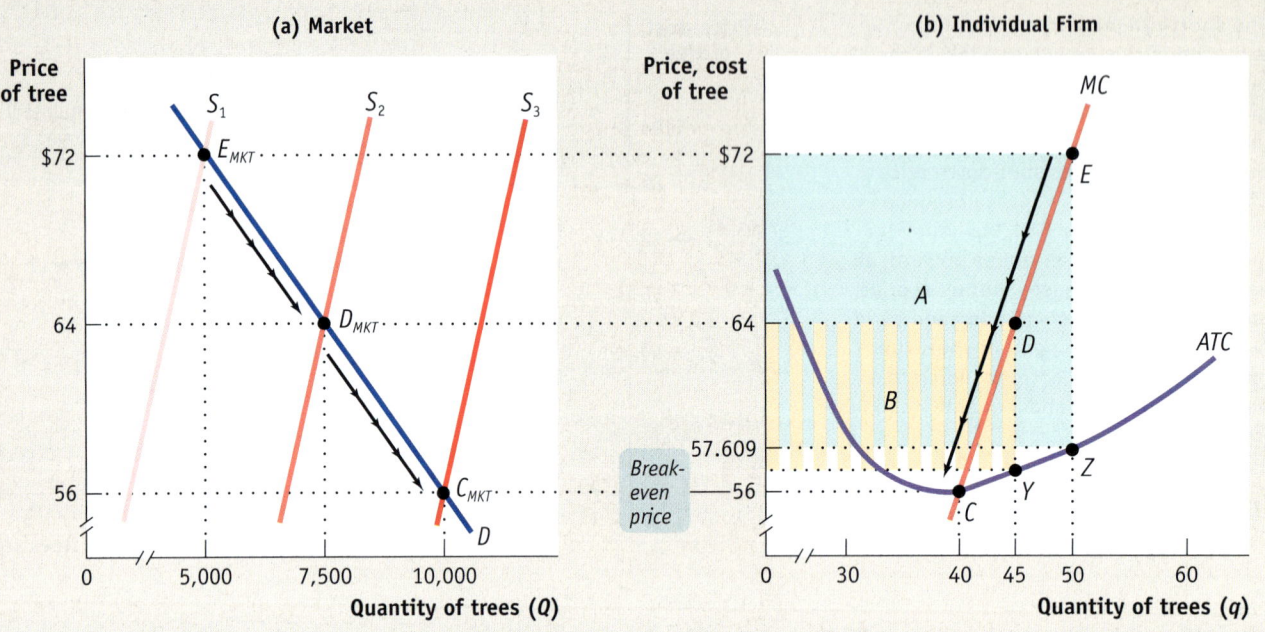

Point E_{MKT} of panel (a) shows the initial short-run market equilibrium. Each of the 100 existing producers makes an economic profit, illustrated in panel (b) by the green rectangle labelled A, the profit of an existing firm. Profits induce entry by additional producers, shifting the short-run industry supply curve outward from S_1 to S_2 in panel (a), resulting in a new short-run equilibrium at point D_{MKT}, at a lower market price of $64 and higher industry output. Existing firms reduce output and profit falls to the area given by the striped rectangle labelled B in panel (b). Entry continues to shift out the short-run industry supply curve, as price falls and industry output increases yet again. Entry of new firms ceases at point C_{MKT} on supply curve S_3 in panel (a). Here market price is equal to the break-even price; existing producers make zero economic profits, and there is no incentive for entry or exit. So C_{MKT} is also a long-run market equilibrium.

D_{MKT}, with a market price of $64 and a quantity of 7,500 trees. At $64, each firm produces 45 trees, so that industry output is $167 \times 45 = 7,500$ trees (rounded).

From panel (b), you can see the effect of the entry of 67 new producers on an existing firm: the fall in price causes it to reduce its output, and its profit falls to the area represented by the striped rectangle labelled B.

Although diminished, the profit of existing firms at D_{MKT} means that entry will continue and the number of firms will continue to rise. If the number of producers rises to 250, the short-run industry supply curve shifts out again to S_3, and the market equilibrium is at C_{MKT}, with a quantity supplied and demanded of 10,000 trees and a market price of $56 per tree.

Like E_{MKT} and D_{MKT}, C_{MKT} is a short-run equilibrium. But it is also something more. Because the price of $56 is each firm's break-even price, an existing producer makes zero economic profit—neither a profit nor a loss, earning only the opportunity cost of the resources used in production—when producing its profit-maximizing output of 40 trees.

At this price there is no incentive either for potential producers to enter or for existing producers to exit the industry. So C_{MKT} corresponds to a **long-run market equilibrium**—a situation in which the quantity supplied equals the quantity demanded given that sufficient time has elapsed for producers to either enter or exit the industry. In a long-run market equilibrium, all existing and potential producers have fully adjusted to their optimal long-run choices; as a result, no producer has an incentive to either enter or exit the industry.

To explore further the significance of the difference between short-run and long-run equilibrium, consider the effect of an increase in demand on an industry

A market is in **long-run market equilibrium** when the quantity supplied equals the quantity demanded, given that sufficient time has elapsed for entry into and exit from the industry to occur.

with free entry that is initially in long-run equilibrium. Panel (b) in Figure 12-7 shows the market adjustment; panels (a) and (c) show how an existing individual firm behaves during the process.

In panel (b) of Figure 12-7, D_1 is the initial demand curve and S_1 is the initial short-run industry supply curve. Their intersection at point X_{MKT} is both a short-run and a long-run market equilibrium because the equilibrium price of $56 leads to zero economic profit—and therefore neither entry nor exit. It corresponds to point X in panel (a), where an individual existing firm is operating at the minimum of its average total cost curve.

Now suppose that the demand curve shifts out for some reason to D_2. As shown in panel (b), in the short run, industry output moves along the short-run industry supply curve S_1 to the new short-run market equilibrium at Y_{MKT}, the intersection of S_1 and D_2. The market price rises to $72 per tree, and industry output increases from Q_X to Q_Y. This corresponds to an existing firm's movement from X to Y in panel (a) as the firm increases its output in response to the rise in the market price.

But we know that Y_{MKT} is not a long-run equilibrium, because $72 is higher than minimum average total cost, so existing producers are making economic profits. This will lead additional firms to enter the industry.

Over time, entry will cause the short-run industry supply curve to shift to the right. In the long run, the short-run industry supply curve will have shifted out

FIGURE 12-7 The Effect of an Increase in Demand in the Short Run and the Long Run

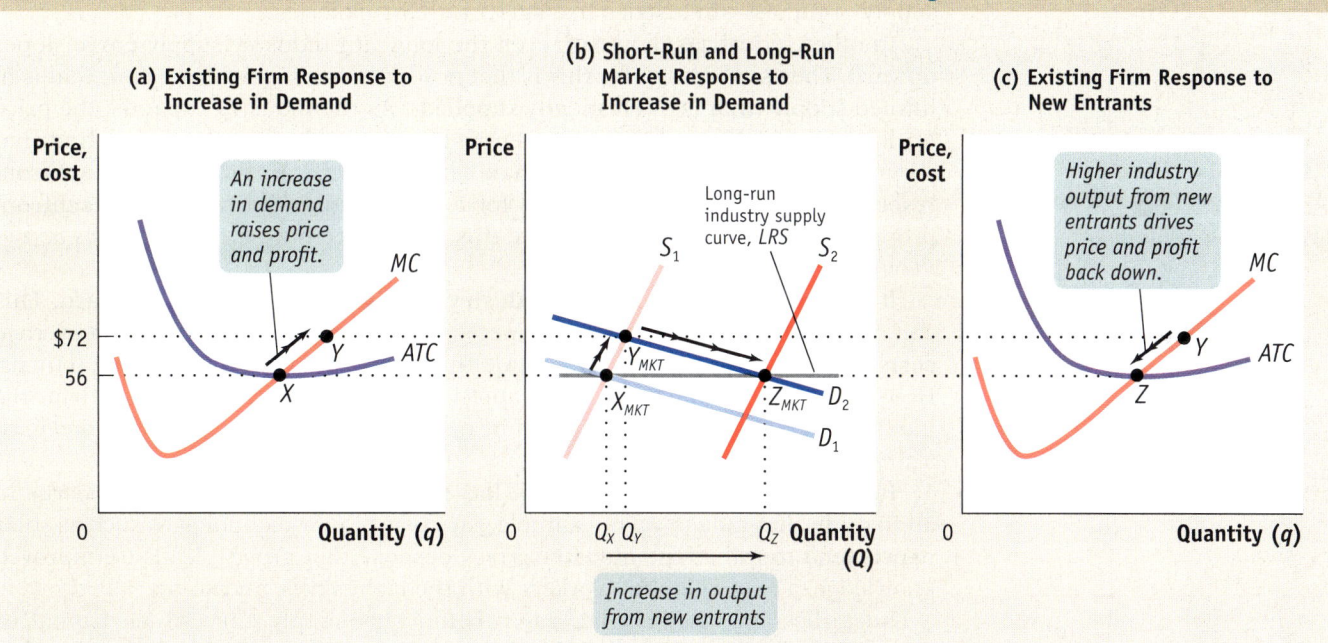

(a) Existing Firm Response to Increase in Demand

(b) Short-Run and Long-Run Market Response to Increase in Demand

(c) Existing Firm Response to New Entrants

Panel (b) shows how an industry adjusts in the short run and long run to an increase in demand; panels (a) and (c) show the corresponding adjustments by an existing firm. Initially the market is at point X_{MKT} in panel (b), a short-run and long-run equilibrium at a price of $56 and industry output of Q_X. An existing firm makes zero economic profit, operating at point X in panel (a) at minimum average total cost. Demand increases as D_1 shifts rightward to D_2 in panel (b), raising the market price to $72. Existing firms increase their output, and industry output moves along the short-run industry supply curve S_1 to a short-run equilibrium at Y_{MKT}. Correspondingly, the existing firm in panel (a) moves from point X to point Y. But at a price of $72 existing firms are profitable. As shown in panel (b), in the long run new entrants arrive and the short-run industry supply curve shifts rightward, from S_1 to S_2. There is a new equilibrium at point Z_{MKT}, at a lower price of $56 and higher industry output of Q_Z. An existing firm responds by moving from Y to Z in panel (c), returning to its initial output level and zero economic profit. Production by new entrants accounts for the total increase in industry output, $Q_Z - Q_X$. Like X_{MKT}, Z_{MKT} is also a short-run and long-run equilibrium: with existing firms earning zero economic profit, there is no incentive for any firms to enter or exit the industry. The horizontal line passing through X_{MKT} and Z_{MKT}, LRS, is the long-run industry supply curve: at the break-even price of $56, producers will produce any amount that consumers demand in the long run.

The **long-run industry supply curve** shows how the quantity supplied responds to the price once producers have had time to enter or exit the industry.

to S_2, and the equilibrium will be at Z_{MKT}—with the price falling back to $56 per tree and industry output increasing yet again, from Q_Y to Q_Z. Like X_{MKT} before the increase in demand, Z_{MKT} is both a short-run and a long-run market equilibrium.

The effect of entry on an existing firm is illustrated in panel (c), in the movement from Y to Z along the firm's individual supply curve. The firm reduces its output in response to the fall in the market price, ultimately arriving back at its original output quantity, corresponding to the minimum of its average total cost curve. In fact, every firm that is now in the industry—the initial set of firms and the new entrants—will operate at the minimum of its average total cost curve, at point Z. This means that the entire increase in industry output, from Q_X to Q_Z, comes from production by new entrants.

The line *LRS* that passes through X_{MKT} and Z_{MKT} in panel (b) is the **long-run industry supply curve.** It shows how the quantity supplied by an industry responds to the price given that producers have had time to enter or exit the industry.

In this particular case, the long-run industry supply curve is horizontal at $56. In other words, in this industry supply is *perfectly elastic* in the long run: given time to enter or exit, producers will supply any quantity that consumers demand at a price of $56. Perfectly elastic long-run supply is actually a good assumption for many industries. In this case we speak of there being *constant costs across the industry:* each firm, regardless of whether it is an incumbent or a new entrant, faces the same cost structure (that is, they each have the same cost curves). Industries that satisfy this condition are those in which there is a perfectly elastic supply of inputs—industries like agriculture or bakeries.

In other industries, however, even the long-run industry supply curve slopes upward. The usual reason for this is that producers must use some input that is in limited supply (that is, inelastically supplied). As the industry expands, the price of that input is driven up. Consequently, later entrants in the industry find that they have a higher cost structure than early entrants. An example is beachfront resort hotels, which must compete for a limited quantity of prime beachfront property. Industries that behave like this are said to have *increasing costs across the industry.*

It is possible for the long-run industry supply curve to slope downward. This can occur when an industry faces increasing returns to scale, in which average costs fall as output rises. Notice we said that the *industry* faces increasing returns. However, when increasing returns apply at the level of the individual firm, the industry usually ends up dominated by a small number of firms (an *oligopoly*) or a single firm (a *monopoly*).

In some cases, the advantages of large scale for an entire industry accrue to all firms in that industry. For example, the costs of new technologies such as solar panels tend to fall as the industry grows because that growth leads to improved knowledge, a larger pool of workers with the right skills, and so on.

Regardless of whether the long-run industry supply curve is horizontal or upward sloping or even downward sloping, the long-run price elasticity of supply is *higher* than the short-run price elasticity whenever there is free entry and exit. As shown in Figure 12-8, the long-run industry supply curve is always flatter than the short-run industry supply curve. The reason is entry and exit: a high price caused by an increase in demand attracts entry by new producers, resulting in a rise in industry output and an eventual fall in price; a low price caused by a decrease in demand induces existing firms to exit, leading to a fall in industry output and an eventual increase in price.

The distinction between the short-run industry supply curve and the long-run industry supply curve is very important in practice. We often see a sequence of events like that shown in Figure 12-7: an increase in demand initially leads to a large price increase, but prices return to their initial level once new firms have entered the industry. Or we see the sequence in reverse: a fall in demand reduces prices in the short run, but they return to their initial level as producers exit the industry.

FIGURE 12-8 Comparing the Short-Run and Long-Run Industry Supply Curves

The long-run industry supply curve may slope upward, but it is always flatter—more elastic—than the short-run industry supply curve. This is because of entry and exit: a higher price attracts new entrants in the long run, resulting in a rise in industry output and a fall in price; a lower price induces existing producers to exit in the long run, generating a fall in industry output and an eventual rise in price.

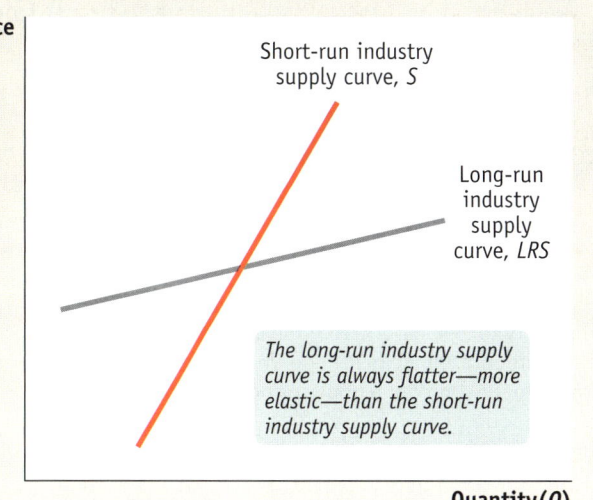

The long-run industry supply curve is always flatter—more elastic—than the short-run industry supply curve.

The Cost of Production and Efficiency in Long-Run Equilibrium

Our analysis leads us to three conclusions about the cost of production and efficiency in the long-run equilibrium of a perfectly competitive industry. These results will be important in our discussion in Chapter 13 of how monopoly gives rise to inefficiency.

1. *In a perfectly competitive industry in equilibrium, the value of marginal cost is the same for all firms.* That's because all firms produce the quantity of output at which marginal cost equals the market price, and as price-takers they all face the same market price.

2. *In a perfectly competitive industry with free entry and exit, each firm will have zero economic profit in long-run equilibrium.* Each firm produces the quantity of output that minimizes its average total cost—corresponding to point Z in panel (c) of Figure 12-7. So the total cost of production of the industry's output is minimized in a perfectly competitive industry.

The exception is an industry with increasing costs across the industry. Given a sufficiently high market price, early entrants make positive economic profits, but the last entrants do not as the market price falls. Average costs are minimized for later entrants, as the industry reaches long-run equilibrium, but not necessarily for the early ones.

3. *The long-run market equilibrium of a perfectly competitive industry is efficient: no mutually beneficial transactions go unexploited.* To understand this, recall a fundamental requirement for efficiency: all consumers who have a willingness to pay greater than or equal to sellers' costs actually get the good. In addition, when a market is efficient (except under certain, well-defined conditions), the market price matches all consumers with a willingness to pay greater than or equal to the market price to all sellers who have a cost of producing the good less than or equal to the market price.

So in the long-run equilibrium of a perfectly competitive industry, production is efficient: costs are minimized and no resources are wasted. In addition, the allocation of goods to consumers is efficient: every consumer willing to pay the cost of producing a unit of the good gets it. Indeed, no mutually beneficial transaction is left unexploited. Moreover, this condition tends to persist over time as the environment changes: the force of competition makes producers responsive to changes in consumers' desires and to changes in technology.

PITFALLS

ECONOMIC PROFIT, AGAIN

Some readers may wonder why a firm would want to enter an industry if the market price is only slightly greater than the break-even price. Wouldn't a firm prefer to go into another business that yields a higher profit?

The answer is that here, as always, when we calculate cost, we mean *opportunity cost*—that is, cost that includes the return a firm could get by using its resources elsewhere. And so the profit that we calculate is *economic profit;* if the market price is above the break-even level, no matter how slightly, the firm can earn more in this industry than they could elsewhere.

A reduction in supply of Chinese pork — combined with hefty taxes on pork from the United States and a temporary ban in 2019 on imported pork from Canada — meant a boon for pork producers in other countries.

ECONOMICS >> *in Action*
A Global Pork Shortage Hits Chinese Diners Hard

Powered by rapidly rising incomes, Chinese consumers have been eating more meat, and their meat of preference has definitely been pork. In the past 20 years, pork consumption per capita in China has nearly doubled. In 2020, the average Chinese consumer ate an estimated 30 kilograms of pork per year, compared to 22 kg for the average Canadian respectively.

However, the market for pork in China hit a devastating supply shock—a leftward shift of the supply curve—in 2018, when African swine fever, a deadly and rapidly spreading disease, first appeared in Chinese pig stocks. Because there was no vaccine against the disease, animals exposed to the disease had to be destroyed immediately to stop the spread. By late 2019, some 40% of Chinese pigs—equivalent to hundreds of millions of animals—had been lost. As a result, China has experienced a chronic shortage of pork and sky-rocketing pork prices. The producer price of pork in China—the price at the farm—has more than doubled, rising by 125%.

The demand and supply reverberations have spread globally. As the world's largest consumer of pork, China "has a major influence on the price and availability of pork worldwide," according to a study commission by the U.S. National Pork Board. In 2019, there was a global surge in pork and bacon prices, registering the steepest rise seen in 15 years. As one market observer commented, "It doesn't matter where you are in the world at the moment, pork prices are up."

Reduction in the supply of Chinese-produced pork has been a boon to pork producers in other countries. Pork producers in Brazil, Australia, Canada, and the European Union have entered the Chinese market on a large scale. By late 2019, imports of foreign pork into China had surged by 150%. In 2019, despite a four-month ban on pork imports from Canada, the value of Canada's exports of pork to China was up 18.5%. Some Canadian industry representatives feel exports to China may be up by 60% in 2020. The import surge increased the supply curve for Chinese consumers relative to the right, dampening the rise in pork prices.

Yet, the gain to non-Chinese pork producers may be short-lived; 50% of China's domestically produced pork comes from small-scale farms—farms which are typically too small to effectively fight against a disease like African swine fever. Decimated by the epidemic, small-scale pork farms are being forced to exit the market, and modern, large-scale pork farms are expanding their share of total output. By modernizing its methods of pork production, China hopes never to be hit with a devastating pork shortage like this again.

>> Quick Review

• The **industry supply curve** corresponds to the supply curve of earlier chapters. In the short run, the time period over which the number of producers is fixed, the **short-run market equilibrium** is given by the intersection of the **short-run industry supply curve** and the demand curve. In the long run, the time period over which producers can enter or exit the industry, the **long-run market equilibrium** is given by the intersection of the **long-run industry supply curve** and the demand curve. In the long-run market equilibrium, no producer has an incentive to enter or exit the industry.

• The long-run industry supply curve is often horizontal, although it may slope upward when a necessary input is in limited supply. It is always more elastic (flatter) than the short-run industry supply curve.

• In the long-run market equilibrium of a perfectly competitive industry, each firm produces at the same marginal cost, which is equal to the market price, and the total cost of production of the industry's output is minimized. It is also efficient.

>> Check Your Understanding 12-3

Solutions appear at back of book.

1. Which of the following events will induce firms to enter an industry? Which will induce firms to exit? When will entry or exit cease? Explain your answers.
   a. A technological advance lowers the fixed cost of production of every firm in the industry.
   b. The wages paid to workers in the industry go up for an extended period of time.
   c. A permanent change in consumer tastes increases demand for the good.
   d. The price of a key input rises due to a long-term shortage of that input.
2. Assume that the egg industry is perfectly competitive and is in long-run equilibrium with a perfectly elastic long-run industry supply curve. Health concerns about cholesterol then lead to a decrease in demand. Construct a figure similar to Figure 12-7, showing the short-run behaviour of the industry and how long-run equilibrium is reestablished.

Retail Wars: Big Box Stores in the Age of Amazon

AP Images/Gerry Broome

The large number of defunct or dying shopping malls littered across Canada and the United States confirms that the brick-and-mortar retail industry has undergone what Robin Lewis, author of *The New Rules of Retail*, describes as "a period that would only be paralleled by the Industrial Revolution." Online shopping has decimated many long-established retailers such as Sears, Zellers, and J.C. Penney, and even newer ones such as Circuit City and Toys "R" Us.

But in the last few years, several brick-and-mortar retailers such as Walmart and Best Buy have put up a vigorous fight. To combat consumers' penchant for *showrooming*—visiting a brick-and-mortar store to inspect the merchandise, and then buying it with a mobile shopping app on their smartphone at a cheaper price—Best Buy stocks some products that manufacturers have slightly modified as Best Buy exclusives, making it harder to find an online comparison. Both Best Buy and Walmart have beefed up their online retail presence, and they send discount alerts and coupons directly to customers' phones. Both stores leveraged their existing infrastructure by pairing digital commerce with brick-and-mortar convenience, allowing customers to order online and pick up (and return) merchandise in stores, a challenge to Amazon's warehouse

and delivery model. Walmart also instituted a price-match guarantee, in which customers receive Walmart gift cards for the value of any price difference.

Yet the most innovative counter-assault is the brainchild of Hubert Joly, the CEO of Best Buy. In 2012, by all appearances Best Buy was soon to follow its rival, electronics superstore Circuit City, into bankruptcy. However, by 2019, Best Buy was consistently beating its Wall Street earnings forecasts. How did Joly deliver? The first and perhaps most necessary strategy was price-matching: "Until I match Amazon's prices, the customers are ours to lose," Mr. Joly said. Second, Best Buy distinguished itself in an area that couldn't be captured by using robots or fast delivery: customer service. To keep its sales associates well-informed and happy, Joly reinstated a much-loved employee discount and instituted an ambitious training program to ensure that employees could answer questions about entirely new categories such as virtual reality headsets. Third, Joly transformed Best Buy's delivery infrastructure, so that it could ship its items nearly as fast as Amazon could. In the end, Joly has found a way to change showroomers into customers.

For brick-and-mortar retailers, today's retail environment is a race for survival. As one analyst said, "Only a couple of retailers can play the lowest-price game. This is going to accelerate the demise of retailers who do not have either competitive pricing or standout store experience."

QUESTIONS FOR THOUGHT

1. From the evidence in the case, what can you infer about whether or not the retail market for electronics satisfied the conditions for perfect competition before the advent of comparison price shopping via mobile app? What was the most important impediment to competition?

2. What effect is the introduction of shopping apps having on competition in the retail market for electronics? On the profitability of brick-and-mortar retailers like Best Buy? What, on average, will be the effect on the consumer surplus of purchasers of these items?

3. Why are some retailers responding by having manufacturers make slightly modified or exclusive versions of products for them? Is this trend likely to increase or diminish?

SUMMARY

1. In a **perfectly competitive market** all producers are **price-taking producers** and all consumers are **price-taking consumers**—no one's actions can influence the market price. Consumers are normally price-takers, but producers often are not. In a **perfectly competitive industry,** all producers are price-takers.

2. There are two necessary conditions for a perfectly competitive industry: there are many producers, none of whom have a large **market share,** and the industry produces a **standardized product** or **commodity**—goods that consumers regard as equivalent. A third condition is often satisfied as well: **free entry and exit** into and from the industry.

3. A producer chooses output according to the **optimal output rule:** produce the quantity at which **marginal revenue** equals marginal cost. For a price-taking firm, marginal revenue is equal to price and its **marginal revenue curve** is a horizontal line at the market price. It chooses output according to the **price-taking firm's optimal output rule:** produce the quantity at which price equals marginal cost. However, a firm that produces the optimal quantity may not be profitable.

4. A firm is profitable if total revenue exceeds total cost or, equivalently, if the market price exceeds its **break-even price**—minimum average total cost. If market price exceeds the break-even price, the firm is profitable; if it is less, the firm is unprofitable; if it is equal, the firm breaks even. When profitable, the firm's per-unit profit is $P - ATC;$ when unprofitable, its per-unit loss is $ATC - P$.

5. Fixed cost is irrelevant to the firm's optimal short-run production decision, which depends on its **shut-down price**—its minimum average variable cost—and the market price. When the market price is equal to or exceeds the shut-down price, the firm produces the output quantity where marginal cost equals the market price. When the market price falls below the shut-down price, the firm ceases production in the short run. This generates the firm's **short-run individual supply curve.**

6. Fixed cost matters over time. If the market price is below minimum average total cost for an extended period of time, firms will exit the industry in the long run. If above, existing firms are profitable and new firms will enter the industry in the long run.

7. The **industry supply curve** depends on the time period. The **short-run industry supply curve** is the industry supply curve given that the number of firms is fixed. The **short-run market equilibrium** is given by the intersection of the short-run industry supply curve and the demand curve.

8. The **long-run industry supply curve** is the industry supply curve given sufficient time for entry into and exit from the industry. In the **long-run market equilibrium**—given by the intersection of the long-run industry supply curve and the demand curve—no producer has an incentive to enter or exit. The long-run industry supply curve is often horizontal. It may slope upward if there is limited supply of an input, resulting in increasing costs across the industry. It may even slope downward, the case of decreasing costs across the industry. But it is always more elastic (flatter) than the short-run industry supply curve.

9. In the long-run market equilibrium of a competitive industry, profit maximization leads each firm to produce at the same marginal cost, which is equal to market price. Free entry and exit means that each firm earns zero economic profit—producing the output corresponding to its minimum average total cost. So the total cost of production of an industry's output is minimized. The outcome is efficient because every consumer with a willingness to pay greater than or equal to marginal cost gets the good.

KEY TERMS

PRACTICE QUESTIONS

1. A recent report found that Christmas trees have doubled in price over the last three years. The price surge is partly due to a glut of trees 10 years prior. During the Great Recession of 2008 many consumers reduced their purchases leading to a surplus of trees and lower prices. Explain how a glut in trees 10 years prior could lead to higher prices today. Focus on how farms changed operations in response to the price decrease.

2. Given the assumptions of a perfectly competitive industry, explain why firms operating in that industry are reluctant to invest in new technological development.

3. Washington state is the largest producer of apples in the United States. In 2018, farms in Washington produced 171 million bushels of apples, nearly five times more than the next highest producing American state, New York, and more than eight times the entire production in Canada. Many apple farms in Washington depend on migrant labour from Mexico and Central America. These countries were once reliable sources of labour, but farmers are now experiencing a large shortage of labour. Most migrant workers are choosing year-round positions in the construction industry instead of the seasonal work offered in agriculture, leaving apple farms relying on undocumented migrant labour. With fewer undocumented workers, labour costs have soared, forcing many farmers to invest in expensive mechanical harvesting devices. Explain how both the labour shortage and investing in mechanical harvesting devices will change the farms' cost structure and industry dynamics.

4. Your roommate is having difficulty understanding how a firm can keep operating despite losing money, earning a negative profit. How will firms respond to losing money?

PROBLEMS

1. For each of the following, is the business a price-taking producer? Explain your answers.

   a. A cappuccino café in a university town where there are dozens of very similar cappuccino cafés

   b. The makers of Pepsi

   c. One of many sellers of zucchini at a local farmers' market

2. For each of the following, is the industry perfectly competitive? Referring to market share, standardization of the product, and/or free entry and exit, explain your answers.

   a. Aspirin

   b. Alicia Keys concerts

   c. SUVs

3. Bob produces flower pots for sale, which he designs and manufactures using 3-D printing technology. Bob rents a building for $30,000 per month and rents machinery for $20,000 a month. Those are his fixed costs. His variable cost per month is given in the accompanying table.

Quantity of flower pots	VC
0	$0
1,000	5,000
2,000	8,000
3,000	9,000
4,000	14,000
5,000	20,000
6,000	33,000
7,000	49,000
8,000	72,000
9,000	99,000
10,000	150,000

   a. Calculate Bob's average variable cost, average total cost, and marginal cost for each quantity of output.

   b. There is free entry into the industry, and anyone who enters will face the same costs as Bob.

Suppose that currently the price of a flower pot is $25. What will Bob's profit be? Is this a long-run equilibrium? If not, what will the price of a flower pot be in the long run?

4. Consider Bob's company described in Problem 3. Assume that flower pot production is a perfectly competitive industry. For each of the following questions, explain your answers.

   a. What is Bob's break-even price? What is his shutdown price?

   b. Suppose the price of a flower pot is $2. What should Bob do in the short run?

   c. Suppose the price of a flower pot is $7. What is the profit-maximizing quantity of flower pots that Bob should produce? What will his total profit be? Will he produce or shut down in the short run? Will he stay in the industry or exit in the long run?

   d. Suppose instead that the price of a flower pot is $20. Now what is the profit-maximizing quantity of flower pots that Bob should produce? What will his total profit be now? Will he produce or shut down in the short run? Will he stay in the industry or exit in the long run?

5. Consider again Bob's company described in Problem 3.

   a. Draw Bob's marginal cost curve.

   b. Over what range of prices will Bob produce no flower pots in the short run?

   c. Draw Bob's individual supply curve. In your graph, plot the price range from $0 to $60 in increments of $10.

6. a. A profit-maximizing business incurs an economic loss of $10,000 per year. Its fixed cost is $15,000 per year. Should it produce or shut down in the short run? Should it stay in the industry or exit in the long run?

   b. Suppose instead that this business has a fixed cost of $6,000 per year. Should it produce or shut down in the short run? Should it stay in the industry or exit in the long run?

7. The first sushi restaurant opens in town. Initially people are very cautious about eating tiny portions of raw fish, as this is a town where large portions of grilled meat have always been popular. Soon, however, an influential health report warns consumers against grilled meat and suggests that they increase their consumption of fish, especially raw fish. The sushi restaurant becomes very popular and its profit increases.

   a. What will happen to the short-run profit of the sushi restaurant? What will happen to the number of sushi restaurants in town in the long run? Will the first sushi restaurant be able to sustain its short-run profit over the long run? Explain your answers.

   b. Local steakhouses suffer from the popularity of sushi and start incurring losses. What will happen to the number of steakhouses in town in the long run? Explain your answer.

8. A perfectly competitive firm has the following short-run total cost:

Quantity	TC
0	$5
1	10
2	13
3	18
4	25
5	34
6	45

   Market demand for the firm's product is given by the following market demand schedule:

Price	Quantity demanded
$12	300
10	500
8	800
6	1,200
4	1,800

   a. Calculate this firm's marginal cost and, for all output levels except zero, the firm's average variable cost and average total cost.

   b. There are 100 firms in this industry that all have costs identical to those of this firm. Draw the short-run industry supply curve. In the same diagram, draw the market demand curve.

   c. What is the market price, and how much profit will each firm make?

9. A new vaccine against a deadly disease has just been discovered. Presently, 55 people die from the disease each year. The new vaccine will save lives, but it is not completely safe. Some recipients of the shots will die from adverse reactions. The projected effects of the inoculation are given in the accompanying table:

Percent of population inoculated	Total deaths due to disease	Total deaths due to inoculation	Marginal benefit of inoculation	Marginal cost of inoculation	"Profit" of inoculation
0	55	0	—	—	—
10	45	0	—	—	—
20	36	1	—	—	—
30	28	3	—	—	—
40	21	6	—	—	—
50	15	10	—	—	—
60	10	15	—	—	—
70	6	20	—	—	—
80	3	25	—	—	—
90	1	30	—	—	—
100	0	35	—	—	—

   a. What are the interpretations of "marginal benefit" and "marginal cost" here? Calculate marginal benefit and marginal cost per each 10% increase in the rate of inoculation. Write your answers in the table.

   b. What proportion of the population should optimally be inoculated?

   c. What is the interpretation of "profit" here? Calculate the profit for all levels of inoculation.

10. Evaluate each of the following statements. If a statement is true, explain why; if it is false, identify the mistake and try to correct it.

   a. A profit-maximizing firm in a perfectly competitive industry should select the output level at which the difference between the market price and marginal cost is greatest.

   b. An increase in fixed cost lowers the profit-maximizing quantity of output produced in the short run.

11. The production of agricultural products like wheat is one of the few examples of a perfectly competitive industry. In this question, we analyze results from a study released by the Saskatchewan Ministry of Agriculture about crop production in the province in 2016–2017.

   a. The average variable cost per hectare planted with durum wheat in 2016 was $209.60 per hectare (in the dark brown soil zone). Assuming an expected yield of 53 bushels per hectare, calculate the average variable cost per bushel of durum wheat.

   b. Suppose prior to the 2016 growing season the expected average price of durum wheat in Saskatchewan was $6.69 per bushel. Do you think the average farm would have exited the (durum wheat) industry in the short run? Explain. Below what price would farms exit the durum wheat industry?

c. In fact, the average price of durum wheat received by a farmer in Saskatchewan in December 2016 was $6.28 per bushel. At this price would farmers be pleased they did not exit or regret not exiting? Explain.

d. According to Ministry of Agriculture estimates in 2016, a farmer with dark brown soil with an estimated yield of 53 bushels per hectare would have total costs of production of $310.58 per hectare. Using these figures determine the average cost of production and determine whether the typical farmer would be profitable or not.

e. Suppose you were told that the latest data from Statistics Canada just arrived and the average durum wheat yield of Saskatchewan farmers in 2016 was actually 60 bushels per hectare. How does this impact the average variable cost and average total cost figures (both per bushel)? Would the average farmer regret not exiting the industry or be pleased that they had remained to produce durum wheat?

12. The accompanying table presents prices for washing and ironing a dress shirt taken from a survey of dry cleaners in three neighbouring towns.

Dry cleaner	City	Price
A-1 Cleaners	Savonville	$1.50
Regal Cleaners	Savonville	1.95
Rush Cleaners	Savonville	1.95
Zippy Dry Cleaners	Savonville	1.95
Effie the Tailor	Savonville	2.00
Magnolia Wash	Laverham	2.00
Master Cleaners	Savonville	2.00
Tidy Cleaners	Laverham	2.00
Sunny Cleaners	Savonville	2.00
Geddy Cleaners	Blanchiston	2.10
Rockwell Cleaners	Blanchiston	2.10
Victoria Cleaners	Savonville	2.15
Kim's Fine Cleaners	Savonville	2.25
York Cleaners	Laverham	2.25
Niko the Tailor	Savonville	2.25
Pressed 4 Time	Laverham	2.50
King's Cleaners	Laverham	2.50

a. What is the average price per shirt washed and ironed in Laverham? In Savonville?

b. Draw typical marginal cost and average total cost curves for York Cleaners in Laverham, assuming it is a perfectly competitive firm but is making a profit on each shirt in the short run. Mark the short-run equilibrium point and shade the area that corresponds to the profit made by the dry cleaner.

c. Assume $2.25 is the short-run equilibrium price in Laverham. Draw a typical short-run demand and supply curve for the market. Label the equilibrium point.

d. Observing profits in the Laverham area, another dry-cleaning service, Diamond Cleaners, enters the market. It charges $1.95 per shirt. What is the new average price of washing and ironing a shirt in Laverham? Illustrate the effect of entry on the average Laverham price by a shift of the short-run supply curve, the demand curve, or both.

e. Assume that York Cleaners now charges the new average price and just breaks even (that is, makes zero economic profit) at this price. Show the likely effect of the entry on your diagram in part b.

f. If the dry-cleaning industry is perfectly competitive, what does the average difference in price between Laverham and Savonville imply about costs in the two areas?

13. This question uses the algebraic method of determining average variable cost from Appendix 11A and the algebraic method of determining equilibrium from Appendix 3A. A firm in a perfectly competitive constant cost industry has total and marginal costs in the short run given by:

$$TC = 0.5 \times q^2 + 2.5 \times q + 72 \qquad \text{Total Cost}$$
$$MC = q + 2.5 \qquad \text{Marginal Cost}$$

where q is the output per day and TC is the total cost in dollars. The firm has fixed costs of $40 (which is already included in the TC equation above). This TC equation generates minimum average total cost of $14.50 at $q = 12$. This firm generates minimum long-run average costs (also at $q = 12$, $LRAC = \$14.50$). (*Hint:* The average total cost curve is at a minimum where it intersects the marginal cost curve (that is, $ATC = MC$). Similarly, the average variable cost curve is at a minimum where $AVC = MC$.)

a. Determine the average variable cost. At what price will the firm shut down in the short run?

b. In the short run, if the firm faces a price of $11.50, how much will the firm produce?

c. In the short run, if the firm faces a price of $20.50, how much profit will the firm earn?

d. In the short run, there are 200 identical firms in the industry. Demand for the output of firms in this industry is given by:

$$P = 32.5 - 0.01 \times Q \qquad \text{Demand Curve}$$

where Q is the total amount sold to consumers. What are the equilibrium price and quantity?

e. Given the demand curve described in part d, how many firms will there be in this industry in the long run?

f. Suppose in the long run, there is technological change that reduces the long-run minimum average cost of the typical business firm to $8.50 at $q = 8$. Now, how many firms will there be in the industry in the long run?

14. Over the last three years, Christmas tree prices have increased from an average of $35 per tree to over $75 per tree. How would a Christmas tree farm and the overall industry respond to the price change under the following circumstances? Be sure to explain how your answer depends on the elasticity of supply:

a. The price increase is a result of an increase in demand from younger generations, mainly millennials, increasing their desire to purchase real Christmas trees.

b. The price increase is a result of fewer Christmas tree farms harvesting trees in response to consumers purchasing more artificial trees.

WORK IT OUT

15. Kate's Katering provides catered meals, and the catered meals industry is perfectly competitive. Kate's machinery costs $100 per day and is the only fixed input. Her variable cost consists of the wages paid to the cooks and the food ingredients. The variable cost per day associated with each level of output is given in the accompanying table.

Quantity of meals	VC
0	0
10	200
20	300
30	480
40	700
50	1,000

a. Calculate the total cost, the average variable cost, the average total cost, and the marginal cost for each quantity of output.

b. What is the break-even price and quantity? What is the shut-down price and quantity?

c. Suppose that the price at which Kate can sell catered meals is $21 per meal. In the short run, will Kate earn a profit? In the short run, should she produce or shut down?

d. Suppose that the price at which Kate can sell catered meals is $17 per meal. In the short run, will Kate earn a profit? In the short run, should she produce or shut down?

e. Suppose that the price at which Kate can sell catered meals is $13 per meal. In the short run, will Kate earn a profit? In the short run, should she produce or shut down? ■

13 Monopoly

"SHINE BRIGHT LIKE A DIAMOND"

RIHANNA, THE SUPERSTAR song-stylist, fashion icon, and makeup mogul, is well known for her association with diamond gemstones. Her 2012 hit song "Diamonds" topped the charts in over 20 countries. In 2018, she became the brand ambassador for one of the oldest and most exclusive purveyors of diamond jewelry, Chopard of Paris. Her annual Diamond Ball raises millions of dollars for charity.

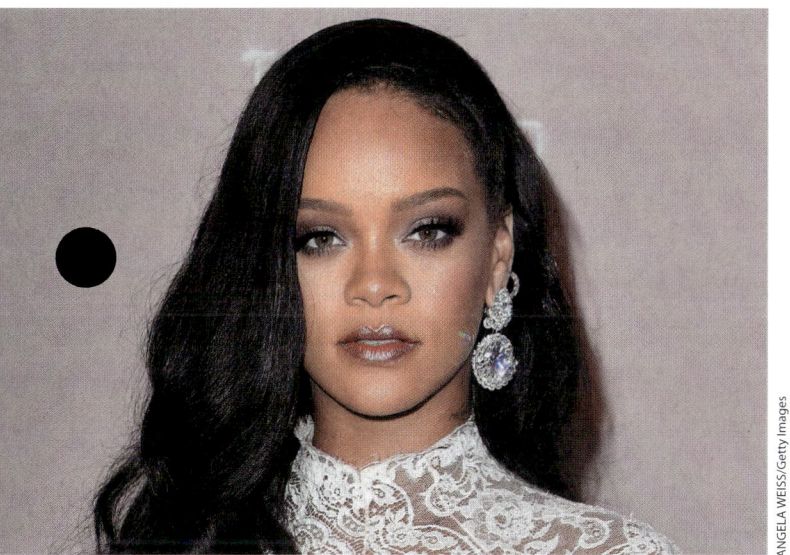

ANGELA WEISS/Getty Images

Got stones?

But why does Rihanna focus on diamonds? Diamonds are a symbol of luxury, valued not only for their appearance but for their perceived rarity.

Yet, as geologists will tell you, diamonds aren't actually all that rare. In fact, according to the *Dow Jones-Irwin Guide to Fine Gems and Jewelry,* diamonds are "more common than any other gem-quality coloured stone. They only seem rarer."

Why do diamonds seem more precious and rare than rubies, emeralds, and other stones? Part of the answer is a brilliant marketing campaign. But the main reason diamonds seem to be rare is the legacy of a company named De Beers which *made* them rare. For 100 years, De Beers controlled most of the world's diamond mines, allowing it to limit the quantity of diamonds supplied to the market.

In previous chapters, we have concentrated exclusively on perfectly competitive markets — markets in which the producers are perfect competitors. But the diamond market has historically been very different. At the height of its power, De Beers controlled the global diamond market and was unlike the producers we've studied so far. It was a *monopolist,* the sole (or almost sole) producer of a good. Monopolists behave differently from producers in perfectly competitive industries: whereas perfect competitors take the price at which they can sell their output as given, monopolists know that their actions affect market prices and take that into account when deciding how much to produce.

Before we begin our analysis, let's step back and look at *monopoly* and perfect competition as parts of a broader system for classifying markets. Perfect competition and monopoly are particular types of *market structure.* They are specific categories in a system economists use to classify markets and industries according to two main dimensions. This chapter begins with a brief overview of types of market structure. It will help us here and in subsequent chapters to understand on a deeper level why markets differ and why producers in those markets behave quite differently. ●

WHAT YOU WILL LEARN

- What is the significance of **monopoly,** a type of industry in which only one producer, a **monopolist,** operates?

- How does being a monopolist affect a firm's price and output decisions?

- Why does the presence of monopoly typically reduce social welfare?

- What tools do policy makers use to address the problem of monopoly?

- How do digital giants like Amazon, Google, and Facebook fit into our model of monopoly and what special challenges do they present?

- What is **price discrimination** and why is it so prevalent in certain industries?

‖ Types of Market Structure

In the real world, there is a mind-boggling array of different markets. We observe widely different behaviour patterns by producers across markets. In some markets, firms are extremely competitive. In others, firms seem somehow to coordinate their actions to avoid competing with one another. And, as we have just described, some markets are monopolies in which there is no competition at all.

To develop principles and make predictions about markets and how producers will behave in them, economists have developed four primary models of market structure: *monopoly, oligopoly, perfect competition,* and *monopolistic competition.* This system of market structures is based on two dimensions:

1. The number of firms in the market (one, few, or many)
2. Whether the goods offered are identical or *differentiated*

Differentiated goods are goods that are different from each other in some ways but considered at least somewhat substitutable by consumers (think Coke versus Pepsi). Whether a market has differentiated products or identical products depends on the nature of the good and consumer preferences. Some goods—soft drinks, economics textbooks, breakfast cereals—can readily be made into different varieties in the eyes and tastes of consumers. Other goods—Christmas trees or pencils, for example—are much less easy to differentiate.

Figure 13-1 provides a simple visual summary of the four types of market structure classified according to the two dimensions. In *monopoly,* a single producer sells a single, undifferentiated product. In *oligopoly,* a few producers—more than one but not a large number—sell products that may be either identical or differentiated. In *perfect competition,* as we know, many firms each sell an identical product. And finally, in *monopolistic competition,* many firms each sell a differentiated product (think of producers of economics textbooks).

Over the course of this chapter and the next two we will see what determines the number of firms in a market: whether there is one (monopoly), a few (oligopoly), or many (perfect competition and monopolistic competition). We will just briefly note that in the long run it depends on whether there are conditions that make it difficult for new firms to enter the market. When these conditions are present, industries tend to be monopolies or oligopolies; when they are not present, industries tend to be perfectly competitive or monopolistically competitive.

FIGURE 13-1 **Types of Market Structure**

The behaviour of any given firm and the market it occupies are analyzed using one of four models of market structure — monopoly, oligopoly, perfect competition, or monopolistic competition. This system for categorizing market structure is based on two dimensions: (1) whether products are differentiated or identical, and (2) the number of producers in the industry — one, a few, or many.

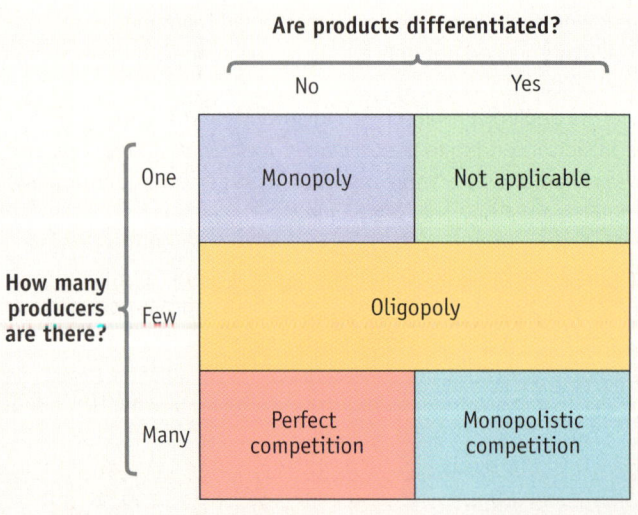

Although this chapter is devoted to monopoly, important aspects of monopoly carry over to oligopoly and monopolistic competition. In the next section, we will define monopoly and review the conditions that make it possible. These same conditions, in less extreme form, also give rise to oligopoly. We then show how a monopolist can increase profit by limiting the quantity supplied to a market—behaviour that also occurs in oligopoly and monopolistic competition.

As we'll see, this kind of behaviour is good for the producer but bad for consumers; it also causes inefficiency. An important topic of study will be the ways in which public policy tries to limit the damage. Finally, we turn to one of the surprising effects of monopoly—one that is very often present in oligopoly and monopolistic competition as well: the fact that different consumers often pay different prices for the same good.

The Meaning of Monopoly

The De Beers monopoly was created in South Africa in the 1880s by Cecil Rhodes, a British imperialist and businessman. At that time, South Africa was the largest single source of diamonds, and South African mines dominated the world's supply of diamonds. There were, however, many mining companies, all competing with each other. Rhodes bought the great majority of those mines and consolidated them into a single company, De Beers. By 1889, De Beers controlled almost all of the world's diamond production.

De Beers, in other words, became a **monopolist.** A producer is a monopolist if it is the sole supplier of a good that has no close substitutes. When a firm is a monopolist, the industry is a **monopoly.**

Monopoly: Our First Departure from Perfect Competition

As we saw in Chapter 12, the supply and demand model of a market is not universally valid. Instead, it's a model of perfect competition, which is only one of several different types of market structure. A market will be perfectly competitive only if there are many producers, all of whom produce the same good. Monopoly is the most extreme departure from perfect competition.

In practice, true monopolies are hard to find in the modern Canadian economy, partly because of legal obstacles. If a contemporary entrepreneur tried to consolidate all the firms in an industry the way that Rhodes did with diamond mining, that person would soon land in court, accused of breaking the Competition Act, Canada's *antitrust* laws, which are intended to prevent monopolies from emerging. Oligopoly, a market structure in which there is a small number of large producers, is much more common. In fact, most of the goods you buy, from cars to airline tickets, are supplied by oligopolies.

Monopolies do, however, play an important role in some sectors of the economy, such as pharmaceuticals. Furthermore, an analysis of monopoly provides a foundation for other departures from perfect competition that we have mentioned, such as oligopoly and monopolistic competition.

What Monopolists Do

Why did Rhodes want to consolidate South African diamond producers into a single company, and what difference did it make to the world diamond market? Figure 13-2 offers a preliminary view of the effects of monopoly. It shows an industry in which the supply curve under perfect competition intersects the demand curve at C, leading to the price P_C and the output Q_C.

Suppose that this industry is consolidated into a monopoly. The monopolist *moves up the demand curve* by reducing quantity supplied to a point like M, at which the quantity produced, Q_M, is lower, and the price, P_M, is higher than under perfect competition.

A **monopolist** is a firm that is the only producer of a good that has no close substitutes. An industry controlled by a monopolist is known as a **monopoly.**

FIGURE 13-2 What a Monopolist Does

Under perfect competition, the price and quantity are determined by supply and demand. Here, the competitive equilibrium is at *C,* where the price is P_C and the quantity is Q_C. A monopolist reduces the quantity supplied to Q_M and moves up the demand curve from *C* to *M,* raising the price to P_M.

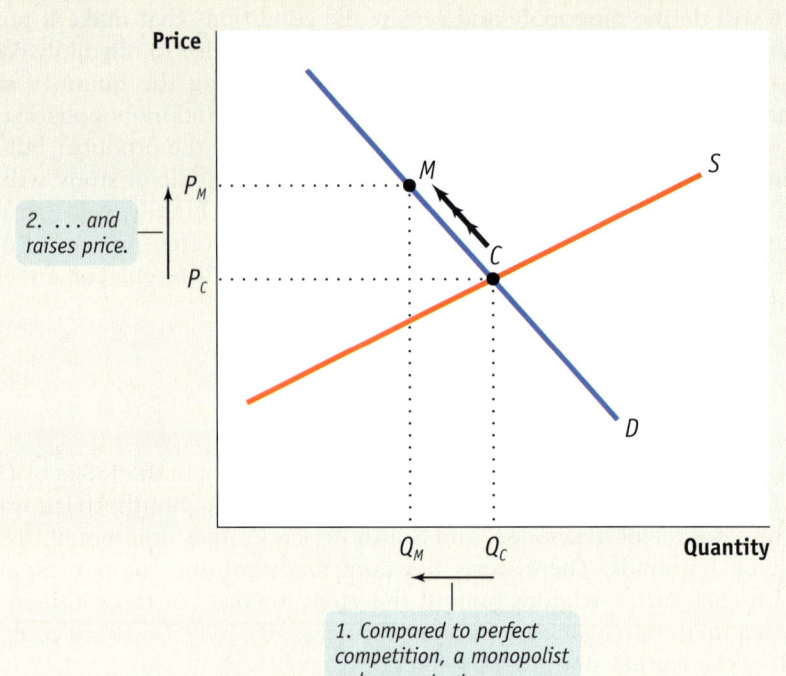

2. ... and raises price.

1. Compared to perfect competition, a monopolist reduces output ...

The ability of a monopolist to raise the price of its product above the competitive level by reducing output is known as **market power.** And market power is what monopoly is all about. A wheat farmer who is 1 of 100,000 wheat farmers has no market power: the farmer must sell wheat at the going market price. However, your local water utility does have market power: it can raise prices and still keep many (though not all) of its customers, because they have no other way to get water. In short, it's a monopolist.

The reason a monopolist reduces output and raises price compared to the perfectly competitive industry levels is to increase profit. Cecil Rhodes consolidated the diamond producers into De Beers because he realized that the whole would be worth more than the sum of its parts—the monopoly would generate more profit than the sum of the profits of the individual competitive firms. Under perfect competition economic profits (revenue over and above the opportunity costs of the firm's resources) normally vanish in the long run as competitors enter the market. Under monopoly the profits don't go away—a monopolist is able to continue earning economic profits in the long run.

In fact, monopolists are not the only types of firms that possess market power. In the next chapter, we will study *oligopolists,* firms that can have market power as well. Under certain conditions, oligopolists can earn positive economic profits in the long run by restricting output like monopolists do.

But why don't profits get competed away? What allows monopolists to be monopolists?

Why Monopolies Exist

A monopolist making profits will not go unnoticed by others. Why don't other firms crash the party, grab a piece of the action, and drive down prices and profits in the long run?

Market power is the ability of a firm to raise prices.

For a monopoly to persist, something must keep others from going into the same business; that "something" is known as a **barrier to entry.** There are five principal types of barriers to entry: control of a scarce resource or input, increasing returns to scale, technological superiority, network externalities, and a government-created barrier to entry.

1. Control of a Scarce Resource or Input

A monopolist that controls a resource or input crucial to an industry can prevent other firms from entering its market. For example, Cecil Rhodes created the De Beers monopoly by establishing control over the mines that produced the great bulk of the world's diamonds. The market for diamonds also offers an example of what happens when a monopolist loses control of its scarce resource or input. De Beers's hold on the market was seriously weakened by the opening of rival diamond mines in Russia, Canada, and Australia in the 1990s. More recently, the advent of high-quality manufactured diamonds has effectively ended De Beers's monopoly position.

2. Increasing Returns to Scale

Many Canadians have natural gas piped into their homes for cooking and heating. Invariably, the local gas company is a monopolist. Why don't rival companies compete to provide gas?

In the early nineteenth century, when the gas industry was starting up, companies did compete for local customers. However, the cost of laying gas lines did not depend on the amount of gas sold and the large fixed costs it required to provide gas lines gave an advantage to companies with a larger volume of sales. Firms with a larger volume of sales had a cost advantage because they were able to spread the fixed costs over a larger volume, and so had lower average total costs than smaller firms. Soon local gas supply became a monopoly in every town.

Local gas supply is an industry in which average cost falls as output increases. As we learned in Chapter 11, this phenomenon is called *increasing returns to scale:* when average total cost falls as output increases, firms tend to grow larger. In an industry characterized by increasing returns to scale, larger companies are more profitable and either buy up or drive out smaller ones. For the same reason, established companies have a cost advantage over any potential entrant—a potent barrier to entry. So increasing returns to scale—also known as *economies of scale*—can both give rise to and sustain monopoly.

A monopoly created and sustained by increasing returns to scale is called a **natural monopoly.** The defining characteristic of a natural monopoly is that it possesses increasing returns to scale over the range of output that is relevant for the industry. This is illustrated in Figure 13-3, showing the firm's average total cost curve and the market demand curve, *D*. Here we can see that the natural monopolist's *ATC* curve declines over the output levels at which price is greater than or equal to average total cost.

So the natural monopolist has increasing returns to scale over the entire range of output for which any firm would want to remain in the industry—the range of output at which the firm would at least break even in the long run. The source of this condition is large fixed costs: when large fixed costs are required to operate, a given quantity of output is produced at lower average total cost by one large firm than by two or more smaller firms.

The most visible natural monopolies in the modern economy are local utilities—water, natural gas, power generation, and fiber optic cable. As we'll see later, natural monopolies pose a special challenge to public policy.

3. Technological Superiority

A firm that maintains a consistent technological advantage over potential competitors can establish itself as a monopolist. For example, from the 1970s through the 1990s, the semiconductor chip manufacturer Intel was able to maintain a consistent advantage over potential competitors in both the design and the production of microprocessors, the chips that run

To earn economic profits, a monopolist must be protected by a **barrier to entry**—something that prevents other firms from entering the industry.

A **natural monopoly** exists when increasing returns to scale provide a large cost advantage to a single firm that produces all of an industry's output.

FIGURE 13-3 Increasing Returns to Scale Lead to Natural Monopoly

A natural monopoly can arise when fixed costs required to operate are very high. When this occurs, the firm's *ATC* curve declines over the range of output at which price is greater than or equal to average total cost. This gives the firm increasing returns to scale over the entire range of output at which the firm would at least break even in the long run. As a result, a given quantity of output is produced more cheaply by one large firm than by two or more smaller firms.

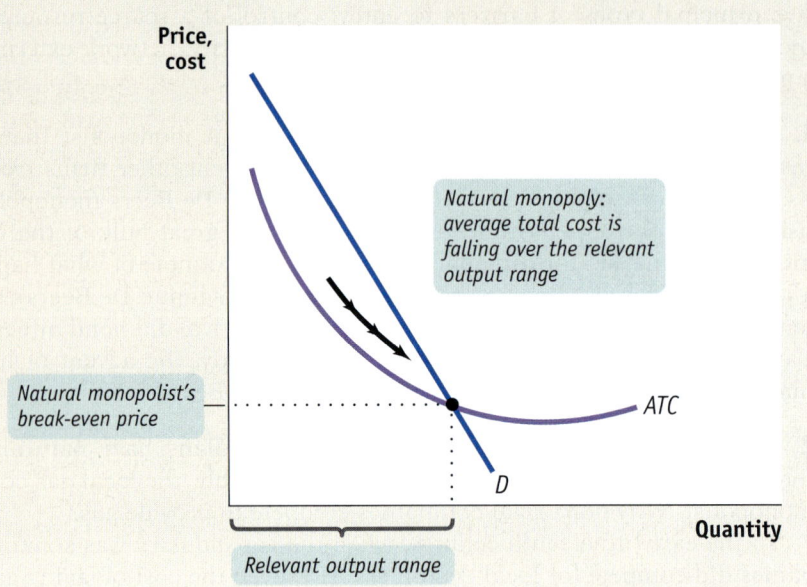

computers. But technological superiority is typically not a barrier to entry over the longer term: over time, competitors will invest in upgrading their technology to match that of the technology leader. In fact, Intel's technological superiority was eventually eroded by a competitor, AMD, which developed chips that are as fast and as powerful as Intel chips.

The fact that technological change can erode monopoly power is also illustrated by the diamond market. As noted earlier, the quality of manufactured diamonds has improved to the point that they rival the real thing, which contributed to the erosion of DeBeers's monopoly position.

4. Network Externalities If you were the only person in the world with an internet connection, what would that connection be worth to you? The answer, of course, is nothing. Your internet connection is valuable only because other people are also connected. And, in general, the more people who are connected, the more valuable your connection is. A **network externality** exists when the value of a good or service to an individual is greater if many others use the same good or service. The value of a network externality derives from enabling its users to participate in a network of other users.

The earliest form of network externalities arose in transportation, when the value of a road or airport increased as the number of people who had access to it rose. Network externalities are especially prevalent in the digital technology and communications sectors of the economy.

How, or why, are network externalities a pervasive feature of the digital economy? The classic case is computer operating systems. Worldwide, most personal computers run on Microsoft Windows. Although many believe that Apple has a superior operating system, the wider use of Windows in the early days of personal computers attracted more software development and technical support, giving it a lasting dominance. More recent examples of firms that have come to dominate their industries through network externalities are Facebook, Amazon, Netflix, Google, Twitter, WeChat, AliPay, and Snapchat.

When a network externality exists, the firm with the largest network of customers using its product has an advantage in attracting new customers, one that may allow it to become a monopolist. At a minimum, the dominant firm can

A **network externality** exists when the value of a good or service to an individual is greater when many other people use the good or service as well.

charge a higher price and so earn higher profits than competitors. Moreover, a network externality gives an advantage to the firm with the deepest pockets, not necessarily the firm with the best technology. Companies with the most money on hand can sell the most goods at a loss with the expectation that doing so will give them the largest customer base and, eventually, a monopoly. The practice of pricing below cost is called predatory pricing. However, in many countries, such as Canada, this pricing strategy illegal under national antitrust laws.

In practice, a network externality behaves a lot like a case of increasing returns to scale: for the larger firm, the cost of accessing a new customer is less than for a smaller firm. Like natural monopoly, network externalities present a difficult problem for public policy makers. We will examine these issues in more detail later in this chapter.

5. Government-Created Barriers The pharmaceutical company Merck introduced Propecia, a drug effective against hair loss, in 1999. Although Propecia was very profitable and other drug companies had the know-how to produce it, no other firms challenged Merck's monopoly. That's because the Canadian government had given Merck the sole legal right to produce the drug in Canada. Propecia is an example of a monopoly protected by government-created barriers.

GLOBAL COMPARISON   WHAT ACCOUNTS FOR AMERICA'S HIGH DRUG PRICES?

Although providing cheap patent-protected drugs to patients in poor countries is a new phenomenon, charging different prices to consumers in different countries is not: it's an example of *price discrimination*.

A monopolist will maximize profits by charging a higher price in the country with a lower price elasticity (the rich country) and a lower price in the country with a higher price elasticity (the poor country). Interestingly, however, drug prices can differ substantially even among countries with comparable income levels. How do we explain this?

The answer is differences in regulation.

This graph shows a price comparison of Advair, an asthma medication, across Canada and four other high-income countries. As you can see, Canadians pay more for this drug than the residents of Norway, Australia, and the United Kingdom, but we are only paying one-fourth of the price paid by our neighbours in the United States. Indeed, the example of Advair is not unusual. Americans consistently pay more for top-selling drugs than residents of other countries.

The reason? The Canadian government and these other countries' governments regulate drug prices more actively than the U.S. government does, helping to keep drug prices affordable for their citizens. So it's not surprising that some Americans travel to Canada and Mexico to purchase their drugs, or buy them from abroad over the internet to save money.

Yet, American drug makers contend that higher drug prices are necessary to cover the high cost of research and development, which can run into the tens of millions of dollars over several years for successful drugs. Critics of the drug companies counter that American drug prices are in excess of what is needed

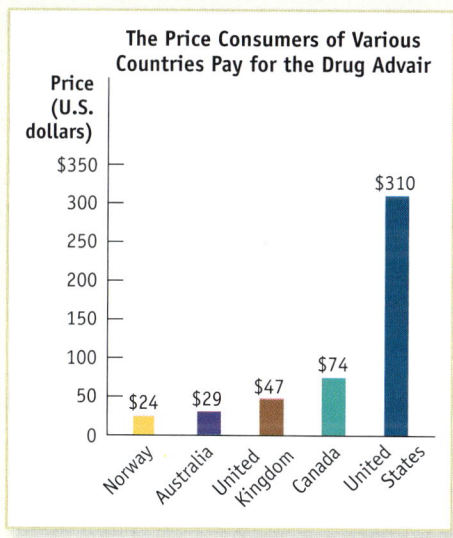

for a socially desirable level of drug innovation. Instead, they say that drug companies are too often focused on developing drugs that generate high profits rather than those that improve health or save lives.

What's indisputable is that some level of profit is necessary to fund innovation.

It is also clear that through the high prices that they pay, Americans effectively subsidize research and development for new drugs that benefit patients worldwide. However, with rising drug prices drawing the attention of policy makers, insurers, and consumers, how long this will continue has become a question.

Data from: Bloomberg News, https://www.bloomberg.com/graphics/2015-drug-prices/.

A **patent** gives an inventor a temporary monopoly in the use or sale of an invention.

A **copyright** gives the creator of a literary or artistic work sole rights to profit from that work.

Most legally created monopolies today arise from *patents* and *copyrights*. A **patent** gives an inventor the sole right to make, use, or sell that invention for a period that in most countries lasts between 14 and 20 years. Patents are given to the creators of new products, such as drugs or mechanical devices. Similarly, a **copyright** gives the creator of a literary or artistic work the sole right to profit from that work, usually for a period equal to the creator's lifetime plus 50 years.

The justification for patents and copyrights is a matter of incentives. If inventors were not protected by patents, they would gain little reward from their efforts: as soon as a valuable invention was made public, others would copy it and sell products based on it. And if inventors could not expect to profit from their inventions, then there would be no incentive to incur the costs of invention in the first place. Likewise for the creators of literary or artistic works. The law allows a monopoly to exist temporarily by granting property rights that encourage invention and creation.

Patents and copyrights are temporary because the law strikes a compromise between the interests of producers and the interests of consumers. The higher price for the good that holds while the legal protection is in effect compensates inventors for the cost of invention; conversely, the lower price that results once the legal protection lapses benefits consumers.

Because the lifetime of the temporary monopoly cannot be tailored to specific cases, this system is imperfect and leads to some missed opportunities. In some cases there can even be significant welfare issues. For example, the violation of multinational drug patents by pharmaceutical companies in poor countries has been a major source of controversy, pitting the needs of poor patients who cannot afford to pay retail drug prices against the interests of the drug manufacturers that have incurred high research costs to discover and test these drugs.

To solve this problem, some multinational drug companies and poor countries have negotiated deals in which the patents are honoured but the multinational companies sell their drugs at deeply discounted prices. (This is an example of *price discrimination,* which we'll learn about shortly.)

ECONOMICS >> *in Action*
The Monopoly That Wasn't: China and the Market for Rare Earths

A quiver of panic shot through much of the world's high-technology and military sectors in 2010. Rare earths, a group of 17 elements that are a critical input in the manufacture of high-tech products like smartphones and military jet components, had suddenly become much harder to obtain.

China controlled 85% to 95% of the global supply of rare earths and, until 2009, made them relatively abundant and cheap on world markets. However, in 2010 China adopted an *export quota*—a limit on the amount of rare earths that could be exported, severely restricting supply on the world market and leading to sharply higher prices. For example, the rare earth dysprosium went from US$166 per kilo in 2010 to nearly US$1,000 per kilo in 2011, a nearly fivefold increase.

But the panic proved to be temporary. China's dominance in rare earths was due to its low cost of production, and not to a monopoly position. In fact, only about a third of the world's rare earth reserves are found in China. Rare earths mines in Canada, Australia, and the United States, which had been mothballed during the period of low prices, were reopened in response to the sharply higher prices. In addition, other sources emerged, such as recovering rare earths from discarded computer equipment.

The episode revealed to government and business leaders outside of China how vulnerable they were to disruptions in the supply of Chinese rare earths. As a result, they committed to keeping the alternative sources operating, even if prices should fall. And China's leaders learned that without control over the global sources of rare earths, what looked like a monopoly position, in fact, wasn't.

>> Check Your Understanding 13-1

Solutions appear at back of book.

1. Suppose Lamplighter New Brunswick is the only natural gas distributor in the province of New Brunswick. Last winter, residents were shocked that the price of natural gas had increased drastically and believed that they were the victims of market power. Explain which of the following pieces of evidence support or contradict that conclusion.
   a. There is a national shortage of natural gas, and Lamplighter New Brunswick could procure only a limited amount.
   b. Last year, Lamplighter New Brunswick and several other competing local natural gas distributing firms merged into a single firm.
   c. The cost to Lamplighter New Brunswick of purchasing natural gas from a natural gas processing plant has gone up significantly.
   d. Recently, some nonlocal firms have begun to offer natural gas to Lamplighter New Brunswick's regular customers at a price much lower than Lamplighter New Brunswick's.
   e. Lamplighter New Brunswick has acquired an exclusive government licence to draw natural gas from the only natural gas pipeline in the province.
2. Suppose the government is considering extending the length of a patent from 20 years to 30 years. How would this change each of the following?
   a. The incentive to invent new products
   b. The length of time during which consumers have to pay higher prices
3. Explain the nature of the network externality in each of the following cases.
   a. A new type of web-based payment system called PayMo
   b. A new type of car engine, which runs on solar cells
   c. A website for trading locally provided goods and services

How a Monopolist Maximizes Profit

Once Cecil Rhodes consolidated the competing diamond producers of South Africa into a single company, the industry's behaviour changed: the quantity supplied fell and the market price rose. We will now learn how a monopolist increases its profit by reducing output. And we will see the crucial role that market demand plays in leading a monopolist to behave differently from a perfectly competitive industry.

The Monopolist's Demand Curve and Marginal Revenue

Recall the firm's optimal output rule: a profit-maximizing firm produces the quantity of output at which the marginal cost of producing the last unit of output equals marginal revenue—the change in total revenue generated by that last unit of output. That is, $MR = MC$ at the profit-maximizing quantity of output.

Although the optimal output rule holds for all firms, we will see shortly that its application leads to different profit-maximizing output levels for a monopolist compared to a firm in a perfectly competitive industry—that is, a price-taking firm. We can see the difference by comparing the demand curve faced by a monopolist to the demand curve faced by an individual perfectly competitive firm.

>> Quick Review

• In a **monopoly,** a single firm uses its **market power** to charge higher prices and produce less output than a competitive industry, generating profits in the short run and long run. For a monopoly to succeed, there must be no close substitutes to the good.

• Monopoly profits will not persist in the long run unless there is a **barrier to entry** such as control of a scarce resource, increasing returns to scale, technological superiority, network externalities, or legal restrictions imposed by governments.

• A **natural monopoly** arises when average total cost declines over the output range relevant for the industry. This creates a barrier to entry because an established **monopolist** has a lower average total cost than an entrant.

• In the digital economy, **network externalities** are prevalent. Because the value of using a good or service is greater as the number of other people using it rises, a network externality can lead to monopoly because rival firms shrink and fail as customers move to the firm with the largest number of customers. Both natural monopolies and network externalities present special challenges to policy makers.

• **Patents** and **copyrights,** government-created barriers, are a source of temporary monopoly that attempt to balance the need for higher prices as compensation to an inventor for the cost of invention against the increase in consumer surplus from lower prices and greater efficiency. Patents and copyrights expire after a certain amount of time. So, like technological superiority, which typically erodes over time, they are not long-term barriers to entry.

FIGURE 13-4 **Comparing the Demand Curves of a Perfectly Competitive Producer and a Monopolist**

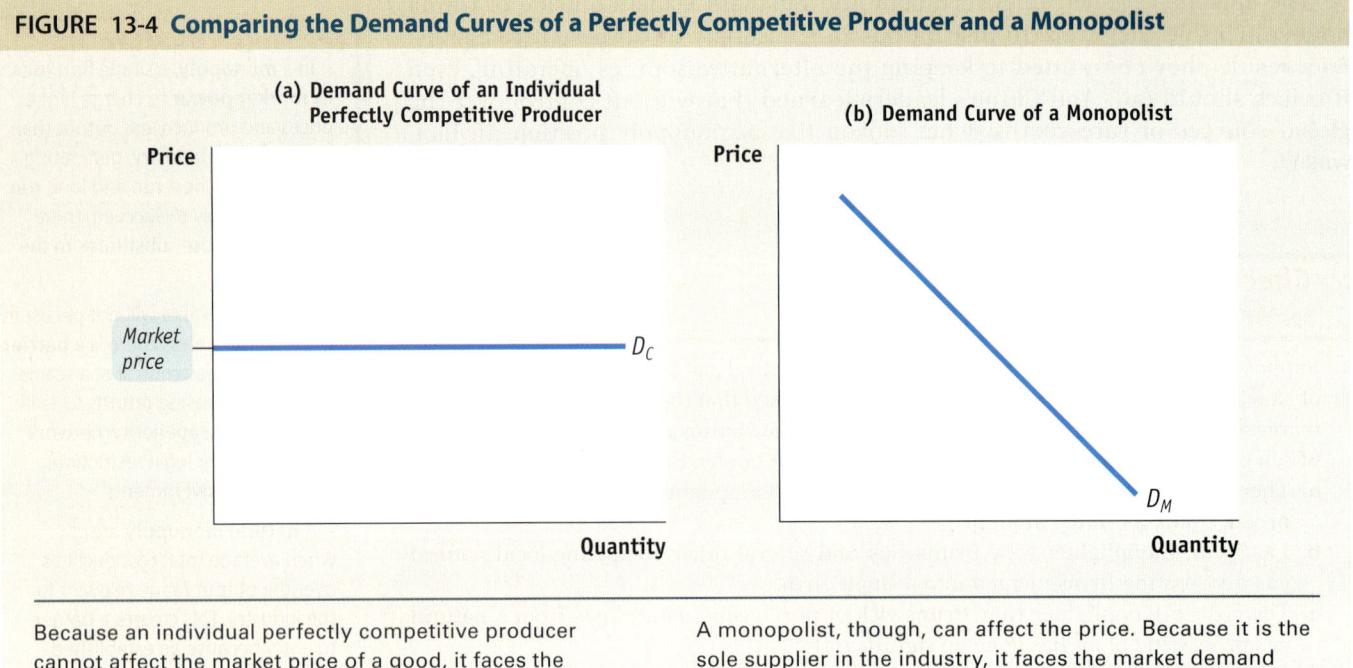

Because an individual perfectly competitive producer cannot affect the market price of a good, it faces the horizontal demand curve D_C, as shown in panel (a), allowing it to sell as much as it wants at the market price.

A monopolist, though, can affect the price. Because it is the sole supplier in the industry, it faces the market demand curve D_M, as shown in panel (b). To sell more output, it must lower the price; by reducing output, it raises the price.

Comparing Demand Curves Recall that each of the firms in a perfectly competitive industry faces a *perfectly elastic* demand curve that is horizontal at the market price, like D_C in panel (a) of Figure 13-4. A perfectly competitive firm can sell as much as it likes at the market price, yet will lose all of its sales if it attempts to charge more. Therefore the marginal revenue of a perfectly competitive producer is simply the market price. As a result, the price-taking firm's optimal output rule is to produce the output level at which the marginal cost of the last unit produced is equal to the market price.

In contrast, a monopolist is the sole supplier of its good. So its demand curve is simply the market demand curve. Like virtually all market demand curves, it slopes downward, like D_M in panel (b) of Figure 13-4. As a result, a monopolist must cut its price to sell more. *This downward slope creates a difference—a "wedge"—between the price of the good and the marginal revenue received by the monopolist for that good.*

Table 13-1 shows this wedge between price and marginal revenue for a monopolist, by calculating the monopolist's total revenue and marginal revenue schedules from its demand schedule.

Comparing Marginal Revenue and Price Now let's examine how the wedge between the monopolist's marginal revenue and price changes according to the quantity of output. The first two columns of Table 13-1 show a hypothetical demand schedule for De Beers diamonds. For the sake of simplicity, we assume that all diamonds are exactly alike. And to make the arithmetic easy, we suppose that the number of diamonds sold is far smaller than is actually the case. For instance, at a price of $500 per diamond, we assume that only 10 diamonds are sold. The demand curve implied by this schedule is shown in panel (a) of Figure 13-5.

The third column of Table 13-1 shows De Beers's total revenue from selling each quantity of diamonds—the price per diamond multiplied by the number of diamonds sold. The last column calculates marginal revenue, the change in total revenue from producing and selling another diamond.

After the first diamond, the marginal revenue a monopolist receives from selling one more unit is less than the price at which that unit is sold. For example, if De Beers sells 10 diamonds, the price at which the 10th diamond is sold is $500. But the marginal revenue— the change in total revenue in going from 9 to 10 diamonds—is only $50.

The marginal revenue from that 10th diamond is less than the price because an increase in production by a monopolist has two opposing effects on revenue:

1. *A quantity effect.* One more unit is sold, increasing total revenue by the price at which the unit is sold (in this case +$500).
2. *A price effect.* To sell the last unit, the monopolist must cut the market price on *all* units sold. This decreases total revenue (in this case, by $9 \times -\$50 = -\$450$).

The quantity effect and the price effect when the monopolist goes from selling 9 diamonds to 10 diamonds are illustrated by the two shaded areas in panel (a) of Figure 13-5. Increasing diamond sales from 9 to 10 means moving down the demand curve from *A* to *B*, reducing the price per diamond from $550 to $500. The green-shaded area represents the quantity effect: De Beers sells the 10th diamond at a price of $500. This is offset, however, by the price effect, represented by the yellow-shaded area. To sell that 10th diamond, De Beers must reduce the price on all its diamonds from $550 to $500. So it loses $9 \times \$50 = \$450$ in revenue, the yellow-shaded area. As point *C* indicates, the total effect on revenue of selling one more diamond—the marginal revenue—derived from an increase in diamond sales from 9 to 10 is only $50.

Point *C* lies on the monopolist's marginal revenue curve, labelled *MR* in panel (a) of Figure 13-5 and taken from the last column of Table 13-1. The crucial point about the monopolist's marginal revenue curve is that it is always *below* the demand curve. That's because of the price effect: a monopolist's marginal revenue from selling an additional unit is always less than the price the monopolist receives for the previous unit. It is the price effect that creates the wedge between the monopolist's marginal revenue curve and the demand curve: to sell an additional diamond, De Beers must cut the market price on all units sold.

In fact, this wedge exists for any firm that possesses market power, such as an oligopolist as well as a monopolist. Having market power means that the firm faces a downward-sloping demand curve. As a result, there will always be a price effect from a change in its output. So for a firm with market power, the marginal revenue curve always lies below its demand curve.

Take a moment to compare the monopolist's marginal revenue curve with the marginal revenue curve for a perfectly competitive firm, one without market power. For such a firm there is no price effect from an increase

TABLE 13-1 Demand, Total Revenue, and Marginal Revenue for the De Beers Monopoly

Price of diamond P	Quantity of diamonds Q	Total revenue $TR = P \times Q$	Marginal revenue $MR = \Delta TR/\Delta Q$
$1,000	0	$0	
			$950
950	1	950	
			850
900	2	1,800	
			750
850	3	2,550	
			650
800	4	3,200	
			550
750	5	3,750	
			450
700	6	4,200	
			350
650	7	4,550	
			250
600	8	4,800	
			150
550	9	4,950	
			50
500	10	5,000	
			−50
450	11	4,950	
			−150
400	12	4,800	
			−250
350	13	4,550	
			−350
300	14	4,200	
			−450
250	15	3,750	
			−550
200	16	3,200	
			−650
150	17	2,550	
			−750
100	18	1,800	
			−850
50	19	950	
			−950
0	20	0	

FIGURE 13-5 A Monopolist's Demand, Total Revenue, and Marginal Revenue Curves

Panel (a) shows the monopolist's demand and marginal revenue curves for diamonds from Table 13-1. The marginal revenue curve lies below the demand curve. To see why, consider point *A* on the demand curve, where 9 diamonds are sold at $550 each, generating total revenue of $4,950. To sell a 10th diamond, the price on all 10 diamonds must be cut to $500, as shown by point *B*. As a result, total revenue increases by the green area (the quantity effect: +$500) but decreases by the yellow area (the price effect: –$450). So the marginal revenue from the 10th diamond is $50 (the difference between the green and yellow areas), which is much lower than its price, $500.

Panel (b) shows the monopolist's total revenue curve for diamonds. As output goes from 0 to 10 diamonds, total revenue increases. It reaches its maximum at 10 diamonds — the level at which marginal revenue is equal to 0 — and declines thereafter. The quantity effect dominates the price effect when total revenue is rising; the price effect dominates the quantity effect when total revenue is falling.

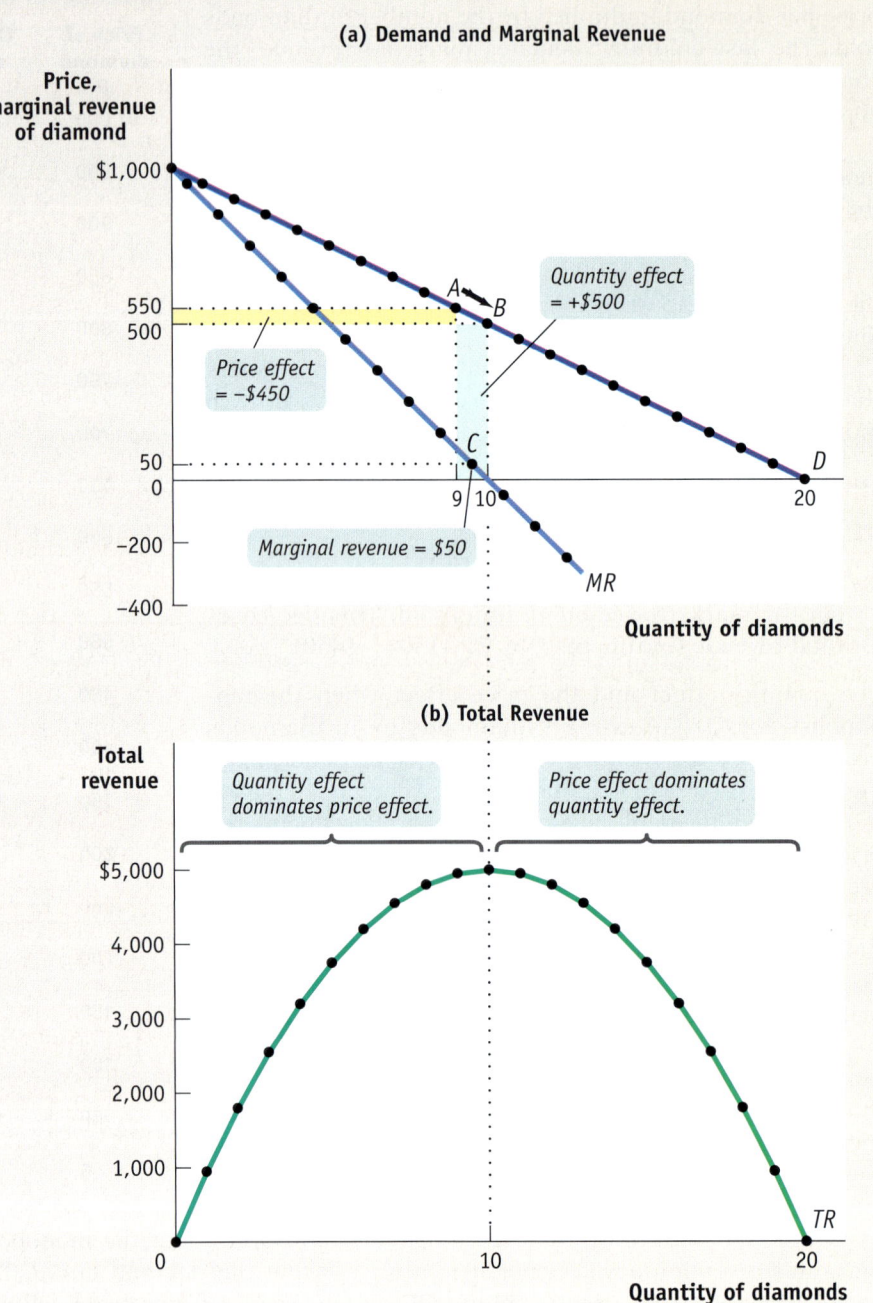

(or decrease) in output: its marginal revenue curve is simply its horizontal demand curve. For a perfectly competitive firm, then, market price and marginal revenue are always equal.

To emphasize how the quantity and price effects offset each other for a firm with market power, De Beers's total revenue curve is shown in panel (b) of Figure 13-5. Notice that it is hill-shaped: as output rises from 0 to 10 diamonds, total revenue increases. This reflects the fact that at *low levels of output, the quantity effect is stronger than the price effect:* as the monopolist sells more, it has to lower the price on only very few units, so the price effect is small. As output rises beyond 10 diamonds, total revenue actually falls. This reflects the fact that *at high levels of output, the price effect is stronger than the quantity effect:* as the monopolist sells more, it now has to lower the price on many units of output, making the price effect very large.

Correspondingly, the marginal revenue curve lies below 0 at output levels above 10 diamonds. For example, an increase in diamond production from 11 to 12 yields only $400 for the 12th diamond, simultaneously reducing the revenue from diamonds 1 through 11 by $550. As a result, the marginal revenue of the 12th diamond is –$150.

The Monopolist's Profit-Maximizing Output and Price

To complete the story of how a monopolist maximizes profit, we now bring in the monopolist's marginal cost. Let's assume that there is no fixed cost of production; we'll also assume that the marginal cost of producing an additional diamond is constant at $200, no matter how many diamonds De Beers produces. Then marginal cost will always equal average total cost, and the marginal cost curve (and the average total cost curve) is a horizontal line at $200, as shown in Figure 13-6.

To maximize profit, the monopolist compares marginal cost with marginal revenue. If marginal revenue exceeds marginal cost, De Beers increases profit by producing more; if marginal revenue is less than marginal cost, De Beers increases profit by producing less. So the monopolist maximizes its profit by using the optimal output rule:

(13-1) $MR = MC$ at the monopolist's profit-maximizing quantity of output

The monopolist's optimal point is shown in Figure 13-6. At point A, the marginal cost curve, MC, crosses the marginal revenue curve, MR. The corresponding

---

FIGURE 13-6 The Monopolist's Profit-Maximizing Output and Price

This figure shows demand, marginal revenue, and marginal cost curves. Marginal cost per diamond is constant at $200, so the marginal cost curve is horizontal at $200. According to the optimal output rule, the profit-maximizing quantity of output for the monopolist is at $MR = MC$, shown by point A, where the marginal cost and marginal revenue curves cross at an output of 8 diamonds. The price De Beers can charge per diamond is found by going to the point on the demand curve directly above point A, which is point B here — a price of $600 per diamond. It makes a profit of $400 \times 8 = \$3,200$. A perfectly competitive industry produces the output level at which $P = MC$, given by point C, where the demand curve and marginal cost curves cross. So a competitive industry produces 16 diamonds, sells at a price of $200, and makes zero profit.

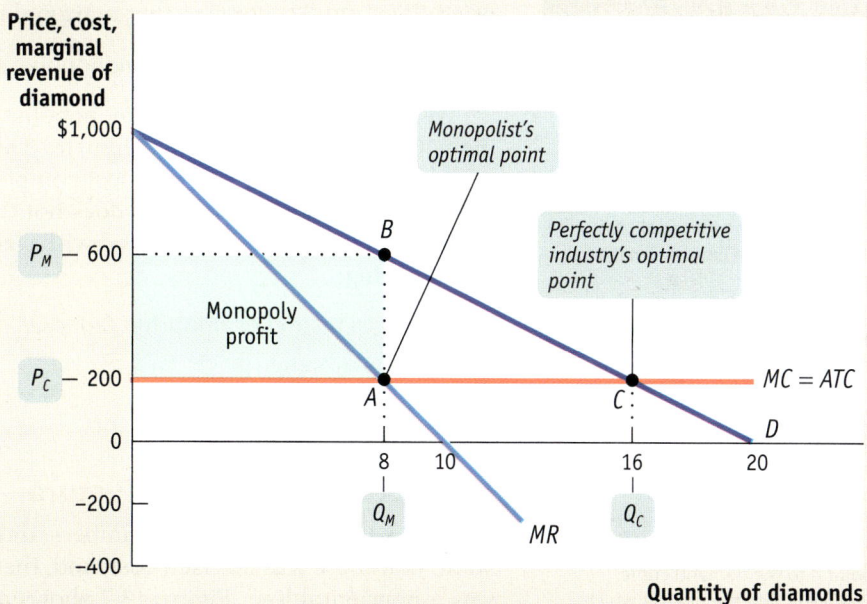

output level, 8 diamonds, is the monopolist's profit-maximizing quantity of output, Q_M. The price at which consumers demand 8 diamonds is $600, so the monopolist's price, P_M, is $600—corresponding to point B. The average total cost of producing each diamond is $200, so the monopolist earns a profit of $600 − $200 = $400 per diamond, and total profit is $8 \times $400 = $3,200, as indicated by the shaded area.

Monopoly versus Perfect Competition

When Cecil Rhodes consolidated many independent diamond producers into De Beers, he converted a perfectly competitive industry into a monopoly. We can now use our analysis to see the effects of such a consolidation.

Let's look again at Figure 13-6 and ask how this same market would work if, instead of being a monopoly, the industry were perfectly competitive. We will continue to assume that there is no fixed cost and that marginal cost is constant, so average total cost and marginal cost are equal.

If the diamond industry consists of many perfectly competitive firms, each of those producers takes the market price as given. For each firm, marginal revenue is equal to the market price. So each firm within the industry uses the price-taking firm's optimal output rule:

(13-2) $P = MC$ at the perfectly competitive firm's profit-maximizing
quantity of output

In Figure 13-6, this corresponds to producing at point C, where the price per diamond, P_C, is $200, equal to the marginal cost of production. So the profit-maximizing output of an industry under perfect competition, Q_C, is 16 diamonds.

But does the perfectly competitive industry earn any profits at point C? No: the price of $200 is equal to the average total cost per diamond. So there are no economic profits for this industry when it produces at the perfectly competitive output level.

We've already seen that once the industry is consolidated into a monopoly, the result is very different. The monopolist's calculation of marginal revenue takes the price effect into account, so that marginal revenue is less than the price. That is:

(13-3) $P > MR = MC$ at the monopolist's profit-maximizing quantity of output

We've also seen that the monopolist produces less than the competitive industry—8 diamonds rather than 16. The price under monopoly is $600, compared with only $200 under perfect competition. The monopolist earns a positive profit, but the competitive firm does not.

As suggested earlier, compared with a competitive industry, a monopolist does the following:

- Produces a smaller quantity: $Q_M < Q_C$
- Charges a higher price: $P_M > P_C$
- Earns a profit

Monopoly: The General Picture

Figure 13-6 involved specific numbers and assumed that marginal cost was constant, that there was no fixed cost, and, therefore, that the average total cost curve was a horizontal line. Figure 13-7 shows a more general picture of monopoly in action: D is the market demand curve; MR, the marginal revenue curve; MC, the marginal cost curve; and ATC, the average total cost curve. Here we return to the usual assumption that the marginal cost curve has a "swoosh" shape and the average total cost curve is U-shaped.

Applying the optimal output rule, we see that the profit-maximizing level of output is the output at which marginal revenue equals marginal cost, indicated

PITFALLS

FINDING THE MONOPOLY PRICE

To find the *profit-maximizing quantity of output* for a monopolist, look for the point where the marginal revenue curve crosses the marginal cost curve. Point A in Figure 13-6 is an example.

However, it's important not to make the mistake of imagining that point A also shows the *price* at which the monopolist sells its output. It doesn't. Instead, it shows the *marginal revenue* received by the monopolist, which is less than the price.

To find the monopoly price, you have to go up vertically from point A to the demand curve. There you find the price at which consumers demand the profit-maximizing quantity. So the profit-maximizing price–quantity combination is always a point on the demand curve, like point B in Figure 13-6.

FIGURE 13-7 The Monopolist's Profit

In this case, the marginal cost curve has a "swoosh" shape and the average total cost curve is U-shaped. The monopolist maximizes profit by producing the level of output at which $MR = MC$, given by point A, generating quantity Q_M. It finds its monopoly price, P_M, from the point on the demand curve directly above point A, point B here. The average total cost of Q_M is shown by point C. Profit is given by the area of the shaded rectangle.

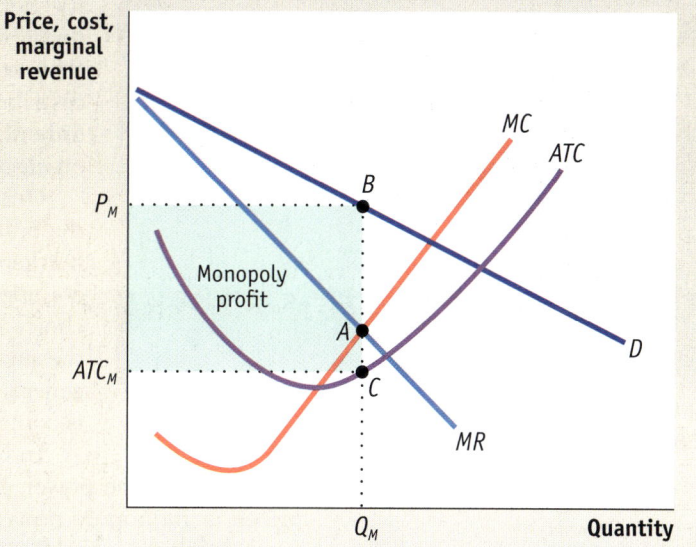

by point A. The profit-maximizing quantity of output is Q_M, and the price charged by the monopolist is P_M. At the profit-maximizing level of output, the monopolist's average total cost is ATC_M, shown by point C.

Recalling how we calculated profit in Equation 12-5, profit is equal to the difference between total revenue and total cost. So we have:

(13-4) $\text{Profit} = TR - TC$

$$= (P_M \times Q_M) - (ATC_M \times Q_M)$$

$$= (P_M - ATC_M) \times Q_M$$

Profit is equal to the area of the shaded rectangle in Figure 13-7, with a height of $P_M - ATC_M$ and a width of Q_M.

From Chapter 12 we know that a perfectly competitive industry can have profits in the *short run but not in the long run*. In the short run, price can exceed average total cost, allowing a perfectly competitive firm to make a profit. But we also know that this cannot persist.

In the long run, any profit in a perfectly competitive industry will be competed away as new firms enter the market. In contrast, barriers to entry allow a monopolist to make profits in *both the short run and the long run*.

ECONOMICS >> *in Action*
Shocked by the High Price of Electricity

Historically, electric utilities in North America were recognized as natural monopolies. A utility serviced a defined geographical area and owned both the plants that generated electricity and the transmission lines that delivered it to retail customers. The rates charged to customers were regulated by the government and were set at a level to cover the utility's cost of operation plus a modest return on capital to its shareholders.

Beginning in the late 1990s, however, there was a move toward deregulation, based on the belief that competition would deliver lower retail electricity prices. Competition occurs at two junctures in the channel from power generation to retail customers: (1) distributors compete to sell electricity to retail customers and (2) power generators compete to supply power to distributors.

Although some electric utilities were deregulated in the 1990s, the current trend is to reregulate them.

That was the theory, at least. At the time of writing, only Alberta and Ontario had instituted some form of electricity deregulation, separating generation and transmission/distribution activities into separate firms. Generators sell their output into a competitive market, while the transmission/distribution firms continue to be a regulated monopoly. Why did only some provinces and territories actually follow through on electricity deregulation?

One major obstacle is the lack of choice in power generators, the bulk of which still entail large up-front fixed costs. In many markets there is only one power generator. Although consumers appear to have a choice in their electricity distributor, the choice is illusory, since everyone must get their electricity from the same source in the end. Even when there is choice in power generators, there is frequently no choice in transmission, which is controlled by monopoly power line companies.

In fact, deregulation can make consumers worse off when there is only one power generator. Unfettered by regulations that set consumer prices, a monopoly power generator can engage in market manipulation. The most shocking example was what happened in California during 2000 and 2001. After California deregulated its electricity market, an "energy crisis" suddenly occurred that brought blackouts and billions of dollars in electricity surcharges to homes and businesses. It turned out that a monopoly power generator intentionally reduced the amount of power supplied to consumers in order to drive up prices. After an investigation, regulators discovered audiotapes on which executives could be heard discussing plans to shut down power plants during times of peak energy demand, joking about how they were "stealing" more than US$1 million a day from California's electricity consumers.

Another problem associated with deregulation of energy markets is it tends to lead to insufficient investment in new power plants. Without regulation, power generators are no longer guaranteed a market price that gives them a profitable rate of return on new power plants. As a result, builders of new power generation capacity are demanding much higher prices before they invest. And in U.S. states with deregulation, capacity has failed to keep up with growing demand. For example, Texas, a deregulated state, has experienced massive blackouts due to insufficient capacity, and in New Jersey and Maryland, regulators have intervened to compel producers to build more power plants.

Lastly, consumers in deregulated states have been subject to big spikes in their electricity bills, often paying much more than consumers in regulated states. Angry customers and exasperated regulators have prompted many governments to shift into reverse. In 2017, following much criticism over rising prices partly due to investments in greener power, the government of Ontario promised to lower residential electricity rates by an average of 25%.

>> Quick Review

• The crucial difference between a firm with market power, such as a monopolist, and a firm in a perfectly competitive industry is that perfectly competitive firms are price-takers that face horizontal demand curves, but a firm with market power faces a downward-sloping demand curve.

• Due to the price effect of an increase in output, the marginal revenue curve of a firm with market power always lies below its demand curve. So a profit-maximizing monopolist chooses the output level at which marginal cost is equal to marginal revenue — *not* to price.

• As a result, the monopolist produces less and sells its output at a higher price than a perfectly competitive industry would. It earns profits in the short run and the long run.

>> Check Your Understanding 13-2

Solutions appear at back of book.

1. Use the accompanying total revenue schedule of Emerald, Inc., a monopoly producer of 10-carat emeralds, to calculate the answers to parts a–d. Then answer part e.
   a. The demand schedule
   b. The marginal revenue schedule
   c. The quantity effect component of marginal revenue per output level
   d. The price effect component of marginal revenue per output level
   e. What additional information is needed to determine Emerald, Inc.'s profit-maximizing output?

Quantity of emeralds demanded	Total revenue
1	$100
2	186
3	252
4	280
5	250

2. Use Figure 13-6 to show what happens to the following when the marginal cost of diamond production rises from \$200 to \$400.
- Marginal cost curve
- Profit-maximizing price and quantity
- Profit of the monopolist
- Perfectly competitive industry profits

‖ Monopoly and Public Policy

It's profitable to be a monopolist, but it's not so beneficial to be a monopolist's customer. A monopolist, by reducing output and raising prices, benefits at the expense of consumers. But buyers and sellers always have conflicting interests: buyers want lower prices while sellers want higher prices. Is the conflict under monopoly any different than it is under perfect competition?

The answer is yes, because monopoly is a source of inefficiency: the losses to consumers from monopoly behaviour are larger than the gains to the monopolist. Because monopoly leads to net losses to society's welfare, governments often try either to prevent the emergence of monopolies or to limit their effects. In this section, we will see why monopoly leads to inefficiency and examine the policies governments adopt in an attempt to prevent this inefficiency.

Welfare Effects of Monopoly

By restricting output below the level at which marginal cost is equal to the market price, a monopolist increases its profit but hurts consumers. When comparing the monopolist's gain in profit to the loss in consumer surplus, we learn that the loss in consumer surplus is larger than the monopolist's gain. As a result, monopoly causes a net loss for society.

To see why, let's return to the case where the marginal cost curve is horizontal, as shown in the two panels of Figure 13-8. Here the marginal cost curve is *MC*, the demand curve is *D*, and, in panel (b), the marginal revenue curve is *MR*.

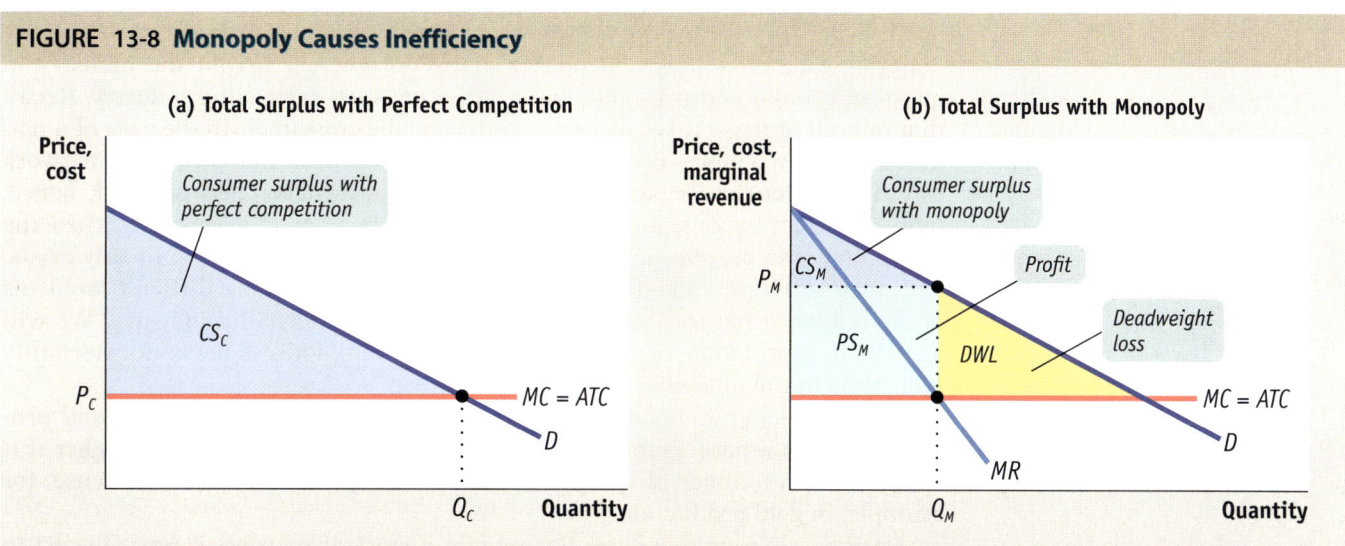

FIGURE 13-8 Monopoly Causes Inefficiency

(a) Total Surplus with Perfect Competition

(b) Total Surplus with Monopoly

Panel (a) depicts a perfectly competitive industry: output is Q_C, and market price, P_C, is equal to *MC*. Since price is exactly equal to each producer's average total cost of production per unit, there is no profit and no producer surplus. So total surplus is equal to consumer surplus, the entire shaded area. Panel (b) depicts the industry under monopoly: the monopolist decreases output to Q_M and charges P_M. Consumer surplus (blue area) has shrunk: a portion of it has been captured as profit (green area), and a portion of it has been lost to deadweight loss (yellow area), the value of mutually beneficial transactions that do not occur because of monopoly behaviour. As a result, total surplus falls.

Panel (a) shows what happens if this industry is perfectly competitive. Equilibrium output is Q_C; the price of the good, P_C, is equal to marginal cost, and marginal cost is also equal to average total cost because there is no fixed cost and marginal cost is constant. Each firm is earning exactly its average total cost per unit of output, so there is no profit and no producer surplus in this equilibrium.

The consumer surplus generated by the market is equal to the area of the blue shaded triangle CS_C shown in panel (a). Since there is no producer surplus when the industry is perfectly competitive, CS_C also represents the total surplus.

Panel (b) shows the results for the same market, but this time assuming that the industry is a monopoly. The monopolist produces the level of output Q_M, at which marginal cost is equal to marginal revenue, and it charges the price P_M. The industry now earns profit—which is also the producer surplus—equal to the area of the green rectangle, PS_M. Note that this profit is surplus captured from consumers as consumer surplus shrinks to the area of the blue triangle, CS_M.

By comparing panels (a) and (b), we see that in addition to the redistribution of surplus from consumers to the monopolist, another important change has occurred: the sum of profit and consumer surplus—total surplus—is *smaller* under monopoly than under perfect competition. That is, the sum of CS_M and PS_M in panel (b) is less than the area CS_C in panel (a). In Chapter 7, we analyzed how taxes generated *deadweight loss* to society. Here we show that monopoly creates a deadweight loss to society equal to the area of the yellow triangle, DWL. So monopoly produces a net loss for society.

This net loss arises because some mutually beneficial transactions do not occur. There are people for whom an additional unit of the good is worth more than the marginal cost of producing it but who don't consume it because they are not willing to pay P_M.

If you recall our discussion of the deadweight loss from the chapter on taxes, you will notice that the deadweight loss from monopoly looks quite similar. Indeed, by driving a wedge between price and marginal cost, monopoly acts much like a tax on consumers and produces the same kind of inefficiency.

So monopoly hurts the welfare of society as a whole and is a source of market failure. Is there anything government policy can do about it?

Policy Remedies to Monopoly

Policy toward monopoly depends crucially on whether or not the industry in question is: (a) a natural monopoly or (b) a network externality industry. Recall that in both of these cases, bigger is better for the consumer. In the case of a natural monopoly, a bigger producer has lower average cost. In the case of a network externality industry, a bigger producer provides a bigger network and, hence, more value for a consumer. If neither one of those conditions apply, then the best policy is to prevent monopoly from arising or break it up if it already exists. Let's focus on these remedies first, before turning to the more difficult problems of dealing with natural monopoly and a network externality industry. We will address natural monopoly later in this section, and address network externality industries in the following section.

The De Beers monopoly on diamonds didn't have to happen. Diamond production is not a natural monopoly: the industry's costs would be no higher if it consisted of a number of independent, competing producers as is the case, for example, in gold production.

De Beers is a unique case. For unique historical reasons, it was allowed to remain a monopoly until it was overtaken by events in the 1990s. But beginning in the late nineteenth century, most similar monopolies have been broken up. Regulators focused on monopolies that had arisen, like De Beers, from the consolidation of rival firms in an industry into common ownership. The most celebrated example in the United States is Standard Oil, founded by John D. Rockefeller in 1870. By 1878 Standard Oil controlled almost all U.S. oil refining; but in 1911 a court order broke the company into a number of smaller units, including the companies that later became Exxon and Mobil (and merged in 1999 to become ExxonMobil). In Canada, in the 1980s the federal government started allowing other firms to enter the telephone business removing Bell Canada's monopoly status in long distance and local phone services over a large part of the country.

The government policies used to prevent or eliminate monopolies are known as *antitrust policies*, which we will discuss in the next chapter.

In **public ownership** of a monopoly, the good is supplied by the government or by a firm owned by the government.

Dealing with Natural Monopoly

Breaking up a monopoly that isn't natural is clearly a good idea: the gains to consumers outweigh the loss to the producer. But it's not so clear whether a natural monopoly, one in which a large producer has lower average total costs than small producers, should be broken up, because this would raise average total cost. For example, a town government that tried to prevent a single company from dominating local gas supply—which, as we've discussed, is almost surely a natural monopoly—would raise the cost of providing gas to its residents.

Yet even in the case of a natural monopoly, a profit-maximizing monopolist acts in a way that causes inefficiency—it charges consumers a price that is higher than marginal cost and, by doing so, prevents some potentially beneficial transactions. Also, it can seem unfair that a firm that has managed to establish a monopoly position earns a large profit at the expense of consumers.

Two policy options can be adopted to deal with the inefficiencies of monopoly: public ownership and regulation.

1. Public Ownership In many countries, the preferred answer to the problem of natural monopoly has been **public ownership.** Instead of allowing a private monopolist to control an industry, the government establishes a public agency to provide the good and protect consumers' interests. In Canada, the government has often assumed control of a monopoly industry by nationalizing it. Publicly owned companies in Canada are called *Crown* corporations. They may be owned by any level of government—federal, provincial, territorial, or municipal government. Federally owned Crown corporations include Canada Post, Atomic Energy of Canada Limited, Via Rail Canada, the Canadian Broadcasting Corporation, and the Bank of Canada. Most electric utilities are Crown corporations at either the provincial level (BC Hydro, Ontario Power Generation, Hydro One, Hydro-Québec, and NB Hydro), territorial level (Northwest Territories Power), or municipal level (Toronto Hydro, EPCOR, ENMAX, London Hydro). In past decades, some governments have privatized some of their Crown corporations, such as Air Canada, Petro Canada, the Canadian National Railway, Potash Corporation of Saskatchewan Inc., and Nova Scotia Power.

Via Rail, a public company, has provided train service, at a loss, to destinations that attract few passengers.

The advantage of public ownership, in principle, is that a publicly owned natural monopoly can set prices based on the criterion of efficiency rather than profit maximization. In a perfectly competitive industry, profit-maximizing behaviour is efficient because producers produce the quantity at which price is equal to marginal cost; that is why there is no economic argument for public ownership of, say, Christmas tree farms.

Experience suggests, however, that public ownership as a solution to the problem of natural monopoly often works badly in practice. One reason is that publicly owned firms are often less eager than private companies to keep costs down or offer high-quality products. Another is that publicly owned companies all too often end up serving political interests—providing contracts or jobs to people with the right connections. For example, Via Rail receives government subsidies to stay in business. The company received $394 million in government subsidies in 2018.

Price regulation limits the price that a monopolist is allowed to charge.

2. Regulation An alternative to operating a natural monopoly as a Crown corporation is to leave the industry in private hands but subject it to regulation. For example, many local utilities such as electricity, natural gas, and others are covered by **price regulation** that limits the prices they can charge.

As we've learned, imposing a *price ceiling* on a competitive industry is a recipe for shortages, black markets, and other nasty side effects. Doesn't imposing a limit on the price that, say, a local gas company can charge have the same effects?

Not necessarily: a price ceiling on a monopolist need not create a shortage—in the absence of a price ceiling, a monopolist would charge a price that is higher than its marginal cost of production. So even if forced to charge a lower price—as long as that price is above *MC* and the monopolist at least breaks even on total output—the monopolist still has an incentive to produce the quantity demanded at that price.

Figure 13-9 shows an example of price regulation of a natural monopoly—a highly simplified version of a local gas company. The company faces a demand curve *D*, with an associated marginal revenue curve *MR*. For simplicity, we assume that the firm's total costs consist of two parts: a fixed cost and variable costs that are incurred at a constant proportion to output. In this case, marginal cost is constant, and the marginal cost curve (which here is also the average variable cost curve) is the horizontal line *MC*.

The average total cost curve is the downward-sloping curve *ATC*; it slopes downward because the higher the output, the lower the average fixed cost (the fixed cost per unit of output). Because average total cost slopes downward over the range of output relevant for market demand, this is a natural monopoly.

Panel (a) illustrates a case of natural monopoly without regulation. The unregulated natural monopolist chooses the monopoly output Q_M and charges the price P_M. Since the monopolist receives a price greater than its average total cost, it earns a profit. This profit is exactly equal to the producer surplus in this market, represented by the green-shaded rectangle. Consumer surplus is given by the blue-shaded triangle.

FIGURE 13-9 Unregulated and Regulated Natural Monopoly

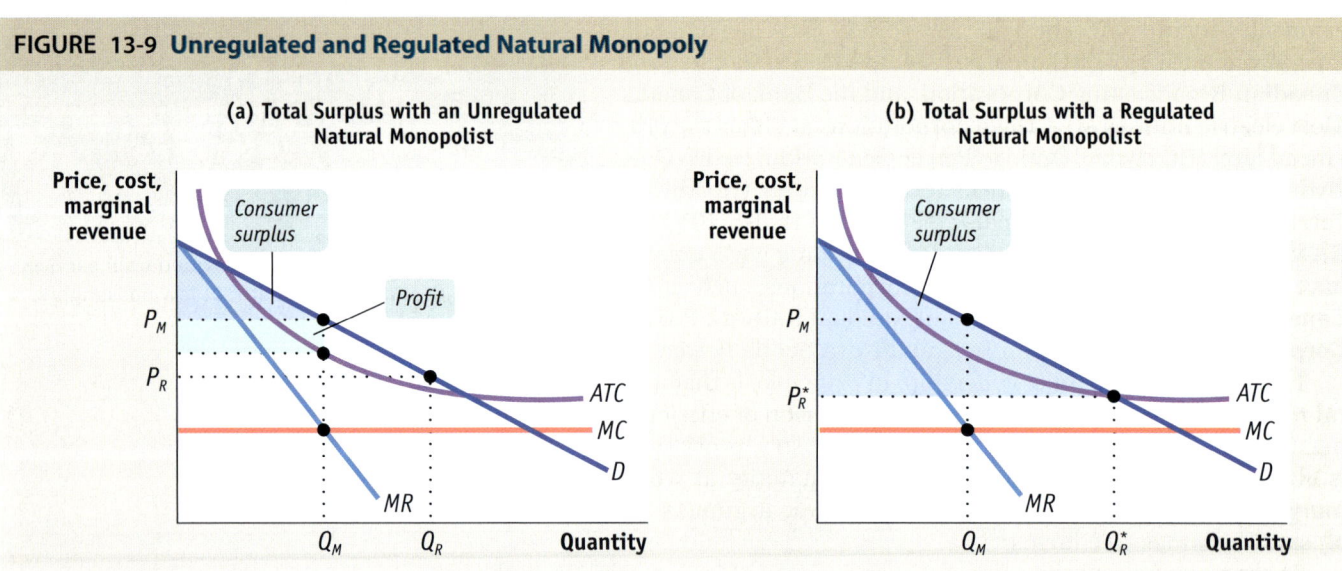

This figure shows the case of a natural monopolist. In panel (a), if the monopolist is allowed to charge P_M, it makes a profit, shown by the green area; consumer surplus is shown by the blue area. If it is regulated and must charge the lower price P_R, output increases from Q_M to Q_R and consumer surplus increases.

Panel (b) shows what happens when the monopolist must charge a price equal to average total cost, the price P_R^*. Output expands to Q_R^*, and consumer surplus is now the entire blue area. The monopolist makes zero profit. This is the greatest total surplus possible when the monopolist is allowed to at least break even, making P_R^* the best regulated price.

Now suppose that regulators impose a price ceiling on local gas deliveries—one that falls below the monopoly price P_M but above ATC, say, at P_R in panel (a). At that price the quantity demanded is Q_R.

Does the company have an incentive to produce that quantity? Yes. If the price at which the monopolist can sell its product is fixed by regulators, the firm's output no longer affects the market price. The monopolist ignores the MR curve and is willing to expand output to meet the quantity demanded as long as the price it receives for the next unit is greater than marginal cost and the monopolist at least breaks even on total output. So with price regulation, the monopolist produces more, at a lower price.

Of course, the monopolist will not be willing to produce at all if the imposed price means producing at a loss. That is, the price ceiling has to be set high enough to allow the firm to cover its average total cost. Panel (b) shows a situation in which regulators have pushed the price down as far as possible, at the level where the average total cost curve crosses the demand curve. This type of regulation is often called **average cost pricing**. Another alternative is to regulate the natural monopoly so as to force it to charge a price equal to its marginal cost of production (**marginal cost pricing**). But this could require the government to provide the firm with a subsidy so that it can cover its fixed costs.

At any lower price the firm loses money. The price here, P_R^*, is the best regulated price: the monopolist is just willing to operate and produces Q_R^*, the quantity demanded at that price. Consumers and society gain as a result.

The welfare effects of this regulation can be seen by comparing the shaded areas in the two panels of Figure 13-9. Consumer surplus is increased by the regulation, with the gains coming from two sources. First, profits are eliminated and added instead to consumer surplus. Second, the larger output and lower price lead to an overall welfare gain—an increase in total surplus. In fact, panel (b) illustrates the largest total surplus possible.

This all looks terrific: consumers are better off, profits are eliminated, and overall welfare increases. Unfortunately, things are rarely that easy in practice. There two main problems. First is the problem of inadequate information: regulators don't have the information required to set the price exactly at the level at which the demand curve crosses the average total cost curve. Sometimes they set it too low, creating shortages; at other times they set it too high. Also, regulated monopolies, like publicly owned firms, tend to exaggerate their costs to regulators and to provide inferior quality to consumers. Second is the problem of *regulatory capture:* because vast sums of money are at stake, regulators can be unduly influenced by the companies they are supposed to oversee.

However, as the Economics in Action of the last section, "Shocked by the High Price of Electricity," shows, some level of regulation and oversight of a natural monopoly is generally much better than none at all.

A New Generation of Market Power

These days, an old-fashioned monopolist like De Beers is hard to find. Except in the cases of monopolies that arise from natural monopoly, government protection, or technological advantage (usually short-lived), examples of industries in which there is truly only one seller that has sole control of a good are found almost exclusively in history books.

There's a reason for that. As we explained earlier, a Canadian company that tried to become a monopolist by acquiring control of a scarce natural resource by buying up rival firms (as Cecil Rhodes did) would soon be accused of breaking Canadian antitrust laws.

Yet the topic of monopoly and antitrust regulation has recently become one of the hottest topics of economic discussion in recent years. Why? It's due to the rise of the digital economy and the network externalities that it creates. Companies such as Microsoft, Apple, Google, eBay, AliPay, WeChat, Amazon, and Uber have

Average cost pricing is a form of price regulation that forces a monopoly to set its price equal to its average total cost.

Marginal cost pricing is a form of price regulation that forces a monopoly to set its price equal to its marginal cost.

transformed the economy. They represent the fastest growing and among the most profitable firms in the economy. However, they represent a unique set of problems in policy making. While the old-fashioned way of becoming a monopolist is no longer viable, network externalities provide a number of ways of gaining market power and, potentially, of becoming a monopolist (or very close to one). In this section, we'll explore the special nature of market power that arises from network externalities. We will also learn about an important variation of market power called monopsony—an industry in which there is only one buyer—which has been on the rise due to the growth of network externalities.

In the past few years, the digital economy and its network externalities have generated significant urgency in answering the questions of how to manage market power, both in the case of monopoly and of monopsony. In this section, we'll learn why and about the special challenges that policy makers now face.

A New Generation of Market Power and Monopoly

As we learned earlier, increasing returns to scale and network externalities share the critical feature that "bigger is better." Recall that when network externalities are present in an industry, the firm with the largest network is preferred by consumers to firms with smaller networks. Hence the biggest firm in the industry gets bigger while smaller firms shrink. Eventually, the biggest firm—the *dominant* firm—will become large enough relative to any rivals to exert market power and behave like a monopolist.

As in standard monopoly, the dominant firm in a network externalities industry creates a deadweight loss to society if it raises price and reduces output in order to capture surplus from consumers. And in fast-moving digital industries, there's another potential inefficiency caused by market power: *stifling innovation.* The dominant firm, by using its size advantage to deter rivals from entering the market or using their network, stifles the innovation that they can bring.

Microsoft is the best example of a network externalities firm that used its size to vanquish rivals and stifle innovation. A U.S. federal court found Microsoft guilty of engaging in "monopolization": using its market dominance in the PC operating systems market to harm Netscape, a rival to Microsoft's Internet Explorer in the internet browser market. The federal court also found that Microsoft had undertaken steps against a number of rival software companies—that possessed superior technology to Microsoft's—to crush any challenge to its near-monopoly position in the operating-system market, the source of the network externality. Rather than breaking Microsoft up into smaller companies, the court mandated that Microsoft open up its operating-system software to allow rival software companies to work with it. However, Microsoft's position was by then so dominant that rival software companies were never able to establish a significant market share. A case in point: after having an initial market share of 90% share of the internet browser market, Netscape eventually disappeared. Not surprisingly, Microsoft's software division remains highly profitable, reporting profits of nearly US$13 billion in 2019.

More recently, in 2018 and in 2019, the EU's antitrust authorities accused Google of engaging in anti-competitive behaviour and stifling innovation by blocking rivals across a number of different platforms, such as online shopping searches and the market for Android phone operating systems, hitting it with over US$9 billion in fines. However, the final verdicts in these cases will probably take years to decide; if history is any judge, by that time Google's dominance will be sealed.

A New Generation of Market Power and Monopsony

Is it possible for the buyer and not the seller to have market power? Put another way, is it possible to have a market in which there is only one buyer but many sellers, so that the buyer can use its power to capture surplus from the sellers? The answer is yes, and that market is called a **monopsony.**

Like a monopolist, a **monopsonist** will distort the competitive market outcome in order to capture more of the surplus, except that the monopsonist will

A **monopsony** exists when there is only one buyer of a good. A **monopsonist** is a firm that is the sole buyer in a market.

do this through quantity purchased and price paid for goods rather than through quantity sold and price charged for goods.

The classic example is a single employer in a small town—say, the local factory—that is purchasing labour services from workers. Recall that a monopolist, realizing that it can affect the price at which its goods are sold, reduces output in order to get a higher price and increase its profits. A monopsonist does much the same thing, but with a twist: realizing that it can affect the wage it pays by moving down the labour supply curve, it reduces the number of employees hired and pays a lower wage in order to increase its profits.

Just as a monopolist creates a deadweight loss by producing too little output, a monopsonist creates a deadweight loss by hiring too few workers and paying wages that are too low. As a result it also produces too little output.

In the past, monopsony was a relatively rare phenomenon as sellers would find a way to offer their goods and services to a rival. For example, workers subject to a local monopsonist employer could in most cases simply move away and find employment elsewhere. However, with the advent of the digital economy, monopsony behaviour appears to be on the rise. Giant e-commerce platforms like Amazon or the Apple App Store can now use their power to win concessions from sellers who use their platforms to sell their merchandise. They can capture surplus from sellers by forcing them to accept lower prices for their merchandise in various ways—such as by charging them high fees, by developing competing in-house brands (i.e., the Amazon Basics brand), and the like. Eventually, sellers will reduce their sales on the platform. Output falls and deadweight loss is incurred.

The recent and ongoing legal case of *Apple v. Pepper* is an example of monopsony behaviour arising from a network externality. In the legal proceedings, consumers and app designers charged that Apple's requirement that all iOS apps be purchased through its Apple App Store allowed Apple to exert monopsony power over app designers. By charging app designers 30% of their sales price, the plaintiffs claimed that Apple was using the dominance of its e-commerce platform to capture surplus from app suppliers. App suppliers, as a result, had to either accept lower surplus or try to pass the 30% "Apple tax" onto consumers. Either way, output falls in comparison to the competitive outcome, in which app suppliers and consumers can freely trade with one another. However, because app designers want to sell on the e-commerce platform visited by the largest number of customers, while customers want to visit the platform with the largest number of apps supplied—dealing with monopsony behaviour based on network externalities presents the same policy difficulty as dealing with monopoly behaviour based on network externalities.

Policies to Address the New Generation of Market Power

The examples discussed here illustrate the thorny challenge that market power arising from network externalities poses to policy makers. Like natural monopoly, the firm with the largest network is likely to become dominant enough to exert market power. And it could, eventually, become a monopolist or a monopsonist as smaller firms disappear. Yet, policy makers have also recognized that, like natural monopoly, welfare will be reduced if the dominant firm was split into smaller firms with smaller networks. In time, the problem of market power would reappear as consumers migrate to the firm with the larger network, repeating the dynamic in which the largest firm grows larger while smaller firms shrink and disappear. And when it comes to fostering innovation, there also lies a conundrum. While with monopoly or monopsony behaviour the digital giants can stifle innovation created by rivals, it's clear that the digital giants themselves are also huge sources of innovation. Thus poorly implemented regulation of the giants can stifle innovation as well. To regulate them on account of their size, these companies argue, is simply to penalize them for their success in delivering to consumers what they want.

Given the explosive growth of the digital economy, it's arguable that the problem of how to manage the new generation of market power is one of the most difficult challenges facing economists and policy makers. As the following Economics in Action shows, as of the time of writing there are few clear answers.

ECONOMICS >> *in Action*

Are North American Antitrust Policy Makers Behind the Digital Times?

The digital giants — Google, Facebook, and Amazon — have presented difficult regulatory challenges for antitrust policy makers.

The digital giants, Amazon, Facebook, and Google, are the quintessential firms of the digital economy. Amazon, which began as an online retailer of books, has grown into a corporate behemoth: a general retailer, a marketing platform, a provider of delivery and logistical services, a payment service, a credit lender, an auction house, a major book publisher, a producer of television and films, a hardware manufacturer, a fashion creator, and a leading provider of cloud services and computing power.

Facebook is the world's dominant social platform, with nearly 2.6 billion active users as of 2020. Google accounts for 92% of global search engine activity. Together, Facebook and Google account for 73% of digital advertising in the United States (51% globally). In 2019, Amazon reported annual revenue of over US$280 billion; Facebook reported nearly US$71 billion; and Google reported US$162 billion. (This data was found using Google, written on a computer purchased on Amazon, while not looking at any open Facebook pages.)

But economists and historians have noted a striking feature of these three companies: each one has relied on practices that, in previous eras, were found to be either anti-competitive, or had created critical large-scale infrastructure that warranted regulation as a natural monopoly.

For example, all three firms have taken actions to eliminate rivals. Amazon has purchased a myriad of e-retailing companies—such as Audible, Diapers. com, and Zappos—to maintain its dominance as the one-stop shopping website. Likewise, Facebook has bought rival social-networking platforms Friendster, Instagram, and WhatsApp. According to EU antitrust authorities, Google has harmed competitors by requiring equipment manufacturers to install its search engine on their products.

Amazon's massive warehouse system of 175 warehouses across the world (with more than 100 in the United States alone), manned by fleets of robots, enables it to provide super-fast delivery. And the volume discounts it receives from delivery companies like UPS aren't available to smaller rivals. So goods suppliers, like Eveready Batteries, find it necessary to list their products on Amazon Marketplace. Yet, this enables Amazon to gather finely detailed data on customers' shopping habits, which they then can use to create their own "Amazon Basics" brand, which directly competes against the goods suppliers at lower prices. Finally, recent revelations about Facebook's use of its users' private data has led to calls for intervention.

So what explains U.S., Canadian and EU policy makers' lack of action?

One explanation for this inaction is that, like in the case of natural monopoly, policy makers understand that there is no easy fix to the problem of market dominance when there are network externalities. A second explanation is that policy makers don't think the firms are exploiting their dominant positions because there is no clear evidence that consumers are being charged monopoly prices and that output is being restricted. And it is certainly true that consumers have gained vast benefits from the three firms. A third explanation is that global policy makers fear that regulation could stifle innovation and thereby reduce society's welfare in the long run.

Yet, others are not so sanguine. According to some economists and historians, policy makers have a view of social welfare that is too restrictive. In the case of Amazon, they assert that the welfare of goods suppliers should also be taken into account along with that of consumers. They argue that Amazon's actions will eventually force some goods suppliers out of their markets, reducing innovation as well as the quality and diversity of products available, and allowing Amazon to eventually raise prices. For example, the parent company of Diapers.com rebuffed an offer from Amazon to buy the company in 2009. Amazon responded by creating its own brand of diapers and baby products, undercutting the prices on Diapers.com. So in 2010, the company gave in and allowed itself to be purchased by Amazon.

Also, economists and historians argue that the antitrust framework of the past doesn't take into account the enormous advantages that Amazon, Facebook, and Google have in acquiring and using their users' data in a way that reinforces their market dominance. In addition, they argue that in Amazon's case, its constantly fluctuating and personalized pricing system simply doesn't allow regulators the ability to monitor if Amazon is indeed inflating its prices. Finally, they raise the concern that the enormous economic weight of the digital giants will translate into outsized political power, making it harder to check their dominance and their exercise of market power. This echoes one of the primary concerns that led to the creation of U.S. and Canadian antitrust laws in the 1890s (which we will discuss in the next chapter).

So far, EU regulators have acted far more aggressively than U.S. and Canadian regulators. As of 2019, the EU had fined Google over US\$9 billion, claiming that it had abused its market dominance in several sectors, such as advertising and the Android operating system. The EU is currently weighing whether to charge Amazon with abusing its market dominance and data gathering ability against small suppliers. And it has moved against Facebook's lax handling of users' private data.

Are U.S. and Canadian policy makers moving too slowly? Or are EU policy makers moving too aggressively? At this point, the answer is unclear. Moreover, some observers say that despite the more active stance by EU policy makers, it's not clear that their actions will ultimately alter the firms' market dominance.

Whatever the ultimate policy stance, it's clear that antitrust policy will be a topic of intense debate for the foreseeable future.

>> Check Your Understanding 13-3

Solutions appear at back of book.

1. What policy should the government adopt in the following cases? Explain.
   a. Internet service in Anytown, Alberta, is provided by cable. Customers feel they are being overcharged, but the cable company claims it must charge prices that allow it to recover the costs of laying cable.
   b. The only two airlines that currently fly to Iqaluit, Nunavut need government approval to merge. Other airlines wish to fly to Iqaluit, Nunavut but need government-allocated landing slots to do so.
2. True or false? Explain your answer.
   a. Society's welfare is lower under monopoly because some consumer surplus is transformed into profit for the monopolist.
   b. A monopolist causes inefficiency because there are consumers who are willing to pay a price greater than or equal to marginal cost but less than the monopoly price.
3. Suppose a monopolist mistakenly believes that its marginal revenue is always equal to the market price. Assuming constant marginal cost and no fixed cost, draw a diagram comparing the level of profit, consumer surplus, total surplus, and deadweight loss for this misguided monopolist compared to a smart monopolist.
4. Some social media industry observers claim that Facebook is so dominant in the social media market that it is now like a utility, such as a water utility. What have you learned about monopoly that might validate this claim? What evidence might invalidate this claim?

>> Quick Review

• By reducing output and raising price above marginal cost, a monopolist captures some of the consumer surplus as profit and causes deadweight loss. To avoid deadweight loss, government policy attempts to curtail monopoly behaviour.

• When monopolies are "created" rather than natural, governments should act to prevent them from forming and break up existing ones.

• One method of managing natural monopoly is by **public ownership.** However, publicly owned companies are often poorly run. Another method is **price regulation.** A price ceiling imposed on a monopolist does not create shortages as long as it is not set too low.

• Owing to the rise of the digital economy, market power arising from network externalities has become a topic of intense debate as digital giants engage in monopoly and **monopsony** behaviour. A **monopsonist** can affect the price of the good it buys: it captures surplus from sellers by reducing how much it purchases and thereby lowers the price paid to the seller. Like a monopoly, it creates deadweight loss as too little output is produced.

• Because consumers benefit from bigger networks, market power arising from network externalities is a difficult challenge for policy makers. The digital giants can exercise market power, creating deadweight loss and stifling innovation by deterring rivals. Yet, the digital giants are also sources of innovation and are successful because consumers prefer them. Moreover, if they are broken up, dominant firms with market power are likely to reemerge.

A **single-price monopolist** offers its product to all consumers at the same price.

Sellers engage in **price discrimination** when they charge different prices to different consumers for the same good.

‖ Price Discrimination

Up to this point, we have considered only the case of a **single-price monopolist,** one that charges all consumers the same price. As the term suggests, not all monopolists do this. In fact, many if not most monopolists find that they can increase their profits by charging different customers different prices for the same good: they engage in **price discrimination.**

One of the most striking examples of price discrimination involves airline tickets. Although there are a number of airlines, most air routes in Canada are serviced by only one or two carriers. As a result, these carriers have market power and can set prices. So any regular airline passenger quickly becomes aware that the question "How much will it cost me to fly there?" rarely has a simple answer.

If you are willing to buy a nonrefundable ticket a month in advance and happen to purchase the ticket on Tuesday or Wednesday evening, the round trip may cost only $150—or less if you are a senior citizen or a student. But if you have to go on a business trip tomorrow, which happens to be Tuesday, and come back on Wednesday, the same round trip might cost $550. Yet the business traveller and the visiting grandparent receive the same product—the same cramped seat, the same awful food (if indeed any food is served).

You might argue that airlines are not usually monopolists—that in most flight markets the airline industry is an oligopoly because there is more than one firm offering flights to most destinations. In fact, price discrimination takes place under oligopoly and monopolistic competition as well as monopoly because these firms have some market power and can therefore influence prices. But it doesn't happen under perfect competition, where firms have no ability to influence prices. And once we've seen why monopolists sometimes price-discriminate, we'll be in a good position to understand why it happens in oligopoly and monopolistic competition, too.

The Logic of Price Discrimination

Let's begin by looking at why price discrimination might be more profitable than charging all consumers the same price. Imagine that Air Sunshine offers the only nonstop flights between Montreal and Toronto. Assume that there are no capacity problems—the airline can fly as many planes as the number of passengers warrants. Also assume that there is no fixed cost. The marginal cost to the airline of providing a seat is $125, however many passengers it carries. Further assume that the airline knows there are two kinds of potential passengers: 2,000 business travellers who want to travel between these destinations each week, and 2,000 students who want to do the same.

Will potential passengers take the flight? It depends on the price. The business travellers it turns out, really need to fly; they will take the plane as long as the price is no more than $550. Since they are flying purely for business, we assume that cutting the price below $550 will not lead to any increase in business travel. The students, however, have less money and more time; if the price goes above $150, they will take the bus. The implied demand curve is shown in Figure 13-10.

So what should the airline do? If it has to charge everyone the same price, its options are limited. It could charge $550; that way it would get as much as possible out of the business travellers but lose the student market. Or it could charge only $150; that way it would get both types of travellers but would make significantly less money from sales to business travellers.

We can quickly calculate the profits from each of these alternatives. If the airline charged $550, it would sell 2,000 tickets to the business travellers earning total revenue of 2,000 × $550 = $1.1 million and incurring costs of 2,000 × $125 = $250,000; so its profit would be $850,000, illustrated by the shaded area *B* in Figure 13-10.

FIGURE 13-10 Two Types of Airline Customers

Air Sunshine has two types of customers, business travellers willing to pay at most $550 per ticket and students willing to pay at most $150 per ticket. There are 2,000 of each kind of customer. Air Sunshine has a constant marginal cost of $125 per seat. If Air Sunshine could charge these two types of customers different prices, it would maximize its profit by charging business travellers $550 and students $150 per ticket. It would capture all of the consumer surplus as profit.

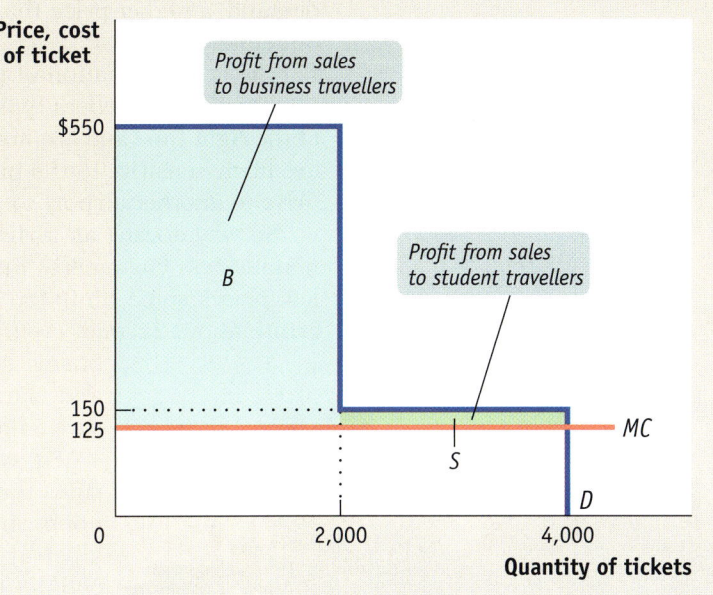

If the airline charged only $150, it would sell 4,000 tickets, receiving revenue of 4,000 × $150 = $600,000 and incurring costs of 4,000 × $125 = $500,000; in this case, its profit would be $100,000. If the airline must charge everyone the same price, charging the higher price and forgoing sales to students is clearly more profitable.

What the airline would really like to do, however, is charge the business travellers the full $550 but offer $150 tickets to the students. That's a lot less than the price paid by business travellers but it's still above marginal cost; so if the airline could sell those extra 2,000 tickets to students, it would make an additional $50,000 in profit. That is, it would make a profit equal to the areas *B* plus *S* in Figure 13-10.

It would be more realistic to suppose that there is some "give" in each group's demand: at a price below $550, there would be some increase in business travel; and at a price above $150, some students would still purchase tickets. But this, it turns out, does not do away with the argument for price discrimination.

The important point is that the two groups of consumers differ in their *sensitivity to price*—that a high price has a larger effect in discouraging purchases by students than purchases by business travellers. As long as different groups of customers respond differently to the price, a monopolist will find that it can capture more consumer surplus and increase its profit by charging them different prices.

Price Discrimination and Elasticity

A more realistic description of the demand that airlines face would not specify particular prices at which different types of travellers would choose to fly. Instead, it would distinguish between the groups on the basis of their sensitivity to the price—their price elasticity of demand.

Suppose that a company sells its product to two easily identifiable groups of people—business travellers and students. It just so happens that business travellers are very insensitive to the price: there is a certain amount of the product they just have to have whatever the price, but they cannot be persuaded to buy much more than that no matter how cheap it is. Students, though, are more flexible: offer a good enough price and they will buy quite a lot, but raise the price too high and they will switch to something else. What should the company do?

The answer is the one already suggested by our simplified example: the company should charge business travellers who have a low price elasticity of demand, a higher price than it charges students, who have a high price elasticity of demand.

The actual situation of the airlines is very much like this hypothetical example. Business travellers typically place a high priority on being at the right place at the right time and are not very sensitive to the price. But nonbusiness travellers are fairly sensitive to the price: faced with a high price, they might take the bus, drive to another airport to get a lower fare, or skip the trip altogether.

So why doesn't an airline simply announce different prices for business and nonbusiness customers? First, this would probably be illegal because Canadian law places some limits on the ability of companies to practice open price discrimination. Second, even if it were legal, it would be a hard policy to enforce: business travellers might be willing to wear casual clothing and claim they were visiting family in Montreal in order to save $400.

On many airline routes, the fare you pay depends on the type of traveller you are.

So what the airlines do—quite successfully—is impose rules that indirectly have the effect of charging business and nonbusiness travellers different fares. Business travellers usually travel during the week and want to be home on the weekend; so the round-trip fare is much higher if you don't stay over a Saturday night. The requirement of a weekend stay for a cheap ticket effectively separates business from nonbusiness travellers.

Similarly, business travellers often visit several cities in succession rather than make a simple round trip; so round-trip fares are much lower than twice the one-way fare. Many business trips are scheduled on short notice; so fares are much lower if you book far in advance. Fares are also lower if you purchase a last-minute ticket, taking your chances on whether you actually get a seat—business travellers have to make it to that meeting; people visiting their relatives don't.

Because customers must show their ID at check-in, airlines make sure there are no resales of tickets between the two groups that would undermine their ability to price-discriminate—students can't buy cheap tickets and resell them to business travellers. Look at the rules that govern ticket-pricing, and you will see an ingenious implementation of profit-maximizing price discrimination.

Perfect Price Discrimination

Let's return to the example of business travellers and students travelling between Toronto and Montreal, illustrated in Figure 13-10, and ask what would happen if the airline could distinguish between the two groups of customers to charge each a different price.

Clearly, the airline would charge each group its willingness to pay—that is, the maximum that each group is willing to pay. For business travellers, the willingness to pay is $550; for students, it is $150. As we have assumed, the marginal cost is $125 and does not depend on output, making the marginal cost curve a horizontal line. As we noted earlier, we can easily determine the airline's profit: it is the sum of the areas of the rectangle *B* and the rectangle *S*.

In this case, the consumers do not get any consumer surplus! The entire surplus is captured by the monopolist in the form of profit. When a monopolist is able to capture the entire surplus in this way, we say that it achieves **perfect price discrimination.**

In general, the greater the number of different prices a monopolist is able to charge, the closer it can get to perfect price discrimination. Figure 13-11 shows a monopolist facing a downward-sloping demand curve, a monopolist who we

Perfect price discrimination takes place when a monopolist charges each consumer their willingness to pay—the maximum that the consumer is willing to pay.

FIGURE 13-11 Price Discrimination

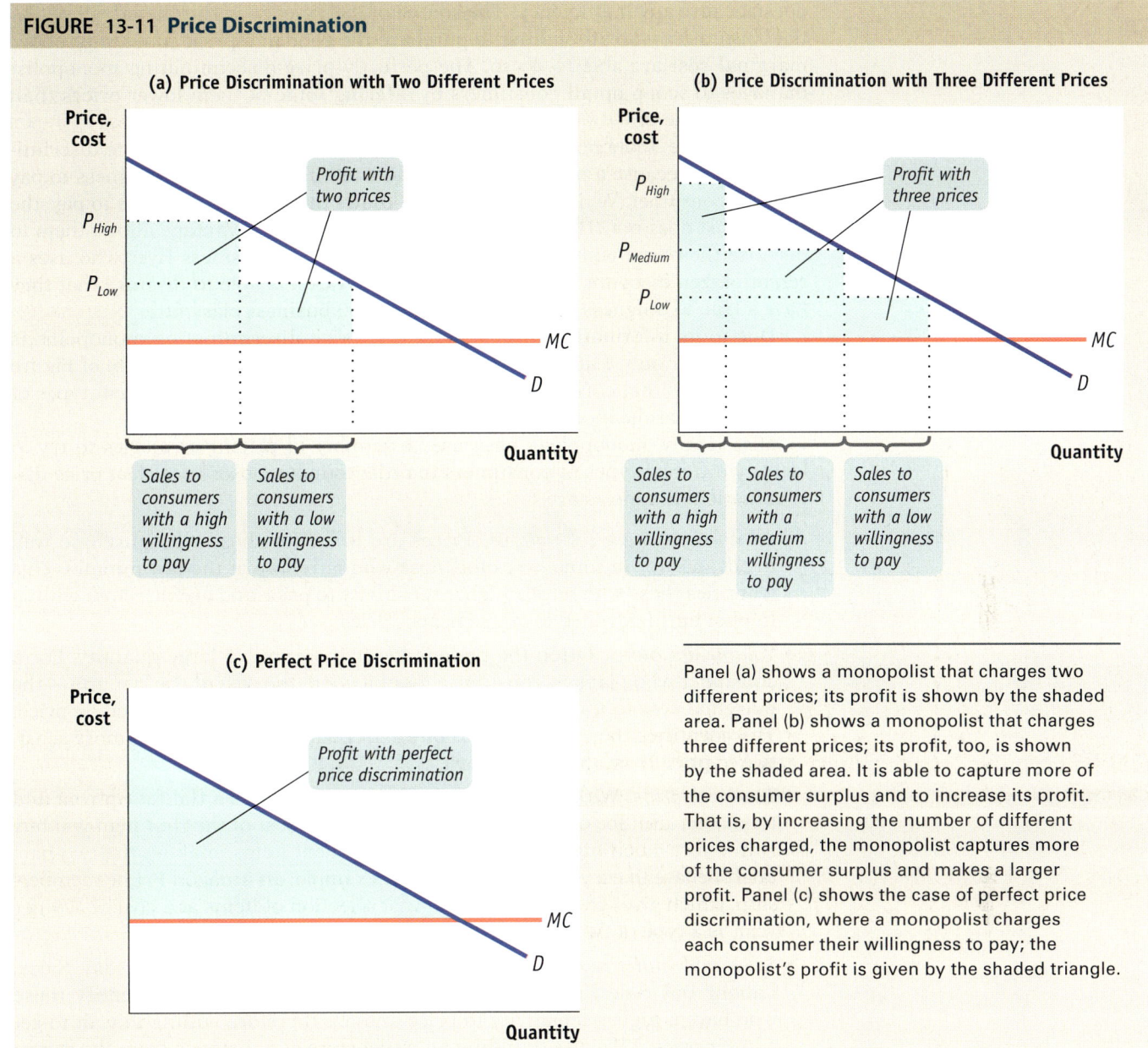

(a) Price Discrimination with Two Different Prices

Profit with two prices

P_{High}

P_{Low}

MC

D

Price, cost

Quantity

Sales to consumers with a high willingness to pay

Sales to consumers with a low willingness to pay

(b) Price Discrimination with Three Different Prices

P_{High}

P_{Medium}

P_{Low}

Profit with three prices

MC

D

Price, cost

Quantity

Sales to consumers with a high willingness to pay

Sales to consumers with a medium willingness to pay

Sales to consumers with a low willingness to pay

(c) Perfect Price Discrimination

Price, cost

Profit with perfect price discrimination

MC

D

Quantity

Panel (a) shows a monopolist that charges two different prices; its profit is shown by the shaded area. Panel (b) shows a monopolist that charges three different prices; its profit, too, is shown by the shaded area. It is able to capture more of the consumer surplus and to increase its profit. That is, by increasing the number of different prices charged, the monopolist captures more of the consumer surplus and makes a larger profit. Panel (c) shows the case of perfect price discrimination, where a monopolist charges each consumer their willingness to pay; the monopolist's profit is given by the shaded triangle.

assume is able to charge different prices to different groups of consumers, with the consumers who are willing to pay the most being charged the most.

In panel (a), the monopolist charges two different prices; in panel (b), the monopolist charges three different prices. Two things are apparent:

1. The greater the number of prices the monopolist charges, the lower the lowest price—that is, some consumers will pay prices that approach marginal cost.

2. The greater the number of prices the monopolist charges, the more money it extracts from consumers.

With a very large number of different prices, the picture would look like panel (c), a case of perfect price discrimination. Here, each consumer is charged their willingness to pay, the last consumer pays marginal cost, and the entire consumer surplus is extracted as profit.

Both our airline example and the example in Figure 13-11 can be used to make another point: a monopolist that can engage in perfect price discrimination doesn't cause any inefficiency! The source of inefficiency is eliminated: all potential consumers who are willing to purchase the good at a price equal to or above marginal cost are able to do so. The perfectly price-discriminating monopolist manages to scoop up all consumers by offering some of them lower prices than it charges others.

In practice, monopolists find it nearly impossible to perfectly price discriminate. That's because a monopolist is not able to know the true willingness to pay of every consumer. While each consumer knows their true willingness to pay, the monopolist does not. Thus the consumer's information advantage allows them to disguise their true willingness to pay. For example, a business flyer who uses a senior citizen discount when purchasing their ticket is able to disguise that they have a true willingness to pay equal to the $550 business class fare.

Due to its information disadvantage, the price-discriminating monopolist is forced to offer only a limited number of different prices (as in panel (b) of Figure 13-11)—prices that correspond to the willingness to pay of the different types of consumers that the monopolist can identify.

Historically, monopolists have used a number of pricing strategies to try to identify different types of consumers in order to move closer to perfect price discrimination. Examples are:

- *Advance purchase restrictions.* Prices are lower for those who purchase well in advance (or in some cases for those who purchase at the last minute). This identifies those who have a higher sensitivity to price and are therefore willing to plan far in advance to get a cheaper price.

- *Volume discounts.* Often the price is lower if you buy a large quantity. For a consumer who plans to consume a lot of a good, the cost of the last unit—the marginal cost to the consumer—is considerably less than the average price. This identifies those who plan to buy a lot and so are likely to be more sensitive to price from those who don't.

- *Two-part tariffs.* With a two-part tariff, a customer pays a flat fee upfront and then a per-unit fee on each item purchased. The cost of the first item you buy is in effect much higher than that of subsequent items, making the two-part tariff behave like a volume discount. For example, an Amazon Prime membership, which gives free shipping on a vast selection of items at a cost of $79 per year, is a type of two-part tariff.

- *Sales and outlet stores.* Holding regular sales such as Black Friday Sales, Labour Day Sales, Boxing Day Sales, and so on, is a way to identify those who have a higher sensitivity to price and are therefore willing to wait to get a lower price. Likewise, building an outlet store at a distance from the centre of the city allows the monopolist to establish a separate market for those customers who have a higher sensitivity to price and are therefore willing to drive a distance to get a lower price.

- *Digital personalized pricing.* The fastest-growing method of price discrimination is digital personalized pricing. By gathering personal data on shoppers' online choices and characteristics, online retailers can greatly reduce the information advantages that shoppers have about their true willingness to pay. For example, the online travel agency Orbitz discovered that Mac computer users spend as much as 30% more a night on hotels. So it shows them a fancier and costlier menu of hotels than it shows to PC users. Digital personalized pricing has the potential to achieve a closer approximation to perfect price discrimination than any other method because of its ability to collect and analyze very precise information about shoppers.

Compared to a single-price monopolist, price discrimination—even when it is not perfect—can increase the efficiency of the market. For example, with price discrimination, firms can sell to consumers who were formerly priced out of the market. Those who are now able to purchase the good at a lower price generate enough surplus to offset the loss in surplus to those now facing a higher price and no longer buying the good. In this way, total surplus increases when price discrimination is introduced. This explanation of price discrimination also helps explain why government policies on monopoly typically focus on preventing deadweight losses, not preventing price discrimination—unless it causes serious issues of equity.

For example, consider a drug that is disproportionately prescribed to senior citizens, who are often on fixed incomes and so are very sensitive to price. A policy that allows a drug company to charge senior citizens a low price and everyone else a high price may indeed increase total surplus. But price discrimination that creates serious concerns about equity is likely to be prohibited—for example, an ambulance service that charges patients based on the severity of their emergency.

>> Check Your Understanding   13-4

Solutions appear at back of book.

1. True or false? Explain your answer.
   a. A single-price monopolist sells to some customers that a price-discriminating monopolist refuses to.
   b. A price-discriminating monopolist creates more inefficiency than a single-price monopolist because it captures more of the consumer surplus.
   c. Under price discrimination, a customer with highly elastic demand will pay a lower price than a customer with inelastic demand.
2. Which of these are cases of price discrimination and which are not? In the cases of price discrimination, identify the consumers with high and those with low price elasticity of demand.
   a. Damaged merchandise is marked down.
   b. Restaurants have senior citizen discounts.
   c. Food manufacturers place discount coupons for their merchandise in newspapers.
   d. Airline tickets cost more during the summer peak flying season.

>> Quick Review

• Not every monopolist is a **single-price monopolist.** Many monopolists, as well as oligopolists and monopolistic competitors, engage in **price discrimination.**

• Price discrimination is profitable when consumers differ in their sensitivity to the price. A price-discriminating monopolist charges higher prices to low-elasticity consumers and lower prices to high-elasticity ones. The most widely used techniques are advance purchase restrictions; volume discounts; two-part tariffs; sales and outlet stores; and digital personalized pricing. Compared to a single-price monopoly, price discrimination reduces deadweight loss.

• Digital personalized pricing comes the closest to achieving **perfect price discrimination,** in which each consumer pays a price equal to their willingness to pay. This allows the monopolist to capture the total surplus in the market. No deadweight loss is incurred because all mutually beneficial transactions occur. Unless it causes serious equity issues, governments tend to focus on preventing deadweight loss and not preventing price discrimination.

Amazon and Hachette Go to War

Horacio Villalobos/Getty Images

In May 2014, all-out war broke out between Amazon, then the third largest U.S. book retailer, and Hachette, the fourth largest book publisher. Suddenly Amazon took weeks to deliver Hachette publications (paper and e-books), including best sellers from authors like Stephen Colbert, Dan Brown, and J. D. Salinger, meanwhile offering shoppers suggestions for non-Hachette books as alternatives. In addition, preorder options for forthcoming Hachette books—including one by J. K. Rowling of Harry Potter fame—disappeared from Amazon's website along with many other Hachette books. These same books were readily available, often at lower prices, at rival book retailers, such as Barnes and Noble.

All publishers pay retailers a share of sales prices. In this case, hostilities were set off by Amazon's demand that Hachette raise that share from 30% to 50%. This was a familiar story: Amazon demanded ever-larger percentages during yearly contract negotiations. Since it won't carry a publisher's books without an agreement, protracted disagreement and the resulting loss of sales are disastrous for publishers. This time, however, Hachette refused to give in and went public with Amazon's demands.

Amazon claimed that the publisher could pay more out of its profit margin—around 75% on e-books, 60% on paperbacks, and 40% on hardcovers. Indeed, Amazon openly admitted that its long-term objective was to displace publishers altogether, and deal directly with authors itself. This model has been popularized by companies like Netflix that are now producing their own media content. Amazon received support from some famous authors, including Dean Koontz and Michael Lewis. Ironically, publishers countered that Amazon's calculations ignored the costs of editing, marketing, advertising, and at times supporting struggling writers until they became successful; yet recently, Amazon has found success in publishing as many large publishers have cut their marketing and editing budgets. Amazon, they claimed, would eventually destroy the book industry, and now the publishing industry.

In the conflict, Amazon faced some very angry authors. Douglas Preston, a best-selling Hachette author of thrillers, saw his sales drop by at least 60%. Speaking of the comfortable lifestyle that his writing supported, Preston observed that if Amazon decided not to sell his books at all, "All this goes away." In the end, the conflict became a public relations disaster for Amazon as writers and even some readers turned against the company. So, Amazon eventually capitulated and agreed to allow Hachette to set the price of its e-books. However, given Amazon's size and influence, authors remain wary about the future.

In fact, a few years later, Amazon became the largest U.S. book retailer. This is largely due to Amazon's costly investments in its website and its vast warehouse and speedy delivery system, despite sometimes charging higher prices than rival websites. These upgrades have been funded by Amazon investors, who waited patiently for 20 years, incurring billions of dollars in losses. But 2015 was a turning point for Amazon. That year, the company made a small profit, and each year since, it has experienced increased profitability. In 2018, Amazon made over US$10 billion. The wait for its investors finally paid off. Over the same time period, Amazon's share price increased by nearly 500%.

QUESTIONS FOR THOUGHT

1. What is the source of surplus in this industry? Who generates it? How is it divided among the various agents (authors, publishers, and retailers)?

2. What are the various sources of market power here? What is at risk for the various parties?

SUMMARY

1. There are four main types of market structure based on the number of firms in the industry and product differentiation: perfect competition, monopoly, oligopoly, and monopolistic competition.

2. A **monopolist** is a producer who is the sole supplier of a good without close substitutes. An industry controlled by a monopolist is a **monopoly.**

3. The key difference between a monopoly and a perfectly competitive industry is that a single perfectly competitive firm faces a horizontal demand curve but a monopolist faces a downward-sloping demand curve. This gives the monopolist **market power,** the ability to raise the market price by reducing output compared to a perfectly competitive firm.

4. To persist, a monopoly must be protected by a **barrier to entry.** This can take the form of control of a natural resource or input, increasing returns to scale that give rise to **natural monopoly,** technological superiority, a **network externality,** or government rules that prevent entry by other firms, such as **patents** or **copyrights.** Neither technological superiority nor patents and copyrights provide long-term barriers to entry.

5. The marginal revenue of a monopolist is composed of a quantity effect (the price received from the additional unit) and a price effect (the reduction in the price at which all units are sold). Because of the price effect, a monopolist's marginal revenue is always less than the market price, and the marginal revenue curve lies below the demand curve.

6. At the monopolist's profit-maximizing output level, marginal cost equals marginal revenue, which is less than market price. At the perfectly competitive firm's profit-maximizing output level, marginal cost equals the market price. So in comparison to perfectly competitive industries, monopolies produce less, charge higher prices, and earn profits in both the short run and the long run.

7. A monopoly creates deadweight losses by charging a price above marginal cost: the loss in consumer surplus exceeds the monopolist's profit. The government should intervene to prevent the formation of monopolies that are created to exploit monopoly power and earn monopoly profits. If they already exist, the government should break them up. Monopolies based on government-created barriers and technological superiority will disappear over time. However, breaking up a natural monopoly will raise costs and reduce welfare.

8. Natural monopolies can still cause deadweight losses. To limit these losses, governments sometimes impose **public ownership** and at other times impose **price regulation.** A price ceiling on a monopolist, as opposed to a perfectly competitive industry, need not cause shortages and can increase total surplus.

9. How to manage market power arising from network externalities is a much-debated topic as digital giants engage in monopoly and **monopsony** behaviour. A **monopsonist**—the single buyer of a good in an industry—captures surplus from sellers by reducing its purchases and lowering the price paid to sellers. Too little output is produced and a deadweight loss is incurred.

10. Market power arising from network externalities poses a difficult policy problem because consumers benefit from bigger networks. On the one hand, market power imposes deadweight loss, and stifles innovation in fast-moving digital industries. On the other hand, the digital giants innovate as well, and are successful because consumers have preferred them. Moreover, given the dynamics of network externalities, if the digital giant is broken up, dominant firms with market power are likely to reemerge.

11. Not all monopolists are **single-price monopolists.** Monopolists, as well as oligopolists and monopolistic competitors, often engage in **price discrimination** to make higher profits, using various techniques to differentiate consumers based on their sensitivity to price, charging those with less elastic demand higher prices. Compared to a single-price monopoly, price discrimination reduces deadweight loss. The most widely used techniques are advance purchase restrictions; volume discounts; two-part tariffs; sales and outlet stores; and digital personalized pricing.

12. Digital personalized pricing comes the closest to achieving **perfect price discrimination,** in which each consumer pays a price equal to their willingness to pay. While the monopolist captures the total surplus in the market, no deadweight loss is incurred because all mutually beneficial transactions occur. Unless it causes serious equity issues, governments tend to focus on preventing deadweight loss and not preventing price discrimination.

KEY TERMS

PRACTICE QUESTIONS

1. Skyscraper City has a subway system, for which a one-way fare is $1.50. There is pressure on the mayor to reduce the fare by one-third, to $1.00. The mayor is dismayed, thinking that this will mean Skyscraper City is losing one-third of its revenue from sales of subway tickets. The mayor's economic adviser reminds her that she is focusing only on the price effect and ignoring the quantity effect. Explain why the mayor's estimate of a one-third loss of revenue is likely to be an overestimate. Illustrate with a diagram.

2. This diagram illustrates your local electric company's natural monopoly. It shows the demand curve for kilowatt-hours (kWh) of electricity, the company's marginal revenue (MR) curve, its marginal cost (MC) curve, and its average total cost (ATC) curve. The government wants to regulate the monopolist by imposing a price ceiling.

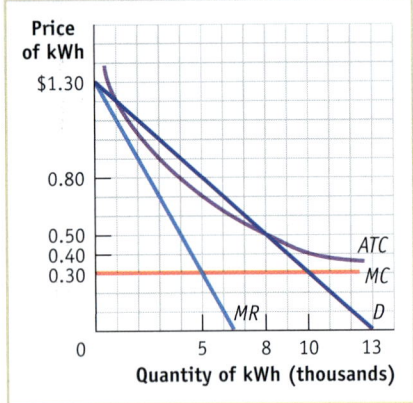

a. If the government does not regulate this monopolist, which price will it charge? Illustrate the inefficiency this creates by shading the deadweight loss from monopoly.

b. If the government imposes a price ceiling equal to the marginal cost, $0.30, will the monopolist make profits or lose money? Shade the area of profit (or loss) for the monopolist. If the government does impose this price ceiling, do you think the firm will continue to produce in the long run?

c. If the government imposes a price ceiling of $0.50, will the monopolist make a profit, lose money, or break even?

3. A monopolist knows that in order to expand the quantity of output it produces from 8 to 9 units it must lower the price of its output from $2 to $1. Calculate the quantity effect and the price effect. Use these results to calculate the monopolist's marginal revenue of producing the 9th unit. The marginal cost of producing the 9th unit is positive. Is it a good idea for the monopolist to produce the 9th unit?

4. Explain the following situations.

a. In Europe, when a service contract is purchased, many cell phone service providers give away for free what would otherwise be very expensive cell service. Why might a company want to do that?

b. In England, the country's antitrust authority prohibited the cell phone service provider Vodafone from offering a plan that gave customers free calls to other Vodafone customers. Why might Vodafone have wanted to offer these calls for free? Why might a government want to step in and ban this practice? Why might it not be a good idea for a government to interfere in this way?

5. For people with life-threatening allergies, carrying a device that can automatically inject epinephrine (called an *autoinjector*) is a necessity. In the summer of 2016, Mylan, the maker of the widely used autoinjector EpiPen, found itself with a virtual monopoly. A year earlier its primary competitor, Auvi-Q, was recalled amid fears that it would malfunction and deliver the wrong dose. In addition, the U.S. Food and Drug Administration (FDA) denied a third drug producer, Teva, from releasing a generic autoinjector. Prior to these events, a two-pack EpiPen sold for approximately US$100. But during that summer, Mylan raised the price to over US$600 per pack, leading to extensive news coverage, popular online petitions, and outrage on the part of consumers. Mylan countered that many consumers received their EpiPens through their medical insurance, hence they were protected from the price increase. For those who didn't have insurance coverage and had to pay the full price, Mylan offered a US$300 savings card.

a. Draw a graph that shows consumer and producer surplus in a competitive market for epinephrine autoinjectors. Assume firms have a constant marginal cost of US$100 per pack.

b. Next, using that graph, show how much consumer surplus, producer surplus, and deadweight loss change after the Auvi-Q recall and the denied entry of Teva by the U.S. FDA.

c. How is the savings card offered to those without insurance an example of price discrimination? (*Hint:* Patients who are covered by medical insurance are like consumers who have high incomes and can therefore afford to pay full price.) Draw a graph showing how consumer and producer surplus will change under the savings card program.

PROBLEMS

1. Each of the following firms possesses market power. Explain its source.

   a. Merck, the producer of the patented cholesterol-lowering drug Zetia

   b. Waterworks, a provider of piped water

   c. Chiquita, a supplier of bananas and owner of most banana plantations

   d. The Walt Disney Company, the creators of Mickey Mouse

2. Bob, Bill, Ben, and Brad Baxter have just made a documentary movie about their basketball team. They are thinking about making the movie available for download on the internet, and they can act as a single-price monopolist if they choose to. Each time the movie is downloaded, their internet service provider charges them a fee of $4. The Baxter brothers are arguing about which price to charge customers per download. The accompanying table shows the demand schedule for their film.

Price of download	Quantity of downloads demanded
$10	0
8	1
6	3
4	6
2	10
0	15

   a. Calculate the total revenue and the marginal revenue per download.

   b. Bob is proud of the film and wants as many people as possible to download it. Which price would he choose? How many downloads would be sold?

   c. Bill wants as much total revenue as possible. Which price would he choose? How many downloads would be sold?

   d. Ben wants to maximize profit. Which price would he choose? How many downloads would be sold?

   e. Brad wants to charge the efficient price. Which price would he choose? How many downloads would be sold?

3. Mateo's room overlooks a major league baseball stadium. He decides to rent a telescope for $50.00 a week and charge his friends to use it to peep at the games for 30 seconds. He can act as a single-price monopolist for renting out "peeps." For each person who takes a 30-second peep, it costs Mateo $0.20 to clean the eyepiece. The accompanying table shows the information Mateo has gathered about the weekly demand for the service.

Price of peep	Quantity of peeps demanded
$1.20	0
1.00	100
0.90	150
0.80	200
0.70	250
0.60	300
0.50	350
0.40	400
0.30	450
0.20	500
0.10	550

   a. For each price in the table, calculate the total revenue from selling peeps and the marginal revenue per peep.

   b. At what quantity will Mateo's profit be maximized? What price will he charge? What will his total profit be?

   c. Mateo's landlady complains about all the visitors and tells him to stop selling peeps. But, if he pays her $0.20 for every peep he sells, she won't complain. What effect does the $0.20-per-peep bribe have on Mateo's marginal cost per peep? What is the new profit-maximizing quantity of peeps? What effect does the $0.20-per-peep bribe have on Mateo's total profit?

4. Suppose that De Beers is a single-price monopolist in the diamond market. De Beers has five potential customers: Raquel, Jackie, Jake, Elijah, and Jordan. Each of these customers will buy at most one diamond—and only if the price is just equal to, or lower than, their willingness to pay. Raquel's willingness to pay is $400; Jackie's, $300; Jake's, $200; Elijah's, $100; and Jordan's, $0. De Beers's marginal cost per diamond is $100. The result is a demand schedule for diamonds as follows:

Price of diamond	Quantity of diamonds demanded
$500	0
400	1
300	2
200	3
100	4
0	5

   a. Calculate De Beers's total revenue and its marginal revenue. From your calculation, draw the demand curve and the marginal revenue curve.

   b. Explain why De Beers faces a downward-sloping demand curve and why the marginal revenue from an additional diamond sale is less than the price of the diamond.

c. Suppose De Beers currently charges $200 for its diamonds. If it lowers the price to $100, how large is the price effect? How large is the quantity effect?

d. Add the marginal cost curve to your diagram from part a and determine which quantity maximizes De Beers's profit and which price De Beers will charge.

5. Use the demand schedule for diamonds given in Problem 4. The marginal cost of producing diamonds is constant at $100. There is no fixed cost.

a. If De Beers charges the monopoly price, how large is the individual consumer surplus that each buyer experiences? Calculate total consumer surplus by summing the individual consumer surpluses. How large is producer surplus?

Suppose that upstart Russian and Asian producers enter the market and it becomes perfectly competitive.

b. What is the perfectly competitive price? What quantity will be sold in this perfectly competitive market?

c. At the competitive price and quantity, how large is the consumer surplus that each buyer experiences? How large is total consumer surplus? How large is producer surplus?

d. Compare your answer to part c to your answer to part a. How large is the deadweight loss associated with monopoly in this case?

6. Use the demand schedule for diamonds given in Problem 4. De Beers is a monopolist, but it can now price-discriminate perfectly among all five of its potential customers. De Beers's marginal cost is constant at $100. There is no fixed cost.

a. If De Beers can price-discriminate perfectly, to which customers will it sell diamonds and at what prices?

b. How large is each individual consumer surplus? How large is total consumer surplus? Calculate producer surplus by summing the producer surplus generated by each sale.

7. Download Records decides to release an album by the group Mary and the Little Lamb. It produces the album with no fixed cost, but the total cost of creating a digital album and paying Mary her royalty is $6 per album. Download Records can act as a single-price monopolist. Its marketing division finds that the demand schedule for the album is as shown in the accompanying table.

Price of album	Quantity of albums demanded
$22	0
20	1,000
18	2,000
16	3,000
14	4,000
12	5,000
10	6,000
8	7,000

a. Calculate the total revenue and the marginal revenue per album.

b. The marginal cost of producing each album is constant at $6. To maximize profit, what level of output should Download Records choose, and which price should it charge for each album?

c. Mary renegotiates her contract and will be paid a higher royalty per album. So the marginal cost rises to be constant at $14. To maximize profit, what level of output should Download Records now choose, and which price should it charge for each album?

8. The Collegetown movie theatre serves 900 students and 100 professors in town. Each student's willingness to pay for a movie ticket is $5. Each professor's willingness to pay is $10. Each will buy only one ticket. The movie theatre's marginal cost per ticket is constant at $3, and there is no fixed cost.

a. Suppose the movie theatre cannot price-discriminate and charges both students and professors the same price per ticket. If the movie theatre charges $5, who will buy tickets and what will the movie theatre's profit be? How large is consumer surplus?

b. If the movie theatre charges $10, who will buy movie tickets and what will the movie theatre's profit be? How large is consumer surplus?

c. Assume the movie theatre can price-discriminate between students and professors by requiring students to show their student ID. If the movie theatre charges students $5 and professors $10, how much profit will the movie theatre make? How large is consumer surplus?

9. In Canada, the Competition Bureau is charged with promoting competition and challenging mergers that would likely lead to higher prices. Several years ago, Staples and Office Depot (the owner of Grand and Toy), two of the largest office supply superstores in North America, announced their agreement to merge.

a. Some critics of the merger argued that, in many parts of the country, a merger between the two companies would create a monopoly in the office supply superstore market. Based on the Competition Bureau's argument and its mission to challenge mergers that would likely lead to higher prices, do you think it allowed the merger?

b. Staples and Office Depot argued that, while in some parts of the country they might create a monopoly in the office supply superstore market, the Competition Bureau should consider the larger market for all office supplies, which includes many smaller stores that sell office supplies (such as grocery stores and other retailers). In that market, Staples and Office Depot would face competition from many other, smaller stores. If the market for all office supplies is the relevant market that the Competition Bureau should consider, would it make the Competition Bureau more or less likely to allow the merger?

10. Prior to 1999, the same company that generated electricity in Ontario also distributed it over high-voltage lines. But then the provincial government separated the generation from the distribution of electricity, allowing competition among electricity generators, while electricity distributors remained regulated.

    a. Assume that the market for electricity distribution was and remains a natural monopoly. Use a graph to illustrate the market for electricity distribution if the government sets price equal to average total cost.

    b. Assume that deregulation of electricity generation creates a perfectly competitive market. Also assume that electricity generation does not exhibit the characteristics of a natural monopoly. Use a graph to illustrate the cost curves in the long-run equilibrium for an individual firm in this industry.

11. In 2014, U.S. telecommunications companies Time Warner and Comcast announced their intention to merge. This prompted questions of monopoly because the combined company would supply cable access to an overwhelming majority of Americans. It also raised questions of monopsony since the combined company would be virtually the only purchaser of programming for broadcast shows. Although the merger was ultimately disallowed, assume that it had occurred. In each of the following, determine whether it is evidence of monopoly, monopsony, or neither.

    a. The monthly cable fee for consumers increases significantly more than the increase in the cost of producing and delivering programs over cable.

    b. Companies that advertise on cable TV find that they must pay higher rates for advertising.

    c. Companies that produce broadcast shows find they must produce more shows for the same amount they were paid before.

    d. Consumers find that there are more shows available for the same monthly cable fee.

12. Walmart is the world's largest retailer. As a consequence, it has sufficient bargaining power to push its suppliers to lower their prices so it can honour its slogan of "Save Money. Live Better" for its customers.

    a. Is Walmart acting like a monopolist or monopsonist when purchasing goods from suppliers? Explain.

    b. How does Walmart affect the consumer surplus of its customers? The producer surplus of its suppliers?

    c. Over time, what is likely to happen to the quality of products produced by Walmart suppliers?

13. The market demand for recorders (a simple musical instrument) in Hamelin is given by the following graph. Currently, Pied Piping is the single seller in Hamelin.

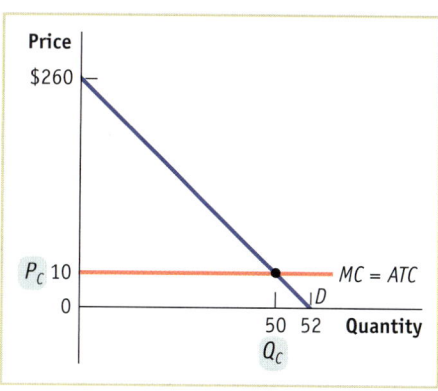

Note: Be sure to show your work and do not round your answers.

    a. At what level of output and price does Pied Piping maximize its profit? What is the deadweight loss in the market for recorders?

    b. In an attempt to increase output, the government decides to regulate the industry through an average cost pricing. What are the price charged and quantity sold by the monopolist after the regulation?

    c. What is the deadweight loss after the regulation? What is the change in consumer surplus?

14. This question uses the algebraic method to solve problems from Appendix 3A and Appendix 6A. The market of widgets is characterized by a single seller. The market demand and the firm's total cost are given by:

$$P = 150 - Q \qquad \text{Demand Curve}$$
$$TC = 475 + 50Q \qquad \text{Cost Function}$$

where P is the price per widget and Q is the number of widgets. The firm has fixed costs of \$475, and a constant variable cost of production equal to \$50 per unit made. The marginal cost is always \$50 for another widget.

    a. Determine the profit maximizing price and quantity. What are the firm's profit, the consumer surplus, and the deadweight loss?

    b. Suppose the government decides to regulate the firm through price regulation. The government is considering either marginal cost pricing or average cost pricing. Calculate the following items under each proposal:

       i. Price charged

       ii. Quantity produced

       iii. Firm's profit

       iv. Consumer surplus

       v. Deadweight loss

    c. You are asked to make a recommendation on which proposal—marginal cost pricing or average cost pricing—the government should adopt. What kind of recommendation would you give? Explain.

15. This question uses the algebraic method to solve problems from Appendix 3A and Appendix 6A. Suppose the Potash Corporation of Saskatchewan (PotashCorp) is the sole producer of the fertilizer, potash, in the Canadian market. The market demand and PotashCorp's total cost are given by:

$$P = 1,750 - 6Q \qquad \text{Demand Curve}$$
$$TC = 11,400 + 550Q \qquad \text{Cost Function}$$

where P is the price per tonne of potash and Q is the quantity in tonnes.

Note: Round your answer to two decimal places where needed. Be sure to show your work.

a. Determine the quantity produced and price charged by PotashCorp if it is an unregulated monopoly.

b. Determine the deadweight loss in the market if PotashCorp is an unregulated monopoly.

c. Suppose the federal government decides to regulate the industry to decrease the deadweight loss associated with this monopoly. The new regulation requires PotashCorp to adopt average cost pricing. What will be the price charged by PotashCorp? What is the change in total surplus?

WORK IT OUT

16. Consider an industry with the demand curve (D) and marginal cost curve (MC) shown in the accompanying diagram. There is no fixed cost. If the industry is a single-price monopoly, the monopolist's marginal revenue curve would be MR. Answer the following questions by naming the appropriate points or areas.

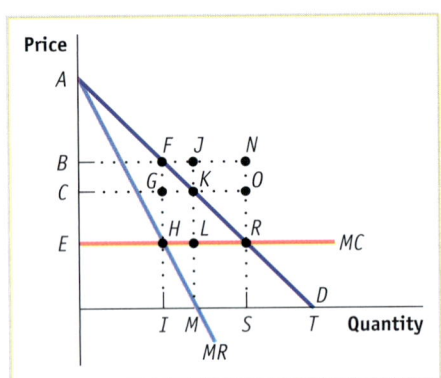

a. If the industry is perfectly competitive, what will be the total quantity produced? At what price?

b. Which area reflects consumer surplus under perfect competition?

c. If the industry is a single-price monopoly, what quantity will the monopolist produce? Which price will it charge?

d. Which area reflects the single-price monopolist's profit?

e. Which area reflects consumer surplus under single-price monopoly?

f. Which area reflects the deadweight loss to society from single-price monopoly?

g. If the monopolist can price-discriminate perfectly, what quantity will the perfectly price-discriminating monopolist produce? ■

14 Oligopoly

DEFLATING THE BREAD DOUGH

WHEN YOU GO GROCERY SHOPPING, you probably find that your grocery bills are getting higher and higher over time. You might also notice some product prices are rising at a much faster rate than others. For example, the price of food purchased from stores rose by a total of 45% between 2001 and 2015; however, the price of bakery products such as bread, rolls, and buns rose by a shocking 96% over the same period. What happened in the bread market? Was there a change in the Canadian diet that we drastically ate more bread? Or, did we experience a shortage of bread? The answer to the last two questions is not really.

In 2015, it was exposed to the public that Canada Bread and Weston Bakeries plus five grocery chains engaged in a price-fixing scheme on bread.

Indeed, what happened in Canada's bread market was the two largest bread producers, Canada Bread and Weston Bakeries, along with five grocery chains (Loblaws, Walmart Canada, Sobeys, Metro, and Giant Tiger) collaborated in an extensive price-fixing scheme that made Canadians pay at least $1.50 more for a loaf of bread over a 14-year period. According to the Competition Bureau, a federal agency that is responsible for Canada's competition policy, these companies agreed to boost the price of bread on at least 15 occasions, and each time they pushed the price up by about 10 cents. These companies were engaging in price-fixing — an arrangement between competing sellers to push prices up and keep them high — an illegal act in Canada.

The deal ended in 2015 when Loblaw, along with its parent company, George Weston, came forward to regulators about their participation in this industry-wide price-fixing scheme and cooperated in the investigation in exchange for immunity from criminal charges or penalties for violating the Competition Act, Canada's antitrust laws. However, when the news got out in late 2017 and early 2018, it sparked significant outrage among Canadians. To calm public anger and make up for its diminished reputation, Loblaw offered a $25 gift card to eligible Canadian households.

What the companies were doing was illegal. To understand why it was illegal and why the companies were doing it anyway, we need to examine the issues posed by industries that are neither perfectly competitive nor purely monopolistic. Oligopoly is a type of market structure in which there are only a few producers. In the real world, oligopoly occurs much more frequently than monopoly. And it is arguably more typical of modern economies than perfect competition.

The problems posed by oligopoly keep the regulators busy. Among other things, firms in an oligopoly are often tempted to engage in the kind of behaviour that got them into trouble with the law. Over the past few years, there have been numerous investigations and some convictions for price-fixing in a variety of industries, from insurance to elevators, and from chocolate bars to computer chips. For example, the Competition Bureau extracted fines totalling $23.2 million from four of the largest chocolate producers (Cadbury, Hershey, Nestlé, and Mars) in Canada for price-fixing.

When there are only a few producers in an industry, as is the case with oligopoly, the issue of *strategic behaviour* arises: how one firm behaves affects the behaviour of other firms. Because firms can affect each other's behaviour, they are tempted to coordinate their actions, or *collude*, in order to stifle competition and raise profits, as Weston Bakeries and its co-conspirators did. As a result of this behaviour, regulators often intervene in oligopolistic industries to protect consumers.

In this chapter, we begin by examining what oligopoly is and why it is so important. Then we turn to the behaviour of oligopolistic industries. Finally, we look at *antitrust policy,* which is adopted by regulators to maintain competition in oligopolistic industries, thereby keeping oligopolies "well behaved." ●

WHAT YOU WILL LEARN

• What is **oligopoly** and why does it occur?

• Why do **oligopolists** benefit from **collusion** and how are consumers hurt by it?

• How do the insights gained from **game theory** help us to understand the strategic behaviour of oligopolists?

• Why is **antitrust policy,** policy which is aimed at preventing collusion among oligopolists, a critical function of government?

An **oligopoly** is an industry with only a small number of producers. A producer in such an industry is known as an **oligopolist.**

When no one firm has a monopoly, but producers nonetheless realize that they can affect market prices, an industry is characterized by **imperfect competition.**

‖ The Prevalence of Oligopoly

At the time of the alleged price-fixing, no one company controlled the Canadian bread industry, but there were only a few major producers. An industry with only a few sellers is known as an **oligopoly;** a firm in such an industry is known as an **oligopolist.**

Oligopolists obviously compete with one another for sales. But neither Weston Bakeries nor Canada Bread was like a firm in a perfectly competitive industry, which takes the price at which it can sell its product as given. Each of these firms knew that its decision about how much to produce would affect the market price. That is, like monopolists, each of the firms had some *market power*. So the competition in this industry wasn't "perfect."

Economists refer to a situation in which firms compete but also possess market power—which enables them to affect market prices—as **imperfect competition.** As we saw in Chapter 13, there are actually two important forms of imperfect competition: oligopoly and *monopolistic competition*. Of these, oligopoly is probably the more important in practice.

The multibillion-dollar bread business is not the only oligopoly in Canada. Many other goods and services—some familiar, others not—are supplied by only a few competing sellers, which means the industries in question are oligopolies. For example, most air routes are served by only two or three airlines: in recent years, regularly scheduled shuttle service between Toronto and Calgary or Vancouver has been provided only by Air Canada and WestJet. Most chocolate bars are produced by Cadbury, Hershey, Nestlé, and Mars. Most cola beverages are sold by Coca-Cola and Pepsi. This list could go on for several more pages.

It's important to realize that an oligopoly isn't necessarily made up of large firms. What matters isn't size per se; the question is how many competitors there are. When a small town has only two grocery stores, grocery service there is just as much an oligopoly as air shuttle service between Toronto and Calgary.

Why are oligopolies so prevalent? Essentially, oligopoly is the result of some of the same factors that sometimes produce monopoly, but in weaker form. The most important source of oligopoly is the existence of *increasing returns to scale*, which give bigger producers a cost advantage over smaller ones. When these effects are very strong, they lead to monopoly; when they are moderately strong, they lead to an industry with a small number of firms.

For example, larger grocery stores typically have lower costs than smaller ones. But the advantages of large scale taper off once grocery stores are reasonably large, which is why two or three stores often survive in small towns.

If oligopoly is so common, why has most of this book focused on competition in industries where the number of sellers is very large? And why did we study monopoly, which is relatively uncommon, first? The answer has two parts.

First, much of what we learn from the study of perfectly competitive markets—about costs, entry and exit, and efficiency—remains valid despite the fact that many industries are not perfectly competitive. Second, the analysis of oligopoly rests on the notion of *interdependence* between firms—in oligopoly, the actions of one firm directly affect other firms within the industry. When firms are interdependent, there are a multitude of different possible outcomes depending upon how the firms behave. This is unlike either perfect competition and monopoly, where there will be one rational choice for a firm and one market equilibrium. So by studying perfect competition and monopoly before oligopoly, we are following a rule that is generally good to follow: first, deal with the questions you can easily answer (perfect competition and monopoly), and then address the harder ones (oligopoly).

ECONOMICS >> *in Action*

Is It a Beer-opoly or Not?

In practice, it's not always easy to determine an industry's market structure by looking solely at the number of producers. The market for beer is one example: although there are dozens of beer brewers, many of them are small niche producers (makers of craft beer), leaving the overall market dominated by two very large brewers. Molson Coors Beverage Company and Anheuser-Busch InBev account for 33.3% and 16.5%, respectively, of Canadian beer sales. You can see the distribution of brewers in Figure 14-1.

So, economists often use a measure called the *Herfindahl–Hirschman Index*, or HHI, to gauge the nature of competition in a given industry. The HHI for an industry is calculated as the square of each firm's market share summed over the firms in the industry. (We defined *market share* in Chapter 12.) For example, according to a survey by IBISWorld, the market shares of the three largest breweries in Canada were 33.3%, 16.5%, and 3.9%, the HHI for the industry is

$$HHI = 33.3^2 + 16.5^2 + 3.9^2 = 1,396$$

By squaring each market share, the HHI is much larger when the industry is dominated by a small number of firms, making it a better measure of how concentrated an industry is.

The HHI is used in the United States by the Justice Department and the Federal Trade Commission (FTC), which have the job of enforcing antitrust policy, a topic we investigate in more detail later in this chapter. The mission of these organizations is to try to ensure that there is adequate competition in an industry by prosecuting price-fixing, breaking up economically inefficient monopolies, and disallowing mergers between firms when it's believed that the merger will reduce competition. According to U.S. Justice Department guidelines, an HHI below 1,500 indicates a strongly competitive market, between 1,500 and 2,500 indicates a somewhat competitive market, and over 2,500 indicates an oligopoly. In an industry with an HHI over 1,500, a merger that results in a significant increase in the HHI will receive special scrutiny and is likely to be disallowed. If applying the U.S. Justice Department guidelines, the Canadian beer industry would be considered a competitive market.

However, defining an industry can be tricky, so rough rules of thumb are not appropriate for all situations. As a result, while the Canadian Competition Bureau may study changes in the HHI as a sign of changes in the level of competition, it does not employ rule-of-thumb ranges of "good" or "bad" levels for the index. Between 2013 and 2015, the government allowed Telus to buy Public Mobile, Rogers to buy Mobilicity, and Shaw to buy Wind Mobile. These mergers were allowed even though these three firms were allowed to enter the Canadian wireless communications market in 2008 to create additional competition in this highly concentrated industry, with an HHI of about 3,155 at that time. Another consideration when deciding whether an industry is an oligopoly is access to the market by external suppliers. For example, in 2009, sugar manufacturing in Ontario had an HHI of 8,569, while for all of Canada the HHI was 4,936. Both denote a high degree of market concentration, which might imply low levels of competition. But thanks to imports of sugar produced outside of Canada, the degree of competition is actually much higher than the HHI might imply, resulting in Canadian sugar prices actually being below those in the United States and Mexico.

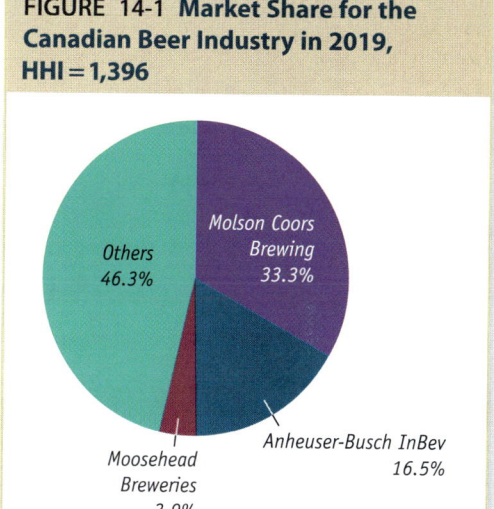

FIGURE 14-1 Market Share for the Canadian Beer Industry in 2019, HHI = 1,396

Others 46.3%

Molson Coors Brewing 33.3%

Moosehead Breweries 3.9%

Anheuser-Busch InBev 16.5%

Data from: IBISWorld.

When a firm's decision significantly affects the profits of other firms in the industry, the firms are in a situation of **interdependence.**

An oligopoly consisting of only two firms is a **duopoly.** Each firm is known as a **duopolist.**

Sellers engage in **collusion** when they cooperate to raise their joint profits. A **cartel** is an agreement among several producers to obey output restrictions in order to increase their joint profits.

>> Check Your Understanding 14-1

Solutions appear at back of book.

1. Explain why each of the following industries is an oligopoly, not a perfectly competitive industry.
   a. The world oil industry, where a few countries near the Persian Gulf control much of the world's oil reserves
   b. The microprocessor industry, where two firms, Intel and its bitter rival AMD, dominate the technology
   c. The wide-body passenger jet industry, composed of the American firm Boeing and the European firm Airbus, where production is characterized by extremely large fixed costs
2. The accompanying table shows the market shares for search engines in 2020 in Canada.
   a. Calculate the HHI in this industry.
   b. If Yahoo! and Bing were to merge, what would the HHI be?

Search engine	Market share
Google	92.0%
Bing/Microsoft	4.7
Yahoo!/Verizon Media	2.2
DuckDuckGo	0.8

‖ Understanding Oligopoly

Oligopolists can behave very differently than firms in other types of market structure because they operate in a state of **interdependence.** This means that the pricing and production decisions of one firm significantly affect the profits of its rivals. To begin to understand how oligopolies think and behave, we will start with an example.

A Duopoly Example

We'll now examine the simplest version of oligopoly, an industry in which there are only two producing firms—a **duopoly**—and each is known as a **duopolist.**

Going back to our opening story, imagine that there are only two producers of loaves of bread, Weston Bakeries and Canada Bread. To make things simpler, suppose that once a company has incurred the fixed cost needed to produce loaves of bread, the marginal cost of producing another loaf of bread is zero. So the companies are concerned only with the revenue they receive from sales, and not with their costs.

Table 14-1 shows a hypothetical demand schedule for loaves of bread and the total revenue of the industry at each price–quantity combination.

If this were a perfectly competitive industry, each firm would have an incentive to produce more as long as the market price was above marginal cost. Since the marginal cost is assumed to be zero, this would mean that at equilibrium loaves of bread would be provided free. Firms would produce until price equals zero, yielding a total output of 120 million loaves of bread and zero revenue for both firms.

Yet, surely the firms would not be that stupid. With only two firms in the industry, each would realize that by producing more, it drives down the market price. So each firm would, like a monopolist, realize that profits would be higher if it and its rival limited their production.

So how much will the two firms produce?

One possibility is that the two companies will engage in **collusion**—they will cooperate to raise their joint profits. The strongest form of collusion is a **cartel,** an arrangement between producers that determines how much each is allowed

TABLE 14-1 Demand Schedule for Bread

Price of loaf	Quantity of loaves demanded (millions)	Total revenue (millions)
$12	0	$0
11	10	110
10	20	200
9	30	270
8	40	320
7	50	350
6	60	360
5	70	350
4	80	320
3	90	270
2	100	200
1	110	110
0	120	0

to produce. The world's most famous cartel is the Organization of the Petroleum Exporting Countries (OPEC), described in an Economics in Action later in the chapter.

As its name indicates, OPEC is actually an agreement among governments rather than firms. There's a reason this cartel is an agreement among governments: cartels among firms are illegal in Canada and many other jurisdictions. But let's ignore the law for a moment (which is, of course, what Weston Bakeries did in real life—to its detriment).

Let's illustrate with an example of a cartel formed by only two firms, Weston Bakeries and Canada Bread. We'll assume that this cartel decided to act as if it were a monopolist, maximizing total industry profits. It's obvious from Table 14-1 that in order to maximize the combined profits of the two firms, the cartel should set total industry output at 60 million loaves of bread, which would sell at a price of $6 per loaf of bread, leading to revenue of $360 million, the maximum possible.

Then the only question would be how much of that 60 million loaves of bread each firm gets to produce. A fair solution might be for each firm to produce 30 million loaves of bread with revenues for each firm of $180 million.

But even if the two firms agreed on such a deal, they might have a problem: each of the firms would have an incentive to break its word and produce more than the agreed-upon quantity.

Collusion and Competition

Suppose that the presidents of Weston Bakeries and Canada Bread were to agree that each would produce 30 million loaves of bread over the next year. Both would understand that this plan maximizes their combined profits. And both would have an incentive to cheat.

To see why, consider what would happen if Canada Bread honoured its agreement, producing only 30 million loaves of bread, but Weston Bakeries ignored its promise and produced 40 million loaves of bread. This increase in total output would drive the price down from $6 to $5 per loaf of bread, the price at which 70 million loaves of bread are demanded. The industry's total revenue would fall from $360 million ($6 × 60 million loaves of bread) to $350 million ($5 × 70 million loaves of bread). However, Weston Bakeries's revenue would *rise*, from $180 million ($6 × 30 million loaves of bread) to $200 million ($5 × 40 million loaves of bread). Since we are assuming a marginal cost of zero, this would mean a $20 million increase in Weston Bakeries's profits.

But Canada Bread's president might make exactly the same calculation. And if both firms were to produce 40 million loaves of bread, the price would drop to $4 per loaf of bread. So each firm's profits would fall, from $180 million to $160 million.

Why do individual firms have an incentive to produce more than the quantity that maximizes their joint profits? Because neither firm has as strong an incentive to limit its output as a true monopolist would.

Let's go back for a minute to the theory of monopoly. We know that a profit-maximizing monopolist sets marginal cost (which in this case is zero) equal to marginal revenue. But what is marginal revenue? Recall that producing an additional unit of a good has two effects:

1. A positive *quantity* effect: one more unit is sold, increasing total revenue by the price at which that unit is sold.

2. A negative *price* effect: in order to sell one more unit, the monopolist must cut the market price on *all* units sold.

The negative price effect is the reason marginal revenue for a monopolist is less than the market price. In the case of oligopoly, when considering the effect of increasing production, a firm is concerned only with the price effect on its *own* units of output, not those of its fellow oligopolists. Both Weston Bakeries and Canada Bread suffer a negative price effect if Weston Bakeries decides to produce extra

When firms ignore the effects of their actions on each others' profits, they engage in **noncooperative behaviour.**

loaves of bread and so drives down the price. But Weston Bakeries cares only about the negative price effect on the units it produces, not about the loss to Canada Bread.

This tells us that an individual firm in an oligopolistic industry faces a smaller price effect from an additional unit of output than does a monopolist; therefore, the marginal revenue that such a firm calculates is higher. So it will seem to be profitable for any one company in an oligopoly to increase production, even if that increase reduces the profits of the industry as a whole. But if everyone thinks that way, the result is that everyone earns a lower profit!

Until now, we have been able to analyze producer behaviour by asking what a producer should do to maximize profits. But even if Weston Bakeries and Canada Bread are both trying to maximize profits, what does this predict about their behaviour? Will they engage in collusion, reaching and holding to an agreement that maximizes their combined profits? Or will they engage in **noncooperative behaviour,** with each firm acting in its own self-interest, even though this has the effect of driving down everyone's profits? Both strategies sound like profit maximization. Which will actually describe their behaviour?

Now you see why oligopoly, with only a small number of players, makes collusion a real possibility. If there were dozens or hundreds of firms, it would be safe to assume they would behave noncooperatively. Yet when there are only a handful of firms in an industry, collusion isn't inevitable. For reasons we explain in the next section, oligopolists are often unable to collude.

Since collusion is ultimately more profitable than noncooperative behaviour, firms do have an incentive to collude if they can. One way to do so is to formalize it—sign an agreement (maybe even draw up a legal contract) or establish some financial incentives for the companies to set their prices high. But in Canada and many other nations, you can't do that—at least not legally. Companies cannot make a legal contract to keep prices high: not only is the contract unenforceable, but writing it is a one-way ticket to jail. Neither can they sign an informal agreement that lacks the force of law but perhaps rests on threats of retaliation—that's illegal, too.

In fact, executives from rival companies rarely meet without lawyers present, who make sure that the conversation does not stray into inappropriate territory. Even hinting at how nice it would be if prices were higher can bring you an unwelcome interview with the Competition Bureau.

For example, in 2013, the Competition Bureau announced that Yazaki, a Japanese supplier of automobile parts, was fined a record $30 million, for participating in a bid-rigging cartel involving vehicle parts. Bid-rigging occurs when two or more firms work together to fix their bids for contracts so as to set prices and allocate the market amongst the group. Yazaki pleaded guilty to the charge that it had coordinated bids with competing suppliers for the Canadian operations of Honda and Toyota. Suppliers Furukawa Electric Co. and JTEKT Corporation each received $5 million fines. In the United States, Yazaki agreed to pay a US$470 million fine for price-fixing and bid-rigging, the second largest criminal fine to that time. Four U.S.-based Yazaki executives were given prison sentences of 15 to 24 months for their roles in this criminal conspiracy.

Sometimes, as we've seen, oligopolistic firms just ignore the rules. But more often they find ways to achieve collusion without a formal agreement, as we'll soon see.

ECONOMICS >> *in Action*
The Case Against Chocolate Producers Melts

In the Weston Bakeries case, company executives admitted to price-fixing, giving investigators indisputable evidence of collusion that was used to prosecute the consirators. However, without solid evidence, the prosecution of price-fixing can be a tricky business. The differing outcomes of price-fixing allegations in the Canadian and the U.S. chocolate industry make that point abundantly clear.

In late 2015, an eight-year-long probe into collusion by the major Canadian chocolate makers finally ended. It started when Cadbury Canada disclosed that it had colluded with Hershey Canada, Nestlé Canada, and Mars Canada. In the ensuing court case, 13 Cadbury Canada executives revealed their contacts with the other companies, including one episode in which a Nestlé Canada executive handed over details about a forthcoming price hike to Cadbury Canada. According to court documents, top executives of Hershey Canada, Nestlé Canada, and Mars Canada secretly met to set prices. After protracted litigation, all four producers settled the case and paid fines totalling more than $23 million that were then distributed among consumers.

Are chocolate makers engaging in price-fixing?

South of the border, several of the largest U.S. grocery chains and snack retailers were convinced that they, too, had been victims of collusion by chocolate makers. In 2010, one of these stores, SuperValu, filed a lawsuit against the U.S. divisions of the four chocolate makers. In contrast to Canada, where the big four controlled a little less than 50% of the market, in the U.S. market they controlled over 75%. SuperValu claimed that the U.S. companies had been fixing prices since 2002, regularly increasing prices by mid-single-digit to double-digit amounts within a few days of one another.

Indeed, over that period the price of chocolate candy in the United States had soared, climbing by 17% from 2008 to 2010, far in excess of the rate of inflation in the United States. U.S. chocolate makers, however, defended their actions, contending that they were simply passing on the higher costs of cocoa beans, dairy products, and sugar. And as antitrust experts pointed out, without solid evidence such as conversations or written agreements between companies, price-fixing can be very difficult to prove because it is not illegal for producers to raise prices at the same time.

In 2014, a U.S. judge threw out the collusion case against the U.S. chocolate producers, stating that closely timed price increases were not sufficient proof of collusion and that there was no evidence that U.S. producers knew of the collusion between their Canadian counterparts. U.S. Federal Judge Christopher Conner concluded that the companies engaged in "rational, competitive behavior" when they increased prices to counter anticipated cost increases. In 2015, Canadian regulators finally closed their books on the case, deciding against bringing further criminal charges against the four companies.

>> Check Your Understanding 14-2

Solutions appear at back of book.

1. Which of the following factors increase the likelihood that an oligopolist will collude with other firms in the industry? Which increase the likelihood that an oligopolist will act noncooperatively and raise output? Explain your answers.
   a. The firm's initial market share is small. (*Hint:* Think about the price effect.)
   b. The firm has a cost advantage over its rivals.
   c. The firm's customers face additional costs when they switch from the use of one firm's product to another firm's product.
   d. The oligopolist has a lot of unused production capacity but knows that its rivals are operating at their maximum production capacity and cannot increase the amount they produce.

>> Quick Review

• Oligopolies operate in a state of **interdependence,** in which a firm's pricing and production decisions directly affect the other firm(s) in the industry.

• Some of the key issues in oligopoly can be understood by looking at the simplest case, a **duopoly**—an industry containing only two firms, called **duopolists.**

• By acting as if they were a single monopolist, oligopolists can maximize their combined profits. So there is an incentive to form a **cartel.**

• However, each firm has an incentive to cheat—to produce more than it is supposed to under the cartel agreement. So there are two principal outcomes: successful **collusion** or behaving **noncooperatively** by cheating.

‖ Games Oligopolists Play

In our duopoly example and in real life, each oligopolistic firm realizes that it is interdependent: its profit depends on what its competitor does and its competitor's profit depends on what it does. Each firm's decisions, then, will

The study of behaviour in situations of interdependence is known as **game theory.**

The reward received by a player in a game, such as the profit earned by an oligopolist, is that player's **payoff.**

A **payoff matrix** shows how the payoff to each of the participants in a two-player game depends on the actions of both. Such a matrix helps us analyze situations of interdependence.

significantly affect the profit of the other firm (or firms, in the case of more than two).

In effect, the two firms are playing a game in which the profit of each player depends not only on its own actions but on those of the other player (or players). In order to understand more fully how oligopolists behave, economists, along with mathematicians, developed the area of study of such games, known as **game theory.** It has many applications, not just to economics but also to military strategy, politics, and other social sciences.

Let's see how game theory helps us understand oligopoly.

The Prisoners' Dilemma

Game theory deals with any situation in which the reward to any one player—the **payoff**—depends not only on their own actions but also on those of other players in the game. In the case of oligopolistic firms, the payoff is simply the firm's profit.

When there are only two players, as in a duopoly, the interdependence between the players can be represented with a **payoff matrix** like that shown in Figure 14-2. Each row corresponds to an action by one player (in this case, Weston Bakeries); each column corresponds to an action by the other (in this case, Canada Bread). For simplicity, let's assume that Weston Bakeries can pick only one of two alternatives: produce 30 million loaves of bread or produce 40 million loaves of bread. Canada Bread has the same pair of choices.

The matrix contains four boxes, each divided by a diagonal line. Each box shows the payoff to the two firms that results from a pair of choices: the number below the diagonal shows Weston Bakeries's profits; the number above the diagonal shows Canada Bread's profits.

These payoffs show what we concluded from our earlier analysis: the combined profit of the two firms is maximized if they each produce 30 million loaves of bread. Either firm can, however, increase its own profit by producing 40 million loaves of bread while the other produces only 30 million loaves of bread. But if both produce the larger quantity, both will have lower profits than if they had both held their output down.

FIGURE 14-2 A Payoff Matrix

Two firms, Weston Bakeries and Canada Bread, must decide how many loaves of bread to produce. The profits of the two firms are *interdependent:* each firm's profit depends not only on its own decision but also on the other's decision. Each row represents an action by Weston Bakeries; each column an action by Canada Bread. Both firms will be better off if they both choose the lower output, but it is in each firm's individual interest to choose the higher output.

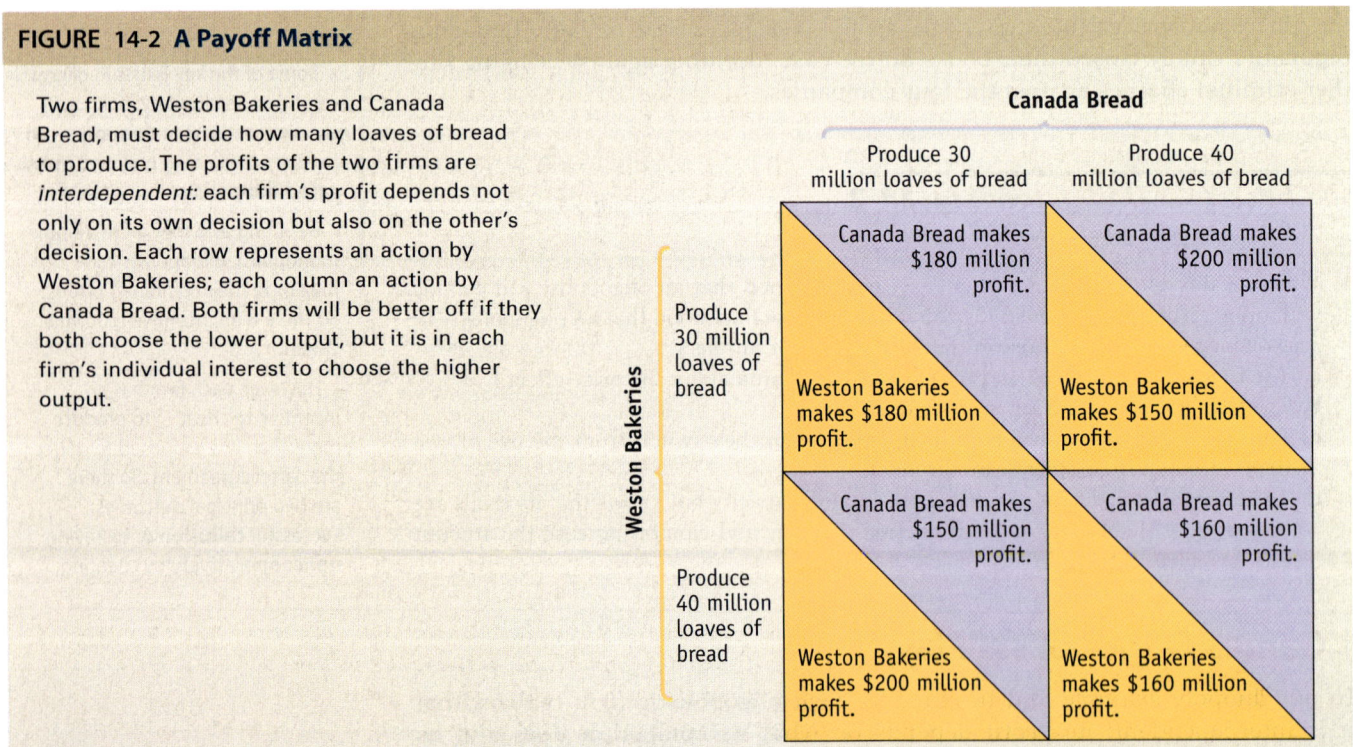

The particular situation shown here is a version of a famous—and seemingly paradoxical—case of interdependence that appears in many contexts. Known as the **prisoners' dilemma,** it is a type of game in which the payoff matrix implies the following:

- Each player has an incentive, regardless of what the other player does, to cheat—to take an action that benefits it at the other's expense.

- When both players cheat, both are worse off than they would have been if neither had cheated.

The original illustration of the prisoners' dilemma occurred in a fictional story about two accomplices in crime—let's call them Thelma and Louise—who have been caught by the police. The police have enough evidence to put them behind bars for 5 years. They also know that the pair have committed a more serious crime, one that carries a 20-year sentence; unfortunately, they don't have enough evidence to convict the women on that charge. To do so, they would need each of the prisoners to implicate the other in the second crime.

So the police put the miscreants in separate cells and say the following to each: "Here's the deal: if neither of you confesses, you know that we'll send you to jail for 5 years. If you confess and implicate your partner, and she doesn't do the same, we'll reduce your sentence from 5 years to 2. But if your partner confesses and you don't, you'll get the maximum 20 years. And if both of you confess, we'll give you both 15 years."

Figure 14-3 shows the payoffs that face the prisoners, depending on the decision of each to remain silent or to confess. (Usually the payoff matrix reflects the players' payoffs, and higher payoffs are better than lower payoffs. This case is an exception: a higher number of years in prison is bad, not good!) Let's assume that the prisoners have no way to communicate and that they have not sworn an oath not to harm each other or anything of that sort. So each acts in her own self-interest. What will they do?

The answer is clear: both will confess. Look at it first from Thelma's point of view: she is better off confessing, regardless of what Louise does. If Louise doesn't confess, Thelma's confession reduces her own sentence from 5 years to 2.

Prisoners' dilemma is a game based on two premises: (1) Each player has an incentive to choose an action that benefits itself at the other player's expense; (2) When both players act in this way, both are worse off than if they had acted cooperatively.

FIGURE 14-3 The Prisoners' Dilemma

Each of two prisoners, held in separate cells, is offered a deal by the police — a light sentence if she confesses and implicates her accomplice but her accomplice does not do the same, a heavy sentence if she does not confess but her accomplice does, and so on. It is in the joint interest of both prisoners not to confess; it is in each one's individual interest to confess.

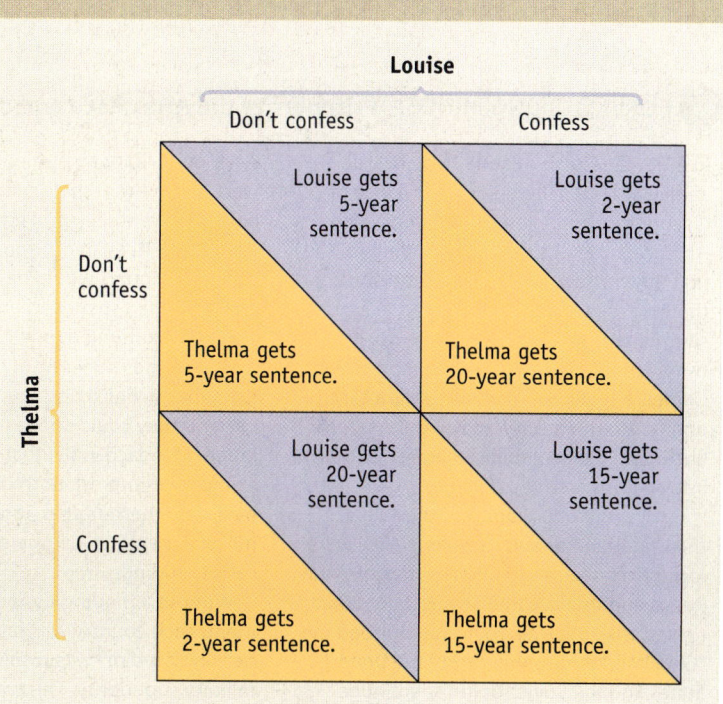

An action is a **dominant strategy** when it is a player's best action regardless of the action taken by the other player.

A **Nash equilibrium,** also known as a **noncooperative equilibrium,** results when each player in a game chooses the action that maximizes their payoff given the actions of other players, ignoring the effects of their action on the payoffs received by those other players.

If Louise *does* confess, Thelma's confession reduces her sentence from 20 to 15 years. Either way, it's clearly in Thelma's interest to confess. And because she faces the same incentives, it's clearly in Louise's interest to confess, too. To confess in this situation is a type of action that economists call a *dominant strategy.* An action is a **dominant strategy** when it is the player's best action regardless of the action taken by the other player.

It's important to note that not all games have a dominant strategy—it depends on the structure of payoffs in the game. But in the case of Thelma and Louise, it is clearly in the interest of the police to structure the payoffs so that confessing is a dominant strategy for each person. So as long as the two prisoners have no way to make an enforceable agreement that neither will confess (something they can't do if they can't communicate, and the police certainly won't allow them to do so because the police want to compel each one to confess), Thelma and Louise will each act in a way that hurts the other.

So if each prisoner acts rationally in her own interest, both will confess. Yet if neither of them had confessed, both would have received a much lighter sentence! In a prisoners' dilemma, each player has a clear incentive to act in a way that hurts the other player—but when both make that choice, it leaves both of them worse off.

When Thelma and Louise both confess, they reach an *equilibrium* of the game. We have used the concept of equilibrium many times; it is an outcome in which no individual or firm has any incentive to change their own action.

In game theory, this kind of equilibrium, in which each player takes the action that is best for her given the actions taken by other players, and vice versa, is known as a **Nash equilibrium,** after the mathematician and Nobel laureate John Nash. (Nash's life was chronicled in the best-selling biography *A Beautiful Mind,* which was made into a movie.) Because the players in a Nash equilibrium do not take into account the effect of their actions on others, this is also known as a **noncooperative equilibrium.**

Now look back at Figure 14-2: Weston Bakeries and Canada Bread are in the same situation as Thelma and Louise. Each firm is better off producing the higher output, regardless of what the other firm does. Yet if both produce 40 million loaves of bread, both are worse off than if they had followed their agreement and produced only 30 million loaves of bread. In both cases, then, the pursuit of individual self-interest—the effort to maximize profits or to minimize jail time—has the perverse effect of hurting both players.

 FOR INQUIRING MINDS **Prisoners of the Arms Race and the Resurgent Cold War**

In 2016, the North Atlantic Treaty Organization, or NATO, the defensive alliance of 28 countries spanning Europe and North America, raised its military spending for the first time in years. Most experts attribute the increase to Russia's newly more aggressive military posture in Europe, evidenced by its 2014 invasion and annexation of the Crimea, a region of Ukraine. It was a case of "back to the future," as NATO members (including Canada) found themselves drawn into an arms race with Russia.

Between World War II and the 1980s, the United States and its allies (NATO) were locked in a seemingly endless struggle with Russia and its allies (the Soviet Union) that never broke out into open war. Dubbed the "Cold War," during this period the United States and the Soviet Union spent huge

sums on military equipment, sums that were a significant drain on the U.S. economy and eventually proved a crippling burden for the Russian economy.

Both countries would have been better off if each had spent less on arms. Yet the arms race continued for 40 years. The arms race illustrates the logic of the prisoner's dilemma, in which both parties would be better if they could cooperate, but it is rational for each individual party to act in its own self-interest. Both countries would have been better off in a stalemate with low military spending, compared to one with high spending.

Without a binding cooperative agreement, each country was rational to spend heavily: if it didn't, its rival would gain military superiority. The two countries tried

to escape this trap by repeatedly negotiating limits on weapons. However, these agreements were hard to negotiate and very difficult to verify. Ultimately, the issue was resolved as heavy military spending hastened the collapse of the Soviet Union in 1991. For the next 20 years, the arms race between the United States and Russia largely faded away.

That is until 2016, when the Russian annexation of the Crimea provided a clear sign that the arms race had returned as Russia had regained its economic footing. Russian military spending climbed 60% from 2008 to 2015, before settling back to earlier levels in 2017 and 2018. The increased NATO spending in response has made it abundantly clear that the logic of the arms race is still very much alive.

Prisoners' dilemmas appear in many situations. Clearly, the players in any prisoners' dilemma would be better off if they had some way of enforcing cooperative behaviour—if Thelma and Louise had both sworn to a code of silence or if Weston Bakeries and Canada Bread had signed an enforceable agreement not to produce more than 30 million loaves of bread.

But in Canada, an agreement setting the output levels of two oligopolists isn't just unenforceable, it's illegal. So it seems that a noncooperative equilibrium is the only possible outcome. Or is it?

Overcoming the Prisoners' Dilemma: Repeated Interaction and Tacit Collusion

Thelma and Louise in their cells are playing what is known as a *one-shot* game—that is, they play the game with each other only once. They get to choose once and for all whether to confess or hang tough, and that's it. However, most of the games that oligopolists play aren't one-shot; instead, they expect to play the game repeatedly with the same rivals.

An oligopolist usually expects to be in business for many years, and it knows that its decision today about whether to cheat is likely to affect the way other firms treat it in the future. So a smart oligopolist doesn't just decide what to do based on the effect on profit in the short run. Instead, it engages in **strategic behaviour,** taking account of the effects of the action it chooses today on the future actions of other players in the game. And under some conditions oligopolists that behave strategically can manage to behave as if they had a formal agreement to collude.

Suppose that Weston Bakeries and Canada Bread expect to be in the bread business for many years and therefore expect to play the game of cheat versus collude shown in Figure 14-2 many times. Would they really betray each other time and again?

Probably not. Suppose that Weston Bakeries considers two strategies. In one strategy it always cheats, producing 40 million loaves of bread each year, regardless of what Canada Bread does. In the other strategy, it starts with good behaviour, producing only 30 million loaves of bread in the first year, and watches to see what its rival does. If Canada Bread also keeps its production down, Weston Bakeries will stay cooperative, producing 30 million loaves of bread again for the next year. But if Canada Bread produces 40 million loaves of bread, Weston Bakeries will take the gloves off and also produce 40 million loaves of bread the next year. This latter strategy—start by behaving cooperatively, but thereafter do whatever the other player did in the previous period—is generally known as **tit for tat.**

Tit for tat is a form of strategic behaviour, which we have just defined as behaviour intended to influence the future actions of other players. Tit for tat offers a reward to the other player for cooperative behaviour—if you behave cooperatively, so will I. It also provides a punishment for cheating—if you cheat, don't expect me to be nice in the future.

The payoff to Weston Bakeries of each of these strategies would depend on which strategy Canada Bread chooses. Consider the four possibilities, shown in Figure 14-4:

1. If Weston Bakeries plays tit for tat and so does Canada Bread, both firms will make a profit of $180 million each year.

2. If Weston Bakeries plays always cheat but Canada Bread plays tit for tat, Weston Bakeries makes a profit of $200 million the first year but only $160 million per year thereafter.

3. If Weston Bakeries plays tit for tat but Canada Bread plays always cheat, Weston Bakeries makes a profit of only $150 million in the first year but $160 million per year thereafter.

4. If Weston Bakeries plays always cheat and Canada Bread does the same, both firms will make a profit of $160 million each year.

Which strategy is better? In the first year, Weston Bakeries does better playing always cheat, whatever its rival's strategy: it assures itself that it will get

A firm engages in **strategic behaviour** when it attempts to influence the future behaviour of other firms.

A strategy of **tit for tat** involves playing cooperatively at first, then doing whatever the other player did in the previous period.

FIGURE 14-4 How Repeated Interaction Can Support Collusion

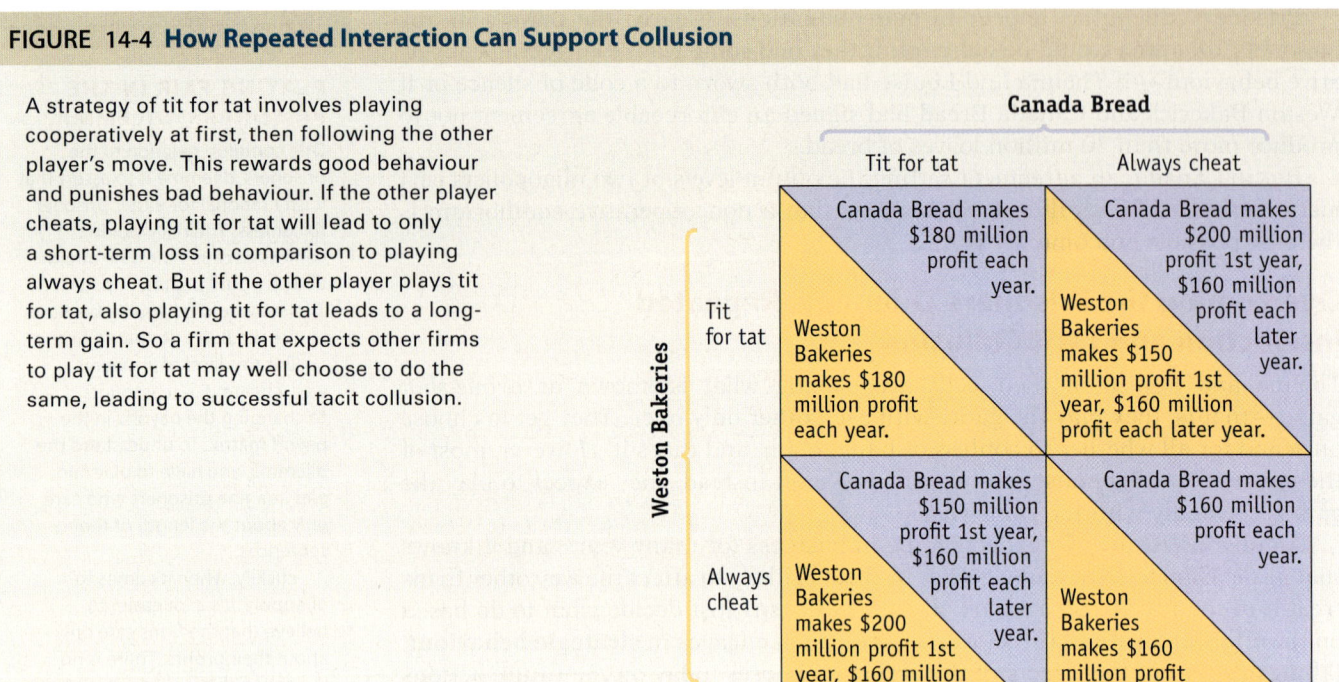

A strategy of tit for tat involves playing cooperatively at first, then following the other player's move. This rewards good behaviour and punishes bad behaviour. If the other player cheats, playing tit for tat will lead to only a short-term loss in comparison to playing always cheat. But if the other player plays tit for tat, also playing tit for tat leads to a long-term gain. So a firm that expects other firms to play tit for tat may well choose to do the same, leading to successful tacit collusion.

Canada Bread

	Tit for tat	Always cheat
Weston Bakeries — Tit for tat	Canada Bread makes $180 million profit each year. / Weston Bakeries makes $180 million profit each year.	Canada Bread makes $200 million profit 1st year, $160 million profit each later year. / Weston Bakeries makes $150 million profit 1st year, $160 million profit each later year.
Weston Bakeries — Always cheat	Canada Bread makes $150 million profit 1st year, $160 million profit each later year. / Weston Bakeries makes $200 million profit 1st year, $160 million profit each later year.	Canada Bread makes $160 million profit each year. / Weston Bakeries makes $160 million profit each year.

either $200 million or $160 million (which of the two payoffs it actually receives depends on whether Canada Bread plays tit for tat or always cheat). This is better than what it would get in the first year if it played tit for tat: either $180 million or $150 million. But by the second year, a strategy of always cheat gains Weston Bakeries only $160 million per year for the second and all subsequent years, regardless of Canada Bread's actions.

Over time, the total amount gained by Weston Bakeries by playing always cheat is less than the amount it would gain by playing tit for tat: for the second and all subsequent years, it would never get any less than $160 million and would get as much as $180 million if Canada Bread played tit for tat as well. Which strategy, always cheat or tit for tat, is more profitable depends on two things: how many years Weston Bakeries expects to play the game and what strategy its rival follows.

If Weston Bakeries expects the bread business to end in the near future, it is in effect playing a one-shot game. So it might as well cheat and grab what it can. Even if Weston Bakeries expects to remain in the bread business for many years (therefore to find itself repeatedly playing this game with Canada Bread) and, for some reason, expects Canada Bread always to cheat, it should also always cheat. That is, Weston Bakeries should follow the old rule "Do unto others before they do unto you."

But if Weston Bakeries expects to be in the business for a long time and thinks Canada Bread is likely to play tit for tat, it will make more profits over the long run by playing tit for tat, too. It could have made some extra short-term profits by cheating at the beginning, but this would provoke Canada Bread into cheating, too, and would, in the end, mean lower profits.

The lesson of this story is that when oligopolists expect to compete with one another over an extended period of time, each individual firm will often conclude that it is in its own best interest to be helpful to the other firms in the industry. So it will restrict its output in a way that raises the profits of the other firms, expecting them to return the favour. Despite the fact that firms have no way of making an enforceable agreement to limit output and raise prices (and are in legal jeopardy if they even discuss prices), they manage to act "as if" they had such an agreement. When this happens, we say that firms engage in **tacit collusion.**

When firms limit production and raise prices in a way that raises one anothers' profits, even though they have not made any formal agreement, they are engaged in **tacit collusion.**

ECONOMICS >> *in Action*
The Ups and Downs of a Cartel: OPEC Hits the Skids on U.S. Shale Oil

The Organization of the Petroleum Exporting Countries (OPEC), composed of the 13 countries of Algeria, Angola, Gabon, Iran, Iraq, Kuwait, Libya, Nigeria, Saudi Arabia, Republic of Congo, Syria, the United Arab Emirates, and Venezuela, is a cartel that controlled 44% of global crude oil output in 2019. The cartel accounts for 72% of proven crude oil reserves and generates 60% of global crude oil exports. Unlike corporations that are legally prohibited from forming cartels, national governments can do whatever they like in setting prices.

For many years OPEC was the largest, most successful, and most economically important cartel in the world. Its members met regularly to set price and production quotas for oil.

Figure 14-5 shows the price of oil (in constant U.S. dollars) since 1947. OPEC first demonstrated its muscle in 1973: during the Yom Kippur War in the Middle East, OPEC produc-

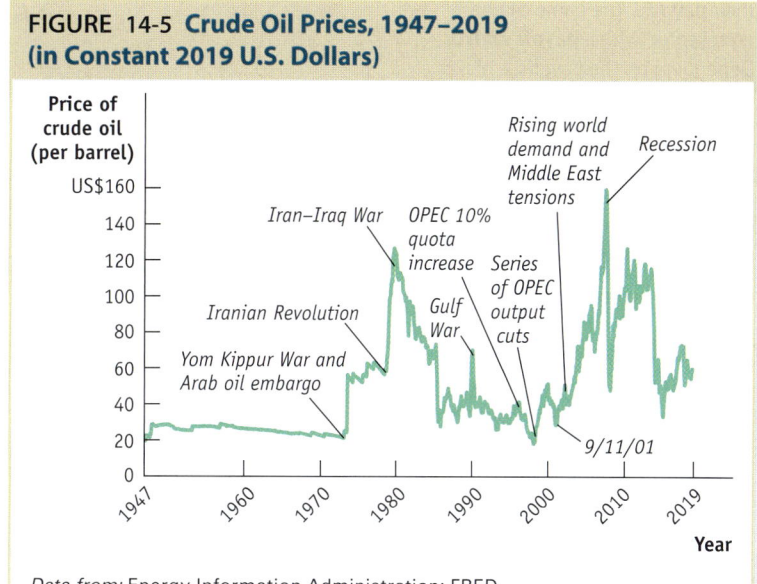

FIGURE 14-5 Crude Oil Prices, 1947–2019 (in Constant 2019 U.S. Dollars)

Data from: Energy Information Administration; FRED.

ers limited their output—and they liked the resulting price increase so much that they decided to continue the practice. Following a second wave of turmoil from the Iran-Iraq War in 1979, output quotas fell further and prices shot even higher.

Higher oil prices spurred more exploration and production, so by the mid-1980s a growing glut of oil on world markets and cheating by cash-strapped OPEC members led to a price collapse. But in the late 1990s, OPEC emerged successful once again, as Saudi Arabia, the largest producer by far, began acting as the "swing producer": allowing other members to produce as much as they wanted, then adjusting its own output to meet the overall production limit. By 2008, the price of oil had soared to US$145 per barrel.

Yet, by late 2015, OPEC was nearly dead as a successful cartel as the price of oil had dropped to under US$30 a barrel, a victim of surging oil exports from Russia, which accounts for the third largest share of reserves and output in the world. After having suffered a huge fall in production in the late 1990s during a period of political instability, Russia ramped up its production enough to precipitate a plunge in prices by 2015. So by late 2016, Russia and OPEC agreed to jointly limit their oil production, sending oil prices surging to above US$55 per barrel.

In fact, few industry observers believe that OPEC (or OPEC plus Russia) will ever regain its glory days, with a consensus of US$60 per barrel as the most likely maximum price for the near future. One important factor is the rising popularity of renewables as more and more countries shift their economies toward green technology and away from fossil fuels like oil. But the most important near-term factor dampening the rise in oil prices is the vast expansion of oil supply from the United States arising from new fracking technologies. Within five years, the United States is expected to overtake Saudi Arabia as the world's largest oil producer. As one analyst said, "U.S. shale is a huge game changer for OPEC. If prices rise to US$60 and a large volume of oil can come back quickly, that's a very significant constraint on the ability of OPEC to manage the oil market." And, unlike Russia, it is virtually impossible that U.S. producers (of whom there are thousands) will ever agree to a voluntary output limitation.

>> Check Your Understanding 14-3

Solutions appear at back of book.

1. Find the Nash (noncooperative) equilibrium actions for the following payoff matrix. Which actions maximize the total payoff of Nikita and Margaret? Why is it unlikely that they will choose those actions without some communication?

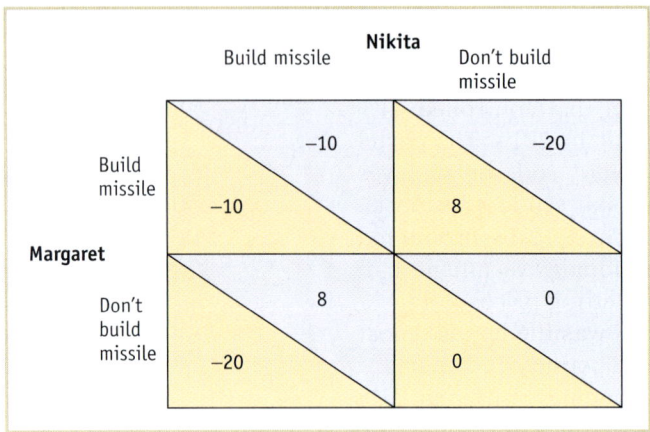

2. Which of the following factors make it more likely that oligopolists will play noncooperatively? Which make it more likely that they will engage in tacit collusion? Explain.
   a. Each oligopolist expects several new firms to enter the market in the future.
   b. It is very difficult for a firm to detect whether another firm has raised output.
   c. The firms have coexisted while maintaining high prices for a long time.

Oligopoly in Practice

In an earlier Economics in Action, we described how the four leading chocolate companies in Canada were colluding to raise prices for many years. Collusion is not, fortunately, the norm. But how do oligopolies usually work in practice? The answer depends both on the legal framework that limits what firms can do and on the underlying ability of firms in a given industry to cooperate without formal agreements.

The Legal Framework

To understand oligopoly pricing in practice, we must be familiar with the legal constraints under which oligopolistic firms operate. In North America, oligopoly first became an issue during the second half of the nineteenth century, when the growth of railroads—themselves an oligopolistic industry—created a national market for many goods.

Large firms producing oil, steel, and many other products soon emerged. The industrialists quickly realized that profits would be higher if they could limit price competition. So, many industries formed cartels—that is, they signed formal agreements to limit production and raise prices. This was perfectly legal until 1889, when the first federal legislation against such cartels (Canada's first competition law) was passed. A similar law in the United States followed in 1890.

However, although these cartels were legal, they weren't legally *enforceable*—members of a cartel couldn't ask the courts to force a firm that was violating its agreement to reduce its production. And firms often did violate their agreements, for the reason already suggested by our duopoly example: there is always a temptation for each firm in a cartel to produce more than it is supposed to.

In the United States 1881, clever lawyers at John D. Rockefeller's Standard Oil Company came up with a solution—the so-called trust. In a trust, shareholders of all the major companies in an industry placed their shares in the hands of a board of trustees who controlled the companies. This, in effect, merged the companies into a single firm that could then engage in monopoly pricing. In this way, the Standard Oil Trust established what was essentially an American monopoly of the oil industry, and it was soon followed by trusts in U.S. sugar, whiskey, lead, cottonseed oil, and linseed oil.

Eventually there was a public backlash, driven partly by concern about the economic effects of the trust movement, partly by fear that the owners of the trusts were simply becoming too powerful. The result was the U.S. Sherman Antitrust Act of 1890, which was intended both to prevent the creation of more monopolies and to break up existing ones. At first this law went largely unenforced. But over the decades that followed, the U.S. federal government became increasingly committed to making it difficult for oligopolistic industries either to become monopolies or to behave like them. Such efforts are known to this day as **antitrust policy.**

One of the most striking early actions of antitrust policy was the breakup of Standard Oil in 1911. (Its components formed the nuclei of many of today's large U.S. oil companies—Standard Oil of New Jersey became Exxon, Standard Oil of New York became Mobil, and so on.) In the 1980s, while Bell Canada was losing its telephone monopoly via government deregulation, a long-running case led to the breakup of Bell Telephone in the United States, which once had a monopoly of both local and long-distance phone service. As we mentioned earlier, the competition and antitrust regulators review proposed mergers between companies in the same industry and will bar mergers that they believe will reduce competition.

Among advanced countries, Canada and the United States are unique in their long tradition of antitrust policy. Until recently, other advanced countries did not have policies against price-fixing, and some had even

Antitrust policy consists of efforts undertaken by the government to prevent oligopolistic industries from becoming or behaving like monopolies.

"Frankly, I'm dubious about amalgamated smelting and refining pleading innocent to their antitrust violation due to insanity."

GLOBAL COMPARISON CONTRASTING APPROACHES TO COMPETITION REGULATION

Like the Competition Bureau in Canada or the FTC in the United States, the European Union's Competition Commission (CC) enforces competition and antitrust regulation for the 27 member nations. It wields the authority to block mergers, force companies to sell subsidiaries, and impose heavy fines if it determines that companies have acted unfairly to inhibit competition.

Although companies are able to dispute charges at a hearing once a complaint has been issued, if the CC feels that its own case is convincing, it rules against the firm and levies a penalty. Companies that believe they have been unfairly treated have only limited recourse. Critics complain that the commission acts as prosecutor, judge, and jury.

In contrast, charges of unfair competition in Canada and the United States must be made in court, where lawyers for the Attorney General of Canada (supported by the Competition Bureau) or, in the United States, the FTC, have to present their evidence to independent judges. Companies employ legions of highly trained and highly paid lawyers to counter the government's case. For Canadian and American regulators, there is no guarantee of success. In fact, judges in many cases have found in favour of companies and against the regulators. Moreover, companies can appeal unfavourable decisions, so reaching a final verdict can take several years. Companies, not surprisingly, prefer the North American system. Between 2015 and 2019, the average criminal fine imposed by the U.S. Department of Justice was about 50 times larger than the average criminal fine imposed by Canada's Competition Bureau. But during the same

period, the average criminal fine imposed by the European Union (EU) was three times larger than the U.S. average.

Observers, however, criticize both systems for their inadequacies. In the slow-moving, litigious, and expensive North American system, consumers and rival companies may wait a very long time to secure protection. And companies often prevail, raising questions about how well consumers are protected. But some charge that the EU system gives inadequate protection to companies that are accused.

Overall, EU regulators have been far more willing than North American regulators to take aim at tech giants, having opened multiple investigations of Apple, Google, and Facebook. In 2017, the EU fined Google US$2.7 billion for anticompetitive behaviour in the internet search market, arguing that it unfairly favoured its own search engine over those of rivals. This was more than double the previous largest penalty in this type of antitrust case. And in 2018, the EU fined Google a record US$5.8 billion for anticompetitive behaviour in the Android software market. While some claim that the EU is unfairly targeting U.S. firms, seeking to give them an advantage over EU firms, others dispute that characterization, saying that consumers need more protection from antitrust behaviour and privacy invasions by tech giants.

And regulators in other jurisdictions are taking notice: Joseph Simons, the chairman of the FTC, said in 2018, "Let me just say we're going to read what the EU put out very closely. We're very interested in what they are doing."

supported the creation of cartels, believing that it would help their own firms against foreign rivals. But the situation has changed radically over the past 30 years, as the EU—a supranational body tasked with enforcing antitrust policy for its member countries—has moved toward North American practices. Today, EU and North American regulators often target the same firms because price-fixing has "gone global" as international trade has expanded.

Many governments around the world have now instituted amnesty programs in which a price-fixer receives much-reduced penalties if it informs on its co-conspirators. The Canadian Competition Bureau introduced its own leniency, or amnesty, program in 2000. It also substantially increased maximum fines levied upon conviction. Now, the maximum monetary fine has been increased to $25 million and the maximum prison sentence has been lengthened to 14 years. These two new policies clearly made informing on your cartel partners a dominant strategy, and it has paid off: in recent years, executives from Belgium, Britain, France, Germany, Italy, Mexico, the Netherlands, South Korea, Switzerland, and the United States, as well as from Canada, have been convicted in courts in Canada and the United States of cartel crimes. As one lawyer commented, "you get a race to the courthouse" as each conspirator seeks to be the first to come clean.

Life has gotten much tougher over the past few years if you want to operate a cartel. So what's an oligopolist to do?

Tacit Collusion and Price Wars

If a real industry were as simple as our bread example, it probably wouldn't be necessary for the company presidents to meet or do anything that could land them in jail. Both firms would realize that it was in their mutual interest to restrict output to 30 million loaves of bread each and that any short-term gains to either firm from producing more would be much less than the later losses as the other firm retaliated. So even without any explicit agreement, the firms would probably achieve the tacit collusion needed to maximize their combined profits.

Real industries are nowhere near that simple. Nonetheless, in most oligopolistic industries, most of the time, the sellers do appear to succeed in keeping prices above their noncooperative level. Tacit collusion, in other words, is the normal state of oligopoly.

Although tacit collusion is common, it rarely allows an industry to push prices all the way up to their monopoly level; collusion is usually far from perfect. As we discuss next, there are four factors that make it hard for an industry to coordinate on high prices.

1. Less Concentration In a less concentrated industry, the typical firm will have a smaller market share than in a more concentrated industry. This tilts firms toward noncooperative behaviour because when a smaller firm cheats and increases its output, it gains for itself all of the profit from the higher output. And if its rivals retaliate by increasing their output, the firm's losses are limited because of its relatively modest market share. A less concentrated industry is often an indication that there are low barriers to entry.

2. Complex Products and Pricing Schemes In our bread example, the two firms produce only one product. In reality, however, oligopolists often sell thousands or even tens of thousands of different products. Under these circumstances, keeping track of what other firms are producing and the prices they are charging is difficult. This makes it hard to determine whether a firm is cheating on the tacit agreement.

3. Differences in Interests In the bread example, a tacit agreement for the firms to split the market equally is a natural outcome, probably acceptable to both firms. In real industries, however, firms often differ both in their perceptions about what is fair and in their real interests.

For example, suppose that Canada Bread was a long-established bread producer and Weston Bakeries a more recent entrant to the industry. Canada Bread might feel that it deserved to continue producing more than Weston Bakeries, but Weston Bakeries might feel that it was entitled to 50% of the business.

Alternatively, suppose that Weston Bakeries's marginal costs were lower than Canada Bread's. Even if they could agree on market shares, they would then disagree about the profit-maximizing level of output.

4. Bargaining Power of Buyers Often oligopolists sell not to individual consumers but to large buyers—other industrial enterprises, nationwide chains of stores, and so on. These large buyers are in a position to bargain for lower prices from the oligopolists: they can ask for a discount from an oligopolist and warn that they will go to a competitor if they don't get it. An important reason why large retailers like Walmart are able to offer lower prices to customers than small retailers is precisely their ability to use their size to extract lower prices from their suppliers.

These difficulties in enforcing tacit collusion have sometimes led companies to defy the law and create illegal cartels. We've already examined the cases of the bread industry and the chocolate industry. Recent examples include the generic drug industry, canned tuna, and the two major credit card companies. An older, classic example is the U.S. electrical equipment conspiracy of the 1950s, which led to the prosecution of and jail sentences for some executives. It provides a classic illustration of the factors that make tacit collusion especially difficult to achieve.

- There were many firms—40 companies were indicted.
- They produced a very complex array of products, often more or less custom-built for particular clients.
- They differed greatly in size, from giants like General Electric to family firms with only a few dozen employees.
- The customers in many cases were large buyers like electrical utilities, which would normally try to force suppliers to compete for their business.

Tacit collusion just didn't seem practical—so executives met secretly and illegally to decide who would bid what price for which contract.

Because tacit collusion is often hard to achieve, most oligopolies charge prices that are well below what the same industry would charge if it were controlled by a monopolist—or what they would charge if they were able to collude explicitly. In addition, sometimes collusion breaks down and there is a **price war.** A price war sometimes involves simply a collapse of prices to their noncooperative level. Sometimes they even go *below* that level, as sellers try to put each other out of business or at least punish what they regard as cheating.

Product Differentiation and Price Leadership

In our hypothetical example of the Canada Bread and Weston Bakeries bread companies, we have assumed that their breads are perfect substitutes. That is, consumers regard them as identical. In many oligopolies, however, firms produce products that consumers regard as similar but not identical. A $10 difference in price won't make many customers switch from a Samsung smartphone to an iPhone, or vice versa.

Sometimes the differences between products are real, like differences between Froot Loops and Wheaties; sometimes, like differences between brands of vodka (which is supposed to be tasteless), they exist mainly in the minds of consumers. Either way, the effect is to reduce the intensity of competition among the firms: consumers will not all rush to buy whichever product is cheapest.

As you might imagine, oligopolists welcome the extra market power that comes when consumers think that their product is different from that of competitors. So in many oligopolistic industries, firms make considerable efforts to create the perception that their product is different—that is, they engage in **product differentiation.**

A **price war** occurs when tacit collusion breaks down and prices collapse.

Product differentiation is an attempt by a firm to convince buyers that its product is different from the products of other firms in the industry.

In **price leadership,** one firm sets its price first, and other firms then follow.

Firms that have a tacit understanding not to compete on price often engage in intense **nonprice competition,** using advertising and other means to try to increase their sales.

A firm that tries to differentiate its product may do so by altering what it actually produces, adding "extras," or choosing a different design. It may also use advertising and marketing campaigns to create a differentiation in the minds of consumers, even though its product is more or less identical to the products of rivals.

A classic case of how products may be perceived as different even when they are really pretty much the same is over-the-counter medication. For many years there have been just a few pain relievers available without a prescription—aspirin, ibuprofen, acetaminophen, and naproxen. These pain relievers are widely available as generic brands yet many consumers choose to spend more for the name brands of Bayer, Advil, Tylenol, and Aleve. Each brand uses a marketing campaign that implies some special superiority over their generic competitors (store brands), which are essentially the same thing (one classic slogan was "contains the pain reliever doctors recommend most"—that is, aspirin).

Whatever the nature of product differentiation, oligopolists producing differentiated products often reach a tacit understanding not to compete on price. For example, during the years when the great majority of cars sold in North America were produced by the Big Three auto companies (General Motors, Ford, and Chrysler), there was an unwritten rule that none of the three companies would try to gain market share by making its cars noticeably cheaper than those of the other two.

But then who would decide on the overall price of cars? The answer was normally General Motors: as the biggest of the three, it would announce its prices for the year first, and the other companies would match it. This pattern of behaviour, in which one company tacitly sets prices for the industry as a whole, is known as **price leadership.**

Interestingly, firms that have a tacit agreement not to compete on price often engage in vigorous **nonprice competition**—adding new features to their products, spending large sums on ads that proclaim the inferiority of their rivals' offerings, and so on.

Perhaps the best way to understand the mix of cooperation and competition in such industries is with a political analogy. During the long Cold War between the United States and the Soviet Union, the two countries engaged in intense rivalry for global influence. They not only provided financial and military aid to their allies; they sometimes supported forces trying to overthrow governments allied with their rival (as the Soviet Union did in Vietnam in the 1960s and early 1970s, and as the United States did in Afghanistan from 1979 until the collapse of the Soviet Union in 1991). They even sent their own soldiers to support allied governments against rebels (as the United States did in Vietnam and the Soviet Union did in Afghanistan). But they did not get into direct military confrontations with each other; open warfare between the two superpowers was regarded by both as too dangerous—and was tacitly avoided.

Price wars aren't as serious as shooting wars, but the principle is the same.

How Important Is Oligopoly?

We have seen that, across industries, oligopoly is far more common than either perfect competition or monopoly. When we try to analyze oligopoly, the economist's usual way of thinking—asking how self-interested individuals would behave, then analyzing their interaction—does not work as well as we might hope because we do not know whether rival firms will engage in noncooperative behaviour or manage to engage in some kind of collusion.

Given the prevalence of oligopoly, then, is the analysis we developed in earlier chapters, which was based on perfect competition, still useful?

The conclusion of the great majority of economists is yes. For one thing, important parts of the economy are fairly well described by perfect competition.

And even though many industries are oligopolistic, in many cases the limits to collusion keep prices relatively close to marginal costs—in other words, the industry behaves "almost" as if it were perfectly competitive.

It is also true that predictions from supply and demand analysis are often valid for oligopolies. For example, in Chapter 5 we saw that price controls will produce shortages. Strictly speaking, this conclusion is certain only for perfectly competitive industries. But in the 1970s, when the U.S. government imposed price controls on the definitely oligopolistic oil industry, the result was indeed to produce shortages and lines at the gas pumps.

So how important is it to take account of oligopoly? Most economists adopt a pragmatic approach. As we have seen in this chapter, the analysis of oligopoly is far more difficult and messy than that of perfect competition; so in situations where they do not expect the complications associated with oligopoly to be crucial, economists prefer to adopt the working assumption of perfectly competitive markets. They always keep in mind the possibility that oligopoly might be important; they recognize that there are important issues, from antitrust policies to price wars, where trying to understand oligopolistic behaviour is crucial.

We will follow the same approach in the chapters that follow.

ECONOMICS >> *in Action*
The Price Wars of Christmas: Amazon and Walmart Slug It Out

It's the Christmas season—and in the aisles and websites of North American retail, there's a slugfest going on. Market observers are carefully watching which retailer will come to dominate the biggest selling season of the year. Online sales, which accounted for nearly one-half of total Christmas sales in 2019, have weaponized head-to-head price competition. Such direct competition creates the potential for a race to the bottom, with big and small retailers, as well as suppliers, suffering the consequences.

If Amazon is the King Kong of retail, then Walmart is the up-and-coming Godzilla, a fight that experts say has the potential to go beyond a conventional price war. On price alone, several studies have shown Amazon to be the low-price leader. Over time, Walmart fell behind Amazon in terms of price-competitiveness as Walmart continued to focus on sales in its physical stores.

There's a price war going on in the toy aisle.

Yet by Christmas of 2019, Walmart was clearly closing the gap. Research from Boomerang Commerce found that "Amazon and Walmart are nearly neck-and-neck on pricing" for popular gifts. Their review of featured U.S. Thanksgiving weekend deals on both sites in 2019, for example, showed Walmart featuring 40 items on its home page, compared to 26 items for Amazon, and discounts at Walmart averaged 33.9%, compared to Amazon's 36.9%. In addition, Walmart began offering lower prices to customers who picked up their online purchases in the store, betting that they would make additional purchases while there.

In order to soften direct price competition, retailers are also using strategies like bundling products with services (such as offering in-home assembly), time-sensitive discounting, and customized products. Yet the competitive pressures are definitely present: the holiday sale season has lengthened over time, as each retailer tries to capture more sales from its rivals by starting its discounting earlier. Not so long ago, Black Friday, the day after U.S. Thanksgiving, marked the start of the selling season. Now, it starts at Halloween, the fourth busiest day of the year for online sales.

As one market commented on the state of the retail industry during the Christmas season, "I don't think it's just a price war. I think it's a strategic price war, or a smart price war. In the end, no retailer wants to lose money."

>> Check Your Understanding 14-4
Solutions appear at back of book.

1. Which of the following factors are likely to support the conclusion that there is tacit collusion in this industry? Which are not? Explain.
   a. For many years the price in the industry has changed infrequently, and all the firms in the industry charge the same price. The largest firm publishes a catalogue containing a "suggested" retail price. Changes in price coincide with changes in the catalogue.
   b. There has been considerable variation in the market shares of the firms in the industry over time.
   c. Firms in the industry build into their products unnecessary features that make it hard for consumers to switch from one company's products to another company's products.
   d. Firms meet yearly to discuss their annual sales forecasts.
   e. Firms tend to adjust their prices upward at the same times.

Virgin Atlantic Blows the Whistle . . . or Blows It?

Ian Waldie/Getty Images

The United Kingdom is home to two long-haul airline carriers (carriers that fly between continents): British Airways and its rival, Virgin Atlantic. Although British Airways is the dominant company, with a market share generally between 50% and 100% on routes between London and various American cities, Virgin has been a tenacious competitor.

The rivalry between the two has ranged from relatively peaceable to openly hostile over the years. In the 1990s, British Airways lost a court case alleging it had engaged in "dirty tricks" to drive Virgin out of business. In April 2010, however, British Airways may well have wondered if the tables had been turned.

It all began in mid-July 2004, when oil prices were rising. British prosecutors alleged that the two airlines had plotted to levy fuel surcharges on passengers. For the next two years, according to the prosecutors, the rivals had established a cartel through which they coordinated increases in surcharges. British Airways first introduced a £5 (US$8.25) surcharge on long-haul flights when a barrel of oil traded at about US$38. It increased the surcharge six times, so that by 2006, when oil was trading at about US$69 a barrel, the surcharge was £70 (US$115). At the same time, Virgin Atlantic also levied a £70 fee. These surcharges increased within days of each other.

Eventually, three Virgin executives decided to blow the whistle in exchange for immunity from prosecution. British Airways immediately suspended its executives under suspicion and paid fines of nearly US$500 million to U.S. and U.K. authorities. And in 2010, four British Airways executives were prosecuted by British authorities for their alleged role in the conspiracy.

The lawyers for the executives argued that although the two airlines had swapped information, this was not proof of a criminal conspiracy. In fact, they argued, Virgin was so fearful of American regulators that it had admitted to criminal behaviour before confirming that it had indeed committed an offence.

One of the defence lawyers, Clare Montgomery, argued that because U.S. laws against anti-competitive behaviour are much tougher than those in the United Kingdom, companies may be compelled to blow the whistle to avoid investigation. "It's a race," she said. "If you don't get to them and confess first, you can't get immunity. The only way to protect yourself is to go to the authorities, even if you haven't [done anything]." The result was that the Virgin executives were given immunity in both the United States and the United Kingdom, but the British Airways executives were subject to prosecution (and possible multiyear jail terms) in both countries.

In late 2011, the case came to a shocking end for Virgin Atlantic and U.K. authorities. Citing e-mails that Virgin was forced to turn over by the court, the judge found insufficient evidence that there was ever a conspiracy between the two airlines. The court was incensed enough to threaten to rescind the immunity granted to the three Virgin executives.

QUESTIONS FOR THOUGHT

1. Explain why Virgin Atlantic and British Airways might collude in response to increased oil prices. Was the market conducive to collusion or not?

2. How would you determine whether illegal behaviour actually occurred? What might explain these events other than illegal behaviour?

3. Explain the dilemma facing the two airlines as well as their individual executives.

SUMMARY

1. Many industries are **oligopolies:** there are only a few sellers. In particular, a **duopoly** has only two sellers. Oligopolies exist for more or less the same reasons that monopolies exist, but in weaker form. They are characterized by **imperfect competition:** firms compete but possess market power.

2. Oligopolists operate in a state of **interdependence** in which the actions of one firm have a significant effect on the profits of its rivals. The firms in an oligopoly could maximize their combined profits by acting as a **cartel,** setting output levels for each firm as if they were a single monopolist; to the extent that firms manage to do this, they engage in **collusion.** But each individual firm has an incentive to produce more than it would in such an arrangement—to engage in **noncooperative behaviour.**

3. The situation of interdependence, in which each firm's profit depends noticeably on what other firms do, is the subject of **game theory.** In the case of a game with two players, the **payoff** of each player depends both on its own actions and on the actions of the other; this interdependence can be represented as a **payoff matrix.** Depending on the structure of payoffs in the payoff matrix, a player may have a **dominant**

strategy—an action that is always the best regardless of the other player's actions.

4. **Duopolists** face a particular type of game known as a **prisoners' dilemma;** if each acts independently in its own interest, the resulting **Nash equilibrium** or **noncooperative equilibrium** will be bad for both. However, firms that expect to play a game repeatedly tend to engage in **strategic behaviour,** trying to influence each other's future actions. A particular strategy that seems to work well in maintaining **tactic collusion** is **tit for tat.**

5. In order to limit the ability of oligopolists to collude and act like monopolists, most governments pursue an **antitrust policy** designed to make collusion more difficult. In practice, however, tacit collusion is widespread.

6. A variety of factors make tacit collusion difficult: large numbers of firms, complex products and pricing, differences in interests, and bargaining power of buyers. When tacit collusion breaks down, there is a **price war.** Oligopolists try to avoid price wars in various ways, such as through **product differentiation** and through **price leadership,** in which one firm sets prices for the industry. Another is through **nonprice competition,** such as advertising.

KEY TERMS

PRACTICE QUESTIONS

1. Epic Games's massively popular online game *Fortnite* starts with 100 players who are dropped onto an island to face off in a game that resembles the one in Suzanne Collins's book series *The Hunger Games.* Each player must scavenge or barter for weapons and eliminate the other players in their path; the last player standing wins. Launched in 2017, today the game boasts more than 350 million users. Players can play for free but often spend money on special skins (costumes) and pay for access to specific battles. However, developers at Epic Games recently noticed a worrying trend: more advanced players were colluding in the game. In response to the collusion, Epic Games is now banning any player that colludes.

   a. What is the incentive for players to collude in *Fortnite*?

   b. Why would Epic Games want to eliminate collusion in *Fortnite*?

2. In George R.R. Martin's novel *A Storm of Swords* (one of the books that inspired HBO's *Game of Thrones*), the young and sadistic King Joffrey has the largest army in the realm at his command. Joffrey is offered the following advice by his grandfather, Lord Tywin, who is also the army commander: "Joffrey, when your enemies defy you, you must serve them steel and fire. When they go to their knees, however, you must help them back to their feet. Elsewise no man will ever bend the knee to you."

a. Assume that King Joffrey has one enemy and can make two choices: serve them steel and fire (violence) or offer them a hand (forgiveness). King Joffrey's enemy must also make a decision to fight or surrender. In a single game, what is the likely outcome between King Joffrey and his enemy?

b. Now suppose King Joffrey faces potential threats from multiple enemies. What is the likely outcome for King Joffrey if he ignores Lord Tywin's advice?

c. What type of strategy does Lord Tywin propose? Explain how it will likely lead to a different outcome?

PROBLEMS

1. The accompanying table presents recent market share data for the global smartphone market.

Company	Market share
Apple	19.9%
Samsung	18.8
Huawei	15.2
Xiaomi	8.9
OPPO	8.3

a. Use the data provided to calculate the Herfindahl–Hirschman Index (HHI) for the market.

b. Based on this HHI, what type of market structure is the global smartphone market?

2. The accompanying table shows the demand schedule for vitamin D. Suppose that the marginal cost of producing vitamin D is zero.

Price of vitamin D (per tonne)	Quantity of vitamin D demanded (tonnes)
$8	0
7	10
6	20
5	30
4	40
3	50
2	60
1	70

a. Assume that BASF is the only producer of vitamin D and acts as a monopolist. It currently produces 40 tonnes of vitamin D at $4 per tonne. If BASF were to produce 10 more tonnes, what would be the price effect for BASF? What would be the quantity effect? Would BASF have an incentive to produce those 10 additional tonnes?

b. Now assume that Roche enters the market by also producing vitamin D and the market is now a duopoly. BASF and Roche agree to produce 40 tonnes of vitamin D in total, 20 tonnes each. BASF cannot be punished for deviating from the agreement with Roche. If BASF, on its own, were to deviate from that agreement and produce 10 more tonnes, what would be the price effect for BASF? What would be the quantity effect for BASF? Would BASF have an incentive to produce those 10 additional tonnes?

3. The market for honey in Winnipeg is controlled by two companies, Busy Bees and Honey Hive. Both companies will ruthlessly eliminate any other company that attempts to enter the Winnipeg honey market. The marginal cost of producing honey is constant and equal to $40 per kilogram. There is no fixed cost. The accompanying table gives the market demand schedule for honey.

Price of honey (per kilogram)	Quantity of honey demanded (kilograms)
$100	1,000
90	1,500
80	2,000
70	2,500
60	3,000
50	3,500
40	4,000
30	4,500
20	5,000
10	5,500

a. Suppose Busy Bees and Honey Hive form a cartel. For each of the quantities given in the table, calculate the total revenue for their cartel and the marginal revenue for each additional kilogram. How many kilograms of honey would the cartel sell in total and at what price? The two companies share the market equally (each produces half of the total output of the cartel). How much profit does each company make?

b. Beatrice Buzz, the CEO of Busy Bees, breaks the agreement and sells 500 more kilograms of honey than under the cartel agreement. Assuming the Honey Hive maintains the agreement, how does this affect the price for honey and the profit earned by each company?

c. Quincy Queen, the CEO of Honey Hive, decides to punish Busy Bees by increasing their sales by 500 kilograms as well. How much profit does each company earn now?

4. In France, the market for bottled water is controlled by two large firms, Perrier and Evian. Each firm has a fixed cost of €1 million and a constant marginal cost of €2 per litre of bottled water (€1 = 1 euro). The following table gives the market demand schedule for bottled water in France.

Price of bottled water (per litre)	Quantity of bottled water demanded (millions of litres)
€10	0
9	1
8	2
7	3
6	4
5	5
4	6
3	7
2	8
1	9

a. Suppose the two firms form a cartel and act as a monopolist. Calculate marginal revenue for the cartel. What will the monopoly price and output be? Assuming the firms divide the output evenly, how much will each produce and what will each firm's profit be?

b. Now suppose Perrier decides to increase production by 1 million litres. Evian doesn't change its production. What will the new market price and output be? What is Perrier's profit? What is Evian's profit?

c. What if Perrier increases production by 3 million litres? Evian doesn't change its production. What would Perrier's output and profit be relative to those in part b?

d. What do your results tell you about the likelihood of cheating on such agreements?

5. To preserve the North Atlantic fish stocks, it is decided that only two fishing fleets, one from North America and the other from the EU, can fish in those waters. Suppose that this fisheries agreement breaks down, so that the fleets behave noncooperatively. Assume that North America and the EU each can send out either one or two fleets. The more fleets in the area, the more fish they catch in total but the lower the catch of each fleet. The accompanying matrix shows the profit (in dollars) per week earned by each side.

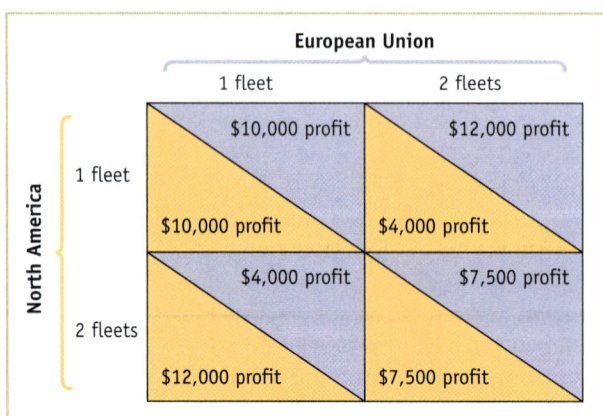

a. What is the noncooperative Nash equilibrium? Will each side choose to send out one or two fleets?

b. Suppose that the fish stocks are being depleted. Each region considers the future and comes to a tit-for-tat agreement whereby each side will send only one fleet out as long as the other does the same. If either of them breaks the agreement and sends out a second fleet, the other will also send out two and will continue to do so until its competitor sends out only one fleet. If both play this tit-for-tat strategy, how much profit will each make every week?

6. Untied and Air "R" Us are the only two airlines operating flights between Petiteville and Bigtown. That is, they operate in a duopoly. Each airline can charge either a high price or a low price for a ticket. The accompanying matrix shows their payoffs, in profits per seat (in dollars), for any choice that the two airlines can make.

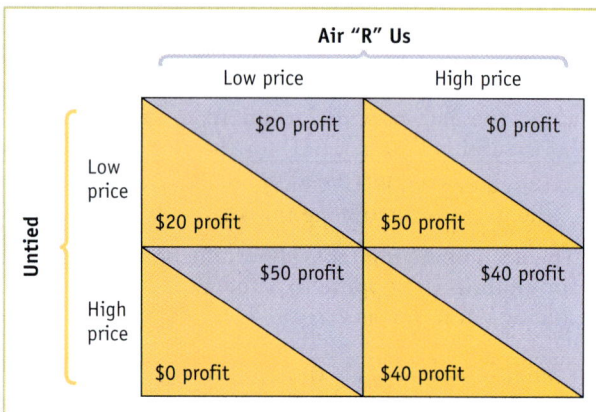

a. Suppose the two airlines play a one-shot game—that is, they interact only once and never again. What will be the Nash (noncooperative) equilibrium in this one-shot game?

b. Now suppose the two airlines play this game twice. And suppose each airline can play one of two strategies: it can play either always charge the low price or tit for tat—that is, it starts off charging the high price in the first period, and then in the second period it does whatever the other airline did in the previous period. Write down the payoffs to Untied from the following four possibilities:

  i. Untied plays always charge the low price when Air "R" Us also plays always charge the low price.

  ii. Untied plays always charge the low price when Air "R" Us plays tit for tat.

  iii. Untied plays tit for tat when Air "R" Us plays always charge the low price.

  iv. Untied plays tit for tat when Air "R" Us also plays tit for tat.

7. Suppose that Coke and Pepsi are the only two producers of cola drinks, making them duopolists. Both companies have zero marginal cost and a fixed cost of $100,000.

  a. Assume first that consumers regard Coke and Pepsi as perfect substitutes. Currently both are sold for

$0.20 per can, and at that price each company sells 4 million cans per day.

   i. How large is Pepsi's profit?

   ii. If Pepsi were to raise its price to $0.30 per can, and Coke did not respond, keeping its price at $0.20 per can, what would happen to Pepsi's profit?

b. Now suppose that each company advertises to differentiate its product from the other company's. As a result of advertising, Pepsi realizes that if it raises or lowers its price, it will sell less or more of its product, as shown by the demand schedule in the accompanying table.

Price of Pepsi (per can)	Quantity of Pepsi demanded (millions of cans)
$0.10	5
0.20	4
0.30	3
0.40	2
0.50	1

If Pepsi now were to raise its price to $0.30 per can, what would happen to its profit?

c. Comparing your answer to part a(i) and to part b, what is the maximum amount Pepsi would be willing to spend on advertising?

8. Second Cup and Starbucks spend huge sums of money each year to advertise their coffee in an attempt to steal customers from each other. Suppose each year Second Cup and Starbucks have to decide whether or not they want to spend money on advertising. If neither firm advertises, each will earn a profit of $2 million. If they both advertise, each will earn a profit of $1.5 million. If one firm advertises and the other does not, the firm that advertises will earn a profit of $2.8 million and the other firm will earn $1 million.

a. Use a payoff matrix to depict this problem.

b. Suppose Second Cup and Starbucks can write an enforceable contract about what they will do. What is the cooperative solution to this game?

c. What is the Nash equilibrium without an enforceable contract? Explain why this is the likely outcome.

9. Over the last 40 years, OPEC has had varied success in forming and maintaining its cartel agreements. Explain how the following factors may contribute to the difficulty of forming and/or maintaining its price and output agreements.

a. New oil fields are discovered and increased drilling is undertaken in the Gulf of Mexico and the North Sea by nonmembers of OPEC.

b. Crude oil is a product that is differentiated by sulfur content: it costs less to refine low-sulfur crude oil into gasoline. Different OPEC countries possess oil reserves of different sulfur content.

c. Cars powered by hydrogen are developed.

10. Suppose you are an economist working for the Competition Bureau. In each of the following cases you are given the task of determining whether the behaviour warrants an antitrust investigation for possible illegal acts or is just an example of undesirable, but not illegal, tacit collusion. Explain your reasoning.

a. Two companies dominate the industry for industrial lasers. Several people sit on the boards of directors of both companies.

b. Three banks dominate the market for banking in a given state. Their profits have been going up recently as they add new fees for customer transactions. Advertising among the banks is fierce, and new branches are springing up in many locations.

c. The two oil companies that produce most of the petroleum for western Canada have decided to forgo building their own pipelines and to share a common pipeline, the only means of transporting petroleum products to that market.

d. The two major companies that dominate the market for herbal supplements have each created a subsidiary that sells the same product as the parent company in large quantities but with a generic name.

e. The two largest credit card companies, Passport and OmniCard, have required all retailers who accept their cards to agree to limit their use of rival credit cards.

11. In 2015, Anheuser-Busch InBev offered US$104.2 billion to acquire SABMiller. The U.S. Justice Department approved the merger, but only after the two beer giants agreed to sell off a number of brands, including Miller Lite, Peroni, and Snow (the world's top-selling beer produced in China). Anheuser-Busch InBev sought the merger to increase its global market share. The accompanying table presents the global market share before and after the merger for the world's 10 largest brewers.

Brewers	Market share	
	Before merger	After merger
AB InBev	21%	29%
SABMiller	10	–
Heineken	9	11
Carlsberg	6	6
China Resource Brewery Ltd.	6	6
Tsingtao Brewery Group	4	4
Molson Coors	3	4
Yanjing	3	3
Kirin	2	2
BGI/Groupe Castel	2	2

a. Using the table, calculate the HHI for the global beer market both before and after the merger.

b. Based on the HHI calculated in part a, how has the market structure for the global beer industry changed?

12. In 2011, the U.S Justice Department rejected AT&T's proposal to purchase T-Mobile for US$39 billion due to anti-competitive concerns. A few years later, Sprint launched its own attempt to purchase T-Mobile. In 2019, Sprint's discussions with T-Mobile about a potential takeover were still ongoing, with a proposed merger close to complete.

a. Use the accompanying table to calculate the HHI before and after the proposed 2011 merger of AT&T and T-Mobile.

b. Use the table to calculate the HHI before and after the proposed merger of Sprint and T-Mobile in 2019.

c. Based on your calculations in parts a and b, do you think the U.S Justice Department is likely to approve a merger between Sprint and T-Mobile?

Carrier	2011	2019
Verizon	34%	29%
AT&T	32	40
Sprint	17	13
T-Mobile	10	16

13. Note: This is a challenging question that uses the algebraic method to solve problems from Appendix 3A and Appendix 6A.

The market for widgets is characterized by many buyers but only two producers, A and B. The market demand for widgets is given by:

$$P = 200 - 5Q^d$$

where Q^d = total demand for widgets and $Q^d = q_A + q_B$.

Both producers face the same production cost, which is $20 in fixed cost and a constant variable cost of $5 per widget. In other words, the cost functions for A and B are:

$$TC_A = 20 + 5q_A$$
$$TC_B = 20 + 5q_B$$

a. Determine the best response functions for producers A and B.

b. Determine the profit-maximizing levels of output by producers A and B if they both choose the quantity of widgets produced simultaneously. What is the profit for each producer?

c. If both producers collude, what is the equilibrium price and quantity? Determine the industry profit under the collusive outcome.

d. Compare your answers to parts b and c. Which outcome (collusive or noncollusive) would the producers prefer? Explain.

e. Which outcome (collusive or noncollusive) is a more stable outcome? Explain.

WORK IT OUT

14. Let's revisit the fisheries agreement introduced in Problem 5 stating that to preserve the North Atlantic fish stocks, only two fishing fleets, one from the North America and the other from the EU, can fish in those waters. The accompanying table shows the market demand schedule per week for fish from these waters. The only costs are fixed costs, so fishing fleets maximize profit by maximizing revenue.

Price of fish (per kilogram)	Quantity of fish demanded (kilograms)
$17	1,800
16	2,000
15	2,100
14	2,200
12	2,300

a. If both fishing fleets collude, what is the revenue-maximizing output for the North Atlantic fishery? What price will a kilogram of fish sell for?

b. If both fishing fleets collude and share the output equally, what is the revenue to the EU fleet? To the North American fleet?

c. Suppose the EU fleet cheats by expanding its own catch by 100 kilograms per week. The North American fleet doesn't change its catch. What is the revenue to the North American fleet? To the EU fleet?

d. In retaliation for the cheating by the EU fleet, the North American fleet also expands its catch by 100 kilograms per week. What is the revenue to the North American fleet? To the EU fleet? ∎

.15 Monopolistic Competition and Product Differentiation

THE FOOD COURT OF CANADA

WITH OVER 800 STORES covering over 5.3 million square feet and catering to over 30.8 million visitors annually, the West Edmonton Mall, located in Alberta is the largest mall in Canada. To make sure that the thousands who visit it daily have plenty of energy to shop, it also contains the largest and most extensive food court in the country, with over 100 dining venues. There you can find Edo Japan, A&W, Jimmy the Greek, New York Fries, Oriental Dim Sum, Taco Time, Thai Express, and many, many more. With its enormous variety, the West Edmonton Mall food court is a microcosm of the Canadian fast-food industry.

So how would you describe the fast-food industry? On the one side, it clearly isn't a monopoly. When you go to a fast-food court, you have a choice among vendors, and there is real competition between them. For example, there is competition between A&W and Burger King for the burger diners, as well as competition between the burger vendors and the pizza vendors. On the other side, in a way, each vendor *does* possess some aspects of a monopoly because each vendor offers a different menu and a different eating experience. For example, Burger King is the "home of the Whopper," a flame-grilled hamburger, but if you prefer a Big Mac, you can only find one at McDonalds. The point is that each fast-food provider offers a product that is *differentiated* from its rivals' products.

In the fast-food industry, many firms compete to satisfy more or less the same demand — the desire of consumers for something tasty and quick. But each firm offers to satisfy that demand with a distinctive, differentiated product — products that

Competing for your taste buds.

consumers typically view as close but not perfect substitutes.

When there are many firms offering competing, differentiated products, as there are in the fast-food industry, economists say that the industry is characterized by *monopolistic competition*. This is the fourth and final market structure that we will discuss (having covered perfect competition, monopoly, and oligopoly in earlier chapters).

We'll start by defining monopolistic competition more carefully and explaining its characteristic features. Then we'll explore how firms differentiate their products; this will allow us to analyze how monopolistic competition works. The chapter concludes with a discussion of some ongoing controversies about product differentiation — in particular, the question of why advertising is effective. ●

WHAT YOU WILL LEARN

- What is **monopolistic competition?**
- Why do oligopolists and monopolistically competitive firms differentiate their products?
- How are prices and profits determined in monopolistic competition in the short run and the long run?
- How does monopolistic competition pose a trade-off between lower prices and greater product diversity?
- What is the economic significance of advertising and **brand names?**

Monopolistic competition is a market structure in which there are many competing producers in an industry, each producer sells a differentiated product, and there is free entry into and exit from the industry in the long run.

‖ The Meaning of Monopolistic Competition

Leo owns the Wonderful Wok stand in the food court of a big shopping mall. He offers the only dim sum and fried rice there, but there are more than a dozen other vendors from Bodacious Burgers to Pizza Paradise. When deciding what to charge for a meal, Leo knows that he must take those alternatives into account: even people who normally prefer fried rice won't order a $20 lunch from Leo when they can get a burger, fries, and drink for $6.

But Leo also knows that he won't lose all his business even if his lunches cost a bit more than the alternatives. Fried rice and dim sum aren't the same things as burgers or pizza. Some people will really be in the mood for fried rice that day, and they will buy from Leo even if they could dine more cheaply on burgers. Of course, the reverse is also true: even if a meal at Wonderful Wok is a bit cheaper, some people will choose burgers instead. In other words, Leo does have some market power: he has *some* ability to set his own price.

So how would you describe Leo's situation? He definitely isn't a price-taker, so he isn't in a situation of perfect competition. But you wouldn't exactly call him a monopolist, either. Although he's the only seller of Chinese food in that food court, he does face competition from other food vendors.

Yet it would also be wrong to call him an oligopolist. Oligopoly, remember, involves competition among a small number of interdependent firms in an industry protected by some—albeit limited—barriers to entry and whose profits are highly interdependent. Because their profits are highly interdependent, oligopolists have an incentive to collude, tacitly or explicitly. But in Leo's case there are *lots* of vendors in the shopping mall, too many to make tacit collusion feasible.

Economists describe Leo's situation as one of **monopolistic competition.** Monopolistic competition is particularly common in service industries like restaurants and gas stations, but it also exists in some manufacturing industries. It involves three conditions: large numbers of competing producers, differentiated products, and free entry into and exit from the industry in the long run.

In a monopolistically competitive industry, each producer has some ability to set the price of their differentiated product. But exactly how high they can set it is limited by the competition they face from other existing and potential producers that produce close, but not identical, products.

Large Numbers

In a monopolistically competitive industry, there are many producers. Such an industry does not look either like a monopoly, where the firm faces no competition, or an oligopoly, where each firm has only a few rivals. Instead, each seller has many competitors. For example, there are many vendors in a big food court, many gas stations along a major highway, and many hotels at a popular ski resort.

Differentiated Products

In a monopolistically competitive industry, each producer has a product that consumers view as somewhat distinct from the products of competing firms; at the same time, though, consumers see these competing products as close substitutes. If Leo's food court contained 15 vendors selling exactly the same kind and quality of food, there would be perfect competition: any seller who tried to charge a higher price would have no customers. But suppose that Wonderful Wok is the only Chinese food vendor, Bodacious Burgers is the only hamburger stand, and so on. The result of this differentiation is that each seller has some ability to set their own price: each producer has some—albeit limited—market power.

Free Entry and Exit in the Long Run

In monopolistically competitive industries, new producers, with their own distinct products, can enter the industry freely in the long run. For example, other food vendors would open outlets in the food court if they thought it would be profitable to do so. In addition, firms will exit the industry if they find they are not covering their costs in the long run.

Monopolistic Competition: In Sum

Monopolistic competition, then, differs from the three market structures we have examined so far. It's not the same as perfect competition: firms have some power to set prices. It's not pure monopoly: firms face some competition. And it's not the same as oligopoly: because there are many firms and free entry, the potential for collusion so important in oligopoly no longer exists.

We'll see in a moment how prices, output, and the number of products available are determined in monopolistically competitive industries. But first, let's look a little more closely at what it means to have differentiated products.

‖ Product Differentiation

Product differentiation often plays an important role in oligopolistic industries because it reduces the intensity of competition between firms when tacit collusion cannot be achieved. Product differentiation plays an even more crucial role in monopolistically competitive industries. Because tacit collusion is virtually impossible when there are many producers, product differentiation is the only way monopolistically competitive firms can acquire some market power.

How do firms in the same industry—such as fast-food vendors, gas stations, or chocolate makers—differentiate their products? Sometimes the difference is mainly in the minds of consumers rather than in the products. We'll discuss the role of advertising and the importance of brand names in achieving this kind of product differentiation later in the chapter. But, in general, firms differentiate their products by—surprise!—actually making them different.

The key to product differentiation is that consumers have different preferences and are willing to pay somewhat more to satisfy those preferences. Each producer can carve out a market niche by producing something that caters to the particular preferences of some group of consumers better than the products of other firms.

There are three important forms of product differentiation:

1. By style or type
2. By location
3. By quality

Differentiation by Style or Type

The other sellers in Leo's food court offer different types of fast food: hamburgers, pizza, tacos, and so on. Each consumer arrives at the food court with some preference for one or another of these offerings. This preference may depend on the consumer's mood, their diet, or what they have already eaten that day. These preferences will not make consumers indifferent to price: if Wonderful Wok were to charge $15 for an egg roll, everybody would go to Bodacious Burgers or Pizza Paradise instead. But some people will choose a more expensive meal if that type of food is closer to their preference. So the products of the different vendors are substitutes, but they aren't *perfect* substitutes—they are *imperfect substitutes*.

Vendors in a food court aren't the only sellers that differentiate their offerings by type. Clothing stores concentrate on women's or men's clothes, on business or casual clothes, on trendy or classic styles, and so on. Auto manufacturers offer sedans, minivans, sport-utility vehicles, and sports cars, each type aimed at drivers with different needs and tastes.

Books offer yet another example of differentiation by type and style. Mysteries are differentiated from romances; among mysteries, we can differentiate among hard-boiled detective stories, whodunits, and police procedurals. And no two writers of fantasy and science fiction are exactly alike: J. K. Rowling and Margaret Atwood each have their devoted fans.

In fact, product differentiation is characteristic of most consumer goods. As long as people differ in their tastes, producers find it possible and profitable to produce a wide variety of goods.

Differentiation by Location

Gas stations along a road offer differentiated products. True, the gas may be exactly the same. But the location of the stations is different, and location matters to consumers: it's more convenient to stop for gas near your home, near your workplace, or near wherever you are when the gas gauge gets low.

In fact, many monopolistically competitive industries supply goods differentiated by location. This is especially true in service industries, from car mechanics to drugstores, where customers often choose the seller who is closest rather than cheapest.

For industries that differentiate by location, proximity is everything.

Differentiation by Quality

Do you have a craving for chocolate? How much are you willing to spend on it? You see, there's chocolate and then there's chocolate: although ordinary chocolate may not be very expensive, gourmet chocolate can cost several dollars per bite.

With chocolate, as with many goods, there is a range of possible qualities. You can get a usable bicycle for less than $100; you can get a much fancier bicycle for 10 times as much. It all depends on how much the additional quality matters to you and how much you will miss the other things you could have purchased with that money.

Because consumers vary in what they are willing to pay for higher quality, producers can differentiate their products by quality—some offering lower-quality, inexpensive products and others offering higher-quality products at a higher price.

Product Differentiation: In Sum

Product differentiation, then, can take several forms. Whatever form it takes, however, there are two important features of industries with differentiated products:

1. *There is competition among sellers:* even though sellers of differentiated products are not offering identical goods, they are to some extent competing for a limited market. If more businesses enter the market, each will find that it sells less quantity at any given price. For example, if a new gas station opens along a particular road, each of the existing gas stations will sell a bit less.

2. *There is value in variety:* consumers benefit from the proliferation of differentiated products. A food court with eight vendors makes consumers happier than one with only six vendors, even if the prices are the same, because some customers will get a meal that is closer to what they had in mind. A road on which there is a gas station every two kilometres is more convenient for drivers than a road where gas stations are five kilometres apart. Likewise, when a product

is available with a range of quality standards, fewer people are forced to pay for higher quality than they need or to settle for lower quality than they want.

As we'll see next, competition among the sellers of differentiated products is the key to understanding how monopolistic competition works.

ECONOMICS >> *in Action*
Abbondanza!

Has the experience of trying to choose a pasta sauce among the dozens of varieties on the shelves in the grocery store ever left you feeling overwhelmed? If so, you have one person to thank and to blame: Howard Moskowitz, an American market researcher and psychophysicist. Thirty years ago, making your selection was much simpler: there was no Newman's Sockarooni, no Barilla's Spicy Marinara with Roasted Garlic, no Emeril's Homestyle, no Classico's Tomato Basil. In fact, there were only two brands available, Prego and Ragú. And they offered only one variety each—plain spaghetti sauce.

In the late 1980s, Prego was in a slump compared to its rival, Ragú. While searching for a way to turn its business around, the company concluded that Prego and Ragú pasta sauces were relatively indistinguishable. But rather than engage in a price war with its rival, Prego hired Moskowitz, who realized that the answer to Prego's dilemma was to find out what appealed to consumers' taste buds and then use this to distinguish Prego from Ragú. Moskowitz proceeded to create 45 varieties of pasta sauces, varied on every conceivable measure: sweetness, spiciness, tartness, saltiness, thickness, and so on. He then taste-tested them around the country. What stood out was consumers' preference for extra chunky sauce—an unavailable option at the time, when both Prego and Ragú offered highly blended, watery sauces.

In 1989, Prego launched its Extra Chunky variety, and it was extraordinarily successful. It's a measure of Moskowitz's success that today it is hard to appreciate the radicalness of his approach. Thirty years ago, the food industry believed it should strive to create a "platonic dish"—some ideal version that would completely satisfy consumers' tastes. Prego and Ragú offered thin pasta sauces because their ideal reflected how sauce was made in Italy. But Prego came to understand the importance of setting itself apart while avoiding head-to-head price competition with Ragú, which would ultimately be self-defeating. Along came Moskowitz, who freed the food industry to indulge consumers' iconoclastic desire for variety and distinctive flavours. So the next time you are puzzling over which pasta sauce to buy, think of Moskowitz and his radical ideas.

A dizzying variety of pasta sauces is available — thanks to monopolistic competition.

>> Check Your Understanding 15-1
Solutions appear at back of book.

1. Each of the following goods and services is a differentiated product. Which are differentiated as a result of monopolistic competition and which are not? Explain your answers.
   a. Ladders
   b. Soft drinks
   c. Clothing stores
   d. Steel

2. You must determine which of two types of market structure better describes an industry, but you are allowed to ask only one question about the industry. What question should you ask to determine if an industry is:
   a. Perfectly competitive or monopolistically competitive?
   b. A monopoly or monopolistically competitive?

>> Quick Review

• In **monopolistic competition** there are many competing producers, each with a differentiated product, and free entry and exit in the long run.

• Product differentiation can occur in oligopolies that fail to achieve tacit collusion as well as in monopolistic competition. It takes three main forms: by style or type, by location, or by quality. The products of competing sellers are considered imperfect substitutes.

• Producers compete for the same market, so entry by more producers reduces the quantity each existing producer sells at any given price. In addition, consumers gain from the increased diversity of products.

‖ Understanding Monopolistic Competition

Suppose an industry is monopolistically competitive: it consists of many producers, all competing for the same consumers but offering differentiated products. How does such an industry behave?

As the term *monopolistic competition* suggests, this market structure combines some features typical of monopoly with others typical of perfect competition. Because each firm is offering a distinct product, it is in a way like a monopolist: it faces a downward-sloping demand curve and has some market power—the ability within limits to determine the price of its product. However, unlike a pure monopolist, a monopolistically competitive firm does face competition: the amount of its product it can sell depends on the prices and products offered by other firms in the industry.

The same, of course, is true of an oligopoly. In a monopolistically competitive industry, however, there are *many* producers, as opposed to the small number that defines an oligopoly. This means that the puzzle of oligopoly—will firms collude or will they behave noncooperatively?—does not arise in the case of monopolistically competitive industries. True, if all the gas stations or all the restaurants in a town could agree—explicitly or tacitly—to raise prices, it would be in their mutual interest to do so.

But such collusion is virtually impossible when the number of firms is large and, by implication, there are no barriers to entry. So in situations of monopolistic competition, we can safely assume that firms behave noncooperatively and ignore the potential for collusion.

Monopolistic Competition in the Short Run

Recall the distinction between short-run and long-run equilibrium. The short-run equilibrium of an industry takes the number of firms as given. The long-run equilibrium, by contrast, is reached only after enough time has elapsed for firms to enter or exit the industry. To analyze monopolistic competition, we focus first on the short run and then on how an industry moves from the short run to the long run.

Panels (a) and (b) of Figure 15-1 show two possible situations that a typical firm in a monopolistically competitive industry might face in the short run. In each case, the firm looks like any monopolist: it faces a downward-sloping demand curve, which implies a downward-sloping marginal revenue curve.

We assume that every firm has an upward-sloping marginal cost curve but that it also faces some fixed costs, so that its average total cost curve is U-shaped. This assumption doesn't matter in the short run, but, as we'll see shortly, it is crucial to understanding the long-run equilibrium.

In each case the firm, in order to maximize profit, sets marginal revenue equal to marginal cost. So how do these two figures differ? In panel (a), the firm is profitable; in panel (b), it is unprofitable. (Recall that we are referring always to economic profit, not accounting profit—that is, a profit given that all factors of production are earning their opportunity costs.)

In panel (a), the firm faces the demand curve D_P and the marginal revenue curve MR_P. It produces the profit-maximizing output q_P, the quantity at which marginal revenue is equal to marginal cost, and sells it at the price P_P. This price is above the average total cost at this output, ATC_P. The firm's profit is indicated by the area of the shaded rectangle.

In panel (b), the firm faces the demand curve D_U and the marginal revenue curve MR_U. It chooses the quantity q_U at which marginal revenue is equal to marginal cost. However, in this case the price P_U is *below* the average total cost ATC_U; so at this quantity the firm loses money. Its loss is equal to the area of the shaded rectangle. Since q_U is the profit-maximizing quantity—which means, in this case, the loss-minimizing quantity—there is no way for a firm in this situation to make a profit.

FIGURE 15-1 The Monopolistically Competitive Firm in the Short Run

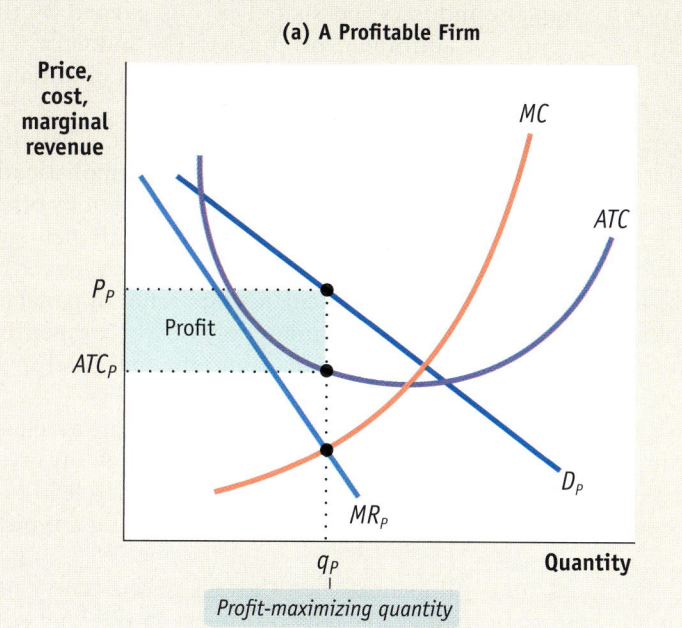

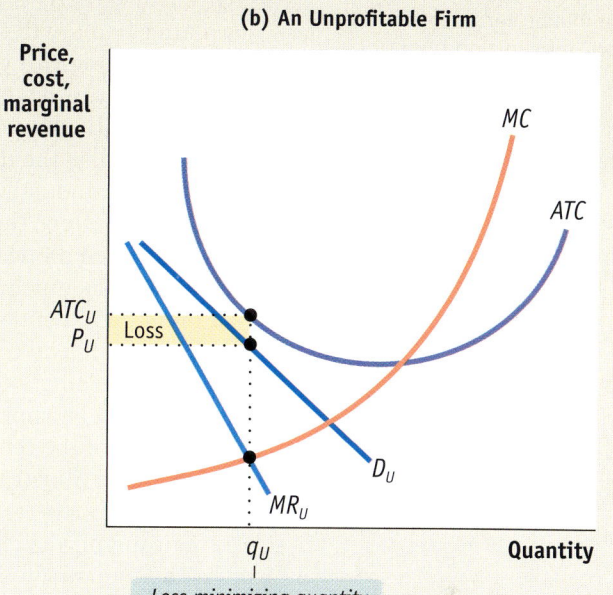

The firm in panel (a) can be profitable for some output quantities: the quantities for which its average total cost curve, *ATC*, lies below its demand curve, *D_P*. The profit-maximizing output quantity is *q_P*, the output at which marginal revenue, *MR_P*, is equal to marginal cost, *MC*. The firm charges price *P_P* and earns a profit, represented by the area of the green-shaded rectangle. The firm in

panel (b), however, can never be profitable because its average total cost curve lies above its demand curve, *D_U*, for every output quantity. The best that it can do if it produces at all is to produce quantity *q_U* and charge price *P_U*. This generates a loss, indicated by the area of the yellow-shaded rectangle. Any other output quantity results in a greater loss.

We can confirm this by noting that at *any* quantity of output, the average total cost curve in panel (b) lies above the demand curve D_U. Because $ATC > P$ at all quantities of output, this firm always suffers a loss.

As this comparison suggests, the key to whether a firm with market power is profitable or unprofitable in the short run lies in the relationship between its demand curve and its average total cost curve. In panel (a) the demand curve D_P crosses the average total cost curve, meaning that some of the demand curve lies above the average total cost curve. So there are some price–quantity combinations available at which price is higher than average total cost, indicating that the firm can choose a quantity at which it makes positive profit.

In panel (b), by contrast, the demand curve D_U does not cross the average total cost curve—it always lies below it. So the price corresponding to each quantity demanded is always less than the average total cost of producing that quantity. There is no quantity at which the firm can avoid losing money.

These figures, showing firms facing downward-sloping demand curves and their associated marginal revenue curves, look just like ordinary monopoly analysis. The "competition" aspect of monopolistic competition comes into play, however, when we move from the short run to the long run.

Monopolistic Competition in the Long Run

Obviously, an industry in which existing firms are losing money, like the one in panel (b) of Figure 15-1, is not in long-run equilibrium. When existing firms are losing money, some firms will *exit* the industry. The industry will not be in long-run equilibrium until the persistent losses have been eliminated by the exit of some firms.

In the long run, a monopolistically competitive industry ends up in **zero-profit equilibrium:** each firm makes zero profit at its profit-maximizing quantity.

It may be less obvious that an industry in which existing firms are earning profits, like the one in panel (a) of Figure 15-1, is also not in long-run equilibrium. Given that there is *free entry* into the industry, persistent profits earned by the existing firms will lead to the entry of additional producers. The industry will not be in long-run equilibrium until the persistent profits have been eliminated by the entry of new producers.

How will entry or exit by other firms affect the profits of a typical existing firm? Because the differentiated products offered by firms in a monopolistically competitive industry compete for the same set of customers, entry or exit by other firms will affect the demand curve facing every existing producer. If new gas stations open along a highway, each of the existing gas stations will no longer be able to sell as much gas as before at any given price. So, as illustrated in panel (a) of Figure 15-2, entry of additional producers into a monopolistically competitive industry will lead to a *leftward* shift of the demand curve and the marginal revenue curve facing a typical existing producer.

Conversely, suppose that some of the gas stations along the highway close. Then each of the remaining stations will be able to sell more gasoline at any given price. So, as illustrated in panel (b), exit of firms from an industry will lead to a *rightward* shift of the demand curve and marginal revenue curve facing a typical remaining producer.

The industry will be in long-run equilibrium when there is neither entry nor exit. This will occur only when every firm earns zero profit. So in the long run, a monopolistically competitive industry will end up in **zero-profit equilibrium,** in which firms just manage to cover their costs at their profit-maximizing output quantities. (The app industry offers an example of this principle, as you will see in the upcoming Economics in Action.)

We have seen that a firm facing a downward-sloping demand curve will earn positive profits if any part of that demand curve lies above its average total cost

FIGURE 15-2 Entry and Exit Shift Existing Firm's Demand Curve and Marginal Revenue Curve

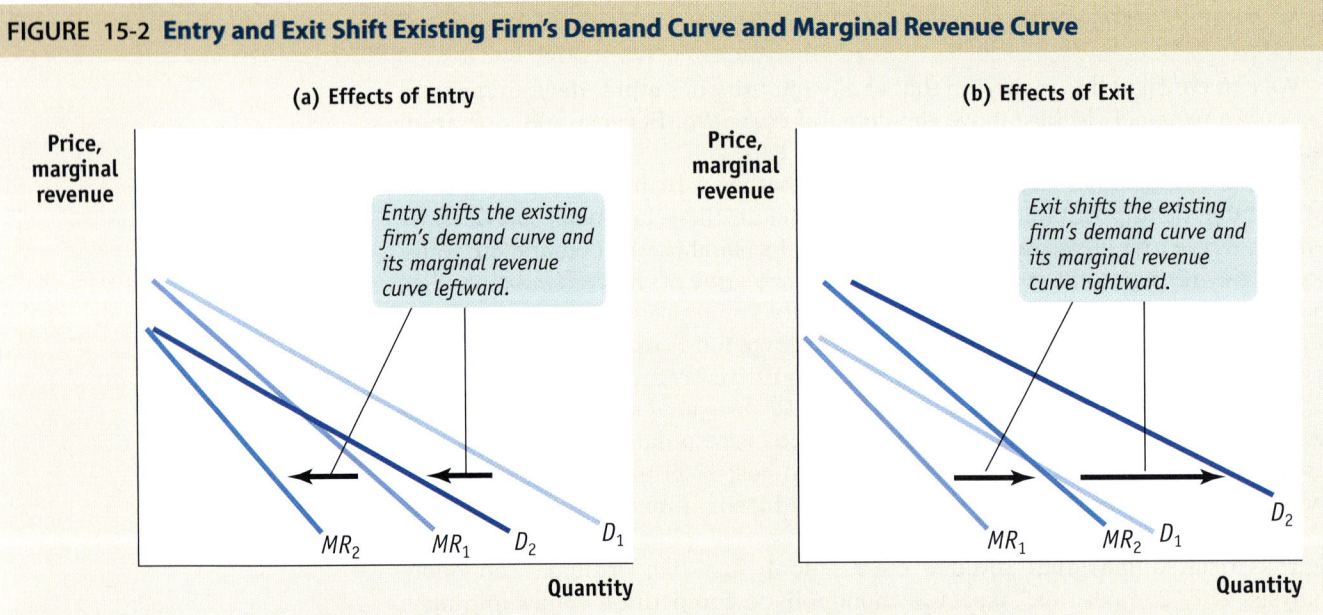

Entry will occur in the long run when existing firms are profitable. In panel (a), entry causes each existing firm's demand curve and marginal revenue curve to shift to the left. The firm receives a lower price for every unit it sells, and its profit falls. Entry will cease when firms make zero profit. Exit will occur in the long run when existing firms are unprofitable. In panel (b), exit from the industry shifts each remaining firm's demand curve and marginal revenue curve to the right. The firm receives a higher price for each unit it sells, and profit rises. Exit will cease when the remaining firms make zero profit.

FIGURE 15-3 The Long-Run Zero-Profit Equilibrium

If existing firms are profitable, entry will occur and shift each existing firm's demand curve leftward. If existing firms are unprofitable, each remaining firm's demand curve shifts rightward as some firms exit the industry. Entry and exit will cease when every existing firm makes zero profit at its profit-maximizing quantity. So, in long-run zero-profit equilibrium, the demand curve of each firm is tangent to its average total cost curve at its profit-maximizing quantity: at the profit-maximizing, q_{MC}, price, P_{MC}, equals average total cost, ATC_{MC}. A monopolistically competitive firm is like a monopolist without monopoly profits.

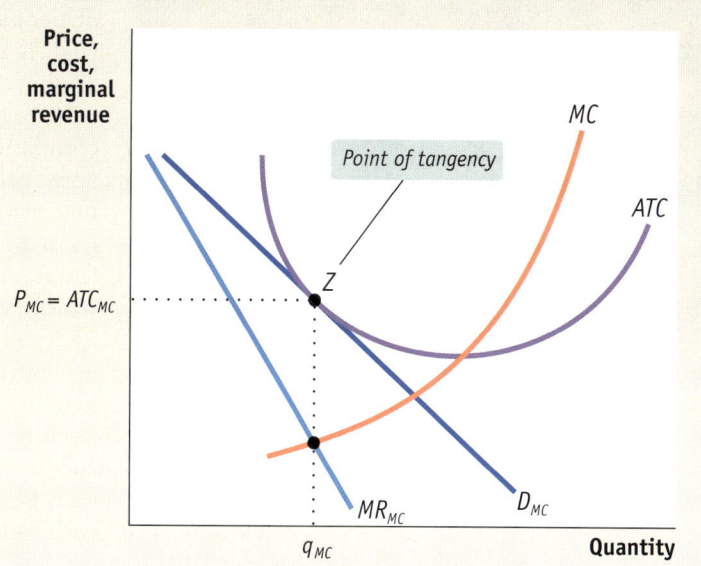

curve; it will incur a loss if its demand curve lies everywhere below its average total cost curve. So in zero-profit equilibrium, the firm must be in a borderline position between these two cases; its demand curve must just touch its average total cost curve. That is, it must be just *tangent* to it at the firm's profit-maximizing output quantity—the output quantity at which marginal revenue equals marginal cost.

If this is not the case, the firm operating at its profit-maximizing quantity will find itself making either a profit or loss, as illustrated in the panels of Figure 15-1. But we also know that free entry and exit means that this cannot be a long-run equilibrium. Why? In the case of a profit, new firms will enter the industry, shifting the demand curve of every existing firm leftward until all profits are extinguished. In the case of a loss, some existing firms will exit and so shift the demand curve of every remaining firm to the right until all losses are extinguished. All entry and exit ceases only when every existing firm makes zero profit at its profit-maximizing quantity of output.

Figure 15-3 shows a typical monopolistically competitive firm in such a zero-profit equilibrium. The firm produces q_{MC}, the output at which $MR_{MC} = MC$, and charges price P_{MC}. At this price and quantity, represented by point Z, the demand curve is just tangent to its average total cost curve. The firm earns zero profit because price, P_{MC}, is equal to average total cost, ATC_{MC}.

The normal long-run condition of a monopolistically competitive industry, then, is that each producer is in the situation shown in Figure 15-3. Each producer acts like a monopolist, facing a downward-sloping demand curve and setting marginal cost equal to marginal revenue so as to maximize profits. But this is just enough to achieve zero economic profit. The producers in the industry are like monopolists without monopoly profits.

ECONOMICS >> *in Action*
Hits and Flops in the App Store

There's no denying that some apps have been extremely lucrative creations. King Digital Entertainment, the company that created the wildly popular game app Candy Crush, was purchased by Activision, owners of Call of Duty, Guitar Hero, and Skylanders, for nearly US$6 billion in 2016. That same year, Uber, the

Although a few apps have been extraordinarily profitable, the app industry can't escape the zero-profit equilibrium.

ride-hailing app, was valued at an astounding US$66 billion. Spurred by these success stories, an unprecedented number of people have rushed to develop mobile apps. But lost in the rush is the fact that the vast majority of apps have flopped or are barely alive.

The app industry looks a lot like an example of monopolistic competition. First, there is free entry in app design. And second, apps are differentiated products. They are differentiated by platform: the iOS (Apple) platform, the Android (Google) platform, or the Microsoft platform. They are also differentiated by function: sharing photos, digital colouring, a virtual koi pond, travel pricing and reservations, personal finance management, and so on. And within each functional subgroup of apps there are variations, each trying to capture a larger share of the market. In 2019, the iOS platform had 2.2 million available apps, slightly less than the 2.6 million apps available from Google Play. The two platforms generated close to 105 billion downloads in 2019. But as one industry observer, Frank Bi, commented, ". . . the easy money is gone."

Hundreds of thousands of apps now languish in obscurity for every breakout hit like TikTok, Snapchat, or Clash of Clans. The original App Store model of selling apps is outdated. Today most apps are downloaded for free or at a minimum expense. In 2011, 63% of apps were paid downloads at an average price of US$3.64; by 2019 that figure dropped to less than 7% with an average price of US$1.01. It's estimated that in 75% of downloads, the app is used once and never again.

At this point, many app developers are struggling to survive, unable to generate enough download revenue to continue operations. In other words, the app creation industry has reached the zero-profit equilibrium state that characterizes monopolistic competition. So, in the end, this cutting edge, high-tech industry cannot escape the consequences of the economics of monopolistic competition.

>> Quick Review

• Like a monopolist, each firm in a monopolistically competitive industry faces a downward-sloping demand curve and marginal revenue curve. In the short run, it may earn a profit or incur a loss at its profit-maximizing quantity.

• If the typical firm earns positive profit, new firms will enter the industry in the long run, shifting each existing firm's demand curve to the left. If the typical firm incurs a loss, some existing firms will exit the industry in the long run, shifting the demand curve of each remaining firm to the right.

• The long-run equilibrium of a monopolistically competitive industry is a **zero-profit equilibrium** in which firms just break even. The typical firm's demand curve is tangent to its average total cost curve at its profit-maximizing quantity.

>> Check Your Understanding 15-2

Solutions appear at back of book.

1. Currently a monopolistically competitive industry, composed of firms with U-shaped average total cost curves, is in long-run equilibrium. Describe how the industry adjusts, in both the short and long run, in each of the following situations.
   a. A technological change that increases fixed cost for every firm in the industry
   b. A technological change that decreases marginal cost for every firm in the industry

2. Why, in the long run, is it impossible for firms in a monopolistically competitive industry to create a monopoly by joining together to form a single firm?

Monopolistic Competition versus Perfect Competition

In a way, long-run equilibrium in a monopolistically competitive industry looks a lot like long-run equilibrium in a perfectly competitive industry. In both cases, there are many firms; in both cases, profits have been competed away; in both cases, the price received by every firm is equal to the average total cost of production.

However, the two versions of long-run equilibrium are different—in ways that are economically significant.

Price, Marginal Cost, and Average Total Cost

Figure 15-4 compares the long-run equilibrium of a typical firm in a perfectly competitive industry with that of a typical firm in a monopolistically competitive

FIGURE 15-4 Comparing Long-Run Equilibrium in Perfect Competition and Monopolistic Competition

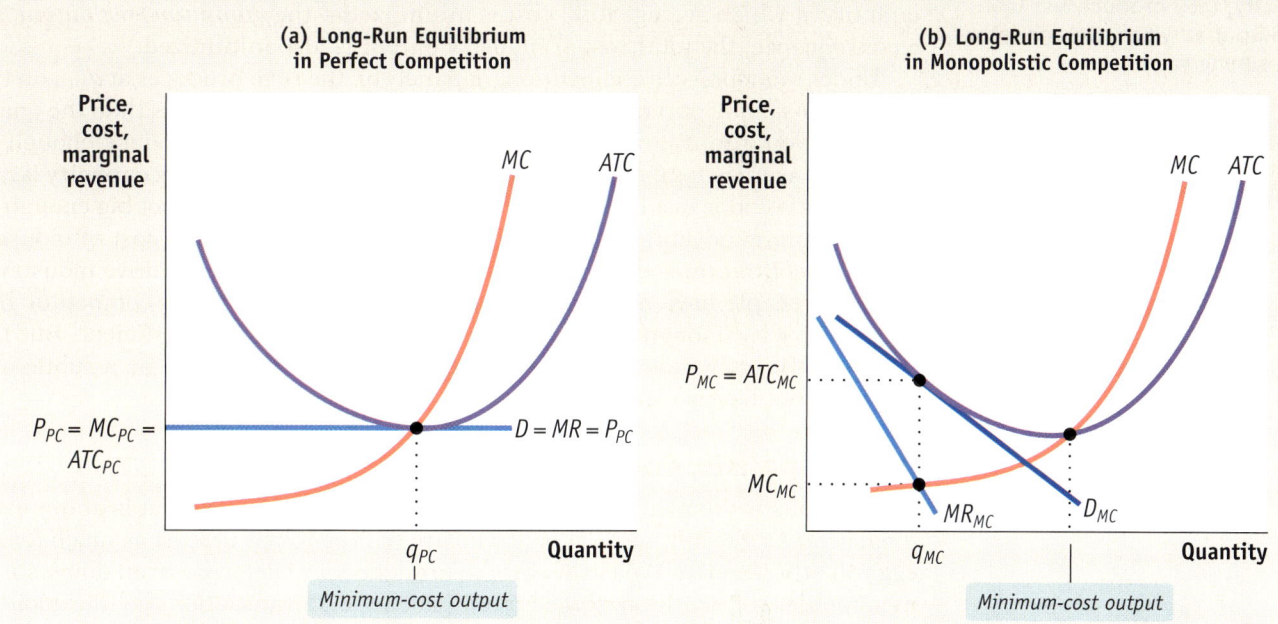

(a) Long-Run Equilibrium in Perfect Competition

(b) Long-Run Equilibrium in Monopolistic Competition

Panel (a) shows the situation of the typical firm in long-run equilibrium in a perfectly competitive industry. The firm operates at the minimum-cost output q_{PC}, sells at the competitive market price P_{PC}, and makes zero profit. It is indifferent to selling another unit of output because P_{PC} is equal to its marginal cost, MC_{PC}. Panel (b) shows the situation of the typical firm in long-run equilibrium in

a monopolistically competitive industry. At q_{MC} it makes zero profit because its price, P_{MC}, just equals average total cost, ATC_{MC}. At q_{MC} the firm would like to sell another unit at price P_{MC} since P_{MC} exceeds marginal cost, MC_{MC}. But it is unwilling to lower price to make more sales. It therefore operates to the left of the minimum-cost output level and has excess capacity.

industry. Panel (a) shows a perfectly competitive firm facing a market price equal to its minimum average total cost; panel (b) reproduces Figure 15-3. Comparing the panels, we see two important differences.

First, in the case of the perfectly competitive firm shown in panel (a), the price, P_{PC}, received by the firm at the profit-maximizing quantity, q_{PC}, is equal to the firm's marginal cost of production, MC_{PC}, at that quantity of output. By contrast, at the profit-maximizing quantity chosen by the monopolistically competitive firm in panel (b), q_{MC}, the price, P_{MC}, is *higher* than the marginal cost of production, MC_{MC}.

This difference translates into a difference in the attitude of firms toward consumers. A wheat farmer, who can sell as much wheat as they like at the going market price, would not get particularly excited if you offered to buy some more wheat at the market price. Since that farmer has no desire to produce more at that price and can sell the wheat to someone else, you are not doing them a favour.

But if you decide to fill up your tank at Jamil's gas station rather than at Katy's, you are doing Jamil a favour. He is not willing to cut his price to get more customers—he's already made the best of that trade-off. But if he gets a few more customers than he expected at the *posted* price, that's good news: an additional sale at the posted price increases his revenue more than it increases his costs because the posted price exceeds marginal cost.

The fact that monopolistic competitors, unlike perfect competitors, want to sell more at the going price is crucial to understanding why they engage in activities like advertising that help increase sales.

The other difference between monopolistic competition and perfect competition that is visible in Figure 15-4 involves the position of each firm on its average

Firms in a monopolistically competitive industry have **excess capacity:** they produce less than the output at which average total cost is minimized.

total cost curve. In panel (a), the perfectly competitive firm produces at point q_{PC}, at the bottom of the U-shaped *ATC* curve. That is, each firm produces the quantity at which average total cost is minimized—the *minimum-cost output*. As a consequence, the total cost of industry output is also minimized.

Under monopolistic competition, in panel (b), the firm produces at q_{MC}, on the *downward-sloping* part of the U-shaped *ATC* curve: it produces less than the quantity that would minimize average total cost. This failure to produce enough to minimize average total cost is sometimes described as the **excess capacity** issue. The typical vendor in a food court or gas station along a road is not big enough to take maximum advantage of available cost savings. So the total cost of industry output is not minimized in the case of a monopolistically competitive industry.

Some people have argued that, because every monopolistic competitor has excess capacity, monopolistically competitive industries are inefficient. But the issue of efficiency under monopolistic competition turns out to be a subtle one that does not have a clear answer.

Is Monopolistic Competition Inefficient?

A monopolistic competitor, like a monopolist, charges a price that is above marginal cost. As a result, some people who are willing to pay at least as much for an egg roll at Wonderful Wok as it costs to produce it are deterred from doing so. In monopolistic competition, some mutually beneficial transactions go unexploited.

Furthermore, it is often argued that monopolistic competition is subject to another kind of inefficiency: that the excess capacity of every monopolistic competitor implies *wasteful duplication* because monopolistically competitive industries offer too many varieties. According to this argument, it would be better if there were only two or three vendors in the food court, not six or seven. If there were fewer vendors, they would each have lower average total costs and so could offer food more cheaply.

Is this argument against monopolistic competition right—that it lowers total surplus by causing inefficiency? Not necessarily. It's true that if there were fewer gas stations along a highway, each gas station would sell more gasoline and so would have lower costs per litre. But there is a drawback: drivers would be inconvenienced because gas stations would be farther apart. The point is that the diversity of products offered in a monopolistically competitive industry is beneficial to consumers. So the higher price consumers pay because of excess capacity is offset to some extent by the value they receive from greater diversity.

There is, in other words, a trade-off: more producers means higher average total costs but also greater product diversity. Does a monopolistically competitive industry arrive at the socially optimal point on this trade-off? Probably not—but it is hard to say whether there are too many firms or too few! Most economists now believe that duplication of effort and excess capacity in monopolistically competitive industries are not important issues in practice.

>> Quick Review

• In the long-run equilibrium of a monopolistically competitive industry, there are many firms, each earning zero profit.

• Price exceeds marginal cost, so some mutually beneficial trades are unexploited.

• Monopolistically competitive firms have **excess capacity** because they do not minimize average total cost. But it is not clear that this is actually a source of inefficiency, since consumers gain from product diversity.

>> Check Your Understanding 15-3

Solutions appear at back of book.

1. True or false? Explain your answers.
   a. Like a firm in a perfectly competitive industry, a firm in a monopolistically competitive industry is willing to sell a good at any price that equals or exceeds marginal cost.
   b. Suppose there is a monopolistically competitive industry in long-run equilibrium that possesses excess capacity. All the firms in the industry would be better off if they merged into a single firm and produced a single product, but whether consumers are made better off by this is ambiguous.
   c. Fads and fashions are more likely to arise in monopolistic competition or oligopoly than in monopoly or perfect competition.

‖ Controversies About Product Differentiation

Up to this point, we have assumed that products are differentiated in a way that corresponds to some real desire of consumers. For example, there is real convenience in having a gas station nearby. Likewise, your taste buds know that Chinese and Mexican cuisines are different from one another.

In the real world, however, some instances of product differentiation can seem puzzling if you think about them. What is the real difference between Crest and Colgate toothpaste? Between Energizer and Duracell batteries? Or a Marriott and a Hilton hotel room? Most people would be hard-pressed to answer any of these questions. Yet the producers of these goods make considerable efforts to convince consumers that their products are different from and better than those of their competitors.

No discussion of product differentiation is complete without spending at least a bit of time on the two related issues—and puzzles—of *advertising* and *brand names*.

The Role of Advertising

Wheat farmers don't advertise their wares online and on billboards, but car dealers do. That's not because farmers are shy and car dealers are outgoing; it's because advertising is worthwhile only in industries in which firms have at least some market power.

The purpose of advertisements is to convince people to buy more of a seller's product at the going price. A perfectly competitive firm, which can sell as much as it likes at the going market price, has no incentive to spend money convincing consumers to buy more. Only a firm that has some market power, and that therefore charges a price above marginal cost, can gain from advertising. Industries that are more or less perfectly competitive, like the milk industry, do advertise—but these ads are sponsored by an association on behalf of the industry as a whole, not on behalf of the milk that comes from the cows on a particular farm.

Given that advertising works, it's not hard to see why firms with market power would spend money on it. But the big question about advertising is *why* it works. A related question is whether advertising is, from society's point of view, a waste of resources.

Not all advertising poses a puzzle. Much of it is straightforward: it's a way for sellers to inform potential buyers about what they have to offer (or, occasionally, for buyers to inform potential sellers about what they want). Nor is there much controversy about the economic usefulness of ads that provide information: the real estate ad that declares "sunny, charming, 2 br, 1 ba, a/c" tells you things you need to know (even if a few euphemisms are involved—"charming," of course, means "small").

But what information is being conveyed when Jay-Z touts Samsung cell phones, or when Gigi Hadid promotes BMW? Surely nobody believes that Jay-Z is personally vouching for the superior operating system of a Samsung phone, or that Gigi Hadid's engineering know-how led her to choose a BMW over a rival car. Yet companies believe, with good reason, that money spent on such promotions increases their sales—and that they would be in big trouble if they stopped advertising but their competitors continued to do so.

Why are consumers influenced by ads and endorsements by media influencers that do not really provide any information about the product? One answer is that consumers are not as rational as economists typically

"The active ingredient is marketing."

Barbara Smaller/CartoonStock

assume. Perhaps consumers' judgments, or even their tastes, can be influenced by things that economists think ought to be irrelevant, such as which company has hired the most attractive and charismatic celebrity to endorse its product. And there is surely some truth to this. As we learned in Chapter 9, consumer rationality is a useful working assumption; it is not an absolute truth.

However, another answer is that consumer response to advertising is not entirely irrational because ads can serve as indirect signals in a world where consumers don't have good information about products. Suppose, to take a common example, that you need to avail yourself of some service that you don't use regularly—finding a dentist or a mover. When searching online, you will see firms with sponsored listings pop up at the top or with larger displays. You know that these listings appear as they do because the firms paid extra for them; still, it may be quite rational to call one of the firms with a big display ad. After all, the big ad probably means that it's a relatively large, successful company—otherwise, the company wouldn't have found it worth spending the money for the larger ad.

The same principle may partly explain why ads feature celebrities. You don't really believe that Justin Bieber prefers one brand of underwear over another. But the fact that Calvin Klein is willing and able to pay the Biebs nearly US$70 million to put his name on its product tells you that it is a major company that is likely to stand behind its product. According to this reasoning, an expensive advertisement serves to establish the quality of a firm's products in the eyes of consumers.

The possibility that it is rational for consumers to respond to advertising also has some bearing on the question of whether advertising is a waste of resources. If ads only work by manipulating the weak-minded, the hundreds of billions of dollars that North American businesses spend annually will have been an economic waste—except to the extent that ads sometimes provide entertainment. To the extent that advertising conveys important information, however, it is an economically productive activity after all.

Brand Names

You've been driving all day, and you decide that it's time to find a place to sleep. On your right, you see a sign for the Bates Motel; on your left, you see a sign for a Days Inn, or a Best Western, or some other national chain. Which one do you choose?

Unless they are familiar with the area, most people would head for the chain. In fact, most motels in Canada are members of major chains; the same is true of most fast-food restaurants and many, if not most, stores in shopping malls.

Motel chains and fast-food restaurants are only one aspect of a broader phenomenon: the role of **brand names,** names owned by particular companies that differentiate their products in the minds of consumers. In many cases, a company's brand name is the most important asset it possesses: clearly, McDonald's is worth far more than the sum of the deep-fat fryers and hamburger grills the company owns.

In fact, companies often go to considerable lengths to defend their brand names, suing anyone else who uses them without permission. You may talk about blowing your nose on a kleenex or using scotch tape to wrap gifts, but unless the product in question comes from Kleenex or Scotch, legally the seller must describe it as a facial tissue or adhesive tape.

As with advertising, with which they are closely linked, the social usefulness of brand names is a source of dispute. Does the preference of consumers for known brands reflect consumer irrationality? Or do brand names convey real information? That is, do brand names create unnecessary market power, or do they serve a real purpose?

As in the case of advertising, the answer is probably some of both. On one side, brand names often do create unjustified market power. Many consumers

A **brand name** is a name owned by a particular firm that distinguishes its products from those of other firms.

will pay more for brand-name goods in the supermarket even though consumer experts assure us that the cheaper store brands are equally good. Similarly, many common medicines, like aspirin, are cheaper—with no loss of quality—in their generic form.

On the other side, for many products the brand name does convey information. A traveller arriving in a strange town can be sure of what awaits in a Holiday Inn or a McDonald's; a tired and hungry traveller may find this preferable to trying an independent hotel or restaurant that might be better—but might be worse.

In addition, brand names offer some assurance that the seller is engaged in repeated interaction with its customers and so has a reputation to protect. If a traveller eats a bad meal at a restaurant in a tourist trap and vows never to eat there again, the restaurant owner may not care, since the chance is small that the traveller will be in the same area again in the future. But if that traveller eats a bad meal at McDonald's and vows never to eat there again, that matters to the company. This gives McDonald's an incentive to provide consistent quality, thereby assuring travellers that quality controls are in place. Not surprisingly, branding has become a feature of peer-to-peer e-commerce as companies recognize that many customers will pay extra for assurances of quality and safety in anonymous, online transactions. Hence Uber created its Premium class of ride, that uses luxury cars driven by drivers with high ratings. Likewise Airbnb created the category of Plus properties, accommodations that are vetted by Airbnb staff and have a record of great reviews.

ECONOMICS >> *in Action*
The Perfume Industry: Leading Consumers by the Nose

The perfume industry has remarkably few barriers to entry: to make a fragrance, it is easy to purchase ingredients, mix them, and bottle the result. Even if you don't think you have a very good "nose," consultants are readily available to help you create something special (or even copy someone else's fragrance). So how is it possible that a successful perfume can generate a profit rate of almost 100%? Why don't rivals enter and compete away those profits?

A clue to the answer is that the most successful perfumes these days are heavily promoted by celebrities. Rihanna, Beyoncé, Taylor Swift, and Zendaya all have perfumes that are marketed by them. Britney Spears has 28! In fact, the cost of producing what is in the bottle is minuscule compared to the total cost of selling a successful perfume—only about 3% of the production cost and less than 1% of the retail price. The remaining 97% of the production cost goes into packaging, marketing, and advertising.

The extravagant bottles that modern perfumes come in—some shaped like spaceships or encrusted with rhinestones—incur a cost of four to six times that of the perfume inside. Top bottle designers earn well over $100,000 for a single design. Add onto that the cost of advertising, in-store employees who spritz and hawk, and commissions to salespeople.

Finally, include the cost of celebrity endorsements that run into the millions of dollars. For example, Beyoncé reportedly has earned more than US$40 million on her fragrance, Heat. Moreover, in comparison to older fragrances that have been around for decades, like Chanel or Dior, modern fragrances are made with much cheaper synthetic ingredients. So while a scent like Chanel would last 24 hours, modern fragrances last only a few hours at best.

In the perfume industry, it's packaging and advertising that generate profits.

>> **Quick Review**

• In industries with product differentiation, firms advertise in order to increase the demand for their products.

• Advertising is not a waste of resources when it gives consumers useful information about products.

• Advertising that simply touts a product is harder to explain. Either consumers are irrational, or expensive advertising communicates that the firm's products are of high quality.

• Some firms create **brand names.** As with advertising, the economic value of brand names can be ambiguous. They convey real information when they assure consumers of product quality.

As one celebrated "nose," Roja Dova, commented, "Studies show that people will say that a particular perfume is one of their favourites, but in a blind test they hate it. The trouble is that most people buy scent for their ego, after seeing an image in an advert and wanting to identify themselves in a certain way."

So here's a metaphysical question: even if perfume buyers really hate a fragrance in a blind test, but advertising convinces them that it smells wonderful, who are we to say that they are wrong to buy it? Isn't the attractiveness of a scent in the mind of the beholder?

>> **Check Your Understanding** 15-4

Solutions appear at back of book.

1. In which of the following cases is advertising likely to be economically useful? Economically wasteful? Explain your answer.
   a. Advertisements on the benefits of aspirin
   b. Advertisements for Bayer aspirin
   c. Advertisements on the benefits of drinking orange juice
   d. Advertisements for Tropicana orange juice
   e. Advertisements that state how long a plumber or an electrician has been in business

2. Some industry analysts have stated that a successful brand name is like a barrier to entry. Explain the reasoning behind this statement.

Harry's and the Dollar Shave Club Nick the Profits of Schick and Gillette

Mary Altaffer/ASSOCIATED PRESS

For 95 years, the historical market leaders of the North American razor industry, Gillette and Schick, had enjoyed a comfortable if competitive long-term relationship. King Gillette invented the safety razor in 1901, and in 1921 Colonel Jacob Schick introduced another version of the safety razor. Now owned by large companies (Procter & Gamble and Energizer, respectively), the razor business has been incredibly profitable. Razor cartridges are the most profitable category of packaged goods. So much so that Gillette and Schick shared a US$20 billion dollar global industry in 2019.

To keep these profits rolling in, Schick and Gillette introduced new feature after new feature, such as hydrating gel reservoirs, multiblade heads, and swivelling ball-hinges. For example, Gillette boasted that its Pro-Glide Shield (which sells for US$20) with FlexBall technology "responds to contours and gets virtually every hair." In addition, both companies spent hundreds of millions of dollars on advertising and celebrity endorsements.

It was the culmination of a long-standing strategy undertaken by both companies: sell cheap razor handles, and make money on expensive cartridge refills. The two rivals created an arms-race dynamic in the market—going from two blades to three, then four and five to six—which forced customers to upgrade their razors every few years.

Then, in 2011 and 2012, came Dollar Shave Club and Harry's, two direct-to-consumer razor brands. For both companies, simplicity was the point: both offer a very limited range of razors, priced around US$2 per cartridge. "The average guy does not like shopping and comparing 27 different things," said Katz-Mayfield, Harry's CEO.

Greg Lesko, a 56-year-old from the Pittsburgh area, said he became "fed up" with Gillette's high prices. "I figured there was nothing to lose so I gave Harry's a try. I wouldn't go back [to Gillette razors] if you paid me."

By 2018, the two startups had captured 14% of U.S. razor blade sales and were growing furiously. Both companies based themselves on a simple premise: a subscriber sets up a regular monthly order online, to be shipped to their home, at a fraction of the US$10 to US$20 retail cost of razors from Schick or Gillette. By the time Dollar Shave Club was purchased by Unilever in 2016, its annual sales were close to US$200 million. It was purchased for US$1 billion, a remarkable price for a five-year-old startup. In 2019, Schick followed, announcing a planned acquisition of Harry's for an even greater sum of US$1.37 billion. However, in early 2020, the FTC sued to block the merger, with the complaint alleging that Harry's has shaken up a "comfortable duopoly." Harry's "has forced its rivals to offer lower prices, and more options, to consumers across the country," according to Daniel Francis, deputy director of the U.S. FTC's Bureau of Competition. Not surprisingly, Gillette and Schick have started their own inexpensive, subscription-based lines of razors.

QUESTIONS FOR THOUGHT

1. What explains the complexity of and high rate of innovation in razors by Gillette and Schick?

2. Why is the razor business so profitable? What explains the size of the advertising budgets of Schick and Gillette?

3. What explains the popularity of Harry's and the Dollar Shave Club? What dilemma do Schick and Gillette face in deciding to create their own lines of inexpensive subscription-based razors? What does this indicate about the welfare value to customers of the innovation in razors?

SUMMARY

1. **Monopolistic competition** is a market structure in which there are many competing producers, each producing a differentiated product, and there is free entry and exit in the long run. Product differentiation takes three main forms: by style or type, by location, or by quality. Products of competing sellers are considered imperfect substitutes, and each firm has its own downward-sloping demand curve and marginal revenue curve.

2. Short-run profits will attract entry of new firms in the long run. This reduces the quantity each existing producer sells at any given price and shifts its demand curve to the left. Short-run losses will induce exit by some firms in the long run. This shifts the demand curve of each remaining firm to the right.

3. In the long run, a monopolistically competitive industry is in **zero-profit equilibrium:** at its profit-maximizing quantity, the demand curve for each existing firm is tangent to its average total cost curve. There are zero profits in the industry and no entry or exit.

4. In long-run equilibrium, firms in a monopolistically competitive industry sell at a price greater than marginal cost. They also have **excess capacity** because they produce less than the minimum-cost output; as a result, they have higher costs than firms in a perfectly competitive industry. Whether or not monopolistic competition is inefficient is ambiguous because consumers value the diversity of products that it creates.

5. A monopolistically competitive firm will always prefer to make an additional sale at the going price, so it will engage in advertising to increase demand for its product and enhance its market power. Advertising and **brand names** that provide useful information to consumers are economically valuable. But they are economically wasteful when their only purpose is to create market power. In reality, advertising and brand names are likely to be some of both: economically valuable and economically wasteful.

KEY TERMS

Monopolistic competition, p. 470
Zero-profit equilibrium, p. 476

Excess capacity, p. 480

Brand name, p. 482

PRACTICE QUESTIONS

1. The market structure of the local gas station industry is monopolistic competition. Suppose that currently each gas station incurs a loss. Draw a diagram for a typical gas station to show this short-run situation. Then, in a separate diagram, show what will happen to the typical gas station in the long run. Explain your reasoning.

2. The local hairdresser industry has the market structure of monopolistic competition. Your hairdresser boasts that they are making a profit and that if they continue to do so, they will be able to retire in five years. Use a diagram to illustrate your hairdresser's current situation. Do you expect this to last? In a separate diagram, draw what you expect to happen in the long run. Explain your reasoning.

3. Magnificent Blooms is a florist in a monopolistically competitive industry. It is a successful operation, producing the quantity that minimizes its average total cost and making a profit. The owner also says that at its current level of output, its marginal cost is above marginal revenue. Illustrate the current situation of Magnificent Blooms in a diagram. Answer the following questions by illustrating with a diagram.

   a. In the short run, could Magnificent Blooms increase its profit?

   b. In the long run, could Magnificent Blooms increase its profit?

PROBLEMS

1. Use the three conditions for monopolistic competition discussed in the chapter to decide which of the following firms are likely to be operating as monopolistic competitors. If they are not monopolistically competitive firms, are they monopolists, oligopolists, or perfectly competitive firms?

   a. A local band that plays for weddings, parties, and so on

   b. Minute Maid, a producer of individual-serving juice boxes

   c. Your local dry cleaner

   d. A farmer who produces soybeans

2. You are thinking of setting up a coffee shop. The market structure for coffee shops is monopolistic competition. There are three Starbucks shops and two other coffee shops very much like Starbucks in your town already. In order for you to have some degree of market power, you may want to differentiate your coffee shop. Thinking about the three different ways in which

products can be differentiated, explain how you would decide whether you should copy Starbucks or whether you should sell coffee in a completely different way.

3. "In the long run, there is no difference between monopolistic competition and perfect competition." Discuss whether this statement is true, false, or ambiguous with respect to the following criteria.

   a. The price charged to consumers

   b. The average total cost of production

   c. The efficiency of the market outcome

   d. The typical firm's profit in the long run

4. "In both the short run and in the long run, the typical firm in monopolistic competition and a monopolist each make a profit." Do you agree with this statement? Explain your reasoning.

5. The market for clothes has the structure of monopolistic competition. What impact will fewer firms in this industry have on you as a consumer? Address the following issues.

   a. Variety of clothes

   b. Differences in quality of service

   c. Price

6. For each of the following situations, decide whether advertising is directly informative about the product or simply an indirect signal of its quality. Explain your reasoning.

   a. Football great American Peyton Manning drives a Buick in a TV commercial and claims that he prefers it to any other car.

   b. A Craigslist ad states, "For sale: 1999 Honda Civic, 160,000 kilometres, new transmission."

   c. McDonald's spends millions of dollars on an advertising campaign that proclaims: "I'm lovin' it."

   d. Subway advertises one of its sandwiches by claiming that it contains 6 grams of fat and fewer than 300 calories.

7. In each of the following cases, explain how the advertisement functions as a signal to a potential buyer. Explain what information the buyer lacks that is being supplied by the advertisement and how the information supplied by the advertisement is likely to affect the buyer's willingness to buy the good.

   a. "Looking for work. Excellent references from previous employers available."

   b. "Electronic equipment for sale. All merchandise carries a one-year, no-questions-asked warranty."

   c. "Car for sale by original owner. All repair and maintenance records available."

8. The accompanying table shows the Herfindahl–Hirschman Index (HHI) for the restaurant, cereal, movie studio, and laundry detergent industries in the United States as well as the advertising expenditures of the top 10 firms in each industry. Use the information in the table to answer the following questions.

Industry	HHI	Advertising expenditures (millions)
Restaurants	179	US$1,784
Cereal	2,598	732
Movie studios	918	3,324
Laundry detergent	2,750	132

   a. Which market structure—oligopoly or monopolistic competition—best characterizes each of the industries?

   b. Based on your answer to part a, which type of market structure has higher advertising expenditures? Use the characteristics of each market structure to explain why this relationship might exist.

9. McDonald's spends millions of dollars each year on legal protection of its brand name, thereby preventing any unauthorized use of it. Explain what information this conveys to you as a consumer about the quality of McDonald's products.

10. Before the existence of food-delivery companies UberEats, Grubhub, DoorDash, and Postmates, many students who attended college or university in small towns faced a pizza dilemma. While up late studying, hungry students had limited food options: in most locations there was only one late night food delivery option, usually pizza. Analyze the short-run and long-run effect of entrance of food-delivery companies in the market for late night delivery in small college or university towns.

11. Have you ever wondered why there are so many mattress stores? There is no question that we value a good night's rest and are willing to spend countless dollars on finding the perfect mattress. Despite an overwhelmingly large number of mattress stores, there seems to be an increasing number of new mattress companies selling online. Companies like Purple, Casper, Puffy, and even Amazon have started selling mattresses online. Assuming the brick-and-mortar mattress stores operated in a monopolistically competitive industry, how would you model the cost curves for these mattress companies in the short run? How have online mattress stores disrupted the industry?

▪ WORK IT OUT

12. The restaurant business in town is a monopolistically competitive industry in long-run equilibrium. One restaurant owner asks for your advice. This owner tells you that, each night, not all tables in the restaurant are full. The owner also tells you that the restaurant would attract more customers if it lowered the prices on the menu and that doing so would lower the average total cost. Should the restaurant lower prices? Draw a diagram showing the demand curve, marginal revenue curve, marginal cost curve, and average total cost curve for this restaurant to explain your advice. Show in your diagram what would happen to the restaurant owner's profit if the restaurant were to lower the price so that it sells at the minimum-cost output. ▪

Externalities

TROUBLE UNDERFOOT

WHEN RESEARCHERS AT DUKE University in North Carolina published a paper with an unassuming title, "Increased stray gas abundance in a subset of drinking water wells near Marcellus shale gas extraction," the effects of that publication were anything but restrained. While its results are not definitive, the paper presented evidence that

Ariel Skelley/DigitalVision/Getty Images

Wichita Eagle/Getty Images

Does pollution from fracking for natural gas endanger underground sources of drinking water? If so, how should society make the trade-off?

fracking — the extraction of natural gas by fracturing underground shale deposits with chemical-laden pressurized jets of water — at the Marcellus gas field in Pennsylvania had contaminated underground drinking water supplies with ethane and propane.

The Duke paper provided support to some critics of fracking who claim that it poses an intolerable pollution threat to drinking water supplies. It also helped fuel an increasingly polarized debate over the costs and benefits of fracking.

You may recall from our discussion in Chapter 3 that fracking from British Columbia to Texas, has dramatically reduced the cost of energy in North America, leading to lower heating bills for homeowners and lower production costs for suppliers. And fracking has the potential to significantly reduce air pollution as consumers and industries move from dirtier-burning gasoline and coal to cleaner-burning natural gas.

However, as anticipated in Chapter 3, the environmental benefits of cleaner air from cheaper natural gas have been challenged by the specter of polluted drinking water from fracking. A key question in assessing the trade-off is the role of government: should regulators do more to protect groundwater supplies? Would more regulatory oversight of how fracking wells are drilled reduce groundwater contamination? What amount of contamination would regulators find acceptable? And how would they enforce it?

The dilemma posed by fracking is just one example of the dilemmas that are caused by *externalities*. An externality occurs when individuals impose costs or deliver benefits to others, but don't have an economic incentive to take those costs or benefits into account when making decisions. We briefly noted the concept of externalities

in Chapters 1 and 4. There we stated that one of the principal sources of market failure is actions that create *side effects* that are not properly taken into account — that is, actions that create externalities.

In this chapter, we'll examine the economics of externalities, seeing how they can get in the way of market efficiency and lead to market failure, why they provide a reason for government intervention in markets, and how economic analysis can be used to guide government policy.

Externalities arise from the side effects of actions. First, we'll study the case of pollution, which generates a *negative externality* — a side effect that imposes costs on others. Whenever a side effect can be directly observed and quantified, it can be regulated: by imposing direct controls on it, taxing it, or subsidizing it. As we will see, government intervention in this case should be aimed directly at moving the market to the right quantity of the side effect. ●

WHAT YOU WILL LEARN

- What are **externalities** and why do they lead to inefficiency and government intervention in the market?

- How do **negative externalities, positive externalities,** and *network externalities* differ?

- What is the **Coase theorem** and how does it explain that private individuals can sometimes remedy externalities?

- Why are some government policies to deal with externalities efficient while others are not?

- Why are network externalities an important feature of high-tech industries?

An **external cost** is an uncompensated cost that an individual or firm imposes on others.

An **external benefit** is a benefit that an individual or firm confers on others without receiving compensation.

External costs and benefits are known as **externalities.** External costs are **negative externalities,** and external benefits are **positive externalities.**

|| Understanding Externalities

The environmental costs of pollution are the best known and most important example of an **external cost**—an uncompensated cost that an individual or firm imposes on others. In a modern economy there are many examples of an external cost that an individual or firm imposes on others. A very familiar one is the external cost of traffic congestion: an individual who chooses to drive during rush hour increases congestion and has no incentive to take into account the inconvenience inflicted on other drivers. Another familiar example is the cost created by people who text while driving, increasing the risk of accidents that will harm others as well as themselves (see the upcoming For Inquiring Minds).

Pollution leads to an external cost because, in the absence of government intervention, those who decide how much pollution to create have no incentive to take into account the costs of pollution that they impose on others. In the case of air pollution from a coal-fired power plant, the power company has no incentive to take into account the health costs imposed upon people who breathe dirty air. Instead, the company's incentives are determined by the private monetary costs and benefits of generating power, such as the price of coal, the price earned for a kilowatt of energy, and so on.

We'll see later in this chapter that there are also important examples of **external benefits,** benefits that individuals or firms confer on others without receiving compensation. For example, when you get a flu shot, you are less likely to pass on the flu virus to your roommates. Yet you alone incur the opportunity cost of getting the vaccination and the painful jab. Businesses that develop new technologies also generate external benefits, because their ideas often contribute to innovation by other firms.

External costs and benefits are jointly known as **externalities,** with external costs called **negative externalities** and external benefits called **positive externalities.** Externalities can lead to private decisions—that is, decisions by individuals or firms—that are not optimal for society as a whole. Let's take a closer look at why by focusing on the case of pollution.

FOR INQUIRING MINDS   Driving While Distracted

Why is that person in the car in front of us driving so erratically? Is the driver drunk? No, the driver is texting or using their cell phone to check social media or make calls.

In a survey by InsuranceHotline.com in 2019, 26% of Canadians admitted they have checked their phone while driving and 41% said they would do that while stopped at a traffic light (which is a form of distracted driving). So it is not surprising that the Insurance Bureau of Canada (IBC) has now declared distracted driving one of the biggest dangers on the road. Traffic safety experts take the risks posed by driving while using a cell phone very seriously: a driver is 23 times more likely to have an accident while texting. For example, the Ontario Provincial Police (OPP), looked at all the car crashes that required them to investigate and found that for four straight years distracted driving caused more casualties (and 65 deaths in 2016) than any other dangerous driving behaviours such as drunk driving and speeding.

Texting while driving kills twice as many people in Canada than impaired drivers.

Using hands-free, voice-activated devices to make a call doesn't seem to help much because the main danger is distraction. As one traffic consultant put it, "It's not where your eyes are; it's where your head is."

The Canadian Automobile Association (CAA) urges people not to use cell phones while driving. Most provinces have some restrictions on cell phone use while driving. But in response to a growing number of accidents, some jurisdictions have banned cell phone use behind the wheel altogether. In all Canadian provinces and territories, except Nunavut, it is illegal to text and drive. Cell phone use while driving is illegal in many other countries as well, including Japan and Israel.

Why not leave the decision up to the driver? Because the risk posed by driving

Using a cell phone while driving makes you a danger to others as well as yourself.

while using a cell phone isn't just a risk to the driver; it's also a safety risk to others—to a driver's passengers, to pedestrians, and to people in other cars. Even if a driver decides that the benefit of using their cell phone while driving is worth the cost, they aren't taking into account the cost to other people. Driving while using a cell phone, in other words, generates a serious—and sometimes fatal—negative externality.

The Economics of a Negative Externality: Pollution

Pollution is a bad thing. Yet most pollution is a side effect of activities that provide us with good things: our air is polluted by power plants generating the electricity that lights our cities, and our rivers are damaged by fertilizer runoff from farms that grow our food. And groundwater contamination may occur from fracking, which also produces cleaner-burning fuel. Why shouldn't we accept a certain amount of pollution as the cost of a good life?

Actually, we do. Even highly committed environmentalists don't think that we can or should completely eliminate pollution—even an environmentally conscious society would accept *some* pollution as the cost of producing useful goods and services. What environmentalists argue is that unless there is a strong and effective environmental policy, our society will generate *too much* pollution—too much of a bad thing. And the great majority of economists agree.

To see why, we need a framework that lets us think about how much pollution a society *should* have. We'll then be able to see why a market economy, left to itself, will produce more pollution than it should. We'll start by adopting the simplest framework to study the problem—assuming that the amount of pollution emitted by a polluter is directly observable and controllable.

The Costs and Benefits of Pollution

How much pollution should society allow? The answer to this question involves comparing the marginal benefit from an additional unit of pollution with the marginal cost of an additional unit of pollution.

The **marginal social cost (*MSC*) of pollution** is the additional cost imposed on society as a whole by an additional unit of pollution.

For example, sulfur dioxide from coal-fired power plants mixes with rainwater to form acid rain, which damages fisheries, crops, and forests, while groundwater contamination, which may be a side effect of fracking, damages health. Typically, the marginal social cost of pollution is increasing—each additional unit of pollution emitted causes a greater level of damage than the unit before. That's because nature can often safely handle low levels of pollution but is increasingly harmed as pollution reaches higher levels.

The marginal social cost of pollution can be expressed as the sum of two terms (*MSC* = *MPC* + *MEC*): **marginal private cost (*MPC*) of pollution**—the additional cost imposed on the polluter if the polluter creates another unit of pollution—and **marginal external cost (*MEC*) of pollution**—the additional cost imposed on others if the polluter creates another unit of pollution. If, as is often the case, creating another unit of pollution imposes zero additional costs on the polluter (i.e., the pollution only harms others in society), then the marginal social cost is equal to the marginal external cost (*MSC* = *MEC*, as *MPC* = 0).

The **marginal social benefit (*MSB*) of pollution** is the benefit to society from an additional unit of pollution. This may seem like a confusing concept—how can there be any benefit to society from pollution? The answer lies in the understanding that pollution can be reduced—but at a cost. For example, air pollution from coal-fired power plants can be reduced by using more-expensive coal and expensive scrubbing technology; contamination of drinking water due to fracking can be limited with more-expensive drilling techniques; wastewater contamination of rivers and oceans can be reduced by building water treatment facilities.

All these methods of reducing pollution have an opportunity cost. That is, avoiding pollution requires using scarce resources that could have been employed to produce other goods and services. So the marginal social benefit of pollution is the goods and services that could be had by society if it tolerated another unit of pollution.

The marginal social benefit is the sum of two terms (*MSB* = *MPB* + *MEB*): **marginal private benefit (*MPB*) of pollution**—the additional benefit the polluter

The **marginal social cost (*MSC*) of pollution** is the additional cost imposed on society as a whole by an additional unit of pollution.

The **marginal private cost (*MPC*) of pollution** is the additional cost imposed on the polluter if the polluter creates another unit of pollution.

The **marginal external cost (*MEC*) of pollution** is the additional cost imposed on others if the polluter creates another unit of pollution.

The **marginal social benefit (*MSB*) of pollution** is the additional gain to society as a whole from an additional unit of pollution.

The **marginal private benefit (*MPB*) of pollution** is the additional benefit for the polluter if the polluter creates another unit of pollution.

The **marginal external benefit (MEB) of pollution** is the additional benefit for others if the polluter creates another unit of pollution.

The **socially optimal quantity of pollution** is the quantity of pollution that society would choose if all the costs and benefits of pollution were fully accounted for.

receives if the polluter creates another unit of pollution—and **marginal external benefit (MEB) of pollution**—the additional benefit others receive if the polluter creates another unit of pollution. If creating another unit of pollution only creates additional benefits for the polluter, the marginal social benefit is equal to the marginal private benefit ($MSB = MPB$, as $MEB = 0$).

Comparisons between the pollution levels tolerated in rich and poor countries illustrate the importance of the level of the marginal social benefit of pollution in deciding how much pollution a society wishes to tolerate. Because poor countries have a higher opportunity cost of resources spent on reducing pollution than richer countries, they tolerate higher levels of pollution. For example, the World Health Organization has estimated that 3.8 million people in poor countries die prematurely from breathing polluted indoor air caused by burning dirty fuels like wood, dung, and coal to heat and cook—a situation that residents of rich countries can afford to avoid.

Using hypothetical numbers, Figure 16-1 shows how we can determine the **socially optimal quantity of pollution**—the quantity of pollution that society would choose if all the social costs and benefits were fully accounted for. The upward-sloping marginal social cost curve, *MSC*, shows how the marginal cost to society of an additional unit of pollution varies with the quantity of pollution. It is typically upward sloping because the harm inflicted by a unit of pollution typically increases since more pollution has already been emitted. In contrast, the marginal social benefit curve, *MSB*, is downward sloping. At high levels of pollution, the cost of achieving a reduction in pollution is fairly small. However, as pollution levels drop, it becomes progressively more costly to engineer a further fall in pollution as more expensive techniques must be used, so the *MSB* is higher at lower levels of pollution.

As we can see from Figure 16-1, the socially optimal quantity of pollution in this example isn't zero. It's Q_{OPT}, the quantity corresponding to point *O*, where *MSB* crosses *MSC*. At Q_{OPT}, the marginal social benefit from an additional unit of pollution and its marginal social cost are equalized at $200.

FIGURE 16-1 The Socially Optimal Quantity of Pollution

Pollution yields both costs and benefits. Here the *MSC* curve shows how the marginal cost to society as a whole from emitting one more unit of pollution emissions depends on the quantity of emissions. The *MSC* curve is upward sloping, so the marginal social cost increases as pollution increases. The *MSB* curve shows how the marginal benefit to society as a whole of emitting an additional unit of pollution emissions depends on the quantity of pollution emissions. The *MSB* curve is downward sloping, so the marginal social benefit falls as pollution increases. The socially optimal quantity of pollution is Q_{OPT}; at that quantity, the marginal social benefit of pollution is equal to the marginal social cost, corresponding to $200.

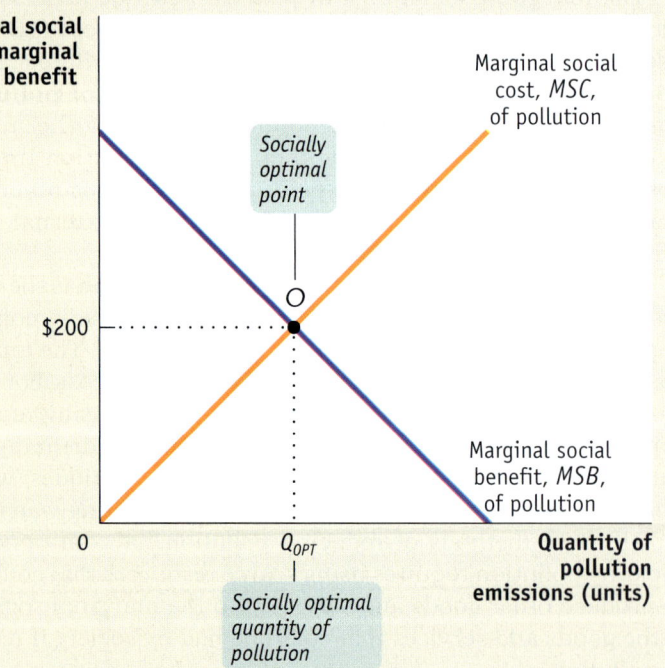

But will a market economy, left to itself, arrive at the socially optimal quantity of pollution? No, it won't.

Why a Market Economy Produces Too Much Pollution

While pollution yields both benefits and costs to society, in a market economy without government intervention too much pollution will be produced. In that case it is polluters alone—owners of power plants or gas-drilling companies, for example—who decide how much pollution is created. And they have no incentive to take into account the cost that pollution inflicts on others. Instead, the company's incentives are determined by the private monetary costs and benefits of generating power, such as the price of coal, the price earned for a kilowatt of energy, and so on.

Figure 16-2 shows the result of this asymmetry between who reaps the benefits and who pays the costs. In a market economy without government intervention, since polluters are the only ones making the decisions, only the private benefits of pollution are taken into account when choosing how much pollution to produce, rather than the costs to society. So instead of producing the socially optimal quantity, Q_{OPT}, the market economy will generate the amount Q_{MKT}. At Q_{MKT}, the marginal social benefit of an additional unit of pollution is zero, while the marginal social cost of an additional unit is much higher—$400.

Why? Well, take a moment to consider what the polluter would do if they were emitting Q_{OPT} of pollution. Remember that the *MSB* curve represents the resources made available by tolerating one more unit of pollution. The polluter would notice that if they increase their emission of pollution by moving down the *MSB* curve from Q_{OPT} to Q_H, they would gain $200 – $100 = $100. That gain of $100 comes from using less-expensive but higher-emission production techniques. Remember, they suffer none of the costs of doing this—only others do. However, it won't stop there. At Q_H, they notice that if emissions are increased from Q_H to Q_{MKT}, they would gain another $100 as they move down the *MSB* curve yet again. This would

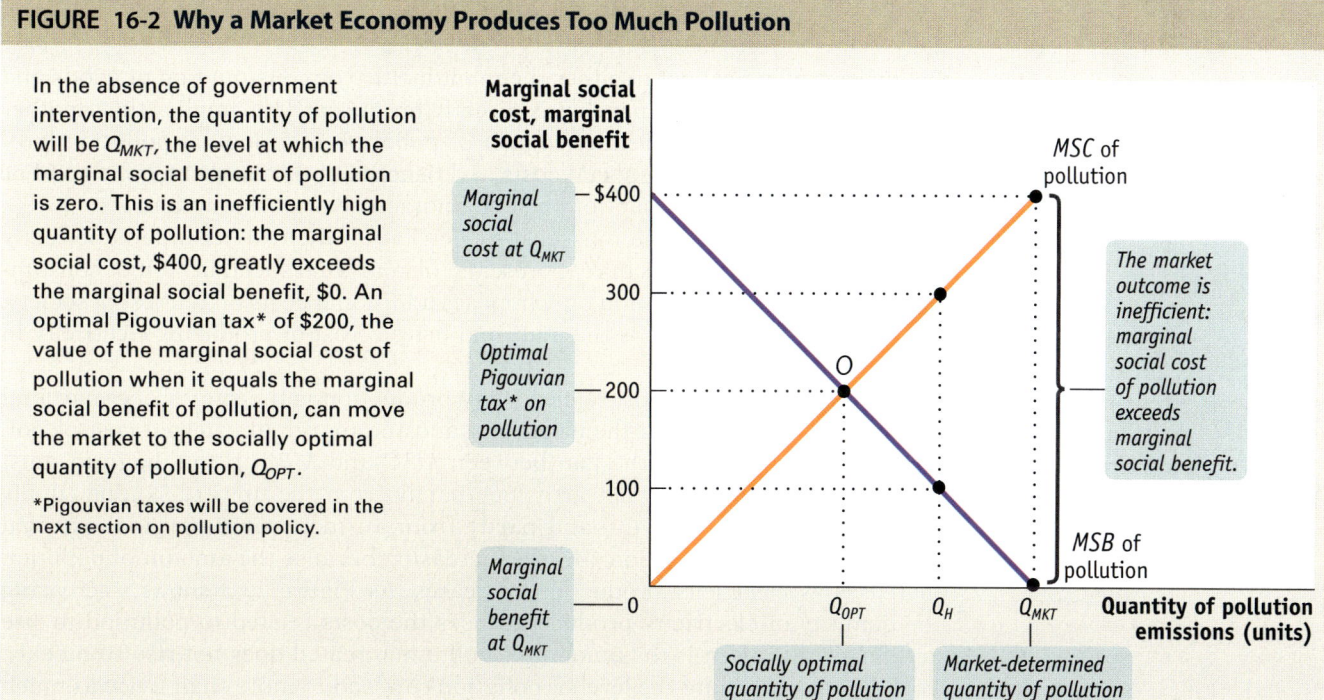

FIGURE 16-2 Why a Market Economy Produces Too Much Pollution

In the absence of government intervention, the quantity of pollution will be Q_{MKT}, the level at which the marginal social benefit of pollution is zero. This is an inefficiently high quantity of pollution: the marginal social cost, $400, greatly exceeds the marginal social benefit, $0. An optimal Pigouvian tax* of $200, the value of the marginal social cost of pollution when it equals the marginal social benefit of pollution, can move the market to the socially optimal quantity of pollution, Q_{OPT}.

*Pigouvian taxes will be covered in the next section on pollution policy.

be achieved by using even cheaper and higher-emission production techniques. They will stop at Q_{MKT} because at this emission level the marginal social benefit of a unit of pollution is zero. That is, at Q_{MKT} they gain nothing by using yet cheaper and dirtier production techniques and emitting more pollution.

As an example, consider the nature of the benefits and costs from air pollution from burning coal. For polluters, the benefits take the form of monetary savings: by emitting an extra tonne of sulphur dioxide, any given polluter saves the cost of buying expensive, low-sulphur coal or installing pollution-control equipment. So the benefits of pollution accrue directly to the polluters. (This means $MEB = 0$, so $MSB = MPB$.)

The costs of (air) pollution, though, fall on people who have no say in the decision about how much pollution takes place: for example, about half of all airborne sulphur dioxide in eastern Canada comes from sources in the United States, especially coal burning power plants in and around the Tennessee Valley. People who fish in Canada do not control the decisions of power plants in Tennessee. (This means $MPC = 0$, so $MSC = MEC > 0$. A competitive market equilibrium will be where $MPB = MPC = 0$, which means too much pollution will be created.)

The market outcome, Q_{MKT}, is inefficient. Recall that an outcome is inefficient if someone could be made better off without someone else being made worse off. At an inefficient outcome, a mutually beneficial trade is being missed. At Q_{MKT}, the benefit accruing to the polluter of the last unit of pollution is very low—virtually zero. But the cost imposed on society of that last unit of pollution is quite high—$400. So by reducing the quantity of pollution at Q_{MKT} by one unit, the total social cost of pollution falls by $400 but the total social benefit falls by virtually zero.

So total surplus rises by approximately $400 if the quantity of pollution at Q_{MKT} is reduced by one unit. At Q_{MKT}, society would be willing to pay the polluter up to $400 not to emit the last unit of pollution, and the polluter would be willing to accept their offer since that last unit gains them virtually nothing. But because there is no means in this market economy for this transaction to take place, an inefficient outcome occurs.

Externalities and the Competitive Market

Pollution is a by-product of either the manufacture or consumption of goods and services—it is not a product that is directly produced. This implies that another way to study the social welfare impact of pollution is to look at pollution indirectly by investigating the social costs and benefits in the market for the good or service that causes the pollution by its manufacture or consumption.

Figure 16-3 depicts the market for electricity, which we assume is perfectly competitive. The demand curve represents the marginal social benefit of consuming electricity. Since pollution only imposes additional costs on the rest of society, the industry supply curve is the marginal private cost of producing electricity in perfect competition.

The marginal social cost of electricity production is the sum of the marginal private cost of generating the electricity and the marginal external cost of pollution. That means that the gap between MSC and MPC in the diagram must equal MEC. MSC gets its upward slope partly from the upward-sloping supply curve—which is also MPC—and partly from an increasing marginal external cost of electricity production. MEC is increasing because the amount of pollution increases as electricity production increases. As Figure 16-3 shows, increasing the quantity of electricity produced causes the costs related to pollution to rise at a faster rate, even if the amount of pollution created does not rise so quickly. For example, doubling the level of pollution can lead to more than twice as much harm resulting from the pollution.

FIGURE 16-3 **Perfect Competition with Externalities**

When externalities are created either in production or consumption of a good or service, a perfectly competitive market is inefficient resulting in a deadweight loss. The market for electricity is plagued by a negative externality as the production of electricity often creates significant amounts of harmful pollution. The competitive equilibrium occurs at the intersection between the supply and demand curves. The socially optimal level of output occurs where the marginal social benefit curve intersects the marginal social cost curve. Since the market ignores the negative externality, perfect competition results in too much electricity being produced (and too much pollution) and in electricity being sold at a price that is too low.

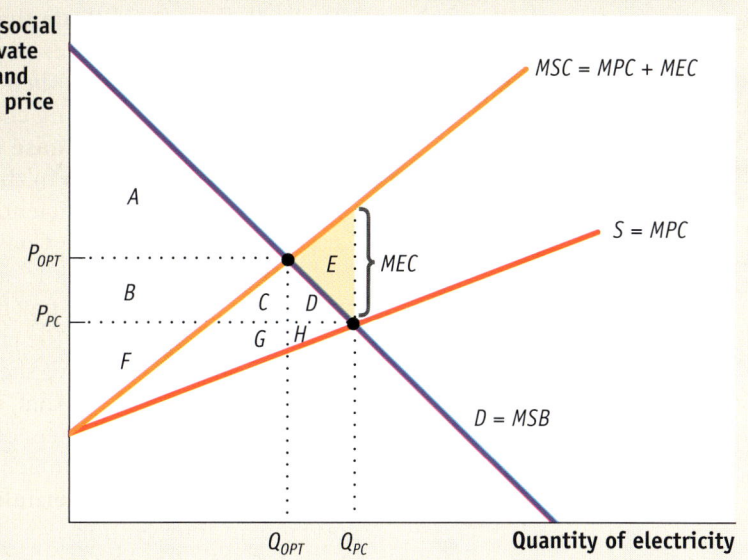

	Perfect Competition Equilibrium	Socially Optimal Production Point
Consumer surplus (*CS*)	$A + B + C + D$	A
Producer surplus (*PS*)	$F + G + H$	$B + C + F + G$
Total external cost (*TEC*)	$C + D + E + G + H$	$C + G$
Total Economic Surplus (Social Welfare = *CS* + *PS* − *TEC*)	$A + B + F − E$	$A + B + F$

The perfectly competitive market for electricity is in equilibrium where supply intersects demand at price P_{PC} and quantity Q_{PC}. The resulting consumer surplus is the triangle above P_{PC} (below the demand curve). Likewise, the producer surplus is the triangle below P_{PC} (above the supply curve). But unlike the used books we examined in Chapter 4, in this market, the sum of the consumer and producer surplus is not the total benefit to society from the production and consumption of the good—as this sum ignores the impact of pollution. The total external cost imposed by electricity production is the area between *MSC* and the supply curve. The total economic surplus is equal to the sum of consumer surplus and producer surplus minus the total external cost.

The socially optimal level of electricity production occurs where *MSB* intersects *MSC*. Figure 16-3 reveals that the perfectly competitive equilibrium is inefficient; perfect competition is not socially optimal when there are externalities—it results in an overproduction of electricity and added pollution. At the socially optimal level of output, the consumer surplus is the triangle above P_{OPT}, the producer surplus is the area below P_{OPT} but above the supply curve, and the total external cost is the area between *MSC* and the supply curve. Thus the total economic surplus at the socially optimal level is greater than that obtained via perfect competition! The table in Figure 16-3 shows this. Perfect competition results in a deadweight loss equal to the shaded area labelled as *E* in Figure 16-3.

According to the **Coase theorem,** the economy can always reach an efficient solution, even in the presence of externalities, provided that the costs of making a deal are sufficiently low. When individuals take externalities into account, they **internalize the externalities.**

Transaction costs—the costs to individuals of making a deal—often prevent a mutually beneficial trade from occurring.

Private Solutions to Externalities

As we've just seen, externalities in a market economy cause inefficiency: there is a mutually beneficial trade that is being missed. So can the private sector solve the problem of externalities without government intervention? Will individuals be able to make that deal on their own? According to the *Coase theorem,* formulated by the Nobel Prize–winning economist Ronald Coase, the answer is yes if certain conditions are met. The **Coase theorem** states that the economy can always reach an efficient solution, even in the presence of externalities, provided that the costs of making a deal are sufficiently low. For example, if fracking is causing groundwater contamination, the Coase theorem says that the problem can be avoided if landowners pay drillers to use drilling technology that creates less pollution. Alternatively, drillers can pay landowners the cost of damage to their groundwater. If drillers legally have the right to pollute, then the first outcome is more likely. If drillers don't legally have the right to pollute, then the second is more likely.

What Coase argued is that, either way, if transaction costs are sufficiently low, then drillers and landowners can make a mutually beneficial deal. When individuals take externalities into account when making decisions, economists say that they **internalize the externality.** In that case the outcome is efficient without government intervention.

So why don't private parties always internalize externalities? The problem is **transaction costs**—the costs of making a deal—often prevent a mutually beneficial trade from occurring. Transaction costs are a barrier particularly when those who are hurt by the externality are widely dispersed, such as in the case of air pollution or *greenhouse gases.* When this happens, the cost of communication and negotiation is simply too high to achieve an efficient outcome.

When transaction costs prevent the private sector from dealing with externalities, it is time to look for government solutions. We turn to public policy in the next section.

ECONOMICS >> *in Action*
How Much Does Your Electricity Really Cost?

Three leading economists, Nicholas Z. Muller, Robert Mendelsohn, and Nobel Prize–winner William Nordhaus, estimated the external cost of pollution by various U.S. industries. The costs took a variety of forms, from harmful effects on health to reduced agricultural yields. In the case of the electricity-generation sector they estimated the costs of carbon dioxide emissions—one of the many greenhouse gases that cause *climate change.*

The authors used a relatively low estimate of the external costs because their valuation is a contentious issue—in part because the external costs will fall on future generations. They compared the total external costs of pollution (TEC) for the coal-fired and natural gas–fired power sector, and compared this to each sectors' value added (VA)—the market value of its output.

The accompanying table shows the TEC to VA ratios and the TEC to kilowatt-hour ratios for the two sectors. As you can see, both modes of electricity generation impose large external costs, exceeding their value added. But the TEC per kilowatt-hour generated with natural gas is much lower than that of one generated with coal, because burning natural gas releases both less carbon dioxide and fewer other pollutants. A conservative estimate is that the external cost of a kilowatt hour is

What is the social cost of carbon?

one-third of the retail price of electricity when generated by coal, and one-twentieth when generated by natural gas.

In 2014, the U.S. Environmental Protection Agency (EPA) issued rules that limited carbon emissions from newly constructed power plants, with the intent of compelling new coal-fired plants to adopt carbon-capture technology. In 2018, the United States significantly relaxed those rules in a bid to revive the coal industry. Yet industry analysts observed that this relaxation of the limits on carbon emissions was unlikely to reverse the coal industry's long-term decline. By 2016, fracking had rendered natural gas–fired plants cheaper to operate than coal-fired plants. In that year, for the first time in history, more U.S. energy was generated by natural gas than by coal. And by 2018, some clean energy plants were even cheaper than natural gas–fired plants.

	TEC/VA	TEC/ Kilowatt-hour
Coal	US$2.83	US$0.039
Natural gas	1.30	0.005

Presently no estimates are available of the external costs of Canadian electricity generation. The good news is greenhouse gas emissions in the electricity generation sector declined 42% between 2000 and 2017 thanks to the increased use of renewable electricity generation.

>> Check Your Understanding 16-1

Solutions appear at back of book.

1. Wastewater runoff from large poultry farms adversely affects their neighbours. Explain the following:
   a. The nature of the external cost imposed
   b. The outcome in the absence of government intervention or a private deal
   c. The socially optimal outcome
2. According to Yasmin, any student who borrows a book from the university library and fails to return it on time imposes a negative externality on other students. She claims that rather than charging a modest fine for late returns, the library should charge a huge fine so that borrowers will never return a book late. Is Yasmin's economic reasoning correct?

‖ Government Policy and Pollution

By the 1960s, vast tracts of ghostly, withered trees in the northeastern United States and southeastern Canada revealed an ominous truth: these great forests were dying. Moreover, the lakes and streams within them were dying too, as the stock of fish and other aquatic life plummeted.

The culprit was acid rain, a phenomenon that occurs when rain mixes with airborne sulfur dioxide pollutants from coal-burning power plants. The result is highly acidic rain that poisons trees and aquatic life. Before 1970, there were no rules governing the amount of sulfur dioxide that coal-burning power plants in North America could emit.

In 1985, Canada passed the Canadian Acid Rain Control Program that set targets to reduce sulphur dioxide emissions in eastern Canada by 50%. And it worked—the acidity of rainfall declined significantly. Economists, however, argued that a more flexible system of rules that exploits the effectiveness of markets could reduce pollution at a lower cost. In 1991, this theory was put into effect with the Canada-U.S. Air Quality Agreement. And guess what? The economists were right!

In this section we'll look at the three types of policies governments typically use to deal with pollution: environmental standards, emissions taxes, and tradable emissions permits.

We will also see how economic analysis has been used to improve those policies. And we will look at the issue of climate change and how government policy can be used to address it.

>> Quick Review

• External costs and benefits are known as **externalities.** Pollution is an example of an **external cost,** or **negative externality;** in contrast, some activities can give rise to **external benefits,** or **positive externalities.**

• The **marginal social cost (MSC) of pollution** is equal to the sum of the **marginal private cost (MPC) of pollution** and the **marginal external cost (MEC) of pollution:** $MSC = MPC + MEC$.

• The **marginal social benefit (MSB) of pollution** is equal to the sum of the **marginal private benefit (MPB) of pollution** and the **marginal external benefit (MEB) of pollution:** $MSB = MPB + MEB$.

• There are costs as well as benefits to reducing pollution, so the optimal quantity of pollution isn't zero. Instead, the **socially optimal quantity of pollution** is the quantity at which the **marginal social cost of pollution** is equal to the **marginal social benefit of pollution.**

• Left to itself, a market economy will typically generate an inefficiently high level of pollution because polluters have no incentive to take into account the costs they impose on others.

• According to the **Coase theorem,** the private sector can sometimes resolve externalities on its own: if transaction costs aren't too high, individuals can reach a deal to **internalize the externality.** When **transaction costs** are too high, government intervention may be warranted.

Environmental Standards

Among the most serious negative externalities we face today are those associated with actions that damage the environment—air pollution, water pollution, habitat destruction, and so on. Protection of the environment has become a major role of government in all developed nations. Environment and Climate Change Canada is the federal agency that implements the environmental agenda of the federal government. It also administers and enforces the country's policies and acts related to environmental protection.

How does a country protect its environment? At present the main policy tools are **environmental standards,** rules that protect the environment by specifying actions by producers and consumers. A familiar example is the law that requires almost all vehicles to have catalytic converters, which reduce the emission of toxic gases and other pollutants that cause smog and lead to health problems. Other rules require communities to treat their sewage or factories to avoid or limit certain kinds of pollution. And as we just saw in the Economics in Action, environmental standards were put in place in 2014, compelling new coal- and gas-fired power plants to adopt cleaner-burning technologies.

Mischa Richter/The New Yorker Collection/The Cartoon Bank

"They have very strict antipollution laws in this state."

Environmental standards came into widespread use in the 1960s and 1970s, and they have had considerable success in reducing pollution. For example, the Canadian Environmental Protection Act, 1999 (CEPA 1999) included provisions to regulate vehicle, engine, and equipment emissions, which encouraged firms to adopt cleaner or greener technologies.

Emissions Taxes

Another policy tool to address pollution is to charge polluters an **emissions tax.** Emissions taxes depend on the amount of pollution a firm emits. As we learned in Chapter 7, a tax imposed on an activity will reduce the level of that activity.

Recall that without government intervention, polluters have an incentive to increase pollution beyond the socially optimal quantity of pollution. In fact, polluters will push pollution up to the quantity Q_{MKT}, shown in Figure 16-2, the point at which marginal social benefit equals zero.

As shown in that figure, if the marginal social benefit and marginal social cost of an additional unit of pollution are equal at $200, a tax on polluters of $200 per unit of pollution will induce them to reduce their emissions to Q_{OPT}, the socially optimal quantity. This illustrates a general result: an emissions tax equal to the marginal social cost at the socially optimal quantity of pollution induces polluters to internalize the externality—to take into account the true cost to society of their actions.

An emissions tax is also a more efficient way to reduce pollution than environmental standards because the tax ensures that the marginal benefit of pollution is equal for all sources of pollution. Environmental standards, by contrast, treat all polluters the same, when they actually differ according to their costs of pollution reduction.

The term *emissions tax* may convey the misleading impression that taxes are a solution to only one kind of negative externality, pollution. In fact, taxes can be used to discourage any activity that generates negative externalities, such as driving (which inflicts environmental damage greater than the cost of producing gasoline) or smoking (which inflicts health costs on society far greater than the cost of making a cigarette).

Environmental standards are rules that protect the environment by specifying actions by producers and consumers.

An **emissions tax** is a tax that depends on the amount of pollution a firm produces.

GLOBAL COMPARISON   ECONOMIC GROWTH AND GREENHOUSE GASES IN SIX COUNTRIES

At first glance, a comparison of the per capita greenhouse gas emissions of various countries, shown in panel (a) of this graph, suggests that Canada, the United States, and Australia are the worst offenders. In 2018, the average Canadian is responsible for 15.3 tonnes of greenhouse gas emissions (measured in carbon dioxide, CO_2, equivalents) — the pollution that causes climate change — compared to only 2.8 tonnes for the average Uzbek, 7.1 tonnes for the average Chinese, and 2.0 tonnes for the average Indian.

Such a conclusion, however, ignores an important factor in determining the level of a country's greenhouse gas emissions: its gross domestic product, or GDP — the total value of a country's domestic output. Output typically cannot be produced without more energy, and more energy usage typically results in more pollution. In fact, some have argued that criticizing a country's level of greenhouse gases without taking account of its level of economic development is misguided. It would be equivalent to faulting a country for being at a more advanced stage of economic development.

A more meaningful way to compare pollution across countries is to measure emissions per US$1 million of a country's GDP, as shown in panel (b). On this basis, the United States, Canada, and Australia are now "green" countries, but China, India, and Uzbekistan are not. What explains the reversal once GDP is accounted for? The answer is scarce resources.

Countries that are poor, such as Uzbekistan, China (historically), and India, have viewed resources spent on pollution reduction as better spent on other things. They have argued that they are too poor to afford the same environmental priorities as wealthy developed countries. To impose a wealthy country's environmental standards on them would, they claimed, jeopardize their economic growth.

However, the scientific evidence pointing to *greenhouse gases* as the cause of *climate change* and the falling price of nonpolluting energy sources has changed attitudes in poorer countries. Realizing that their citizens are likely to suffer disproportionately more from climate change, poor countries joined forces with rich countries to sign the *Paris Agreement* in 2015, an agreement between 196 countries to limit their greenhouse gas emissions, to keep global temperatures from increasing less than 2 degrees Celsius, the temperature at which the effects of climate change are considered to be catastrophic and irreversible. The United States has announced its intent to withdraw from the agreement in November 2020, the only country in the world to reject the agreement.

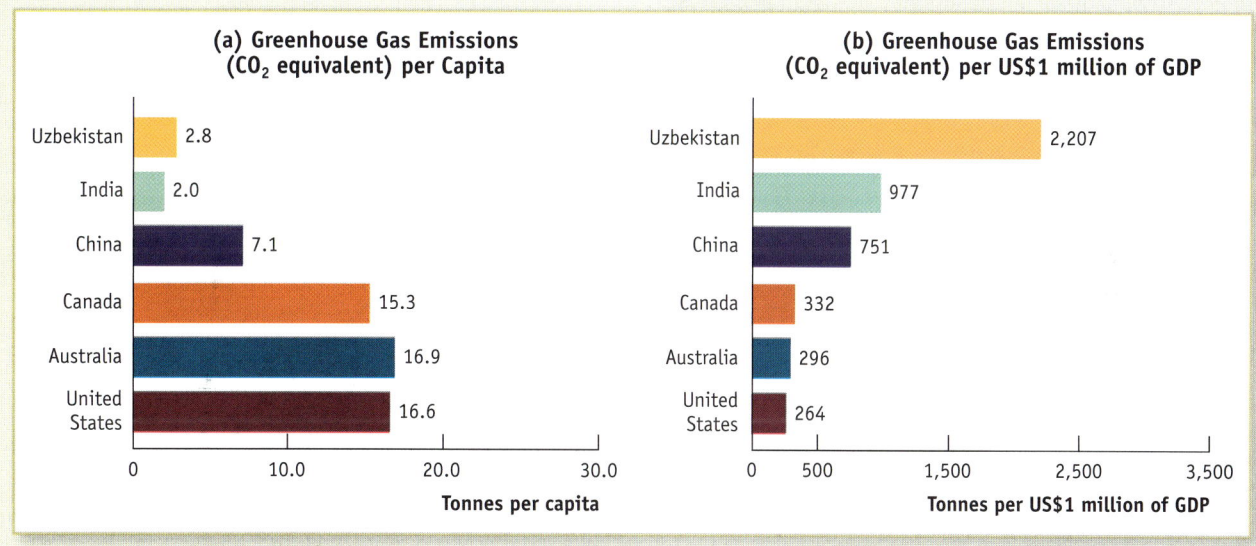

Data from: Global Carbon Atlas; IMF – World Economic Outlook.

In general, taxes designed to reduce the costs imposed on society from a negative externality are known as **Pigouvian taxes,** after the economist A. C. Pigou, who emphasized their usefulness in his classic 1920 book, *The Economics of Welfare.* In our example, the optimal Pigouvian tax is $200. As you can see from Figure 16-2, this corresponds to the marginal social cost of pollution at the optimal output quantity, Q_{OPT}.

The main shortcoming of emissions taxes compared to environmental standards is that government officials usually aren't sure how high the tax should be set. If they set it too low, pollution reduction would be insufficient. If they set it too high, emissions will be reduced by more than is efficient. This uncertainty

Taxes designed to reduce the costs imposed on society from a negative externality are known as **Pigouvian taxes.**

around the optimal level of the emissions tax can't be eliminated, but the nature of the risks can be changed by using an alternative policy, issuing tradable emissions permits. However, emissions taxes can have political advantages: voters may be more willing to approve of them when the tax revenue is rebated back to consumers.

The Pigouvian Tax in the Competitive Market

Rather than levy a tax directly on pollution, it is possible to impose the tax on the production of the good whose production or consumption results in the creation of the pollution. Figure 16-4 below revisits the competitive market for electricity with an optimal Pigouvian tax.

Suppose an excise tax is imposed on electricity producers. This per-unit tax raises the marginal private cost of suppliers by T, effectively shifting the supply curve up. If the tax is set equal to the size of the marginal external cost of electricity at the socially optimal level of output, then the tax results in the socially optimal point being reached. The socially optimal level of electricity (Q_{OPT}) will be produced, consumers will be charged the socially optimal price (P_{OPT}), and firms will receive a price of ($P_{OPT} - T$). Of course, as we discussed in Chapter 7, if the per-unit tax is applied to consumers the same result will occur.

FIGURE 16-4 Applying a Pigouvian Tax to Perfect Competition with Externalities

If instead of directly taxing pollution, an excise tax, T, is applied on the production of the good causing the pollution, then the optimal per-unit Pigouvian tax on output is equal to its marginal external cost at the socially optimal quantity of output. The tax eliminates the deadweight loss of perfect competition by forcing the market to internalize the costs generated by the externality.

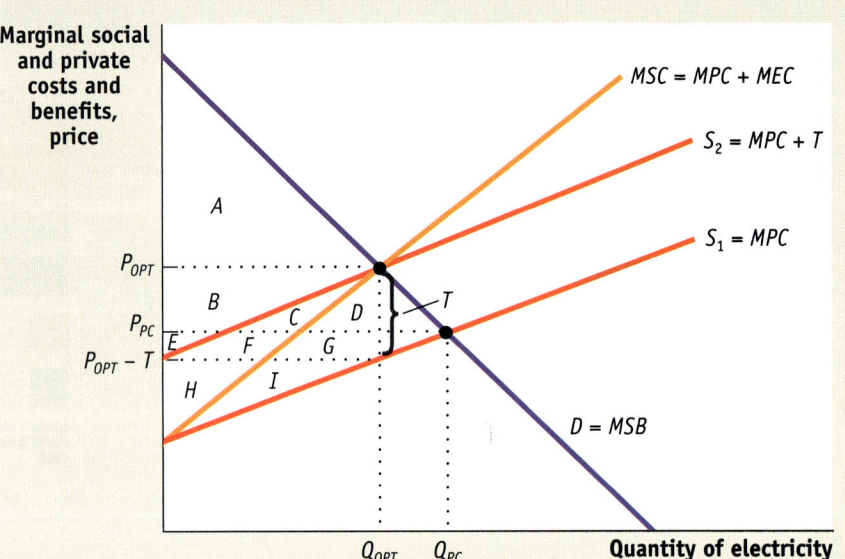

	Optimal Pigouvian Tax	Socially Optimal Production Point
Consumer surplus (CS)	A	A
Producer surplus (PS)	H + I	B + C + D + E + F + G + H + I
Tax revenue (T × Q_OPT)	B + C + D + E + F + G	0
Total external cost (TEC)	D + G + I	D + G + I
Total Economic Surplus (Social Welfare = CS + PS + T × Q_OPT − TEC)	A + B + C + E + F + H	A + B + C + E + F + H

After the tax is applied, the consumer surplus is equal to area A, the producer surplus is equal to the sum of areas *H* and *I*, while the government tax revenue is the rectangle made up of *B, C, D, E, F,* and *G*. Since the total external cost is the area between the *MSC* and supply curves it equals the sum of the areas *D, G,* and *I*. So with the tax, the total economic surplus is equal to the sum of the areas *A, B, C, E, F,* and *H*. The calculations in the table in Figure 16-4 show that this outcome is socially efficient. By charging a per-unit tax on electricity equal to the marginal external cost at the socially optimal level, the market fully internalizes the cost generated by the externality, which eliminates the deadweight loss of perfect competition.

Tradable Emissions Permits

Tradable emissions permits are licences to emit limited quantities of pollutants that can be bought and sold by polluters. Tradable emissions permits work in practice much like the tradable quotas (discussed in Chapter 5) in which regulators created a system of tradable licences to fish for crabs. The tradable licences resulted in an efficient way to allocate the right to fish—boat owners with the safest and lowest cost of operation purchase the rights of owners with less safe, higher cost boats. Although tradable emissions permits involve trading a "bad" like pollution instead of a "good" like crab, both systems work to allocate an activity efficiently because the permits, like licences, are *tradable*.

Here's why this system works in the case of pollution. Firms that pollute typically have different costs of reducing pollution—for example, it will be more costly for plants using older technology to reduce pollution than plants using newer technology. Regulators begin the system by issuing polluters with permits to pollute based on some formula—say, for example, equal to 50% of a given firm's historical level of emissions. Firms then have the right to trade permits among themselves.

Under this system, a market in permits to pollute will emerge. Polluters who place a higher value on the right to pollute—those with older technology—will purchase permits from polluters who place a lower value on the right to pollute—those with newer technology. As a result, a polluter with a higher value for a unit of emissions will pollute more than a polluter with a lower value.

In the end, those with the lowest cost of reducing pollution will reduce their pollution the most, while those with the highest cost of reducing pollution will reduce their pollution the least. The total effect is to allocate pollution reduction efficiently—that is, in the least costly way.

Just like emissions taxes, tradable emissions permits provide polluters with an incentive to take the marginal social cost of pollution into account. To see why, suppose that the market price of a permit to emit one unit of pollution is $200. Every polluter now has an incentive to limit its emissions to the point where its marginal benefit of one unit of pollution is $200. Why?

If the marginal benefit of one more unit of pollution is greater than $200 then it is cheaper to pollute more than to pollute less. In that case the polluter will buy a permit and emit another unit. And if the marginal benefit of one more unit of pollution is less than $200, then it is cheaper to reduce pollution than to pollute more. In that scenario, the polluter will reduce pollution rather than buy the $200 permit.

From this example we can see how an emissions permit leads to the same outcome as an emissions tax when they are the same amount: a polluter who pays $200 for the right to emit one unit faces the same incentives as a polluter who faces an emissions tax of $200 per unit. And it's equally true for polluters who have received more permits from regulators than they plan to use: by not emitting one unit of pollution, a polluter frees up a permit that it can sell for $200. In other words, the opportunity cost of a unit of pollution to this firm is $200, regardless of whether it is used.

Tradable emissions permits are licences to emit limited quantities of pollutants that can be bought and sold by polluters.

Recall that when using emissions taxes to arrive at the optimal level of pollution, the problem arises of finding the right amount of the tax: if the tax is too low, too much pollution is emitted; if the tax is too high, too little pollution is emitted (in other words, too many resources are spent reducing pollution). A similar problem with tradable emissions permits is getting the quantity of permits right, which is much like the flip-side of getting the level of the tax right.

Because it is difficult to determine the optimal quantity of pollution, regulators can find themselves either issuing too many permits, so that there is insufficient pollution reduction, or issuing too few, so that there is too much pollution reduction.

In the case of sulfur dioxide pollution, the U.S. government first relied on environmental standards, but then turned to a system of tradable emissions permits. Currently the largest emissions permit trading system is the European Union system for controlling emissions of carbon dioxide.

Comparing Environmental Policies with an Example

Figure 16-5 shows a hypothetical industry consisting of only two plants, plant A and plant B. We'll assume that plant A uses newer technology, giving it a

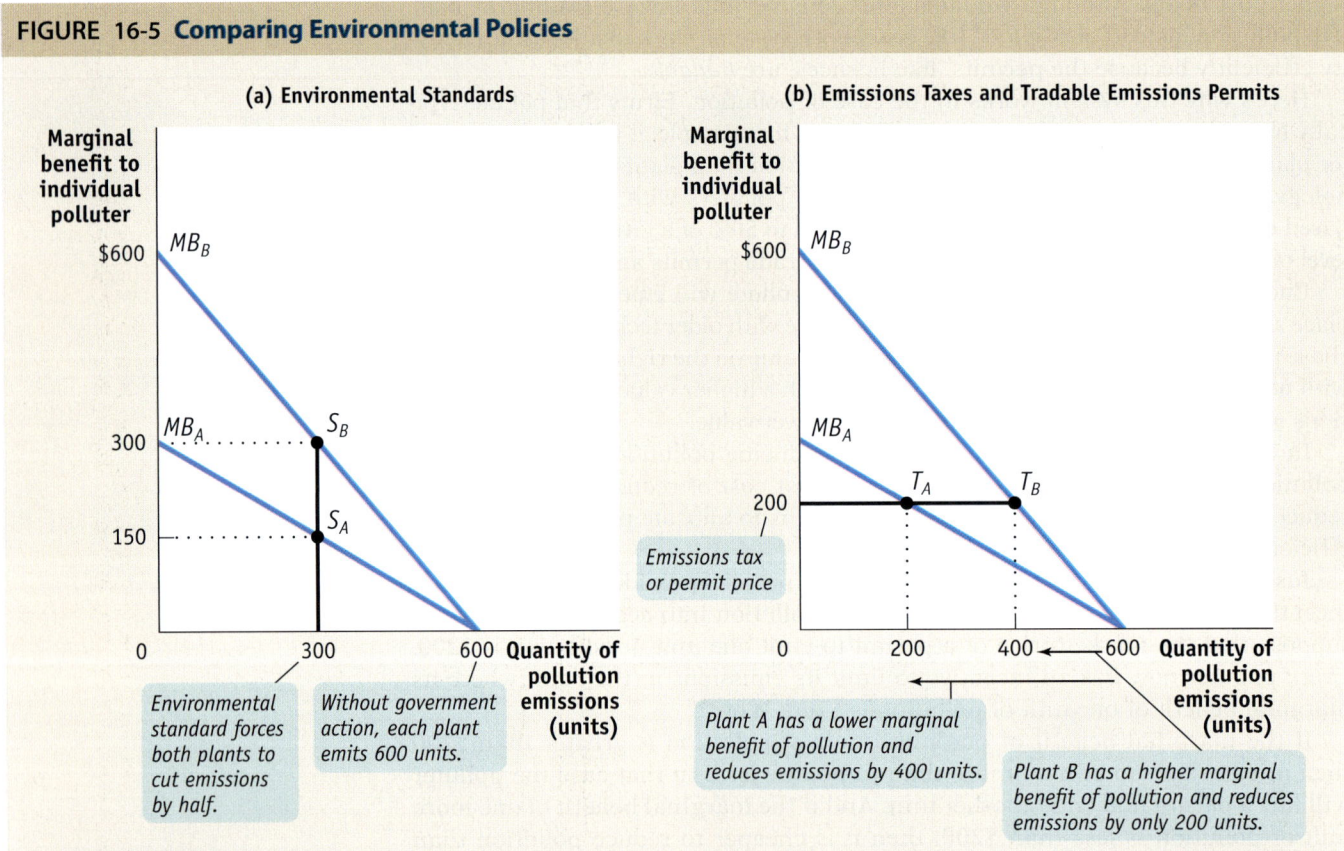

FIGURE 16-5 Comparing Environmental Policies

(a) Environmental Standards

(b) Emissions Taxes and Tradable Emissions Permits

Environmental standard forces both plants to cut emissions by half.

Without government action, each plant emits 600 units.

Plant A has a lower marginal benefit of pollution and reduces emissions by 400 units.

Plant B has a higher marginal benefit of pollution and reduces emissions by only 200 units.

In both panels, MB_A shows the marginal benefit of pollution to plant A and MB_B shows the marginal benefit of pollution to plant B. In the absence of government intervention, each plant would emit 600 units. However, the cost of reducing emissions is lower for plant A, as shown by the fact that MB_A lies below MB_B. Panel (a) shows the result of an environmental standard that requires both plants to cut emissions in half; this is inefficient, because it leaves the marginal benefit of pollution higher for plant B than for plant A. Panel (b) shows that an emissions tax as well as a system of tradable permits achieves the same quantity of overall pollution efficiently. Faced with either an emissions tax of $200 per unit, or a market price of a permit of $200 per unit, each plant reduces pollution to the point where its marginal benefit is $200.

lower cost of pollution reduction, while plant B uses older technology and has a higher cost of pollution reduction. Reflecting this difference, plant A's marginal benefit of pollution curve, MB_A, lies below plant B's marginal benefit of pollution curve, MB_B. Because it is more costly for plant B to reduce its pollution at any output quantity, an additional unit of pollution is worth more to plant B than to plant A.

In the absence of government action, we know that polluters will pollute until the marginal social benefit of a unit of pollution is equal to zero. As a result, without government intervention each plant will pollute until its own marginal benefit of pollution is equal to zero. This corresponds to an emissions quantity of 600 units for each plant—the quantities of pollution at which MB_A and MB_B are equal to zero. So although plant A and plant B have different costs of pollution reduction, they will each choose to emit the same amount of pollution.

Now suppose that regulators decide that the overall pollution from this industry should be cut in half, from 1,200 units to 600 units. Panel (a) of Figure 16-5 shows this might be achieved with an environmental standard that requires each plant to cut its emissions in half, from 600 to 300 units. The standard has the desired effect of reducing overall emissions from 1,200 to 600 units but accomplishes it inefficiently.

As you can see from panel (a), the environmental standard leads plant A to produce at point S_A, where its marginal benefit of pollution is $150, but plant B produces at point S_B, where its marginal benefit of pollution is twice as high, $300.

This difference in marginal benefits between the two plants tells us that the same quantity of pollution can be achieved at lower total cost by allowing plant B to pollute more than 300 units but inducing plant A to pollute less. In fact, the efficient way to reduce pollution is to ensure that at the industry-wide outcome, the marginal benefit of pollution is the same for all plants. When each plant values a unit of pollution equally, there is no way to rearrange pollution reduction among the various plants that achieves the optimal quantity of pollution at a lower total cost.

We can see from panel (b) how an emissions tax achieves exactly that result. Suppose both plant A and plant B pay an emissions tax of $200 per unit, so that the marginal cost of an additional unit of emissions to each plant is now $200 rather than zero. As a result, plant A produces at T_A and plant B produces at T_B. So plant A reduces its pollution more than it would under an inflexible environmental standard, cutting its emissions from 600 to 200 units. Meanwhile, plant B reduces its pollution less, going from 600 to 400 units.

In the end, total pollution—600 units—is the same as under the environmental standard, but total surplus is higher. That's because the reduction in pollution has been achieved efficiently, allocating most of the reduction to plant A, the plant that can reduce emissions at a lower cost. (Remember that producer surplus is the area below the supply curve and above the price line. So there is more total producer surplus in panel (b) than in panel (a).)

Panel (b) also illustrates why a system of tradable emissions permits also achieves an efficient allocation of pollution among the two plants. Assume that in the market for permits, the market price of a permit is $200 and each plant has 300 permits to start the system. Plant B, with the higher cost of pollution reduction, will buy 100 permits from plant A, enough to allow it to emit 400 units. Correspondingly, plant A, with the lower cost, will sell 100 of its permits to plant B and emit only 200 units. Provided that the market price of a permit is the same as the optimal emissions tax, the two systems arrive at the same outcome.

Emissions Taxes versus Tradable Emissions Permits

It turns out that a tax on emissions of greenhouse gases, like the carbon tax in British Columbia, can have the exact same outcome as a system of tradable emissions permit. Figure 16-6 below helps to convey this point.

Suppose we have a product whose production results in the emission of greenhouse gases. Panel (a) of Figure 16-6 shows the impact of a tax on greenhouse gas emissions that is levied on the suppliers of this product. Imposing an excise tax, T, per unit shifts the supply curve up to $(S + T)$ and moves the market equilibrium from A to B. In the new equilibrium, the quantity exchanged has declined (from Q_E to Q_T), the price paid by consumers has increased (from P_E to P_C), and the price received by producers will decline (from P_E to P_P, where $P_P = P_C - T$). The tax revenue is equal to the area shaded in green in Figure 16-6 (Tax revenue = $T \times Q_T$).

Now what if the government decides to impose a system of tradable emissions permits instead? Such a system is described in panel (b) of Figure 16-6: the government creates a volume limit or "cap" on the total quantity of the product that can be supplied. In effect, this makes the supply curve perfectly vertical and shifts it to the left to the new (lower) government-imposed upper bound on production. This new supply curve is labelled S_2 in the diagram. In the new equilibrium at B, the quantity exchanged has declined (from Q_E to Q_{Cap}) and the price paid by consumers has increased (from P_E to P_C). If the government issues permits freely, the firms receiving them capture the shaded area as profit since the price earned by firms (P_C) exceeds their cost of production (P_P). Alternatively, if the government sells the permits, then the green-shaded area is equal to the governments permit revenue and firms earn zero profit.

FIGURE 16-6 Comparing Emissions Taxes and Tradable Emissions Permits

(a) Emissions Tax

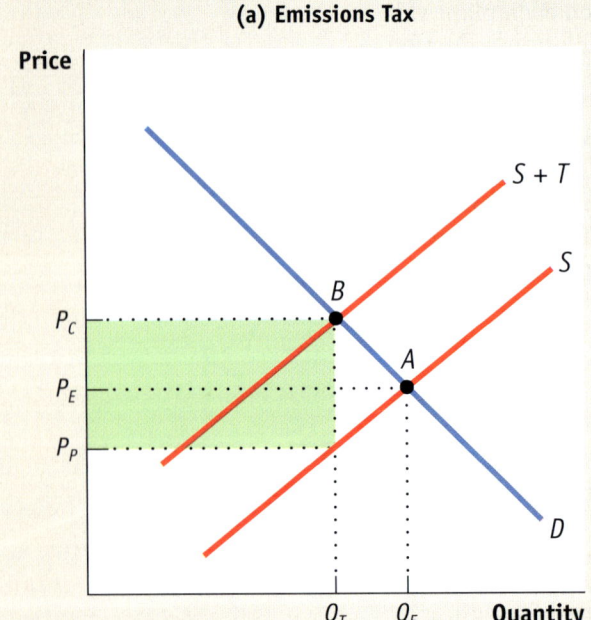

(b) Tradable Emissions Permits

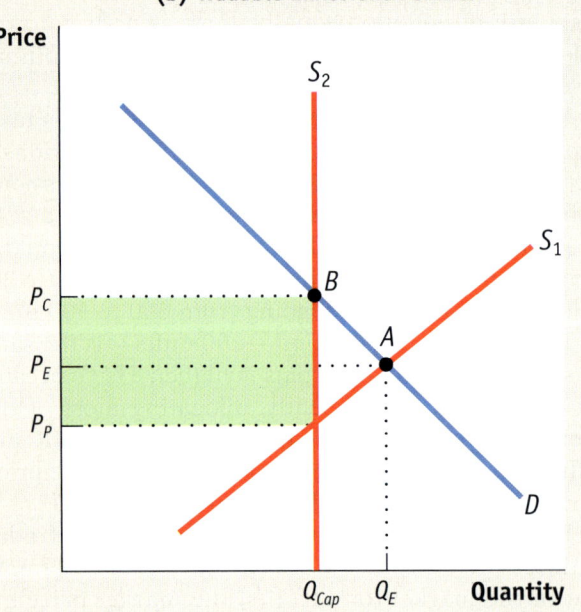

As shown in panel (a), a per-unit emissions tax collected from suppliers shifts the supply curve up. This reduces the quantity of the product exchanged, raises the price that consumers pay, lowers the price that suppliers receive, and results in tax revenue for the government (equal to the green-shaded area).

Using a system of tradable emissions permits makes the supply curve perfectly vertical at the government-imposed maximum level of output, as shown in panel (b). This reduces the quantity of the product exchanged and raises the price that consumers pay. If the permits are free, the green-shaded area represents profits captured by firms. If permits are sold by the government, this area represents the revenue for the government.

The lesson is simple. It does not matter whether the government uses an emissions tax or a tradable emissions system; if properly designed both can result in exactly the same outcome for society.

ECONOMICS >> *in Action*
Carbon Pricing

Tradable emissions permit systems for greenhouse gases are examples of cap-and-trade systems: the government sets a cap (a maximum amount of pollutant that can be emitted), issues tradable emissions permits, and enforces a yearly rule that a polluter must hold a number of permits equal to the amount of pollutant emitted. The goal is to set the cap low enough to generate environmental benefits, while giving polluters flexibility in meeting environmental standards and motivating them to adopt new technologies that will lower the cost of reducing pollution.

In response to climate change and to meet the country's international commitment—a 30% emissions reduction from 2005 levels by 2030, the Canadian federal government announced a national policy for carbon pricing in the fall of 2016 with a minimum carbon price starting at $10 per tonne in 2018, and rising to $50 per tonne in 2022. According to the announced plan, each province was given the flexibility to choose which method, carbon tax or cap-and-trade, to achieve the target set by the federal government.

Currently, different provinces have adopted different carbon pricing options—some provinces have set their own standards that meet the federal standards, while some have not (or refuse to). For example, British Columbia went with its own carbon tax and a cap-and-trade system, and Québec belongs to a tradable emissions permit scheme with California. Both Ontario and Alberta opted not to impose a provincial carbon tax, and so residents of these two provinces are charged a carbon tax levied by the federal government. The following table shows the 2019 price of greenhouse gas emission per tonne in these provinces (the federal carbon tax in 2019 was $20).

British Columbia	Alberta	Ontario	Québec
$40	pay the federal levy	pay the federal levy	Trading at $20.82

As you can see, the federal carbon pricing announced by the federal government will not have any impact on British Columbia and Québec in the meantime as the prices are already higher than the introductory price set by the federal government. Given this, it is no wonder that some have urged the federal government to do more about greenhouse gas emissions.

Although carbon trading and carbon taxes can be efficient ways to reduce greenhouse emissions, they are not silver bullets for all pollution problems. They are appropriate for pollution that's geographically dispersed, like greenhouse gases; they don't work for pollution that's localized, like groundwater contamination. And there must be vigilant monitoring of compliance for the system to work. In addition, they have become a difficult political issue for governments trying to run an effective environmental policy.

The political problems stem from the fact that a lower cap imposes higher costs on companies, because they must either achieve great pollution reductions or because they must purchase permits that command a higher market price. Similarly, if the carbon tax is set too high, this too will also raise production costs. So companies lobby governments to set higher caps or a lower tax level. Carbon trading and carbon taxes can be a hard sell to consumers as well. Fearing higher gasoline prices and heating costs, there will be resistance to these policies because most people don't want to pay the full (social) cost of the

>> Quick Review

• Governments often limit pollution with **environmental standards.** Generally, such standards are an inefficient way to reduce pollution because they are inflexible.

• Environmental goals can be achieved efficiently in two ways: **emissions taxes** and **tradable emissions permits.** These methods are efficient because they are flexible, allocating more pollution reduction to those who can do it more cheaply. They also motivate polluters to adopt new pollution-reducing technology. An emissions tax is a form of **Pigouvian tax.** The optimal Pigouvian tax is equal to the marginal social cost of pollution at the socially optimal quantity of pollution.

products/services they consume. As one energy economist noted, "It is politically difficult to get carbon prices to levels that have an effect."

>> Check Your Understanding 16-2

Solutions appear at back of book.

1. Some opponents of tradable emissions permits object to them on the grounds that polluters that sell their permits benefit monetarily from their contribution to polluting the environment. Assess this argument.

2. Explain the following.
   a. Why an emissions tax smaller than or greater than the marginal social cost at Q_{OPT} leads to a smaller total surplus compared to the total surplus generated if the emissions tax had been set optimally
   b. Why a system of tradable emissions permits that sets the total quantity of allowable pollution higher or lower than Q_{OPT} leads to a smaller total surplus compared to the total surplus generated if the number of permits had been set optimally
   c. How a carbon tax, which is a tax on carbon emissions, would encourage consumers to use more renewable energy sources

‖ The Economics of Climate Change

It is safe to say that one of the most challenging problems that the world will face during your lifetime is **climate change.** Science has conclusively shown that emissions of *greenhouse gases* are changing Earth's climate. On a global scale, **greenhouse gases** trap heat in Earth's atmosphere, leading to extreme weather patterns around the world—drought, flooding, extreme temperatures, destructive storm activity, and rising sea levels. Climate change inflicts huge costs and suffering, as crops fail, homes are washed away, tropical diseases spread, animal species are lost, and areas become uninhabitable. Moreover, the burden of this cost will fall more heavily on poorer countries, which have fewer resources to cope with the change.

In 2019, the Network of Central Banks and Supervisors for Greening the Financial System warned that unmitigated climate change could lower Canadian GDP per capita by 1.5 to 23% by 2100. One study estimated that 20% of world GDP would be lost under the same conditions. Economists and scientists widely recognize that the direct cost of fossil-fuel consumption greatly underestimates the social cost. In a World Bank study, Nobel prize–winning economists Joseph Stiglitz and Nicholas Stern estimated that the true environmental cost of carbon emissions ranges from US$50 to US$100 per tonne as of 2017, and may climb as high as US$400 by 2050. According to industry observers, the plunge in American electricity demand caused by the coronavirus pandemic of 2020 is likely to hasten the permanent closure of many U.S.-based coal plants.

The Causes of Climate Change

The rise in Earth's temperature began in the first half of the nineteenth century and has accelerated since the 1980s as Figure 16-7 shows. The source of the vast majority of greenhouse gases is human

An accumulation of greenhouse gases caused by the use of fossil fuels has led to changes in Earth's climate, known as **climate change.**

Greenhouse gases are gas emissions that trap heat in Earth's atmosphere.

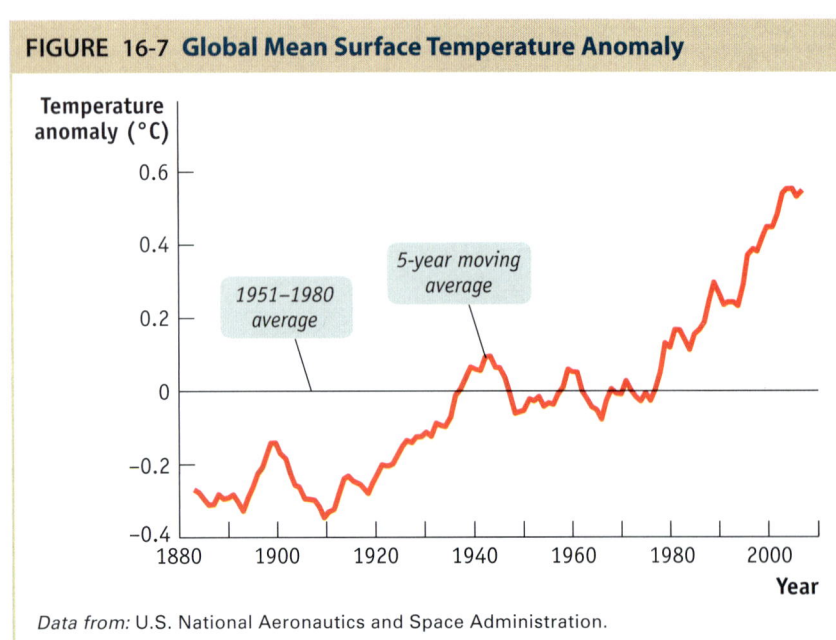

FIGURE 16-7 Global Mean Surface Temperature Anomaly

Data from: U.S. National Aeronautics and Space Administration.

activity—specifically, the burning of **fossil fuels** such as coal, oil, and natural gas, which are derived from fossil sources and are used to generate electricity or power vehicles. Burning fossil fuels releases carbon into the atmosphere, which turns into greenhouse gases. While fossil fuels are in limited supply, **renewable energy sources** are inexhaustible. Examples are solar and wind-generated power. Unlike fossil fuels, renewables are **clean energy sources** because they do not emit greenhouse gases.

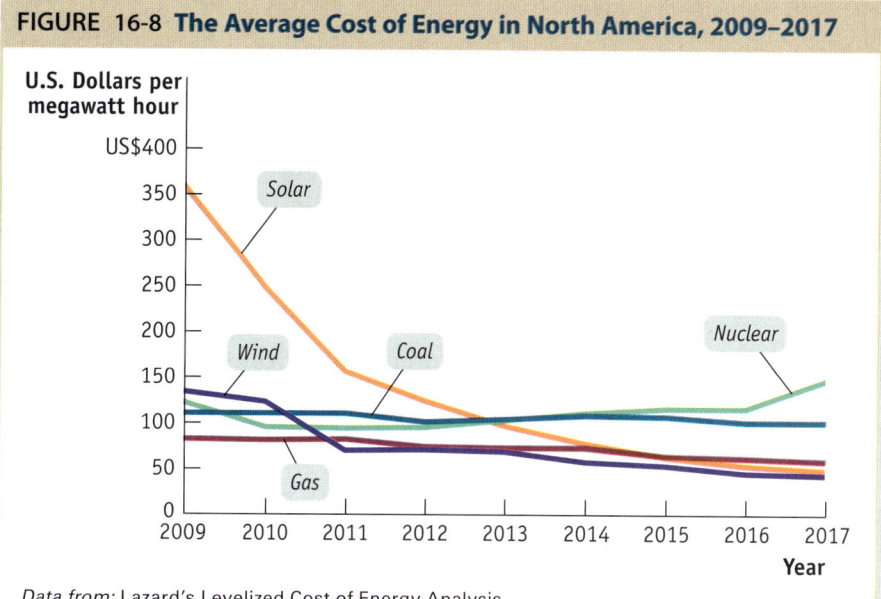

FIGURE 16-8 **The Average Cost of Energy in North America, 2009–2017**

Data from: Lazard's Levelized Cost of Energy Analysis.

Over the past decade, government subsidies, environmental regulation, and the threat of emissions taxes have spurred huge investments in clean energy sources, leading to dramatic cost reductions for renewables. In 2014, the government of Ontario put an end to the use of coal (the most polluting fossil fuel) for power generation. Among the plants that closed was the largest coal fired generation facility in North America. In the United States, coal was once the energy source of choice, accounting for nearly 60% of power generation; environmental restrictions and technological innovations have rendered it more costly than natural gas or renewables. By 2019, in the United States, the use of coal as a power source had fallen to 20%, which is even lower than the 23% share accounted for by renewables. In fact, in many instances, prices for industrial-scale solar power and wind power have become even cheaper than cleaner-burning natural gas power as Figure 16-8 shows.

Despite these advances, world energy consumption remains overwhelmingly dependent upon fossil fuels. In 2018, they accounted for approximately 85% of total consumption, while renewables accounted for only 10.8%. (Nuclear energy accounts for the difference of approximately 4%.) Why? It's dollars and cents. Historically, fossil fuels have been a cheaper source of energy than renewables. In much of the world, energy is generated by aging power plants that run on coal. This is true of both China and India where 70% or more of the electricity is generated by coal.

Policies to Address Climate Change

Earlier in this chapter, we learned about government policies aimed at achieving an efficient level of greenhouse gas emissions. These included regulations or mandates, emissions taxes, and cap-and-trade systems.

However, history has shown that to solve a complex and global negative externality problem like greenhouse gas emissions, other policies are needed. These include both government subsidies to research and development (R&D) and multilateral agreements.

Government Subsidies to R&D   Since the 1980s, the Canadian and U.S. governments have provided billions of dollars in subsidies for R&D dedicated

Fossil fuels such as coal and oil are fuels derived from fossil sources.

Renewable energy sources such as solar and wind power are inexhaustible sources of energy (unlike fossil-fuel sources, which are exhaustible).

Clean energy sources are those that do not emit greenhouse gases. Renewable energy sources are also clean energy sources.

The **Paris Agreement** is an international agreement by 196 countries to reduce their greenhouse gas emissions.

to lowering the cost of clean energy sources. These subsidies were critical in kick-starting innovation in the clean energy sector that has become increasingly cost competitive with the fossil-fuel industry. The 2017 federal budget allocated almost $1.7 billion over four years for spending on renewable energy R&D and demonstration and commercialization programs, and another $2.4 billion over four years to promote the production and use of "clean energy." These subsidies have the advantage of allowing the government to encourage energy innovation while avoiding imposing additional taxes on fossil fuels or regulating them—both less popular policies that have the potential to provoke a political backlash.

Multilateral Agreements Most countries would be disinclined to undertake costly policies to reduce greenhouse gas emissions if other countries refuse to do the same. To encourage cooperation, *multilateral agreements* set common objectives and allocate burden-sharing across countries, significantly increasing the chances of success in tackling climate change. In 2015, 196 countries came together under the **Paris Agreement,** committing to reduce emissions of greenhouse gases, with a common goal of limiting the increase in Earth's temperature to 2° Celsius, the level beyond which the effects of climate change are considered to be catastrophic and irreversible. Another example of a successful multilateral agreement was the *Montreal Protocol* of 1987. By setting limits on the production of ozone-depleting chemicals around the world, this agreement is credited with saving the Earth's ozone layer, a part of the upper atmosphere that protects Earth from the harmful effects of ultraviolet radiation coming from the sun.

Incentives for Individual Choices Incentives aimed at individual choices have an important role to play in addressing climate change. For example, through smart-metering, individuals are motivated to conserve energy, a fast and cost-effective way to reduce greenhouse gases. Higher gasoline taxes and wider availability of charging stations can motivate drivers to switch to electrically-powered cars. Individuals can also privately alter their choices, such as using less air conditioning, taking public transportation, or eating less meat (an emissions-heavy source of nutrition).

Climate Change Mitigation: Costs and Benefits

Reducing greenhouse gas emissions to sustainable levels requires a major structural shift in the economy that will inevitably affect growth rates and consumption. Consequently, some have claimed that attempts to mitigate climate change should be abandoned because the costs to consumers are too high.

However, that argument fails under a cost-benefit analysis. In a review of the latest scientific evidence, the Intergovernmental Panel on Climate Change concluded that meeting the Paris Agreement goals would mean that global consumption would shrink by 3–11% by 2100 compared to the status quo. But this number is quite a modest loss given that the world economy will continue growing, with an average growth rate of around 3% over the last several years. And as mentioned earlier, global losses by 2100 from runaway climate change are estimated at 20% of world GDP.

Moreover, when the direct health costs from fossil-fuel air pollution are taken into account, the losses from runaway climate change climb significantly. The World Health Organization estimates that 4.6 million people die annually from air pollution caused by burning fossil fuels.

Nearly 1.25 million "excess" deaths are estimated to occur each year in China, alone, from fossil-fuel fouled air. The health benefits of switching to clean energy is estimated to be as much as 5% of global GDP. In addition, the estimates of the costs of mitigating climate change don't incorporate the rapidly dropping price of clean energy sources as technology advances.

So claims that the costs of addressing climate change are too high don't withstand scrutiny. That's why, as the next Economics in Action describes, over 3,500 economists have advocated for a carbon tax to combat climate change.

ECONOMICS >> *in Action*
Over 3,500 Economists Agree: Tax Greenhouse Gas Emissions

In 2019, 3,558 economists from across the ideological spectrum—4 former chairs of the U.S. Federal Reserve System, 27 Nobel laureates, 15 former chairs of the U.S. Council of Economic Advisers, and 2 former U.S. Secretaries of the Department of Treasury—signed a joint statement calling for a tax on greenhouse gas emissions to fight climate change, with the proceeds of the tax to be distributed to American consumers. In their words, "Global climate change is a serious problem calling for immediate national action." Published in the *Wall Street Journal*, it was the largest public statement by economists in history.

According to the statement, an emissions tax is needed to quickly reduce emissions, and it should be raised every year until emissions reductions goals are set. A tax, they argue, is more efficient that regulations. By distributing the tax revenues to American consumers in the form of a "carbon dividend," they also believe that this system is politically more viable and more equitable than a cap and trade system. Finally, they argue that imports from abroad should also be taxed according to their true environmental cost, so that American firms aren't put at a cost-disadvantage relative to foreign firms. For the economics profession, it was an indisputable show of support for the validity of the economics of climate change.

>> Check Your Understanding 16-3
Solutions appear at back of book.

1. What are the types of fossil fuels? What are the main clean energy sources? What are their relationships to climate change?
2. What market failure led to climate change? What are the estimated losses to GDP from unmitigated climate change?
3. Why are government subsidies an important policy tool in addressing climate change? Multilateral agreements? Incentives to individual choice?
4. How would you respond to the argument that the structural change to the economy required to address climate change is too costly?

‖ Positive Externalities

Stretching from Niagara Falls through Hamilton and the Greater Toronto Area, the Golden Horseshoe region is probably the most densely populated region in the country, containing a large portion of Canada's industry and about 9.2 million residents. Yet a drive through this region reveals a surprising feature: farm after farm, growing everything from corn to peaches to the famous Niagara grapes for ice wine. This situation is no accident: the federal and provincial governments have passed laws that give tax subsidies to farmers who permanently preserve their farmland rather than sell it to developers. These subsidies have helped preserve thousands of hectares of open space.

Why have Canadian citizens voted to raise their own taxes to subsidize the preservation of farmland? Because they believe that preserved farmland provides external benefits, such as natural beauty, access to fresh food, and the conservation of wild bird populations. In addition, preservation alleviates the external

>> Quick Review

• **Climate change** is the result of burning fossil fuels that release **greenhouse gases** into the atmosphere. Climate change inflicts huge costs and suffering, especially on residents of poorer countries. Under unmitigated climate change, a federal report estimates losses as high as 23% of Canadian GDP in 2100; another study estimates losses as high as 20% of world GDP.

• Unlike fossil fuels (coal, oil, and natural gas), **renewable energy sources,** such as solar and wind power, are inexhaustible. They are **clean energy sources** because they do not emit greenhouse gases. In Canada, environmental restrictions and subsidies have combined to spur innovation in clean energy sources, which are now cheaper than fossil fuels in many applications.

• World energy consumption is currently highly dependent on fossil fuels, a legacy of fossil fuel's historically lower cost compared to clean energy resources. However, economists and scientists estimate that the true cost of greenhouse gas emissions is far higher than the current market price.

• In addition to the standard set of tools for achieving the efficient level of greenhouse gas emissions (mandates, emissions tax, or cap and trade system), other policies can be of critical importance for addressing climate change. They are government subsidies to R&D in clean energy sources; multilateral agreements such as the **Paris Agreement;** and incentives to individual choice, particularly energy conservation.

• While addressing climate change will require a structural shift in the economy away from fossil fuels and toward clean energy sources, claims that addressing climate change is too costly fail under a cost-benefit analysis.

Canadians understand that preserving local farmland makes them better off.

costs that come with more development, such as pressure on roads, water supplies, and municipal services—and, inevitably, more pollution. Ducks Unlimited Canada (DUC), a private, nonprofit organization dedicated to conserving, restoring, and managing wetlands, estimated that for every $1 invested in their conservation work, the social return on their investment was $22.

In this section, we'll explore the topics of external benefits and positive externalities. They are, in many ways, the mirror images of external costs and negative externalities. Left to its own, the market will produce too little of a good (in this case, preserved Ontario farmland) that confers external benefits on others. But society as a whole is better off when policies are adopted that increase the supply of such a good.

Preserved Farmland: An External Benefit

Preserved farmland yields both benefits and costs to society. In the absence of government intervention, the farmer who wants to sell their land incurs all the costs of preservation—namely, the forgone profit to be made from selling the farmland to a developer. But the benefits of preserved farmland accrue not to the farmer but to neighbouring residents, who have no right to influence how the farmland is disposed of.

Figure 16-9 illustrates society's problem. The marginal social cost of preserved farmland, shown by the MSC curve, is the additional cost imposed on society by an additional hectare of such farmland. This represents the forgone profits that would have accrued to farmers if they had sold their land to developers. The line is upward sloping because when very few hectares are preserved and there is

FIGURE 16-9 Why a Market Economy Preserves Too Little Farmland

Without government intervention, the quantity of preserved farmland will be zero, the level at which the marginal social cost of preservation is zero. This is an inefficiently low quantity of preserved farmland: the marginal social benefit is $20,000, but the marginal social cost is zero. An optimal Pigouvian subsidy of $10,000, the value of the marginal social benefit of preservation when it equals the marginal social cost, can move the market to the socially optimal level of preservation, Q_{OPT}.

In this case, there is no marginal external cost ($MEC = 0$). Therefore, the marginal social cost is simply equal to the marginal private cost ($MSC = MPC$). Similarly, in the absence of government intervention, since there is no marginal private benefit of preserving farmland ($MPB = 0$), the marginal social benefit is simply equal to the marginal external benefit ($MSB = MEB$).

The competitive market outcome occurs where $MPC = MPB$. Since MPB is zero in the present case, the market outcome is at zero. In the absence of government intervention, no farmland is preserved ($Q_{MKT} = 0$). This is much less than the socially optimal level, which occurs where $MSC = MSB > 0$; society wants some positive quantity of farmland preserved.

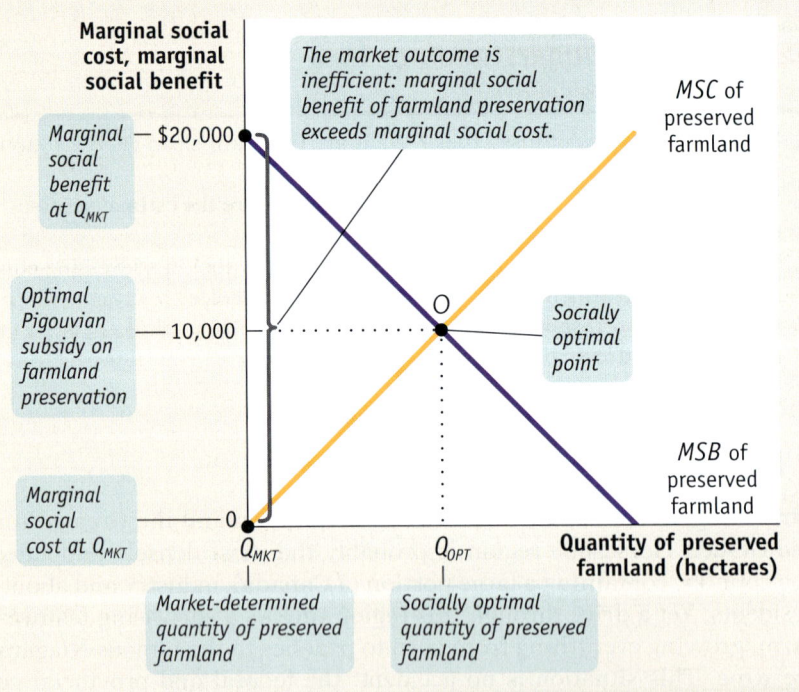

plenty of land available for development, the profit that could be made from selling a hectare to a developer is small. But as the number of preserved hectares increases and few are left for development, the amount a developer is willing to pay for them, and therefore the forgone profit, increases as well.

The *MSB* curve represents the marginal social benefit of preserved farmland. It is the additional benefit that accrues to society—in this case, the farmer's neighbours—when an additional hectare of farmland is preserved. The curve is downward sloping because as more farmland is preserved, the benefit to society of preserving another hectare falls.

As Figure 16-9 shows, the socially optimal point, *O*, occurs when the marginal social cost and the marginal social benefit are equalized—here, at a price of $10,000 per hectare. At the socially optimal point, Q_{OPT} hectares of farmland are preserved.

The market alone will not provide Q_{OPT} hectares of preserved farmland. Instead, in the market outcome no hectares will be preserved; the level of preserved farmland, Q_{MKT}, is equal to zero. That's because farmers will set the marginal social cost of preservation—their forgone profits—at zero and sell all their hectares to developers. Because farmers bear the entire cost of preservation but gain none of the benefits, an inefficiently low quantity of hectares will be preserved in the market outcome.

This is clearly inefficient because at zero hectares preserved, the marginal social benefit of preserving an hectare of farmland is $20,000 which exceeds the (zero) marginal social cost of preserving a hectare. So how can the economy be induced to produce Q_{OPT} hectares of preserved farmland, the socially optimal level? The answer is a **Pigouvian subsidy:** a payment designed to encourage activities that yield external benefits. The optimal Pigouvian subsidy, as shown in Figure 16-9, is equal to the marginal social benefit of preserved farmland at the socially optimal level, Q_{OPT}—that is, $10,000 per hectare.

So Canadians are indeed implementing the right policy to raise their social welfare—taxing themselves in order to provide subsidies for farmland preservation.

Positive Externalities in Today's Economy

In the overall Canadian economy, the single most important source of external benefits is the creation of knowledge. In high-tech industries such as semiconductors, software design, green technology, and bioengineering, innovations by one firm are quickly emulated and improved upon by rival firms. Such spreading of knowledge across individuals and firms is known as a **technology spillover.** In today's economy, the greatest sources of technology spillovers are major universities and research institutes.

In technologically advanced countries such as Canada, the United States, Japan, the United Kingdom, Germany, France, and Israel, there is an ongoing exchange of people and ideas among private industries, major universities, and research institutes located in close proximity. The dynamic interplay that occurs in these *research clusters* spurs innovation and competition, theoretical advances, and practical applications.

One of Canada's best known and most successful research clusters is located in the Waterloo region in Ontario, anchored by several universities and colleges, the Perimeter Institute for Theoretical Physics, the Institute for Quantum Computing, a number of other research parks and incubators, plus companies such as BlackBerry, OpenText, and Google Canada. Ultimately, the areas of technology spillover increase the economy's productivity and raise living standards.

But research clusters don't appear out of thin air. Except in a few instances in which firms have funded basic research on a long-term basis, research clusters have grown up around major universities. And like farmland preservation, major

A **Pigouvian subsidy** is a payment designed to encourage activities that generate positive externalities.

A **technology spillover** is a positive externality that results when knowledge spreads among individuals and firms.

universities and their research activities are subsidized by government. In fact, government policy makers in advanced countries have long understood that the external benefits generated by knowledge, stemming from basic education to high-tech research, are key to the economy's growth over time.

fatihhoca/Getty Images

Early-childhood intervention programs focusing on education and health offer many benefits to society.

ECONOMICS >> *in Action*
The Impeccable Economic Logic of Early-Childhood Intervention Programs

One of the most vexing problems facing any society is how to break what researchers call the *cycle of poverty:* children who grow up in disadvantaged socioeconomic circumstances are far more likely to remain trapped in poverty as adults, even after we account for differences in ability. They are more likely to be unemployed or underemployed, to engage in crime, and to suffer chronic health problems.

Early-childhood intervention programs offer hope for breaking the cycle. A study by the RAND Corporation found that high-quality early-childhood programs that focus on education and health care lead to significant social, intellectual, and financial advantages for kids who would otherwise be at risk of dropping out of high school and of engaging in criminal behaviour. Children in programs like Head Start were less likely to engage in such destructive behaviours and more likely to end up with a job and to earn a high salary later in life.

Another study by researchers at the University of Toronto looked at early-childhood intervention programs from a dollars-and-cents perspective, estimating that a national child-care program launched in Canada could provide annual benefits worth $10.2 billion at a cost of $7.9 billion; a 29% return on investment.

>> *Check Your Understanding* 16-4
Solutions appear at back of book.

1. In 2016–2017, government grants to Canadian universities and colleges totalled $13.9 billion. The federal, provincial, and territorial governments also provided grants and loans to postsecondary students. Explain why this can be an optimal policy to encourage the creation of knowledge.
2. In each of the following cases, determine whether a negative or positive externality is imposed and what an appropriate policy response would be.
   a. Trees planted in urban areas improve air quality and lower summer temperatures.
   b. Water-saving toilets reduce the need to pump water from rivers and aquifers. The cost of a litre of water to homeowners is virtually zero.
   c. Bottled drinks are packaged in plastic that does not decompose when discarded. As a result, they take up vast amounts of landfill space or must be burned, releasing pollutants.

‖ Network Externalities

As explained in Chapter 13, a *network externality* exists when the value of a good or service increases as the number of other people who also use the good or service increases. Although network externalities are common in technology-driven and communication-driven sectors of the economy, the phenomenon is considerably more widespread than that.

Consider the case of a car. You might not think that the value of having a car depends on how many others also have cars, but in the early days of car consumerism it certainly did. That's because when very few cars existed, service stations and repair shops were few and far between, and local governments had little or no incentive to upgrade roads to make them car-worthy. However, as more people purchased cars, service stations and repair shops sprang up, and roads were improved. As a result, owning a car became even more valuable.

What a network externality shares with positive and negative externalities is an external effect: one person's actions affect the payoff to another person's actions. Network externalities play a key role both in the economy and in a number of regulatory policy controversies.

The External Benefits of a Network Externality

We can now deepen our understanding of network externalities by noting that a network externality involves an external benefit: one person's adoption of a good or service extends an external benefit to another person who also adopts that good or service. As a result, the marginal benefit of the good or service to any one person depends on the number of other people who also use it.

Although the most common network externalities involve methods of communication—the internet, cell phones, social media, and so on—they are also frequently present in transportation. For example, the value to a traveller of a given airport increases as more travellers use that airport as well, making more airlines and more destinations available from it. A marketplace website like eBay is more valuable to use, either to buy or to sell, the greater the number of other people also using that site. Similarly, many of us value banking with a particular bank because of the number of ATMs it has, and it will have more ATMs if it has a larger customer base.

The classic case of network externalities in the tech industry arises from computer operating systems. Most personal computers around the world run on Windows by Microsoft rather than on Apple's competing system. In 2019, nearly 6 new PCs that run Windows were sold for every Apple Mac sold. Why does Windows dominate personal computers? There are two answers to the question, both involving network externalities. First, there is a direct effect: it is easier for a Windows user to get help and advice from other Windows users. Second, is an indirect effect: Windows' early dominance attracted more software developers, so more programs were developed to run on Windows than on a competing system. (This second effect has largely vanished now, but it was important in the early days of making PCs dominant.)

When a network externality arises from the use of a good or service, it leads to **positive feedback,** also known as a *bandwagon effect:* if large numbers of people use it, other people become more likely to use it, too. And if fewer people use the good or service, others become less likely to use it as well. This leads to a chicken-versus-egg problem: if one person's value of the good depends on whether another person also uses the good, how do you get anyone to buy the good in the first place?

Not surprisingly, producers of goods and services with network externalities are aware of this problem. They understand that of two competing products, the one with the largest network—not necessarily the one that's the better product—will win in the end. The product with the larger network will continue to grow and dominate the market, while its rival will shrink and eventually disappear.

An important way to gain an advantage at the early stages of a market with network externalities is to sell the product cheaply, perhaps at a loss, in order to increase the size of the network of users. For example, Skype, the first widely successful internet calling company, allows free calls only between members. This builds Skype's network of users, who will then pay for using Skype to call a non-Skype contact or to place a call to a landline phone. Today, Skype is used heavily for international calling. Newer companies such as WhatsApp and Snapchat likewise increase the size of their network by allowing free interaction

A good is subject to **positive feedback** when success breeds greater success and failure breeds further failure.

between members, allowing them to generate more revenue from selling ads and user data. And as we explain in the following Economics in Action, the fact that all web browsers—including Internet Explorer, Chrome, and Firefox—are free to download is a legacy of Microsoft's early strategy of providing Internet Explorer free on its computers in order to buttress its Windows operating-system dominance.

Network externalities present special challenges for antitrust regulators because the antitrust laws do not, strictly speaking, forbid monopoly. Rather, they only prohibit *monopolization*—efforts to create a monopoly. If you just happen to end up ruling an industry, that's okay, but if you take actions designed to drive out competition, that's not okay. So we could argue that monopolies in goods with network externalities, because they occur naturally, should not pose legal problems.

Unfortunately, it isn't that simple. Firms investing in new technologies are clearly trying to establish monopoly positions. Furthermore, in the face of positive feedback, firms have an incentive to engage in aggressive strategies to push their goods in order to increase their network size and tip the market in their favour. So what is the dividing line between legal and illegal actions? In the Microsoft antitrust case, described in the next Economics in Action, reasonable economists and legal experts disagreed sharply about whether the company had broken the law.

ECONOMICS >> *in Action*
The Microsoft Case

Stephen Brashear/Getty Images

The Microsoft case was a good example of the pros and cons raised by goods with network externalities.

A consent decree between Microsoft and the U.S. government prohibiting certain business practices expired in 2011, marking the end of an era for the company. Beginning in 1998, the U.S. Justice Department, as well as 20 states and the District of Columbia sued Microsoft, alleging predatory practices against competitors to protect the monopoly position held by its Windows operating system.

At the time, Microsoft was by any reasonable definition a monopoly, as just about all personal computers in the late 1990s ran Windows. And the key feature supporting this dominance was a network externality: people used Windows because other people used Windows.

Despite urging by some economists, the U.S. Justice Department did not challenge the Windows monopoly itself, as most experts agreed that monopoly was the natural outcome of an industry with network externalities. What U.S. Justice Department lawyers did claim, however, was that Microsoft had used the monopoly position of its Windows operating system to give its other products an unfair advantage over competitors.

For example, by bundling Internet Explorer free as part of Windows, it was alleged that Microsoft had given itself an unfair advantage over rival web browser Netscape, because it prevented Netscape from charging customers for its use. The U.S. government argued that this was harmful because it discouraged innovation: potential software innovators were unwilling to invest large sums out of fear that Microsoft would bundle equivalent software with Windows for free. Microsoft, in contrast, argued that by setting the precedent that companies would be punished for success, the government was the real opponent of innovation.

After many years of legal wrangling, the consent decree was signed in 2002, which barred Microsoft from excluding rivals from its computers and forced the company to make Windows seamlessly interoperable with non-Microsoft software. This eliminated any advantage Microsoft had through free bundling of its own programs into the Windows package.

Although the case against Microsoft consumed many tens of millions of U.S. dollars in legal costs and is considered one of the most significant antitrust cases of its generation, its long-term effects are hotly debated. Some say that the case essentially had no effect, as the cutting edge of technology moved into mobile devices like smartphones and tablets, leaving Microsoft and its PC-centred business behind. Others argue that, although the case may not have dampened overall innovation as Microsoft claimed, it changed the culture of Microsoft itself, making it more cautious and therefore unable to explore and capitalize on new technological trends.

Two effects, however, are beyond dispute. Because of Microsoft's example, products with network externalities are often priced at a loss or even at zero—as in the case of today's web browsers, Chrome and Firefox, which are available for free. Second, rival tech companies now routinely charge one another with predatory behaviour that exploits a network externality advantage—as in Microsoft's charges against Google for its advantage in the search engine market.

>> Check Your Understanding 16-5

Solutions appear at back of book.

1. For each of the following goods, explain the nature of the network externality present.
   a. Appliances using a particular voltage, such as 110 volts versus 220 volts
   b. 8½-by-11-inch paper versus 8-by-12½-inch paper
2. Suppose there are two competing companies in an industry that has a network externality. Explain why it is likely that the company able to sustain the largest initial losses will eventually dominate the market.

Xcel Energy Goes for a Win-Win

iurii/Shutterstock

Historically, renewables have been more expensive than fossil fuels, and federal subsidies to the renewable energy industry have been critical in bringing costs to consumers down as well as in funding innovation. However, over the years, those subsidies have frequently been at risk. For example, from 2012 to 2013, newly installed wind capacity in the United States plunged by 93% from when federal subsidies ended. In 2014 and 2015, wind capacity revived when those subsidies were restored. But in 2017 a new pattern appeared: when American federal subsidies for renewable energy were again at risk as the U.S. Congress debated whether to cut them, the percentage of newly installed power capacity that was accounted for by renewables fell only modestly—from nearly 50% in 2017 to 48% in 2018. In 2020, the future of the American subsidies are again unclear: without congressional action, they will largely expire at the end of 2021. However, by 2020 renewables are projected to account for 78% of newly installed American power capacity. Will the threat to end subsidies stall their meteoric rise?

Benjamin Fowke, the CEO of Xcel Energy of Colorado, thinks not and is undeterred. He is trained in finance and accounting, so it's safe to say that he is no starry-eyed dreamer. Xcel Energy has announced that across its eight-state system, 60% of its energy will be generated by renewables and its carbon emissions will be reduced by 80% by 2030.

Fowke is positioning Xcel Energy to take advantage of the *learning curve* associated with the cost of renewable energy. The term is used to describe the dramatic fall in costs that is often achieved after a new technology is introduced. Adoption of the new technology spreads because scientists, innovators, and manufacturers get better at exploiting it. A virtuous cycle is generated as costs fall and adoption of the new technology increases, spurring further investment and additional reductions in costs.

An example is solar energy: the price to consumers of a watt of solar energy has dropped by more than 75% since 1998. The learning curve has been steepest in the last decade, with solar prices dropping by 60%. In the case of wind energy, prices have dropped by more than 90% since 1980.

According to Fowke, it is now cheaper to build new wind turbines than to operate its lowest-cost existing coal plants. For example, in 2017 Xcel purchased wind energy at a cost of US$15 to US$20 per megawatt-hour, compared to US$25 to US$35 for natural gas–generated power, the main energy source competing with renewables.

Unsurprisingly, competition with conventional fossil-fuel producers encourages the solar and wind industries, along with producers of other renewables, to keep improving their product and prices to stay ahead of the competition.

QUESTIONS FOR THOUGHT

1. Explain how subsidies affect the future adoption of a new technology that is subject to steep learning curve effects. Relate this to the role of government intervention when externalities are present.

2. Is Fowke right or wrong to persist in the adoption of renewables when federal subsidies are under threat? Analyze the investment decision that a CEO like Fowke must make in deciding whether and when to invest more capacity in renewables instead of in fossil-fuel sources.

3. How does this case illustrate the way in which business and government can work together in a market economy?

SUMMARY

1. When pollution can be directly observed and controlled, government policies should be geared directly to producing the **socially optimal quantity of pollution,** the quantity at which the **marginal social cost of pollution** is equal to the **marginal social benefit of pollution.** In the absence of government intervention, a market produces too much pollution because polluters take only their benefit from polluting into account, not the costs imposed on others.

2. The costs to society of pollution are an example of an **external cost;** in some cases, however, economic activities yield **external benefits.** External costs and benefits are jointly known as **externalities,** with external costs called **negative externalities** and external benefits called **positive externalities.**

3. According to the **Coase theorem,** individuals can find a way to **internalize the externality,** making government intervention unnecessary, as long as **transaction costs**—the costs of making a deal—are sufficiently low. However, in many cases transaction costs are too high to permit such deals.

4. Governments often deal with pollution by imposing **environmental standards,** a method, economists argue, that is usually an inefficient way to reduce pollution. Two efficient (cost-minimizing) methods for reducing pollution are **emissions taxes,** a form of **Pigouvian tax,** and **tradable emissions permits.** The optimal Pigouvian tax on pollution is equal to its marginal social cost at the socially optimal quantity of pollution. These methods also provide incentives for the creation and adoption of production technologies that cause less pollution.

5. A history of heavy reliance on **fossil fuels** that emit **greenhouse gases** has led to problems created by **climate change.** Unlike fossil fuels, **renewable energy sources** are inexhaustible. Policies such as taxes, tax credits, subsidies, and mandates, as well as consumer use of smart metering and industrial commitments, can help ensure a wide-scale shift toward renewable **clean energy sources.** Multilateral agreements such as the **Paris Agreement** commit many countries to common objectives and allocate burden-sharing across countries in order to tackle climate change.

6. When a good or activity yields positive externalities, such as **technology spillovers,** then an optimal **Pigouvian subsidy** to producers moves the market to the socially optimal quantity of production.

7. Communications, transportation, and high-technology goods are frequently subject to *network externalities,* which arise when the value of a good or service increases as the number of other people who use the good or service increases. Such goods are likely to be subject to **positive feedback:** if large numbers of people buy the good, other people are more likely to buy it, too. So success breeds greater success and failure breeds further failure: the good with the larger network will eventually dominate, and rival goods will disappear. As a result, producers have an incentive to take aggressive action in the early stages of the market to increase the size of their network. Markets with network externalities tend to be monopolies. They are especially challenging for antitrust regulators because differentiating between the natural progression of the network externality and illegal monopolization efforts by producers can be hard to do.

KEY TERMS

External cost, p. 490
External benefit, p. 490
Externalities, p. 490
Negative externalities, p. 490
Positive externalities, p. 490
Marginal social cost (*MSC*) of pollution, p. 491
Marginal private cost (*MPC*) of pollution, p. 491
Marginal external cost (*MEC*) of pollution, p. 491
Marginal social benefit (*MSB*) of pollution, p. 491

Marginal private benefit (*MPB*) of pollution , p. 491
Marginal external benefit (*MEB*) of pollution, p. 492
Socially optimal quantity of pollution, p. 492
Coase theorem, p. 496
Internalize the externality, p. 496
Transaction costs, p. 496
Environmental standards, p. 498
Emissions tax, p. 498
Pigouvian taxes, p. 499

Tradable emissions permits, p. 501
Climate change, p. 506
Greenhouse gases, p. 506
Fossil fuels, p. 507
Renewable energy sources, p. 507
Clean energy sources, p. 507
Paris Agreement, p. 508
Pigouvian subsidy, p. 511
Technology spillover, p. 511
Positive feedback, p. 513

PRACTICE QUESTIONS

1. To recline or not to recline? In early 2020, a passenger on an American Airlines flight was caught on video continuously punching the back of the seat in front of him, in which another passenger sat in the reclined position. The video went viral and sparked a national debate on whether passengers should recline their seats. Who is entitled to more space directly behind the airplane seat? Using the Coase theorem, recommend one remedy that can provide an efficient solution to this problem.

2. The Global Carbon Project brings together the international science community to "establish a common and mutually agreed knowledge base to support policy debate and action to slow down and ultimately stop the increase of greenhouse gases in the atmosphere." Go to its website, Global Carbon Atlas, www.globalcarbonatlas.org, and find the data map by selecting the tab "CO2 Emissions" on the top of the page. The default map will present $MtCO_2$ (metric tonnes of CO_2) by country. What countries produced the most carbon emissions? What do you notice about the high-carbon-emitting countries? Next, in the left-hand tool bar, change the units to tCO_2 (total CO_2) per person. What do you notice about the disparity across countries? What happened with the high-emitting countries you identified previously?

PROBLEMS

1. What type of externality (positive or negative) is present in each of the following examples? Is the marginal social benefit of the activity greater than or equal to the marginal benefit to the individual? Is the marginal social cost of the activity greater than or equal to the marginal cost to the individual? Without intervention, will there be too little or too much (relative to what would be socially optimal) of this activity?

   a. Mr. Chau plants lots of colourful flowers in his front yard.

   b. Your next-door neighbour likes to build bonfires in their backyard, and sparks often drift onto your house.

   c. Maija, who lives next to an apple orchard, decides to keep bees to produce honey.

   d. Justine buys a large SUV that consumes a lot of gasoline.

2. Some Canadian dairy farmers are adopting a new technology that allows them to produce their own electricity from methane gas captured from animal waste. (One cow can produce up to 2 kilowatts a day.) This practice reduces the amount of methane gas released into the atmosphere. In addition to reducing their own utility bills, the farmers are allowed to sell any electricity they produce at favourable rates.

   a. Explain how the ability to earn money from capturing and transforming methane gas behaves like a Pigouvian tax on methane gas pollution and can lead dairy farmers to emit the efficient amount of methane gas pollution.

   b. Suppose some dairy farmers have lower costs of transforming methane into electricity than others. Explain how this system of capturing and selling methane gas leads to an efficient allocation of emissions reduction among farmers.

3. Voluntary environmental programs were extremely popular in Canada, the United States, Europe, and Japan in the 1990s. Part of their popularity stems from the fact that these programs do not require legislative authority, which is often hard to obtain. The voluntary Memorandum of Understanding (MOU) between Transport Canada and Canadian airlines in 2005 is an example of such a program. With this agreement, Transport Canada sought to reduce emissions of greenhouse gases. Companies were asked to voluntarily commit to reducing emissions by improving fuel efficiency from their 1990 levels by 24% by 2012. The program actually exceeded its target resulting in a 31% cumulative improvement. In 2012, a new voluntary agreement was signed between these parties that would see fuel efficiency improve by at least 2% per year until 2020. For this question assume that fuel efficiency improvements result in an equal percent reduction in greenhouse gas emissions.

   a. As in Figure 16-5, draw marginal benefit curves for pollution generated by two airlines, A and B, in 1990. Assume that without government intervention, each airline emits the same amount of pollution, but that at all levels of pollution less than this amount, airline A's marginal benefit of polluting is less than that of airline B (perhaps due to using a different type of aircraft). Label the vertical axis "Marginal benefit to individual polluter" and the horizontal axis "Quantity of pollution emissions." Mark the quantity of pollution each plant produces without government action.

   b. Do you expect the total quantity of pollution before the programme was put in place to have been less than or more than the optimal quantity of pollution? Why?

   c. Suppose the airlines whose marginal benefit curves you depicted in part a were participants in this MOU. In a replica of your graph from part a, mark targeted levels of pollution in 2012 for the two airlines. Which airline was required to reduce emissions more? Was this solution necessarily efficient?

d. What kind of environmental policy does this MOU most closely resemble? What is the main shortcoming of such a policy? Compare it to two other types of environmental policies discussed in this chapter.

4. According to a report from the Association of Universities and Colleges of Canada, "University graduates will on average earn $1.3 million more during their careers [lifetime earnings] than a high school graduate and $1 million more than a college grad." This indicates that there is a considerable benefit to a graduate from investing in their own education. Tuition at Canadian universities in 2014–2015 covered only about 27% of the cost, so the government applies a Pigouvian subsidy to university education.

If a Pigouvian subsidy is appropriate, is the externality created by a university education a positive or a negative externality? What does this imply about the differences between the costs and benefits that accrue privately to students compared to social costs and benefits? What are some reasons for the differences?

5. The district municipality of Delta, south of Vancouver, provides free trees planted on municipal property adjacent to the side or front of homeowners' yards when requested.

a. Using concepts in the chapter, explain why a municipality would subsidize planting trees on private property, but near the street.

b. Draw a diagram similar to Figure 16-9 that shows the marginal social benefit, the marginal social cost, and the optimal Pigouvian subsidy on planting trees.

6. Fishing for sablefish had been so intensive that sablefish were threatened with extinction. After considering banning such fishing, Fisheries and Oceans Canada introduced individual tradable quotas in 1990, each of which entitles its holder to a catch of a certain size. Explain how uncontrolled fishing generates a negative externality and how the voucher scheme may overcome the inefficiency created by this externality.

7. The two dry-cleaning companies in Collegetown, College Cleaners and Big Green Cleaners, are a major source of air pollution. Together they currently produce 350 units of air pollution, which the town wants to reduce to 200 units. The accompanying table shows the current pollution level produced by each company and each company's marginal cost of reducing its pollution. The marginal cost is constant.

Companies	Initial pollution level (units)	Marginal cost of reducing pollution (per unit)
College Cleaners	230	$5
Big Green Cleaners	120	$2

a. Suppose that Collegetown passes an environmental standards law that limits each company to 100 units of pollution. What would be the total cost to the two companies of each reducing its pollution emissions to 100 units?

Suppose instead that Collegetown issues 100 pollution vouchers to each company, each entitling the company to one unit of pollution, and that these vouchers can be traded.

b. How much is each pollution voucher worth to College Cleaners? To Big Green Cleaners? (That is, how much would each company, at most, be willing to pay for one more voucher?)

c. Who will sell vouchers and who will buy them? How many vouchers will be traded?

d. What is the total cost to the two companies of the pollution controls under this voucher system?

8. a. EAuction and EMarketplace are two competing internet auction sites, where buyers and sellers transact goods. Each auction site earns money by charging sellers for listing their goods. EAuction has decided to eliminate fees for the first transaction for sellers that are new to its site. Explain why this is likely to be a good strategy for EAuction in its competition with EMarketplace.

b. EMarketplace complained to the Competition Bureau that EAuction's practice of eliminating fees for new sellers was anti-competitive and would lead to monopolization of the internet auction industry. Is EMarketplace correct? How should the Competition Bureau respond?

c. EAuction stopped its practice of eliminating fees for new sellers. But since it provided much better technical service than its rival, EMarketplace, buyers and sellers came to prefer EAuction. Eventually, EMarketplace closed down, leaving EAuction as a monopolist. Should the Competition Bureau intervene to break EAuction into two companies? Explain.

d. EAuction is now a monopolist in the internet auction industry. It also owns a site that handles payments over the internet, called PayForIt. It is competing with another internet payment site, called PayBuddy. EAuction has now stipulated that any transaction on its auction site must use PayForIt, rather than PayBuddy, for the payment. Should the Competition Bureau intervene? Explain.

9. Which of the following are characterized by network externalities? Which are not? Explain.

a. The choice between installing 110-volt electrical current in structures rather than 220-volt

b. The choice between purchasing a Toyota versus a Ford

c. The choice of a printer, where each printer requires its own specific type of ink cartridge

d. The choice of whether to purchase an iPad Air or an iPad Mini.

WORK IT OUT

10. The loud music coming from the sorority next to your dorm is a negative externality that can be directly quantified. The accompanying table shows the marginal social benefit and the marginal social cost per decibel (dB, a measure of volume) of music.

Volume of music (dB)	Marginal social benefit of dB	Marginal social cost of dB
90		
	$36	$0
91		
	30	2
92		
	24	4
93		
	18	6
94		
	12	8
95		
	6	10
96		
	0	12
97		

a. Draw the marginal social benefit curve and the marginal social cost curve. Use your diagram to determine the socially optimal volume of music.

b. Only the members of the sorority benefit from the music, and they bear none of the cost. Which volume of music will they choose?

c. The university imposes a Pigouvian tax of $3 per decibel of music played. From your diagram, determine the volume of music the sorority will now choose. ∎

.17 Public Goods and Common Resources

 ## THE GREAT STINK

BY THE MIDDLE OF THE NINETEENTH century, London had become the world's largest city, with close to 2.5 million inhabitants. Unfortunately, all those people produced a lot of waste — and there was no place for it to go except into the Thames, the river flowing through the city. Nobody with a working nose could ignore the results. And the river didn't just smell bad — it carried dangerous waterborne diseases like cholera and typhoid. London neighbourhoods close to the Thames had death rates from cholera more than six times greater than the neighbourhoods farthest

London's River Thames, in the nineteenth century (top) and now. Government intervention turned it from an open sewer to a pristine waterway.

away. And the great majority of Londoners drew their drinking water from the Thames.

What the city needed, said reformers, was a sewage system to carry waste away from the river. Yet no private individual was willing to build such a system, and influential people were opposed to the idea that the government should take responsibility for the problem.

But the hot summer of 1858 brought what came to be known as the Great Stink, which was so bad that one health journal reported "men struck down with the stench." Even the privileged and powerful suffered: Parliament met in a building next to the river. After unsuccessful efforts to stop the smell by covering the windows with chemical-soaked curtains, Parliament finally approved a plan for an immense system of sewers and pumping stations to direct sewage away from the city.

The system, opened in 1865, brought dramatic improvement in the city's quality of life; cholera and typhoid epidemics, which had been regular occurrences, completely disappeared. The Thames was turned from the filthiest to the cleanest metropolitan river in the world, and the sewage system's principal engineer, Sir Joseph Bazalgette, was lauded as having "saved more lives than any single Victorian public official." It was estimated at the time that his sewer system added 20 years to the life span of the average Londoner.

The story of the Great Stink and the policy response that followed illustrate two important reasons for government intervention in the economy. London's new sewage system was a clear example of a *public good* — a good that benefits many people, whether or not they have paid for it, and whose benefits to any one individual do not depend on how many others also benefit. As we will see, public goods differ in important ways from the *private goods* we have studied so far — and these differences mean that public goods cannot be efficiently supplied by the market.

In addition, clean water in the Thames is an example of a *common resource,* a good that many people can consume whether

or not they have paid for it but whose consumption by each person reduces the amount available to others. Such goods tend to be overused by individuals in a market system unless the government takes action.

In earlier chapters, we saw that markets sometimes fail to deliver efficient levels of production and consumption of a good or activity. We saw how inefficiency can arise from market power, which allows monopolists and colluding oligopolists to charge prices that are higher than marginal cost, thereby preventing mutually beneficial transactions from occurring. We also saw how inefficiency can arise from positive and negative externalities, which cause a divergence between the costs and benefits of an individual's or industry's actions and the costs and benefits of those actions borne by society as a whole.

In this chapter, we will take a somewhat different approach to the question of why markets sometimes fail. Here we focus on how *the characteristics of goods often determine whether markets can deliver them efficiently.* When goods have the "wrong" characteristics, the resulting market failures resemble those associated with externalities or market power. This alternative way of looking at sources of inefficiency deepens our understanding of why markets sometimes don't work well and how government can take actions that increase society's welfare. ●

WHAT YOU WILL LEARN

- What is a **public good** and how is it different from a **private good**?

- What is a **common resource** and why is it overused?

- What is an **artificially scarce good** and why is it underconsumed?

- Why do markets typically fail to supply these types of goods efficiently?

- How can government intervention make society better off in the production and consumption of these types of goods?

521

A good is **excludable** if the supplier of that good can prevent people who do not pay from consuming it.

A good is **rival in consumption** if the same unit of the good cannot be consumed by more than one person at the same time.

A good that is both excludable and rival in consumption is a **private good.**

When a good is **nonexcludable,** the supplier cannot prevent consumption by people who do not pay for it.

A good is **nonrival in consumption** if more than one person can consume the same unit of the good at the same time.

‖ Private Goods — and Others

What's the difference between installing a new bathroom in a house and building a municipal sewage system? What's the difference between growing wheat and fishing in the open ocean?

These aren't trick questions. In each case there is a basic difference in the characteristics of the goods involved. Bathroom fixtures and wheat have the characteristics necessary to allow markets to work efficiently. Public sewage systems and fish in the sea do not.

Let's look at these crucial characteristics and why they matter.

Characteristics of Goods

Goods like bathroom fixtures or wheat have two characteristics that, as we'll soon see, are essential if a good is to be efficiently provided by a market economy.

- They are **excludable:** suppliers of the good can prevent people who don't pay from consuming it.
- They are **rival in consumption:** the same unit of the good cannot be consumed by more than one person at the same time.

When a good is both excludable and rival in consumption, it is called a **private good.** Wheat is an example of a private good. It is *excludable:* the farmer can sell a bushel to one consumer without having to provide wheat to everyone in the county. And it is *rival in consumption:* if I eat bread baked with a farmer's wheat, that wheat cannot be consumed by someone else.

But not all goods possess these two characteristics. Some goods are **nonexcludable**—the supplier cannot prevent consumption of the good by people who do not pay for it. Fire protection is one example: a fire department that puts out fires before they spread protects the whole city, not just people who have made contributions to the Firemen's Benevolent Association. An improved environment is another: the city of London couldn't have ended the Great Stink for some residents while leaving the River Thames foul for others.

Nor are all goods rival in consumption. Goods are **nonrival in consumption** if more than one person can consume the same unit of the good at the same time. TV shows are nonrival in consumption: your decision to watch a show does not prevent other people from watching the same show.

Because goods can be either excludable or nonexcludable, rival or nonrival in consumption, there are four types of goods, illustrated by the matrix in Figure 17-1:

- *Private goods,* which are excludable and rival in consumption, like wheat
- *Public goods,* which are nonexcludable and nonrival in consumption, like a public sewer system
- *Common resources,* which are nonexcludable but rival in consumption, like clean water in a river
- *Artificially scarce goods,* which are excludable but nonrival in consumption, like on-demand movies on Amazon Prime

There are, of course, many other characteristics that distinguish between types of goods—necessities versus luxuries, normal versus inferior, and so on. Why focus on whether goods are excludable and rival in consumption?

FIGURE 17-1 Four Types of Goods

	Rival in consumption	Nonrival in consumption
Excludable	**Private goods** • Wheat • Bathroom fixtures	**Artificially scarce goods** • On-demand movies • Computer software
Non-excludable	**Common resources** • Clean water • Biodiversity	**Public goods** • Public sanitation • National defence

There are four types of goods. The type of a good depends on (1) whether or not it is excludable — whether a producer can prevent someone from consuming it; and (2) whether or not it is rival in consumption — whether it is impossible for the same unit of a good to be consumed by more than one person at the same time.

Why Markets Can Supply Only Private Goods Efficiently

As we learned in earlier chapters, markets are typically the best means for a society to deliver goods and services to its members; that is, markets are efficient except in the case of the well-defined problems of market power, externalities, or other instances of market failure. But there is yet another condition that must be met, one rooted in the nature of the good itself: markets cannot supply goods and services efficiently unless they are private goods—excludable and rival in consumption.

To see why excludability is crucial, suppose that a farmer had only two choices: either produce no wheat or provide a bushel of wheat to every resident of the county who wants it, whether or not that resident pays for it. It seems unlikely that anyone would grow wheat under those conditions.

Yet the operator of a municipal sewage system faces pretty much the same problem as our hypothetical farmer. A sewage system makes the whole city cleaner and healthier—but that benefit accrues to all the city's residents, whether or not they pay the system operator. That's why no private entrepreneur came forward with a plan to end London's Great Stink.

The general point is that if a good is nonexcludable, self-interested consumers won't be willing to pay for it—they will take a "free ride" on anyone who *does* pay. So there is a **free-rider problem.** Examples of the free-rider problem are familiar from daily life. One you may have encountered is when students are required to do a group project. There is often a tendency for some group members to shirk, relying on others in the group to get the work done. The shirkers *free-ride* on someone else's effort.

Because of the free-rider problem, the forces of self-interest alone do not lead to an efficient level of production for a nonexcludable good. Even though consumers would benefit from increased production of the good, no one individual is willing to pay for more, and so no producer is willing to supply it. The result is that nonexcludable goods suffer from *inefficiently low production.* That is, they are undersupplied in a market economy. In fact, in the face of the free-rider problem, self-interest may not ensure that any amount of the good—let alone the efficient quantity—is produced.

Goods that are excludable and nonrival in consumption, like on-demand movies, suffer from a different kind of inefficiency. As long as a good is excludable, it is possible to earn a profit by making it available only to those who pay. Therefore producers are willing to supply an excludable good. But the marginal cost of letting an additional viewer watch an on-demand movie is zero because it is nonrival in consumption. So the efficient price to the consumer is also zero—or, to put it another way, individuals should watch movies up to the point where their marginal benefit is zero.

But if Amazon actually charges viewers $4 for on-demand movies, viewers will consume the good only up to the point where their marginal benefit is $4. When consumers must pay a price greater than zero for a good that is nonrival in consumption, the price they pay is higher than the marginal cost of allowing them to consume that good, which is zero. So in a market economy, goods that are nonrival in consumption suffer from *inefficiently low consumption*—they are underconsumed.

Now we can see why private goods are the only goods that can be efficiently produced and consumed in a competitive market. (That is, a private good will be efficiently produced and consumed in a market free of market power, externalities, or other instances of market failure.) Because private goods are excludable, producers can charge for them and so have an incentive to produce them. And because they are also rival in consumption, it is efficient for consumers to pay a positive price—a price equal to the marginal cost of production. If one or both of these characteristics are lacking, a market economy will not lead to efficient production and consumption of the good.

Fortunately for the market system, most goods are private goods. Food, clothing, shelter, and most other desirable things in life are excludable and rival in consumption, so markets can provide us with most things. Yet there are crucial goods that don't meet these criteria—and in most cases, that means that the government must step in.

Goods that are nonexcludable suffer from the **free-rider problem:** many individuals are unwilling to pay for their own consumption and instead will take a "free ride" on anyone who does pay.

The emergence of institutions to maintain law and order laid the foundation for the flowering of the Renaissance.

ECONOMICS >> *in Action*
From Mayhem to Renaissance

Life during the European Middle Ages—from approximately 1100 to 1500—was difficult and dangerous, with high rates of violent crime, banditry, and war casualties. According to researchers, murder rates in Europe in 1200 were 30 to 40 per 100,000 people. But by 1500 the rate had been halved to around 20 per 100,000; today, it is less than 1 per 100,000. What accounts for the sharp decrease in mayhem over the last 900 years?

Think public goods, as the history of medieval Italian city-states illustrates.

Starting around the year 900 in Venice and 1100 in other city-states like Milan and Florence, citizens began to organize and create institutions for protection. In Venice, citizens built a defensive fleet to battle the pirates who regularly attacked them. Other city-states built strong defensive walls to encircle their cities and formed defensive militias. Institutions were created to maintain law and order: cadres of guards, watchmen, and magistrates were hired; courthouses and jails were built.

As a result, trade, commerce, and banking flourished, as well as literacy, numeracy, and the arts. By 1300, the leading cities of Venice, Milan, and Florence had each grown to over 100,000 people. As resources and the standard of living increased, the rate of violent deaths diminished.

The Republic of Venice became known as *La Serenissima*—the Most Serene One—because of its enlightened governance, overseen by a council of leading citizens. Owing to its stability, diplomatic prowess, and prodigious fleet of vessels, Venice became enormously wealthy in the fifteenth and sixteenth centuries.

The provision of public goods brought stability, high literacy, and numeracy that made Florence the banking centre of Italy. During the fifteenth century it was ruled by the Medici, an immensely wealthy banking family. It was their patronage of artists such as Leonardo da Vinci and Michelangelo that ushered in the Renaissance.

So Western Europe was able to move from mayhem to Renaissance through the creation of public goods, like good governance and defence, that benefited everyone and could not be diminished by any one person's use.

>> Check Your Understanding 17-1
Solutions appear at back of book.

1. Classify each of the following goods according to whether they are excludable and whether they are rival in consumption. What kind of good is each?
   a. Use of a public space such as a park
   b. A cheese burrito
   c. Information from a website that is password-protected
   d. Publicly announced information on the path of an incoming hurricane

2. Which of the goods in Question 1 will be provided by a competitive market? Which will not be? Explain your answer.

>> Quick Review

• Goods can be classified according to two attributes: whether they are **excludable** and whether they are **rival in consumption.**

• Goods that are both excludable and rival in consumption are **private goods.** Private goods can be efficiently produced and consumed in a competitive market.

• When goods are **nonexcludable,** there is a **free-rider problem:** consumers will not pay producers, leading to inefficiently low production.

• When goods are **nonrival in consumption,** the efficient price for consumption is zero. But if a positive price is charged to compensate producers for the cost of production, the result is inefficiently low consumption.

A **public good** is both nonexcludable and nonrival in consumption.

‖ Public Goods

A **public good** is the exact opposite of a private good: it is a good that is both nonexcludable and nonrival in consumption. A public sewer system is an example of a public good: you can't keep a river clean without making it clean for everyone who lives near its banks, and my protection from great stinks does not come at my neighbour's expense.

Here are some other examples of public goods:

- *Disease prevention.* When doctors act to stamp out an epidemic before it can spread, they protect people around the world.
- *National defence.* A strong military protects all citizens.
- *Scientific research.* More knowledge benefits everyone.

Because these goods are nonexcludable, they suffer from the free-rider problem, so no private firm would be willing to produce them. And because they are nonrival in consumption, it would be inefficient to charge people for consuming them. As a result, society must find nonmarket methods for providing these goods.

Providing Public Goods

Public goods are provided through a variety of means. The government doesn't always get involved—in many cases a nongovernmental solution has been found for the free-rider problem. But these solutions are usually imperfect in some way.

Some public goods are supplied through voluntary contributions. For example, private donations support a considerable amount of scientific research. But they are insufficient to finance huge, socially important projects like basic medical research.

Some public goods are supplied by self-interested individuals or firms because those producing the goods are able to make money in an indirect way. The classic example is broadcast television, which in most of Canada is supported entirely by advertising. The downside of such indirect funding is that it skews the nature and quantity of the public goods that are supplied, as well as imposing additional costs on consumers. TV stations show the programs that yield the most advertising revenue (that is, programs best suited for selling prescription drugs, weight-loss remedies, and the like to the segment of the population that buys them), which are not necessarily the programs people most want to see. And viewers must also endure many commercials.

Some potentially public goods are deliberately made excludable and therefore subject to charge, like on-demand movies. In the United Kingdom, where most television programming is paid for by a yearly licence fee assessed on every television owner (£154.50, or about $262 in 2019), television viewing is made artificially excludable by the use of television detection vans that roam neighbourhoods in an attempt to locate televisions in nonlicenced households and fine the residents. However, as noted earlier, when suppliers charge a price greater than zero for a nonrival good, consumers will consume an inefficiently low quantity of that good.

In small communities, a high level of social encouragement or pressure can be brought to bear on people to contribute money or time to provide the efficient level of a public good. Volunteer fire departments, which depend both on the volunteered services of the firefighters themselves and on contributions from local residents, are a good example. But as communities grow larger and more anonymous, social pressure is increasingly difficult to apply, compelling larger towns and cities to tax residents to provide salaried firefighters for fire protection services.

As this last example suggests, when these other solutions fail, it is up to the government to provide public goods. Indeed, the most important public goods—national defence, the legal system, disease control, fire protection in municipalities, and so on—are provided by government and paid for by taxes. Economic theory tells us that the provision of public goods is one of the crucial roles of government.

How Much of a Public Good Should Be Provided?

In some cases, provision of a public good is an "either–or" decision: London would either have a sewage system—or not. But in most cases, governments must decide not only whether to provide a public good but also *how much* of that public good to provide. For example, street cleaning is a public good—but how often should the streets be cleaned? Once a month? Twice a month? Every other day?

Imagine a city in which there are only two residents, Theo and Abby. Assume that the public good in question is street cleaning and that Theo and Abby truthfully tell the government how much they value a unit of the public good, where a unit is equal to one street cleaning per month. Specifically, each of them tells the government *their willingness to pay for another unit of the public good supplied*—an amount that corresponds to that *individual's marginal benefit* of another unit of the public good.

Using this information plus information on the cost of providing the good, the government can use marginal analysis to find the efficient level of providing the public good: the level at which the *marginal social benefit* of the public good is equal to the marginal cost of producing it. Recall from Chapter 16 that the marginal social benefit of a good is the benefit that accrues to society as a whole from the consumption of one additional unit of the good.

Telekhovskyi/Shutterstock

We all benefit when someone does the cleaning up.

But what is the marginal social benefit of another unit of a public good—a unit that generates utility for *all* consumers, not just one consumer, because it is non-excludable and nonrival in consumption? This question leads us to an important principle: *In the special case of a public good, the marginal social benefit of a unit of the good is equal to the sum of the individual marginal benefits that are enjoyed by all consumers of that unit.*

Or to consider it from a slightly different angle, if a consumer could be compelled to pay for a unit before consuming it (the good is made excludable), then the marginal social benefit of a unit is equal to the *sum* of each consumer's willingness to pay for that unit. Using this principle, the marginal social benefit of an additional street cleaning per month is equal to Theo's individual marginal benefit from that additional cleaning *plus* Abby's individual marginal benefit.

Why? Because a public good is nonrival in consumption—Theo's benefit from a cleaner street does not diminish Abby's benefit from that same clean street, and vice versa. Because people can all simultaneously consume the same unit of a public good, the marginal social benefit of an additional unit of that good is the *sum* of the individual marginal benefits of all who enjoy the public good. And the efficient quantity of a public good is the quantity at which the marginal social benefit is equal to the marginal cost of providing it.

FOR INQUIRING MINDS Voting as a Public Good

It's a sad fact that many Canadians who are eligible to vote don't bother to. As a result, their interests tend to be ignored by politicians. Yet what is self-defeating on a public level is completely rational on an individual level.

As economist Mancur Olson pointed out in a famous book titled *The Logic of Collective Action,* voting is a public good, one that suffers from severe free-rider problems.

Imagine that you are one of a million people who would stand to gain the equivalent of $100 each if some plan is passed in a provincewide referendum—say, a plan to improve public schools. And suppose that

the opportunity cost of the time it would take you to vote is $10. Will you be sure to go to the polls and vote for the referendum? If you are rational, the answer is no because it is very unlikely that your vote will decide the issue, either way. If the measure passes, you benefit, even if you didn't bother to vote—the benefits are nonexcludable. If the measure doesn't pass, your vote would not have changed the outcome. By not voting and free-riding on those who do vote you save $10.

Of course, many people do vote out of a sense of civic duty. But because political action is a public good, typically people

devote too little effort to defending their own interests.

The result, Olson pointed out, is that when a large group of people share a common political interest, they are likely to exert too little effort promoting their cause and so will be ignored. Conversely, small, well-organized interest groups that act on issues narrowly targeted in their favour tend to have disproportionate power.

Is this a reason to distrust democracy? Winston Churchill said it best: "Democracy is the worst form of government, except for all the other forms that have been tried."

Figure 17-2 illustrates the efficient provision of a public good, showing three marginal benefit curves. Panel (a) shows Theo's individual marginal benefit curve from street cleaning, MB_T: he would be willing to pay $25 for the city to clean its streets once a month, an additional $18 to have it done a second time, and so on. Panel (b) shows Abby's individual marginal benefit curve from street cleaning, MB_A. Panel (c) shows the marginal social benefit curve from street cleaning, *MSB:* it is the vertical sum of Theo and Abby's individual marginal benefit curves, MB_T and MB_A.

To maximize society's welfare, the government should clean the street up to the level at which the marginal social benefit of an additional cleaning is

FIGURE 17-2 A Public Good

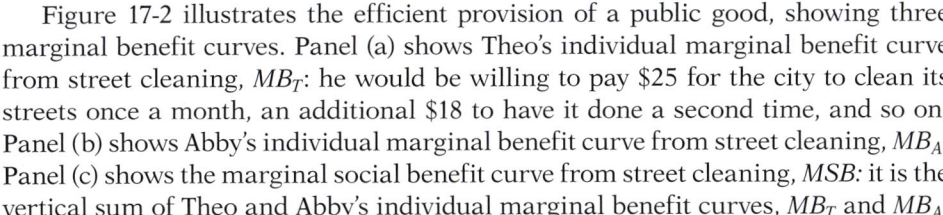

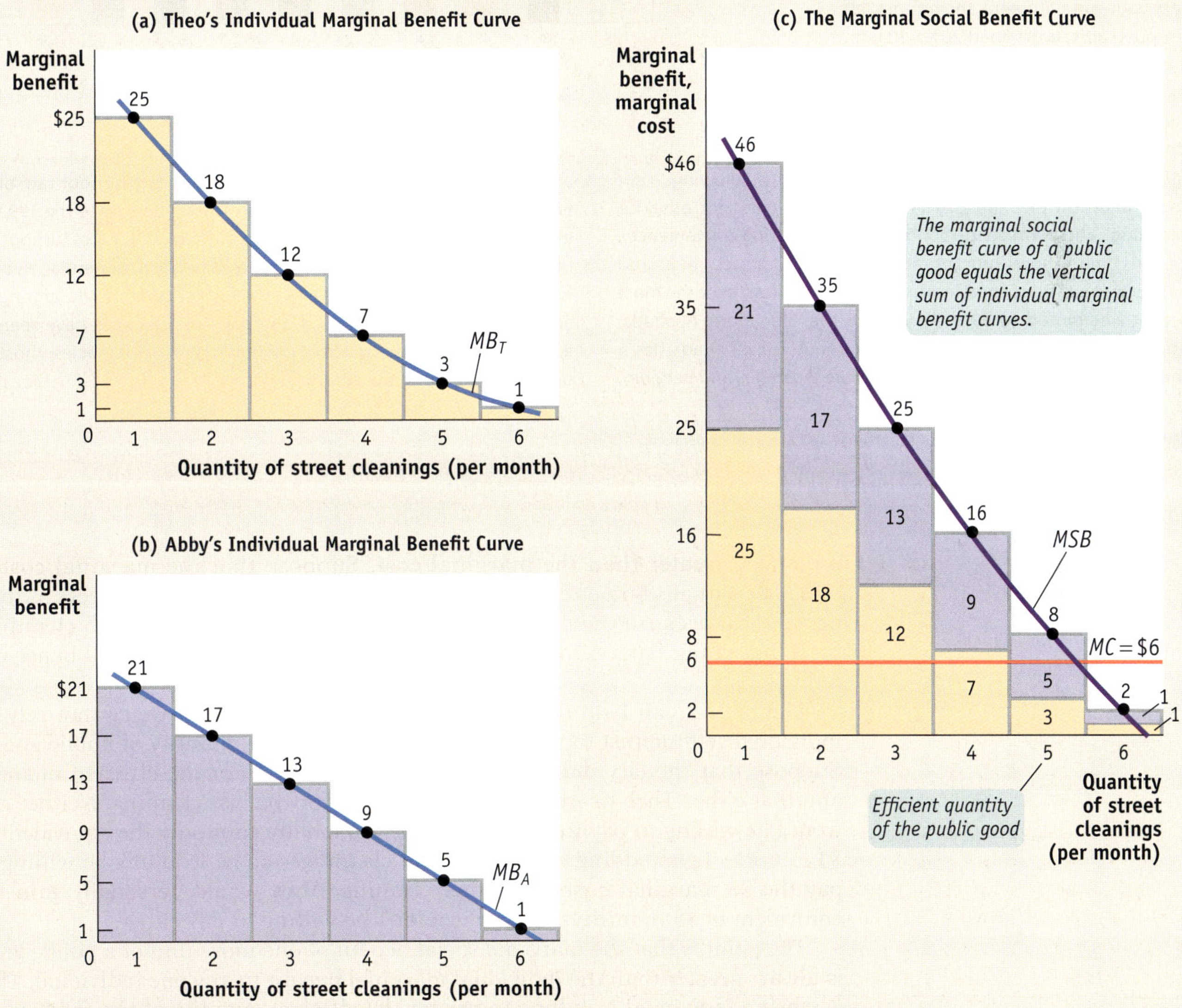

Panel (a) shows Theo's individual marginal benefit curve of street cleanings per month, MB_T, and panel (b) shows Abby's individual marginal benefit curve, MB_A. Panel (c) shows the marginal social benefit of the public good, equal to the sum of the individual marginal benefits to all consumers (in this case, Theo and Abby). The marginal social benefit curve,

MSB, is the vertical sum of the individual marginal benefit curves MB_T and MB_A. At a constant marginal cost of $6, there should be 5 street cleanings per month, because the marginal social benefit of going from 4 to 5 cleanings is $8 ($3 for Theo plus $5 for Abby), but the marginal social benefit of going from 5 to 6 cleanings is only $2.

Despite the fact that choosing not to vote can be an entirely rational choice, many countries consistently achieve astonishingly high turnout rates in their elections by adopting policies that encourage voting. In Singapore, Australia, and Belgium, voting is compulsory; eligible voters are penalized if they fail to do their civic duty by casting their ballots. These penalties are effective at getting out the vote. When Venezuela dropped its mandatory voting requirement, the turnout rate dropped 30%; it dropped 20% when the Netherlands did the same.

Other countries have policies that reduce the cost of voting; for example, declaring election day a work holiday (giving citizens ample time to cast their ballots), allowing voter registration on election day (eliminating the need for advance planning), and permitting voting by mail (increasing convenience).

This figure shows turnout rates in several countries, measured as the percentage of eligible voters who cast ballots, over the most recent election up to 2019. As you can see, Singapore, Australia, and Belgium have the highest voter turnout rates. Canada has a lower turnout rate compared to Singapore, Australia, and Belgium,

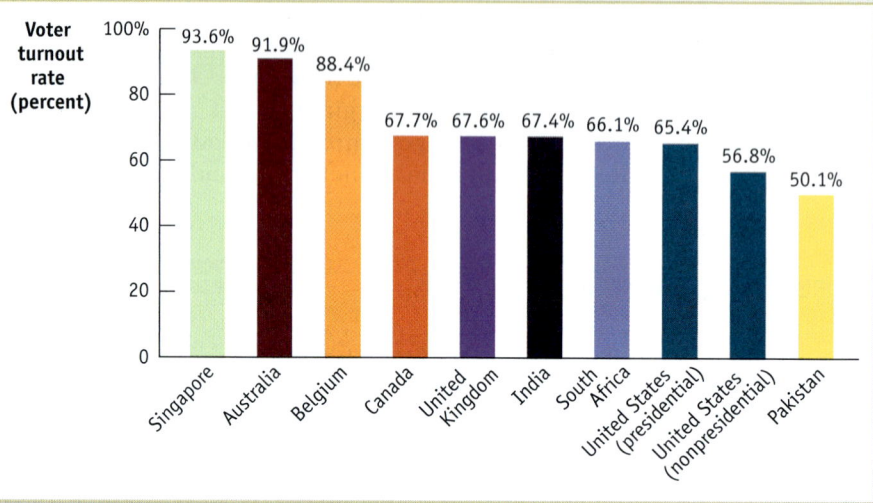

and this rate is trending downward (although the turnout rate of 68.3% in the 2015 federal election was the highest since the 1993 election). The the United States has an even lower level of turnout. In fact, voter turnout drops significantly in nonpresidential elections, when the United States has the lowest turnout rate among advanced countries. In general, the past four decades have seen a decline in voter turnout rates in the major democracies, most dramatically among the youngest voters.

Data from: International Institute for Democracy and Electoral Assistance.

no longer greater than the marginal cost. Suppose that the marginal cost of street cleaning is $6 per cleaning. Then the city should clean its streets 5 times per month, because the marginal social benefit of going from 4 to 5 cleanings is $8, but going from 5 to 6 cleanings would yield a marginal social benefit of only $2.

Figure 17-2 can help reinforce our understanding of why we cannot rely on individual self-interest to yield provision of an efficient quantity of public goods. Suppose that the city did one fewer street cleaning than the efficient quantity and that either Theo or Abby was asked to pay for the last cleaning. Neither one would be willing to pay for it! Theo would personally gain only the equivalent of $3 in utility from adding one more street cleaning—so he wouldn't be willing to pay the $6 marginal cost of another cleaning. Abby would personally gain the equivalent of $5 in utility—so she wouldn't be willing to pay either.

The point is that the marginal social benefit of one more unit of a public good is always greater than the individual marginal benefit to any one individual. That is why no individual is willing to pay for the efficient quantity of the good.

Does this description of the public good problem, in which the marginal social benefit of an additional unit of the public good is greater than any individual's marginal benefit, sound a bit familiar? It should: we encountered a somewhat similar situation in our discussion of *positive externalities*. Remember that in the case of a positive externality, the marginal social benefit accruing to all consumers of another unit of the good is greater than the price that the producer receives for that unit; as a result, the market produces too little of the good.

In the case of a public good, the individual marginal benefit of a consumer plays the same role as the price received by the producer in the case of positive externalities: both cases create insufficient incentive to provide an efficient amount of the good.

The problem of providing public goods is very similar to the problem of dealing with positive externalities; in both cases there is a market failure that calls for government intervention. One basic rationale for the existence of government is that it provides a way for citizens to tax themselves in order to provide public goods—particularly a vital public good like national defence.

Of course, if society really consisted of only two individuals, they would probably manage to strike a deal to provide the good. But imagine a city with a million residents, each of whose individual marginal benefit from provision of the good is only a tiny fraction of the marginal social benefit. It would be impossible for people to reach a voluntary agreement to pay for the efficient level of street cleaning—the potential for free-riding makes it too difficult to make and enforce an agreement among so many people. But they could and would vote to tax themselves to pay for a citywide sanitation department.

> **Cost-benefit analysis** is the estimation and comparison of the social costs and social benefits of providing a public good.

Cost-Benefit Analysis

How do governments decide in practice how much of a public good to provide? Sometimes policy makers just guess—or do whatever they think will get them reelected. However, responsible governments try to estimate and compare both the social benefits and the social costs of providing a public good, a process known as **cost-benefit analysis.**

It's straightforward to estimate the cost of supplying a public good. Estimating the benefit is harder. In fact, it is a very difficult problem.

Now you might wonder why governments can't figure out the marginal social benefit of a public good just by asking people their willingness to pay for it (their individual marginal benefit). But it turns out that it's hard to get an honest answer.

This is not a problem with private goods: we can determine how much an individual is willing to pay for one more unit of a private good by looking at that individual's actual choices. But because people don't actually pay for public goods, the question of willingness to pay is always hypothetical.

Worse yet, it's a question that people have an incentive not to answer truthfully. People naturally want more rather than less. Because they cannot be made to pay for whatever quantity of the public good they use, people are apt to overstate their true feelings when asked how much they desire a public good. For example, if street cleaning were scheduled according to the stated wishes of homeowners alone, the streets would be cleaned every day—an inefficient level of provision.

So governments must be aware that they cannot simply rely on the public's statements when deciding how much of a public good to provide—if they do, they are likely to provide too much. In contrast, as the preceding For Inquiring Minds explains, relying on the public to indicate how much of the public good they want through voting has problems as well—and is likely to lead to too little of the public good being provided.

ECONOMICS >> *in Action*
Canadian Infrastructure is "At Risk"

On a daily basis, Canadians depend on the infrastructure that helps sustain our quality of life and supports our standard of living. Thousands take public transit to get to school, work, or other places. Others depend on roadways and bridges to get to where they're going. But even if we are not out driving on roadways, we still consume goods and services that would not be possible without such infrastructure. Public infrastructure doesn't end there. It also includes all of the public buildings, like libraries, community centres, and sports facilities, as well as all of the infrastructure used to process and pipe clean water into, and waste water out of, our homes and workplaces.

Every year, Canada gets a report card on its infrastructure—the Canadian Infrastructure Report Card (CIRC). The CIRC assesses the condition of municipally-owned infrastructure. It notes: "Municipal infrastructure gets people and goods moving, provides safe drinking water, handles our waste, creates spaces for sport and recreation, and helps protect our homes against flooding and other natural disasters. It is the foundation that the daily life of Canadians is built upon."

Unfortunately, not all of the news is good. Some of the key findings of the 2019 CIRC are:

- Roads and bridges: About 40% are in fair, poor or very poor condition, and only 20% of these assets were built in last 20 years.

- Cultural, recreational, and sport facilities: Approximately 30% to 35% are in fair, poor, or very poor condition. For some facilities, such as swimming pools, libraries, and community centres, more than 60% were built 20 or more years ago.

- Water infrastructure such as watermains and sewers: About 30% of these assets are in fair, poor, or very poor condition, and a significant percentage of these assets are 50 to 100 years old.

The results indicate that much of Canada's public infrastructure is aging and in poor shape. This increases the risk that Canadians will face a failure of some these public assets they depend on. In addition, there is an urgent need for long-term investments in infrastructure renewal to meet the needs of our growing population. The report also notes that investing in additional preventative maintenance and regular repair will not only prolong the asset service life, it will help avoid premature and costly reconstruction and service disruptions.

Of course most Canadians, if asked, would argue that we need more public transit, clean water, community/sports facilities, and other public infrastructure, not less. But this will not happen without a significantly higher investment into these areas.

So why are we not investing enough? One overly simplistic answer is that our municipalities just can't afford it. Despite the fact that every year the federal Gas Tax Fund delivers $2 billion directly to 3,600 municipalities for infrastructure renewal, these municipalities often find it difficult to come up with the funds needed to properly maintain the existing infrastructure, let alone consider growing the stock of such assets. This helps to explain why you often hear local politicians calling on the provincial, territorial, and/or federal government for increased funding to help foot the bill. But these governments too face their own fiscal constraints, so they fail to provide a high and steady-enough stream of funding to help address this issue.

>> Quick Review

- A **public good** is both nonexcludable and nonrival in consumption.

- Because most forms of public-good provision by the private sector have serious defects, they are typically provided by the government and paid for with taxes.

- The marginal social benefit of an additional unit of a public good is equal to the sum of each consumer's individual marginal benefit from that unit. At the efficient quantity, the marginal social benefit equals the marginal cost of providing the good.

- No individual has an incentive to pay for providing the efficient quantity of a public good because each individual's marginal benefit is less than the marginal social benefit. This is a primary justification for the existence of government.

- Although governments should rely on **cost-benefit analysis** to determine how much of a public good to supply, doing so is problematic because individuals tend to overstate the good's value to them.

>> Check Your Understanding 17-2

Solutions appear at back of book.

1. The town of Centreville, population 16, has two types of residents, Homebodies and Revellers. Using the accompanying table, the town must decide how much to spend on its New Year's Eve party. No individual resident expects to directly bear the cost of the party.

a. Suppose there are 10 Homebodies and 6 Revellers. Determine the marginal social benefit schedule of money spent on the party. What is the efficient level of spending?

b. Suppose there are 6 Homebodies and 10 Revellers. How do your answers to part a change? Explain.

c. Suppose that the individual marginal benefit schedules are known but no one knows the true proportion of Homebodies versus Revellers. Individuals are asked their preferences. What is the likely outcome if each person assumes that others will pay for any additional amount of the public good? Why is it likely to result in an inefficiently high level of spending? Explain.

Money spent on party	Individual marginal benefit of additional $1 spent on party	
	Homebody	Reveller
$0		
	$0.05	$0.13
1		
	0.04	0.11
2		
	0.03	0.09
3		
	0.02	0.07
4		

‖ Common Resources

A **common resource** is a good that is nonexcludable but is rival in consumption. An example is the stock of fish in a limited fishing area, like the fisheries off the coast of Nova Scotia. Traditionally, anyone who had a boat could go out to sea and catch fish—fish in the sea were a nonexcludable good. Yet because the total number of fish is limited, the fish that one person catches are no longer available to be caught by someone else. So fish in the sea are rival in consumption.

Other examples of common resources are clean air and water, as well as the diversity of animal and plant species on the planet (biodiversity). In each of these cases the fact that the good, though rival in consumption, is nonexcludable poses a serious problem.

The Problem of Overuse

Because common resources are nonexcludable, individuals cannot be charged for their use. Yet because they are rival in consumption, an individual who uses a unit depletes the resource by making that unit unavailable to others. As a result, a common resource is subject to **overuse:** an individual will continue to use it until that individual's marginal benefit of its use is equal to their own individual marginal cost, ignoring the cost that this action inflicts on society as a whole. As we will see shortly, the problem of overuse of a common resource is similar to a problem we studied in Chapter 16: the problem of a good that generates a negative externality, such as groundwater contamination from fracking or climate change from greenhouse gas emissions.

Fishing is a classic example of a common resource. In heavily fished waters, my fishing imposes a cost on others by reducing the fish population and making it harder for others to catch fish. But I have no personal incentive to take this cost into account, since I cannot be charged for fishing. As a result, from society's point of view, I catch too many fish.

Traffic congestion is another example of overuse of a common resource. A major highway during rush hour can accommodate only a certain number of vehicles per hour. If I decide to drive to work alone rather than carpool or work at home, I make the commute of many other people a bit longer; but I have no incentive to take these consequences into account.

In the case of a common resource, the *marginal social cost* of my use of that resource is higher than my *individual marginal cost,* the cost to me of using an additional unit of the good.

A **common resource** is nonexcludable and rival in consumption: you can't stop me from consuming the good, and more consumption by me means less of the good available for you.

Common resources left to the market suffer from **overuse:** individuals ignore the fact that their use depletes the amount of the resource remaining for others.

FIGURE 17-3 A Common Resource

The supply curve S, which shows the marginal cost of production of the fishing industry, is composed of the individual supply curves of the individual fisher. But each fisher's individual marginal cost does not include the cost that their actions impose on others: the depletion of the common resource. As a result, the marginal social cost curve, MSC, lies above the supply curve; in an unregulated market, the quantity of the common resource used, Q_{MKT}, exceeds the efficient quantity of use, Q_{OPT}.

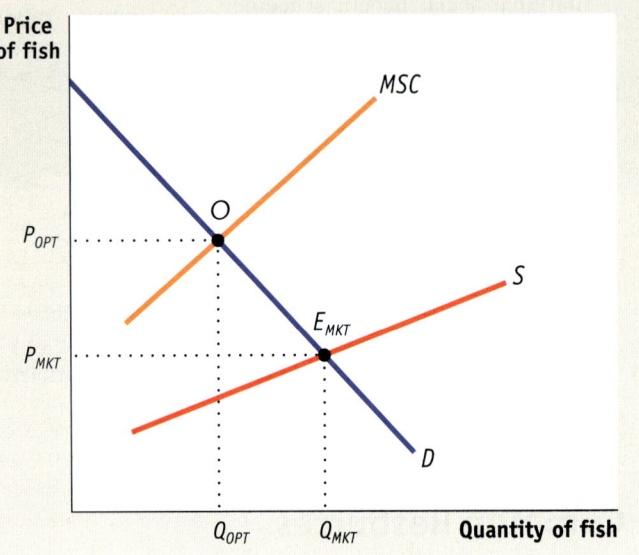

Figure 17-3 illustrates this point. It shows the demand curve for fish, which measures the marginal benefit of fish—the benefit to consumers when an additional unit of fish is caught and consumed. It also shows the supply curve for fish, which measures the marginal cost of production of the fishing industry. We know that the industry supply curve is the horizontal sum of each individual fisher's supply curve—equivalent to their individual marginal cost curve. The fishing industry supplies the quantity where its marginal cost is equal to the price, the quantity Q_{MKT}.

But the efficient outcome is to catch the quantity Q_{OPT}, the quantity of output that equates the marginal benefit to the marginal social cost, not to the fishing industry's marginal cost of production. The market outcome results in overuse of the common resource.

As we noted, there is a close parallel between the problem of managing a common resource and the problem posed by negative externalities. In the case of an activity that generates a negative externality, the marginal social cost of production is greater than the industry's marginal cost of production, the difference being the marginal external cost imposed on society. Here, the loss to society arising from a fisher's depletion of the common resource plays the same role as the external cost plays when there is a negative externality. In fact, many negative externalities (such as pollution) can be thought of as involving common resources (such as clean air).

The Efficient Use and Maintenance of a Common Resource

Because common resources pose problems similar to those created by negative externalities, the solutions are also similar. To ensure efficient use of a common resource, society must find a way of getting individual users of the resource to take into account the costs they impose on other users. This is basically the same principle as that of getting individuals to internalize a negative externality that arises from their actions.

There are three fundamental ways to induce people who use common resources to internalize the costs they impose on others.

- Tax or otherwise regulate the use of the common resource
- Create a system of tradable licences for the right to use the common resource

FOR INQUIRING MINDS   **Taking Water for Granted**

Canada is known for its water — we have the world's largest fresh water lakes and plenty of rivers and lakes. Since water access is easy and plentiful and the cost of usage is so low compared to other developed countries, many Canadians take our water for granted. Sadly, we rank among the top in the world when it comes to per capita water consumption. A study showed that, for residential use of water, the average Canadian used 220 litres of water per day, while in Newfoundland and Labrador daily residential water usage per person was 474 litres.

However, the growing use of water for agriculture and industry, combined with climate change and urbanization, has begun to put pressure on one of the country's most valuable natural resources. The Fraser Valley relies heavily on groundwater aquifers for its water. However, the hot and dry summer, combined with the lack of rainfall in recent years, made some of the region's shallower wells dry up by early summer. Homeowners were forced to purchase water from water providers or had to dig deeper wells to get better access to water. Similar events happened in other parts of British Columbia.

This experience changed people's attitudes and thinking toward water supply. Although water is still plentiful now, concern about long-term water use is growing and people now take water conservation more seriously. Nathan Goltz, a fourth generation farmer and now a vineyard manager in the Okanagan Valley, found that he has to be more efficient than previous generations when it comes to water use for growing crops. He recalled stories from his father that farmers would just let water run for 12 hours a day during growing seasons. However, things are much different now. "Nowadays we measure how much water we're putting in the soil, how far down is it going and when do I need to water again," said Goltz.

Long before the hot and dry summers, various measures and incentives have been implemented to lower water consumption. These measures and incentives range from building and repairing water infrastructure to installing water meters, switching to volume-based pricing, limiting the day and time for watering residential landscaping in the summer, switching to drought-resistant plants, and others. Hopefully, with a change in people's thinking toward water supply, we will be able to see more efficient use of our valuable resource.

- Make the common resource excludable and assign property rights to some individuals

Like activities that generate negative externalities, use of a common resource can be reduced to the efficient quantity by imposing a Pigouvian tax. For example, some countries have imposed congestion charges on those who drive during rush hour, in effect charging them for use of the common resource of city streets. Likewise, visitors to national parks must pay a fee, and the number of visitors to any one park is restricted.

A second way to correct the problem of overuse is to create a system of tradable licences for the use of the common resource much like the systems designed to address negative externalities. The policy maker issues the number of licences that corresponds to the efficient level of use of the good. Making the licences tradable ensures that the right to use the good is allocated efficiently — that is, those who end up using the good (those willing to pay the most for a licence) are those who gain the most from its use.

But when it comes to common resources, often the most natural solution is simply to assign property rights. At a fundamental level, common resources are subject to overuse because *nobody owns them*. The essence of ownership of a good — the *property right* over the good — is that you can limit who can and cannot use the good as well as how much of it can be used.

When a good is nonexcludable, in a very real sense no one owns it because a property right cannot be enforced — and consequently no one has an incentive to use it efficiently. So one way to correct the problem of overuse is to make the good excludable and assign property rights over it to someone. The good then has an owner who has an incentive to protect the value of the good — to use it efficiently rather than overuse it.

As the following Economics in Action shows, a system of tradable licences, called individual transferable quotas, or ITQs, has been a successful strategy in some fisheries.

ECONOMICS >> *in Action* 🌎
Saving the Oceans with ITQs

The world's oceans are in serious trouble. According to a study by the International Program on the State of the Oceans, there is an imminent risk of widespread extinctions of multiple species of fish. As of 2019, 40% of North Atlantic fish stocks and 87% of Mediterranean fish stocks are in danger of collapse. In the North Sea, 93% of cod are fished before they can breed. And bluefin tuna, a favourite in Japanese sushi, are in danger of imminent extinction, with current stocks at less than 97% of their natural, unfished levels.

Not surprisingly, the principal culprit is overfishing. The decline of fishing stocks has worsened as fishers trawl in deeper waters with their very large nets to catch the remaining fish, unintentionally killing many other marine animals in the process.

The fishing industry is in crisis, too, as fishers's incomes decline and they are compelled to fish for longer periods of time and in more dangerous waters in order to make a living.

Valentina Photo/Shutterstock

Will ITQs help save the North Sea cod?

But ITQs, may provide a solution to both crises. Under an ITQ scheme, individual fishers receive a licence entitling them to catch an annual quota within a given fishing ground. The ITQ is given for a long period of time, sometimes indefinitely. Because it is transferable, the owner can sell or lease it.

Researchers who analyzed 121 established ITQ schemes around the world concluded that ITQs can help reverse the collapse of fisheries because each ITQ holder has a financial interest in the long-term maintenance of their particular fishery. This view is endorsed by Arne Fuglvog, a commercial fisher, who explained that owning part of the resource has led to more careful oversight of it: "We want to keep the resource healthy. We don't want to overfish it. We want to keep making a living at it for as long as we can and keep it for future generations."

ITQ schemes (also called catch-share schemes) are common in New Zealand, Australia, Iceland, and increasingly in the United States and Canada. (The quota share program for lobster fishing in Atlantic Canada, analyzed in Chapter 5, is an example of a Canadian ITQ.) The Alaskan halibut fishery is one example of a successful ITQ scheme. Before it was implemented, the annual fishing season had shrunk from four months to two or three days, resulting in dangerous races by the boats. Now the season lasts nearly eight months. Steve Gaines, director of the Marine Science Institute at the University of California at Santa Barbara says, "Halibut fishers were barely squeaking by—but now the fishery is insanely profitable."

>> Quick Review

• A **common resource** is rival in consumption but nonexcludable.

• The problem with common resources is **overuse:** a user depletes the amount of the common resource available to others but does not take this cost into account when deciding how much to use the common resource.

• Like negative externalities, a common resource can be efficiently managed by Pigouvian taxes, by the creation of a system of tradable licences for its use, or by making it excludable and assigning property rights.

>> Check Your Understanding 17-3

Solutions appear at back of book.

1. Rocky Mountain Forest is a government-owned forest in which private citizens were allowed in the past to harvest as much timber as they wanted free of charge. State in economic terms why this is problematic from society's point of view.

2. You are an advisor to the Minister of Natural Resources and have been instructed to come up with ways to preserve the forest for the general public. Name three different methods you could use to maintain the efficient level of tree harvesting and explain how each would work. For each method, what information would you need to know in order to achieve an efficient outcome?

‖ Artificially Scarce Goods

An **artificially scarce good** is a good that is excludable but nonrival in consumption. As we've already seen, on-demand movies are a familiar example. The marginal cost to society of allowing an individual to watch the movie is zero, because one person's viewing doesn't interfere with other people's viewing. Yet Amazon and companies like it prevent individuals from seeing on-demand movies if they haven't paid. Goods like software, video games, or digital books, which are valued for the information they embody (and are sometimes called *information goods*), are also artificially scarce.

> An **artificially scarce good** is excludable but nonrival in consumption.

As we've already seen, markets will supply artificially scarce goods: because they are excludable, the producers can charge people for consuming them.

But artificially scarce goods are nonrival in consumption, which means that the marginal cost of an individual's consumption is zero. So the price that the supplier of an artificially scarce good charges exceeds marginal cost. Because the efficient price is equal to the marginal cost of zero, the good is "artificially scarce," and consumption of the good is inefficiently low. However, unless the producer can somehow earn revenue for producing and selling the good, the producer will be unwilling to produce at all—an outcome that leaves society even worse off than it would otherwise be with positive but inefficiently low consumption.

Figure 17-4 illustrates the loss in total surplus caused by artificial scarcity. The demand curve shows the quantity of on-demand movies watched at any given price. The marginal cost of allowing an additional person to watch the movie is zero, so the efficient quantity of movies viewed is Q_{OPT}. Amazon charges a positive price, in this case $4 to watch the movie, and as a result only Q_{MKT} on-demand movies will be watched. This leads to a deadweight loss equal to the area of the shaded triangle.

Does this look familiar? Like the problems that arise with public goods and common resources, the problem created by artificially scarce goods is similar to the problem of *natural monopoly*. A natural monopoly, you will recall, is an industry in which average total cost is above marginal cost for the relevant output range. In order to be willing to produce output, the producer must charge a price at least as high as average total cost—that is, a price above marginal cost. But a price above marginal cost leads to inefficiently low consumption.

FIGURE 17-4 An Artificially Scarce Good

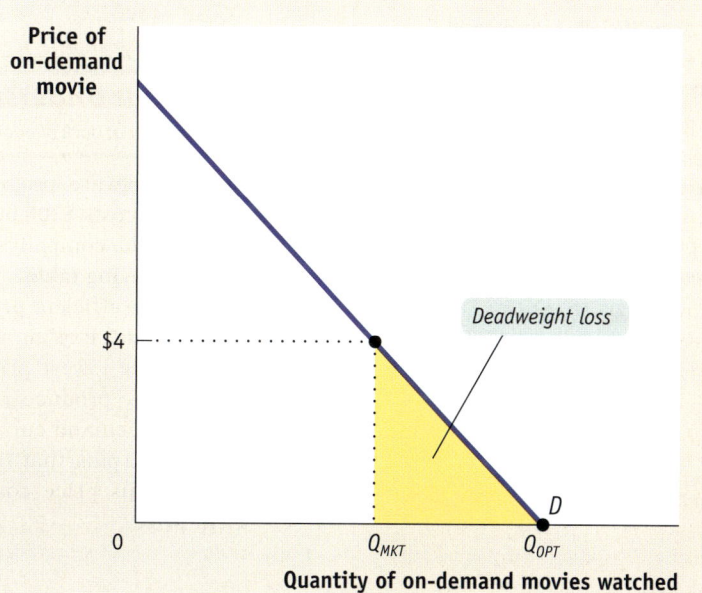

An artificially scarce good is excludable and nonrival in consumption. It is made artificially scarce because producers charge a positive price, but the marginal cost of allowing one more person to consume the good is zero. In this example, the market price of an on-demand movie is $4 and the quantity demanded at that price is Q_{MKT}. But the efficient level of consumption is Q_{OPT}, the quantity demanded when the price is zero. The efficient quantity, Q_{OPT}, exceeds the quantity demanded in an unregulated market, Q_{MKT}. The shaded area represents the loss in total surplus from charging a price of $4.

Price of on-demand movie

Deadweight loss

$4

D

0   Q_{MKT} Q_{OPT}

Quantity of on-demand movies watched

ECONOMICS >> in Action
Twenty-First Century Piracy

heshphoto/AGE Fotostock

Intellectual property goods, like video games, must be made artificially scarce, which creates an incentive to pirate them.

Intellectual property piracy, or IPP, is the illegal copying, distribution, or use of intellectual property. The most common forms include the piracy of software, sophisticated digital hardware, counterfeit goods, movies, music, and games. It is a global industry that has cost the owners of intellectual property rights—musicians, actors, movie studios, software companies, and creators of software and games—$1.33 trillion in 2019. For example, Torrentfreak.com, a website that tracks illegal downloads, found that the final episode of *Game of Thrones* was illegally downloaded 1.5 million times within eight hours of its airing. And the Business Software Alliance estimates that 36% of all software in use is pirated.

Authorities have stepped up their efforts to combat IPP. In Canada, ISPs (internet service providers) now keep track of illegal downloads, with fines up to $5,000 per illegal download. In the United States, the Federal Bureau of Investigation (FBI) has now teamed up with Interpol, the international crime-fighting agency, to find, charge, and extradite to the United States individuals who run large-scale pirating operations abroad.

What is the connection to artificially scarce goods? It stems from the fact that, once an intellectual property good is created, the marginal cost to deliver another unit to a consumer is virtually zero—it involves only a few seconds-long internet download. And because intellectual property goods are nonrival in consumption, my consumption of a bootleg version of the movie *The Avengers* or a computer game doesn't impede or reduce your consumption of them.

However, if movie and game creators are unable to charge for the right to use their products, they won't produce them in the first place. (This explains why free versions of software or games are knock-offs of commercial versions and are of inferior quality.) So, intellectual property goods must be made artificially scarce. However, this creates the incentive to pirate them. So you can be sure that law enforcement agencies are engaged in their own version of the game whack-a-mole in their efforts to stop intellectual property piracy.

>> Quick Review

• An **artificially scarce good** is excludable but nonrival in consumption.

• Because the good is nonrival in consumption, the efficient price to consumers is zero. However, because it is excludable, sellers charge a positive price, which leads to inefficiently low consumption.

• The problems of artificially scarce goods are similar to those posed by a natural monopoly.

>> Check Your Understanding 17-4
Solutions appear at back of book.

1. Xena is a software program produced by Xenoid. Each year, Xenoid produces an upgrade that costs $300,000 to produce. It costs nothing to allow customers to download it from the company's website. The demand schedule for the upgrade is shown in the accompanying table.
   a. What is the efficient price to a consumer of this upgrade? Explain your answer.
   b. What is the lowest price at which Xenoid is willing to produce and sell the upgrade? Draw the demand curve and show the loss of total surplus that occurs when Xenoid charges this price compared to the efficient price.

Price of upgrade	Quantity of upgrades demanded
$180	1,700
150	2,000
120	2,300
90	2,600
0	3,500

Saving the "Beast": Ecotourism Protects the Jaguars of Brazil

Hal Beral/VW Pics/Universal Images Group via Getty Images

"It's *Fera*—that's 'Beast' in Portuguese. She's almost four now, 145 pounds," whispered Haberfeld to a jeep full of gawking humans, as they stared at a lounging jaguar a mere 20 yards away. Just a few years ago, Fera's life would have been in great danger if she had allowed human beings to come so close to her. Now, thanks to the work of Mario Haberfeld and his Onçafari Project, Fera and her offspring are thriving.

Today, jaguars are the superstars of Caiman Ecological Refuge, a 131,000-acre luxury ecotourism property in Brazil. Jaguars used to range from the Grand Canyon to Argentina. But having lost half of their natural range, Caiman refuge is now a crucial bastion for the big cats. It's located in the world's largest tropical wetland, a vast savanna larger than England. In the rainy season, it brims with wildlife; in the dry season, it's home to a robust free-range cattle industry. At Caiman refuge, more than 100 jaguars—with males weighing as much as 135 kilograms—cross paths with 30,000 head of cattle.

And there's the rub. Although it is illegal to hunt jaguars in Brazil, the law was routinely flouted as cowboys and landowners shot the apex predators on sight. As the project biologist commented, "People associate jaguars with losing money. They are seen as the villain." Haberfeld's insight was not to attempt to enforce existing law. Rather, it was to make ranchers start to see jaguars as profit-drivers rather than loss-makers.

To accomplish that, Haberfeld presented a clear cost-benefit proposition to them. Jaguars kill about 1% of ranchers' stock in a year. "So for him [the rancher], it's nothing," in Haberfeld's words. But by adding high-end jaguar-focused ecotourism lodges to their vast ranches, landowners could make money both on cattle and the big cats, he argued. Once he convinced ranchers to spare the animals, he worked with biologists to habituate them to nearby human presence.

And it worked. In 2012, only 7% of Caiman refuge visitors saw jaguars, and often expressed disappointment in not seeing them. By 2016, 72% of guests saw the big cats, rising to 95% in the dry season. And the economic impact is real: surveys show that 85% of Caiman refuge visitors choose a lodge according to its rate of jaguar sightings, with the most successful lodges earning about $7,000 per visitor. The key, according to Haberfeld, was to understand that ranchers are above all businessmen and that the bottom line will ultimately prevail. Haberfeld sees his mission in shifting the attitudes of ranchers. That is, to create the conditions so that, as Haberfeld says of the ranchers: "then the guy will understand, 'Wow, I'm losing money by killing jaguars.'"

QUESTIONS FOR THOUGHT

1. Using the concepts you learned in this chapter, explain the economic incentives behind the loss of jaguars' natural habitat and the killing of the animals.

2. Also using the concepts from this chapter, explain the change in incentives that led to the protection of the jaguars of the Caiman Ecological Refuge.

SUMMARY

1. Goods may be classified according to whether or not they are **excludable** and whether or not they are **rival in consumption.**

2. Free markets can deliver efficient levels of production and consumption for **private goods,** which are both excludable and rival in consumption. When goods are nonexcludable or nonrival in consumption, or both, free markets cannot achieve efficient outcomes.

3. When goods are **nonexcludable,** there is a **free-rider problem:** some consumers will not pay for the good, consuming what others have paid for and leading to inefficiently low production. When goods are **nonrival in consumption,** they should be free, and any positive price leads to inefficiently low consumption.

4. A **public good** is nonexcludable and nonrival in consumption. In most cases a public good must be supplied by the government. The marginal social benefit of a public good is equal to the sum of the individual marginal benefits to each consumer. The efficient quantity of a public good is the quantity at which marginal social benefit equals the marginal cost of providing the good. Like a positive externality, marginal social benefit is greater than any one individual's marginal benefit, so no individual is willing to provide the efficient quantity.

5. One rationale for the presence of government is that it allows citizens to tax themselves in order to provide public goods. Governments use **cost-benefit analysis** to determine the efficient provision of a public good. Such analysis is difficult, however, because individuals have an incentive to overstate the good's value to them.

6. A **common resource** is rival in consumption but nonexcludable. It is subject to **overuse,** because an individual does not take into account the fact that their use depletes the amount available for others. This is similar to the problem of a negative externality: the marginal social cost of an individual's use of a common resource is always higher than the individual marginal cost. Pigouvian taxes, the creation of a system of tradable licences, or the assignment of property rights are possible solutions.

7. **Artificially scarce goods** are excludable but nonrival in consumption. Because no marginal cost arises from allowing another individual to consume the good, the efficient price is zero. A positive price compensates the producer for the cost of production but leads to inefficiently low consumption. The problem of an artificially scarce good is similar to that of a natural monopoly.

KEY TERMS

PRACTICE QUESTIONS

1. Prior to 2003, the city of London was often one big parking lot. Traffic jams were common, and it could take hours to travel a couple of kilometres. Each additional commuter contributed to the congestion, which can be measured by the total number of cars on London roads. Although each commuter suffered by spending valuable time in traffic, none of them paid for the inconvenience they caused others. The total cost of travel includes the opportunity cost of time spent in traffic and any fees levied by London authorities.

   a. Draw a graph illustrating the overuse of London roads, assuming that there is no fee to enter London in a vehicle and that roads are a common resource. Put the cost of travel on the vertical axis and the quantity of cars on the horizontal axis. Draw typical demand, individual marginal cost (*MC*), and marginal social cost (*MSC*) curves and label the equilibrium point. (*Hint:* The marginal cost takes into account the opportunity cost of spending time on the road for individual drivers but not the inconvenience they cause to others.)

   b. In February 2003, the city of London began charging a £5 congestion fee on all vehicles travelling in central London. Illustrate the effects of this congestion charge on your graph and label the new equilibrium point. Assume the new equilibrium point is not optimally set (that is, assume that the £5 charge is too low relative to what would be efficient).

   c. The congestion fee was raised to £9 in January 2011. Illustrate the new equilibrium point on your graph, assuming the new charge is now optimally set.

2. Butchart Gardens is a very large garden in Victoria, British Columbia, renowned for its beautiful plants. It is so large that it could hold many times more visitors than currently visit it. The garden charges an admission fee of $30. At this price, 1,000 people visit the garden each day. If admission were free, 2,000 people would visit each day.

a. Are visits to Butchart Gardens excludable or nonex-cludable? Are they rival in consumption or nonrival? What type of good is it?

b. In a diagram, illustrate the demand curve for visits to Butchart Gardens. Indicate the situation when Butchart Gardens charges an admission fee of $30. Also indicate the situation when Butchart Gardens charges no admission fee.

c. Illustrate the deadweight loss from charging a $30 admission fee. Explain why charging a $30 admission fee is inefficient.

3. In developing a vaccine for the COVID-19 virus, a pharmaceutical company incurs a very high fixed cost. The marginal cost of delivering the vaccine to patients, however, is negligible (consider it to be equal to zero). The pharmaceutical company holds the exclusive patent to the vaccine. You are a regulator who must decide what price the pharmaceutical company is allowed to charge.

a. Draw a diagram that shows the price for the vaccine that would arise if the company is unregulated, and label it P_M. What is the efficient price for the vaccine? Show the deadweight loss that arises from the price P_M.

b. On another diagram, show the lowest price that the regulator can enforce that would still induce the pharmaceutical company to develop the vaccine. Label it P^*. Show the deadweight loss that arises from this price. How does it compare to the deadweight loss that arises from the price P_M?

c. Suppose you have accurate information about the pharmaceutical company's fixed cost. How could you use price regulation of the pharmaceutical company, combined with a subsidy to the company, to have the efficient quantity of the vaccine provided at the lowest cost to the government?

PROBLEMS

1. The government is involved in providing many goods and services. For each of the goods or services listed, determine whether it is rival or nonrival in consumption and whether it is excludable or nonexcludable. What type of good is it? Without government involvement, would the quantity provided be efficient, inefficiently low, or inefficiently high?

a. Street signs

b. Via rail service

c. Regulations limiting pollution

d. A congested interstate highway without tolls

e. A lighthouse on the coast

2. An economist gives the following advice to a museum director: "You should introduce 'peak pricing.' At times when the museum has few visitors, you should admit visitors for free. And at times when the museum has many visitors, you should charge a higher admission fee."

a. When the museum is quiet, is it rival or nonrival in consumption? Is it excludable or nonexcludable? What type of good is the museum at those times? What would be the efficient price to charge visitors during that time, and why?

b. When the museum is busy, is it rival or nonrival in consumption? Is it excludable or nonexcludable? What type of good is the museum at those times? What would be the efficient price to charge visitors during that time, and why?

3. In many planned communities, various aspects of community living are subject to regulation by a homeowners' association. These rules can regulate house architecture; require snow removal from sidewalks; exclude outdoor equipment, such as backyard swimming pools; require appropriate conduct in shared spaces such as the community clubhouse; and so on.

Suppose there has been some conflict in one such community because some homeowners feel that some of the regulations mentioned above are overly intrusive. You have been called in to mediate. Using what you have learned about public goods and common resources, how would you decide what types of regulations are warranted and what types are not?

4. The accompanying table shows Tanisha's and Ari's individual marginal benefit of different amounts of street cleanings per month. Suppose that the marginal cost of street cleanings is constant at $9 each.

Quantity of street cleanings per month	Tanisha's individual marginal benefit	Ari's individual marginal benefit
0		
	$10	$8
1		
	6	4
2		
	2	1
3		

a. If Tanisha had to pay for street cleaning on her own, how many street cleanings would there be?

b. Calculate the marginal social benefit of street cleaning. What is the optimal number of street cleanings?

c. Consider the optimal number of street cleanings. The last street cleaning of the optimal number of street cleanings costs $9. Is Tanisha willing to pay for that last cleaning on her own? Is Ari willing to pay for that last cleaning on his own?

5. Anyone with a radio receiver can listen to public radio, which is funded largely by donations.

a. Is public radio excludable or nonexcludable? Is it rival in consumption or nonrival? What type of good is it?

b. Should the government support public radio? Explain your reasoning.

c. In order to finance itself, public radio decides to transmit only to satellite radios, for which users have to pay a fee. What type of good is public radio then? Will the quantity of radio listening be efficient? Why or why not?

6. Your economics professor assigns a group project for the course. Describe the free-rider problem that can lead to a suboptimal outcome for your group. To combat this problem, the instructor asks you to evaluate the contribution of your peers in a confidential report. Will this evaluation have the desired effects?

7. The village of Upper Bigglesworth has a village "commons," a piece of land on which each villager, by law, is free to graze cows. Use of the commons is measured in units of the number of cows grazing on it. Assume that the marginal private cost curve of cow-grazing on the commons is upward sloping (say due to more time spent herding). There is also a marginal social cost curve of cow-grazing on the commons: each additional cow grazed means less grass available for others, and the damage done by overgrazing of the commons increases as the number of cows grazing increases. Finally, assume that the private benefit to the villagers of each additional cow grazing on the commons declines as more cows graze, since each additional cow has less grass to eat than the previous one.

a. Is the commons excludable or nonexcludable? Is it rival in consumption or nonrival? What kind of good is the commons?

b. Draw a diagram showing the marginal social cost, marginal private cost, and the marginal private benefit of cow-grazing on the commons, with the quantity of cows that graze on the commons on the horizontal axis. How does the quantity of cows grazing in the absence of government intervention compare to the efficient quantity? Show both in your diagram.

c. The villagers hire you to tell them how to achieve an efficient use of the commons. You tell them that there are three possibilities: a Pigouvian tax, the assignment of property rights over the commons, and a system of tradable licences for the right to graze a cow. Explain how each one of these options would lead to an efficient use of the commons. In the assignment of property rights, assume that one person is assigned the rights to the commons and the rights to all the cows. Draw a diagram that shows the Pigouvian tax.

8. The accompanying table shows six consumers' willingness to pay (their individual marginal benefit) to download a Jay-Z album. The marginal cost of making the file accessible to one additional consumer is constant, at zero.

Consumer	Individual marginal benefit
Adriana	$2
Bhagesh	15
Chizuko	1
Denzel	10
Emma	5
Frank	4

a. What would be the efficient price to charge for a download of the file?

b. All six consumers are able to download the file for free from a file-sharing service, Pantster. Which consumers will download the file? What will be the total consumer surplus to those consumers?

c. Pantster is shut down for copyright law infringement. In order to download the file, consumers now have to pay $4.99 at a commercial music site. Which consumers will download the file? What will be the total consumer surplus to those consumers? How much producer surplus accrues to the commercial music site? What is the total surplus? What is the deadweight loss from the new pricing policy?

9. Software has historically been an artificially scarce good—it is nonrival because the cost of replication is negligible once the investment to write the code is made, but software companies make it excludable by charging for user licences. But then open-source software emerged, most of which is free to download and can be modified and maintained by anyone.

a. Discuss the free-rider problem that might exist in the development of open-source software. What effect might this have on quality? Why does this problem not exist for proprietary software, such as the products of a company like Microsoft or Adobe?

b. Some argue that open-source software serves an unsatisfied market demand that proprietary software ignores. Draw a typical diagram that illustrates how proprietary software may be underproduced. Put the price and marginal cost of software on the vertical axis and the quantity of software on the horizontal axis. Draw a typical demand curve and a marginal cost curve (*MC*) that is always equal to zero. Assume that the software company charges a positive price, *P*, for the software. Label the equilibrium point and the efficient point.

10. Canadians have become passionate consumers of the Asian hot sauce Sriracha. Sriracha is produced by Huy Fong Foods in Irwindale, California. Each year the company processes over 45 million kilograms of chili peppers to make its delectable sauce. But roasting all of those chili peppers has had an unintended consequence: pollution. Recently, local residents began complaining about a pungent odour from the plant that they believed led to heartburn, nosebleeds, and coughing.

The hypothetical table shows the estimated marginal social benefit (*MSB*) and marginal social cost (*MSC*) of pollution that arises from odour emissions.

Quantity of odour emissions (thousands of odour units)	Marginal social benefit ($ per odour unit)	Marginal social cost ($ per odour unit)
0	$80	$0
1	72	8
2	64	16
3	56	24
4	48	32
5	40	40
6	32	48
7	24	56
8	16	64
9	8	72
10	0	80

a. How can the pollution that results from Sriracha production have a marginal social benefit?

b. Graph the marginal social cost and marginal social benefit of odour.

c. What is the market-determined quantity of odour?

d. What is the social gain from reducing the market-determined quantity of odour by one odour unit?

 WORK IT OUT

11. A residential community has 100 residents who are concerned about security. The accompanying table gives the total cost of hiring a 24-hour security service as well as each individual resident's total benefit.

Quantity of security guards	Total cost	Total individual benefit to each resident
0	$0	$0
1	150	10
2	300	16
3	450	18
4	600	19

a. Explain why the security service is a public good for the residents of the community.

b. Calculate the marginal cost, the individual marginal benefit for each resident, and the marginal social benefit.

c. If an individual resident were to decide about hiring and paying for security guards on their own, how many guards would that resident hire?

d. If the residents act together, how many security guards will they hire? ■

18

The Economics of the Welfare State

FREE MEDICATION FOR ONTARIO'S YOUTH

AS CANADIANS, the cost of seeking medical help is much lower than our American counterparts. This can be attributed to the provision of the Canadian universal health care program — most of our health care spending is paid by the provincial and territorial governments. Despite having universal health care, Canadians still have to pay for their drug prescriptions.

FatCamera/Getty Images

Implementation of OHIP+ was a major expansion of the Canadian welfare state.

Acknowledging that it can be very costly to pay for medication, in particular for poor families, Ontario became the first province in Canada to offer free prescription drugs to residents under age 25. On January 1, 2018, the government of Ontario began providing free access to more than 4,400 approved prescription medications to children and youth through the OHIP+ program. At the time of the program's launch, the provincial government expected OHIP+ would benefit 4 million children and youth.

The idea of OHIP+ was well-received by residents, as a poll by Campaign Research in January 2018 found that 72% of respondents

approved of the idea, with only 18% opposed to it. However, it is a costly program; at launch, it was expected to cost about $500 million a year. When the new provincial government was sworn in in June 2018, it reformed OHIP+. Effective April 1, 2019, free prescription medication was available only to Ontarians under age 25 without private insurance coverage. The revised program was expected to save the provincial government $250 million.

The provision of OHIP+ is an attempt to limit economic insecurity and reduce economic inequality. This is an example of the welfare state, the collection of government programs that serve this purpose. Modern governments, especially in wealthy countries, devote a large chunk of their budgets to welfare such as health care, income support for the elderly, aid to the poor, and other programs.

There are intense political disputes about the appropriate size and role of the welfare state. Indeed, you can argue that these disputes are what politics is mainly about, with liberals seeking to expand the welfare state's reach and conservatives seeking to scale it back. Yet there is broad political consensus that troubled families should receive some help. And they do: even conservatives generally accept a fairly extensive welfare state as a fact of life.

We start this chapter by discussing the underlying rationale for welfare state programs. Then we describe and analyze the two main kinds of programs operating in Canada: income support programs, such as support for seniors via the Canada Pension Plan (CPP)/Québec Pension Plan (QPP), Old Age Security (OAS), and Guaranteed Income Supplement (GIS) payments, and health care programs — Canada's largest area of social spending by far. ●

WHAT YOU WILL LEARN

- What is the **welfare state** and how does it benefit society?
- What are the causes and consequences of poverty?
- How has income inequality in Canada changed over time?
- How do **social insurance programs** like OAS affect poverty and income inequality?
- Why is there debate over the size of the welfare state?
- What are the special concerns of **private health insurance** and how have governments acted to address them?

The **welfare state** is the collection of government programs designed to alleviate economic hardship.

A **government transfer** is a government payment to an individual or a family.

A **social welfare program** is a government program designed to provide payments based on need.

A **social insurance program** is a government program designed to provide protection against unpredictable financial distress.

‖ Poverty, Inequality, and Public Policy

The term **welfare state** has come to refer to the collection of government programs that are designed to alleviate economic hardship. A large share of government spending for all wealthy countries consists of **government transfers**—payments by the government to individuals and families—that provide financial aid to the poor, assistance to unemployed workers, guaranteed income for the elderly, and assistance in paying medical bills for those with large health care expenses.

The Logic of the Welfare State

There are three major economic rationales for the creation of the welfare state. We'll turn now to a discussion of each.

1. Alleviating Income Inequality Suppose that the Taylor family, which has an income of only $15,000 a year, were to receive a government cheque for $1,500. This cheque might allow the Taylors to afford a better place to live, eat a more nutritious diet, or in other ways significantly improve their quality of life. Also suppose that the Fisher family, which has an income of $300,000 a year, were to face an extra tax of $1,500. This probably wouldn't make much difference to their quality of life: at worst, they might have to give up a few minor luxuries.

This hypothetical exchange illustrates the first major rationale for the welfare state: *alleviating income inequality*. Because a marginal (or additional) dollar is worth more to a poor person than a rich one, modest transfers from the rich to the poor will do the rich little harm but benefit the poor a lot. So, according to this argument, a government that plays Robin Hood, taking from the rich to give to those in need, does more good than harm. Programs that are designed to provide payments based on need are known as **social welfare programs.**

2. Alleviating Economic Insecurity The second major rationale for the welfare state is *alleviating economic insecurity*. When bad things happen, such as a flood or an illness, they almost always happen to a limited number of people. For example, the flood in southern Alberta in 2013 forced thousands to flee their homes and caused around $6 billion in damage, but the flood left the rest of Canada unscathed.

Imagine 10 families, each of which can expect an income next year of $50,000 if nothing goes wrong. But suppose the odds are that something *will* go wrong for one of the families, although nobody knows which one. For example, suppose each of the families has a one in 10 chance of experiencing a sharp drop in income because one family member is laid off or their home is badly flooded. And assume that this event will produce severe hardship for the family—a family member will have to drop out of school or the family will lose its home.

Now suppose there's a government program that provides aid to families in distress, paying for that aid by taxing families that are having a good year. Arguably, this program will make all the families better off, because even families that don't currently receive aid from the program might need it at some point in the future. Each family will therefore feel safer knowing that the government stands ready to help when disaster strikes. Programs designed to provide protection against unpredictable financial distress are known as **social insurance programs.**

These two rationales for the welfare state, alleviating income inequality and alleviating economic insecurity, are closely related to the *ability-to-pay principle* we learned about in Chapter 7. Recall how the ability-to-pay principle is used to justify progressive taxation: it says that people with low incomes, for whom an additional dollar makes a big difference to economic well-being, should pay a smaller fraction of their income in taxes than people with higher incomes, for whom an additional dollar makes much less difference. The same principle suggests that those with very low incomes should actually get money back from the tax system.

3. Reducing Poverty and Providing Access to Health Care The third and final major rationale for the welfare state involves *the social benefits of poverty reduction and access to health care*, especially when applied to children of poor households. Researchers have documented that such children, on average, suffer lifelong disadvantages. Children from economically disadvantaged backgrounds, even after adjusting for ability, are more likely to be underemployed or unemployed, engage in crime, and suffer chronic health problems—all of which impose significant social costs. So, according to the evidence, programs that help to alleviate poverty and provide access to health care generate external benefits to society.

More broadly, as the following For Inquiring Minds explains, some political philosophers argue that principles of social justice demand that society take care of the poor and unlucky. Others disagree, arguing that welfare state programs go beyond the proper role of government. To an important extent, the difference between those two philosophical positions defines what we mean in politics by "liberalism" and "conservatism."

But before we get carried away, it's important to realize that things aren't quite that cut and dried. Even conservatives who believe in limited government typically support some welfare state programs. And even economists who support the goals of the welfare state are concerned about the effects of large-scale aid to the poor and unlucky on their incentives to work and save. Like taxes, welfare state programs can create substantial deadweight losses, so their true economic costs can be considerably larger than the direct monetary cost.

We'll turn to the costs and benefits of the welfare state later in this chapter. First, however, let's examine the problems the welfare state is supposed to address.

The Problem of Poverty

What, exactly, do we mean by poverty? Any definition is somewhat arbitrary. In Canada, the **poverty line** (or **poverty threshold**) is the minimum level of income considered adequate to purchase the necessities of life. Anyone who falls below the poverty line is considered to be in a state of poverty. Although there is no official definition of the poverty line, Statistics Canada constructs the low income cut-offs (LICOs) to study poverty. The LICOs are income thresholds below which a family will likely devote too large a share of its income to the necessities as compared to the average family. According to the LICOs measures, if a family is expected to spend 20 percentage points more than an average family on necessities, then that family is considered to be living below the poverty line. Since the LICOs compare individual or family spending to that of the average person or family, they are a *relative measure*. To address issues related to differences in family sizes and the types of communities they live in, Statistics Canada calculates 35 LICOs for seven different family sizes and five different community sizes, using before-tax and after-tax income.

Although the LICOs are the most commonly used criterion to measure poverty in Canada, other measures such as the low-income measure (LIM) are also used, especially for international comparisons. The LIM is defined as 50% of median adjusted household income in which household size is taken into account—a larger household needs more income to meet its needs. The LIM is another relative measure of poverty: households with income below a certain percentage of the median, usually 50%, are deemed poor. If median income declines, then the LIM threshold declines too.

An *absolute measure*, which defines an amount of money a family or individual needs, is the alternative to a relative measure. The market basket measure (MBM),

The **poverty line** (or **poverty threshold**) is the annual income below which a family is considered poor.

The **poverty rate** is the percentage of the population living below the poverty line.

developed by Employment and Social Development Canada (ESDC), is an absolute measure of poverty. The MBM is a measure of low income based on the cost of a specified quality and quantity of food, clothing, footwear, transportation, shelter, and other expenses for a family with two adults and two children.

The poverty line depends on the size of a family and the size of the community. Using the before-tax LICOs measure, in 2018, the poverty line for a family of four living in a community of at least 500,000 residents was $48,167 (the after-tax LICOs measure was $40,614).

Trends in Poverty Based on conventional wisdom, you might expect that as the economy grows and becomes more prosperous, and as average income rises, the percentage of the population living below the poverty line would decline steadily. Is that the case in Canada? Let's see. Panel (a) of Figure 18-1 shows the **poverty rate**—the percentage of the population below the poverty line—from 1976 to 2018, using the different measures mentioned above. As you can see, the poverty rate fluctuated during that period and it began to show a declining trend starting in 1996.

Panel (b) shows the poverty rate by age group using the after-tax LICOs. The poverty rate for seniors shows a clear declining trend, dropping from 30% to 5% in recent years. The poverty rate for those under age 18 was above the overall poverty rate for most of the years during the period. The picture for those aged between 18 and 64 was a bit gloomier; their poverty rate moved from below the overall poverty rate in earlier years to just above the overall rate in recent years.

Who Are the Poor? Who are the poor in Canada? Obvious answers are likely to be the single-parent families, families with a female as the primary breadwinner,

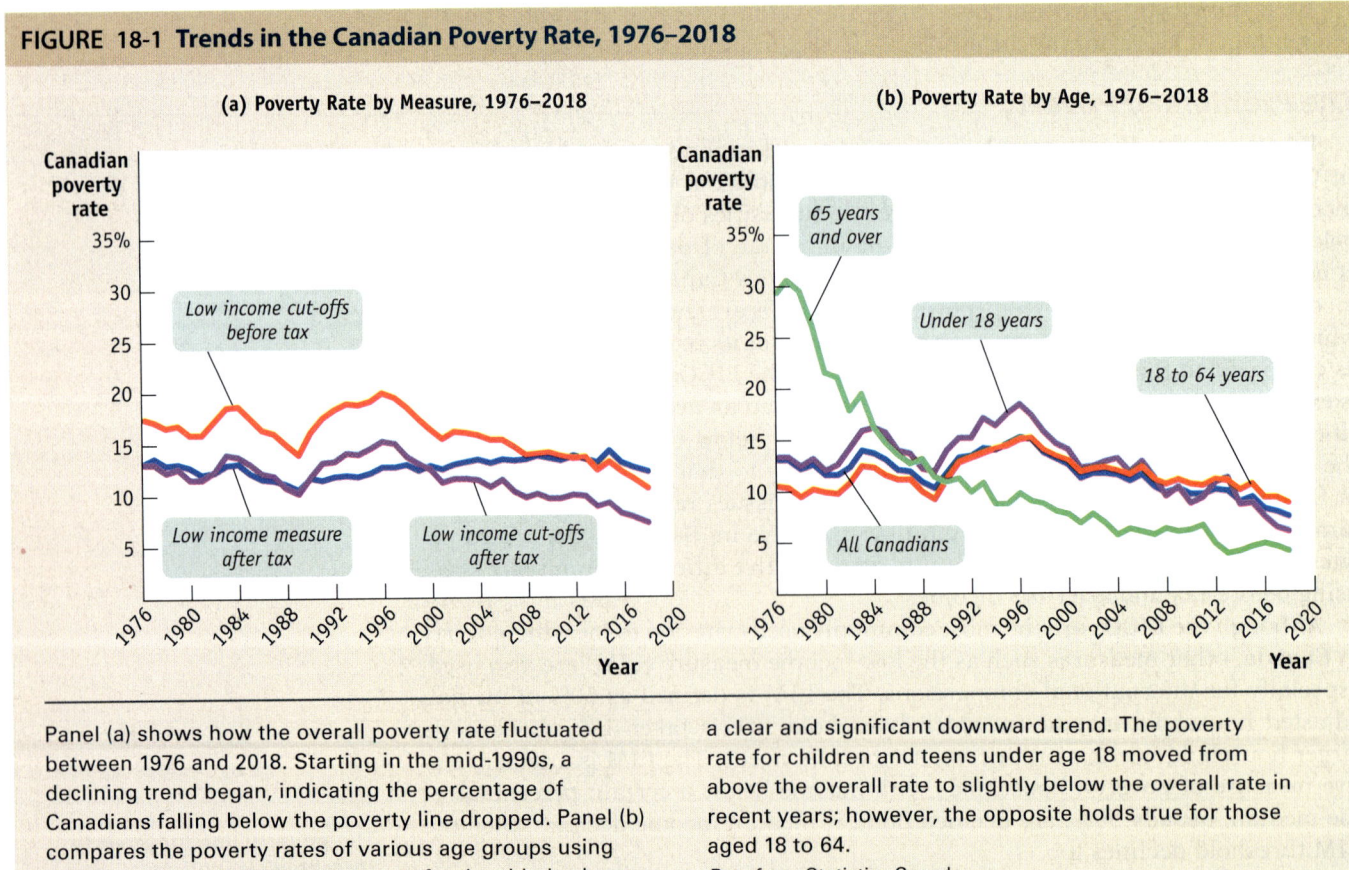

FIGURE 18-1 Trends in the Canadian Poverty Rate, 1976–2018

(a) Poverty Rate by Measure, 1976–2018

(b) Poverty Rate by Age, 1976–2018

Panel (a) shows how the overall poverty rate fluctuated between 1976 and 2018. Starting in the mid-1990s, a declining trend began, indicating the percentage of Canadians falling below the poverty line dropped. Panel (b) compares the poverty rates of various age groups using the after-tax LICOs. The poverty rate for the elderly shows a clear and significant downward trend. The poverty rate for children and teens under age 18 moved from above the overall rate to slightly below the overall rate in recent years; however, the opposite holds true for those aged 18 to 64.

Data from: Statistics Canada.

Aboriginals, and visible minorities. Is this true? Let's take a look of how these groups fare.

In 2018, according to the after-tax LICOs as a measure of poverty, about 2.67 million Canadians were in poverty—about 7.3% of the population, or about one in 14 Canadians. The incidence of poverty was equally split between females (1.31 million) and males (1.36 million). About 1.425 million unattached individuals were considered to be poor in 2018 and 86% of those individuals (about 1.224 million) were under age 65.

There is a correlation between family makeup and poverty: single-parent families had a higher chance of living in poverty (with a poverty rate of 15.6% in 2018). Of the single-parent families living in poverty, 93% of them were led by a single mother. Although married couples with children were much less likely to be poor, with a poverty rate of 3.8%, about 18% of the poor were in families with children and both parents present.

According to data from the 2016 Census, the poverty rate of Indigenous people living off reserves was 14.1%. Recent immigrants, those who immigrated to Canada between 2011 and 2016, and visible minority are more vulnerable; their poverty rates were 31.4% and 16.4%, respectively.

What really stands out in the data is the persistence or duration of low income and the mobility of the low-income group. The good news is that most Canadians are poor only for a short period of time and most of them can increase their income within a year. During the 2010–2017 period, 61.6% of those considered to have low income would leave the pool within a year and 6.6% of the poor continued to be poor for five years more. The bad news is that it is getting more difficult for low-income Canadians to move up to higher income groups. One study showed that the percentage of the bottom 10% of income earners to climb up the income ladder over five years had dropped from 73% in the late 1980s to about 62% in recent years. This may be caused by changes in the structure of the Canadian economy and, in the period of 2007–2012, the Canadian economy was hit by the Great Recession. Many worry the coronavirus pandemic would hit the low-income group more severely.

What Causes Poverty? Poverty is often blamed on lack of education and educational attainment clearly has a strong positive effect on income level—those with more education earn, on average, higher incomes than those with less education. A 2019 study by Statistics Canada looked at the return on education over a 15-year study period. The study found that the median cumulative earnings of a male worker with a bachelor's degree was 1.8 times that of male high school graduates from 1990 to 2010. The difference in (median) earnings was even more profound among women; women with a bachelor's degree earned 2.4 times more than high school graduates.

Lack of proficiency in English or French is also a barrier to higher income. For example, immigrants to Alberta with poor English skills are more likely to work for minimum wage in industries like retail and manufacturing, which offer temporary jobs and are more susceptible to economic fluctuations. Even for immigrants who are proficient in English, finding a decent job may not be easy if they lack connections and Canadian experience.

And it's important not to overlook the role of racial and gender discrimination; although less pervasive today than 50 years ago, discrimination still erects formidable barriers to advancement for many Canadians. Visible minorities earn

Canada's poverty rate is near the middle of the pack when compared to other rich countries.

Denis Tangney Jr/Getty Images

less and are less likely to be employed than whites with comparable levels of education. Studies find that visible minorities and Aboriginals suffer persistent discrimination by employers. Women earn lower incomes than men with similar qualifications.

In addition, one important source of poverty that should not be overlooked is bad luck. Many families find themselves impoverished when a wage-earner loses a job or a family member falls seriously ill.

Consequences of Poverty The consequences of poverty are often severe, particularly for children. Poverty is often associated with lack of access to a nutritious diet, which can lead to higher risk of suffering health problems, developmental delays, and behavioural problems. Child poverty can also result in lower attainment in education and is more likely to lead to adult poverty when the children grow up. Recent medical studies have shown that children raised in severe poverty tend to suffer from lifelong learning disabilities. As a result, Canadian children growing up in or near poverty don't have an equal chance at the starting line: they tend to be at a disadvantage throughout their lives. Even talented children who come from poor families are unlikely to finish college or university.

To make things worse, the problems of child poverty do not hit the country evenly. Some provinces have higher child poverty rates than others. Table 18-1 shows the provincial child poverty rates in 2018 using the after-tax LICOs. Manitoba had the highest child poverty rates, sitting at 9.6%. The high rate in Manitoba caused lots of concern among advocacy groups and others. Sid Frankel, an associate professor of social work at the University of Manitoba, claimed that child poverty has become a "a chronic nightmare." The advocacy groups urged the provincial government to take action including increasing the Manitoba Child Benefit, developing a plan to reduce child poverty in indigenous communities, and increasing the minimum wage.

TABLE 18-1 Provincial Poverty Rates for Canadians Under Age 18, 2018

	Poverty rate, persons under age 18
Canada	5.9%
Atlantic provinces (Newfoundland, Labrador, Prince Edward Island, Nova Scotia, New Brunswick)	5.3
Québec	5.3
Ontario	6.8
Manitoba	9.6
Saskatchewan	6.1
Alberta	4.7
British Columbia	4

Data from: Statistics Canada.
Note: Separate data for Newfoundland and Prince Edward Island were not available; the child poverty rates for Nova Scotia and New Brunswick were 8.5% and 3.4% respectively.

Similarly, some ethnic groups are more likely to live in poverty than others. A report released by the Canadian Centre for Policy Alternatives in 2019 found that for prime-age workers the average employment income of racialized Canadians was only 74% of that paid to non-racialized workers. Also a 2016 report by the same research institute found that 60% of First Nations children lived in poverty. This disturbingly high child poverty rate explains, to some extent, why Aboriginal children were behind non-Aboriginal children in other measures of well-being such as educational attainment and overall health, while dealing with higher rates of substance abuse, suicide, and homelessness. Unfortunately, disadvantages from childhood can carry forward to adulthood, making it more likely that a First Nations person will suffer lifelong poverty.

Economic Inequality

Canada is a rich country. The average income for a Canadian household with at least two people was $116,400 (measured in 2018 dollars), far exceeding the poverty line. How is it possible, then, that so many Canadians still live in poverty? The answer is that income is unequally distributed, with many households earning much less than the average and others earning much more.

Table 18-2 shows the distribution of pre-tax (total) income in 2018 among Canadian families, as estimated by Statistics Canada. Households are grouped into *deciles*, each containing 10%, or one-tenth, of the population. The first, or lowest, decile contains households whose income places them below the 10th percentile in income, the second decile contains households whose income places them between the 10th and 20th percentiles, and so on.

For each group, Table 18-2 shows three numbers. The second column shows the income ranges that define the group. For example, in 2018, the lowest decile consisted of households with annual incomes of less than $39,000; the next decile of households had incomes between $39,001 and $54,700, and so on. The third column shows the average level of family income in each group; families in the highest decile had an average income of $305,000, 11.1 times the average level of income of families in the lowest decile. The fourth column shows the percentage of total Canadian income received by each group.

TABLE 18-2 Canada's Income Distribution in 2018

Income group	Income range	Average income	Percent of total income
Lowest decile	$39,000 and under	$27,500	2.4%
Second decile	$39,001 to $54,700	$46,900	4.0
Third decile	$54,701 to $68,300	$61,500	5.3
Fourth decile	$68,301 to $82,800	$74,400	6.5
Fifth decile	$82,801 to $97,400	$90,000	7.7
Sixth decile	$97,401 to $114,000	$105,500	9.1
Seventh decile	$114,001 to $134,800	$123,700	10.6
Eighth decile	$134,801 to $161,500	$147,300	12.7
Ninth decile	$161,501 to $207,000	$181,400	15.6
Highest decile	More than $207,000	$305,000	26.2
Mean income = $116,400		**Median income = $97,400**	

Data from: Statistics Canada.

Mean versus Median Household Income At the bottom of Table 18-2 are two useful numbers for thinking about the incomes of Canadian households. **Mean household income,** also called average household income, is the total income of all Canadian households divided by the number of households. **Median household income** is the income of a household in the exact middle of the income distribution—the level of income at which half of all households have lower income and half have higher income. It's very important to realize that these two numbers do not measure exactly the same thing.

Economists often illustrate the difference by asking people first to imagine a room containing several dozen more or less ordinary wage-earners, and then to think about what happens to the mean and median incomes of the people in the room if a Bay Street CEO, some of whom earn millions of dollars a year, walks in. The mean income soars, because the CEO's income pulls up the average, but median income hardly rises at all.

This example helps explain why economists generally regard median income as a better guide to the economic status of typical families than mean income: mean income is strongly affected by the incomes of a relatively small number of very high-income Canadians, who are not representative of the population as a whole; median income is not.

What we learn from Table 18-2 is that income in Canada is quite unequally distributed. The average income earned by the poorest decile of families is about 30% of the average income earned by families in the fifth decile, and the average income of the richest decile is 3.4 times the average income earned by those in the fifth decile. The Economics in Action at the end of this section discusses long-term trends in Canada's income inequality.

It's important to note that the data in Table 18-2 overstate the true degree of inequality in Canada to some degree, for two reasons:

- Household incomes vary from year to year. In any given year, many households at the bottom of the income distribution are having a particularly bad year, just as many at the top are having a particularly good year. Their average incomes over a number of years aren't as unequal as those in a single year.

- Household incomes vary over a lifetime. Young people and retired people, on average, have lower income than people in their prime working years. So data that mix people of different ages will show more income inequality than data that make comparisons among people of similar ages.

Mean household income is the average income across all households.

Median household income is the income of the household lying at the exact middle of the income distribution.

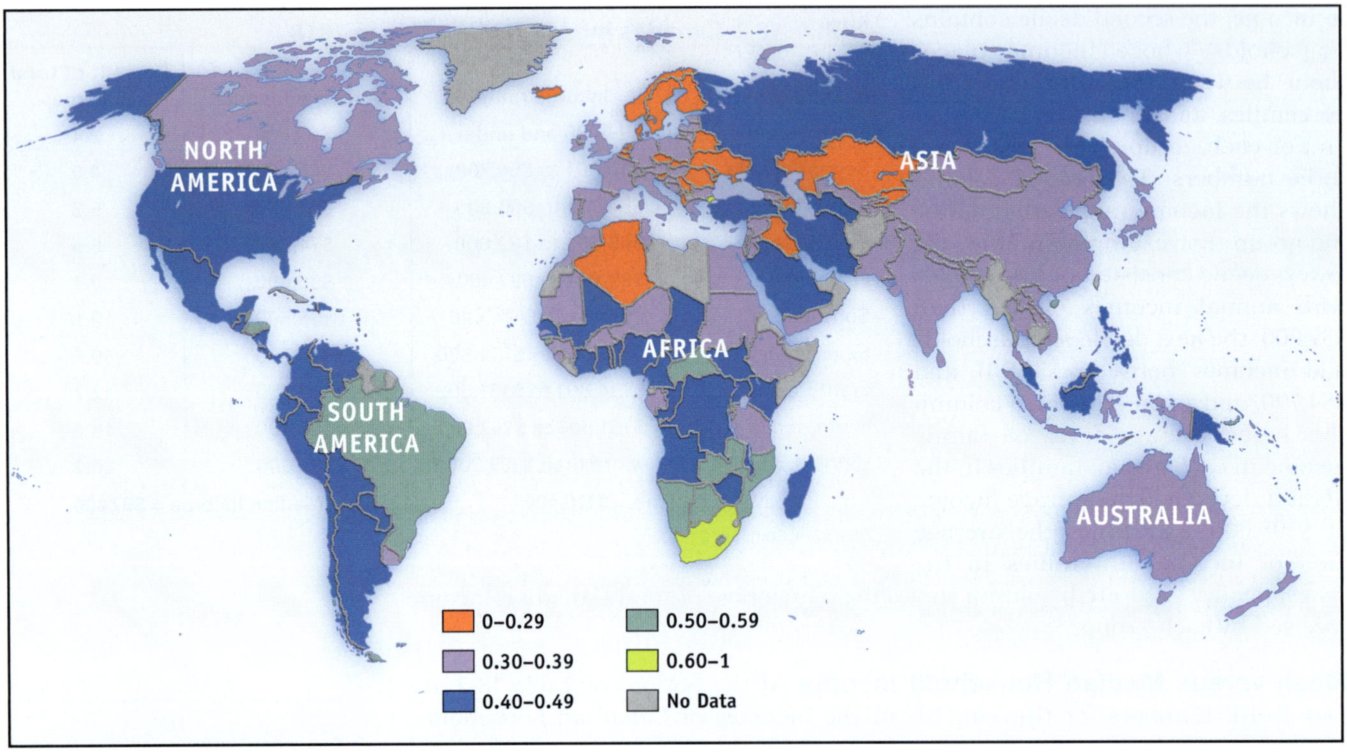

■ 0–0.29	■ 0.50–0.59
■ 0.30–0.39	■ 0.60–1
■ 0.40–0.49	■ No Data

FIGURE 18-2 Income Inequality Around the World

The highest levels of income inequality are found in Africa and Latin America. The most equal distributions of income are in Europe, especially in Scandinavia. Compared to other wealthy countries, Canada, with a Gini coefficient of 0.35, high income inequality (though not as high as the United Kingdom or the United States).

Data from: World Bank, *World Development Indicators* 2018; Statistics Canada.

The **Gini coefficient** is a number that summarizes a country's level of income inequality based on how unequally income is distributed across quintiles.

Despite those qualifications, there is a considerable amount of genuine income inequality in Canada, and income has become considerably more unequal since 1980.

International Comparisons of Inequality

A good way to gain some perspective on the level of income inequality in Canada is to compare it to levels in other countries. To do that, economists created the **Gini coefficient,** a measure of income inequality based on the type of data found in Table 18-1. Mathematically, a country's Gini coefficient can range from 0, indicating a perfectly equal distribution of income, to 1, indicating the most unequal distribution of income possible—one in which all the income goes to a single person.

Figure 18-2 shows recent estimates of the Gini coefficient for many of the world's countries. Countries with a high degree of income inequality have a Gini coefficient close to 0.5. Aside from a few countries in Africa, the highest levels of income inequality are found in Latin America, especially Brazil. Countries with a very equal income distribution have Gini coefficients around 0.25. The most equal distributions of income are in Europe, especially in Scandinavia. According to the most recent data (as shown in Figure 18-2), Canada has a Gini coefficient of 0.34. So, compared to other wealthy countries, Canada has high inequality, though not as unequal as other countries in North and South America.

When Is Inequality a Problem?

Some level of income inequality in an economy is desirable. In a market-based economy, a significant share of the observed inequality will represent the economic reward to skill, effort, innovation, and education. Without such a reward, incentives would suffer and the economy would stagnate.

Yet high income inequality is a problem because it means that a significant share of a country's population is not sharing in the country's overall prosperity. Although the poverty rate in Canada has declined somewhat in the past two decades, the Gini coefficient has been relatively stable, indicating that income inequality still persists. A further concern is how inequality is perpetuated across generations. The children of poor parents are much more likely to be poor than the children of affluent parents—a correlation that is stronger in Canada and the United States than in other rich countries.

Extreme inequality can hurt a nation's long-term economic prospects if, as is often the case, it limits opportunities. Those born into low-income families may fail to receive adequate nutrition and health care, limiting their productivity as adults; they may also lack access to education and job opportunities, limiting their ability to make contributions to economic growth. In some cases, high inequality also contributes to social and political instability, which further damages a nation's economic performance.

Economic Insecurity

As we stated earlier, although the rationale for the welfare state rests partly on the social benefits of reducing poverty and inequality, it also rests in part on the benefits of reducing economic insecurity, which afflicts even relatively well-off families.

One form economic insecurity takes is the risk of a sudden loss of income, which usually happens when a family member loses a job and either spends an extended period without work or is forced to take a new job that pays considerably less. For example, according to Statistics Canada, in the wake of the coronavirus

---

GLOBAL COMPARISON **INCOME, REDISTRIBUTION, AND INEQUALITY IN RICH COUNTRIES**

Spend some time travelling around Canada, then spend some more time travelling around Denmark. You'll almost surely come away with the impression that Denmark has substantially less income inequality than Canada, that the rich aren't as rich and the poor aren't as poor. And the numbers confirm this impression: the Gini coefficient for Denmark, and indeed for most of Western Europe, is lower than in Canada.

But why?

The answer, to an important extent, is the role of government, which, in Canada, plays a significant role in redistributing income away from those with the highest incomes to those who earn the least. But European nations have substantially bigger welfare states than Canada does, and do a lot more income redistribution.

The accompanying figure shows two measures of the Gini coefficient for a number of rich countries. (The figure focuses on households in which everyone is under age 60, because differences in retirement ages skew results among older families.)

A country with a perfectly equal income distribution—one in which every household had the same income—would have a Gini coefficient of zero. At the other extreme, a country in which all of the income goes to one household would have a Gini coefficient of 1. For each country, the purple bars show the actual Gini, a measure of the observed inequality in income before taxes and transfers are made. The orange bars show what each country's Gini would be after taxes and transfers are made. It turns out that the inequality of market incomes in Denmark is somewhat lower than that in Canada, but much of the difference in observed inequality is the result of Denmark's bigger welfare state.

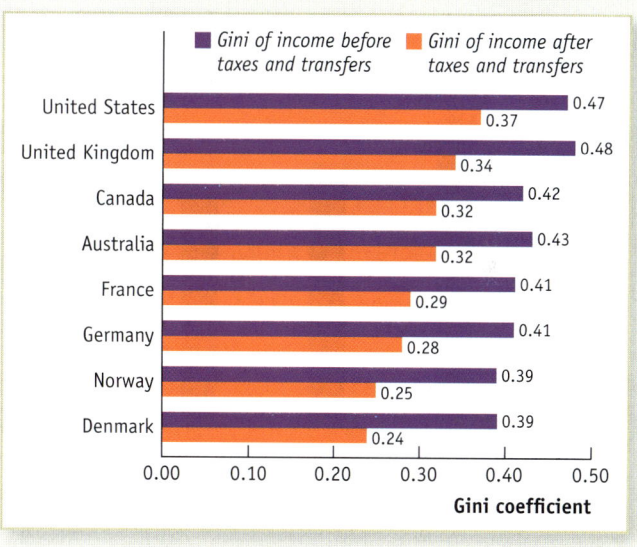

There are some caveats to this conclusion. On one side, the data probably don't do a very good job of tracking very high incomes, which are probably a bigger factor in the United States and Canada than elsewhere. On the other side, European welfare states may indirectly increase measured income inequality through their effects on incentives. Still, the data strongly suggest that differences in inequality among rich countries reflect different policies as well as differences in the underlying economic situation.

Data from: Janet C. Gornick and Branko Milanovic, "Income Inequality in the United States in Cross-National Perspective: Redistribution Revisited," Luxembourg Income Study Center, May 4, 2015.

pandemic in March and April 2020, the employment in low-wage jobs fell by 38%, compared to 13% in other paid jobs. In addition, young people, and those without Bachelor's degrees, faced a higher layoff rate.

Even if a family doesn't face a loss in income, lower-income families might face another type of risk—health risk. Families with higher educational attainment are more likely to have jobs that allow them to work from home. Estimates show that 65% of families that have a breadwinner with a Bachelor's degree or higher have jobs that can be done remotely, while only 23.6% of families whose primary earners have a high school diploma can do the same. Thus, families with primary earners with lower levels of education might have a higher chance of getting COVID-19 as it's more difficult for them to practice social distancing.

ECONOMICS >> *in Action*
Trends in Income Inequality in Canada

Does inequality tend to rise, fall, or stay the same over time? Let's take a look. Detailed Canadian data on income by deciles, as shown in Table 18-2, are only available starting in 1976. Panel (a) of Figure 18-3 shows the annual growth rate of average after-tax income for economic families, measured in 2018 dollars, for the five quintiles over two periods: from 1980 to 2000 and from 2001 to 2018. There is a clear difference between the two periods. In the first period, there were larger differences in the growth rates of average real after-tax income.

Canadian households in higher after-tax income groups found their real income increasing between 1980 and 2000; however, households in the middle three quintiles experienced the lowest growth rates in that period. People in the lowest quintile experienced the second highest average growth rate of real after-tax income of the quintiles, meaning they were gaining on those in the middle three quintiles (the middle class). But this average growth rate of 0.56% per year was almost one percentage point lower than the growth rate experienced during this period by those in the top quintile, so those at the top were pulling ahead of all those in every other quintile. The good news is that after 2000, average real after-tax income within each group grew at a faster rate for all groups, and the lowest quintile experienced the highest growth rate of average real income of 3.69% per year. So during this period the poorest 20% of families were gaining on the rest of the income distribution—inequality was declining.

Panel (b) of Figure 18-3 shows the share of total income earned by the top 10% of Canadians between 1982 and 2017. Again we can see that inequality in Canada was rising in the 1980s and 1990s when the share of total income earned by the top 10% of Canadians rose from 30% to 35%, but it

FIGURE 18-3 **Trends in Canadian Income Inequality**

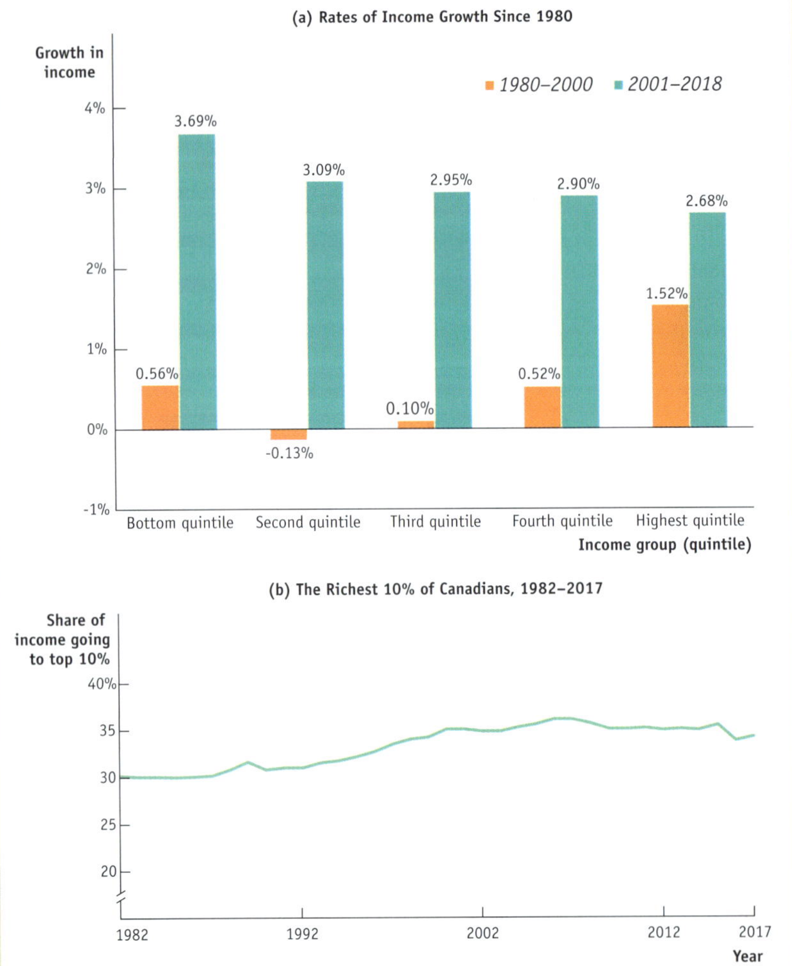

(a) Rates of Income Growth Since 1980

(b) The Richest 10% of Canadians, 1982–2017

Data from: Statistics Canada.

then stabilized after 2000 (fluctuating around 35%). The average income earned by the top 10% of Canadians, measured in 2018 dollars, rose from $149,600 in 1982 to $228,800 in 2018, with an annual growth rate of 1.1% between 1982 and 2000 and 1.2% between 2000 and 2018. The lower growth rate of real income after 2000 helps explain why the share of total income earned by the top 10% of Canadians had stabilized in later years.

Many believe the persistence of income inequality is caused by rapid technological change. The demand for highly skilled or talented workers increases more rapidly than the demand for other workers, leading to a rise in the wage gap between the highly skilled and other workers. Growing international trade may also have contributed by allowing Canada to import labour-intensive products from low-wage countries rather than making them domestically, reducing the demand for less skilled Canadian workers and depressing their wages. Rising immigration may be yet another source—on average, immigrants earn lower wages than workers born in Canada.

All these explanations, however, fail to account for one key feature: much of the rise in inequality doesn't reflect a rising gap between highly educated workers and those with less education, but rather growing differences among highly educated workers themselves. For example, teachers and top business executives have similarly high levels of education, but executive paycheques have risen dramatically and teachers' salaries have not. For some reason, a few "superstars"—a group that includes literal superstars in the entertainment world, but also such groups as Bay Street traders and top corporate executives—now earn much higher incomes than was the case a generation ago. It's still unclear what caused this change.

>> Check Your Understanding 18-1

Solutions appear at back of book.

1. Indicate whether each of the following programs is a social welfare program or a social insurance program.
   a. A pension guarantee program, which provides pensions for retirees if they have lost their employment-based pension due to their employer's bankruptcy
   b. The federal program known as the Canada Child Benefit (CCB), which is a tax-free monthly payment made to eligible families with children under the age of 18

   Note: The monthly CCB payment received by families depends on the tax return. As family income increases, the amount of CCB received will be reduced gradually until it reaches zero.

   c. The federal flood program, which provides financial help to communities hit by major floods
   d. The Canada Mortgage and Housing Corporation (CMHC), which provides affordable housing to low-income families under the framework

2. Is the poverty line, as defined by an after-tax LICO, a relative or an absolute measure of poverty? That is, does it define poverty according to how poor someone is relative to others or according to some fixed measure that doesn't change over time? Explain.

3. The accompanying table gives the distribution of income for a very small economy.
   a. What is the mean income? What is the median income? Which measure is more representative of the income of the average person in the economy? Why?
   b. What income range defines the first quintile? The third?

	Income
Sephora	$39,000
Kelly	17,500
Raul	900,000
Vijay	15,000
Oskar	28,000

4. Which of the following statements more accurately reflects the principal source of rising inequality in Canada today?
   a. The salary of the manager of the local branch of Sunrise Bank has risen relative to the salary of the neighbourhood gas station attendant.
   b. The salary of the CEO of Sunrise Bank has risen relative to the salary of the local branch bank manager, who has similar education levels.

>> Quick Review

• **Welfare state** programs, which include **government transfers,** absorb a large share of government spending in wealthy countries.

• The ability-to-pay principle explains one rationale for the welfare state: alleviating income inequality. **Social welfare programs** do this by aiding those in need. **Social insurance programs** address the second rationale: alleviating economic insecurity. The external benefits to society of poverty reduction and access to health care, especially for children, is a third rationale for the welfare state.

• The **poverty rate** describes the percentage of people who are below the **poverty line** (sometimes called the **poverty threshold**). Although the poverty line is not officially defined in Canada, common measures include LICOs, the LIM, and the MBM.

• The causes of poverty can include lack of education, the legacy of racial and gender discrimination, and bad luck. The consequences of poverty are dire especially for children and Aboriginals.

• **Median household** income is a better indicator of typical household income than **mean household** income. A comparison of **Gini coefficients** across countries shows that Canada has less income inequality than poor countries but more than some rich countries.

• The level of income inequality in Canada has fluctuated over time. The period of 1980 to 2000 saw increased inequality in Canada, but since 2000 the level of inequality has stabilized and declined somewhat.

‖ The Welfare State in Canada

The welfare state in Canada consists of three huge programs (health care, social security/OAS, and child care benefits) and a number of smaller programs. Table 18-3 shows one useful way to categorize the major welfare state programs in Canada.

The spending on these welfare state programs varies and comes from different levels of government. For example, in the 2018–2019 fiscal year, the federal government of Canada spent $53.4 billion on elderly benefits such as OAS, $23.9 billion on family allowance/children's benefits, and $18.9 billion on Employment Insurance benefits. In addition, the federal government transfers to other levels of government reached $75.9 billion in the same fiscal year. Pension benefits payments from the CPP/QPP reached $62 billion in the 2018–2019 fiscal year. Last, but not least, the largest component in Canada's welfare state program is the provision of health care services:

TABLE 18-3 Major Welfare State Programs in Canada

	Monetary transfers	In-kind
Means-tested	Social services National Child Benefit Supplement (NCBS) Old Age Security (OAS) Canada Child Benefit (CCB)	Affordable housing Provincial drug plans (for low-income families)
Not means-tested	Canada Pension Plan/Québec Pension Plan (CPP/QPP) Employment Insurance (EI)	Health care

doctors, hospitals, prescription medicine, and other specialized services, with a total cost in 2019 of $264 billion (shared by all levels of government). The federal government provided $52.7 billion in 2018–2019 through the Canada Health and Social Transfer to lower levels of government to assist with the provision of health care and other social services by these governments. Table 18-3 distinguishes between programs that are **means-tested** and those that are not. In means-tested programs, benefits are available only to families or individuals whose income and/or wealth falls below some minimum. Basically, means-tested programs are social welfare programs designed to help only those with low incomes. By contrast, non-means-tested programs provide their benefits to everyone, although, as we'll see, they tend in practice to reduce income inequality.

Table 18-3 also distinguishes between programs that provide monetary transfers that beneficiaries can spend as they choose and those that provide **in-kind benefits,** which are given in the form of goods or services rather than money. The largest in-kind benefits are dominated by federal, provincial, and territorial spending on health care. We'll discuss health care in the next section of this chapter. For now, let's examine the other major programs.

Means-Tested Programs

When people speak of welfare, they are often referring to monetary aid to poor families. The main source of such monetary aid in Canada is social services. Social services programs include social assistance, workers' compensation benefits, veterans' benefits, and other social services. These programs are exclusively for low-income families. Some means-tested programs, such as GIS, CCB, and affordable housing are designated for specific groups of the population.

Old Age Security or OAS is a major part of Canada's public pension system. It has two parts: the OAS pension, which is a monthly payment to Canadians who are age 65 or above, and the OAS benefits (GIS, Allowance, and Allowance for the Survivor, which are additional payments to low-income seniors). At the time of writing, the monthly OAS pension payment was $613.53. Although the OAS pension was originally designed to be paid to all seniors, it now has a clawback feature. This essentially makes it a means-tested program. The clawback raises the marginal effective tax rate by 15 percentage points so that the maximum income to receive the OAS pension in 2020 was $128,137.

Economists use the term **negative income tax** for a program that supplements the earnings of low-income working families. While several countries do have a negative income tax program, Canada does not, though support for the idea is growing across the political spectrum. In the United States, the program is known as the

A **means-tested** program is a program available only to individuals or families whose incomes fall below a certain level.

An **in-kind benefit** is a benefit given in the form of goods or services.

A **negative income tax** is a program that supplements the income of low-income working families.

Earned Income Tax Credit (EITC). The EITC provides additional income to millions of American workers. Under the EITC program, only workers who earn income are eligible for it; over a specific range of incomes, the more a worker earns, the higher the EITC. That is, the EITC acts as a negative income tax for low-wage workers.

Non-Means-Tested Programs

Non-means-tested programs are available to individuals and families regardless of income. The largest non-means-tested program in Canada is the provision of health care, which will be discussed in detail in the latter part of this chapter. CPP/QPP, a major component of the country's public retirement income system, is also a significant non-means-tested program.

The CPP was established in 1965 by the Pearson government with the goal of providing financial security in the case of retirement, disability, or death. Québec is the only province to have opted out of the CPP and instead has its own public pension (QPP). CPP/QPP was made mandatory to force workers to save some of their current income for retirement. The goal is to overcome the shortsightedness of workers, especially younger Canadians, who do not save enough money to support themselves after retirement.

CPP/QPP initially had a "pay-as-you-go" structure, similar to how the OAS works. However, in 1997 an agreement among the federal, provincial, and territorial governments raised CPP contributions for both employers and employees and lowered future payouts to ensure CPP/QPP was partially funded and sustainable for at least the next half century. Once CPP/QPP contributors reach the age of 65, they can receive their full (earned) pension. In this way, CPP/QPP is a savings program, unlike OAS, which is financed out of current tax revenue with the aim of bringing the income of elderly Canadians above a threshold income.

Prime Minister Lester B. Pearson introduced the Canada Pension Plan (CPP) in 1965.

CP Photo/Lynn Ball

Like CPP/QPP, the provision of free (and mandatory) education up to Grade 12 in Canada also helps to alleviate the problem of shortsightedness—in this case, underinvesting in education. As mentioned previously, education plays an important role in an individual's financial well-being. Education not only helps raise people's standard of living—on average the poor tend to have lower levels of education—but higher average levels of education in a country tend to result in fewer social problems and improved health outcomes. Although education can have high returns, households have an incentive to underinvest in it because it takes a long time to see the benefits (see Chapter 16 for the external benefits of education). To reduce the problem of underinvestment in education and to encourage the accumulation of human capital, all levels of government in Canada cooperate to provide free education at elementary and secondary levels and subsidize post-secondary education. The governments are, in effect, making education less expensive to encourage (or force) more people to get educated.

Employment insurance, or EI, although normally a smaller portion of government transfers than social pensions, is another key social insurance program. EI provides qualifying workers who lose their jobs with up to 55% of their insured income up to a yearly maximum insurable amount—$54,200 as of January 2020—for 14 to 45 weeks, depending on the unemployment rate in the region. (In response to the recession of 2008–2009, the federal government temporarily increased the maximum length by five weeks.) In Canada, both employers and employees are required to pay a payroll tax that finances the operation of EI programs. In 2020, the maximum annual employee premium was $853.36, while employers were required to pay 1.4 times their employees' contributions.

In light of the outbreak of coronavirus pandemic, the federal government rolled out the Canada Emergency Response Benefit (CERB) as a supplementary, temporary income support program for laid-off workers. At the time of writing, the CERB provides $500 per week for up to 24 weeks or until October 3, 2020, whichever comes first.

The Effects of the Welfare State on Poverty and Inequality

Because the people who receive government transfers tend to be different from those who are taxed to pay for those transfers, the welfare state in Canada has the effect of redistributing income from some people to others. Each year Statistics Canada computes the amount and share of government transfers provided to the Canadians.

Table 18-4 shows the average total income, average government transfers received, and average income tax paid by different types of economic families in 2018. It is not surprising that there is an inverse relationship between average income earned and average government transfers received. Regarding the family types, families with higher income will be less reliant on government assistance, so the amount of government transfers received falls.

TABLE 18-4 Taxes and Transfers by Economic Family Types, 2018

Economic family type	Average total income	Average government transfers	Average income tax
All Canadians	$89,900	$11,600	$14,800
Economic families	116,400	13,800	19,400
Elderly families	88,200	28,400	12,500
Non-elderly families	123,700	10,000	21,200
Unattached individuals	43,800	7,900	6,800
Unattached elderly persons	41,600	18,000	5,300
Unattached non-elderly persons	44,800	3,500	7,400

Data from: Statistics Canada.

According to Table 18-4, the amount of transfers received as a fraction of total income is higher for seniors. Families with breadwinners aged 65 or above found that government transfers received reached 32% of their income in 2018, while transfers received by unattached seniors was equal to 43% of their income. Similarly, taxes as a share of income were also lower for seniors (about 14% for senior families and 13% for unattached seniors). This shows that the design of the welfare state programs and tax system in Canada is aimed at helping the low-income groups.

ECONOMICS >> *in Action*
Welfare State Programs and Poverty Rates in the Great Recession, 2008–2009

In 2008, Canada entered a deep economic downturn. At that time, it was considered the worst recession the nation had experienced since the 1930s, and the unemployment rate shot up significantly in a short period of time. Recovery started in 2010, and it was not until 2017 that the country's unemployment rate returned to the pre-Great Recession level.

Given that, you might have expected to see a sharp rise in poverty; the official poverty rate did in fact move up, as you can see in Figure 18-4. But while the Great Recession and its aftermath certainly hurt many Canadian families, the country never seemed as desperate as it did during the Great Depression, or even during the previous recessions in the early 1980s and early 1990s. But why?

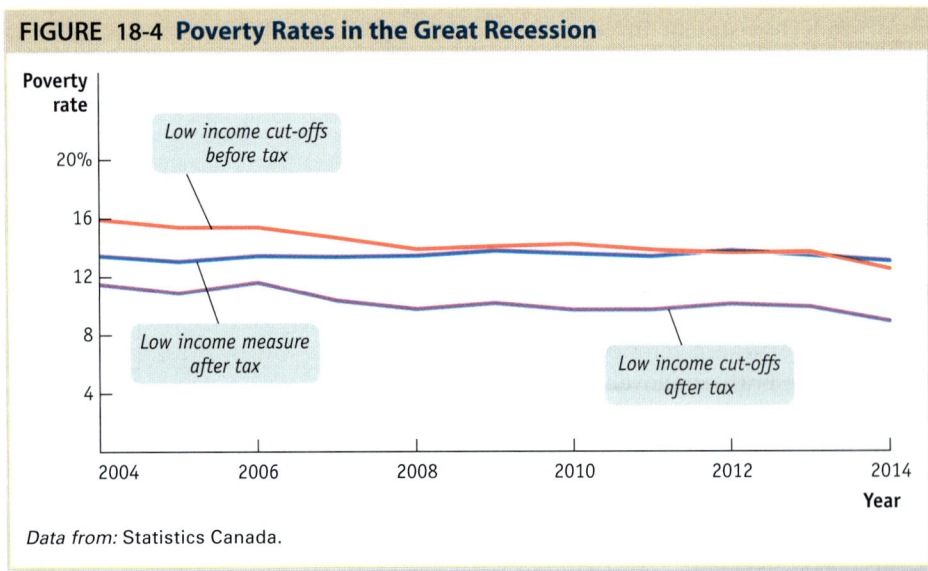

FIGURE 18-4 Poverty Rates in the Great Recession

Data from: Statistics Canada.

The main answer, it turns out, was the welfare state programs, which automatically expanded during the slump and were further reinforced by legislation that temporarily expanded EI and other forms of aid. Figure 18-4 shows the percentage of persons in poverty using different measures for poverty between 2004 and 2014. The figure shows that while the percentage of Canadians living in poverty rose a little bit in 2009, poverty levels remained relatively stable during the period of 2008–2010, an indication that the provision of welfare programs might help limit the rise in poverty.

>> Check Your Understanding 18-2

Solutions appear at back of book.

1. Explain how the negative income tax avoids the disincentive to work that characterizes social welfare programs that simply give benefits based on low income.
2. According to Table 18-4, what effect does the Canadian welfare state have on the overall poverty rate?

‖ The Economics of Health Care

A large part of the welfare state in Canada and in other wealthy countries is devoted to paying for health care. In most wealthy countries, the government pays between 70% and 80% of all medical costs for its citizens and permanent residents. In Canada, the public sector picks up 70% of all health care costs—slightly below the OECD average of about 73%—although it is more like 77% when the impact of the tax system is taken into account. The private sector, which covers the remaining 30% of costs in Canada, plays a much larger role in the U.S. health care system, paying 56% of all medical costs.

Figure 18-5 shows who paid for Canadian health care in 2019. Only 14.4% of health care spending was expenses "out of pocket"—that is, paid directly by individuals. Most health care spending, 70%, was paid for by the public sector—provincial and territorial governments covered 65.3% of all health care costs, and the other 5.1% came from the federal government, municipal governments, and social security spending. Private health insurance covered 12.3% of all health care spending, often for things such as drug and vision care coverage. The final 2.9% of all health care spending is a category called non-consumption. This refers to a mixed bag of private spending on things such as hospital non-patient revenue, capital spending for privately owned facilities, and health research.

Insurance of some form or another paid for the majority of all Canadian health care costs. To understand why, we need to examine the special economics of health care.

The Need for Health Insurance

In 2019, Canadian personal health care expenses were about $7,068 per person—11.6% of GDP (above the OECD average of 8.8% of GDP, but well below the United States at 16.9% of GDP). This did not, however, mean that the typical Canadian spent $7,068 on medical treatment. In fact, in any given year, half the population incurs only minor medical expenses. But a small percentage of the population faces huge medical bills, with 10% of the population typically accounting for almost two-thirds of medical costs.

>> **Quick Review**

• **Means-tested** programs are designed to reduce poverty, but non-means-tested programs do so as well. Programs are classified according to whether they provide monetary or **in-kind benefits.**

• A **negative income tax** is a program that supplements the earnings of low-income working families. Though several countries use a negative income tax program, Canada does not.

• Health care, the largest program in the Canadian welfare state, is a non-means-tested program that provides health care services to all Canadians (independent of their income). EI is also a key social insurance program that is not means-tested.

• Overall, the Canadian welfare state is redistributive. It increases the share of income going to the poorest 80%, while reducing the share going to the richest 20%.

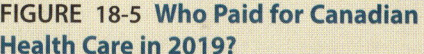

FIGURE 18-5 Who Paid for Canadian Health Care in 2019?

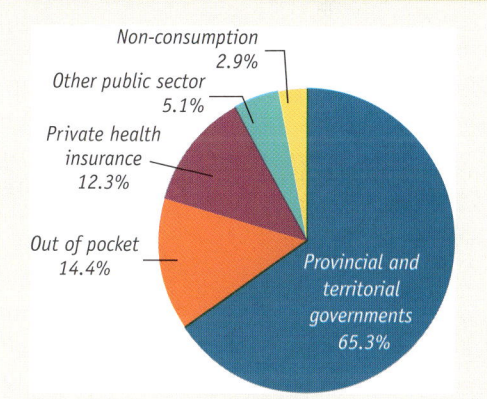

Non-consumption 2.9%
Other public sector 5.1%
Private health insurance 12.3%
Out of pocket 14.4%
Provincial and territorial governments 65.3%

In Canada in 2019, insurance paid for about 82.7% of health care costs: the sum of 12.3% (private insurance), 65.3% (provincial and territorial governments), and part of the 5.1% (other public sector—mainly spending by social security funds such as workers compensation).

Data from: Canadian Institute for Health Information, National Health Expenditure Trends, 1975 to 2019.

Under **private health insurance,** each member of a large pool of individuals pays a fixed amount annually to a private company that agrees to pay most of the medical expenses of the pool's members.

Is it possible to predict who will have high medical costs? To a limited extent, yes: there are broad patterns to illness. For example, the elderly are more likely to need expensive surgery and/or drugs than the young. But the fact is that anyone can suddenly find themself needing very expensive medical treatment, costing many thousands of dollars in a very short time—far beyond what most families can easily afford. Yet nobody wants to be unable to afford (and obtain) such treatment if it becomes necessary.

Private Health Insurance   Market economies have an answer to this problem: health insurance. Under **private health insurance,** each member of a large pool of individuals agrees to pay a fixed amount annually (called a *premium*) into a common fund (or *pool*) that is managed by a private company, which then pays most of the medical expenses of the pool's members. Although members must pay fees even in years in which they don't have large medical expenses, they benefit from the reduction in risk: if they do turn out to have high medical costs, the pool will take care of those expenses.

There are, however, inherent problems with the market for private health insurance. These problems arise from the fact that medical expenses, although basically unpredictable, aren't *completely* unpredictable. That is, people often have some idea whether or not they are likely to face large medical bills over the next few years. This creates a serious problem for private health insurance companies.

Suppose that an insurance company offers a "one-size-fits-all" health care policy, under which customers pay an annual premium equal to the average Canadian's annual medical expenses, plus a bit more to cover the company's operating expenses and a normal rate of profit. In return, the insurance company pays the policyholder's medical bills, whatever they are.

If all potential customers had an equal risk of incurring high medical expenses for the year, this might be a workable business proposition. In reality, however, people often have very different risks of facing high medical expenses—and, crucially, they often know this ahead of time. This reality would quickly undermine any attempt by an insurance company to offer one-size-fits-all health insurance. The policy would be a bad deal for healthy people, who don't face a significant risk of high medical bills: on average, they would pay much more in insurance premiums than the cost of their actual medical bills. But it would be a very good deal for people with chronic, costly conditions, who would on average pay less in premiums than the cost of their care.

As a result, some healthy people are likely to take their chances and go without insurance. This would make the insurance company's average customer less healthy than the average Canadian. This raises the medical bills the company will have to pay and raises the company's costs per customer. That is, the insurance company would face a problem called *adverse selection*, which is discussed in detail in Chapter 20. Because of adverse selection, a company that offers health insurance to everyone at a price reflecting average medical costs of the general population, and that gives people the freedom to decline coverage, would find itself losing a lot of money.

The insurance company could respond by charging more—raising its premium to reflect the higher-than-average medical bills of its customers. But this would drive off even more healthy people, leaving the company with an even sicker, higher-cost clientele, forcing it to raise the premium even more, driving off even more healthy people, and so on. This phenomenon is known as the *adverse selection death spiral*, which ultimately leads the health insurance company to fail.

This description of the problems with health insurance might lead you to believe that private health insurance can't work. In fact, however, most working Canadians do have some private health insurance that supplements the public coverage available to all. Insurance companies are able, to some extent, to overcome the problem of adverse selection two ways: by carefully *screening* people who apply for coverage and through employment-based health insurance. With screening (which we'll learn more about in Chapter 20), people who are likely to have high medical expenses are charged higher-than-average premiums—or in many cases, refused coverage entirely. The next section explains how employment-based health insurance, a unique feature of the Canadian workplace, also allows private health insurance to work.

A **single-payer system** is a health care system in which the government is the principal payer of medical bills funded through taxes.

Employment-Based Health Insurance For the most part, insurance companies overcome adverse selection by selling insurance indirectly, to peoples' employers rather than to individuals. The big advantage of *employment-based health insurance*—insurance that a company provides to its employees—is that these employees are likely to contain a representative mix of healthy and less healthy people, rather than a selected group of people who want insurance because they expect to pay high medical bills. This is especially true if the employer is a large company with thousands or tens of thousands of workers. Employers require their employees to participate in the company health insurance plan because allowing employees to opt out (which healthier ones will be tempted to do) raises the cost of providing insurance for everyone else.

There's another reason employment-based insurance is widespread in Canada: it gets special, favourable tax treatment. Workers pay taxes on their paycheques, but workers who receive health insurance from their employers don't pay taxes on the value of the benefit. Also, employers' contributions to these health insurance plans are not a taxable benefit for employees, but are a tax-deductible expense for the employer. So employment-based health insurance is, in effect, subsidized by the Canadian tax system. Economists estimate the value of this subsidy at about $5 billion each year.

In spite of this subsidy, however, many working Canadians don't receive employment-based health insurance. Those who aren't covered include most older Canadians (because relatively few employers offer workers insurance that continues after they retire), the many workers whose employers don't offer coverage (especially part-time workers), and the unemployed.

Government Health Insurance

Canada operates a publicly funded, privately provided, universal, comprehensive, accessible and portable, single-payer, provincially administered national health care system. Let's examine each of these facets in more detail.

Under public health insurance, sometimes called publicly funded health insurance, each member of the public (citizens and permanent residents) qualifies for free access to certain health care services, which are paid for by the government. Canada's public health care system is a **single-payer system** with the government acting as the single insurer and paying the entire cost of all medically insured health care services. Although the public does not directly face any payment, this health care spending is financed through taxes, in some cases including special levies geared toward collecting funding specifically for health care.

Canada's health care system is administered by the provinces and territories according to the constitution. Nevertheless, the federal government plays a key role in the public provision of health care: it sends transfer payments to provinces to help cover health care costs. The *Canada Health Act*, which was unanimously enacted by Parliament in 1984, established five national principles as to how the provision of public health care should operate (otherwise federal transfer payments may be withheld). As described by Parliament these five national principles are:

- *Universality*, meaning the public health care insurance must be provided to all Canadians.
- *Comprehensiveness*, meaning that all medically necessary hospital and doctor services are covered by public health insurance.

- *Accessibility*, meaning that financial or other barriers to the provision of publicly funded health services are discouraged, so that health services are available to all Canadians when they need them.

- *Portability*, meaning that all Canadians are covered under public health care insurance, even when they travel internationally or move within Canada.

- *Public administration*, which requires provincial and territorial health care insurance plans be managed by a public agency on a not-for-profit basis.

According to the federal government, there are two overarching objectives of federal health care policy: (1) to ensure that every Canadian has *timely* access to all medically necessary health services *regardless* of their ability to pay for those services; and (2) to ensure that *no* Canadian suffers *undue* financial hardship as a result of having to pay health care bills.

While publicly funded, Canada's health care is largely provided by private doctors and not-for-profit private hospitals. Provinces and territories determine lists of insured medical services provided by physicians and hospitals and negotiate with the providers of these services to set fee schedules. Should doctors or hospitals attempt to charge additional fees for insured services (sometimes called "user charges," "co-payments," or "extra-billing"), the federal government reserves the right to reduce transfer payments to their jurisdiction by an offsetting amount. This in essence makes such additional user fees illegal and keeps the system a single-payer model free and accessible to all. The public administration of the system helps keep total costs down, which allows for the affordable provision of good quality health care.

For decades, Canada's health care was privately funded, resulting in access to care based on ability to pay. But in 1947, Saskatchewan introduced Canada's first publicly funded health insurance plan covering hospital services. In 1956, the federal government offered to share the costs with any province setting up a provincially funded health insurance plan. By 1961, all provinces and territories had signed agreements with the federal government and had set up provincial health insurance plans covering hospital care that qualified for federal cost sharing. The public health care system has since evolved into a provincial or territorial provision of many doctor and hospital health care services to all Canadians, plus a prescription drug benefit. These drug benefit plans are generally targeted to seniors, recipients of social assistance, and individuals with illnesses or conditions that are associated with high drug costs. All other Canadians have to pay for prescription drugs either out of their own pockets or via private supplemental health insurance. The same goes for any non-insured health care services or medication.

Health Care in Other Countries

Health care is one area where Canada is very different from the United States. In fact, when it comes to health care, the United States is very different from most other wealthy countries in three distinct ways. First, the United States relies much more on private health insurance than any other wealthy country does. Second, it spends much more on health care per person. Third, it's the only wealthy nation where large numbers of people lack health insurance.

The U.S. government runs three health insurance programs: Medicare, Medicaid, and military health care. Medicare covers hospitalizations and some other medical costs. It is financed by payroll taxes and is available to all Americans age 65 and older, regardless of their income and wealth. Medicaid is a means-tested program for low-income Americans, paid for with federal and state government revenues. Millions of Americans receive health insurance as a consequence of military service. Unlike Medicare and Medicaid, which pay medical bills but don't deliver health care directly, the Veterans Health Administration runs hospitals and clinics throughout the United States, in a similar system to the British National Health Service.

Table 18-5 shows the breakdown of health insurance coverage across the U.S. population in 2018. A majority of Americans—more than 178 million people—received health insurance through their employers. The majority of those without private insurance was covered by Medicare and Medicaid. (The numbers in Table 18-5 don't add up because some people have more than one form of coverage. For example, many recipients of Medicare also have supplemental coverage either through Medicaid or private policies.)

So the U.S. health care system offers a mix of private insurance, mainly from employers, and public insurance of various forms. Most Americans have health insurance either from private insurance companies or through various forms of government insurance. However, in 2012, before the implementation of the Affordable Care Act (ACA or "ObamaCare"), almost 48 million Americans, 15.4% of the population, had no health insurance at all. At the time of writing, President Donald J. Trump and his administration are rolling out changes to the ACA and aiming to repeal it.

Table 18-6 compares four wealthy countries: Canada, France, Britain, and the United States. The United States is the only one of the four countries that relies on private health insurance to cover most people. As a result, it is the only one in which private spending on health care is (slightly) larger than public spending on health care.

As previously mentioned, Canadian doctors are generally not employed directly by the government, and hospitals, although they are not-for-profit, are usually privately run. The British system is extended to everyone: a government agency, the British National Health Service, directly employs health care workers and runs hospitals and clinics that are available free of charge to the public. France is somewhere in between the Canadian and British systems. In France, the government acts as a single-payer, providing health insurance to everyone, and French citizens can receive treatment from private doctors and hospitals; but they also have the choice of receiving care from a sizable health care system run directly by the French government.

All three non-U.S. systems provide health insurance to all of their citizens; yet all three spend much less on health care per person than the United States. Many Americans assume this must mean that foreign health care is inferior in quality. But many health care experts disagree with the claim. As they point out, Britain, Canada, and France generally match or exceed the United States in terms of many measures of health care provision, such as the number of doctors, nurses, and hospital beds per 100,000 people. It's true that U.S. medical care includes more advanced technology in some areas and many more expensive surgical procedures. U.S. patients also have shorter waiting times for elective surgery than patients in Canada or Britain. France, however, also has very short waiting times.

TABLE 18-5 Number of Americans Covered by Health Insurance, 2018 (millions)

Covered by private health insurance	**217.8**
Employment-based	178.4
Direct purchase	34.9
Covered by government insurance	**111.3**
Medicaid	57.7
Medicare	57.8
Military health care	11.4
Not covered	**27.5**

Data from: U.S. Census Bureau.

TABLE 18-6 Health Care Systems in Advanced Countries, 2018

	Government share of health care spending	Health care spending per capita (C$, purchasing power parity)	Life expectancy (total population at birth, years)	Infant mortality (deaths per 1,000 live births)
Canada	69.7%	$6,448	82.8	4.30
France	83.4	6,436	82.6	3.40
Britain	77.1	5,275	81.4	3.64
United States	40.4	13,722	78.5	5.60

Data from: OECD, World Bank, and Canadian Institute for Health Information.

Surveys of patients seem to suggest that there are no significant differences in the quality of care received by patients in Canada, Europe, and the United States. And as Table 18-6 shows, the United States does considerably worse than other advanced countries in terms of basic measures such as life expectancy and infant mortality, although their poor performance on these measures may have causes other than the quality of medical care—notably, relatively high levels of poverty and income inequality in the United States.

So why does the United States spend so much more on health care than other wealthy countries do? Some of the disparity is the result of higher doctors' salaries, but most studies suggest that this is a secondary factor. Another possibility is that Americans are getting better care than their counterparts abroad, but in ways that don't show up either surveys of patient experiences or statistics on health performance.

However, the most likely explanation is that the U.S. system suffers from serious inefficiencies that other countries manage to avoid. Critics of the U.S. system emphasize the system's reliance on private insurance companies, which expend resources on such activities as marketing and trying to identify and weed out high-risk patients, leading to high operating costs. On average, the operating costs of private health insurers eat up 14% of the premiums clients pay, leaving only 86% to spend on providing health care.

By contrast, U.S. Medicare spends only 3% of its funds on operating costs, leaving 97% to spend on health care. In Canada, administration accounted for only 1.8% of public health insurance spending in 2019. A study by the McKinsey Global Institute found that the United States was spending almost six times as much per person on health care administration as other wealthy countries. Americans also pay higher prices for prescription drugs—or some travel to Canada to buy lower-priced prescription medication—because in other countries government agencies bargain with pharmaceutical companies to get lower drug prices. The higher drug prices also arise from the pharmaceutical companies' need to charge higher prices to recoup the cost of developing the drugs.

Is Canadian Health Care Spending Sustainable?

The Canadian health care system is a key part of Canada's welfare state. A recent Nanos Research poll found that 94% of Canadians were in favour of preserving public health care. In fact, health care is often cited as the biggest issue for voters, beating out issues like taxes, job creation, retirement security, and the environment. But as Table 18-7 clearly shows, Canadian health care spending as a percentage of total income has been rising. Canadians are right to be concerned about whether the public health care system is sustainable. Can the system survive? In what form? And what, if anything, can Canadians do to help keep the system running?

Between 1970 and 2018, per capita (nominal) health care costs experienced a 32-fold rise in the United States and an 18-fold increase in Canada. Canada's public system experienced much smaller cost increases than the U.S. system with its dependence on for-profit health insurance and health care providers.

But you might ask if this is a fair comparison—what about other industrialized nations? As it turns out, health care costs are rising throughout the developed world. Table 18-7 shows total health care spending as a percentage of total income and the percentage growth of this amount between 1998 and 2018 for a number of major OECD countries. Canada's total health care spending, at 10.7% of total income in 2018, is by no means on the low end for these countries. But at the same time it is

TABLE 18-7 Health Expenditure (1998–2018 data unless indicated)

	Total health expenditure (percent of GDP)	Percent change of health spending
Australia	9.3%	272%
Britain	9.8	326
Canada	10.7	226
Finland	9.1	278
France	11.2	214
Germany	11.2	234
Ireland	7.1	352
Japan	10.9	304
Netherlands	9.9	239
Norway	10.2	261
Switzerland	12.2	233
United States	16.9	259

Data from: OECD Health Statistics 2019.

TABLE 18-8 Health Care Expenditure Shares, by Funder and Type, 1989 and 2019

	Public		Private		Total	
	1989	**2019**	**1989**	**2019**	**1989**	**2019**
Hospitals	48.4%	34.1%	14.1%	8.8%	39.7%	26.6%
Other institutions	9.1	11.1	9.3	10.5	9.2	10.9
Physicians	20.1	21.0	0.6	0.8	15.2	15.1
Other professionals	2.1	1.8	35.7	32.8	10.6	10.9
Drugs	4.7	8.0	30.1	32.7	11.1	15.3
Capital	4.1	3.9	2.8	2.4	3.7	3.4
Public health	4.7	7.7	0	0	3.5	5.4
Administration	2.1	1.8	4.7	5.7	2.7	2.9
Other health spending	4.8	10.8	2.9	6.3	4.3	9.5
Total	100.0	100.0	100.0	100.0	100.0	100.0
Percent of GDP	**6.3**	**8.2**	**2.1**	**3.4**	**8.4**	**11.6**

Data from: Canadian Institute for Health Information, National Health Expenditure Trends, 1975–2019.

not the highest either, nor has it grown any faster than health care costs in these other nations. According to the 2001 Romanov Commission report on the future of health care in Canada, publicly funded health care is both feasible and efficient. The much-publicized problems of Canada's health care system stem from the fact that it is chronically underfunded.

Table 18-8 attempts to address what exactly is driving health care costs up. This table compares Canadian health care spending in 1989 and 2019. It tabulates spending over major categories and shows the percentage of public, private, and total health care spending in each category. For example, in 1989, 20.1% of public health care spending went to physicians and rose slightly to 21.0% in 2019. In 1989, 0.6% of all private health care spending went to physicians and this share rose to 0.8% of all private health care spending. The table also presents the health care spending as a percentage of GDP, showing that health care costs rose from 8.4% of GDP in 1989 to 11.6% in 2019.

Interestingly, while health care costs now represent a larger share of GDP, the total share spent on hospitals has shrunk. The shares spent on doctors and other professionals have remained stable. What we see instead is that the greatest cost pressures are coming from prescription drugs (both publicly and private funded), public health, and rising administration costs in the private sector.

The reason spending on drugs rose so quickly lies in two related areas. Medical progress offers new drugs for previously untreatable conditions, though often at great expense. Also, the aging population drives up drug costs since older citizens are much more likely to need prescription drugs than younger, healthier patients. This is exactly why some have called on the federal government to take the lead in negotiating with brand name pharmaceutical companies for price concessions, either in return for longer patent protection or through the bulk buying of drugs at the national scale. If this can be achieved, the health care system costs should be more sustainable for the long run. But is this feasible and will it be enough? Sadly, there are no easy answers to these questions.

In 2014, when the health care accord that set the funding and health care service delivery agreements between the federal, provincial, and territorial governments expired, the previous (Conservative) government sought to reduce the 6% annual escalation factor built into the Canada Health Transfer (CHT) to 3%. While 6% exceeds the rate of inflation for health care spending, this reduction would have removed about $60 billion in funding over the next decade. Supporters of public not-for-profit health care were left scrambling to fight against what they saw as the next big threat to Canadian health care and another push toward the end of a single-payer system with for-profit health care. The Liberal government refused to reverse the decline and refused to negotiate with all the provinces and territories simultaneously. Instead, it chose unilateral negotiations with each. In the end, the provinces that reached agreements were assured that their federal transfers for health care would grow by a minimum of 3% per year (or the growth rate of nominal GDP if this exceeds 3%).

Unfortunately, in 2017, the Canadian and Ontario Health Coalitions noted that "Three highly credible and independent organizations—the Parliamentary Budget Office, the Conference Board of Canada, and the Financial Accountability Office of Ontario—had previously released analyses showing that in order to maintain today's basket of health care services for the next 10-years, a CHT escalator of approximately 5.2% would be required based, roughly, on a projection of 2+% increase needed to meet population growth and aging, and an additional 3% needed for inflation, income growth, and enrichment." They go on to note that over the coming decade the impact of the deals negotiated with the Liberal government would see a cumulated health care funding shortfall of $31 billion versus the amount needed to maintain existing programs and services.

ECONOMICS >> *in Action*
Tommy Douglas, the Greatest Canadian

Tommy Douglas is one the most prominent Canadians of the past century. In 1935, Douglas was elected to Parliament as a member of the Co-operative Commonwealth Federation (CCF), Canada's first national social democratic party. In 1944, Douglas's CCF won a huge majority in the Saskatchewan provincial election. So Douglas became not only the premier of Saskatchewan (a post he held for 17 years), but also leader of the first socialist government in North America. Douglas introduced many measures geared toward improving the welfare of society. Some of the most lasting measures were in the field of health care services.

Kiefer Sutherland unveils a statue of his grandfather Tommy Douglas in Weyburn, Saskatchewan.

Starting in 1944, free medical, hospital, and dental services were introduced for pensioners. Treatment of severe diseases such as cancer, tuberculosis, and sexually transmitted infections was made free for all.

In 1947, Douglas introduced a universal hospitalization insurance plan paid for by the provincial treasury, with a $5 levy per person. In 1959, Douglas announced plans to introduce Medicare: a universal, prepaid, publicly administered medical insurance plan to cover hospital and doctor's services, including preventative care. His proposal was aided by Prime Minister John Diefenbaker's 1958 promise that the federal government would pay 50% of the cost of any provincial hospital plan. In 1961, after 17 years in office, Douglas resigned from his position as premier to become the leader of the federal New Democratic Party. The next year, Saskatchewan's Medicare plan came into force on July 1, 1962. Over the next decade, all provinces adopted their own provincial plans, similar in design to Saskatchewan's Medicare, and half paid for by the federal government.

For his contributions as the father of universal health care in Canada and for his other works, Douglas was voted the greatest Canadian of all time in a CBC survey in 2004.

>> **Check Your Understanding** **18-3**
Solutions appear at back of book.

1. Jiro is an international student enrolled in a four-year degree program. He is required to enrol in a health insurance program run by his school.
   a. Explain how Jiro and his parents benefit from this health insurance program even though, given his age, it is unlikely that he will need expensive medical treatment.
   b. Explain how his school's health insurance program avoids the adverse selection death spiral.
2. According to its critics, what accounts for the higher costs of the U.S. health care system compared to those of other wealthy countries?

The Debate Over the Welfare State

The goals of the welfare state seem laudable: to help the poor, to protect against severe economic hardship, and to ensure access to essential health care. But good intentions don't always make for good policy. There is an intense debate about how large the welfare state should be, a debate that partly reflects differences in philosophy but also reflects concern about the possibly counter-productive effects on incentives of welfare state programs. Disputes about the size of the welfare state are also one of the defining issues of modern Canadian politics.

Problems with the Welfare State

There are two different arguments against the welfare state. One, which we described earlier in this chapter, is based on philosophical concerns about the proper role of government. As we learned, some political theorists believe that redistributing income is not a legitimate role of government. Rather, they believe that government's role should be limited to maintaining the rule of law, providing public goods, and managing externalities.

The more conventional argument against the welfare state involves the tradeoff between efficiency and equity. As we've learned, the *ability-to-pay-principle*—the argument that an extra dollar of income matters more to a less well-off individual than to a more well-off individual—implies that the government can help the poor at relatively little cost to the well-off. But this redistribution of income requires that high-income taxpayers pay a higher fraction of their income in taxes than those with lower incomes. This is the principle behind progressive taxation.

But this must be balanced against the efficiency costs of high marginal tax rates. Consider an extremely progressive tax system that imposes a marginal rate of 90% on very high incomes. The problem is that such a high marginal rate reduces the incentive to increase a family's income by working hard or making risky investments. As a result, an extremely progressive tax system tends to make society as a whole poorer, which could hurt even those the system was intended to benefit. That's why even economists who strongly favour progressive taxation don't support a return to the extremely progressive system that prevailed in 1948, when the top Canadian marginal income tax rate was 80%. So, the design of the tax system involves a trade-off between equity and efficiency.

A similar trade-off between equity and efficiency implies that there should be a limit to the size of the welfare state. A government that operates a large welfare state requires more revenue than one that restricts itself mainly to provision of public goods such as building highways. A large welfare state requires higher tax revenue and higher marginal tax rates than a smaller welfare state.

Table 18-9 shows "social expenditure," a measure that roughly corresponds to total welfare state spending, as a percentage of GDP in Canada, the United

TABLE 18-9 Social Expenditure and Marginal Tax Rates		
	Social expenditure in 2018 (percent of GDP)	Top marginal tax rate in 2018
Canada	17.3%	53.5%
United States	18.7	43.7
Denmark	28.0	55.9
Britain	20.6	45.0
France	31.2	55.4

Data from: OECD. Marginal tax rate is defined as a percentage of total labour costs.

States, Denmark, Britain, and France. It also compares this with an estimate of the top marginal tax rate faced by an average single wage-earner, including payroll taxes paid by employers and provincial and municipality taxes. As you can see, France's large welfare state goes along with a high marginal rate of taxation. As the upcoming Economics in Action explains, some but not all economists believe that this high rate of taxation is a major reason the Danes work substantially fewer hours per year than North Americans.

One way to hold down the costs of the welfare state is to means-test benefits: make them available only to those who need them. But means-testing benefits creates a different kind of trade-off between equity and efficiency. Consider the following example: Suppose there is some means-tested benefit, worth $2,000 per year, that is available only to families with incomes of less than $20,000 per year. Now suppose that a family currently has an income of $19,500 but that one family member is deciding whether to take a new job that will raise the family's income to $20,500. Well, taking that job will actually make the family worse off, because it will gain $1,000 in earnings but lose the $2,000 government benefit.

This feature of means-tested benefits, which makes a family worse off if it earns more is known as a *notch*. It is a well-known problem with programs that aid the poor and behaves much like a high marginal tax rate on income. Most welfare state programs are designed to avoid a notch by setting a sliding scale for benefits. With a sliding scale, benefits diminish gradually as the recipient's income rises rather than come to an abrupt end.

Even so, the combined effect of the major means-tested programs shown in Table 18-3, plus additional means-tested programs such as welfare and housing aid that are offered by provincial, territorial, and municipal governments, is to create very high effective marginal tax rates. For example, a 2013 study by the C.D. Howe Institute found that an Ontario family consisting of two adults and two children that raised its income from $40,000 a year—just above the poverty line in 2012—to $41,000 would lose $0.68 of every additional dollar of income earned to taxes and lost means-tested social benefits.

The Politics of the Welfare State

In 1791, in the early phase of the French Revolution, French citizens convened a congress, the Legislative Assembly, in which representatives were seated according to social class: the upper classes, who pretty much liked the way things were, sat on the right; commoners, who wanted big changes, sat on the left. Ever since, political commentators refer to politicians as being on the "right" (more conservative) or on the "left" (more liberal).

But what do modern politicians on the left and right disagree about? In Canada, besides concerns over the environment and globalization, they mainly disagree about the appropriate size of the welfare state. The debate over the need for a national child care program is a case in point, with support split almost entirely according to party lines—Liberals and New Democratic Party (on the left) in favour of a national program and Conservatives (on the right) opposed.

You might think that saying that political debate is really about just one thing—how big to make the welfare state—is a huge oversimplification. But anyone can see that most members of Parliament and members of the Provincial Parliament vote along party lines. Politicians on the left tend to favour a larger welfare state and those on the right to oppose it. This left–right distinction is central to today's politics. In recent decades, it has become much clearer where the members of the major federal political parties stand on the left–right spectrum.

Can economic analysis help resolve this political conflict? Only up to a point. Some of the political controversy involves differences in opinion about the trade-offs we have just discussed: if you believe that the disincentive effects of generous benefits and high taxes are very large, you will look less favourably on welfare state programs than if you believe they're fairly small. Economic analysis, by improving our knowledge of the facts, can help resolve some of these differences. Yet some of the disagreements over the welfare state are the result of a misunderstanding of economics; for example, how health insurance markets work.

To an important extent, however, differences of opinion on the welfare state reflect differences in values and philosophy. And those are differences economics can't resolve.

ECONOMICS >> *in Action*
The Not-So Melancholy Danes?

The United States has the smallest welfare state of any major advanced economy. Denmark has one of the largest. As a result, Denmark has much higher social spending than the United States as a percentage of total national income, and Danish citizens face much higher tax rates than Americans. One argument against a large welfare state is that it has negative effects on efficiency. Does Danish experience support this argument?

On the face of it, the answer would seem to be a clear yes. Table 18-10 shows that Danish GDP per capita—the total value of the economy's output, divided by the total population—is about 16% lower than GDP per capita in the United States. But is the size of the Danish welfare state responsible for that difference, and is lower Danish GDP per capita a sign of trouble?

With one of the largest welfare states in the world, Denmark guarantees health care for all its citizens.

Not necessarily. Once one looks at the sources of relatively low Danish GDP, a more nuanced picture emerges.

As a matter of basic arithmetic, GDP per capita reflects three factors:

- The fraction of the population that is employed
- How much the average worker produces in an hour
- The number of hours each worker work

TABLE 18-10 **Difference Between Denmark and the United States, in Percent (2017)**	
GDP per capita	−16%
Employed share of population	+7%
Productivity	−1%
Hours worked	−20%

Data from: Total Economy Database.

So Danes are actually slightly more likely to be employed than Americans (7% more likely) and they basically have the same productivity (1% less productive). The reason Denmark has lower GDP per capita than Americans do (16% lower) is that employed Danes work fewer hours over the course of a year (20% fewer). This in turn largely reflects deliberate policy: where Americans take fewer vacations than citizens of any other wealthy country, Danish employers are legally required to give employees 5 weeks of paid leave each year, and the country's strong union movement has in many cases negotiated additional time off.

This deliberate choice puts a different spin on Denmark's lower GDP per capita, since it's not at all clear that trading off somewhat less income for more time with one's family or other pursuits is a bad deal. For what it's worth, surveys that ask how satisfied people are with their lives rank Denmark consistently high—and consistently above the United States.

To be fair, it's not clear that every country would do as well with a huge welfare state as Denmark appears to. But in Denmark, the welfare state seems to work.

>> **Check Your Understanding** 18-4

Solutions appear at back of book.

1. Explain how each of the following policies creates a disincentive to work or undertake a risky investment.
   a. A high sales tax on consumer items
   b. The complete loss of a housing subsidy when yearly income rises above $25,000
2. Over the past 40 years, has the polarization in the Canadian Parliament increased, decreased, or stayed the same?

Welfare State Entrepreneurs

Pawel Gaul/Getty Images

"Wiggo Dalmo is a classic entrepreneurial type: the Working Class Kid Made Good." So began a profile in the January 2011 issue of *Inc.* magazine. Dalmo began as an industrial mechanic who worked for a large company, repairing mining equipment. Eventually, however, he decided to strike out on his own and start his own business. Momek, the company he founded, eventually grew into a $44 million, 150-employee operation that does a variety of contract work on oil rigs and in mines.

You can read stories like this all the time in business magazines. What was unusual about this particular article is that Dalmo and his company are Norwegian—and Norway, like other Scandinavian countries, has a very generous welfare state, supported by high levels of taxation. So what does Dalmo think of that system? He approves, saying that Norway's tax system is "good and fair," and he thinks the system is good for business. In fact, the *Inc.* article was titled, "In Norway, Start-Ups Say Ja to Socialism."

Why? After all, the financial rewards for being a successful entrepreneur are more limited in a country like Norway, with its high taxes. But there are other considerations. For example, a Canadian thinking of leaving a large company to start a new business needs to worry about whether they will be able to get supplementary health insurance, whereas a Norwegian in the same position is assured of health care regardless of employment. And the downside of failure is larger in North America, where minimal aid is offered to the unemployed.

Still, is Wiggo Dalmo an exceptional case? Table 18-11 shows the nations with the highest level of entrepreneurial activity, according to a study financed by the U.S. Small Business Administration, which tried to quantify the level of entrepreneurial activity in different nations. Canada and the United States made it into the top 10, but so did Norway. And the list also includes Denmark, New Zealand, Sweden, and Australia—all nations with high taxes and extensive social insurance programs.

The moral is that when comparing how business-friendly different welfare state systems really are, you have to think a bit past the obvious question of the level of taxes.

TABLE 18-11 The Top 10 Entrepreneurial Countries	
Rank	Country
1	Denmark
2	New Zealand
3	Ireland
4	Puerto Rico
5	Sweden
6	Canada
7	Australia
8	United States
9	Norway
10	Belgium

Data from: Zoltan Acs and Laszlo Serb (2011), *The Global Entrepreneurship and Development Index 2010.*

QUESTIONS FOR THOUGHT

1. Why does Norway have to have higher taxes overall than Canada?

2. This case suggests that government-paid health care helps entrepreneurs. How does this relate to the arguments we made for social insurance in the text?

3. How would the incentives of people like Wiggo Dalmo be affected if Norwegian health care was means-tested instead of available to all?

4. Briefly explain how this case influences the care one should use when making international comparisons of competitiveness based on a single indicator such as labour costs (hourly wages) or (highest marginal) personal income tax rates.

SUMMARY

1. The **welfare state** absorbs a large share of government spending in all wealthy countries. **Government transfers** are the payments made by the government to individuals and families. **Social welfare programs** alleviate income inequality by helping those in need; **social insurance programs** alleviate economic insecurity. Welfare state programs also deliver external benefits to society through poverty reduction and improved access to health care, particularly for children.

2. The **poverty line** (or **poverty threshold**) is not officially defined in Canada. The most commonly used criteria to measure poverty in Canada are the LICOs, a relative measure. The LIM, another relative measure, and the MBM, an absolute measure, are also used to measure poverty. In Canada, the **poverty rate,** the percentage of the population with an income below the poverty threshold, fluctuates over time. There are various causes of poverty: lack of education, the legacy of discrimination, and bad luck. The consequences of poverty are particularly harmful for children, resulting in more chronic disease, lower lifetime earnings, and higher rates of criminality.

3. **Median household income,** the income of a family at the centre of the income distribution, is a better indicator of the income of the typical household than **mean household income** because it is not distorted by the inclusion of a small number of very wealthy households. The **Gini coefficient,** a number that summarizes a country's level of income inequality based on how unequally income is distributed across quintiles, is used to compare income inequality across countries.

4. Both **means-tested** and non-means-tested programs reduce poverty. The largest means-tested programs in Canada include social services, OAS, and the CCB. The major **in-kind benefits** program is health care. Some countries also have **negative income tax** programs that supplement the income of the working poor.

5. Canada's health care system is universal (a **single-payer system** paid for by provincial/territorial governments) and guarantees free access to all Canadians for all insured services.

6. Compared to other countries, the United States relies more heavily on **private health insurance** and has substantially higher health care costs per person without clearly providing better care. Throughout the developed world, health care costs are rising, largely due to advances in technology. The U.S. ACA has the objectives of reducing the number of uninsured Americans and reducing the rate of growth of U.S. health care costs. President Trump has sought to end the ACA and to replace it with a new health care law.

7. Debates over the size of the welfare state are based on philosophical and equity-versus-efficiency considerations. The equity-versus-efficiency debate arises from the fact that an extensive welfare state requires high taxes on the well-off, which can diminish society's wealth by reducing their incentive to work and make risky investments. Means-testing of benefits can reduce the cost of the welfare state but must be carefully designed to avoid reducing the incentive to work by the poor.

8. Politicians on the left tend to favour a bigger welfare state and those on the right to oppose it. This left–right distinction is central to today's politics. Canada's three major federal political parties have become more polarized in recent decades, with a much clearer distinction than in the past about where their members stand on the left–right spectrum.

KEY TERMS

Welfare state, p. 544
Government transfers, p. 544
Social welfare programs, p. 544
Social insurance programs, p. 544
Poverty line (or poverty threshold), p. 545

Poverty rate, p. 546
Mean household income, p. 549
Median household income, p. 549
Gini coefficient, p. 550
Means-tested, p. 554

In-kind benefits, p. 554
Negative income tax, p. 554
Private health insurance, p. 558
Single-payer system, p. 559

PRACTICE QUESTIONS

1. In this problem you are going to explore the trends in income inequality across countries. Go to the World Inequality Database, wid.world, and select "Country Graphs." Open up the data for Finland and the Netherlands.

   a. Compare the income shares in each country for the most recent year of data. What do you notice?

   b. How has inequality changed over time?

   c. How does the after-tax income distribution differ from the pre-tax distribution?

   d. How does the trend compare with the United States?

   e. Explore other countries in the database.

2. Using the World Inequality Database, wid.world, from the previous question, select the data for China. In the upper left corner of the page is an option to "select a subregion" or state. Select the data for Rural China and Urban China.

   a. What are the current values of the income share for the top 10%, top 1%, and bottom 50% of earners for each region?

   b. How has share of income going to the top income earners changed over time for each region?

   c. What are the likely factors that explain the increase in income going to the top of the distribution across these two regions? What factors explain the difference across these two regions today?

PROBLEMS

1. The accompanying table contains data on the Canadian economy for the years 1988 and 2018. The second column shows the poverty threshold using the low income measures. The third column shows Canada's GDP per capita, a measure of the standard of living.

Year	Poverty threshold (low income measures, 1 person, total income, 2018 constant dollars)	Real GDP per capita (2018 dollars)
1988	$18,073	$42,593
2018	24,183	59,583

Data from: Statistics Canada.

   a. By what factor has the poverty threshold increased from 1988 to 2018? That is, has it doubled, tripled, and so on?

   b. By what factor has GDP per capita (a measure of the standard of living) increased from 1988 to 2018? That is, has it doubled, tripled, and so on?

   c. What do your results tell you about how those people classified as "poor" have done economically relative to other Canadian citizens?

2. In the city of Metropolis, there are 100 residents, each of whom lives until age 75. Residents of Metropolis have the following incomes over their lifetime: Through age 14, they earn nothing. From age 15 until age 29, they earn 200 metros (the currency of Metropolis) per year. From age 30 to age 49, they earn 400 metros. From age 50 to age 64, they earn 300 metros. Finally, at age 65, they retire and are paid a pension of 100 metros per year until they die at age 75. Each year, everyone consumes whatever their income is that year (that is, there is no saving and no borrowing). Currently, 20 residents are 10 years old, 20 residents are 20 years old, 20 residents are 40 years old, 20 residents are 60 years old, and 20 residents are 70 years old.

   a. Study the income distribution among all residents of Metropolis. Split the population into quintiles according to their income. How much income does a resident in the lowest quintile have? In the second, third, fourth, and top quintiles? What share of total income of all residents goes to the residents in each quintile? Construct a table showing the share of total income that goes to each quintile. Does this income distribution show inequality?

   b. Now look only at the 20 residents of Metropolis who are currently 40 years old, and study the income

distribution among only those residents. Split those 20 residents into quintiles according to their income. How much income does a resident in the lowest quintile have? In the second, third, fourth, and top quintiles? What share of total income of all 40-year-olds goes to the residents in each quintile? Does this income distribution show inequality?

   c. What is the relevance of these examples for assessing data on the distribution of income in any country?

3. The accompanying table presents data from Statistics Canada on median and mean income of male workers for the years 1976 and 2018. The income figures are adjusted to eliminate the effect of inflation.

Year	Median income	Mean income
	(2018 dollars)	
1976	$47,300	$53,500
2018	43,100	56,500

Data from: Statistics Canada.

   a. By what percentage has median income changed over this period? By what percentage has mean income changed over this period?

   b. Between 1976 and 2018, has the income distribution become less or more unequal? Explain.

4. There are 100 households in the economy of Equalor. Initially, 99 of them have an income of $10,000 each and one household has an income of $1,010,000.

   a. What is the median income in this economy? What is the mean income?

   Through its social welfare programs, the government of Equalor now redistributes income: it takes $990,000 away from the richest household and distributes it equally among the remaining 99 households.

   b. What is the median income in this economy now? What is the mean income? Has the median income changed? Has the mean income changed? Which indicator (mean or median household income) is a better indicator of the typical Equalorian household's income? Explain.

5. The country of Marxland has the following income tax and social insurance system. Each citizen's income is taxed at an average tax rate of 100%. A social insurance system then provides transfers to each citizen

such that each citizen's after-tax income is exactly equal. That is, each citizen gets (through a government transfer payment) an equal share of the income tax revenue. What is the incentive for one individual citizen to work and earn income? What will the total tax revenue in Marxland be? What will be the after-tax income (including the transfer payment) for each citizen? Do you think such a tax system that creates perfect equality will work?

6. The tax system in Taxilvania includes a negative income tax. For all incomes below $10,000, individuals pay an income tax of 40% (that is, they receive a payment of 40% of their income). For any income above the $10,000 threshold, the tax rate on that additional income is 10%. For the first three scenarios below, calculate the amount of income tax to be paid and after-tax income.

Scenarios	
1	Lowani earns income of $8,000
2	Midram earns income of $40,000
3	Hi-Wan earns income of $100,000

a. Can you find a notch in this tax system? That is, can you find a situation where earning more pre-tax income actually results in less after-tax income?

7. In the city of Notchingham, each worker is paid a wage rate of $10 per hour. Notchingham administers its own unemployment benefit, which is structured as follows: If you are unemployed (that is, if you do not work at all), you get unemployment benefits (a transfer from the government) of $50 per day. As soon as you work for only one hour, the unemployment benefit is completely withdrawn. That is, there is a notch in the benefit system.

a. How much income does an unemployed person have per day? How much daily income does an individual who works four hours per day have? How many hours do you need to work to earn just the same as if you were unemployed?

b. Will anyone ever accept a part-time job that requires working four hours per day, rather than being unemployed?

c. Suppose that Notchingham now changes the way in which the unemployment benefit is withdrawn. For each additional dollar an individual earns, $0.50 of the unemployment benefit is withdrawn. How much daily income does an individual who works four hours per day now have? Is there an incentive now to work four hours per day rather than being unemployed?

8. In a private insurance market, there are two different kinds of people: some who are more likely to require expensive medical treatment and some who are less likely to require medical treatment and who, if they do, require less expensive treatment. One health insurance policy is offered, tailored to the average person's health care needs: the premium is equal to the average person's medical expenses (plus the insurer's expenses and normal profit).

a. Explain why such an insurance policy is unlikely to be feasible.

In an effort to avoid the adverse selection death spiral, a private health insurer offers two health insurance policies: one that is intended for those who are more likely to require expensive treatment (and therefore charges a higher premium) and one that is intended for those who are less likely to require treatment (and therefore charges a lower premium).

b. Could this system overcome the problem created by adverse selection?

c. How do provincial and territorial governments in Canada, the U.S. Veterans Health Administration, and the British National Health Service (NHS) avoid these problems?

19 Factor Markets and the Distribution of Income

THE VALUE OF A DEGREE

DOES HIGHER EDUCATION PAY? Yes, it does: in the modern economy, employers are willing to pay a premium for workers with more education. And the size of that premium has increased a lot over the last few decades. A report by Statistics Canada shows that education does pay off! Using the 2016 Census data, Statistics Canada found that the median earnings of both men and women with a bachelor's degree were higher than those with a lower level of education. Men with a bachelor's degree had median earnings of $82,082 in 2015, and they earned about 13% more than men with an apprenticeship certificate. Also these men with a four-year bachelor's degree earned about 21% and 47% more than men with a college diploma, or a high school diploma, respectively. In the same report, similarly results were found for women. Women

with a bachelor's degree had median earnings of $68,342 in 2015. Women with a bachelor's degree earned about 79%, 41%, and 58% more than women with an apprenticeship certificate, with a college diploma or with a high school diploma, respectively.

Who decided that the wages of workers with a four-year university degree would be so much more than for workers without one? The answer, of course, is that nobody decided it. Wage rates are prices, the prices of different kinds of labour; and they are decided, like other prices, by supply and demand.

Still, there is a qualitative difference between the wage rate of high school grads and the price of used textbooks: the wage rate isn't the price of a *good*, it's the price of a *factor of production*. And although markets for factors of production are in many ways similar to those for goods, there are also some important differences.

In this chapter, we examine *factor markets*, the markets in which the factors of production such as labour, land, and capital are traded. Factor markets, like markets for goods and services, play a crucial role in the economy: they allocate productive resources to producers and help ensure that those resources are used efficiently.

We begin by describing the major factors of production and the demand for factors of production, which leads to a crucial insight: the *marginal productivity theory of income distribution*. We then consider some challenges to the marginal productivity theory and examine the markets for capital and for land. The chapter concludes with a discussion of the supply of the most important factor, labour. ●

Calaimage/Sam Edwards/Getty Images

If you have doubts about completing university, consider this: not getting a university degree will cost you about half a million dollars over your lifetime.

WHAT YOU WILL LEARN

- How are resources like land, labour, **physical capital**, and **human capital** traded in factor markets, and how does this determine the **factor distribution of income**?

- What is the **marginal productivity theory of income distribution**?

- What are the sources of wage disparities, and what is the role of discrimination?

- How does market power affect labour markets?

- How do decisions about **time allocation** determine labour supply?

Physical capital—often referred to simply as *capital*—consists of manufactured productive resources such as equipment, buildings, tools, and machines.

Human capital is the improvement in labour created by education and knowledge that is embodied in the workforce.

The Economy's Factors of Production

You may recall that we have already defined a factor of production in Chapter 2 in the context of the circular-flow diagram of the economy: it is any resource that is used by firms to produce goods and services for consumption by households. Factors of production are bought and sold in *factor markets,* and the prices in factor markets are known as *factor prices.*

What are these factors of production, and why do factor prices matter?

The Factors of Production

Economists divide factors of production into four principal classes: land, labour, physical capital, and human capital. Land is a resource provided by nature; labour is the work done by human beings.

In Chapter 9, we defined *capital:* it is the value of the assets that are used by a firm in producing its output. There are two broad types of capital. **Physical capital**—often referred to simply as *capital*—consists of manufactured resources such as equipment, buildings, tools, and machines.

In the modern economy, **human capital,** the improvement in labour created by education and knowledge, and embodied in the workforce, is at least equally significant. The importance of human capital has increased greatly because of the progress of technology, which has made a high level of technical knowledge essential to many jobs—one cause of the increased premium paid for workers with advanced degrees.

Why Factor Prices Matter: The Allocation of Resources

Factor markets and factor prices play a key role in one of the most important processes that must take place in any economy: the allocation of resources among producers. As we will see, it is through the allocation of resources that an economy decides what and how much to produce.

To see how factor markets operate in the allocation of an economy's resources, consider Alberta. Starting in 2015, the world oil price dropped significantly, and this had an adverse impact on Alberta as many oil production facilities shut down because they were no longer profitable to operate. The level of employment in the mining, quarrying, and oil and gas extraction industry in the province dropped from its all time high of 175,300 in 2014 to 141,700 in 2019. What caused the drop in the level of employment in the oil and gas extraction industry in Alberta? The factor market: with the decline in oil prices, the demand for labour had softened a lot and put downward pressure on workers' wages. In this sense, factor markets are similar to goods markets, which allocate goods among consumers. But there are two features that make factor markets special. The first is that demand in a factor market is called *derived demand;* that is, demand for the factor is derived from a firm's output choice. This is different from demand in a market for goods. The second feature is that factor markets are where most of us get the largest shares of our income (government transfers being the next largest source of income in the economy).

Factor Incomes and the Distribution of Income

Most Canadian families get most of their income in the form of wages and salaries—that is, they get their income by selling their own labour. Some people, however, get most of their income from physical capital: when you own stock in a company, what you really own is a share of that company's physical capital. And some people get much of their income from rents earned on land they own.

As a consequence, then, the prices of factors of production have a major impact on how the economic pie is sliced among different groups. For example, a higher wage rate, other things equal, means that a larger proportion of the economy's total income goes to people who derive their income from labour, and less goes to those who derive their income from capital or land. Economists refer to how the economic pie is sliced as the *distribution of income*. Specifically, factor prices determine the **factor distribution of income**—how the total income of the economy is divided among labour, land, and capital.

As the following Economics in Action explains, the factor distribution of income in Canada has been relatively stable over the past few decades. In other times and places, however, large changes have taken place in the factor distribution. One notable example: during the Industrial Revolution, the share of total income earned by English landowners fell sharply, while the share earned by English capital owners rose. As explained in the For Inquiring Minds, this shift had a profound effect on society.

> The **factor distribution of income** is the division of total income among labour, land, and capital.

ECONOMICS >> *in Action*
The Factor Distribution of Income in Canada

When we talk about the factor distribution of income, what are we talking about in practice?

In Canada, as in all advanced economies, payments to labour account for most of the economy's total income. Figure 19-1 shows the factor distribution of income in Canada in 2019: in that year, 57.1% of total income in the economy took the form of *compensation of employees*—a number that includes both wages and benefits such as social insurance. This number was slightly lower than the average between 1981 and 2019 (57.6%) and was higher than the average between 2000 and 2016 (56.3%).

However, measured wages and benefits don't capture the full income of "labour" because a significant fraction of total income in Canada is "proprietors' income"—the earnings of people who own their own businesses. The category gross mixed income includes gross operating income from unincorporated businesses, farms, and rentals.

But much of what we call compensation of employees is really a return on human capital. A surgeon isn't just supplying the services of a pair of ordinary hands (at least the patient hopes not!): that individual is also supplying the result of many years and hundreds of thousands of dollars invested in training and experience. We can't directly measure what fraction of wages is really a payment for education and training, but many economists believe that human capital has become *the* most important factor of production in modern economies.

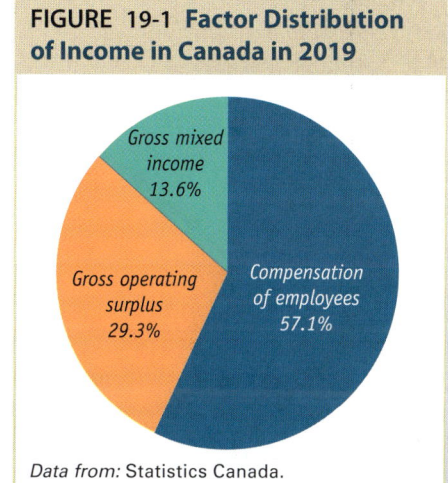

FIGURE 19-1 Factor Distribution of Income in Canada in 2019

Gross mixed income 13.6%

Gross operating surplus 29.3%

Compensation of employees 57.1%

Data from: Statistics Canada.

>> Check Your Understanding 19-1

Solutions appear at back of book.

1. Suppose that the government places price controls on the market for university professors, imposing a wage that is lower than the market wage. Describe the effect of this policy on the production of university degrees. What sectors of the economy do you think will be adversely affected by this policy? What sectors of the economy might benefit?

‖ Marginal Productivity and Factor Demand

All economic decisions are based on comparing costs to benefits—and usually about comparing marginal costs to marginal benefits. This goes both for a consumer, deciding whether to undertake another year of schooling, and for a producer, deciding whether to hire an additional worker.

Although there are some important exceptions, most factor markets in the modern Canadian economy are perfectly competitive, meaning that buyers and sellers of a given factor are price-takers. And in a competitive labour market, it's clear how to define an employer's marginal cost of a worker: it is simply the worker's wage rate. But what is the benefit of that worker? To answer that question, we return to a concept first introduced in Chapter 11: the *production function*, which relates inputs to output. And as in Chapter 12, we will assume throughout this chapter that all producers are price-takers in their output markets—that is, they operate in a perfectly competitive industry.

Value of the Marginal Product

Figure 19-2 reproduces Figures 11-1 and 11-2, which showed the production function for wheat on Riley and Tyler's farm. Panel (a) uses the total product curve to show how total wheat production depends on the number of workers employed on the farm; panel (b) shows how the *marginal product* of labour, the increase in output from employing one more worker, depends on the number of

FIGURE 19-2 The Production Function and Marginal Product of Labour Curve for Riley and Tyler's Farm

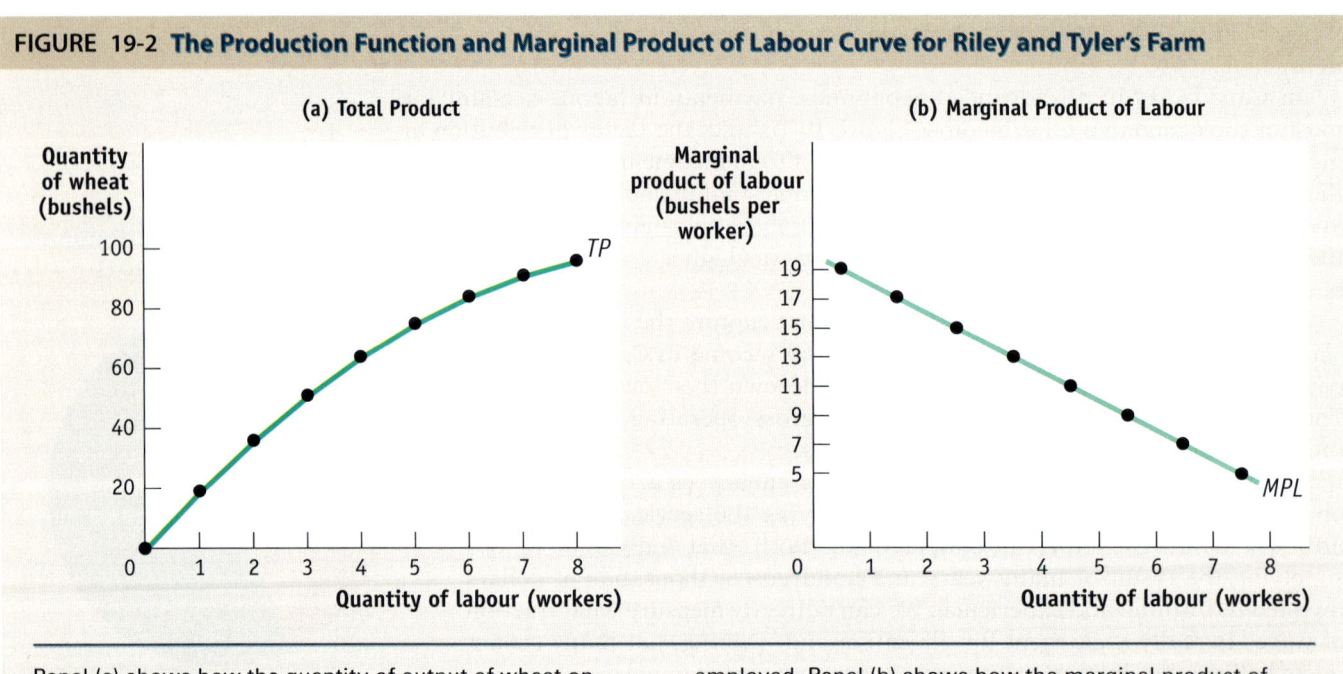

Panel (a) shows how the quantity of output of wheat on Riley and Tyler's farm depends on the number of workers

employed. Panel (b) shows how the marginal product of labour depends on the number of workers employed.

workers employed. Table 19-1, which reproduces the table in Figure 11-1, shows the numbers behind the figure.

Assume that Riley and Tyler want to maximize their profit, that workers must be paid $200 each, and that wheat sells for $20 per bushel. What is their optimal number of workers? That is, how many workers should they employ to maximize profit?

Riley and Tyler use marginal analysis to answer this question in several steps (which we showed in Chapters 11 and 12).

- In Chapter 11, we used information from the producer's production function to derive the firm's total cost and its marginal cost.

- In Chapter 12, we derived the *price-taking firm's optimal output rule:* a price-taking firm's profit is maximized by producing the quantity of output at which the marginal cost of the last unit produced is equal to the market price.

- Having determined the optimal quantity of output, we can go back to the production function and find the optimal number of workers—it is simply the number of workers needed to produce the optimal quantity of output.

TABLE 19-1 Employment and Output for Riley and Tyler's Farm

Quantity of labour L (workers)	Quantity of wheat q (bushels)	Marginal product of labour $MPL = \dfrac{\Delta q}{\Delta L}$ (bushels per worker)
0	0	
		19
1	19	
		17
2	36	
		15
3	51	
		13
4	64	
		11
5	75	
		9
6	84	
		7
7	91	
		5
8	96	

There is, however, another way to use marginal analysis to find the number of workers that maximizes a producer's profit. We can go directly to the question of what level of employment maximizes profit. This alternative approach is equivalent to the approach we outlined in the preceding list—it's just a different way of looking at the same thing. But it gives us more insight into the demand for factors as opposed to the supply of goods.

To see how this alternative approach works, let's suppose that Riley and Tyler are considering whether or not to employ an additional worker. At each level of employment, they would compare the cost to the benefit of hiring. The increase in *cost* from employing that additional worker is the wage rate, W. The *benefit* to Riley and Tyler from employing that extra worker is the value of the extra output that worker can produce. What is this value? It is the marginal product of labour, MPL, multiplied by the price per unit of output, P. This amount—the extra value of output that is generated by employing one more unit of labour—is known as the **value of the marginal product** of labour, or $VMPL$:

(19-1) Value of the marginal product of labour $= VMPL = P \times MPL$

So should Riley and Tyler hire that extra worker? The answer is yes if the value of the extra output is more than the cost of the worker—that is, if $VMPL > W$. Otherwise they shouldn't hire that worker.

So the decision to hire labour is a marginal decision, in which the marginal benefit to the producer from hiring an additional worker ($VMPL$) should be compared with the marginal cost to the producer (W). And as with any marginal decision, the optimal choice is where marginal benefit is just equal to marginal cost. That is, to maximize profit Riley and Tyler will employ workers up to the point at which, for the last worker employed:

(19-2) $VMPL = W$ at the profit-maximizing level of employment

This rule doesn't apply only to labour; it applies to any factor of production. The value of the marginal product of any factor is its marginal product times the price of the good it produces. Applying this rule to all factors of production gives

The **value of the marginal product** of a factor is the value of the additional output generated by employing one more unit of that factor.

The **price-taking producer's optimal employment rule** says that a price-taking producer's profit is maximized by employing each factor of production up to the level at which the value of the marginal product is equal to the factor's price.

The **value of the marginal product curve** of a factor shows how the value of the marginal product of that factor depends on the quantity of the factor employed.

us the **price-taking producer's optimal employment rule:** *a profit-maximizing price-taking producer employs each factor of production up to the level at which the value of the marginal product is equal to that factor's price.*

It's important to realize that this rule doesn't conflict with our analysis in Chapters 11 and 12. There we saw that a profit-maximizing producer of a good chooses the level of output at which the price of that good is equal to the marginal cost of production. It's just a different way of looking at the same rule. If the level of output is chosen so that price equals marginal cost, then it is also true that at that output level the value of the marginal product of labour will equal the wage rate.

Now let's look more closely at why choosing the level of employment at which the value of the marginal product of the last worker employed is equal to the wage rate is the right method, and how it helps us understand factor demand.

Value of the Marginal Product and Factor Demand

Table 19-2 calculates the value of the marginal product of labour on Riley and Tyler's farm, on the assumption that the price of wheat is $20 per bushel. In Figure 19-3, the horizontal axis shows the number of workers employed; the vertical axis measures the value of the marginal product of labour *and* the wage rate. The curve shown is the **value of the marginal product curve** of labour. This curve, like the marginal product of labour curve, slopes downward because of diminishing returns to labour in production. That is, the value of the marginal product of each worker is less than that of the preceding worker, because the marginal product of each worker is less than that of the preceding worker.

We have just seen that to maximize profit, Riley and Tyler must hire workers up to the point at which the wage rate is equal to the value of the marginal product of the last worker employed. Let's use the example to see how this principle really works.

Assume that Riley and Tyler currently employ 3 workers and that workers must be paid the market wage rate of $200. Should they employ an additional worker?

Looking at Table 19-2, we see that if Riley and Tyler currently employ 3 workers, the value of the marginal product of an additional worker is $260. So if they employ an additional worker, they will increase the value of their production by $260 but increase their cost by only $200, yielding an increased profit of $60. In fact, a producer can always increase total profit by employing one more unit of a factor of production as long as the value of the marginal product produced by that unit exceeds its factor price.

Alternatively, suppose that Riley and Tyler employ 8 workers. By reducing the number of workers to 7, they can save $200 in wages. In addition, the value of the marginal product of the last one, the 8th worker, was only $100. So, by reducing employment by one worker, they can increase profit by $200 – $100 = $100. In other words, a producer can always increase total profit by employing one less unit of a factor of production as long as the value of the marginal product produced by that unit is less than the factor price.

Using this method, we can see from Table 19-2 that the profit-maximizing employment level is 5 workers given a wage rate of $200. The value of the marginal product of the 5th worker is $220, so adding the 5th worker results in $20 of additional profit. But Riley and Tyler should not hire more than 5 workers: the value of the marginal product of the 6th worker is only $180, $20 less than the cost

TABLE 19-2 Value of the Marginal Product of Labour for Riley and Tyler's Farm

Quantity of labour L (workers)	Marginal product of labour MPL (bushels per worker)	Value of the marginal product of labour $VMPL = P \times MPL$
0		
	19	$380
1		
	17	340
2		
	15	300
3		
	13	260
4		
	11	220
5		
	9	180
6		
	7	140
7		
	5	100
8		

FIGURE 19-3 The Value of the Marginal Product Curve

This curve shows how the value of the marginal product of labour depends on the number of workers employed. It slopes downward because of diminishing returns to labour in production. To maximize profit, Riley and Tyler choose the level of employment at which the value of the marginal product of labour is equal to the market wage rate. For example, at a wage rate of $200 the profit-maximizing level of employment is 5 workers, shown by point A. The value of the marginal product curve of a factor is the producer's individual demand curve for that factor.

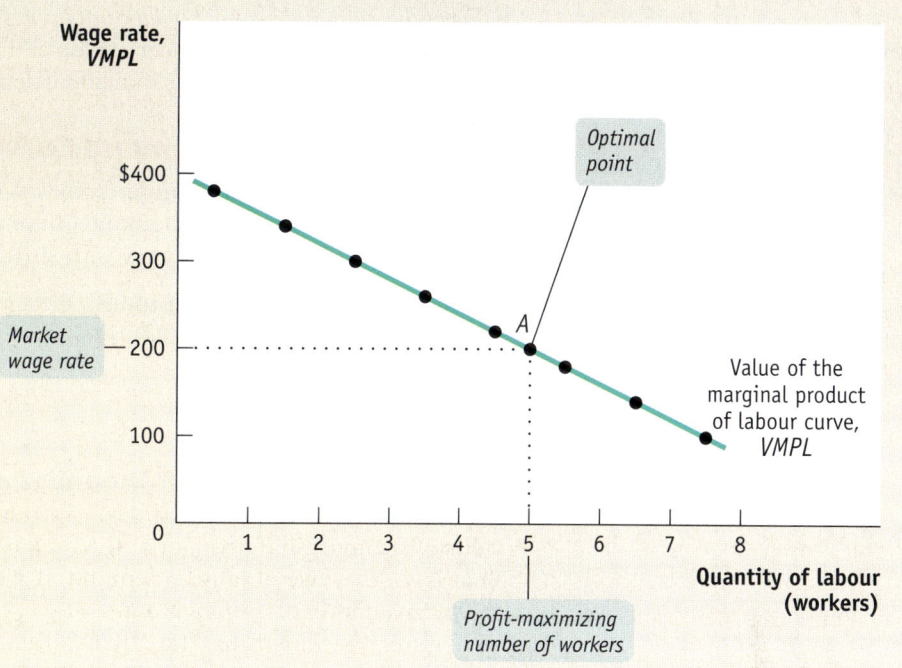

of that worker. So, to maximize total profit, Riley and Tyler should employ workers up to, but not beyond the point at which the value of the marginal product of the last worker employed is equal to the wage rate.

Now look again at the value of the marginal product curve in Figure 19-3. To determine the profit-maximizing level of employment, we set the value of the marginal product of labour equal to the price of labour—a wage rate of $200 per worker. This means that the profit-maximizing level of employment is at point A, corresponding to an employment level of 5 workers. If the wage rate were higher than $200, we would simply move up the curve and reduce the number of workers employed; if the wage rate were lower than $200, we would move down the curve and increase the number of workers employed.

In this example, Riley and Tyler have a small farm in which the potential employment level varies from 0 to 8 workers, and they hire workers up to the point at which the value of the marginal product of the last worker is greater than or equal to the wage rate. (To go beyond this point and hire workers for which the wage exceeds the value of the marginal product would reduce Riley and Tyler's profit.)

Suppose, however, that the producer in question is large and has the potential of hiring many workers. When there are many employees, the value of the marginal product of labour falls only slightly when an additional worker is employed. As a result, there will be some worker whose value of the marginal product almost exactly equals the wage rate. (In keeping with the Riley and Tyler example, this means that some worker generates a value of the marginal product of approximately $200.) In this case, the producer maximizes profit by choosing a level of employment at which the value of the marginal product of the last worker hired *equals* (to a very good approximation) the wage rate.

Firms continue to hire workers until the value of the marginal product of the last worker hired equals the wage rate.

In the interest of simplicity, we will assume from now on that producers use this rule to determine the profit-maximizing level of employment. *This means that the value of the marginal product of labour curve is the individual producer's labour demand curve.* And, in general, a producer's value of the marginal product curve for any factor of production is that producer's individual demand curve for that factor of production.

Shifts of the Factor Demand Curve

As in the case of ordinary demand curves, it is important to distinguish between movements along the factor demand curve and shifts of the factor demand curve. What causes factor demand curves to shift? There are three main causes:

1. Changes in the price of output
2. Changes in the supply of other factors
3. Changes in technology

Let's look at each in detail.

1. Changes in the Price of Output Remember that factor demand is derived demand: if the price of a good that is produced with a factor changes, so will the value of the marginal product of the factor that is employed to produce that good. That is, in the case of labour demand, if P changes, $VMPL = P \times MPL$ will change at any given level of employment.

Figure 19-4 illustrates the effects of changes in the price of wheat, assuming that $200 is the current wage rate. Panel (a) shows the effect of an *increase* in the price of wheat. This shifts the value of the marginal product of labour curve upward, because $VMPL$ rises at any given level of employment. If the wage rate remains unchanged at $200, the optimal point moves from point A to point B: the profit-maximizing level of employment rises.

Panel (b) shows the effect of a *decrease* in the price of wheat. This shifts the value of the marginal product of labour curve downward. If the wage rate

FIGURE 19-4 Shifts of the Value of the Marginal Product Curve

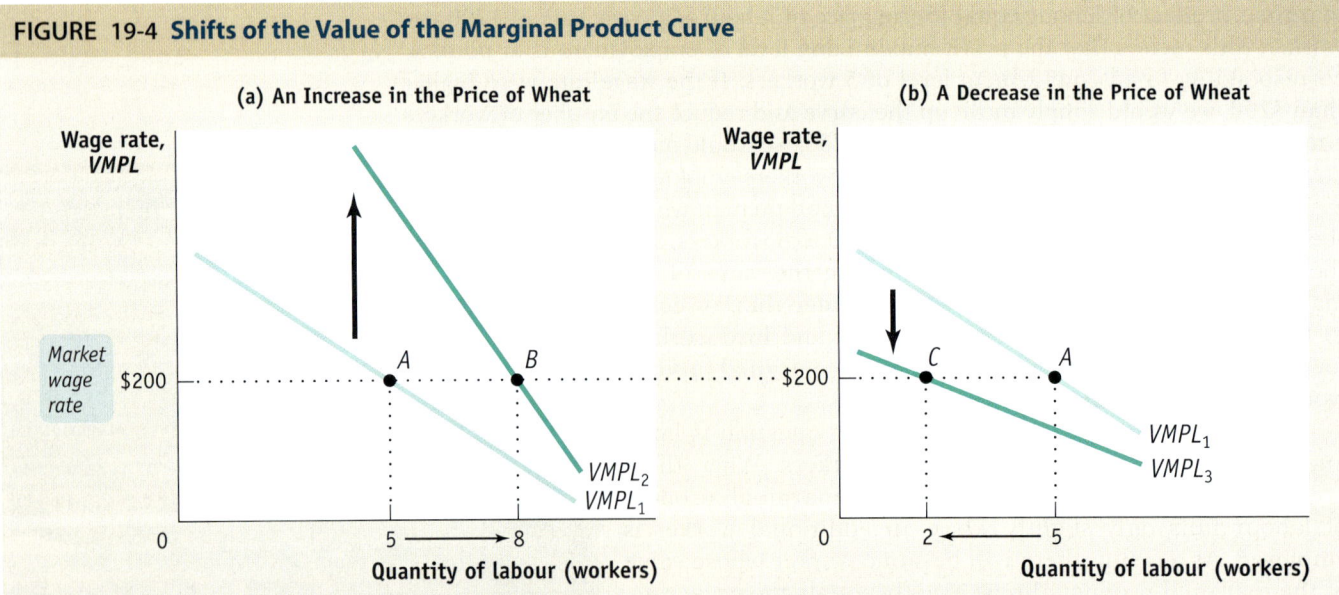

Panel (a) shows the effect of an increase in the price of wheat on Riley and Tyler's demand for labour. The value of the marginal product of labour curve shifts upward, from $VMPL_1$ to $VMPL_2$. If the market wage rate remains at $200, profit-maximizing employment rises from 5 workers to 8 workers, shown by the movement from point A to point B.

Panel (b) shows the effect of a decrease in the price of wheat. The value of the marginal product of labour curve shifts downward, from $VMPL_1$ to $VMPL_3$. At the market wage rate of $200, profit-maximizing employment falls from 5 workers to 2 workers, shown by the movement from point A to point C.

remains unchanged at $200, the optimal point moves from point *A* to point *C:* the profit-maximizing level of employment falls.

2. Changes in the Supply of Other Factors Suppose that Riley and Tyler acquire more land to cultivate—say, by clearing a woodland on their property. Each worker now produces more wheat because each one has more land to work with. As a result, the marginal product of labour on the farm rises at any given level of employment. This has the same effect as an increase in the price of wheat, which is illustrated in panel (a) of Figure 19-4: the value of the marginal product of labour curve shifts upward, and at any given wage rate the profit-maximizing level of employment rises.

In contrast, suppose Riley and Tyler cultivate less land. This leads to a fall in the marginal product of labour at any given employment level. Each worker produces less wheat because each has less land to work with. As a result, the value of the marginal product of labour curve shifts downward—as in panel (b) of Figure 19-4—and the profit-maximizing level of employment falls.

3. Changes in Technology In general, the effect of technological progress on the demand for any given factor can go either way: improved technology can either increase or reduce the demand for a given factor of production. And, frequently, a decrease in one factor leads to an increase in another.

How can technological progress reduce factor demand? Consider horses, which were once an important factor of production. The development of substitutes for horse power, such as cars and tractors, greatly reduced the demand for horses. At the same time, however, demand increased for other factors such as drivers, manufacturers, and skilled auto mechanics.

In today's economy, the expanding use of automation and robots as a substitute for human labour has some analysts predicting that the factor demand for human workers will decrease in certain industries in the coming decades. Robots can collect goods from warehouse shelves and lay bricks at construction sites, eliminating the need for humans to perform these tasks. And, as you might predict, at the same time, the demand for other factors such as software developers and robotics engineers will increase.

The usual effect of technological progress is to increase the demand for a given factor by raising its productivity. So despite persistent fears that machinery and automation would reduce the demand for labour, over the long term the Canadian economy has seen both large wage increases and large increases in employment. That's because technological progress has raised labour productivity, and as a result increased the demand for labour.

The Marginal Productivity Theory of Income Distribution

We've now seen that each perfectly competitive producer in a perfectly competitive factor market maximizes profit by hiring labour up to the point at which its value of the marginal product is equal to its price—in the case of labour, to the point where $VMPL = W$. What does this tell us about labour's share in the factor distribution of income? To answer that question, we need to examine equilibrium in the labour market. From that vantage point we will go on to learn about the markets for land and capital and about how they also influence the factor distribution of income.

Let's start by assuming that the labour market is in equilibrium: at the current market wage rate, the number of workers that producers want to employ is equal to the number of workers willing to work. Thus, all employers pay the *same* wage rate, and *each* employer, whatever they are producing, employs labour up to the point at which the value of the marginal product of the last worker hired is equal to the market wage rate.

This situation is illustrated in Figure 19-5, which shows the value of the marginal product curves of two producers—Farmer Garcia, who produces wheat, and Farmer Freeman, who produces corn. Despite the fact that they produce

FIGURE 19-5 All Producers Face the Same Wage Rate

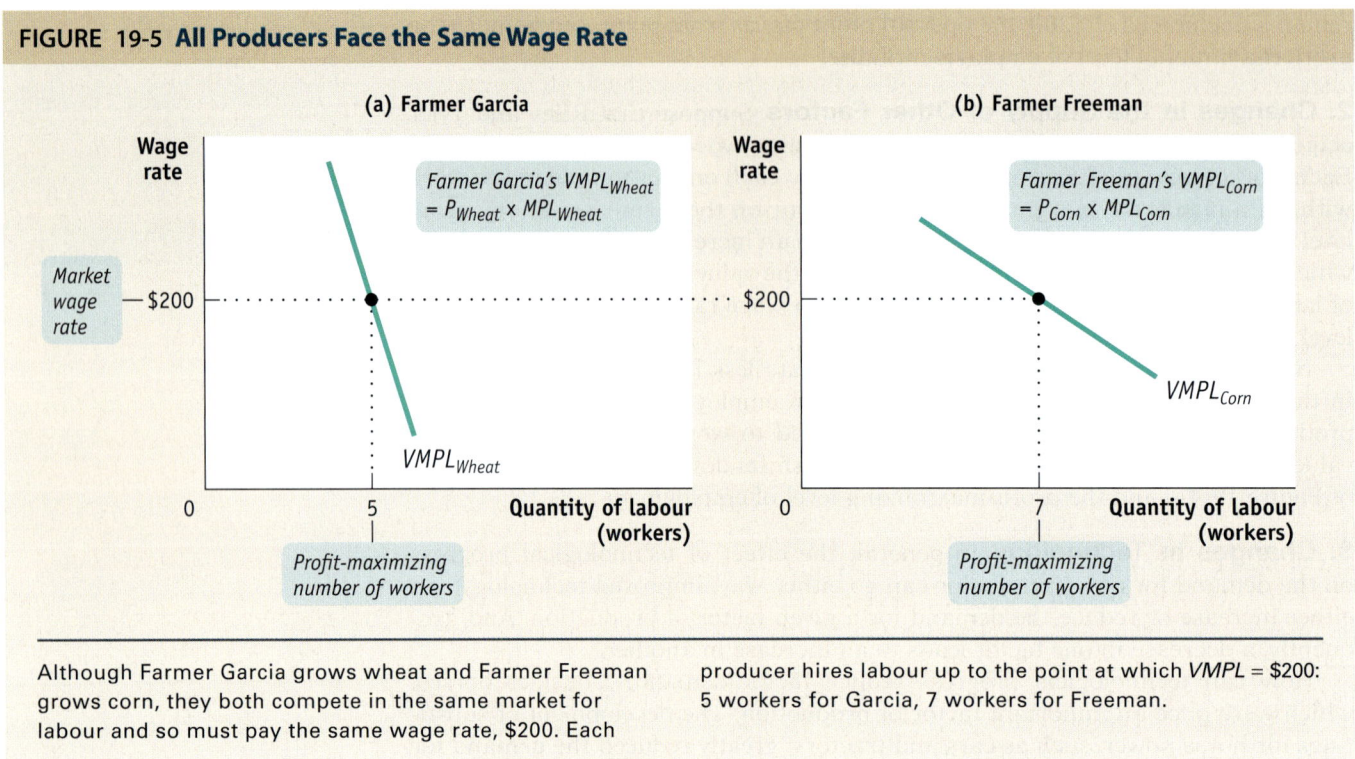

Although Farmer Garcia grows wheat and Farmer Freeman grows corn, they both compete in the same market for labour and so must pay the same wage rate, $200. Each producer hires labour up to the point at which *VMPL* = $200: 5 workers for Garcia, 7 workers for Freeman.

different products, they compete for the same workers and so must pay the same wage rate, $200. When both farmers maximize profit, both hire labour up to the point at which its value of the marginal product is equal to the wage rate. In the figure, this corresponds to employment of 5 workers by Garcia and 7 by Freeman.

Figure 19-6 illustrates the labour market as a whole. The *market labour demand curve*, like the market demand curve for a good (shown in Figure 3-5),

FIGURE 19-6 Equilibrium in the Labour Market

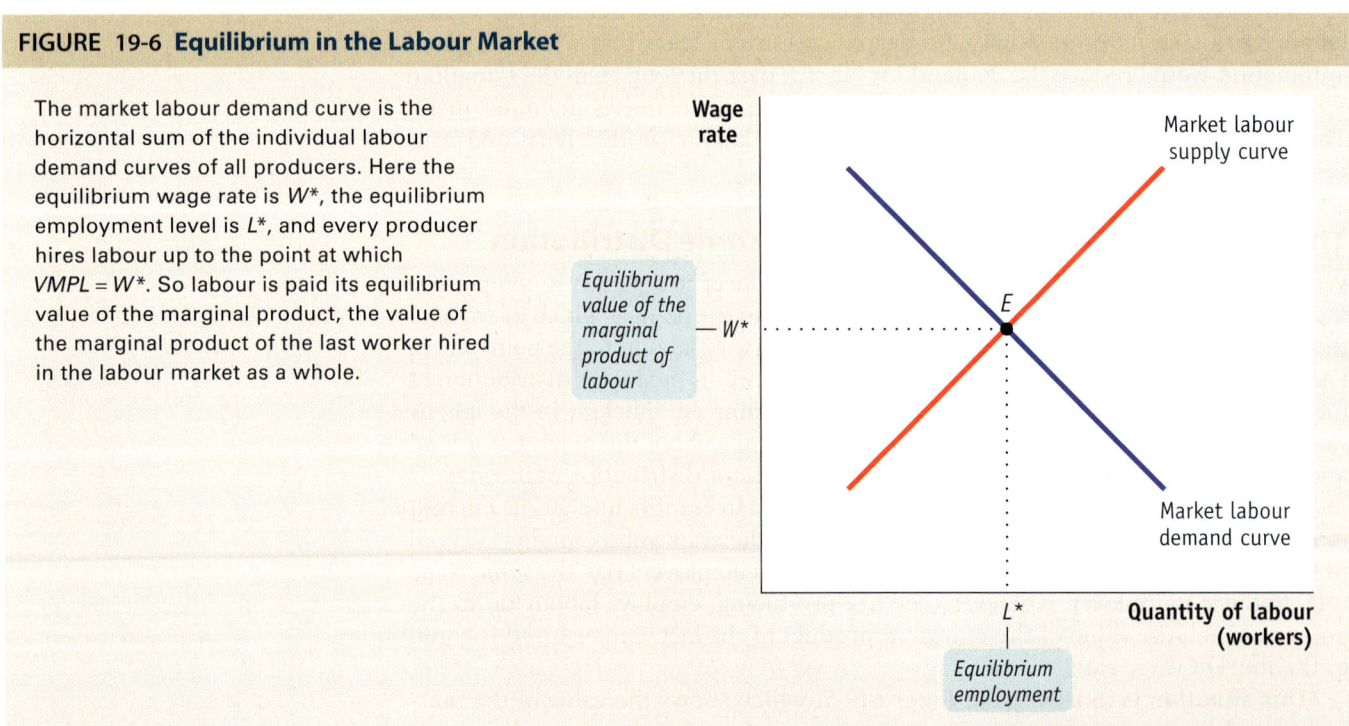

The market labour demand curve is the horizontal sum of the individual labour demand curves of all producers. Here the equilibrium wage rate is *W**, the equilibrium employment level is *L**, and every producer hires labour up to the point at which *VMPL* = *W**. So labour is paid its equilibrium value of the marginal product, the value of the marginal product of the last worker hired in the labour market as a whole.

is the horizontal sum of all the individual labour demand curves of all the producers who hire labour. And recall that each producer's individual labour demand curve is the same as their value of the marginal product of labour curve. For now, let's simply assume an upward-sloping labour supply curve; we'll discuss labour supply later in this chapter. Then the equilibrium wage rate is the wage rate at which the quantity of labour supplied is equal to the quantity of labour demanded. In Figure 19-6, this leads to an equilibrium wage rate of W^* and the corresponding equilibrium employment level of L^*. (The equilibrium wage rate is also known as the market wage rate.)

And as we showed in the examples of the farms of Riley and Tyler and of Farmer Garcia and Farmer Freeman (where the equilibrium wage rate is $200), each farm hires labour up to the point at which the value of the marginal product of labour is equal to the equilibrium wage rate. Therefore, in equilibrium, the value of the marginal product of labour is the same for all employers. So the equilibrium (or market) wage rate is equal to the **equilibrium value of the marginal product** of labour—the additional value produced by the last unit of labour employed in the labour market as a whole. It doesn't matter where that additional unit is employed, since equilibrium *VMPL* is the same for all producers.

What we have just learned, then, is that the market wage rate is equal to the equilibrium value of the marginal product of labour. And the same is true of each factor of production: in a perfectly competitive market economy, the market price of each factor is equal to its equilibrium value of the marginal product. Let's examine the markets for land and (physical) capital now. (From this point on, we'll refer to physical capital as simply *capital*.)

The Markets for Land and Capital

If we maintain the assumption that the markets for goods and services are perfectly competitive, the result that we derived for the labour market also applies to other factors of production. Suppose, for example, that a farmer is considering whether to rent an additional hectare of land for the next year. The farmer will compare the cost of renting that hectare with the value of the additional output generated by employing an additional hectare—the value of the marginal product of a hectare of land. To maximize profit, the farmer must employ land up to the point at which the value of the marginal product of a hectare of land is equal to the rental rate per hectare.

What if the farmer already owns the land? We already saw the answer in Chapter 9, which dealt with economic decisions: even if you own land, there is an implicit cost—the opportunity cost—of using it for a given activity, because it could be used for something else, such as renting it out to other farmers at the market *rental rate*. So a profit-maximizing producer employs additional hectares of land up to the point at which the cost of the last hectare employed, explicit or implicit, is equal to the value of the marginal product of that hectare.

The same is true for capital. The explicit or implicit cost of using a unit of land or capital for a set period of time is called its **rental rate.** In general, a unit of land or capital is employed up to the point at which that unit's value of the marginal product is equal to its rental rate over that time period. How are the rental rates for land and capital determined? By the equilibria in the land market and the capital market, of course. Figure 19-7 illustrates those outcomes.

Panel (a) shows the equilibrium in the market for land. Summing over the individual demand curves for land of all producers gives us the market demand curve for land. Due to diminishing returns, the demand curve slopes downward, like the demand curve for labour. As we have drawn it, the supply curve of land is relatively steep and therefore relatively inelastic. This reflects the fact that finding new supplies of land for production is typically difficult and expensive—for example, creating new farmland through expensive irrigation. The equilibrium rental rate for land, R^*_{Land}, and the equilibrium quantity of land employed in production, Q^*_{Land}, are given by the intersection of the two curves.

The **equilibrium value of the marginal product** of a factor is the additional value produced by the last unit of that factor employed in the factor market as a whole.

The **rental rate** of either land or capital is the cost, explicit or implicit, of using a unit of that asset for a given period of time.

FIGURE 19-7 Equilibria in the Land and Capital Markets

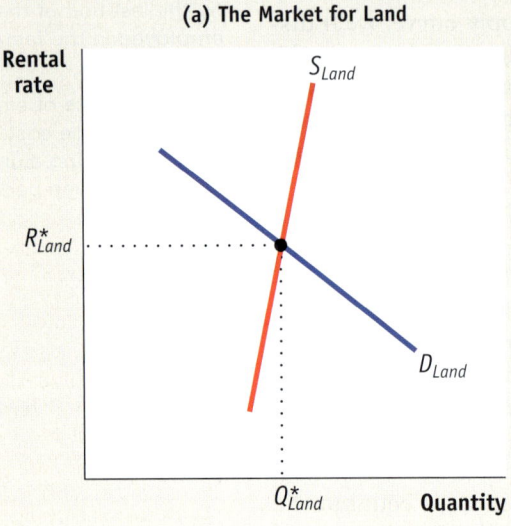

(a) The Market for Land

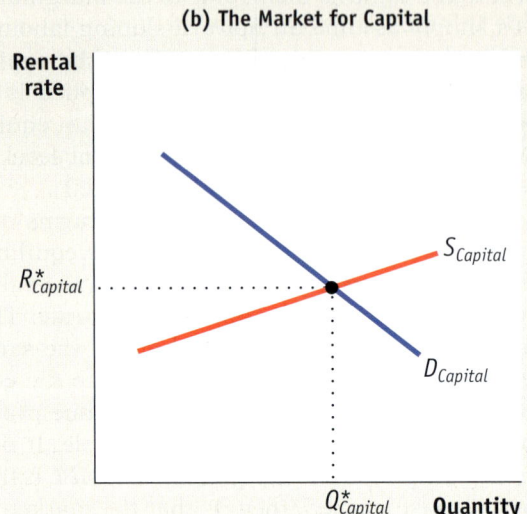

(b) The Market for Capital

Panel (a) illustrates equilibrium in the market for land; panel (b) illustrates equilibrium in the market for capital. The supply curve for land is relatively steep, reflecting the high cost of increasing the quantity of productive land. The supply curve for capital, in contrast, is relatively flat, due to the relatively high responsiveness of savings to changes in the rental rate for capital. The equilibrium rental rates for land and capital, as well as the equilibrium quantities transacted, are given by the intersections of the demand and supply curves. In a competitive land market, each unit of land will be paid the equilibrium value of the marginal product of land, R^*_{Land}. Likewise, in a competitive capital market, each unit of capital will be paid the equilibrium value of the marginal product of capital, $R^*_{Capital}$.

Panel (b) shows the equilibrium in the market for capital. In contrast to the supply curve for land, the supply curve for capital is relatively elastic. That's because the supply of capital is relatively responsive to price: capital construction is paid for with funds that come from the savings of financial investors, and the amount of savings that financial investors make available is relatively responsive to the rental rate for capital. The equilibrium rental rate for capital, $R^*_{Capital}$, and the equilibrium quantity of capital employed in production, $Q^*_{Capital}$, are given by the intersection of the two curves.

The Marginal Productivity Theory of Income Distribution

So we have learned that when the markets for goods and services and the factor markets are perfectly competitive, a factor of production will be employed up to the point at which its value of the marginal product is equal to its market equilibrium price. That is, it will be paid its equilibrium value of the marginal product.

What does this say about the factor distribution of income? It leads us to the **marginal productivity theory of income distribution,** which says that each factor is paid the value of the output generated by the last unit of that factor employed in the factor market as a whole—its equilibrium value of the marginal product.

To understand why the marginal productivity theory of income distribution is important, look back at Figure 19-1, which shows the factor distribution of income in Canada, and ask yourself this question: who or what decided that labour would get 57.1% of total Canadian income? Why not 90% or 30%?

The answer, according to the marginal productivity theory of income distribution, is that the division of income among the economy's factors of production isn't arbitrary: it is determined by each factor's marginal productivity at the economy's equilibrium. The wage rate earned by *all* workers in the economy is equal to

According to the **marginal productivity theory of income distribution,** every factor of production is paid its equilibrium value of the marginal product.

the increase in the value of output generated by the last worker employed in the economy-wide labour market.

So far we have treated factor markets as if every unit of each factor were identical. That is, as if all land were identical, all labour were identical, and all capital were identical. But in reality, factors differ considerably with respect to productivity. For example, workers have different skills and abilities.

Rather than thinking of one land market for all land resources in an economy, and similarly one capital market and one labour market, think, instead, of different markets for different types of land, physical capital, human capital, and labour. For example, the market for computer programmers is different from the market for pastry chefs.

When we consider that there are separate factor markets for different types of factors, we can still apply the marginal productivity of income distribution. That is, when the labour market for software programmers is in equilibrium, the theory says that the wage rate earned by all software programmers is equal to the market's equilibrium value of the marginal product—the value of the marginal product of the last computer programmer hired in that market.

The marginal productivity theory of income distribution rests on the assumption that factor markets as well as goods and services markets are perfectly competitive. Yet, as we discuss in the next section, many markets don't satisfy that criterion. So it is useful as a benchmark, but not as an exact representation of the real world.

And it's important to note that to the extent the marginal productivity theory of income distribution works, it's an explanation of what markets do, not a statement about what is fair or right. That is, it doesn't tell us what the income distribution "ought" to be. Rather, the marginal productivity theory of income distribution can serve as a benchmark to help society decide what is the right trade-off between equity and efficiency.

ECONOMICS >> *in Action*
Help Wanted!

Canada's manufacturing sector, led by the changes in technology and the drive to exploit our vast fossil fuel reserves, has created labour shortages in many occupations. Highly skilled machinists working to manufacture machinery for the resource extraction sector are better paid compared to many other workers in the country, earning an average of nearly $60,600 in 2018, excluding benefits. Like most skilled labour in Canada, these machinists are very productive: according to Statistics Canada, in 2018, the average worker employed in the mining and oil and gas field machinery manufacturing sector generated approximately $189,100 in value added.

Thus, there is an $128,500 difference between the salary paid to these skilled workers and the value added they generate. Does this mean that the marginal productivity theory of income distribution doesn't hold? Doesn't the theory imply that machinists should be paid $189,100, the average value added that each one generates?

The marginal productivity theory of income distribution holds for skilled machinists.

The answer is no, for two reasons. First, the $189,100 figure is averaged over *all Canadian machinists currently employed in this sector*. The theory says that machinists will be paid the value of the marginal product of the *last machinist hired*, and due to diminishing returns to labour, that value will be lower than the average over all machinists currently employed. Second, a worker's equilibrium wage rate includes other costs, such as employee benefits, that have to be added to the $60,600 salary. The marginal productivity theory of income distribution says that workers are paid a wage rate, *including all benefits*, equal to the value of the marginal product.

All of these additional costs are covered in Canada's machinery manufacturing sector. The machinists have good benefits and job security, which add to their salaries. Including these benefits, machinists' total compensation will be equal to the value of the marginal product of the last machinist employed.

There is yet another factor that explains the $128,500 gap: there are not enough machinists at the current wage rate. According to the government of Canada, the employment outlook for machinists in 2019–2021 remains fair in some provinces (Alberta, Manitoba, Ontario, Québec, and Nova Scotia) and good in other provinces (British Columbia, Saskatchewan, New Brunswick, and Prince Edward Island), indicating there is demand for the position.

Why don't these companies just raise their wages in order to attract more skilled machinists and technicians? The problem is that the work they do is so specialized that it is hard to hire from the outside, even when these companies raise wages as an inducement. To address this problem, the 2017 federal budget allocated an additional $1.8 billion in spending over the next six years to help ensure more Canadians get the skills training they need to get new and better jobs. In the end, it does appear that the marginal productivity theory of income distribution holds.

>> Check Your Understanding 19-2

Solutions appear at back of book.

1. In the following cases, state the direction of the shift of the demand curve for labour and what will happen, other things equal, to the market equilibrium wage rate and quantity of labour employed as a result.
   a. Service industries, such as retailing and banking, experience an increase in demand. These industries use relatively more labour than nonservice industries.
   b. Due to overfishing, there is a fall in the amount of fish caught per day by commercial fishers; this decrease affects their demand for workers.
2. Explain the following statement: "When producers in different industries all compete for the same workers, then the value of the marginal product of the last worker hired will be equal across all producers regardless of whether they are in different industries."

Is the Marginal Productivity Theory of Income Distribution Really True?

Although the marginal productivity theory of income distribution is a well-established part of economic theory, closely linked to the analysis of markets in general, it is a source of some controversy. There are two main objections to it.

First, in the real world we see large disparities in income between factors of production that, in the eyes of some observers, should receive the same payment. Perhaps the most conspicuous examples in Canada are the large differences in the average wages between women and men and among various racial and ethnic groups. Do these wage differences really reflect differences in marginal productivity, or is something else going on?

Second, many people wrongly believe that the marginal productivity theory of income distribution gives a *moral* justification for the distribution of income, implying that the existing distribution is fair and appropriate. This misconception sometimes leads other people, who believe that the current distribution of income is unfair, to reject marginal productivity theory.

To address these controversies, we'll start by looking at income disparities across gender and ethnic groups. Then we'll ask what factors might account for these disparities and whether these explanations are consistent with the marginal productivity theory of income distribution.

Wage Disparities in Practice

Wage rates in Canada cover a very wide range. At the beginning of 2020, more than one million Canadian workers received the legal minimum wage, a rate that varied from $11.32 per hour in Saskatchewan to $15 per hour in Alberta. At the other extreme, Canada's top 100 highest-paid CEOs had an average compensation of $11.8 million in 2019, which was 227 times the wage of an average Canadian worker. Even leaving out these extremes, there is a huge range of wage rates. Are people really that different in their marginal productivities?

A particular source of concern is the existence of systematic wage differences across gender and immigration status. Figure 19-8 compares annual median earnings in 2016 of workers aged 15 or older classified by gender and immigration status. As a group, males (averaging across all ethnicities and places of birth) had the highest earnings. The data show that women (averaging across all ethnicities and places of birth) earned only about 71% as much as men. Indeed, regardless of their immigration status, women earn less than their counterparts. Perhaps it is not surprising that immigrants earn less, as they lack local experience; however, the situation is worse for refugees and newly arrived immigrants who landed in Canada more recently.

Marginal Productivity and Wage Inequality

A large part of the observed inequality in wages can be explained by considerations that are consistent with the marginal productivity theory of income distribution. In particular, there are three well-understood sources of wage differences across occupations and individuals.

First is the existence of **compensating differentials:** across different types of jobs, wages are often higher or lower depending on how attractive or unattractive the job is. Workers with unpleasant or dangerous jobs demand a higher wage in comparison to workers with jobs that require the same skill and effort but lack the unpleasant or dangerous qualities. For example, truckers who haul hazardous loads are paid more than truckers who haul non-hazardous loads. But for any *given* job, the marginal productivity theory of income distribution generally holds true. For example, hazardous-load truckers are paid a wage equal to the

Compensating differentials are wage differences across jobs that reflect the fact that some jobs are less pleasant than others.

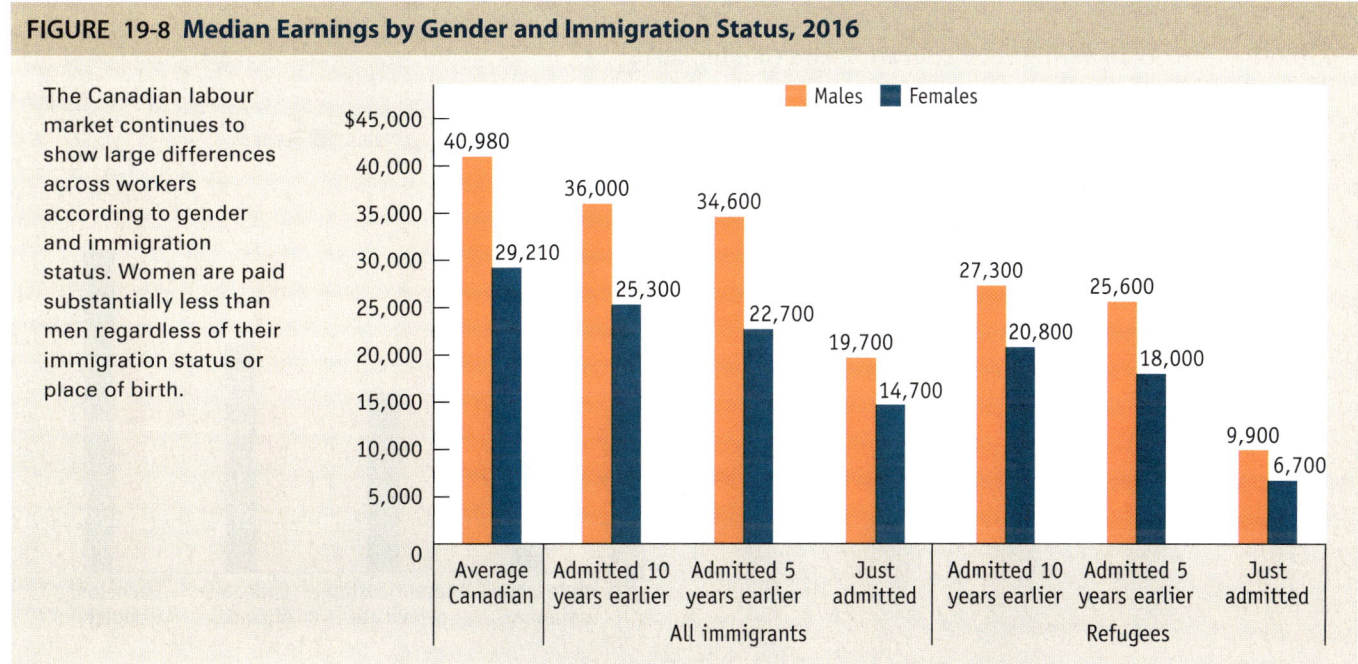

FIGURE 19-8 Median Earnings by Gender and Immigration Status, 2016

The Canadian labour market continues to show large differences across workers according to gender and immigration status. Women are paid substantially less than men regardless of their immigration status or place of birth.

equilibrium value of the marginal product of the last person employed in the labour market for hazardous-load truckers.

A second reason for wage disparities that is consistent with marginal productivity theory is differences in ability. A higher-ability person, by producing a better product, commands a higher price than a person with lower abilities. The person with higher abilities also generates a higher value of the marginal product, and this difference in the value of the marginal product translates into differences in earning potential. Professional sports is a good example: practice is important, but most of the population doesn't have what it takes to score goals like Sidney Crosby or hit tennis balls like Milos Raonic. The same is true in other fields of endeavour.

A third reason for wage differences is differences in the quantity of human capital. Recall that human capital—education and training—is at least as important in the modern economy as physical capital in the form of buildings and machines. Different people embody quite different quantities of human capital, and a person with a higher quantity of human capital typically generates a higher value of the marginal product by producing a product that commands a higher price. So differences in human capital account for substantial differences in wages. People with high levels of human capital, such as skilled surgeons or engineers, who undergo many years of education and training, generally receive high wages. In 2016, surgeons earned an average of $461,000.

The most direct way to see the effect of human capital on wages is to look at the relationship between educational levels and earnings. Figure 19-9 shows earnings differentials by gender and four educational levels for people aged 15 or older in 2015. As you can see, regardless of gender, higher education is associated with higher median earnings. For example, in 2015, females without a high school diploma had median earnings 37% less than those with a high school diploma and 59% less than those with a post-secondary degree or diploma below a bachelor's degree—and similar patterns exist for males.

Because men typically have had more years of education than women, differences in levels of education are part of the explanation for the earnings differences shown in Figure 19-8.

It's also important to realize that formal education is not the only source of human capital; on-the-job training and experience are also very important.

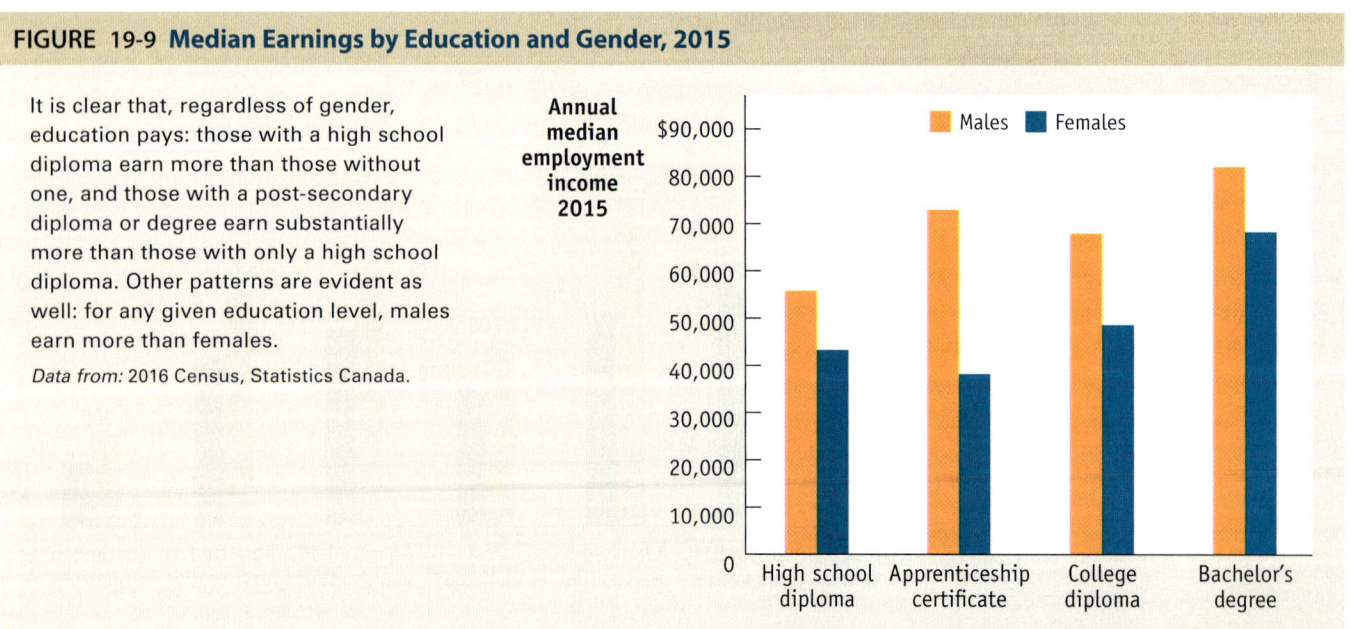

FIGURE 19-9 Median Earnings by Education and Gender, 2015

It is clear that, regardless of gender, education pays: those with a high school diploma earn more than those without one, and those with a post-secondary diploma or degree earn substantially more than those with only a high school diploma. Other patterns are evident as well: for any given education level, males earn more than females.

Data from: 2016 Census, Statistics Canada.

This point was highlighted by a 2010 Library of Parliament Background Paper. The study was motivated by concerns over the presence of a *gender-wage gap* despite the fact that women have caught up with men in terms of both labour force participation and education attainment. In the Canadian labour market, researchers found that the gender gap was largely explained by differences in:

- human capital (women tended to have lower levels of it)
- choice of occupation (women tended to choose occupations such as nursing and teaching, in which they earned less)
- career interruptions (women moved in and out of the labour force more frequently)
- part-time status (women were more likely to work part-time instead of full-time)
- overtime status (women were less likely to work overtime)

The study showed that the average hourly wage of women between the ages of 25 and 54 was 15% below that of their male counterparts. Indeed, the gender wage gap varies across occupations: the female-to-male earnings ratio ranged from 70% for occupations unique to primary industry to 99% for occupations in art, culture, recreation, and sport.

But it's also important to emphasize that earnings differences arising from these factors are not necessarily fair. Canada lags behind some advanced countries in providing government or legal support for child care. As a result, Canadian women face more career interruptions than men and are also less able to work full-time than men. Similarly, a society where Aboriginal and immigrant children typically receive a poor education because they live in underfunded school districts, then go on to earn low wages because they are poorly educated, may have labour markets that are well described by marginal productivity theory. Yet many people would still consider the resulting distribution of income unfair.

Still, many observers think that actual wage differentials cannot be entirely explained by compensating differentials, differences in talent, differences in human capital, or differences in job status. They believe that market power, *efficiency wages*, and discrimination also play an important role. We will examine these forces next.

Market Power

The marginal productivity theory of income distribution is based on the assumption that factor markets are perfectly competitive. In such markets we can expect workers to be paid the equilibrium value of their marginal product, regardless of who they are. But how valid is this assumption?

We studied markets that are *not* perfectly competitive in preceding chapters. Now let's touch briefly on the ways in which labour markets may deviate from the competitive assumption. One undoubted source of differences in wages between otherwise similar workers is the role of **unions**—organizations that try to raise wages and improve working conditions for their members. Unions are a source of power in factor markets. When they are successful, unions replace one-on-one wage deals between workers and employers with *collective bargaining*, in which the employer must negotiate wages with union representatives. Without question, this leads to higher wages for those workers who are represented by unions. In 2019, the median weekly earnings of union members in Canada was $1,140, compared to $962 for workers not represented by unions—more than a 15% difference. Studies have shown that unionization helps reduce the wage differences between White men and women, as well as between White and non-White workers.

Unions are organizations of workers that try to raise wages and improve working conditions for their members by bargaining collectively with employers.

According to the **efficiency-wage model,** some employers pay an above-equilibrium wage as an incentive for better performance.

How much does collective action, either by workers or by employers, affect wages in Canada now? Canada's unionization rates have remained relatively stable in the past few decades, falling from 34% in 1997 to 30% in 2020. Unions in Canada still exert a significant upward effect on wages. About 70% of all unionized employees working belong to national unions. Also, many unionized workers work in the public sector, balancing the market power governments possesses as employers. However, with deregulation, outsourcing, and globalization, the power of unions has eroded slightly, especially their bargaining power over wages. Nonetheless, they still play an important role in the negotiations of job security, better working conditions, and benefits for their members.

Efficiency Wages

Another source of wage differentials is the phenomenon of *efficiency wages*—a type of incentive scheme used by employers to motivate workers to work hard and to reduce worker turnover. Suppose a worker performs a job that is extremely important but that the employer can observe how well the job is being performed only at infrequent intervals—say, serving as a caregiver for the employer's child. Then it makes sense for the employer to pay more than the worker could earn in an alternative job—that is, more than the equilibrium wage. Why? Because earning a premium makes losing this job quite costly for the worker.

The **efficiency-wage model** states that when it is difficult to observe a worker's performance, it may be economically rational for an employer to pay a wage greater than the market equilibrium level as an incentive for better performance. The threat of losing a job that pays a premium motivates the worker to do the job well and avoid being fired. Likewise, paying a premium also reduces worker turnover—the frequency with which an employee leaves a job voluntarily. Despite the fact that it may take no more effort and skill to be a child's caregiver than to be a hospital care aide, efficiency wages show why it often makes economic sense for a parent to pay a caregiver more than the equilibrium wage of hospital care aides.

Like price floors and, in particular, much like the minimum wage—efficiency wages lead to a surplus of labour in labour markets where they are used. This surplus of labour translates into unemployment—some workers are actively searching for a high-paying efficiency-wage job but are unable to get one, and other more fortunate but no more deserving workers are able to acquire one.

As a result, two workers with exactly the same profile—the same skills and same job history—may earn unequal wages: the worker who is lucky enough to get an efficiency-wage job earns more than the worker who gets a standard job (or who remains unemployed while searching for a higher-paying job).

Efficiency wages are a response to a type of market failure that arises when some employees are able to hide the fact that they don't always perform as well as they should. As a result, employers use nonequilibrium wages to motivate their employees, leading to an inefficient outcome.

Discrimination

Workplace discrimination has been a long-standing feature of the Canadian economy. Although formal discrimination on the basis of gender or race was made illegal nearly 70 years ago, researchers find that informal discrimination still exists. For example, researchers in a U.S. study found that when they submit fictitious job applications using identical resumes but with ethnically identifiable names, White-identified applicants receive 36% more call-backs than African-American–identified applicants, and 24% more than Hispanic-identified applicants.

It is a real and ugly fact that throughout history there has been discrimination against workers who are considered to be of the wrong race, ethnicity, gender, or other characteristics. How does this fit into our economic models?

Discrimination is *not* a natural consequence of market competition. On the contrary, market forces tend to work against discrimination. To see why, consider the incentives that would exist if social convention dictated that women be paid 30% less than men with equivalent qualifications and experience. Companies would be able to reduce their costs by hiring women rather than men. The result would be to create an excess demand for female workers, which would eventually drive up their wages.

But if market competition works against discrimination, how is it that so much discrimination has taken place? The answer is twofold.

First, when labour markets don't work well, employers may have the ability to discriminate without hurting their profits. For example, market interferences (such as unions or minimum-wage laws) or market failures (such as efficiency wages) can lead to wages that are above their equilibrium levels. In these cases, there are more job applicants than there are jobs, leaving employers free to discriminate among applicants. In 2012, with unemployment over 7%, the Canadian Human Rights Commission, the federal agency tasked with investigating discrimination charges in the federal government and federally regulated industries (e.g., banking, transportation, and communication), reported that complaints from workers and jobseekers had hit an all-time high, the most logged in the agency's 35-year history.

Second, discrimination has sometimes been institutionalized in government policy. This institutionalization of discrimination has made it easier to maintain it against market pressure, and historically it is the form that discrimination has typically taken. For example, in Canada in the late 1800s and early 1900s, Asians faced immigration barriers (including exclusion from entry) and laws restricting the jobs they could have and forcing their wages to be less than what other employees earned.

Although market competition tends to work against *current* discrimination, it is not a remedy for past discrimination, which typically has had an impact on the education and experience of its victims and thereby reduces their income.

FOR INQUIRING MINDS How Labour Works the German Way

Germany is home to some of the most well-known manufacturing firms in the world. From the automotive sector to beer brewing, and from home appliances to chemical engineering and pharmaceuticals, German products are considered among the highest quality available. And unlike in Canada, blue-collar jobs — those that don't require university degrees — pay high enough wages that they are still prized. If you ask Germans what accounts for their ability to combine a highly successful manufacturing sector with well-paying blue-collar jobs, two overlapping institutions will top their lists: Germany's works councils system and their apprenticeship system.

Enshrined in the German constitution, works councils exist in every factory to encourage management and employees to work together on issues like work conditions, productivity, and wages, with the goal of discouraging costly conflict. Workers are given seats in management organizations such as a company's board of directors. This collabourative environment, in turn, supports higher levels of unionization within German manufacturing. As a result, German unions are more successful at raising the wages of their members.

But what allows German manufacturing to compete successfully while paying higher wages? One explanation is the German apprentice system, which is promoted and accredited by the German government. These programs provide hands-on training to young workers in specific skills from automotive electronics to hairdressing. About 60% of German high school students train in an apprenticeship program, graduating with a formal certificate, and often landing a permanent job at the company where they were trained. As a result, the typical German manufacturing worker starts a job with higher levels of job-specific human capital than their North American counterpart.

So integral is the apprenticeship system to the success of German manufacturing that German companies have been replicating it at their plants in the United States. In South Carolina, where BMW and Tognum, a German engine maker, are located, apprenticeship programs have been created in partnership with local and state governments to assure that young workers are trained in the skills that the companies need. And, needless to say, the apprentices welcome such training and the well-paying jobs that it will bring.

So Does Marginal Productivity Theory Work?

The main conclusion you should draw from this discussion is that the marginal productivity theory of income distribution is not a perfect description of how factor incomes are determined, but that it is still a very useful tool for economic analysis. The deviations are important. But, by and large, in a modern economy with well-functioning labour markets, factors of production are paid the equilibrium value of the marginal product—the value of the marginal product of the last unit employed in the market as a whole.

It's important to emphasize, once again, that this does not mean that the factor distribution of income is morally justified.

ECONOMICS >> *in Action*
Marginal Productivity and the Minimum Wage Puzzle

The U.S. government, like many other governments, puts a floor under wages: nationally, employers aren't allowed to pay workers less than US$7.25 an hour. However, many states and some cities impose their own minimum wages, in some cases well above the national standard. For example, Arizona requires that employers pay at least US$12.00 an hour. Seattle requires payment of US$16.39 an hour.

Labour economists have devoted a lot of attention to U.S. state and local minimum wages, both because they affect millions of workers and because they serve as "natural experiments": by looking at what happens when a U.S. state increases its minimum wage, and especially by comparing the results with developments in neighbouring U.S. states, economists can gather important information about how labour markets actually work in the real world.

The results of such an experiment may seem readily apparent: a U.S. state that increases its minimum wage, say from US$7.25 to US$16.39, raises the cost of labour. Minimum-wage workers, like employees at fast-food restaurants, are now more expensive to hire. Wouldn't these higher costs lead employers to reduce employment and workers to lose their jobs? But that's not what seems to happen, according to many labour economists (although there are some dissenters). Instead, even significant minimum-wage hikes, while they do raise wages for many workers, appear to have no effect on employment. How is this possible?

The answer, suggest some of the economists who have pioneered this line of research, is *monopsony:* because large employers use their market power to hold down wages, paying workers less than their marginal product, moderate increases in the minimum wage do not discourage hiring because even the new higher wage is still below labour's marginal product, so employing workers is still profitable.

If correct, this analysis has implications well beyond minimum wage policy, because it casts doubt on how well the marginal productivity theory of income distribution works for the economy as a whole.

>> Quick Review

• Existing large disparities in wages both among individuals and across groups lead some to question the marginal productivity theory of income distribution.

• **Compensating differentials,** as well as differences in the values of the marginal products of workers that arise from differences in talent, job experience, job status, and human capital, account for some wage disparities.

• Market power, in the form of **unions** or monopsony behaviour by employers, as well as the **efficiency-wage model,** in which employers pay an above-equilibrium wage to induce better performance, also explain how some wage disparities arise.

• Discrimination has historically been a major factor in wage disparities. Market competition tends to work against discrimination. But discrimination can leave a long-lasting legacy of diminished human capital acquisition.

>> Check Your Understanding 19-3
Solutions appear at back of book.

1. Assess each of the following statements. Do you think they are true, false, or ambiguous? Explain.
   a. The marginal productivity theory of income distribution is inconsistent with the presence of income disparities associated with gender, race, or ethnicity.
   b. Companies that engage in workplace discrimination but whose competitors do not are likely to have lower profits as a result of their actions.
   c. Workers who are paid less because they have less experience are not the victims of discrimination.
   d. Walmart moves into a small, rural town forcing many small businesses to close. Workers are the victims of discrimination as they take lower paying jobs at Walmart.

‖ The Supply of Labour

Up to this point we have focused on the demand for factors, which determines the quantities demanded of labour, capital, or land by producers as a function of their factor prices. What about the supply of factors?

In this section, we focus exclusively on the supply of labour. We do this for two reasons. First, in the modern Canadian economy, labour is the most important factor of production, accounting for most of factor income. Second, as we'll see, labour supply is the area in which factor markets look most different from markets for goods and services.

Decisions about labour supply result from decisions about **time allocation:** how many hours to spend on different activities.

Leisure is time available for purposes other than earning money to buy marketed goods.

Work versus Leisure

In the labour market, the roles of firms and households are the reverse of what they are in markets for goods and services. A good such as wheat or smartphones is supplied by firms and demanded by households; labour, though, is demanded by firms and supplied by households. How do people decide how much labour to supply?

As a practical matter, most people have limited control over their work hours: either you take a job that involves working a set number of hours per week, or you don't get the job at all. To understand the logic of labour supply, however, it helps to put realism to one side for a bit and imagine an individual who can choose to work as many or as few hours as they like.

Why wouldn't such an individual work as many hours as possible? Because workers are human beings, too, and have other uses for their time. An hour spent on the job is an hour not spent on other, presumably more pleasant, activities. So the decision about how much labour to supply involves making a decision about **time allocation**—how many hours to spend on different activities.

By working, people earn income that they can use to buy goods. The more hours an individual works, the more goods that individual can afford to buy. But this increased purchasing power comes at the expense of a reduction in **leisure,** the time spent not working. (Leisure doesn't necessarily mean time spent goofing off. It could mean time spent with one's family, pursuing hobbies, exercising, and so on.) And though purchased goods yield utility, so does leisure. Indeed, we can think of leisure itself as a normal good, which most people would like to consume more of as their incomes increase.

How does a rational individual decide how much leisure to consume? By making a marginal comparison, of course. In analyzing consumer choice, we asked how a utility-maximizing consumer uses a marginal *dollar*. In analyzing labour supply, we ask how an individual uses a marginal *hour*.

Consider Jaden, an individual who likes both leisure and the goods money can buy. Suppose that his wage rate is $10 per hour. In deciding how many hours he wants to work, he must compare the marginal utility of an additional hour of leisure with the additional utility he gets from $10 worth of goods. If $10 worth of goods adds more to his total utility than an additional hour of leisure, he can increase his total utility by giving up an hour of leisure to work an additional hour. If an extra hour of leisure adds more to his total utility than $10 worth of goods, he can increase his total utility by working one fewer hour in order to gain an hour of leisure.

At Jaden's optimal labour supply choice, then, his marginal utility of one hour of leisure is equal to the marginal utility he gets from the goods that his hourly wage can purchase. This is very similar to the *optimal consumption rule* we encountered in Chapter 10, except that it is a rule about time rather than money.

Every worker faces a trade-off between leisure and work.

Kevin Kozicki/Image Source/Getty Images

The **individual labour supply curve** shows how the quantity of labour supplied by an individual depends on that individual's wage rate.

Our next step is to ask how Jaden's decision about time allocation is affected when his wage rate changes.

Wages and Labour Supply

Suppose that Jaden's wage rate doubles, from $10 to $20 per hour. How will he change his time allocation?

You could argue that Jaden will work longer hours, because his incentive to work has increased: by giving up an hour of leisure, he can now gain twice as much money as before. But you could equally well argue that he will work less, because he doesn't need to work as many hours to generate the income to pay for the goods he wants.

As these opposing arguments suggest, the quantity of labour Jaden supplies can either rise or fall when his wage rate rises. To understand why, let's recall the distinction between *substitution effects* and *income effects* that we learned in Chapter 10 and its appendix. We saw there that a price change affects consumer choice in two ways: by changing the opportunity cost of a good in terms of other goods (the substitution effect) and by making the consumer richer or poorer (the income effect).

Now think about how a rise in Jaden's wage rate affects his demand for leisure. The opportunity cost of leisure—the amount of money he gives up by taking an hour off instead of working—rises. That substitution effect gives him an incentive, other things equal, to consume *less* leisure and work *longer* hours. Conversely, a higher wage rate makes Jaden richer—and this income effect leads him, other things equal, to want to consume *more* leisure and work *fewer* hours, because leisure is a normal good.

So in the case of labour supply, the substitution effect and the income effect work in opposite directions. If the substitution effect is so powerful that it dominates the income effect, an increase in Jaden's wage rate leads him to supply *more* hours of labour. If the income effect is so powerful that it dominates the substitution effect, an increase in the wage rate leads him to supply *fewer* hours of labour.

We see, then, that the **individual labour supply curve**—the relationship between the wage rate and the number of hours of labour supplied by an individual worker—does not necessarily slope upward. If the income effect dominates, a higher wage rate will reduce the quantity of labour supplied.

Figure 19-10 illustrates the two possibilities for labour supply. If the substitution effect dominates the income effect, the individual labour supply curve slopes upward; panel (a) shows an increase in the wage rate from $10 to $20 per hour leading to a *rise* in the number of hours worked from 40 to 50. However, if the income effect dominates, the quantity of labour supplied goes down when the wage rate increases. Panel (b) shows the same rise in the wage rate leading to a *fall* in the number of hours worked from 40 to 30. (Economists refer to an individual labour supply curve that contains both upward-sloping and downward-sloping segments as a "backward-bending labour supply curve"—a concept that we analyze in detail in this chapter's appendix.)

Is a negative response of the quantity of labour supplied to the wage rate a real possibility? Yes: many labour economists believe that income effects on the supply of labour may be somewhat stronger than substitution effects. The most compelling piece of evidence for this belief comes from Canadians' increasing consumption of leisure over the past century. At the end of the nineteenth century, wages adjusted for inflation were only about one-eighth what they are today; the typical workweek was 70 hours, and very few workers retired at age 65. Today the typical workweek is less than 40 hours, and most people retire at age 65 or earlier. So it seems that Canadians have chosen to take advantage of higher wages in part by consuming more leisure.

FIGURE 19-10 The Individual Labour Supply Curve

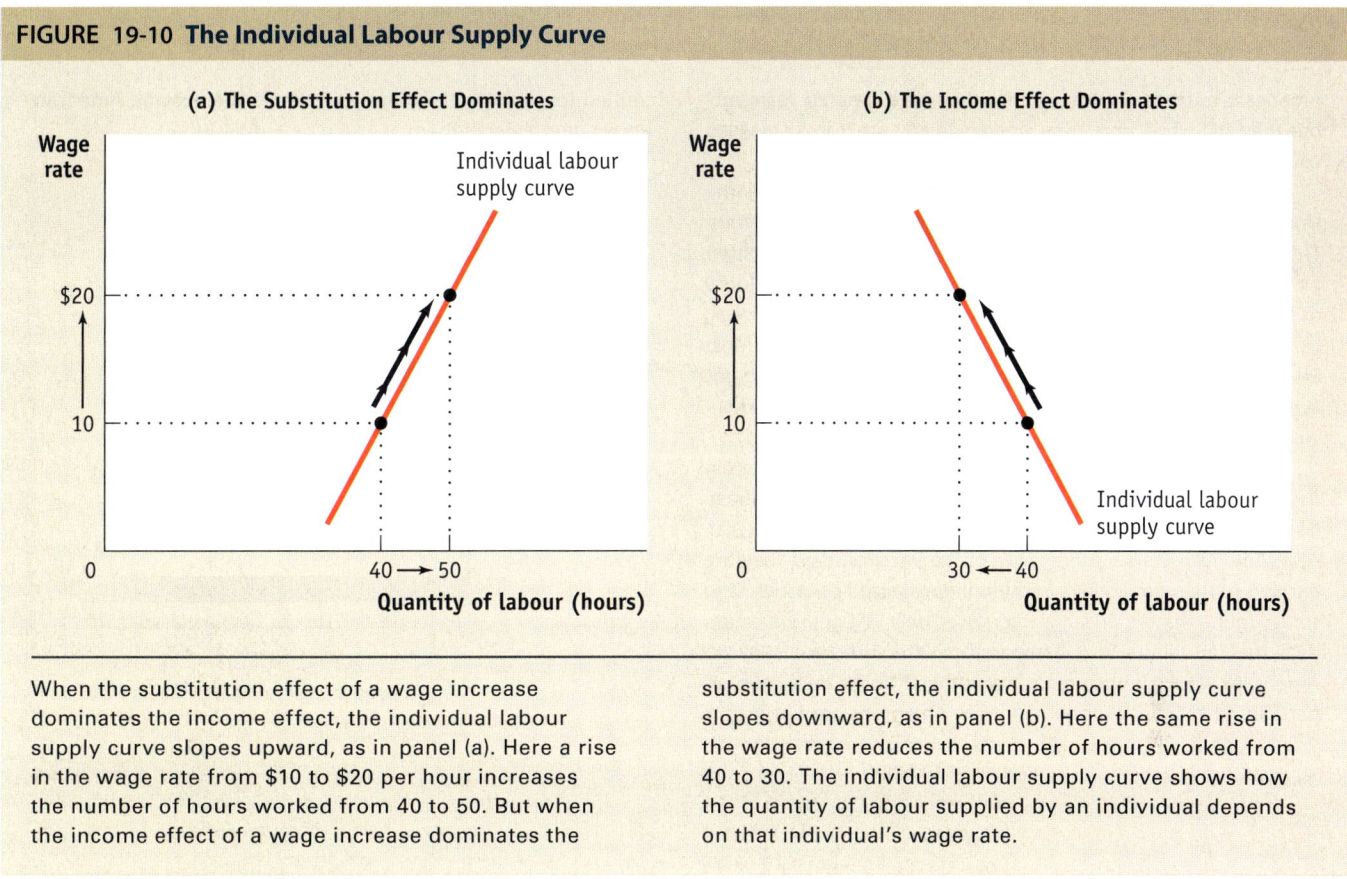

When the substitution effect of a wage increase dominates the income effect, the individual labour supply curve slopes upward, as in panel (a). Here a rise in the wage rate from $10 to $20 per hour increases the number of hours worked from 40 to 50. But when the income effect of a wage increase dominates the substitution effect, the individual labour supply curve slopes downward, as in panel (b). Here the same rise in the wage rate reduces the number of hours worked from 40 to 30. The individual labour supply curve shows how the quantity of labour supplied by an individual depends on that individual's wage rate.

Shifts of the Labour Supply Curve

Now that we have examined how income and substitution effects shape the individual labour supply curve, we can turn to the market labour supply curve. In any labour market, the market supply curve is the horizontal sum of the individual labour supply curves of all workers in that market. A change in any factor *other than the wage* that alters workers' willingness to supply labour causes a shift of the labour supply curve. A variety of factors can lead to such shifts, including changes in preferences and social norms, changes in population, changes in opportunities, and changes in wealth.

Changes in Preferences and Social Norms Changes in preferences and social norms can lead workers to increase or decrease their willingness to work at any given wage. A striking example of this phenomenon is the large increase in the number of employed women—particularly married employed women—that has occurred in Canada and the United States since the 1960s. Until that time, women who could afford to largely did not work outside the home. Changes in preferences and norms in post–World War II North America (helped along by the invention of labour-saving home appliances such as washing machines, increasing urbanization of the population, and higher female education levels) have induced large numbers of North American women to join the workforce—a phenomenon often repeated in other countries that experience similar social and technological forces.

Changes in Population Changes in the population size generally lead to shifts of the labour supply curve. A larger population tends to shift the labour supply curve rightward as more workers are available at any given wage; a smaller population tends to shift the labour supply curve leftward. From 1990 to 2019,

GLOBAL COMPARISON   THE OVERWORKED AMERICAN?

Americans today may work less than they did a hundred years ago, but they still work more than workers in any other industrialized country.

This figure compares average annual hours worked in the United States with those worked in other industrialized countries. The differences result from a combination of Americans' longer workweeks and shorter vacations. For example, the great majority of full-time American workers put in at least 40 hours per week. Until recently, however, a government mandate limited most French workers to a 35-hour workweek; collective bargaining has achieved a similar reduction in the workweek for many German workers.

In 2019, American workers got, on average, 10 paid vacation days, but 24% of American workers got none at all. In contrast, German workers are guaranteed six weeks of paid vacation a year. Also, American workers use fewer of the vacation days they are entitled to than do workers in other industrialized countries. One survey found that American workers used only 51% of the vacation days they are entitled to, compared to 90% in France. Why do Americans work so much more than others? Unlike their counterparts in other industrialized countries, Americans are not legally entitled to paid vacation days; as a result, the average American worker gets fewer of them.

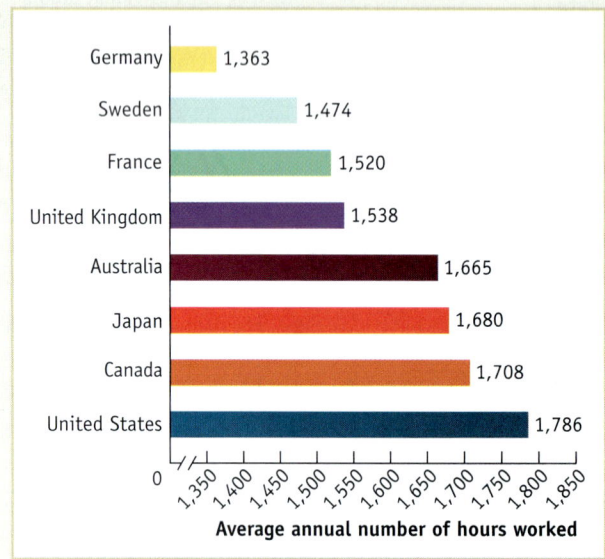

Data from: OECD.

the Canadian labour force grew approximately 1.21% per year, generated largely by immigration. As a result, from 1987 to a 2019, the Canadian labour market had a rightward-shifting labour supply curve. However, while the population continued to grow in the recession years 1992 and 2009, the growth rate of the labour force slowed as workers, disillusioned by bad job prospects, left the labour force. As a result, in 1992 the Canadian labour supply curve did not shift right at all.

Changes in Opportunities At one time, teaching was the only occupation considered suitable for university-educated women. However, as opportunities in other professions opened up to women starting in the 1960s, many women left teaching and potential female teachers chose other careers. This generated a leftward shift of the supply curve for teachers, reflecting a fall in the willingness to work at any given wage and forcing schools to pay more to maintain an adequate teaching staff. These events illustrate a general result: when superior alternatives arise for workers in another labour market, the supply curve in the original labour market shifts leftward as workers move to the new opportunities. Similarly, when opportunities diminish in one labour market—say, layoffs in the manufacturing industry due to increased foreign competition—the supply in alternative labour markets increases as workers move to these other markets.

Changes in Wealth A person whose wealth increases will buy more normal goods, including leisure. So when a class of workers experiences a general rise in their wealth levels—say, due to a stock market boom—the income effect from the wealth increase will shift the labour supply curve associated with those workers leftward as workers consume more leisure and work less. Note that *the income effect caused by a change in wealth shifts the labour supply curve,* but *the income effect from a wage rate increase*—as we discussed in the case of the individual labour supply curve—*is a movement along the labour supply curve.*

ECONOMICS >> *in Action*
The Real Housewives of the United States

If you watch old American TV shows, you might think that the United States in the 1950s was a land of traditional families, with a male breadwinner and a stay-at-home housewife. The reality wasn't that stark: even in 1960, more than 40% of American women in their prime working years (ages 25–54) were in the paid labour force. But that compared with 97% labour force participation for American men in the same age group.

The high cost of child care in the United States depresses American women's labour supply in comparison to other wealthy countries.

Over the 35 years that followed, American women moved in large numbers into jobs outside the home: by the mid-1990s, more than 75% of American prime-working-age women were in the paid workforce. But over the next few decades women's employment in the United States stagnated, or even declined a bit.

The funny thing is that this didn't happen in other wealthy countries, where women's employment continued to rise. By 2019, around 85% of prime-working-age women in northern European countries and Canada were in the workforce, while the United States was still at 75%. Even Japan, which used to be famous for blatant gender discrimination, had higher female employment than the United States.

Why did the United States diverge? The most likely explanation is public policy that affects labour supply decisions. Most other wealthy countries either directly provide day care for children of working mothers, or subsidize and regulate private day care. The United States doesn't have a comparable policy, so the costs of going to work are much higher for U.S. women with children than for their counterparts abroad.

One implication of this explanation is that changing policy could have large implications for labour supply. Some U.S. politicians are now advocating creation of a national program that subsidizes child care. They argue that such a program would partly (not completely) pay for itself, because more women would take paying jobs, and would as a result pay higher taxes. The logic of labour supply says that these claims are probably right.

>> Check Your Understanding 19-4

Solutions appear at back of book.

1. Formerly, Jaden was free to work as many or as few hours per week as he wanted. But a new law limits the maximum number of hours he can work per week to 35. Explain under what circumstances, if at all, he is made:
   a. Worse off
   b. Equally as well off
   c. Better off
2. Explain in terms of the income and substitution effects how a fall in Jaden's wage rate can induce him to work more hours than before.

>> Quick Review

• The choice of how much labour to supply is a problem of **time allocation:** a choice between work and **leisure.**

• A rise in the wage rate causes both an income and a substitution effect on an individual's labour supply. The substitution effect of a higher wage rate induces more hours of work supplied, other things equal. This is countered by the income effect: higher income leads to a higher demand for leisure, a normal good. If the income effect dominates, a rise in the wage rate can actually cause the individual labour supply curve to slope the "wrong" way: downward.

• The market labour supply curve is the horizontal sum of the **individual labour supply curves** of all workers in that market. It shifts for four main reasons: changes in preferences and social norms, changes in population, changes in opportunities, and changes in wealth.

Belinda Howell/Getty Images

Walmart Revolutionizes Its Labour Practices

AP Images/David J. Phillip

With 2.2 million employees in 2019—roughly 1.5% of the U.S. working population—Walmart is America's largest private employer. The big-box retail chain is so large that Walmart's employee policies are considered a barometer of the current state of the labour market for retail workers.

Yet in the 1990s and early-to-mid 2000s, Walmart was considered a notoriously bad place to work. It was known for failing to provide workers with consistent schedules, for offering few benefits, and for paying wages so low that some employees qualified for food stamps and other antipoverty programs. During this period, Walmart was hit with several lawsuits alleging overtime violations, sexual harassment by managers, and gender discrimination.

Not only were Walmart employees unsatisfied—customers were too. They complained of dirty bathrooms, empty shelves, endless checkout lines, and impossible-to-find sales help. "Walmart's relentless focus on costs does seem to have taken some toll on in-store conditions and stock levels," an analyst explained, adding "If an item is not on the shelf, then you cannot sell it." As of 2015, only 16% of Walmart stores were meeting the company's own customer service goals.

But in 2015, Walmart suddenly began to overhaul its labour practices. At first the changes were fairly modest: higher wages and more consistent work scheduling. By 2016, Walmart's average pay for a nonmanagerial full-time worker was US$13.69 per hour, up 16% from 2014 (but still below Costco's hourly rate of nearly US$20 per hour).

The changes produced clear results. Customer feedback improved markedly: by 2016, 75% of Walmart stores were hitting their customer service targets. Walmart sales, which had been sliding relative to those of competitors, rose.

The changes didn't stop there. In 2018, in the midst of a strong economy, the company raised starting pay, introduced a year-end bonus to employees, and added 10 weeks of fully paid maternity leave for full-time employees. As one market observer said, "Those are 'sticky benefits'—the kind that might keep you from leaving Walmart just to earn 50 cents or $1 an hour more, or might woo you to Walmart in the first place."

At the same time, in order to counter the threat from rival retailer Amazon, Walmart has been investing more in worker training while investing heavily in its own e-commerce capabilities. Now customers can "click and collect" in their local Walmart store. When an item isn't on the shelf, customers can order it online. If necessary, a Walmart sales associate will walk a customer through that process. The company has created "Walmart Academies," located in the back of stores, where associates can expand their skills by learning about management responsibilities and mobile shopping apps.

Yes, indeed, a revolution is underway in Aisle 6.

QUESTIONS FOR THOUGHT

1. Use the marginal productivity theory of income distribution to explain how companies like Walmart can pay workers so little that they fall below the poverty line.

2. Use the case to explain how similar workers in the same labour market can end up being paid different wages in equilibrium. Also explain why Walmart believed it could improve its profitability by raising its labour costs.

3. Some politicians want to encourage more companies to adopt a high-wage strategy. What are the possible positive and negative effects of such a policy?

4. When an employer introduces "sticky benefits," like generous child-care benefits, what does that imply about the costs of worker turnover to employer?

5. What factors do you think compelled Walmart to change its labour practices? Be specific.

SUMMARY

1. Just as there are markets for goods and services, there are markets for factors of production, including labour, land, and both **physical capital** and **human capital.** These markets determine the **factor distribution of income.**

2. According to the **price-taking producer's optimal employment rule,** a price-taking producer's profit is maximized by employing each factor of production up to the level at which its **value of the marginal product** is equal to the factor's price. The value of the marginal product of a factor is equal to its marginal product multiplied by the price of the output it produces. The **value of the marginal product curve** is therefore the individual price-taking producer's demand curve for a factor.

3. The market demand curve for labour is the horizontal sum of the individual demand curves of producers in that market. It shifts for three main reasons: changes in output price, changes in the supply of other factors, and technological changes.

4. When a competitive labour market is in equilibrium, the market wage is equal to the **equilibrium value of the marginal product** of labour, the additional value produced by the last worker hired in the labour market as a whole. The same principle applies to other factors of production: the **rental rate** of land or capital is equal to the equilibrium value of the marginal products. This insight leads to the **marginal productivity theory of income distribution,** according to which each factor is paid the value of the marginal product of the last unit of that factor employed in the factor market as a whole.

5. Large disparities in wages raise questions about the validity of the marginal productivity theory of income distribution. Many disparities can be explained by **compensating differentials** and by differences in talent, job experience, job status, and human capital across workers. Market interference in the forms of **unions** and collective action by employers also creates wage disparities. The **efficiency-wage model,** which arises from a type of market failure, shows how wage disparities can result from employers' attempts to increase worker performance. Free markets tend to diminish discrimination, but discrimination remains a real source of wage disparity, especially through its effects on human capital acquisition. Discrimination is typically maintained either through problems in labour markets or (historically) through institutionalization in government policies.

6. Labour supply is the result of decisions about **time allocation,** where each worker faces a trade-off between **leisure** and work. An increase in the hourly wage rate tends to increase work hours via the substitution effect but to reduce work hours via the income effect. If the net result is that a worker increases the quantity of labour supplied in response to a higher wage, the **individual labour supply curve** slopes upward. If the net result is that a worker reduces work hours, the individual labour supply curve—unlike supply curves for goods and services—slopes downward.

7. The market labour supply curve is the horizontal sum of the individual labour supply curves of all workers in that market. It shifts for four main reasons: changes in preferences and social norms, changes in population, changes in opportunities, and changes in wealth.

KEY TERMS

Physical capital, p. 574
Human capital, p. 574
Factor distribution of income, p. 575
Value of the marginal product, p. 577
Price-taking producer's optimal employment rule, p. 578

Value of the marginal product curve, p. 578
Equilibrium value of the marginal product, p. 583
Rental rate, p. 583
Marginal productivity theory of income distribution, p. 584

Compensating differentials, p. 587
Unions, p. 589
Efficiency-wage model, p. 590
Time allocation, p. 593
Leisure, p. 593
Individual labour supply curve, p. 594

PRACTICE QUESTIONS

1. The market for school teachers appears to be very competitive, but similar to nursing, many cities have only a few employers. Most regions have one or two school districts that employ the majority of teachers. How can monopsony power within school districts contribute to lower wages and gender wage discrimination?

2. The OECD (Organization for Economic Cooperation and Development) presents average wage data across developed countries. The database also includes data on the gender wage gap and share of low- and high-wage workers. For this problem go to the website: data.oecd.org/earnwage/average-wages.htm. In the left sidebar, select the tab for gender wage gap.

a. What is the definition of the gender wage gap?

b. What is the gender wage gap for Canada? Provide an interpretation of the value.

c. What are the primary factors that explain the gender wage gap? Do these factors rule out discrimination?

3. A recent study by economists at Northwestern University and UCLA researched the wage and employment effects of economic consolidation in the hospital industry across the United States. The authors looked at three distinct groups of workers:

i. Unskilled workers whose occupations are not constricted to the health care industry, such as custodial and cafeteria workers

ii. Skilled workers whose skills are not specific to the industry, such as human resources personnel and U.S. Equal Employment Opportunity Commission compliance officers

iii. Skilled health care professionals such as nurses or pharmacy workers

Which group of workers do you think was most affected by the consolidations? Why?

PROBLEMS

1. In 2019, national income in Canada was $2,051 billion. In the same year, 19.06 million workers were employed, at an average wage, excluding employers' social contributions, of $52,995 per worker per year.

   a. How much direct compensation was paid to Canadian employees in 2019?

   b. Analyze the factor distribution of income. What percentage of national income was received in the form of direct compensation to employees in 2019 (excluding employers' social contributions)? In light of Figure 19-1, what percentage of national income do employers' social contributions represent?

   c. Suppose that a huge wave of corporate downsizing leads many terminated employees to open their own businesses. What is the effect on the factor distribution of income?

   d. Suppose the supply of labour rises due to an increase in the retirement age. What happens to the percentage of national income received in the form of compensation of employees?

2. Marty's Frozen Yogurt has the production function per day shown in the accompanying table. The equilibrium wage rate for a worker is $80 per day. Each cup of frozen yogurt sells for $2.

Quantity of labour (workers)	Quantity of frozen yogurt (cups)
0	0
1	110
2	200
3	270
4	300
5	320
6	330

   a. Calculate the marginal product of labour for each worker and the value of the marginal product of labour per worker.

   b. How many workers should Marty employ?

3. The production function for Patty's Pizza Parlor is given in the table in Problem 12. The price of pizza is $2, but the hourly wage rate rises from $10 to $15. Use a diagram to determine how Patty's demand

for workers responds as a result of this wage rate increase.

4. Jameel runs a driver education school. The more driving instructors he hires, the more driving lessons he can sell. But because he owns a limited number of training automobiles, each additional driving instructor adds less to Jameel's output of driving lessons. The accompanying table shows Jameel's production function per day. Each driving lesson can be sold at $35 per hour.

Quantity of labour (driving instructors)	Quantity of driving lessons (hours)
0	0
1	8
2	15
3	21
4	26
5	30
6	33

Determine Jameel's labour demand schedule (his demand schedule for driving instructors) for each of the following daily wage rates for driving instructors: $160, $180, $200, $220, $240, and $260.

5. Dale and Dana work at a self-service gas station and convenience store. Dale opens up every day, and Dana arrives later to help stock the store. They are both paid the current market wage of $9.50 per hour. But Dale feels he should be paid much more because the revenue generated from the gas pumps he turns on every morning is much higher than the revenue generated by the items that Dana stocks. Assess this argument.

6. A *New York Times* article observed that the wage of farmworkers in Mexico was $11 an hour but the wage of immigrant Mexican farmworkers in California was $9 an hour.

   a. Assume that the output sells for the same price in the two countries. Does this imply that the marginal product of labour of farmworkers is higher in Mexico or in California? Explain your answer, and illustrate with a diagram that shows the demand and supply curves for labour in the respective markets. In your diagram, assume that the quantity supplied of labour for any given wage rate is the same for Mexican farmworkers as it is for immigrant Mexican farmworkers in California.

b. Now suppose that farmwork in Mexico is more arduous and more dangerous than farmwork in California. As a result, the quantity supplied of labour for any given wage rate is not the same for Mexican farmworkers as it is for immigrant Mexican farmworkers in California. How does this change your answer to part a? What concept best accounts for the difference between wage rates for Mexican farmworkers and immigrant Mexican farmworkers in California?

c. Illustrate your answer to part b with a diagram. In this diagram, assume that the quantity of labour demanded for any given wage rate is the same for Mexican employers as it is for Californian employers.

7. Kendra is the owner of Wholesome Farms, a commercial dairy. Kendra employs labour, land, and capital. In her operations, Kendra can substitute between the amount of labour she employs and the amount of capital she employs. That is, to produce the same quantity of output she can use more labour and less capital; similarly, to produce the same quantity of output she can use less labour and more capital. Let w^* represent the annual cost of labour in the market, let r_L^* represent the annual cost of a unit of land in the market, and let r_k^* represent the annual cost of a unit of capital in the market.

a. Suppose that Kendra can maximize her profits by employing less labour and more capital than she is currently using but the same amount of land. What three conditions must now hold for Kendra's operations (involving her value of the marginal product of labour, land, and capital) for this to be true?

b. Kendra believes that she can increase her profits by renting and using more land. However, if she uses more land, she must use more of both labour and capital; if she uses less land, she can use less of both labour and capital. What three conditions must hold (involving her value of the marginal product of labour, land, and capital) for this to be true?

8. For each of the following situations in which similar workers are paid different wages, give the most likely explanation for these wage differences.

a. Test pilots for new jet aircraft earn higher wages than airline pilots.

b. University graduates usually have higher earnings in their first year on the job than workers without University degrees have in their first year on the job.

c. Full professors command higher salaries than assistant professors for teaching the same class.

d. Unionized workers are generally better paid than non-unionized workers.

9. Research consistently finds that despite nondiscrimination policies, non-white workers on average receive lower wages than White workers do. What are the possible reasons for this? Are these reasons consistent with marginal productivity theory?

10. Greta is an enthusiastic amateur gardener and spends a lot of her free time working in her yard. She also has

a demanding and well-paid job as a freelance advertising consultant. Because the advertising business is going through a difficult time, the hourly consulting fee Greta can charge falls. Greta decides to spend more time gardening and less time consulting. Explain her decision in terms of income and substitution effects.

11. You are the premier's economic policy adviser. The premier wants to put in place policies that encourage employed people to work more hours at their jobs and that encourage unemployed people to find and take jobs. Assess each of the following policies in terms of reaching that goal. Explain your reasoning in terms of income and substitution effects, and indicate when the impact of the policy may be ambiguous.

a. The provincial income tax rate is lowered, which has the effect of increasing workers' after-tax wage rate.

b. The provincial income tax rate is increased, which has the effect of decreasing workers' after-tax wage rate.

c. The provincial property tax rate is increased, which reduces workers' after-tax income.

 WORK IT OUT

12. Patty's Pizza Parlor has the production function per hour shown in the accompanying table. The hourly wage rate for each worker is $10. Each pizza sells for $2.

Quantity of labour (workers)	Quantity of pizza
0	0
1	9
2	15
3	19
4	22
5	24

a. Calculate the marginal product of labour for each worker and the value of the marginal product of labour per worker.

b. Draw the value of the marginal product of labour curve. Use your diagram to determine how many workers Patty should employ.

c. The price of pizza increases to $4. Calculate the value of the marginal product of labour per worker, and draw the new value of the marginal product of labour curve in your diagram. Use your diagram to determine how many workers Patty should employ now.

Now let's assume that Patty buys a new high-tech pizza oven that allows her workers to become twice as productive as before. That is, the first worker now produces 18 pizzas per hour instead of 9, and so on.

d. Calculate the new marginal product of labour and the new value of the marginal product of labour at the original price of $2 per pizza.

e. Use a diagram to determine how Patty's hiring decision responds to this increase in the productivity of her workforce. ■

Indifference Curve Analysis of Labour Supply

In the chapter, you learned why the labour supply curve can slope downward instead of upward: the substitution effect of a higher wage rate, which provides an incentive to work longer hours, can be outweighed by the income effect of a higher wage rate, which may lead individuals to consume more leisure. In this appendix, we will see how this analysis can be carried out using the *indifference curves* introduced in the Chapter 10 appendix.

The Time Allocation Budget Line

Let's return to the example of Jaden, who likes leisure but also likes having money to spend. We now assume that Jaden has a total of 80 hours per week that he could spend either working or enjoying as leisure time. (The remaining hours in his week, we assume, are taken up with necessary activities, mainly sleeping.) Let's also assume, initially, that his hourly wage rate is $10.

His consumption possibilities are defined by the **time allocation budget line** in Figure 19A-1, a budget line that shows Jaden's trade-offs between consumption of leisure and income. Hours of leisure per week are measured on the horizontal axis, and the money he earns from working is measured on the vertical axis.

The horizontal intercept, point *X*, is at 80 hours: if Jaden didn't work at all, he would have 80 hours of leisure per week but would not earn any money. The vertical intercept, point *Y*, is at $800: if Jaden worked all the time, he would earn $800 per week.

Why can we use a budget line to describe Jaden's time allocation choice? The budget lines found in Chapter 10 and its appendix represent the trade-offs facing consumers deciding how to allocate their income among different goods. Here, instead of asking how Jaden allocates his income, we ask how he allocates his

A **time allocation budget line** shows an individual's trade-off between consumption of leisure and the income that allows consumption of marketed goods.

FIGURE 19A-1 The Time Allocation Budget Line

Jaden's time allocation budget line shows his trade-off between work, which pays a wage rate of $10 per hour, and leisure. At point *X* he allocates all his time, 80 hours, to leisure but has no income. At point *Y* he allocates all his time to work, earning $800, but consumes no leisure. His hourly wage rate of $10, the opportunity cost of an hour of leisure, is equal to minus the slope of the time allocation budget line. We have assumed that point *A*, at 40 hours of leisure and $400 in income, is Jaden's optimal time allocation choice. It obeys the optimal time allocation rule: the additional utility Jaden gets from one more hour of leisure must equal the additional utility he gets from the goods he can purchase with one hour's wages.

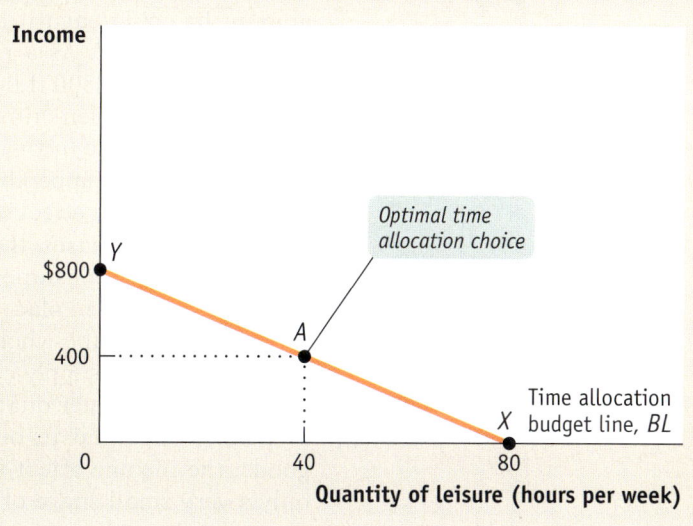

The **optimal time allocation rule** says that an individual should allocate time so that the marginal utility gained from the income earned from an additional hour worked is equal to the marginal utility of an additional hour of leisure.

time. But the principles underlying the allocation of income and the allocation of time are the same: each involves allocating a fixed amount of a resource (80 hours of time in this case) with a constant trade-off (Jaden must forgo $10 for each additional hour of leisure). So using a budget line is just as appropriate for time allocation as it is for income allocation.

As in the case of ordinary budget lines, opportunity cost plays a key role. The opportunity cost of an hour of leisure is what Jaden must forgo by working one less hour—$10 in income. This opportunity cost is, of course, Jaden's hourly wage rate and is equal to minus the slope of his time allocation budget line. You can verify this by noting that the slope is equal to minus the vertical intercept, point *Y*, divided by the horizontal intercept, point *X*—that is, –$800/(80 hours) = –$10 per hour.

To maximize his utility, Jaden must choose the optimal point on the time allocation budget line in Figure 19A-1. In Chapter 10, we saw that a consumer who allocates spending to maximize utility finds the point on the budget line that satisfies the *utility-maximizing principle of marginal analysis:* the marginal utility per dollar spent on two goods must be equal. Although Jaden's choice involves allocating time rather than money, the same principles apply.

Since Jaden "spends" time rather than money, the counterpart of the utility-maximizing principle of marginal analysis is the **optimal time allocation rule:** the marginal utility Jaden gets from the extra money earned from an additional hour spent working must equal the marginal utility of an additional hour of leisure.

‖ The Effect of a Higher Wage Rate

Depending on his tastes, Jaden's utility-maximizing choice of hours of leisure and income could lie anywhere on the time allocation budget line in Figure 19A-1. Let's assume that his optimal choice is point *A*, at which he consumes 40 hours of leisure and earns $400. Now we are ready to link the analysis of time allocation to labour supply.

When Jaden chooses a point like *A* on his time allocation budget line, he is also choosing the quantity of labour he supplies to the labour market. By choosing to consume 40 of his 80 available hours as leisure, he has also chosen to supply the other 40 hours as labour.

Now suppose that Jaden's wage rate doubles, from $10 to $20 per hour. The effect of this increase in his wage rate is shown in Figure 19A-2. His time allocation budget line rotates outward: the vertical intercept, which represents the amount he could earn if he devoted all 80 hours to work, shifts upward from point *Y* to point *Z*. As a result of the doubling of his wage, Jaden would earn $1,600 instead of $800 if he devoted all 80 hours to working.

But how will Jaden's time allocation actually change? As we saw in the chapter, this depends on the *income effect* and *substitution effect* that we learned about in Chapter 10 and its appendix.

The substitution effect of an increase in the wage rate works as follows. When the wage rate increases, the opportunity cost of an hour of leisure increases; this induces Jaden to consume less leisure and work more hours—that is, to substitute hours of work in place of hours of leisure as the wage rate rises. If the substitution effect were the whole story, the individual labour supply curve would look like any ordinary supply curve and would always slope upward—a higher wage rate leads to a greater quantity of labour supplied.

What we learned in our analysis of demand was that for most consumer goods, the income effect isn't very important because most goods account for only a very small share of a consumer's spending. In addition, in the few cases of goods where the income effect is significant—for example, major purchases like housing—it usually reinforces the substitution effect: most goods are

FIGURE 19A-2 An Increase in the Wage Rate

The two panels show Jaden's initial optimal choice, point A or BL_1, the time allocation budget line corresponding to a wage rate of $10. After his wage rate rises to $20, his budget line rotates out to the new budget line, BL_2: if he spends all his time working, the amount of money he earns rises from $800 to $1,600, reflected in the movement from point Y to point Z. This generates two opposing effects: the substitution effect pushes him to consume less leisure and to work more hours; the income effect pushes him to consume more leisure and to work fewer hours. Panel (a) shows the change in time allocation when the substitution effect is stronger: Jaden's new optimal choice is point B, representing a decrease in hours of leisure to 30 hours and an increase in hours of labour to 50 hours. In this case, the individual labour supply curve slopes upward. Panel (b) shows the change in time allocation when the income effect is stronger: point C is the new optimal choice, representing an increase in hours of leisure to 50 hours and a decrease in hours of labour to 30 hours. Now the individual labour supply curve slopes downward.

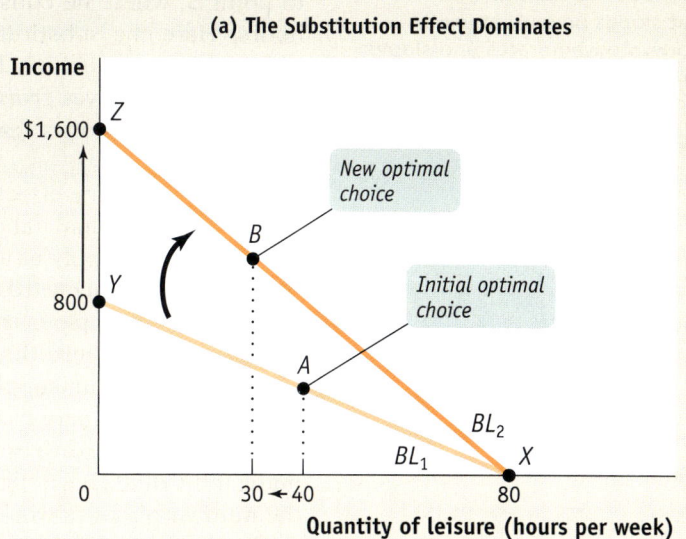

(a) The Substitution Effect Dominates

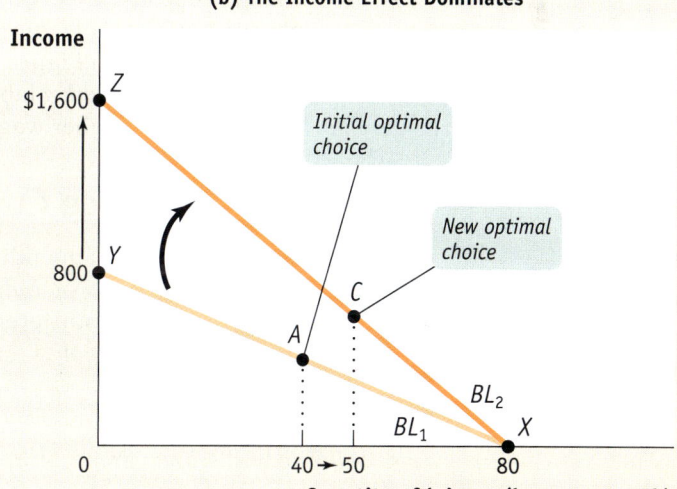

(b) The Income Effect Dominates

normal goods, so when a price increase makes a consumer poorer, that consumer buys less of that good.

In the labour/leisure choice, however, the income effect takes on a new significance, for two reasons. First, most people get the great majority of their income from wages. This means that the income effect of a change in the wage rate is *not* small: an increase in the wage rate will generate a significant increase in income. Second, leisure is a normal good: when income rises, other things equal, people tend to consume more leisure and work fewer hours.

So the income effect of a higher wage rate tends to *reduce* the quantity of labour supplied, working in opposition to the substitution effect, which tends to *increase* the quantity of labour supplied. So the net effect of a higher wage rate on the quantity of labour Jaden supplies could go either way—depending on his preferences, he might choose to supply more labour, or he might choose to supply less labour. The two panels of Figure 19A-2 illustrate these two outcomes. In each panel, point A represents Jaden's initial consumption choice.

A **backward-bending individual labour supply curve** is an individual labour supply curve that slopes upward at low to moderate wage rates and slopes downward at higher wage rates.

Panel (a) shows the case in which Jaden works more hours in response to a higher wage rate. An increase in the wage rate induces him to move from point A to point B, where he consumes less leisure than at A and therefore works more hours. Here the substitution effect prevails over the income effect. Panel (b) shows the case in which Jaden works fewer hours in response to a higher wage rate. Here, he moves from point A to point C, where he consumes more leisure and works *fewer* hours than at A. Here the income effect prevails over the substitution effect.

When the income effect of a higher wage rate is stronger than the substitution effect, the individual labour supply curve, which shows how much labour an individual will supply at any given wage rate will have a segment that slopes the "wrong" way—downward: a higher wage rate leads to a smaller quantity of labour supplied. An example is the segment connecting points B and C in Figure 19A-3.

Economists believe that the substitution effect usually dominates the income effect in the labour supply decision when an individual's wage rate is low. An individual labour supply curve typically slopes upward for lower wage rates as people work more in response to rising wage rates. But they also believe that many individuals have stronger preferences for leisure and will choose to cut back the number of hours worked as their wage rate continues to rise.

For these individuals, the income effect eventually dominates the substitution effect as the wage rate rises, leading their individual labour supply curves to change slope and to "bend backward" at high wage rates. An individual labour supply curve with this feature, called a **backward-bending individual labour supply curve,** is shown in Figure 19A-3. Although an *individual* labour supply curve may bend backward, *market* labour supply curves almost always slope upward over their entire range as higher wage rates draw more new workers into the labour market.

‖ Indifference Curve Analysis

In the Chapter 10 appendix, we learned that consumer choice can be represented using the concept of *indifference curves,* which provide a "map" of consumer preferences. But indifference curves are also especially useful for addressing the issue of labour supply.

FIGURE 19A-3 A Backward-Bending Individual Labour Supply Curve

At lower wage rates, the substitution effect dominates the income effect for Clive. This is illustrated by the movement along the individual labour supply curve from point A to point B: a rise in the wage rate from W_1 to W_2 leads the quantity of labour supplied to increase from L_1 to L_2. But at higher wage rates, the income effect dominates the substitution effect, shown by the movement from point B to point C: here, a rise in the wage rate from W_2 to W_3 leads the quantity of labour supplied to decrease from L_2 to L_3.

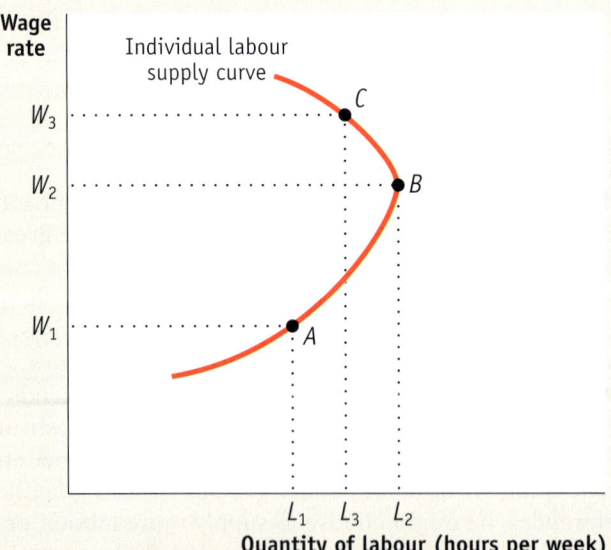

FIGURE 19A-4 Labour Supply Choice: The Indifference Curve Approach

Point *A*, on *BL*₁, is Jaden's initial optimal choice. After a wage rate increase, his income and utility level increase: his new time allocation budget line is *BL*₂ and his new optimal choice is point *C*. This change can be decomposed into the substitution effect, the fall in the hours of leisure from point *A* to point *S*, and the income effect, the increase in the number of hours of leisure from point *S* to point *C*. As shown here, the income effect dominates the substitution effect: the net result of an increase in the wage rate is an increase in the hours of leisure consumed and a decrease in the hours of labour supplied.

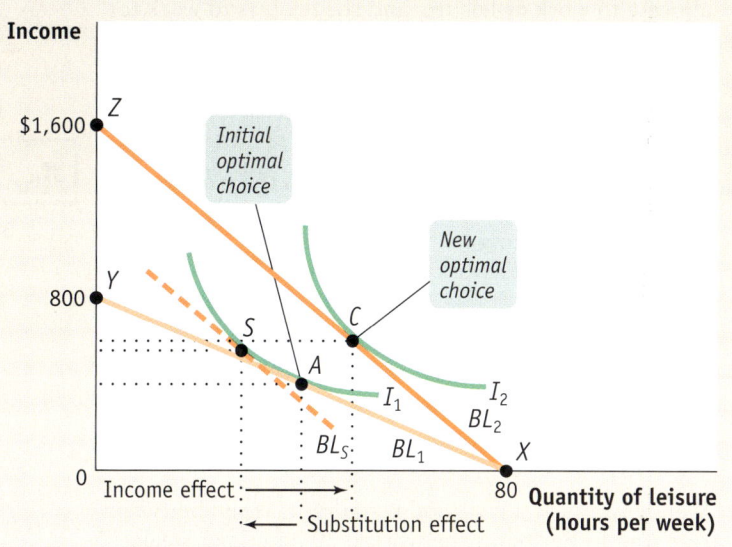

Using indifference curves, Figure 19A-4 shows how an increase in the wage rate can lead to a fall in the quantity of labour supplied. Point *A* is Jaden's initial optimal choice, given an hourly wage rate of $10. It is the same as point *A* in Figure 19A-1; this time, however, we include an indifference curve to show that it is a point at which the budget line is tangent to the highest possible indifference curve.

Now consider the effect of a rise in the wage rate to $20. Imagine, for a moment, that at the same time Jaden was offered a higher wage, he was told that he had to start repaying his student loan and that the combination of good and bad news left his utility unchanged. Then he would find himself at point *S*: on the same indifference curve as at *A*, but tangent to a steeper budget line, the dashed line *BL*ₛ in Figure 19A-4, which is parallel to *BL*₂. The move from point *A* to point *S* is the substitution effect of his wage increase: it leads him to consume less leisure and therefore supply more labour.

But now cancel the repayment on the student loan, and Jaden is able to move to a higher indifference curve. His new optimum is at point *C*, which corresponds to *C* in panel (b) of Figure 19A-2. The move from point *S* to point *C* is the income effect of his wage increase. And we see that this income effect can outweigh the substitution effect: at *C* he consumes more leisure, and therefore supplies less labour, than he did at *A*.

PROBLEMS

1. Leandro has 16 hours per day that he can allocate to work or leisure. His job pays a wage rate of $20. Leandro decides to consume 8 hours of leisure. His indifference curves have the usual shape: they slope downward, they do not cross, and they have the characteristic convex shape.

   a. Draw Leandro's time allocation budget line for a typical day. Then illustrate the indifference curve at his optimal choice.

   Now Leandro's wage rate falls to $10.

   b. Draw Leandro's new budget line.

   c. Suppose that Leandro now works only 4 hours as a result of his reduced wage rate. Illustrate the indifference curve at his new optimal choice.

   d. Leandro's decision to work less as the wage rate falls is the result of a substitution effect and an income effect. In your diagram, show the income effect and the substitution effect from this reduced wage rate. Which effect is stronger?

2. Florence is a highly paid fashion consultant who earns $100 per hour. She has 16 hours per day that she can allocate to work or leisure, and she decides to work for 12 hours.

   a. Draw Florence's time allocation budget line for a typical day, and illustrate the indifference curve at her optimal choice.

   One of Florence's clients is featured on the front page of *Vague*, an influential fashion magazine. As a result, Florence's consulting fee now rises to $500 per hour. Florence decides to work only 10 hours per day.

   b. Draw Florence's new time allocation budget line, and illustrate the indifference curve at her optimal choice.

   c. In your diagram, show the income effect and the substitution effect from this increase in the wage rate. Which effect is stronger?

3. Wendy works at a fast-food restaurant. When her wage rate was $5 per hour, she worked 30 hours per week. When her wage rate rose to $6 per hour, she decided to work 40 hours. But when her wage rate rose further to $7, she decided to work only 35 hours.

   a. Draw Wendy's individual labour supply curve.

   b. Is Wendy's behaviour irrational, or can you find a rational explanation? Explain your answer.

4. According to Statistics Canada, the amount of free time activities enjoyed by the average Canadian fell from 5 hours 46 minutes per day in 1998 to 5 hours 27 minutes per day in 2010. Another study by Statistics Canada showed that during the same time period, Canadian workers experienced an increase in real wage rates.

   a. Use the income and substitution effects to describe the labour supply for the average Canadian. Which effect dominates?

   b. In addition to increasing wages, the labour force participation for women had increased from 58.4%

in 1998 to 62.4% in 2010. For the average woman who had entered the labour force, which effect dominates?

   c. Draw typical individual labour supply curves that illustrate your answers to part a and part b above.

WORK IT OUT

5. Tamara has 80 hours per week that she can allocate to work or leisure. Her job pays a wage rate of $20 per hour, but Tamara is being taxed on her income in the following way. On the first $400 that Tamara makes, she pays no tax. That is, for the first 20 hours she works, her net wage—what she takes home after taxes—is $20 per hour. On all income above $400, Tamara pays a 75% tax. That is, for all hours above the first 20 hours, her net wage rate is only $5 per hour. Tamara decides to work 30 hours. Her indifference curves have the usual shape.

   a. Draw Tamara's time allocation budget line for a typical week. Also illustrate the indifference curve at her optimal choice.

   The government changes the tax scheme. Now only the first $100 of income is tax-exempt. That is, for the first 5 hours she works, Tamara's net wage rate is $20 per hour. But the government reduces the tax rate on all other income to 50%. That is, for all hours above the first 5 hours, Tamara's net wage rate is now $10. After these changes, Tamara finds herself exactly equally as well off as before. That is, her new optimal choice is on the same indifference curve as her initial optimal choice.

   b. Draw Tamara's new time allocation budget line on the same diagram. Also illustrate her optimal choice. Bear in mind that she is equally as well off (on the same indifference curve) as before the tax changes occurred.

   c. Will Tamara work more or less than before the changes to the tax scheme? Why? ■

Uncertainty, Risk, and Private Information

EXTREME WEATHER

IN 2019, the Ottawa River Flood topped the list of 2019 weather stories from Environment Canada and was considered to be the flood of the century. Between April 10 and May 10, Ottawa had an accumulated rainfall of 150mm, twice the amount during normal times. According to the National Capital Commission, the cost of repairing damage done to the nation's capital's bridges, pathways, and shorelines would range from $6 million to $10 million. The flood costs would be much higher if the damages to personal property were included. While eastern Canada had floods, the west was ravaged by fires. The 2019 Alberta wildfires scorched more than 800,000 hectares of land, and more than 10,000 Albertans had to evacuate.

These natural disasters are not foreign to us. When it comes to natural disasters, flooding is the one that causes the most damage in dollar terms in Canada. In recent years, the spending by the federal government on disaster relief caused by fires and floods has increased significantly. The average annual disaster relief cost $430 million between 2016 and 2019, up from $360 million in the 2011–2015 period while the clean-up spending between the 2011–2015 period was triple the average annual bill in the five years before that. Flooding and major rainstorms accounted for more than 75% of the relief spending. Due to climate change, Canada has experienced more severe weather in recent decades. Property damage from extreme weather costs millions to households and billions to the economy. According to the Insurance Bureau of Canada, for 11 years in a row, the insured losses related to extreme weather are more than a billion dollars.

As these extreme weather events illustrate, uncertainty is a feature of the real world. Up to this point we have assumed that people make decisions with knowledge of exactly how the future will unfold. (The exception is our coverage of health insurance decisions.) Yet, as anyone who lives in an area threatened by natural disasters realizes, making decisions when the future is uncertain carries with it the *risk of loss*. In fact, both climatologists and the property insurance industry largely agree that extreme weather events have become more frequent as a result of climate change.

It is often possible for individuals to use markets to reduce their risk. For example, hurricane victims who had insurance were able to receive some, if not complete, compensation for their losses. In fact, through insurance and other devices, the modern economy offers many ways for individuals to reduce their exposure to risk.

However, a market economy cannot always solve the problems created by uncertainty. Markets do very well at coping with risk when two conditions hold: (1) when risk can be reasonably well *diversified*, and (2) when the probability of loss is equally well known by everyone. However, the increase in extreme weather events over the past several years has led many insurers to stop relying on *diversification* for weather-related losses and instead to sharply reduce their coverage of such losses.

In practice, the second condition is often the more limiting one. Markets run into trouble when some people know things that others do not — a situation that involves what is called *private information*. We'll see that private information can cause inefficiency by preventing mutually beneficial transactions from occurring — especially in insurance markets.

In this chapter, we'll examine why most people dislike risk. Then we'll explore how a market economy allows people to reduce risk at a price. Finally, we'll turn to the special problems created for markets by private information. •

The Ottawa River flood in 2019 illustrated that uncertainty is an important feature of the real world.

WHAT YOU WILL LEARN

- Why is **risk** a key feature of the economy?
- Why does diminishing marginal utility make people **risk-averse** and how does it determine what they are willing to pay to reduce risk?
- How do insurance markets lead to mutually beneficial trades of risk?
- What is **private information** and what special problems does it pose for markets?

A **random variable** is a variable with an uncertain future value.

The **expected value** of a random variable is the weighted average of all possible values, where the weights on each possible value correspond to the probability of that value occurring.

A **state of the world** is a possible future event.

Risk is uncertainty about future outcomes. When the uncertainty is about monetary outcomes, it becomes **financial risk.**

‖ The Economics of Risk Aversion

In general, people don't like risk and are willing to pay a price to avoid it. Just ask the Canadian insurance industry.

In 2019, private Canadian insurers collected $65.3 billion in premiums for insurance on homes, cars, and businesses, and another $69 billion in premiums on life and disability insurance policies. But what exactly is *risk?* And why don't most people like it? To answer these questions, we need to look briefly at the concept of *expected value* and the meaning of *uncertainty.* Then we can turn to why people dislike risk.

Expectations and Uncertainty

The Lee family doesn't know how big its medical bills will be next year. If all goes well, they won't have any medical expenses at all. Let's assume that there's a 50% chance of that happening. But if a family member requires hospitalization or expensive drugs, they will face medical expenses of $10,000. Let's assume that there's also a 50% chance that these high medical expenses will materialize.

In this example—which is designed to illustrate a point, rather than to be realistic—the Lees' medical expenses for the coming year are a **random variable,** a variable that has an uncertain future value. No one can predict which of its possible values, or outcomes, a random variable will take. But that doesn't mean we can say nothing about the Lees' future medical expenses. On the contrary, an actuary (a person trained in evaluating uncertain future events) could calculate the **expected value** of expenses next year—the weighted average of all possible values, where the weights on each possible value correspond to the probability of that value occurring. In this example, the expected value of the Lees' medical expenses is $(0.5 \times \$0) + (0.5 \times \$10,000) = \$5,000$.

To derive the general formula for the expected value of a random variable, we imagine that there are a number of different **states of the world,** possible future events. Each state is associated with a different realized value—the value that actually occurs—of the random variable. You don't know which state of the world will actually occur, but you can assign probabilities, one for each state of the world.

Let's assume that P_1 is the probability of state 1, P_2 the probability of state 2, and so on. And you know the realized value of the random value in each state of the world: S_1 in state 1, S_2 in state 2, and so on. Let's also assume that there are N possible states. Then the expected value of a random variable is:

(20-1) *Expected value of a random variable*
$$EV = (P_1 \times S_1) + (P_2 \times S_2) + \ldots + (P_N \times S_N)$$

In the case of the Lee family, there are only two possible states of the world, each with a probability of 0.5.

Notice, however, that the Lee family doesn't actually expect to pay $5,000 in medical bills next year. That's because in this example there is no state of the world in which the family pays exactly $5,000. Either the family pays nothing, or it pays $10,000. So the Lees face considerable uncertainty about their future medical expenses.

But what if the Lee family can buy supplemental health insurance that will cover any medical expenses they face that are not covered by a government health insurance plan, whatever they turn out to be? Suppose, in particular, that the family can pay $5,000 up front in return for full coverage of whatever medical expenses actually arise during the coming year. Then the Lees' future medical expenses are no longer uncertain *for them:* in return for $5,000—an amount equal to the expected value of the medical expenses—the insurance company assumes all responsibility for paying those medical expenses. Would this be a good deal from the Lees' point of view?

Yes, it would—or at least most families would think so. Most people prefer, other things equal, to reduce **risk**—uncertainty about future outcomes. (We'll focus here on **financial risk,** in which the uncertainty is about monetary outcomes, as opposed to uncertainty about outcomes that can't be assigned a monetary value.) In fact, most people are willing to pay a substantial price to reduce their risk; that's why we have an insurance industry.

But before we study the market for insurance, we need to understand why people feel that risk is a bad thing, an attitude that economists call *risk aversion.* The source of risk aversion lies in a concept we first encountered in our analysis of consumer demand, back in Chapter 10: *diminishing marginal utility.*

The Logic of Risk Aversion

To understand how diminishing marginal utility gives rise to risk aversion, we need to look not only at the Lees' medical costs but also at how those costs affect the income the family has left after medical expenses. Let's assume the family knows that it will have an income of $30,000 next year. If the family has no medical expenses, it will be left with all of that income. If its medical expenses are $10,000, its income after medical expenses will be only $20,000. Since we have assumed that there is an equal chance of these two outcomes, the expected value of the Lees' income after medical expenses is $(0.5 \times \$30,000) + (0.5 \times \$20,000) = \$25,000$. At times we will simply refer to this as expected income.

But as we'll now see, if the family's utility function has the shape typical of most families', its **expected utility**—the expected value of its total utility given uncertainty about future outcomes—is less than it would be if the family didn't face any risk and knew with certainty that its income after medical expenses would be $25,000.

To see why, we need to look at how total utility depends on income. Panel (a) of Figure 20-1 shows a hypothetical utility function for the Lee family, where total utility depends on income—the amount of money the Lees have available for consumption of goods and services (after they have paid any medical bills). The table within the figure shows how the family's total utility varies over the income range of $20,000 to $30,000. As usual, the utility function slopes upward, because more income leads to higher total utility. Notice as well that the curve gets flatter as we move up and to the right, which reflects diminishing marginal utility.

In Chapter 10, we applied the principle of diminishing marginal utility to individual goods and services: each successive unit of a good or service that a consumer purchases adds less to their total utility. The same principle applies to income used for consumption: each successive dollar of income adds less to total utility than the previous dollar.

Panel (b) shows how marginal utility varies with income, confirming that marginal utility of income falls as income rises. As we'll see in a moment, diminishing marginal utility is the key to understanding the desire of individuals to reduce risk.

To analyze how a person's utility is affected by risk, economists start from the assumption that individuals facing uncertainty maximize their *expected* utility. We can use the data in Figure 20-1 to calculate the Lee family's expected utility. We'll first do the calculation assuming that the Lees have no supplemental insurance, and then we'll recalculate it assuming that they have purchased supplemental insurance.

Without supplemental insurance, if the Lees are lucky and don't incur any medical expenses, they will have an income of $30,000, generating total utility of 1,080 utils. But if they have no supplemental insurance and are unlucky, incurring $10,000 in medical expenses, they will have just $20,000 of their income to spend on consumption and total utility of only 920 utils. So *without supplemental insurance,* the family's expected utility is $(0.5 \times 1,080) + (0.5 \times 920) = 1,000$ utils.

Now let's suppose that an insurance company offers to pay whatever medical expenses the family incurs during the next year in return for a **premium**—a payment to the insurance company—of $5,000. Note that the amount of the premium in this case is equal to the expected value of the Lees' medical expenses—the

Expected utility is the expected value of an individual's total utility given uncertainty about future outcomes.

A **premium** is a payment to an insurance company in return for the insurance company's promise to pay a claim in certain states of the world.

FIGURE 20-1 The Utility Function and Marginal Utility Curve of a Risk-Averse Family

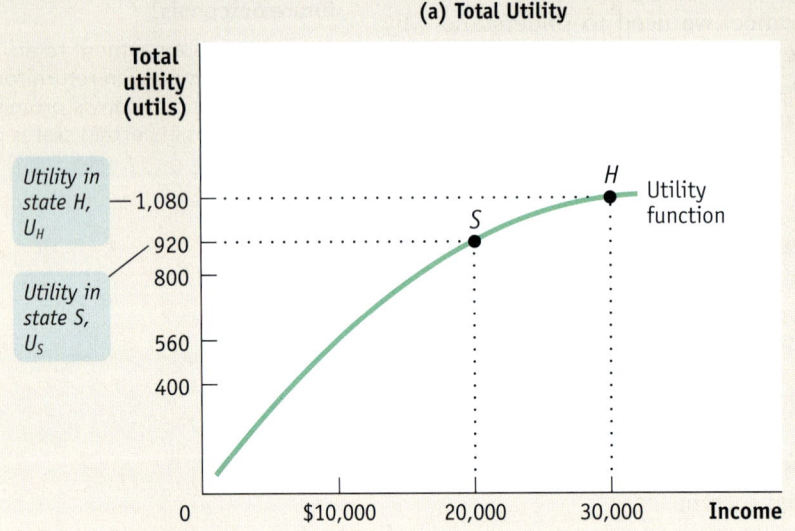

(a) Total Utility

Income	Total utility (utils)
$20,000	920
21,000	945
22,000	968
23,000	989
24,000	1,008
25,000	1,025
26,000	1,040
27,000	1,053
28,000	1,064
29,000	1,073
30,000	1,080

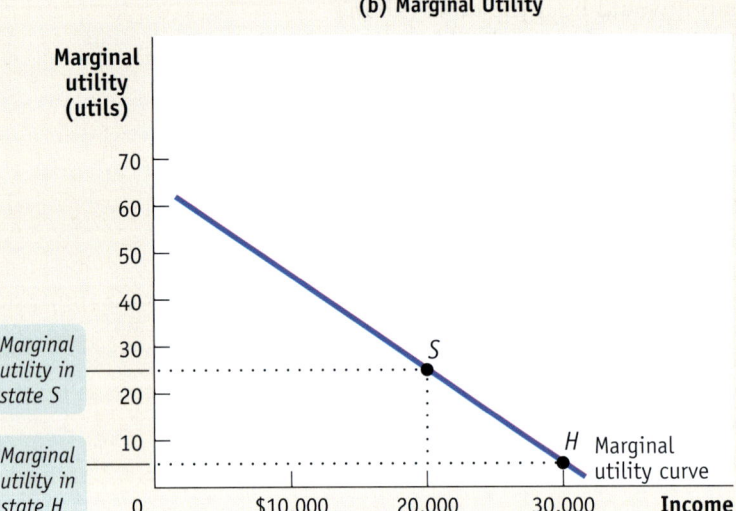

(b) Marginal Utility

Panel (a) shows how the total utility of the Lee family depends on its income available for consumption (that is, its income after medical expenses). The curve slopes upward: more income leads to higher total utility. But it gets flatter as we move up it and to the right, reflecting diminishing marginal utility. Panel (b) reflects the negative relationship between income and marginal utility when there is risk aversion: the marginal utility from each additional $1,000 of income is lower the higher your income. So the marginal utility of income is higher when the family has high medical expenses and therefore low income (point S) than when it has low medical expenses and therefore high income (point H).

expected value of their future claim against the policy. An insurance policy with this feature, for which the premium is equal to the expected value of the claim, has a special name—a **fair insurance policy.**

If the family purchases this fair insurance policy, the expected value of its income available for consumption is the *same* as it would be without insurance: $25,000—that is, $30,000 minus the $5,000 premium. But the family's risk has been eliminated: the family has an income available for consumption of $25,000 *for sure,* which means that it receives the utility level associated with an income of $25,000.

Reading from the table in Figure 20-1, we see that this utility level is 1,025 utils. Or to put it a slightly different way, their expected utility with supplemental insurance is $1 \times 1,025 = 1,025$ utils, because with supplemental insurance they will receive a utility of 1,025 utils with a probability of 1. And this is higher than the level of expected utility without supplemental insurance—only 1,000 utils. So by eliminating risk through the purchase of a fair insurance policy, the family increases its expected utility even though its expected income hasn't changed.

A **fair insurance policy** is an insurance policy for which the premium is equal to the expected value of the claim.

TABLE 20-1 The Effect of Fair Insurance on the Lee Family's Income Available for Consumption and Expected Utility

	Income in different states of the world		Expected value of income available for consumption	Expected utility
	$0 in extra/ supplemental medical expenses (0.5 probability)	$10,000 in extra/ supplemental medical expenses (0.5 probability)		
Without supplemental insurance	$30,000	$20,000	(0.5 × $30,000) + (0.5 × $20,000) = $25,000	(0.5 × 1,080 utils) + (0.5 × 920 utils) = 1,000 utils
With fair supplemental insurance	$25,000	$25,000	(0.5 × $25,000) + (0.5 × $25,000) = $25,000	(0.5 × 1,025 utils) + (0.5 × 1,025 utils) = 1,025 utils

The calculations for this example are summarized in Table 20-1. This example shows that the Lees, like most people in real life, are **risk-averse:** they will choose to reduce the risk they face when the cost of that reduction leaves the expected value of their income or wealth unchanged. So the Lees, like most people, will be willing to buy fair insurance.

You might think that this result depends on the specific numbers we have chosen. In fact, however, the proposition that purchase of a fair insurance policy increases expected utility depends on only one assumption: diminishing marginal utility. The reason is that *with diminishing marginal utility, a dollar gained when income is low adds more to utility than a dollar gained when income is high.*

That is, having an additional dollar matters more when you are facing hard times than when you are facing good times. And as we will shortly see, a fair insurance policy is desirable because it transfers a dollar from high-income states (where it is valued less) to low-income states (where it is valued more).

But first, let's see how diminishing marginal utility leads to risk aversion by examining expected utility more closely. In the case of the Lee family, there are two states of the world; let's call them H and S, for healthy and sick. In state H, the family has no medical expenses; in state S, it has $10,000 in medical expenses. We'll use the symbols U_H and U_S to represent the Lee family's total utility in each state. Then the family's expected utility is:

(20-2) Expected utility = (Probability of state H × Total utility in state H) + (Probability of state S × Total utility in state S)

$$= (0.5 \times U_H) + (0.5 \times U_S)$$

The fair (supplemental) insurance policy *reduces* the family's income available for consumption in state H by $5,000, but it *increases* it in state S by the same amount. As we've just seen, we can use the utility function to directly calculate the effects of these changes on expected utility. But as we have also seen in many other contexts, we gain more insight into individual choice by focusing on *marginal* utility.

To use marginal utility to analyze the effects of fair (supplemental) insurance, let's imagine introducing the supplemental insurance a bit at a time, say in 5,000 small steps. At each of these steps, we reduce income in state H by $1 and simultaneously increase income in state S by $1. At each of these steps, total utility in state H falls by the marginal utility of income in that state but total utility in state S rises by the marginal utility of income in that state.

Now look again at panel (b) of Figure 20-1, which shows how marginal utility varies with income. Point S shows marginal utility when the Lee family's income is $20,000; point H shows marginal utility when income is $30,000. Clearly, marginal utility is higher when income after medical expenses is low. Because of diminishing marginal utility, an additional dollar of income adds more to total utility when the family has low income (point S) than when it has high income (point H).

This tells us that the gain in expected utility from increasing income in state S is larger than the loss in expected utility from reducing income in state H by the same

Risk-averse individuals will choose to reduce the risk they face when that reduction leaves the expected value of their income or wealth unchanged.

amount. So at each step of the process of reducing risk, by transferring $1 of income from state *H* to state *S*, expected utility increases. This is the same as saying that the family is risk-averse. That is, risk aversion is a result of diminishing marginal utility.

Almost everyone is risk-averse, because almost everyone has diminishing marginal utility. But the degree of risk aversion varies among individuals—some people are more risk-averse than others. To illustrate this point, Figure 20-2 compares two individuals, Danny and Mel. We suppose that each of them earns the same income now but is confronted with the possibility of earning either $1,000 more or $1,000 less.

Panel (a) of Figure 20-2 shows how each individual's total utility would be affected by the change in income. Danny would gain very few utils from a rise in income, which moves him from *N* to H_D, but lose a large number of utils from a fall in income, which moves him from *N* to L_D. That is, he is highly risk-averse. This is reflected in panel (b) by his steeply declining marginal utility curve.

FIGURE 20-2 Differences in Risk Aversion

As shown in panel (a), Danny and Mel have different utility functions. Danny is highly risk-averse: a gain of $1,000 in income, which moves him from *N* to H_D, adds only a few utils to his total utility, but a $1,000 fall in income, which moves him from *N* to L_D, reduces his total utility by a large number of utils. By contrast, Mel gains almost as many utils from a $1,000 rise in income (the movement from *N* to H_M) as he loses from a $1,000 fall in income (the movement from *N* to L_M). Panel (b) illustrates this difference using the two men's marginal utility curves. The slope of Danny's marginal utility curve is steeper than Mel's, which means that Danny would be willing to pay much more for insurance than Mel.

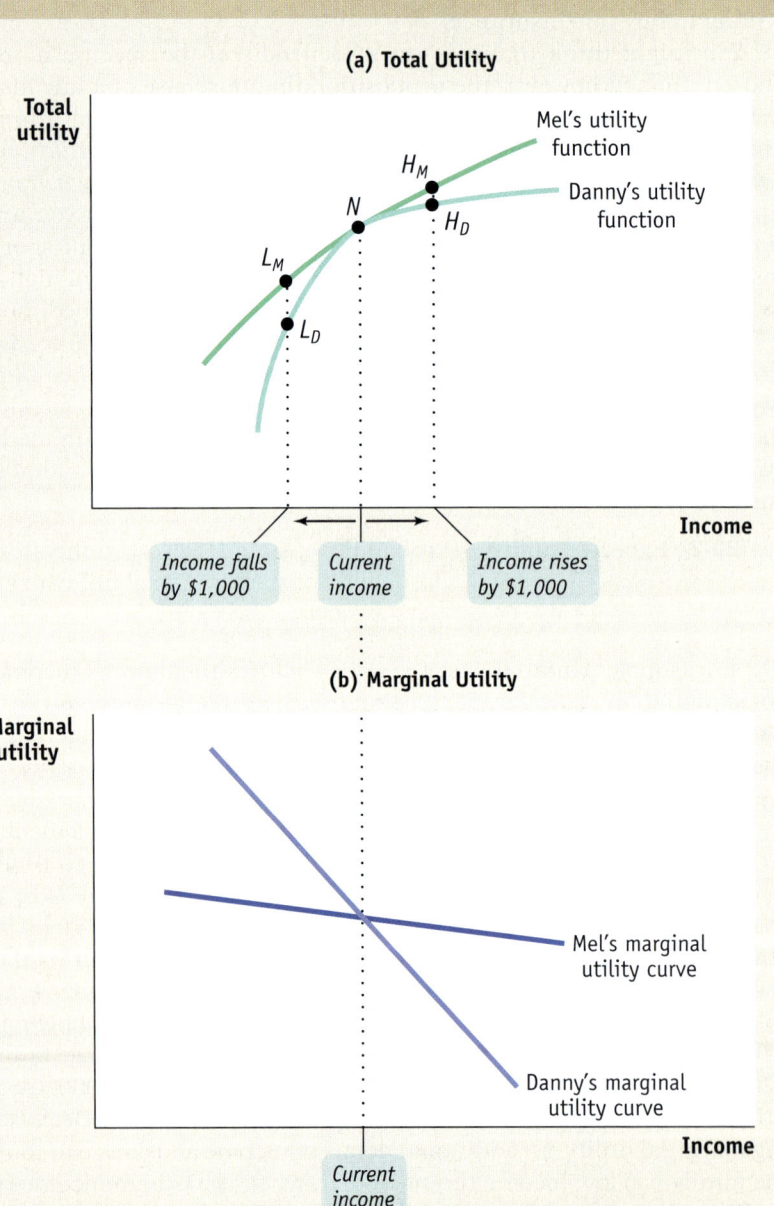

(a) Total Utility

(b) Marginal Utility

Mel, though, as shown in panel (a), would gain almost as many utils from higher income, which moves him from N to H_M, as he would lose from lower income, which moves him from N to L_M. He is barely risk-averse at all. This is reflected in his marginal utility curve in panel (b), which is almost horizontal. So, other things equal, Danny will gain a lot more utility from insurance than Mel will. Someone who is completely insensitive to risk is called **risk-neutral.**

Individuals differ in risk aversion for two main reasons: differences in preferences and differences in initial income or wealth.

A **risk-neutral** person is completely insensitive to risk.

1. *Differences in preferences.* Other things equal, people simply differ in how much their marginal utility is affected by their level of income. Someone whose marginal utility is relatively unresponsive to changes in income will be much less sensitive to risk. In contrast, someone whose marginal utility depends greatly on changes in income will be much more risk-averse.

2. *Differences in initial income or wealth.* The possible loss of $1,000 makes a big difference to a family living below the poverty threshold; it makes very little difference to someone who earns $1 million a year. In general, people with high incomes or high wealth will be less risk-averse.

Differences in risk aversion have an important consequence: they affect how much an individual is willing to pay to avoid risk.

Paying to Avoid Risk

The risk-averse Lee family is clearly better off taking out a fair insurance policy—a policy that leaves their expected income unchanged but eliminates their risk. Unfortunately, real insurance policies are rarely fair: because insurance companies have to cover other costs, such as salaries for salespeople and actuaries, they charge more than they expect to pay in claims.

Will the Lee family still want to purchase an "unfair" supplemental insurance policy—one for which the premium is larger than the expected claim?

It depends on the size of the premium. Look again at Table 20-1. We know that without supplemental insurance expected utility is 1,000 utils and that supplemental insurance costing $5,000 raises expected utility to 1,025 utils. If the premium were $6,000, the Lees would be left with an income of $24,000, which, as you can see from Figure 20-1, would give them a total utility of 1,008 utils—which is still higher than their expected utility if they had no supplemental insurance at all. So the Lees would be willing to buy supplemental insurance with a $6,000 premium. But they wouldn't be willing to pay $7,000, which would reduce their income to $23,000 and their total utility to 989 utils.

This example shows that risk-averse individuals are willing to make deals that reduce their expected income but also reduce their risk: they are willing to pay a premium that exceeds their expected claim.

PITFALLS

BEFORE OR AFTER THE FACT?

Why is an insurance policy different from a doughnut?

No, it's not a riddle. Although the supply and demand for insurance behave like the supply and demand for any good or service, the payoff is very different. When you buy a doughnut, you know what you're going to get. When you buy insurance, by definition you *don't* know what you're going to get. If you bought car insurance and then didn't have an accident, you got nothing from the policy, except peace of mind, and might wish that you hadn't bothered. But if you did have an accident, you probably would be glad that you bought insurance that covered the cost.

This means we have to be careful in assessing the rationality of insurance purchases (or, for that matter, any decision made in the face of uncertainty). *After the fact*—after the uncertainty has been resolved—such decisions are almost always subject to second-guessing. But that doesn't mean that the decision was wrong *before the fact,* given the information available at the time.

One highly successful Wall Street investor told the authors that he never looks back—as long as he believes he made the right decision given what he knew when he made it, he never reproaches himself if things turn out badly. That's the right attitude, and it almost surely contributes to his success.

The more risk-averse they are, the higher the premium they are willing to pay. That willingness to pay is what makes the insurance industry possible. In contrast, a risk-neutral person is unwilling to pay at all to reduce their risk.

"Call me when you invent the warranty."

ECONOMICS >> *in Action*

Warranties

Many expensive consumer goods—electronics, major appliances, cars—come with some form of *warranty*. Typically, the manufacturer guarantees to repair or replace the item if something goes wrong with it during some specified period after purchase—usually six months or one year.

Why do manufacturers offer warranties? Part of the answer is that warranties *signal* to consumers that the goods are of high quality. But mainly warranties are a form of consumer insurance. For many people, the cost of repairing or replacing an expensive item like a smartphone or a car would be a serious burden. If they were obliged to come up with the cash, their consumption of other goods would be restricted; as a result, their marginal utility of income would be higher than if they didn't have to pay for repairs.

So a warranty that covers the cost of repair or replacement increases the consumer's expected utility, even if the cost of the warranty is greater than the expected future claim paid by the manufacturer.

>> Quick Review

- The **expected value** of a **random variable** is the weighted average of all possible values, where the weight corresponds to the probability of a given value occurring.

- Uncertainty about **states of the world** entails **risk,** or **financial risk** when there is an uncertain monetary outcome. When faced with uncertainty, consumers choose the option yielding the highest level of **expected utility.**

- Most people are **risk-averse:** they would be willing to purchase a **fair insurance policy** in which the premium is equal to the expected value of the claim.

- Risk aversion arises from diminishing marginal utility. Differences in preferences and in income or wealth lead to differences in risk aversion.

- Depending on the size of the **premium,** a risk-averse person may be willing to purchase an "unfair" insurance policy with a premium larger than the expected claim. The greater your risk aversion, the greater the premium you are willing to pay. A **risk-neutral** person is unwilling to pay any premium to avoid risk.

>> Check Your Understanding 20-1

Solutions appear at back of book.

1. Compare two families who own homes near the floodplain of the Red River in Manitoba. Which family is likely to be more risk-averse—(i) a family with income of $2 million per year, or (ii) a family with income of $60,000 per year? Would either family be willing to buy an "unfair" insurance policy to cover losses to their Red River home?

2. Karma's income next year is uncertain: there is a 60% probability she will make $22,000 and a 40% probability she will make $35,000. The accompanying table shows some income and utility levels for Karma.

Income	Total utility (utils)
$22,000	850
25,000	1,014
26,000	1,056
35,000	1,260

   a. What is Karma's expected income? Her expected utility?

   b. What certain income level leaves her as well off as her uncertain income? What does this imply about Karma's attitudes toward risk? Explain.

   c. Would Karma be willing to pay some amount of money greater than zero for an insurance policy that guarantees her an income of $26,000? Explain.

Buying, Selling, and Reducing Risk

Lloyd's of London is the oldest existing commercial insurance company, and it is an institution with an illustrious past. Originally formed in the eighteenth century to help merchants cope with the risks of commerce, it grew in the heyday of the British Empire into a mainstay of imperial trade.

The basic idea of Lloyd's was simple. In the eighteenth century, shipping goods on sailing vessels was risky: the chance that a ship would sink in a storm or be captured by pirates was fairly high. The merchant who owned the ship and its cargo could easily be ruined financially by such an event. Lloyd's matched shipowners seeking insurance with wealthy investors who promised to compensate a merchant if his ship were lost. In return, the merchant paid the investor a fee in advance. If his ship *didn't* sink, the investor still kept the fee.

In effect, the merchant paid a price to relieve himself of risk. By matching people who wanted to purchase insurance with people who wanted to provide it, Lloyd's performed the functions of a market. The fact that British merchants could use Lloyd's to reduce their risk made many more Brits willing to undertake merchant trade.

Insurance companies have changed quite a lot from the early days of Lloyd's. But asking why Lloyd's worked to the mutual benefit of merchants and investors is a good way to understand how the market economy as a whole "trades" and thereby transforms risk.

The insurance industry rests on these two principles, which we will consider in turn.

1. Trade in risk, like trade in any good or service, can produce mutual gains. In this case, the gains come when those less willing to bear risk transfer it to people who are more willing to bear it.
2. Some risk can be made to disappear through *diversification*.

Trading Risk

It may seem a bit strange to talk about "trading" risk. After all, risk is a bad thing—and aren't we supposed to be trading goods and services?

But people often trade away things they don't like to other people who dislike them less. Suppose you have just bought a house for $300,000, the average price for a house in your community. But you have now learned, to your horror, that the building next door is being turned into a nightclub. You want to sell the house immediately and are willing to accept $285,000 for it. But who will now be willing to buy it? The answer: a person who doesn't really mind late-night noise. Such a person might be willing to pay up to $300,000. So there is an opportunity here for a mutually beneficial deal—you are willing to sell for as little as $285,000, and the other person is willing to pay as much as $300,000, so any price in between will benefit both of you.

The key point is that the two parties have different sensitivities to noise, which enables those who most dislike noise, in effect, to pay other people to make their lives quieter. Trading risk works exactly the same way: people who want to reduce the risk they face can pay other people who are less sensitive to risk to take some of their risk away.

As we saw in the previous section, individual preferences account for some of the variations in people's attitudes toward risk, but differences in income and wealth are probably the principal reason behind different risk sensitivities. Lloyd's made money by matching wealthy investors who were more risk-tolerant with less wealthy and therefore more risk-averse shipowners.

Suppose, staying with our Lloyd's of London story, that a merchant whose ship went down would lose £1,000 and that there was a 10% chance of such a disaster. The expected loss in this case would be $0.10 \times £1,000 = £100$. But the merchant, whose whole livelihood was at stake, might have been willing to pay £150 to be compensated in the amount of £1,000 if the ship sank. Meanwhile, a wealthy investor for whom the loss of £1,000 was no big deal would have been willing to take this risk for a return only slightly better than the expected loss—say, £110.

Clearly, there is room for a mutually beneficial deal here: the merchant pays something less than £150 and more than £110—say, £130—in return for compensation if the ship goes down. In effect, they have paid a less risk-averse individual to bear the burden of their risk. Everyone has been made better off by this transaction.

The funds that an insurer places at risk when providing insurance are called the insurer's **capital at risk.**

An **efficient allocation of risk** is an allocation of risk in which those who are most willing to bear risk are those who end up bearing it.

The funds that an insurer places at risk when providing insurance are called the insurer's **capital at risk.** In our example, the wealthy Lloyd's investor places capital of £1,000 at risk in return for a premium of £130. In general, the amount of capital that potential insurers are willing to place at risk depends, other things equal, on the premium offered. If every ship is worth £1,000 and has a 10% chance of going down, nobody would offer insurance for less than a £100 premium, equal to the expected claim. In fact, only an investor who isn't risk-averse at all—that is, who is risk-neutral—would be willing to offer a policy at that price, because accepting a £100 premium would leave the insurer's expected income unchanged while increasing that insurer's risk.

Suppose there is one investor who is risk-neutral. But the next most willing investor is slightly risk-averse and insists on a £105 premium. The next investor, being somewhat more risk-averse, demands a premium of £110, and so on. By varying the premium and asking how many insurers would be willing to provide insurance at that premium, we can trace out a supply curve for insurance, as shown in Figure 20-3. As the premium increases as we move up the supply curve, more risk-averse investors are induced to provide coverage.

Meanwhile, potential buyers will consider their willingness to pay a given premium, defining the demand curve for insurance. In Figure 20-4, the highest premium that any shipowner is willing to pay is £200. Who's willing to pay this? The most risk-averse shipowner, of course. A slightly less risk-averse shipowner might be willing to pay £190, an even slightly less risk-averse shipowner is willing to pay £180, and so on.

Now imagine a market in which there are thousands of shipowners and potential insurers, so that the supply and demand curves for insurance are smooth lines. In this market, as in markets for ordinary goods and services, there will be an equilibrium price and quantity. Figure 20-5 illustrates such a market equilibrium at a premium of £130, with a total quantity of 5,000 policies bought and sold, representing a total capital at risk of £5,000,000.

Notice that in this market risk is transferred from the people who most want to get rid of it (the most risk-averse shipowners) to the people least bothered by risk (the least risk-averse investors). So just as markets for goods and services typically produce an efficient allocation of resources, markets for risk also typically lead to an **efficient allocation of risk**—an allocation of risk in which those who

FIGURE 20-3 The Supply of Insurance

This is the supply of insurance policies to provide £1,000 in coverage to a merchant ship that has a 10% chance of being lost. Each investor has £1,000 of capital at risk. The lowest possible premium at which a policy is offered is £100, equal to the expected claim, and only a risk-neutral investor is willing to supply this policy. As the premium increases, investors who are more risk-averse are induced to supply policies to the market, increasing the quantity of policies supplied.

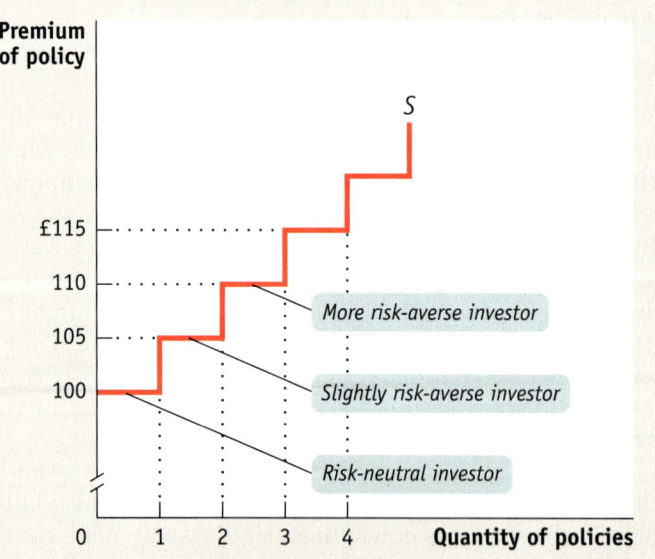

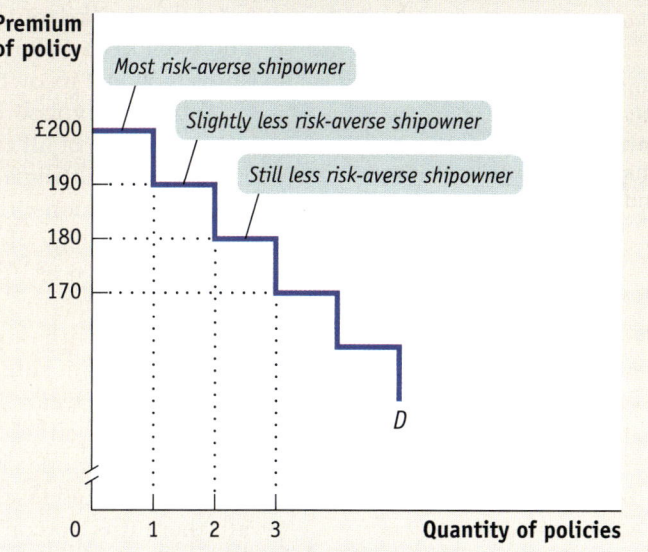

FIGURE 20-4 The Demand for Insurance

This is the demand for insurance policies for £1,000 in coverage of a merchant ship that has a 10% chance of being lost. In this example, the highest premium at which anyone demands a policy is £200, which only the most risk-averse shipowners will desire. As the premium falls, shipowners who are less risk-averse are induced to demand policies, increasing the quantity of policies demanded.

are most willing to bear risk are those who end up bearing it. But as in the case of the markets for goods and services, there is an important qualification to this result: there are well-defined cases in which the market for risk fails to achieve efficiency. These arise from the presence of *private information*, which we will discuss in the next section.

The trading of risk between individuals who differ in their degree of risk aversion plays an extremely important role in the economy, but it is not the only way that markets can help people cope with risk. Under some circumstances, markets can perform a sort of magic trick: they can make some (though rarely all) of the risk that individuals face simply disappear.

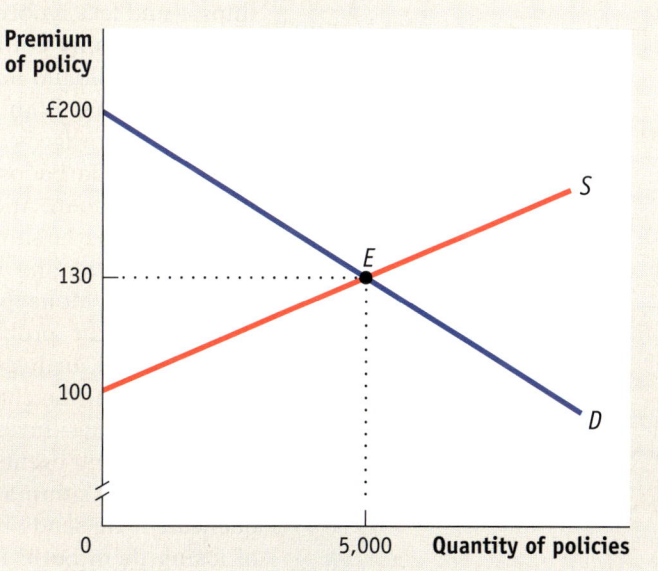

FIGURE 20-5 Insurance Market

Here we represent the hypothetical market for insuring a merchant ship, where each ship requires £1,000 in coverage. The demand curve is made up of shipowners who wish to buy insurance, and the supply curve is made up of wealthy investors who wish to supply insurance. In this example, at a premium of £200, only the most risk-averse shipowners will purchase insurance; at a premium of £100, only risk-neutral investors are willing to supply insurance. The equilibrium is at a premium of £130 with 5,000 policies bought and sold. In the absence of *private information* (explained in the next section), the insurance market leads to an efficient allocation of risk.

Two possible events are **independent events** if each of them is neither more nor less likely to happen if the other one happens.

An individual can engage in **diversification** by investing in several different things, so that the possible losses are independent events.

Making Risk Disappear: The Power of Diversification

In the early days of Lloyd's, British merchant ships traversed the world, trading spices and silk from Asia, tobacco and rum from the New World, and textiles and wool from Britain, among other goods. Each of the many routes that British ships took had its own unique risks—pirates in the Caribbean, gales in the North Atlantic, and typhoons in the Indian Ocean.

In the face of all these risks, merchants were able to survive by reducing their risks by not putting all their eggs in one basket: by sending different ships to different destinations, they could reduce the probability that all their ships would be lost. A strategy of investing in such a way to reduce the probability of severe losses is known as *diversification,* which can often make some of the economy's risk disappear.

Let's stay with our shipping example. It was all too likely that a pirate might seize a merchant ship in the Caribbean or that a typhoon might sink another ship in the Indian Ocean. But the key point here is that the various threats to shipping didn't have much to do with each other. So it was considerably less likely that a merchant with one ship in the Caribbean and another in the Indian Ocean in a given year would lose them both, one to a pirate and the other to a typhoon. After all, there was no connection: the actions of cutthroats in the Caribbean had no influence on weather in the Indian Ocean, or vice versa.

Statisticians refer to such unconnected events as **independent events**—one is no more likely to happen if the other does than if it does not. Many unpredictable events are independent of each other. If you toss a coin twice, the probability that it will come up heads on the second toss is the same whether it came up heads or tails on the first toss. If your house burns down today, it does not affect the probability that my house will burn down the same day (unless we live next door to each other or employ the services of the same incompetent electrician).

There is a simple rule for calculating the probability that two independent events will both happen: multiply the probability that one event would happen on its own by the probability that the other event would happen on its own. If you toss a coin once, the probability that it will come up heads is 0.5. If you toss the coin twice, the probability that it will come up heads *both* times is $0.5 \times 0.5 = 0.25$.

But what did it matter to shipowners or Lloyd's investors that ship losses in the Caribbean and ship losses in the Indian Ocean were independent events? The answer is that by spreading their investments across different parts of the world, they could make some of the riskiness of the shipping business simply disappear.

Let's suppose that Joseph Moneypenny, Esq., is wealthy enough to outfit two ships—and let's ignore for a moment the possibility of insuring his ships. Should Mr. Moneypenny equip two ships for the Caribbean trade and send them off together? Or should he send one ship to Barbados and one to Calcutta?

Assume that both voyages will be equally profitable if successful, yielding £1,000 if the voyage is completed. Also assume that there is a 10% chance both that a ship sent to Barbados will run into a pirate and that a ship sent to Calcutta will be sunk by a typhoon. And if two ships travel to the same destination, we will assume that they share the same fate. So if Mr. Moneypenny were to send both his ships to either destination, he would face a probability of 10% of losing all his investment.

But if Mr. Moneypenny were instead to send one ship to Barbados and one to Calcutta, the probability that he would lose both of them would be only $0.1 \times 0.1 = 0.01$, or just 1%. As we will see shortly, his expected payoff would be the same—but the chance of losing it all would be much less. So by engaging in **diversification**—investing in several different things, where the possible losses are independent events—he could make some of his risk disappear.

Table 20-2 summarizes Mr. Moneypenny's options and their possible consequences. If he sends both ships to the same destination, he runs a 10% chance of losing them both. If he sends them to different destinations, there are three possible outcomes.

TABLE 20-2 How Diversification Reduces Risk

If both ships are sent to the same destination			
State	Probability	Payoff	Expected payoff
Both ships arrive	0.9 = 90%	£2,000	$(0.9 \times £2,000) + (0.1 \times £0) = £1,800$
Both ships lost	0.1 = 10%	0	

If one ship is sent east, the other west			
State	Probability	Payoff	Expected payoff
Both ships arrive	$0.9 \times 0.9 = 81\%$	£2,000	$(0.81 \times £2,000) + (0.01 \times £0) +$
Both ships lost	$0.1 \times 0.1 = 1\%$	0	$(0.18 \times £1,000) = £1,800$
One ship arrives	$(0.9 \times 0.1 + (0.1 \times 0.9) = 18\%$	1,000	

1. Both ships could arrive safely: because there is a 0.9 probability of either one making it, the probability that both will make it is $0.9 \times 0.9 = 81\%$.
2. Both could be lost—but the probability of that happening is only $0.1 \times 0.1 = 1\%$.
3. Only one ship can arrive. The probability that the first ship arrives and the second ship is lost is $0.9 \times 0.1 = 9\%$. The probability that the first ship is lost but the second ship arrives is $0.1 \times 0.9 = 9\%$. So the probability that only one ship makes it is $9\% + 9\% = 18\%$.

You might think that diversification is a strategy available only to the wealthy. But there are ways for even small investors to diversify. Even if Mr. Moneypenny can only afford to equip one ship, he can enter a partnership with another merchant. They can jointly outfit two ships, agreeing to share the profits equally, and then send those ships to different destinations. That way each investor faces less risk than if he equips one ship alone.

In the modern economy, diversification is made much easier for investors by the fact that they can easily buy shares in many companies by using the *stock market*. The owner of a **share** in a company is the owner of part of that company—typically a very small part, one-millionth or less. An individual who put all of their wealth in shares of a single company would lose all of that wealth if the company went bankrupt. But most investors hold shares in many companies, which makes the chance of losing all their investment very small.

In fact, Lloyd's of London wasn't just a way to trade risks; it was also a way for investors to diversify. To see how this worked, let's introduce Lady Penelope, a wealthy aristocrat, who decides to increase her income by placing £1,000 of her capital at risk via Lloyd's. She could use that capital to insure just one ship. But more typically she would enter a *syndicate,* a group of investors, who would jointly insure a number of ships going to different destinations, agreeing to share the cost if any one of those ships went down. Because it would be much less likely for all the ships insured by the syndicate to sink than for any one of them to go down, Lady Penelope would be at much less risk of losing her entire capital.

In some cases, an investor can make risk almost entirely disappear by taking a small share of the risk in many independent events. This strategy is known as **pooling.**

Consider the case of a supplemental health insurance company, which has millions of policyholders, with thousands of them requiring expensive treatment each year. The insurance company can't know whether any given individual will, say, require a heart bypass operation. But heart problems for two different individuals are pretty much independent events. And when there are many possible independent events, it is possible, using statistical analysis, to predict with great accuracy *how many* events of a given type will happen. For example, if you toss a coin 1,000 times, it will come up heads about 500 times—and it is very unlikely to be more than a percent or two off that figure.

A **share** in a company is a partial ownership of that company.

Pooling is a strong form of diversification in which an investor takes a small share of the risk in many independent events. This produces a payoff with very little total overall risk.

FOR INQUIRING MINDS   Those Pesky Emotions

For a small investor (someone investing less than several hundred thousand dollars), financial economists agree that the best strategy for investing in stocks is to buy an index fund.

Why index funds? Because they contain a wide range of stocks that reflect the overall market, they achieve diversification, and they have low management fees. In addition, financial economists agree that it's a losing strategy to try to "time" the market: to buy when the stock market is low and sell when it's high. Instead, small investors should buy a fixed dollar amount of stocks and other financial assets every year, regardless of the state of the market.

Yet many, if not most, small investors don't follow this advice. Instead, they buy individual stocks or funds that charge high fees. They spend endless hours online chasing the latest hot tip or sifting through data trying to discern patterns in stocks' behaviour. They try to time the market but invariably buy when stocks are high and

"Your mother called to remind you to diversify."

refuse to sell losers. And they fail to diversify, instead concentrating too much money in a few stocks they think are winners.

So why are humans so dense when it comes to investing? According to experts, the culprit is emotion. In his book *Your Money and Your Brain*, Jason Zweig states, "the brain is not an optimal tool for making financial decisions." As he explains it, the

problem is that the human brain evolved to detect and interpret simple patterns. (Is there a lion lurking in that bush?) As a consequence, "when it comes to investing, our incorrigible search for patterns leads us to assume that order exists where it often doesn't." In other words, investors fool themselves into believing that they've discovered a lucrative stock market pattern when, in fact, stock market behaviour is largely random.

Not surprisingly, financial decision making is a major topic of study in the area of behavioural economics, a branch of economics that studies why human beings often fail to behave rationally.

So, what's the typical twenty-first-century investor to do? According to Mr. Zweig, there's hope: if you recognize the influence of your emotions, then you can tame them.

So a company offering fire insurance can predict very accurately how many of its clients' homes will burn down in a given year; a company offering supplemental health insurance can predict very accurately how many of its clients will need heart surgery in a given year; a life insurance company can predict how many of its clients will . . . Well, you get the idea.

When an insurance company is able to take advantage of the predictability that comes from aggregating a large number of independent events, it is said to engage in *pooling of risks*. And this pooling often means that even though insurance companies protect people from risk, the owners of the insurance companies may not themselves face much risk.

Lloyd's of London wasn't just a way for wealthy individuals to get paid for taking on some of the risks of less wealthy merchants. It was also a vehicle for pooling some of those risks. The effect of that pooling was to shift the supply curve in Figure 20-5 rightward: to make investors willing to accept more risk, at a lower price, than would otherwise have been possible.

The Limits of Diversification

Diversification can reduce risk. In some cases it can eliminate it. But these cases are not typical, because there are important limits to diversification. We can see the most important reason for these limits by returning to Lloyd's one more time.

In Lloyd's early days, there was one important hazard facing British shipping other than pirates or storms: war. Between 1690 and 1815, Britain fought a series of wars, mainly with France (which, among other things, led to the British takeover of New France during the Seven Years' War). Each time, France would sponsor privateers—basically pirates with official backing—to raid British shipping and thus indirectly damage Britain's war effort.

Whenever war broke out between Britain and France, losses of British merchant ships would increase. Unfortunately, merchants could not protect themselves against this eventuality by sending ships to different ports: the privateers would prey on British ships anywhere in the world. So the loss of a ship to French privateers in the Caribbean and the loss of another ship to French privateers in the Indian Ocean would *not* be independent events. It would be quite likely that they would happen in the same year.

When an event is more likely to occur if some other event occurs, these two events are said to be **positively correlated.** And like the risk of having a ship seized by French privateers, many financial risks are, alas, positively correlated.

> Two events are **positively correlated** if each event is more likely to occur if the other event also occurs.

Here are some of the positively correlated financial risks that investors in the modern world face:

- *Severe weather.* Within any given region, losses due to weather are definitely not independent events. When an ice storm hits Québec, a lot of Québec homes will get damaged. To some extent, insurance companies can diversify away this risk by insuring homes in many provinces. But events like El Niño (a recurrent temperature anomaly in the Pacific Ocean that disrupts weather around the world) can cause simultaneous flooding across North America and elsewhere. And as we have seen, over the past several years, there has been a significant increase in extreme weather.

- *Political events.* Modern governments do not, thankfully, licence privateers. Even today, however, some kinds of political events such as a war or revolution in a key raw-material-producing area—can damage business around the globe.

- *Business cycles.* The causes of *business cycles,* fluctuations in the output of the economy as a whole, are a subject for macroeconomics. What we can say here is that if one company suffers a decline in business because of a nationwide economic slump, many other companies will also suffer such declines. So these events will be positively correlated.

When events are positively correlated, the risks they pose cannot be diversified away. An investor can protect herself from the risk that any one company will do badly by investing in many companies; this investor cannot use the same technique to protect against an economic slump in which *all* companies do badly.

An insurance company can protect itself against the risk of losses from local flooding by insuring houses in many different places. But a global weather pattern that produces floods in many places will defeat this strategy. Not surprisingly, insurers pulled back from writing policies when it became clear that extreme weather patterns had become worse. They could no longer be confident that profits from policies written in good weather areas would be sufficient to compensate for losses incurred on policies in hurricane and drought-prone areas.

So institutions like insurance companies and stock markets cannot make risk go away completely. There is always an irreducible core of risk that cannot be diversified. Markets for risk, however, do accomplish two things: First, they enable the economy to eliminate the risk that can be diversified. Second, they allocate the risk that remains to the people most willing to bear it.

ECONOMICS >> *in Action*
When Lloyd's Almost Lost It

At the end of the 1980s, Lloyd's found itself in severe trouble. Investors who had placed their capital at risk, believing that the risks were small and the return on their investments more or less assured, found themselves required to make large payments to satisfy enormous claims. A number of investors, including members of some very old aristocratic families, found themselves pushed into bankruptcy.

Insurance companies cannot completely eliminate risk, as the overwhelming number of asbestos claims faced by Lloyd's made clear.

What happened? Part of the answer is that ambitious managers at Lloyd's had persuaded investors to take on risks that were much larger than the investors realized. (Or to put it a different way, the premiums the investors accepted were too small for the true level of risk contained in the policies.)

But the biggest single problem was that many of the events against which Lloyd's had become a major insurer were *not* independent. In the 1970s and 1980s, Lloyd's had become a major provider of corporate liability insurance in the United States: it protected American corporations against the possibility that they might be sued for selling defective or harmful products. Everyone expected such suits to be more or less independent events. Why should one company's legal problems have much to do with another's?

The answer turned out to lie in one word: asbestos. For decades, this fireproofing material had been used in many products, which meant that many companies were responsible for its use. Then it turned out that asbestos can cause severe damage to the lungs, especially in children. The result was a torrent of lawsuits by people who believed they were injured by asbestos and billions of dollars in damage awards—many of them ultimately paid by Lloyd's investors.

>> **Check Your Understanding 20-2**

Solutions appear at the back of book.

1. Explain how each of the following events would change the equilibrium premium and quantity of insurance in the market, indicating any shifts in the supply and demand curves.
   a. An increase in the number of ships travelling the same trade routes and so facing the same kinds of risks
   b. An increase in the number of trading routes, with the same number of ships travelling a greater variety of routes and so facing different kinds of risk
   c. An increase in the degree of risk aversion among the shipowners in the market
   d. An increase in the degree of risk aversion among the investors in the market
   e. An increase in the risk affecting the economy as a whole
   f. A fall in the wealth levels of investors in the market

Private Information: What You Don't Know Can Hurt You

Markets do very well at dealing with diversifiable risk and with risk due to uncertainty: situations in which nobody knows what is going to happen, whose house will be flooded, or who will get sick. However, markets have much more trouble with situations in which *some people know things that other people don't know*—situations of **private information.**

As we will see, private information can distort economic decisions and sometimes prevent mutually beneficial economic transactions from taking place. (Sometimes economists use the term *asymmetric information* rather than *private information,* but they are equivalent.)

Why is some information private? The main reason is that people generally know more about themselves than other people do. For example, you know whether or not you are a careful driver. But unless you have already been in several accidents, your auto insurance company does not. You are more likely to have a better estimate than your insurance company of whether or not you will need an expensive medical procedure. And if you are selling me your used car, you are more likely to be aware of any problems with it than I am.

But why are such differences in who knows what a problem? It turns out that there are two distinct sources of trouble: *adverse selection,* which arises from having private information about the way things are, and *moral hazard,* which arises from having private information about what people do.

Private information is information that some people have but others do not.

Adverse Selection: The Economics of Lemons

How do I know whether or not this used car is a lemon?

Suppose that someone offers to sell you an almost brand-new car—purchased just three months ago, with only 2,000 kilometres on the odometer and no dents or scratches. Will you be willing to pay almost the same for it as for a car direct from the dealer?

Probably not, for one main reason: you cannot help but wonder why this car is being sold. Is it because the owner has discovered something wrong with it—that it is a "lemon"? Having driven the car for a while, the owner knows more about it than you do—and people are more likely to sell cars that give them trouble.

You might think that sellers of used cars are at an advantage because they know more about them than buyers do. But potential buyers know that potential sellers are likely to offer them lemons—they just don't know which car is a lemon. For this reason, buyers will offer a lower price than they would if they had a guarantee of the car's quality. And this poor opinion of used cars tends to be self-reinforcing, precisely because it depresses the prices that buyers offer. Used cars sell at a significant discount because buyers expect a disproportionate share of those cars to be lemons.

Even a used car that is not a lemon would sell only at a large discount because buyers don't know whether it's a lemon or not. But potential sellers who have good cars ("plums") are unwilling to sell them at a deep discount, except under exceptional circumstances. So good used cars are rarely offered for sale, and used cars that are offered for sale have a strong tendency to be lemons. (This is why people who have a compelling reason to sell a car, such as moving overseas, make a point of revealing that information to potential buyers—as if to say "This car is not a lemon!")

The end result, then, is not only that used cars sell for low prices and that there are a large number of them with hidden problems. Equally important, many potentially beneficial transactions—sales of good cars by people who would like to get rid of them to people who would like to buy them—end up being frustrated by the inability of potential sellers to convince potential buyers that their cars are actually worth the higher price being asked. So some mutually beneficial trades between those who want to sell used cars and those who want to buy them go unexploited.

Although economists sometimes refer to situations like this as the *lemons problem,* the more formal name of the problem is **adverse selection.** The reason for the name is obvious: because the potential sellers know more about the quality of what they are selling than the potential buyers, they have an incentive to select the worst things to sell.

Adverse selection does not apply only to used cars. It is a problem for many parts of the economy—notably for insurance companies, and most notably for health insurance companies.

Suppose that a health insurance company were to offer a standard supplemental health policy to everyone with the same premium. The premium would reflect the *average* risk of incurring a medical expense not covered by a provincial health insurance plan. But that would make the policy look very expensive to healthy people, who know that they are less likely than the average person to incur medical expenses. So healthy people would be less likely than less healthy people to buy the policy, leaving the health insurance company with exactly the customers it doesn't want: people with a higher-than-average risk of needing medical care, who would find the premium to be a good deal.

In order to cover its expected losses from this sicker customer pool, the health insurance company is compelled to raise premiums, driving away more of the remaining healthier customers, and so on. Because the insurance company can't determine who is healthy and who is not, it must charge everyone the same premium, thereby discouraging healthy people from purchasing policies and encouraging unhealthy people to buy policies.

As we discussed in Chapter 18, adverse selection could lead to a phenomenon called an *adverse selection death spiral* as the market for supplemental health

Adverse selection occurs when an individual knows more about the way things are than other people do. Private information leads buyers to expect hidden problems in items offered for sale, leading to low prices and the best items being kept off the market.

Adverse selection can be reduced through **screening:** using observable information about people to make inferences about their private information.

Adverse selection can be diminished by people **signalling** their private information through actions that credibly reveal what they know.

A long-term **reputation** allows an individual to reassure others that they are not concealing adverse private information.

insurance collapses: insurance companies refused to offer policies because there was no premium at which the company could cover its losses. Because of the severe adverse selection problems, governments in many advanced countries have assumed the role of providing health insurance to their citizens. As we saw in Chapter 18, provincial and territorial governments, through their health services insurance plans and drug benefit programs like the Québec Health Insurance Plan and the Québec Drug Insurance Fund, now disburse 70% of the total payments for medical care in Canada. Canadian public health care programs are available to all residents, healthy or not, and are financed by taxes which people can not opt out of—thereby avoiding the adverse selection (death spiral) problem.

However, adverse selection still exists in other insurance markets such as auto insurance. In general, people or firms faced with the problem of adverse selection follow one of several well-established strategies for dealing with it. One strategy is **screening:** using observable information to make inferences about private information. If you apply to purchase auto insurance, you'll find that the insurance company will ask about your driving record in an attempt to "screen out" unsafe drivers—people they will refuse to insure or will insure only at very high premiums.

Auto insurance companies provide a very good example of the use of statistics in screening to reduce adverse selection. They may not know whether you are a careful driver, but they have statistical data on the accident rates of people who resemble your profile—and use those data in setting premiums. A 19-year-old male who drives a sports car and has already had a fender-bender is likely to pay a much higher premium than a 40-year-old female who drives an SUV and has never had an accident.

In some cases, this may be unfair: some adolescent males are very careful drivers, and some women drive SUVs as if they were F-16s. But nobody can deny that the insurance companies are right on average.

Another strategy to counter the problems caused by adverse selection is for good prospects to do some **signalling** of their private information—taking some action that wouldn't be worth taking unless they were indeed good prospects. For example, reputable used-car dealers often offer warranties—promises to repair any problems with the cars they sell that arise within a given amount of time. This isn't just a way of insuring their customers against possible expenses; it's a way of credibly showing that they are not selling lemons. As a result, more sales occur and dealers can command higher prices for their used cars.

Finally, in the face of adverse selection, it can be very valuable to establish a good **reputation:** a used-car dealership will often advertise how long it has been in business to show that it has continued to satisfy its customers. As a result, new customers will be willing to purchase cars and pay more for that dealer's cars.

Moral Hazard

In the late 1970s, major North American cities experienced an epidemic of suspicious fires that appeared to be deliberately set. Investigators eventually became aware of patterns in a number of the fires. Particular landlords who owned several buildings seemed to have an unusually large number of their buildings burn down. Although it was difficult to prove, police suspected that most of these fire-prone landlords were hiring professional arsonists to torch their own properties.

Why burn your own building? These buildings were typically in neighbourhoods where rising crime and middle-class flight had led to a decline in property values. But the insurance policies on the buildings were written to compensate owners based on historical property values, and so would pay the owner of a destroyed building more than the building was worth in the current market. For an unscrupulous landlord who knew the right people, this presented a profitable opportunity.

The arson epidemic became less severe during the 1980s, partly because insurance companies began making it difficult to overinsure properties, and partly because a boom in real estate values made many previously arson-threatened buildings worth more unburned.

The arson episodes make it clear that it is a bad idea for insurance companies to let customers insure buildings for more than their value—it gives the customers some destructive incentives. You might think, however, that the incentive problem would go away as long as the insurance is no more than 100% of the value of what is being insured.

But, unfortunately, anything close to 100% insurance still distorts incentives by inducing policyholders to behave differently than they would in the absence of insurance. The reason is that preventing fires requires effort and cost on the part of a building's owner. Fire alarms and sprinkler systems have to be kept in good repair, and fire safety rules have to be strictly enforced. All of this takes time and money that the owner may not find worth spending if the insurance policy will provide close to full compensation for any losses.

Of course, the insurance company could specify in the policy that it won't pay if basic safety precautions were unmet. But it isn't always easy to tell how careful a building's owner has been—the owner knows, but the insurance company does not.

The point is that the building's owner has private information about their own actions: whether they have really taken all appropriate precautions. As a result, the insurance company is likely to face more claims than if it were able to determine exactly how much effort a building owner exerts to prevent a loss. The problem of distorted incentives that arises when an individual has private information about their own actions but someone else bears the costs of a lack of care or effort is known as **moral hazard.**

To deal with moral hazard, individuals with private information need to be given some personal stake in what happens so they have a reason to exert effort even if others cannot verify that they have done so. Moral hazard is the reason salespeople in many stores receive a commission on sales: it's hard for managers to be sure how hard salespeople are really working, and if they were paid only a straight salary, they would not have an incentive to exert effort to make those sales.

Insurance companies deal with moral hazard by requiring a **deductible:** they compensate for losses only above a certain amount, so that coverage is always less than 100%. The insurance on your car, for example, may pay for repairs only after the first $500 in loss. This means that a careless driver who gets into a fender-bender will end up paying $500 for repairs even if they are insured, which provides at least some incentive to be careful and reduces moral hazard.

In addition to reducing moral hazard, deductibles provide a partial solution to the problem of adverse selection. Your insurance premium often drops substantially if you are willing to accept a large deductible. This is an attractive option to people who know they are low-risk customers; it is less attractive to people who know they are high-risk—and are likely to have an accident and end up paying the deductible. By offering a menu of policies with different premiums and deductibles, insurance companies can screen their customers, inducing them to sort themselves out on the basis of their private information.

As the example of deductibles suggests, moral hazard limits the ability of the economy to allocate risks efficiently. You generally can't get full (100%) insurance on your home or car, even though you would like to buy it, and you bear the risk of large deductibles, even though you would prefer not to. The following Economics in Action illustrates how in some cases moral hazard limits the ability of investors to diversify their investments.

Moral hazard occurs when an individual knows more about their own actions than other people do. This leads to a distortion of incentives to take care or to exert effort when someone else bears the costs of the lack of care or effort.

A **deductible** in an insurance policy is a sum that the insured individual must pay before being compensated for a claim.

ECONOMICS >> *in Action*
Franchise Owners Try Harder

Franchise owners face risk, which motivates them to work harder than salaried managers.

When Canadians go out for a quick meal, they often end up at one of the fast-food chains—McDonald's, Harvey's, Taco Bell, and so on. Because these are large corporations, customers may assume that the people who serve them are employees of large corporations. But usually they aren't. Most fast-food restaurants—for example, 99.5% of Tim Hortons outlets and 85% of McDonald's outlets—are franchises. That is, some individual has paid the parent company for the right to operate a restaurant selling its product. This person may look like an arm of a giant company but is in fact a small-business owner.

Becoming a franchisee is not a guarantee of success. You must put up a large amount of money, both to buy the licence and to set up the restaurant itself. For example, in 2019 it cost between US$1 million and US$2.2 million to open a McDonald's franchise. And although McDonald's takes care that its franchises are not too close to each other, they often face stiff competition from rival chains and even from a few truly independent restaurants. Becoming a franchise owner, in other words, involves taking on a lot of risk.

But why should people be willing to take these risks? Didn't we just learn that it is better to diversify, to spread your wealth among many investments?

The logic of diversification would seem to say that it's better for someone with US$1.7 million to invest in a wide range of stocks rather than put it all into one Taco Bell. This implies that Taco Bell would find it hard to attract franchisees: nobody would be willing to be a franchisee unless they expected to earn considerably more than they would as a hired manager with their wealth invested in a diversified portfolio of stocks. So wouldn't it be more profitable for Pizza Hut or Taco Bell simply to hire managers to run their restaurants?

It turns out that it isn't, because the success of a restaurant depends a lot on how hard the manager works, on the effort they put into choosing the right employees, on keeping the place clean and attractive to customers, and so on. The problem is moral hazard: the manager knows how effectively they are running their restaurant, but company headquarters—which bears the costs of a poorly run restaurant—does not. So a salaried manager, who gets paid even without doing everything possible to make the restaurant a success, does not have the incentive to do that extra bit—an incentive the owner does have because they have a substantial personal stake in the restaurant's success.

In other words, there is a moral hazard problem when a salaried manager runs a Pizza Hut, where the private information is how hard the manager works. Franchising solves this problem. A franchisee, whose wealth is tied up in the business and who stands to profit personally from its success, has every incentive to work extremely hard.

The result is that fast-food chains rely mainly on franchisees to operate their restaurants, even though the contracts with these owner-managers allow the franchisees on average to make much more than it would have cost the companies to employ store managers. The higher earnings of franchisees compensate them for the risk they accept, and the companies are compensated by higher sales that lead to higher licence fees.

In addition, licencing agreements forbid franchisees from taking actions that reduce their risk exposure to their business, such as selling shares of the franchise to others. It's an illustration of the fact that given a manager's action is subject to moral hazard, the parent company won't allow them to eliminate their risk through diversification.

>> *Check Your Understanding* 20-3

Solutions appear at the back of book.

1. Your car insurance premiums are lower if you have had no moving violations for several years. Explain how this feature tends to decrease the potential inefficiency caused by adverse selection.

2. A common feature of home construction contracts is that when it costs more to construct a building than was originally estimated, the contractor must absorb the additional cost. Explain how this feature reduces the problem of moral hazard but also forces the contractor to bear more risk than the contractor would like.

3. True or false? Explain your answer, stating what concept analyzed in this chapter accounts for the feature.

    People with higher deductibles on their auto insurance:
    a. Generally drive more carefully
    b. Pay lower premiums
    c. Generally are wealthier

>> *Quick Review*

• **Private information** can distort incentives and prevent mutually beneficial transactions from occurring. One source is **adverse selection:** sellers have private information about their goods and buyers offer low prices, leading the sellers of quality goods to drop out and leaving the market dominated by "lemons."

• Adverse selection can be reduced by revealing private information through **screening** or **signalling,** or by cultivating a long-term **reputation.**

• Another source of problems is **moral hazard.** In the case of insurance, it leads individuals to exert too little effort to prevent losses. This gives rise to features like **deductibles,** which limit the efficient allocation of risk.

PURE—An Insurance Company That Withstands Hurricanes

ntzolov/Getty Images

Ross Buchmueller went where few others dared to go: he went to Florida to underwrite homeowner insurance policies soon after Hurricane Katrina and Hurricane Rita hit the American Gulf Coast in 2005 (An *underwriter* "produces" insurance by measuring the risk, calculating the premium, and writing the insurance contract.) Katrina alone was the most expensive natural disaster in U.S. history: 1,800 people were killed and US$41 billion in insured losses were incurred, enough to wipe out 25 years' worth of insurance industry premiums. And with more bad weather to come, by the end of 2005, insurers had incurred US$71 billion in losses, the worst year on record.

In the years after Katrina, major national insurers significantly reduced their policy writing in hurricane-prone coastal areas. And for homeowners in those areas who could still obtain insurance, both premiums and deductibles sky-rocketed. Millions of Americans who built or purchased homes in hurricane-prone coastal areas with the expectation of being able to buy affordable insurance faced a costly and risky dilemma.

So in 2007, some industry professionals were skeptical when Privilege Underwriters Reciprocal Exchange (PURE), the company created by Ross Buchmueller, began underwriting policies in Florida. Michael Koziol, an insurance industry analyst, observed "Like any new company, there's a certain risk. More new companies go under than old companies." The common industry view was that although Florida insurance premiums were at record highs, they were still too low to offset the potential costs from extreme weather events.

However, Buchmueller had a two-pronged strategy for making a profit. First, after studying industry statistics on past hurricane-related claims, he limited his sales to homes worth more than US$1 million that were fairly new, solidly built, and equipped with strong shutters and high-grade windows that repelled flying debris. Second, Buchmueller purchased policies from big, global insurance companies that covered 75% of his potential losses. The size and global reach of their portfolios allowed these companies to treat the exposure to Florida hurricane losses as a relatively small risk.

Buchmueller was confident in his approach: for his select group of customers, not only did he offer policies at lower premiums than competitors, he often offered policies to homeowners that no one else would cover. One of PURE's first customers, Ellis Kern, who had previously been insured by Lloyd's of London, saw his premium fall by nearly 55%.

So how has PURE fared over time? As of 2019, not only had PURE survived, it had thrived, growing by 30% to 40% in *each* of the 10 years prior. PURE's successes in Florida allowed it to expand nationwide, so that it now offers coverage in 49 U.S. states plus the District of Columbia. In early 2020, the international insurance company, Tokio Marine, purchased PURE for US$3.1 *billion*.

QUESTIONS FOR THOUGHT

1. What is one example of moral hazard by homeowners in hurricane-prone areas? Explain.

2. How does the case illustrate market failure due to adverse selection?

3. What were the sources of Buchmueller's innovation that allowed him to succeed in the presence of moral hazard and adverse selection?

4. Why did Buchmueller purchase insurance policies from big, global insurance companies to cover up to 75% of his own losses? What principle does this illustrate?

SUMMARY

1. The **expected value** of a **random variable** is the weighted average of all possible values, where the weight corresponds to the probability of a given value occurring.

2. **Risk** is uncertainty about future events or **states of the world.** It is **financial risk** when the uncertainty is about monetary outcomes.

3. Under uncertainty, people maximize **expected utility.** A **risk-averse** person will choose to reduce risk when that reduction leaves the expected value of their income or wealth unchanged. A **fair insurance policy** has that feature: the **premium** is equal to the expected value of the claim. A **risk-neutral** person is completely insensitive to risk and therefore unwilling to pay any premium to avoid it.

4. Risk aversion arises from diminishing marginal utility: an additional dollar of income generates higher marginal utility in low-income states than in high-income states. A fair insurance policy increases a risk-averse person's utility because it transfers a dollar from a high-income state (a state when no loss occurs) to a low-income state (a state when a loss occurs).

5. Differences in preferences and income or wealth lead to differences in risk aversion. Depending on the size of the premium, a risk-averse person is willing to purchase "unfair" insurance, a policy for which the premium exceeds the expected value of the claim. The greater your risk aversion, the higher the premium you are willing to pay.

6. There are gains from trade in risk, leading to an **efficient allocation of risk:** those who are most willing to bear risk put their **capital at risk** to cover the losses of those least willing to bear risk.

7. Risk can also be reduced through **diversification,** investing in several different things that correspond to **independent events.** The stock market, where **shares** in companies are traded, offers one way to diversify. Insurance companies can engage in **pooling,** insuring many independent events so as to eliminate almost all risk. But when the underlying events are **positively correlated,** all risk cannot be diversified away.

8. **Private information** can cause inefficiency in the allocation of risk. One problem is **adverse selection,** private information about the way things are. It creates the "lemons problem" in used-car markets, where sellers of high-quality cars drop out of the market. Adverse selection can be limited in several ways—through **screening** of individuals, through the **signalling** that people use to reveal their private information, and through the building of a **reputation.**

9. A related problem is **moral hazard:** individuals have private information about their actions, which distorts their incentives to exert effort or care when someone else bears the costs of that lack of effort or care. It limits the ability of markets to allocate risk efficiently. Insurance companies try to limit moral hazard by imposing **deductibles,** placing more risk on the insured.

KEY TERMS

Random variable, p. 610
Expected value, p. 610
State of the world, p. 610
Risk, p. 610
Financial risk, p. 610
Expected utility, p. 611
Premium, p. 611
Fair insurance policy, p. 612

Risk-averse, p. 613
Risk-neutral, p. 615
Capital at risk, p. 618
Efficient allocation of risk, p. 618
Independent events, p. 620
Diversification, p. 620
Share, p. 621
Pooling, p. 621

Positively correlated, p. 623
Private information, p. 624
Adverse selection, p. 625
Screening, p. 626
Signalling, p. 626
Reputation, p. 626
Moral hazard, p. 627
Deductible, p. 627

PRACTICE QUESTIONS

1. Insurance companies are using technology to learn more about their customer's behaviour. Explain how each of the following devices reduces the adverse selection problem. Which customers are most likely to use the devices?

   a. GPS car trackers that monitor speed, time of day, and erratic driving

   b. Fitness and diet health trackers

2. Many star university athletes are faced with the difficult decision of going pro and earning millions or choosing to stay in school to complete their degree. What are the financial risks faced by the university athlete? How can insurance be used to mitigate these risks?

PROBLEMS

1. For each of the following situations, calculate the expected value.

   a. Tanisha owns one share of IBM stock, which is currently trading at $80. There is a 50% chance that the share price will rise to $100 and a 50% chance that it will fall to $70. What is the expected value of the future share price?

   b. Sharon buys a ticket in a small lottery. There is a probability of 0.7 that she will win nothing, of 0.2 that she will win $10, and of 0.1 that she will win $50. What is the expected value of Sharon's winnings?

   c. Aaron is a farmer whose rice crop depends on the weather. If the weather is favourable, he will make a profit of $100. If the weather is unfavourable, he will make a profit of –$20 (that is, he will lose money). The weather forecast reports that the probability of weather being favourable is 0.9 and the probability of weather being unfavourable is 0.1. What is the expected value of Aaron's profit?

2. Vicky is considering investing some of her money in a startup company. She currently has income of $4,000, and she is considering investing $2,000 of that in the company. There is a 0.5 probability that the company will succeed and will pay out $8,000 to Vicky (her original investment of $2,000 plus $6,000 of the company's profits). And there is a 0.5 probability that the company will fail and Vicky will get nothing (and lose her investment). The accompanying table illustrates Vicky's utility function.

Income	Total utility (utils)
$0	0
1,000	50
2,000	85
3,000	115
4,000	140
5,000	163
6,000	183
7,000	200
8,000	215
9,000	229
10,000	241

   a. Calculate Vicky's marginal utility of income for each income level. Is Vicky risk-averse?

   b. Calculate the expected value of Vicky's income if she makes this investment.

   c. Calculate Vicky's expected utility from making the investment.

   d. What is Vicky's utility from not making the investment? Will Vicky therefore invest in the company?

Income	Total utility(utils)	Marginal utility (utils)
$0	0	
		50
1,000	50	
		35
2,000	85	
		30
3,000	115	
		25
4,000	140	
		23
5,000	163	
		20
6,000	183	
		17
7,000	200	
		15
8,000	215	
		14
9,000	229	
		12
10,000	241	

3. Vicky's utility function was given in Problem 2. As in Problem 2, Vicky currently has income of $4,000. She is considering investing in a startup company, but the investment now costs $4,000 to make. If the company fails, Vicky will get nothing from the company. But if the company succeeds, she will get $10,000 from the company (her original investment of $4,000 plus $6,000 of the company's profits). Each event has a 0.5 probability of occurring. Will Vicky invest in the company?

4. You have $1,000 that you can invest. If you buy Ford stock, you face the following returns and probabilities from holding the stock for one year: with a probability of 0.2 you will get $1,500; with a probability of 0.4 you will get $1,100; and with a probability of 0.4 you will get $900. If you put the money into the bank, in one year's time you will get $1,100 for certain.

   a. What is the expected value of your earnings from investing in Ford stock?

   b. Suppose you are risk-averse. Can we say for sure whether you will invest in Ford stock or put your money into the bank?

5. Wilbur is an airline pilot who currently has income of $60,000. If he gets sick and loses his flight medical certificate, he loses his job and has only $10,000 income. His probability of staying healthy is 0.6, and his probability of getting sick is 0.4. Wilbur's utility function is given in the accompanying table.

Income	Total utility (utils)
$0	0
10,000	60
20,000	110
30,000	150
40,000	180
50,000	200
60,000	210

a. What is the expected value of Wilbur's income?

b. What is Wilbur's expected utility?

Wilbur thinks about buying "loss-of-licence" insurance that will compensate him if he loses his flight medical certificate.

c. One insurance company offers Wilbur full compensation for his income loss (that is, the insurance company pays Wilbur $50,000 if he loses his flight medical certificate), and it charges a premium of $40,000. That is, regardless of whether he loses his flight medical certificate, Wilbur's income after insurance will be $20,000. What is Wilbur's utility? Will he buy the insurance?

d. What is the highest premium Wilbur would be willing to pay for full insurance (insurance that completely compensates him for the income loss)?

6. According to the Insurance Bureau of Canada, there were 232 cars stolen per 100,000 people in Canada in 2018. Beth owns a car worth $20,000 and is considering purchasing an insurance policy to protect herself from car theft. For the following questions, assume that the chance of car theft is the same in all regions and across all car models.

a. What should the premium for a fair insurance policy have been in 2018 for a policy that replaces Beth's car if it is stolen? (*Hint:* In your calculation, round up to three decimal places.)

b. Suppose an insurance company charges 0.6% of the car's value for a policy that pays for replacing a stolen car. How much will the policy cost Beth?

c. Will Beth purchase the insurance in part b if she is risk-neutral?

d. Discuss a possible moral hazard problem facing Beth's insurance company if she purchases the insurance.

7. Hugh's income is currently $5,000. His utility function is shown in the accompanying table.

Income	Total utility (utils)
$0	0
1,000	100
2,000	140
3,000	166
4,000	185
5,000	200
6,000	212
7,000	222
8,000	230
9,000	236
10,000	240

a. Calculate Hugh's marginal utility of income. What is his attitude toward risk?

b. Hugh is thinking about gambling in a casino. With a probability of 0.5 he will lose $3,000, and with a probability of 0.5 he will win $5,000. What is the

expected value of Hugh's income? What is Hugh's expected utility? Will he decide to gamble? (Suppose that he gets no extra utility from going to the casino.)

c. Suppose that the "spread" (how much he can win versus how much he can lose) of the gamble narrows, so that with a probability of 0.5 Hugh will lose $1,000, and with a probability of 0.5 he will win $3,000. What is the expected value of Hugh's income? What is his expected utility? Is this gamble better for him than the gamble in part b? Will he decide to gamble?

8. Eva is risk-averse. Currently she has $50,000 to invest. She faces the following choice: she can invest in the stock of a startup company, or she can invest in IBM stock. If she invests in the startup company, then with a probability of 0.5 she will lose $30,000, but with a probability of 0.5 she will gain $50,000. If she invests in IBM stock, then with a probability of 0.5 she will lose $10,000, but with a probability of 0.5 she will gain $30,000. Can you tell which investment she will prefer to make?

9. Suppose you have $1,000 that you can invest in Ted and Larry's Ice Cream Parlor and/or Ethel's House of Cocoa. The price of a share of stock in either company is $100. The fortunes of each company are closely linked to the weather. When it is warm, the value of Ted and Larry's stock rises to $150 but the value of Ethel's stock falls to $60. When it is cold, the value of Ethel's stock rises to $150 but the value of Ted and Larry's stock falls to $60. There is an equal chance of the weather being warm or cold.

a. If you invest all your money in Ted and Larry's, what is your expected stock value? What if you invest all your money in Ethel's?

b. Suppose you diversify and invest half of your $1,000 in each company. How much will your total stock be worth if the weather is warm? What if it is cold?

c. Suppose you are risk-averse. Would you prefer to put all your money in Ted and Larry's, as in part a? Or would you prefer to diversify, as in part b? Explain your reasoning.

10. Canadian Bond Fund and New Canada Fund are two portfolios constructed and managed by Mawer Investment Management Ltd. of Calgary. They comprise bonds and debentures (bond-like securities) of Canadian government and corporate issuers and stocks of smaller Canadian companies. The accompanying table shows the expected value of the annual percentage returns associated with these portfolios based on returns for the 10-year period ending May 29, 2020.

Portfolio	Expected value of return (percent)
Mawer Canadian Bond Fund	4.0%
Mawer New Canada Fund	12.8

a. Which portfolio would a risk-neutral investor prefer?

b. Jing, a risk-averse investor, chooses to invest in the Canadian Bond Fund portfolio. What can be inferred about the risk of the two portfolios from Jing's choice of investment? Based on historical performance, would a risk-neutral investor ever choose Canadian Bond Fund?

c. Jing is aware that diversification can reduce risk. She considers a portfolio in which half her investment is in units of the Canadian Bond Fund and the other half in New Canada Fund units. What is the expected value of the return for this combined portfolio? Would you expect this combined portfolio to be more risky or less risky than the New Canada Fund portfolio? Why or why not?

11. You are considering buying a second-hand Volkswagen. From reading car magazines, you know that half of all Volkswagens have problems of some kind (they are "lemons") and the other half run just fine (they are "plums"). If you knew that you were getting a plum, you would be willing to pay $10,000 for it: this is how much a plum is worth to you. You would also be willing to buy a lemon, but only if its price was no more than $4,000: this is how much a lemon is worth to you. And someone who owns a plum would be willing to sell it at any price above $8,000. Someone who owns a lemon would be willing to sell it for any price above $2,000.

a. For now, suppose that you can immediately tell whether the car that you are being offered is a lemon or a plum. Suppose someone offers you a plum. Will there be trade?

Now suppose that the seller has private information about the car they are selling: the seller knows whether they have a lemon or a plum. But when the seller offers you a Volkswagen, you do not know whether it is a lemon or a plum. So this is a situation of adverse selection.

b. Since you do not know whether you are being offered a plum or a lemon, you base your decision on the expected value to you of a Volkswagen, assuming you are just as likely to buy a lemon as a plum. Calculate this expected value.

c. Suppose, from driving the car, the seller knows they have a plum. However, you don't know whether this particular car is a lemon or a plum, so the most you are willing to pay is your expected value. Will there be trade?

12. You own a company that produces chairs, and you are thinking about hiring one more employee. Each chair produced gives you revenue of $10. There are two potential employees, Fred and Sylvia. Fred is a fast worker who produces 10 chairs per day, creating revenue for you of $100. Fred knows that he is fast and so will work for you only if you pay him more than $80 per day. Sylvia is a slow worker who produces only five chairs per day, creating revenue for you of $50. Sylvia knows that she is slow and so will work for you if you pay her more than $40 per day. Although Sylvia knows she is slow and Fred knows he is fast, you do

not know who is fast and who is slow. So this is a situation of adverse selection.

a. Since you do not know which type of worker you will get, you think about what the expected value of your revenue will be if you hire one of the two. What is that expected value?

b. Suppose you offered to pay a daily wage equal to the expected revenue you calculated in part a. Whom would you be able to hire: Fred, or Sylvia, or both, or neither?

c. If you know whether a worker is fast or slow, which one would you prefer to hire and why? Can you devise a compensation scheme to guarantee that you employ only the type of worker you prefer?

13. For each of the following situations, do the following: first describe whether it is a situation of moral hazard or of adverse selection. Then explain what inefficiency can arise from this situation and explain how the proposed solution reduces the inefficiency.

a. When you buy a second-hand car, you do not know whether it is a lemon (low quality) or a plum (high quality), but the seller knows. A solution is for sellers to offer a warranty with the car that pays for repair costs.

b. Some people are prone to see doctors unnecessarily for minor complaints like headaches, and health insurance providers do not know how urgently you need a doctor. A solution is for insurees to have to make a co-payment of a certain dollar amount (for example, $10) each time they visit a health care provider. All insurees are risk-averse.

c. When airlines sell tickets, they do not know whether a buyer is a business traveller (who is willing to pay a lot for a seat) or a leisure traveller (who has a low willingness to pay). A solution for a profit-maximizing airline is to offer an expensive ticket that is very flexible (it allows date and route changes) and a cheap ticket that is very inflexible (it has to be booked in advance and cannot be changed).

d. A company does not know whether workers on an assembly line work hard or whether they slack off. A solution is to pay the workers "piece rates," that is, pay them according to how much they have produced each day. All workers are risk-averse, but the company is not risk-neutral.

e. When making a decision about hiring you, prospective employers do not know whether you are a productive or unproductive worker. A solution is for productive workers to provide potential employers with references from previous employers.

14. Kory owns a house that is worth $300,000. If the house burns down, she loses all $300,000. If the house

does not burn down, she loses nothing. Her house burns down with a probability of 0.02. Kory is risk-averse.

a. What would a fair insurance policy cost?

b. Suppose an insurance company offers to insure her fully against the loss from the house burning down, at a premium of $1,500. Can you say for sure whether Kory will or will not take the insurance?

c. Suppose an insurance company offers to insure her fully against the loss from the house burning down, at a premium of $6,000. Can you say for sure whether Kory will or will not take the insurance?

d. Suppose that an insurance company offers to insure her fully against the loss from the house burning down, at a premium of $9,000. Can you say

for sure whether Kory will or will not take the insurance?

WORK IT OUT

15. You have $1,000 that you can invest. If you buy Imperial Oil stock, then, in one year's time: with a probability of 0.4 you will get $1,600; with a probability of 0.4 you will get $1,100; and with a probability of 0.2 you will get $800. If you put the money into the bank, in one year's time you will get $1,100 for certain.

a. What is the expected value of your earnings from investing in Imperial Oil stock?

b. Suppose you prefer putting your money into the bank to investing it in Imperial Oil stock. What does that tell us about your attitude toward risk? ■

Solutions to *Check Your Understanding* Questions

This section offers suggested answers to the *Check Your Understanding* questions found within chapters.

‖ CHAPTER ONE

1-1 Check Your Understanding

1. **a.** This illustrates the concept of opportunity cost. Given that a person can only eat so much at one sitting, having a slice of chocolate cake requires that you forgo eating something else, such as a slice of coconut cream pie.

    b. This illustrates the concept that resources are scarce. Even if there were more resources in the world, the total amount of those resources would be limited. As a result, scarcity would still arise. For there to be no scarcity, there would have to be unlimited amounts of everything (including unlimited time in a human life), which is clearly impossible.

    c. This illustrates the concept that people usually exploit opportunities to make themselves better off. Students will seek to make themselves better off by signing up for the tutorials of teaching assistants with good reputations and avoiding those teaching assistants with poor reputations. It also illustrates the concept that resources are scarce. If there were unlimited spaces in tutorials with good teaching assistants, they would not fill up.

    d. This illustrates the concept of marginal analysis. Your decision about allocating your time is a "how much" decision: how much time spent exercising versus how much time spent studying. You make your decision by comparing the benefit of an additional hour of exercising to its cost, the effect on your grades of one less hour spent studying.

2. **a.** Yes. The increased time spent commuting is a cost you will incur if you accept the new job. That additional time spent commuting—or equivalently, the benefit you would get from spending that time doing something else—is an opportunity cost of the new job.

    b. Yes. One of the benefits of the new job is that you will be making $50,000. But if you take the new job, you will have to give up your current job; that is, you have to give up your current salary of $45,000. So $45,000 is one of the opportunity costs of taking the new job.

    c. No. A more spacious office is an additional benefit of your new job and does not involve forgoing something else. So it is not an opportunity cost.

1-2 Check Your Understanding

1. **a.** This illustrates the concept that there are gains from trade. Students trade tutoring services based on their different abilities in academic subjects.

    b. This illustrates the concept that when markets don't achieve efficiency, government intervention can improve society's welfare. In this case, the market, left alone, will permit bars and nightclubs to impose costs on their neighbours in the form of loud music, costs that the bars and nightclubs have no incentive to take into account. This is an inefficient outcome because society as a whole can be made better off if bars and nightclubs are induced to reduce their noise.

    c. This illustrates the concept that resources should be used as efficiently as possible to achieve society's goals. By closing neighbourhood clinics and shifting funds to the main hospital, better health care can be provided at a lower cost.

    d. This illustrates the concept that markets move toward equilibrium. Here, because books with the same amount of wear and tear sell for about the same price, no buyer or seller can be made better off by engaging in a different trade than they undertook. This means that the market for used textbooks has moved to an equilibrium.

2. **a.** This does not describe an equilibrium situation. Many students should want to change their behaviour and switch to eating at the restaurants. An equilibrium will be established when students are equally as well off eating at the restaurants as eating at the dining hall—which would happen if, say, prices at the dining hall were higher than at the restaurants.

    b. This does describe an equilibrium situation. By changing your behaviour and riding the bus, you would not be made better off. Therefore, you have no incentive to change your behaviour.

1-3 Check Your Understanding

1. **a.** This illustrates the principle that increases in the economy's potential lead to economic growth over time. Cheaper solar panels will lower the cost of energy, increasing the economy's potential and economic growth. Solar panel manufacturers will be better off but firms producing competing energy will be worse off.

    b. This illustrates the principle that overall spending sometimes gets out of line with the economy's productive capacity; when it does, government policy can change spending. The tax cut would increase people's after-tax incomes, leading to higher consumer spending.

    c. This illustrates the principle that one person's spending is another person's income. As oil companies decrease their spending on labour by laying off workers and paying remaining workers lower wages, those workers' incomes fall. In turn, those workers decrease their consumer spending, causing restaurants and other consumer businesses to lose income.

‖ CHAPTER TWO

2-1 Check Your Understanding

1. **a.** False. An increase in the resources available to Bombardier for use in producing private business jets and subway trains changes the production possibility frontier by shifting it outward. This is because Bombardier can now produce more jets and subway trains than before. In the accompanying figure, the line labelled "Bombardier's original *PPF*" represents Bombardier's original production possibility frontier, and the line labelled "Bombardier's new *PPF*" represents the new production possibility frontier that results from an increase in resources available to Bombardier.

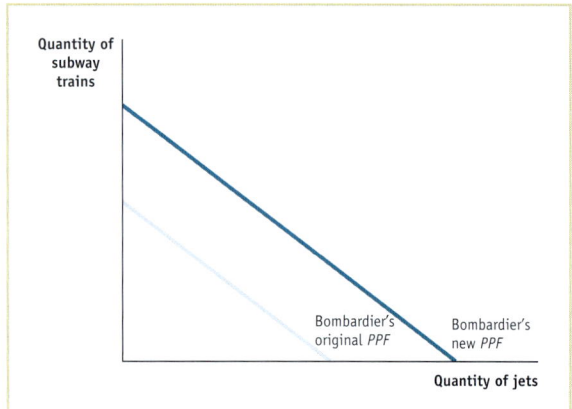

b. True. A technological change that allows Bombardier to build more small jets for any amount of private business jets built results in a change in its production possibility frontier. This is illustrated in the accompanying figure: the new production possibility frontier is represented by the line labelled "Bombardier's new *PPF*," and the original production frontier is represented by the line labelled "Bombardier's original *PPF*." Since the maximum quantity of jets that Bombardier can build is the same as before, the new production possibility frontier intersects the vertical axis at the same point as the original frontier. But since the maximum possible quantity of small jets is now greater than before, the new frontier intersects the horizontal axis to the right of the original frontier.

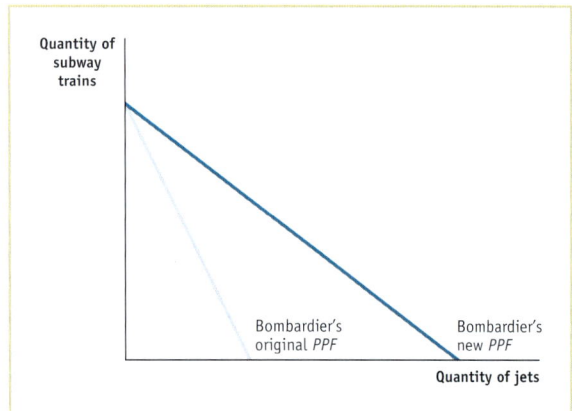

c. False. The production possibility frontier illustrates how much of one good an economy must give up to get more of another good only when resources are used efficiently in production. If an economy is producing inefficiently—that is, inside the frontier—then it does not have to give up a unit of one good in order to get another unit of the other good. Instead, by becoming more efficient in production, this economy can have more of both goods.

2. **a.** Canada has an absolute advantage in automobile production because it takes fewer Canadians (6) to produce a car in one day than Italians (8). Canada also has an absolute advantage in washing machine production because it takes fewer Canadians (2) to produce a washing machine in one day than Italians (3).

b. In Italy, the opportunity cost of a washing machine in terms of an automobile is $\frac{3}{8}$: $\frac{3}{8}$ of a car can be produced with the same number of workers and in the same time it takes to produce one washing machine. In Canada, the opportunity cost of a washing machine in terms of an automobile is $\frac{2}{6} = \frac{1}{3}$: $\frac{1}{3}$ of a car can be produced with the same number of workers and in the same time it takes to produce one washing machine. Since $\frac{1}{3} < \frac{3}{8}$, Canada has a comparative advantage in the production of washing machines: to produce a washing machine, only $\frac{1}{3}$ of a car must be given up in Canada but $\frac{3}{8}$ of a car must be given up in Italy. This means that Italy has a comparative advantage in automobiles. This can be checked as follows. The opportunity cost of an automobile in terms of a washing machine in Italy is $\frac{8}{3}$, equal to $2\frac{2}{3}$: $2\frac{2}{3}$ washing machines can be produced with the same number of workers and in the time it takes to produce one car in Italy. And the opportunity cost of an automobile in terms of a washing machine in Canada is $\frac{6}{2}$, equal to 3:3 washing machines can be produced with the same number of workers and in the time it takes to produce one car in Canada. Since $2\frac{2}{3} < 3$, Italy has a comparative advantage in producing automobiles.

c. The greatest gains are realized when each country specializes in producing the good for which it has a comparative advantage. Therefore, Canada should specialize in washing machines and Italy should specialize in automobiles.

3. At a trade of 7 Canadian jets for 29 Brazilian subway trains, Brazil gives up less for a jet than it would if it were building the jets itself. Without trade, Brazil gives up 6 subway trains for each jet it produces. With trade, Brazil gives up only 29/7 subway trains for each jet from Canada. Likewise, Canada gives up less for a subway train that it would if it were producing subway trains itself. Without trade, Canada gives up 2/7 of jet for each subway train. With trade, Canada gives up only 7/29 a jet for each subway train from Brazil.

4. An increase in the amount of money spent by households results in an increase in the flow of goods to households. This, in turn, generates an increase in demand for factors of production by firms. So, there is an increase in the number of jobs in the economy.

2-2 Check Your Understanding

1. **a.** This is a normative statement because it stipulates what should be done. In addition, it may have no "right" answer. That is, should people be prevented from all dangerous personal behaviour if they enjoy that behaviour—like skydiving? Your answer will depend on your point of view.

b. This is a positive statement because it is a description of fact.

2. a. True. Economists often have different value judgments about the desirability of a particular social goal. But despite those differences in value judgments, they will tend to agree that society, once it has decided to pursue a given social goal, should adopt the most efficient policy to achieve that goal. Therefore, economists are likely to agree on adopting policy choice B.

b. False. Disagreements between economists are more likely to arise because they base their conclusions on different models or because they have different value judgments about the desirability of the policy.

|| CHAPTER THREE

3-1 Check Your Understanding

1. a. The quantity of umbrellas demanded is higher at any given price on a rainy day than on a dry day. This is a rightward shift of the demand curve, since at any given price the quantity demanded rises. This implies that any specific quantity can now be sold at a higher price.

b. The quantity of summer Caribbean cruises demanded rises in response to a price reduction. This is a movement along the demand curve for summer Caribbean cruises.

c. The demand for roses increases the week of Valentine's Day. This is a rightward shift of the demand curve.

d. The quantity of gasoline demanded falls in response to a rise in price. This is a movement along the demand curve.

3-2 Check Your Understanding

1. a. The quantity of houses supplied rises as a result of an increase in prices. This is a movement along the supply curve.

b. The quantity of strawberries supplied is higher at any given price. This is a rightward shift of the supply curve.

c. The quantity of labour supplied is lower at any given wage. This is a leftward shift of the supply curve compared to the supply curve during school vacation. So, in order to attract workers, fast-food chains have to offer higher wages.

d. The quantity of labour supplied rises in response to a rise in wages. This is a movement along the supply curve.
   Alternatively, if we consider submarkets, the quantity of labour supplied temporarily rises in the local labour market at any given wage. This is a rightward shift of the local labour supply curve.

e. The quantity of cabins supplied is higher at any given price. This is a rightward shift of the supply curve.

3-3 Check Your Understanding

1. a. The supply curve shifts rightward. At the original equilibrium price of the year before, the quantity of grapes supplied exceeds the quantity demanded. This is a case of surplus. The price of grapes will fall.

b. The demand curve shifts leftward. At the original equilibrium price, the quantity of hotel rooms supplied exceeds the quantity demanded. This is a case of surplus. The rates for hotel rooms will fall.

c. The demand curve for second-hand snowblowers shifts rightward. At the original equilibrium price, the quantity of second-hand snowblowers demanded exceeds the

quantity supplied. This is a case of shortage. The equilibrium price of second-hand snowblowers will rise.

3-4 Check Your Understanding

1. a. The market for large cars: this is a rightward shift in demand caused by a decrease in the price of a complement, gasoline. As a result of the shift, the equilibrium price of large cars will rise and the equilibrium quantity of large cars bought and sold will also rise.

b. The market for fresh paper made from recycled stock: this is a rightward shift in supply due to a technological innovation. As a result of this shift, the equilibrium price of fresh paper made from recycled stock will fall and the equilibrium quantity bought and sold will rise.

c. The market for movies at a local movie theatre: this is a leftward shift in demand caused by a fall in the price of a substitute, on-demand films. As a result of this shift, the equilibrium price of movie tickets will fall and the equilibrium number of people who go to the movies will also fall.

2. Upon the announcement of the new chip, the demand curve for computers using the earlier chip shifts leftward, as demand decreases, and the supply curve for these computers shifts rightward, as supply increases.

a. If demand decreases relatively more than supply increases, then the equilibrium quantity falls, as shown here:

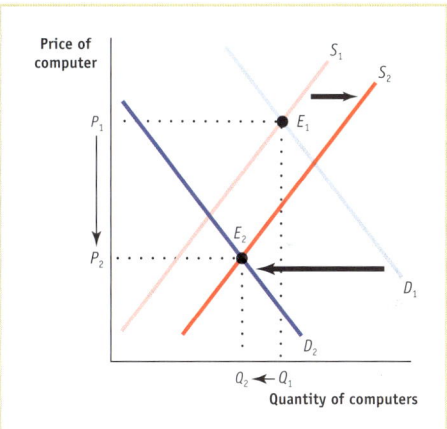

If supply increases relatively more than demand decreases, then the equilibrium quantity rises, as shown here:

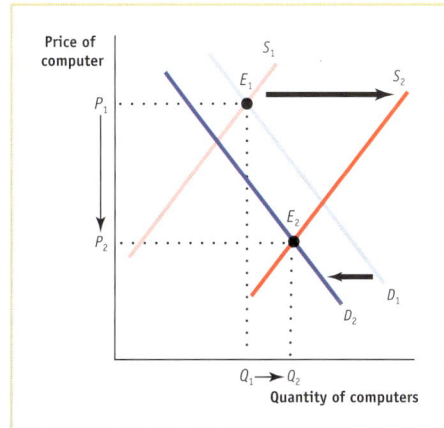

b. In both cases, the equilibrium price falls.

‖ CHAPTER FOUR

4-1 Check Your Understanding

1. A consumer buys each pepper if the price is less than (or just equal to) the consumer's willingness to pay for that pepper. The demand schedule is constructed by asking how many peppers will be demanded at any given price. The accompanying table illustrates the demand schedule.

Price of pepper	Quantity of peppers demanded	Quantity of peppers demanded by Teresa	Quantity of peppers demanded by Azar
$0.90	1	1	0
0.80	2	1	1
0.70	3	2	1
0.60	4	2	2
0.50	5	3	2
0.40	6	3	3
0.30	8	4	4
0.20	8	4	4
0.10	8	4	4
0.00	8	4	4

When the price is $0.40, Teresa's consumer surplus from the first pepper is $0.50, from her second pepper $0.30, from her third pepper $0.10, and she does not buy any more peppers. Teresa's individual consumer surplus is therefore $0.90. Azar's consumer surplus from her first pepper is $0.40, from her second pepper $0.20, from her third pepper $0.00 (since the price is exactly equal to her willingness to pay, she buys the third pepper but receives no consumer surplus from it), and she does not buy any more peppers. Azar's individual consumer surplus is therefore $0.60. Total consumer surplus at a price of $0.40 is therefore $0.90 + $0.60 = $1.50.

4-2 Check Your Understanding

1. **a.** A producer supplies each pepper if the price is greater than (or just equal to) the producer's cost of producing that pepper. The supply schedule is constructed by asking how many peppers will be supplied at any price. The accompanying table illustrates the supply schedule.

   b. When the price is $0.70, Cara's producer surplus from the first pepper is $0.60, from her second pepper $0.60, from her third pepper $0.30, from her fourth pepper $0.10, and she does not supply any more peppers. Cara's individual producer surplus is therefore $1.60. Jamie's producer surplus from his first pepper is $0.40, from his second pepper $0.20, from his third pepper $0.00 (since the price is exactly equal to his cost, he sells the third pepper but receives no producer surplus from it), and he does not supply any more peppers. Jamie's individual producer surplus is therefore $0.60. Total producer surplus at a price of $0.70 is therefore $1.60 + $0.60 = $2.20.

Price of pepper	Quantity of peppers supplied	Quantity of peppers supplied by Cara	Quantity of peppers supplied by Jamie
$0.90	8	4	4
0.80	7	4	3
0.70	7	4	3
0.60	6	4	2
0.50	5	3	2
0.40	4	3	1
0.30	3	2	1
0.20	2	2	0
0.10	2	2	0
0.00	0	0	0

4-3 Check Your Understanding

1. The quantity demanded equals the quantity supplied at a price of $0.50, the equilibrium price. At that price, a total quantity of five peppers will be bought and sold. Teresa will buy three peppers and receive consumer surplus of $0.40 on her first, $0.20 on her second, and $0.00 on her third pepper. Azar will buy two peppers and receive consumer surplus of $0.30 on her first and $0.10 on her second pepper. Total consumer surplus is therefore $1.00. Cara will supply three peppers and receive producer surplus of $0.40 on her first, $0.40 on her second, and $0.10 on her third pepper. Jamie will supply two peppers and receive producer surplus of $0.20 on his first and $0.00 on his second pepper. Total producer surplus is therefore $1.10. Total surplus in this market is therefore $1.00 + $1.10 = $2.10.

2. **a.** If Azar consumes one fewer pepper, she loses $0.60 (her willingness to pay for her second pepper); if Teresa consumes one more pepper, she gains $0.30 (her willingness to pay for her fourth pepper). This results in an overall loss of consumer surplus of $0.60 – $0.30 = $0.30.

   b. Cara's cost of the last pepper she supplied (the third pepper) is $0.40, and Jamie's cost of producing one more (his third pepper) is $0.70. Total producer surplus therefore falls by $0.70 – $0.40 = $0.30.

   c. Azar's willingness to pay for her second pepper is $0.60; this is what she would lose if she were to consume one fewer pepper. Cara's cost of producing her third pepper is $0.40; this is what she would save if she were to produce one fewer pepper. If we therefore reduced quantity by one pepper, we would lose $0.60 – $0.40 = $0.20 of total surplus.

3. The new guideline is likely to reduce the total life span of kidney recipients because recipients with small children are more likely to get a kidney compared to the original guideline. As a result, total surplus is likely to fall. However, this new policy can be justified as an acceptable sacrifice of efficiency for fairness because it's a desirable goal to reduce the chance of a small child losing a parent.

4-4 Check Your Understanding

1. When these rights are separated, someone who owns both the above-ground and the mineral rights can sell each of these separately in the market for above-ground rights and the market for mineral rights. And each of these markets will achieve efficiency: if the market price for above-ground rights is higher than the seller's cost, the seller will sell those rights and total surplus increases. If the market price for mineral rights is higher than the seller's cost, the seller will sell those rights and total surplus increases. If the two rights, however, cannot be sold separately, a seller can only sell both rights or none at all. Imagine a situation in which the seller values the mineral rights highly (that is, has a high cost of selling it) but values the above-ground rights much less. If the two rights are separate, the owner may sell the above-ground rights (increasing total surplus) but not the mineral rights. If, however, the two rights cannot be sold separately, and the owner values the mineral rights sufficiently highly, they may not sell either of the two rights. In this case, surplus could have been created through the sale of the above-ground rights but goes unrealized because the two rights could not be sold separately.

2. There will be many sellers willing to sell their books but only a few buyers who want to buy books at that price. As a result, only a few transactions will actually occur, and many transactions that would have been mutually beneficial will not take place. This, of course, is inefficient.

3. Markets, alas, do not always lead to efficiency. When there is market failure, the market outcome may be inefficient. This can occur for three main reasons. Markets can fail when, in an attempt to capture more surplus, one party—a monopolist, for instance—prevents mutually beneficial transactions from occurring. Markets can also fail when one individual's actions have side effects—externalities—on the welfare of others. Finally, markets can fail when the goods themselves—such as goods about which some relevant information is private—are unsuited for efficient management by markets. And when markets don't achieve efficiency, government intervention can improve society's welfare.

|| CHAPTER FIVE

5-1 Check Your Understanding

1. **a.** Fewer homeowners are willing to rent out their driveways because the price ceiling has reduced the payment they receive. This is an example of a fall in price leading to a fall in the quantity supplied. It is shown in the accompanying diagram by the movement from point E to point A along the supply curve, a reduction in quantity of 400 parking spaces.

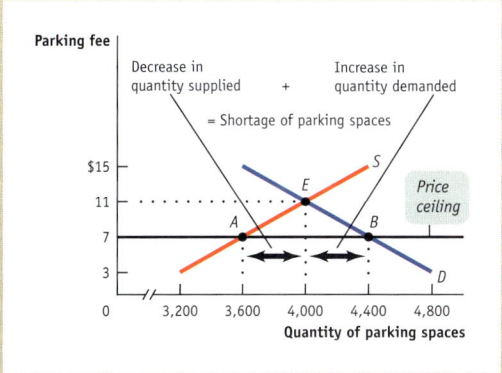

b. The quantity demanded increases by 400 spaces as the price decreases. At a lower price, more fans are willing to drive and rent a parking space. It is shown in the diagram by the movement from point E to point B along the demand curve.

c. Under a price ceiling, the quantity demanded exceeds the quantity supplied; as a result, shortages arise. In this case, there will be a shortage of 800 parking spaces. It is shown by the horizontal distance between points A and B.

d. Price ceilings result in wasted resources. The additional time fans spend to guarantee a parking space is wasted time.

e. Price ceilings lead to inefficient allocation of a good—here, the parking spaces—to consumers.

f. Price ceilings lead to black markets.

2. **a.** False. By lowering the price that producers receive, a price ceiling leads to a decrease in the quantity supplied.

b. True. A price ceiling leads to a lower quantity supplied than in an efficient, unregulated market. As a result, some people who would have been willing to pay the market price, and so would have gotten the good in an unregulated market, are unable to obtain it when a price ceiling is imposed.

c. True. Those producers who still sell the product now receive less for it and are therefore worse off. Other producers will no longer find it worthwhile to sell the product at all and so will also be made worse off.

3. **a.** Since the apartment is rented quickly at the same price, there is no change (either gain or loss) in producer surplus. So any change in total surplus comes from changes in consumer surplus. When you are evicted, the amount of consumer surplus you lose is equal to the difference between your willingness to pay for the apartment and the rent-controlled price. When the apartment is rented to someone else at the same price, the amount of consumer surplus the new renter gains is equal to the difference between their willingness to pay and the rent-controlled price. So this will be a pure transfer of surplus from one person to another only if both your willingness to pay and the new renter's willingness to pay are the same. Since under rent control apartments are not always allocated to those who have the highest willingness to pay, the new renter's willingness to pay may be either equal to, lower than, or higher than your willingness to pay. If the new renter's willingness to pay is lower than yours, this will create additional deadweight loss: there is some additional consumer surplus that is lost. However, if the new renter's willingness to pay is higher than yours, this will create an increase in total surplus, as the new renter gains more consumer surplus than you lost.

b. This creates deadweight loss: if you were able to give the ticket away, someone else would be able to obtain consumer surplus, equal to their willingness to pay for the ticket. You neither gain nor lose any surplus, since you cannot go to the concert whether or not you give the ticket away. If you were able to sell the ticket, the buyer would obtain consumer surplus equal to the difference between their willingness to pay for the ticket and the price at which you sell the ticket. In addition, you would obtain producer surplus equal to the difference between the price at which you sell the ticket and your cost of selling the ticket (which, since you won the ticket, is presumably zero). Since the restriction to neither sell nor give away the ticket means that this surplus cannot be obtained by anybody, it creates deadweight loss. If you could give the ticket away, as just described, there would be consumer surplus that accrues to the recipient of the ticket; and if you give the ticket to the person with the highest willingness to pay, there would be no deadweight loss.

c. This creates deadweight loss. If students buy ice cream on campus, they obtain consumer surplus: their willingness to pay must be higher than the price of the ice cream. Your college obtains producer surplus: the price is higher than your college's cost of selling the ice cream. Prohibiting the sale of ice cream on campus means that these two sources of total surplus are lost: there is deadweight loss.

d. Given that your dog values ice cream equally as much as you do, this is a pure transfer of surplus. As you lose consumer surplus, your dog gains equally as much consumer surplus.

5-2 Check Your Understanding

1. **a.** Some gas station owners will benefit from getting a higher price. Q_F indicates the sales made by these owners. But some will lose; there are those who make sales at the market equilibrium price of P_E but do not make sales at the regulated price of P_F. These missed sales are indicated on the graph by the fall in the quantity demanded along the demand curve, from point E to point A.

b. Those who buy gas at the higher price of P_F will probably receive better service; this is an example of *inefficiently high quality* caused by a price floor as gas station owners compete on quality rather than price. But opponents are correct to claim that consumers are generally worse off—those who buy at P_F would have been happy to buy at P_E, and many who were willing to buy at a price between P_E and P_F are now unwilling to buy. This is indicated on the graph by the fall in the quantity demanded along the demand curve, from point E to point A.

c. Proponents are wrong because consumers and some gas station owners are hurt by the price floor, which creates "missed opportunities"—desirable transactions between consumers and station owners that never take place. The deadweight loss, the amount of total surplus lost because of missed opportunities, is indicated by the shaded area in the accompanying figure. Moreover, the inefficiency of wasted resources arises as consumers spend time and money driving to other jurisdictions. The price floor also tempts people to engage in black market activity. With the price floor, only Q_F units are sold. But at prices between P_E and P_F, there are drivers who cumulatively want to buy more than Q_F and owners who are willing to sell to them, a situation likely to lead to illegal activity.

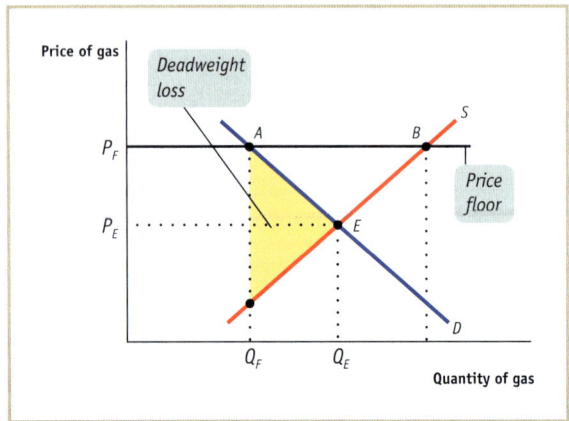

5-3 Check Your Understanding

1. **a.** The price of a ride is $7 since the quantity demanded at this price is 6 million: $7 is the *demand price* of 6 million rides. This is represented by point A in the accompanying figure.

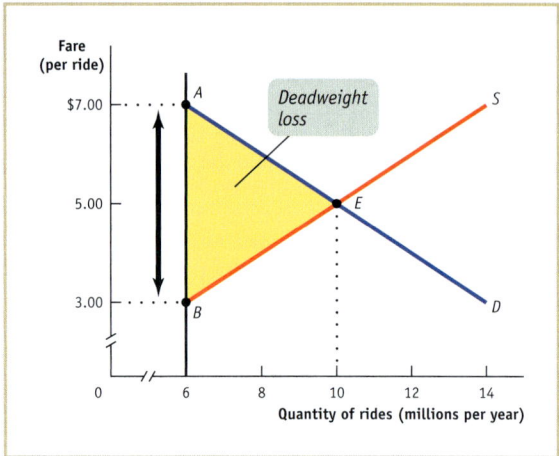

b. At 6 million rides, the supply price is $3 per ride, represented by point B in the figure. The wedge between the demand price of $7 per ride and the supply price of $3 per ride is the quota rent per ride, $4. This is represented in the figure above by the vertical distance between points A and B.

c. The quota discourages 4 million mutually beneficial transactions. The shaded triangle in the figure represents the deadweight loss.

d. At 9 million rides, the demand price is $5.50 per ride, indicated by point C in the accompanying figure, and the supply price is $4.50 per ride, indicated by point D. The quota rent is the difference between the demand price and the supply price: $1. The deadweight loss is represented by the shaded triangle in the figure. As you can see, the deadweight loss is smaller when the quota is set at 9 million rides than when it is set at 6 million rides.

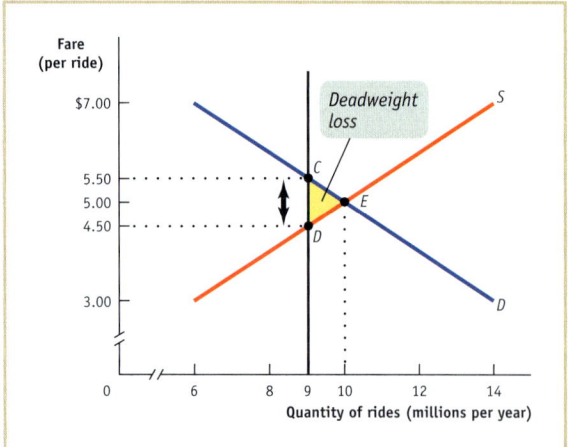

2. The accompanying figure shows a decrease in demand by 4 million rides, represented by a leftward shift of the demand curve from D_1 to D_2: at any given price, the quantity demanded falls by 4 million rides. (For example, at a price of $5, the quantity demanded falls from 10 million to 6 million rides per year.) This eliminates the effect of a quota limit of 8 million rides. At point E_2, the new market equilibrium, the equilibrium quantity is equal to the quota limit; as a result, the quota has no effect on the market.

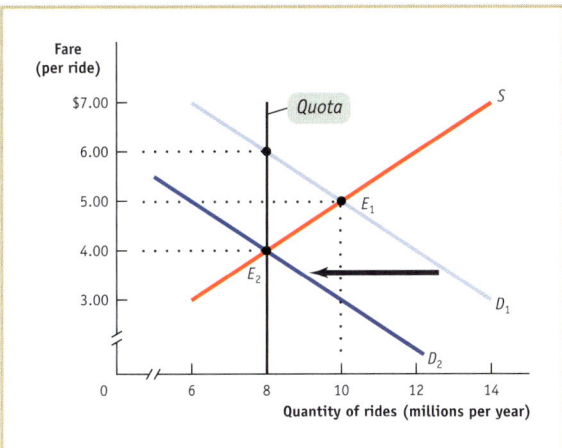

‖ CHAPTER SIX

6-1 Check Your Understanding

1. By the midpoint method, the percent change in the price of strawberries is:

$$\frac{\$1.00 - \$1.50}{(\$1.50 + \$1.00)/2} \times 100 = \frac{-\$0.50}{\$1.25} \times 100 = -40\%$$

Similarly, the percent change in the quantity of strawberries demanded is:

$$\frac{200,000 - 100,000}{(100,000 + 200,000)/2} \times 100 = \frac{100,000}{150,000} \times 100 = 67\%$$

Dropping the minus sign, the price elasticity of demand using the midpoint method is 67%/40% = 1.675.

2. By the midpoint method, the percent change in the quantity of movie tickets demanded in going from 4,000 tickets to 5,000 tickets is:

$$\frac{5,000 - 4,000}{(4,000 + 5,000)/2} \times 100 = \frac{1,000}{4,500} \times 100 = 22\%$$

Since the price elasticity of demand is 1 at the current consumption level, it will take a 22% reduction in the price of movie tickets to generate a 22% increase in quantity demanded.

3. Since price rises, we know that quantity demanded must fall. Given the current price of $0.50, a $0.05 increase in price represents a 10% change, using the method in Equation 6-2. So the price elasticity of demand is:

$$\frac{\text{change in quantity demanded}}{10\%} = 1.2$$

so that the change in quantity demanded (10% × 1.2) equals 12%. A 12% decrease in quantity demanded represents 100,000 × 0.12, or 12,000 sandwiches.

6-2 Check Your Understanding

1. a. Elastic demand. Consumers are highly responsive to changes in price. For a rise in price, the quantity effect (which tends to reduce total revenue) outweighs the price effect (which tends to increase total revenue). Overall, this leads to a fall in total revenue.

b. Unit-elastic demand. Here the revenue lost to the fall in price is exactly equal to the revenue gained from higher sales. The quantity effect exactly offsets the price effect.

c. Inelastic demand. Consumers are relatively unresponsive to changes in price. For consumers to purchase a given percent increase in output, the price must fall by an even greater percent. The price effect of a fall in price (which tends to reduce total revenue) outweighs the quantity effect (which tends to increase total revenue). As a result, total revenue decreases.

d. Inelastic demand. Consumers are relatively unresponsive to price, so the percent fall in output is smaller than the percent rise in price. The price effect of a rise in price (which tends to increase total revenue) outweighs the quantity effect (which tends to reduce total revenue). As a result, total revenue increases.

2. a. The demand of an accident victim for a blood transfusion is very likely to be perfectly inelastic because there is no substitute and it is necessary for survival. The demand curve will be vertical, at a quantity equal to the needed transfusion quantity.

b. Students' demand for green erasers is likely to be perfectly elastic because there are easily available substitutes: nongreen erasers. The demand curve will be horizontal, at a price equal to that of nongreen erasers.

6-3 Check Your Understanding

1. By the midpoint method, the percent increase in Charlotte's income is:

$$\frac{\$18,000 - \$12,000}{(\$12,000 + \$18,000)/2} \times 100 = \frac{\$6,000}{\$15,000} \times 100 = 40\%$$

Similarly, the percent increase in her consumption of albums is:

$$\frac{40 - 10}{(10 + 40)/2} \times 100 = \frac{30}{25} \times 100 = 120\%$$

So Charlotte's income elasticity of demand for movies is 120%/40% = 3.

2. Sanjay's consumption of expensive restaurant meals will fall more than 10% because a given percent change in income (a fall of 10% here) induces a larger percent change in consumption of an income-elastic good.

3. The cross-price elasticity of demand is 5%/20% = 0.25. Since the cross-price elasticity of demand is positive, the two goods are substitutes.

6-4 Check Your Understanding

1. By the midpoint method, the percent change in the number of hours of web-design services contracted is:

$$\frac{500,000 - 300,000}{(300,000 + 500,000)/2} \times 100 = \frac{200,000}{400,000} \times 100 = 50\%$$

Similarly, the percent change in the price of web-design services is:

$$\frac{\$150 - \$100}{(\$100 + \$150)/2} \times 100 = \frac{\$50}{\$125} \times 100 = 40\%$$

The price elasticity of supply is 50%/40% = 1.25. So supply is elastic.

2. **a.** True. An increase in demand raises price. If the price elasticity of supply of milk is low, then relatively little additional quantity supplied will be forthcoming as the price rises. As a result, the price of milk will rise substantially to satisfy the increased demand for milk. If the price elasticity of supply is high, then there will be a relatively large increase in quantity supplied when the price rises. As a result, the price of milk will rise only by a little to satisfy the higher demand for milk.

   b. False. It is true that long-run price elasticities of supply are generally larger than short-run elasticities of supply. But this means that the short-run supply curves are generally steeper, not flatter, than the long-run supply curves.

   c. True. When supply is perfectly elastic, the supply curve is a horizontal line. So a change in demand has no effect on price; it affects only the quantity bought and sold.

|| CHAPTER SEVEN

7-1 Check Your Understanding

1. The following figure shows that, after introduction of the excise tax, the price paid by consumers rises to $1.20; the price received by producers falls to $0.90. Consumers bear $0.20 of the $0.30 tax per kilogram of butter; producers bear $0.10 of the $0.30 tax per kilogram of butter. The tax drives a wedge of $0.30 between the price paid by consumers and the price received by producers. As a result, the quantity of butter bought and sold is now 9 million kilograms.

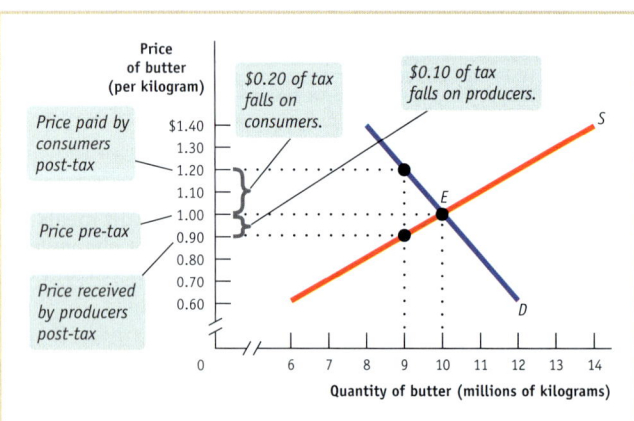

2. The fact that demand is very inelastic means that consumers will reduce their demand for textbooks very little in response to an increase in the price caused by the tax. The fact that supply is somewhat elastic means that suppliers will respond to the fall in the price by reducing supply. As a result, the incidence of the tax will fall heavily on consumers of economics textbooks

and very little on publishers, as shown in the accompanying figure.

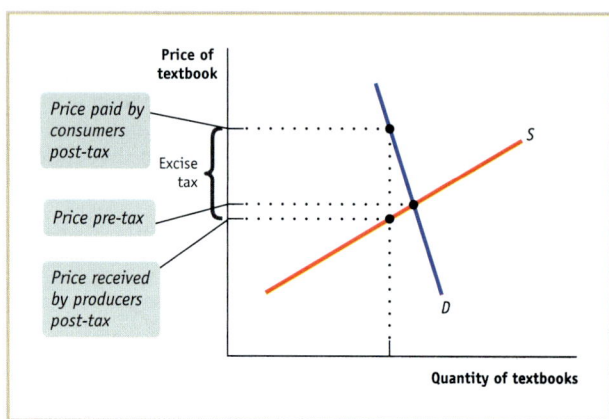

3. True. When a substitute is readily available, demand is elastic. This implies that producers cannot easily pass on the cost of the tax to consumers because consumers will respond to an increased price by switching to the substitute. Furthermore, when producers have difficulty adjusting the amount of the good produced, supply is inelastic. That is, producers cannot easily reduce output in response to a lower price net of tax. So the tax burden will fall more heavily on producers than consumers.

4. The fact that supply is very inelastic means that producers will reduce their supply of bottled water very little in response to the fall in price caused by the tax. Demand, on the other hand, will fall in response to an increase in price because demand is somewhat elastic. As a result, the incidence of the tax will fall heavily on producers of bottled spring water and very little on consumers, as shown in the accompanying figure.

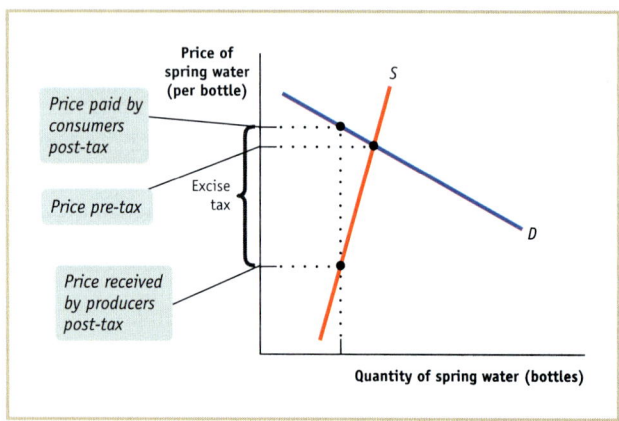

5. True. The lower the elasticity of supply, the more the burden of a tax will fall on producers rather than consumers, other things equal.

7-2 Check Your Understanding

1. **a.** Without the excise tax, Zachary, Yves, Xavier, and William sell, and Ana, Brianna, Chizuko, and Dylan buy one can of pop each, at $0.40 per can. So the quantity bought and sold is 4.

b. At a price to consumers of $0.60, only Ana and Brianna are willing to buy a can of pop. At a price paid to producers of only $0.20, only Zachary and Yves are willing to sell. So the quantity bought and sold is 2.

c. Without the excise tax, Ana's individual consumer surplus is $0.70 − $0.40 = $0.30, Brianna's is $0.60 − $0.40 = $0.20, Chizuko's is $0.50 − $0.40 = $0.10, and Dylan's is $0.40 − $0.40 = $0.00. Total consumer surplus is $0.30 + $0.20 + $0.10 + $0.00 = $0.60. With the tax, Ana's individual consumer surplus is $0.70 − $0.60 = $0.10 and Brianna's is $0.60 − $0.60 = $0.00. Total consumer surplus post-tax is $0.10 + $0.00 = $0.10. So the total consumer surplus lost because of the tax is $0.60 − $0.10 = $0.50.

d. Without the excise tax, Zachary's individual producer surplus is $0.40 − $0.10 = $0.30, Yves's is $0.40 − $0.20 = $0.20, Xavier's is $0.40 − $0.30 = $0.10, and William's is $0.40 − $0.40 = $0.00. Total producer surplus is $0.30 + $0.20 + $0.10 + $0.00 = $0.60. With the tax, Zachary's individual producer surplus is $0.20 − $0.10 = $0.10 and Yves's is $0.20 − $0.20 = $0.00. Total producer surplus post-tax is $0.10 + $0.00 = $0.10. So the total producer surplus lost because of the tax is $0.60 − $0.10 = $0.50.

e. With the tax, two cans of pop are sold, so the government tax revenue from this excise tax is 2 × $0.40 = $0.80.

f. Total surplus without the tax is $0.60 + $0.60 = $1.20. With the tax, total surplus is $0.10 + $0.10 = $0.20, and government tax revenue is $0.80. So deadweight loss from this excise tax is $1.20 − ($0.20 + $0.80) = $0.20.

2. a. The demand for gasoline is inelastic because there is no close substitute for gasoline itself and it is difficult for drivers to arrange substitutes for driving, such as taking public transportation. As a result, the deadweight loss from a tax on gasoline would be relatively small, as shown in the accompanying diagram.

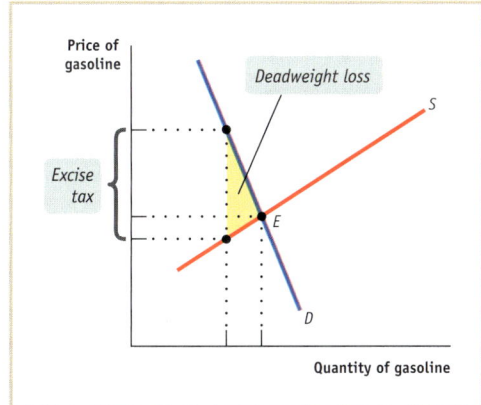

b. The demand for milk chocolate bars is elastic because there are close substitutes: dark chocolate bars, milk chocolate kisses, and so on. As a result, the deadweight loss from a tax on milk chocolate bars would be relatively large, as shown in the accompanying diagram.

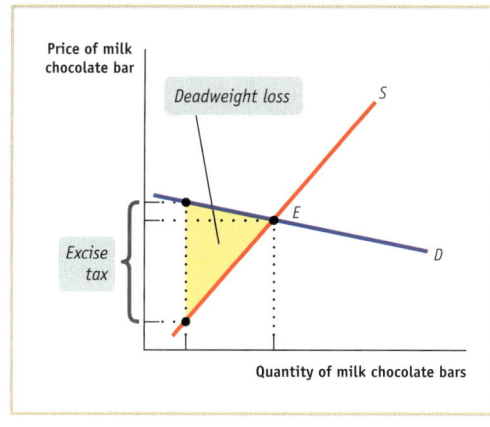

7-3 Check Your Understanding

1. a. Since drivers are the beneficiaries of highway safety programs, this tax performs well according to the benefits principle. But since the level of the tax does not depend on ability to pay the tax, it does not perform well according to the ability-to-pay principle. Since higher-income car purchasers are likely to spend more on a new car, a tax assessed as a percentage of the purchase price of the car would perform better on the ability-to-pay principle. A $500-per-car tax will cause people to buy fewer new cars, but a percentage-based tax will cause people to buy fewer cars and less expensive cars.

b. This tax does not perform well according to the benefits principle because the payers are nonresidents of the local area, but the beneficiaries are local residents who will enjoy greater government services. But to the extent that people who stay in hotels have higher income compared to those who don't, the tax performs well according to the ability-to-pay principle. It will distort the action of staying in a hotel room in this area, resulting in fewer nights of hotel room stays.

c. This tax performs well according to the benefits principle because local homeowners are the users of local schools. It also performs well according to the ability-to-pay principle because it is assessed as a percentage of home value: higher-income residents, who own more expensive homes, will pay higher taxes. It will distort the action of buying a house in this area versus another area with a lower property tax rate. It could also distort the action of making improvements to a house that would increase its assessed value.

d. This tax performs well according to the benefits principle because food consumers are the beneficiaries of government food safety programs. It does not perform well according to the ability-to-pay principle because food is a necessity, and lower-income people will pay approximately as much as higher-income people. This tax will distort the action of buying food, leading people to purchase cheaper varieties of food.

7-4 Check Your Understanding

1. a. The marginal tax rate for someone with income of $5,000 is 1%: for each additional $1 in income, $0.01 or 1%, is taxed away. This person pays total tax of $5,000 × 1% = $50, which is ($50/$5,000) × 100 = 1% of their income.

b. The marginal tax rate for someone with income of $20,000 is 2%: for each additional $1 in income, $0.02 or 2%, is taxed away. This person pays total tax of $10,000 × 1% + $10,000 × 2% = $300, which is ($300/$20,000) × 100 = 1.5% of their income.

c. Since the high-income taxpayer pays a larger percentage of their income than the low-income taxpayer, this tax is progressive.

2. A 1% tax on consumption spending means that a family earning $15,000 and spending $10,000 will pay a tax of 1% × $10,000 = $100, equivalent to 0.67% of its income; ($100/$15,000) × 100 = 0.67%. But a family earning $10,000 and spending $8,000 will pay a tax of 1% × $8,000 = $80, equivalent to 0.80% of its income; ($80/$10,000) × 100 = 0.80%. The tax is regressive, since the lower-income family pays a higher percentage of its income in tax than the higher-income family.

3. a. False. Recall that a seller always bears some burden of a tax as long as their supply of the good is not perfectly elastic. Since the supply of labour a worker offers is not perfectly elastic, some of the payroll tax will be borne by the worker, and therefore the tax will affect the person's incentive to take a job.

b. False. Under a proportional tax, the percentage of the tax base is the same for everyone. Under a lump-sum tax, the total tax paid is the same for everyone, regardless of income.

|| CHAPTER EIGHT

8-1 Check Your Understanding

1. a. To determine comparative advantage, we must compare the two countries' opportunity costs for a given good. Take the opportunity cost of 1 tonne of corn in terms of bicycles. In China, the opportunity cost of 1 bicycle is 0.01 tonne of corn; so the opportunity cost of 1 tonne of corn is 1/0.01 bicycles = 100 bicycles. Canada has the comparative advantage in corn since its opportunity cost in terms of bicycles is 50, a smaller number. Similarly, the opportunity cost in Canada of 1 bicycle in terms of corn is 1/50 tonne of corn = 0.02 tonne of corn. This is greater than 0.01, the Chinese opportunity cost of 1 bicycle in terms of corn, implying that China has a comparative advantage in bicycles.

b. Given that Canada can produce 200,000 bicycles if no corn is produced, it can produce 200,000 bicycles × 0.02 tonne of corn/bicycle = 4,000 tonnes of corn when no bicycles are produced. Likewise, if China can produce 3,000 tonnes of corn if no bicycles are produced, it can produce 3,000 tonnes of corn × 100 bicycles/tonne of corn = 300,000 bicycles if no corn is produced. These points determine the vertical and horizontal intercepts of Canadian and Chinese production possibility frontiers, as shown in the accompanying diagram.

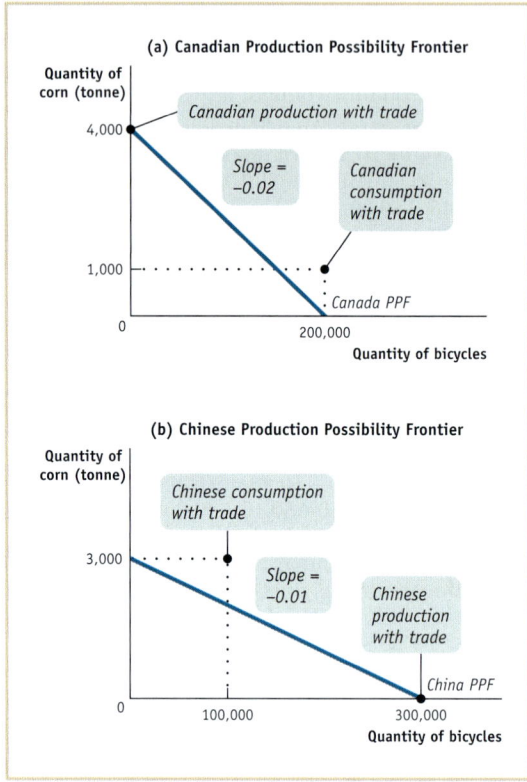

(a) Canadian Production Possibility Frontier

Quantity of corn (tonne)

Canadian production with trade

4,000

Slope = −0.02

Canadian consumption with trade

1,000

Canada PPF

0   200,000

Quantity of bicycles

(b) Chinese Production Possibility Frontier

Quantity of corn (tonne)

Chinese consumption with trade

3,000

Slope = −0.01

Chinese production with trade

China PPF

0   100,000   300,000

Quantity of bicycles

c. The diagram shows the production and consumption points of the two countries. Each country is clearly better off with international trade because each now consumes a bundle of the two goods that lies outside its own production possibility frontier, indicating that these bundles were unattainable in autarky.

2. a. According to the Heckscher–Ohlin model, this pattern of trade occurs because Canada has a relatively larger endowment of factors of production, such as human capital and physical capital, that are suited to the production of lumber, but France has a relatively larger endowment of factors of production suited to wine-making, such as vineyards and the human capital of vintners.

b. According to the Heckscher–Ohlin model, this pattern of trade occurs because Canada has a relatively larger endowment of factors of production, such as human and physical capital, that are suited to making machinery, but Brazil has a relatively larger endowment of factors of production suited to shoe-making, such as unskilled labour and leather.

8-2 Check Your Understanding

1. In the accompanying diagram, P_A is the Canadian price of grapes in autarky and P_W is the world price of grapes under international trade. With trade, Canadian consumers pay a price of P_W for grapes and consume quantity Q_D, Canadian grape producers produce quantity Q_S, and the difference, $Q_D − Q_S$, represents imports of Mexican grapes. As a consequence of the strike by truckers, imports are halted, the price paid by Canadian consumers rises to the autarky price, P_A, and Canadian consumption falls to the autarky quantity, Q_A.

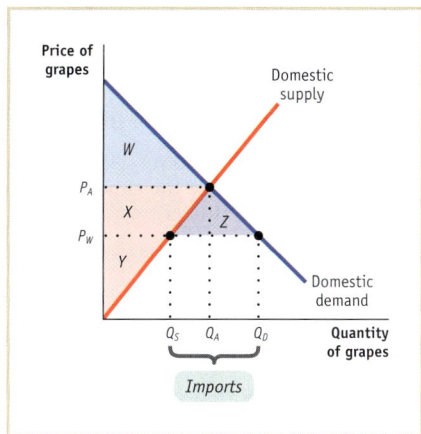

a. Before the strike, Canadian consumers enjoyed consumer surplus equal to areas $W + X + Z$. After the strike, their consumer surplus shrinks to W. So consumers are worse off, losing consumer surplus represented by $X + Z$.

b. Before the strike, Canadian producers had producer surplus equal to the area Y. After the strike, their producer surplus increases to $Y + X$. So Canadian producers are better off, gaining producer surplus represented by X.

c. Canadian total surplus falls as a result of the strike by an amount represented by area Z, the loss in consumer surplus that does not accrue to producers.

2. Mexican grape producers are worse off because they lose sales of exported grapes to Canada, and Mexican grape pickers are worse off because they lose the wages that were associated with the lost sales. The lower demand for Mexican grapes caused by the strike implies that the price Mexican consumers pay for grapes falls, making them better off. Canadian grape pickers are better off because their wages increase as a result of the increase of $Q_A - Q_S$ in Canadian sales.

8-3 Check Your Understanding

1. a. If the tariff is $0.50, the price paid by domestic consumers for a kilogram of imported butter is $0.50 + $0.50 = $1.00, the same price as a kilogram of domestic butter. Imported butter will no longer have a price advantage over domestic butter, imports will cease, and domestic producers will capture all the feasible sales to domestic consumers, selling amount Q_A in the accompanying figure. If the tariff is $0.25, the price paid by domestic consumers for a kilogram of imported butter is $0.50 + $0.25 = $0.75, $0.25 cheaper than a kilogram of domestic butter. American butter producers will gain sales in the amount of $Q_2 - Q_1$ as a result of the $0.25 tariff. But this is smaller than the amount they would have gained under the $0.50 tariff, the amount $Q_A - Q_1$.

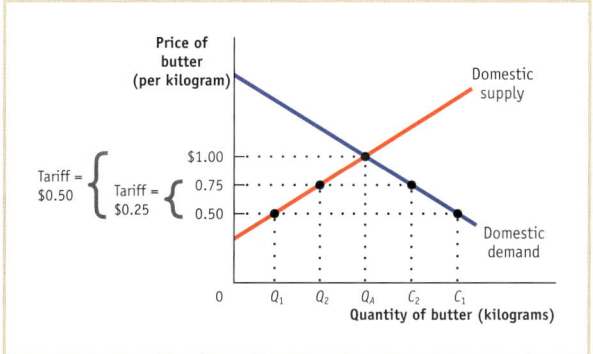

b. As long as the tariff is at least $0.50, increasing it more has no effect. At a tariff of $0.50, all imports are effectively blocked.

2. All imports are effectively blocked at a tariff of $0.50. So such a tariff corresponds to an import quota of 0.

8-4 Check Your Understanding

1. There are many fewer businesses that use steel as an input than there are consumers who buy sugar or clothing. So it will be easier for such businesses to communicate and coordinate among themselves to lobby against tariffs than it will be for consumers. In addition, each business will perceive that the cost of a steel tariff is quite costly to its profits, but an individual consumer is either unaware of or perceives little loss from tariffs on sugar or clothing.

2. Countries are often tempted to protect domestic industries by claiming that an import poses a quality, health, or environmental danger to domestic consumers. A WTO official should examine whether domestic producers are subject to the same stringency in the application of quality, health, or environmental regulations as foreign producers. If they are, then it is more likely that the regulations are for legitimate, non–trade protection purposes; if they are not, then it is more likely that the regulations are intended as trade protection measures.

‖ CHAPTER NINE

9-1 Check Your Understanding

1. a. Supplies are an explicit cost because they require an outlay of money.

   b. If the basement could be used in some other way that generates money, such as renting it to a student, then the implicit cost is that money forgone. Otherwise, the implicit cost is zero.

   c. Wages are an explicit cost.

   d. By using the van for their business, Marisol and Logan forgo the money they could have gained by selling it. So use of the van is an implicit cost.

   e. Marisol's forgone wages from her job are an implicit cost.

2. We need only compare the choice of becoming a machinist to the choice of taking a job in another city in order to make the right choice. We can discard the choice of acquiring a pharmacology degree because we already know that taking a job in another city is always superior to it. Now let's compare the remaining two alternatives: becoming a skilled machinist versus immediately taking a job in another city. As an apprentice machinist, Adam will earn only $30,000 over the first two years, versus $57,000 in the out-of-city job. So he has an implicit cost of $30,000 − $57,000 = −$27,000 by becoming a machinist instead of immediately moving out of city to work. However, two years from now the value of his lifetime earnings as a machinist is $725,000 versus $600,000 in advertising, giving him an accounting profit of $125,000 by choosing to be a machinist. Summing, his economic profit from choosing a career as a machinist over his other career is $125,000 − $27,000 = $98,000. In contrast, his economic profit from choosing the alternative, a career out of city over a career as a machinist, is −$125,000 + $27,000 = −$98,000. By the principle of "either–or" decision making, Adam should choose to be a machinist because that career has a positive economic profit.

3. You can discard alternative A because both B and C are superior to it. But you must now compare B versus C. You should then choose the alternative—B or C—that carries a positive economic profit.

9-2 Check Your Understanding

1. **a.** The marginal cost of doing your laundry is any monetary outlays plus the opportunity cost of your time spent doing laundry today—that is, the value you would place on spending time today on your next best alternative activity, like seeing a movie. The marginal benefit is having more clean clothes today to choose from.

   b. The marginal cost of changing your oil is the opportunity cost of time spent changing your oil now as well as the explicit cost of the oil change. The marginal benefit is the improvement in your car's performance.

   c. The marginal cost is the unpleasant feeling of a burning mouth that you receive from it plus any explicit cost of the jalapeno. The marginal benefit of another jalapeno on your nachos is the pleasant taste that you receive from it.

   d. The marginal cost is the wage you must pay that worker. The marginal benefit of hiring another worker in your company is the value of the output that worker produces.

   e. The marginal cost is the value lost due to the increased side effects from this additional dose. The marginal benefit of another dose of the drug is the value of the reduction in the patient's disease.

   f. The marginal cost is the opportunity cost of your time—what you would have gotten from the next best use of your time. The marginal benefit is the probable increase in your grade.

2. The accompanying table shows Alexa's new marginal cost and her new profit. It also reproduces Alexa's marginal benefit from Table 9-5.

Years of schooling	Total cost	Marginal cost	Marginal benefit	Profit
0	$0			
		$90,000	$300,000	$210,000
1	90,000			
		30,000	150,000	120,000
2	120,000			
		50,000	90,000	40,000
3	170,000			
		80,000	60,000	–20,000
4	250,000			
		120,000	50,000	–70,000
5	370,000			

Alexa's marginal cost is decreasing until she has completed two years of schooling, after which marginal cost increases because of the value of her forgone income. The optimal amount of schooling is still three years. For less than three years of schooling, marginal benefit exceeds marginal cost; for more than three years, marginal cost exceeds marginal benefit.

9-3 Check Your Understanding

1. **a.** Your sunk cost is $8,000 because none of the $8,000 spent on the truck is recoverable.

   b. Your sunk cost is $4,000 because 50% of the $8,000 spent on the truck is recoverable.

2. **a.** This is an invalid argument because the time and money already spent are a sunk cost at this point.

   b. This is also an invalid argument because what you should have done two years ago is irrelevant to what you should do now.

   c. This is a valid argument because it recognizes that sunk costs are irrelevant to what you should do now.

   d. This is a valid argument given that you are concerned about disappointing your parents. But your parents' views are irrational because they do not recognize that the time already spent is a sunk cost.

9-4 Check Your Understanding

1. **a.** Jenny is exhibiting loss aversion. She has an oversensitivity to loss, leading to an unwillingness to ignore sunk costs and move on.

   b. This is an example of framing bias. Retailers are using the multiple-item offers to induce shoppers to buy more under the perception that they are getting a good deal. But it is not a good deal for Leo because he buys more than he needs.

   c. Danilo may have unrealistic expectations of future behaviour. Even if he does not want to participate in the plan now, he should find a way to commit to participating at a later date.

   d. Emma is showing signs of status quo bias. She is avoiding making a decision altogether; in other words, she is sticking with the status quo.

2. You would determine whether a decision was rational or irrational by first accurately accounting for all the costs and benefits of the decision. In particular, you must accurately measure all opportunity costs. Then calculate the economic payoff of the decision relative to the next best alternative. If you would still make the same choice after this comparison, then you have made a rational choice. If not, then the choice was irrational.

‖ CHAPTER TEN

10-1 Check Your Understanding

1. Consuming a unit that generates negative marginal utility leaves the consumer with lower total utility than not consuming that unit at all. A rational consumer, a consumer who maximizes utility, would not do that. For example, from Figure 10-1 you can see that Cassie receives 64 utils if she consumes 8 clams; but if she consumes the ninth clam, she loses a util, netting her a total utility of only 63 utils. So whenever consuming a unit generates negative marginal utility, the consumer is made better off by not consuming that unit, even when that unit is free.

2. Since Marta has diminishing marginal utility of coffee, her first cup of coffee of the day generates the greatest increase in total utility. Her third and last cup of the day generates the least.

3. a. Mabel does not have diminishing marginal utility of exercising since each additional unit consumed brings more additional enjoyment than the previous unit.

b. Mei does not have diminishing marginal utility of vinyl records because each additional unit generates the same additional enjoyment as the previous unit.

c. Dexter has diminishing marginal utility of restaurant meals since the additional utility generated by a good restaurant meal is less when he consumes lots of them than when he consumed few of them.

10-2 Check Your Understanding

1. a. The accompanying table shows the consumer's consumption possibilities, *A* through *C*. These consumption possibilities are plotted in the accompanying diagram, along with the consumer's budget line, *BL*.

Consumption bundle	Quantity of popcorn (buckets)	Quantity of movie tickets
A	0	2
B	2	1
C	4	0

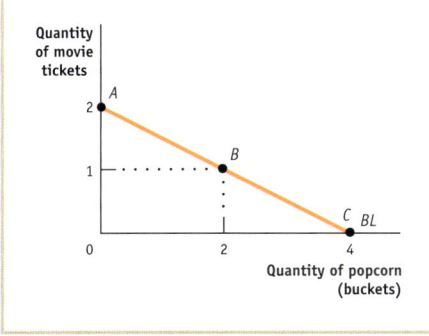

b. The accompanying table shows the consumer's consumption possibilities, *A* through *D*. These consumption possibilities are plotted in the accompanying diagram, along with the consumer's budget line, *BL*.

Consumption bundle	Quantity of underwear (pairs)	Quantity of socks (pairs)
A	0	6
B	1	4
C	2	2
D	3	0

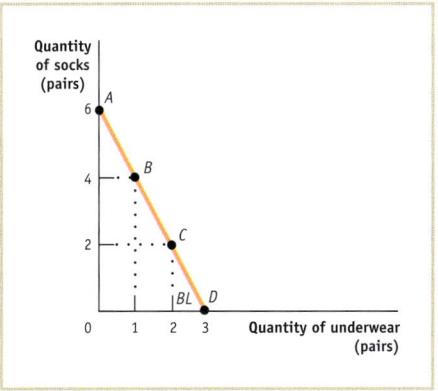

10-3 Check Your Understanding

1. From Table 10-3 you can see that Sammy's marginal utility per dollar from increasing his consumption of egg rolls from 3 rolls to 4, and his marginal utility per dollar from increasing his consumption of Coke from 9 bottles to 10 are the same, 0.75 utils. But a consumption bundle consisting of 4 egg rolls and 10 bottles of Coke is not Sammy's optimal consumption bundle because it is not affordable given his income of $20; 4 egg rolls and 10 bottles of Coke cost $4 × 4 + $2 × 10 = $36, $16 more than Sammy's income. This can be illustrated with Sammy's budget line from panel (a) of Figure 10-3: a bundle of 4 egg rolls and 10 bottles of Coke is represented by point *X* in the accompanying diagram, a point that lies outside Sammy's budget line. If you look at the horizontal axis of panel (a) of Figure 10-3, it is quite clear that there is no such thing in Sammy's consumption possibilities as a bundle consisting of 4 egg rolls and 10 bottles of Coke.

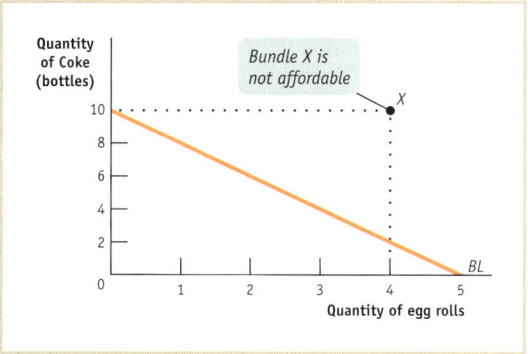

2. Sammy's maximum utility per dollar is generated when he goes from consuming 0 to 1 egg roll (3.75 utils) and as he goes from 0 to 1 bottle of Coke (5.75 utils). But this bundle consisting of 1 egg roll and 1 bottle of Coke generates only 26.5 utils for him. Instead, Sammy should choose the consumption bundle that satisfies his budget constraint and for which the marginal utility per dollar for both goods is equal.

10-4 Check Your Understanding

1. a. Since spending on orange juice is a small share of Clare's spending, the income effect from a rise in the price of orange juice is insignificant. Only the substitution effect, represented by the substitution of lemonade in place of orange juice, is significant.

b. Since rent is a large share of Delia's expenditures, the increase in rent generates a significant income effect, making Delia feel poorer. Since housing is a normal good for Delia, the income and substitution effects move in the same direction, leading her to reduce her consumption of housing by moving to a smaller apartment.

c. Since a meal ticket is a significant share of the students' living costs, an increase in its price will generate a significant income effect. Because cafeteria meals are an inferior good, the substitution effect (which would induce students to substitute restaurant meals in place of cafeteria meals) and the income effect (which would induce them to eat in the cafeteria more often because they are poorer) move in opposite directions.

2. In order to determine whether any good is a Giffen good, you must first establish whether it is an inferior good. In other words, if students' incomes decrease, other things equal, does the quantity of cafeteria meals demanded increase? Once you have established that the good is an inferior good, you must then establish that the income effect outweighs the substitution effect. That is, as the price of cafeteria meals rises, other things equal, does the quantity of cafeteria meals demanded increase? Be careful that, in fact, all other things remain equal. But if the quantity of cafeteria meals demanded truly increases in response to a price rise, you have found a Giffen good.

‖ CHAPTER ELEVEN

11-1 Check Your Understanding

1. **a.** The fixed input is the 10-tonne machine, and the variable input is electricity.

   b. As you can see from the declining numbers in the third column of the accompanying table, electricity does indeed exhibit diminishing returns: the marginal product of each additional kilowatt of electricity is less than that of the previous kilowatt.

Quantity of electricity (kilowatts per hour)	Quantity of ice (kilograms)	Marginal product of electricity (kilograms per kilowatt)
0	0	
		1,000
1	1,000	
		800
2	1,800	
		600
3	2,400	
		400
4	2,800	

   c. As you can see from the table below, the average product of the variable input falls as the quantity of variable input used increases.

Quantity of electricity (kilowatts per hour)	Quantity of ice (kilograms)	Average product of the variable input (kilograms of ice per kilowatts of electricity)
0	0	0
1	1,000	1,000
2	1,800	900
3	2,400	800
4	2,800	700

   d. A 50% increase in the size of the fixed input means that Bernie now has a 15-tonne machine. So the fixed input is now the 15-tonne machine. Since it generates a 100% increase in output for any given amount of electricity, the quantity of output and marginal product are now as shown in the accompanying table.

Quantity of electricity (kilowatts)	Quantity of ice (kilograms)	Marginal product of electricity (kilograms per kilowatt)
0	0	
		2,000
1	2,000	
		1,600
2	3,600	
		1,200
3	4,800	
		800
4	5,600	

11-2 Check Your Understanding

1. **a.** As shown in the accompanying table, the marginal cost for each pie is found by multiplying the marginal cost of the previous pie by 1.5. Variable cost for each output level is found by summing the marginal cost for all the pies produced to reach that output level. So, for example, the variable cost of three pies is $1.00 + $1.50 + $2.25 = $4.75. Average fixed cost for Q pies is calculated as $9.00/Q$ since fixed cost is $9.00. Average variable cost for Q pies is equal to variable cost for the Q pies divided by Q; for example, the average variable cost of five pies is $13.19/5, or approximately $2.64. Finally, average total cost can be calculated in two equivalent ways: as TC/Q or as $AVC + AFC$.

Quantity of pies	Marginal cost of pie	Variable cost	Average fixed cost of pie	Average variable cost of pie	Average total cost of pie
0		$0.00	—	—	—
	$1.00				
1		1.00	$9.00	$1.00	$10.00
	1.50				
2		2.50	4.50	1.25	5.75
	2.25				
3		4.75	3.00	1.58	4.58
	3.38				
4		8.13	2.25	2.03	4.28
	5.06				
5		13.19	1.80	2.64	4.44
	7.59				
6		20.78	1.50	3.46	4.96

   b. The spreading effect dominates the diminishing returns effect when average total cost is falling: the fall in AFC dominates the rise in AVC for pies 1 to 4. The diminishing returns effect dominates when average total cost is rising: the rise in AVC dominates the fall in AFC for pies 5 and 6.

c. Aidy's minimum-cost output is 4 pies; this generates the lowest average total cost, $4.28. When output is less than 4, the marginal cost of a pie is less than the average total cost of the pies already produced. So making an additional pie lowers average total cost. For example, the marginal cost of pie 3 is $2.25, whereas the average total cost of pies 1 and 2 is $5.75. So making pie 3 lowers average total cost to $4.58, equal to $(2 \times \$5.75 + \$2.25)/3$. When output is more than 4, the marginal cost of a pie is greater than the average total cost of the pies already produced. Consequently, making an additional pie raises average total cost. So, although the marginal cost of pie 6 is $7.59, the average total cost of pies 1 through 5 is $4.44. Making pie 6 raises average total cost to $4.96, equal to $(5 \times \$4.44 + \$7.59)/6$.

11-3 Check Your Understanding

1. a. The accompanying table shows the average total cost of producing 12,000, 22,000, and 30,000 units for each of the three choices of fixed cost. For example, if the firm makes choice 1, the total cost of producing 12,000 units of output is $\$8,000 + 12,000 \times \$1.00 = \$20,000$. The average total cost of producing 12,000 units of output is therefore $\$20,000/12,000 = \$1.67$. The other average total costs are calculated similarly. So if the firm wanted to produce 12,000 units, it would make choice 1 because this gives it the lowest average total cost. If it wanted to produce 22,000 units, it would make choice 2. If it wanted to produce 30,000 units, it would make choice 3.

	12,000 units	22,000 units	30,000 units
Average total cost from choice 1	$1.67	$1.36	$1.27
Average total cost from choice 2	1.75	1.30	1.15
Average total cost from choice 3	2.25	1.34	1.05

b. Having historically produced 12,000 units, the firm would have adopted choice 1. When producing 12,000 units, the firm would have had an average total cost of $1.67. When output jumps to 22,000 units, the firm cannot alter its choice of fixed cost in the short run, so its average total cost in the short run will be $1.36. In the long run, however, it will adopt choice 2, making its average total cost fall to $1.30.

c. If the firm believes that the increase in demand is temporary, it should not alter its fixed cost from choice 1 because choice 2 generates higher average total cost as soon as output falls back to its original quantity of 12,000 units: $1.75 versus $1.67.

2. a. This firm is likely to experience constant returns to scale. To increase output, the firm must hire more workers, purchase more computers, and pay additional telephone charges. Because these inputs are easily available, their long-run average total cost is unlikely to change as output increases.

b. This firm is likely to experience decreasing returns to scale. As the firm takes on more projects, the costs of communication and coordination required to implement the expertise of the firm's owner are likely

to increase. As a result, the firm's long-run average total cost will increase as output increases.

c. This firm is likely to experience increasing returns to scale. Because diamond mining requires a large initial set-up cost for excavation equipment, long-run average total cost will fall as output increases.

3. The accompanying diagram shows the long-run average total cost curve (*LRATC*) and the short-run average total cost curve corresponding to a long-run output choice of 5 cases of salsa (*ATC*$_5$). The curve *ATC*$_5$ shows the short-run average total cost for which the level of fixed cost minimizes average total cost at an output of 5 cases of salsa. This is confirmed by the fact that at 5 cases per day, *ATC*$_5$ touches *LRATC*, the long-run average total cost curve.

If Selena's Gourmet Salsas expects to produce only 4 cases of salsa for a long time, the firm should change its fixed cost. If it does not change its fixed cost and produces 4 cases of salsa, the firm's average total cost in the short run is indicated by point *B* on *ATC*$_5$; it is no longer on the *LRATC*. If it changes its fixed cost, though, its average total cost could be lower, at point *A*.

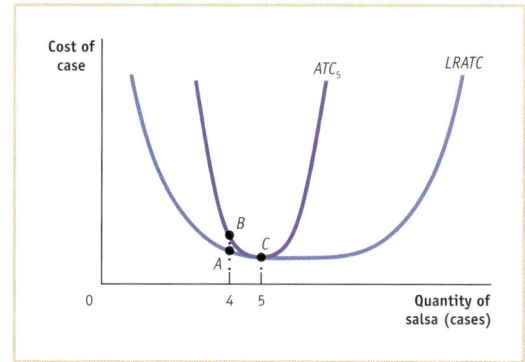

CHAPTER TWELVE

12-1 Check Your Understanding

1. a. With only two producers in the world, each producer will represent a sizeable share of the market. So the industry will not be perfectly competitive.

b. Because each producer of natural gas from the North Sea has only a small market share of total world supply of natural gas, and since natural gas is a standardized product, the natural gas industry will be perfectly competitive.

c. Because each designer has a distinctive style, high-fashion clothes are not a standardized product. So the industry will not be perfectly competitive.

d. The market described here is the market in each city for tickets to hockey games. Since there are only one or two teams in each major city, each team will represent a sizeable share of the market. So the industry will not be perfectly competitive.

12-2 Check Your Understanding

1. a. The firm should shut down immediately when price is less than minimum average variable cost, the shut-down price. In the accompanying diagram, this is optimal for prices in the range 0 to P_1.

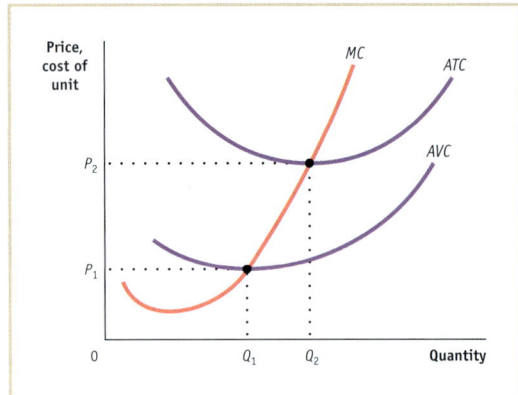

b. When price is greater than minimum average variable cost (the shut-down price) but less than minimum average total cost (the break-even price), the firm should continue to operate in the short run even though it is making a loss. This is optimal for prices in the range P_1 to P_2 and for quantities Q_1 to Q_2.

c. When price exceeds minimum average total cost (the break-even price), the firm makes a profit. This happens for prices in excess of P_2 and results in quantities greater than Q_2.

2. This is an example of a temporary shut-down by a firm when the market price lies below the shut-down price, the minimum average variable cost. In this case, the market price is the price of a lobster meal and variable cost is the variable cost of serving such a meal, such as the cost of the lobster, employee wages, and so on. In this example, however, it is the average variable cost curve rather than the market price that shifts over time, due to seasonal changes in the cost of lobsters. Atlantic Canada lobster shacks have relatively low average variable cost during the summer, when cheap Atlantic Canada lobsters are available. During the rest of the year, their average variable cost is relatively high due to the high cost of imported lobsters. So the lobster shacks are open for business during the summer, when their minimum average variable cost lies below price. But they close during the rest of the year, when price lies below their minimum average variable cost.

12-3 Check Your Understanding

1. a. A fall in the fixed cost of production generates a fall in the average total cost of production and, in the short run, an increase in each firm's profit at the current output

level. So in the long run new firms will enter the industry. The increase in supply drives down price and profits. Once profits are driven back to zero, entry will cease.

b. An increase in wages generates an increase in the average variable and the average total cost of production at every output level. In the short run, firms incur losses at the current output level, and so in the long run some firms will exit the industry. (If the average variable cost rises sufficiently, some firms may even shut down in the short run.) As firms exit, supply decreases, price rises, and losses are reduced. Exit will cease once losses return to zero.

c. Price will rise as a result of the increased demand, leading to a short-run increase in profits at the current output level. In the long run, firms will enter the industry, generating an increase in supply, a fall in price, and a fall in profits. Once profits are driven back to zero, entry will cease.

d. The shortage of a key input causes that input's price to increase, resulting in an increase in average variable and average total costs for producers. Firms incur losses in the short run, and some firms will exit the industry in the long run. The fall in supply generates an increase in price and decreased losses. Exit will cease when losses have returned to zero.

2. In the accompanying diagram, point X_{MKT} in panel (b), the intersection of S_1 and D_1, represents the long-run industry equilibrium before the change in consumer tastes. When tastes change, demand falls and the industry moves in the short run to point Y_{MKT} in panel (b), at the intersection of the new demand curve D_2 and S_1, the short-run supply curve representing the same number of egg producers as in the original equilibrium at point X_{MKT}. As the market price falls, an individual firm reacts by producing less—as shown in panel (a)—as long as the market price remains above the minimum average variable cost. If market price falls below minimum average variable cost, the firm would shut down immediately. At point Y_{MKT}, the price of eggs is below minimum average total cost, creating losses for producers. This leads some firms to exit, which shifts the short-run industry supply curve leftward to S_2. A new long-run equilibrium is established at point Z_{MKT}. As this occurs, the market price rises again, and, as shown in panel (c), each remaining producer reacts by increasing output (here, from point Y to point Z). All remaining producers again make zero profits. The decrease in the quantity of eggs supplied in the industry comes entirely from the exit of some producers from the industry. The long-run industry supply curve is the curve labelled LRS in panel (b).

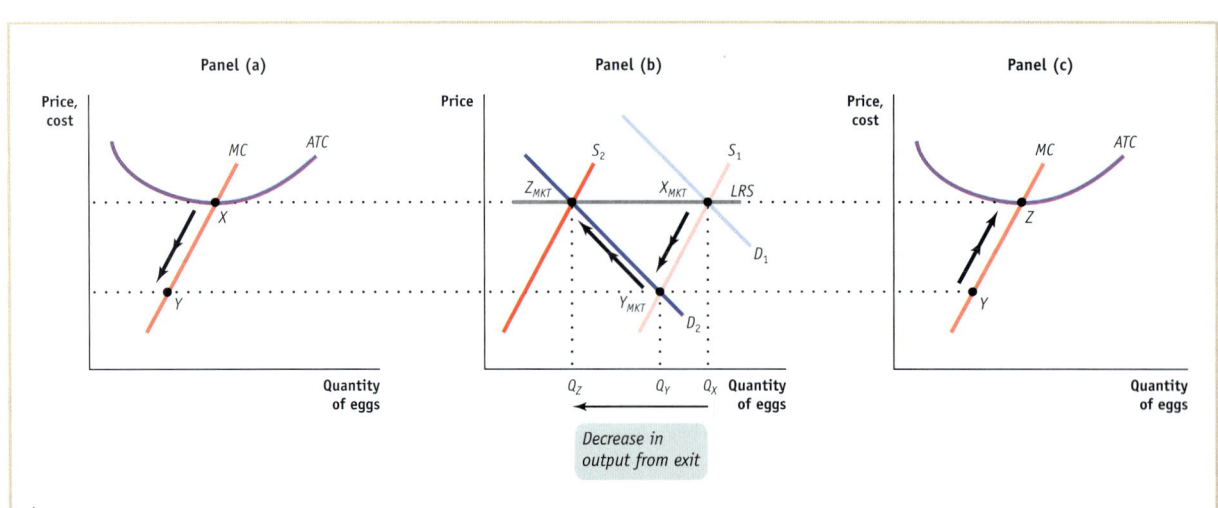

|| CHAPTER THIRTEEN

13-1 Check Your Understanding

1. **a.** This does not support the conclusion. Lamplighter New Brunswick has a limited amount of natural gas, and the price has risen in order to equalize supply and demand.

    b. This supports the conclusion because the market for natural gas has become monopolized, and a monopolist will reduce the quantity supplied and raise price to generate profit.

    c. This does not support the conclusion. Lamplighter New Brunswick has raised its price to consumers because the price of its input, natural gas, has increased.

    d. This supports the conclusion. The fact that other firms have begun to supply natural gas at a lower price implies that Lamplighter New Brunswick must have earned sufficient profits to attract the others to New Brunswick.

    e. This supports the conclusion. It indicates that Lamplighter New Brunswick enjoys a barrier to entry because it controls access to the only natural gas pipeline.

2. **a.** Extending the length of a patent increases the length of time during which the inventor can reduce the quantity supplied and increase the market price. Since this increases the period of time during which the inventor can earn economic profits from the invention, it increases the incentive to invent new products.

    b. Extending the length of a patent also increases the period of time during which consumers have to pay higher prices. So determining the appropriate length of a patent involves making a trade-off between the desirable incentive for invention and the undesirable high price to consumers.

3. **a.** When a large number of other people use PayMo, then any one merchant is more likely to accept it for payment. So the larger the customer base, the more likely PayMo will be accepted for payment.

    b. When a large number of people own a car with a new type of engine, it will be easier to find a knowledgeable mechanic who can repair it.

    c. When a large number of people use such a website, it is more likely that you will be able to find a buyer for something you want to sell or a seller for something you want to buy.

13-2 Check Your Understanding

1. **a.** The price at each output level is found by dividing the total revenue by the number of emeralds produced; for example, the price when 3 emeralds are produced is $252/3 = $84. The price at the various output levels is then used to construct the demand schedule in the accompanying table.

    b. The marginal revenue schedule is found by calculating the change in total revenue as output increases by one unit. For example, the marginal revenue generated by increasing output from 2 to 3 emeralds is ($252 − $186) = $66.

    c. The quantity effect component of marginal revenue is the additional revenue generated by selling one more unit of the good at the market price. For example, as shown in the accompanying table, at 3 emeralds, the

market price is $84; so when going from 2 to 3 emeralds, the quantity effect is equal to $84.

    d. The price effect component of marginal revenue is the decline in total revenue caused by the fall in price when one more unit is sold. For example, as shown in the table, when only 2 emeralds are sold, each emerald sells at a price of $93. However, when Emerald, Inc. sells an additional emerald, the price must fall by $9 to $84. So the price effect component in going from 2 to 3 emeralds is (−$9) × 2 = −$18. That's because 2 emeralds can only be sold at a price of $84 when 3 emeralds in total are sold, although they could have been sold at a price of $93 when only 2 in total were sold.

Quantity of emeralds demanded	Price of emerald	Marginal revenue	Quantity effect component	Price effect component
1	$100			
		$86	$93	−$7
2	93			
		66	84	−18
3	84			
		28	70	−42
4	70			
		−30	50	−80
5	50			

    e. In order to determine Emerald, Inc.'s profit-maximizing output level, you must know its marginal cost at each output level. Its profit-maximizing output level is the one at which marginal revenue is equal to marginal cost.

2. As the accompanying diagram shows, the marginal cost curve shifts upward to $400. The profit-maximizing price rises and quantity falls. Profit falls from $3,200 to $300 × 6 = $1,800. Competitive industry profits, though, are unchanged at zero.

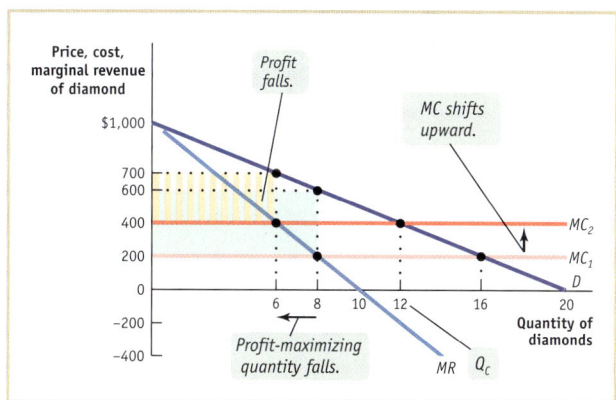

13-3 Check Your Understanding

1. **a.** Cable internet service is a natural monopoly. So the government should intervene only if it believes that price exceeds average total cost, where average total cost is based on the cost of laying the cable. In this case it should impose a price ceiling equal to average total cost. Otherwise, it should do nothing.

    b. The government should approve the merger only if it fosters competition by transferring some of the company's landing slots to another, competing airline.

2. **a.** False. As can be seen from Figure 13-8, panel (b), the inefficiency arises from the fact that some of the consumer surplus is transformed into deadweight loss (the yellow area), not that it is transformed into profit (the green area).

    b. True. If a monopolist sold to all customers who have a valuation greater than or equal to marginal cost, all mutually beneficial transactions would occur and there would be no deadweight loss.

3. As shown in the accompanying diagram, a profit-maximizing monopolist produces Q_M, the output level at which $MR = MC$. A monopolist who mistakenly believes that $P = MR$ produces the output level at which $P = MC$ (when, in fact, $P > MR$, and at the true profit-maximizing level of output, $P > MR = MC$). This misguided monopolist will produce the output level Q_C, where the demand curve crosses the marginal cost curve—the same output level produced if the industry were perfectly competitive. It will charge the price P_C, which is equal to marginal cost, and make zero profit. The entire shaded area is equal to the consumer surplus, which is also equal to total surplus in this case (since the monopolist receives zero producer surplus). There is no deadweight loss since every consumer who is willing to pay as much as or more than marginal cost gets the good. A smart monopolist, however, will produce the output level Q_M and charge the price P_M. Profit equals the green area, consumer surplus corresponds to the blue area, and total surplus is equal to the sum of the green and blue areas. The yellow area is the deadweight loss generated by the monopolist.

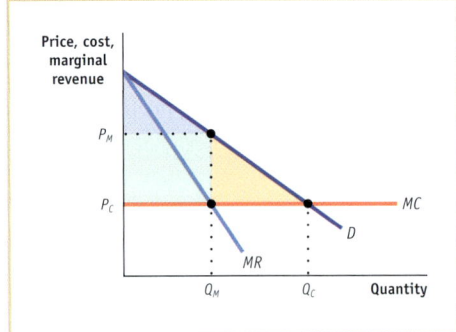

4. Facebook has over 2.6 billion users, which has created a network externality. At this point, Facebook is experiencing increasing returns to scale. But at the same time, there are many social media networks, including Twitter, Instagram, and Snapchat, which have reduced Facebook's market share.

13-4 Check Your Understanding

1. **a.** False. A price-discriminating monopolist will sell to some customers that a single-price monopolist will refuse to—namely, customers with a high price elasticity of demand who are willing to pay only a relatively low price for the good.

    b. False. Although a price-discriminating monopolist does indeed capture more of the consumer surplus, inefficiency is lower: more mutually beneficial transactions occur because the monopolist makes more sales to customers with a low willingness to pay for the good.

    c. True. Under price discrimination consumers are charged prices that depend on their price elasticity

of demand. A consumer with highly elastic demand will pay a lower price than a consumer with inelastic demand.

2. **a.** This is not a case of price discrimination because all consumers, regardless of their price elasticities of demand, value the damaged merchandise less than undamaged merchandise. So the price must be lowered to sell the merchandise.

    b. This is a case of price discrimination. Senior citizens have a higher price elasticity of demand for restaurant meals (their demand for restaurant meals is more responsive to price changes) than other patrons. Restaurants lower the price to high-elasticity consumers (senior citizens). Consumers with low price elasticity of demand will pay the full price.

    c. This is a case of price discrimination. Consumers with a high price elasticity of demand will pay a lower price by collecting and using discount coupons. Consumers with a low price elasticity of demand will not use coupons.

    d. This is not a case of price discrimination; it is simply a case of supply and demand.

‖ CHAPTER FOURTEEN

14-1 Check Your Understanding

1. **a.** The world oil industry is an oligopoly because a few countries control a necessary resource for production, oil reserves.

    b. The microprocessor industry is an oligopoly because two firms possess superior technology and so dominate industry production.

    c. The wide-body passenger jet industry is an oligopoly because there are increasing returns to scale in production.

2. **a.** The HHI in this industry is $92^2 + 4.7^2 + 2.2^2 + 0.8^2 = 84,971.57$.

    b. If Yahoo! and Bing were to merge, making their combined market share $4.7\% + 2.2\% = 6.9\%$. The HHI in this industry would be $92^2 + 6.9^2 + 0.8^2 = 8,512$.

14-2 Check Your Understanding

1. **a.** The firm is likely to act noncooperatively and raise output, which will generate a negative price effect. But because the firm's current market share is small, the negative price effect will fall much more heavily on its rivals' revenues than on its own. At the same time, the firm will benefit from a positive quantity effect.

    b. The firm is likely to act noncooperatively and raise output, which will generate a fall in price. Because its rivals have higher costs, they will lose money at the lower price while the firm continues to make profits. So the firm may be able to drive its rivals out of business by increasing its output.

    c. The firm is likely to collude. Because it is costly for consumers to switch products, the firm would have to lower its price quite substantially (by increasing quantity a lot) to induce consumers to switch to its product. So increasing output is likely to be unprofitable given the large negative price effect.

    d. The firm is likely to act noncooperatively because it knows its rivals cannot increase their output in retaliation.

14-3 Check Your Understanding

1. When Margaret builds a missile, Nikita's payoff from building a missile as well is –10; it is –20 if he does not. The same set of payoffs holds for Margaret when Nikita builds a missile: her payoff is –10 if she builds one as well, –20 if she does not. So it is a Nash (or noncooperative) equilibrium for both Margaret and Nikita to build missiles, and their total payoff is $(-10) + (-10) = -20$. But their total payoff is greatest when neither builds a missile: their total payoff is $0 + 0 = 0$. But this outcome—the cooperative outcome—is unlikely. If Margaret builds a missile but Nikita does not, Margaret gets a payoff of +8, rather than the 0 she gets if she doesn't build a missile. So Margaret is better off if she builds a missile but Nikita doesn't. Similarly, Nikita is better off if he builds a missile but Margaret doesn't: he gets a payoff of +8, rather than the 0 he gets if he doesn't build a missile. So both players have an incentive to build a missile. Both will build a missile, and each gets a payoff of –10. So unless Nikita and Margaret are able to communicate in some way to enforce cooperation, they will act in their own individual interests and each will build a missile.

2. **a.** Future entry by several new firms will increase competition and drive down industry profits. As a result, there is less future profit to protect by behaving cooperatively today. So each oligopolist is more likely to behave noncooperatively today.

   b. When it is very difficult for a firm to detect if another firm has raised output, then it is very difficult to enforce cooperation by playing tit for tat. So it is more likely that a firm will behave noncooperatively.

   c. When firms have coexisted while maintaining high prices for a long time, each expects cooperation to continue. So the value of behaving cooperatively today is high, and it is likely that firms will engage in tacit collusion.

14-4 Check Your Understanding

1. **a.** This is likely to be interpreted as evidence of tacit collusion. Firms in the industry are able to tacitly collude by setting their prices according to the published "suggested" price of the largest firm in the industry. This is a form of price leadership.

   b. This is not likely to be interpreted as evidence of tacit collusion. Considerable variation in market shares indicates that firms have been competing to capture one another's business.

   c. This is not likely to be interpreted as evidence of tacit collusion. These features make it more unlikely that consumers will switch products in response to lower prices. So this is a way for firms to avoid any temptation to gain market share by lowering price. This is a form of product differentiation used to avoid direct competition.

   d. This is likely to be interpreted as evidence of tacit collusion. In the guise of discussing sales targets, firms can create a cartel by designating quantities to be produced by each firm.

   e. This is likely to be interpreted as evidence of tacit collusion. By raising prices together, each firm in the industry is refusing to undercut its rivals by leaving its price unchanged or lowering it. Because it could gain market share by doing so, refusing to do it is evidence of tacit collusion.

CHAPTER FIFTEEN

15-1 Check Your Understanding

1. **a.** Ladders are not differentiated as a result of monopolistic competition. A ladder producer makes different ladders (tall ladders versus short ladders) to satisfy different consumer needs, not to avoid competition with rivals. So two tall ladders made by two different producers will be indistinguishable by consumers.

   b. Soft drinks are an example of product differentiation as a result of monopolistic competition. For example, several producers make colas; each is differentiated in terms of taste, which fast-food chains sell it, and so on.

   c. Clothing stores are an example of product differentiation as a result of monopolistic competition. They serve different clienteles that have different price sensitivities and different tastes. They also offer different levels of customer service and are situated in different locations.

   d. Steel is not differentiated as a result of monopolistic competition. Different types of steel (beams versus sheets) are made for different purposes, not to distinguish one steel manufacturer's products from another's.

2. **a.** Perfectly competitive industries and monopolistically competitive industries both have many sellers. So it may be hard to distinguish between them solely in terms of number of firms. And in both market structures, there is free entry into and exit from the industry in the long run. But in a perfectly competitive industry, one standardized product is sold; in a monopolistically competitive industry, products are differentiated. So you should ask whether products are differentiated in the industry.

   b. In a monopoly there is only one firm, but a monopolistically competitive industry contains many firms. So you should ask whether or not there is a single firm in the industry.

15-2 Check Your Understanding

1. **a.** An increase in fixed cost raises average total cost and shifts the average total cost curve upward. In the short run, firms incur losses. In the long run, some will exit the industry, resulting in a rightward shift of the demand curves for those firms that remain in the industry, since each one now serves a larger share of the market. Long-run equilibrium is reestablished when the demand curve for each remaining firm has shifted rightward to the point where it is tangent to the firm's new, higher average total cost curve. At this point each firm's price just equals its average total cost, and each firm makes zero profit.

   b. A decrease in marginal cost lowers average total cost and shifts the average total cost curve and the marginal cost curve downward. Because existing firms now make profits, in the long run new entrants are attracted into the industry. In the long run, this results in a leftward shift of each existing firm's demand curve since each firm now has a smaller share of the market. Long-run equilibrium is reestablished when each firm's demand curve has shifted leftward to the point where it is tangent to the new, lower average total cost curve. At this point each firm's price just equals average total cost, and each firm makes zero profit.

2. If all the existing firms in the industry joined together to create a monopoly, they would achieve monopoly profits. But this would induce new firms to create new, differentiated products and then enter the industry and capture some of the monopoly profits. So in the long run it would be impossible to maintain a monopoly. The problem arises from the fact that because new firms can create new products, there is no barrier to entry that can maintain a monopoly.

15-3 Check Your Understanding

1. **a.** False. As can be seen from panel (b) of Figure 15-4, a monopolistically competitive firm produces at a point where price exceeds marginal cost—unlike a perfectly competitive firm, which produces where price equals marginal cost (at the point of minimum average total cost). A monopolistically competitive firm will refuse to sell at marginal cost. This would be below average total cost and the firm would incur a loss.

   b. True. Firms in a monopolistically competitive industry could achieve higher profits (monopoly profits) if they all joined together and produced a single product. In addition, since the industry possesses excess capacity, producing a larger quantity of output would lower the firm's average total cost. The effect on consumers, however, is ambiguous. They would experience less choice. But if consolidation substantially reduces industry-wide average total cost and therefore substantially increases industry-wide output, consumers may experience lower prices under monopoly.

   c. True. Fads and fashions are created and promulgated by advertising, which is found in oligopolies and monopolistically competitive industries but not in monopolies or perfectly competitive industries.

15-4 Check Your Understanding

1. **a.** This is economically useful because such advertisements are likely to focus on the medical benefits of aspirin.

   b. This is economically wasteful because such advertisements are likely to focus on promoting Bayer aspirin versus a rival's aspirin product. The two products are medically indistinguishable.

   c. This is economically useful because such advertisements are likely to focus on the health and enjoyment benefits of orange juice.

   d. This is economically wasteful because such advertisements are likely to focus on promoting Tropicana orange juice versus a rival's product. The two are likely to be indistinguishable by consumers.

   e. This is economically useful because the longevity of a business gives a potential customer information about its quality.

2. A successful brand name indicates a desirable attribute, such as quality, to a potential buyer. So, other things equal—such as price—a firm with a successful brand name will achieve higher sales than a rival with a comparable product but without a successful brand name. This is likely to deter new firms from entering an industry in which an existing firm has a successful brand name.

‖ CHAPTER SIXTEEN

16-1 Check Your Understanding

1. **a.** The external cost is the pollution caused by the wastewater runoff, an uncompensated cost imposed by the poultry farms on their neighbours.

   b. Since poultry farmers do not take the external cost of their actions into account when making decisions about how much wastewater to generate, they will create more runoff than is socially optimal in the absence of government intervention or a private deal. They will produce runoff up to the point at which the marginal social benefit of an additional unit of runoff is zero; however, their neighbours experience a high, positive level of marginal social cost of runoff from this output level. So the quantity of wastewater runoff is inefficient: reducing runoff by one unit would reduce total social benefit by less than it would reduce total social cost.

   c. At the socially optimal quantity of wastewater runoff, the marginal social benefit is equal to the marginal social cost. This quantity is lower than the quantity of wastewater runoff that would be created in the absence of government intervention or a private deal.

2. Yasmin's reasoning is not correct: allowing some late returns of books is likely to be socially optimal. Although you impose a marginal social cost on others every day that you are late in returning a book, there is some positive marginal social benefit to you of returning a book late—for example, you get a longer period to use it in working on a term paper.

   The socially optimal number of days that a book is returned late is the number at which the marginal social benefit equals the marginal social cost. A fine so stiff that it prevents any late returns is likely to result in a situation in which people return books although the marginal social benefit of keeping them another day is greater than the marginal social cost—an inefficient outcome. In that case, allowing an overdue patron another day would increase total social benefit more than it would increase total social cost. So charging a moderate fine that reduces the number of days that books are returned late to the socially optimal number of days is appropriate.

16-2 Check Your Understanding

1. This is a misguided argument. Allowing polluters to sell emissions permits makes polluters face the cost of polluting in the form of the opportunity cost of the permit. If a polluter chooses not to reduce its emissions, it cannot sell its emissions permits. As a result, it forgoes the opportunity of making money from the sale of the permits. So despite the fact that the polluter receives a monetary benefit from selling the permits, the scheme has the desired effect: to make polluters internalize the externality of their actions.

2. **a.** If the emissions tax is smaller than the marginal social cost at Q_{OPT}, a polluter will face a marginal cost of polluting (equal to the amount of the tax) that is less than the marginal social cost at the socially optimal quantity of pollution. Since a polluter will produce emissions up

to the point where the marginal social benefit is equal to its marginal cost, the resulting amount of pollution will be larger than the socially optimal quantity. As a result, there is inefficiency: if the amount of pollution is larger than the socially optimal quantity, the marginal social cost exceeds the marginal social benefit. A reduction in emissions levels will increase social surplus.

If the emissions tax is greater than the marginal social cost at Q_{OPT}, a polluter will face a marginal cost of polluting (equal to the amount of the tax) that is greater than the marginal social cost at the socially optimal quantity of pollution. This will lead the polluter to reduce emissions below the socially optimal quantity. This also is inefficient: whenever the marginal social benefit is greater than the marginal social cost, an increase in emissions levels will raise social surplus.

b. If the total amount of allowable pollution is set too high, the supply of emissions permits will be high and so the equilibrium price at which permits trade will be low. That is, polluters will face a marginal cost of polluting (the price of a permit) that is "too low"—lower than the marginal social cost at the socially optimal quantity of pollution. As a result, pollution will be greater than the socially optimal quantity. This is inefficient and lowers total surplus.

If the total level of allowable pollution is set too low, the supply of emissions permits will be low and so the equilibrium price at which permits trade will be high. That is, polluters will face a marginal cost of polluting (the price of a permit) that is "too high"—higher than the marginal social cost at the socially optimal quantity of pollution. As a result, pollution will be lower than the socially optimal quantity. This also is inefficient and lowers total surplus.

c. A carbon tax will increase the cost of using fossil fuels, including the prices of gasoline and coal. As the cost of fossil fuels increases, consumers will reduce their use of fossil fuels as energy sources. They will be increasingly likely to purchase more fuel-efficient cars and invest in solar technology for their homes.

16-3 Check Your Understanding

1. Types of fossil fuels are coal, oil, and gas. The main clean energy sources are wind and solar. The burning of fossil fuels creates greenhouse gas emissions, which cause climate change. Clean energy sources do not create greenhouse gas emissions, so do not contribute to climate change.

2. The market failure that led to climate change was the historical underpricing of fossil-fuel consumption. That is, the market price of fossil fuel was too low compared to the true cost of greenhouse gas emissions that they generated. The estimated loss to U.S. GDP from unmitigated climate change is 10%; the estimated loss to world GDP is 20%.

3. Government subsidies to innovations in clean energy are an important policy tool because it is unlikely that the clean energy sector would have become cost competitive with fossil fuels without them. Multilateral agreements between countries are an important policy tool because a country is likely to be unwilling to cut its emissions

without a commitment by other countries to do the same. Individual incentives are important because they can lead to fast and effective ways to conserve energy and thus reduce greenhouse gas emissions.

4. Although the structural change required to address climate change will require some loss of GDP, it is small (1) compared to the costs of unmitigated climate change; and (2) compared to the projected growth rate of GDP over time. Also, the direct health costs of unmitigated climate change are significant, resulting in millions of excess deaths and as much as 5% of world GDP.

16-4 Check Your Understanding

1. College education provides external benefits through the creation of knowledge. And student aid acts like a Pigouvian subsidy on higher education. If the marginal social benefit of higher education is indeed $120 billion, then student aid is an optimal policy.

2. **a.** Planting trees generates an external benefit since many people (not just those who plant the trees) benefit from the increased air quality and lower summer temperatures. Without a subsidy, people will plant too few trees, setting the marginal social cost of planting a tree—what they forgo by planting a tree—too low. (Although too low, it may still be more than zero since a homeowner gains some personal benefit from planting a tree.) A Pigouvian subsidy will induce people to plant more trees, bringing the marginal social benefit of planting a tree in line with the marginal social cost.

b. Water-saving toilets generate an external benefit because they discourage wasting water, thereby reducing the need to pump water from rivers and aquifers. Without a subsidy, homeowners will use water until the marginal social cost of water usage is equal to zero since water is costless to them. A Pigouvian subsidy on water-saving toilets will induce homeowners to reduce their water usage so that the marginal social benefit of water is in line with the marginal social cost.

c. Discarded plastic drink bottles impose an external cost by degrading the environment. Without a tax, people will discard plastic bottles freely—until the marginal social cost of discarding a bottle (what they must forgo in discarding a bottle) is zero. A Pigouvian tax or subsidy on drink bottles will bring the marginal social benefit of a drink bottle in line with its marginal social cost. This can be done two ways: via a tax or a subsidy. A tax will induce drink manufacturers to shift away from polluting plastic bottles to less polluting containers, like paper cartons. A subsidy for disposing of the containers in an environmentally sound way, such as recycling, will induce drink consumers to dispose of the bottles in a way that reduces the external costs.

16-5 Check Your Understanding

1. **a.** The voltage of an appliance must be consistent with the voltage of the electrical outlet it is plugged into. Consumers will want to have 110-volt appliances when houses are wired for 110-volt outlets, and builders will want to install 110-volt outlets when most prospective

homeowners use 110-volt appliances. So a network externality arises because a consumer will want to use appliances that operate with the same voltage as the appliances used by most other consumers.

   b. Printers, copy machines, fax machines, and so on are designed for specific paper sizes. Consumers will want to purchase paper of a size that can be used in these machines, and machine manufacturers will want to manufacture their machines for the size of paper that most consumers use. So a network externality arises because a consumer will want to use the size of paper used by most other consumers—namely, 8½-by-11-inch paper rather than 8-by-12½-inch paper.

2. Of the two competing companies, the company able to achieve the higher number of sales is likely to dominate the market. In a market with a network externality, new consumers will base their buying decisions on the number of existing consumers of a specific product. In other words, the more consumers a company can attract initially, the more consumers will choose to buy that company's product; therefore, the good exhibits *positive feedback*. So it is important for a company to make a large number of sales early on. It can do this by pricing its good cheaply and taking a loss on each unit sold. The company that can best afford to subsidize a large number of sales early on is likely to be the winner of this competition.

‖ CHAPTER SEVENTEEN

17-1 Check Your Understanding

1. **a.** Use of a public park is nonexcludable, but it may or may not be rival in consumption, depending on the circumstances. For example, if both you and I use the park for jogging, then your use will not prevent my use—use of the park is nonrival in consumption. In this case, the public park is a public good. But use of the park is rival in consumption if there are many people trying to use the jogging path at the same time or when my use of the public tennis court prevents your use of the same court. In those cases, the public park is a common resource.

   b. A cheese burrito is both excludable and rival in consumption. Hence it is a private good.

   c. Information from a password-protected website is excludable but nonrival in consumption. So it is an artificially scarce good.

   d. Publicly announced information on the path of an incoming hurricane is nonexcludable and nonrival in consumption. So it is a public good.

2. A private producer will supply only a good that is excludable; otherwise, the producer won't be able to charge a price for it that covers the costs of production. So a private producer would be willing to supply a cheese burrito and information from a password-protected website but unwilling to supply a public park or publicly announced information about an incoming hurricane.

17-2 Check Your Understanding

1. **a.** With 10 Homebodies and 6 Revellers, the marginal social benefit schedule of money spent on the party is as shown in the accompanying table.

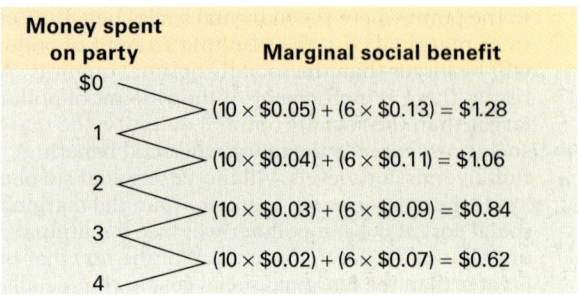

The efficient spending level is $2, the highest level for which the marginal social benefit is greater than the marginal cost ($1).

   b. With 6 Homebodies and 10 Revellers, the marginal social benefit schedule of money spent on the party is as shown in the accompanying table.

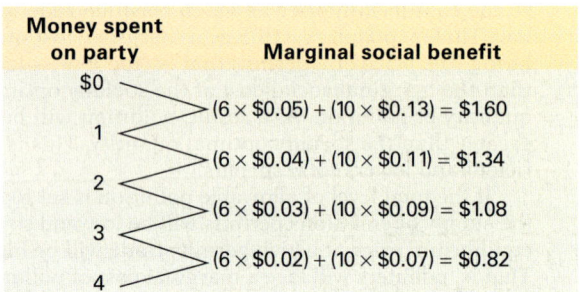

The efficient spending level is now $3, the highest level for which the marginal social benefit is greater than the marginal cost ($1). The efficient level of spending has increased from that in part a because with relatively more Revellers than Homebodies, an additional dollar spent on the party generates a higher level of social benefit compared to when there are relatively more Homebodies than Revellers.

   c. When the numbers of Homebodies and Revellers are unknown but residents are asked their preferences, Homebodies will pretend to be Revellers to induce a higher level of spending on the public party. That's because a Homebody still receives a positive individual marginal benefit from an additional $1 spent, despite the fact that the individual's marginal benefit is lower than that of a Reveller for every additional $1. In this case the "reported" marginal social benefit schedule of money spent on the party will be as shown in the accompanying table.

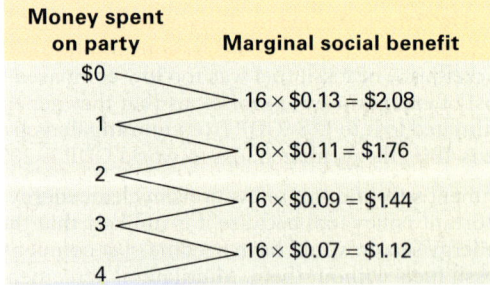

As a result, $4 will be spent on the party, the highest level for which the "reported" marginal social benefit is greater than the marginal cost ($1). Regardless of whether there are 10 Homebodies and 6 Revellers (part a) or 6 Homebodies and 10 Revellers (part b), spending $4 in total on the party is clearly inefficient because marginal cost exceeds marginal social benefit at this spending level.

As a further exercise, consider how much Homebodies gain by this misrepresentation. In part a, the efficient level of spending is $2. So by misrepresenting their preferences, the 10 Homebodies gain, in total, $10 \times (\$0.03 + \$0.02) = \$0.50$—that is, they gain the marginal individual benefit in going from a spending level of $2 to $4. The 6 Revellers also gain from the misrepresentations of the Homebodies; they gain $6 \times (\$0.09 + \$0.07) = \$0.96$ in total. This outcome is clearly inefficient—when $4 in total is spent, the marginal cost is $1 but the marginal social benefit is only $0.62, indicating that too much money is being spent on the party.

In part b, the efficient level of spending is actually $3. The misrepresentation by the 6 Homebodies gains them, in total, $6 \times \$0.02 = \$0.12$, but the 10 Revellers gain $10 \times \$0.07 = \$0.70$ in total. This outcome is also clearly inefficient—when $4 is spent, marginal social benefit is only $\$0.12 + \$0.70 = \$0.82$ but marginal cost is $1.

17-3 Check Your Understanding

1. When individuals are allowed to harvest freely, the government-owned forest becomes a common resource, and individuals will overuse it—they will harvest more trees than is efficient. In economic terms, the marginal social cost of harvesting a tree is greater than a private logger's individual marginal cost.

2. The three methods consistent with economic theory are (i) Pigouvian taxes, (ii) a system of tradable licences, and (iii) allocation of property rights.

   i. *Pigouvian taxes.* You would enforce a tax on loggers that equals the difference between the marginal social cost and the individual marginal cost of logging a tree at the socially efficient harvest amount. In order to do this, you must know the marginal social cost schedule and the individual marginal cost schedule.

   ii. *System of tradable licences.* You would issue tradable licences, setting the total number of trees harvested equal to the socially efficient harvest number. The market that arises in these licences will allocate the right to log efficiently when loggers differ in their costs of logging: licences will be purchased by those who have a relatively lower cost of logging. The market price of a licence will be equal to the difference between the marginal social cost and the individual marginal cost of logging a tree at the socially efficient harvest amount. In order to implement this, you need to know the socially efficient harvest amount.

   iii. *Allocation of property rights.* Here you would sell or give the forest to a private party. This party will have the right to exclude others from harvesting trees. Harvesting is now a private good—it is excludable and rival in consumption. As a result, there is no longer any divergence between social and private costs, and the private party will harvest the efficient level of trees. You need no additional information to use this method.

17-4 Check Your Understanding

1. a. The efficient price to a consumer is $0, since the marginal cost of allowing a consumer to download it is $0.

b. Xenoid will not produce the software unless it can charge a price that allows it at least to make back the $300,000 cost of producing it. So the lowest price at which Xenoid is willing to produce it is $150. At this price, it makes a total revenue of $\$150 \times 2,000 = \$300,000$; at any lower price, Xenoid will not cover its cost. The shaded area in the accompanying diagram shows the deadweight loss when Xenoid charges a price of $150.

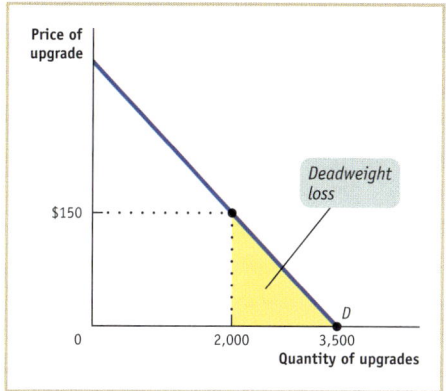

CHAPTER EIGHTEEN

18-1 Check Your Understanding

1. a. A pension guarantee program is a social insurance program. The possibility of an employer declaring bankruptcy and defaulting on its obligation to pay employee pensions creates insecurity. By providing pension income to those employees, such a program alleviates this source of economic insecurity.

   b. The CCB program is a social welfare program. By providing funding to children in eligible households, it targets its spending specifically to low-income families.

   c. The federal flood program is a social insurance program. For many people, the majority of their wealth is tied up in the home they own. The potential for a loss of that wealth creates economic insecurity. By providing assistance to those hit by a major flood, the program alleviates this source of insecurity.

   d. The IAH program is a social welfare program. By targeting support to low-income households, it specifically helps the poor.

2. An after-tax LICO is a relative measure of poverty. The LICOs are income thresholds below which a family is expected to spend too large a share of its income to acquire necessities compared to the average family. The LICOs estimate an income threshold at which families are expected to spend 20 percentage points more than the average family on food, shelter, and clothing. For example, in 2018, using the after-tax LICOs measure, the poverty line for a family of four in a community of at least 500,000 residents was $$40,614.

3. a. To determine mean (or average) income, we take the total income of all individuals in this economy and divide it by the number of individuals. Mean income is $(\$39,000 + \$17,500 + \$900,000 + \$15,000 + \$28,000)/5 = \$999,500/5 = \$199,900$. To determine median income, look at the accompanying table, which ranks the five individuals in order of their income.

	Income
Vijay	$15,000
Kelly	17,500
Oskar	28,000
Sephora	39,000
Raul	900,000

The median income is the income of the individual in the exact middle of the income distribution: Oskar, with an income of $28,000. So the median income is $28,000.

Median income is more representative of the income of individuals in this economy: almost everyone earns income between $15,000 and $39,000, close to the median income of $28,000. Only Raul is the exception: it is his income that raises the mean income to $199,900, which is not representative of most incomes in this economy.

b. The first quintile is made up of the 20% (or one-fifth) of individuals with the lowest incomes in the economy. Vijay makes up the 20% of individuals with the lowest incomes. His income is $15,000, so that is the average income of the first quintile. Oskar makes up the 20% of individuals with the third-lowest incomes. His income is $28,000, so that is the average income of the third quintile.

4. As the Economics in Action pointed out, much of the rise in inequality reflects growing differences among highly educated workers. That is, workers with similar levels of education earn very dissimilar incomes. As a result, the principal source of rising inequality in Canada today is reflected by statement b: the rise in the bank CEO's salary relative to that of the branch manager.

18-2 Check Your Understanding

1. A negative income tax applies only to those workers who earn income; over a certain (low) range of incomes, the more a worker earns, the higher the credit received. A person who earns no income receives no income tax credit. By contrast, social welfare programs that pay individuals based solely on low income still make those payments even if the individual does not work at all; once the individual earns a certain amount of income, these programs discontinue payments. As a result, such programs contain an incentive not to work and earn income, since earning more than a certain amount makes individuals ineligible for their benefits. The negative income tax, however, provides an incentive to work and earn income because its payments increase the more an individual works.

2. According to the data in Table 18-4, the Canadian welfare state reduces the poverty rate. It does so by sending significantly more transfers to low-income families than it takes via income taxes.

18-3 Check Your Understanding

1. a. The program benefits Jiro and his parents because the pool of all university students contains a representative mix of healthy and less healthy people, rather than a selected group of people who want insurance because they expect to pay high medical bills. In that respect, this insurance is like *employment-based health insurance*. Because no student can opt out, the school can offer health insurance based on the health care costs of its

average student. If each student had to buy their own health insurance, some students would not be able to obtain any insurance and many would pay more than they do to the school's insurance program.

b. Since all students are required to enrol in its health insurance program, even the healthiest students cannot leave the program in an effort to obtain cheaper insurance tailored specifically to healthy people. If this were to happen, the school's insurance program would be left with an adverse selection of less healthy students and so would have to raise premiums, beginning the adverse selection death spiral. But since no student can leave the insurance program, the school's program can continue to base its premiums on the average student's probability of requiring health care, avoiding the adverse selection death spiral.

2. According to critics, part of the reason the U.S. health care system is so much more expensive than those of other countries is its fragmented nature. Since each of the many insurance companies has significant administrative (overhead) costs—in part because each insurance company incurs marketing costs and exerts significant effort in weeding out high-risk insureds—the system tends to be more expensive than one in which there is only a single medical insurer. Another part of the explanation is that U.S. medical care includes many more expensive treatments than found in other wealthy countries, pays higher physician salaries, and has higher drug prices.

18-4 Check Your Understanding

1. a. Recall one of the principles from Chapter 1: one person's spending is another person's income. A high sales tax on consumer items is the same as a high marginal tax rate on income. As a result, the incentive to earn income by working or by investing in risky projects is reduced, since the payoff, after taxes, is lower.

b. If you lose a housing subsidy as soon as your income rises above $25,000, your incentive to earn more than $25,000 is reduced. If you earn exactly $25,000, you obtain the housing subsidy; however, as soon as you earn $25,001, you lose the entire subsidy, making you worse off than if you had not earned the additional dollar.

2. Over the past 40 years, polarization in Canadian politics has increased. Forty years ago, some Conservatives were to the left of some Liberals. Today, the rightmost Liberals and NDP politicians appear to be to the left of the leftmost Conservatives.

‖ CHAPTER NINETEEN

19-1 Check Your Understanding

1. Many university professors will depart for other lines of work if the government imposes a wage that is lower than the market wage. Fewer professors will result in fewer courses taught and therefore fewer university degrees produced. It will adversely affect sectors of the economy that depend directly on universities, such as the local shopkeepers who sell goods and services to students and faculty, university textbook publishers, and so on. It will also adversely affect firms that use the "output" produced by universities: new university graduates. Firms that need to hire new employees with university degrees will be hurt as a smaller supply results in a higher market wage for university graduates. Ultimately, the reduced supply of university-educated workers will result in a lower level of human capital in the entire economy relative to what it would have been without the policy. And this will hurt all sectors of the economy that depend on human capital. The sectors of the economy that might benefit are firms that compete with universities in the hiring of would-be university professors. For example, accounting firms will find it easier to hire people who would otherwise have been professors of accounting, and publishers will find it easier to hire people who would otherwise have been professors of English (easier in the sense that the firms can recruit would-be professors with a lower wage than before). In addition, workers who already have university degrees will benefit; they will command higher wages as the supply of university-educated workers falls.

19-2 Check Your Understanding

1. **a.** As the demand for services increases, the price of services will rise. And as the price of the output produced by the industries increases, this shifts the *VMPL* curve upward—that is, the demand for labour rises. This results in an increase in both the equilibrium wage rate and the quantity of labour employed.

   b. The fall in the catch per day means that the marginal product of labour in the industry declines. The *VMPL* curve shifts downward, generating a fall in the equilibrium wage rate and the equilibrium quantity of labour employed.

2. When producers from different industries compete for the same workers, then each worker in the various industries will be paid the same equilibrium wage rate, *W*. And since, by the marginal productivity theory of income distribution, $VMPL = P \times MPL = W$ for the last worker hired in equilibrium, the last worker hired in each of these different industries will have the same value of the marginal product of labour.

19-3 Check Your Understanding

1. **a.** False. Income disparities associated with gender, race, or ethnicity can be explained by the marginal productivity theory of income distribution provided that differences in marginal productivity across people are correlated with gender, race, or ethnicity. One possible source for such correlation is past discrimination. Such discrimination can lower individuals' marginal productivity by, for example, preventing them from acquiring the human capital that would raise their productivity. Another possible source of the correlation is differences in work experience that are associated with gender, race, or ethnicity. For example, in jobs where work experience or length of tenure is important, women may earn lower wages because on average more women than men take child-care-related absences from work.

   b. True. Companies that discriminate when their competitors do not are likely to hire less able workers because they discriminate against more able workers who are considered to be of a different gender, race, ethnicity, or other characteristic. And with less able workers, such companies are likely to earn lower profits than their competitors that don't discriminate.

   c. Ambiguous. In general, workers who are paid less because they have less experience may or may not be the victims of discrimination. The answer depends on the reason for the lack of experience. If workers have less experience because they are young or have chosen to do something else rather than gain experience, then they are not victims of discrimination if they are paid less. But if workers lack experience because previous job discrimination prevented them from gaining experience, then they are indeed victims of discrimination when they are paid less.

   d. False. This is not an example of wage discrimination. As long as Walmart doesn't offer differing wages based on gender, age, or race, all workers will be treated the same. This is an example of firms exploiting monopsony power in the labour market. In a small town, Walmart would be the predominant employer for most entry level, lower-skill jobs.

19-4 Check Your Understanding

1. **a.** Jaden is made worse off if, before the new law, he had preferred to work more than 35 hours per week. As a result of the law, he can no longer choose his preferred time allocation; he now consumes fewer goods and more leisure than he would like.

   b. Jaden's utility is unaffected by the law if, before the law, he had preferred to work 35 or fewer hours per week. The law has not changed his preferred time allocation.

   c. Jaden can never be made better off by a law that restricts the number of hours he can work. He can only be made worse off (case a) or equally as well off (case b).

2. The substitution effect would induce Jaden to work fewer hours and consume more leisure after his wage rate falls—the fall in the wage rate means the price of an hour of leisure falls, leading Jaden to consume more leisure. But a fall in his wage rate also generates a fall in Jaden's income. The income effect of this is to induce Jaden to consume less leisure and therefore work more hours, since he is now poorer and leisure is a normal good. If the income effect dominates the substitution effect, Jaden will in the end work more hours than before.

‖ CHAPTER TWENTY

20-1 Check Your Understanding

1. The family with the lower income is likely to be more risk-averse. In general, higher income or wealth results in lower degrees of risk aversion, due to diminishing marginal utility. Both families may be willing to buy an "unfair" insurance policy. Most insurance policies are "unfair" in that the expected claim is less than the premium. The degree to which a family is willing to pay more than an expected claim for insurance depends on the family's degree of risk aversion.

2. **a.** Karma's expected income is the weighted average of all possible values of her income, weighted by the probabilities with which she earns each possible value of her income. Since she makes $22,000 with a probability of 0.6 and $35,000 with a probability of 0.4, her expected income is $(0.6 \times \$22,000) + (0.4 \times \$35,000) = \$13,200 + \$14,000 = \$27,200$. Her expected utility is simply the expected value of the total utilities she will experience. Since with a probability of 0.6 she

will experience a total utility of 850 utils (the utility to her from making $22,000), and with a probability of 0.4 she will experience a total utility of 1,260 utils (the utility to her from making $35,000), her expected utility is $(0.6 \times 850 \text{ utils}) + (0.4 \times 1,260 \text{ utils}) = 510 \text{ utils} + 504 \text{ utils} = 1,014 \text{ utils}$.

b. If Karma makes $25,000 for certain, she experiences a utility level of 1,014 utils. From the answer to part a, we know that this leaves her equally as well off as when she has a risky expected income of $27,200. Since Karma is indifferent between a risky expected income of $27,200 and a certain income of $25,000, you can conclude that she would prefer a certain income of $25,000 to a risky expected income of $27,200. That is, she would definitely be willing to reduce the risk she faces when this reduction in risk leaves her expected income unchanged. In other words, Karma is risk-averse.

c. Yes. Karma experiences a utility level of 1,056 utils when she has a certain income of $26,000. This is higher than the expected utility level of 1,014 utils generated by a risky expected income of $27,200. So Karma is willing to pay a premium to guarantee a certain income of $26,000.

20-2 Check Your Understanding

1. a. An increase in the number of ships implies an increase in the quantity of insurance demanded at any given premium. This is a rightward shift of the demand curve, resulting in a rise in both the equilibrium premium and the equilibrium quantity of insurance bought and sold.

b. An increase in the number of trading routes means that investors can diversify more. In other words, they can reduce risk further. At any given premium, there are now more investors willing to supply insurance. This is a rightward shift of the supply curve for insurance, leading to a fall in the equilibrium premium and a rise in the equilibrium quantity of insurance bought and sold.

c. If shipowners in the market become even more risk-averse, they will be willing to pay even higher premiums for insurance. That is, at any given premium, there are now more people willing to buy insurance. This is a rightward shift of the demand curve for insurance, leading to a rise in both the equilibrium premium and the equilibrium quantity of insurance bought and sold.

d. If investors in the market become more risk-averse, they will be less willing to accept risk at any given premium. This is a leftward shift of the supply curve for insurance, leading to a rise in the equilibrium premium and a fall in the equilibrium quantity of insurance bought and sold.

e. As the overall level of risk increases, those willing to buy insurance will be more willing to buy insurance at any given premium; the demand curve for insurance shifts to the right. But since overall risk cannot be diversified away, those ordinarily willing to take on risk will be less willing to do so, leading to a leftward shift in the supply curve for insurance. As a result, the equilibrium premium will rise; the effect on the equilibrium quantity of insurance is uncertain.

f. If the wealth levels of investors fall, investors will become more risk-averse and so less willing to supply insurance at any given premium. This is a leftward shift of the supply curve for insurance, leading to a rise in the equilibrium premium and a fall in the equilibrium quantity of insurance bought and sold.

20-3 Check Your Understanding

1. The inefficiency caused by adverse selection is that an insurance policy with a premium based on the average risk of all drivers will attract only an adverse selection of bad drivers. Good (that is, safe) drivers will find this insurance premium too expensive and so will remain uninsured. This is inefficient. However, safe drivers are also those drivers who have had fewer moving violations for several years. Lowering premiums for only those drivers allows the insurance company to screen its customers and sell insurance to safe drivers, too. This means that at least some of the good drivers now are also insured, which decreases the inefficiency that arises from adverse selection. In a way, having no moving violations for several years is building a reputation for being a safe driver.

2. The moral hazard problem in home construction arises from private information about what the contractor does: whether the contractor takes care to reduce the cost of construction or allows costs to increase. The homeowner cannot, or can only imperfectly, observe the cost-reduction effort of the contractor. If the contractor were fully reimbursed for all costs incurred during construction, the contractor would have no incentive to reduce costs. Making the contractor responsible for any additional costs above the original estimate means that the contractor now has an incentive to keep costs low. However, this imposes risk on the contractor. For instance, if the weather is bad, home construction will take longer, and will be more costly, than if the weather had been good. Since the contractor pays for any additional costs (such as weather-induced delays) above the original estimate, the contractor now faces risk that they cannot control.

3. a. True. Drivers with higher deductibles have more incentive to be more careful while driving, to avoid paying the deductible. This is a moral hazard phenomenon.

b. True. Suppose you know that you are a safe driver. You have a choice of a policy with a high premium but a low deductible or one with a lower premium but a higher deductible. In this case, you would be more likely to choose the cheap policy with the high deductible because you know that you will be unlikely to have to pay the deductible. When there is adverse selection, insurance companies use screening devices such as this to make inferences about people's private information about how skillful they are as drivers.

c. True. The wealthier you are, the less risk-averse you are. If you are less risk-averse, you are more willing to bear risk yourself. Having an insurance policy with a high deductible means that you are exposed to more risk: you have to pay more of any insurance claim yourself. This is an implication of how risk aversion changes with a person's income or wealth.

Glossary

A

ability-to-pay principle the principle of tax fairness by which those with greater ability to pay a tax should pay more tax.

absolute advantage the advantage a country has in producing a good or service if the country can produce more output per worker than other countries. Likewise, an individual has an absolute advantage in producing a good or service if they are better at producing it than other people. Having an absolute advantage is not the same thing as having a comparative advantage.

absolute value the value of a number without regard to a plus or minus sign.

accounting profit revenue minus explicit cost.

administrative costs (of a tax) the resources used for its collection, for the method of payment, and for any attempts to evade the tax.

adverse selection the case in which an individual knows more about the way things are than other people do. Adverse selection problems can lead to market problems: private information leads buyers to expect hidden problems in items offered for sale, leading to low prices and the best items being kept off the market.

antitrust policy legislative and regulatory efforts undertaken by the government to prevent oligopolistic industries from becoming or behaving like monopolies.

artificially scarce good a good that is excludable but nonrival in consumption.

autarky a situation in which a country does not trade with other countries.

average cost an alternative term for average total cost; the total cost divided by the quantity of output produced.

average cost pricing a form of price regulation that forces a monopoly to set its price equal to its average total cost.

average fixed cost the fixed cost per unit of output.

average product the amount of output produced per unit of an input.

average total cost total cost divided by quantity of output produced. Also referred to as average cost.

average variable cost the variable cost per unit of output.

B

backward-bending individual labour supply curve an individual labour supply curve that slopes upward at low to moderate wage rates and slopes downward at higher wage rates.

bar graph a graph that uses bars of varying heights or lengths to show the comparative sizes of different observations of a variable.

barrier to entry something that prevents other firms from entering an industry. Crucial in protecting the profits of a monopolist. There are five types of barriers to entry: control over scarce resources or inputs, increasing returns to scale, technological superiority, network externalities, and government-created barriers.

barter trade in the form of the direct exchange of goods or services for other goods or services that people want.

behavioural economics a branch of economics that combines economic modelling with insights from human psychology to understand how people actually make decisions.

benefits principle the principle of tax fairness by which those who benefit from public spending should bear the burden of the tax that pays for that spending.

black market a market in which goods or services are bought and sold illegally, either because it is illegal to sell them at all or because the prices charged are legally prohibited by a price ceiling.

bounded rationality a basis for decision making that leads to a choice that is close to but not exactly the one that leads to the best possible economic outcome; the "good enough" method of decision making.

brand name a name owned by a particular firm that distinguishes its products from those of other firms.

break-even price the market price at which a price-taking firm earns zero profits.

budget constraint the limitation that the cost of a consumer's consumption bundle be no more than the consumer's income.

budget line all the consumption bundles available to a consumer who spends all of their income.

C

capital the total value of assets owned by an individual or firm—physical assets plus financial assets.

capital at risk funds that an insurer places at risk when providing insurance.

cartel an agreement among several producers to obey output restrictions in order to increase their joint profits.

causal relationship the relationship between two variables in which the value taken by one variable directly influences or determines the value taken by the other variable.

circular-flow diagram a diagram that represents the transactions in an economy by two kinds of flows around a circle: flows of physical things such as goods or labour in one direction and flows of funds to pay for these physical things in the opposite direction.

clean energy sources energy sources that do not emit greenhouse gases. Renewable energy sources are also clean energy sources.

climate change the man-made change in Earth's climate from the accumulation of greenhouse gases caused by the use of fossil fuels.

Coase theorem the proposition that even in the presence of externalities an economy can always reach an efficient solution provided that the costs of making a deal are sufficiently low.

collusion cooperation among producers to limit production and raise prices so as to raise one another's profits.

commodity output of different producers regarded by consumers as the same good; also referred to as a standardized product.

common resource a resource that is non-excludable and rival in consumption.

comparative advantage the advantage a country has in producing a good or service if its opportunity cost of producing the good or service is lower than other countries' cost. Likewise, an individual has a comparative advantage in producing a good or service if their opportunity cost of producing the good or service is lower than it is for other people.

compensating differentials wage differences across jobs that reflect the fact that some jobs are less pleasant or more dangerous than others.

competitive market a market in which there are many buyers and sellers of the same good or service, none of whom can influence the price at which the good or service is sold.

complements pairs of goods for which a rise in the price of one good leads to a decrease in the demand for the other good.

constant marginal cost each additional unit costs the same to produce as the previous one.

constant returns to scale long-run average total cost is constant as output increases.

consumer surplus a term often used to refer both to individual consumer surplus and to total consumer surplus.

consumption bundle (of an individual) the collection of all the goods and services consumed by a given individual.

consumption possibilities the set of all consumption bundles that can be consumed given a consumer's income and prevailing prices.

copyright the exclusive legal right of the creator of a literary or artistic work to profit from that work; like a patent, it is a temporary monopoly.

cost (of seller) the lowest price at which a seller is willing to sell a good.

cost-benefit analysis an estimation and comparison of the costs and benefits of providing a good. When governments use cost-benefit analysis, they estimate the social costs and social benefits of providing a public good.

cross-price elasticity of demand a measure of the effect of the change in the price of one good on the quantity demanded of the other; it is equal to the percent change in the quantity demanded of one good divided by the percent change in the price of another good.

curve a line on a graph, which may be curved or straight, that depicts a relationship between two variables.

D

deadweight loss the loss in total surplus that occurs whenever an action or a policy reduces the quantity transacted below the efficient market equilibrium quantity.

decreasing marginal benefit each additional unit of an activity yields less benefit than the previous unit.

decreasing marginal cost each additional unit costs less to produce than the previous one.

decreasing returns to scale long-run average total cost increases as output increases (also known as diseconomies of scale).

deductible a sum specified in an insurance policy that the insured individual must pay before being compensated for a claim; deductibles reduce moral hazard.

demand curve a graphical representation of the demand schedule. It shows the relationship between quantity demanded and price.

demand price the price of a given quantity at which consumers will demand that quantity.

demand schedule a list or table showing how much of a good or service consumers will want to buy at different prices.

dependent variable the determined variable in a causal relationship.

diminishing marginal rate of substitution the principle that the more of one good that is consumed in proportion to another, the less of the second good the consumer is willing to substitute for another unit of the first good; the more of good R a person consumes in proportion to good M, the less they are willing to substitute for another unit of R.

diminishing returns to an input the effect observed when an increase in the quantity of an input, while holding the levels of all other inputs and the state of technology fixed, leads to a decline in the marginal product of that input.

diversification reducing risk by investing in several different things, so that the possible losses are independent events.

domestic demand curve a demand curve that shows how the quantity of a good demanded by domestic consumers depends on the price of that good.

domestic supply curve a supply curve that shows how the quantity of a good supplied by domestic producers depends on the price of that good.

dominant strategy in game theory, an action that is a player's best action regardless of the action taken by the other player.

duopolist one of the two firms in a duopoly.

duopoly an oligopoly consisting of only two firms.

E

economic growth the growing ability of the economy to produce goods and services, leading to higher living standards.

economic profit revenue minus the opportunity cost of resources used; usually less than the accounting profit.

economic signal any piece of information that helps people make better economic decisions.

economics the social science that studies the production, distribution, and consumption of goods and services.

economy a system for coordinating society's productive activities.

efficiency-wage model a model in which some employers pay an above-equilibrium wage as an incentive for better performance.

efficient description of a market or economy that takes all opportunities to make some people better off without making other people worse off.

efficient allocation of risk an allocation of risk in which those most willing to bear risk are those who end up bearing it.

elastic demand the case in which the price elasticity of demand is greater than 1.

emissions tax a tax that depends on the amount of pollution a firm produces.

environmental standards rules established by a government to protect the environment by specifying actions by producers and consumers.

equilibrium an economic situation in which no individual would be better off doing something different.

equilibrium price the price at which the market is in equilibrium, that is, the quantity of a good or service demanded equals the quantity of that good or service supplied; also referred to as the market-clearing price.

equilibrium quantity the quantity of a good or service bought and sold at the equilibrium (or market-clearing) price.

equilibrium value of the marginal product the additional value produced by the last unit of that factor employed in the factor market as a whole.

equity fairness; everyone gets their fair share. Since people can disagree about what is "fair," equity is not as well defined a concept as efficiency.

European Union (EU) a customs union among 27 European nations.

excess capacity the failure to produce enough to minimize average total cost; characteristic of monopolistically competitive firms.

excise tax a tax on sales of a good or service.

excludable referring to a good, describes the case in which the supplier can prevent those who do not pay from consuming the good.

expected utility the expected value of an individual's total utility given uncertainty about future outcomes.

expected value in reference to a random variable, the weighted average of all possible values, where the weights on each possible value correspond to the probability of that value occurring.

explicit cost a cost that requires an outlay of money.

exporting industries industries that produce goods and services that are sold abroad.

exports goods and services sold to other countries.

external benefit an uncompensated benefit that an individual or firm confers on others; also known as positive externality.

external cost an uncompensated cost that an individual or firm imposes on others; also known as negative externality.

externalities external benefits and external costs.

F

factor distribution of income the division of total income among labour, land, and capital.

factor intensity a measure of which factor is used in relatively greater quantities than other factors in production. For example, oil refining is capital-intensive compared to auto seat production because oil refiners use a higher ratio of capital to labour than do producers of auto seats.

factor markets markets in which firms buy the resources they need to produce goods and services.

factors of production the resources used to produce goods and services.

fair insurance policy an insurance policy for which the premium is equal to the expected value of the claim.

financial risk uncertainty about monetary outcomes.

firm an organization that produces goods and services for sale.

fixed cost a cost that does not depend on the quantity of output produced; the cost of a fixed input.

fixed input an input whose quantity is fixed for a period of time and cannot be varied (for example, land).

forecast a simple prediction of the future.

fossil fuel fuel derived from fossil sources such as coal and oil.

framing bias the tendency to make decisions based on how choices are presented rather than on a comparison of their true values.

free entry and exit describes an industry that potential producers can easily enter or current producers can easily leave.

free trade occurs in an economy when the government does not attempt either to reduce or to increase the levels of exports and imports that occur naturally as a result of supply and demand.

free-rider problem problem that results when individuals who have no incentive to pay for their own consumption of a good take a "free ride" on anyone who does pay; a problem with goods that are nonexcludable.

G

gains from trade gains achieved by dividing tasks and trading; in this way people can get more of what they want through trade than they could if they tried to be self-sufficient.

game theory the study of behaviour in situations of interdependence. Used to explain the behaviour of an oligopoly.

Giffen good the hypothetical inferior good for which the income effect outweighs the substitution effect and the demand curve slopes upward.

Gini coefficient a number that summarizes a country's level of income inequality based on how unequally income is distributed across quintiles.

globalization the phenomenon of growing economic linkages among countries.

government transfers a government payment to an individual or a family for which no good or service is provided in return.

greenhouse gases gas emissions that trap heat in Earth's atmosphere.

H

Heckscher–Ohlin model a model of international trade in which a country has a comparative advantage in a good whose production is intensive in the factors that are abundantly available in that country.

horizontal axis the horizontal number line of a graph along which values of the x-variable are measured; also referred to as the x-axis.

horizontal intercept the point at which a curve hits the horizontal axis; it indicates the value of the x-variable when the value of the y-variable is zero.

household a person or a group of people that share their income.

human capital the improvement in labour created by education and knowledge that is embodied in the workforce.

hyperglobalization the phenomenon of extremely high levels of international trade.

I

imperfect competition a market structure in which no firm has a monopoly, but producers nonetheless have market power they can use to affect market prices.

implicit cost a cost that does not require the outlay of money; it is measured by the value, in dollar terms, of benefits that are forgone.

implicit cost of capital the opportunity cost of the use of one's own capital— the income earned if the capital had been employed in its next best alternative use.

import quota a legal limit on the quantity of a good that can be imported.

import-competing industries industries that produce goods and services that are also imported.

imports goods and services purchased from other countries.

incentive anything that offers rewards to people to change their behaviour.

incidence (of a tax) a measure of who really pays a tax.

income distribution the way in which total income is divided among the owners of the various factors of production in an economy.

income effect the change in the quantity of a good consumed that results from the change in a consumer's purchasing power due to the change in the price of the good.

income elasticity of demand the percent change in the quantity of a good demanded when a consumer's income changes divided by the percent change in the consumer's income.

income tax a tax on an individual's or family's income.

income-elastic demand the case in which the income elasticity of demand for a good is greater than 1.

income-inelastic demand the case in which the income elasticity of demand for a good is positive but less than 1.

increasing marginal cost each additional unit costs more to produce than the previous one.

increasing returns to scale long-run average total cost declines as output increases (also referred to as economies of scale).

independent events events for which the occurrence of one does not affect the likelihood of occurrence of any of the others.

independent variable the determining variable in a causal relationship.

indifference curve a contour line that shows all consumption bundles that yield the same amount of total utility for an individual.

indifference curve map a collection of indifference curves for a given individual that represents the individual's entire utility function; each curve corresponds to a different total utility level.

individual choice the decision by an individual of what to do, which necessarily involves a decision of what not to do.

individual consumer surplus the net gain to an individual buyer from the purchase of a good; equal to the difference between the buyer's willingness to pay and the price paid.

individual demand curve a graphical representation of the relationship between quantity demanded and price for an individual consumer.

individual labour supply curve a graphical representation that shows how the quantity of labour supplied by an individual depends on that individual's wage rate.

individual producer surplus the net gain to an individual seller from selling a good; equal to the difference between the price received and the seller's cost.

individual supply curve a graphical representation of the relationship between quantity supplied and price for an individual producer.

industry supply curve a graphical representation that shows the relationship between the price of a good and the total output of the industry for that good.

inefficient describes a market or economy in which there are missed opportunities: some people could be made better off without making other people worse off.

inefficient allocation of sales among sellers a form of inefficiency in which sellers who would be willing to sell a good at the lowest price are unable to make sales while sales go to sellers who are only willing to sell at a higher price; often the result of a price floor.

inefficient allocation to consumers a form of inefficiency in which some people who want the good badly and are willing to pay a high price don't get it, and some who care relatively little about the good and are only willing to pay a low price do get it; often a result of a price ceiling.

inefficiently high quality a form of inefficiency in which sellers offer high-quality goods at a high price even though buyers would prefer a lower quality at a lower price; often the result of a price floor.

inefficiently low quality a form of inefficiency in which sellers offer low-quality goods at a low price even though buyers would prefer a higher quality at a higher price; often a result of a price ceiling.

inelastic demand the case in which the price elasticity of demand is less than 1.

inferior good a good for which a rise in income decreases the demand for the good.

in-kind benefit a benefit given in the form of goods or services.

input a good or service used to produce another good or service.

interaction (of choices) my choices affect your choices, and vice versa; a feature of most economic situations. The results of this interaction are often quite different from what the individuals intend.

interdependence a relationship among firms in which their decisions significantly affect one another's profits; characteristic of oligopolies.

internalize the externality when individuals take into account external costs and external benefits.

interest rate the price, calculated as a percentage of the amount borrowed, charged by the lender.

international trade agreements treaties in which a country promises to engage in less trade protection against the exports of other countries in return for a promise by other countries to do the same for its own exports.

invisible hand a phrase used by Adam Smith to refer to the way in which an individual's pursuit of self-interest can lead, without the individual intending it, to good results for society as a whole.

irrational describes a decision maker who chooses an option that leaves them worse off than choosing another available option.

L

law of demand the principle that a higher price for a good or service, other things equal, leads people to demand a smaller quantity of that good or service.

leisure the time available for purposes other than earning money to buy marketed goods.

licence the right, conferred by the government or an owner, to supply a good.

linear relationship the relationship between two variables in which the slope is constant and therefore is depicted on a graph by a curve that is a straight line.

long run the time period in which all inputs can be varied.

long-run average total cost curve a graphical representation showing the relationship between output and average total cost when fixed cost has been chosen to minimize average total cost for each level of output.

long-run industry supply curve a graphical representation that shows how quantity supplied responds to price once producers have had time to enter or exit the industry.

long-run market equilibrium an economic balance in which, given that sufficient time has elapsed for entry into and exit from the industry to occur, the quantity supplied equals the quantity demanded.

loss aversion oversensitivity to loss, leading to unwillingness to recognize a loss and move on.

lump-sum tax a tax that is the same for everyone, regardless of any actions people take.

M

macroeconomics the branch of economics that is concerned with the overall ups and downs in the economy.

marginal analysis the study of marginal decisions.

marginal benefit the additional benefit derived from producing one more unit of a good or service.

marginal benefit curve a graphical representation showing how the benefit from producing one more unit depends on the quantity that has already been produced.

marginal cost the additional cost incurred by producing one more unit of that good or service.

marginal cost curve a graphical representation showing how the cost of producing one more unit depends on the quantity that has already been produced.

marginal cost pricing a form of price regulation that forces a monopoly to set its price equal to its marginal cost.

marginal decision a decision made at the "margin" of an activity to do a bit more or a bit less of that activity.

marginal external benefit (*MEB*) of pollution the additional benefit for others if the polluter creates another unit of pollution.

marginal external cost (*MEC*) of pollution the additional cost imposed on others if the polluter creates another unit of pollution.

marginal private benefit (*MPB*) of pollution the additional benefit for the polluter if the polluter creates an other unit of pollution.

marginal private cost (*MPC*) of pollution the additional cost imposed on the polluter if the polluter creates another unit of pollution.

marginal product the additional quantity of output produced by using one more unit of that input, holding other inputs and the production technology fixed.

marginal productivity theory of income distribution the proposition that every factor of production is paid its equilibrium value of the marginal product.

marginal rate of substitution (*MRS*) the ratio of the marginal utility of one good to the marginal utility of another; if a good R in place of good M is equal to MU_R/MU_M, the ratio of the marginal utility of R to the marginal utility of M.

marginal revenue the change in total revenue generated by an additional unit of output.

marginal revenue curve a graphical representation showing how marginal revenue varies as output varies.

marginal social benefit of pollution the additional gain to society as a whole from an additional unit of pollution.

marginal social cost of pollution the additional cost imposed on society as a whole by an additional unit of pollution.

marginal tax rate the percentage of an increase in income that is taxed away.

marginal utility the change in total utility generated by consuming one additional unit of a good or service.

marginal utility curve a graphical representation showing how marginal utility depends on the quantity of the good or service consumed.

marginal utility per dollar the additional utility gained from spending one more dollar on a good or service.

market economy an economy in which decisions about production and consumption are made by individual producers and consumers.

market failure the failure of a market to be efficient.

market power the ability of a firm to raise prices.

market share the fraction of the total industry output accounted for by producer's output.

market-clearing price the price at which the market is in equilibrium, that is, the quantity of a good or service demanded equals the quantity of that good or service supplied; also referred to as the equilibrium price.

markets for goods and services markets in which firms sell goods and services that they produce to households.

maximum the highest point on a nonlinear curve, where the slope of the curve changes from positive to negative.

mean household income the average income across all households.

means-tested describes a program in which benefits are available only to individuals or families whose incomes fall below a certain level.

median household income the average income across all households.

mental accounting the habit of mentally assigning dollars to different accounts so that some dollars are worth more than others.

microeconomics the branch of economics that studies how people make decisions and how these decisions interact.

midpoint method a technique for calculating the percent change in which changes in a variable are compared with the average, or midpoint, of the starting and final values.

minimum the lowest point on a nonlinear curve, where the slope of the curve changes from negative to positive.

minimum wage a legal floor on the wage rate, which is the market price of labour.

minimum-cost output the quantity of output at which the average total cost is lowest—the bottom of the U-shaped average total cost curve.

model a simplified representation of a real situation that is used to better understand real-life situations.

monopolist a firm that is the only producer of a good that has no close substitutes.

monopolistic competition a market structure in which there are many competing producers in an industry, each producer sells a differentiated product, and there is free entry and exit into and from the industry in the long run.

monopoly an industry controlled by a monopolist.

monopsonist a firm that is the sole buyer in a market.

monopsony a market in which there is only one buyer but many sellers of a good.

moral hazard the situation that can exist when an individual knows more about their own actions than other people do. This leads to a distortion of incentives to take care or to expend effort when someone else bears the costs of the lack of care or effort.

movement along the demand curve a change in the quantity demanded of a good that results from a change in the good's price.

movement along the supply curve a change in the quantity supplied of a good that results from a change in the good's price.

N

NAFTA-USMCA The current version of the trade agreement among the United States, Canada, and Mexico.

Nash equilibrium in game theory, the equilibrium that results when all players choose the action that maximizes their payoffs given the actions of other players, ignoring the effect of that action on the payoffs of other players; also known as noncooperative equilibrium.

natural monopoly a monopoly that exists when increasing returns to scale provide a large cost advantage to a single firm that produces all of an industry's output.

negative externalities external costs.

negative income tax a government program that supplements the income of low-income working families.

negative relationship a relationship between two variables in which an increase in the value of one variable is associated with a decrease in the value of the other variable. It is illustrated by a curve that slopes downward from left to right.

network externality the increase in the value of a good or service to an individual is greater when a large number of others own or use the same good or service.

noncooperative behaviour actions by firms that ignore the effects of those actions on the profits of other firms.

noncooperative equilibrium in game theory, the equilibrium that results when all players choose the action that maximizes their payoffs given the actions of other players, ignoring the effect of that action on the payoffs of other players; also known as Nash equilibrium.

nonexcludable referring to a good, describes the case in which the supplier cannot prevent consumption by people who do not pay for it.

nonlinear curve a curve in which the slope is not the same between every pair of points.

nonlinear relationship the relationship between two variables in which the slope is not constant and therefore is depicted on a graph by a curve that is not a straight line.

nonmonetary rewards benefits or payoffs that are not financial in nature; examples include increased leisure time and "feel-good" experiences.

nonprice competition competition in areas other than price to increase sales, such as new product features and advertising; especially engaged in by firms that have a tacit understanding not to compete on price.

nonrival in consumption referring to a good, describes the case in which the same unit can be consumed by more than one person at the same time.

normal good a good for which a rise in income increases the demand for that good—the "normal" case.

normative economics the branch of economic analysis that makes prescriptions about the way the economy should work.

North American Free Trade Agreement (NAFTA) a trade agreement among the United States, Canada, and Mexico. Revised in 2018 as the USMCA.

nudge a formulation of the status quo choice intended to shift people to more rational choices when they are prone to status quo bias.

O

offshore outsourcing the practice in which businesses hire people in another country to perform various tasks.

oligopolist a firm in an industry with only a small number of producers.

oligopoly an industry with only a small number of producers.

omitted variable an unobserved variable that, through its influence on other variables, creates the erroneous appearance of a direct causal relationship among those variables.

opportunity cost the real cost of an item: what you must give up in order to get it.

optimal consumption bundle the consumption bundle that maximizes a consumer's total utility given that consumer's budget constraint.

optimal consumption rule the principle that the optimal consumption bundle is on the budget line and the marginal utility per dollar spent on each good in the bundle is equal.

optimal output rule the principle that profit is maximized by producing the quantity of output at which the marginal revenue of the last unit produced is equal to its marginal cost.

optimal quantity the quantity that generates the highest possible total profit.

optimal time allocation rule the principle that an individual should allocate time so that the marginal utility gained from the income earned from an additional hour worked is equal to the marginal utility of an additional hour of leisure.

ordinary goods in a consumer's utility function, those for which additional units of one good are required to compensate for fewer units of another, and vice versa; and for which the consumer experiences a diminishing marginal rate of substitution when substituting one good in place of another.

origin the point where the axes of a two-variable graph meet.

other things equal assumption in the development of a model, the assumption that all other relevant factors remain unchanged.

overuse the depletion of a common resource that occurs when individuals ignore the fact that their use depletes the amount of the resource remaining for others.

P

Paris Agreement an international agreement by 196 countries to reduce their greenhouse gas emissions.

patent a temporary monopoly given by the government to an inventor for the use or sale of an invention.

payoff in game theory, the reward received by a player (for example, the profit earned by an oligopolist).

payoff matrix in game theory, a diagram that shows how the payoffs to each of the participants in a two-player game depend on the actions of both; a tool in analyzing interdependence.

payroll tax a tax on the earnings an employer pays to an employee.

perfect complements goods a consumer wants to consume in the same ratio, regardless of their relative price.

perfect price discrimination the price discrimination that results when a monopolist charges each consumer the maximum that the consumer is willing to pay.

perfect substitutes goods for which the indifference curves are straight lines; the marginal rate of substitution of one good in place of another good is constant, regardless of how much of each an individual consumes.

perfectly competitive industry an industry in which all producers are price-takers.

perfectly competitive market a market in which all participants are price-takers.

perfectly elastic demand the case in which any price increase will cause the quantity demanded to drop to zero; the demand curve is a horizontal line.

perfectly elastic supply the case in which even a tiny increase or reduction in the price will lead to very large changes in the quantity supplied, so that the price elasticity of supply is infinite; the perfectly elastic supply curve is a horizontal line.

perfectly inelastic demand the case in which the quantity demanded does not respond at all to changes in the price; the demand curve is a vertical line.

perfectly inelastic supply the case in which the price elasticity of supply is zero, so that changes in the price of the good have no effect on the quantity supplied; the perfectly inelastic supply curve is a vertical line.

physical capital manufactured productive resources, such as equipment, buildings, tools, and machines; often referred to simply as "capital."

pie chart a circular graph that shows how some total is divided among its components, usually expressed in percentages.

Pigouvian subsidy a payment designed to encourage activities that generate external benefits.

Pigouvian taxes taxes designed to reduce the costs imposed on society from a negative externality.

pooling a strong form of diversification in which an investor takes a small share of the risk in many independent events, so the payoff has very little total overall risk.

positive economics the branch of economic analysis that describes the way the economy actually works.

positive externalities external benefits.

positive feedback put simply, success breeds success, failure breeds failure; the effect is seen with goods that are subject to network externalities.

positive relationship a relationship between two variables in which an increase in the value of one variable is associated with an increase in the value of the other variable. It is illustrated by a curve that slopes upward from left to right.

positively correlated describes a relationship between events such that each event is more likely to occur if the other event also occurs.

poverty line (or **poverty threshold**) the annual income below which a family is officially considered poor.

poverty program a government program designed to aid the poor.

poverty rate the percentage of the population with incomes below the poverty line.

premium a payment to an insurance company in return for the promise to pay a claim in certain states of the world.

present value (of X) the amount of money needed today in order to receive X at a future date given the interest rate.

price ceiling a maximum price sellers are allowed to charge for a good or service; a form of price control.

price controls legal restrictions on how high or low a market price may go.

price discrimination charging different prices to different consumers for the same good.

price elasticity of demand the ratio of the percent change in the quantity demanded to the percent change in the price as we move along the demand curve.

price elasticity of supply a measure of the responsiveness of the quantity of a good supplied to the price of that good; the ratio of the percent change in the quantity supplied to the percent change in the price as we move along the supply curve.

price floor a minimum price buyers are required to pay for a good or service; a form of price control.

price leadership a pattern of behaviour in which one firm sets its price and other firms in the industry follow.

price regulation limits the price that a monopolist is allowed to charge.

price war a collapse of prices when tacit collusion breaks down.

price-taking consumer a consumer whose actions have no effect on the market price of the good or service that the consumer buys.

price-taking firm's optimal output rule the principle that a price-taking firm's profit is maximized by producing the quantity of output at which the market price is equal to the marginal cost of the last unit produced.

price-taking producer a producer whose actions have no effect on the market price of the good or service it sells.

price-taking producer's optimal employment rule a price-taking producer's profit is maximized by employing each factor of production up to the level at which the value of the marginal product is equal to the factor's price.

principle of diminishing marginal utility the proposition that each successive unit of a good or service consumed adds less to total utility than did the previous unit.

principle of "either–or" decision making the principle that, when faced with an "either-or" choice between two activities, choose the one with the positive economic profit.

prisoner's dilemma a game based on two premises: (1) each player has an incentive to choose an action that benefits itself at the other player's expense; and (2) both players are then worse off than if they had acted cooperatively.

private good a good that is both excludable and rival in consumption.

private health insurance a program in which each member of a large pool of individuals pays a fixed amount to a private company that agrees to pay most of the medical expenses of the pool's members.

private information information that some people have, but others do not.

producer surplus a term often used to refer both to individual producer surplus and to total producer surplus.

product differentiation the attempt by firms to convince buyers that their products are different from those of other firms in the industry. If firms can so convince buyers, they can charge a higher price.

production function the relationship between the quantity of inputs a firm uses and the quantity of output it produces.

production possibility frontier a model that illustrates the trade-offs facing an economy that produces only two goods. It shows the maximum quantity of one good that can be produced for any given quantity produced of the other.

profit-maximizing principle of marginal analysis the proposition that in a profit-maximizing "how much" decision the optimal quantity is the largest quantity at which marginal benefit is greater than or equal to marginal cost.

profits tax a tax on a firm's profits.

progressive tax a tax that takes a larger share of the income of high-income taxpayers than of low-income taxpayers.

property rights the rights of owners of valuable items, whether resources or goods, to dispose of those items as they choose.

property tax a tax on the value of property, such as the value of a home.

proportional tax a tax that is the same percentage of the tax base regardless of the taxpayer's income or wealth.

protection an alternative term for trade protection; policies that limit imports.

public good a good that is both nonexcludable and nonrival in consumption.

public ownership the case in which goods are supplied by the government or by a firm owned by the government to protect the interests of the consumer in response to natural monopoly.

Q

quantity control an upper limit, set by the government, on the quantity of some good that can be bought or sold; also referred to as a quota.

quantity demanded the actual amount of a good or service consumers are willing to buy at some specific price.

quantity supplied the actual amount of a good or service producers are willing to sell at some specific price.

quota an upper limit, set by the government, on the quantity of some good that can be bought or sold; also referred to as a quantity control.

quota limit the total amount of a good under a quota or quantity control that can be legally transacted.

quota rent the difference between the demand price and the supply price at the quota limit; this difference, the earnings that accrue to the licence-holder from ownership of the right to sell the good, is equal to the market price of the licence when the licences are traded.

R

random variable a variable with an uncertain future value.

rational describes a decision maker who chooses the available option that leads to the outcome they most prefer.

recession a downturn in the economy.

regressive tax a tax that takes a smaller share of the income of high-income taxpayers than of low-income taxpayers.

relative price the ratio of the price of one good to the price of another.

relative price rule at the optimal consumption bundle, the marginal rate of substitution of one good in place of another is equal to the relative price.

renewable energy sources energy sources, such as solar and wind power, that are inexhaustible, unlike fossil fuel sources, which are exhaustible.

rental rate the cost, implicit or explicit, of using a unit of land or capital for a given period of time.

reputation a long-term standing in the public regard that serves to reassure others that private information is not being concealed; a valuable asset in the face of adverse selection.

resource something that can be used to produce something else; includes natural resources (from the physical environment) and human resources (labour, skill, intelligence).

reverse causality the error committed when the true direction of causality between two variables is reversed, and the independent variable and the dependent variable are incorrectly identified.

Ricardian model of international trade a model that analyzes international trade under the assumption that opportunity costs are constant.

risk uncertainty about future outcomes.

risk-averse describes individuals who choose to reduce risk when that reduction leaves the expected value of their income or wealth unchanged.

risk aversion the willingness to sacrifice some economic payoff in order to avoid a potential loss.

risk-neutral describes individuals who are completely insensitive to risk.

rival in consumption referring to a good, describes the case in which one unit cannot be consumed by more than one person at the same time.

S

sales tax a tax on the value of goods sold.

scarce in short supply; a resource is scarce when there is not enough of the resource available to satisfy all the various ways a society wants to use it.

scatter diagram a graph that shows points that correspond to actual observations of the x- and y-variables; a curve is usually fitted to the scatter of points to indicate the trend in the data.

screening using observable information about people to make inferences about their private information; a way to reduce adverse selection.

share a partial ownership of a company.

shift of the demand curve a change in the quantity demanded at any given price, represented graphically by the shift of the original demand curve to a new position, denoted by a new demand curve.

shift of the supply curve a change in the quantity supplied of a good or service at any given price. It is represented by the change of the original supply curve to a new position, denoted by a new supply curve.

short run the time period in which at least one input is fixed.

short-run individual supply curve a graphical representation that shows how an individual producer's profit-maximizing output quantity depends on the market price, taking fixed cost as given the firm's marginal cost curve at or above its average variable cost curve (and zero output for prices below the minimum of average variable cost).

short-run industry supply curve a graphical representation that shows how the quantity supplied by an industry depends on the market price given a fixed number of producers.

short-run market equilibrium an economic balance that results when the quantity supplied equals the quantity demanded, taking the number of producers as given.

shortage the insufficiency of a good or service that occurs when the quantity demanded exceeds the quantity supplied; shortages occur when the price is below the equilibrium price.

shut-down price the price at which a firm will cease production in the short run if the market price falls below the minimum average variable cost.

signalling taking some action to establish credibility despite possessing private information; a way to reduce adverse selection.

single-payer system a health care system in which the government is the principal payer of medical bills funded through taxes.

single-price monopolist a monopolist that offers its product to all consumers at the same price.

slope a measure of how steep a line or curve is. The slope of a line is measured by "rise over run"—the change in the y-variable between two points on the line divided by the change in the x-variable between those same two points.

social insurance program a government program designed to provide protection against unpredictable financial distress.

social welfare program a government program designed to provide payments based on need.

socially optimal quantity of pollution the quantity of pollution that society would choose if all the costs and benefits of pollution were fully accounted for.

specialization the situation in which each person specializes in the task that they are good at performing.

standardized product output of different producers regarded by consumers as the same good; also referred to as a commodity.

state of the world a possible future event.

status quo bias the tendency to avoid making a decision and sticking with the status quo.

strategic behaviour actions taken by a firm that attempt to influence the future behaviour of other firms.

substitutes pairs of goods for which a rise in the price of one of the goods leads to an increase in the demand for the other good.

substitution effect the change in the quantity of a good consumed as the consumer substitutes other goods that are now relatively cheaper in place of the good that has become relatively more expensive.

sunk cost a cost that has already been incurred and is not recoverable. A sunk cost should be ignored in decisions about future actions.

sunk cost fallacy the mistaken belief that a sunk cost represents an opportunity cost.

supply and demand model a model of how a competitive market behaves.

supply curve a graphical representation of the supply schedule, showing the relationship between quantity supplied and price.

supply price the price of a given quantity at which producers will supply that quantity.

supply schedule a list or table showing how much of a good or service producers will supply at different prices.

surplus the excess of a good or service that occurs when the quantity supplied exceeds the quantity demanded; surpluses occur when the price is above the equilibrium price.

T

tacit collusion cooperation among producers, without a formal agreement, to limit production and raise prices so as to raise one another's profits.

tangency condition on a graph of a consumer's budget line and available indifference curves of available consumption bundles, the point at which an indifference curve and the budget line just touch. When the indifference curves have the typical convex shape, this point determines the optimal consumption bundle.

tangent line a straight line that just touches, or is tangent to, a nonlinear curve at a particular point; the slope of the tangent line is equal to the slope of the nonlinear curve at that point.

tariff a tax levied on imports.

tax base the measure or value, such as income or property value, that determines how much tax an individual or firm pays.

tax rate the amount of tax people are required to pay per unit of whatever is being taxed.

tax structure specifies how a tax depends on the tax base; usually expressed in percentage terms.

technology the technical means for producing goods and services.

technology spillover an external benefit, or positive externality, that results when knowledge spreads among individuals and firms.

time allocation the decision about how many hours to spend on different activities, which leads to a decision about how much labour to supply.

time allocation budget line an individual's possible trade-off between consumption of leisure and the income that allows consumption of marketed goods.

time-series graph a two-variable graph that has dates on the horizontal axis and values of a variable that occurred on those dates on the vertical axis.

tit for tat in game theory, a strategy that involves playing cooperatively at first, then doing whatever the other player did in the previous period.

total consumer surplus the sum of the individual consumer surpluses of all the buyers of a good in a market.

total cost the sum of the fixed cost and the variable cost of producing a given quantity of output.

total cost curve a graphical representation of the total cost, showing how total cost depends on the quantity of output.

total producer surplus the sum of the individual producer surpluses of all the sellers of a good in a market.

total product curve a graphical representation of the production function, showing how the quantity of output depends on the quantity of the variable input for a given quantity of the fixed input and production technology.

total revenue the total value of sales of a good or service (the price of the good or service multiplied by the quantity sold).

total surplus the total net gain to consumers and producers from trading in a market; it is the sum of the producer surplus and the consumer surplus.

tradable emissions permits licences to emit limited quantities of pollutants that can be bought and sold by polluters.

trade the practice, in a market economy, in which individuals provide goods and services to others and receive goods and services in return.

trade protection policies that limit imports.

trade war occurs when countries deliberately try to impose pain on their trading partners, as a way to extract policy concessions.

trade-off a comparison of costs and benefits of doing something.

trade-off between equity and efficiency the dynamic whereby a well-designed tax system can be made more efficient only by making it less fair, and vice versa.

transaction costs the costs to individuals of making a deal that often prevent a mutually beneficial trade from occurring.

truncated cut; in a truncated axis, some of the range of values are omitted, usually to save space.

U

U-shaped average total cost curve a distinctive graphical representation of the relationship between output and average total cost; the average total cost curve at first falls when output is low and then rises as output increases.

unions organizations of workers that try to raise wages and improve working conditions for their members by bargaining collectively with their employers.

unit-elastic demand the case in which the price elasticity of demand is exactly 1.

util a unit of utility.

utility (of a consumer) a measure of the satisfaction derived from consumption of goods and services.

utility function (of an individual) the total utility generated by an individual's consumption bundle.

utility-maximizing principle of marginal analysis the principle that the marginal utility per dollar spent must be the same for all goods and services in the optimal consumption bundle.

V

value of the marginal product the value of the additional output generated by employing one more unit of a given factor, such as labour.

value of the marginal product curve a graphical representation showing how the value of the marginal product of a factor depends on the quantity of the factor employed.

variable a quantity that can take on more than one value.

variable cost a cost that depends on the quantity of output produced; the cost of a variable input.

variable input an input whose quantity the firm can vary at any time (for example, labour).

vertical axis the vertical number line of a graph along which values of the y-variable are measured; also referred to as the y-axis.

vertical intercept the point at which a curve hits the vertical axis; it shows the value of the y-variable when the value of the x-variable is zero.

W

wasted resources a form of inefficiency in which people expend money, effort, and time to cope with the shortages caused by a price ceiling.

wealth tax a tax on an individual's wealth.

wedge the difference between the demand price of the quantity transacted and the supply price of the quantity transacted for a good when the supply of the good is legally restricted. Often created by a quantity control, or quota. The price paid by buyers ends up being higher than that received by sellers.

welfare state the collection of government programs designed to alleviate economic hardship.

willingness to pay the maximum price at which a consumer is prepared to pay for a good.

world price the price at which that good can be bought or sold abroad.

World Trade Organization (WTO) an international organization of member countries that oversees international trade agreements and rules on disputes between countries over those agreements.

X

x-axis the horizontal number line of a graph along which values of the x-variable are measured; also referred to as the horizontal axis.

Y

y-axis the vertical number line of a graph along which values of the y-variable are measured; also referred to as the vertical axis.

Z

zero-profit equilibrium an economic balance in which each firm makes zero profit at its profit-maximizing quantity; a long-run result of a monopolistically competitive industry.

Index

Note: Key terms appear in **boldface** type.

Pricing and bundling options are available at the Macmillan student store: **store.macmillanlearning.com**

Engage Every Economics Student

Achieve is a comprehensive set of interconnected teaching and assessment tools that supports students and instructors at each stage in the learning path, from pre-class to in-class and post-class. Our resources were co-designed with instructors and students, using a foundation of learning research and rigorous testing, and offer unparalleled data and analytics on student performance.

Engaging students for better outcomes

Pre-built assignments include a variety of activities to engage students both inside and outside of class. Research shows that the more engagement a student has with Achieve, the higher their final exam scores by a full letter grade.

Supporting students of all levels

Achieve is designed for all students, from high achievers to those who need extra support. Students less academically prepared who engage in 80% or more of their assigned Achieve activities close the performance gap with more prepared peers by about half. Students more academically prepared see a boost of about nine percentage points on final exam scores at 80% or higher engagement with Achieve activities.

ACHIEVE FOR ECONOMICS INCLUDES

- Insights and Reporting
- Powerful Assessment including Intuitive Graphing Activities
- Interactive e-book
- LearningCurve Adaptive Quizzing
- Gradebook
- Integration Options

In Achieve

- **Animated Pre-lecture Tutorials** help students gain a base-level understanding of core economic topics before classtime begins.
- A robust **e-book** with notetaking, highlighting, and search functions. It is mobile-friendly and accessibility-compliant.
- **Step-by-Step Graphs** break the graphing process down into manageable components, much as an instructor does in the classroom. Also available in Lecture Slides.
- **iClicker** student response system can help bring class to life—in person or virtual—and give every student a voice. Student confidence and end-of-course grades increase with the use of iClicker.
- **LearningCurve Adaptive Quizzing** offers individualized question sets and feedback tailored to each student based on correct and incorrect responses. Questions link to the e-book, encouraging students to read and use the resources at hand.
- **Work It Out** activities pair sample end-of-chapter problems with targeted feedback and video explanations to help students solve problems one step at a time.

BUDGET **B**OOKS This book does not have a traditional binding; its pages are loose and 3-hole punched to provide flexibility and a low price to students.

AUTHENTIC

macmillan learning

worth publishers
Macmillan Learning

macmillanlearning.com

ISBN-13: 978-1-319-33284-6
ISBN-10: 1-319-33284-6

90000

9 781319 332846